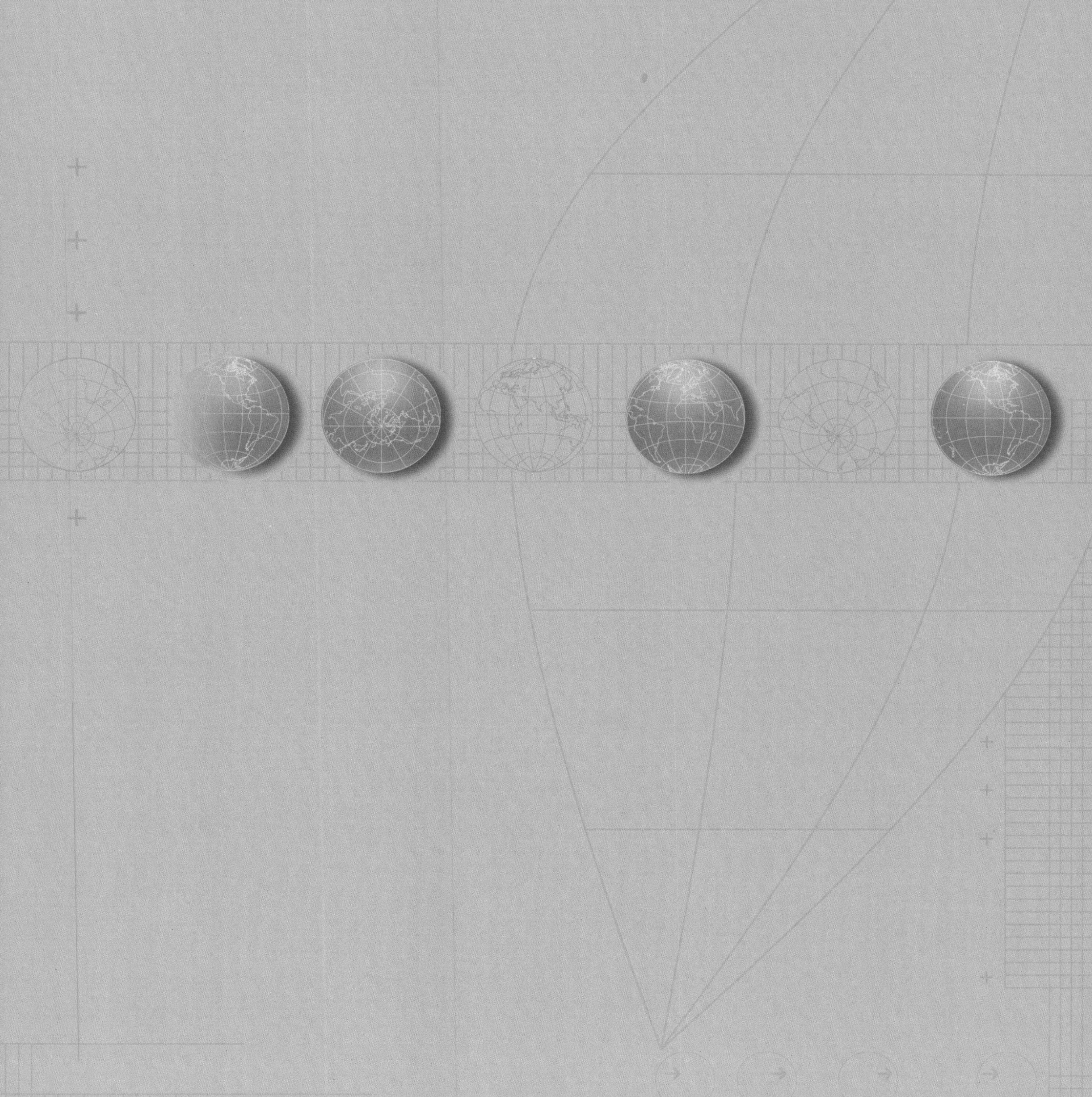

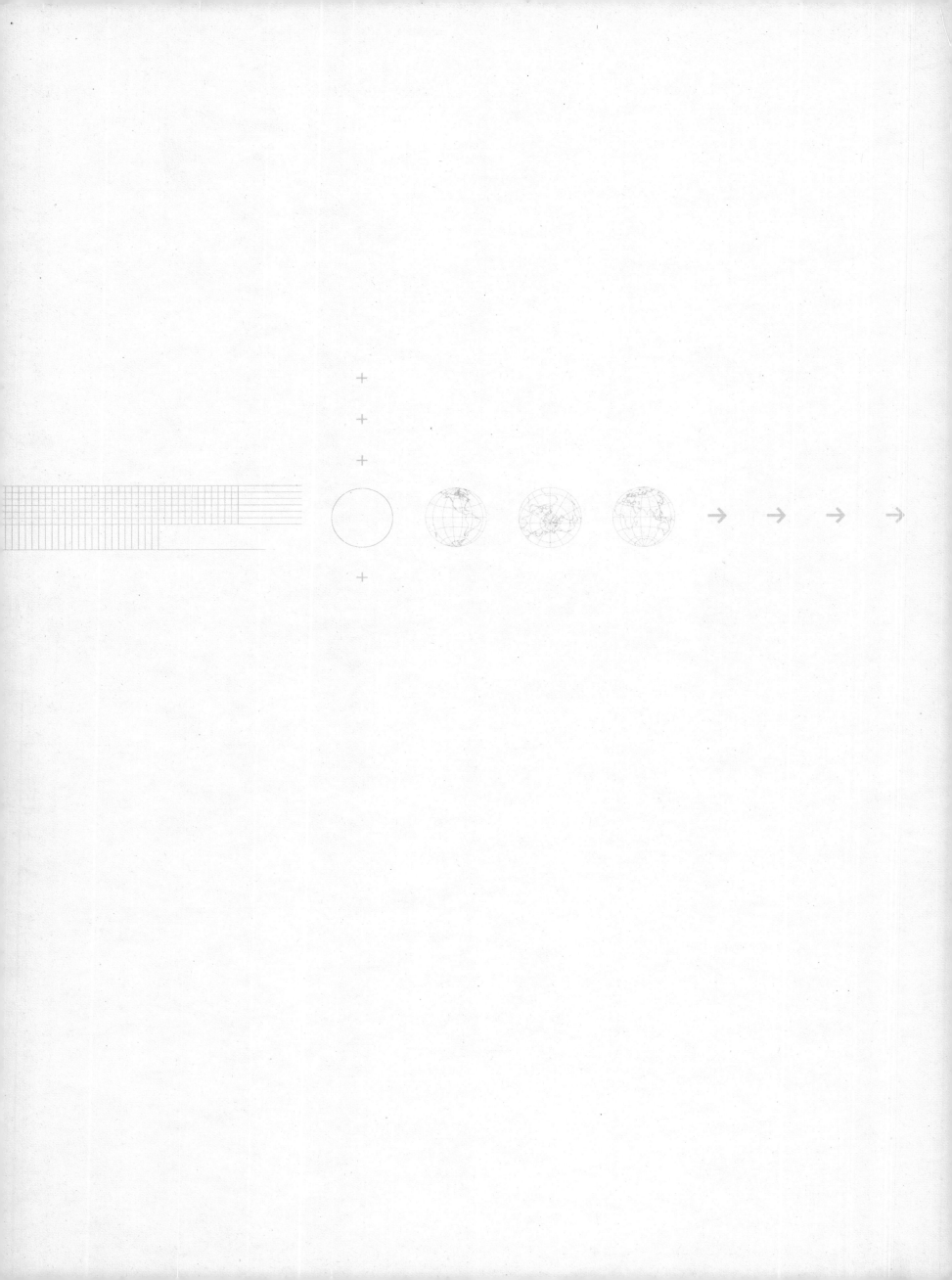

HarperCollins [NEW]
WORLDATLAS

HARPERCOLLINS NEW WORLD ATLAS. Copyright © 2001 by HarperCollins*Publishers*. All rights reserved. Printed in the United States of America. No part of this book may be used or reproduced in any manner whatsoever without written permission except in the case of brief quotations embodied in critical articles and reviews. For information address Harpercollins Publishers Inc., 10 East 53rd Street, New York, NY 10022.

HarperCollins books may be purchased for educational, business, or sales promotional use. For information please write: Special Markets Department, HarperCollins Publishers Inc., 10 East 53rd Street, New York, NY 10022.

First Published 2001 by HarperCollins*Publishers* Ltd

Maps © Bartholomew Ltd 2001

Collins® is a registered trademark of HarperCollins*Publishers* Ltd

Printed in Italy

Library of Congress Cataloging-in-Publication Data has been applied for.

ISBN 0 06 052120 1

The maps in this product are also available for purchase in digital format from Bartholomew Mapping Solutions. For details and information visit
http://www.bartholomewmaps.com
or contact
Bartholomew Mapping Solutions
Tel: +44 (0) 141 306 3162
Fax: +44 (0) 141 306 3104
e-mail: bartholomew@harpercollins.co.uk

HarperCollins [NEW]
WORLDATLAS

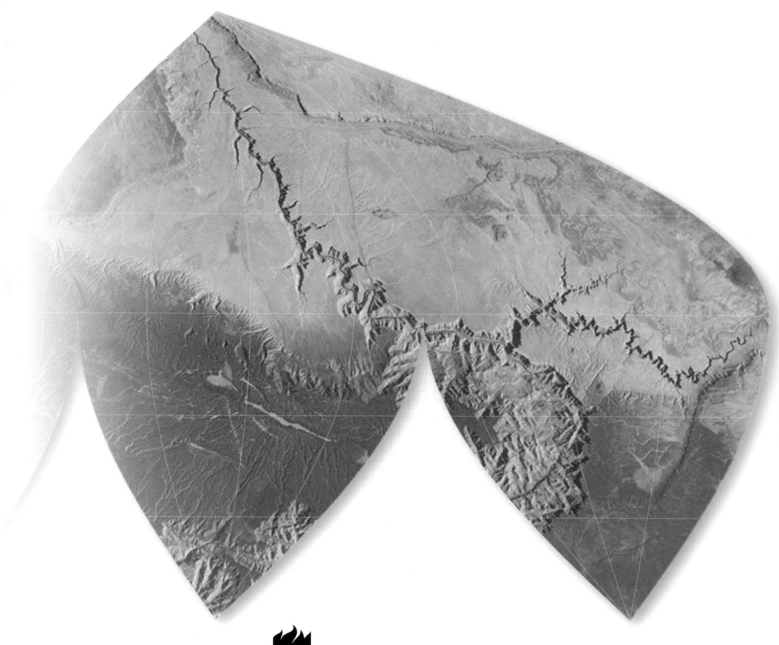

HarperResource
An Imprint of HarperCollinsPublishers

introduction

CONTENTS

The atlas is arranged into a world thematic section and continental sections as defined in the contents list below. Full details of the contents of each section can be found on the introductory spread within the section. As indicated on the contents list, each section is distinctively colour-coded to allow easy identification.

The continental sections contain detailed, comprehensive reference maps of the continent, which are preceded by introductory pages consisting of a mixture of statistical and thematic maps, geographical statistics, and photographs and images illustrating specific themes. Each map and thematic spread contains a 'connections' box, which indicates links to other pages in the atlas containing related information.

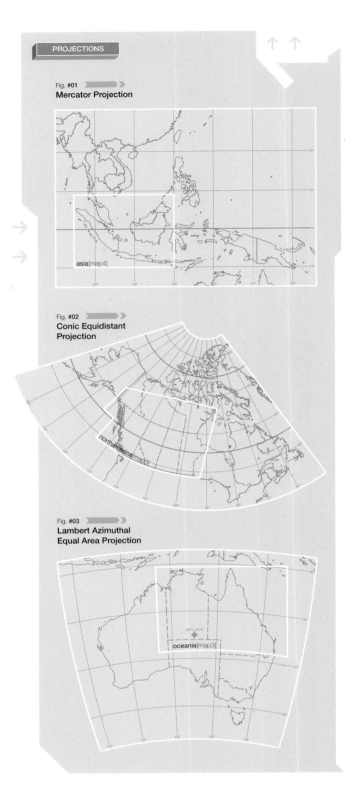

title	pages
world	6–7
[physical features]	8–9
[countries]	10–11
[land images]	12–13
[earthquakes and volcanoes]	14–15
[climate and weather]	16–17
[land cover]	18–19
[changes]	20–21
[population]	22–23
[cities]	24–25
[communications]	26–27
europe	28–29
[landscapes]	30–31
[countries]	32–33
[countries/issues]	34–35
[environments]	36–37
[reference maps]	38–59
asia	60–61
[landscapes]	62–63
[countries]	64–65
[countries/issues]	66–67
[changes]	68–69
[threats]	70–71
[reference maps]	72–109
africa	110–111
[landscapes]	112–113
[countries]	114–115
[countries/issues]	116–117
[locations]	118–119
[reference maps]	120–133

title	pages
oceania	134–135
[landscapes]	136–137
[countries]	138–139
[threats]	140–141
[features]	142–143
[reference maps]	144–153
northamerica	154–155
[landscapes]	156–157
[countries]	158–159
[threats]	160–161
[environments]	162–163
[reference maps]	164–187
southamerica	188–189
[landscapes]	190–191
[countries]	192–193
[contrasts]	194–195
[impacts]	196–197
[reference maps]	198-207
oceans and poles	208–209
oceans [features]	210–211
antarctica [features]	212–213
the arctic [features]	214–215
oceans and poles [reference maps]	216–224
index	225–335
acknowledgements	336

REFERENCE MAPS

Symbols and generalization

Maps show information by using signs, or symbols, which are designed to reflect the features on the Earth which they represent. Symbols can be in the form of points, lines, or areas and variations in the size, shape and colour of the symbols allow a great range of information to be shown. The symbols used on the reference maps are explained opposite.

Not all features on the ground can be shown, nor can all characteristics of a feature be depicted. Much detail has to be generalized to be clearly shown on the maps, the degree of generalization being determined largely by the scale of the map. As map scale decreases, fewer features can be shown, and their depiction becomes less detailed. The most common generalization techniques are selection and simplification. Selection is the inclusion of some features and the omission of others of less importance. Smaller scale maps can show fewer features than larger scales, and therefore only the more important features are selected. Simplification is the process of smoothing lines, combining areas, or slightly displacing symbols to add clarity. Smaller scale maps require more simplification. These techniques are carried out in such a way that the overall character of the area mapped is retained.

Scale

The amount of detail shown on a map is determined by its scale – the relationship between the size of an area shown on the map and the actual size of the area on the ground. Larger scales show more detail, smaller scales require more generalization and show less. The scale can be used to measure the distance between two points and to calculate comparative areas.

Scales used for the reference maps range from 1:3M (large scale) to 1:48M (small scale). Insets are used to show areas of the world of particular interest or which cannot be included in the page layouts in their true position. The scale used is indicated in the margin of each map.

Map projections

The 'projection' of the three-dimensional globe onto a two-dimensional map is always a problem for cartographers. All map projections introduce distortions to either shape, area or distances. Projections for the maps in this atlas have been specifically selected to minimize these distortions. The diagrams above illustrate three types of projection used. The red lines represent the 'centres' of the projections where there is no distortion and scale is correct.

Each reference map is cut to the shape of the graticule (the lines of latitude and longitude), which is determined by the projection used. This gives each map a unique shape, suggesting its position on the globe, as illustrated by the examples on the diagrams.

Geographical names

There is no single standard way of spelling names or of converting them from one alphabet, or symbol set, to another. Instead, conventional ways of spelling have evolved, and the results often differ significantly from the original name in the local language. Familiar examples in English include Munich (München in German), Florence (Firenze in Italian) and Moscow (Moskva from Russian). A further complication is that in many countries different languages are in use in different regions.

These factors, and any changes in official languages, have to be taken into account when creating maps. The policy in this atlas is generally to use local name forms which are officially recognized by the governments of the countries concerned. This is a basic principle laid down by the Permanent Committee on Geographical Names (PCGN) – the body responsible for determining official UK government policy on place names around the world. PCGN rules are also applied to the conversion of non-roman alphabet names, for example in the Russian Federation, into the roman alphabet used in English.

However, English conventional name forms are used for the most well-known places for which such a form is in common use. In these cases, the local form is included in brackets on the map and appears as a cross-reference in the index. Other alternative names, such as well-known historical names or those in other languages, may also be included in brackets. All country names and those for international physical features appear in their English forms.

Boundaries

The status of nations and their boundaries, and the names associated with them, are shown in this atlas as they are in reality at the time of going to press, as far as can be ascertained. All recent changes of the status of nations and their boundaries have been taken into account. Where international boundaries are the subject of dispute, the aim is to take a strictly neutral viewpoint and every reasonable attempt is made to show where an active territorial dispute exists. Generally, prominence is given to the situation as it exists on the ground (the *de facto* situation). The depiction on the maps of boundaries and their current status varies accordingly.

International boundaries are shown on all the reference maps, and those of a large enough scale also include internal administrative boundaries of selected countries. The delineation of international boundaries in the sea is often a very contentious issue, and in many cases an official alignment is not defined. Boundaries in the sea are generally only shown where they are required to clarify the ownership of specific islands or island groups.

Indexing

All names appearing on the reference maps are included in the index and can be easily found from the information included in the index entry. Details of all alternative name forms are included in the index entries and as cross-references. Gazetteer entries, with important geographical information, are included for selected places and features. Full details of index policies and content can be found in the Introduction to the Index on page 225.

SETTLEMENTS

Population	National Capital	Administrative Capital	Other City or Town
over 5 million	**BEIJING** ✡	**Tianjin** ◉	**New York** ◉
1 million to 5 million	**KĀBUL** ✡	**Sydney** ◉	**Kaohsiung** ◉
500 000 to 1 million	BANGUI ✡	Trujillo ◎	Jeddah ◎
100 000 to 500 000	WELLINGTON ✡	Mansa ⊙	Apucarana ⊙
50 000 to 100 000	PORT OF SPAIN ✡	Potenza ○	Arecibo ○
10 000 to 50 000	MALABO ✪	Chinhoyi ○	Ceres ○
1 000 to 10 000	VALLETTA ✪	Ati ○	Venta ○
under 1000		Chhukha ○	Shapki ○

Built-up area

BOUNDARIES

━◆━◆━	International boundary
▫▫▫▫▫	Disputed international boundary or alignment unconfirmed
━━━━	Administrative boundary
• • • • •	Ceasefire line

MISCELLANEOUS

----------	National park
———	Reserve or Regional park
✿	Site of specific interest
▭▭▭▭▭	Wall

LAND AND SEA FEATURES

	Desert
	Oasis
	Lava field
¹²³⁴ △	Volcano *height in metres*
	Marsh
	Ice cap / Glacier
	Escarpment
	Coral reef
¹²³⁴	Pass *height in metres*

LAKES AND RIVERS

	Lake
	Impermanent lake
	Salt lake or lagoon
	Impermanent salt lake
	Dry salt lake or salt pan
¹²³	Lake height *surface height above sea level, in metres*
———	River
-------	Impermanent river or watercourse
‖	Waterfall
—	Dam
∣	Barrage

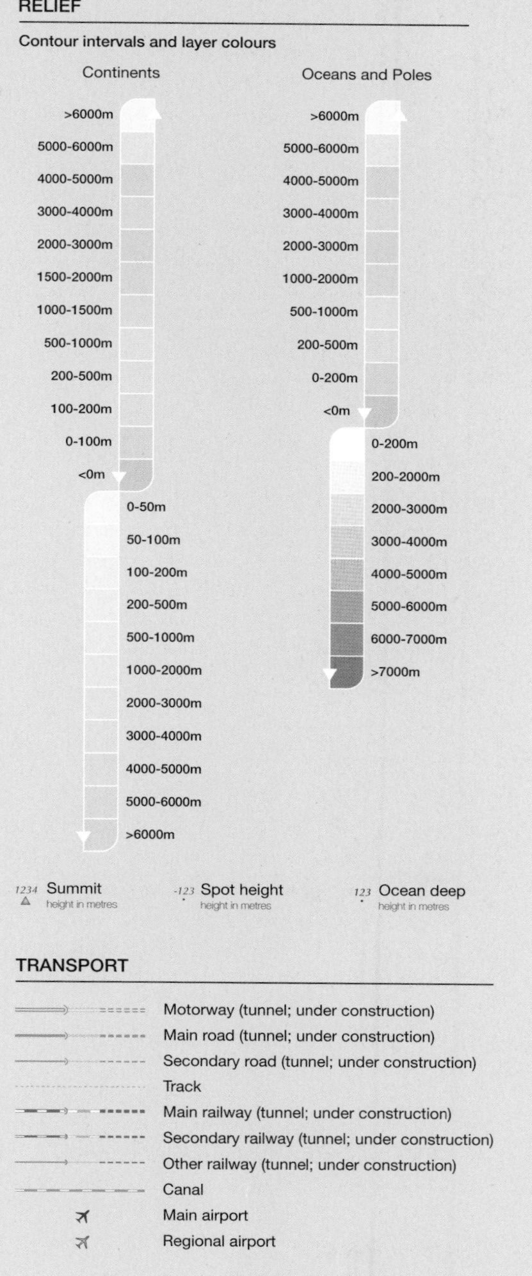

RELIEF

Contour intervals and layer colours

Continents

>6000m
5000-6000m
4000-5000m
3000-4000m
2000-3000m
1500-2000m
1000-1500m
500-1000m
200-500m
100-200m
0-100m
<0m
0-50m
50-100m
100-200m
200-500m
500-1000m
1000-2000m
2000-3000m
3000-4000m
4000-5000m
5000-6000m
>6000m

Oceans and Poles

>6000m
5000-6000m
4000-5000m
3000-4000m
2000-3000m
1000-2000m
500-1000m
200-500m
0-200m
<0m
0-200m
200-2000m
2000-3000m
3000-4000m
4000-5000m
5000-6000m
6000-7000m
>7000m

¹²³⁴ △ Summit *height in metres*	·¹²³ Spot height *height in metres*	₁₂₃ Ocean deep *height in metres*

TRANSPORT

━━━ ═════	Motorway (tunnel; under construction)
━━━ -------	Main road (tunnel; under construction)
━━━ -------	Secondary road (tunnel; under construction)
·········	Track
━┥━┝━ -------	Main railway (tunnel; under construction)
━━━ -------	Secondary railway (tunnel; under construction)
━━━ -------	Other railway (tunnel; under construction)
━━━	Canal
✈	Main airport
✈	Regional airport

SATELLITE IMAGERY

MAIN SATELLITES/SENSORS

satellite/sensor name	launch dates	owner	aims and applications	wavelengths	resolution of imagery	web address
Landsat 4, 5, 7	July 1972-April 1999	National Aeronautics and Space Administration (NASA), USA	The first satellite to be designed specifically for observing the Earth's surface. Originally set up to produce images of use for agriculture and geology. Today is of use for numerous environmental and scientific applications.	Visible, near-infrared, short-wave and thermal infrared wavelength bands.	15m in the panchromatic band (only on Landsat 7), 30m in the six visible, near and short-wave infrared bands and 60m in the thermal infrared band.	geo.arc.nasa.gov ls7pm3.gsfc.nasa.gov
SPOT 1, 2, 3, 4 (Satellite Pour l'Observation de la Terre)	February 1986-March 1998	Centre National d'Etudes Spatiales (CNES) and Spot Image, France	Particularly useful for monitoring land use, water resources research, coastal studies and cartography.	Visible and near infrared.	Panchromatic 10m. Multispectral 20m.	www.cnes.fr www.spotimage.fr
Space Shuttle	Regular launches from 1981	NASA, USA	Each shuttle mission has separate aims. Astronauts take photographs with high specification hand held cameras. The Shuttle Radar Topography Mission (SRTM) in 2000 obtained the most complete near-global high-resolution database of the earth's topography.	Visible with hand held cameras. Radar on SRTM Mission.	SRTM: 30m for US and 90m for rest of the world.	science.ksc.nasa.gov/shuttle/countdown www.jpl.nasa.gov/srtm
IKONOS	September 1999	Space Imaging	First commercial high-resolution satellite. Useful for a variety of applications mainly Cartography, Defence, Urban Planning, Agriculture, Forestry and Insurance.	Visible and near infrared.	Panchromatic 1m. Multispectral 4m.	www.spaceimaging.com

ADDITIONAL IMAGERY

satellite/sensor name	web address
ASTER	asterweb.jpl.nasa.gov www.nasda.go.jp
SeaWIFS	seawifs.gsfc.nasa.gov
Radarsat	www.rsi.ca
MODIS	modis.gsfc.nasa.gov
TOPEX/Poseidon	topex.www.jpl.nasa.gov
ERS-1 (European Space Agency) Earth Resources Satellite	earthnet.esrin.esa.it

PHOTOGRAPHS AND IMAGES

The thematic pages of the atlas contain a wide variety of photographs and images. These are a mixture of 3-D perspective views, terrestrial and aerial photographs and satellite imagery. All are used to illustrate specific themes and to give an indication of the variety of imagery, and different means of visualizing the Earth, available today. The main types of imagery used in the atlas are described in the table above.

Satellite imagery, and the related science of satellite remote sensing – the acquisition, processing and interpretation of images captured by satellites – is a particularly valuable tool in observing and monitoring the Earth. Satellite sensors can capture electromagnetic radiation in a variety of wavelengths, including those visible to the eye (colours), infrared wavelengths and microwave and radio radiation as detected by radar sensors. The data received by the sensors can be processed in different ways to allow detailed interpretation of the landscape and environmental conditions. Panchromatic images represent a single wavelength in values of grey (black and white) while multispectral sensors can combine several wavelengths in a single image. Imagery also varies in the amount of detail it can show. The ability to distinguish visual detail, and the size of the smallest feature which can be detected, is known as the image's resolution, and is usually expressed in metres.

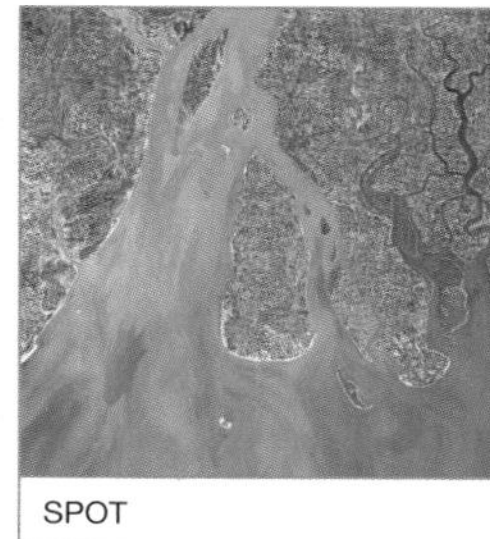

SPOT

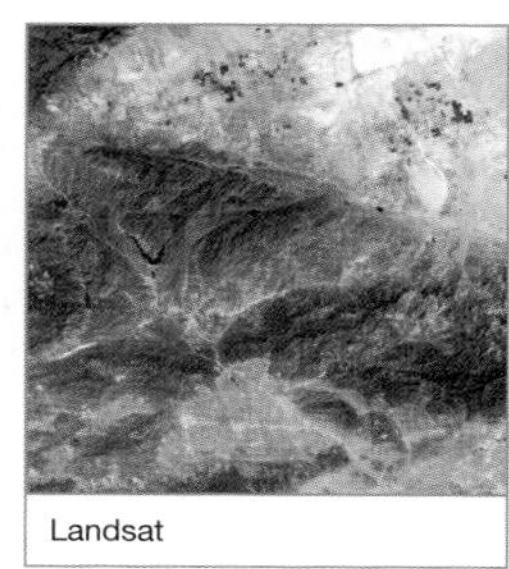

Landsat

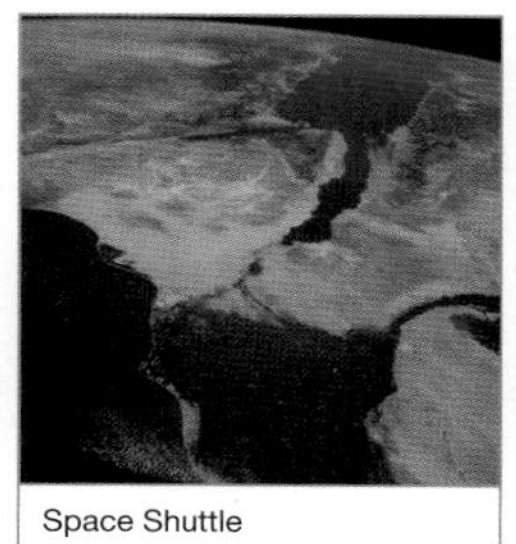

Space Shuttle

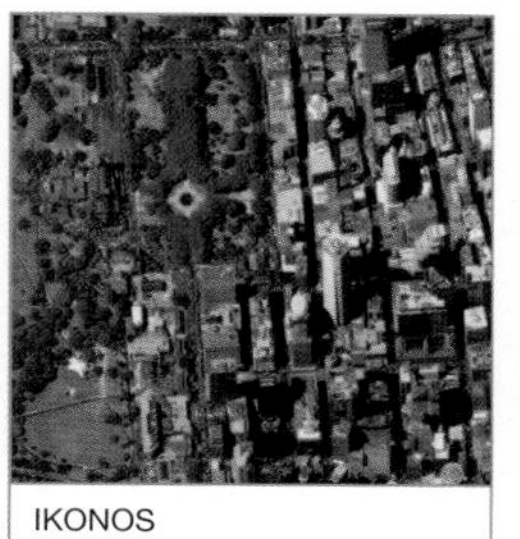

IKONOS

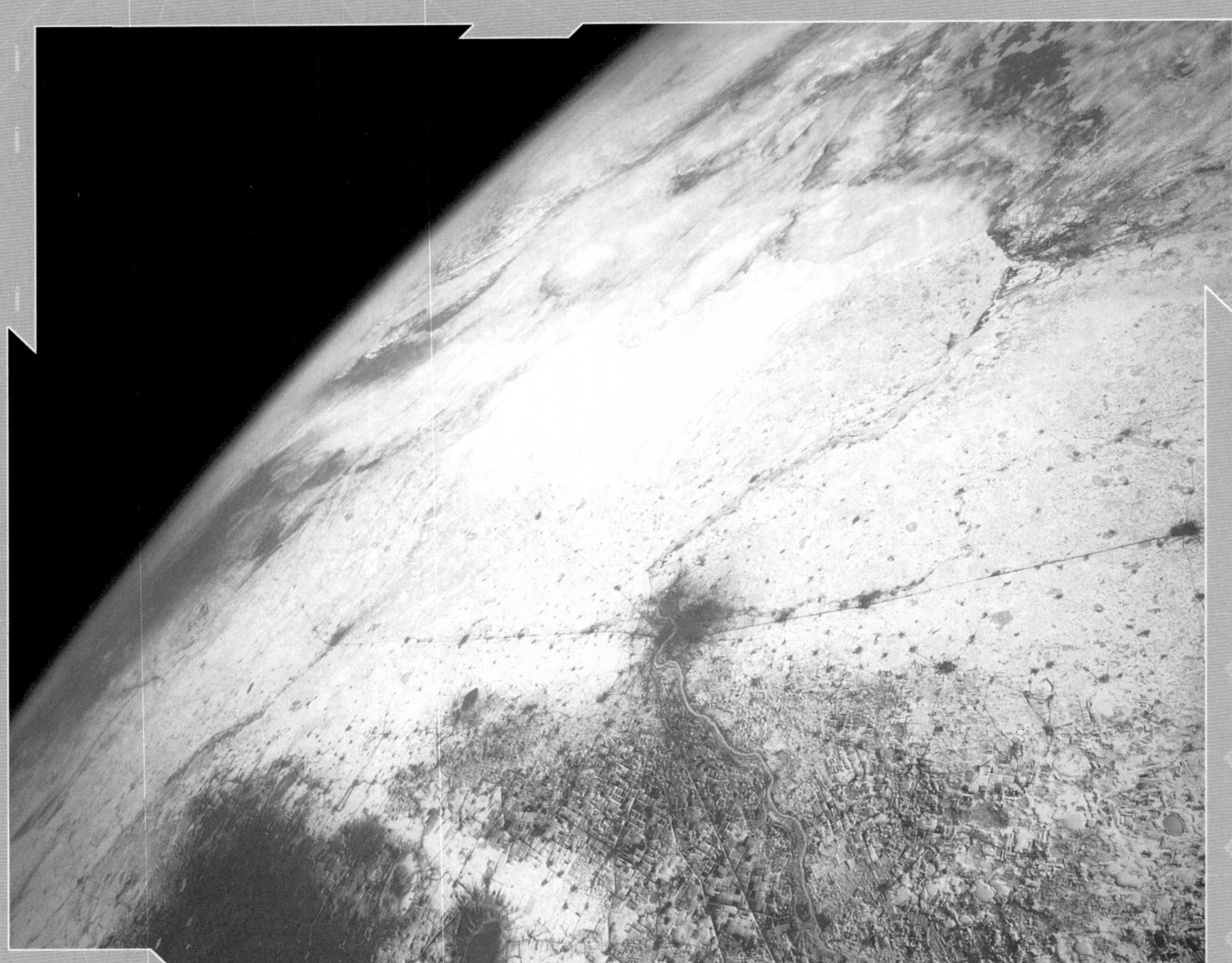

Omsk, *Russian Federation*

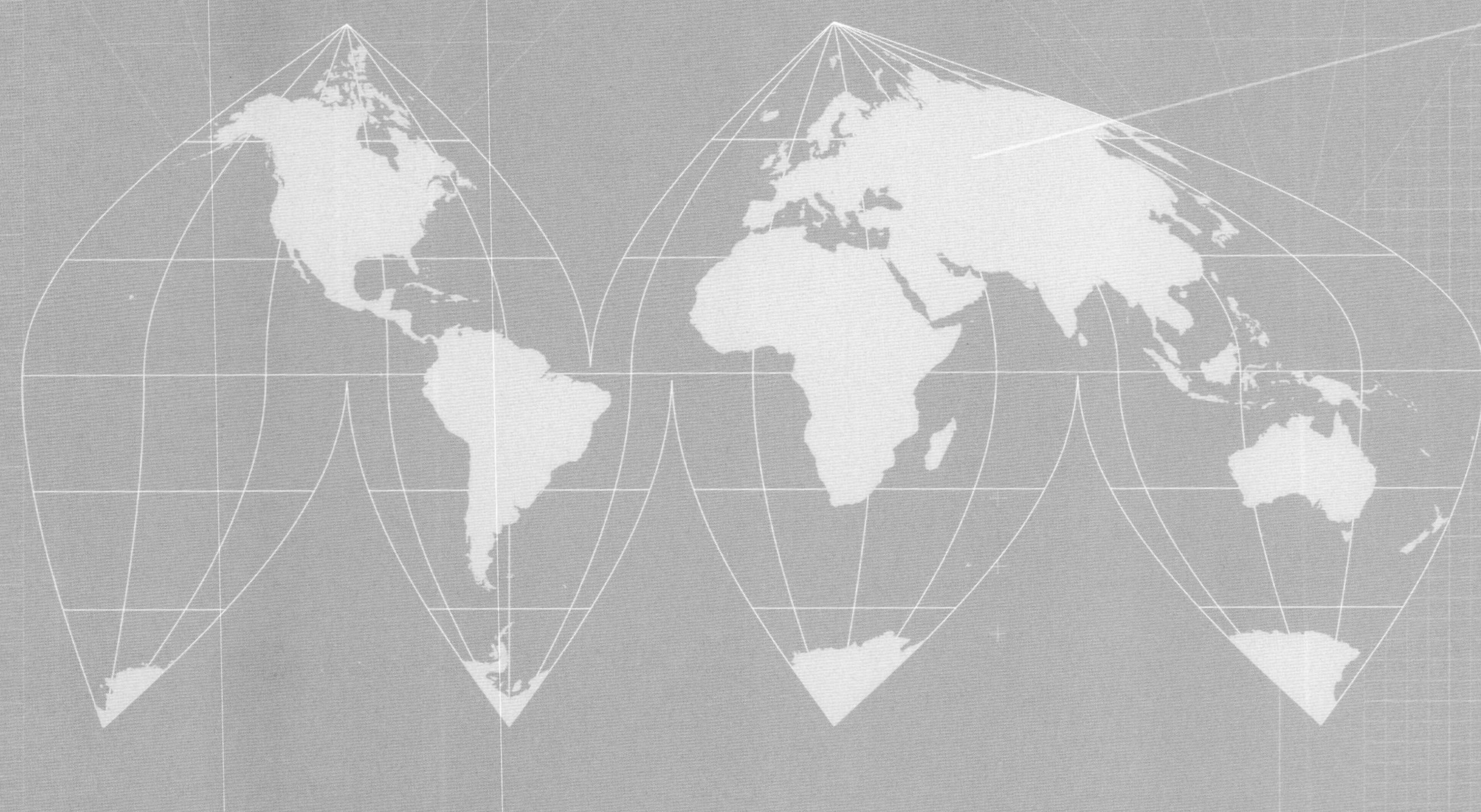

world

[contents]

world[physical features]

1 Nile Delta and Sinai Peninsula, *Africa/Asia*

Several distinct physical features can be seen in this oblique Shuttle photograph which looks southeast from above the Mediterranean Sea over northeast Africa and southwest Asia. The dark, triangular area at the bottom of the photograph is the Nile delta. The Sinai peninsula in the centre of the image is flanked by the two elongated water bodies of the Gulf of Aqaba on the left, and the Gulf of Suez on the right. These gulfs merge to form the Red Sea. The Dead Sea is also visible on the left edge of the image.

Satellite/Sensor : Space Shuttle

2 Himalayas, *Asia*

The Himalayan mountain chain forms a major physical barrier across Jammu and Kashmir, northern India, Nepal and Bhutan and contains the world's highest mountains. This Space Shuttle photograph looks west along the mountains. The low plains on the left contain three major rivers, the Ganges, Indus and Brahmaputra. To the right of the permanently snow-capped mountains is the Plateau of Tibet, a vast barren area over 4 000 m above sea level.

Satellite/Sensor : Space Shuttle

Fig. #01
World physical features

>6000m
5000-6000m
4000-5000m
3000-4000m
2000-3000m
1000-2000m
500-1000m
200-500m
0-200m
<0m

0-200m
200-2000m
2000-3000m
3000-4000m
4000-5000m
5000-6000m
6000-7000m
>7000m

HIGHEST MOUNTAINS

	m	ft	location	map
Mt Everest	8 848	29 028	China/Nepal	97 E4
K2	8 611	28 251	China/Jammu and Kashmir	96 C2
Kangchenjunga	8 586	28 169	India/Nepal	97 F4
Lhotse	8 516	27 939	China/Nepal	97 E3
Makalu	8 463	27 765	China/Nepal	97 E4
Cho Oyu	8 201	26 906	China/Nepal	97 E3
Dhaulagiri	8 167	26 794	Nepal	97 D3
Manaslu	8 163	26 781	Nepal	97 E3
Nanga Parbat	8 126	26 660	Jammu and Kashmir	96 B2
Annapurna I	8 091	26 545	Nepal	97 D3

LONGEST RIVERS

	km	miles	continent	map
Nile	6 695	4 160	Africa	121 F2
Amazon	6 516	4 049	South America	202 B1
Yangtze	6 380	3 964	Asia	87 G2
Mississipi-Missouri	5 969	3 709	North America	179 E7
Ob'-Irtysh	5 568	3 459	Asia	38 G3-39 I5
Yenisey-Angara-Selenga	5 550	3 448	Asia	39 I2-K4
Yellow	5 464	3 395	Asia	85 H4
Congo	4 667	2 900	Africa	127 B6
Rio de la Plata - Parana	4 500	2 796	South America	204 F3
Irtysh	4 440	2 759	Asia	38 G3

LARGEST ISLANDS

	sq km	sq miles	location	map
Greenland	2 175 600	840 004	North America	165 O3
New Guinea	808 510	312 167	Oceania	73 J8
Borneo	745 561	287 863	Asia	77 F2
Madagascar	587 040	266 657	Africa	131 J3
Baffin Island	507 451	195 927	North America	165 L2
Sumatra	473 606	182 860	Asia	76 C3
Honshu	227 414	87 805	Asia	91 F6
Great Britain	218 476	84 354	Europe	47 J9
Victoria Island	217 291	83 897	North America	165 H2
Ellesmere Island	196 236	75 767	North America	165 K2

LARGEST LAKES

	sq km	sq miles	continent	map
Caspian Sea	371 000	143 243	Asia / Europe	102 B4
Lake Superior	82 100	31 698	North America	172 D3
Lake Victoria	68 800	26 563	Africa	128 B5
Lake Huron	59 600	23 011	North America	173 I6
Lake Michigan	57 800	22 316	North America	172 E7
Aral Sea	33 640	12 988	Asia	102 D3
Lake Tanganyika	32 900	12 702	Africa	129 A6
Great Bear Lake	31 328	12 095	North America	166 F1
Lake Baikal	30 500	11 776	Asia	39 K4
Lake Nyasa	30 044	11 600	Africa	129 B7

EARTH'S DIMENSIONS

Equatorial diameter	12 756.274 km (7 926.381 miles)
Polar diameter	12 713.505 km (7 899.806 miles)
Mass	5.974 X 10²¹ tonnes
Total area	509 450 000 sq km/196 672 000 sq miles
Land area	149 450 000 sq km/57 688 000 sq miles
Water area	360 000 000 sq km/138 984 000 sq miles
Volume	1 083 207 X 10⁶ cubic km/259 875 X 10⁶ cubic miles

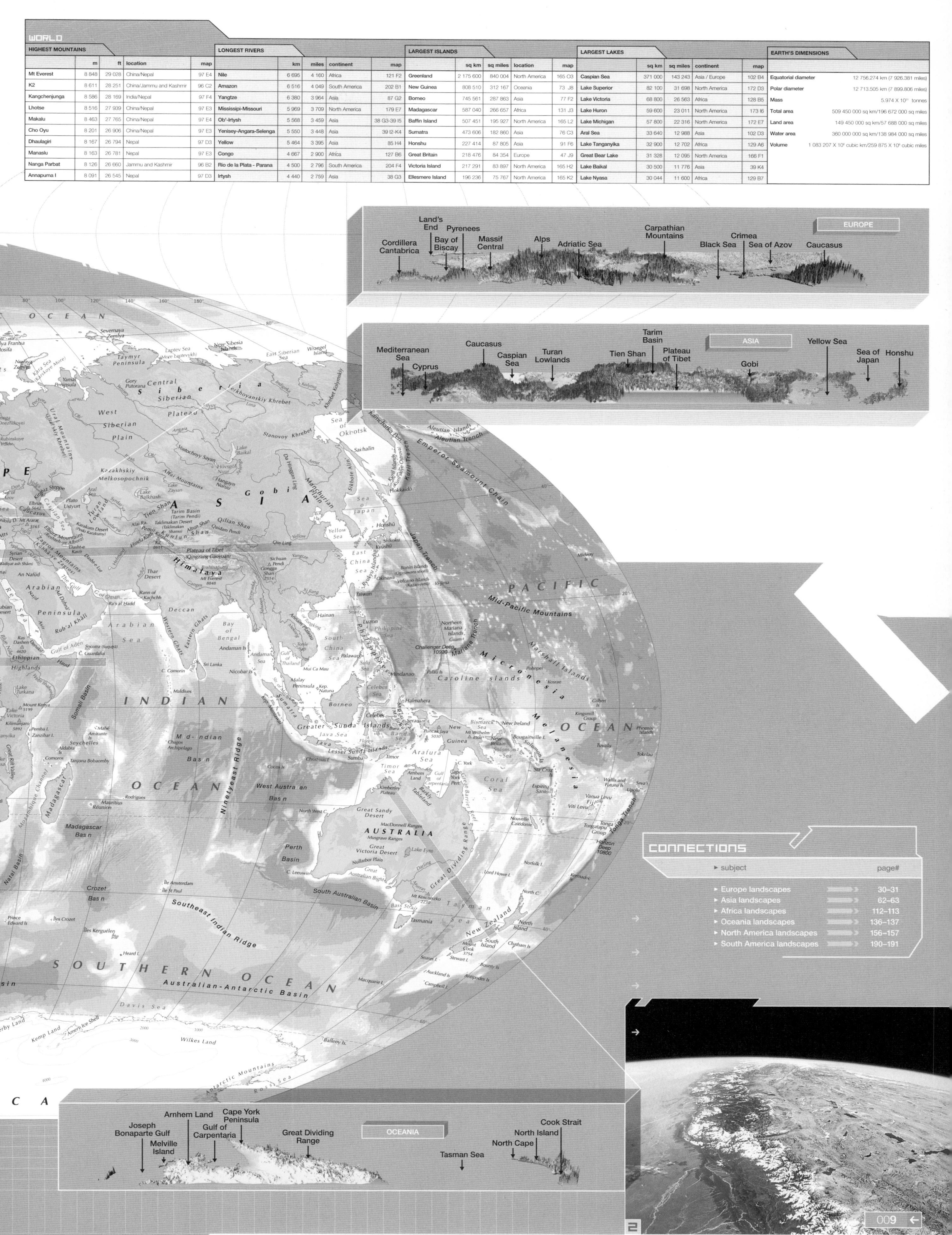

EUROPE

Cordillera Cantabrica · Land's End · Pyrenees · Bay of Biscay · Massif Central · Alps · Adriatic Sea · Carpathian Mountains · Black Sea · Crimea · Sea of Azov · Caucasus

ASIA

Mediterranean Sea · Cyprus · Caucasus · Caspian Sea · Turan Lowlands · Tien Shan · Tarim Basin · Plateau of Tibet · Gobi · Yellow Sea · Sea of Japan · Honshu

OCEANIA

Joseph Bonaparte Gulf · Melville Island · Arnhem Land · Gulf of Carpentaria · Cape York Peninsula · Great Dividing Range · Tasman Sea · North Cape · North Island · Cook Strait

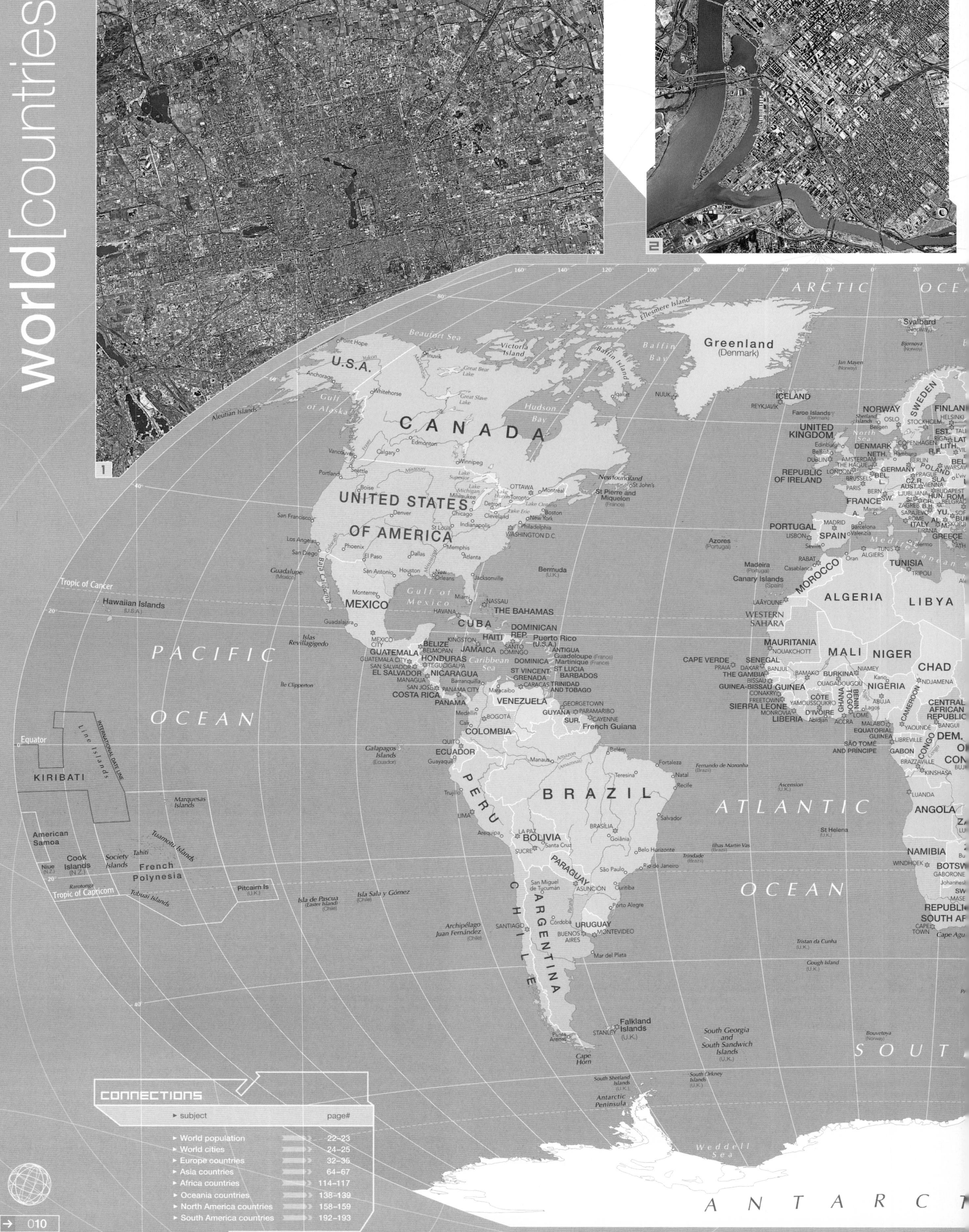

world[countries]

CONNECTIONS

Point Hope
Beaufort Sea
Ellesmere Island
Svalbard (Norway)

Inuvik
Greenland (Denmark)
Victoria Island
Baffin Island
Bjørnøya (Norway)

ARCTIC OCEAN

Jan Mayen (Norway)

U.S.A.
Anchorage
Whitehorse
Great Bear Lake
Baffin Bay
NUUK
REYKJAVÍK
ICELAND
Faroe Islands (Denmark)
NORWAY
SWEDEN
FINLAND
HELSINKI
OSLO
STOCKHOLM

Aleutian Islands
Gulf of Alaska

Great Slave Lake
Iqaluit
Shetland Islands
Bergen
EST. TALL
UNITED KINGDOM
RIGA LAT.
COPENHAGEN LITH.

CANADA

Edmonton
Calgary
Vancouver
Seattle
Portland
Boise

Hudson Bay

Winnipeg
Lake Superior
Lake Michigan
Lake Huron
OTTAWA
Montréal
Toronto
Lake Ontario
Lake Erie

Newfoundland
St Pierre and Miquelon (France)
St John's
Edinburgh
DUBLIN
REPUBLIC OF IRELAND
THE HAGUE
LONDON
BRUSSELS
AMSTERDAM
NETH.
BERLIN
DENMARK
GERMANY
POLAND
WARSAW
BEL.
PRAGUE
CZ. R.

UNITED STATES OF AMERICA

San Francisco
San Diego
Los Angeles
Phoenix
El Paso
Denver
St Louis
Milwaukee
Chicago
Detroit
Cleveland
Indianapolis
New York
Boston
Philadelphia
WASHINGTON D.C.
PARIS
FRANCE
Marseille
BERN
LJUBLJANA
ZAGREB
BUDAPEST
HUN. ROM.
VIENNA
SLVK.
SARAJEVO
YU.
BELGRADE
ITALY
ROME
SKOPJE
TIRANA

Dallas
Memphis
Atlanta
Jacksonville

PORTUGAL
LISBON
MADRID
SPAIN
Barcelona
Valencia
Sevilla

Azores (Portugal)

Bermuda (U.K.)

GREECE
ATH

Tropic of Cancer

San Antonio
Houston
New Orleans
Monterrey
Guadalupe (Mexico)

Gulf of Mexico
Miami
NASSAU
THE BAHAMAS

Madeira (Portugal)
Canary Islands (Spain)
RABAT
Casablanca
Oran
TUNIS
ALGIERS
TUNISIA
TRIPOLI

MOROCCO

Hawaiian Islands (U.S.A.)

MEXICO
Guadalajara
MEXICO CITY
HAVANA
CUBA

LAÂYOUNE
WESTERN SAHARA
ALGERIA
LIBYA

Islas Revillagigedo

BELIZE
BELMOPAN
GUATEMALA
GUATEMALA CITY
HONDURAS
TEGUCIGALPA
SAN SALVADOR
EL SALVADOR
NICARAGUA
MANAGUA

DOMINICAN REP.
HAITI
KINGSTON
JAMAICA
SANTO DOMINGO
PUERTO RICO (U.S.A.)
ANTIGUA
Guadeloupe (France)
Martinique (France)
DOMINICA
ST LUCIA
BARBADOS
ST VINCENT
GRENADA

CAPE VERDE
PRAIA
MAURITANIA
NOUAKCHOTT
SENEGAL
DAKAR
THE GAMBIA
BANJUL
BISSAU
GUINEA-BISSAU
CONAKRY
GUINEA
FREETOWN
SIERRA LEONE
MONROVIA
LIBERIA

MALI
NIGER

BAMAKO
OUAGADOUGOU
BURKINA
NIAMEY
Kano
NIGERIA
ABUJA
NDJAMENA
CHAD

CÔTE D'IVOIRE
YAMOUSSOUKRO
Abidjan
ACCRA
GHANA
BENIN
TOGO
LOMÉ
PORTO-NOVO

PACIFIC OCEAN

SAN JOSÉ
COSTA RICA
PANAMA CITY
PANAMA

Ile Clipperton

Barranquilla
Maracaibo
CARACAS
VENEZUELA
TRINIDAD AND TOBAGO
GEORGETOWN
GUYANA
PARAMARIBO
SUR.
CAYENNE
French Guiana

MALABO
EQUATORIAL GUINEA
LIBREVILLE
GABON
SÃO TOMÉ AND PRÍNCIPE
YAOUNDÉ
CAMEROON
BANGUI
CENTRAL AFRICAN REPUBLIC

Medellín
Cali
BOGOTÁ
COLOMBIA

BRAZZAVILLE
CONGO
KINSHASA
DEM.
CON
BUJ

Equator

Galapagos Islands (Ecuador)
QUITO
ECUADOR
Guayaquil

Manaus
Amazon
BRAZIL

Belém
Fortaleza
Fernando de Noronha (Brazil)
Natal
Recife

LUANDA
ANGOLA
Z

KIRIBATI

Line Islands
INTERNATIONAL DATE LINE

Marquesas Islands
Tuamotu Islands

PERU
Trujillo
LIMA
Teresina
BRASÍLIA
Goiânia

Ascension (U.K.)

ATLANTIC

Arequipa
LA PAZ
BOLIVIA
Santa Cruz
SUCRE

Belo Horizonte
São Paulo
Rio de Janeiro

St Helena (U.K.)

NAMIBIA
WINDHOEK

BOTSW
GABORONE

American Samoa
Cook Islands (N.Z.)
Niue
Society Islands
Tahiti
French Polynesia

PARAGUAY
ASUNCIÓN

Ilhas Martin Vas (Brazil)
Trindade (Brazil)

OCEAN

Johannesburg
SW
MASE

Rarotonga
Tubuai Islands
Pitcairn Is (U.K.)
Tropic of Capricorn

San Miguel de Tucumán
Córdoba
URUGUAY
Curitiba
Pôrto Alegre

REPUBLI
SOUTH AF
CAPE TOWN
Cape Agu

Isla de Pascua (Easter Island) (Chile)
Isla Sala y Gómez (Chile)

Archipiélago Juan Fernández (Chile)
SANTIAGO
ARGENTINA
CHILE
BUENOS AIRES
MONTEVIDEO
Mar del Plata

Tristan da Cunha (U.K.)

Gough Island (U.K.)

Bouvetøya (Norway)

Falkland Islands (U.K.)
STANLEY
Punta Arenas
Cape Horn

South Georgia and South Sandwich Islands (U.K.)

SOUT

South Shetland Islands (U.K.)
South Orkney Islands (U.K.)
Antarctic Peninsula

Weddell Sea

ANTARCTI

1 Beijing, *China*

This infrared SPOT satellite image of Beijing shows the extent of the capital city of China spreading out from the Forbidden City and Tiananmen Square, just to the right of the lake in the centre. The central city has a very marked grid-iron street pattern, with very densely packed low-rise buildings. On the outskirts, areas of intensive cultivation are represented in shades of red.

Satellite/Sensor : SPOT

2 Washington, D.C., *United States of America*

The capital of the United States, Washington, D.C., is shown in this infrared aerial photograph. The city is situated on the confluence of the Potomac and Anacostia rivers, seen here to the left and bottom of the photograph respectively. It has become a leading political, educational and research centre. The Pentagon, home of the US Department of Defense is at the far left of the photograph and The Mall, the Capitol, the White House and Union Station can all be seen in the centre.

3 La Paz, *Bolivia*

This infrared satellite image shows the highest capital in the world, La Paz, which lies at a height of over 3 500 metres above sea level. It is located at the edge of the Altiplano between two mountain belts within the Andes mountains. The mountains seen at the top of the image have year-round snow cover. The grey-blue area to the right of centre is the urban area of La Paz, with the city's airport clearly visible to the west.

Satellite/Sensor : SPOT

4 Mauritania/Senegal, *Africa*

The Senegal river creates a natural border between the northeast African countries of Mauritania and Senegal. The top of this infrared satellite image shows the southern edge of the Sahara desert in Mauritania. The semi-desert southern fringe of the Sahara, the Sahel, stretches east from Mauritania to Chad. The orange-red colour in the bottom half of the image represents mixed scrub and bush savanna vegetation of Senegal.

Satellite/Sensor : SPOT

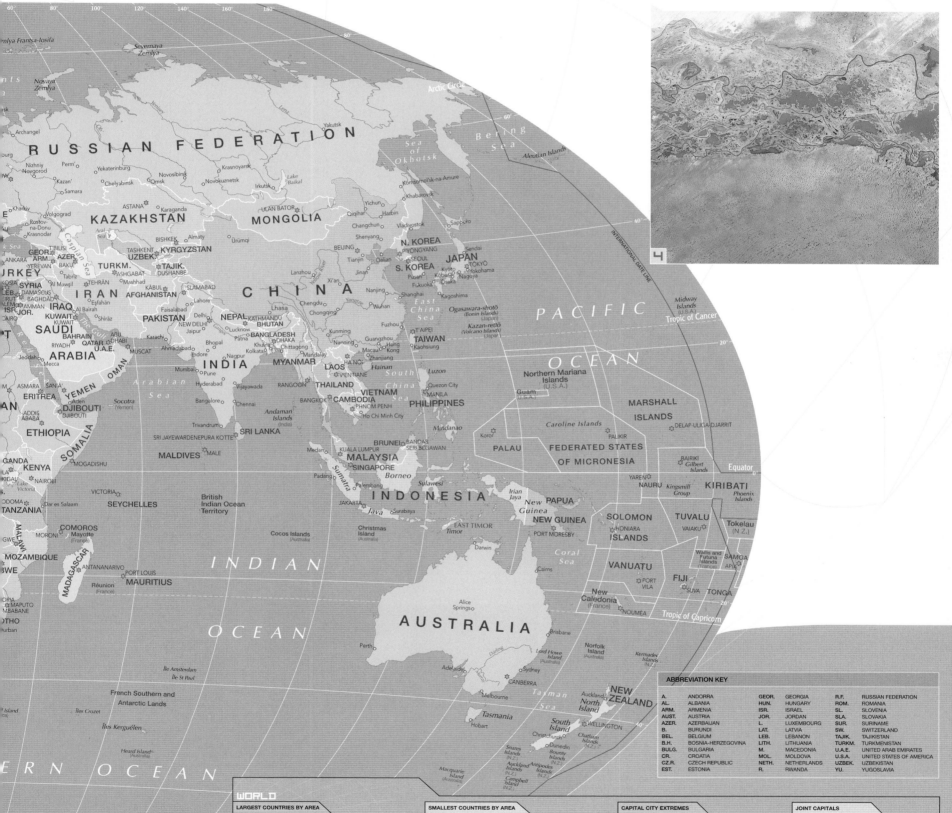

ABBREVIATION KEY

A.	ANDORRA	GEOR.	GEORGIA	R.F.	RUSSIAN FEDERATION
AL.	ALBANIA	HUN.	HUNGARY	ROM.	ROMANIA
ARM.	ARMENIA	ISR.	ISRAEL	SL.	SLOVENIA
AUST.	AUSTRIA	JOR.	JORDAN	SLA.	SLOVAKIA
AZER.	AZERBAIJAN	L.	LUXEMBOURG	SUR.	SURINAME
B.	BURUNDI	LAT.	LATVIA	SW.	SWITZERLAND
BEL.	BELGIUM	LEB.	LEBANON	TAJIK.	TAJIKISTAN
B.H.	BOSNIA-HERZEGOVINA	LITH.	LITHUANIA	TURKM.	TURKMENISTAN
BULG.	BULGARIA	M.	MACEDONIA	U.A.E.	UNITED ARAB EMIRATES
CR.	CROATIA	MOL.	MOLDOVA	U.S.A.	UNITED STATES OF AMERICA
CZ.R.	CZECH REPUBLIC	NETH.	NETHERLANDS	UZBEK.	UZBEKISTAN
EST.	ESTONIA	R.	RWANDA	YU.	YUGOSLAVIA

WORLD

LARGEST COUNTRIES BY AREA

country	sq km	sq miles	map
1. Russian Federation	17 075 400	6 592 849	38–39
2. Canada	9 970 610	3 849 674	164–165
3. United States of America	9 809 378	3 787 422	170–171
4. China	9 584 492	3 700 593	80–81
5. Brazil	8 547 379	3 300 161	202–203
6. Australia	7 682 395	2 966 189	144–145
7. India	3 065 027	1 183 414	92–93
8. Argentina	2 766 889	1 068 302	204–205
9. Kazakhstan	2 717 300	1 049 155	102–103
10. Sudan	2 505 813	967 500	120–121

SMALLEST COUNTRIES BY AREA

country	sq km	sq miles	map
1. Vatican City	0.5	0.2	56
2. Monaco	2	1	51
3. Nauru	21	8	145
4. Tuvalu	25	10	145
5. San Marino	61	24	56
6. Liechtenstein	160	62	51
7. St Kitts and Nevis	261	101	187
8. Maldives	298	115	93
9. Grenada	378	146	187
10. St Vincent and the Grenadines	389	150	187

CAPITAL CITY EXTREMES

			map
Most populous	Tōkyō, Japan	26 444 000	91 F7
Least populous	Yaren, Nauru	600	145 F2
Highest	La Paz, Bolivia	3 636m / 11 910ft	200 C4
Lowest	Manama, Bahrain and Male, Maldives	0.9m / 3ft	100 B5 / 93 D10
Furthest north	Nuuk, Greenland	64° 11'N	165 N3
Furthest south	Wellington, New Zealand	41° 18'S	152 I9
Furthest east	Funafuti, Tuvalu	179° 13'E	145 G2
Furthest west	Nuku'alofa, Tonga	175° 12'W	145 H4

JOINT CAPITALS

cities	country	map
Amsterdam/The Hague	Netherlands	48 C3 / 48 B3
La Paz/Sucre	Bolivia	200 C4 / 200 D4
Pretoria/Cape Town	South Africa	133 M2 / 132 C10

world[land images]

1 Orinoco River, *South America*

The Orinoco river flows from right to left in this Shuttle photograph which looks towards the southeast. The upper section of the image shows the dense forests of the western edge of the Guiana Highlands. The main tributary joining the Orinoco is the Meta river with the town of Puerto Páez at the confluence. The Orinoco and the Meta form part of the boundary between Colombia and Venezuela.

Satellite/Sensor : Space Shuttle

2 Zaskar Mountains, *Asia*

The brackish waters of Tso Morari lake, surrounded by the Zaskar Mountains, can be seen at the left hand edge of this Shuttle photograph. North is to the right of the image. The mountains form one of the ranges at the western end of the Himalayas in the disputed area of Jammu and Kashmir. The lake is more than 4 000 m above sea level, the surrounding mountains rise to over 6 000 m.

Satellite/Sensor : Space Shuttle

3 Altiplano, *South America*

The Altiplano is a high plateau which stretches from western Bolivia to southern Peru. It has an average height of over 3 600 m and is bordered to the west and east by two main ridges of the Andes mountains. This Shuttle photograph shows part of Lake Coipasa. Unusually, the water level is high. The lake is normally a dry lakebed for the majority of the year. The photograph shows individual volcanoes which are common in this region.

Satellite/Sensor : Space Shuttle

4 French Polynesia, *Oceania*

This view of Bora-Bora, an island group within the Society Islands of French Polynesia in the southern Pacific Ocean, is typical of this area which consists of many scattered groups of islands. The main island, just visible at the top of the photograph, lies in a large lagoon surrounded by numerous coral reefs and small islands.

5 Greenland, *North America*

Icebergs are usually formed either by sections breaking off glaciers which flow into the sea, or from the breaking up of ice-sheets as temperatures start to rise in spring. This one, off the northwest coast of Greenland in the Arctic Ocean, is surrounded by flat sections of broken up sea ice.

6 Namib Desert, *Africa*

This satellite image of the west coast of Africa clearly shows the natural barrier formed by the Kuiseb river at the northern edge of the Namib Desert in Namibia. To the north of the river are the Khomas Highlands which are rich in minerals, including uranium, to the south are the extensive dunes within the desert. The town of Walvis Bay is at the mouth of the river with the area's capital of Swakopmund just to the north.

Satellite/Sensor : Landsat

7 Canyonlands, *North America*

In this infrared satellite image of the Canyonlands region of the USA, vegetation shows as red, and forests as brown. The pale colours to the lower left of the image mark the area known as the Painted Desert. North is at the bottom. The image shows the upper reaches of the Grand Canyon, formed as a result of erosion by the Colorado River. The canyon ranges from six to twenty nine kilometres across.

Satellite/Sensor : SPOT

8 Taklimakan Desert, *Asia*

This image looks east over the Kunlun Shan mountains towards the Taklimakan Desert in the Tarim Pendi basin in China. The mountains mark the northern edge of the Plateau of Tibet. The southern edge of the plateau is the Himalayas. The dark areas in the desert at the top and on the left edge of the image are fertile areas, fed by intermittent rivers, around the towns of Hotan and Shache.

Satellite/Sensor : Space Shuttle

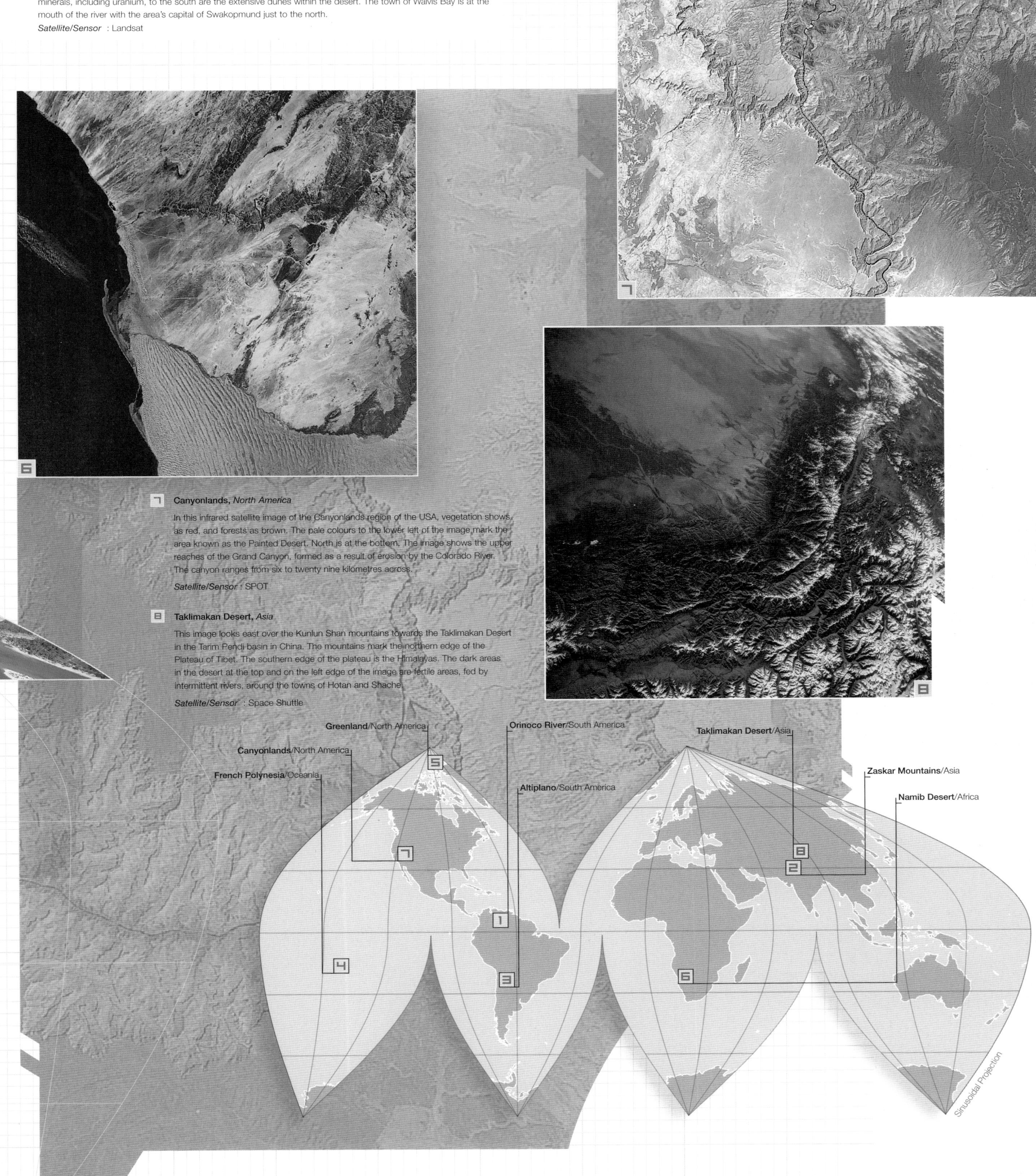

Greenland/North America
Canyonlands/North America
French Polynesia/Oceania
Orinoco River/South America
Altiplano/South America
Taklimakan Desert/Asia
Zaskar Mountains/Asia
Namib Desert/Africa

Sinusoidal Projection

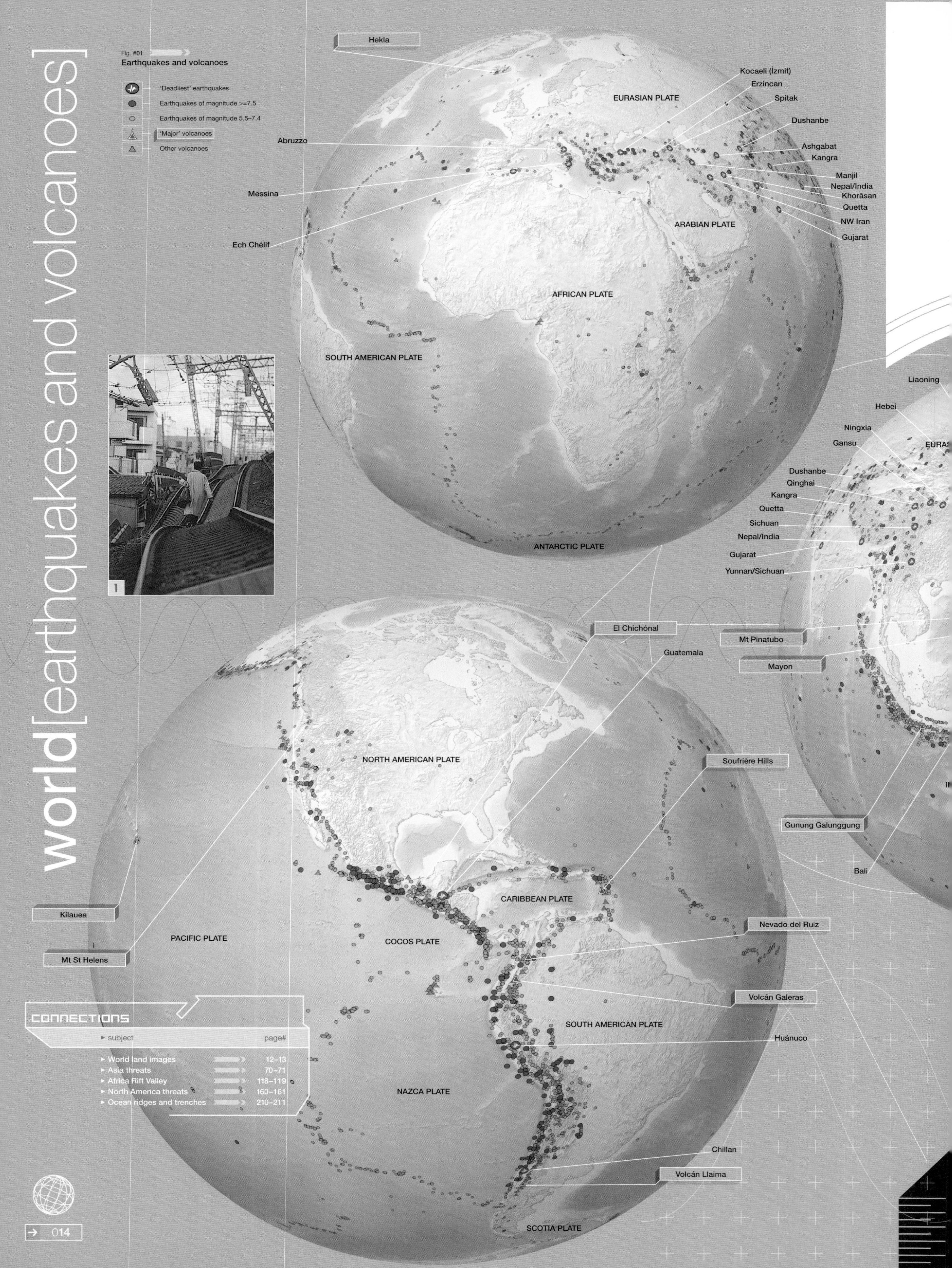

world[earthquakes and volcanoes]
Fig. #01
Earthquakes and volcanoes
'Deadliest' earthquakes
Earthquakes of magnitude >=7.5
Earthquakes of magnitude 5.5–7.4
'Major' volcanoes
Other volcanoes
Hekla
Kocaeli (İzmit)
Erzincan
Spitak
Dushanbe
Ashgabat
Kangra
Manjil
Nepal/India
Khorāsan
Quetta
NW Iran
Gujarat
Abruzzo
Messina
Ech Chélif
EURASIAN PLATE
ARABIAN PLATE
AFRICAN PLATE
SOUTH AMERICAN PLATE
ANTARCTIC PLATE
1
Liaoning
Hebei
Ningxia
Gansu
EURAS
Dushanbe
Qinghai
Kangra
Quetta
Sichuan
Nepal/India
Gujarat
Yunnan/Sichuan
El Chichónal
Guatemala
Mt Pinatubo
Mayon
Soufrière Hills
Gunung Galunggung
Bali
NORTH AMERICAN PLATE
CARIBBEAN PLATE
PACIFIC PLATE
COCOS PLATE
Kilauea
Mt St Helens
Nevado del Ruiz
Volcán Galeras
SOUTH AMERICAN PLATE
Huánuco
NAZCA PLATE
Chillan
Volcán Llaima
SCOTIA PLATE
CONNECTIONS
subject page#
World land images 12–13
Asia threats 70–71
Africa Rift Valley 118–119
North America threats 160–161
Ocean ridges and trenches 210–211
014

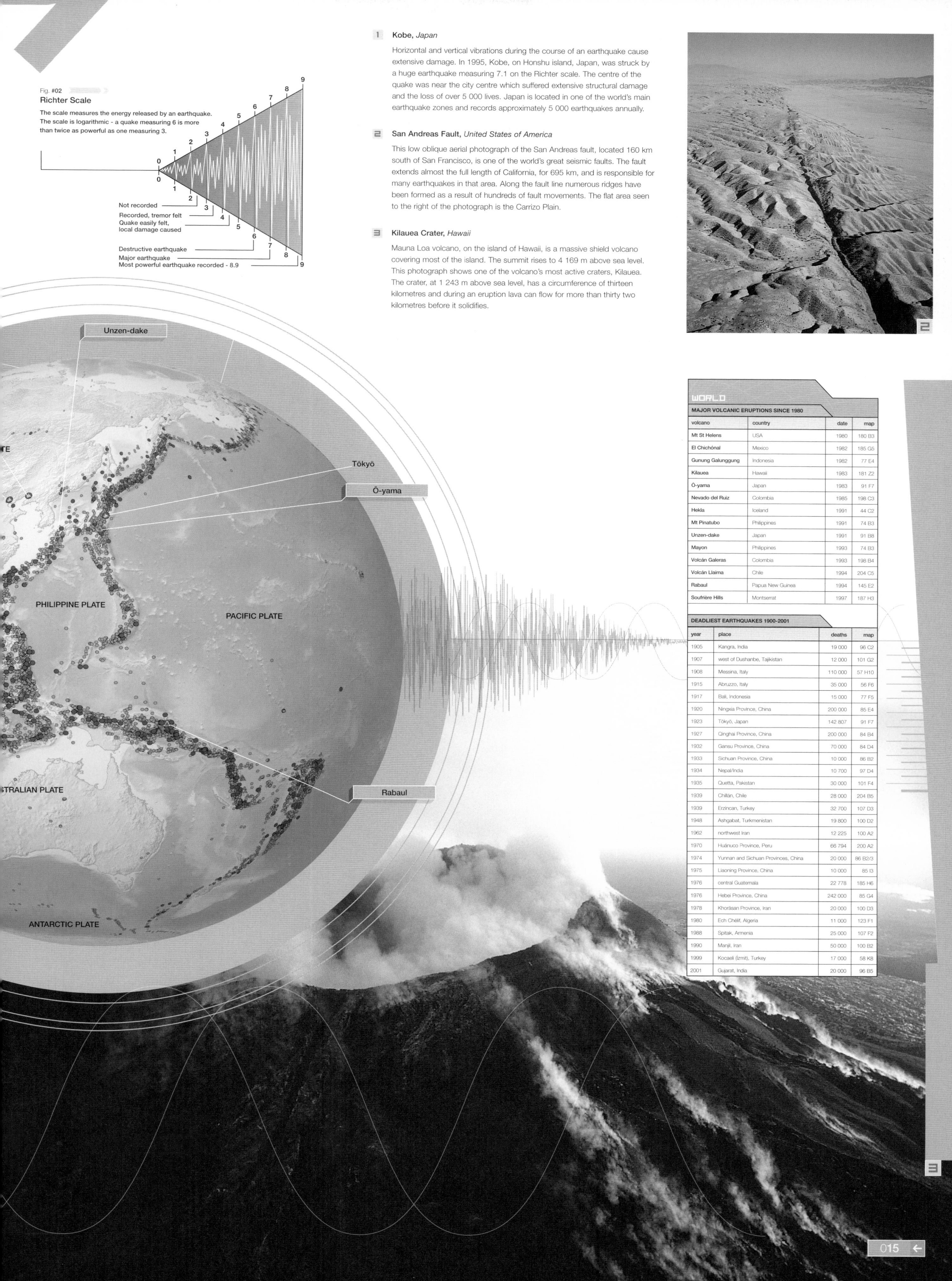

Fig. #02

Richter Scale

The scale measures the energy released by an earthquake.
The scale is logarithmic - a quake measuring 6 is more
than twice as powerful as one measuring 3.

Not recorded
Recorded, tremor felt
Quake easily felt,
local damage caused
Destructive earthquake
Major earthquake
Most powerful earthquake recorded - 8.9

1   Kobe, *Japan*

Horizontal and vertical vibrations during the course of an earthquake cause
extensive damage. In 1995, Kobe, on Honshu island, Japan, was struck by
a huge earthquake measuring 7.1 on the Richter scale. The centre of the
quake was near the city centre which suffered extensive structural damage
and the loss of over 5 000 lives. Japan is located in one of the world's main
earthquake zones and records approximately 5 000 earthquakes annually.

2   San Andreas Fault, *United States of America*

This low oblique aerial photograph of the San Andreas fault, located 160 km
south of San Francisco, is one of the world's great seismic faults. The fault
extends almost the full length of California, for 695 km, and is responsible for
many earthquakes in that area. Along the fault line numerous ridges have
been formed as a result of hundreds of fault movements. The flat area seen
to the right of the photograph is the Carrizo Plain.

3   Kilauea Crater, *Hawaii*

Mauna Loa volcano, on the island of Hawaii, is a massive shield volcano
covering most of the island. The summit rises to 4 169 m above sea level.
This photograph shows one of the volcano's most active craters, Kilauea.
The crater, at 1 243 m above sea level, has a circumference of thirteen
kilometres and during an eruption lava can flow for more than thirty two
kilometres before it solidifies.

Unzen-dake
Tōkyō
Ō-yama
Rabaul

PHILIPPINE PLATE
PACIFIC PLATE
AUSTRALIAN PLATE
ANTARCTIC PLATE

WORLD

MAJOR VOLCANIC ERUPTIONS SINCE 1980

volcano	country	date	map
Mt St Helens	USA	1980	180 B3
El Chichónal	Mexico	1982	185 G5
Gunung Galunggung	Indonesia	1982	77 E4
Kilauea	Hawaii	1983	181 Z2
Ō-yama	Japan	1983	91 F7
Nevado del Ruiz	Colombia	1985	198 C3
Hekla	Iceland	1991	44 C2
Mt Pinatubo	Philippines	1991	74 B3
Unzen-dake	Japan	1991	91 B8
Mayon	Philippines	1993	74 B3
Volcán Galeras	Colombia	1993	198 B4
Volcán Llaima	Chile	1994	204 C5
Rabaul	Papua New Guinea	1994	145 E2
Soufrière Hills	Montserrat	1997	187 H3

DEADLIEST EARTHQUAKES 1900-2001

year	place	deaths	map
1905	Kangra, India	19 000	96 C2
1907	west of Dushanbe, Tajikistan	12 000	101 G2
1908	Messina, Italy	110 000	57 H10
1915	Abruzzo, Italy	35 000	56 F6
1917	Bali, Indonesia	15 000	77 F5
1920	Ningxia Province, China	200 000	85 E4
1923	Tōkyō, Japan	142 807	91 F7
1927	Qinghai Province, China	200 000	84 B4
1932	Gansu Province, China	70 000	84 D4
1933	Sichuan Province, China	10 000	86 B2
1934	Nepal/India	10 700	97 D4
1935	Quetta, Pakistan	30 000	101 F4
1939	Chillán, Chile	28 000	204 B5
1939	Erzincan, Turkey	32 700	107 D3
1948	Ashgabat, Turkmenistan	19 800	100 D2
1962	northwest Iran	12 225	100 A2
1970	Huánuco Province, Peru	66 794	200 A2
1974	Yunnan and Sichuan Provinces, China	20 000	86 B2/3
1975	Liaoning Province, China	10 000	85 I3
1976	central Guatemala	22 778	185 H6
1976	Hebei Province, China	242 000	85 G4
1978	Khorāsan Province, Iran	20 000	100 D3
1980	Ech Chélif, Algeria	11 000	123 F1
1988	Spitak, Armenia	25 000	107 F2
1990	Manjil, Iran	50 000	100 B2
1999	Kocaeli (İzmit), Turkey	17 000	58 K8
2001	Gujarat, India	20 000	96 B5

world [climate and weather]

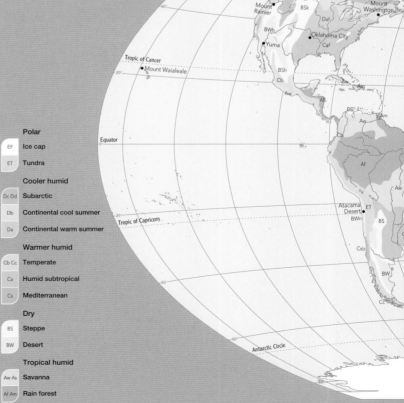

Fig. #01
Pacific Ocean surface winds
August 1999

Wind speed (m per second): >15, 12, 6, 0

Fig. #02
Atlantic Ocean surface winds
August 1999

Fig. #03
Indian Ocean surface winds
August 1999

Fig. #04
Satellite Image of Earth

Fig. #01-#03 Ocean surface winds

Winds play a major role in every aspect of weather on Earth. They affect the exchanges of heat, moisture and greenhouse gases between Earth's atmosphere and the oceans. These images were taken on 1 August 1999 from the QuikSCAT satellite carrying a radar instrument called a scatterometer which can record surface wind speeds in the oceans. In the image of the Pacific Ocean yellow spirals representing typhoon Olga can be seen moving around South Korea and the East China Sea. Intense winter storms can also be seen around Antarctica in all three images.

Satellite/Sensor : QuikSCAT/SeaWinds

Fig. #10-#11 Climate change in the future

Future climate change will depend to a large extent on the effect human activities have on the chemical composition of the atmosphere. As greenhouse gases and aerosol emissions increase the atmospheric temperatures rise. The map of predicted temperature in the 2050s shows that average annual temperatures may rise by as much as 5°C in some areas if current emission rates continue. The map of precipitation change shows some areas are likely to experience a significant increase in precipitation of over 3 mm per day, while others will experience a decrease. Such changes are likely to have significant impacts on sea level which could rise by as much as 50 cm in the next century. The changes would also have implications for water resources, food production and health.

Fig. #04 Satellite image of Earth

Images such as this from the Meteosat satellite provide valuable meteorological information on a global scale. Dense clouds appear white, thinner cloud cover as pink . A swirling frontal weather system is clearly seen in the Atlantic Ocean to the west of Europe.

Satellite/Sensor : Meteosat

Fig. #05
Major climatic regions and sub-types

Köppen classification system

- A Rainy climate with no winter: coolest month above 18°C (64.4°F).
- B Dry climates; limits are defined by formulae based on rainfall effectiveness:
  BS Steppe or semi-arid climate.
  BW Desert or arid climate.
- *C Rainy climates with mild winters: coolest month above 0°C (32°F), but below 18°C (64.4°F); warmest month above 10°C (50°F).
- *D Rainy climates with severe winters: coldest month below 0°C (32°F); warmest month above 10°C (50°F).
- E Polar climates with no warm season: warmest month below 10°C (50°F).
  ET Tundra climate: warmest month below 10°C (50°F) but above 0°C (32°F).
  EF Perpetual frost: all months below 0°C (32°F).
- a Warmest month above 22°C (71.6°F).
- b Warmest month below 22°C (71.6°F).
- c Less than four months over 10°C (50°F).
- d As 'c', but with severe cold: coldest month below -38°C (-36.4°F).
- f Constantly moist rainfall throughout the year.
- *h Warmer dry: all months above 0°C (32°F).
- *k Cooler dry: at least one month below 0°C (32°F).
- m Monsoon rain: short dry season, but is compensated by heavy rains during rest of the year.
- n Frequent fog.
- s Dry season in summer.
- w Dry season in winter.

* Modification of Köppen definition

CONNECTIONS

subject	page#
Asia threats	70–71
Africa issues	116–117
North America threats	160–161
South America impacts	196–197
Antarctica features	212–213
Arctic features	214–215

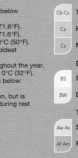

Fig. #06
Tracks of tropical storms
Wind speeds often over
160km per hour

→ Cyclone track → Willy-willies ▨ Source area of tropical storms
→ Typhoon track → Hurricane track ● Major tropical storm (1994-2000)

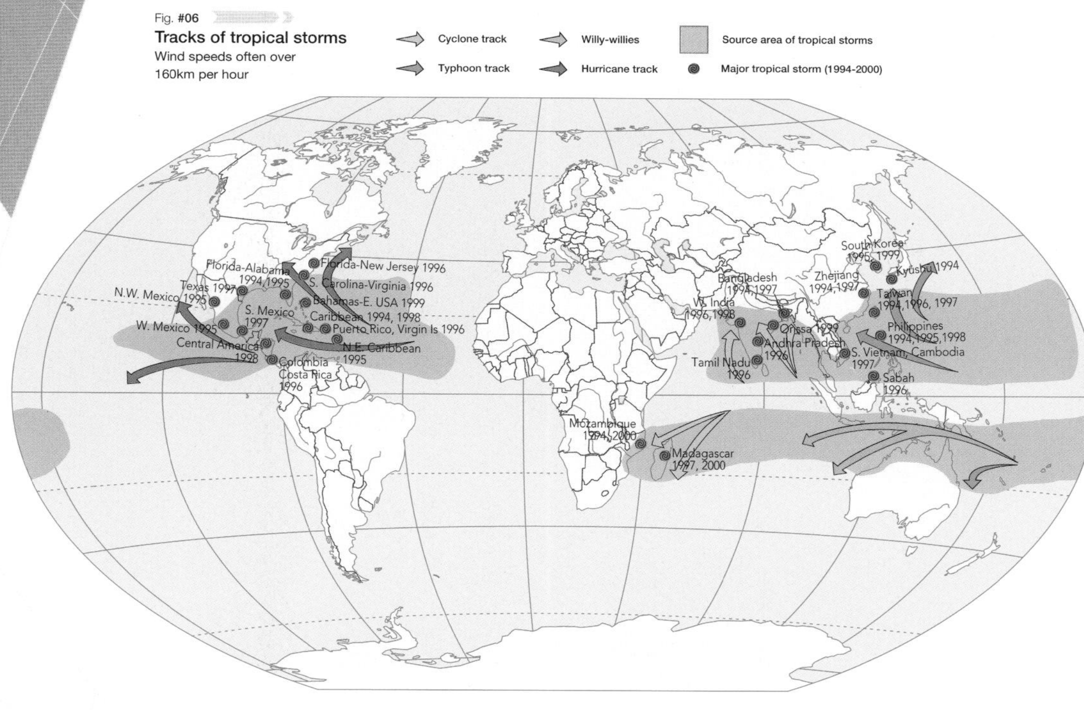

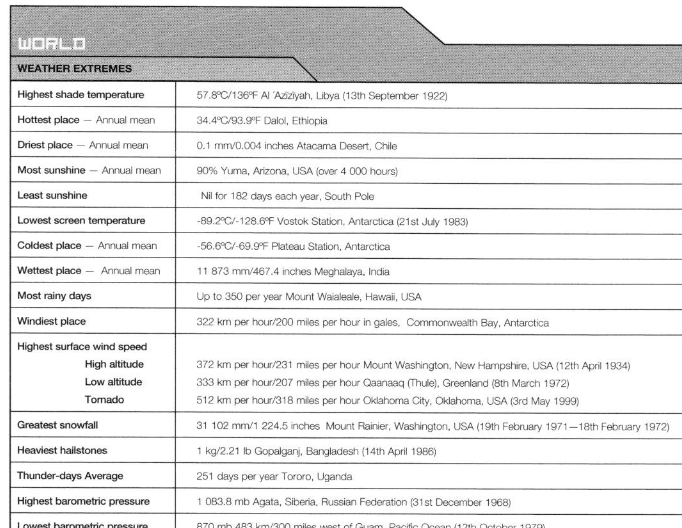

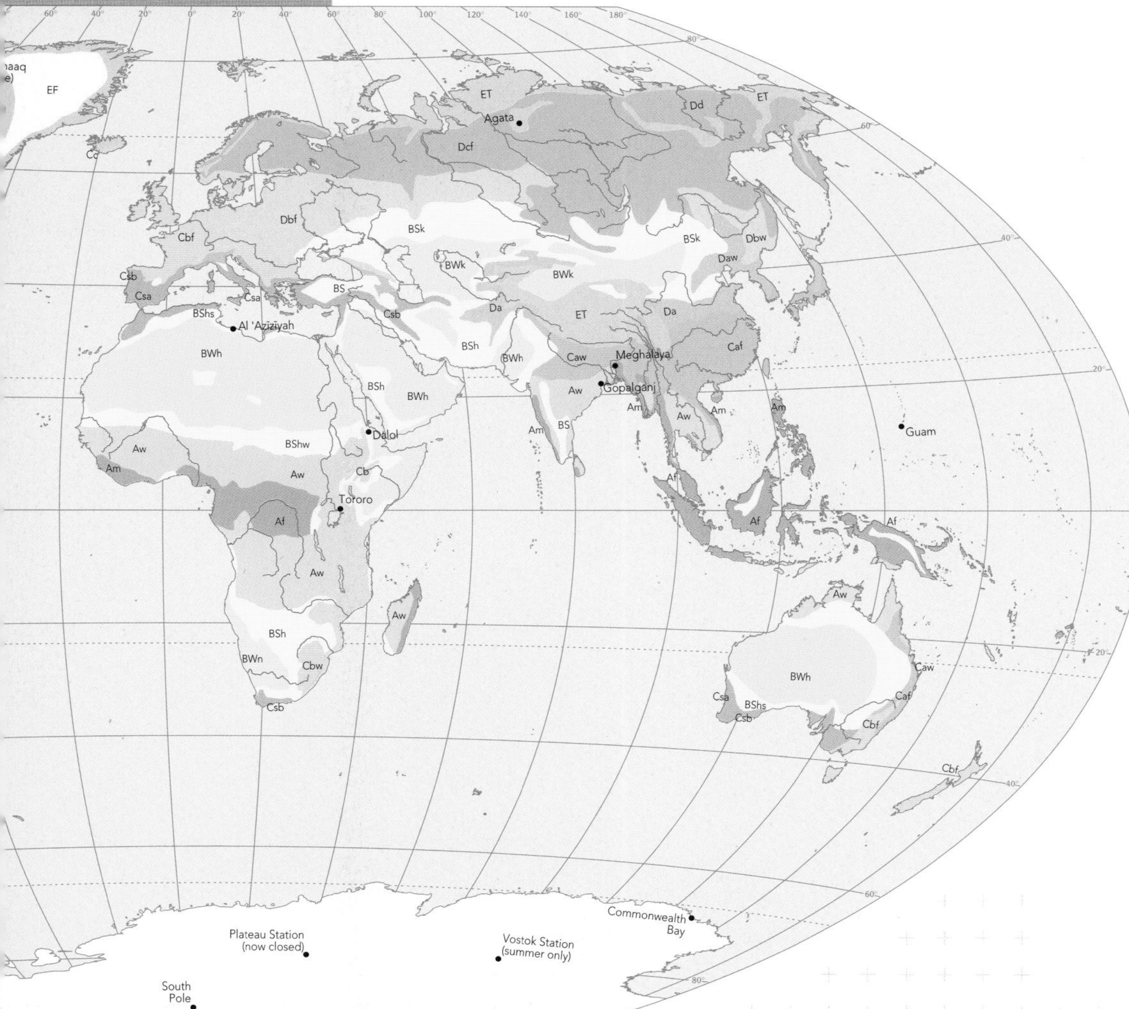

Fig. #07
Actual surface temperature
January

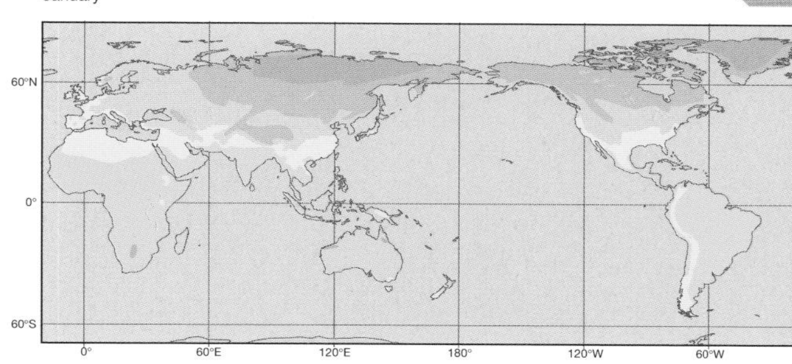

Fig. #08
Actual surface temperature
July

−32   −16   0   16   32 °C

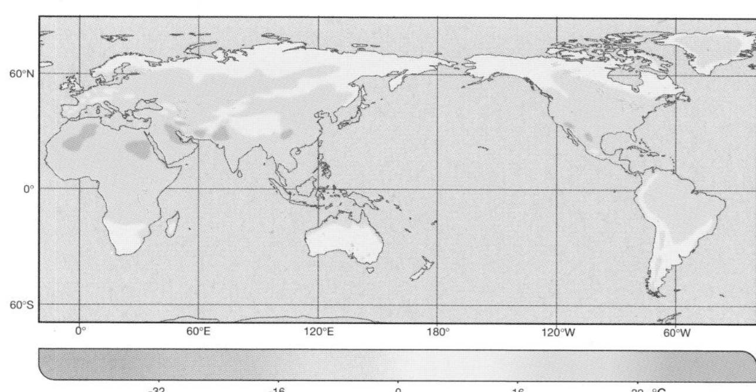

Fig. #09
Average annual precipitation

0   2.5   5   7.5   10
Precipitation (mm per day)

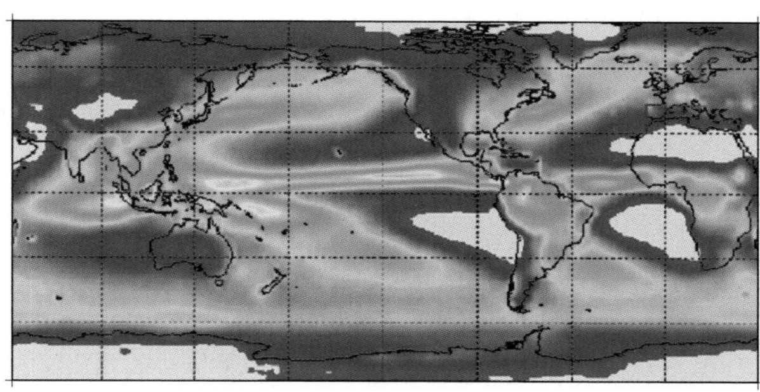

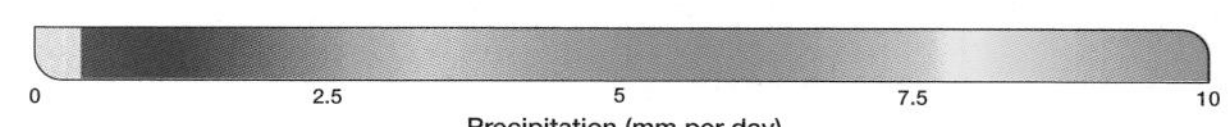

Fig. #10 - #11
Climate changes in the future

#10 Precipitation in 2050s
Predicted average precipitation change

−2   −1   0   1   2   3
Average precipitation change (mm per day)

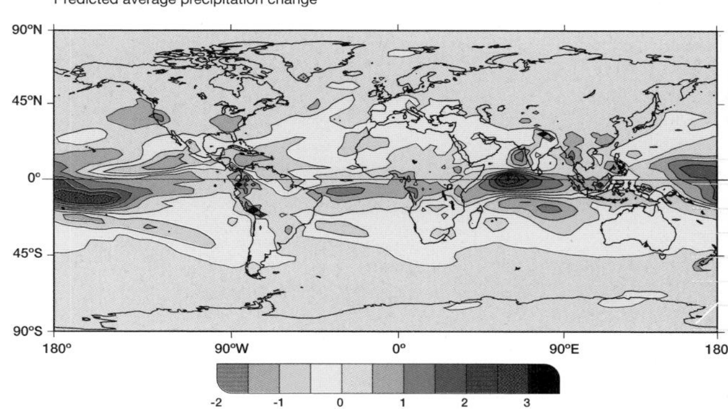

#11 Temperature in 2050s
Predicted annual mean temperature change

0   1   2   3   4   5
Annual mean temperature change (°C)

WORLD

WEATHER EXTREMES

Highest shade temperature	57.8°C/136°F Al 'Azīzīyah, Libya (13th September 1922)
Hottest place — Annual mean	34.4°C/93.9°F Dalol, Ethiopia
Driest place — Annual mean	0.1 mm/0.004 inches Atacama Desert, Chile
Most sunshine — Annual mean	90% Yuma, Arizona, USA (over 4 000 hours)
Least sunshine	Nil for 182 days each year, South Pole
Lowest screen temperature	-89.2°C/-128.6°F Vostok Station, Antarctica (21st July 1983)
Coldest place — Annual mean	-56.6°C/-69.9°F Plateau Station, Antarctica
Wettest place — Annual mean	11 873 mm/467.4 inches Meghalaya, India
Most rainy days	Up to 350 per year Mount Waialeale, Hawaii, USA
Windiest place	322 km per hour/200 miles per hour in gales, Commonwealth Bay, Antarctica
Highest surface wind speed	
High altitude	372 km per hour/231 miles per hour Mount Washington, New Hampshire, USA (12th April 1934)
Low altitude	333 km per hour/207 miles per hour Qaanaaq (Thule), Greenland (8th March 1972)
Tornado	512 km per hour/318 miles per hour Oklahoma City, Oklahoma, USA (3rd May 1999)
Greatest snowfall	31 102 mm/1 224.5 inches Mount Rainier, Washington, USA (19th February 1971 — 18th February 1972)
Heaviest hailstones	1 kg/2.21 lb Gopalganj, Bangladesh (14th April 1986)
Thunder-days Average	251 days per year Tororo, Uganda
Highest barometric pressure	1 083.8 mb Agata, Siberia, Russian Federation (31st December 1968)
Lowest barometric pressure	870 mb 483 km/300 miles west of Guam, Pacific Ocean (12th October 1979)

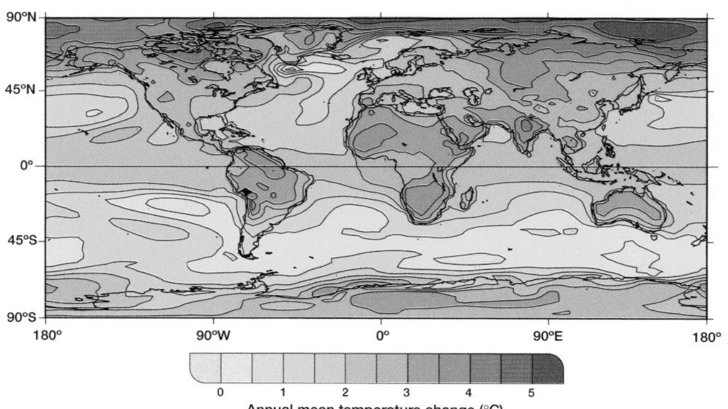

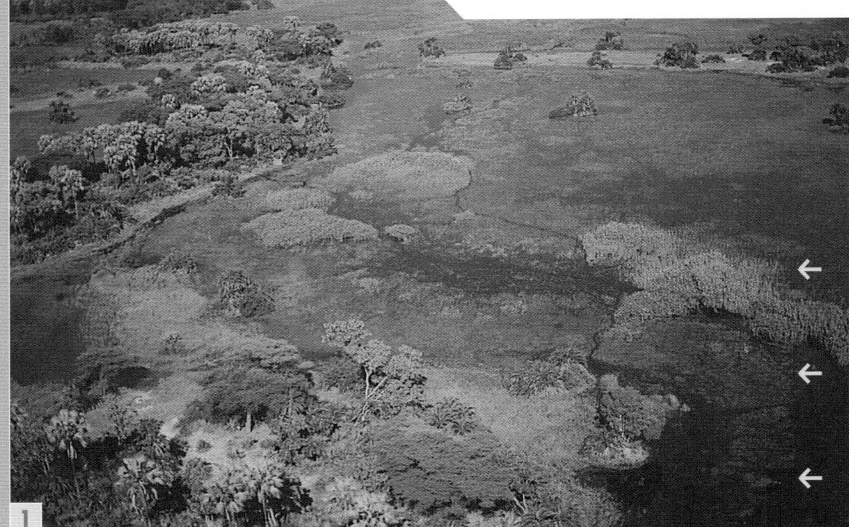

1 Wetland

Wetland areas make up less than 1 per cent of world land cover. This aerial photograph of the Okavango Delta in Botswana shows an unusual environment. Set in the centre of southern Africa, the Okavango river drains into this low lying area, not into the sea. The extent of the wetland varies with the amount of rainfall in the catchment area. The high water table allows for a wide diversity of vegetation to grow in an area surrounded by grassland.

2 Crops/Mosaic

Fertile land which is cultivated by man often produces geometric patterns. The infrared satellite image shows part of the Everglades swamp in Florida, USA, east of Lake Okeechobee. Bare fields appear as dark pink and planted fields as green. The pattern continues into the urban areas depicted in blue. Regular field systems such as these enable mechanized agriculture and crop diversification. The dark mottled area to the top right of the image is an undeveloped part of the Everglades.

Satellite/Sensor : Landsat

3 Urban

Representing approximately 0.2 per cent of total world land cover, the urban environment is probably the farthest removed from the Earth's original, natural land cover. This aerial view of Manhattan in New York, USA, shows the 'grid iron' street pattern typical of many modern cities. Major natural features, such as the Hudson River in this image, interrupt this regular plan. Parkland areas, such as that appearing at the top left of the image, are manufactured rather than natural.

4 Grass/Savanna

This view of Ngorongoro, Tanzania is typical of tropical savanna grasslands. Over 25 per cent of Africa's land cover falls within this category. Large areas of tropical grasslands also occur in South America and northern Australia, with temperate grasslands in North America (prairie) and Asia (steppe). Seasonal rainfall provides a regular cycle of lush, tall grass interspersed by scattered trees and shrubs. The savanna areas of east Africa support large numbers of wild animals.

5 Forest/Woodland

The type of woodland coverage in this photograph is tropical rainforest or jungle. This accounts for over 40 per cent of land cover in South America. Dense coverage includes tall hardwood trees which provide a high canopy over smaller trees and shrubs capable of surviving with little direct sunlight. Natural forest or woodland areas such as the Amazon are under continuous threat from the external pressures of agriculture, mineral exploration or urbanization.

6 Barren

The Hoggar region of Algeria is part of the 30 per cent of barren land in Africa, the most extensive land cover type on the continent. This area is a plateau of bare rock lying at a height of over 2 000 m above sea level. It is surrounded by the sandy desert of the Sahara. Rainfall is negligible and the extreme temperatures result in little, or no vegetation and wildlife.

7 Shrubland

Shrubland areas, shown here around Ayers Rock in central Australia, develop on the fringes of desert regions. Sporadic rainfall and less severe temperatures than in the deserts, are enough for hardy plants and shrubs to grow in the thin soil. Moving away from the desert areas, as conditions become less harsh, the vegetation changes and the range of plants increases.

8 Snow/Ice

The continent of Antarctica is almost completely covered by snow and ice. In the northern hemisphere, Spitsbergen, shown here, is one of a large group of islands within the Arctic Circle which is also permanently covered. There is no vegetation on land and any wildlife must survive on food caught in the sea. Although inhospitable areas at the polar extremes see little human interaction, they are affected by global increases in temperature. Resultant melting of glaciers and icecaps threatens a rise in sea level.

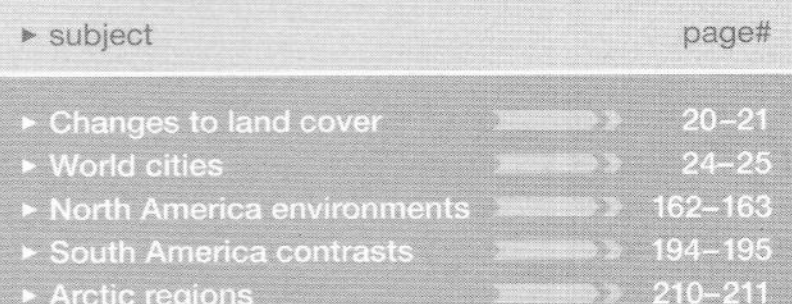

Fig. #01
Continental land cover composition

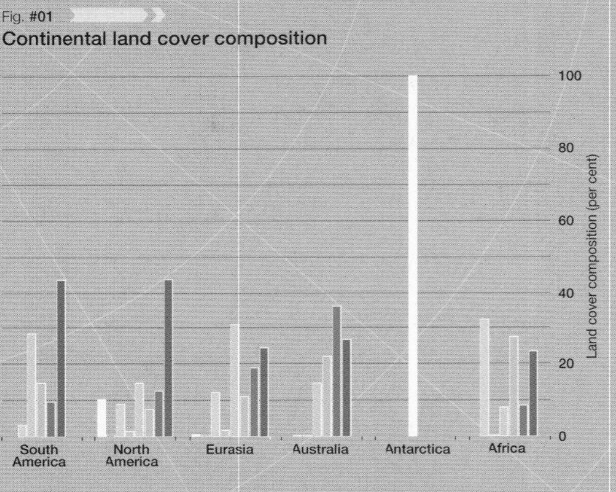

Land cover composition (per cent)

South America · North America · Eurasia · Australia · Antarctica · Africa

Legend:
- Urban
- Wetland
- Snow/Ice
- Barren
- Grass/Savanna
- Shrubland
- Crops/Mosaic
- Forest/Woodland

Fig. #02
Global land cover composition

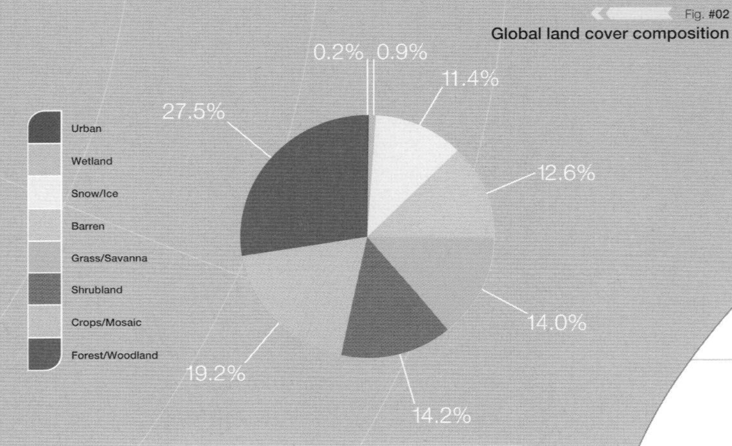

0.2% 0.9% 11.4% 12.6% 14.0% 14.2% 19.2% 27.5%

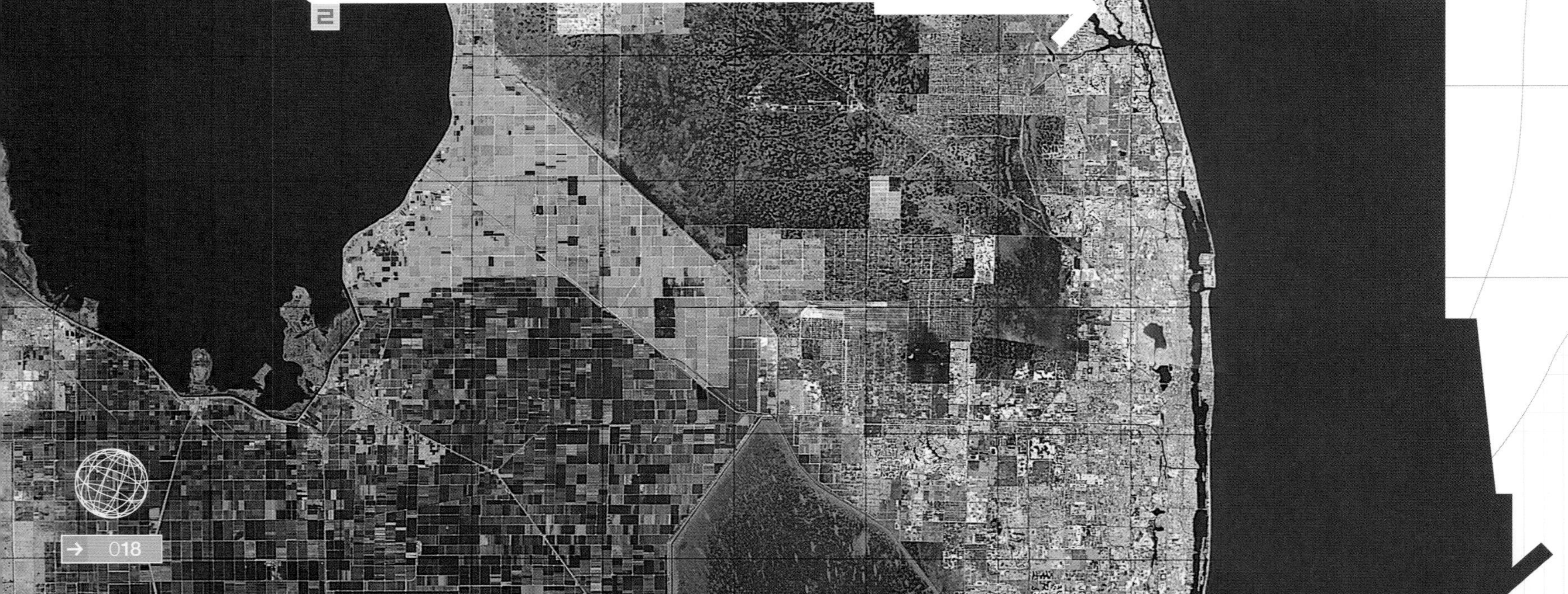

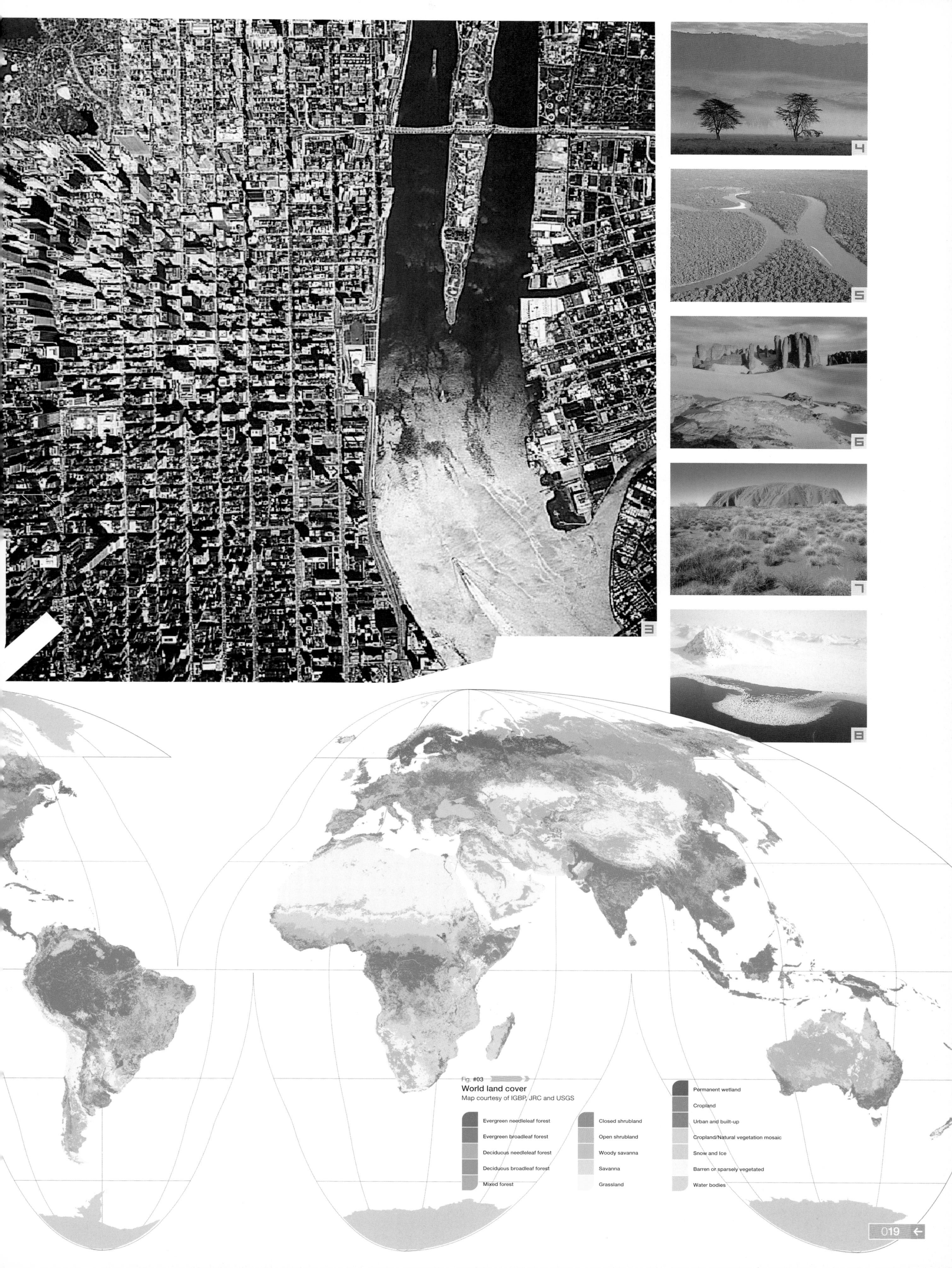

Fig. #03

World land cover
Map courtesy of IGBP, JRC and USGS

Evergreen needleleaf forest	Closed shrubland	Permanent wetland
Evergreen broadleaf forest	Open shrubland	Cropland
Deciduous needleleaf forest	Woody savanna	Urban and built-up
Deciduous broadleaf forest	Savanna	Cropland/Natural vegetation mosaic
Mixed forest	Grassland	Snow and Ice
		Barren or sparsely vegetated
		Water bodies

world[changes]

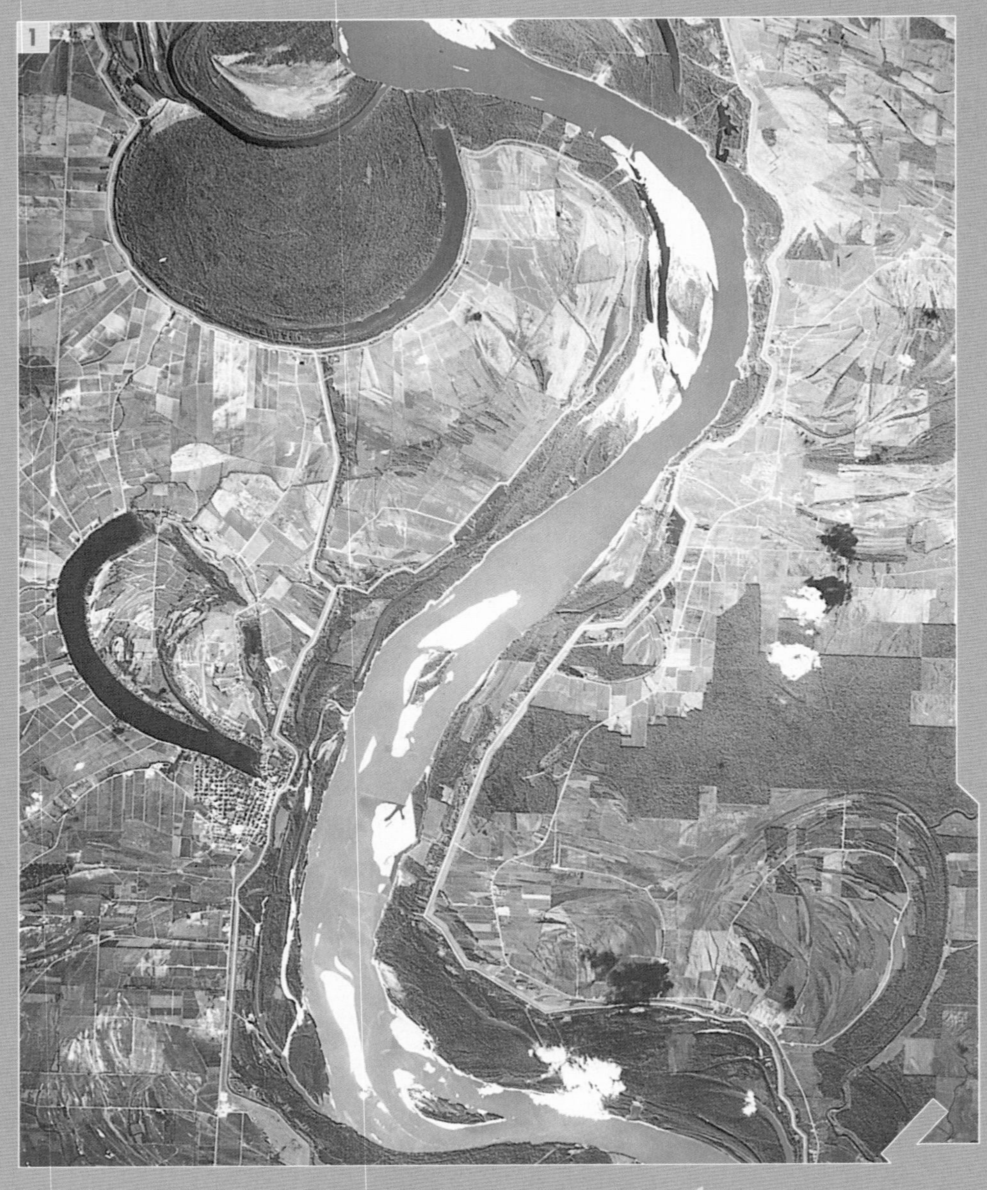

2 Changing Land Use

The changes in land use between Alberta, Canada (top) and Montana, USA (bottom) can be seen on this infrared satellite image. The straight international boundary runs diagonally from centre left to upper right. Intense cultivation on the US side has created regular field patterns, whereas on the Canadian side plantations of forest and thick mountain vegetation cover extensive areas.

Satellite/Sensor : Landsat

3 Deforestation

This aerial photograph shows the dramatic effect the clearcut logging method of deforestation can have on a landscape. The change in appearance and the effects on the immediate environment can be dramatic. It shows part of the northwest US state of Washington, which has large areas of thick forest, particularly on the western slopes of the Cascade mountain range. More than half of the state is forested and lumber and lumber-related products form the basis of much of the state's economic activity.

1 Changing River Courses

This aerial infrared photograph shows a small section of the Mississippi river near Lake Providence in Louisiana state. The pattern of old loops and bends identifies old courses of the river, showing changes which have occurred over many years. Some loops have become isolated 'oxbow' lakes as shown on the west bank of the river in the left of the image. At the bottom right one former loop of the river can be identified within the cultivated area.

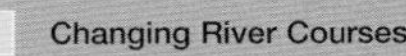

4 Urban Growth

These Landsat images illustrate how such imagery can be used to monitor environmental change. They show the rapid urban growth which has taken place in and around Shenzhen, China, between 1988 (left) and 1996 (right). This city has benefited greatly from its location adjacent to Hong Kong. One of the most obvious changes is the development along the coastline, where huge off-shore structures and large areas of reclaimed land can be seen in the 1996 image. Much of the vegetation (red) in the left image has been cleared and replaced by urban development, leaving only scattered patches of the original vegetation.

Satellite/Sensor : Landsat

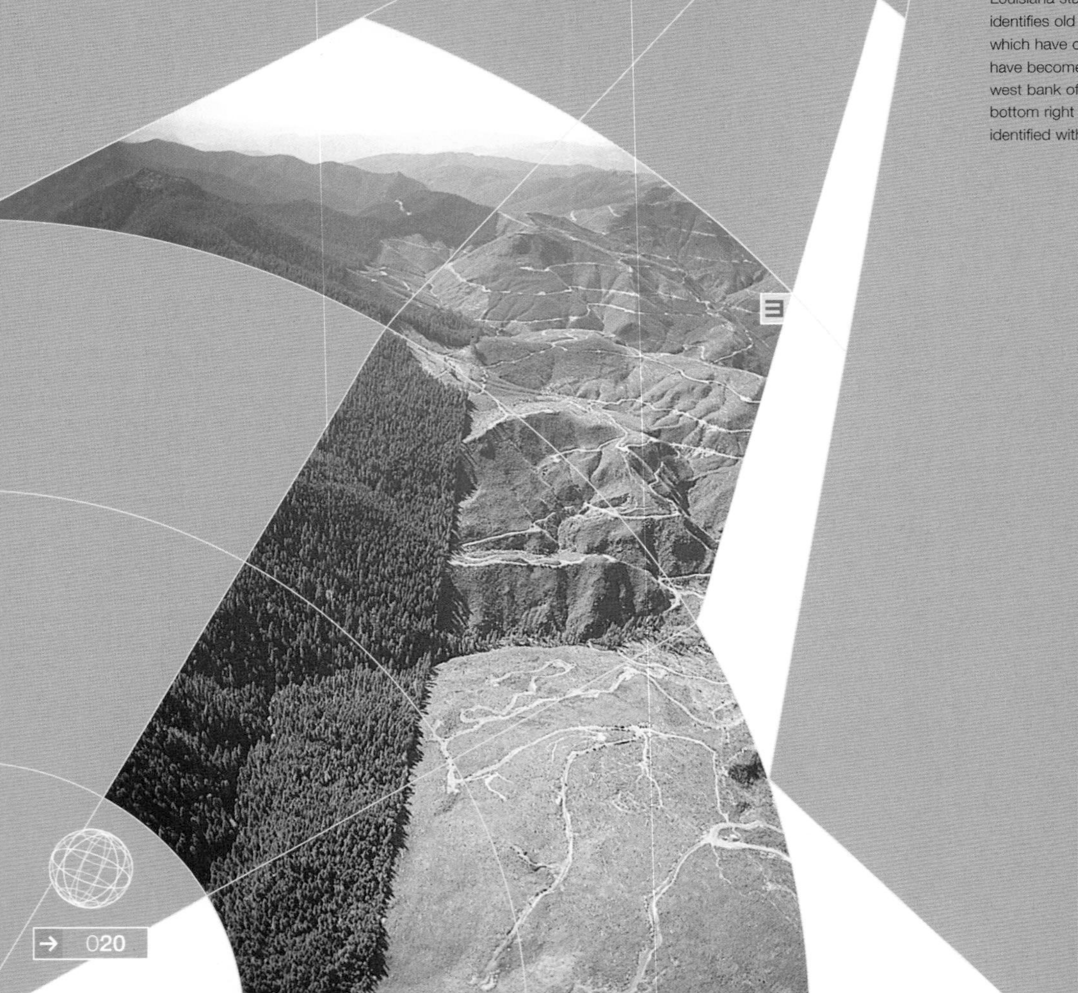

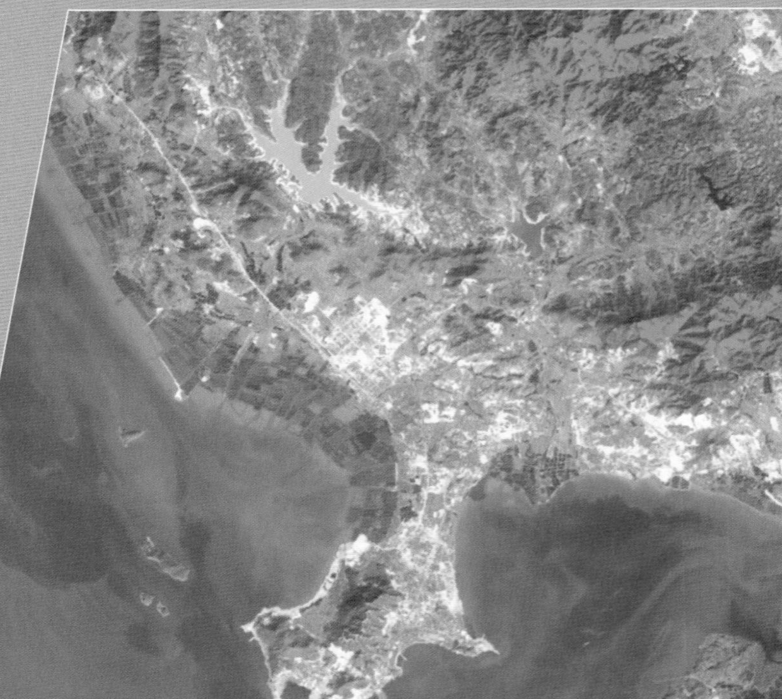

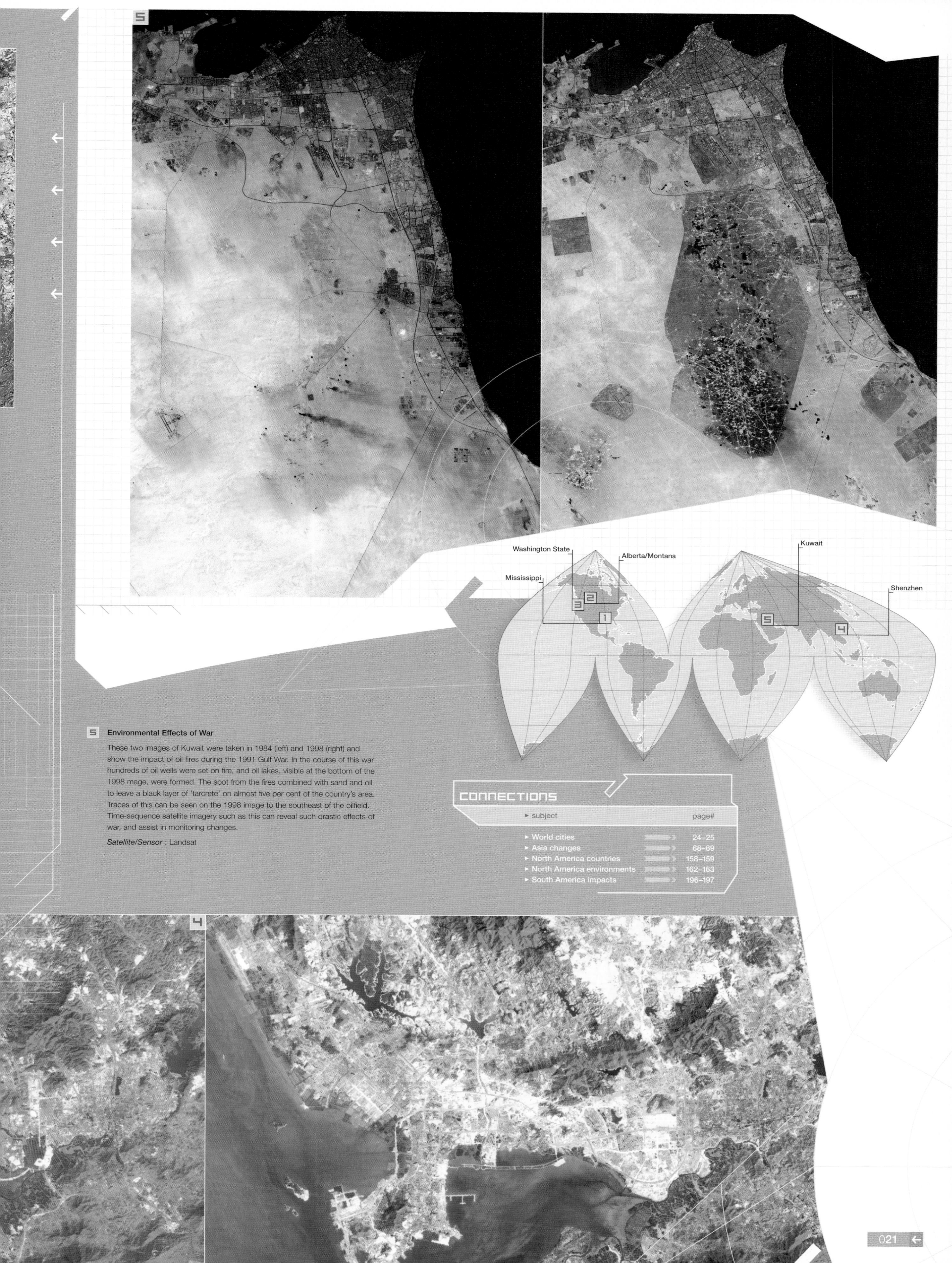

5 Environmental Effects of War

These two images of Kuwait were taken in 1984 (left) and 1998 (right) and show the impact of oil fires during the 1991 Gulf War. In the course of this war hundreds of oil wells were set on fire, and oil lakes, visible at the bottom of the 1998 mage, were formed. The soot from the fires combined with sand and oil to leave a black layer of 'tarcrete' on almost five per cent of the country's area. Traces of this can be seen on the 1998 image to the southeast of the oilfield. Time-sequence satellite imagery such as this can reveal such drastic effects of war, and assist in monitoring changes.

Satellite/Sensor : Landsat

Washington State
Alberta/Montana
Mississippi
Kuwait
Shenzhen

CONNECTIONS

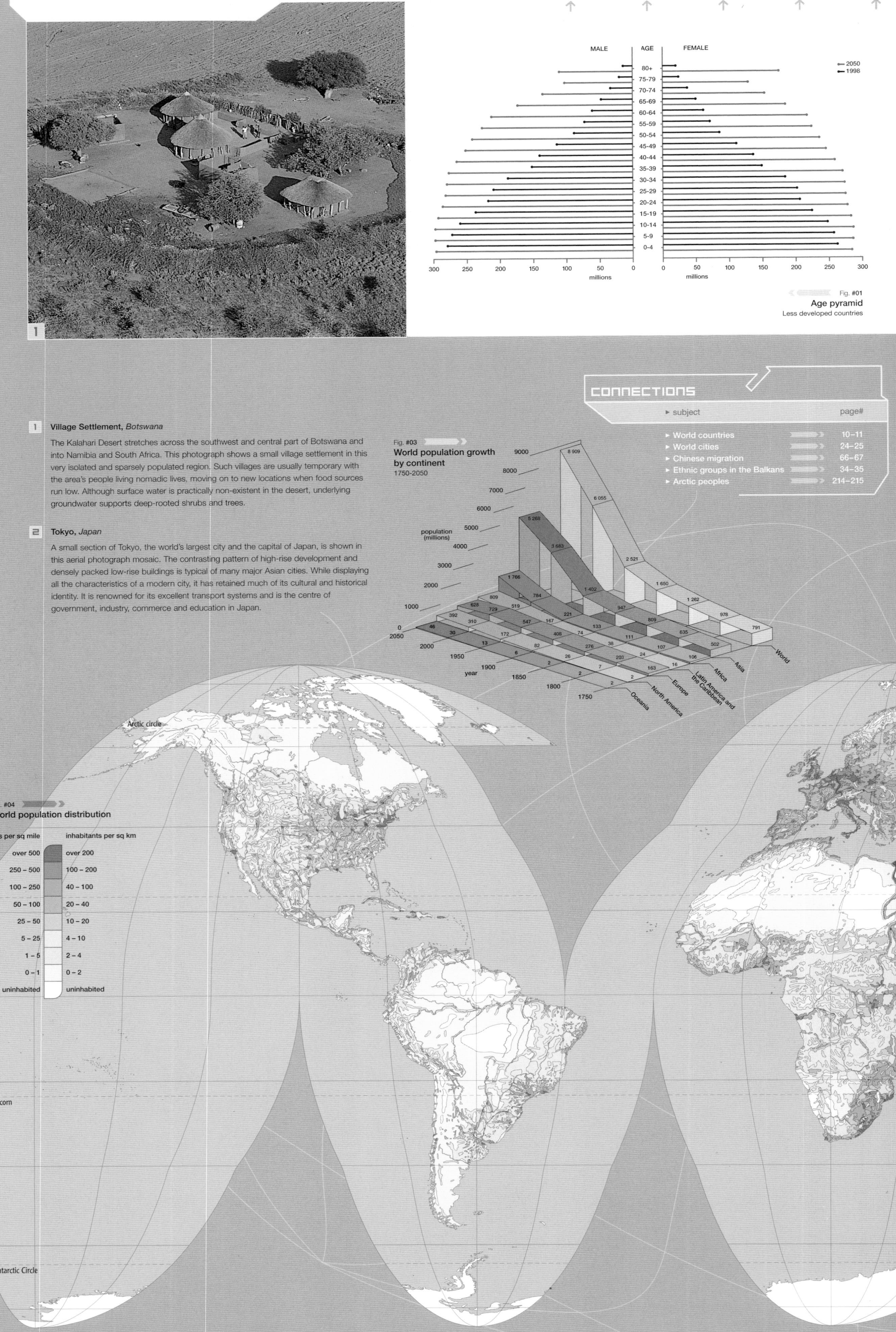

world[population]

Fig. #01
Age pyramid
Less developed countries

MALE	AGE	FEMALE
	80+	
	75-79	
	70-74	
	65-69	
	60-64	
	55-59	
	50-54	
	45-49	
	40-44	
	35-39	
	30-34	
	25-29	
	20-24	
	15-19	
	10-14	
	5-9	
	0-4	

300 250 200 150 100 50 0   0 50 100 150 200 250 300
millions   millions

— 2050
— 1998

1   Village Settlement, *Botswana*

The Kalahari Desert stretches across the southwest and central part of Botswana and into Namibia and South Africa. This photograph shows a small village settlement in this very isolated and sparsely populated region. Such villages are usually temporary with the area's people living nomadic lives, moving on to new locations when food sources run low. Although surface water is practically non-existent in the desert, underlying groundwater supports deep-rooted shrubs and trees.

2   Tokyo, *Japan*

A small section of Tokyo, the world's largest city and the capital of Japan, is shown in this aerial photograph mosaic. The contrasting pattern of high-rise development and densely packed low-rise buildings is typical of many major Asian cities. While displaying all the characteristics of a modern city, it has retained much of its cultural and historical identity. It is renowned for its excellent transport systems and is the centre of government, industry, commerce and education in Japan.

CONNECTIONS

► subject	page#
► World countries	10–11
► World cities	24–25
► Chinese migration	66–67
► Ethnic groups in the Balkans	34–35
► Arctic peoples	214–215

Fig. #03
World population growth by continent
1750-2050

population (millions)

Fig. #04
World population distribution

inhabitants per sq mile	inhabitants per sq km
over 500	over 200
250 – 500	100 – 200
100 – 250	40 – 100
50 – 100	20 – 40
25 – 50	10 – 20
5 – 25	4 – 10
1 – 5	2 – 4
0 – 1	0 – 2
uninhabited	uninhabited

Arctic circle

Equator

Tropic of Capricorn

Antarctic Circle

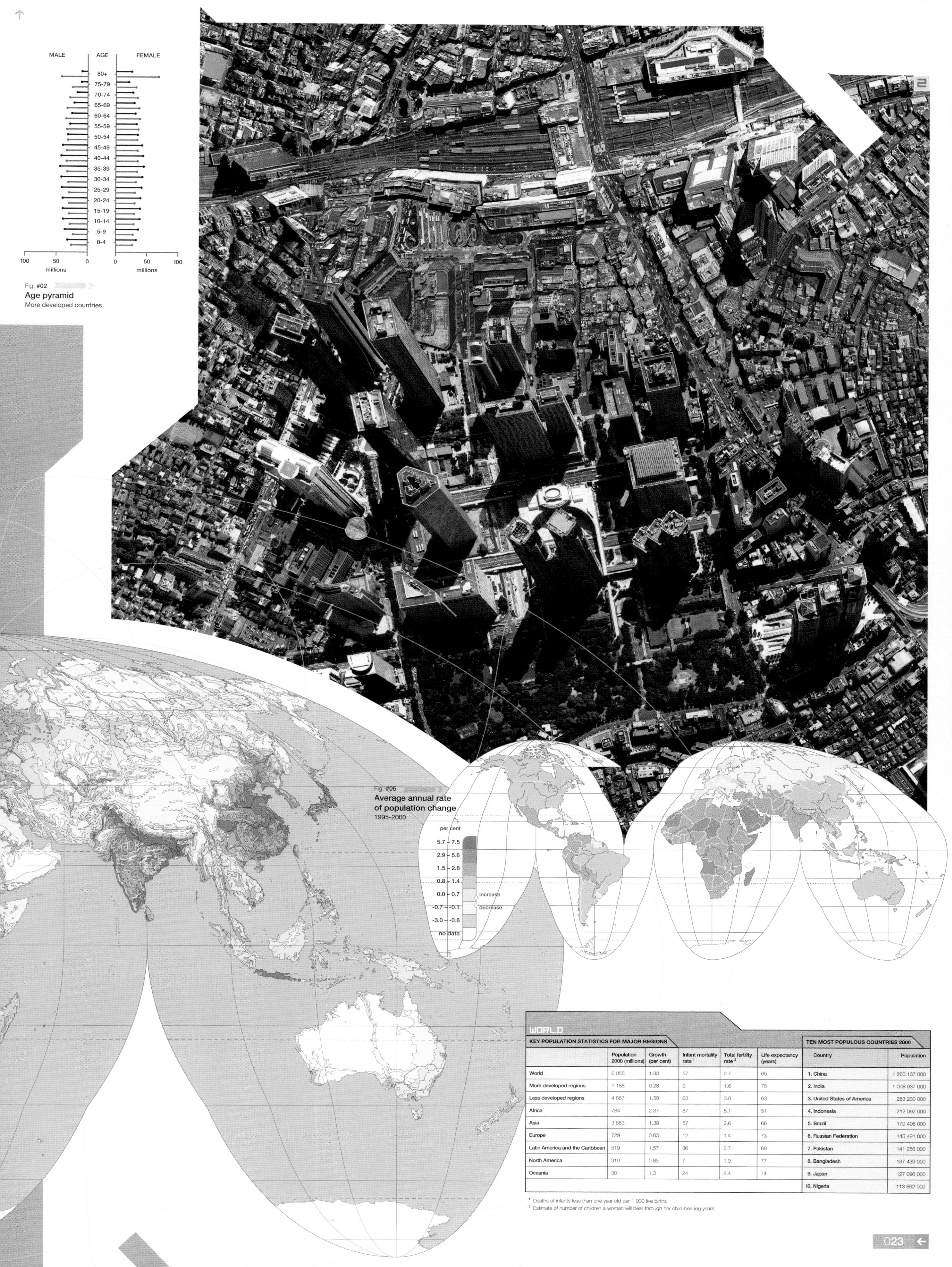

MALE AGE FEMALE

80+
75-79
70-74
65-69
60-64
55-59
50-54
45-49
40-44
35-39
30-34
25-29
20-24
15-19
10-14
5-9
0-4

100   50   0   0   50   100
millions   millions

Fig. #02
Age pyramid
More developed countries

Fig. #05
**Average annual rate
of population change**
1995-2000

per cent

5.7 – 7.5
2.9 – 5.6
1.5 – 2.8
0.8 – 1.4
0.0 – 0.7   increase
-0.7 – -0.1   decrease
-3.0 – -0.8
no data

WORLD

KEY POPULATION STATISTICS FOR MAJOR REGIONS

	Population 2000 (millions)	Growth (per cent)	Infant mortality rate [1]	Total fertility rate [2]	Life expectancy (years)
World	6 055	1.33	57	2.7	65
More developed regions	1 188	0.28	9	1.6	75
Less developed regions	4 867	1.59	63	3.0	63
Africa	784	2.37	87	5.1	51
Asia	3 683	1.38	57	2.6	66
Europe	729	0.03	12	1.4	73
Latin America and the Caribbean	519	1.57	36	2.7	69
North America	310	0.85	7	1.9	77
Oceania	30	1.3	24	2.4	74

TEN MOST POPULOUS COUNTRIES 2000

Country	Population
1. China	1 260 137 000
2. India	1 008 937 000
3. United States of America	283 230 000
4. Indonesia	212 092 000
5. Brazil	170 406 000
6. Russian Federation	145 491 000
7. Pakistan	141 256 000
8. Bangladesh	137 439 000
9. Japan	127 096 000
10. Nigeria	113 862 000

[1] Deaths of infants less than one year old per 1 000 live births
[2] Estimate of number of children a woman will bear through her child-bearing years

world[cities]

1 San Francisco, *United States of America*

The city of San Francisco is situated on the peninsula which lies to the western side of San Francisco Bay. The Golden Gate, upper left, bridges the entrance to the bay and three other bridges are visible in the image. San Francisco has frequently suffered extensive damage from earthquakes and the two lakes south of the city mark the line of the San Andreas fault. The southern end of the bay is surrounded by a green patchwork of salt beds.

Satellite/Sensor : Landsat

2 Hong Kong, *China*

A British colony until 1997, Hong Kong is now a Special Administrative Region of China. This high resolution satellite image is centred on Hong Kong Harbour, with the Kowloon Peninsula to the north (top) and Hong Kong Island to the south. Much of the coastline shown is reclaimed land, including the old Kai Tak airport, seen in the top right of the image. This airport has been closed since the completion of the new Hong Kong International airport 25 kilometres west of the harbour.

Satellite/Sensor : IKONOS

3 Cairo, *Egypt*

This oblique aerial photograph looks north across the suburbs of southwest Cairo. There has been a major expansion of the city and its suburbs over the last fifty years and the city now has a population of over 10 million. The urban expansion brings the city up against the important historical site of the Giza Pyramids. The Pyramid of Khufu and the Great Sphinx can be seen at the left of the photograph.

4 Tokyo, *Japan*

This false-colour infrared image of Tokyo shows the northwest edge of Tokyo Bay. It shows just a small part of the vast expanse of Tokyo, the world's largest city with over 26 million inhabitants. The amount of land reclamation in the bay is obvious, and the reclaimed land includes Tokyo International (Haneda) Airport, at the bottom of the image. Vegetation shows as red, making the grounds of the Imperial Palace clearly visible in the top left.

Satellite/Sensor : Terra/ASTER

CONNECTIONS

▶ subject	page#
▶ World countries	10–11
▶ World land cover	18–19
▶ Urban growth	20–21
▶ World population	22–23
▶ Oceania capitals	138–139

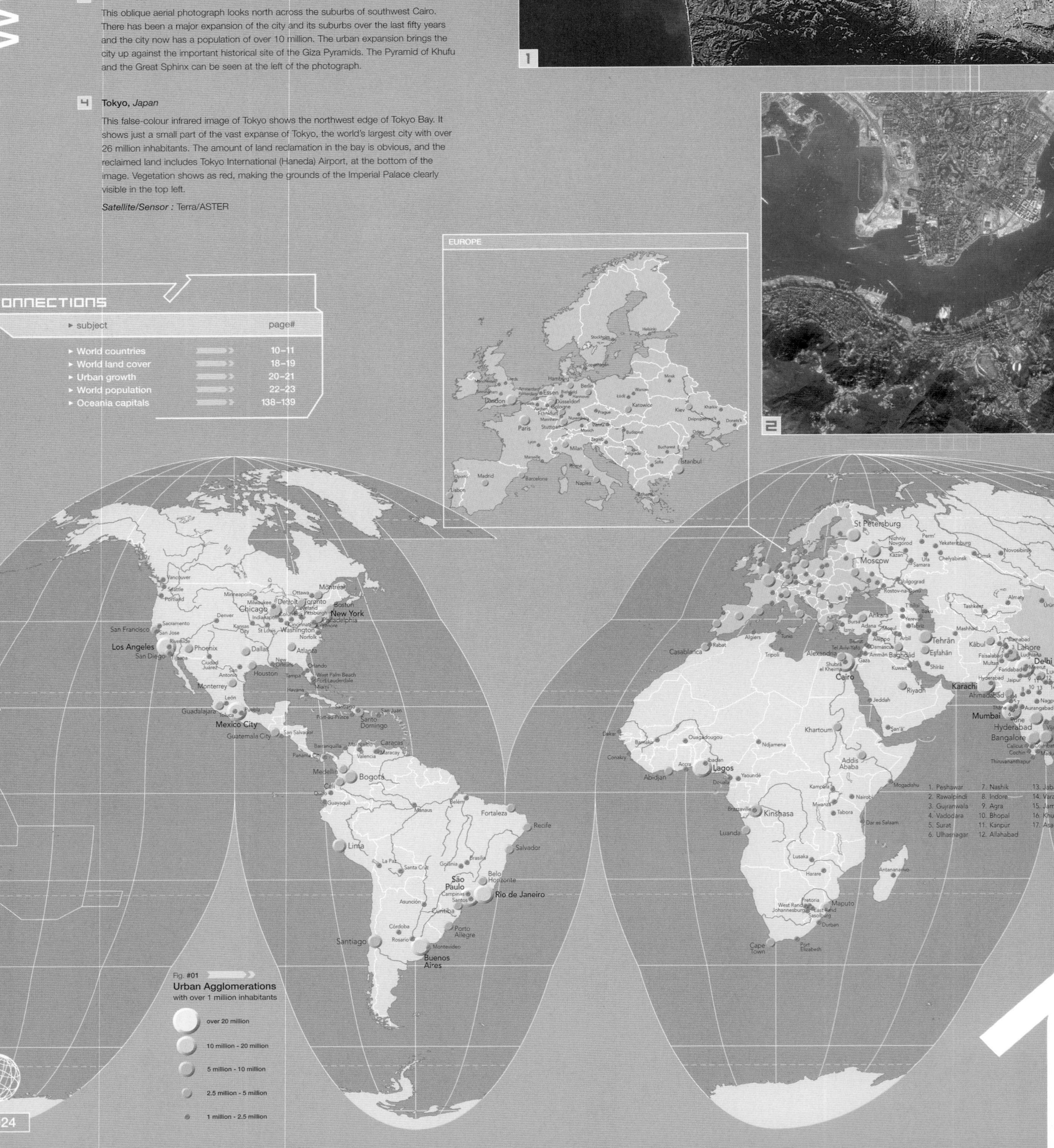

Fig. #01
Urban Agglomerations
with over 1 million inhabitants

- over 20 million
- 10 million - 20 million
- 5 million - 10 million
- 2.5 million - 5 million
- 1 million - 2.5 million

1. Peshawar
2. Rawalpindi
3. Gujranwala
4. Vadodara
5. Surat
6. Ulhasnagar
7. Nashik
8. Indore
9. Agra
10. Bhopal
11. Kanpur
12. Allahabad
13. Jabalpur
14. Varanasi
15. Jamshedpur
16. Khulna
17. Asansol

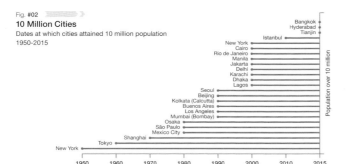

Fig. #02

10 Million Cities
Dates at which cities attained 10 million population
1950-2015

Population over 10 million

Bangkok
Hyderabad
Tianjin
New York
Cairo
Rio de Janeiro
Manila
Jakarta
Delhi
Karachi
Dhaka
Lagos
Istanbul
Seoul
Beijing
Kolkata (Calcutta)
Buenos Aires
Los Angeles
Mumbai (Bombay)
Osaka
São Paulo
Mexico City
Shanghai
Tokyo
New York

1950   1960   1970   1980   1990   2000   2010   2015

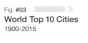

Fig. #03

World Top 10 Cities
1900-2015

World Rank

1
2
3
4
5
6
7
8
9
10

1900   1930   1950   1960   1970   1980   1990   2000   2010   2015

- London
- New York
- Berlin
- Chigago
- Wuhan
- Tokyo
- Philadelphia
- St Petersburg
- Paris
- Moscow
- Shanghai
- Osaka
- Buenos Aires
- Essen
- Kolkata (Calcutta)
- Beijing
- Los Angeles
- Mexico City
- São Paulo
- Mumbai (Bombay)
- Lagos
- Dhaka
- Karachi
- Jakarta

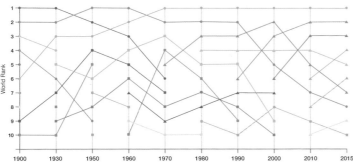

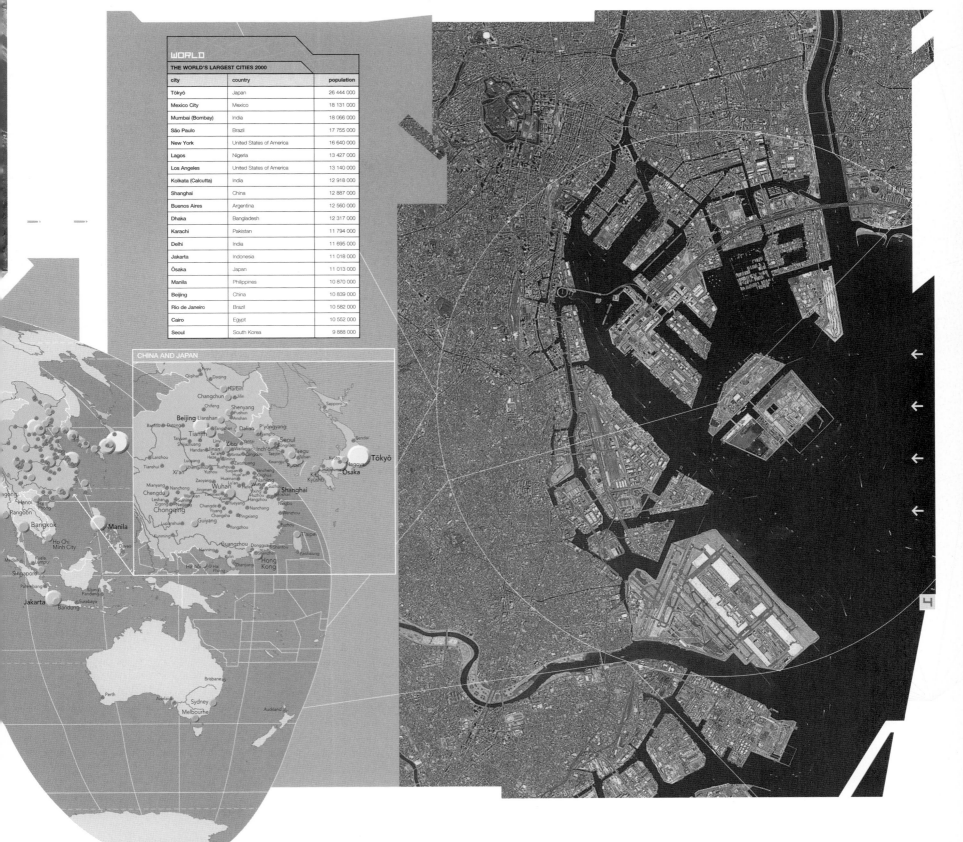

WORLD

THE WORLD'S LARGEST CITIES 2000

city	country	population
Tōkyō	Japan	26 444 000
Mexico City	Mexico	18 131 000
Mumbai (Bombay)	India	18 066 000
São Paulo	Brazil	17 755 000
New York	United States of America	16 640 000
Lagos	Nigeria	13 427 000
Los Angeles	United States of America	13 140 000
Kolkata (Calcutta)	India	12 918 000
Shanghai	China	12 887 000
Buenos Aires	Argentina	12 560 000
Dhaka	Bangladesh	12 317 000
Karachi	Pakistan	11 794 000
Delhi	India	11 695 000
Jakarta	Indonesia	11 018 000
Ōsaka	Japan	11 013 000
Manila	Philippines	10 870 000
Beijing	China	10 839 000
Rio de Janeiro	Brazil	10 582 000
Cairo	Egypt	10 552 000
Seoul	South Korea	9 888 000

CHINA AND JAPAN

world[communications]

Fig. #01
**Communications
satellites**

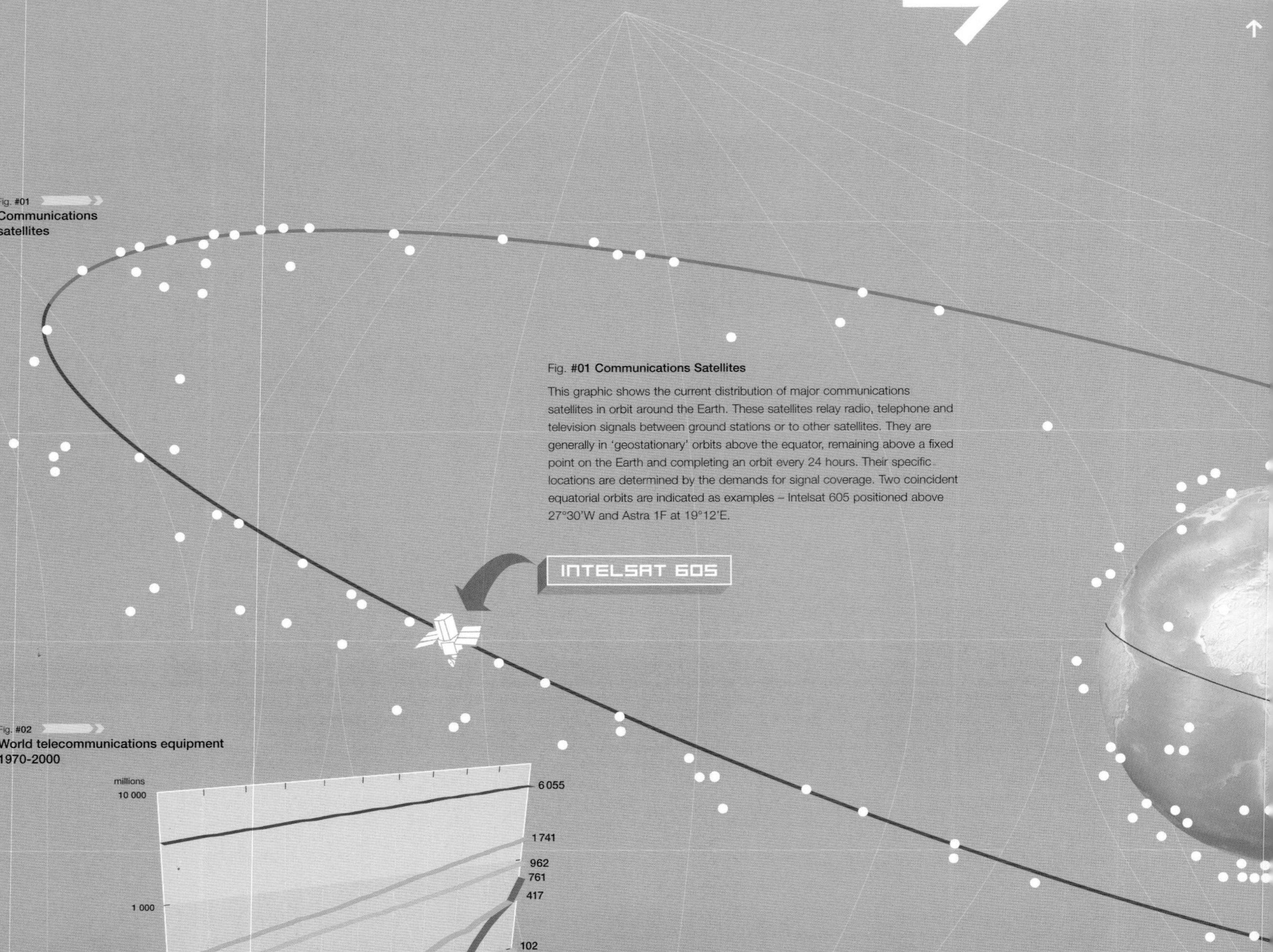

Fig. #01 Communications Satellites

This graphic shows the current distribution of major communications
satellites in orbit around the Earth. These satellites relay radio, telephone and
television signals between ground stations or to other satellites. They are
generally in 'geostationary' orbits above the equator, remaining above a fixed
point on the Earth and completing an orbit every 24 hours. Their specific
locations are determined by the demands for signal coverage. Two coincident
equatorial orbits are indicated as examples – Intelsat 605 positioned above
27°30'W and Astra 1F at 19°12'E.

INTELSAT 605

Fig. #02
**World telecommunications equipment
1970-2000**

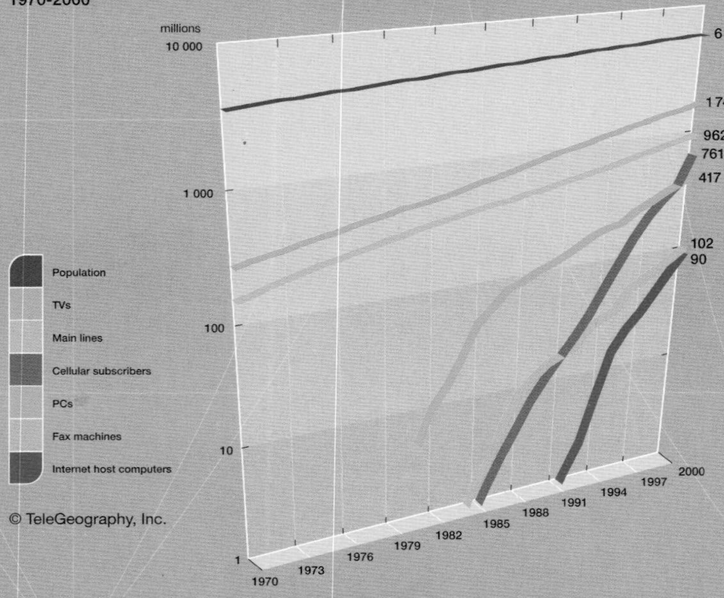

millions
10 000

6 055

1 741

962
761
417

102
90

1 000

- Population
- TVs
- Main lines
- Cellular subscribers
- PCs
- Fax machines
- Internet host computers

100

10

1

© TeleGeography, Inc.

1970 1973 1976 1979 1982 1985 1988 1991 1994 1997 2000

Fig. #03
International telecommunications traffic 1999
Each band is proportional to the total annual traffic on the
public telephone network in both directions

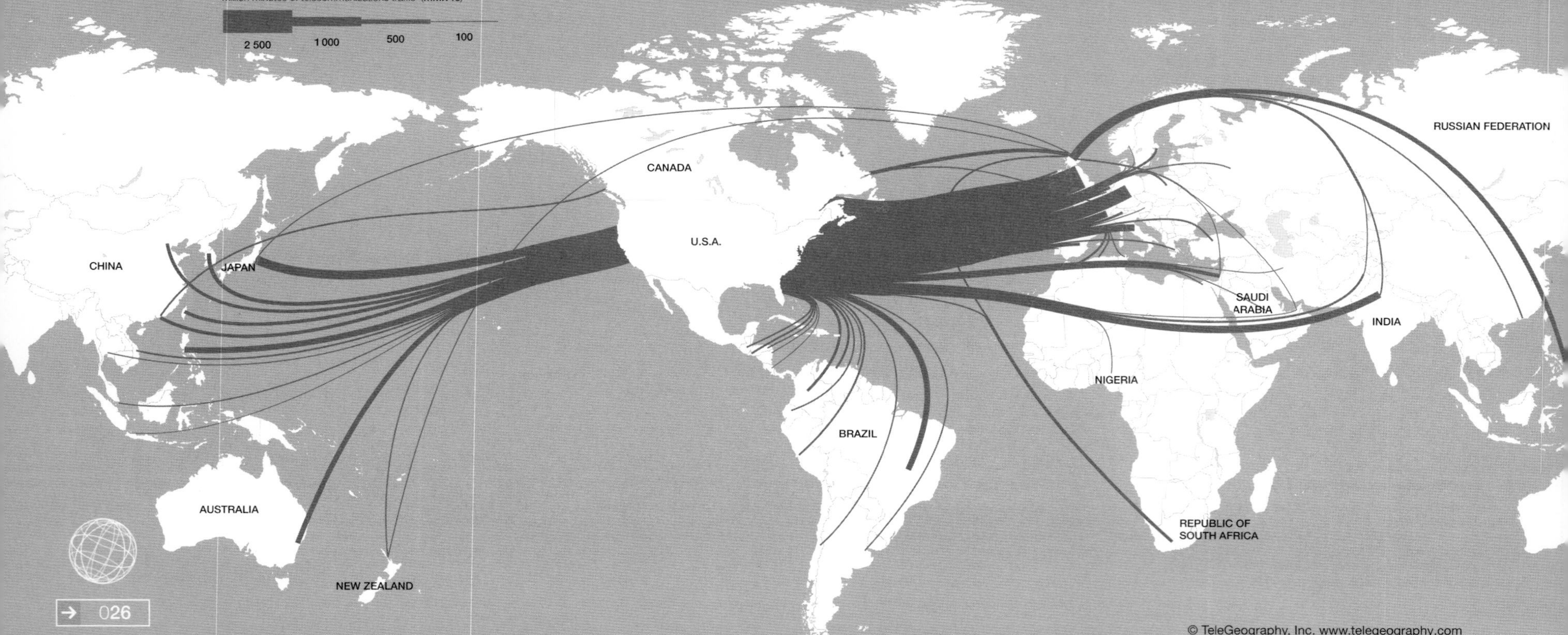

Million minutes of telecommunications traffic (mMiTTs)

2 500   1 000   500   100

CANADA

U.S.A.

RUSSIAN FEDERATION

CHINA

JAPAN

SAUDI
ARABIA

INDIA

NIGERIA

BRAZIL

AUSTRALIA

REPUBLIC OF
SOUTH AFRICA

NEW ZEALAND

© TeleGeography, Inc. www.telegeography.com

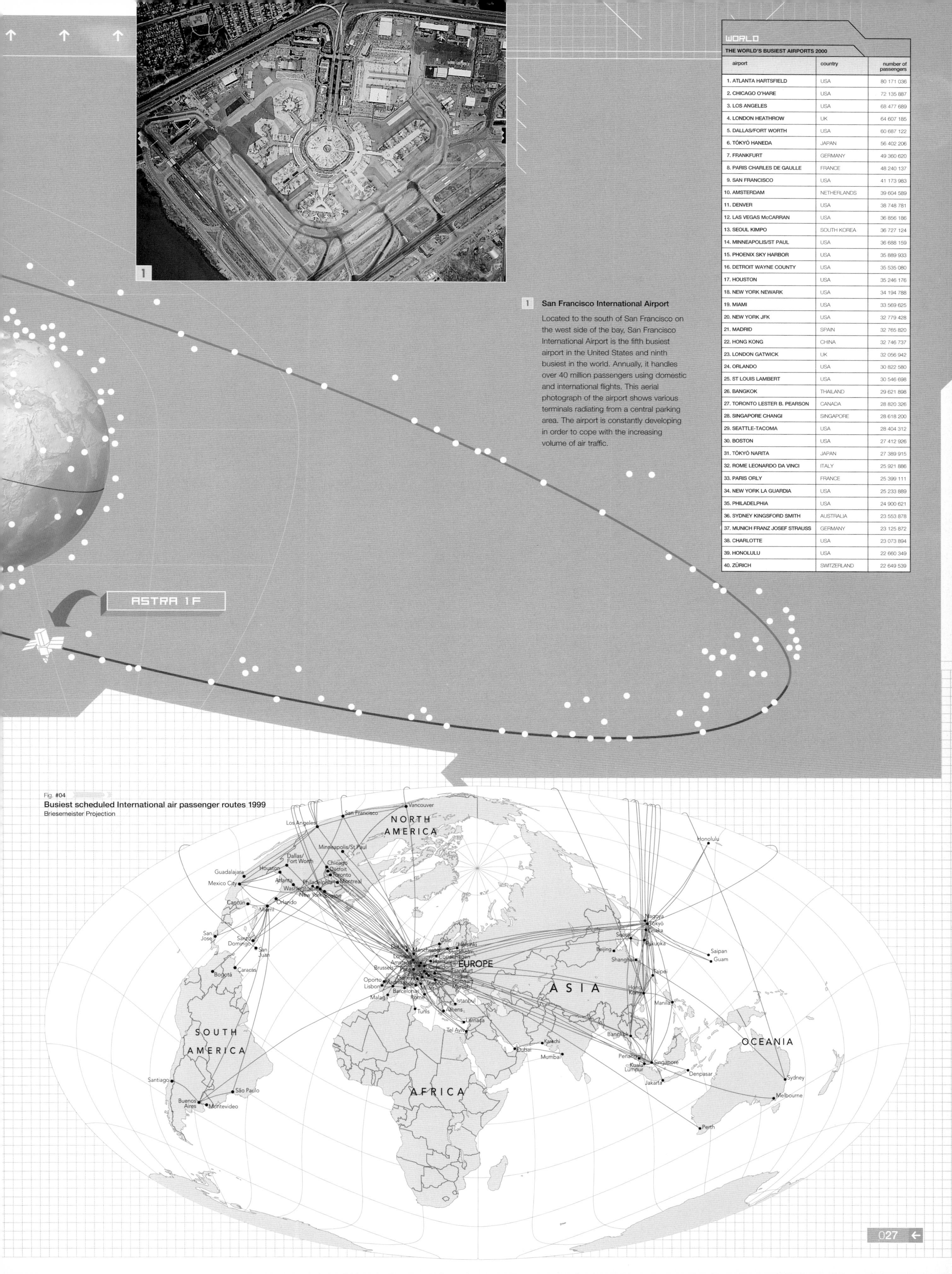

THE WORLD'S BUSIEST AIRPORTS 2000

airport	country	number of passengers
1. ATLANTA HARTSFIELD	USA	80 171 036
2. CHICAGO O'HARE	USA	72 135 887
3. LOS ANGELES	USA	68 477 689
4. LONDON HEATHROW	UK	64 607 185
5. DALLAS/FORT WORTH	USA	60 687 122
6. TŌKYŌ HANEDA	JAPAN	56 402 206
7. FRANKFURT	GERMANY	49 360 620
8. PARIS CHARLES DE GAULLE	FRANCE	48 240 137
9. SAN FRANCISCO	USA	41 173 983
10. AMSTERDAM	NETHERLANDS	39 604 589
11. DENVER	USA	38 748 781
12. LAS VEGAS McCARRAN	USA	36 856 186
13. SEOUL KIMPO	SOUTH KOREA	36 727 124
14. MINNEAPOLIS/ST PAUL	USA	36 688 159
15. PHOENIX SKY HARBOR	USA	35 889 933
16. DETROIT WAYNE COUNTY	USA	35 535 080
17. HOUSTON	USA	35 246 176
18. NEW YORK NEWARK	USA	34 194 788
19. MIAMI	USA	33 569 625
20. NEW YORK JFK	USA	32 779 428
21. MADRID	SPAIN	32 765 820
22. HONG KONG	CHINA	32 746 737
23. LONDON GATWICK	UK	32 056 942
24. ORLANDO	USA	30 822 580
25. ST LOUIS LAMBERT	USA	30 546 698
26. BANGKOK	THAILAND	29 621 898
27. TORONTO LESTER B. PEARSON	CANADA	28 820 326
28. SINGAPORE CHANGI	SINGAPORE	28 618 200
29. SEATTLE-TACOMA	USA	28 404 312
30. BOSTON	USA	27 412 926
31. TŌKYŌ NARITA	JAPAN	27 389 915
32. ROME LEONARDO DA VINCI	ITALY	25 921 886
33. PARIS ORLY	FRANCE	25 399 111
34. NEW YORK LA GUARDIA	USA	25 233 889
35. PHILADELPHIA	USA	24 900 621
36. SYDNEY KINGSFORD SMITH	AUSTRALIA	23 553 878
37. MUNICH FRANZ JOSEF STRAUSS	GERMANY	23 125 872
38. CHARLOTTE	USA	23 073 894
39. HONOLULU	USA	22 660 349
40. ZÜRICH	SWITZERLAND	22 649 539

1 San Francisco International Airport

Located to the south of San Francisco on the west side of the bay, San Francisco International Airport is the fifth busiest airport in the United States and ninth busiest in the world. Annually, it handles over 40 million passengers using domestic and international flights. This aerial photograph of the airport shows various terminals radiating from a central parking area. The airport is constantly developing in order to cope with the increasing volume of air traffic.

ASTRA 1F

Fig. #04
Busiest scheduled International air passenger routes 1999
Briesemeister Projection

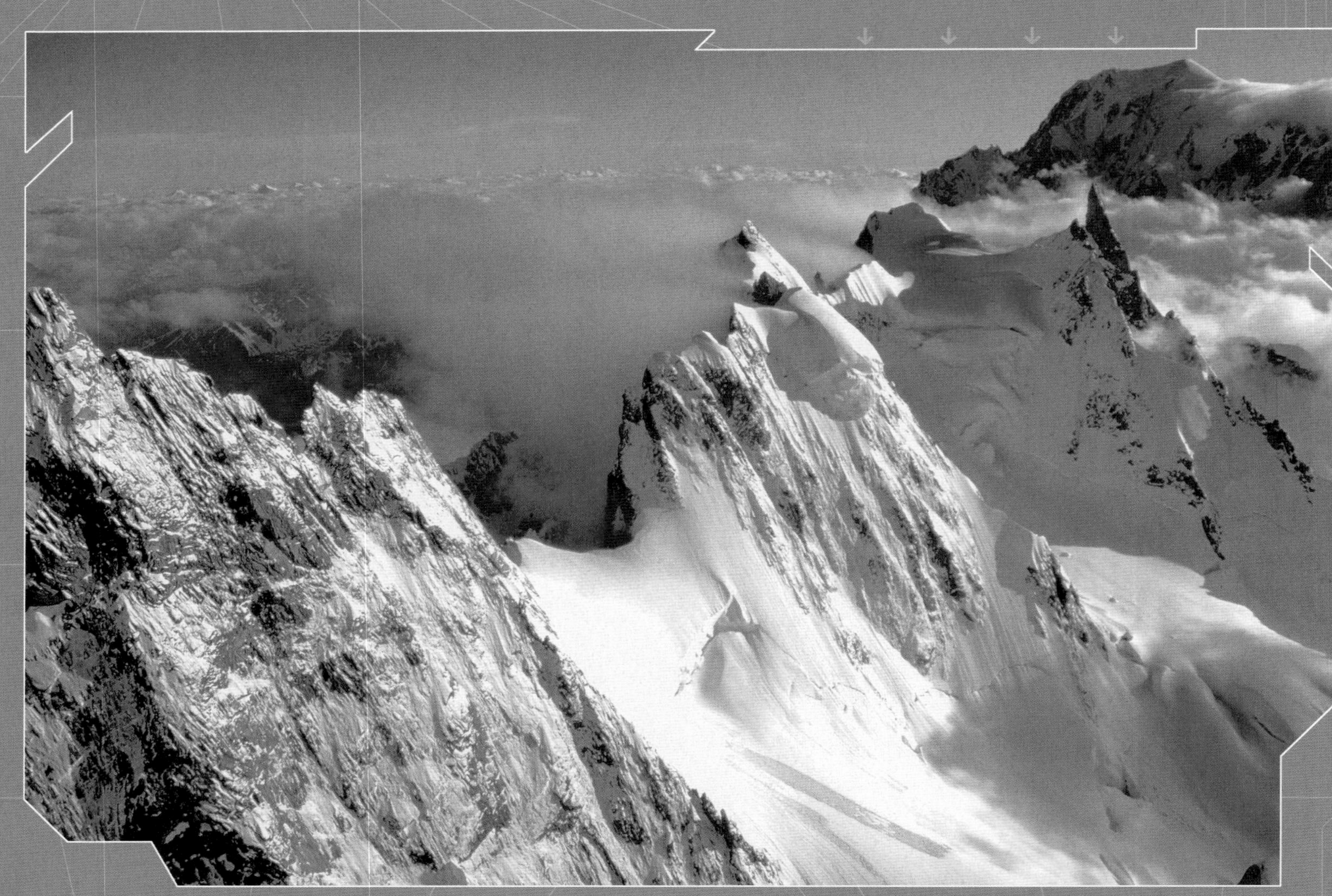

Alps, *France*

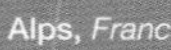

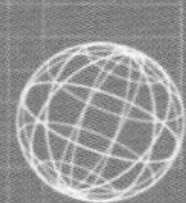

europe

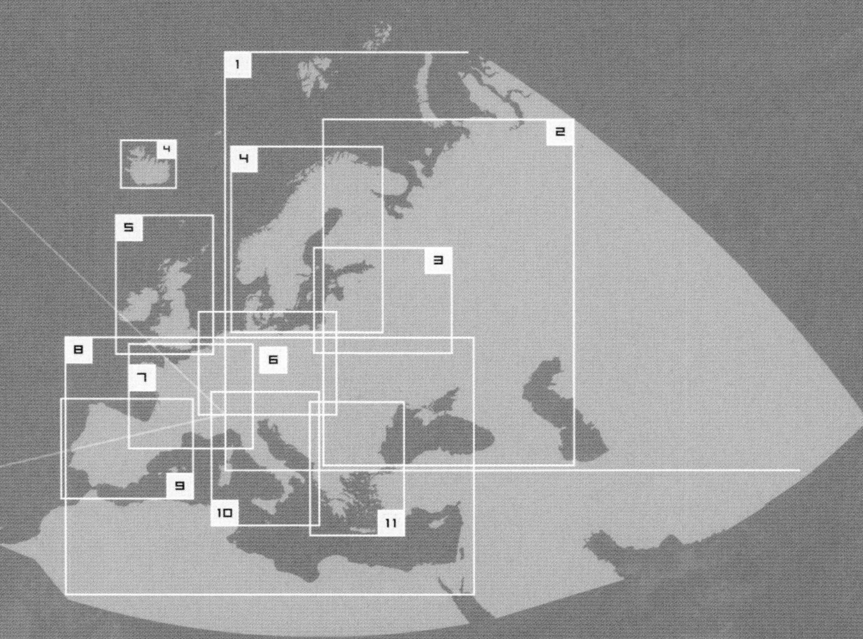

[contents]

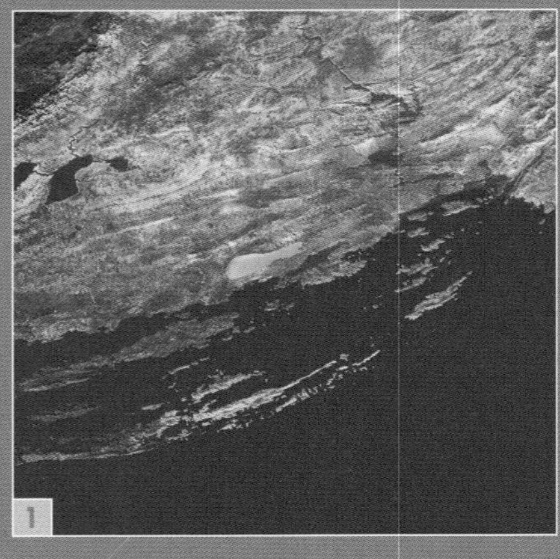

1 Dalmatia, *Croatia*

The Dalmatian coast of Croatia joins the Adriatic Sea in a series of mountainous limestone ridges running parallel to the coast. The mountains continue into the sea leaving strings of long, thin fragmented islands. The Krka river, to the right of this image, is one of a very few rivers which cross this remote region. The soil is thin and patchy but such a coastline provides many sheltered harbours. The large lake which appears green has a high salt content which has seeped through from the sea.

Satellite/Sensor : Space Shuttle

Europe, the world's second smallest continent, is located on the western tip of the vast Eurasian landmass. The curve of mountain ranges, which includes the Alps, the Pyrenees and the Carpathians divides the north of the continent from the south. The highest peak in Europe, Mt Elbrus (5 642 m) lies in the Caucasus, the mountain range between the Black Sea and the Caspian Sea. North of these mountains, the rolling plains of Ukraine and European Russia extend to the Ural Mountains which, together with the Caucasus and the Bosporus in Turkey, form the physical boundary between Europe and Asia.

The Mediterranean Sea, in the south, is a large inland sea which is enclosed by mainland Europe to the north and west, Africa to the south, and Asia to the east. The Strait of Gibraltar connects the Mediterranean to the Atlantic Ocean on the west and in the southeast the Suez canal is the seaway to the Red Sea.

Spitsbergen

Norwegian Sea

Scandinavia

G
Bo

Faroe Islands

Largest island
Great Britain
218 476 sq km / 84 354 sq miles
Map reference 47 J7

North Sea

Elbe River

Rhine River

Ireland

Great Britain

Seine River

English Channel

Loire River

Massif Central

Bay of Biscay

Pyrenees

Bale

Atlantic Ocean

Iberian Peninsula

Tagus River

Strait of Gibraltar

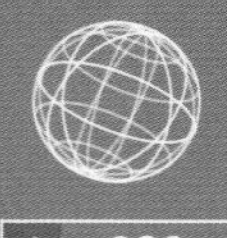

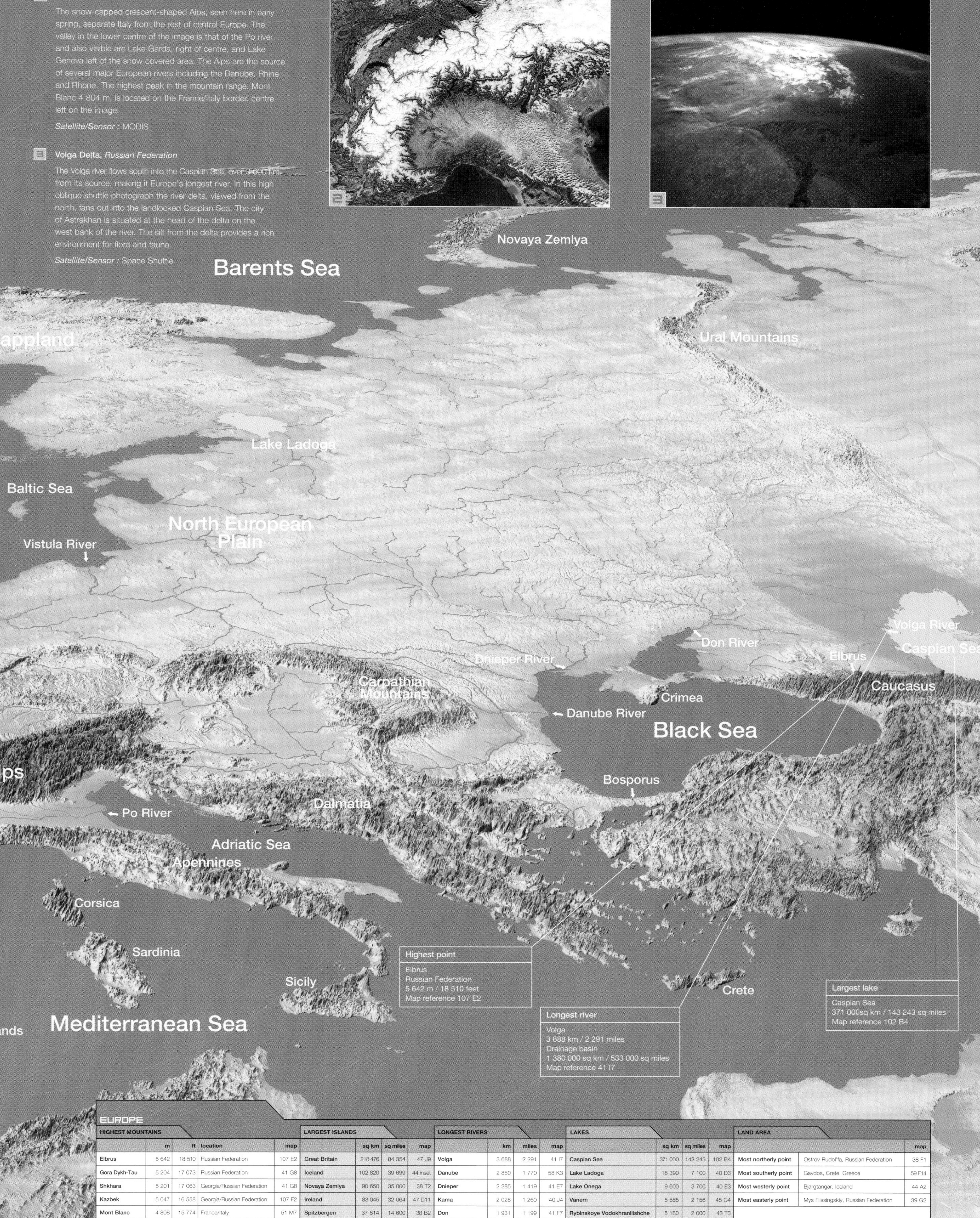

Alps, *Europe*

The snow-capped crescent-shaped Alps, seen here in early spring, separate Italy from the rest of central Europe. The valley in the lower centre of the image is that of the Po river and also visible are Lake Garda, right of centre, and Lake Geneva left of the snow covered area. The Alps are the source of several major European rivers including the Danube, Rhine and Rhone. The highest peak in the mountain range, Mont Blanc 4 804 m, is located on the France/Italy border, centre left on the image.

Satellite/Sensor : MODIS

Volga Delta, *Russian Federation*

The Volga river flows south into the Caspian Sea, over 3 690 km from its source, making it Europe's longest river. In this high oblique shuttle photograph the river delta, viewed from the north, fans out into the landlocked Caspian Sea. The city of Astrakhan is situated at the head of the delta on the west bank of the river. The silt from the delta provides a rich environment for flora and fauna.

Satellite/Sensor : Space Shuttle

Barents Sea

Novaya Zemlya

Lappland

Ural Mountains

Lake Ladoga

Baltic Sea

North European Plain

Vistula River

Volga River

Don River

Elbrus

Caspian Sea

Dnieper River

Caucasus

Carpathian Mountains

Crimea

Danube River

Black Sea

Alps

Bosporus

Po River

Dalmatia

Adriatic Sea

Apennines

Corsica

Sardinia

Sicily

Crete

Mediterranean Sea

ands

Highest point

Elbrus
Russian Federation
5 642 m / 18 510 feet
Map reference 107 E2

Longest river

Volga
3 688 km / 2 291 miles
Drainage basin
1 380 000 sq km / 533 000 sq miles
Map reference 41 I7

Largest lake

Caspian Sea
371 000sq km / 143 243 sq miles
Map reference 102 B4

EUROPE

HIGHEST MOUNTAINS	m	ft	location	map
Elbrus	5 642	18 510	Russian Federation	107 E2
Gora Dykh-Tau	5 204	17 073	Russian Federation	41 G8
Shkhara	5 201	17 063	Georgia/Russian Federation	41 G8
Kazbek	5 047	16 558	Georgia/Russian Federation	107 F2
Mont Blanc	4 808	15 774	France/Italy	51 M7
Durfourspitze	4 634	15 203	Italy/Switzerland	51 N7

LARGEST ISLANDS	sq km	sq miles	map
Great Britain	218 476	84 354	47 J9
Iceland	102 820	39 699	44 inset
Novaya Zemlya	90 650	35 000	38 T2
Ireland	83 045	32 064	47 D11
Spitzbergen	37 814	14 600	38 B2
Sicily	25 426	9 817	57 F1

LONGEST RIVERS	km	miles	map
Volga	3 688	2 291	41 I7
Danube	2 850	1 770	58 K3
Dnieper	2 285	1 419	41 E7
Kama	2 028	1 260	40 J4
Don	1 931	1 199	41 F7
Pechora	1 802	1 119	38 F3

LAKES	sq km	sq miles	map
Caspian Sea	371 000	143 243	102 B4
Lake Ladoga	18 390	7 100	40 D3
Lake Onega	9 600	3 706	40 E3
Vanern	5 585	2 156	45 C4
Rybinskoye Vodokhranilishche	5 180	2 000	43 T3

LAND AREA		map
Most northerly point	Ostrov Rudol'fa, Russian Federation	38 F1
Most southerly point	Gavdos, Crete, Greece	59 F14
Most westerly point	Bjargtangar, Iceland	44 A2
Most easterly point	Mys Flissingskiy, Russian Federation	39 G2
Total land area: 9 908 599 sq km / 3 825 731 sq miles		

EUROPE
COUNTRIES

		area sq km	area sq miles	population	capital	languages	religions	currency	map
ALBANIA		28 748	11 100	3 134 000	Tirana (Tiranë)	Albanian, Greek	Sunni Muslim, Albanian Orthodox, Roman Catholic	Lek	58–59
ANDORRA		465	180	86 000	Andorra la Vella	Spanish, Catalan, French	Roman Catholic	French franc, Spanish peseta	55
AUSTRIA		83 855	32 377	8 080 000	Vienna (Wien)	German, Croatian, Turkish	Roman Catholic, Protestant	Schilling, Euro	48–49
BELARUS		207 600	80 155	10 187 000	Minsk	Belorussian, Russian	Belorussian Orthodox, Roman Catholic	Rouble	42–43
BELGIUM		30 520	11 784	10 249 000	Brussels (Bruxelles)	Dutch (Flemish), French (Walloon), German	Roman Catholic, Protestant	Franc, Euro	51
BOSNIA–HERZEGOVINA		51 130	19 741	3 977 000	Sarajevo	Bosnian, Serbian, Croatian	Sunni Muslim, Serbian Orthodox, Roman Catholic, Protestant	Marka	56
BULGARIA		110 994	42 855	7 949 000	Sofia (Sofiya)	Bulgarian, Turkish, Romany, Macedonian	Bulgarian Orthodox, Sunni Muslim	Lev	58
CROATIA		56 538	21 829	4 654 000	Zagreb	Croatian, Serbian	Roman Catholic, Serbian Orthodox, Sunni Muslim	Kuna	56
CZECH REPUBLIC		78 864	30 450	10 272 000	Prague (Praha)	Czech, Moravian, Slovak	Roman Catholic, Protestant	Koruna	49
DENMARK		43 075	16 631	5 320 000	Copenhagen (København)	Danish	Protestant	Krone	45
ESTONIA		45 200	17 452	1 393 000	Tallinn	Estonian, Russian	Protestant, Estonian and Russian Orthodox	Kroon	42
FINLAND		338 145	130 559	5 172 000	Helsinki (Helsingfors)	Finnish, Swedish	Protestant, Greek Orthodox	Markka, Euro	44–45
FRANCE		543 965	210 026	59 238 000	Paris	French, Arabic	Roman Catholic, Protestant, Sunni Muslim	Franc, Euro	50–51
GERMANY		357 028	137 849	82 017 000	Berlin	German, Turkish	Protestant, Roman Catholic	Mark, Euro	48–49
GREECE		131 957	50 949	10 610 000	Athens (Athina)	Greek	Greek Orthodox, Sunni Muslim	Drachma	58–59
HUNGARY		93 030	35 919	9 968 000	Budapest	Hungarian	Roman Catholic, Protestant	Forint	49
ICELAND		102 820	39 699	279 000	Reykjavik	Icelandic	Protestant	Króna	44
IRELAND, REPUBLIC OF		70 282	27 136	3 803 000	Dublin (Baile Átha Cliath)	English, Irish	Roman Catholic, Protestant	Punt, Euro	46–47
ITALY		301 245	116 311	57 530 000	Rome (Roma)	Italian	Roman Catholic	Lira, Euro	56–57
LATVIA		63 700	24 595	2 421 000	Riga	Latvian, Russian	Protestant, Roman Catholic, Russian Orthodox	Lat	42
LIECHTENSTEIN		160	62	33 000	Vaduz	German	Roman Catholic, Protestant	Swiss franc	51
LITHUANIA		65 200	25 174	3 696 000	Vilnius	Lithuanian, Russian, Polish	Roman Catholic, Protestant, Russian Orthodox	Litas	42
LUXEMBOURG		2 586	998	437 000	Luxembourg	Letzeburgish, German, French	Roman Catholic	Franc, Euro	51
MACEDONIA (F.Y.R.O.M.)		25 713	9 928	2 034 000	Skopje	Macedonian, Albanian, Turkish	Macedonian Orthodox, Sunni Muslim	Denar	58
MALTA		316	122	390 000	Valletta	Maltese, English	Roman Catholic	Lira	57
MOLDOVA		33 700	13 012	4 295 000	Chişinău (Kishinev)	Romanian, Ukrainian, Gagauz, Russian	Romanian Orthodox, Russian Orthodox	Leu	41
MONACO		2	1	33 000	Monaco-Ville	French, Monegasque, Italian	Roman Catholic	French franc	51
NETHERLANDS		41 526	16 033	15 864 000	Amsterdam/The Hague	Dutch, Frisian	Roman Catholic, Protestant, Sunni Muslim	Guilder, Euro	48
NORWAY		323 878	125 050	4 469 000	Oslo	Norwegian	Protestant, Roman Catholic	Krone	44–45

CONNECTIONS

► subject	page#
► World countries	10–11
► Europe landscapes	30–31
► Europe issues	34–35
► Reference maps of Europe	38–59
► Atlantic Ocean	216–217

1 Rock of Gibraltar, *Gibraltar, Europe*

The narrow passage of water, appearing as a horizontal band of blue across the centre of this photograph is the 13 km wide Strait of Gibraltar which connects the Atlantic Ocean to the Mediterranean Sea. The strait forms a physical boundary between the continents of Europe and Africa. The photograph shows the 426 m high Rock of Gibraltar, viewed from Ceuta, a small Spanish enclave in Morocco, on the northern coast of Africa.

2 Bosporus, *Turkey, Europe/Asia*

The continents of Europe and Asia are physically separated by a narrow strait of water, the Bosporus, in Turkey. The strait, which at its narrowest point is less than 1 km wide, is 31 km long and connects the Sea of Marmara in the north to the Black Sea in the south. It is straddled by the city of Istanbul. The strait and the city are clearly shown in this SPOT satellite image. Istanbul airport is located near the coast toward the lower left of the image.

Satellite/Sensor : SPOT

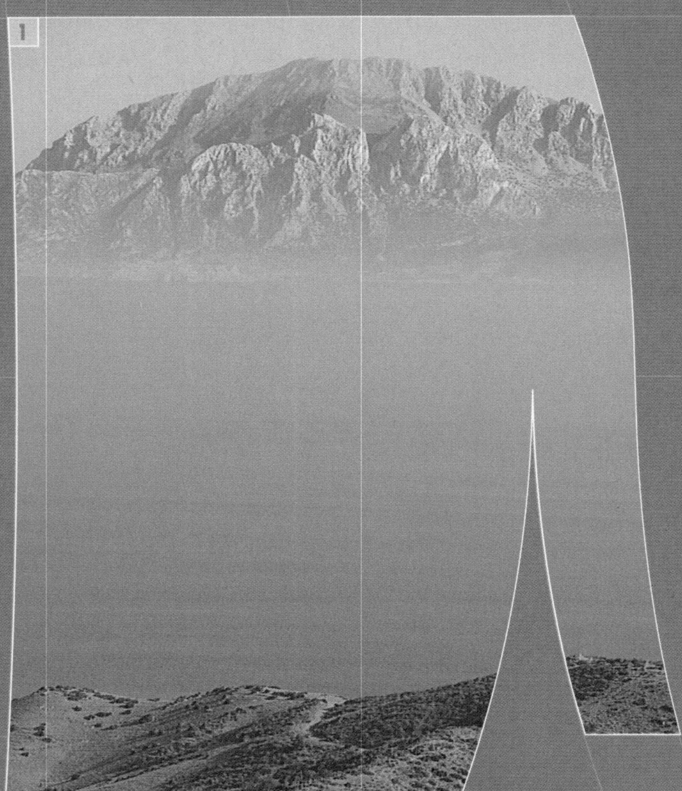

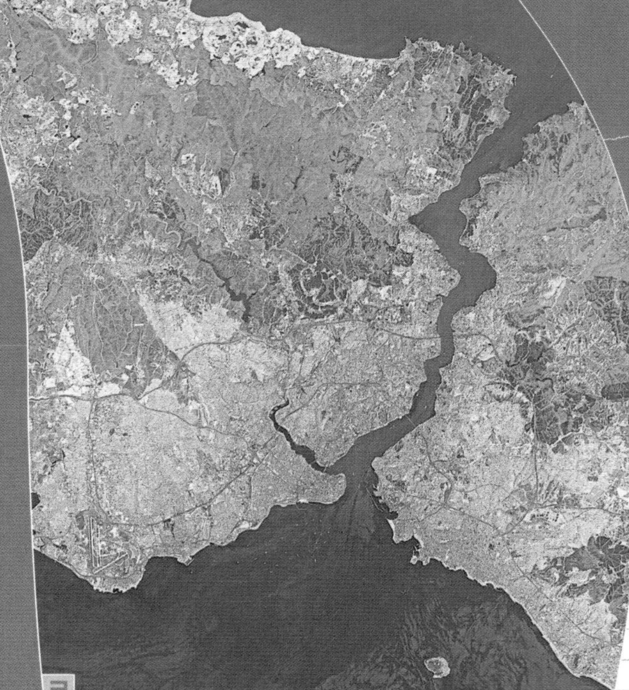

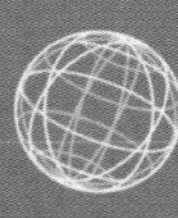

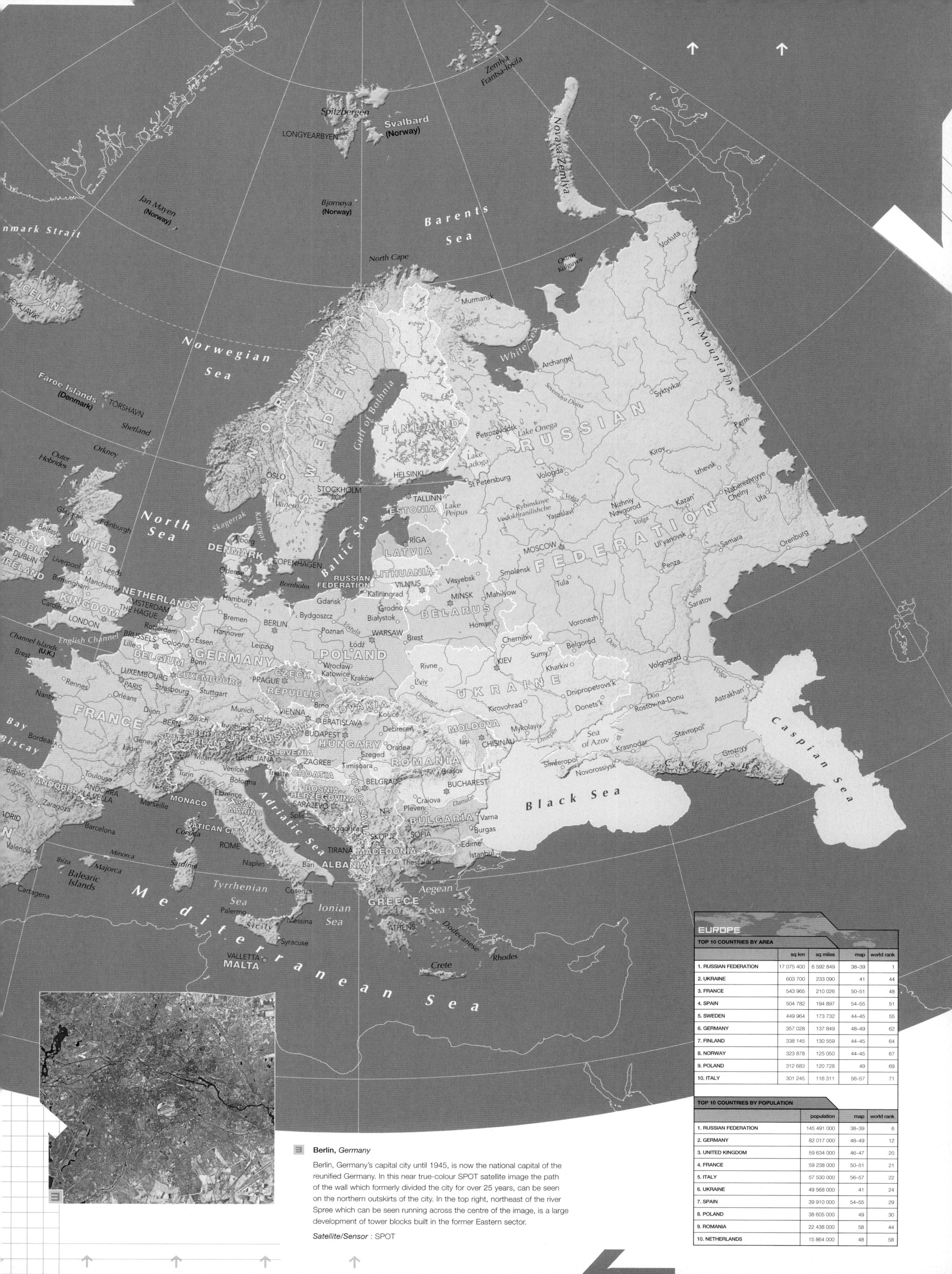

Berlin, *Germany*

Berlin, Germany's capital city until 1945, is now the national capital of the reunified Germany. In this near true-colour SPOT satellite image the path of the wall which formerly divided the city for over 25 years, can be seen on the northern outskirts of the city. In the top right, northeast of the river Spree which can be seen running across the centre of the image, is a large development of tower blocks built in the former Eastern sector.

Satellite/Sensor : SPOT

EUROPE

TOP 10 COUNTRIES BY AREA

	sq km	sq miles	map	world rank
1. RUSSIAN FEDERATION	17 075 400	6 592 849	38–39	1
2. UKRAINE	603 700	233 090	41	44
3. FRANCE	543 965	210 026	50–51	48
4. SPAIN	504 782	194 897	54–55	51
5. SWEDEN	449 964	173 732	44–45	55
6. GERMANY	357 028	137 849	48–49	62
7. FINLAND	338 145	130 559	44–45	64
8. NORWAY	323 878	125 050	44–45	67
9. POLAND	312 683	120 728	49	69
10. ITALY	301 245	116 311	56–57	71

TOP 10 COUNTRIES BY POPULATION

	population	map	world rank
1. RUSSIAN FEDERATION	145 491 000	38–39	6
2. GERMANY	82 017 000	48–49	12
3. UNITED KINGDOM	59 634 000	46–47	20
4. FRANCE	59 238 000	50–51	21
5. ITALY	57 530 000	56–57	22
6. UKRAINE	49 568 000	41	24
7. SPAIN	39 910 000	54–55	29
8. POLAND	38 605 000	49	30
9. ROMANIA	22 438 000	58	44
10. NETHERLANDS	15 864 000	48	58

EUROPE

COUNTRIES

		area sq km	area sq miles	population	capital	languages	religions	currency	map
POLAND		312 683	120 728	38 605 000	Warsaw (Warszawa)	Polish, German	Roman Catholic, Polish Orthodox	Zloty	49
PORTUGAL		88 940	34 340	10 016 000	Lisbon (Lisboa)	Portuguese	Roman Catholic, Protestant	Escudo, Euro	54
ROMANIA		237 500	91 699	22 438 000	Bucharest (București)	Romanian, Hungarian	Romanian Orthodox, Protestant, Roman Catholic	Leu	58
RUSSIAN FEDERATION		17 075 400	6 592 849	145 491 000	Moscow (Moskva)	Russian, Tatar, Ukrainian, local languages	Russian Orthodox, Sunni Muslim, Protestant	Rouble	38–39
SAN MARINO		61	24	27 000	San Marino	Italian	Roman Catholic	Italian lira	56
SLOVAKIA		49 035	18 933	5 399 000	Bratislava	Slovak, Hungarian, Czech	Roman Catholic, Protestant, Orthodox	Koruna	49
SLOVENIA		20 251	7 819	1 988 000	Ljubljana	Slovene, Croatian, Serbian	Roman Catholic, Protestant	Tolar	56
SPAIN		504 782	194 897	39 910 000	Madrid	Castilian, Catalan, Galician, Basque	Roman Catholic	Peseta, Euro	54–55
SWEDEN		449 964	173 732	8 842 000	Stockholm	Swedish	Protestant, Roman Catholic	Krona	44–45
SWITZERLAND		41 293	15 943	7 170 000	Bern (Berne)	German, French, Italian, Romansch	Roman Catholic, Protestant	Franc	51
UKRAINE		603 700	233 090	49 568 000	Kiev (Kyiv)	Ukrainian, Russian	Ukrainian Orthodox, Ukrainian Catholic, Roman Catholic	Hryvnia	41
UNITED KINGDOM		244 082	94 241	59 634 000	London	English, Welsh, Gaelic	Protestant, Roman Catholic, Muslim	Pound	46–47
VATICAN CITY		0.5	0.2	480	Vatican City	Italian	Roman Catholic	Italian lira	56
YUGOSLAVIA		102 173	39 449	10 552 000	Belgrade (Beograd)	Serbian, Albanian, Hungarian	Serbian Orthodox, Montenegrin Orthodox, Sunni Muslim	Dinar	58

DEPENDENT TERRITORIES

		territorial status	area sq km	area sq miles	population	capital	languages	religions	currency	map
Azores (Arquipélago dos Açores)		Autonomous Region of Portugal	2 300	888	243 600	Ponta Delgada	Portuguese	Roman Catholic, Protestant	Port. Escudo	216
Faroe Islands		Self-governing Danish Territory	1 399	540	46 000	Tórshavn (Thorshavn)	Faroese, Danish	Protestant	Danish krone	46
Gibraltar		United Kingdom Overseas Territory	7	3	27 000	Gibraltar	English, Spanish	Roman Catholic, Protestant, Sunni Muslim	Pound	54
Guernsey		United Kingdom Crown Dependency	78	30	64 555	St Peter Port	English, French	Protestant, Roman Catholic	Pound	50
Isle of Man		United Kingdom Crown Dependency	572	221	77 000	Douglas	English	Protestant, Roman Catholic	Pound	47
Jersey		United Kingdom Crown Dependency	116	45	89 136	St Helier	English, French	Protestant, Roman Catholic	Pound	50

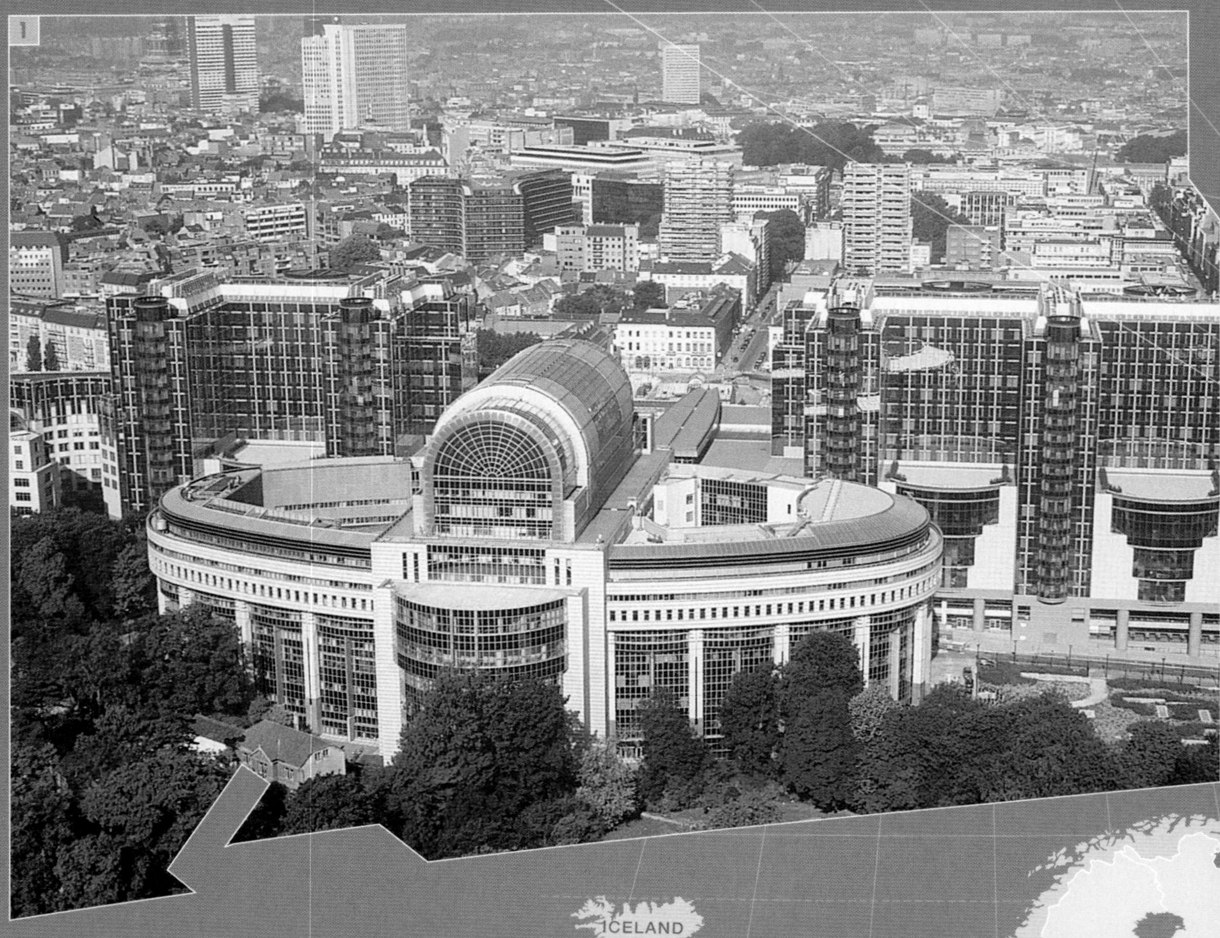

1 The European Union

The European Union (EU) is a union of fifteen independent European states. It was founded as the European Economic Commission by the Treaty of Rome in 1957. Its purpose is to enhance political, economic and social cooperation. As shown on the map, the EU has grown from six to fifteen members and thirteen new applicants are currently negotiating for membership. The headquarters of the EU, in the Belgian capital Brussels, is the curved glass roofed building, known as the Hémicycle Européen, shown in the photograph.

Fig. #01
The European Union

- Founder members (1957)
- Joined in 1973
- Joined in 1981
- Joined in 1986
- Joined in 1995
- Current applicant
- Non-member

ICELAND
NORWAY
SWEDEN
FINLAND
ESTONIA
LATVIA
LITHUANIA
RUS. FED.
DENMARK
BELARUS
UNITED KINGDOM
REPUBLIC OF IRELAND
NETHERLANDS
GERMANY
POLAND
UKRAINE
BELGIUM
Brussels
LUXEMBOURG
CZECH REPUBLIC
SLOVAKIA
FRANCE
AUSTRIA
HUNGARY
MOLDOVA
SWITZERLAND
SLOVENIA
CROATIA
ROMANIA
BOSNIA-HERZEGOVINA
YUGOSLAVIA
ANDORRA
ITALY
BULGARIA
MACEDONIA
PORTUGAL
SPAIN
ALBANIA
GREECE
TURKEY
MALTA
CYPRUS

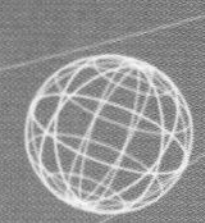

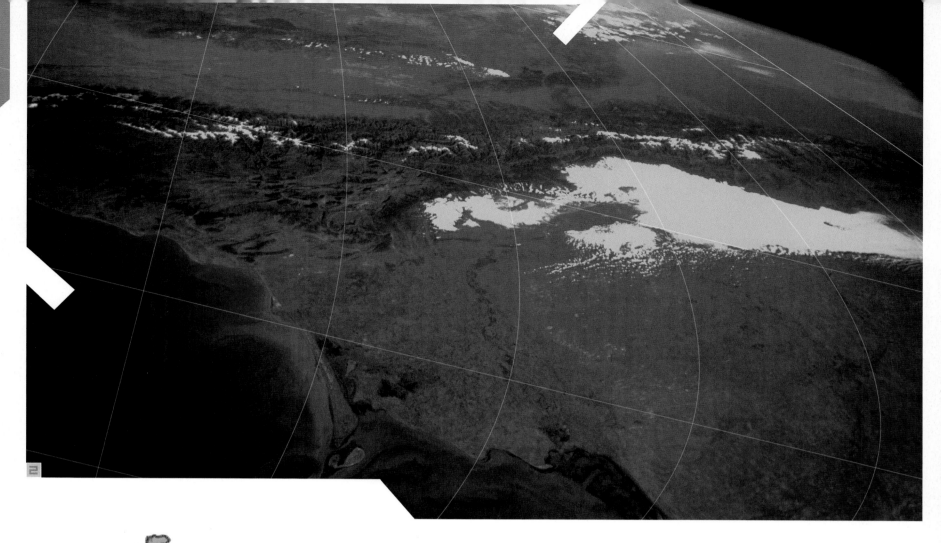

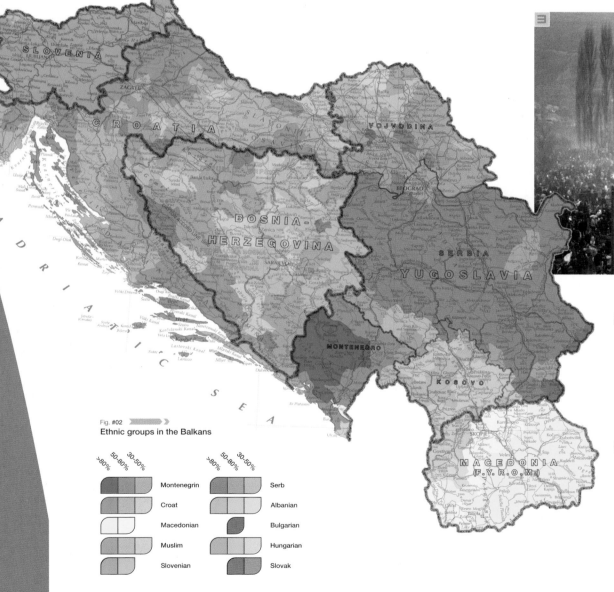

Fig. #02
Ethnic groups in the Balkans

Caucasus, *Europe/Asia*

The Caucasus mountains extend from the eastern shores of the Black Sea to the southwest coast of the Caspian Sea and form an almost impenetrable barrier between Europe in the north, and Asia in the south. Europe's highest mountain, Elbrus, reaches 5 642 m in the western end of the range. The plains lying north of the Caucasus, seen in the lower half of this Shuttle photograph, are part of the Russian Federation and include the region of Chechnia. On the southern slopes of the mountains are the countries of Georgia and Azerbaijan.

Satellite/Sensor : Space Shuttle

The Balkans, *Europe*

The region of the Balkans has a long history of instability and ethnic conflict. The map shows the underlying complexity of the ethnic composition of the former country of Yugoslavia. The 1990 Yugoslav elections uncovered these divisions and over the next three years, four of the six Yugoslav republics – Croatia, Slovenia, Bosnia-Herzegovina and Macedonia – each declared their independence. The civil war continued until 1995 when the Dayton Peace Accord was established. In Kosovo, a sub-division of the Yugoslav republic of Serbia, the majority population of Muslim Albanians were forced to accept direct Serbian rule, and as a result support grew for the independence-seeking rebel Kosovo Liberation Army. In 1998 and 1999 the Serbs reacted through 'ethnic cleansing' of Kosovo, when many Kosovans were killed and, as shown in the photograph, thousands were forced to flee their homes. After NATO action, an agreement for Serb withdrawal was reached in June 1999.

CONNECTIONS

subject	page#
World physical features	8–9
World countries	10–11
Europe landscapes	30–31
Europe countries	32–33
Reference maps of Europe	38–59

europe[environments]

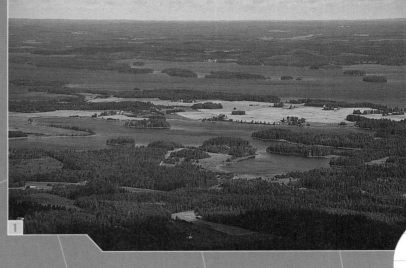

1 Lakelands, ***Finland***

This aerial photograph, taken to the east of Kuopio, shows an environment typical of the lakeland areas of central Finland. The country is mostly lowland, with many lakes, marshes, and low hills. The vast forested interior plateau includes approximately 60 000 lakes, many of which are linked by short rivers, or canals to form commercial waterways.

2 Volcanic Environment, ***Iceland***

The steam rising from the mountain side in this photograph is a result of volcanic activity. Iceland is a country with nearly 200 volcanoes, many of them still active. These create, and have created, great lava fields and rough mountainous terrain. Perhaps the most notable volcano is Hekla which rises to 1 491 m and had a major eruption in 1991. Hot springs and geysers are also common, and their geothermal energy is commonly used for domestic heating.

3 Mediterranean Island, ***Europe***

This satellite image of the French island of Corsica in the Mediterranean Sea shows a mountainous island with some flat areas in the form of lagoons and marshes on the eastern coast. The highest point of the island is Monte Cinto, 2 706 m, which is towards the north of the pale, mountainous area.

Satellite/sensor : SPOT

4 Agricultural Region, ***Italy***

The numerous rectangles in this satellite image are a patchwork of fields found in the Fucino plain, to the east of Avezzano, Italy. This area was formerly a lake which was drained in the mid-nineteenth century and now provides over 160 square kilometres of fertile farmland. Today the area is intensely cultivated with a variety of crops being grown, including cereals, potatoes, sugar beet, grapes and fruit.

Satellite/Sensor : Landsat

5 Planned Village, ***The Netherlands***

This aerial photograph shows the village of Bourtange located in the extreme south-east of Groningen province in the Netherlands, less than 2 km from the German border. The star-shaped fortress dates back to the late sixteenth century. The old core of the village was restored in 1967 and has since been protected as a national monument.

6 Mountainous Coastline, ***United Kingdom***

This satellite image of the west coast of Scotland clearly shows the effect of the last ice age on this landscape. Retreating glaciers left long, deep valleys, high mountains and a very rugged, indented coastline. The barren mountains are clearly identified as the white areas of bare rock. Water appears as darker areas with Loch Maree being the largest loch in the centre of the image.

Satellite/Sensor : Landsat

7 Urban Environment, ***United Kingdom***

This aerial photograph shows part of the centre of London, the capital city of the United Kingdom. Westminster, the seat of the British government, is located on the left bank of the River Thames at the bottom of the photograph. Other notable features are Buckingham Palace (bottom left), St James's Park, Waterloo Station (bottom right) and the London Eye observation wheel in its flat construction position over the river, prior to its final erection and completion.

1

2

3

5

4

CONNECTIONS

▸ subject	page#
▸ World land cover types	18–19
▸ World cities	24–25
▸ Europe landscapes	30–31
▸ Reference maps of Europe	38–59
▸ North America environments	162–163

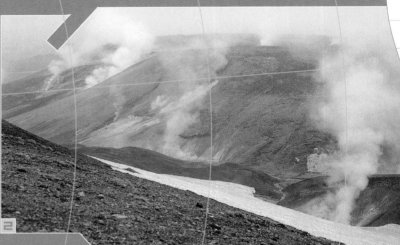

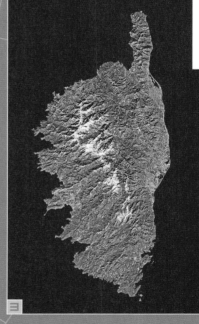

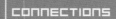

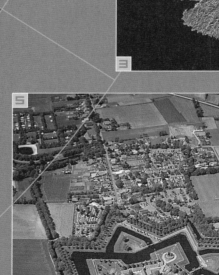

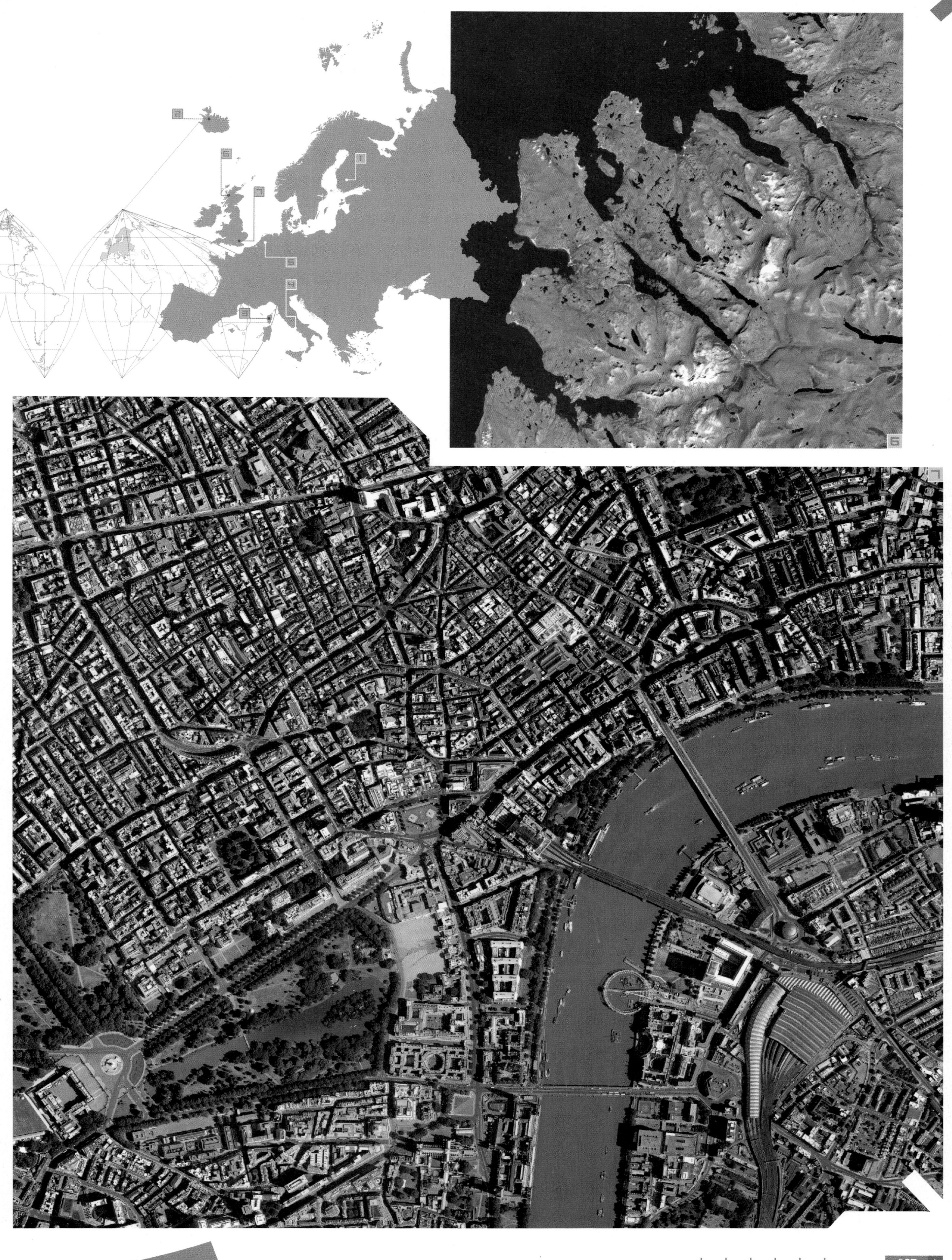

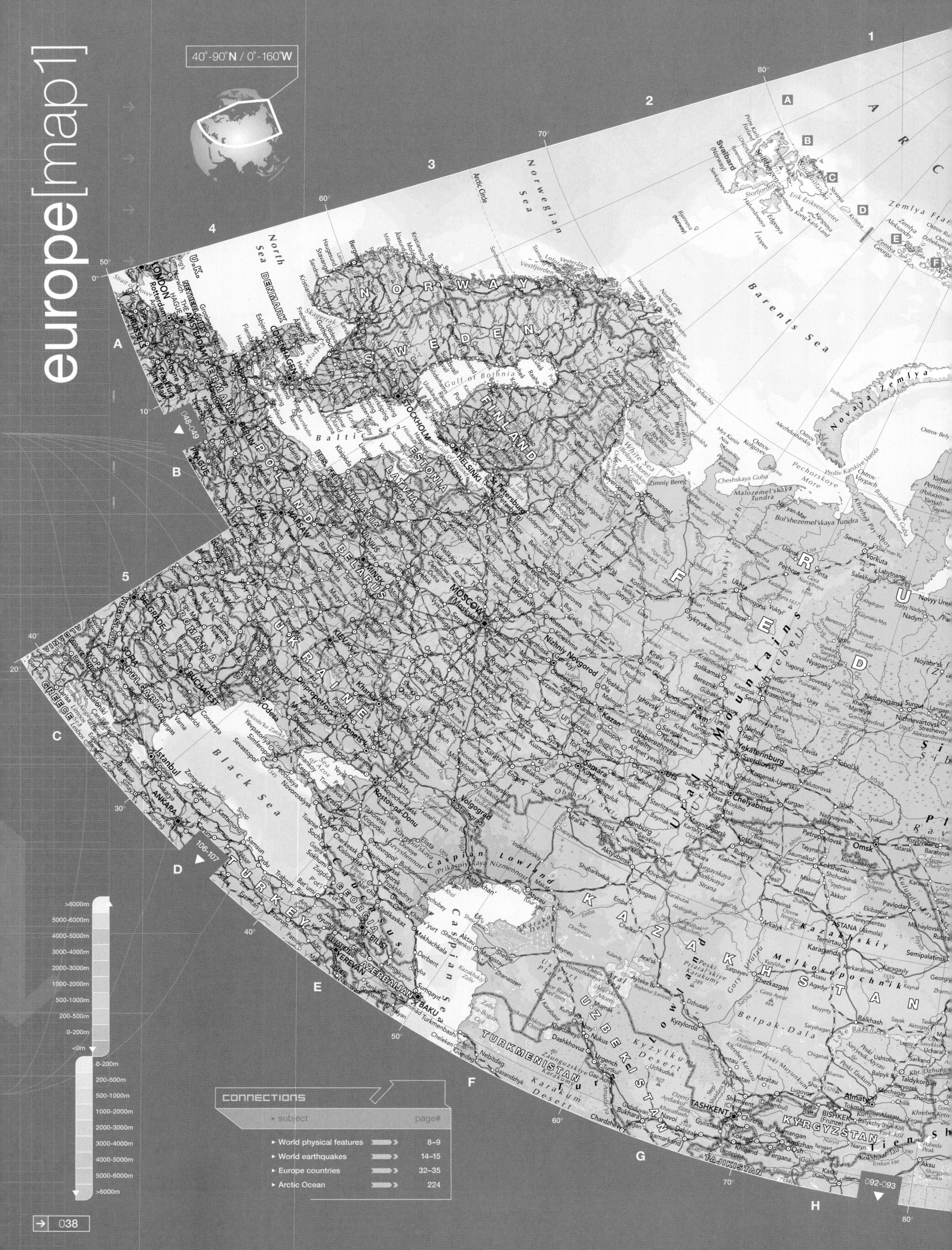
europe[map1]
40°-90°N / 0°-160°W
NORWAY
SWEDEN
FINLAND
DENMARK
U.K.
NETHERLANDS
GERMANY
POLAND
ESTONIA
LATVIA
LITHUANIA
BELARUS
UKRAINE
MOLDOVA
ROMANIA
BULGARIA
YUGOSLAVIA
ALBANIA
MACEDONIA
GREECE
TURKEY
GEORGIA
ARMENIA
AZERBAIJAN
KAZAKHSTAN
UZBEKISTAN
TURKMENISTAN
KYRGYZSTAN
TAJIKISTAN
RUSSIAN FEDERATION
LONDON
AMSTERDAM
BRUSSELS
COPENHAGEN
OSLO
STOCKHOLM
HELSINKI
BERLIN
PRAGUE
WARSAW
VILNIUS
RIGA
MINSK
KIEV
MOSCOW (Moskva)
St Petersburg
CHIŞINĂU
BUCHAREST
BELGRADE
SOFIA
Istanbul
ANKARA
TBILISI
YEREVAN
BAKU
ASTANA (Akmola)
TASHKENT
BISHKEK (Frunze)
Almaty
Norwegian Sea
North Sea
Baltic Sea
Gulf of Bothnia
Barents Sea
White Sea
Black Sea
Sea of Azov
Caspian Sea
Aral Sea
Arctic Circle
Svalbard (Norway)
Novaya Zemlya
Zemlya Frantsa-Iosifa
Ural Mountains
Caspian Lowland
Kyzylkum Desert
Karakum Desert
Betpak-Dala
>6000m
5000-6000m
4000-5000m
3000-4000m
2000-3000m
1000-2000m
500-1000m
200-500m
0-200m
<0m
0-200m
200-500m
500-1000m
1000-2000m
2000-3000m
3000-4000m
4000-5000m
5000-6000m
>6000m
048-049
106-107
092-093
CONNECTIONS
subject page#
World physical features 8–9
World earthquakes 14–15
Europe countries 32–35
Arctic Ocean 224

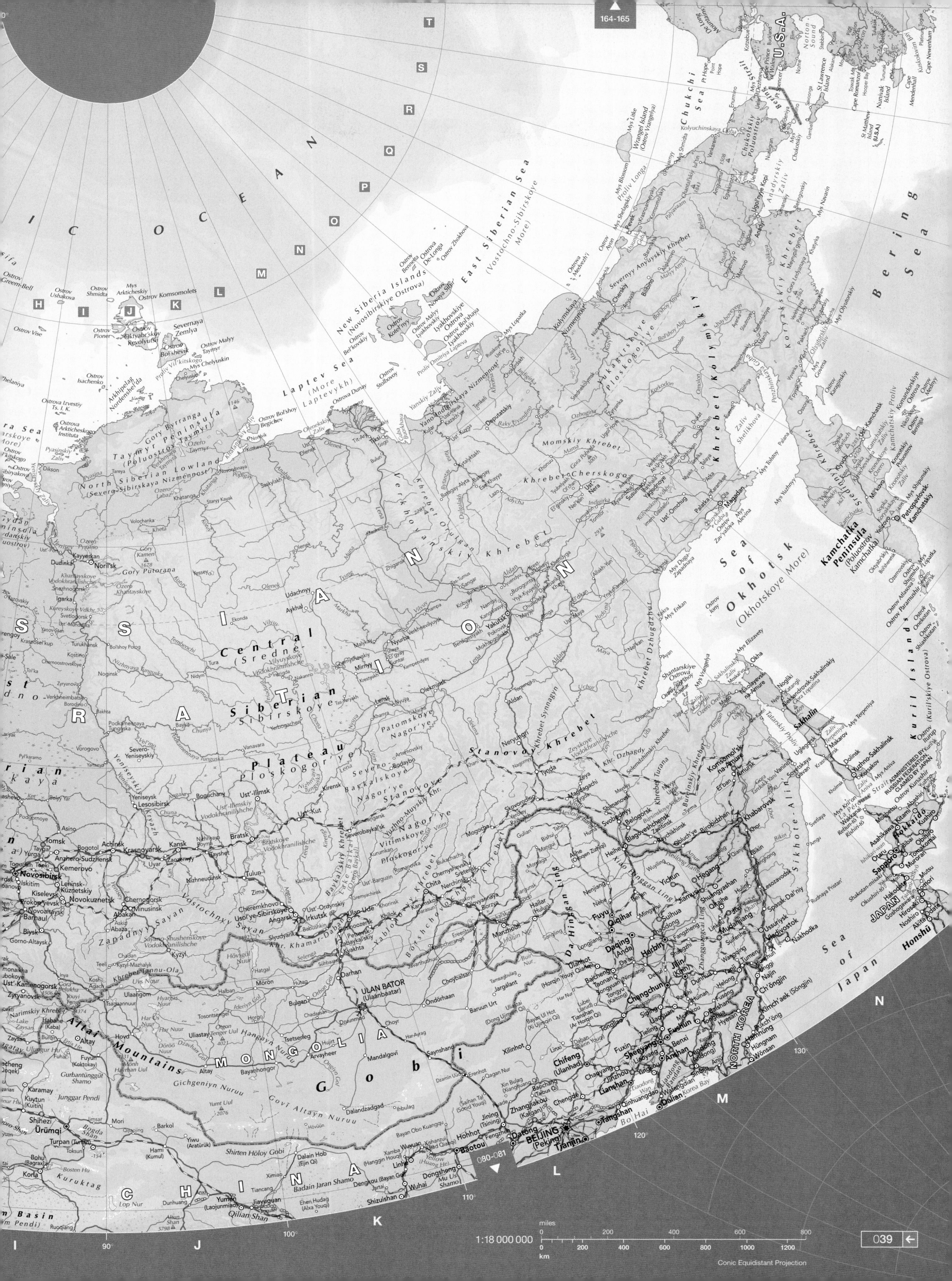

164-165
ARCTIC OCEAN
East Siberian Sea
(Vostochno-Sibirskoye More)
Laptev Sea
(More Laptevykh)
Chukchi Sea
Bering Sea
Sea of Okhotsk
(Okhotskoye More)
Sea of Japan
Korea Bay
Bo Hai
New Siberia Islands
(Novosibirskiye Ostrova)
Wrangel Island
(Ostrov Vrangelya)
Severnaya Zemlya
Ostrov Komsomolets
Ostrov Oktyabr'skoy Revolyutsii
Ostrov Bol'shevik
Taymyr Peninsula
(Poluostrov Taymyr)
North Siberian Lowland
(Severo-Sibirskaya Nizmennost')
Central Siberian Plateau
(Sredne-Sibirskoye Ploskogor'ye)
Verkhoyanskiy Khrebet
Khrebet Cherskogo
Momskiy Khrebet
Kolymskiy Khrebet
Koryakskiy Khrebet
Stanovoy Khrebet
Kamchatka Peninsula
(Poluostrov Kamchatka)
Kuril Islands
(Kuril'skiye Ostrova)
Sakhalin
Hokkaido
Honshu
JAPAN
U.S.A.
NORTH KOREA
RUSSIAN FEDERATION
MONGOLIA
CHINA
Gobi
Altai Mountains
Da Hinggan Ling
Xiao Hinggan Ling
Sikhote-Alin'
Vostochnyy Sayan
Zapadnyy Sayan
ULAN BATOR
(Ulaanbaatar)
BEIJING
(Peking)
Tianjin
Harbin
Changchun
Shenyang
Dalian
Vladivostok
Khabarovsk
Yakutsk
Magadan
Petropavlovsk-Kamchatskiy
Irkutsk
Krasnoyarsk
Novosibirsk
Noril'sk
Ürümqi
Baotou
Hohhot
Datong
Qiqihar
Sapporo
Qilian Shan
080-081
N
M
L
K
J
I
90°
100°
110°
120°
130°
1:18 000 000
miles
0
200
400
600
800
0
200
400
600
800
1000
1200
km
Conic Equidistant Projection

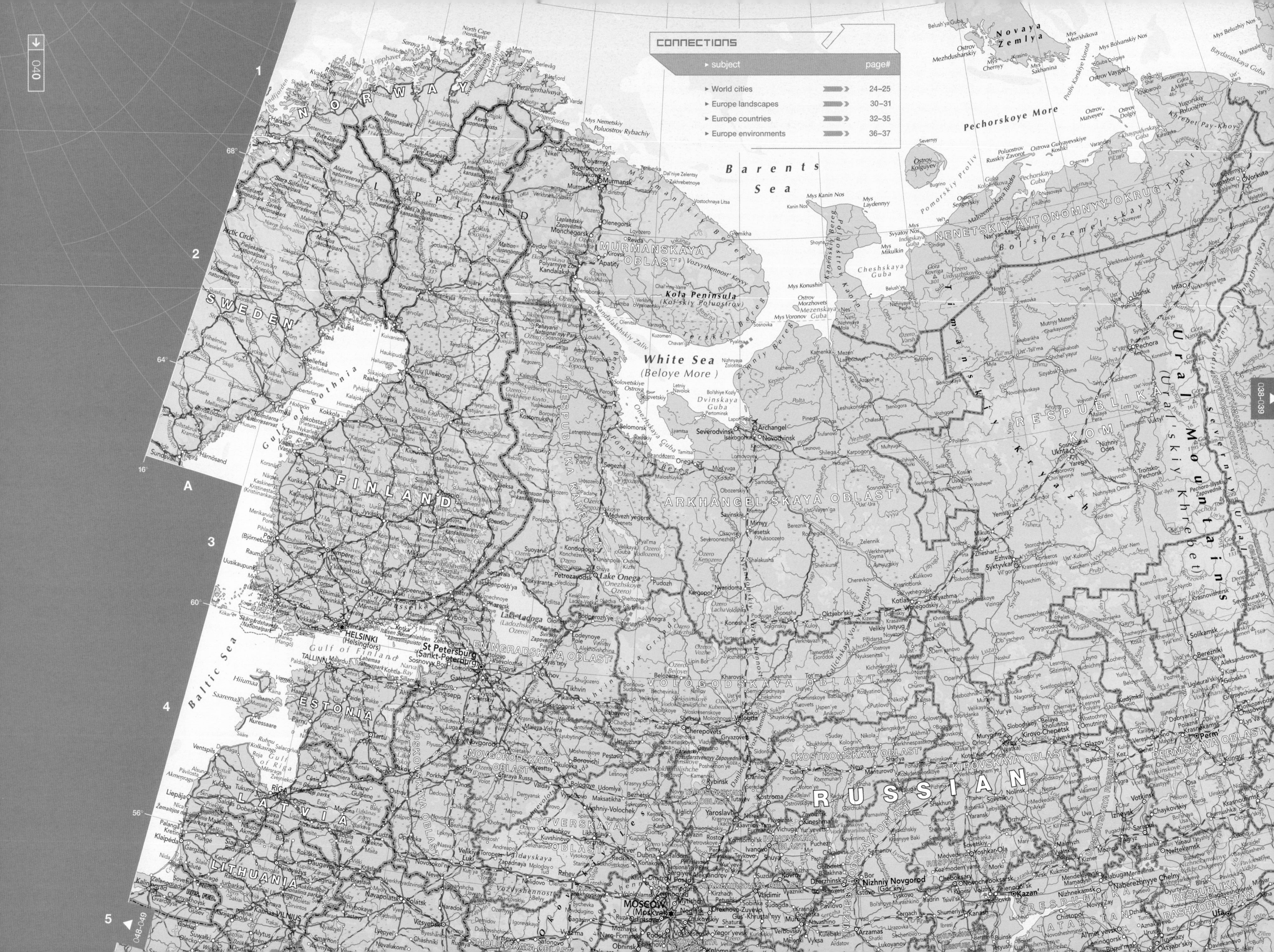

CONNECTIONS

▶ subject	page#
▶ World cities	24-25
▶ Europe landscapes	30-31
▶ Europe countries	32-35
▶ Europe environments	36-37

Ural Mountains
(Ural'skiy Khrebet)

RUSSIAN

Barents Sea

Pechorskoye More

Novaya Zemlya

White Sea
(Beloye More)

Kola Peninsula
(Kol'skiy Poluostrov)

MURMANSKAYA OBLAST

NENETSKIY AVTONOMNYY OKRUG

RESPUBLIKA KOMI

ARKHANGEL'SKAYA OBLAST

VOLOGODSKAYA OBLAST

RESPUBLIKA KARELIYA

LENINGRADSKAYA OBLAST

PSKOVSKAYA OBLAST

NOVGORODSKAYA OBLAST

TVERSKAYA OBLAST

MOSCOW
(Moskva)

N O R W A Y

S W E D E N

F I N L A N D

ESTONIA

LATVIA

LITHUANIA

Lake Ladoga
(Ladozhskoye Ozero)

Lake Onega
(Onezhskoye Ozero)

St Petersburg
(Sankt-Peterburg)

HELSINKI
(Helsingfors)

TALLINN

Gulf of Finland

Gulf of Bothnia

Baltic Sea

Arctic Circle

europe[map2]

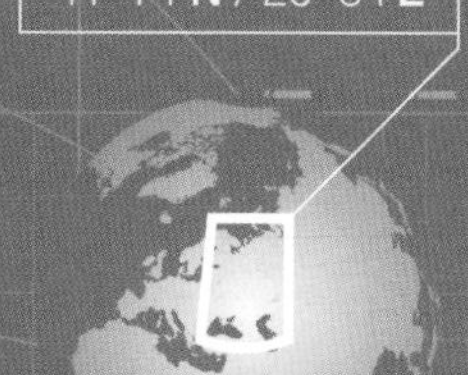

41°-71°N / 20°-54°E

1:7 500 000

Conic Equidistant Projection

Administrative divisions in Russian
Federation numbered on the map:

1. RESPUBLIKA ADYGEYA (G7)
2. CHECHENSKAYA RESPUBLIKA (CHECHNIA) (H8)
3. RESPUBLIKA INGUSHETIYA (INGUSHETIA) (H8)
4. KABARDINO-BALKARSKAYA RESPUBLIKA (G8)
5. KARACHAYEVO-CHERKESSKAYA RESPUBLIKA (G8)
6. RESPUBLIKA SEVERNAYA OSETIYA-ALANIYA
   (NORTH OSSETIA) (H8)

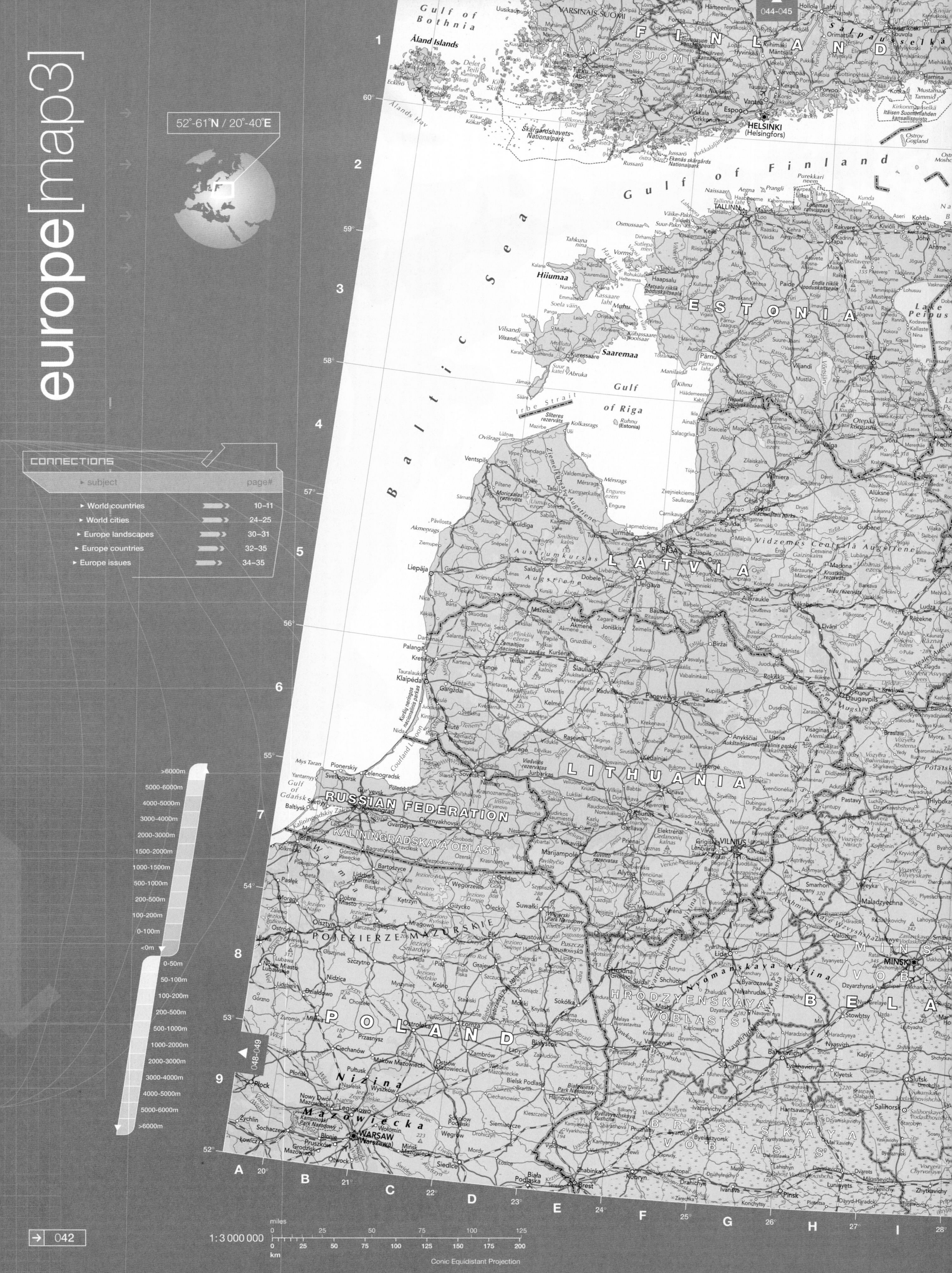

europe[map3]
52°-61°N / 20°-40°E
CONNECTIONS
subject
page#
World countries 10–11
World cities 24–25
Europe landscapes 30–31
Europe countries 32–35
Europe issues 34–35
>6000m
5000-6000m
4000-5000m
3000-4000m
2000-3000m
1500-2000m
1000-1500m
500-1000m
200-500m
100-200m
0-100m
<0m
0-50m
50-100m
100-200m
200-500m
500-1000m
1000-2000m
2000-3000m
3000-4000m
4000-5000m
5000-6000m
>6000m
044-045
048-049
Gulf of Bothnia
Åland Islands
FINLAND
HELSINKI (Helsingfors)
Gulf of Finland
TALLINN
ESTONIA
Hiiumaa
Saaremaa
Baltic Sea
Gulf of Riga
Lake Peipus
LATVIA
RIGA
LITHUANIA
VILNIUS
RUSSIAN FEDERATION
KALININGRADSKAYA OBLAST'
POLAND
WARSAW (Warszawa)
MINSK
HRODZYENSKAYA VOBLASTS'
BRESTSKAYA VOBLASTS'
1:3 000 000
miles
km
Conic Equidistant Projection

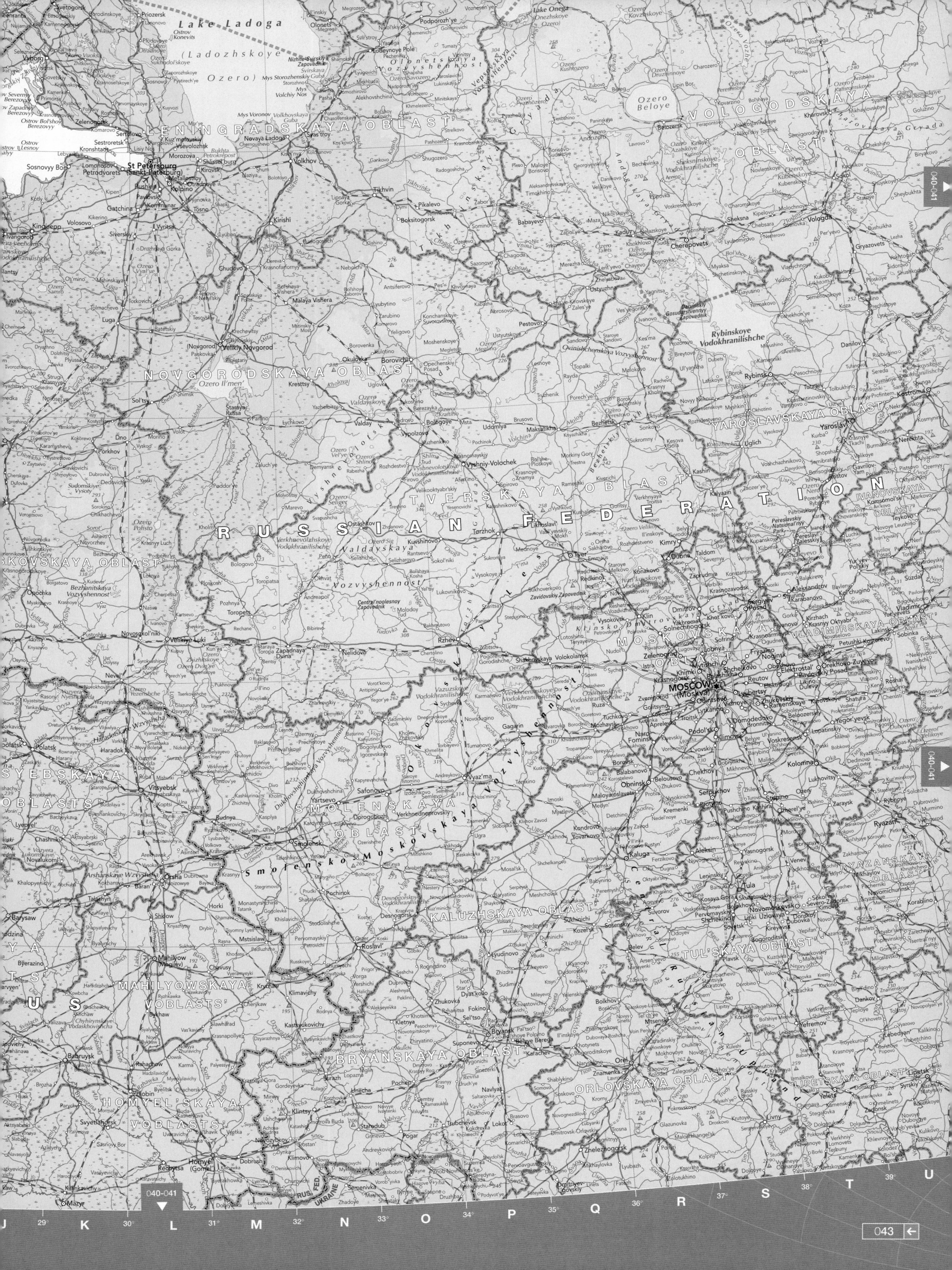

Lake Ladoga
(Ladozhskoye
Ozero)
Lake Onega
(Onezhskoye
Ozero)
Ozero
Beloye
Rybinskoye
Vodokhranilishche
Ozero Il'men'
LENINGRADSKAYA OBLAST
VOLOGODSKAYA
OBLAST
NOVGORODSKAYA OBLAST
YAROSLAVSKAYA OBLAST
TVERSKAYA OBLAST
RUSSIAN FEDERATION
IVANOVSKAYA
OBLAST
MOSKOVSKAYA
OBLAST
VLADIMIRSKAYA OBLAST
SMOLENSKAYA
OBLAST
KALUZHSKAYA OBLAST
TUL'SKAYA OBLAST
RYAZANSKAYA
OBLAST
BRYANSKAYA OBLAST
ORLOVSKAYA OBLAST
LIPETSKAYA OBLAST
VITSYEBSKAYA
VOBLASTS
MAHILYOWSKAYA
VOBLASTS
HOMYEL'SKAYA
VOBLASTS
St Petersburg
(Sankt-Peterburg)
MOSCOW
(Moskva)
Vologda
Yaroslavl'
Kostroma
Tver'
Velikiy Novgorod
Smolensk
Bryansk
Kaluga
Tula
Ryazan'
Orel
Vitsyebsk
Mahilyow
Homyel'
Babruysk
Rybinsk
Cherepovets
Pskov
040-041
J
K
L
M
N
O
P
Q
R
S
T
U
29°
30°
31°
32°
33°
34°
35°
36°
37°
38°
39°

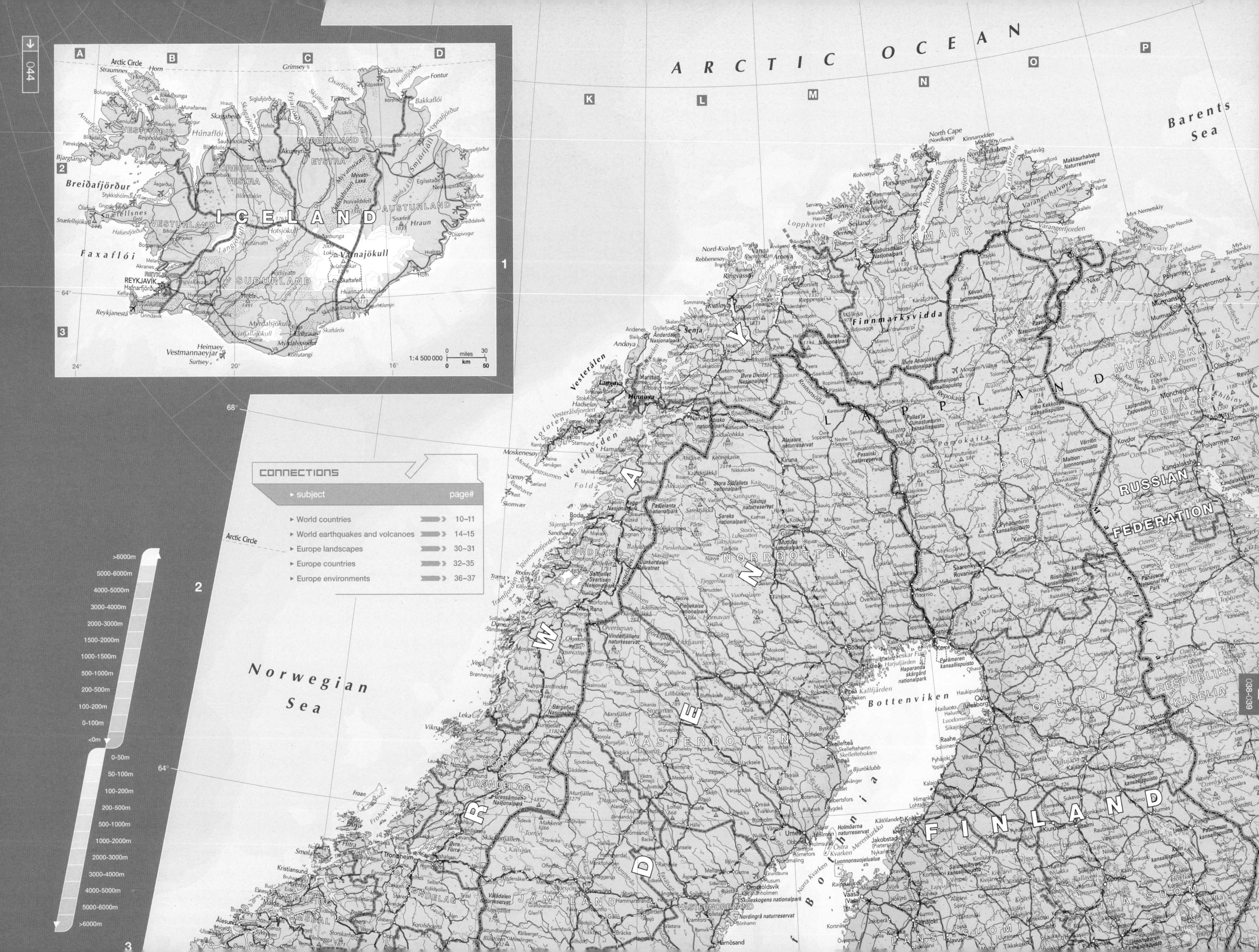

Barents Sea

ARCTIC OCEAN

P

O

N

M

L

K

RUSSIAN FEDERATION

FINLAND

NORWAY

SWEDEN

Norwegian Sea

Faxaflói

Breiðafjörður

ICELAND

1:4 500 000

miles 30
km 50

Arctic Circle

CONNECTIONS

▶ subject   page#

▶ World countries   10–11
▲ World earthquakes and volcanoes 14–15
▲ Europe landscapes   30–31
▲ Europe countries   32–35
▲ Europe environments   36–37

>6000m
5000–6000m
4000–5000m
3000–4000m
2000–3000m
1500–2000m
1000–1500m
500–1000m
200–500m
50–200m
0–50m
<0m
0–10m
10–50m
50–100m
100–200m
200–500m
500–1000m
1000–2000m
2000–3000m
3000–4000m
4000–5000m
5000–6000m
>6000m

europe[map4]

048-049 ▶

54°-72°N / 4°-28°E

1:4 500 000

Conic Equidistant Projection

miles
km

RUSSIAN FEDERATION

BELARUS

FINLAND

ESTONIA

LATVIA

LITHUANIA

RUSSIAN FEDERATION

POLAND

GERMANY

DENMARK

NORWAY

SWEDEN

Gulf of Finland

Gulf of Riga

Baltic Sea

Gulf of Bothnia

Skagerrak

Kattegat

St Petersburg (Sankt-Peterburg)

HELSINKI (Helsingfors)

TALLINN

RIGA

STOCKHOLM

OSLO

COPENHAGEN

Åland Islands

Gotland (Sweden)

Öland

Bornholm (Denmark)

Saaremaa

Jutland

Zealand

Vänern

Vättern

North Frisian Islands

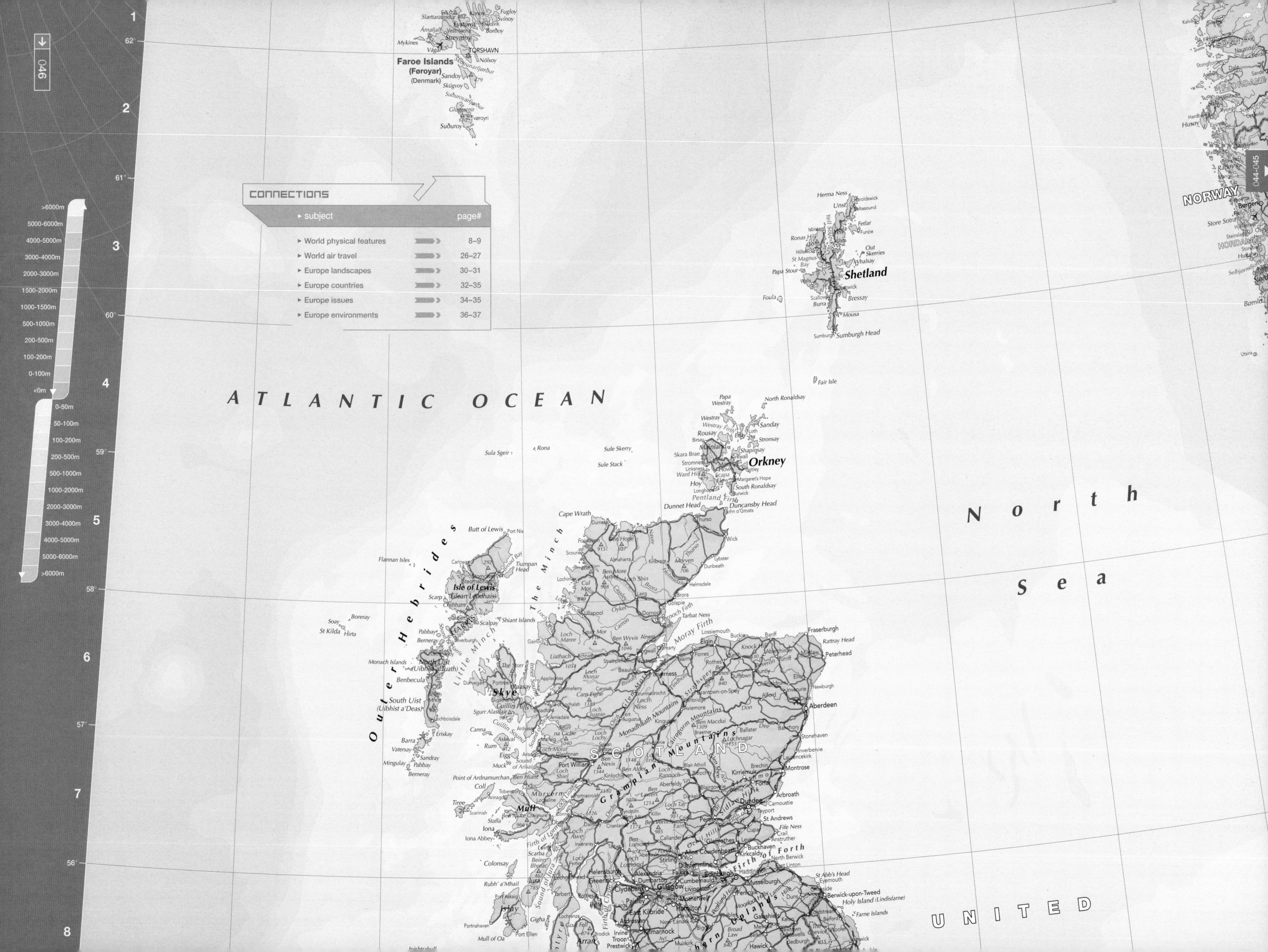

NORWAY

Bergen
Stord Sotra
Huvik
Bomlo

North Sea

U N I T E D

SCOTLAND

Shetland
Herma Ness
Unst
Fetlar
Out Skerries
Whalsay
Bressay
Mousa
Yell Sound
Scalloway
Burra
Sumburgh Head

Fair Isle

Foula

Orkney
North Ronaldsay
Westray
Papa Westray
Sanday
Stronsay
Rousay
Shapinsay
Mainland
Hoy
South Ronaldsay
Stromness
Duncansby Head
Pentland Firth
John o'Groats
Skara Brae

Dunnet Head
Thurso
Wick

Cape Wrath

Sule Skerry
Sule Stack

Sula Sgeir

Rona

Butt of Lewis
Port Nis

Fraserburgh
Rattray Head
Peterhead

Aberdeen
Stonehaven
Montrose
Arbroath
Carnoustie
St Andrews
Fife Ness
Crail
Anstruther
North Berwick

St Abb's Head
Eyemouth

Berwick-upon-Tweed
Holy Island (Lindisfarne)
Farne Islands

Isle of Lewis

Inner Sound

Skye

Mull

Tiree
Coll

Iona
Staffa
Iona Abbey

Colonsay

Jura
Islay
Gigha

Rum
Eigg
Muck

Barra
Vatersay
Mingulay
Berneray

St Kilda
Hirta
Soay
Boreray

Monach Islands
Benbecula
South Uist

Outer Hebrides

The Minch

Little Minch

A T L A N T I C   O C E A N

Faroe Islands
(Foroyar)
(Denmark)

TORSHAVN

5000-6000m
4000-5000m
3000-4000m
2000-3000m
1500-2000m
1000-1500m
500-1000m
200-500m
100-200m
50-100m
0-50m
<0m

0-50m
50-100m
100-200m
200-500m
500-1000m
1000-2000m
1500-2000m
2000-3000m
3000-4000m
4000-5000m
5000-6000m
>6000m

europe[map5]

050-051

1:3 000 000

50°-62°N / 11°W-3°E

Conic Equidistant Projection

europe[map6]

46°-55°N / 4°-22°E

North Sea

>6000m
5000-6000m
4000-5000m
3000-4000m
2000-3000m
1500-2000m
1000-1500m
500-1000m
200-500m
100-200m
0-100m
<0m

0-50m
50-100m
100-200m
200-500m
500-1000m
1000-2000m
2000-3000m
3000-4000m
4000-5000m
5000-6000m
>6000m

DENMARK

NETHERLANDS

BELGIUM

LUXEMBOURG

GERMANY

FRANCE

SWITZERLAND

miles
0   25   50   75   100   125
0 25 50 75 100 125 150 175 200
km

1 : 3 000 000

Conic Equidistant Projection

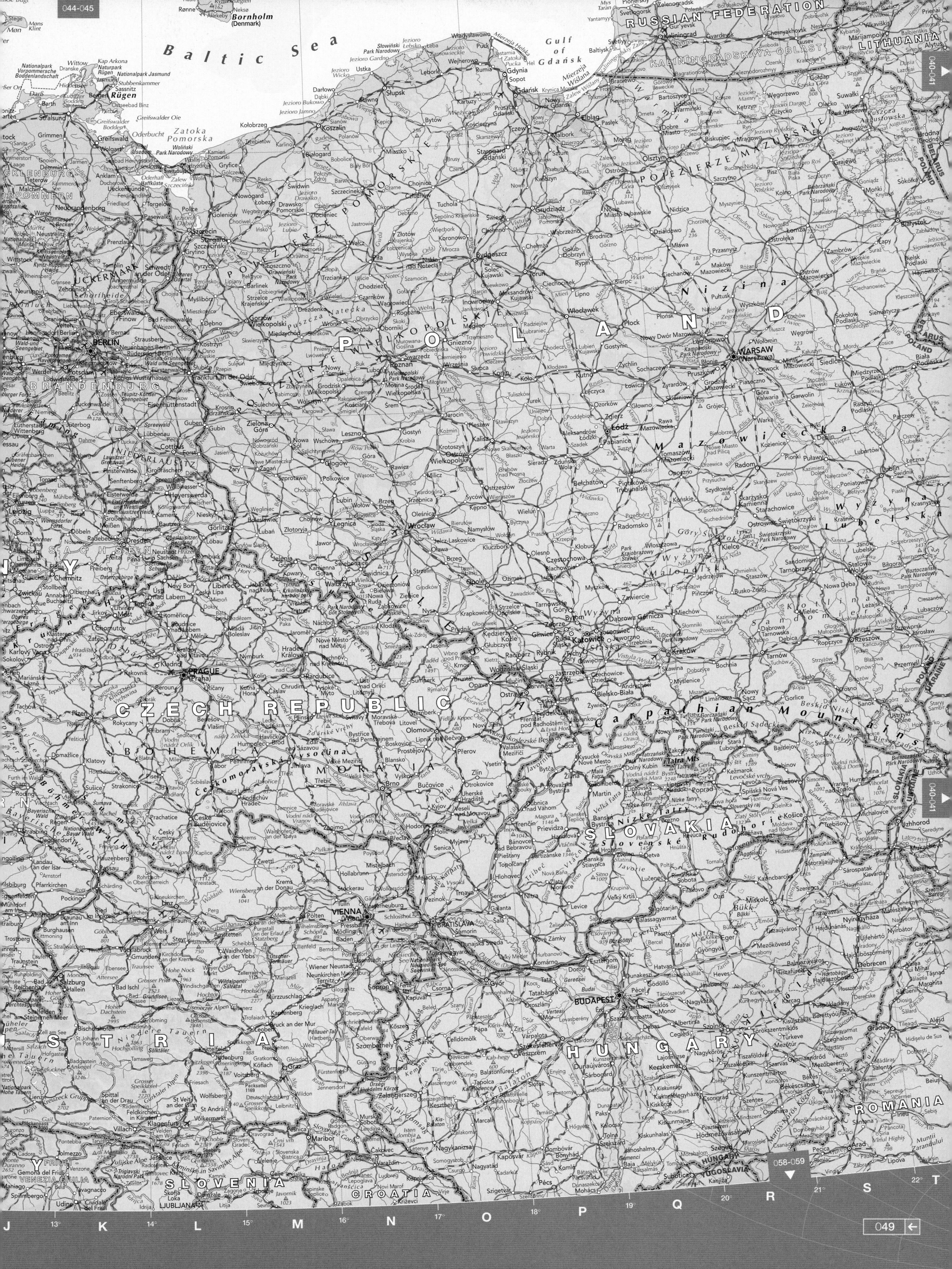

044-045
Baltic Sea
Bornholm (Denmark)
RUSSIAN FEDERATION
LITHUANIA
KALININGRADSKAYA OBLAST'
Kaliningrad
Gulf of Gdańsk
Gdańsk
Gdynia
Rügen
Zatoka Pomorska
Szczecin
POJEZIERZE POMORSKIE
POJEZIERZE MAZURSKIE
POJEZIERZE WIELKOPOLSKIE
BELARUS
POLAND
BERLIN
Potsdam
BRANDENBURG
Frankfurt an der Oder
Poznań
Bydgoszcz
Toruń
Olsztyn
Białystok
WARSAW (Warszawa)
Łódź
Nizina Mazowiecka
Wyżyna Lubelska
Lublin
Kielce
Radom
Wrocław
Dresden
Leipzig
SACHSEN
Chemnitz
Katowice
Kraków
Częstochowa
Opole
Rzeszów
Przemyśl
UKRAINE
PRAGUE (Praha)
CZECH REPUBLIC
BOHEMIA
MORAVIA
Českomoravská Vysočina
Brno
Olomouc
Ostrava
Plzeň
Carpathian Mountains
Tatra Mts
Vysoké Tatry
Nízke Tatry
SLOVAKIA
Košice
Žilina
Banská Bystrica
Nitra
BRATISLAVA
VIENNA (Wien)
Linz
Salzburg
Graz
Klagenfurt
AUSTRIA
Hohe Tauern
Niedere Tauern
BUDAPEST
HUNGARY
Debrecen
Miskolc
Szeged
Győr
Pécs
Lake Balaton
Danube (Duna)
ROMANIA
Oradea
Arad
SLOVENIA
LJUBLJANA
Maribor
CROATIA
YUGOSLAVIA
VENEZIA GIULIA
040-041
058-059
J
13°
K
14°
L
15°
M
16°
N
17°
O
18°
P
19°
Q
20°
R
21°
S
22°
T
049

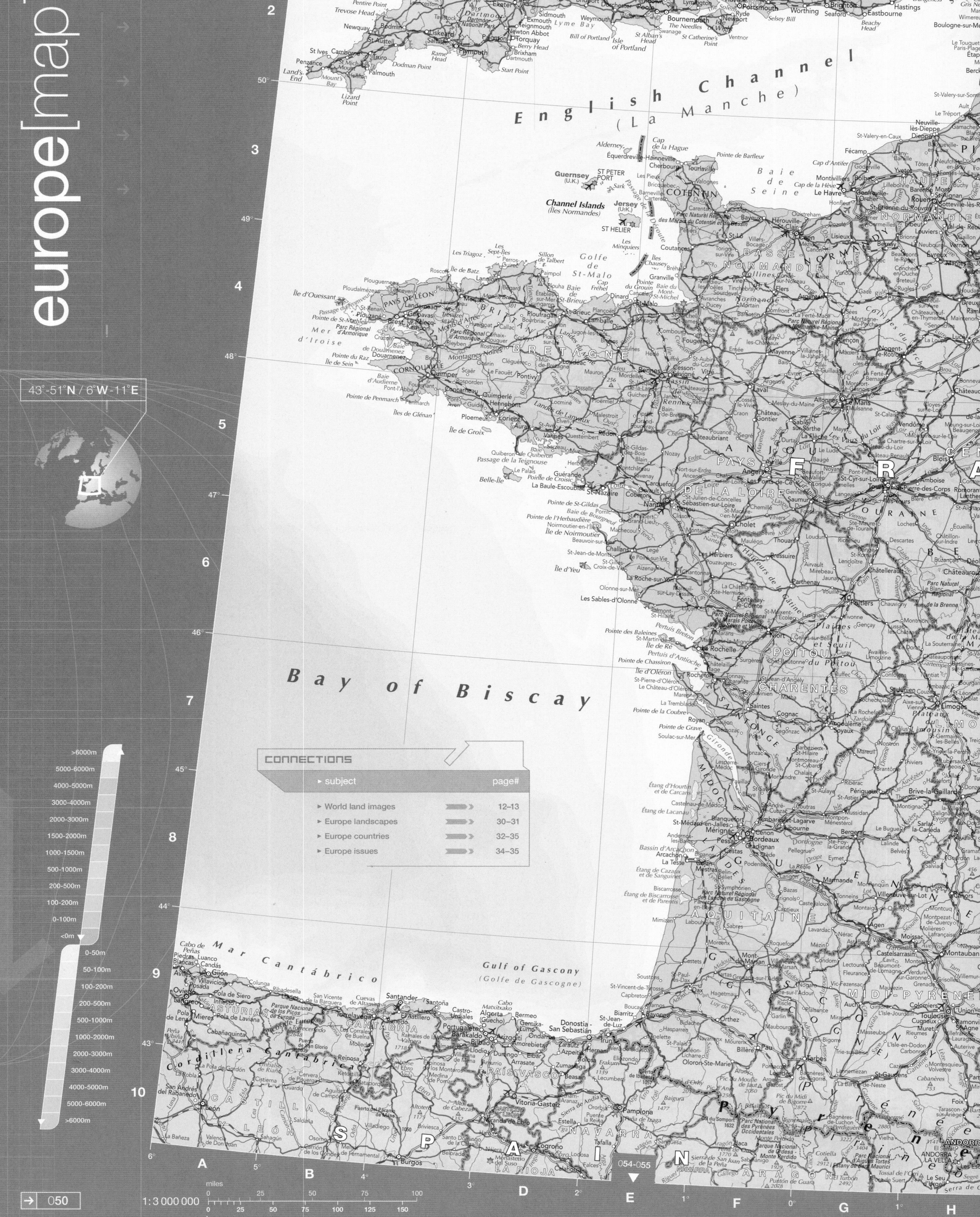

europe[map7

43°-51°N / 6°W-11°E

CONNECTIONS

E n g l i s h   C h a n n e l
(La Manche)

B a y   o f   B i s c a y

Gulf of Gascony
(Golfe de Gascogne)

Mar Cantábrico

UNITED KINGDOM

FRANCE

SPAIN

BRETAGNE

NORMANDIE

BASSE NORMANDIE

PAYS DE LA LOIRE

POITOU

CHARENTES

AQUITAINE

MIDI-PYRÉNÉES

ASTURIAS

CANTABRIA

Cordillera Cantábrica

PYRÉNÉES

LONDON

>6000m
5000-6000m
4000-5000m
3000-4000m
2000-3000m
1500-2000m
1000-1500m
500-1000m
200-500m
100-200m
0-100m
<0m

0-50m
50-100m
100-200m
200-500m
500-1000m
1000-2000m
2000-3000m
3000-4000m
4000-5000m
5000-6000m
>6000m

miles
0   25   50   75   100
km
0   25   50   75   100   125   150
1:3 000 000

Conic Equidistant Projection

054-055

048-049
048-049
056-057

BELGIUM
LUXEMBOURG
GERMANY
FRANCE
SWITZERLAND
LIECHTENSTEIN
AUSTRIA
ITALY
MONACO

NORD-PAS-DE-CALAIS
PICARDIE
CHAMPAGNE
ARDENNE
LORRAINE
ALSACE
FRANCHE-COMTÉ
BOURGOGNE
AUVERGNE
RHÔNE-ALPES
PROVENCE-ALPES
CÔTE-D'AZUR
LANGUEDOC-ROUSSILLON
RHEINLAND-PFALZ
SAARLAND
HESSEN
THÜRINGEN
SACHSEN
BADEN
WÜRTTEMBERG
BAYERN
BAVARIA
TRENTINO
ALTO ADIGE
VENETO
LOMBARDIA
PIEMONTE
VALLE D'AOSTA
LIGURIA
EMILIA-ROMAGNA
TOSCANA
TUSCANY

Massif Central
Alps
Jura
Vosges
Black Forest
Schwäbische Alb
Berner Alpen
Alpi Pennine
Alpi Lepontine
Maritime Alps
Cottian Alps
Appennino Tosco-Emiliano

Gulf of Genoa
Ligurian Sea
Golfe du Lion
Corsica (Corse) (France)
Riviera di Levante
Riviera di Ponente
Côte d'Azur
Arcipelago Toscano

PARIS
BRUSSELS (Bruxelles)
LUXEMBOURG
BERN
VADUZ
Lyon
Marseille
Strasbourg
Frankfurt am Main
Stuttgart
Munich (München)
Nuremberg (Nürnberg)
Zürich
Genève
Milan (Milano)
Turin (Torino)
Genoa (Genova)
Nice

I J K L M N O P Q R
3° 4° 5° 6° 7° 8° 9° 10° 11°

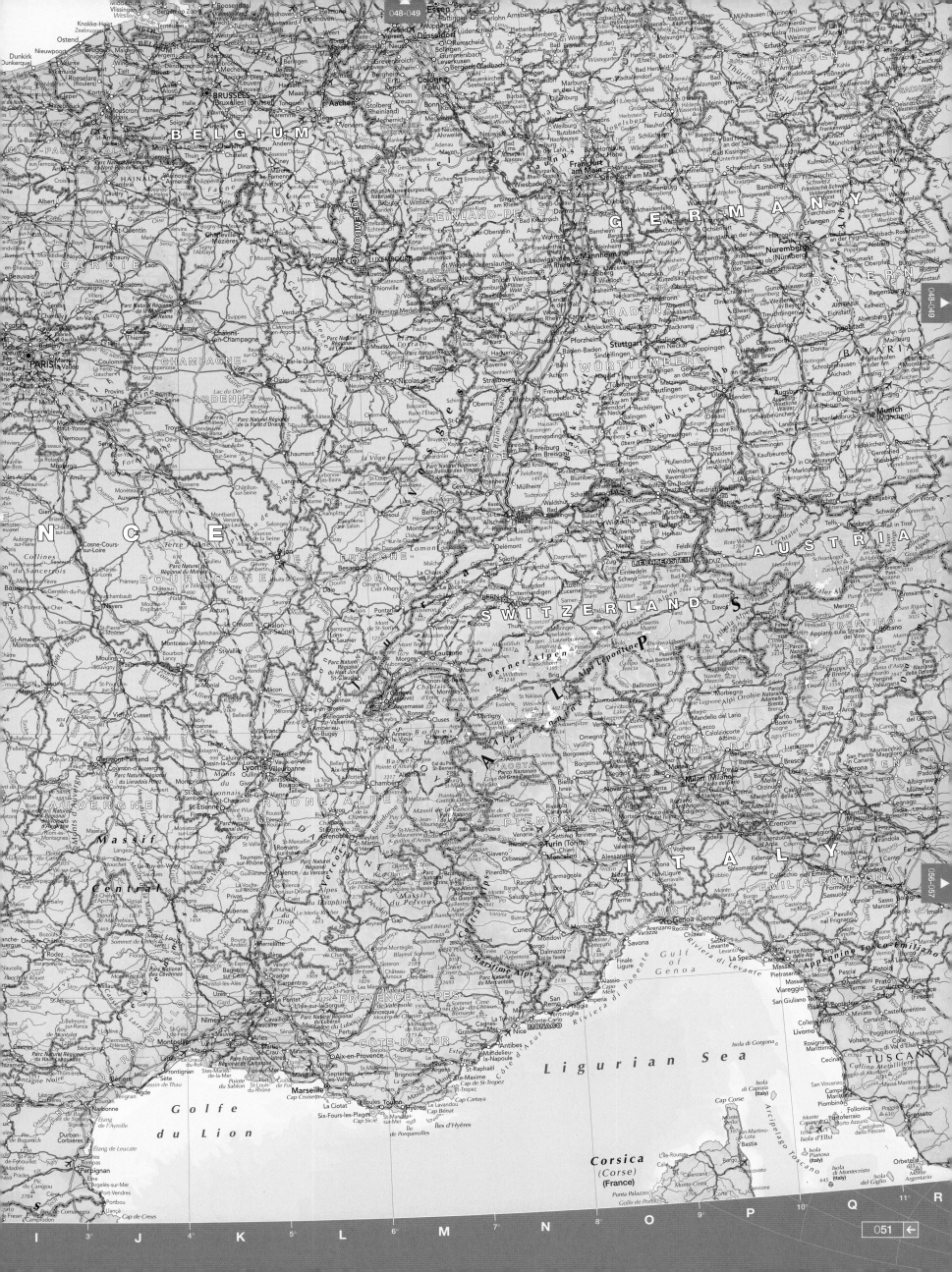

europe[map8]

26°-52°N / 10°W-35°E

Elevation legend:

>6000m
5000-6000m
4000-5000m
3000-4000m
2000-3000m
1000-2000m
500-1000m
200-500m
0-200m
<0m

0-200m
200-500m
500-1000m
1000-2000m
2000-3000m
3000-4000m
4000-5000m
5000-6000m
>6000m

Major labels

REPUBLIC OF IRELAND · UNITED KINGDOM · NETHERLANDS · AMSTERDAM · THE HAGUE · Rotterdam · GERMANY · LONDON · BRUSSELS · BELGIUM · LUXEMBOURG · FRANCE · PARIS · LIECHTENSTEIN · SWITZERLAND · BERN · MONACO · Corsica (Corse) (France) · Sardinia (Sardegna) (Italy) · SPAIN · MADRID · PORTUGAL · LISBON (Lisboa) · Oporto (Porto) · ANDORRA · ANDORRA LA VELLA · Barcelona · Zaragoza · Valencia · Balearic Islands (Islas Baleares) · Majorca · Minorca · Ibiza (Eivissa) · Formentera · GIBRALTAR (U.K.) · MOROCCO · RABAT · Casablanca · Marrakech · High Atlas · Middle Atlas · Anti Atlas · Atlas Mountains · ALGERIA · ALGIERS (Alger) · TUNISIA · TUNIS · MAURITANIA · Sahara · Grand Erg Occidental · Grand Erg Oriental · Hammada du Drâa

Bay of Biscay · English Channel (La Manche) · Mar Cantábrico · Gulf of Gascony · Golfe du Lion · Ligurian Sea · Gulf of Genoa · Mediterranean · Strait of Gibraltar · Golfo de Cádiz · Sierra Morena · Sierra Nevada · Cordillera Cantábrica · Massif Central

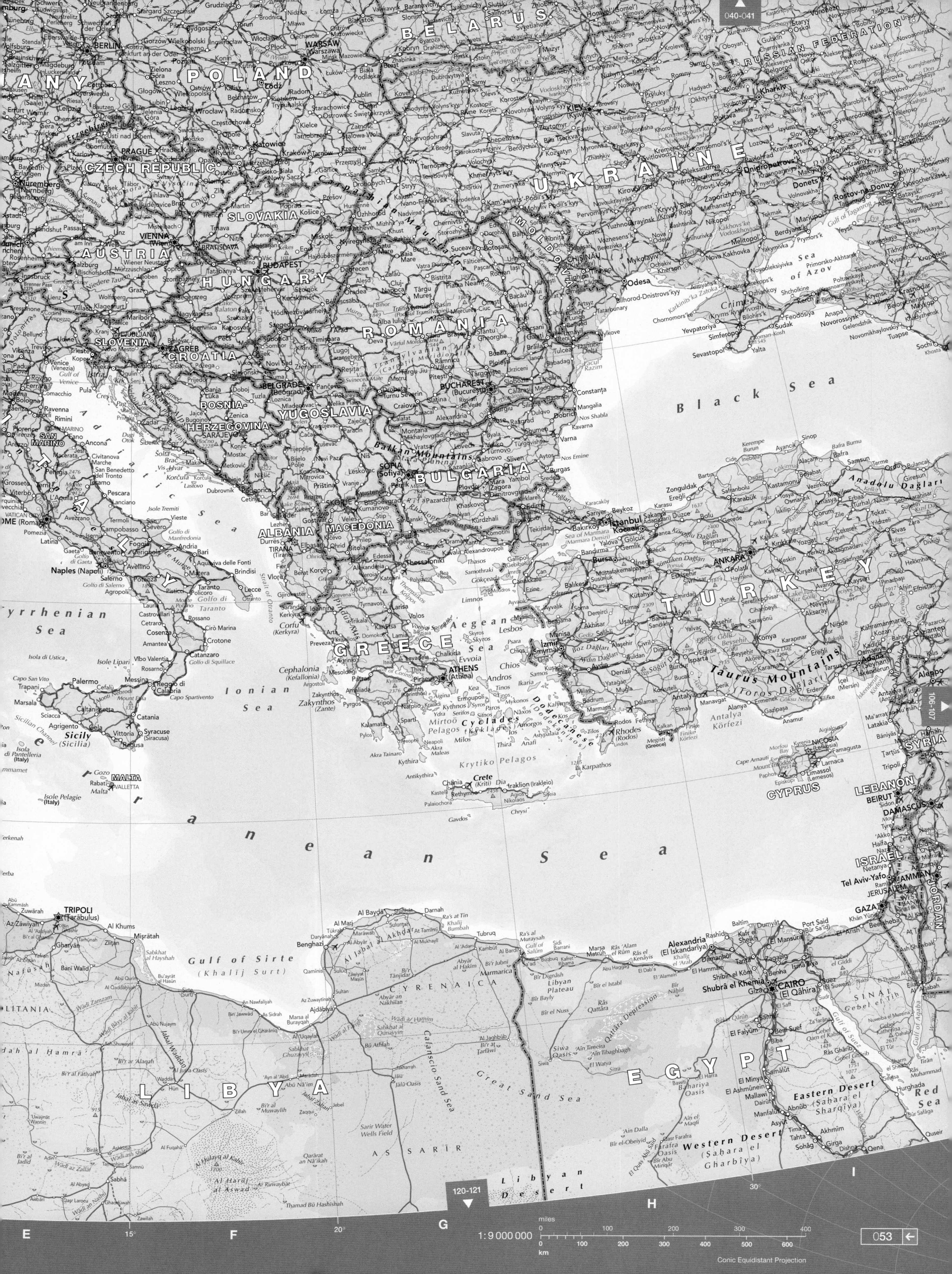
040-041
BELARUS
POLAND
RUSSIAN FEDERATION
UKRAINE
CZECH REPUBLIC
SLOVAKIA
AUSTRIA
HUNGARY
MOLDOVA
ROMANIA
SLOVENIA
CROATIA
BOSNIA HERZEGOVINA
YUGOSLAVIA
SAN MARINO
BULGARIA
ALBANIA
MACEDONIA
ITALY
GREECE
TURKEY
CYPRUS
SYRIA
LEBANON
ISRAEL
JORDAN
LIBYA
EGYPT
MALTA
BERLIN
WARSAW
PRAGUE
VIENNA
BRATISLAVA
BUDAPEST
LJUBLJANA
ZAGREB
SARAJEVO
BELGRADE
BUCHAREST
SOFIA
SKOPJE
TIRANA
ATHENS
KIEV
CHIŞINĂU
NICOSIA
BEIRUT
DAMASCUS
AMMAN
JERUSALEM
CAIRO (El Qâhira)
TRIPOLI (Tarābulus)
VALLETTA
Istanbul
Ankara
Naples (Napoli)
Alexandria (El Iskandarîya)
Tel Aviv-Yafo
Black Sea
Sea of Azov
Aegean Sea
Ionian Sea
Tyrrhenian Sea
Adriatic Sea
Mediterranean Sea
Gulf of Sirte (Khalīj Surt)
Red Sea
Carpathian Mountains
Balkan Mountains
Taurus Mountains
Crete
Rhodes (Rodos)
Cyclades (Kyklades)
Sicily (Sicilia)
Libyan Desert
Western Desert (Şaḩara el Gharbîya)
Eastern Desert (Şaḩara el Sharqîya)
Great Sand Sea
Qattâra Depression
CYRENAICA
106-107
120-121
E
F
G
H
I
15°
20°
30°
1:9 000 000
miles
0
100
200
300
400
km
0
100
200
300
400
500
600
Conic Equidistant Projection
053

CONNECTIONS

Elevation legend:
>6000m
5000-6000m
4000-5000m
3000-4000m
2000-3000m
1500-2000m
1000-1500m
500-1000m
200-500m
100-200m
0-100m
<0m

0-50m
50-100m
100-200m
200-500m
500-1000m
1000-2000m
2000-3000m
3000-4000m
4000-5000m
5000-6000m
>6000m

ATLANTIC OCEAN

Mar Cantábrico

PORTUGAL ESPAÑA MOROCCO

LISBON (Lisboa) Oporto (Porto)

1:3 000 000

Conic Equidistant Projection

50-51

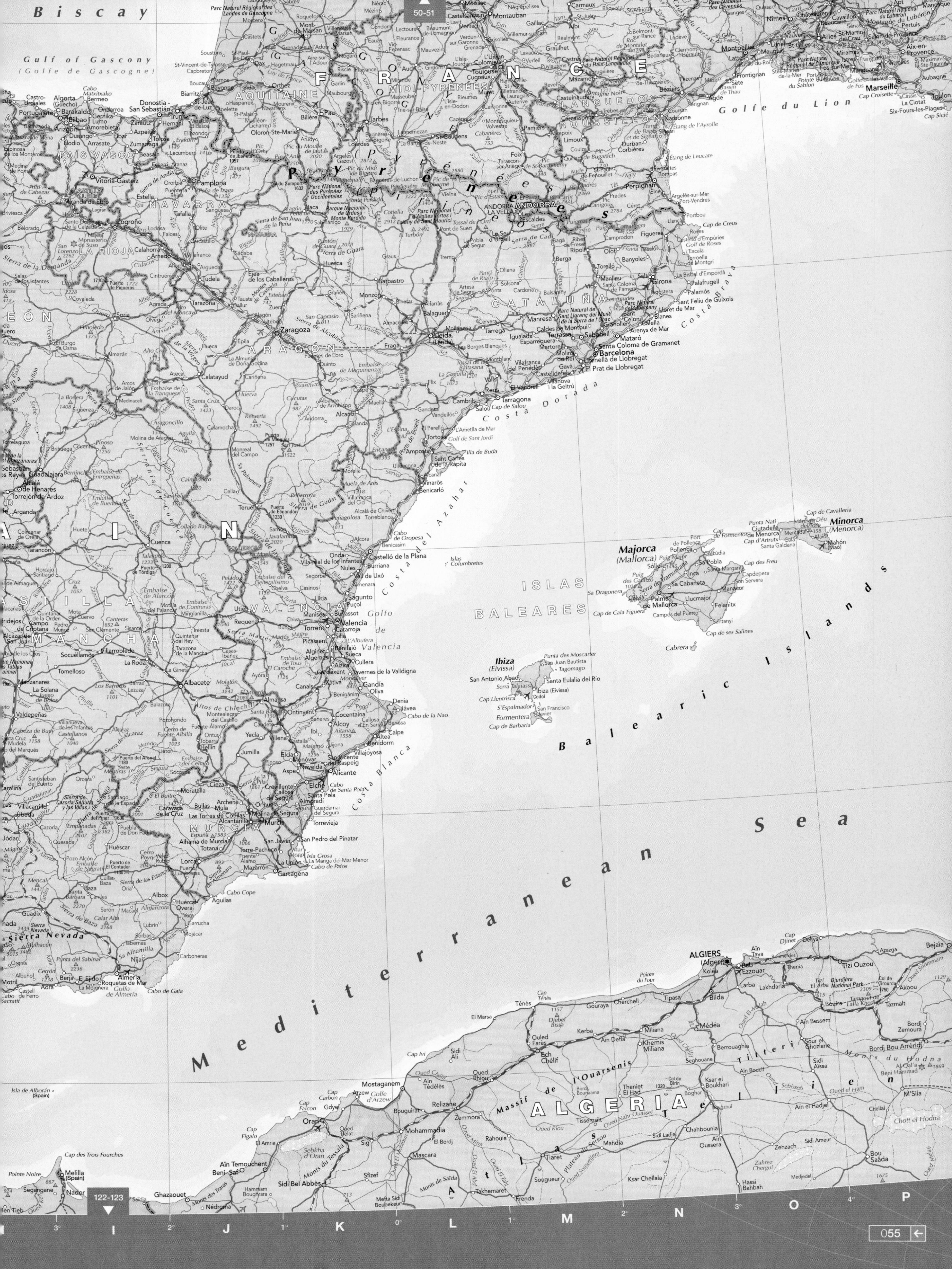
Biscay
Gulf of Gascony
(Golfe de Gascogne)
FRANCE
AQUITAINE
MIDI-PYRÉNÉES
LANGUEDOC
ROUSSILLON
Golfe du Lion
Marseille
Montpellier
Toulouse
Perpignan
Pyrénées
ANDORRA
ANDORRA LA VELLA
NAVARRA
PAÍS VASCO
LA RIOJA
ARAGÓN
CATALUÑA
Costa Brava
Barcelona
Zaragoza
Lleida
Tarragona
Costa Dorada
VALENCIA
Valencia
Golfo de Valencia
Costa del Azahar
Castelló de la Plana
Alicante
Costa Blanca
MURCIA
Murcia
Cartagena
Almería
Sierra Nevada
Albacete
Cuenca
Teruel
Pamplona
Vitoria-Gasteiz
Bilbao
Donostia - San Sebastián
ISLAS BALEARES
Majorca (Mallorca)
Palma de Mallorca
Minorca (Menorca)
Ibiza (Eivissa)
Formentera
Cabrera
Balearic Islands
Mediterranean Sea
ALGERIA
ALGIERS (Alger)
Oran
Mostaganem
Blida
Tizi Ouzou
Bejaïa
Atlas Tellien
Melilla (Spain)
Isla de Alborán (Spain)
I
J
K
L
M
N
O
P

122-123

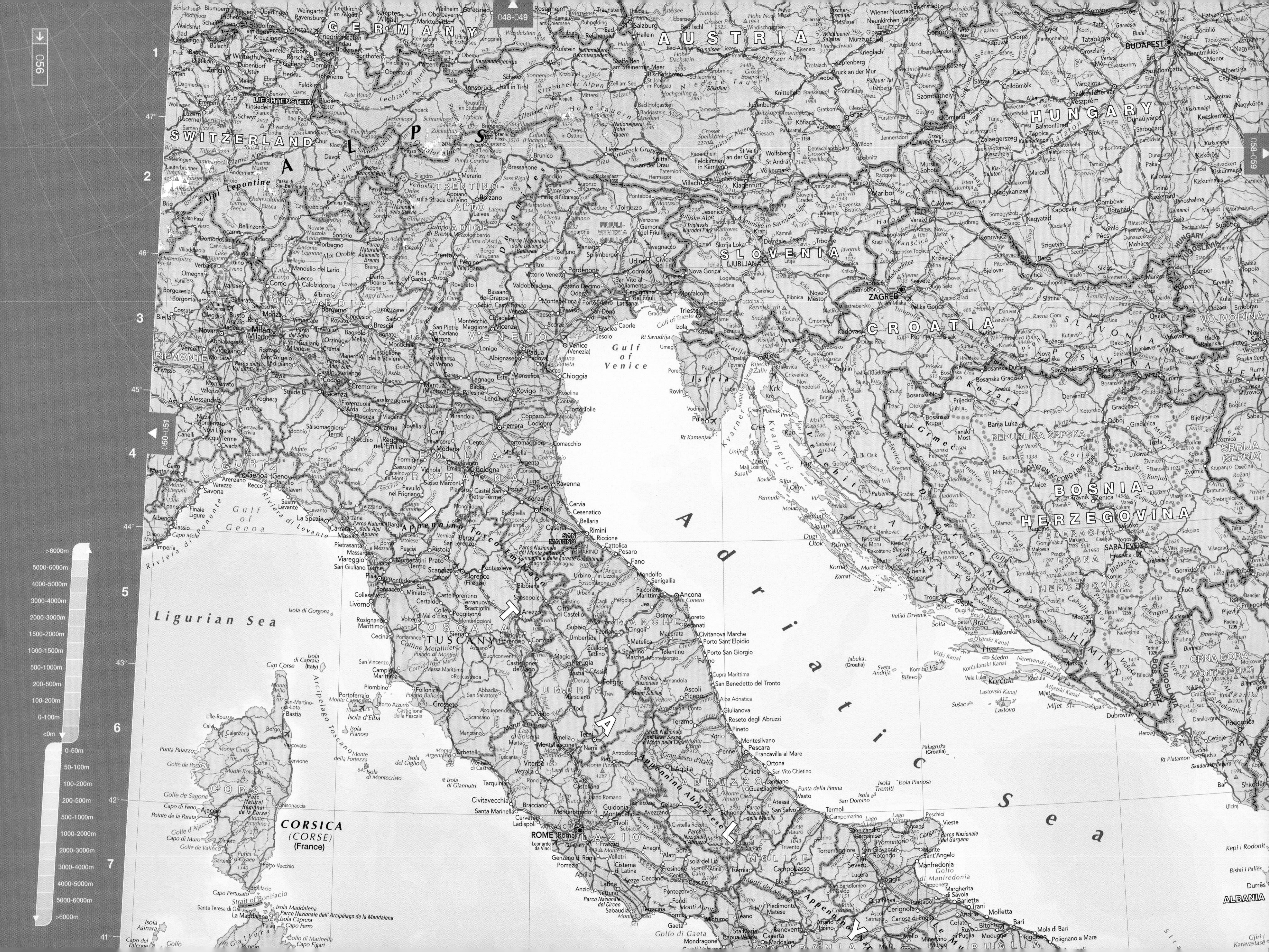

GERMANY
AUSTRIA
HUNGARY
SWITZERLAND
LIECHTENSTEIN
ALPS
SLOVENIA
CROATIA
BOSNIA-HERZEGOVINA
REPUBLIKA SRPSKA
FEDERACIJA BOSNA I HERCEGOVINA
DAYTON ACCORD LINE 1995
SRBIJA (SERBIA)
VOJVODINA
CRNA GORA (MONTENEGRO)
YUGOSLAVIA
ALBANIA
ITALY
Adriatic Sea
Ligurian Sea
Gulf of Venice
Gulf of Genoa
CORSICA (CORSE) (France)
TRENTINO-ALTO ADIGE
VENETO
LOMBARDIA
PIEMONTE
LIGURIA
EMILIA-ROMAGNA
TOSCANA
TUSCANY
UMBRIA
MARCHE
LAZIO
ABRUZZO
MOLISE
PUGLIA
FRIULI-VENEZIA GIULIA
SAN MARINO
Appennino Tosco-Emiliano
Appennino Abruzzese
Arcipelago Toscano
Strait of Bonifacio
BUDAPEST
ZAGREB
LJUBLJANA
SARAJEVO
ROME (Roma)
Milan (Milano)
Venice (Venezia)
Florence (Firenze)
Genoa (Genova)
Bologna
Trieste
Rijeka
Split
Dubrovnik
Ancona
Pescara
Bari
048-049
050-051
058-059
1
2
3
4
5
6
7
47°
46°
45°
44°
43°
42°
41°
>6000m
5000-6000m
4000-5000m
3000-4000m
2000-3000m
1500-2000m
1000-1500m
500-1000m
200-500m
100-200m
0-100m
<0m
0-50m
50-100m
100-200m
200-500m
500-1000m
1000-2000m
2000-3000m
3000-4000m
4000-5000m
5000-6000m
>6000m

35°48'N / 8°19'E

1:3 000 000   Conic Equidistant Projection

miles   25   50   75   100   125
km   25   50   75   100   125   150   175   200

CONNECTIONS

▶ subject   page#

▲ World physical features   8-9
▲ World cities   24-25
▲ Europe landscapes   30-31
▲ Europe countries   32-35
▲ Europe issues   34-35
▲ Europe environments   36-37

Tyrrhenian Sea

Ionian Sea

Mediterranean Sea

Sicilian Channel

SARDINIA
(SARDEGNA)
(Italy)

SICILY
(SICILIA)

MALTA
VALLETTA

TUNISIA
TUNIS

ALGERIA

BASILICATA

CALABRIA

Golfo di Taranto

Golfe de Tunis

Golfe de Hammamet

Isole Lipari

Isole Egadi

Isole Pelagie (Italy)

Reggio di Calabria

Catania

Siracusa (Syracuse)

Messina

Palermo

Marsala

Trapani

Agrigento

Gela

Ragusa

Bizerte

Sousse

Kairouan

Sfax

Gabès

122-123

8   9   10   11   12   13

A   B   C   D   E   F   G   H   I   J   K

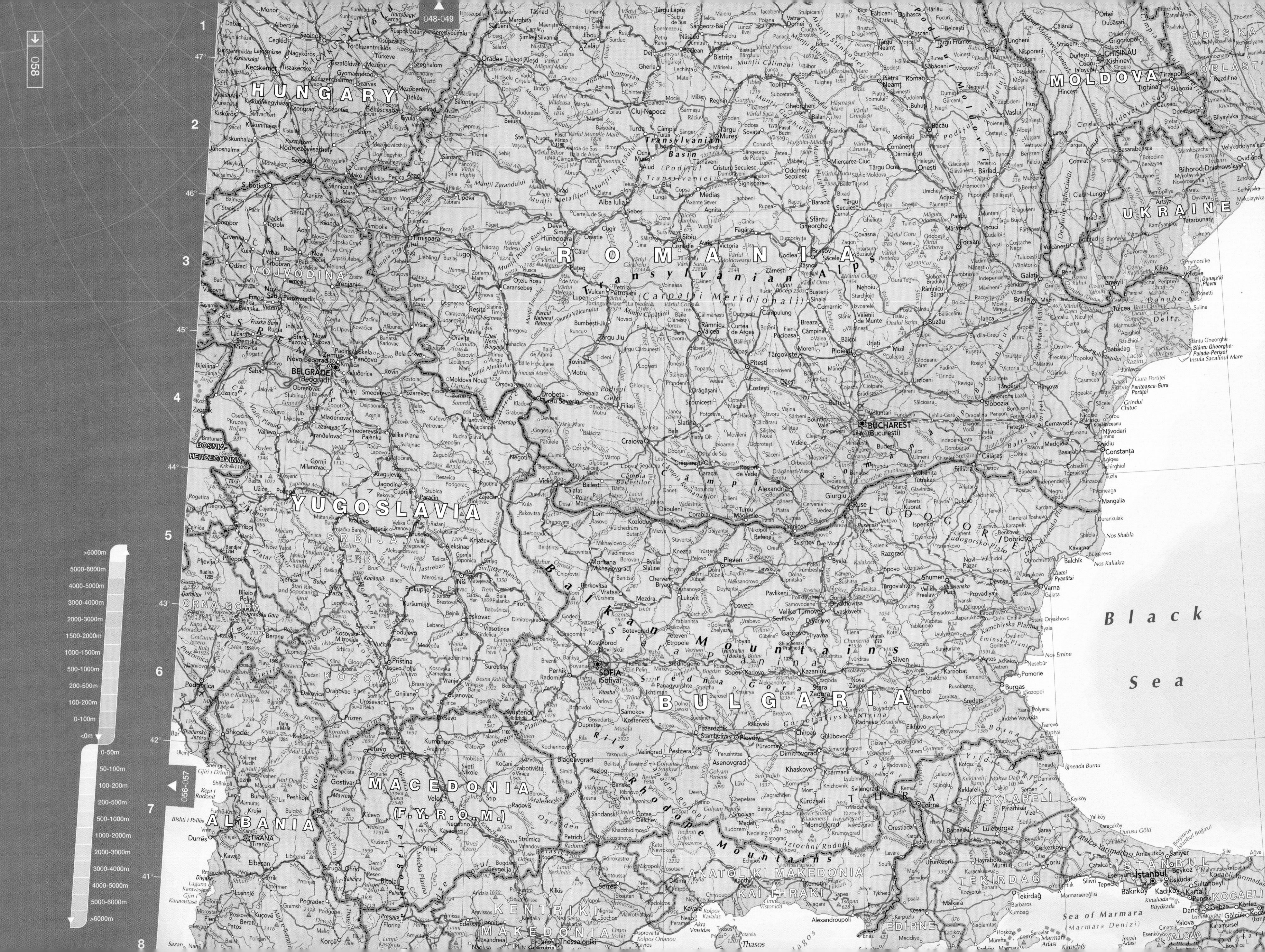

HUNGARY
ROMANIA
MOLDOVA
UKRAINE
YUGOSLAVIA
BULGARIA
MACEDONIA (F.Y.R.O.M.)
ALBANIA
BOSNIA HERZEGOVINA
CRNA GORA (MONTENEGRO)
SRBIJA (SERBIA)
VOJVODINA
KOSOVO
ISTANBUL
KIRKLARELI
TEKIRDAĞ
EDIRNE
KOCAELI
YALOVA
ANATOLIKI MAKEDONIA KAI THRAKI
KENTRIKI MAKEDONIA
ODES'KA OBLAST'
Black Sea
Sea of Marmara (Marmara Denizi)
Transylvanian Alps (Carpaţii Meridionali)
Transylvanian Basin (Podişul Transilvaniei)
Balkan Mountains
Rhodope Mountains
Sredna Gora
LUDOGORIE
THRACE
Danube Delta
Câmpia Română
BUCHAREST (Bucureşti)
BELGRADE (Beograd)
SOFIA (Sofiya)
CHIŞINĂU (Kishinev)
SKOPJE
TIRANA (Tiranë)
>6000m
5000-6000m
4000-5000m
3000-4000m
2000-3000m
1500-2000m
1000-1500m
500-1000m
200-500m
100-200m
0-100m
<0m
0-50m
50-100m
100-200m
200-500m
500-1000m
1000-2000m
2000-3000m
3000-4000m
4000-5000m
5000-6000m
>6000m
048-049
056-057

europe[map 11]

35°-47'N / 19°-29°E

1:3 000 000

Conic Equidistant Projection

Countries / Regions

TURKEY

GREECE

Provinces / Regions (Turkey)

BURSA

BALIKESIR

KÜTAHYA

MANISA

UŞAK

İZMİR

AYDIN

DENİZLİ

MUĞLA

ÇANAKKALE

LYDIA

CARIA

Provinces / Regions (Greece)

IPEIROS

THESSALIA

STEREA ELLAS

DYTIKI ELLAS

ATTIKI

PELOPONNISOS

Voreioi Sporades

VOREIO AIGAIO

NOTIO AIGAIO

KRITI

Seas

Aegean Sea

Mediterranean Sea

Ionian Sea

Krytiko Pelagos

Mirtoö Pelagos

Thrak

Islands

Lesbos (Lesvos)

Limnos

Chios

Ikaria

Samos

Psara

Skyros

Evvoia

Andros

Tinos

Mykonos

Naxos

Paros

Cyclades (Kyklades)

Ios

Amorgos

Santorini (Thira)

Milos

Sifnos

Serifos

Kea

Dodecanese (Dodekanisos)

Rhodes (Rodos)

Kos

Kalymnos

Leros

Patmos

Karpathos

Kasos

Crete (Kriti)

Kythira

Antikythira

Zakynthos (Zante)

Cephalonia (Kefallinia)

Corfu (Kerkyra)

Ionian Islands

Gökçeada

Cities

Bursa

İzmir / Smyrna

ATHENS (Athína)

Piraeus

Patras

Volos

Ioannina

Chalkida

Megara

Salamina

Canakkale

Bandırma

Bergama

Denizli

Nazilli

Mountains / Features

Pindus Mountains

Tavgetos

Gulf of Corinth

Argolikos Kolpos

Saronikos Kolpos

Pagasitikos Kolpos

Thermaikos Kolpos

İzmir Körfezi

Güllük Körfezi

Gökova Körfezi

Steno Karpathou

Menteşe Dağları

Muğla Dağları

Boz Dağları

CONNECTIONS

subject — page#

Europe landscapes — 30–31

Europe countries — 32–33

Europe issues — 34–35

Mediterranean Sea — 52–53

miles 0 25 50 75 100 125

km 0 25 50 75 100 125 150 175 200

Osaka, *Japan*

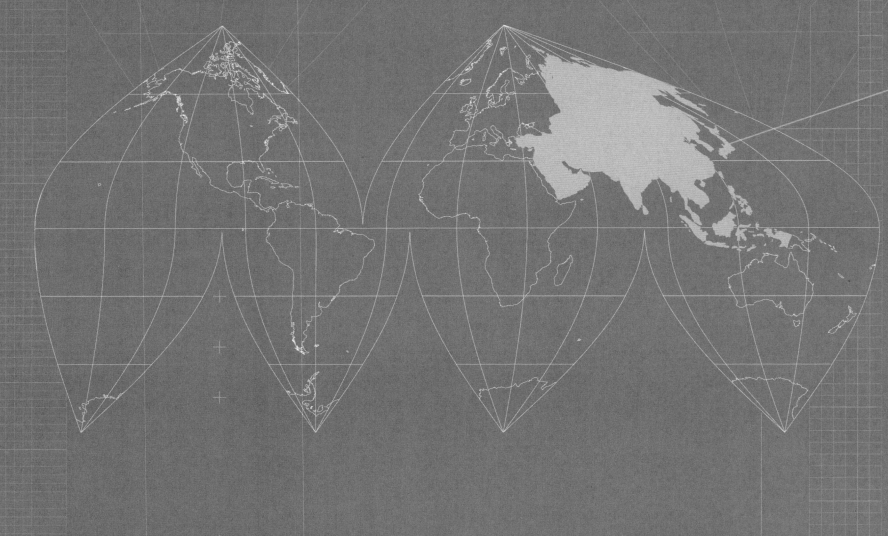

asia

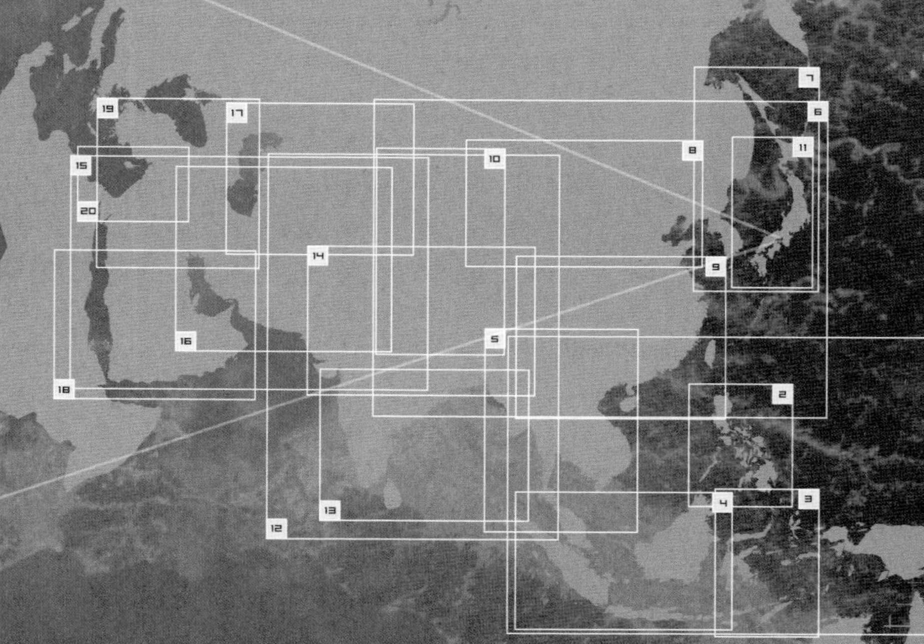

[contents]

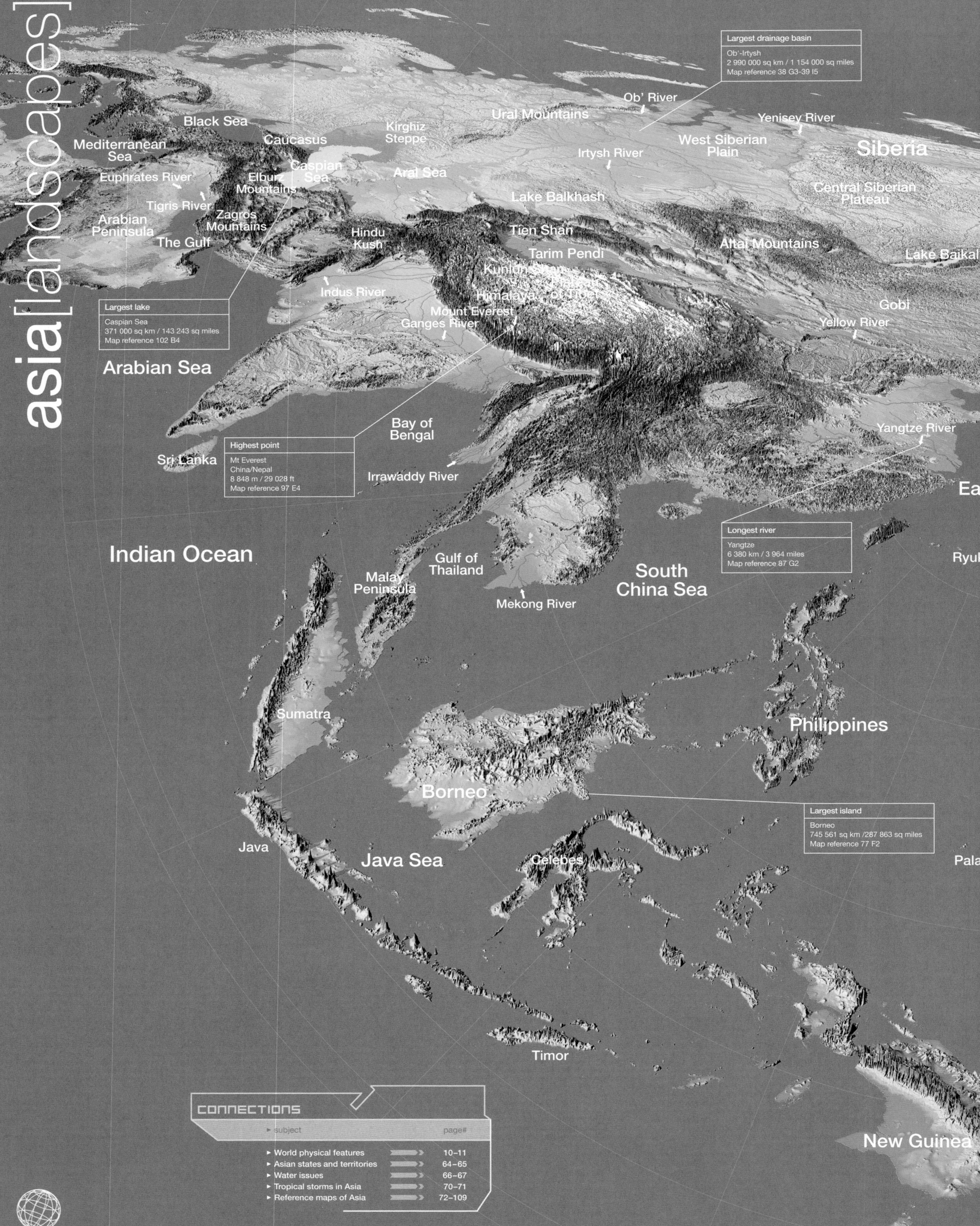

asia[landscapes]

Largest drainage basin
Ob'-Irtysh
2 990 000 sq km / 1 154 000 sq miles
Map reference 38 G3-39 I5

Ob' River
Ural Mountains
Yenisey River
Black Sea
Kirghiz
Steppe
West Siberian
Plain
Siberia
Mediterranean
Sea
Caucasus
Caspian
Sea
Irtysh River
Euphrates River
Elburz
Mountains
Aral Sea
Lake Balkhash
Central Siberian
Plateau
Tigris River
Tien Shan
Altai Mountains
Arabian
Peninsula
Zagros
Mountains
Hindu
Kush
Tarim Pendi
Lake Baikal
The Gulf
Kunlun Shan
Himalaya   of Tibet
Gobi
Indus River
Yellow River

Largest lake
Caspian Sea
371 000 sq km / 143 243 sq miles
Map reference 102 B4

Mount Everest
Ganges River

Arabian Sea

Bay of
Bengal

Yangtze River

Highest point
Mt Everest
China/Nepal
8 848 m / 29 028 ft
Map reference 97 E4

Sri Lanka

Irrawaddy River

Ea

Indian Ocean

Longest river
Yangtze
6 380 km / 3 964 miles
Map reference 87 G2

Ryuk

Gulf of
Thailand
South
China Sea
Malay
Peninsula
Mekong River

Sumatra

Philippines

Borneo
Pala

Largest island
Borneo
745 561 sq km /287 863 sq miles
Map reference 77 F2

Java
Java Sea
Celebes

Timor

New Guinea

Arctic Ocean

Lena River

Argun River

Heilong Jiang River

Sea of Okhotsk

Kamchatka Peninsula

Sea of Japan

Honshu

Pacific Ocean

Northern Mariana Islands

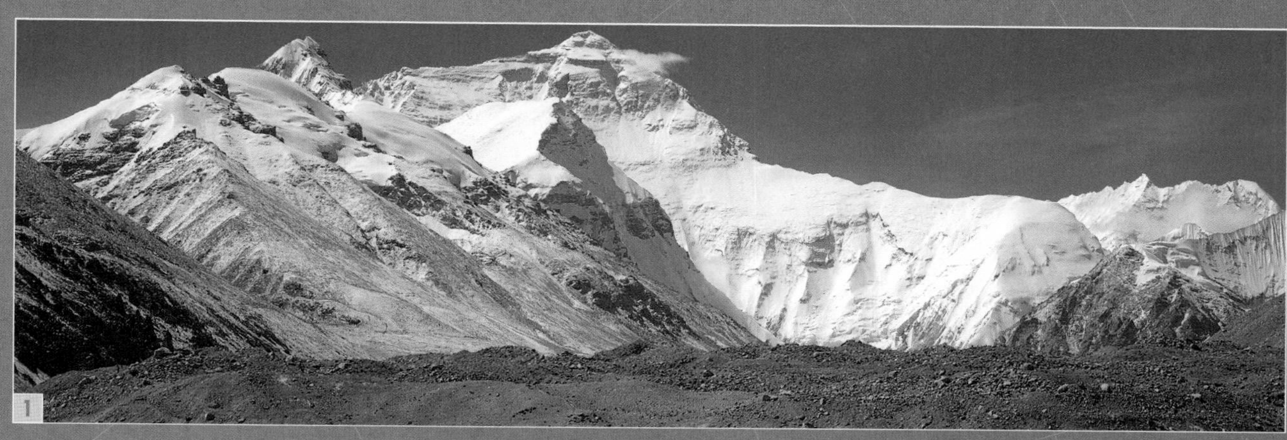

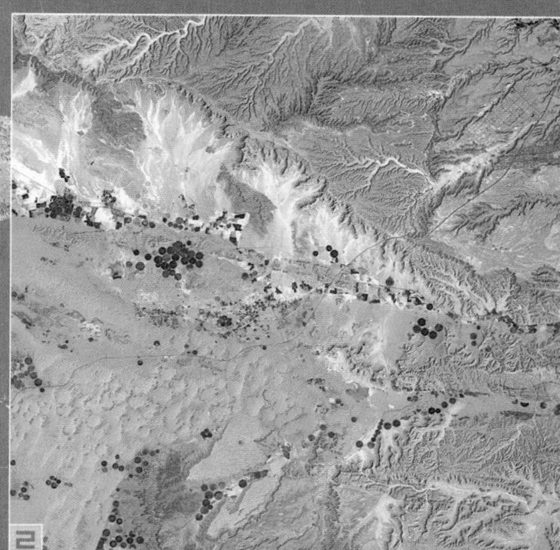

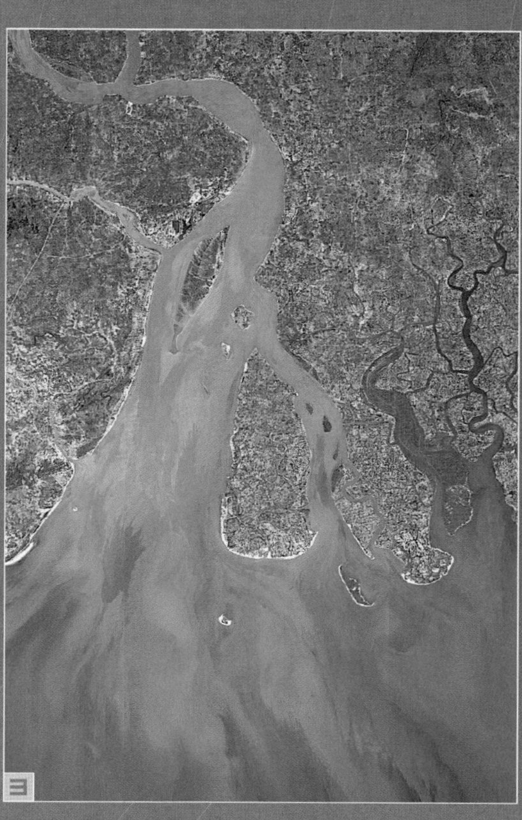

Asia is the world's largest continent and its huge range of physical features is evident in this perspective view from the southeast. These include in southwest Asia the Arabian Peninsula, in southern Asia the Indian subcontinent, in southeast Asia the vast Indonesian archipelago, in central Asia the Plateau of Tibet and the Gobi desert and in east Asia the volcanic islands of Japan and the Kamchatka Peninsula.

North to south, the continent extends over 76 degrees of latitude from the Arctic Ocean in the north to the southern tip of Indonesia in the south. The Ural Mountains and the Caucasus in the west form the boundary with Europe. Asia's most impressive mountain range is the Himalaya, which contains the world's highest peaks. The continent is drained by some of the world's longest rivers and the Caspian Sea is the world's largest lake or inland sea.

1 Himalayas, *China/Nepal*

This view of the Himalayas shows Mount Everest, at 8 848 m the world's highest mountain. The photograph looks south from the Plateau of Tibet, with its typical barren landscape in the foreground. The plateau lies at a height of over 4 000 m. The Himalayas mark the southern limit of the plateau and stretch for over 2 000 km, forming the northern limit of the Indian sub-continent.

2 Arabian Desert, *Saudi Arabia*

The arid desert areas to the southwest of Riyadh, Saudi Arabia are shown in this infrared satellite image. Sand shows as yellow and bare rock as grey. Extensive drainage patterns belie the fact that this area only receives 100 mm of rain each year. These are dry river beds for most of the year. The red dots are circular fields with centre-pivot irrigation systems. Water is fed through large revolving sprinklers.

Satellite/Sensor : SPOT

3 Ganges Delta, *India*

This infrared satellite image shows the Hugli river in the western part of the Ganges delta, flowing into the Bay of Bengal. Vegetation shows as red in the image and the pale blue areas depict water full of sediment. The strong red indicates areas of mangrove swamp. The delta is a huge area, over 300 km across. The fertile soil is intensively farmed but the area is often flooded, particularly as a result of tropical cyclones.

Satellite/Sensor : SPOT

ASIA

HIGHEST MOUNTAINS

	m	ft	location	map
Mt Everest	8 848	29 028	China/Nepal	97 E4
K2	8 611	28 251	China/Jammu and Kashmir	96 C2
Kangchenjunga	8 586	28 169	India/Nepal	97 F4
Lhotse	8 516	27 939	China/Nepal	97 E3
Makalu	8 463	27 765	China/Nepal	97 E4
Cho Oyu	8 201	26 906	China/Nepal	97 E3
Dhaulagiri	8 167	26 794	Nepal	97 D3
Manaslu	8 163	26 781	Nepal	97 E3
Nanga Parbat	8 126	26 660	Jammu and Kashmir	96 B2
Annapurna 1	8 091	26 545	Nepal	97 D3

LARGEST ISLANDS

	sq km	sq miles	map
Borneo	745 561	287 863	77 F2
Sumatra	473 606	182 860	76 C3
Honshu	227 414	87 805	91 F6
Celebes	189 216	73 057	75 B3
Java	132 188	51 038	77 E4
Luzon	104 690	40 421	76 B2
Mindanao	94 630	36 537	74 C6
Hokkaido	78 073	30 144	90 H3
Sakhalin	76 400	29 498	82 F2
Sri Lanka	65 610	25 332	94 D5
Kyushu	36 554	14 114	91 B8
Taiwan	35 873	13 851	87 G4

LONGEST RIVERS

	km	miles	map
Yangtze	6 380	3 964	87 G2
Ob'-Irtysh	5 568	3 459	38 G3 –39 I5
Yenisey-Angara -Selenga	5 550	3 448	39 I2–K4
Yellow	5 464	3 395	85 H4
Irtysh	4 440	2 759	38 G3
Mekong	4 425	2 749	79 D6
Heilong Jiang -Argun'	4 416	2 744	81 M3
Lena-Kirenga	4 400	2 734	39 M2 –K4
Yenisey	4 090	2 541	39 I2
Ob'	3 701	2 300	38 H3

LAKES

	sq km	sq miles	map
Caspian Sea	371 000	143 243	102 B4
Aral Sea	33 640	12 988	102 D3
Lake Baikal	30 500	11 776	39 K4
Lake Balkhash	17 400	6 718	103 H3
Ysyk-Köl	6 200	2 393	103 I4

LAND AREA

		map
Most northerly point	Mys Arkticheskiy, Russian Federation	39 J1
Most southerly point	Pamana, Indonesia	75 B5
Most westerly point	Bozcaada, Turkey	59 H9
Most easterly point	Mys Dezhneva, Russian Federation	39 T3

Total land area: 45 036 492 sq km / 17 388 686 sq miles

ASIA
COUNTRIES

		area sq km	area sq miles	population	capital	languages	religions	currency	map
AFGHANISTAN		652 225	251 825	21 765 000	Kābul	Dari, Pushtu, Uzbek, Turkmen	Sunni Muslim, Shi'a Muslim	Afghani	101
ARMENIA		29 800	11 506	3 787 000	Yerevan (Erevan)	Armenian, Azeri	Armenian Orthodox	Dram	107
AZERBAIJAN		86 600	33 436	8 041 000	Baku	Azeri, Armenian, Russian, Lezgian	Shi'a Muslim, Sunni Muslim, Russian and Armenian Orthodox	Manat	107
BAHRAIN		691	267	640 000	Manama (Al Manāmah)	Arabic, English	Shi'a Muslim, Sunni Muslim, Christian	Dinar	105
BANGLADESH		143 998	55 598	137 439 000	Dhaka (Dacca)	Bengali, English	Sunni Muslim, Hindu	Taka	97
BHUTAN		46 620	18 000	2 085 000	Thimphu	Dzongkha, Nepali, Assamese	Buddhist, Hindu	Ngultrum	97
BRUNEI		5 765	2 226	328 000	Bandar Seri Begawan	Malay, English, Chinese	Sunni Muslim, Buddhist, Christian	Dollar	77
CAMBODIA		181 000	69 884	13 104 000	Phnom Penh	Khmer, Vietnamese	Buddhist, Roman Catholic, Sunni Muslim	Riel	79
CHINA		9 584 492	3 700 593	1 260 137 000	Beijing (Peking)	Mandarin, Wu, Cantonese, Hsiang, regional languages	Confucian, Taoist, Buddhist, Christian, Sunni Muslim	Yuan	80–81
CYPRUS		9 251	3 572	784 000	Nicosia (Lefkosia)	Greek, Turkish, English	Greek Orthodox, Sunni Muslim	Pound	108
GEORGIA		69 700	26 911	5 262 000	T'bilisi	Georgian, Russian, Armenian, Azeri, Ossetian, Abkhaz	Georgian Orthodox, Russian Orthodox, Sunni Muslim	Lari	107
INDIA		3 065 027	1 183 414	1 008 937 000	New Delhi	Hindi, English, many regional languages	Hindu, Sunni Muslim, Shi'a Muslim, Sikh, Christian	Rupee	92–93
INDONESIA		1 919 445	741 102	212 092 000	Jakarta	Indonesian, local languages	Sunni Muslim, Protestant, Roman Catholic, Hindu, Buddhist	Rupiah	72–73
IRAN		1 648 000	636 296	70 330 000	Tehrān	Farsi, Azeri, Kurdish, regional languages	Shi'a Muslim, Sunni Muslim	Rial	100–101
IRAQ		438 317	169 235	22 946 000	Baghdād	Arabic, Kurdish, Turkmen	Shi'a Muslim, Sunni Muslim, Christian	Dinar	107
ISRAEL		20 770	8 019	6 040 000	Jerusalem (Yerushalayim) (El Quds)	Hebrew, Arabic	Jewish, Sunni Muslim, Christian, Druze	Shekel	108
JAPAN		377 727	145 841	127 096 000	Tōkyō	Japanese	Shintoist, Buddhist, Christian	Yen	90–91
JORDAN		89 206	34 443	4 913 000	'Ammān	Arabic	Sunni Muslim, Christian	Dinar	108–109
KAZAKHSTAN		2 717 300	1 049 155	16 172 000	Astana (Akmola)	Kazakh, Russian, Ukrainian, German, Uzbek, Tatar	Sunni Muslim, Russian Orthodox, Protestant	Tenge	102–103
KUWAIT		17 818	6 880	1 914 000	Kuwait (Al Kuwayt)	Arabic	Sunni Muslim, Shi'a Muslim, Christian, Hindu	Dinar	107
KYRGYZSTAN		198 500	76 641	4 921 000	Bishkek (Frunze)	Kyrgyz, Russian, Uzbek	Sunni Muslim, Russian Orthodox	Som	103
LAOS		236 800	91 429	5 279 000	Vientiane (Viangchan)	Lao, local languages	Buddhist, traditional beliefs	Kip	78–79
LEBANON		10 452	4 036	3 496 000	Beirut (Beyrouth)	Arabic, Armenian, French	Shi'a Muslim, Sunni Muslim, Christian	Pound	108–109
MALAYSIA		332 965	128 559	22 218 000	Kuala Lumpur	Malay, English, Chinese, Tamil, local languages	Sunni Muslim, Buddhist, Hindu, Christian, traditional beliefs	Ringgit	76–77
MALDIVES		298	115	291 000	Male	Divehi (Maldivian)	Sunni Muslim	Rufiyaa	93
MONGOLIA		1 565 000	604 250	2 533 000	Ulan Bator (Ulaanbaatar)	Khalka (Mongolian), Kazakh, local languages	Buddhist, Sunni Muslim	Tugrik	84–85
MYANMAR		676 577	261 228	47 749 000	Rangoon (Yangôn)	Burmese, Shan, Karen, local languages	Buddhist, Christian, Sunni Muslim	Kyat	78–79
NEPAL		147 181	56 827	23 043 000	Kathmandu	Nepali, Maithili, Bhojpuri, English, local languages	Hindu, Buddhist, Sunni Muslim	Rupee	96–97
NORTH KOREA		120 538	46 540	22 268 000	P'yŏngyang	Korean	Traditional beliefs, Chondoist, Buddhist	Won	82–83
OMAN		309 500	119 499	2 538 000	Muscat (Masqaṭ)	Arabic, Baluchi, Indian languages	Ibadhi Muslim, Sunni Muslim	Rial	105

1 Middle East Boundaries

International boundaries are often visible from space because of differences in land use. In this Shuttle photograph the borders between Egypt, Gaza and Israel can be clearly identified. Grazing is the predominant agricultural activity in this part of Egypt, to the bottom of the image, and in Gaza in the centre, and has removed much of the vegetation. In contrast, Israel, to the east of the boundary, appears darker and more cultivated because of irrigation from the Jordan river.

Satellite/Sensor : Space Shuttle

2 Egypt/Gaza Border, *Middle East*

Borders between countries frequently follow the alignment of natural physical features, such as rivers, mountains or lake shores. Some borders, however, are demarcated only by man-made features, such as this fence at Rafah on the boundary between Egypt and Gaza. Gaza is a small semi-autonomous region on the southeast shore of the Mediterranean Sea. It is home to about 1 million Palestinian Arabs and was formerly under complete Israeli control.

3 The Great Wall, *China*

The Great Wall of China was built in various stages and forms over a period of 1 000 years from the third century BC. It is one of China's most distinctive and spectacular features. The wall is visible in this aerial photograph as a light coloured line running across the hills from lower right to upper left. Stretching a total length of over 2 400 km from the coast east of Beijing, to the Gobi desert in Gansu province, the wall was first built to protect China from the Mongols and nomadic peoples to the north of the country.

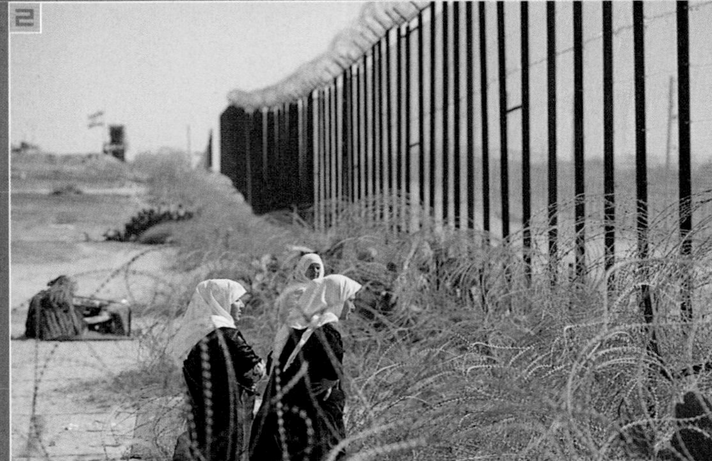

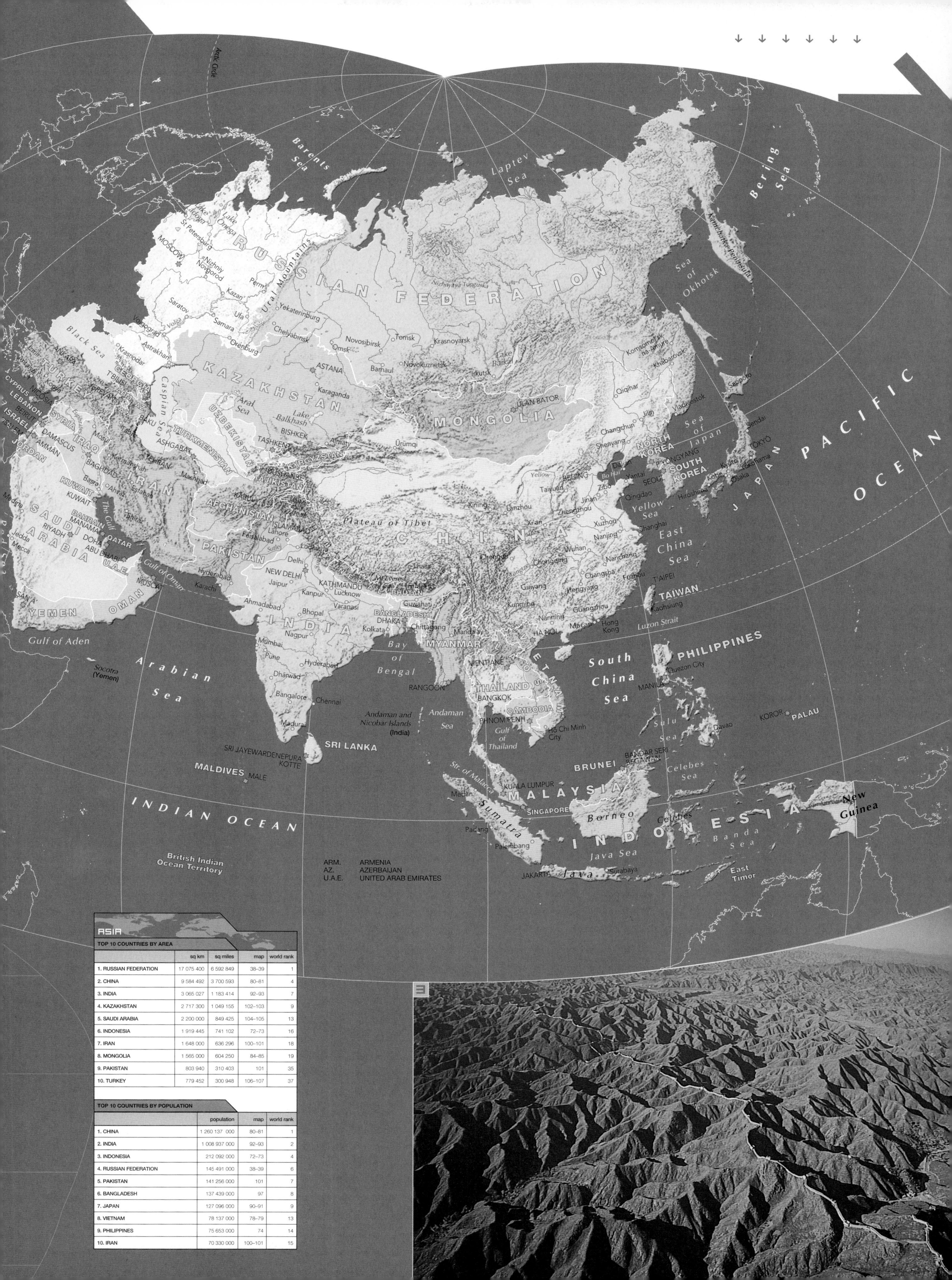

ARM.   ARMENIA
AZ.   AZERBAIJAN
U.A.E. UNITED ARAB EMIRATES

ASIA

TOP 10 COUNTRIES BY AREA

	sq km	sq miles	map	world rank
1. RUSSIAN FEDERATION	17 075 400	6 592 849	38–39	1
2. CHINA	9 584 492	3 700 593	80–81	4
3. INDIA	3 065 027	1 183 414	92–93	7
4. KAZAKHSTAN	2 717 300	1 049 155	102–103	9
5. SAUDI ARABIA	2 200 000	849 425	104–105	13
6. INDONESIA	1 919 445	741 102	72–73	16
7. IRAN	1 648 000	636 296	100–101	18
8. MONGOLIA	1 565 000	604 250	84–85	19
9. PAKISTAN	803 940	310 403	101	35
10. TURKEY	779 452	300 948	106–107	37

TOP 10 COUNTRIES BY POPULATION

	population	map	world rank
1. CHINA	1 260 137 000	80–81	1
2. INDIA	1 008 937 000	92–93	2
3. INDONESIA	212 092 000	72–73	4
4. RUSSIAN FEDERATION	145 491 000	38–39	6
5. PAKISTAN	141 256 000	101	7
6. BANGLADESH	137 439 000	97	8
7. JAPAN	127 096 000	90–91	9
8. VIETNAM	78 137 000	78–79	13
9. PHILIPPINES	75 653 000	74	14
10. IRAN	70 330 000	100–101	15

ASIA
COUNTRIES

		area sq km	area sq miles	population	capital	languages	religions	currency	map
PAKISTAN		803 940	310 403	141 256 000	Islamabad	Urdu, Punjabi, Sindhi, Pushtu, English	Sunni Muslim, Shi'a Muslim, Christian, Hindu	Rupee	101
PALAU		497	192	19 000	Koror	Palauan, English	Roman Catholic, Protestant, traditional beliefs	US dollar	73
PHILIPPINES		300 000	115 831	75 653 000	Manila	English, Pilipino, Cebuano, local languages	Roman Catholic, Protestant, Sunni Muslim, Aglipayan	Peso	74
QATAR		11 437	4 416	565 000	Doha (Ad Dawḥah)	Arabic	Sunni Muslim	Riyal	105
RUSSIAN FEDERATION		17 075 400	6 592 849	145 491 000	Moscow (Moskva)	Russian, Tatar, Ukrainian, local languages	Russian Orthodox, Sunni Muslim, Protestant	Rouble	38–39
SAUDI ARABIA		2 200 000	849 425	20 346 000	Riyadh (Ar Riyāḍ)	Arabic	Sunni Muslim, Shi'a Muslim	Riyal	104–105
SINGAPORE		639	247	4 018 000	Singapore	Chinese, English, Malay, Tamil	Buddhist, Taoist, Sunni Muslim, Christian, Hindu	Dollar	76
SOUTH KOREA		99 274	38 330	46 740 000	Seoul (Sŏul)	Korean	Buddhist, Protestant, Roman Catholic	Won	83
SRI LANKA		65 610	25 332	18 924 000	Sri Jayewardenepura Kotte	Sinhalese, Tamil, English	Buddhist, Hindu, Sunni Muslim, Roman Catholic	Rupee	94
SYRIA		185 180	71 498	16 189 000	Damascus (Dimashq)	Arabic, Kurdish, Armenian	Sunni Muslim, Shi'a Muslim, Christian	Pound	108–109
TAIWAN		36 179	13 969	22 300 000	T'aipei	Mandarin, Min, Hakka, local languages	Buddhist, Taoist, Confucian, Christian	Dollar	87
TAJIKISTAN		143 100	55 251	6 087 000	Dushanbe	Tajik, Uzbek, Russian	Sunni Muslim	Rouble	101
THAILAND		513 115	198 115	62 806 000	Bangkok (Krung Thep)	Thai, Lao, Chinese, Malay, Mon-Khmer languages	Buddhist, Sunni Muslim	Baht	78–79
TURKEY		779 452	300 948	66 668 000	Ankara	Turkish, Kurdish	Sunni Muslim, Shi'a Muslim	Lira	106–107
TURKMENISTAN		488 100	188 456	4 737 000	Ashgabat (Ashkhabad)	Turkmen, Uzbek, Russian	Sunni Muslim, Russian Orthodox	Manat	102–103
UNITED ARAB EMIRATES		83 600	32 278	2 606 000	Abu Dhabi (Abū Ẓabī)	Arabic, English	Sunni Muslim, Shi'a Muslim	Dirham	105
UZBEKISTAN		447 400	172 742	24 881 000	Tashkent	Uzbek, Russian, Tajik, Kazakh	Sunni Muslim, Russian Orthodox	Sum	102–103
VIETNAM		329 565	127 246	78 137 000	Ha Nôi	Vietnamese, Thai, Khmer, Chinese, local languages	Buddhist, Taoist, Roman Catholic, Cao Dai, Hoa Hao	Dong	78–79
YEMEN		527 968	203 850	18 349 000	Şan'ā'	Arabic	Sunni Muslim, Shi'a Muslim	Rial	104–105

DEPENDENT AND DISPUTED TERRITORIES

		territorial status	area sq km	area sq miles	population	capital	languages	religions	currency	map
British Indian Ocean Territory		United Kingdom Overseas Territory	60	23	uninhabited					219
Christmas Island		Australian External Territory	135	52	2 195	The Settlement	English	Buddhist, Sunni Muslim, Protestant, Roman Catholic	Australian dollar	72
Cocos Islands (Keeling Islands)		Australian External Territory	14	5	637	West Island	English	Sunni Muslim, Christian	Australian dollar	218
East Timor		under UN Transitional Administration	14 874	5 743	737 000	Dili	Portuguese, Tetun, English	Roman Catholic		75
French Southern and Antarctic Lands		French Overseas Territory	439 580	169 723	uninhabited					219
Gaza		semi-autonomous region	363	140	3 191 000*	Gaza	Arabic	Sunni Muslim, Shi'a Muslim	Israeli shekel	108
Heard and McDonald Islands		Australian External Territory	412	159	uninhabited					219
Jammu and Kashmir		Disputed territory (India/Pakistan)	222 236	85 806	13 000 000					96–97
West Bank		Disputed territory	5 860	2 263			Arabic, Hebrew	Sunni Muslim, Jewish, Shi'a Muslim, Christian		108

*includes occupied West Bank

1 Tigris and Euphrates Rivers

The availability of water in generally arid regions can cause international disputes or, in already unstable regions such as the Middle East, can fuel existing conflicts and animosities. The Tigris and Euphrates rivers originate in Turkey, meet in southeast Iraq and flow into the Gulf through the Shaṭṭ al 'Arab waterway, seen in the satellite image as a dark grey streak from centre left. They have been important sources of water since the times of the ancient civilizations of Mesopotamia and continue to be vital for Iraq, as well as for the countries where the vast majority of their water is generated – Turkey and Syria. As shown on the map, numerous dams have been built, particularly in Turkey, which affect the overall volume and flow of water through Syria and Iraq. Numerous attempts have been made to formulate treaties between these nations but the issue remains a source of tension. The problems of water supply in Iraq are complicated by internal irrigation schemes and the politically- and environmentally-sensitive draining of large areas of marsh.

Satellite/Sensor : Space Shuttle

Fig. #01
Tigris and Euphrates

- - - Tigris-Euphrates catchment area

Ataturk 🔺 Dam

] Barrage

Mesopotamia

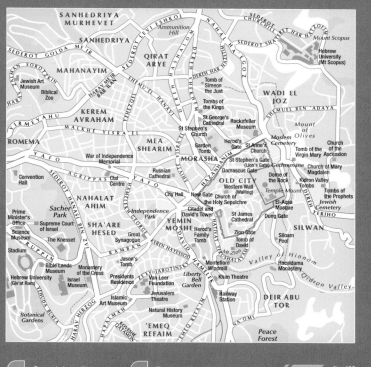

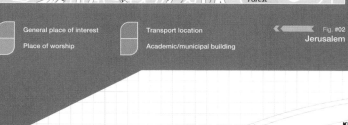

General place of interest
Place of worship
Transport location
Academic/municipal building

Fig. #02
Jerusalem

Jerusalem

The city of Jerusalem is a holy city for Jews, Muslims and Christians alike, and remains a focus of the ongoing conflicts between Israelis and Palestinians. This aerial photograph shows the Old City outlined by the city walls, the full outline of which is shown on the map. The Old City is divided into the Jewish, Muslim, Christian and Armenian quarters. The Muslim quarter, seen on the right of this photograph, is the busiest and most densely populated area. Just left of centre is the distinctive golden-roofed Dome of the Rock and to the left of this the El-Aqsa Mosque.

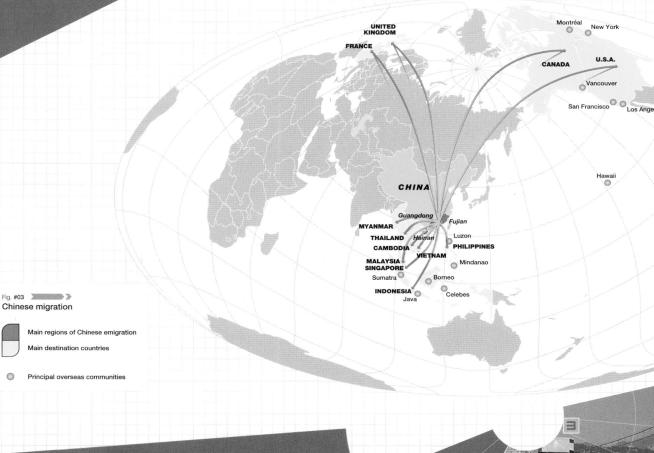

Fig. #03
Chinese migration

Main regions of Chinese emigration
Main destination countries
Principal overseas communities

CONNECTIONS

subject	page#
World countries	10–11
Asia landscapes	62–63
Asia countries	64–65
Reference maps of Asia	72–109

Chinese migration

There has been a pattern of population migration from China since the early nineteenth century. This has resulted in a large overseas Chinese population, or *diaspora*, today estimated at over 30 million. Historically, the most common reasons for this population movement have been economic hardship, famine and political instability. As can be seen from the map, the majority of migrants settle in southeast Asia, mainly in Indonesia, Thailand, Malaysia and Singapore. In some countries this can create tensions between ethnic groups. Over eighty per cent of the Chinese overseas population lives in Asia, with most of them living in Chinese communities within the major cities. Europe and North America have also been important destinations, where the immigrants have again created distinctive communities in large cities, such as Chinatown in San Francisco, part of which is shown in the photograph.

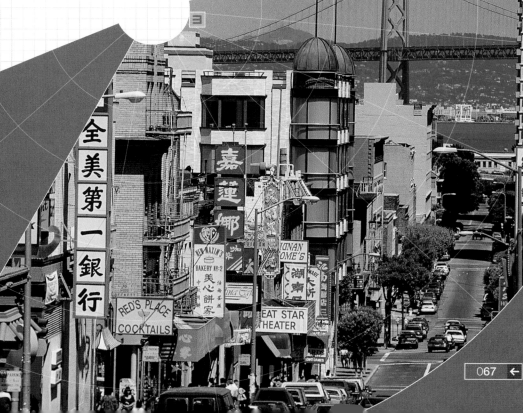

1 **Three Gorges Dam Project,** *China*

The Three Gorges Dam Project on the Yangtze river is the world's largest
hydroelectric project. The term refers to a 190 km stretch of the Yangtze river
where it flows through the precipitous Quitang, Wu and Xiling gorges, as shown
on the satellite image and map. The photograph at the top shows part of the
project area before construction began in 1997. The centre photograph shows
part of the construction work and gives some idea of the effect it will have on
the landscape. When complete, the dam will be over two kilometres wide and
will create a 620 km long reservoir which will engulf over 400 sq km of
farmland, thirteen cities, hundreds of villages, and archaeological sites.
While the project, due for completion in 2009, will improve flood management,
generate electricity and transfer water to dry areas further north, it raises many
social and environmental issues, including the resettlement of between 1–2
million people, the potential accumulation of pollutants and the destruction of
precious natural habitats.

Satellite/Sensor : Landsat (bottom)

Fig. #01
Three Gorges Dam project

miles
0 ————— 50
0 ————— 100
kilometres

Area to be inundated

Area affected by Three Gorges Dam project

Three Gorges Dam

Gorge

Inundated town

Provincial boundary

SHAANXI

HUBEI

SICHUAN

Wuxi

Daning He

Xiang *A*   Xingshan

Kaixian

Wushan

Zigui

Fengjie

Badong   *Xiling*   *Gorge*

Quitang   *Wu*

Yunyang   *Gorge*   *Gorge*   Sandouping   Gezhouba

Wanxian   *Yangtze*   Dam

Yichang

Dong He

Zhongxian

Fengdu   Shizhu

Changshou

Jiangbei   Fuling

CHONGQING

Chongqing   Mudong

Wu Jiang

Ba Xian   Wulong

GUIZHOU

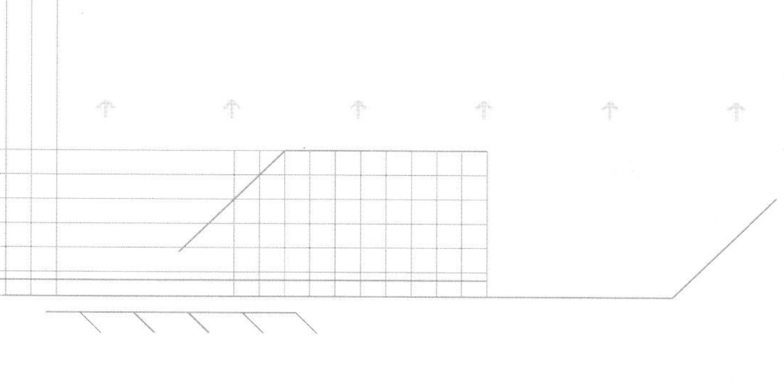

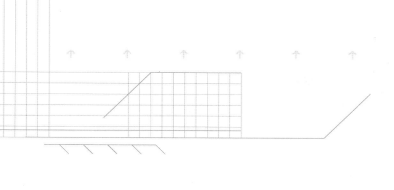

Lake Level Variations

A natural evaporation basin, the Kara-Bogaz-Gol is located in a semi-arid region of Turkmenistan on the eastern shore of the Caspian Sea. In these northwest-looking oblique Shuttle photographs the difference in water level, due to both evaporation and variation in the flow of water from the Caspian Sea into the basin, is striking. The 1985 image (top) shows water in only a small section near the western end. In contrast to this, the 1995 image (bottom) shows the water level to be high in the whole basin. The level of the Caspian Sea is normally approximately three metres above that of the basin, and water flows from one to the other through a dyke built in the late 1970s. However, low rainfall in the region can result in exceptionally low water levels in the Caspian Sea, which dramatically affect the amount of water flowing into the basin.

Satellite/Sensor : Space Shuttle

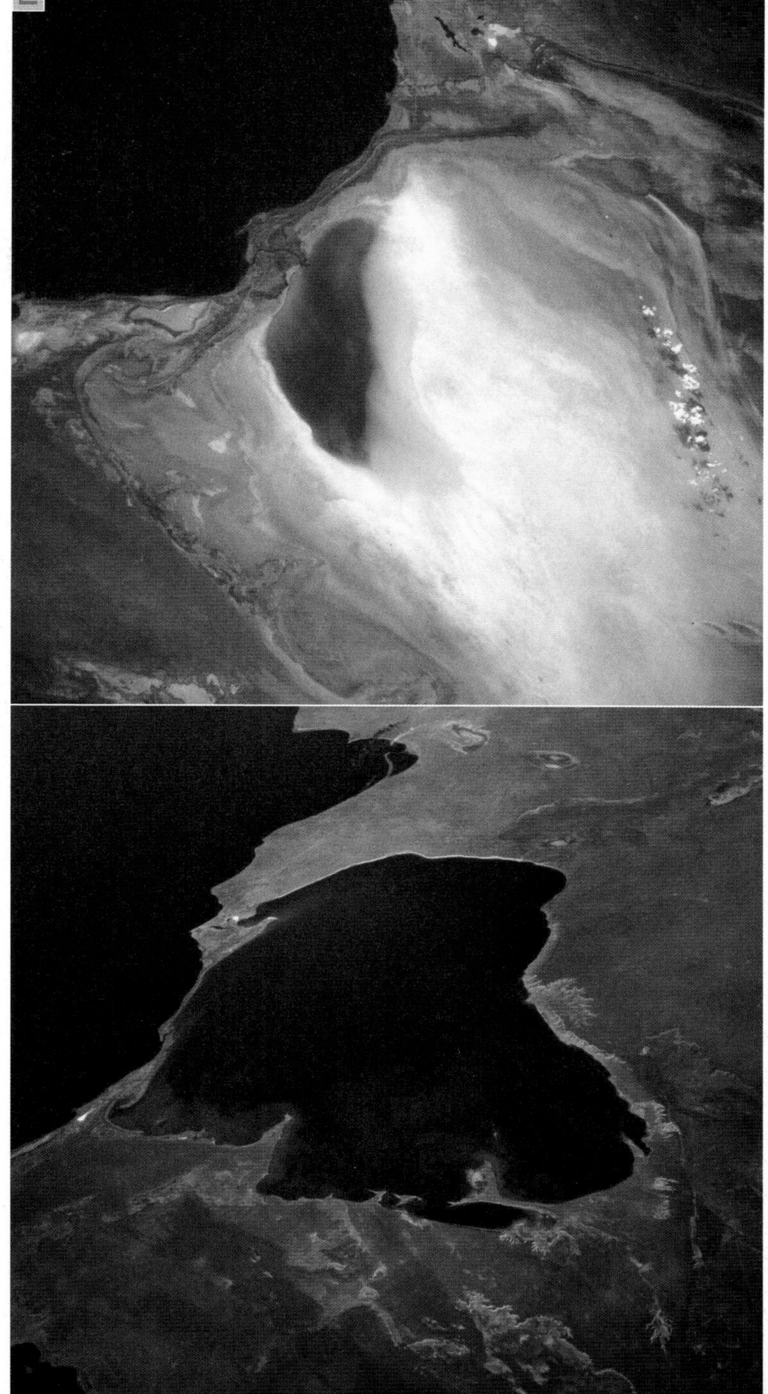

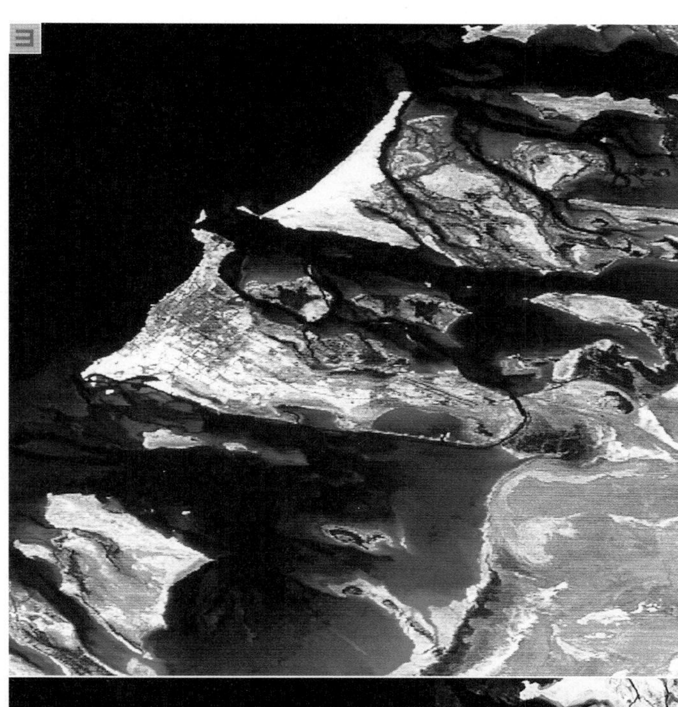

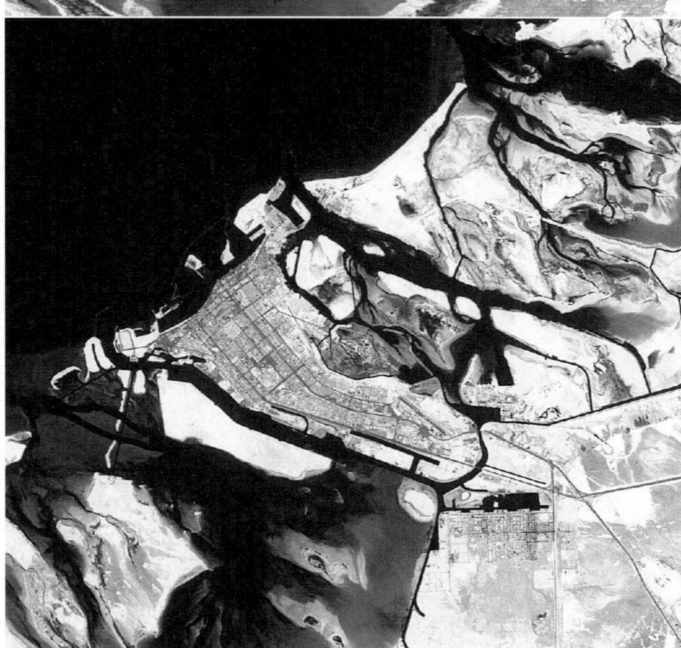

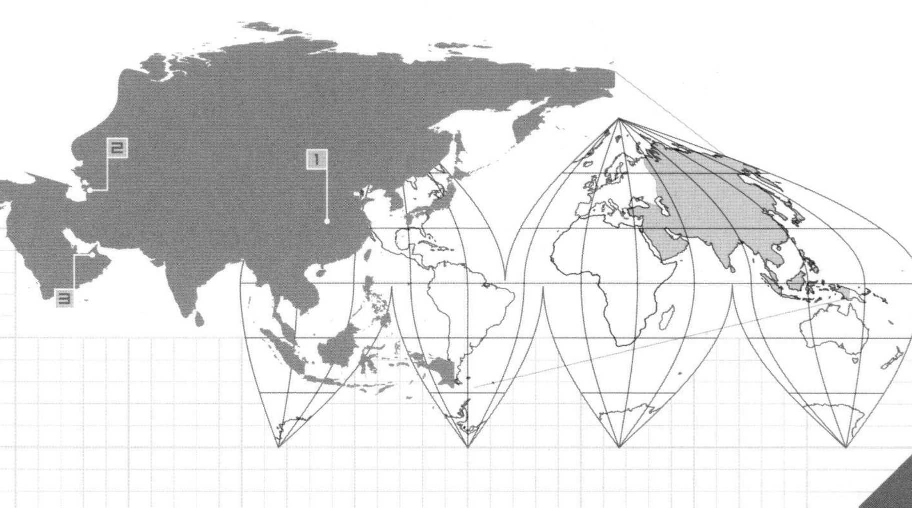

Urban Development and Land Reclamation

These satellite images show the development of the capital of the United Arab Emirates, Abu Dhabi. In the 1950s the town was little more than a small fishing village, but this changed after the discovery of offshore oil in the early 1960s. The changes, particularly to the extent of the city and to the coastline, in the period between the image at the top (1972) and the one below (1989), are dramatic. A national development program was implemented to help improve the city's harbour and to construct buildings, roads, and an international airport.

Satellite/Sensor : Landsat

CONNECTIONS

▸ subject	page#
▸ World earthquakes and volcanoes	14–15
▸ World tropical storms	16–17
▸ Mozambique floods	116–117
▸ North America threats	160–161

1 Tropical Storms

Tropical storms are among the most powerful and destructive weather systems on Earth. Worldwide between eighty and one hundred develop over tropical oceans each year. The northwest Pacific area experiences an average of thirty one typhoons annually and most of these occur between July and October. If they reach land they can cause extensive damage to property or loss of life as a result of high winds and heavy rain. This image gives an idea of the overall size of a typhoon as it moves westwards across the Pacific Ocean towards the island of Guam. Wind speeds in this typhoon reached over 370 km per hour.

Satellite/Sensor : GOES

2 Tropical Cyclone Hudah, *Southwest Indian Ocean*

Tropical cyclone Hudah was one of the most powerful storms ever seen in the Indian Ocean and was typical of the storms which frequently occur in the Pacific and Indian Oceans and which threaten the coasts of Asia and Africa. At the end of March 2000 the storm began a fairly straight westerly track across the entire south Indian Ocean, as shown on the map, struck Madagascar as an intense tropical cyclone, weakened, then regained intensity in the Mozambique Channel before making a final landfall in Mozambique on 9 April. This image was taken just before the cyclone hit the coast of Madagascar where wind gusts reached over 296 km per hour causing the destruction of 90% of the city of Antalaha.

Satellite/Sensor : MODIS

3 Bangladesh Cyclone Damage

Bangladesh, lying at the northern edge of the Bay of Bengal often experiences extreme climatic conditions which can wreak havoc. Cyclones regularly occur in the Bay of Bengal often having devastating effects on the flat coastal regions as shown in this photograph. In 1991 the country was hit by a massive cyclone which killed more than 140 000 people.

4 Klyuchevskaya Volcano, *Russian Federation*

Klyuchevskaya is the highest mountain in eastern Russian Federation and one of the most active volcanoes on the Kamchatka Peninsula. This view shows the major eruption of 1994 when the eruption cloud reached 18 300 m above sea level and the winds carried ash as far as 1 030 km to the southeast. The Kamchatka Peninsula is a sparsely populated area and the volcano's threat to human life is not serious. However, it lies on a major airline route and volcanic eruptions frequently cause aircraft to divert around the region.

Satellite/Sensor : Space Shuttle

Fig. #01

Tracks of tropical cyclones in the southwest Indian Ocean 2000

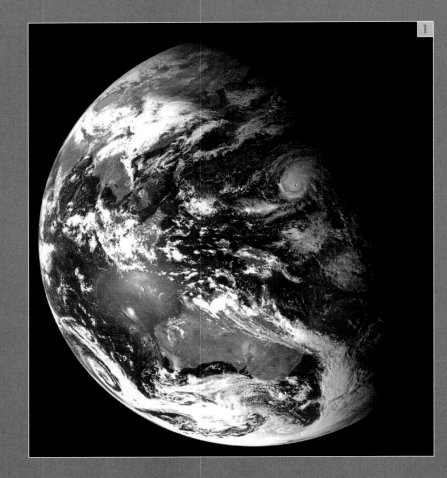

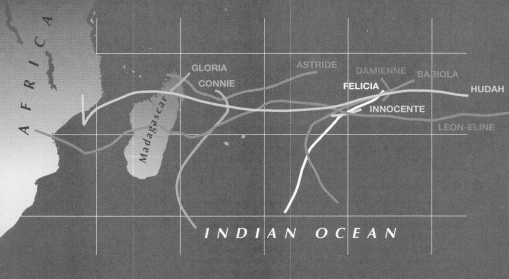

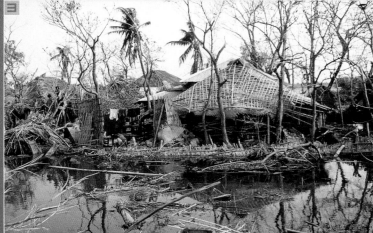

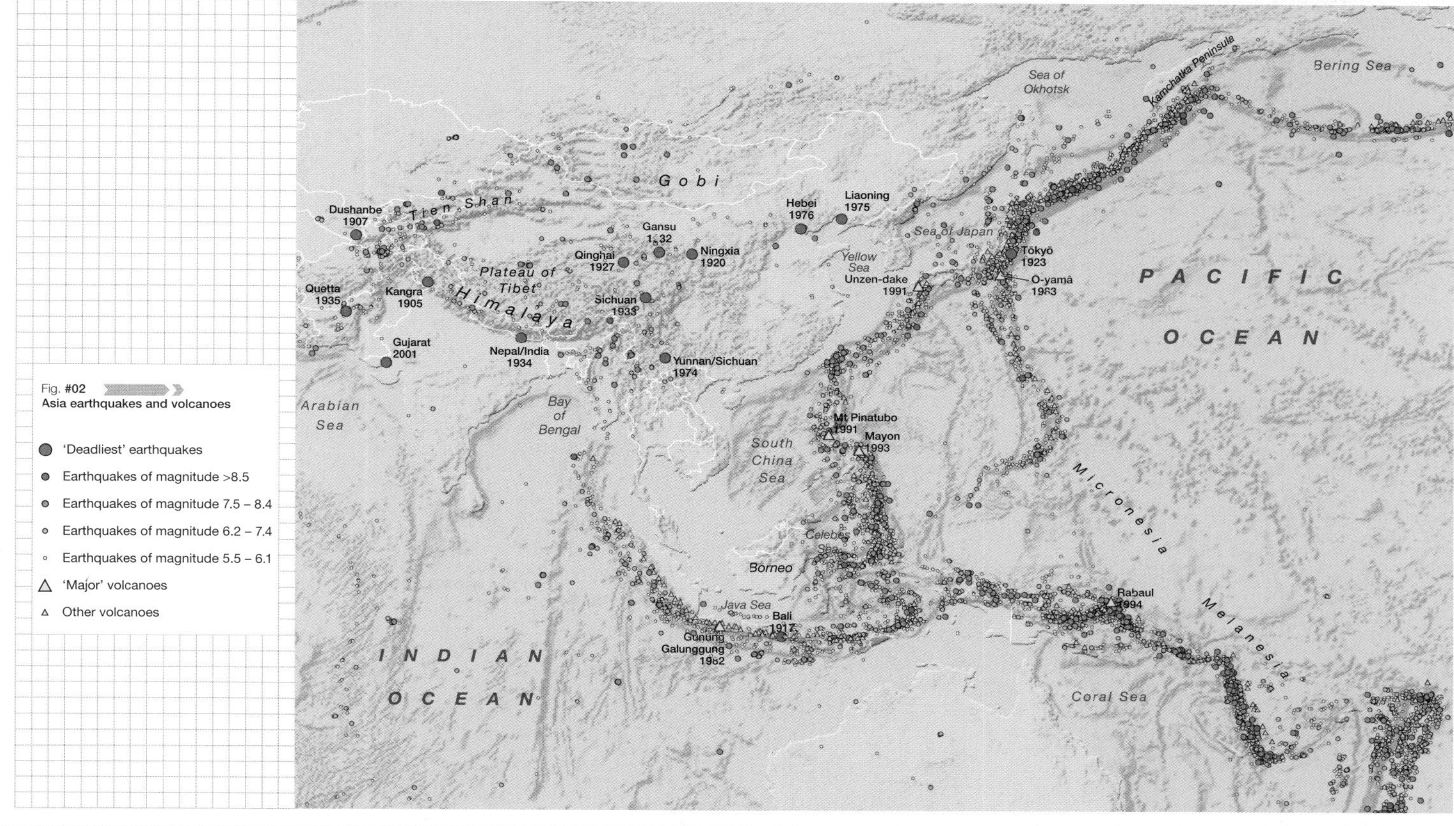

Fig. #02
Asia earthquakes and volcanoes

- ● 'Deadliest' earthquakes
- ● Earthquakes of magnitude >8.5
- ● Earthquakes of magnitude 7.5 – 8.4
- ∘ Earthquakes of magnitude 6.2 – 7.4
- ∘ Earthquakes of magnitude 5.5 – 6.1
- △ 'Major' volcanoes
- ▵ Other volcanoes

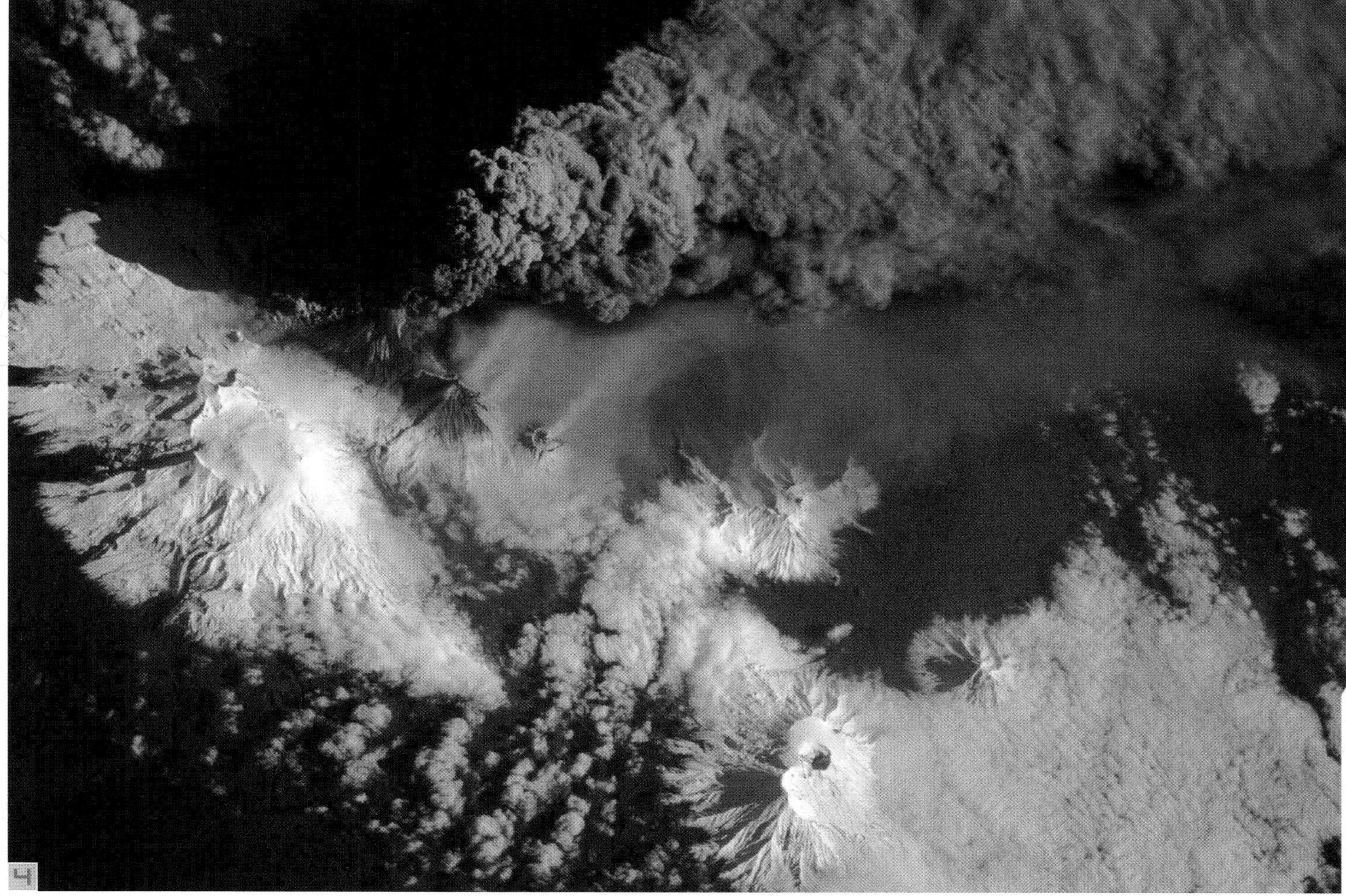

5 **Kamchatka Peninsula,** *Russian Federation*

The Kamchatka Peninsula in the eastern Russian Federation is a volcanic landscape
between the Sea of Okhotsk and the Bering Sea. This near-horizontal perspective view
shows the western side of the peninsula with the Sea of Okhotsk in the foreground.
Inland from the coast, vegetated floodplains and low hills rise towards the snow-capped
volcanoes of the Sredinnyy Khrebet mountain range which forms the spine of the
peninsula. The image was generated using topographic data from the Shuttle Radar
Topography Mission and a Landsat 7 satellite image.

Satellite/Sensor : SRTM/Landsat

asia [map 1]

11°S-26°N / 95°-147°E

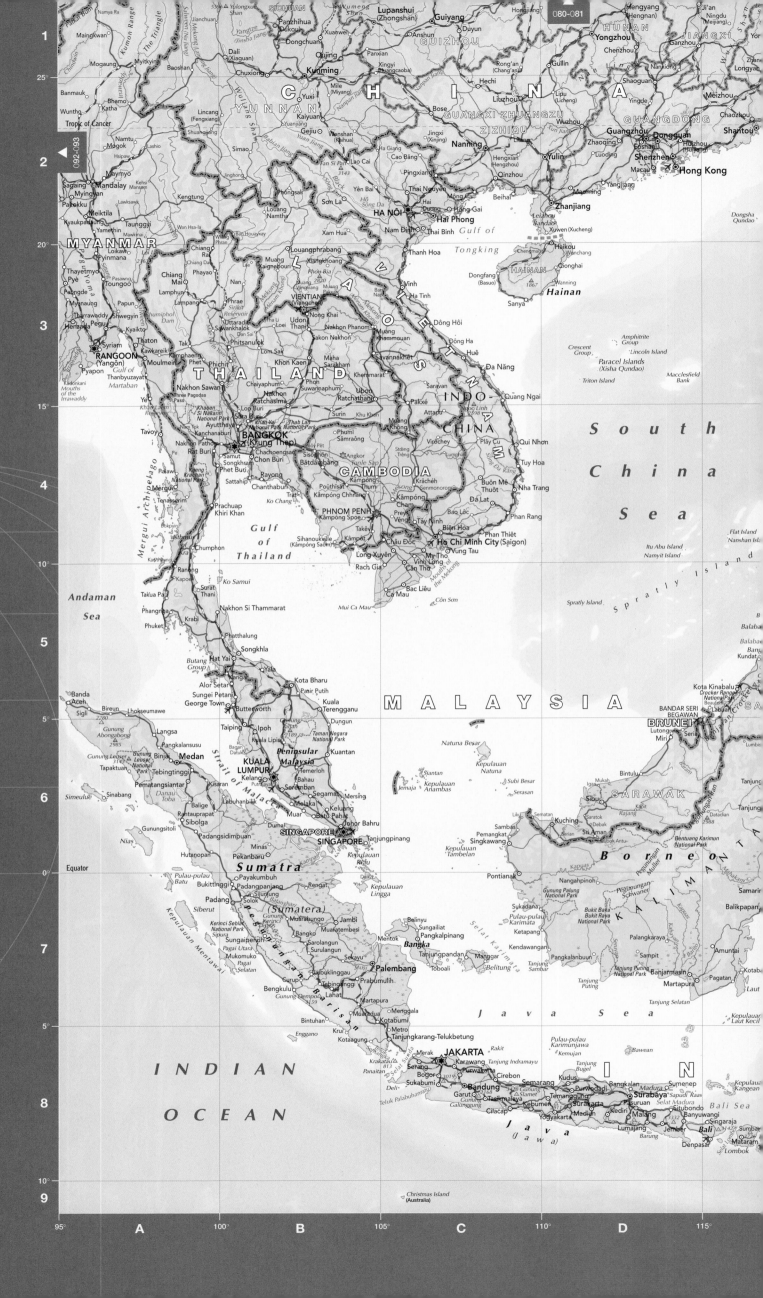

092-093

080-081

CHINA

YUNNAN

GUIZHOU

HUNAN

JIANGXI

GUANGXI ZHUANGZU ZIZHIQU

GUANGDONG

HAINAN

MYANMAR

LAOS

VIETNAM

THAILAND

CAMBODIA

INDO-CHINA

MALAYSIA

BRUNEI

SARAWAK

SINGAPORE

KALIMANTAN

Sumatra (Sumatera)

Borneo

Java (Jawa)

Peninsular Malaysia

Andaman Sea

Gulf of Thailand

Gulf of Tongking

South China Sea

Strait of Malacca

Java Sea

INDIAN OCEAN

Tropic of Cancer

Equator

HA NÔI

BANGKOK (Krung Thep)

RANGOON (Yangôn)

VIENTIANE (Viangchan)

PHNOM PENH

KUALA LUMPUR

BANDAR SERI BEGAWAN

JAKARTA

Hong Kong

Ho Chi Minh City (Saigon)

Christmas Island (Australia)

Land
>6000m
5000-6000m
4000-5000m
3000-4000m
2000-3000m
1000-2000m
500-1000m
200-500m
0-200m
<0m

Sea
0-200m
200-500m
500-1000m
1000-2000m
2000-3000m
3000-4000m
4000-5000m
5000-6000m
>6000m

1 2 3 4 5 6 7 8 9

A B C D

95° 100° 105° 110° 115°

25° 20° 15° 10° 5° 0° 5° 10°

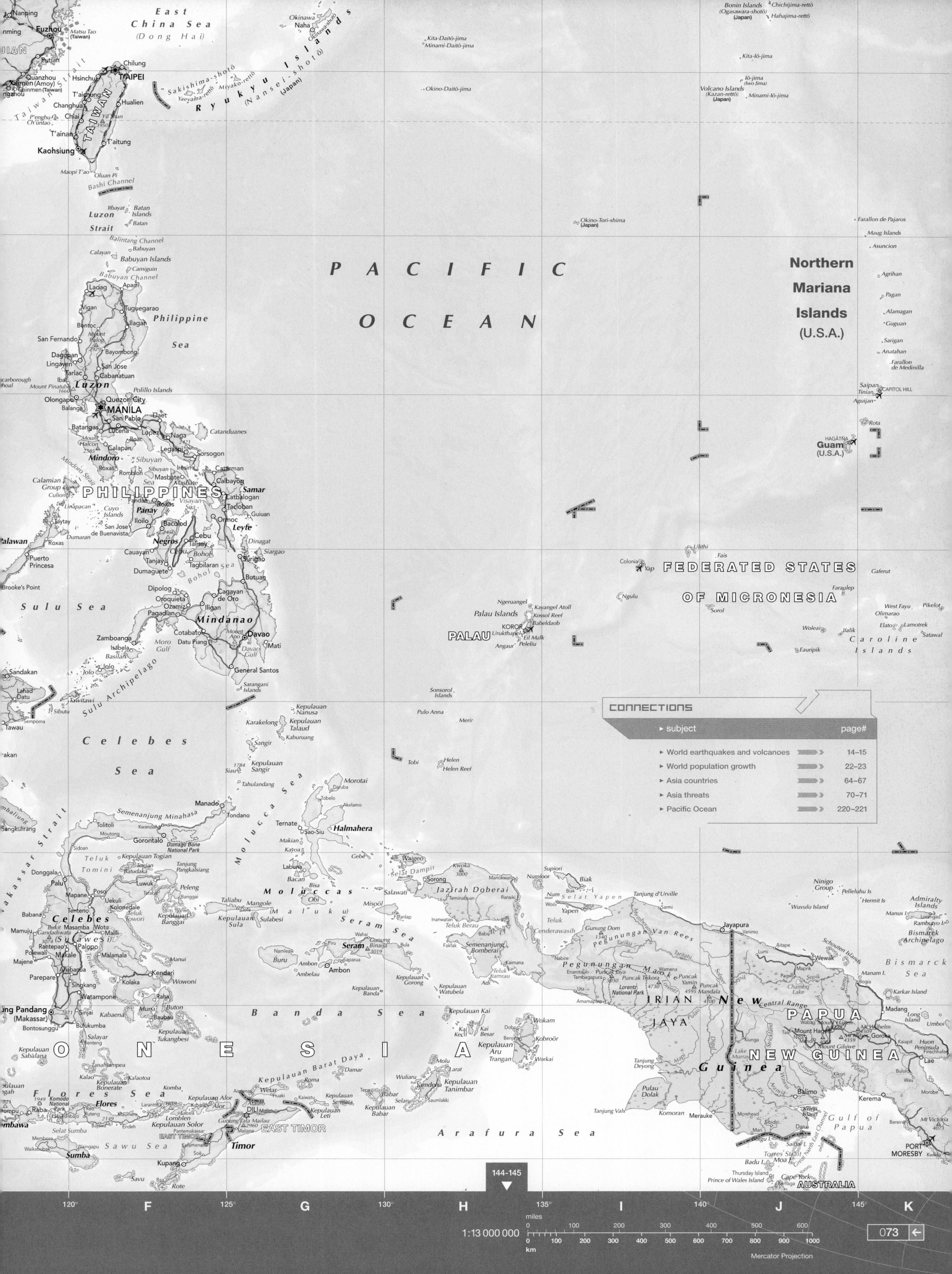
East China Sea
(Dong Hai)
Okinawa
Naha
Ryukyu Islands
(Nansei-shotō)
(Japan)
Sakishima-shotō
Miyako-rettō
Yaeyama-rettō
Kita-Daitō-jima
Minami-Daitō-jima
Oki-Daitō-jima
Bonin Islands
(Ogasawara-shotō)
(Japan)
Chichijima-rettō
Hahajima-rettō
Kita-Iō-jima
Iō-jima
(Iwo Jima)
Volcano Islands
(Kazan-rettō)
(Japan)
Minami-Iō-jima
Fuzhou
Matsu Tao
(Taiwan)
Putian
Quanzhou
Xiamen (Amoy)
Chinmen (Taiwan)
Taiwan Strait
Chilung
T'AIPEI
Hsinchu
T'aichung
Changhua
Chiai
Hualien
P'enghu
Ch'üntao
T'ainan
TAIWAN
T'aitung
Kaohsiung
Maopi T'ao
Oluan Pi
Bashi Channel
Itbayat
Batan Islands
Batan
Luzon Strait
Balintang Channel
Calayan
Babuyan
Babuyan Islands
Camiguin
Babuyan Channel
Laoag
Aparri
Vigan
Tuguegarao
Philippine Sea
Bontoc
Ilagan
San Fernando
Mount Pulog
Dagupan
Lingayen
Bayombong
San Jose
Tarlac
Cabanatuan
Scarborough Shoal
Iba
Mount Pinatubo
Luzon
Polillo Islands
Olongapo
Quezon City
Balanga
MANILA
San Pablo
Daet
Batangas
Lucena
Lopez
Naga
Catanduanes
Mount Halcon
Calapan
Legaspi
Sorsogon
Mindoro
Sibuyan
Mindoro Strait
Roxas
Romblon
Sibuyan Sea
Masbate
Catarman
Calbayog
Samar
Calamian Group
Culion
PHILIPPINES
Catbalogan
Cuyo Islands
Panay
Roxas
Tacloban
Guiuan
Visayan Sea
Linapacan
Taytay
Iloilo
Bacolod
Ormoc
Leyte
San Jose de Buenavista
Dumaran
Negros
Cebu
Dinagat
Palawan
Roxas
Talisay
Siargao
Puerto Princesa
Cauayan
Tanjay
Bohol
Surigao
Dumaguete
Tagbilaran
Bohol Sea
Butuan
Brooke's Point
Dipolog
Cagayan de Oro
Sulu Sea
Oroquieta
Ozamiz
Iligan
Pagadian
Mindanao
Zamboanga
Cotabato
Datu Piang
Mount Apo
Davao
Isabela
Moro Gulf
Davao Gulf
Mati
Basilan
Jolo
Jolo
General Santos
Sandakan
Sulu Archipelago
Sarangani Islands
Lahad Datu
Tawitawi
Sibutu
Tawau
Semporna
Celebes Sea
Kepulauan Nanusa
Karakelong
Kepulauan Talaud
Kaburuang
Sangir
Kepulauan Sangir
Siau
Tahulandang
Molucca Sea
Morotai
Daruba
Tobelo
Akelamo
Manado
Tondano
Semenanjung Minahasa
Tolitoli
Kwandang
Gorontalo
Moutong
Dumoga Bone National Park
Ternate
Soa-Siu
Halmahera
Makian
Kayoa
Makassar Strait
Sangkulirang
Teluk Tomini
Kepulauan Togian
Batudaka
Tanjung Pangkalsiang
Donggala
Palu
Labuha
Bacan
Bisa
Obi
Gebe
Waigeo
Selat Dampir
Sorong
Kwoka
Manokwari
Supiori
Biak
Numfoor
Jazirah Doberai
Teminabuan
Ransiki
Salawati
Misoöl
Molucca
(Maluku)
Taliabu
Mangole
Kepulauan Sula
Sulabesi
Poso
Luwuk
Peleng
Banggai
Kepulauan Banggai
Mapane
Uekuli
Kolonedale
Teluk Towori
Tentena
Celebes
(Sulawesi)
Babana
Mamuju
Bukit Masamba
Wotu
Malili
Rantepao
Palopo
Polewali
Makale
Majene
Malamala
Teluk Bone
Manui
Parepare
Kendari
Wowoni
Kolaka
Watampone
Singkang
Kabaena
Muna
Raha
Buton
Baubau
Ujung Pandang
(Makassar)
Sinjai
Bulukumba
Bontosunggu
Salayar
Benteng
Kepulauan Tukangbesi
Kepulauan Sabalana
INDONESIA
Tanahjampea
Kalao
Kalaotoa
Kepulauan Bonerate
Flores Sea
Komba
Flores
Komodo National Park
Ruteng
Ende
Larantuka
Lomblen
Kepulauan Solor
Kepulauan Alor
Alor
Wetar
Atauro
DILI
Tata Mailau
EAST TIMOR
Maliana
Pantemakassar
Kefamenanu
Soë
Timor
Kupang
Savu
Rote
Roti
Sawu Sea
Selat Sumba
Sumba
Waingapu
Waikabubak
Bima
Sumbawa
Seram Sea
Seram
Wahai
Gunung Binaiya
Bula
Namlea
Buru
Ambon
Ambelau
Saparua
Ambon
Banda Sea
Kepulauan Gorong
Kepulauan Watubela
Kepulauan Banda
Kepulauan Kai
Kai Kecil
Kai Besar
Kepulauan Aru
Dobo
Trangan
Wokam
Kobroör
Workai
Molu
Larat
Yamdena
Kepulauan Tanimbar
Saumlaki
Wuliaru
Selaru
Babar
Kepulauan Babar
Damar
Roma
Kisar
Kepulauan Barat Daya
Kepulauan Sermata
Kepulauan Leti
Arafura Sea
Inanwatan
Teluk Berau
Fakfak
Semenanjung Bomberai
Kaimana
Teluk Kamrau
Adi
Teluk Cenderawasih
Nabire
Num
Selat Yapen
Yapen
Waren
Gunung Dom
Pegunungan Van Rees
Tanjung d'Urville
Sarmi
Jayapura
Vanimo
Pegunungan Maoke
Puncak Jaya
Puncak Trikora
Puncak Yamin
Puncak Mandala
Lorentz National Park
Tembagapura
Enarotali
Uta
Amamapare
IRIAN JAYA
New Guinea
Tanjung Deyong
Pulau Dolak
Tanjung Vals
Komoran
Merauke
PAPUA NEW GUINEA
Aitape
Wewak
Lumi
Schouten Islands
Maprik
Pagwi
Sepik
Chambri Lake
Mount Hagen
Mount Wilhelm
Mount Giluwe
Wabag
Mendi
Tari
Goroka
Madang
Lake Murray
Kiunga
Kikori
Balimo
Kerema
Morehead
Daru
Saibai I.
Kiwai Island
Gulf of Papua
Bereina
Mt Victoria
PORT MORESBY
Boigu I.
Badu I.
Moa I.
Torres Strait
Great North East Channel
Thursday Island
Prince of Wales Island
Cape York
Bamaga
AUSTRALIA
Huon Peninsula
Finschhafen
Lae
Bulolo
Wau
Morobe
Kaiapit
Long Island
Umboi
Karkar Island
Bogia
Manam I.
Bismarck Sea
Bismarck Archipelago
Admiralty Islands
Manus I.
Lorengau
Rambutyo I.
Ninigo Group
Pelleluhu Is
Hermit Is
Wuvulu Island
PACIFIC OCEAN
Okino-Tori-shima
(Japan)
Northern Mariana Islands
(U.S.A.)
Farallon de Pajaros
Maug Islands
Asuncion
Agrihan
Pagan
Alamagan
Guguan
Sarigan
Anatahan
Farallon de Medinilla
Saipan
Tinian
CAPITOL HILL
Aguijan
Rota
HAGÅTÑA
Guam
(U.S.A.)
Ulithi
Fais
Colonia
Yap
FEDERATED STATES OF MICRONESIA
Gaferut
Faraulep
Ngulu
Sorol
West Fayu
Pikelot
Olimarao
Elato
Lamotrek
Woleai
Ifalik
Satawal
Eauripik
Caroline Islands
Ngeruangel
Kayangel Atoll
Palau Islands
Kossol Reef
Babeldaob
KOROR
Urukthapel
Eil Malk
Peleliu
Angaur
PALAU
Sonsorol Islands
Pulo Anna
Merir
Tobi
Helen
Helen Reef
CONNECTIONS
subject page#
World earthquakes and volcanoes 14–15
World population growth 22–23
Asia countries 64–67
Asia threats 70–71
Pacific Ocean 220–221
144-145
120° F 125° G 130° H 135° I 140° J 145° K
1:13 000 000
miles 0 100 200 300 400 500 600
km 0 100 200 300 400 500 600 700 800 900 1000
Mercator Projection

5°-21°N / 117°-128°E

Seas and regions

Luzon Strait

Philippine Sea

South China Sea

Mindoro Sea

PHILIPPINES

Luzon

Mindoro

Panay

Negros

Cebu

Samar

Leyte

Bohol Sea

Sulu Sea

Celebes Sea

Moro Gulf

MALAYSIA

Mindanao

INDONESIA

MANILA ★

Elevation legend

>6000m
5000-6000m
4000-5000m
3000-4000m
2000-3000m
1000-2000m
500-1000m
200-500m
0-200m
<0m

0-200m
200-500m
500-1000m
1000-2000m
2000-3000m
3000-4000m
4000-5000m
5000-6000m
>6000m

076-077

075

miles
0 50 100 150 200 250

km
0 50 100 150 200 250 300 350 400

1:6 000 000

Mercator Projection

PHILIPPINES

Celebes Sea

CONNECTIONS

MALAYSIA
PHILIPPINES

Sulu Archipelago

Mindanao

Sarangani Strait
Sarangani Islands

Miangas (Philippines)

Kepulauan Nanusa
Marampit

Meares
Kawio
Ariaga
Anda
Armadores
Matutuang

Kepulauan Karkaralong

Karakelong

Kepulauan Talaud

Kalalusu
Dumarchen
Pulutan

Salibabu
Lirung
Kaburuang
Damar

Buang

Bukide
Tahuna

Awu

Sangir
Ngalipaeng
Kaloma

Tanjung Sopi

Karangetang
Makalehi
Siau

Rau
Wayabula
Berebere
Morotai
Gosobuso

Biaro

Kepulauan Loloda Utara

Daruba
Tanjung Gila
Sangowo

Tahulandang

Semenanjung Minahasa

Muaras Reef

KALIMANTAN TIMUR

Makassar Strait

Borneo

Tanjung Mangkalihat

Simatang

Tolitoli

Manado
Tondano
Bitung
Lembeh

Gunung Soputan

Amurang

Kahatola
Loloda
Obelo
Tanjung Lelai

Gunung Gamkonora

Ternate
Tidore
Sao-Sio

Halmahera

Kao
Teluk Buli

Wayamli

Makian

Bacan

Kepulauan Widi

Tanjung Libobo

Kepulauan Rajaampat

Kawe

Wayag

Equator

Tanjung Manimbaya

SULAWESI TENGAH

Teluk Tomini

Kepulauan Togian

Unauna
Togian

Gorontalo

Damago Bone National Park

Poso

Kepulauan Banggai

Peleng
Banggai

Taliabu
Sulabesi

Kepulauan Sula

Mangole

Obilatu
Kepulauan Obi
Obi

Misoöl

Tubalai

Moluccas (Maluku)

Halmahera Sea

Seram Sea

INDONESIA

MALUKU

Seram

Buru

Ambon

Banda Sea

SULAWESI SELATAN

Makale

Celebes (Sulawesi)

Palu

Palopo

Mamuju

SULAWESI TENGGARA

Kendari

Kolaka

Buton

Muna

Baubau

Kepulauan Tukangbesi

Kepulauan Banda

Kepulauan Penyu

Kepulauan Lucipara

Parepare

Pinrang

Watampone

Teluk Bone

jung Pandang (Makassar)

Bulukumba

Selayar

Kepulauan Taka'Bonerate

Laut Taka Bonerate National Park

Kepulauan Bonerate

Flores Sea

Kepulauan Sabalana

Sabalana

Tanahjampea

Kakabia

Batuata

Moromaho

Gunungapi

Kepulauan Barat Daya

Serua
Nila

Dai

Dawera

Roma

Damar
Wulur
Teun
Layeni

Komba

Kepulauan Alor

Wetar

Babar

Kisar
Sermata
Kepulauan Sermata

Kepulauan Babar

Kepulauan Leti

Masela

Flores

Komodo

Komodo National Park

Sumbawa

Bima
Raba

Sumba

NUSA TENGGARA TIMUR

Kepulauan Solor

DILI

EAST TIMOR

Timor

Kupang

Sawu Sea

Timor Sea

Rote

AUSTRALIA
Bathurst Island
Gordon Bay

12°S–5°N / 119°–130°E

IRIAN JAYA

076-077
072-073

>6000m	
5000-6000m	
4000-5000m	
3000-4000m	
2000-3000m	
1000-2000m	
500-1000m	
200-500m	
0-200m	
<0m	

0-200m	
200-500m	
500-1000m	
1000-2000m	
2000-3000m	
3000-4000m	
4000-5000m	
5000-6000m	
>6000m	

asia[map3]

miles
0 50 100 150 200 250

1 : 6 000 000

km
0 50 100 150 200 250 300 350 400

Mercator Projection

asia[map4]

8°N-10°S / 95°-120°E

Elevation scale:
>6000m
5000-6000m
4000-5000m
3000-4000m
2000-3000m
1000-2000m
500-1000m
200-500m
0-200m
<0m

0-200m
200-500m
500-1000m
1000-2000m
2000-3000m
3000-4000m
4000-5000m
5000-6000m
>6000m

THAILAND

Ko Phuket · Laem Mum Nouk · Khao Pu-Khao I National Park · Phatthalung · Thale Luang
Trang · Ko Lanta · Ko Lanta · Kantang · Khao Banthat Wildlife Reserve · Khao Phayun · Songkhla
Ko Libong · Thung Wa · Hat Yai · Ghana · Laem Pho
Terutao National Park · Teruto · Sadao · Sai Buri · Pattani · Nakhon
Butang Kawi Group · Ladang · Kangar · Yala · Narathiwat · Tak Bai
Langkawi · Jitra · Betong · Kota Bharu · Perhentian Besar
Sabang · Pulau We · Alor Setar · KEDAH · Redang
Pulau Breueh · Sungei Petani · Kuala Kerai · Kuala Terengganu
Pulau Penasi · Butterworth · KELANTAN
Banda Aceh · George Town · PINANG · TERENGGANU
Sigli · Taiping · PERAK · Dungun
Gunung Bateemeucica · Tanjong Penunjok
ACEH · Kuala Lumpur · Cukai
Gunung Leuser National Park · MALAYSIA
Medan · PAHANG · Kuantan
SUMATERA UTARA · Peninsular Malaysia
Pematangsiantar · SELANGOR · NEGERI SEMBILAN
Prapat · Melaka · JOHOR
Padang · Port Dickson · Muar · Batu Pahat
Nias · Johor Bahru · SINGAPORE
Sibolga · RIAU · Bintan
Padangsidimpuan · Pekanbaru · Kepulauan Riau
Natal · Bukittinggi · Jambi · JAMBI
Padang · SUMATERA BARAT
Siberut · Siberut National Park · SUMATERA SELATAN
Kepulauan Mentawai · Palembang
BENGKULU · Lahat
Bengkulu · LAMPUNG
Krui · Enggano

INDIAN OCEAN

Inset map (1:360 000)

MALAYSIA
Johor Bahru · Pasir Gudang
SEMBAWANG · WOODLANDS · Pulau Selatar · Selat Johor
Pulau Buloh · YISHUN · Pulau Ubin · Tanjong Chek Jawa
Kranji Reservoir · MANDAI · PUNGGOL · Pulau Tekong Kechil
Murai Reservoir · Lim Chu Kang · JALAN KAYU · Pulau Serangoon (Coney I.)
Tanjong Murai · BUKIT PANJANG · SELETAR · Serangoon Harbour
SINGAPORE
Jurong · Bukit Batok · Bukit Timah · ANG MO KIO · HOUGANG · CHANGI
CLEMENTI · TOA PAYOH · BEDOK · TAMPINES
QUEENSTOWN · GEYLANG · KATONG · SIGLAP
Sentosa · Strait of Singapore

1:360 000

miles 0 3
km 0 5

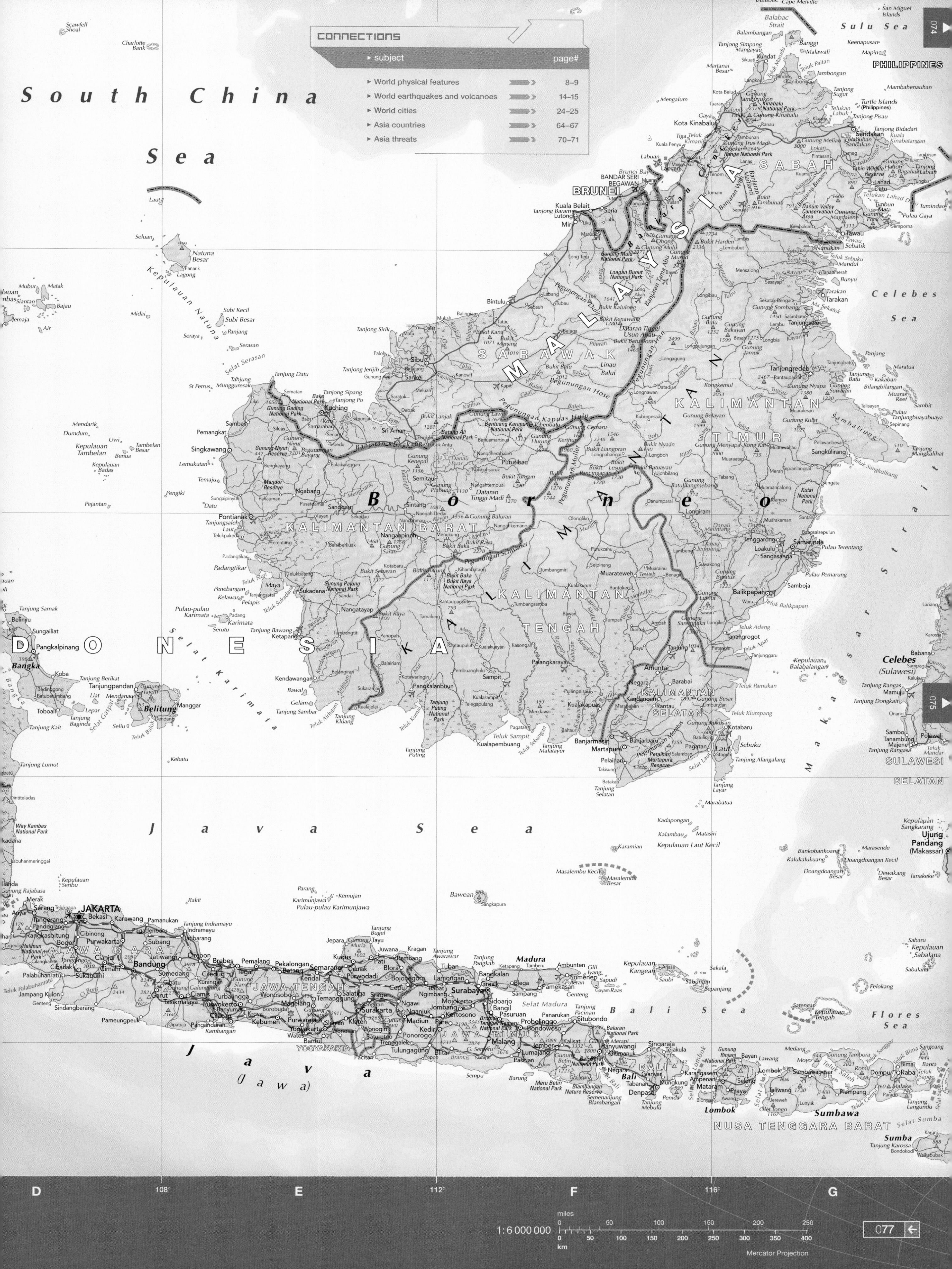

South China

Sea

CONNECTIONS

PHILIPPINES

Sulu Sea

Celebes
Sea

BRUNEI

MALAYSIA

SABAH

SARAWAK

KALIMANTAN
TIMUR

Borneo

KALIMANTAN
BARAT

KALIMANTAN
TENGAH

KALIMANTAN
SELATAN

DONESIA

Celebes
(Sulawesi)

SULAWESI
SELATAN

Java Sea

Ujung
Pandang
(Makassar)

JAKARTA

JAWA
BARAT

JAWA TENGAH

JAWA TIMUR

Bandung

Surabaya

Madura

YOGYAKARTA

Java
(Jawa)

Bali Sea

Flores
Sea

Bali

Lombok

Sumbawa

NUSA TENGGARA BARAT

Sumba

D   108°   E   112°   F   116°   G

miles
0   50   100   150   200   250

1:6 000 000
km
0 50 100 150 200 250 300 350 400

077 ←

Mercator Projection

075

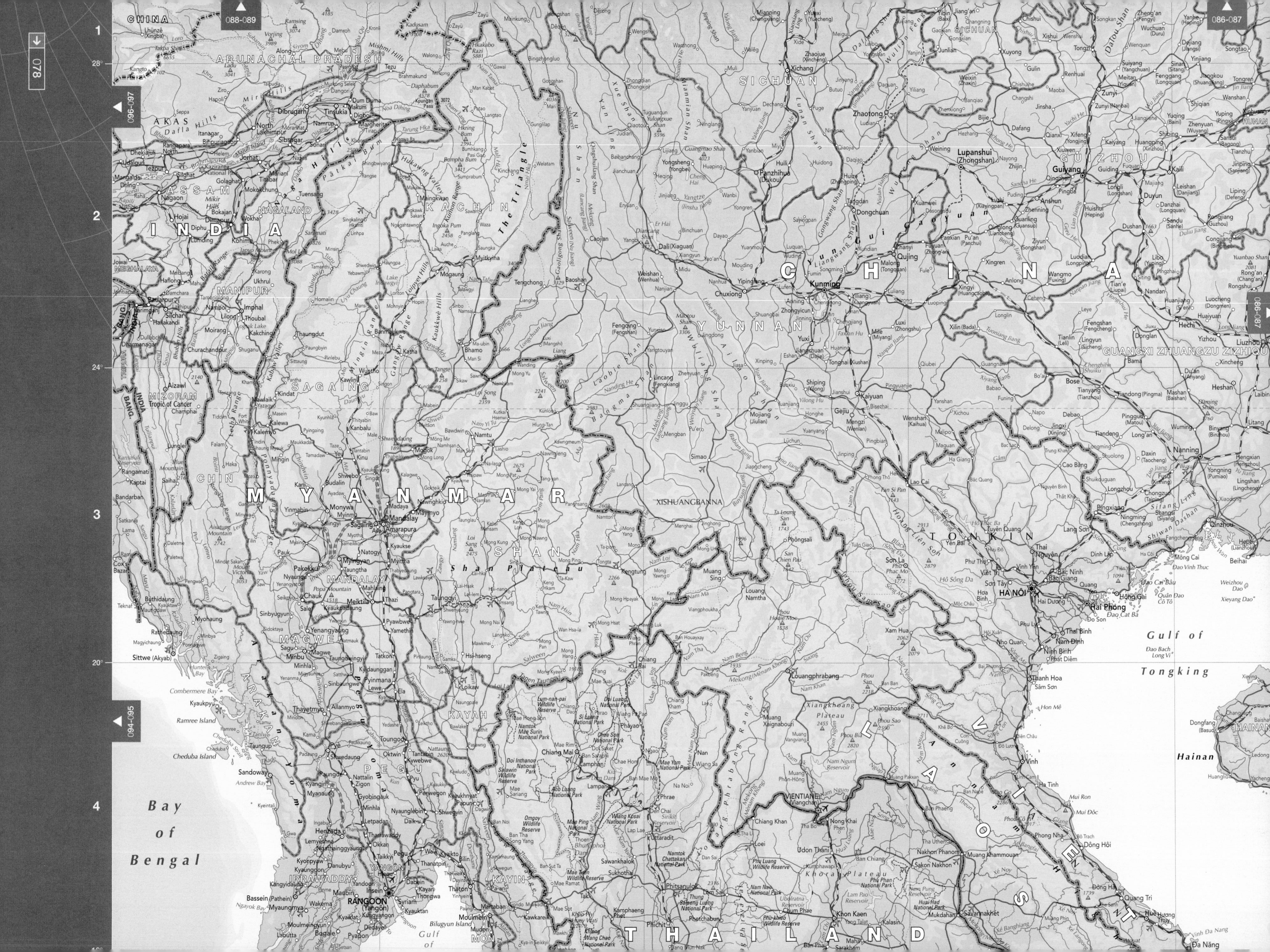
CHINA
INDIA
MYANMAR
LAOS
VIETNAM
THAILAND
SICHUAN
GUIZHOU
YUNNAN
GUANGXI ZHUANGZU ZIZHIQU
HAINAN
ARUNACHAL PRADESH
ASSAM
NAGALAND
MANIPUR
MIZORAM
MEGHALAYA
TRIPURA
BANG.
KACHIN
SAGAING
CHIN
MAGWE
MANDALAY
SHAN
KAYAH
KAYIN
MON
PEGU
IRRAWADDY
YANGON
ARAKAN
TONKIN
XISHUANGBANNA
Shan Plateau
Gulf of Tongking
Bay of Bengal
Kunming
Guiyang
Nanning
HA NOI
Hai Phong
VIENTIANE (Viangchan)
RANGOON (Yangon)
Mandalay
Chiang Mai
Louangphrabang
086-087
088-089
094-095
096-097
1
2
3
4
28°
24°
20°

asia[map5]

5°-29°N / 92°-110°E

A B C D E

92° 96° 100° 104° 108°

5 6 7

12° 8°

CONNECTIONS

subject	page#
Asia landscapes	62–63
Asia countries	64–67
Chinese migration	66–67
Asia threats	70–71
Indian Ocean	218–219

076-077

>6000m
5000-6000m
4000-5000m
3000-4000m
2000-3000m
1000-2000m
500-1000m
200-500m
0-200m
<0m
0-200m
200-500m
500-1000m
1000-2000m
2000-3000m
3000-4000m
4000-5000m
5000-6000m
>6000m

1:6 000 000

miles 0 50 100 150 200 250

km 0 50 100 150 200 250 300 350 400

Mercator Projection

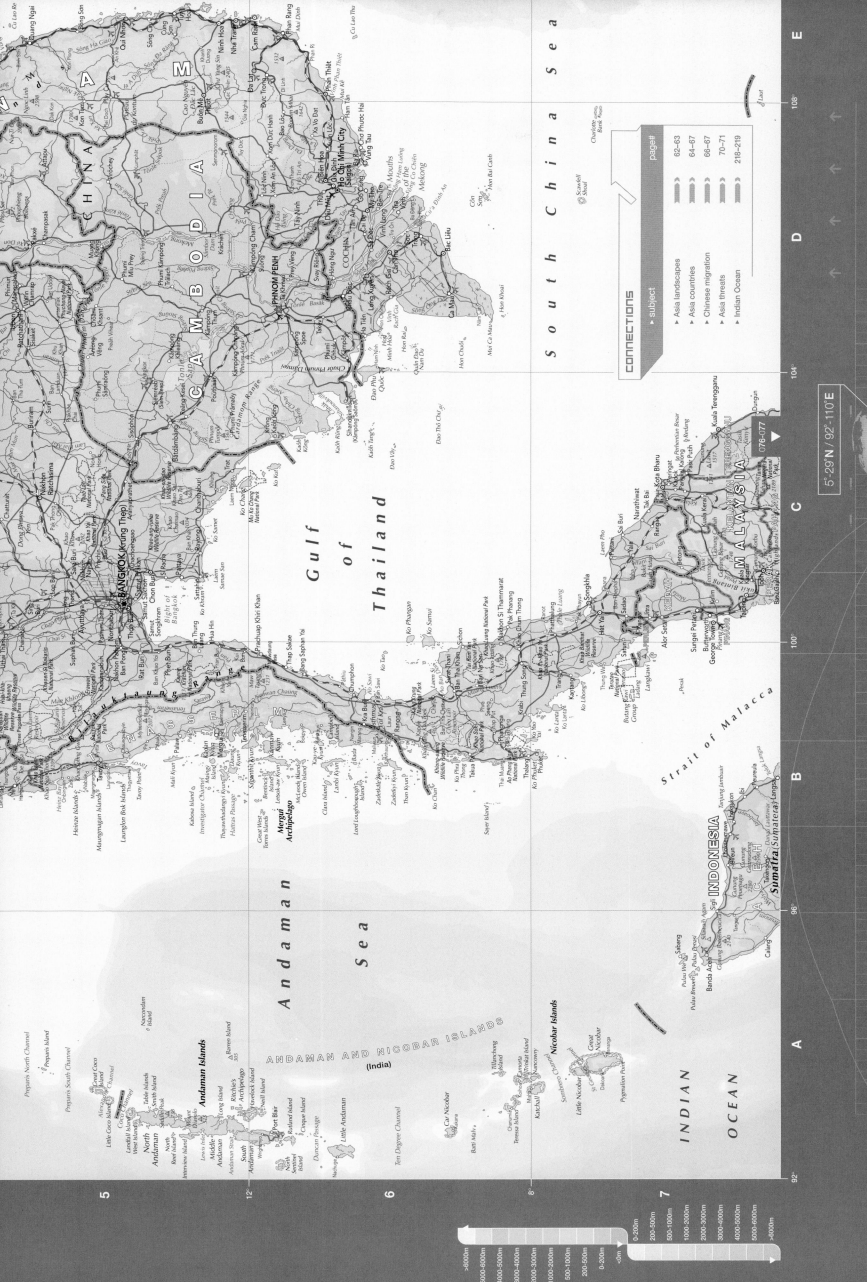

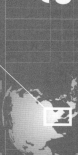

asia[map6]

18°-55°N / 73°-140°E

>6000m
5000-6000m
4000-5000m
3000-4000m
2000-3000m
1000-2000m
500-1000m
200-500m
0-200m
<0m

0-200m
200-500m
500-1000m
1000-2000m
2000-3000m
3000-4000m
4000-5000m
5000-6000m
>6000m

092-93

RUSSIA

KAZAKHSTAN

KYRGYZSTAN

TAJIKISTAN

AFGHANISTAN

MONGOLIA

Omsk
Novosibirsk
Barnaul
Biysk
Rubtsovsk
Semipalatinsk
Ust'-Kamenogorsk
Krasnoyarsk
Bratsk
Irkutsk
Angarsk
Tomsk
Kemerovo
Novokuznetsk
Abakan
Minusinsk
Kyzyl

Karaganda
Balkhash
Almaty
BISHKEK (Frunze)
Osh
Jalal-Abad

Ürümqi
Turpan (Turfan)
Hami (Kumul)
Aksu
Korla
Kashi (Kashgar)
Hotan
Kuqa

XINJIANG UYGUR ZIZHIQU (SINKIANG)

Tarim Basin (Tarim Pendi)

Taklimakan Desert (Taklimakan Shamo)

JAMMU AND KASHMIR
LINE OF CONTROL
AKSAI CHIN
CLAIMED BY INDIA UNDER CHINESE ADMIN.

ISLAMABAD
Rawalpindi
Lahore
Faisalabad
Amritsar
Jalandhar
Srinagar

Karakoram

Kunlun Shan

Altun Shan

Qaidam Pendi

Hoh Xil Shan

CHINA

QINGHAI

Plateau of Tibet (Qing Zang Gaoyuan)

XIZANG ZIZHIQU (TIBET)

Lhasa
Xigazê

Lanzhou (Lanchow)
Xining
Golmud

GANSU

SICHUAN
Chengdu
Leshan
Zigong
Yibin
Xichang

NEPAL
KATHMANDU
Pokhara

BHUTAN
THIMPHU

Mount Everest

UTTAR PRADESH
Agra
Lucknow
Kanpur
Allahabad
Varanasi
Gwalior

BIHAR
Patna

INDIA

MADHYA PRADESH
Jabalpur
Nagpur

JHARKHAND
Ranchi
Jamshedpur

WEST BENGAL
Kolkata (Calcutta)

BANGLADESH
DHAKA (Dacca)
Khulna
Chittagong

ORISSA
Cuttack
Bhubaneshwar
Puri

ANDHRA PRADESH
Visakhapatnam

MEGHALAYA
ASSAM
Guwahati
ARUNACHAL PRADESH
NAGALAND
MANIPUR
MIZORAM
TRIPURA

MYANMAR
Mandalay
Meiktila

YUNNAN
Kunming
Dali (Xiaguan)

LAOS
VIENTIANE (Vngchan)

THAILAND
Chiang Mai

VIETNAM

Bay of Bengal

Mouths of the Ganges

Tropic of Cancer

2 3 4 5 6 7 8 9

A B C D E F G

55° 50° 45° 40° 35° 30° 25° 20°

75° 80° 85° 90° 95° 100°

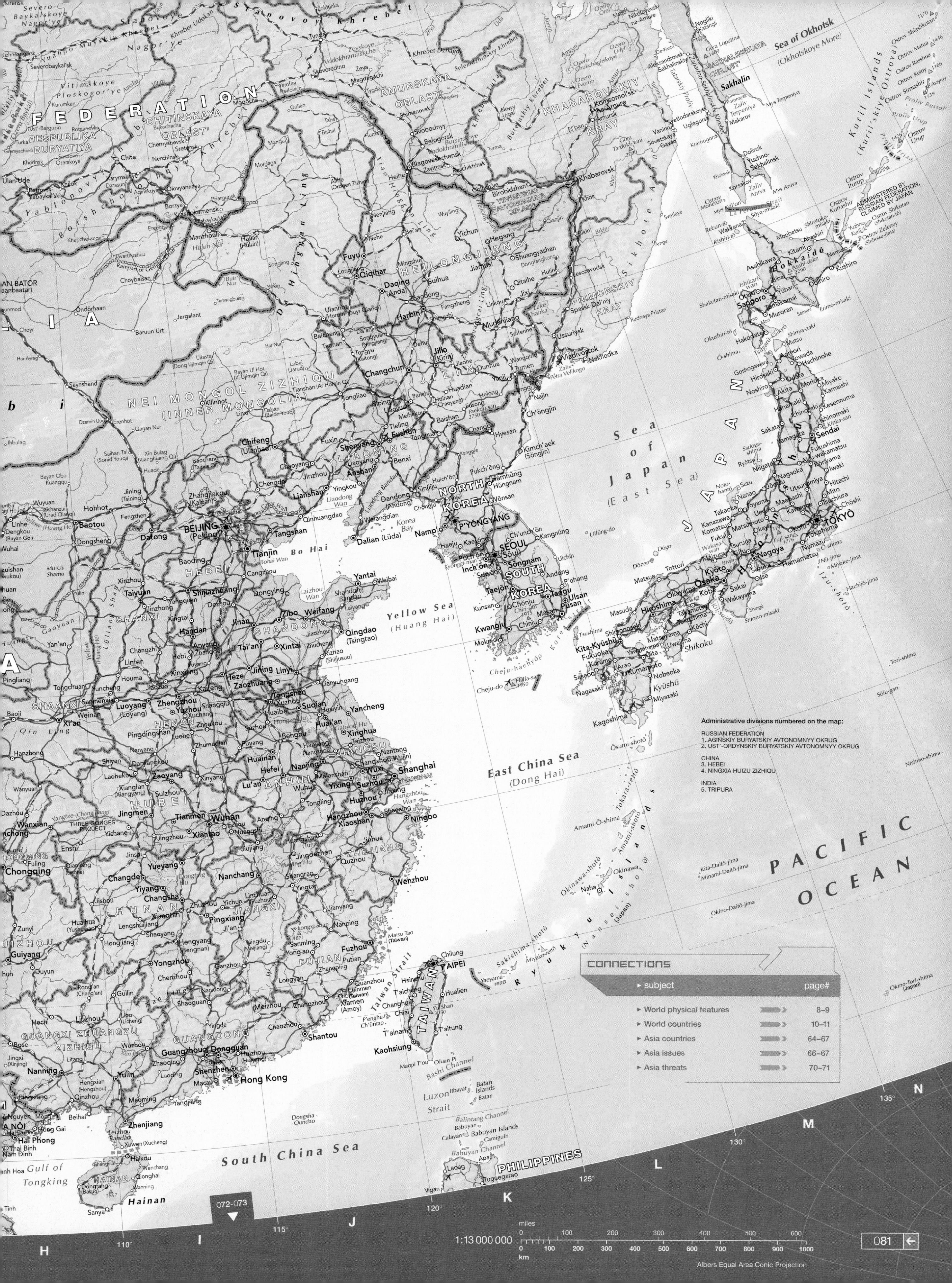

CONNECTIONS

subject	page#
World physical features	8–9
World countries	10–11
Asia countries	64–67
Asia issues	66–67
Asia threats	70–71

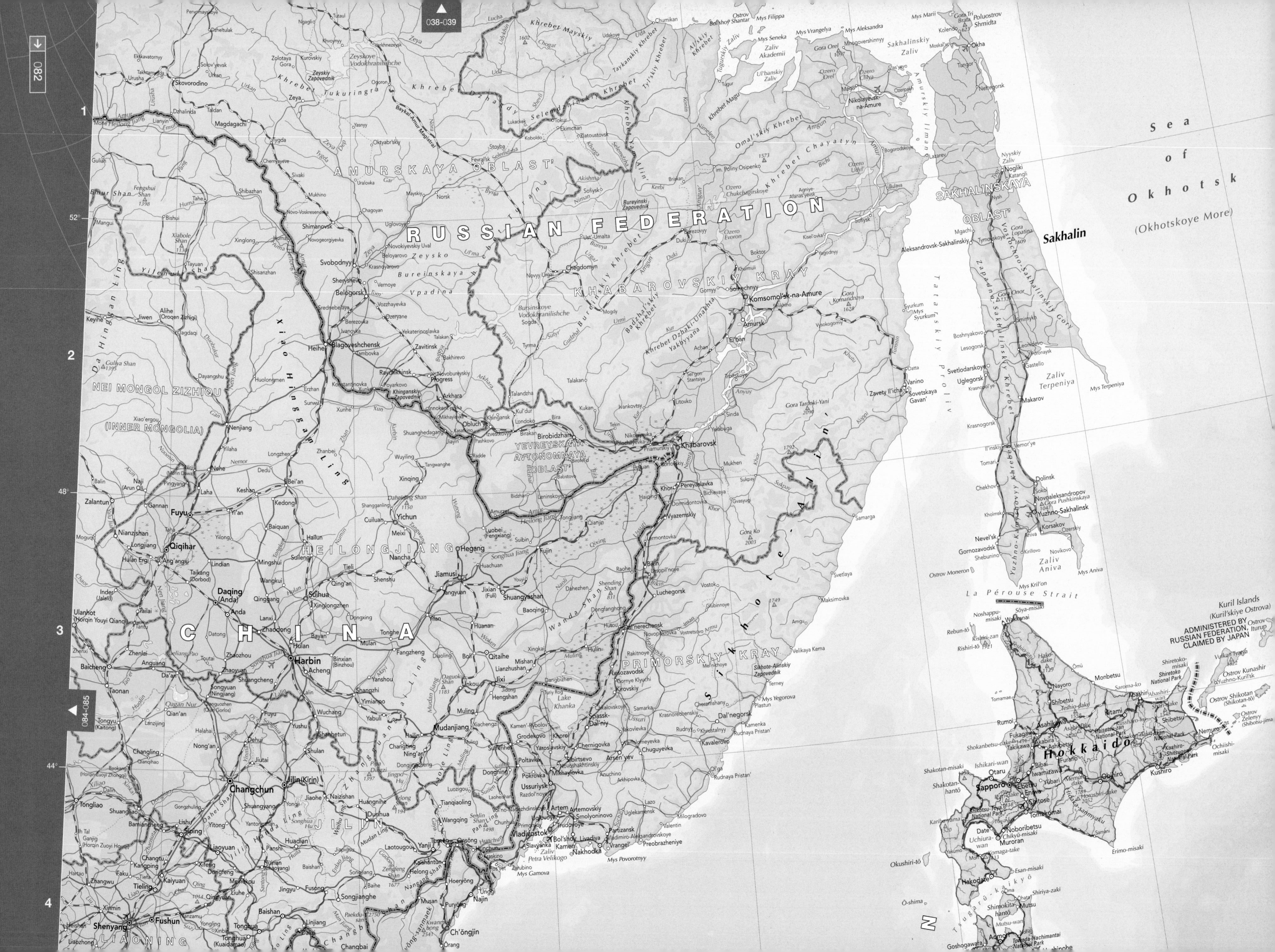
RUSSIAN FEDERATION
CHINA
Sea of Okhotsk
(Okhotskoye More)
Sakhalin
SAKHALINSKAYA OBLAST'
KHABAROVSKIY KRAY
AMURSKAYA OBLAST'
YEVREYSKAYA AVTONOMNAYA OBLAST'
PRIMORSKIY KRAY
HEILONGJIANG
JILIN
LIAONING
NEI MONGOL ZIZHIQU
(INNER MONGOLIA)
Hokkaido
Tatarskiy Proliv
La Pérouse Strait
Kuril Islands
(Kuril'skiye Ostrova)
ADMINISTERED BY RUSSIAN FEDERATION, CLAIMED BY JAPAN
Sikhote-Alin'
Xiao Hinggan Ling
Da Hinggan Ling
Khabarovsk
Vladivostok
Harbin
Changchun
Shenyang
Sapporo
Yuzhno-Sakhalinsk
Komsomol'sk-na-Amure
Blagoveshchensk
Qiqihar
Jilin (Kirin)
038-039
084-085

29° 55'N / 122° 148°E

CONNECTIONS

▶ subject	page#
▶ World population	22–23
▶ World cities	24–25
▶ Asia landscapes	62–63
▶ Asia countries	64–67
▶ Pacific Ocean	220–221

PACIFIC

OCEAN

Sea

of

Japan

(East Sea)

NORTH KOREA

PYONGYANG

SOUTH KOREA

SEOUL

Yellow
Sea
(Huang Hai)

Korea
Bay

East China
Sea
(Dong Hai)

Cheju-haehyŏp

Honshū

TOKYO

Shikoku

Kyūshū

Kita-Kyūshū

Fukuoka

Kagoshima

Nagoya

Osaka

Kyoto

Hiroshima

Matsuyama

Sendai

Izu-shotō

1 : 6 000 000
Conic Equidistant Projection

| miles | 0 | 50 | 100 | 150 | 200 | 250 |
| km | 0 | 50 | 100 | 150 | 200 | 250 | 300 | 350 | 400 |

>6000m
5000-6000m
4000-5000m
3000-4000m
2000-3000m
1000-2000m
500-1000m
200-500m
0-200m
<0m

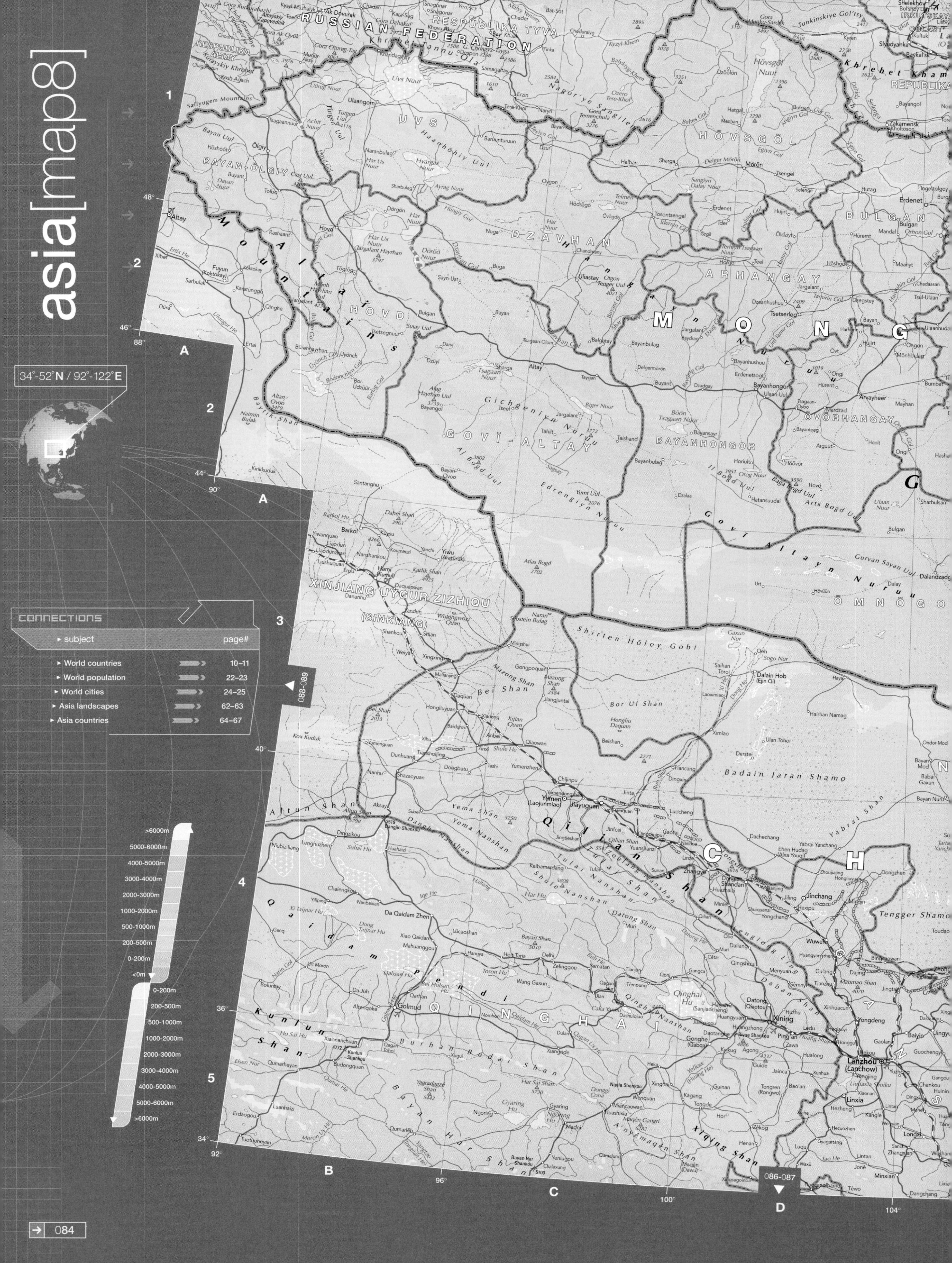

asia[map8]

34°–52°N / 92°–122°E

088–089

086–087

Elevation scale:
>6000m
5000–6000m
4000–5000m
3000–4000m
2000–3000m
1000–2000m
500–1000m
200–500m
0–200m
<0m

<0m
0–200m
200–500m
500–1000m
1000–2000m
2000–3000m
3000–4000m
4000–5000m
5000–6000m
>6000m

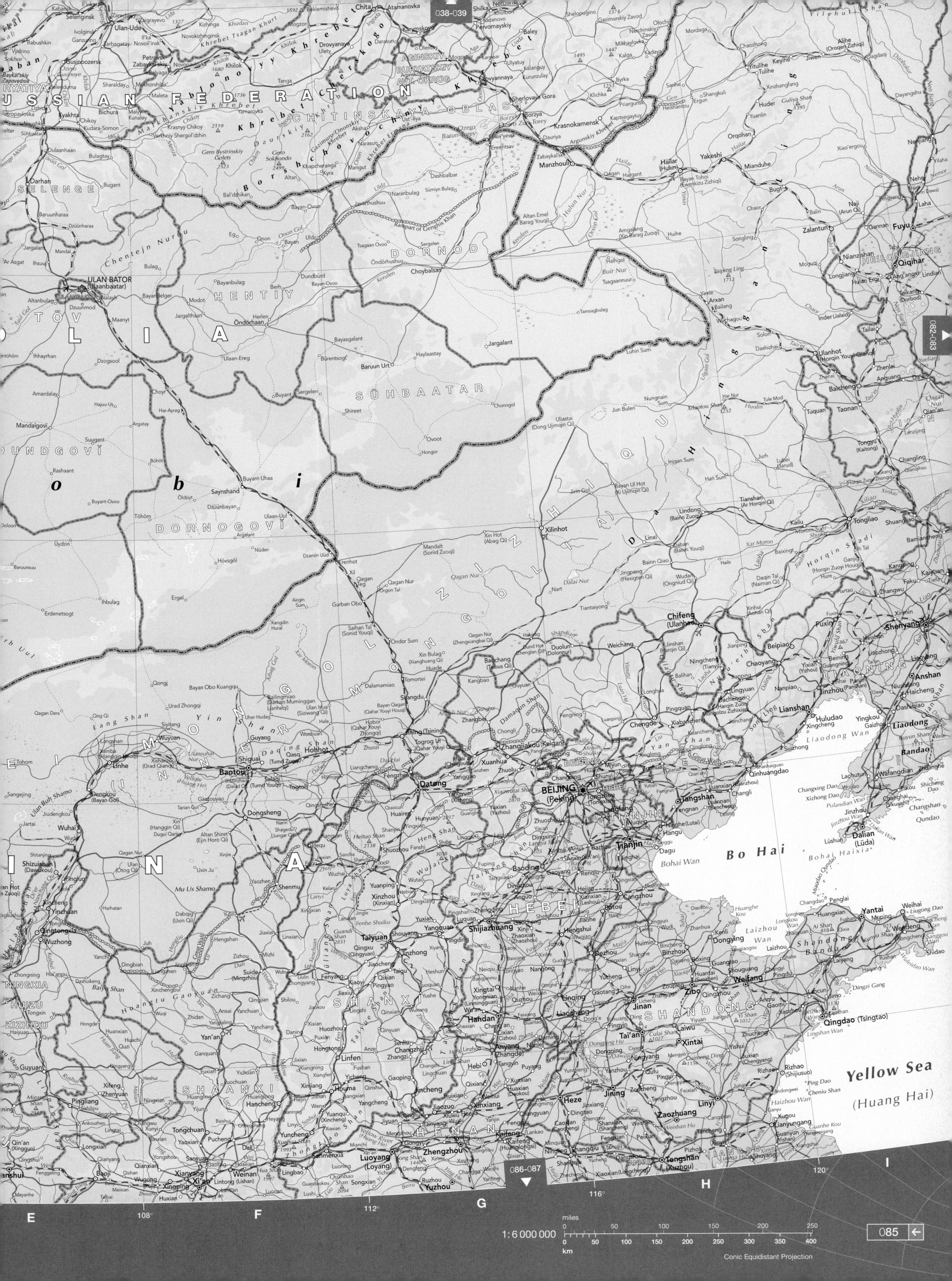

038-039
082-083
086-087
RUSSIAN FEDERATION
CHITINSKAYA OBLAST'
AGINSKIY BURYATSKIY AVT. OKRUG
SELENGE
TÖV
HENTIY
DORNOD
SÜHBAATAR
DUNDGOVĬ
DORNOGOVĬ
MONGOLIA
Gobi
NEI MONGOL (INNER MONGOLIA)
HEILONGJIANG
JILIN
LIAONING
HEBEI
BEIJING
TIANJIN
SHANXI
SHAANXI
HENAN
SHANDONG
NINGXIA HUIZU ZIZHIQU
ULAN BATOR (Ulaanbaatar)
Chita
Ulan-Ude
Qiqihar
Shenyang
BEIJING (Peking)
Tianjin
Datong
Baotou
Hohhot
Taiyuan
Shijiazhuang
Jinan
Qingdao (Tsingtao)
Dalian (Lüda)
Zhengzhou
Luoyang
Xi'an
Bo Hai
Bohai Wan
Liaodong Wan
Laizhou Wan
Yellow Sea (Huang Hai)
Da Hinggan Ling
E
F
G
H
I
108°
112°
116°
120°
1: 6 000 000
miles
0
50
100
150
200
250
km
0
50
100
150
200
250
300
350
400
Conic Equidistant Projection

asia[map9]

18°-36°N / 96°-122°E

miles
1:6 000 000

km

Conic Equidistant Projection

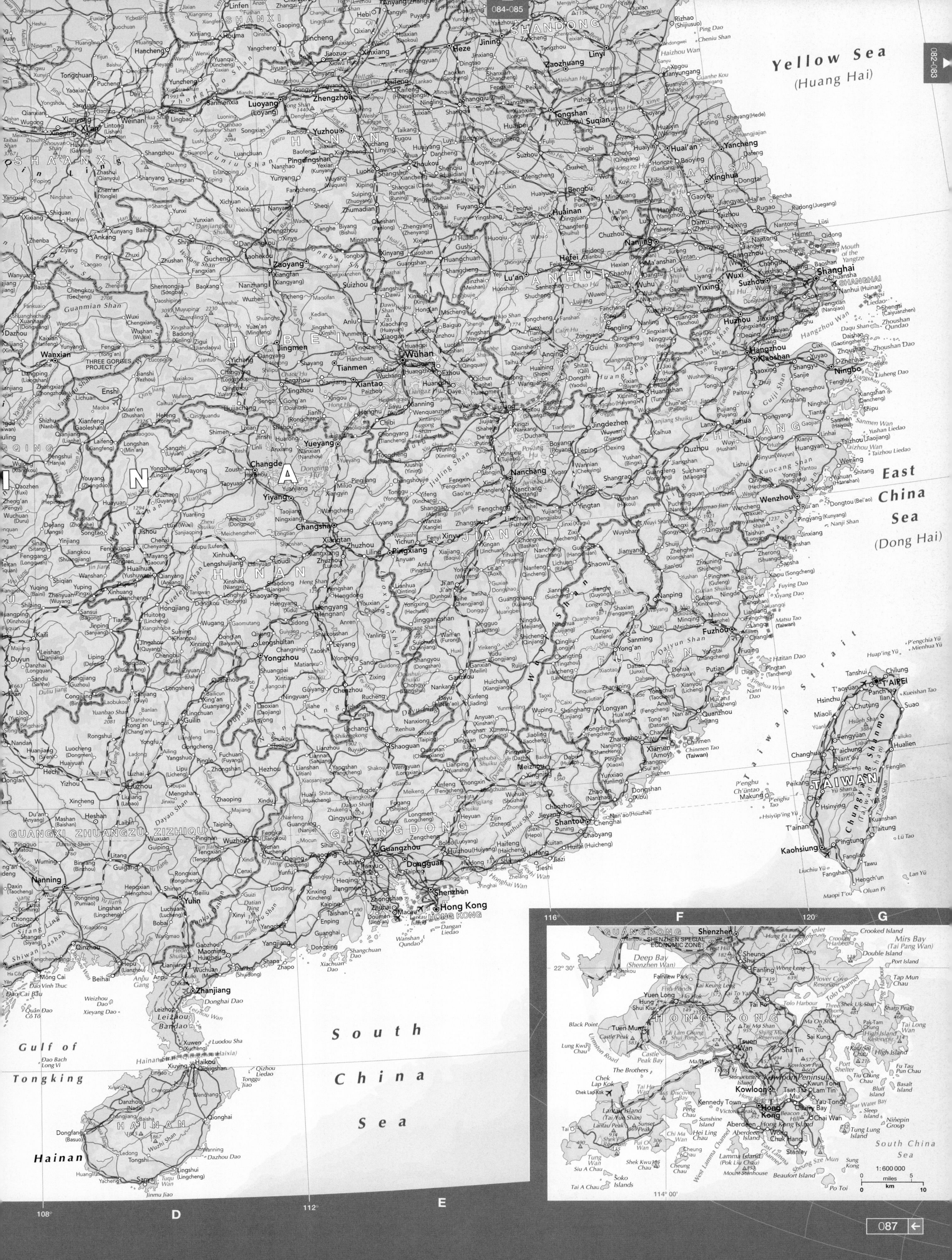

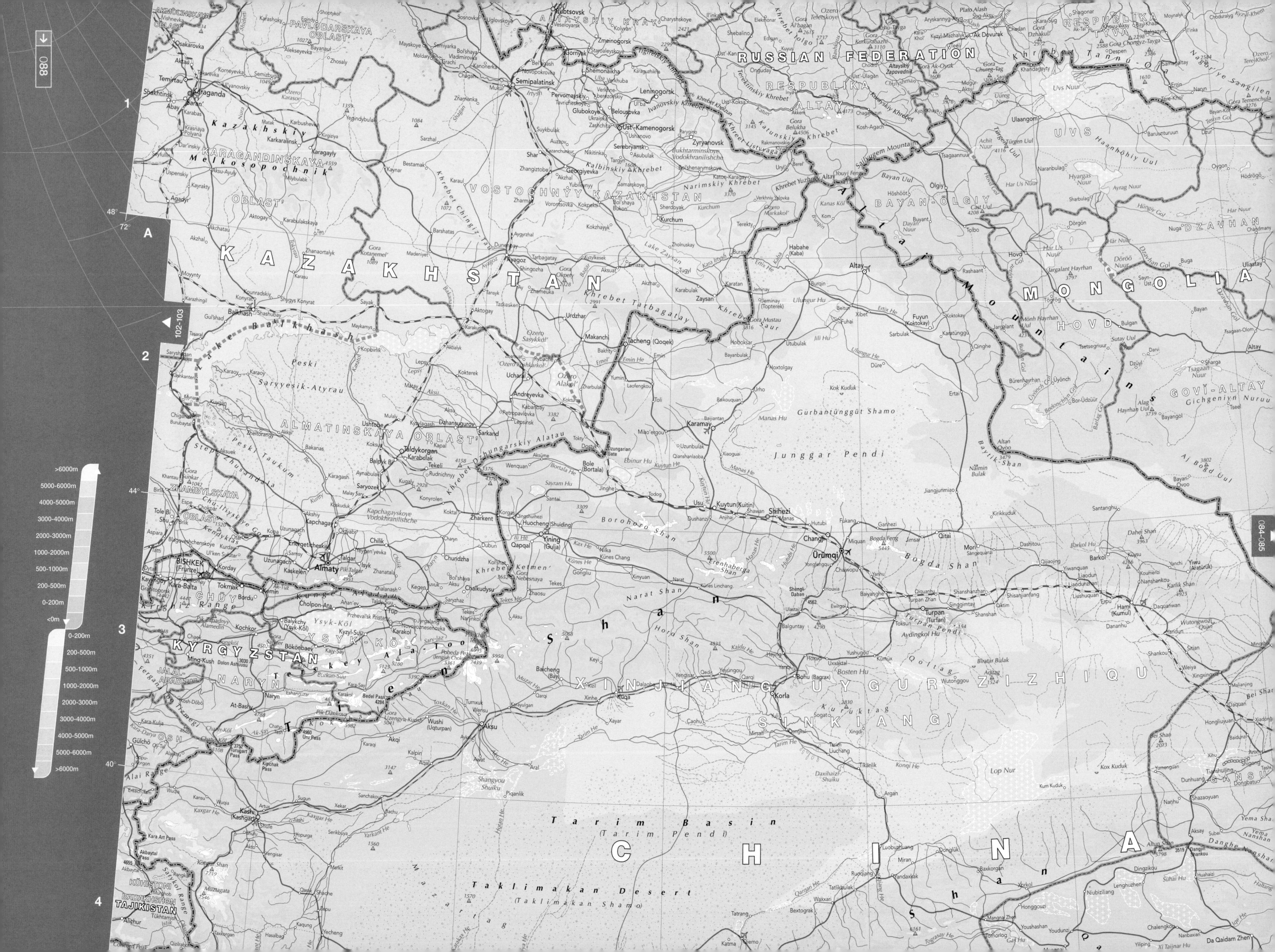

084-085
102-103
RUSSIAN FEDERATION
RESPUBLIKA ALTAY
RESPUBLIKA TYVA
ALTAYSKIY KRAY
MONGOLIA
UVS
BAYAN-ÖLGIY
HOVD
DZAVHAN
GOVĬ-ALTAY
Altai Mountains
KAZAKHSTAN
VOSTOCHNYY KAZAKHSTAN
KARAGANDINSKAYA OBLAST'
PAVLODARSKAYA OBLAST'
ALMATINSKAYA OBLAST'
ZHAMBYLSKAYA OBLAST'
Kazakhskiy Melkosopochnik
Lake Balkhash
Lake Zaysan
Ozero Alakol'
KYRGYZSTAN
CHÜY
YSYK-KÖL
NARYN
JALAL-ABAD
OSH
Ysyk-Köl
KÜHISTONI BADAKHSHON
TAJIKISTAN
CHINA
XINJIANG UYGUR ZIZHIQU (SINKIANG)
GANSU
Tian Shan
Junggar Pendi
Gurbantünggüt Shamo
Tarim Basin (Tarim Pendi)
Taklimakan Desert (Taklimakan Shamo)
Lop Nur
Bosten Hu
Bogda Shan
Ürümqi
Almaty
BISHKEK (Frunze)
Semipalatinsk
Ust'-Kamenogorsk
Karaganda
Balkhash
Kashi (Kashgar)
Aksu
Korla
Turpan (Turfan)
Hami (Kumul)
Karamay
Yining (Gulja)
Hovd
Ölgiy
Altay
A
1
2
3
4
48°
72°
44°
40°
>6000m
5000-6000m
4000-5000m
3000-4000m
2000-3000m
1000-2000m
500-1000m
200-500m
0-200m
<0m
0-200m
200-500m
500-1000m
1000-2000m
2000-3000m
3000-4000m
4000-5000m
5000-6000m
>6000m

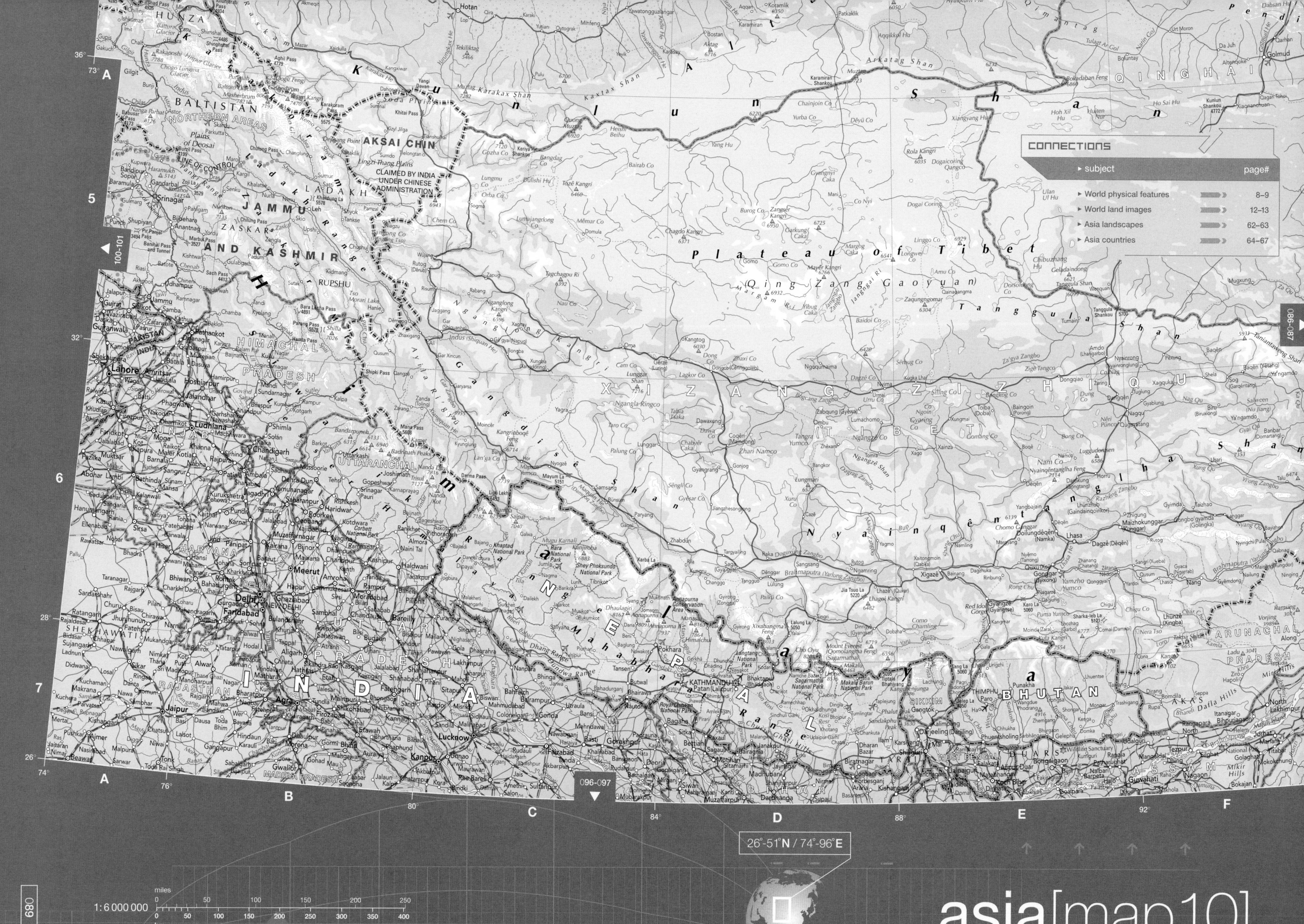

asia[map10]
26°-51°N / 74°-96°E
1:6 000 000
miles
km
Conic Equidistant Projection
CONNECTIONS
subject
page#
World physical features 8–9
World land images 12–13
Asia landscapes 62–63
Asia countries 64–67
100-101
096-097
086-087
Plateau of Tibet
(Qing Zang Gaoyuan)
XIZANG ZIZHIQU
(TIBET)
QINGHAI
Kunlun Shan
Tanggula Shan
Nyainqêntanglha Shan
Gangdisê Shan
Himalaya
AKSAI CHIN
CLAIMED BY INDIA UNDER CHINESE ADMINISTRATION
JAMMU AND KASHMIR
LADAKH
BALTISTAN
NORTHERN AREAS
LINE OF CONTROL
HIMACHAL PRADESH
PUNJAB
HARYANA
UTTARANCHAL
UTTAR PRADESH
RAJASTHAN
INDIA
NEPAL
BHUTAN
SIKKIM
ASSAM
ARUNACHAL PRADESH
WEST BENGAL
BIHAR
Lhasa
Delhi
NEW DELHI
Lahore
Amritsar
Srinagar
Leh
Agra
Jaipur
Lucknow
Kanpur
KATHMANDU
THIMPHU
Xigazê
Hotan
Golmud

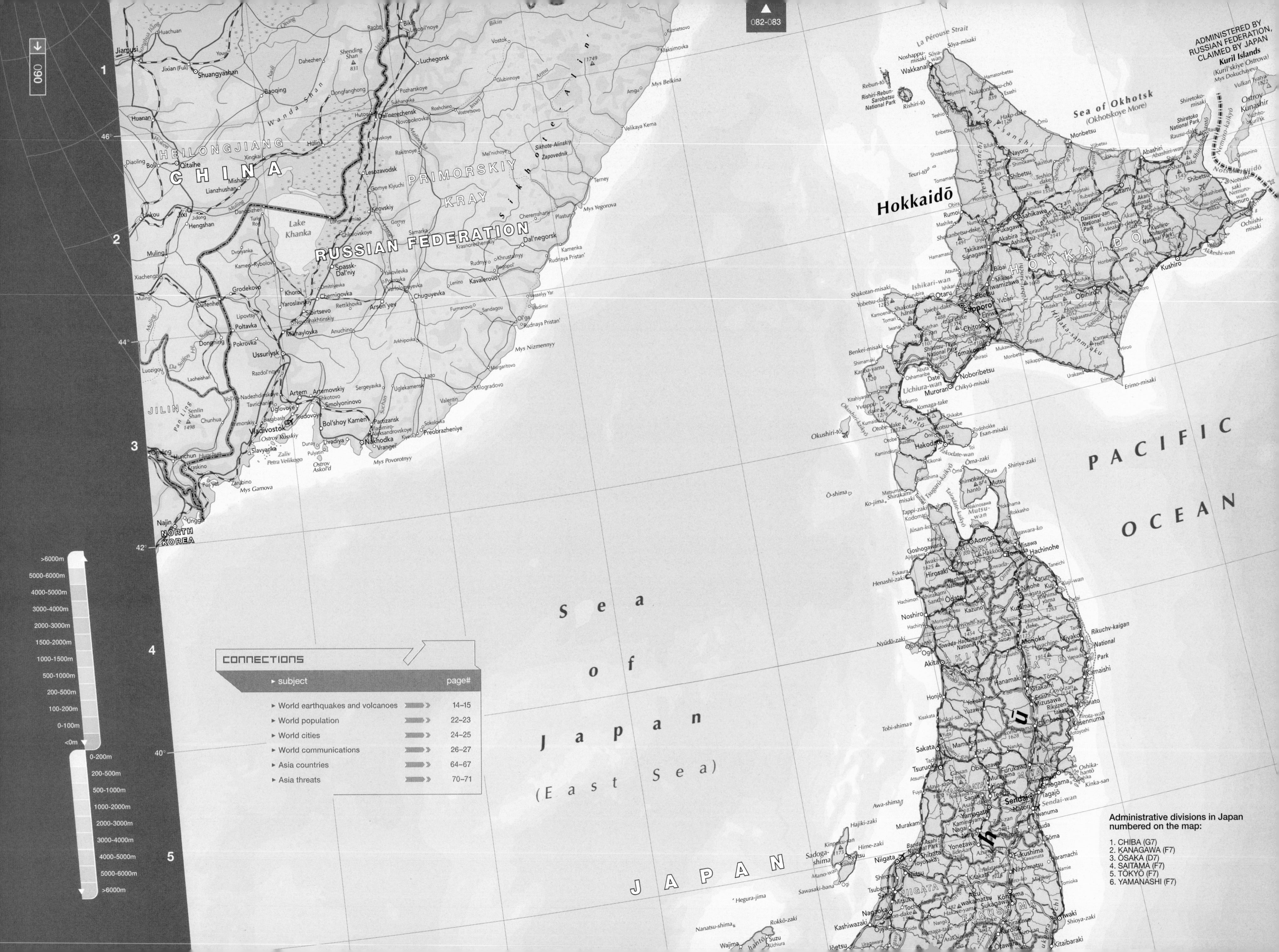

ADMINISTERED BY
RUSSIAN FEDERATION,
RUSSIAN BY JAPAN
CLAIMED BY JAPAN

Kuril Islands
(Kuril'skiye Ostrova)

Hokkaidō

HOKKAIDŌ

Sapporo

Hakodate

Sea of Okhotsk
(Okhotskoye More)

La Pérouse Strait

P A C I F I C

O C E A N

S e a

o f

J a p a n

(E a s t   S e a)

RUSSIAN FEDERATION

PRIMORSKIY
KRAY

Lake
Khanka

Vladivostok

Ussurisk

HEILONGJIANG

C H I N A

J I L I N

NORTH
KOREA

J A P A N

Sendai

CONNECTIONS

▸ subject		page#
▸ World earthquakes and volcanoes		14–15
▸ World population		22–23
▸ World cities		24–25
▸ World communications		26–27
▸ Asia countries		64–67
▸ Asia threats		70–71

Administrative divisions in Japan
numbered on the map:

1. CHIBA (G7)
2. KANAGAWA (F7)
3. OSAKA (D7)
4. SAITAMA (F7)
5. TOKYO (F7)
6. YAMANASHI (F7)

1 2 3 4 5

>6000m
5000-6000m
4000-5000m
3000-4000m
2000-3000m
1500-2000m
1000-1500m
500-1000m
200-500m
100-200m
0-100m
<0m
0-200m
200-500m
500-1000m
1000-2000m
2000-3000m
3000-4000m
4000-5000m
5000-6000m
>6000m

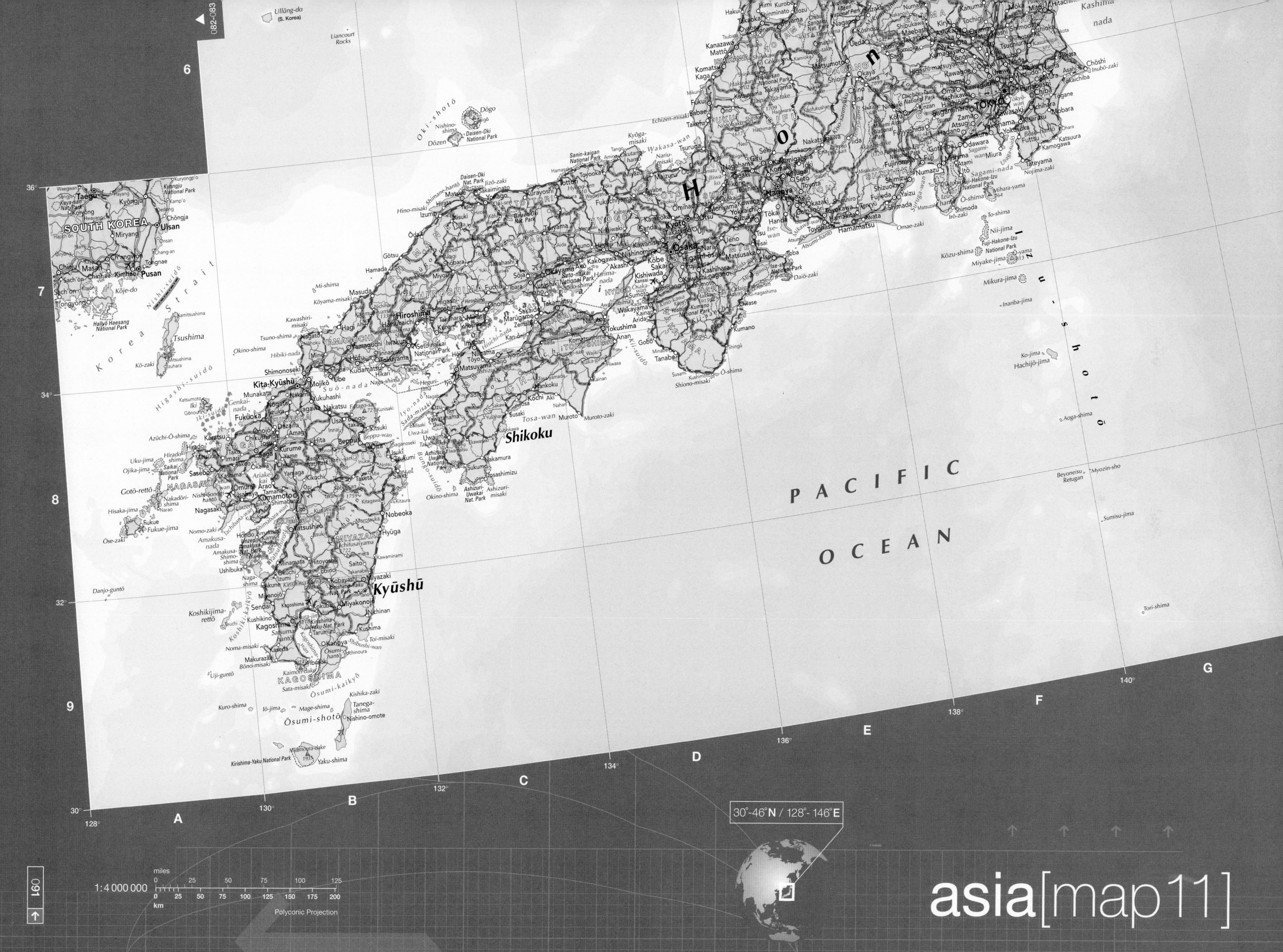

asia[map11]
30°-46°N / 128°-146°E
1:4 000 000
miles
km
Polyconic Projection
082-083
PACIFIC OCEAN
Honshū
Shikoku
Kyūshū
SOUTH KOREA
Korea Strait
Tsushima
Oki-shotō
Izu-shotō
Ōsumi-shotō
Ullŭng-do (S. Korea)
Liancourt Rocks
Tōkyō
Ōsaka
Kyōto
Nagoya
Kōbe
Hiroshima
Kita-Kyūshū
Fukuoka
Nagasaki
Kumamoto
Kagoshima
Miyazaki
Matsuyama
Takamatsu
Tokushima
Kōchi
Okayama
Wakayama
Hamamatsu
Shizuoka
Yokohama
Chiba
Kanazawa
Pusan
Ulsan
Taegu
Shimonoseki
Tanega-shima
Yaku-shima
Hachijō-jima
Tori-shima
Sumisu-jima
Danjo-guntō
Koshikijima-rettō
Gotō-rettō

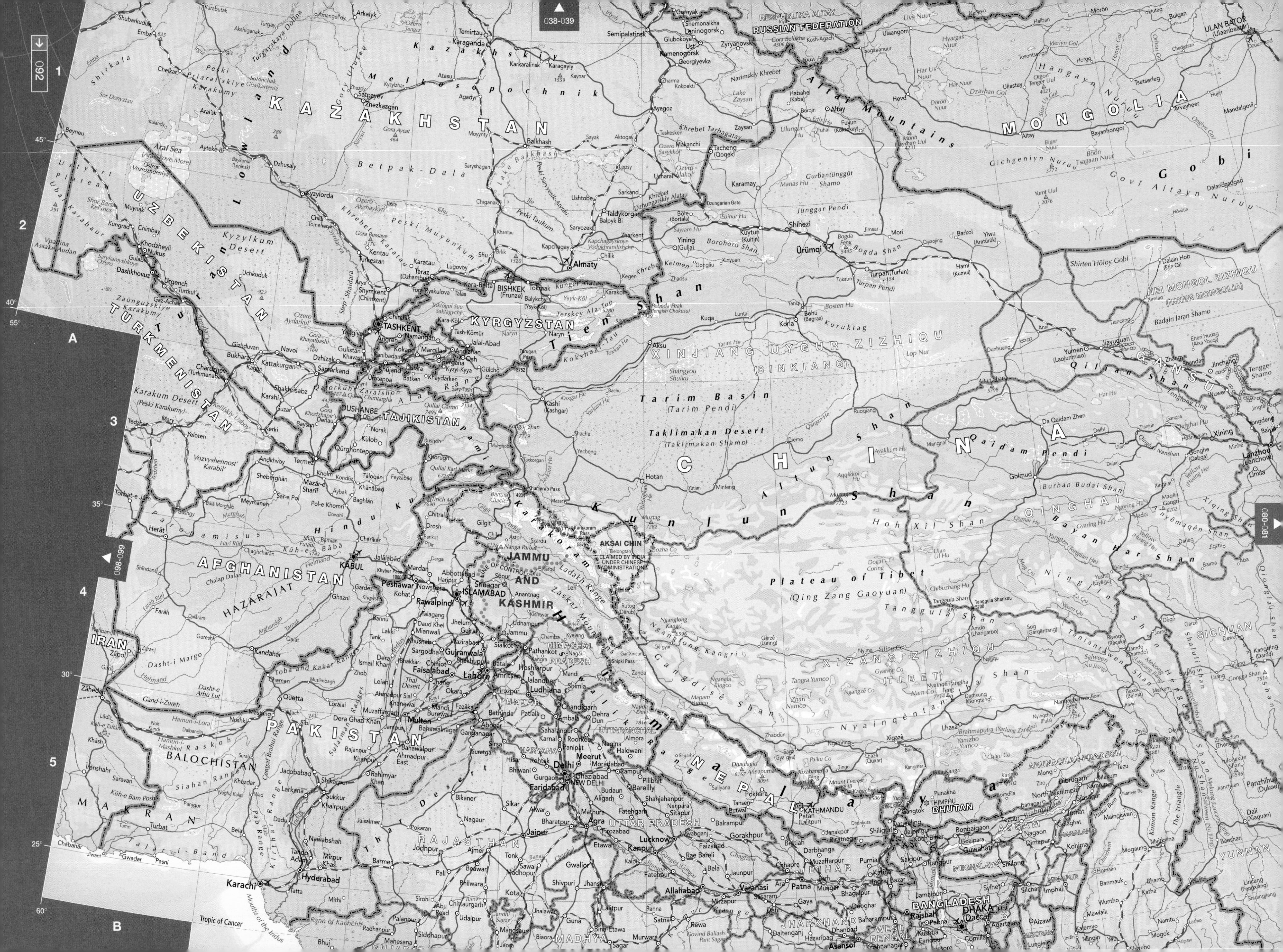

038-039
080-081
098-099
092
KAZAKHSTAN
UZBEKISTAN
TURKMENISTAN
KYRGYZSTAN
TAJIKISTAN
AFGHANISTAN
PAKISTAN
IRAN
CHINA
MONGOLIA
RUSSIAN FEDERATION
NEPAL
BHUTAN
BANGLADESH
JAMMU AND KASHMIR
AKSAI CHIN
XINJIANG UYGUR ZIZHIQU (SINKIANG)
XIZANG ZIZHIQU (TIBET)
QINGHAI
GANSU
SICHUAN
YUNNAN
NEI MONGOL ZIZHIQU (INNER MONGOLIA)
Tarim Basin (Tarim Pendi)
Taklimakan Desert (Taklimakan Shamo)
Plateau of Tibet (Qing Zang Gaoyuan)
Gobi
Tien Shan
Kunlun Shan
Altay Mountains
Hindu Kush
Himalaya
Karakoram
Thar Desert
Tropic of Cancer

asia[map12]

1°S-50°N / 60°-97°E

CONNECTIONS

▶ subject	page#
▲ World physical features	8–9
▲ World land images	12–13
▲ World population	22–23
▲ World cities	24–25
▲ Asia landscapes	62–63
▲ Asia countries	64–67
▲ Asia threats	70–71

Administrative divisions in India numbered on the map:

1. DADRA AND NAGAR HAVELI (D6)
2. DAMAN AND DIU (D6)
3. TRIPURA (H6)

1:12 000 000

Albers Equal Area Conic Projection

miles 100 200 300 400 500
km 100 200 300 400 500 600 700 800

INDIAN OCEAN

Arabian Sea

BAY of BENGAL

Andaman Sea

MYANMAR

THAILAND

INDONESIA

Sumatra

SRI LANKA

MALDIVES

LAKSHADWEEP (India)

ANDAMAN AND NICOBAR ISLANDS (India)

Andaman Islands

Nicobar Islands

MAHARASHTRA

ANDHRA PRADESH

KARNATAKA

KERALA

TAMIL NADU

ORISSA

CHHATTISGARH

Deccan

Coromandel Coast

Malabar Coast

Mouths of the Ganges

Mouths of the Irrawaddy

Mergui Archipelago

Mumbai (Bombay)
Pune (Poona)
Hyderabad
Bangalore
Chennai (Madras)
Calicut (Kozhikode)
Cochin (Kochi)
Trivandrum (Thiruvananthapuram)
Madurai
Coimbatore
Nagpur
Vijayawada
Vishakhapatnam
RANGOON (Yangon)
SRI JAYEWARDENEPURA KOTTE
Colombo
MALÉ

Cape Comorin

Gulf of Mannar

Palk Strait

Equator

>6000m
5000–6000m
4000–5000m
3000–4000m
2000–3000m
1000–2000m
500–1000m
200–500m
0–200m
<0m
0–200m
200–500m
500–1000m
1000–2000m
2000–3000m
3000–4000m
4000–5000m
5000–6000m
>6000m

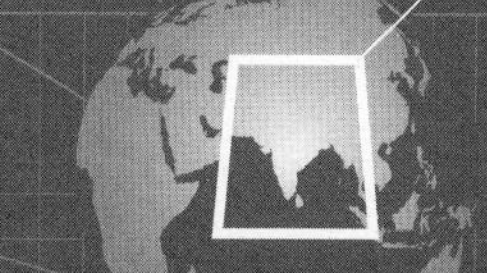

asia[map13]

5°-22°N / 70°-96°E

Arabian Sea

MADHYA PRADESH

MAHARASHTRA

I N D I A

D e c c a n

KARNATAKA

ANDHRA PRADESH

TAMIL NADU

KERALA

Nagpur

Surat
Vadodara (Baroda)
Indore
Nashik
Aurangabad
Thane
Ulhasnagar
Mumbai (Bombay)
Pune (Poona)
Solapur
Hyderabad
Secunderabad
Vijayawada
Kolhapur
Belgaum
GOA
Dharwad
Hubli
Chennai (Madras)
Bangalore
Mangalore
Mysore
Coimbatore
Calicut (Kozhikode)
Cochin (Kochi)
Madurai
Alleppey (Alappuzha)
Quilon (Kollam)
Trivandrum (Thiruvananthapuram)
Pondicherry (Puducherry)
Cape Comorin

Laccadive Islands
Amindivi Islands
Cannanore Islands

LAKSHADWEEP (India)

Kavaratti
Minicoy

Nine Degree Channel
Eight Degree Channel

MALDIVES

Ihavandhippolhu Atoll
Thiladhunmathee Atoll
Miladhunmadulu Atoll
Maalhosmadulu Atoll
Faadhippolhu Atoll
North Maalhosmadulu Atoll
Makunudhoo
Kelai

SRI LANKA

Colombo
SRI JAYEWARDENEPURA KOTTE
Kandy
Jaffna
Trincomalee
Galle

Gulf of Mannar
Palk Strait
Coromandel Coast
Malabar Coast
Gulf of Khambhat

Bassas de Pedro Padua Bank
Sesostris Bank
Byramgore Reef
Cherbaniani Reef
Diu

→ 094

>6000m
5000-6000m
4000-5000m
3000-4000m
2000-3000m
1000-2000m
500-1000m
200-500m
0-200m
<0m

0-200m
200-500m
500-1000m
1000-2000m
2000-3000m
3000-4000m
4000-5000m
5000-6000m
>6000m

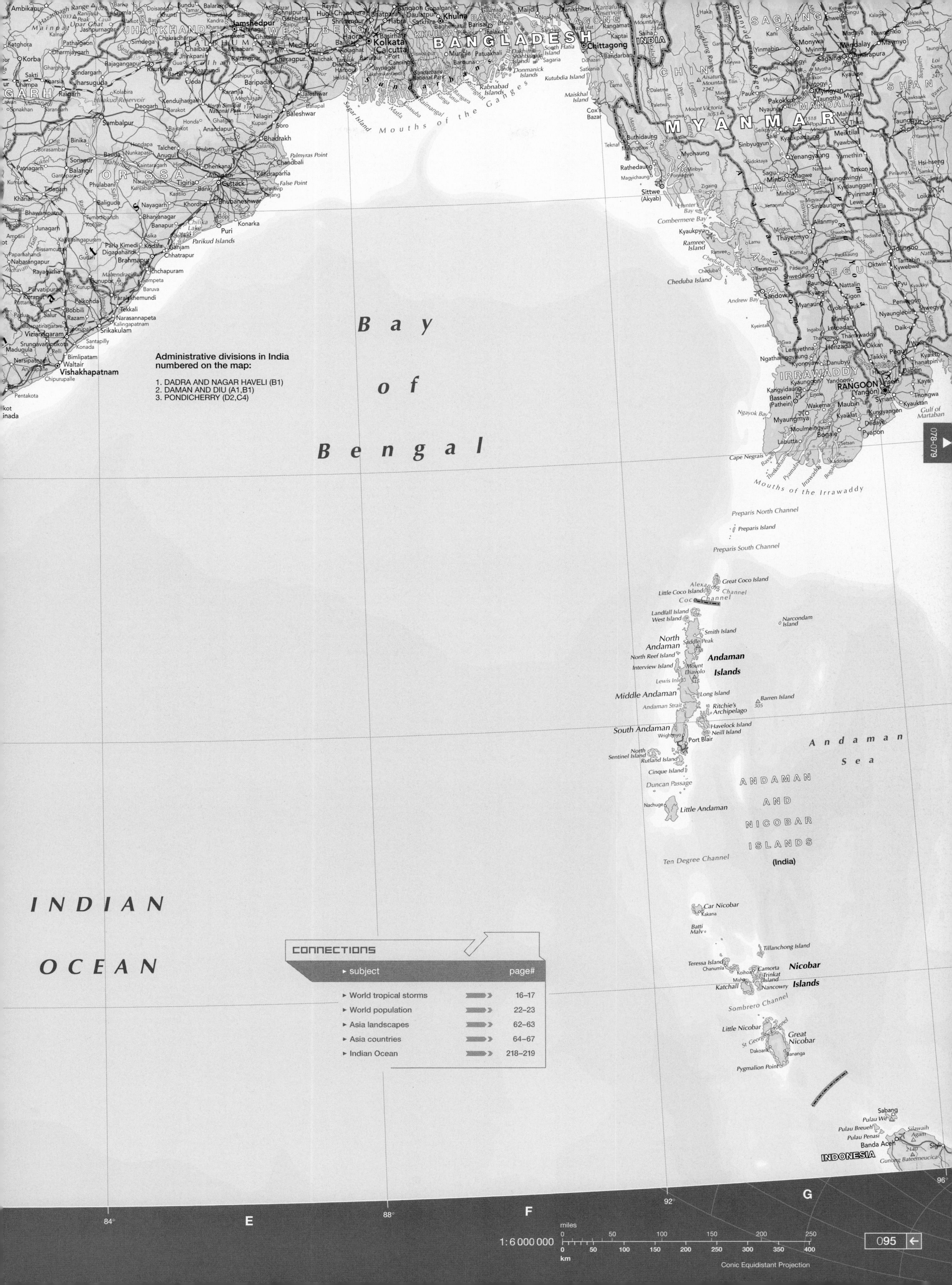
Bay of Bengal
INDIAN OCEAN
Andaman Sea
BANGLADESH
INDIA
MYANMAR
INDONESIA
JHARKHAND
WEST BENGAL
ORISSA
CHITTAGONG
BARISAL
KHULNA
SAGAING
MANDALAY
MAGWE
PEGU
IRRAWADDY
RANGOON
SHAN
CHIN
ANDAMAN AND NICOBAR ISLANDS
(India)
Kolkata (Calcutta)
Chittagong
Jamshedpur
Cuttack
Bhubaneshwar
Puri
Vishakhapatnam
Mandalay
RANGOON (Yangon)
Bassein (Pathein)
Sittwe (Akyab)
Port Blair
Mouths of the Ganges
Mouths of the Irrawaddy
Andaman Islands
North Andaman
Middle Andaman
South Andaman
Little Andaman
Ten Degree Channel
Car Nicobar
Nicobar Islands
Great Nicobar
Little Nicobar
Great Coco Island
Preparis Island
Cheduba Island
Ramree Island
Gulf of Martaban
Administrative divisions in India numbered on the map:
1. DADRA AND NAGAR HAVELI (B1)
2. DAMAN AND DIU (A1,B1)
3. PONDICHERRY (D2,C4)
CONNECTIONS
subject page#
World tropical storms 16–17
World population 22–23
Asia landscapes 62–63
Asia countries 64–67
Indian Ocean 218–219
078–079
84° 88° 92° 96°
E F G
1:6 000 000
miles 0 50 100 150 200 250
km 0 50 100 150 200 250 300 350 400
Conic Equidistant Projection
095

20°-38°N / 68°-96°E

AFGHANISTAN

TAJIKISTAN

PAKISTAN

NORTHERN
AREAS

BALTISTAN

AKSAI CHIN
CLAIMED BY INDIA
UNDER CHINESE
ADMINISTRATION

LINE OF CONTROL

JAMMU
AND KASHMIR

LADAKH

KÂBUL

ISLAMABAD
Rawalpindi

Srinagar

HIMACHAL
PRADESH

PUNJAB

PUNJAB

Lahore
Faisalabad

Multan

HARYANA

UTTARANCHAL

Delhi
NEW DELHI
Faridabad

Meerut

Hyderabad

SINDH

RAJASTHAN

Jodhpur

Jaipur

Agra

UTTAR

Lucknow

Kanpur

Gwalior

I N D

MALWA

Bhopal

Indore

MADHYA PRADESH

GUJARAT

Ahmadabad

Vadodara

Surat

Nagpur

Gulf of Kachchh

Rann of Kachchh

Little
Rann

Gulf of Khambhat

Tropic of Cancer

Arabian Sea

>6000m
5000-6000m
4000-5000m
3000-4000m
2000-3000m
1000-2000m
500-1000m
200-500m
0-200m
<0m

0-200m
200-500m
500-1000m
1000-2000m
2000-3000m
3000-4000m
4000-5000m
5000-6000m
>6000m

Administrative divisions in India
numbered on the map:

1. DADRA AND NAGAR HAVELI (B5)
2. DAMAN AND DIU (A5,B5)

100-101

094-095

1
2
3
4
5

A
B
C

36°
32°
28°
24°

68°
72°
76°
80°

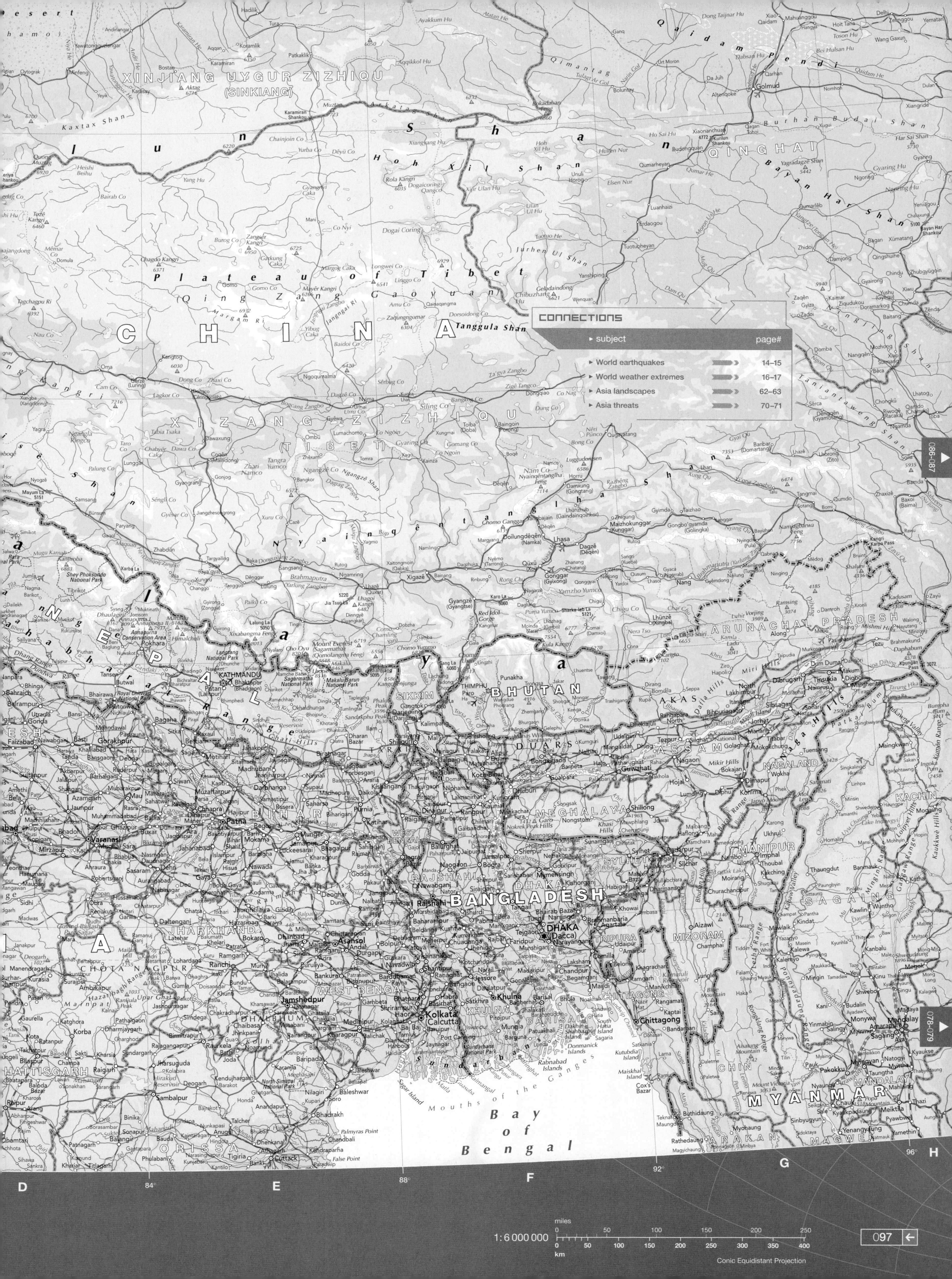

1:6 000 000

miles
0   50   100   150   200   250

km
0   50   100   150   200   250   300   350   400

Conic Equidistant Projection

13°-42°N / 30°-80°E

040-041

052-053

120-121

128-129

Elevation scale:
>6000m
5000-6000m
4000-5000m
3000-4000m
2000-3000m
1000-2000m
500-1000m
200-500m
0-200m
<0m
0-200m
200-500m
500-1000m
1000-2000m
2000-3000m
3000-4000m
4000-5000m
5000-6000m
>6000m

Black Sea

Mediterranean Sea

Red Sea

Gulf of Aden

RUSSIAN FEDERATION
GEORGIA
ARMENIA
AZERBAIJAN
TURKEY
CYPRUS
SYRIA
LEBANON
ISRAEL
JORDAN
IRAQ
KUWAIT
SAUDI ARABIA
EGYPT
SUDAN
ERITREA
ETHIOPIA
YEMEN

ANKARA
NICOSIA (Lefkosia)
BEIRUT
DAMASCUS (Dimashq)
Tel Aviv-Yafo
JERUSALEM
GAZA
'AMMAN
BAGHDAD
KUWAIT (Al Kuwayt)
CAIRO (El Qâhira)
RIYADH (Ar Riyad)
Mecca (Makkah)
Medina (Al Madinah)
Jeddah (Jiddah)
KHARTOUM
Omdurman
ASMARA
ŞAN'A'
Hodeidah

BAKU
YEREVAN
T'BILISI
Tabrīz
Mosul
Arbīl
Basra
Aleppo (Halab)
Homs
Hamah
Adana
Konya
Antalya
Luxor (El Uqsur)
Aswân

An Nafūd
Nubian Desert
Syrian Desert
Rub' al Kh...
Taurus Mountains
Eastern Desert
Tropic of Cancer

098

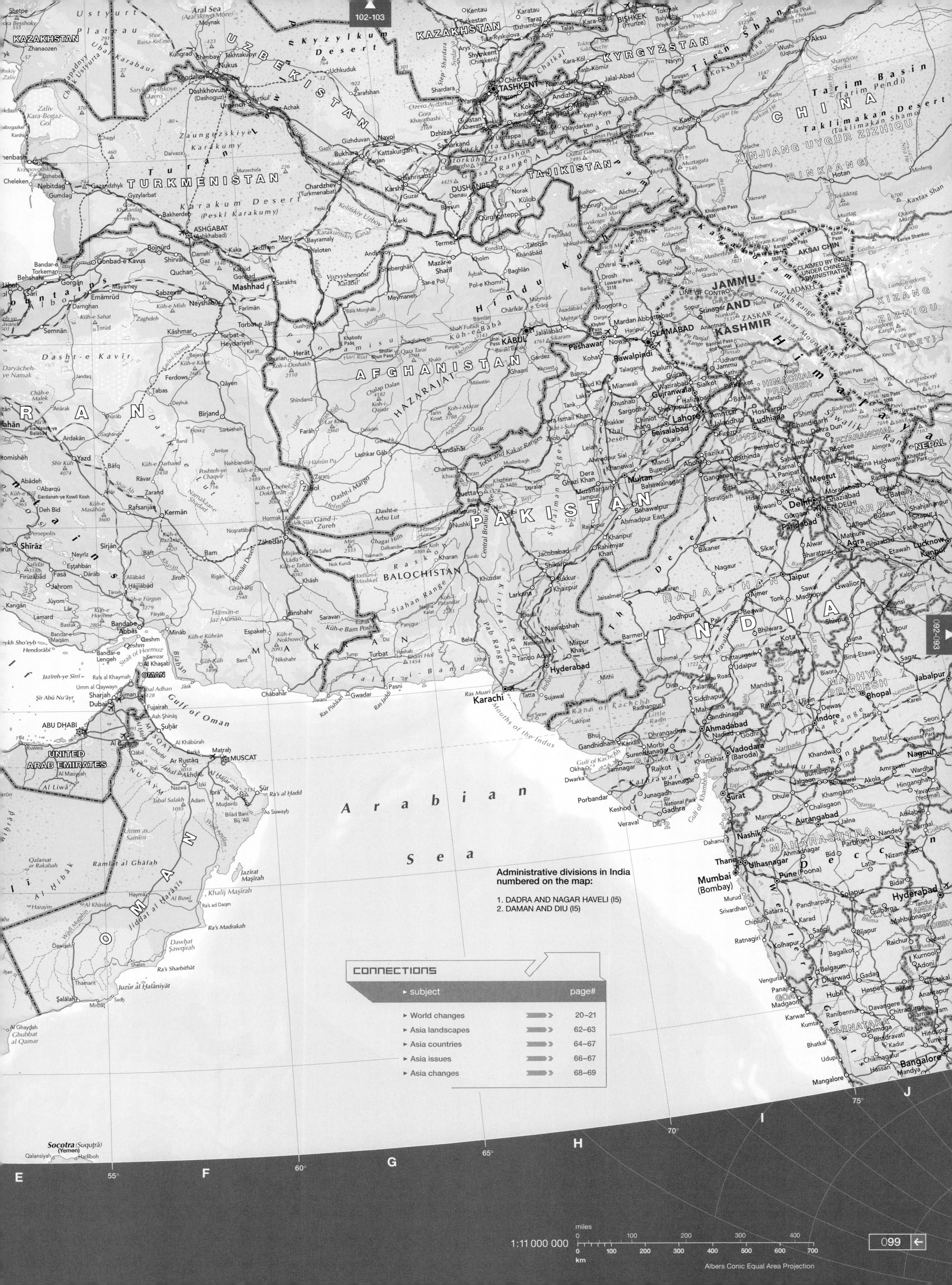

Administrative divisions in India numbered on the map:

1. DADRA AND NAGAR HAVELI (I5)
2. DAMAN AND DIU (I5)

miles
0   100   200   300   400

1:11 000 000

km
0   100   200   300   400   500   600   700

Albers Conic Equal Area Projection

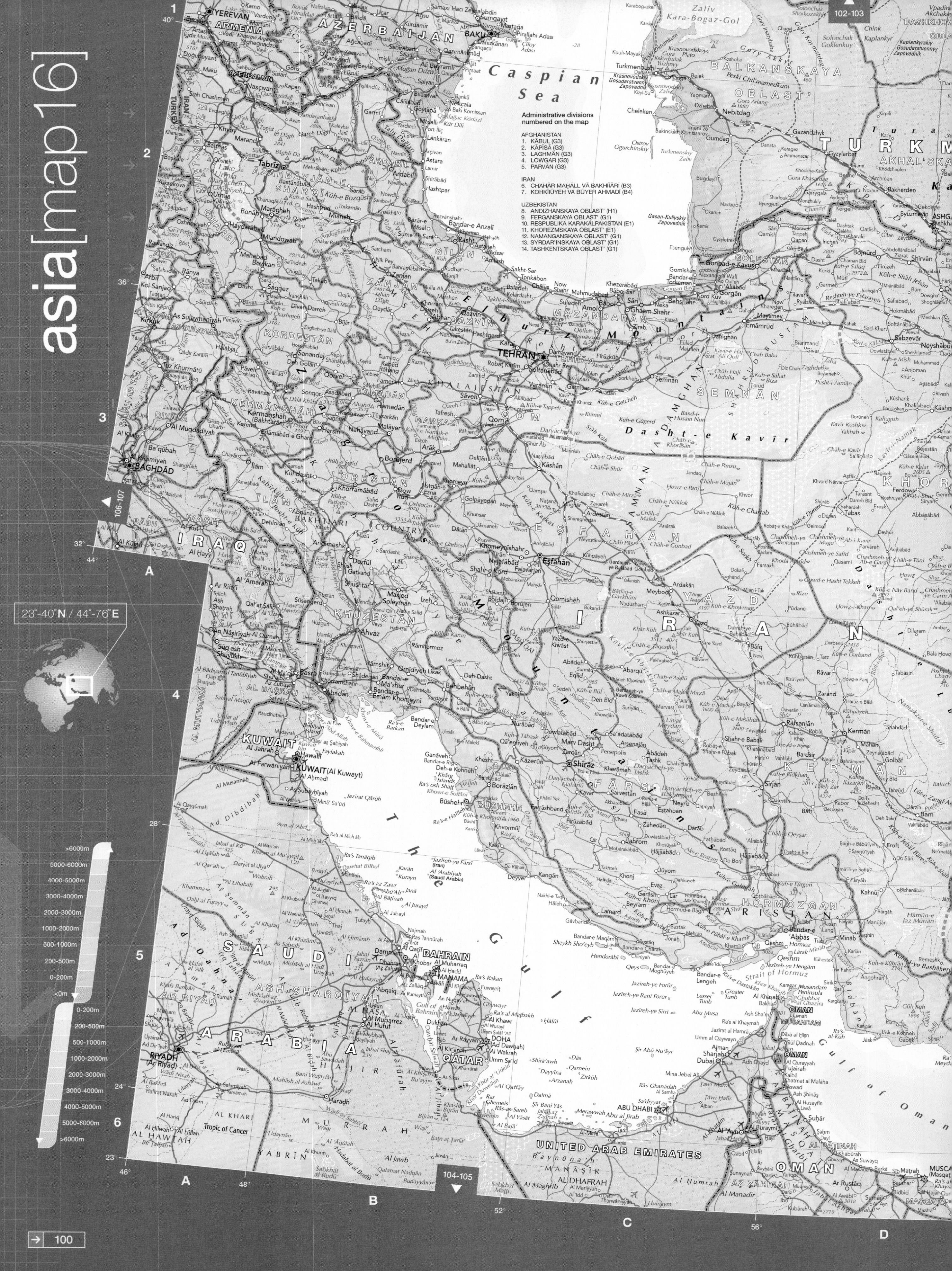

asia[map16]
23°-40°N / 44°-76°E
102-103
106-107
104-105
Caspian Sea
Administrative divisions numbered on the map
AFGHANISTAN
1. KĀBUL (G3)
2. KĀPĪSĀ (G3)
3. LAGHMĀN (G3)
4. LOWGAR (G3)
5. PARVĀN (G3)
IRAN
6. CHAHĀR MAḤĀLL VĀ BAKHTĪĀRĪ (B3)
7. KOHKĪLŪYEH VA BŪYER AHMADĪ (B4)
UZBEKISTAN
8. ANDIZHANSKAYA OBLAST' (H1)
9. FERGANSKAYA OBLAST' (G1)
10. RESPUBLIKA KARAKALPAKSTAN (E1)
11. KHOREZMSKAYA OBLAST' (E1)
12. NAMANGANSKAYA OBLAST' (G1)
13. SYRDAR'INSKAYA OBLAST' (G1)
14. TASHKENTSKAYA OBLAST' (G1)
AZERBAIJAN
ARMENIA
YEREVAN
BAKU
TURKMENISTAN
IRAN
IRAQ
BAGHDĀD
KUWAIT
KUWAIT (Al Kuwayt)
SAUDI ARABIA
RIYADH (Ar Riyāḍ)
BAHRAIN
MANAMA
QATAR
DOHA (Ad Dawḥah)
UNITED ARAB EMIRATES
ABU DHABI
OMAN
TEHRAN
Elburz Mountains
Zagros Mountains
Dasht-e Kavīr
The Gulf
Gulf of Oman
Strait of Hormuz
Tropic of Cancer
>6000m
5000-6000m
4000-5000m
3000-4000m
2000-3000m
1000-2000m
500-1000m
200-500m
0-200m
<0m
0-200m
200-500m
500-1000m
1000-2000m
2000-3000m
3000-4000m
4000-5000m
5000-6000m
>6000m
A
B
C
D
1
2
3
4
5
6

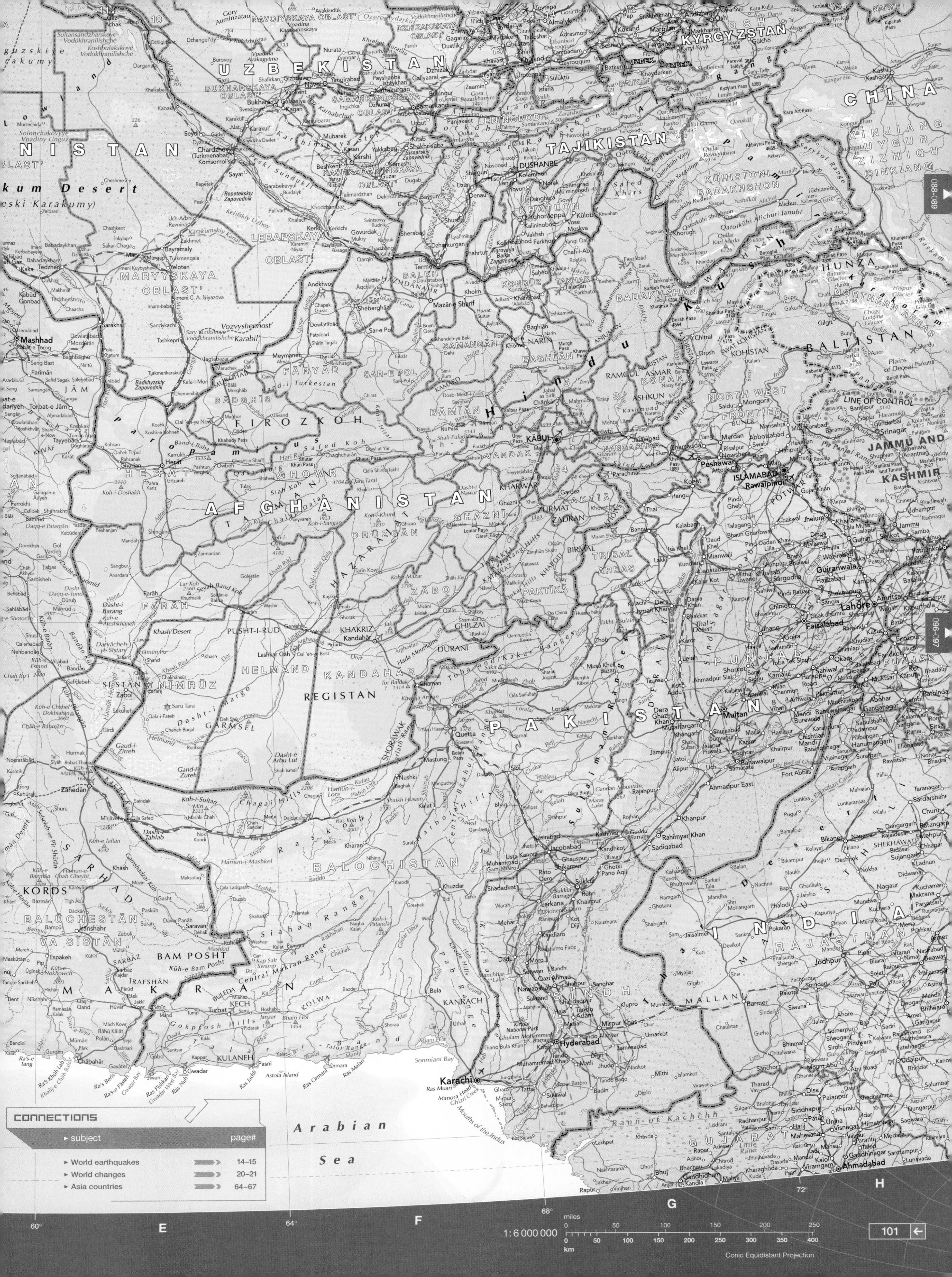
UZBEKISTAN
KYRGYZSTAN
TAJIKISTAN
CHINA
AFGHANISTAN
PAKISTAN
INDIA
JAMMU AND KASHMIR
LINE OF CONTROL
NORTHERN AREAS
NORTH WEST FRONTIER
BALOCHISTAN
PUNJAB
SINDH
RAJASTHAN
GUJARAT
Arabian Sea
DUSHANBE
KĀBUL
ISLAMABAD
Karachi
Lahore
Peshawar
Rawalpindi
Kandahār
Herāt
Quetta
Hyderabad
Multan
Faisalabad
Ahmadabad
Mazār-e Sharīf
Mashhad
Thar Desert
Registan
Hindu Kush
Arabian
Sea
CONNECTIONS
▸ subject
page#
▸ World earthquakes 14–15
▸ World changes 20–21
▸ Asia countries 64–67
1:6 000 000
miles
km
Conic Equidistant Projection
E
F
G
H
60°
64°
68°
72°
088–089
096–097

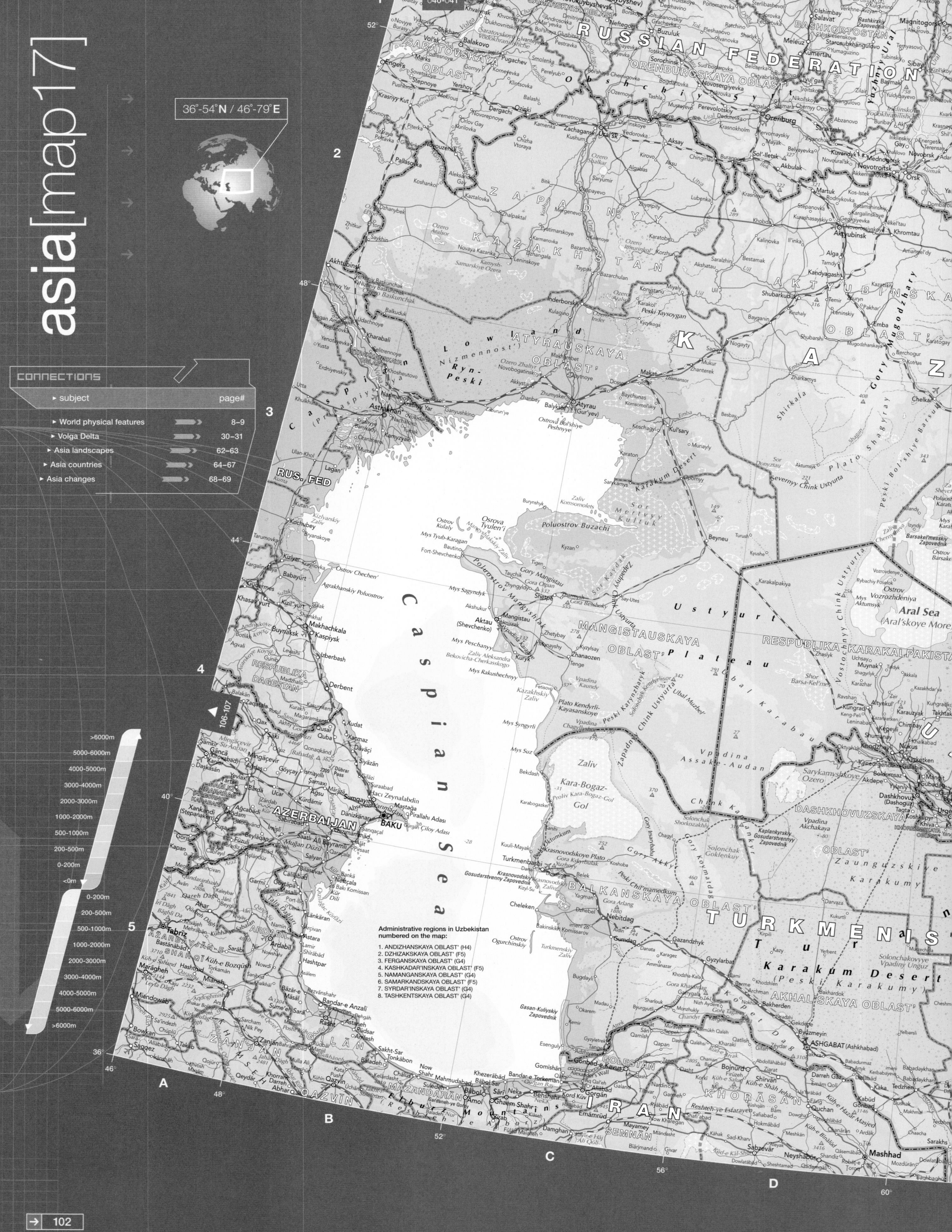

asia[map17]

36°-54°N / 46°-79°E

CONNECTIONS

Administrative regions in Uzbekistan numbered on the map:

1. ANDIZHANSKAYA OBLAST' (H4)
2. DZHIZAKSKAYA OBLAST' (F5)
3. FERGANSKAYA OBLAST' (G4)
4. KASHKADAR'INSKAYA OBLAST' (F5)
5. NAMANGANSKAYA OBLAST' (G4)
6. SAMARKANDSKAYA OBLAST' (F5)
7. SYRDAR'INSKAYA OBLAST' (G4)
8. TASHKENTSKAYA OBLAST' (G4)

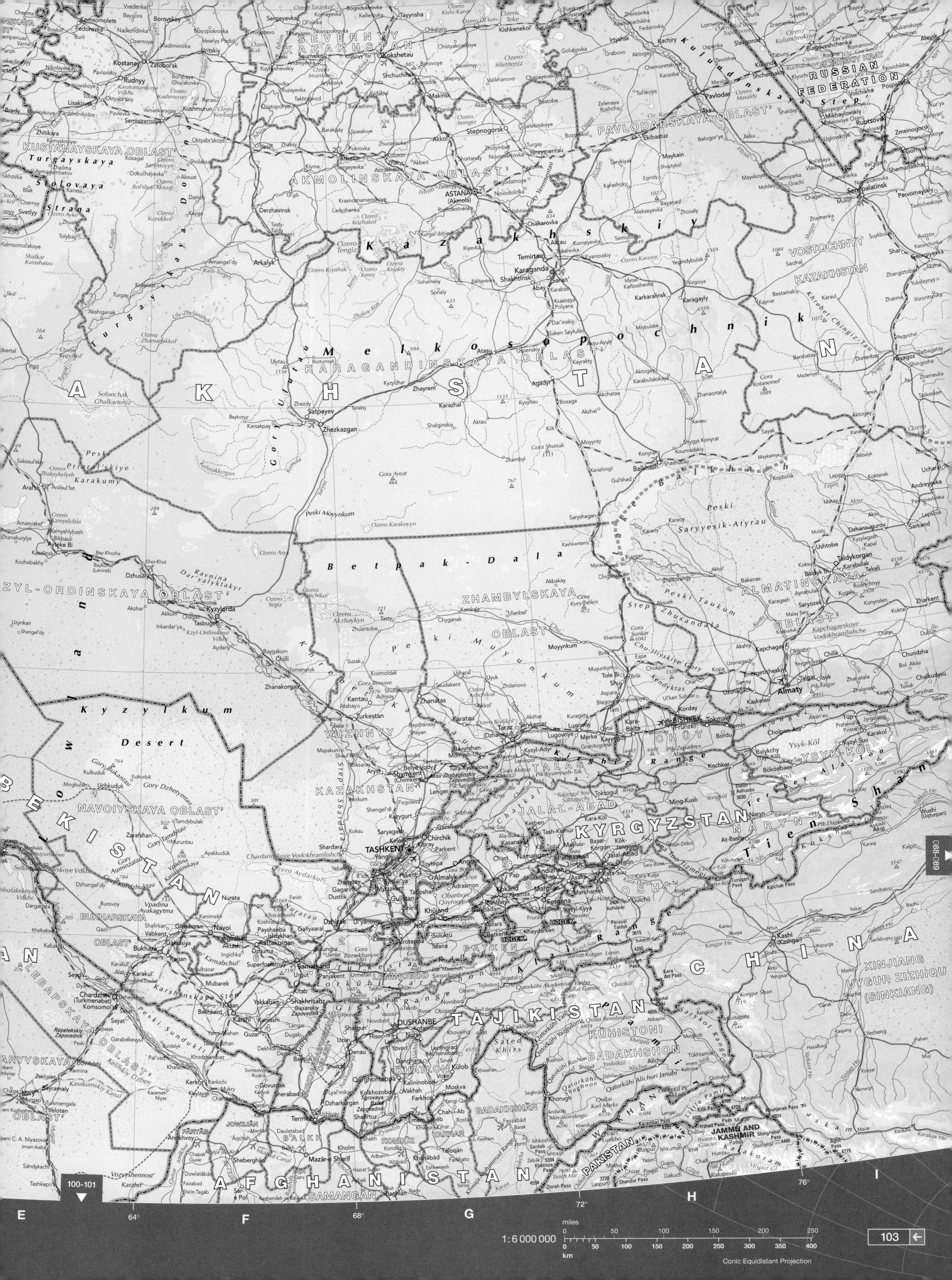

asia[map18]

12°-29°N / 33°-60°E

120-121

Elevation scale:
>6000m
5000-6000m
4000-5000m
3000-4000m
2000-3000m
1000-2000m
500-1000m
200-500m
0-200m
<0m

0-200m
200-500m
500-1000m
1000-2000m
2000-3000m
3000-4000m
4000-5000m
5000-6000m
>6000m

EGYPT
JORDAN
SINAI
JANŪB SĪNĀ
Gulf of Suez
Gulf of Aqaba
Hurghada
Quseir
Al Wajh
QENA
EL BAHR EL AHMAR
EGYPT
Tropic of Cancer
ASWAN
HALAIB TRIANGLE UNDER SUDANESE ADMINISTRATION
Halaib
Port Sudan (Būr Sudan)
Suakin
Nubian Desert
RED SEA
SUDAN
Atbara
Berber
Baiyuda Desert
KHARTOUM
KASSALA
Kassala
EL GEZIRA
Wad Medani
GEDAREF
Gedaref
SENNAR
BLUE NILE
Dinder National Park
Gonder
AMHARA
ETHIOPIA
TIGRAY
Ādwa
Āksum
Mek'elē
Simēn Mountains National Park
Lake Tana
Ādīs Zemen
ERITREA
ASMARA
Massawa
Keren
BARKA
SENHIT
GASH AND SETIT
SERAE
AKELE GUZAI
Dekemhare
Dahlak Marine National Park
Dahlak Archipelago
Suakin Archipelago
DANKALIA
AFAR
Afar Depression
DJIBOUTI
128-129

SAUDI ARABIA
TABŪK
AL JAWF
AL HUDŪD ASH SHAMĀLIYAH
An Nafūd
HĀ'IL
JABAL SHAMMAR
Hā'il
Buraydah
AL QAŞĪM
NAJD
Medina (Al Madīnah)
Yanbu' al Bahr
AL MADĪNAH
'UTAYBAH
MAKKAH
Jeddah (Jiddah)
Mecca (Makkah)
Aţ Ţā'if
'ASĪR
AL BĀHAH
Al Bāhah
BISHAH
ASMAR
Abha
Khamis Mushayt
Al Qunfidhah
Farasān Islands
Jīzān
JĪZĀN
SAADAH
HAJJAH
SAN'Ā'
AL MAHWIT
Hodeidah (Al Ḩudaydah)
Ta'izz
Mocha (Al Mukhā)
LAHIJ
SUBAYHĪ
Aden (Adan)
Bāb al Mandab

104

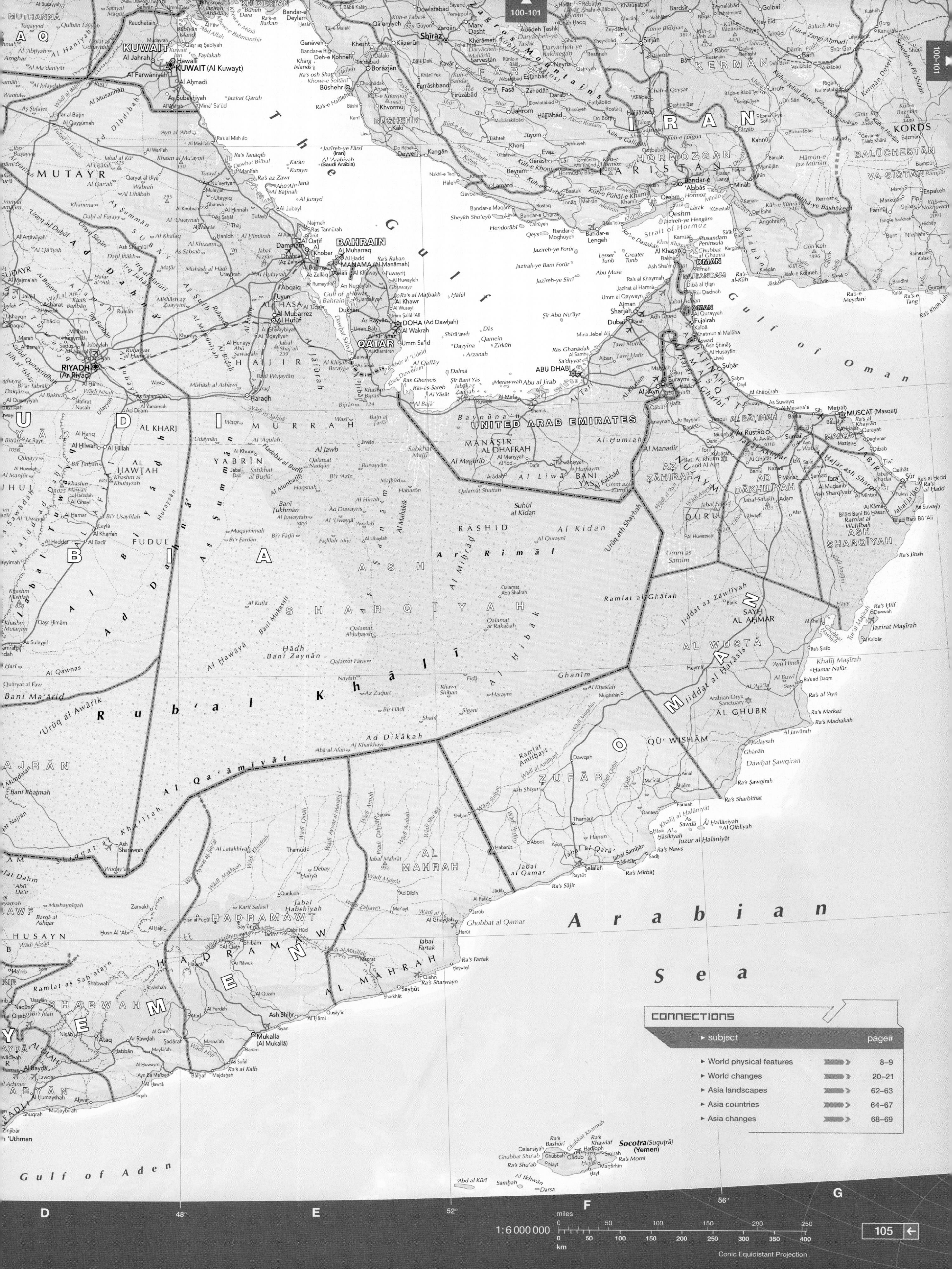

D   48°   E   52°   F   56°   G

miles
0   50   100   150   200   250

1:6 000 000

0 50 100 150 200 250 300 350 400
km

105 ←

Conic Equidistant Projection

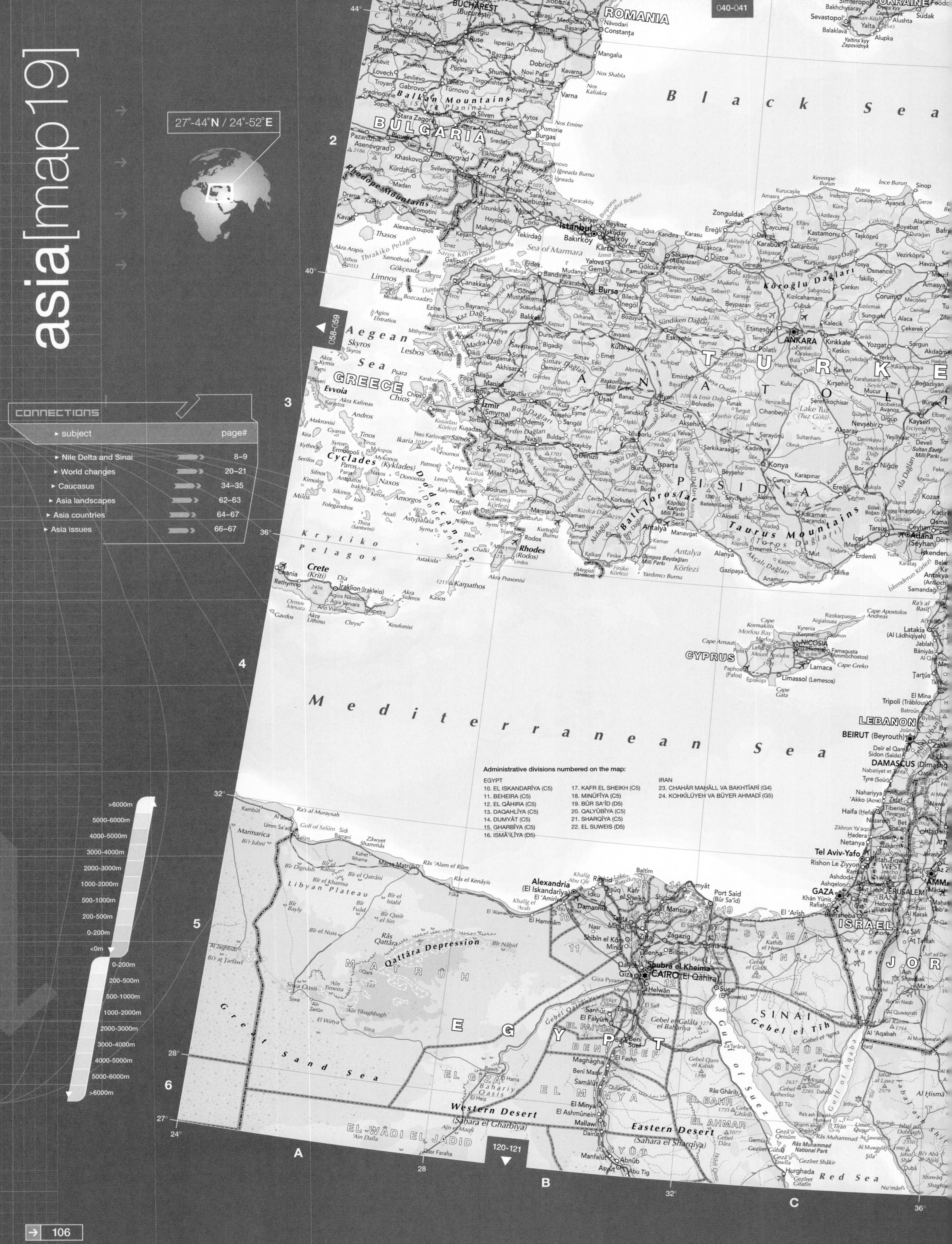
asia[map19]
27°-44°N / 24°-52°E
CONNECTIONS
▸ subject page#
▸ Nile Delta and Sinai 8–9
▸ World changes 20–21
▸ Caucasus 34–35
▸ Asia landscapes 62–63
▸ Asia countries 64–67
▸ Asia issues 66–67
040-041
058-059
120-121
ROMANIA
BULGARIA
GREECE
TURKEY
CYPRUS
LEBANON
ISRAEL
EGYPT
Black Sea
Aegean Sea
Mediterranean Sea
Red Sea
Administrative divisions numbered on the map:
EGYPT
10. EL ISKANDARÎYA (C5)
11. BEHEIRA (C5)
12. EL QÂHIRA (C5)
13. DAQAHLÎYA (C5)
14. DUMYÂT (C5)
15. GHARBÎYA (C5)
16. ISMÂ'ILÎYA (D5)
17. KAFR EL SHEIKH (C5)
18. MINÛFÎYA (C5)
19. BÛR SA'ÎD (D5)
20. QALYÛBÎYA (C5)
21. SHARQÎYA (C5)
22. EL SUWEIS (D5)
IRAN
23. CHAHĀR MAḨĀLL VA BAKHTĪARĪ (G4)
24. KOHKĪLŪYEH VA BŪYER AHMADĪ (G5)
>6000m
5000-6000m
4000-5000m
3000-4000m
2000-3000m
1000-2000m
500-1000m
200-500m
0-200m
<0m
0-200m
200-500m
500-1000m
1000-2000m
2000-3000m
3000-4000m
4000-5000m
5000-6000m
>6000m

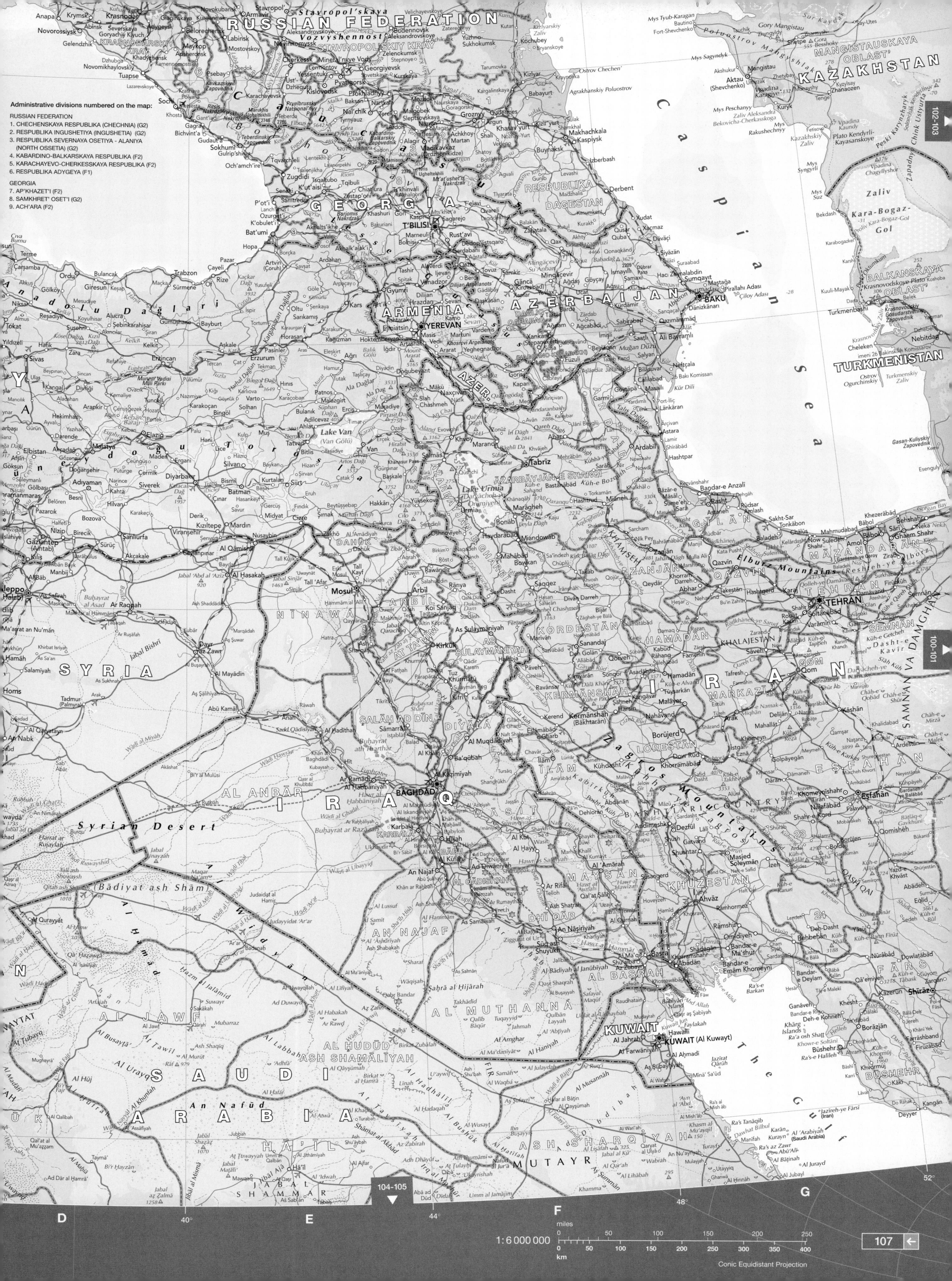

RUSSIAN FEDERATION
Administrative divisions numbered on the map:
RUSSIAN FEDERATION
1. CHECHENSKAYA RESPUBLIKA (CHECHNIA) (G2)
2. RESPUBLIKA INGUSHETIYA (INGUSHETIA) (G2)
3. RESPUBLIKA SEVERNAYA OSETIYA - ALANIYA (NORTH OSSETIA) (G2)
4. KABARDINO-BALKARSKAYA RESPUBLIKA (F2)
5. KARACHAYEVO-CHERKESSKAYA RESPUBLIKA (F2)
6. RESPUBLIKA ADYGEYA (F1)
GEORGIA
7. AP'KHAZET'I (F2)
8. SAMKHRET' OSET'I (G2)
9. ACH'ARA (F2)
KRASNODARSKIY KRAY
STAVROPOL'SKIY KRAY
GEORGIA
T'BILISI
ARMENIA
YEREVAN
AZERBAIJAN
BAKU
KAZAKHSTAN
MANGISTAUSKAYA OBLAST'
TURKMENISTAN
BALKANSKAYA OBLAST'
Caspian Sea
SYRIA
IRAQ
BAGHDAD
IRAN
TEHRAN
KUWAIT
KUWAIT (Al Kuwayt)
SAUDI ARABIA
Syrian Desert
The Gulf
Zagros Mountains
Elburz Mountains
Lake Van
Lake Urmia
102-103
100-101
104-105
D
E
F
G
40°
44°
48°
52°
1:6 000 000
miles
0 50 100 150 200 250
km
0 50 100 150 200 250 300 350 400
Conic Equidistant Projection

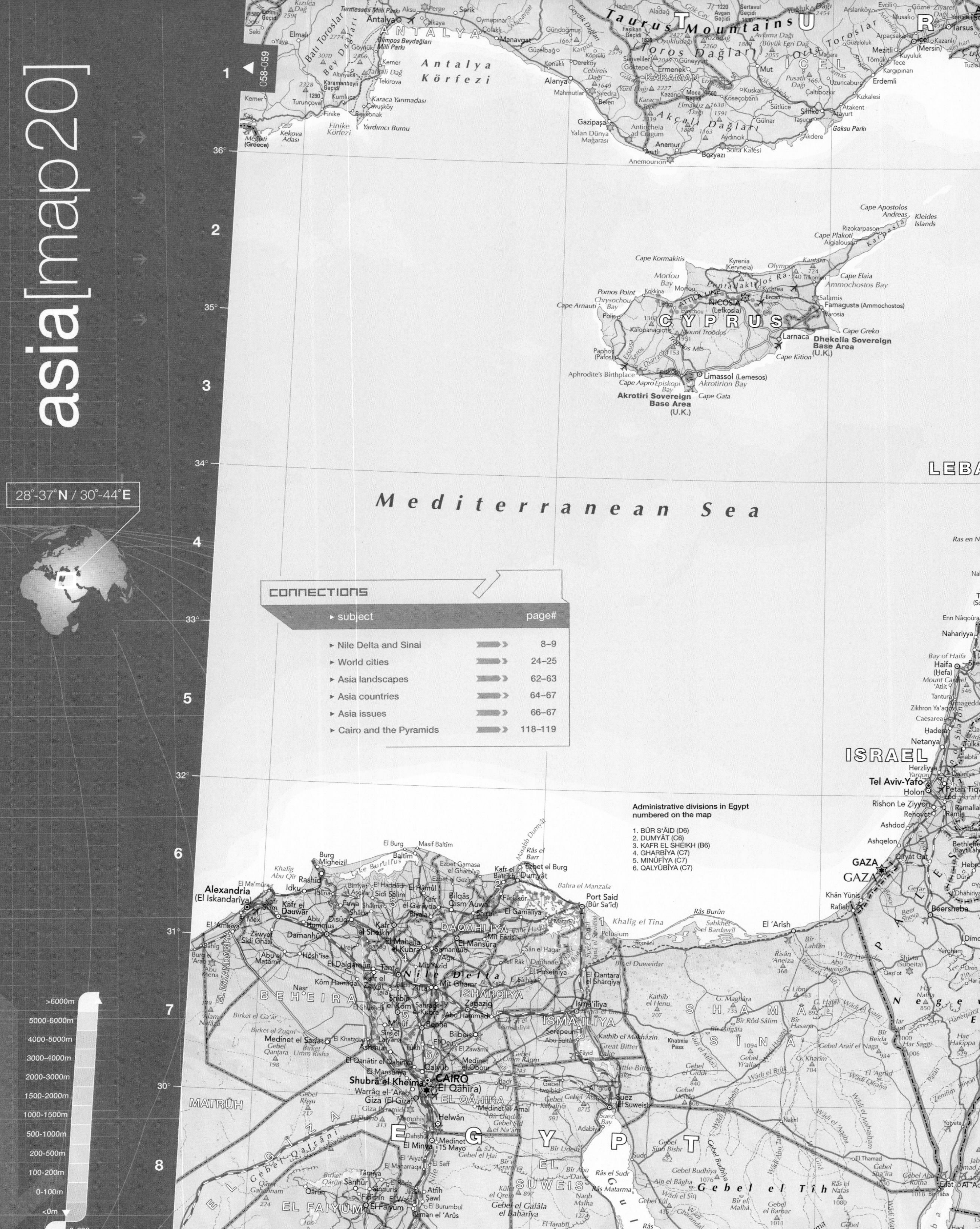

28°-37°N / 30°-44°E

Administrative divisions in Egypt
numbered on the map

1. BÛR S'ÂID (D6)
2. DUMYÂT (C6)
3. KAFR EL SHEIKH (B6)
4. GHARBÎYA (C7)
5. MINÛFÎYA (C7)
6. QALYÛBÎYA (C7)

>6000m
5000-6000m
4000-5000m
3000-4000m
2000-3000m
1500-2000m
1000-1500m
500-1000m
200-500m
100-200m
0-100m
<0m

0-200m
200-500m
500-1000m
1000-2000m
2000-3000m
3000-4000m
4000-5000m
5000-6000m
>6000m

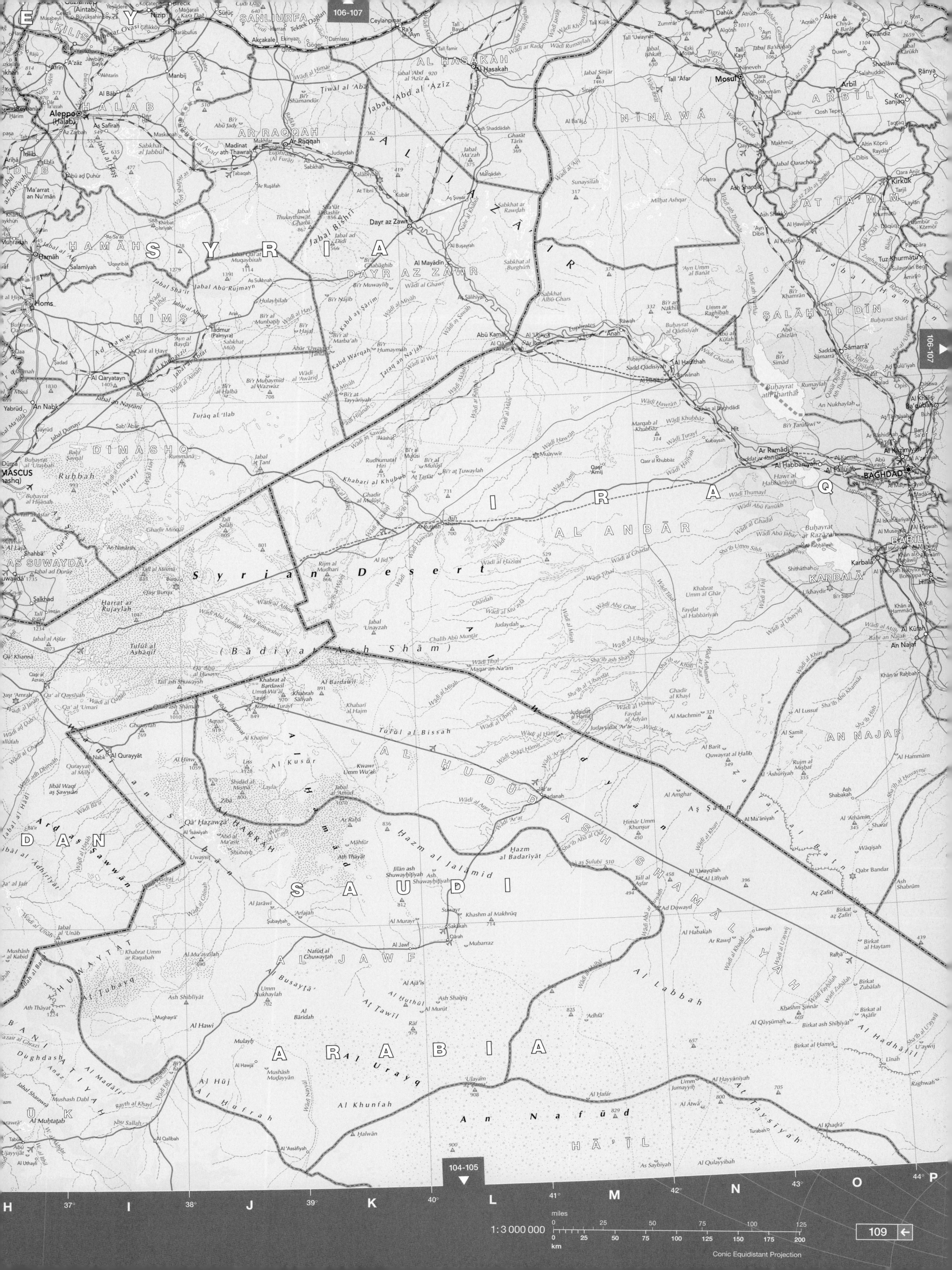

106-107
SYRIA
IRAQ
SAUDI ARABIA
HALAB
IDLIB
HAMAH
HIMS
DIMASHQ
AS SUWAYDA
AR RAQQAH
AL HASAKAH
DAYR AZ ZAWR
NINAWA
ARBIL
AT TA'MIM
SALAH AD DIN
AL ANBAR
BABIL
KARBALA'
AN NAJAF
AL HUDUD ASH SHAMALIYAH
AL JAWF
HA'IL
AL JAZA'IR
Syrian Desert
(Badiyat Ash Sham)
An Nafud
Aleppo (Halab)
Ar Raqqah
Al Hasakah
Mosul
Arbil
Kirkuk
Hamah
Homs
Tadmur (Palmyra)
Dayr az Zawr
Abu Kamal
Al Mayadin
Ar Ramadi
Al Fallujah
BAGHDAD
Karbala'
An Najaf
Al Kufah
Hillah
Samarra'
Tikrit
Hit
Al Hadithah
'Anah
Ar Rutbah
Al Qurayyat
Al Jawf
Sakakah
Tall 'Afar
Nineveh
Tuz Khurmatu
Buhayrat ath Tharthar
Buhayrat ar Razazah
Euphrates
Wadi Hawran
Wadi Sirhan
Al Hamad
Al Harrah
Jabal Bishri
Jabal 'Abd al 'Aziz
Jabal Sinjar
Ceylanpinar
Sanliurfa
Kilis
Manbij
Al Bab
Idlib
Ma'arrat an Nu'man
Salamiyah
Al Qaryatayn
An Nabk
Yabrud
Rafha'
'Ar'ar
Badanah
Turayf
Linah
104-105
H I J K L M N O P
37° 38° 39° 40° 41° 42° 43° 44°
1:3 000 000
miles 0 25 50 75 100 125
km 0 25 50 75 100 125 150 175 200
Conic Equidistant Projection

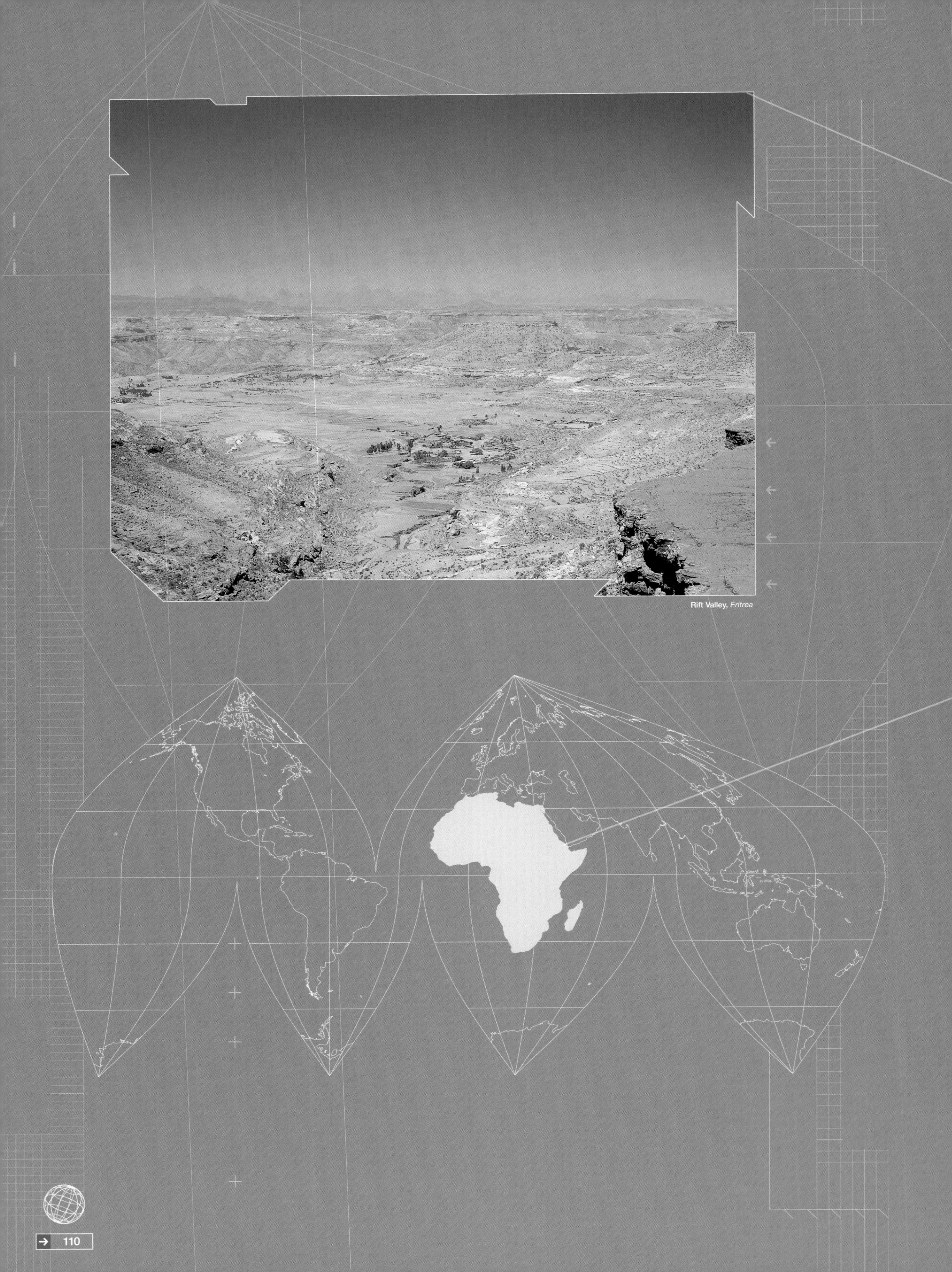

Rift Valley, *Eritrea*

africa

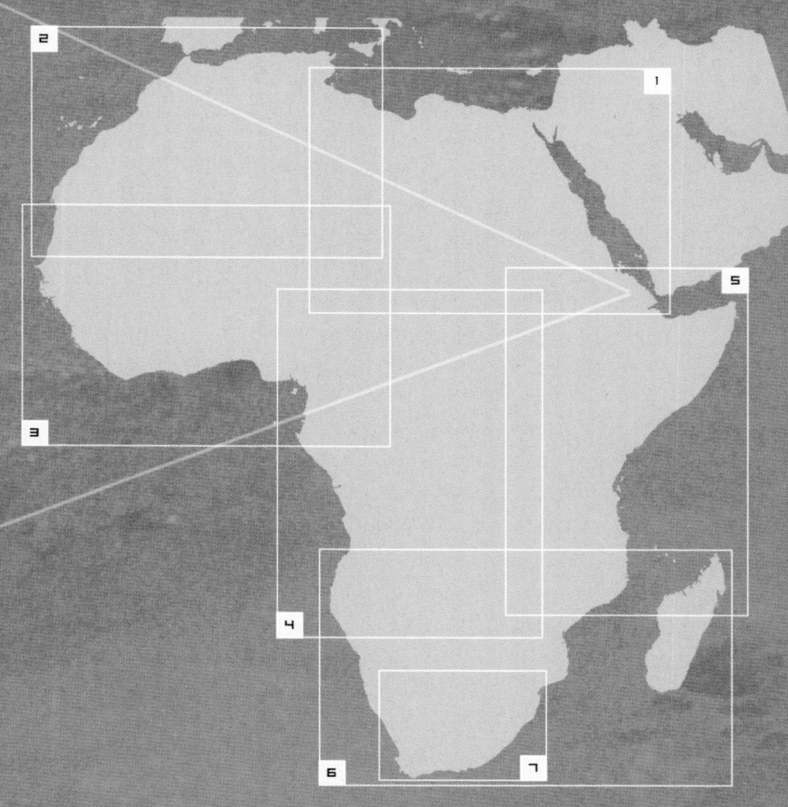

[contents]

africa[landscapes]

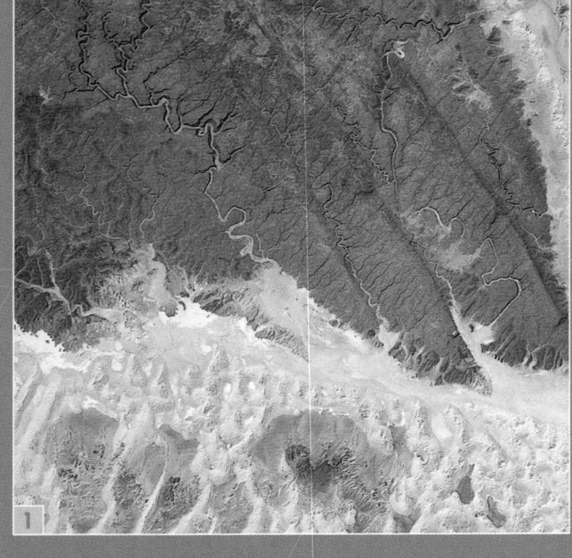

Africa, viewed here from above the southern Indian Ocean, is dominated by several striking physical features. The Sahara desert extends over most of the north and in the east the geological feature, known as the Great Rift Valley, extends from the valley of the river Jordan in Southwest Asia to Mozambique. The valley contains a string of major lakes including Lake Turkana, Lake Tanganyika and Lake Nyasa.

The river basin of the Congo, in central Africa draining into the Atlantic Ocean, is the second largest river basin in the world. The land south of the equator is higher than in the north and forms a massive plateau dissected by several large rivers which flow east to the Indian Ocean or west to the Atlantic. The most distinctive feature in the south is the Drakensberg, a range of mountains which run southwest to northeast through Lesotho and South Africa. The large island separated from Africa by the Mozambique Channel is Madagascar, the fourth largest island in the world.

1 **Sahara Desert,** *Algeria*

The Sahara desert crosses the continent of Africa from the Atlantic Ocean to the Red Sea. Within this vast area there is a great variety in topography with heights from 30 m below sea level to mountains over 3 300 m. This satellite image of east central Algeria shows the sand dunes stopping at the higher ground of the dark base rock. Although rain is scarce, dry river beds can be seen cutting through the rock.

Satellite/Sensor : SPOT

2 **Congo River,** *Democratic Republic of Congo*

This satellite image shows broken clouds above a heavily braided Congo river in Congo. The river is over 4 600 km long and has many long tributaries which result in a drainage basin of approximately 3 700 000 sq km. In this tropical area the river acts as a highway between communities where roads do not exist. The river flows into the Atlantic Ocean, forming the boundary between Angola and the Democratic Republic of Congo.

Satellite/Sensor : Space Shuttle

3 **Atlas Mountains,** *Morocco*

The Atlas Mountains of Morocco in northwest Africa form a major boundary between the Sahara desert and the fertile coastal plain. They are a composite of several ranges created from extensive fault movements and earthquakes, resulting in distinct rock layers and folds, as seen in this image. The dark areas are sandy beds of a seasonal river system.

Satellite/Sensor : SIR-C/X-SAR

Canary Islands

Atlas Mountains

Cape Verde Islands

Sahara

Lake Volta

Benue River

Niger River

Gulf of Guinea

Bioco

São Tomé

Largest desert in the world
Sahara 9 065 000 sq km / 3 500 000 sq miles Map reference 123 F4

Atlantic Ocean

Congo River

Largest drainage basin
Congo Basin 3 700 000 sq km / 1 429 000 sq miles Map reference 126 C5

Bié Plateau

Victoria Falls

Namib Desert

Okavango Delta

Orange River

Kalahari Desert

Great Karoo

Drakensberg

Limpo

Cape of Good Hope

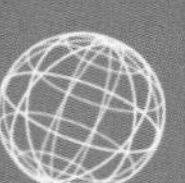

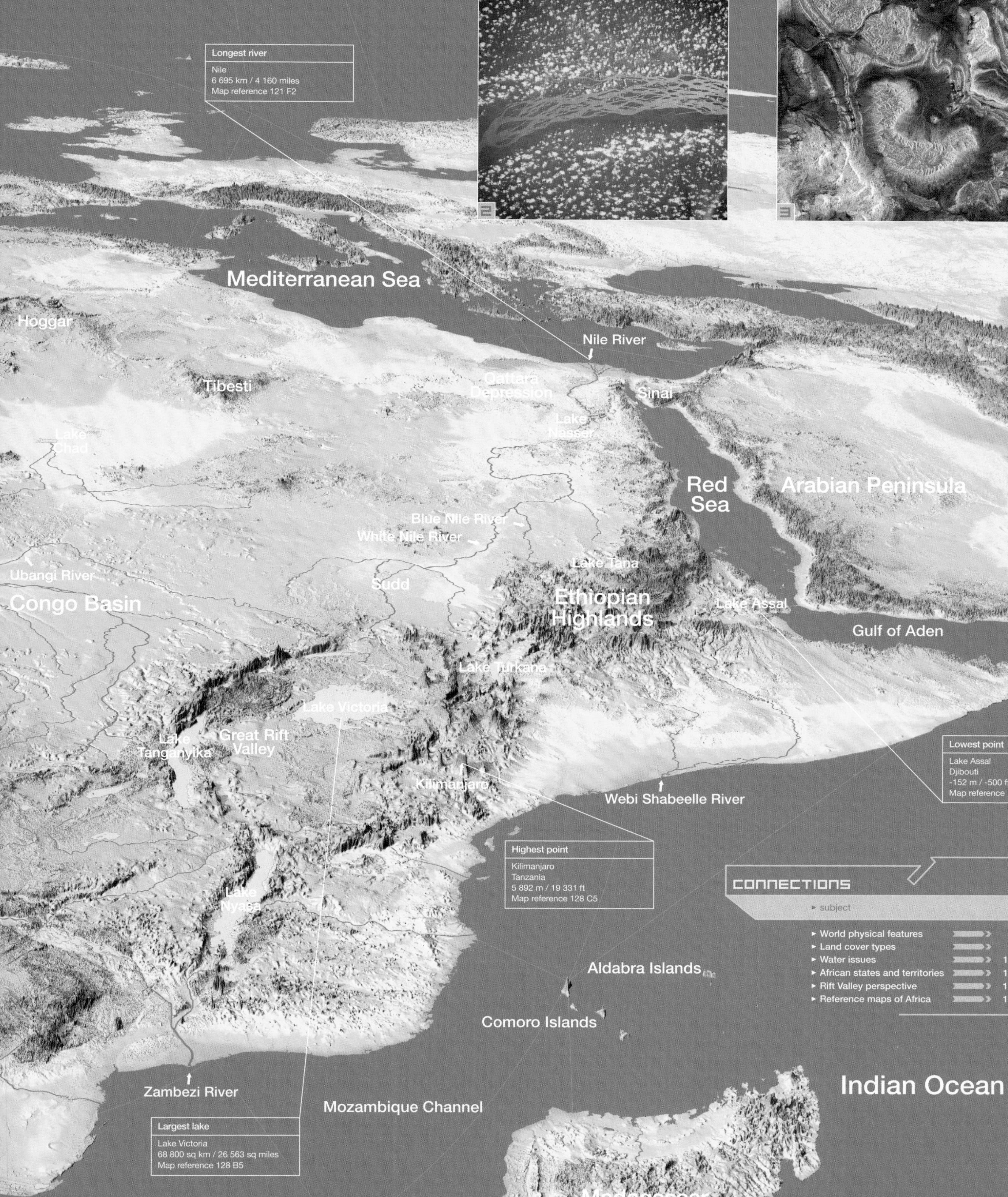

Longest river
Nile
6 695 km / 4 160 miles
Map reference 121 F2

Mediterranean Sea
Hoggar
Tibesti
Lake Chad
Nile River
Qattara Depression
Lake Nasser
Sinai
Red Sea
Arabian Peninsula
Blue Nile River
White Nile River
Lake Tana
Ethiopian Highlands
Lake Assal
Gulf of Aden
Ubangi River
Congo Basin
Sudd
Lake Turkane
Lake Victoria
Great Rift Valley
Lake Tanganyika
Kilimanjaro
Webi Shabeelle River
Lake Nyasa
Aldabra Islands
Comoro Islands
Zambezi River
Mozambique Channel
Madagascar
Indian Ocean

Lowest point
Lake Assal
Djibouti
-152 m / -500 ft
Map reference 128 D2

Highest point
Kilimanjaro
Tanzania
5 892 m / 19 331 ft
Map reference 128 C5

Largest lake
Lake Victoria
68 800 sq km / 26 563 sq miles
Map reference 128 B5

AFRICA

HIGHEST MOUNTAINS	m	ft	location	map
Kilimanjaro	5 892	19 331	Tanzania	128 C5
Mt Kenya	5 199	17 057	Kenya	128 C5
Margherita Peak	5 110	16 765	Democratic Republic of Congo/Uganda	126 F4
Meru	4 565	14 977	Tanzania	128 C5
Ras Dashen	4 533	14 872	Ethiopia	128 C1
Mt Karisimbi	4 510	14 796	Rwanda	126F5

LARGEST ISLANDS	sq km	sq miles	map
Madagascar	587 040	226 657	131 J3

LONGEST RIVERS	km	miles	map
Nile	6 695	4 160	121 F2
Congo	4 667	2 900	127 B6
Niger	4 184	2 599	125 F5
Zambezi	2 736	1 700	131 H2
Webi Shabeelle	2 490	1 547	128 D5
Ubangi	2 250	1 398	126 C5

LAKES	sq km	sq miles	map
Lake Victoria	68 800	26 563	128 B5
Lake Tanganyika	32 900	12 702	129 A6
Lake Nyasa	30 044	11 600	129 B7
Lake Chad	10 000-26 000	3 861-10 039	125 I3
Lake Volta	8 485	3 276	124 F5
Lake Turkana	6 475	2 500	128 C4

LAND AREA		map
Most northerly point	La Galite, Tunisia	123 H1
Most southerly point	Cape Agulhas, South Africa	130 C7
Most westerly point	Santo Antao, Cape Verde	122 inset
Most easterly point	Raas Xaafuun, Somalia	128 F2
Total 30 343 578 sq km / 11 715 721 sq miles		

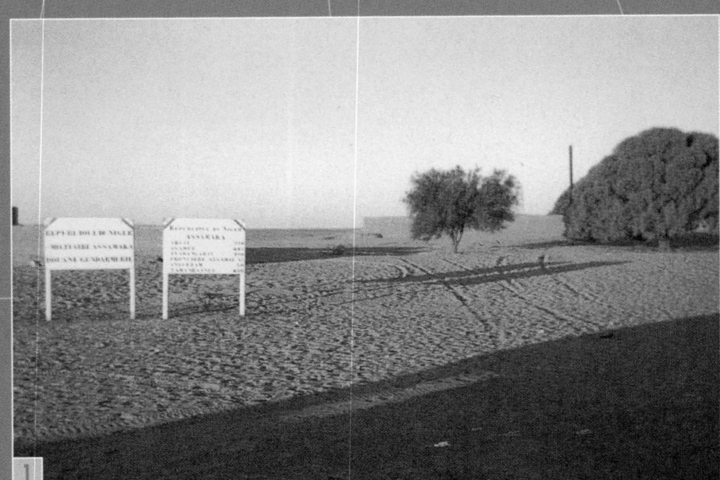

1 Border Post, *Algeria/Niger*

The border between Algeria and Niger lies in the centre of the Sahel region of Africa. Both countries have largely geometric borders in the relatively featureless landscape which offers no obvious physical boundaries. As a result simple indicators of the presence of a border such as the marker shown in this photograph taken south of the actual boundary line, are the only features which advise of the passage from one country to the other.

2 Refugee Camp, *Tanzania*

Much internal migration in Africa has been instigated by war, ethnic conflict, economic disparities and famine. In 1994 over 2 million Rwandans fled to the neighbouring countries of Tanzania and the Democratic Republic of Congo to escape tribal war between Hutus and Tutsis. This photograph shows a refugee camp in Tanzania just across the border from Rwanda and gives an indication of the difficult conditions in such centres. Tanzania is currently one of East Africa's important host countries with a refugee population of nearly half a million.

AFRICA
COUNTRIES

		area sq km	area sq miles	population	capital	languages	religions	currency	map
ALGERIA		2 381 741	919 595	30 291 000	Algiers (Alger)	Arabic, French, Berber	Sunni Muslim	Dinar	122–123
ANGOLA		1 246 700	481 354	13 134 000	Luanda	Portuguese, Bantu, local languages	Roman Catholic, Protestant, traditional beliefs	Kwanza	127
BENIN		112 620	43 483	6 272 000	Porto-Novo	French, Fon, Yoruba, Adja, local languages	Traditional beliefs, Roman Catholic, Sunni Muslim	CFA franc	125
BOTSWANA		581 370	224 468	1 541 000	Gaborone	English, Setswana, Shona, local languages	Traditional beliefs, Protestant, Roman Catholic	Pula	130–131
BURKINA		274 200	105 869	11 535 000	Ouagadougou	French, Moore (Mossi), Fulani, local languages	Sunni Muslim, traditional beliefs, Roman Catholic	CFA franc	124–125
BURUNDI		27 835	10 747	6 356 000	Bujumbura	Kirundi (Hutu, Tutsi), French	Roman Catholic, traditional beliefs, Protestant	Franc	126
CAMEROON		475 442	183 569	14 876 000	Yaoundé	French, English, Fang, Bamileke, local languages	Roman Catholic, traditional beliefs, Sunni Muslim, Protestant	CFA franc	126
CAPE VERDE		4 033	1 557	427 000	Praia	Portuguese, creole	Roman Catholic, Protestant	Escudo	124
CENTRAL AFRICAN REPUBLIC		622 436	240 324	3 717 000	Bangui	French, Sango, Banda, Baya, local languages	Protestant, Roman Catholic, traditional beliefs, Sunni Muslim	CFA franc	126
CHAD		1 284 000	495 755	7 885 000	Ndjamena	Arabic, French, Sara, local languages	Sunni Muslim, Roman Catholic, Protestant, traditional beliefs	CFA franc	120
COMOROS		1 862	719	706 000	Moroni	Comorian, French, Arabic	Sunni Muslim, Roman Catholic	Franc	129
CONGO		342 000	132 047	3 018 000	Brazzaville	French, Kongo, Monokutuba, local languages	Roman Catholic, Protestant, traditional beliefs, Sunni Muslim	CFA franc	126–127
CONGO, DEMOCRATIC REPUBLIC OF		2 345 410	905 568	50 948 000	Kinshasa	French, Lingala, Swahili, Kongo, local languages	Christian, Sunni Muslim	Franc	126–127
CÔTE D'IVOIRE		322 463	124 504	16 013 000	Yamoussoukro	French, creole, Akan, local languages	Sunni Muslim, Roman Catholic, traditional beliefs, Protestant	CFA franc	124
DJIBOUTI		23 200	8 958	632 000	Djibouti	Somali, Afar, French, Arabic	Sunni Muslim, Christian	Franc	128
EGYPT		1 000 250	386 199	67 884 000	Cairo (El Qâhira)	Arabic	Sunni Muslim, Coptic Christian	Pound	120–121
EQUATORIAL GUINEA		28 051	10 831	457 000	Malabo	Spanish, French, Fang	Roman Catholic, traditional beliefs	CFA franc	125
ERITREA		117 400	45 328	3 659 000	Asmara	Tigrinya, Tigre	Sunni Muslim, Coptic Christian	Nakfa	121
ETHIOPIA		1 133 880	437 794	62 908 000	Addis Ababa (Ädis Äbeba)	Oromo, Amharic, Tigrinya, local languages	Ethiopian Orthodox, Sunni Muslim, traditional beliefs	Birr	128
GABON		267 667	103 347	1 230 000	Libreville	French, Fang, local languages	Roman Catholic, Protestant, traditional beliefs	CFA franc	126
THE GAMBIA		11 295	4 361	1 303 000	Banjul	English, Malinke, Fulani, Wolof	Sunni Muslim, Protestant	Dalasi	124
GHANA		238 537	92 100	19 306 000	Accra	English, Hausa, Akan, local languages	Christian, Sunni Muslim, traditional beliefs	Cedi	124–125
GUINEA		245 857	94 926	8 154 000	Conakry	French, Fulani, Malinke, local languages	Sunni Muslim, traditional beliefs, Christian	Franc	124
GUINEA–BISSAU		36 125	13 948	1 199 000	Bissau	Portuguese, crioulo, local languages	Traditional beliefs, Sunni Muslim, Christian	CFA franc	124
KENYA		582 646	224 961	30 669 000	Nairobi	Swahili, English, local languages	Christian, traditional beliefs	Shilling	128–129
LESOTHO		30 355	11 720	2 035 000	Maseru	Sesotho, English, Zulu	Christian, traditional beliefs	Loti	133
LIBERIA		111 369	43 000	2 913 000	Monrovia	English, creole, local languages	Traditional beliefs, Christian, Sunni Muslim	Dollar	124
LIBYA		1 759 540	679 362	5 290 000	Tripoli (Tarābulus)	Arabic, Berber	Sunni Muslim	Dinar	120
MADAGASCAR		587 041	226 658	15 970 000	Antananarivo	Malagasy, French	Traditional beliefs, Christian, Sunni Muslim	Franc	131
MALAWI		118 484	45 747	11 308 000	Lilongwe	Chichewa, English, local languages	Christian, traditional beliefs, Sunni Muslim	Kwacha	129
MALI		1 240 140	478 821	11 351 000	Bamako	French, Bambara, local languages	Sunni Muslim, traditional beliefs, Christian	CFA franc	124–125
MAURITANIA		1 030 700	397 955	2 665 000	Nouakchott	Arabic, French, local languages	Sunni Muslim	Ouguiya	122
MAURITIUS		2 040	788	1 161 000	Port Louis	English, creole, Hindi, Bhojpuri, French	Hindu, Roman Catholic, Sunni Muslim	Rupee	218
MOROCCO		446 550	172 414	29 878 000	Rabat	Arabic, Berber, French	Sunni Muslim	Dirham	122–123
MOZAMBIQUE		799 380	308 642	18 292 000	Maputo	Portuguese, Makua, Tsonga, local languages	Traditional beliefs, Roman Catholic, Sunni Muslim	Metical	131
NAMIBIA		824 292	318 261	1 757 000	Windhoek	English, Afrikaans, German, Ovambo, local languages	Protestant, Roman Catholic	Dollar	130
NIGER		1 267 000	489 191	10 832 000	Niamey	French, Hausa, Fulani, local languages	Sunni Muslim, traditional beliefs	CFA franc	125
NIGERIA		923 768	356 669	113 862 000	Abuja	English, Hausa, Yoruba, Ibo, Fulani, local languages	Sunni Muslim, Christian, traditional beliefs	Naira	125
RWANDA		26 338	10 169	7 609 000	Kigali	Kinyarwanda, French, English	Roman Catholic, traditional beliefs, Protestant	Franc	126
SÃO TOMÉ AND PRÍNCIPE		964	372	138 000	São Tomé	Portuguese, creole	Roman Catholic, Protestant	Dobra	125
SENEGAL		196 720	75 954	9 421 000	Dakar	French, Wolof, Fulani, local languages	Sunni Muslim, Roman Catholic, traditional beliefs	CFA franc	124
SEYCHELLES		455	176	80 000	Victoria	English, French, creole	Roman Catholic, Protestant	Rupee	218
SIERRA LEONE		71 740	27 699	4 405 000	Freetown	English, creole, Mende, Temne, local languages	Sunni Muslim, traditional beliefs	Leone	124
SOMALIA		637 657	246 201	8 778 000	Mogadishu (Muqdisho)	Somali, Arabic	Sunni Muslim	Shilling	128
SOUTH AFRICA, REPUBLIC OF		1 219 090	470 693	43 309 000	Pretoria/Cape Town	Afrikaans, English, nine official local languages	Protestant, Roman Catholic, Sunni Muslim, Hindu	Rand	130–131
SUDAN		2 505 813	967 500	31 095 000	Khartoum	Arabic, Dinka, Nubian, Beja, Nuer, local languages	Sunni Muslim, traditional beliefs, Christian	Dinar	120–121
SWAZILAND		17 364	6 704	925 000	Mbabane	Swazi, English	Christian, traditional beliefs	Lilangeni	133
TANZANIA		945 087	364 900	35 119 000	Dodoma	Swahili, English, Nyamwezi, local languages	Shi'a Muslim, Sunni Muslim, traditional beliefs, Christian	Shilling	128–129
TOGO		56 785	21 925	4 527 000	Lomé	French, Ewe, Kabre, local languages	Traditional beliefs, Christian, Sunni Muslim	CFA franc	125
TUNISIA		164 150	63 379	9 459 000	Tunis	Arabic, French	Sunni Muslim	Dinar	123
UGANDA		241 038	93 065	23 300 000	Kampala	English, Swahili, Luganda, local languages	Roman Catholic, Protestant, Sunni Muslim, traditional beliefs	Shilling	128
ZAMBIA		752 614	290 586	10 421 000	Lusaka	English, Bemba, Nyanja, Tonga, local languages	Christian, traditional beliefs	Kwacha	127
ZIMBABWE		390 759	150 873	12 627 000	Harare	English, Shona, Ndebele	Christian, traditional beliefs	Dollar	131

Equator

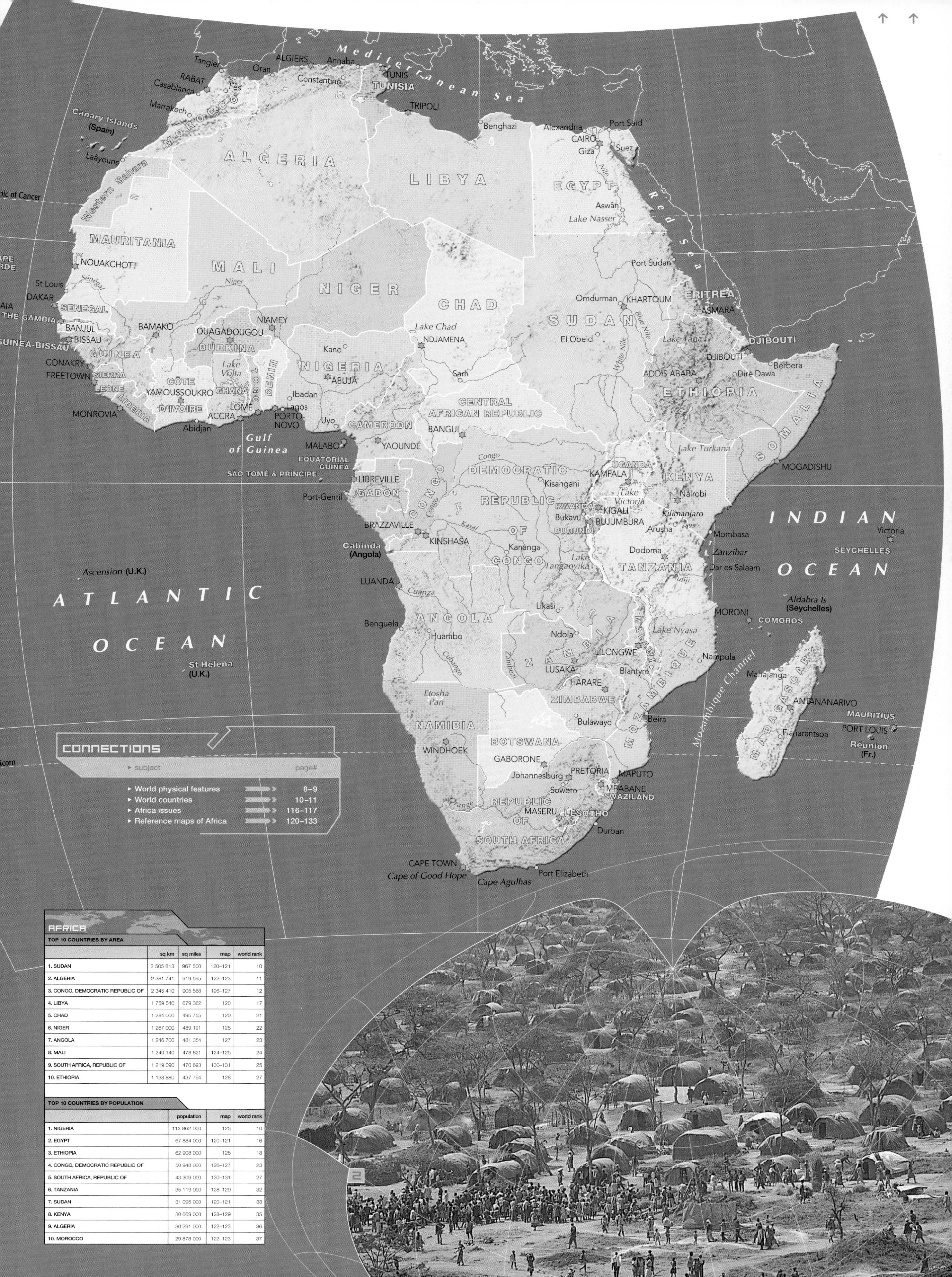

▶ subject	page#
▶ World physical features	8–9
▶ World countries	10–11
▶ Africa issues	116–117
▶ Reference maps of Africa	120–133

AFRICA

TOP 10 COUNTRIES BY AREA

	sq km	sq miles	map	world rank
1. SUDAN	2 505 813	967 500	120–121	10
2. ALGERIA	2 381 741	919 595	122–123	11
3. CONGO, DEMOCRATIC REPUBLIC OF	2 345 410	905 568	126–127	12
4. LIBYA	1 759 540	679 362	120	17
5. CHAD	1 284 000	495 755	120	21
6. NIGER	1 267 000	489 191	125	22
7. ANGOLA	1 246 700	481 354	127	23
8. MALI	1 240 140	478 821	124–125	24
9. SOUTH AFRICA, REPUBLIC OF	1 219 090	470 693	130–131	25
10. ETHIOPIA	1 133 880	437 794	128	27

TOP 10 COUNTRIES BY POPULATION

	population	map	world rank
1. NIGERIA	113 862 000	125	10
2. EGYPT	67 884 000	120–121	16
3. ETHIOPIA	62 908 000	128	18
4. CONGO, DEMOCRATIC REPUBLIC OF	50 948 000	126–127	23
5. SOUTH AFRICA, REPUBLIC OF	43 309 000	130–131	27
6. TANZANIA	35 119 000	128–129	32
7. SUDAN	31 095 000	120–121	33
8. KENYA	30 669 000	128–129	35
9. ALGERIA	30 291 000	122–123	36
10. MOROCCO	29 878 000	122–123	37

DEPENDENT AND DISPUTED TERRITORIES		territorial status	area sq km	area sq miles	population	capital	languages	religions	currency	map
Canary Islands (Islas Canarias)		Autonomous Community of Spain	7 447	2 875	1 606 522	Santa Cruz de Tenerife, Las Palmas	Spanish	Roman Catholic	Peseta	122
Ceuta		Spanish Territory	19	7	68 796	Ceuta	Spanish, Arabic	Roman Catholic, Muslim	Peseta	122
Madeira		Autonomous Region of Portugal	779	301	259 000	Funchal	Portuguese	Roman Catholic, Protestant	Port. escudo	122
Mayotte		French Territorial Collectivity	373	144	144 944	Dzaoudzi	French, Mahorian	Sunni Muslim, Christian	French franc	129
Melilla		Spanish Territory	13	5	59 576	Melilla	Spanish, Arabic	Roman Catholic, Muslim	Peseta	123
Réunion		French Overseas Department	2 551	985	721 000	St-Denis	French, creole	Roman Catholic	French franc	218
St Helena and Dependencies		United Kingdom Overseas Territory	121	47	6 000	Jamestown	English	Protestant, Roman Catholic	Pound sterling	216
Western Sahara		Disputed territory (Morocco)	266 000	102 703	252 000	Laâyoune	Arabic	Sunni Muslim	Moroccan dirham	122

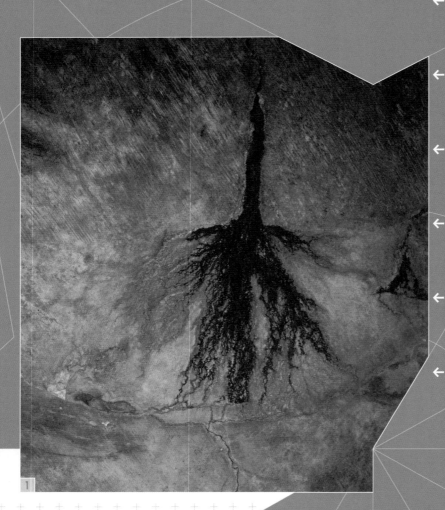

1

1 Okavango Delta, *Botswana*

This Shuttle photograph shows the world's largest inland delta, the Okavango Delta in Botswana. The Okavango river originates in southeast Angola and ends in this spectacular and unique alluvial plain covering 10 000 square kilometres. The river is fed by rains from October to March which produce rich seasonal vegetation and support great numbers of wildlife. Scientists have identified this to be one of the most ecologically sensitive areas on Earth.

Satellite/Sensor : Space Shuttle

CONNECTIONS

2 Nile Valley, *Egypt*

The Nile river winds through Egypt in this satellite image, ending in the distinctive triangular delta on the Mediterranean coast. The dark blue water and green vegetation of the irrigated valley and delta provide a striking contrast to the surrounding desert. Thick layers of silt carried downstream for thousands of years provide the delta with the most fertile soil in Africa. The Suez Canal is also visible on the image, providing a link between the Mediterranean Sea at the top of the image and the Gulf of Suez and the Red Sea to the right.

Satellite/Sensor : MODIS

3 Flooded Village, *Kenya*

This village near Garsen was flooded when the Tana river burst its banks. An increase in extreme weather patterns occurred throughout the world in 1998. Some cases were blamed on the periodic warming of Pacific Ocean waters known as El Niño. In east Africa the regular problems of drought were replaced by excessive rainfall which led to the destruction of crops and the threat of famine. This village felt the affect of Kenya's annual rainfall increasing by over 1000mm in 1998.

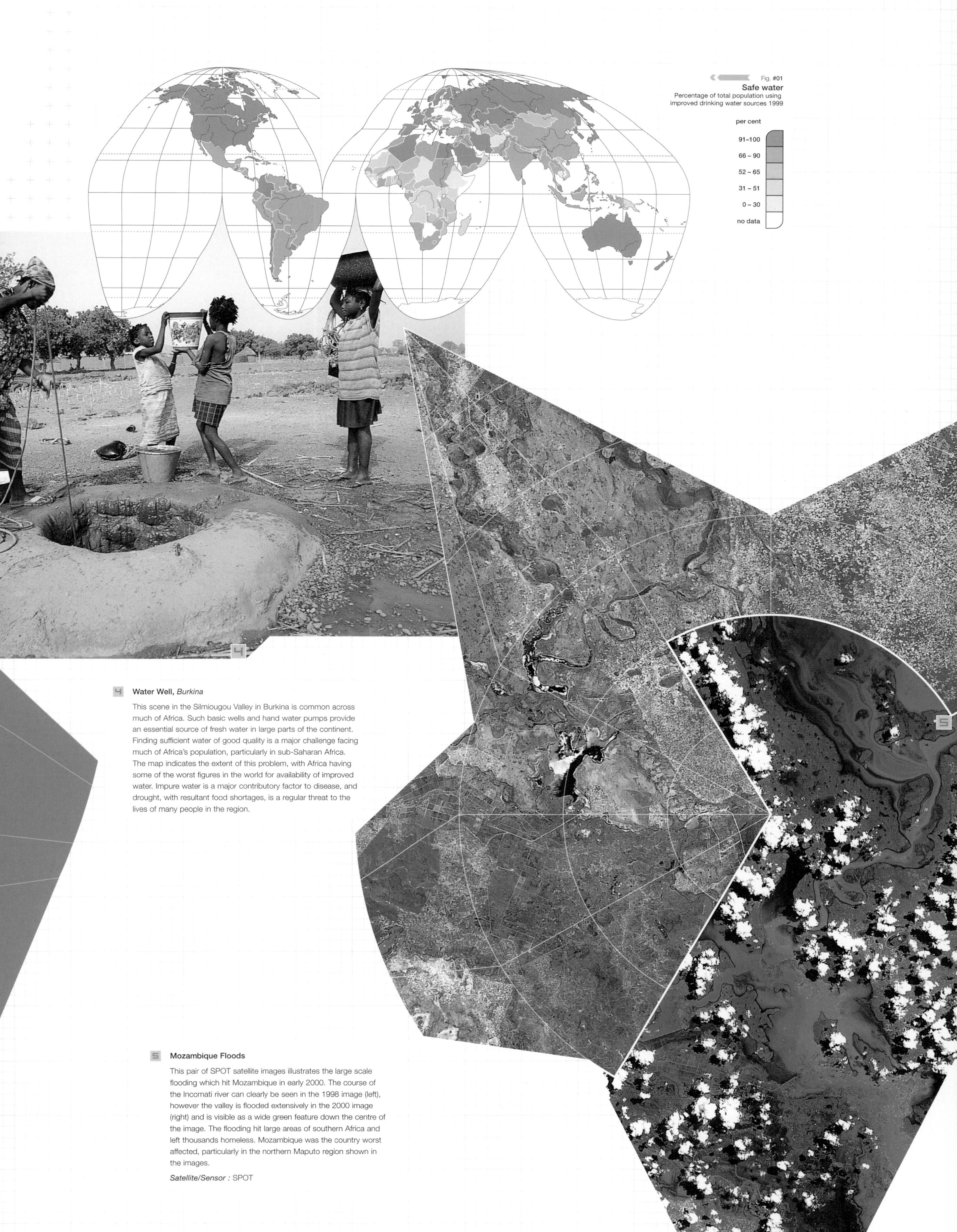

Fig. #01

Safe water
Percentage of total population using
improved drinking water sources 1999

per cent

91–100
66 – 90
52 – 65
31 – 51
0 – 30
no data

4   Water Well, *Burkina*

This scene in the Silmiougou Valley in Burkina is common across
much of Africa. Such basic wells and hand water pumps provide
an essential source of fresh water in large parts of the continent.
Finding sufficient water of good quality is a major challenge facing
much of Africa's population, particularly in sub-Saharan Africa.
The map indicates the extent of this problem, with Africa having
some of the worst figures in the world for availability of improved
water. Impure water is a major contributory factor to disease, and
drought, with resultant food shortages, is a regular threat to the
lives of many people in the region.

5   Mozambique Floods

This pair of SPOT satellite images illustrates the large scale
flooding which hit Mozambique in early 2000. The course of
the Incomati river can clearly be seen in the 1998 image (left),
however the valley is flooded extensively in the 2000 image
(right) and is visible as a wide green feature down the centre of
the image. The flooding hit large areas of southern Africa and
left thousands homeless. Mozambique was the country worst
affected, particularly in the northern Maputo region shown in
the images.

Satellite/Sensor : SPOT

africa[locations]

1 Cape Town, *Republic of South Africa*

Cape Town is the legislative capital of South Africa, the capital city of Western Cape Province and is located 40 km from the Cape of Good Hope. This view from Table Mountain shows the full extent of the city spreading out to the waterfront area on the shores of Table Bay.

2 Cairo, *Egypt*

The largest city in Africa and capital of Egypt, Cairo is situated on the right bank of the river Nile. The main built-up area appears grey in this image. The famous pyramids and the suburb of Giza are visible to the lower left where the city meets the desert. Cairo airport can be seen at the upper right. Agricultural areas, achieved by extensive irrigation, show as deep red around the city.

Satellite/Sensor : SPOT

3 The Great Rift Valley, *Africa*

The Great Rift Valley is a huge, linear depression which marks a series of geological faults resulting from tectonic activity. The section of the valley shown in this 3-D perspective view extends from Lake Nyasa in the south to the Red Sea coast in the north. The valley splits into two branches north of Lake Nyasa and then combines again through the Ethiopian Highlands. The western branch is very prominent in the image and contains several lakes, including Lake Tanganyika. The eastern branch passes to the west of Kilimanjaro, the highest mountain to the right of the image, and contains Lake Turkana on the northern border of Kenya.

4 Victoria Falls, *Zambia/Zimbabwe*

The Victoria Falls are located in the Zambezi river on the Zambia/Zimbabwe border near the town of Livingstone. The river is over 1.7 km wide at the point where the falls drop 108 m over a precipice into a narrow chasm. The volume of water in the falls varies with the seasons. Land on the Zimbabwe side of the falls is preserved as a national park.

5 Sahara Desert, *Africa*

This photograph was taken in the eastern Sahara in Libya and illustrates sharp contrasts in the landscape. At the top are huge sand dunes which have been shaped by the wind. The area in the middle view has been planted with trees, to prevent the movement of sand and soil, and the irrigated area in the near view is typical of a fertile oasis, where the land has been worked to produce crops and to support livestock.

6 The Pyramids, *Egypt*

The suburbs of Giza, shown on the left of this satellite image, spread out from the city of Cairo to an arid plateau on which stand the famous Great Pyramids. The largest, shown at the bottom centre of the image, is the Great Pyramid of Cheops. To the left of this are three small pyramids collectively known as the Pyramids of Queens. Above them is the Great Sphinx. The pyramid at the centre right of the image is Chephren and the small one at the top right is Mycerinus.

Satellite/Sensor : IKONOS

CONNECTIONS

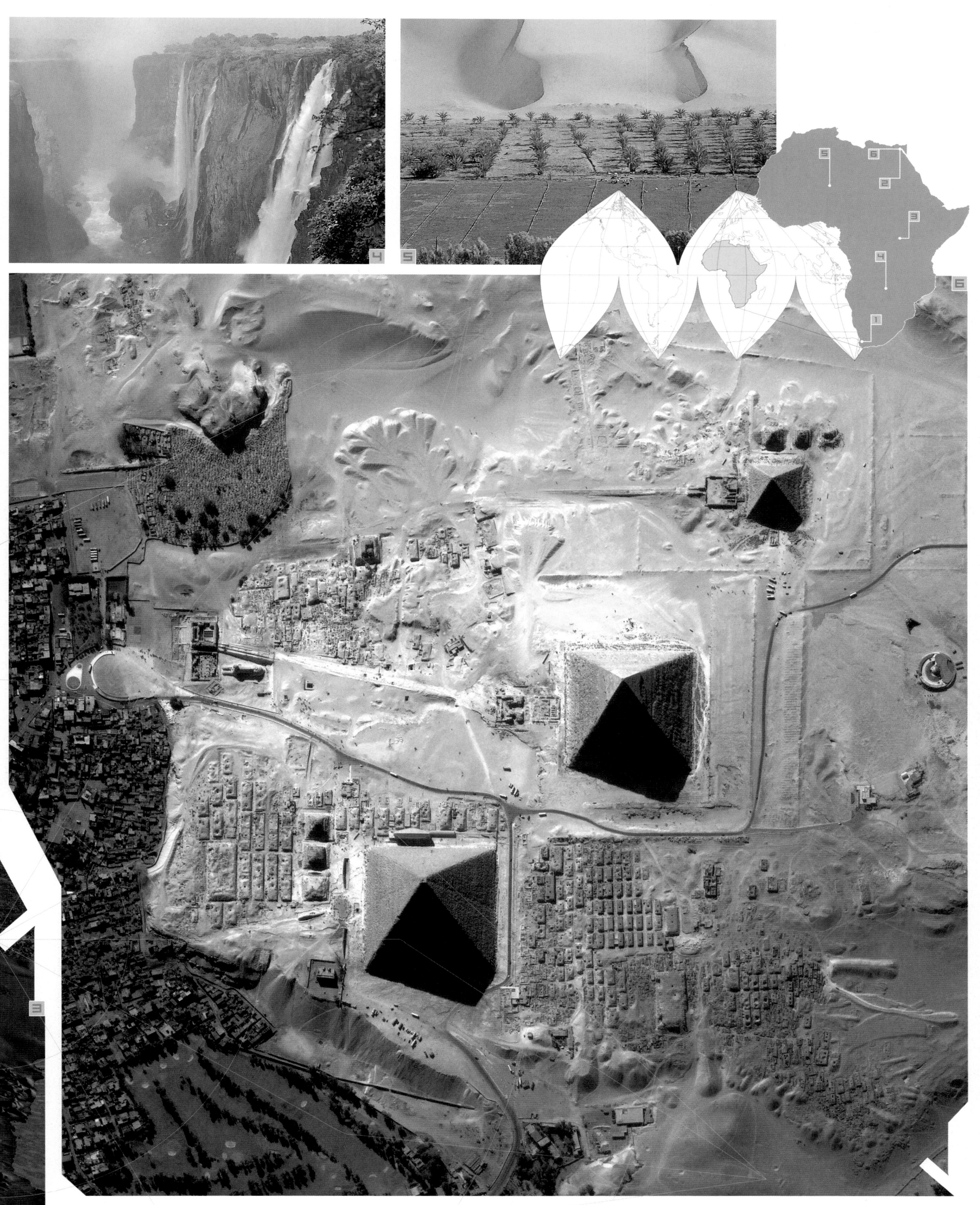

11°-34°N / 9°-44°E

122-123

126-127

>6000m
5000-6000m
4000-5000m
3000-4000m
2000-3000m
1000-2000m
500-1000m
200-500m
0-200m
<0m

0-200m
200-500m
500-1000m
1000-2000m
2000-3000m
3000-4000m
4000-5000m
5000-6000m
>6000m

Mediterranean Sea

Gulf of Sirte
(Khalīj Surt)

TUNISIA

TRIPOLI
(Tarābulus)

LIBYA

Sahara

ALGERIA

Tropic of Cancer

TRIPOLITANIA

CYRENAICA

Benghazi

Tubruq

AS SARĪR

Tibesti

NIGER

AGADEZ

DIFFA

ZINDER

Zinder

NIGERIA

JIGAWA

YOBE

BORNO

Lake Chad

NDJAMENA

CAMEROON

CHAD

KANEM

LAC

BATHA

BILTINE

BORKOU-ENNEDI-TIBESTI

Dépression du Mourdi

Erg du Djourab

BODÉLÉ

CHARI-BAGUIRMI

GUÉRA

SALAMAT

OUADDAÏ

WESTERN DARFUR

Marra Plateau

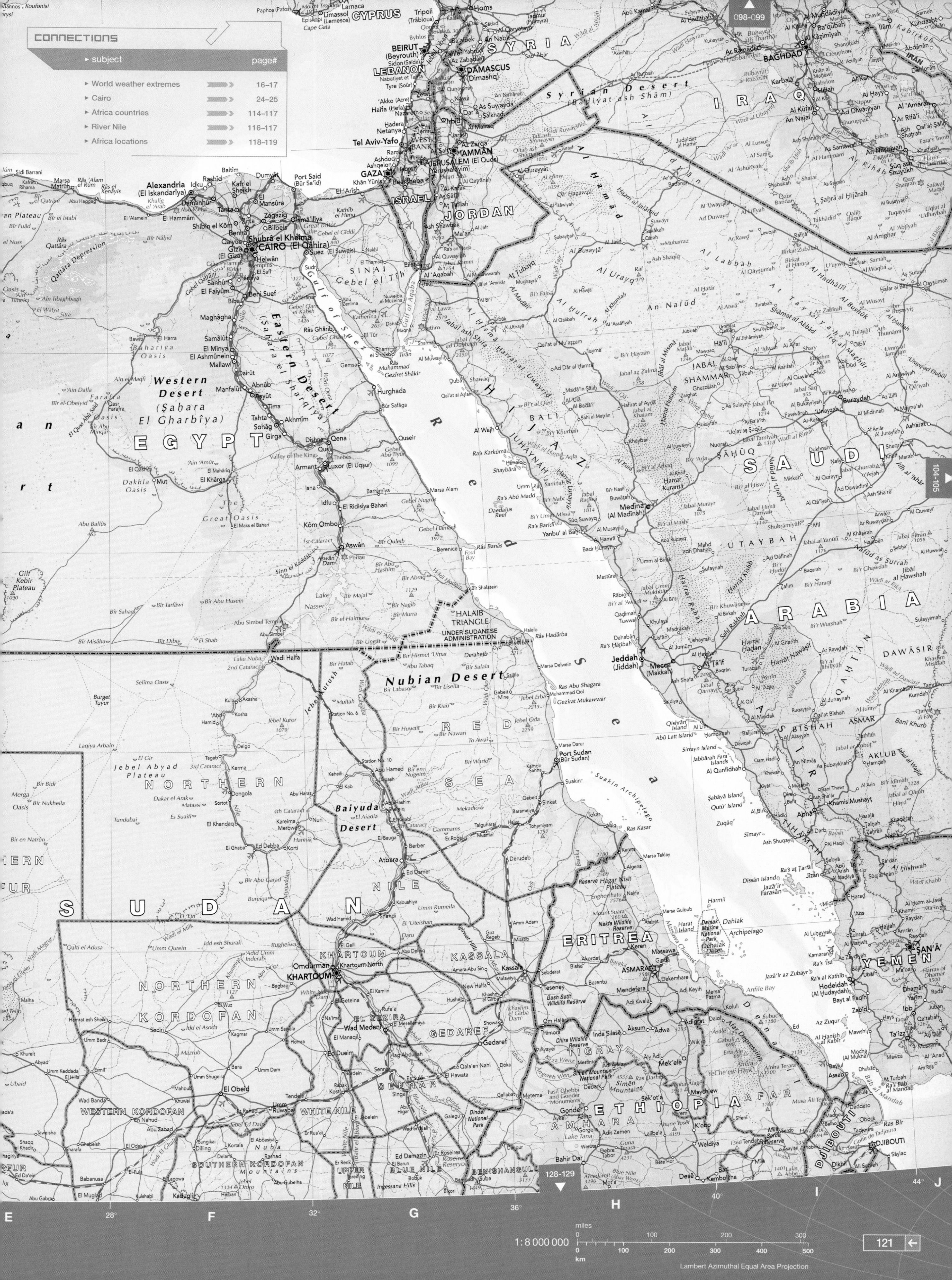

CONNECTIONS
subject
page#
World weather extremes 16–17
Cairo 24–25
Africa countries 114–117
River Nile 116–117
Africa locations 118–119
098-099
104-105
128-129
CYPRUS
SYRIA
LEBANON
BEIRUT (Beyrouth)
DAMASCUS (Dimashq)
Tel Aviv-Yafo
JERUSALEM (El Quds)
AMMAN
ISRAEL
JORDAN
GAZA
WEST BANK
IRAQ
BAGHDAD
IRAN
Syrian Desert (Badiyat ash Shām)
Alexandria (El Iskandarîya)
Port Said (Bûr Sa'îd)
CAIRO (El Qâhira)
Suez (El Suweis)
SINAI
Gulf of Suez
Gulf of Aqaba
Qattâra Depression
Western Desert (Şaḥara El Gharbîya)
Eastern Desert (Şaḥara el Sharqîya)
EGYPT
Luxor (El Uqşur)
Aswân
Lake Nasser
HALAIB TRIANGLE
UNDER SUDANESE ADMINISTRATION
Wadi Halfa
Nubian Desert
RED SEA
Port Sudan (Bûr Sudan)
Bayuda Desert
NORTHERN
NILE
SUDAN
KHARTOUM
Omdurman
Khartoum North
KASSALA
NORTHERN KORDOFAN
WESTERN KORDOFAN
SOUTHERN KORDOFAN
WHITE NILE
EL GEZIRA
SENNAR
GEDAREF
BLUE NILE
UPPER NILE
BENISHANGUL
Red Sea
ERITREA
ASMARA
Massawa
Dahlak Archipelago
TIGRAY
AMHARA
AFAR
ETHIOPIA
Lake Tana
Bahir Dar
Gonder
DJIBOUTI
YEMEN
SAN'A'
SAUDI ARABIA
Medina (Al Madinah)
Mecca (Makkah)
Jeddah (Jiddah)
HIJAZ
An Nafūd
JABAL SHAMMAR
ASIR
TIHAMAH
Farasān
28°
32°
36°
40°
44°
E
F
G
H
I
J
1: 8 000 000
miles
0
100
200
300
km
0
100
200
300
400
500
Lambert Azimuthal Equal Area Projection

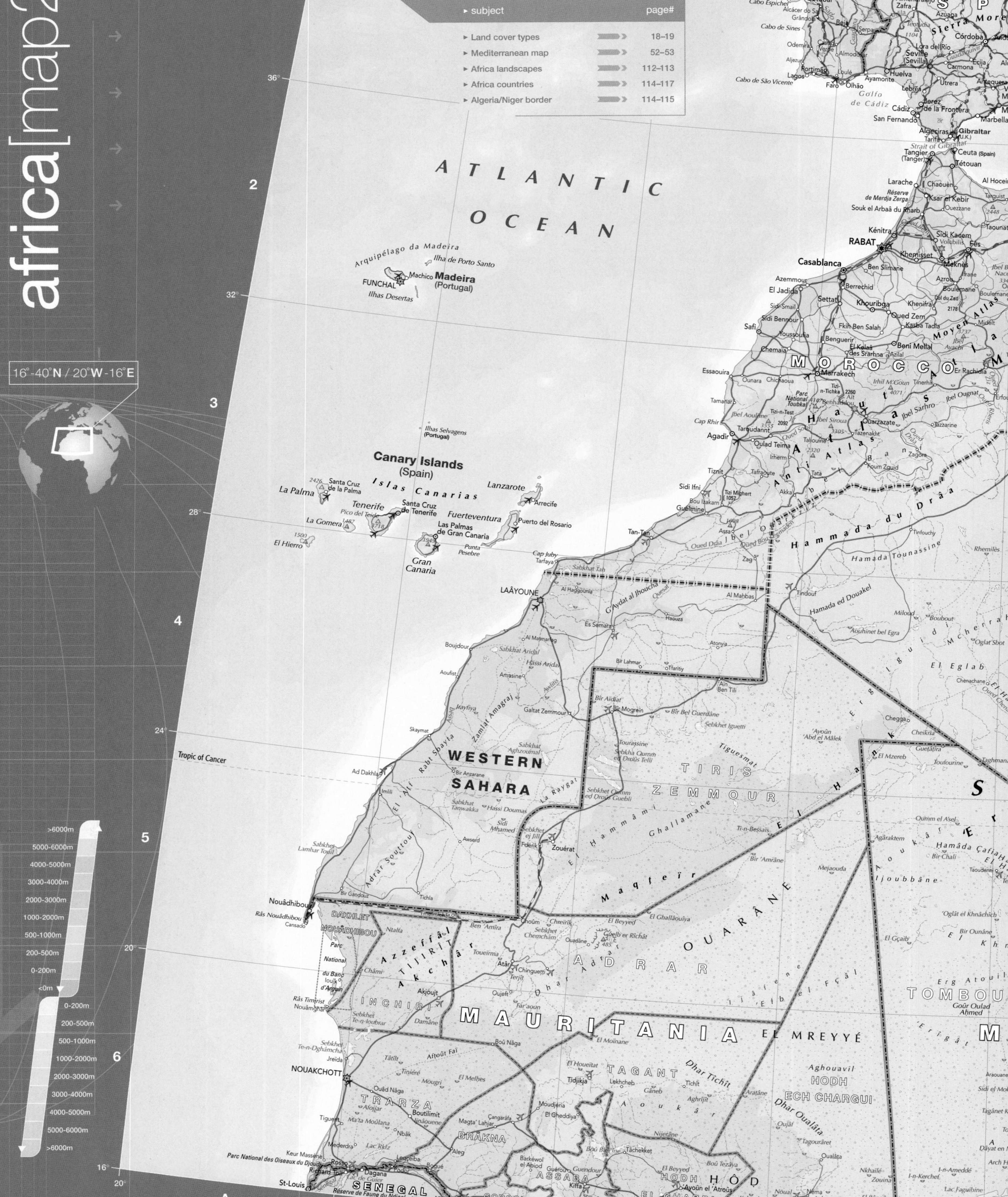

africa[map2]

16°-40°N / 20°W-16°E

CONNECTIONS

► subject   page#

► Land cover types   ➤ 18–19
► Mediterranean map   ➤ 52–53
► Africa landscapes   ➤ 112–113
► Africa countries   ➤ 114–117
► Algeria/Niger border   ➤ 114–115

ATLANTIC

OCEAN

Arquipélago da Madeira
Ilha de Porto Santo
Machico **Madeira**
FUNCHAL   (Portugal)
Ilhas Desertas

Ilhas Selvagens
(Portugal)

Canary Islands
(Spain)
Islas Canarias   Lanzarote
La Palma   Santa Cruz   Arrecife
de la Palma
Tenerife   Santa Cruz   Fuerteventura
La Gomera   de Tenerife   Puerto del Rosario
Pico del Teide   Las Palmas
El Hierro   de Gran Canaria
Punta
Pesebre
Gran
Canaria

PORTUGAL
LISBON
(Lisboa)

RABAT
Casablanca

MOROCCO

Agadir

WESTERN

SAHARA

LAÂYOUNE

Tropic of Cancer
Ad Dakhla

Nouâdhibou

NOUAKCHOTT

MAURITANIA

SENEGAL
St-Louis

>6000m
5000-6000m
4000-5000m
3000-4000m
2000-3000m
1000-2000m
500-1000m
200-500m
0-200m
<0m
0-200m
200-500m
500-1000m
1000-2000m
2000-3000m
3000-4000m
4000-5000m
5000-6000m
>6000m

1
2
3
4
5
6

36°
32°
28°
24°
20°
16°

A   B   C   D

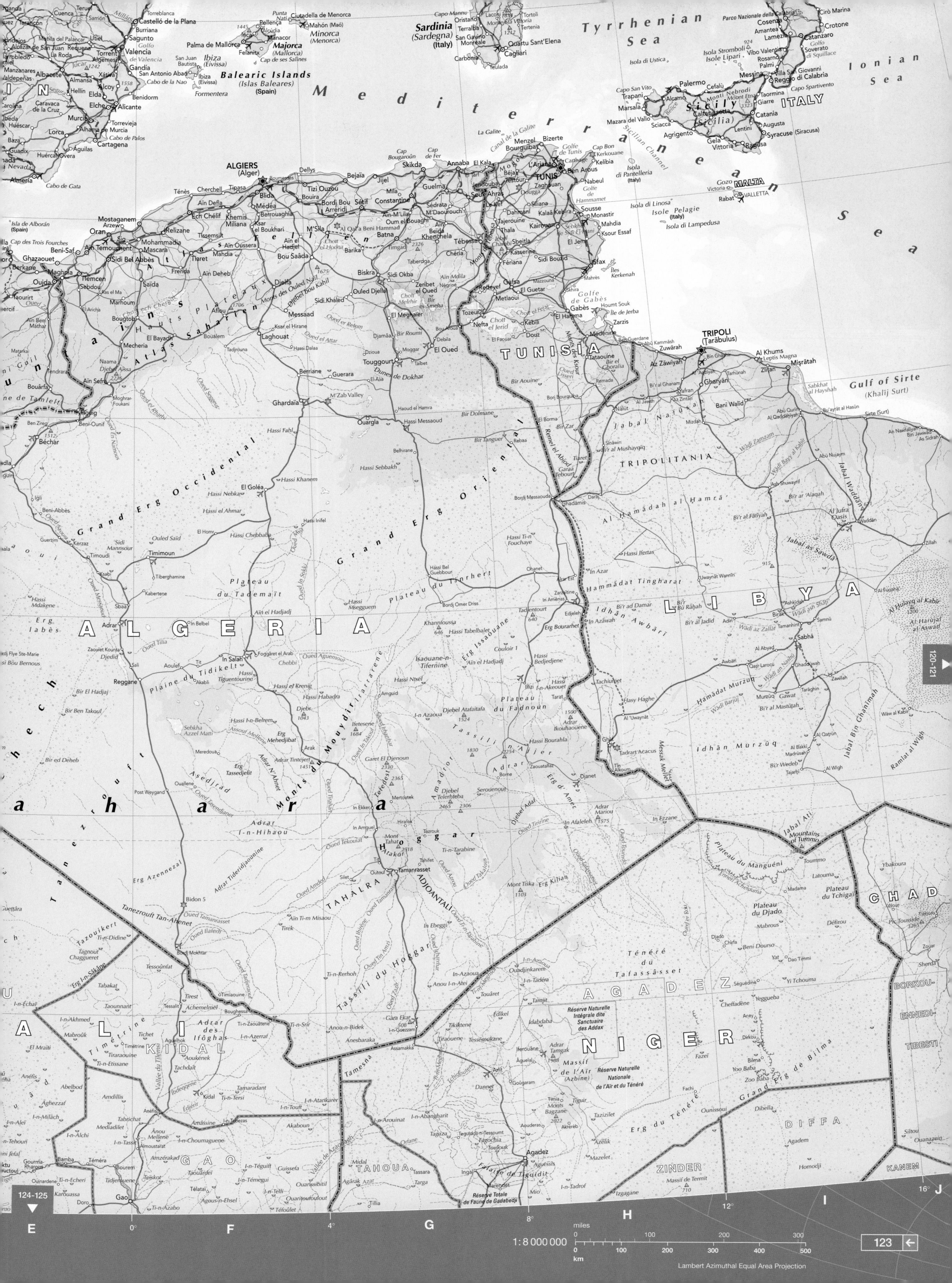

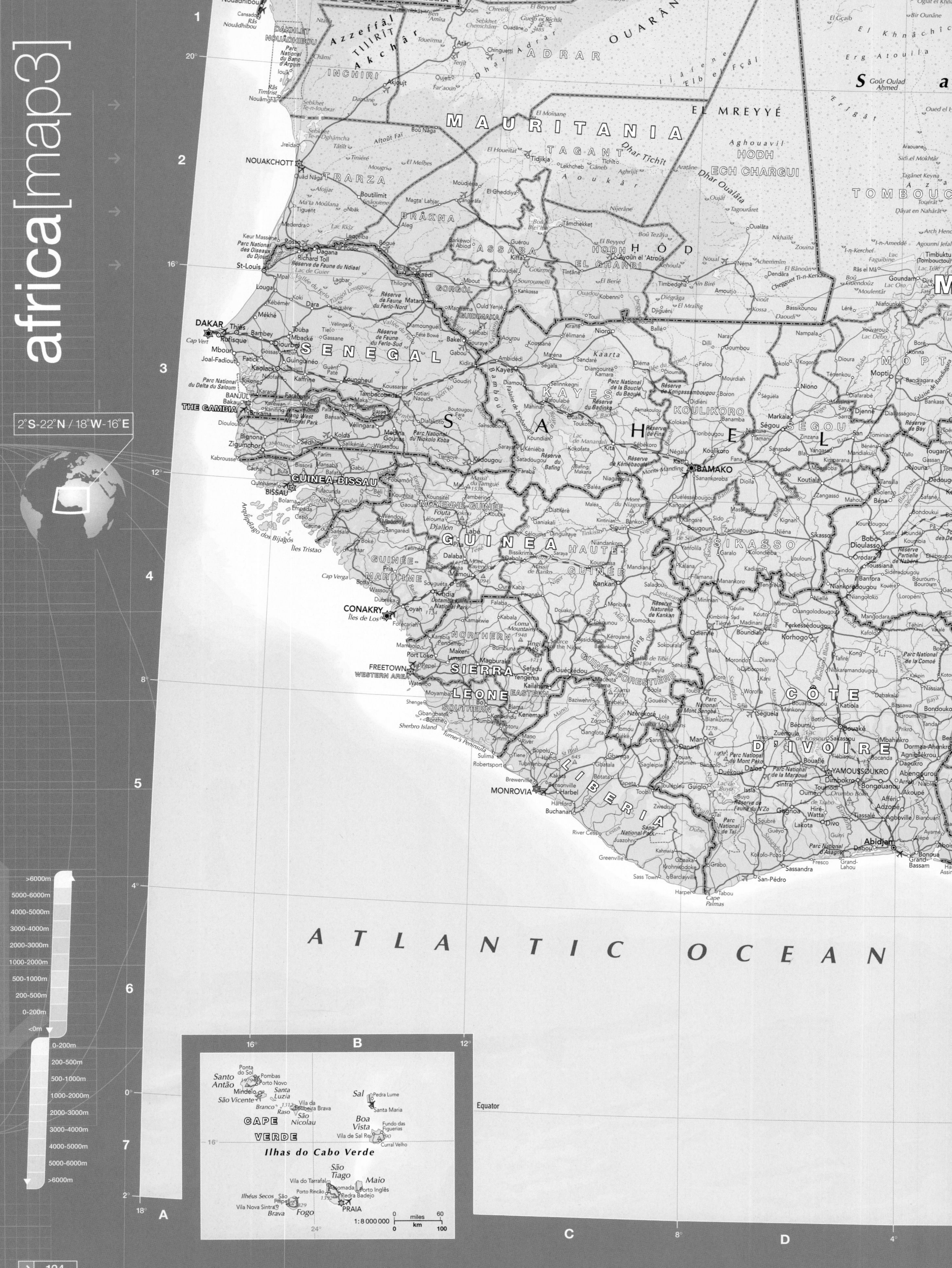

africa[map3]
2°S-22°N / 18°W-16°E
WESTERN SAHARA
MAURITANIA
NOUAKCHOTT
Nouâdhibou
DAKHLET NOUÂDHIBOU
INCHIRI
ADRAR
TAGANT
TRARZA
BRAKNA
ASSABA
GORGOL
GUIDIMAKA
HODH EL GHARBI
HODH ECH CHARGUI
OUARÂNE
EL MREYYÉ
TOMBOUCTOU
MOPTI
SÉGOU
KOULIKORO
KAYES
SIKASSO
BAMAKO
SAHEL
SENEGAL
DAKAR
St-Louis
THE GAMBIA
BANJUL
GUINEA-BISSAU
BISSAU
Arquipélago dos Bijagós
GUINEA
CONAKRY
GUINÉE-MARITIME
MOYENNE-GUINÉE
HAUTE-GUINÉE
GUINÉE-FORESTIÈRE
SIERRA LEONE
FREETOWN
WESTERN AREA
NORTHERN
EASTERN
SOUTHERN
LIBERIA
MONROVIA
CÔTE D'IVOIRE
YAMOUSSOUKRO
Abidjan
ATLANTIC OCEAN
Equator
CAPE VERDE
Ilhas do Cabo Verde
Santo Antão
São Vicente
Santa Luzia
São Nicolau
Sal
Boa Vista
Maio
São Tiago
Fogo
Brava
PRAIA
1:8 000 000
miles
km
>6000m
5000-6000m
4000-5000m
3000-4000m
2000-3000m
1000-2000m
500-1000m
200-500m
0-200m
<0m

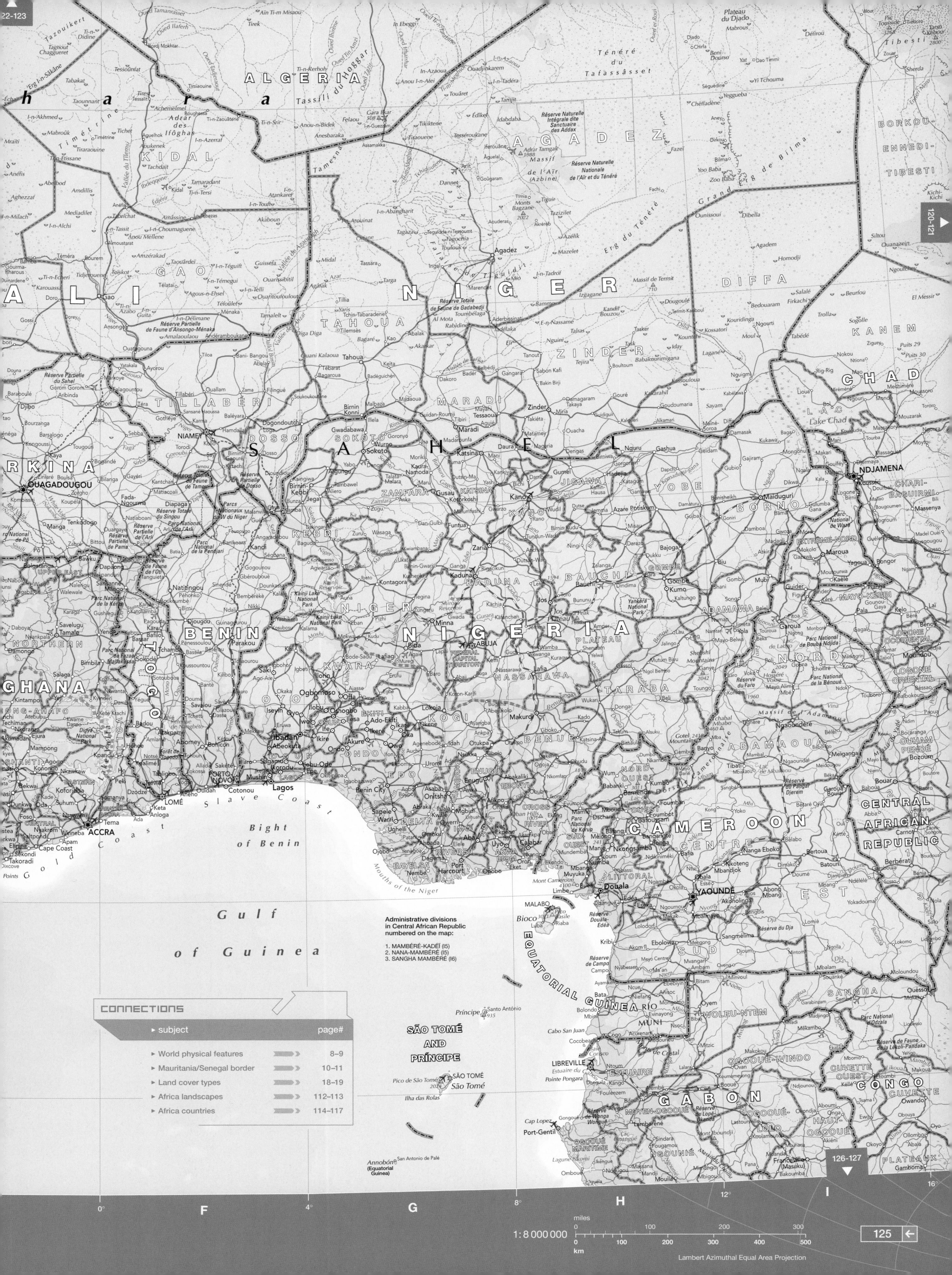

CONNECTIONS

Administrative divisions
in Central African Republic
numbered on the map:

1. MAMBÉRÉ-KADÉÏ (I5)
2. NANA-MAMBÉRÉ (I5)
3. SANGHA MAMBÉRÉ (I6)

Gulf

of Guinea

SÃO TOMÉ
AND
PRÍNCIPE

miles

100   200   300

km
100   200   300   400   500

1 : 8 000 000

Lambert Azimuthal Equal Area Projection

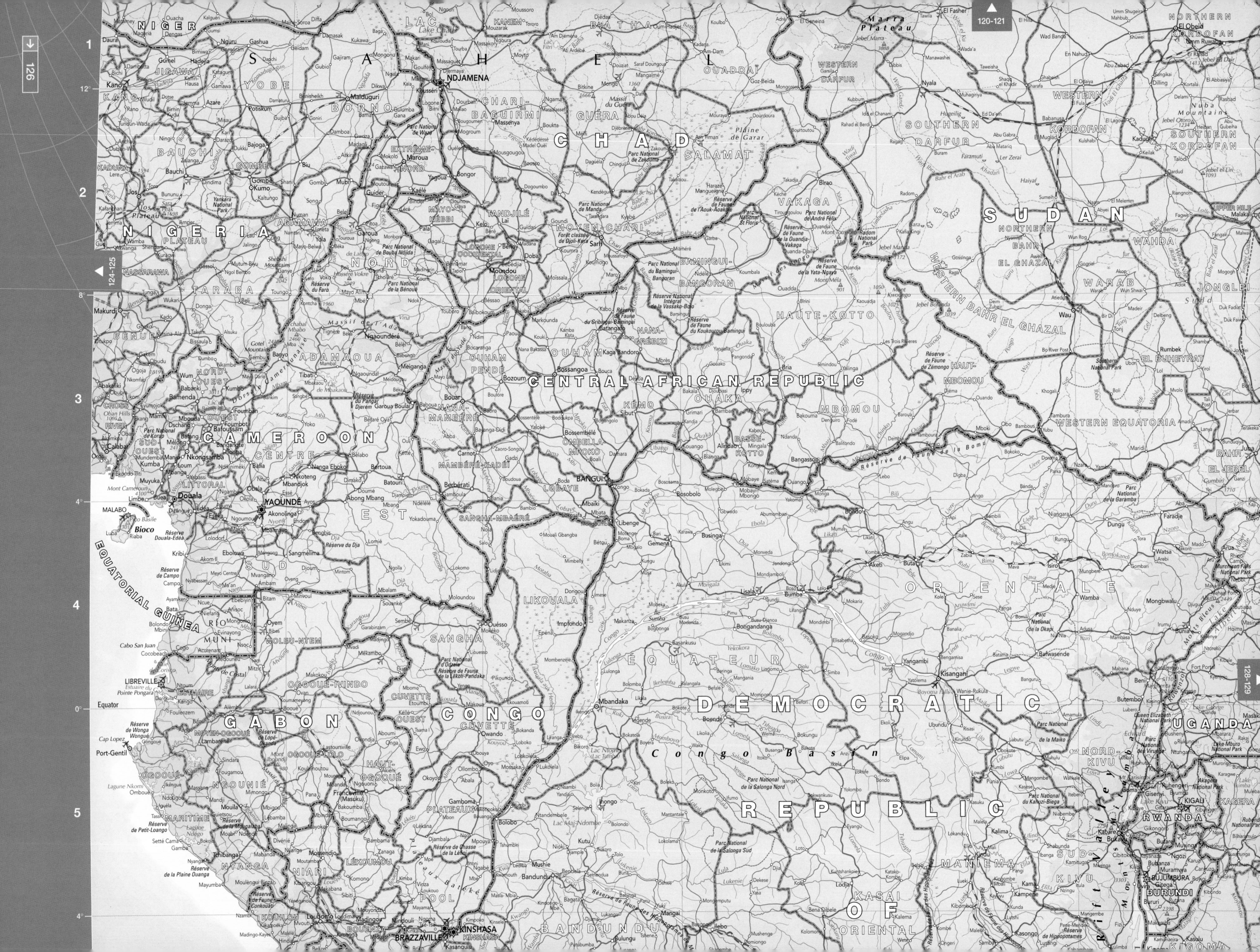

SUDAN
CHAD
CENTRAL AFRICAN REPUBLIC
DEMOCRATIC REPUBLIC OF
CONGO
GABON
CAMEROON
NIGERIA
EQUATORIAL GUINEA
UGANDA
RWANDA
BURUNDI
NDJAMENA
BANGUI
YAOUNDÉ
LIBREVILLE
MALABO
BRAZZAVILLE
KINSHASA
KIGALI
BUJUMBURA
120-121
124-125
128-129

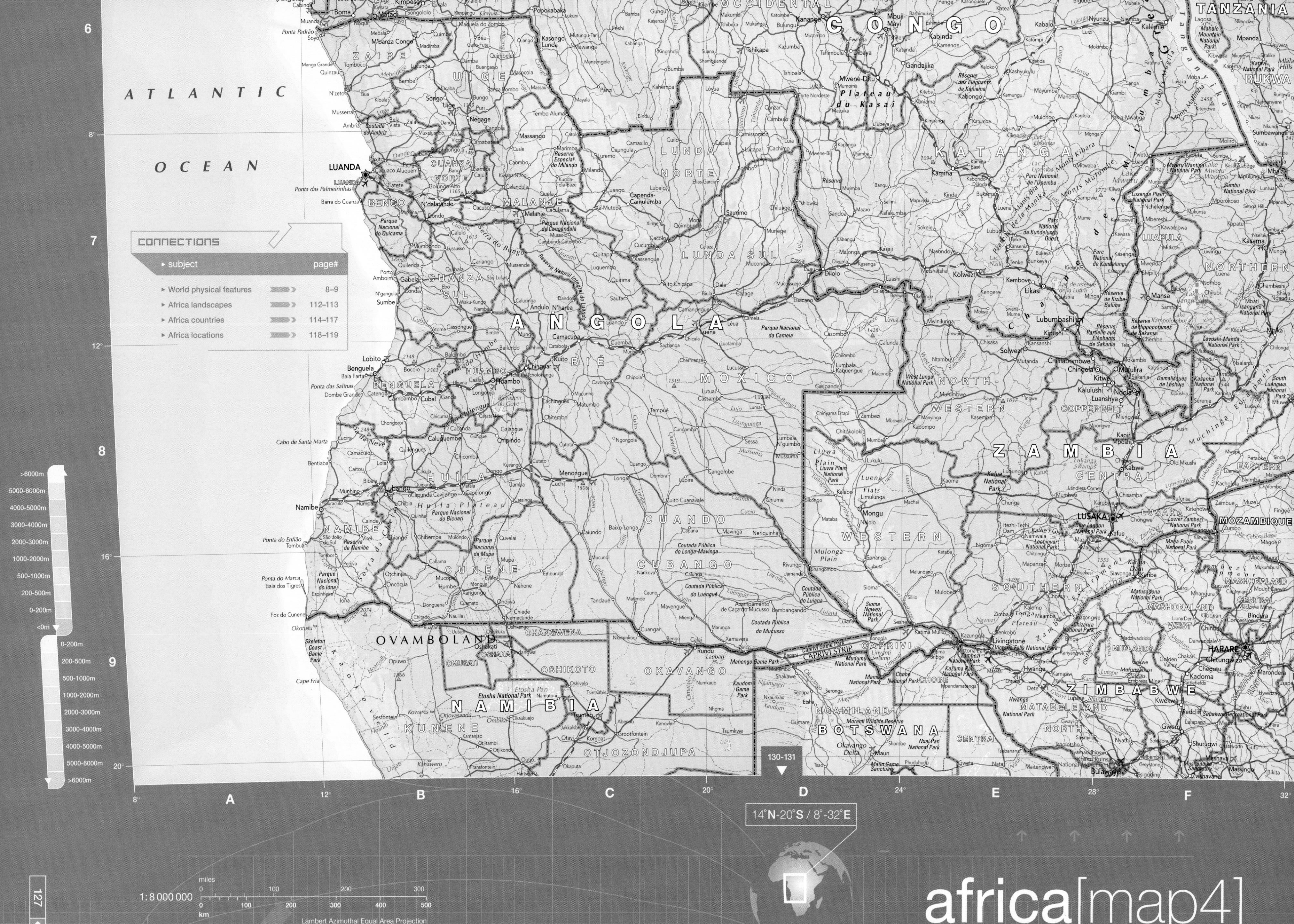

africa[map4]

14°N-20°S / 8°-32°E

130-131

1:8 000 000

Lambert Azimuthal Equal Area Projection

CONNECTIONS

► subject	page#
▲ World physical features	8–9
▲ Africa landscapes	112–113
▲ Africa countries	114–117
▲ Africa locations	118–119

>6000m
5000–6000m
4000–5000m
3000–4000m
2000–3000m
1000–2000m
500–1000m
200–500m
0–200m
<0m

ATLANTIC OCEAN

TANZANIA

CONGO OCCIDENTAL

KATANGA

ANGOLA

LUANDA

ZAMBIA

NAMIBIA

BOTSWANA

ZIMBABWE

MOZAMBIQUE

HARARE

BULAWAYO

LUSAKA

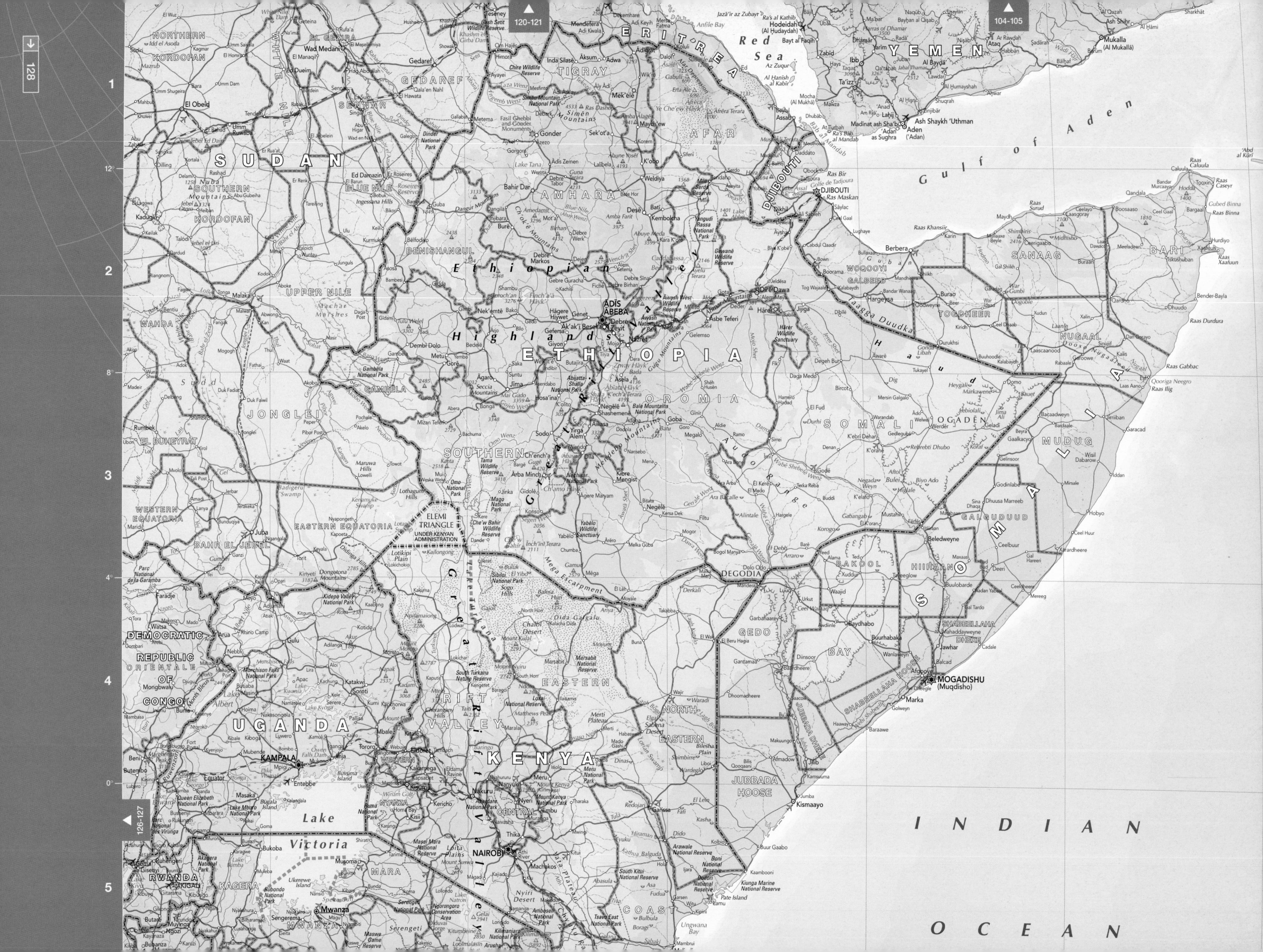

CONNECTIONS

▶ subject	page#
World weather extremes	16–17
Savanna land cover	18–19
Africa countries	114–117
Africa locations	118–119
Indian Ocean map	218–219

Administrative regions in Tanzania numbered on the map:

1. PEMBA NORTH (C6)
2. PEMBA SOUTH (C6)
3. ZANZIBAR NORTH (C6)
4. ZANZIBAR NORTH (C6)
5. ZANZIBAR WEST (C6)

1:8 000 000

18'S–16'N / 29–52'E

Lambert Azimuthal Equal Area Projection

miles / km scale: 100 200 300 400 500

Elevation legend:
>6000m
5000–6000m
4000–5000m
3000–4000m
2000–3000m
1000–2000m
500–1000m
200–500m
0–200m
<0m

130–131

Countries / regions labeled:
TANZANIA, ZAMBIA, MALAWI, MOZAMBIQUE, ZIMBABWE, MADAGASCAR, COMOROS, DEM. REP. CONGO

Selected labels:
Tabora, Dodoma, Dar es Salaam, Zanzibar Island, Pemba Island, Mafia Island, HARARE, LILONGWE, MORONI, MAYOTTE (France), ANTANANARIVO, Toamasina, Mahajanga, Nampula, Nacala, Pemba, Quelimane, Blantyre, Great Rift Valley, Lake Tanganyika, Lake Malawi, Mozambique Channel, Selous Game Reserve, Aldabra Islands (Seychelles), Farquhar Islands (Seychelles), Providence Atoll, St Pierre, Cosmoledo Atoll

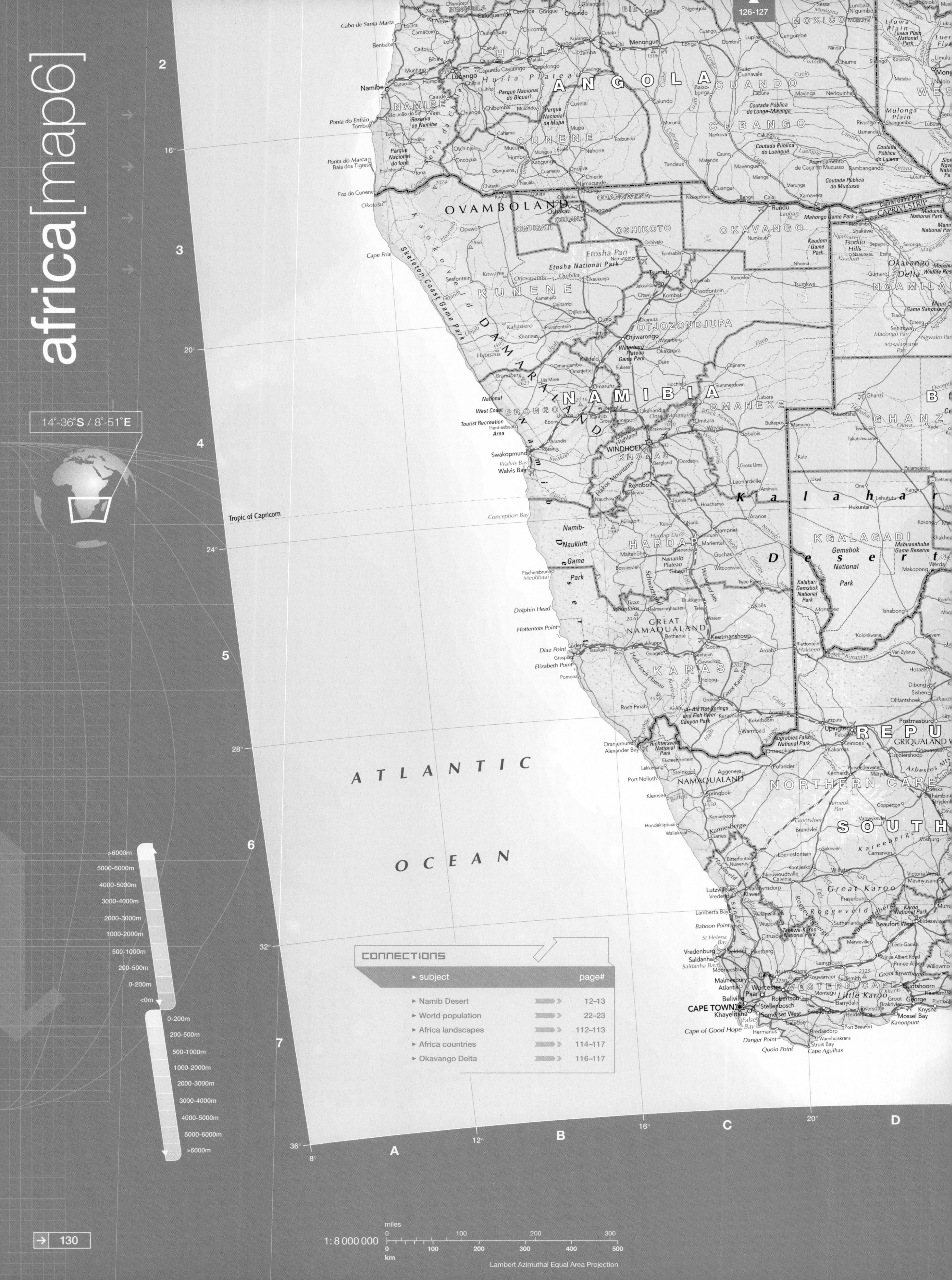

ATLANTIC

OCEAN

ANGOLA

NAMIBIA

Tropic of Capricorn

WINDHOEK

Swakopmund
Walvis Bay

CAPE TOWN
Cape of Good Hope

>6000m
5000-6000m
4000-5000m
3000-4000m
2000-3000m
1000-2000m
500-1000m
200-500m
0-200m
<0m

0-200m
200-500m
500-1000m
1000-2000m
2000-3000m
3000-4000m
4000-5000m
5000-6000m
>6000m

miles
100   200   300
1 : 8 000 000
km   100   200   300   400   500

Lambert Azimuthal Equal Area Projection

128-129

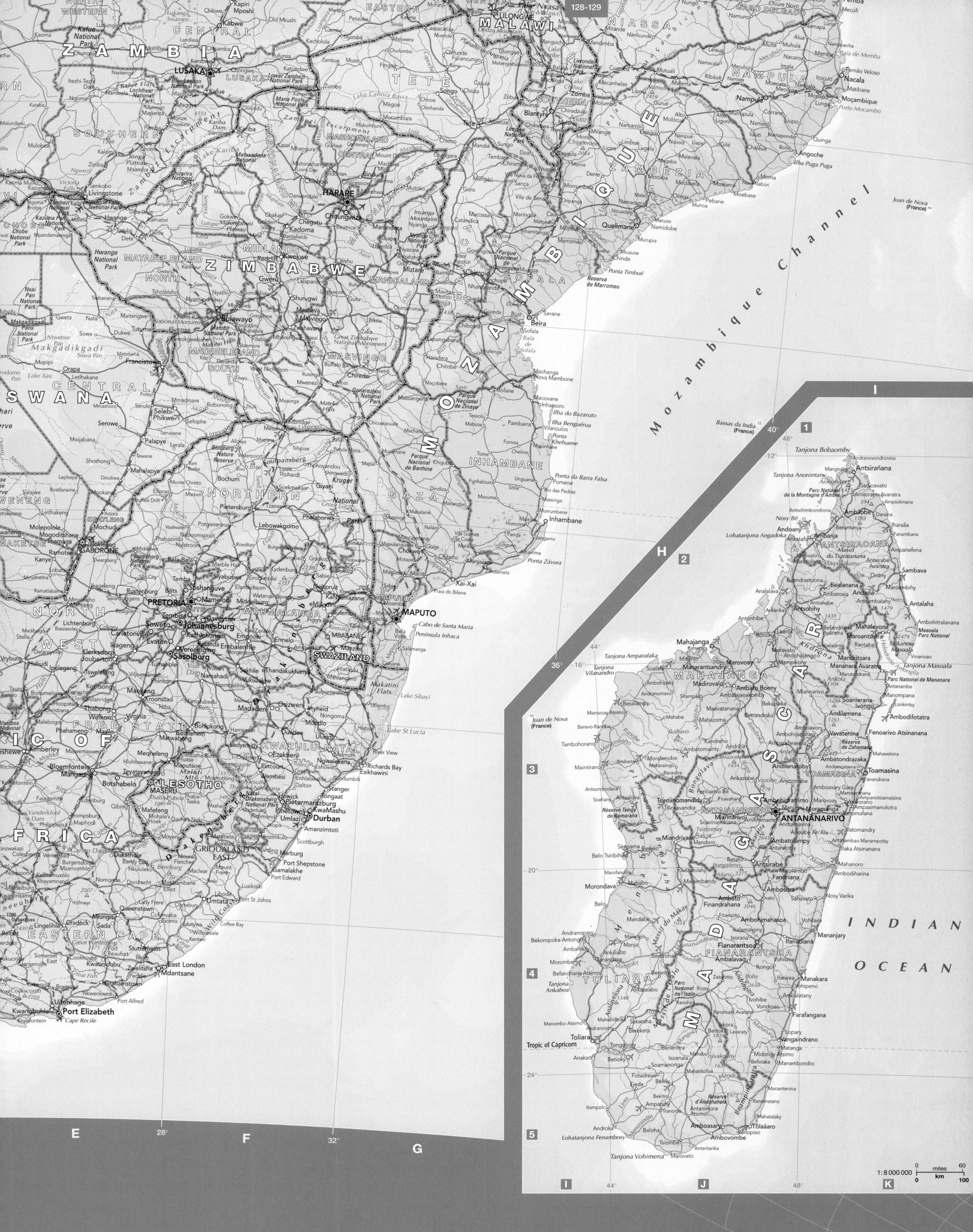
ZAMBIA
LUSAKA
MALAWI
LILONGWE
NIASSA
CABO DELGADO
NAMPULA
TETE
ZAMBEZIA
MOZAMBIQUE
MOZAMBIQUE
Mozambique Channel
HARARE
ZIMBABWE
MASHONALAND CENTRAL
MASHONALAND EAST
MASHONALAND WEST
MIDLANDS
MANICALAND
MASVINGO
MATABELELAND NORTH
MATABELELAND SOUTH
Bulawayo
SOFALA
Beira
INHAMBANE
Inhambane
GAZA
MAPUTO
Juan de Nova (France)
Bassas da India (France)
BOTSWANA
GABORONE
PRETORIA
Johannesburg
NORTHERN
NORTH WEST
MPUMALANGA
SWAZILAND
MBABANE
FREE STATE
KWAZULU NATAL
LESOTHO
MASERU
Durban
Pietermaritzburg
Richards Bay
Bloemfontein
SOUTH AFRICA
EASTERN CAPE
East London
Port Elizabeth
Kimberley
Mahajanga
MAHAJANGA
ANTSIRANANA
Antsirañana
TOAMASINA
Toamasina
ANTANANARIVO
FIANARANTSOA
Fianarantsoa
TOLIARA
Toliara
MADAGASCAR
Morondava
Tropic of Capricorn
INDIAN OCEAN
1:8 000 000
miles
km
E
F
G
H
I
J
K

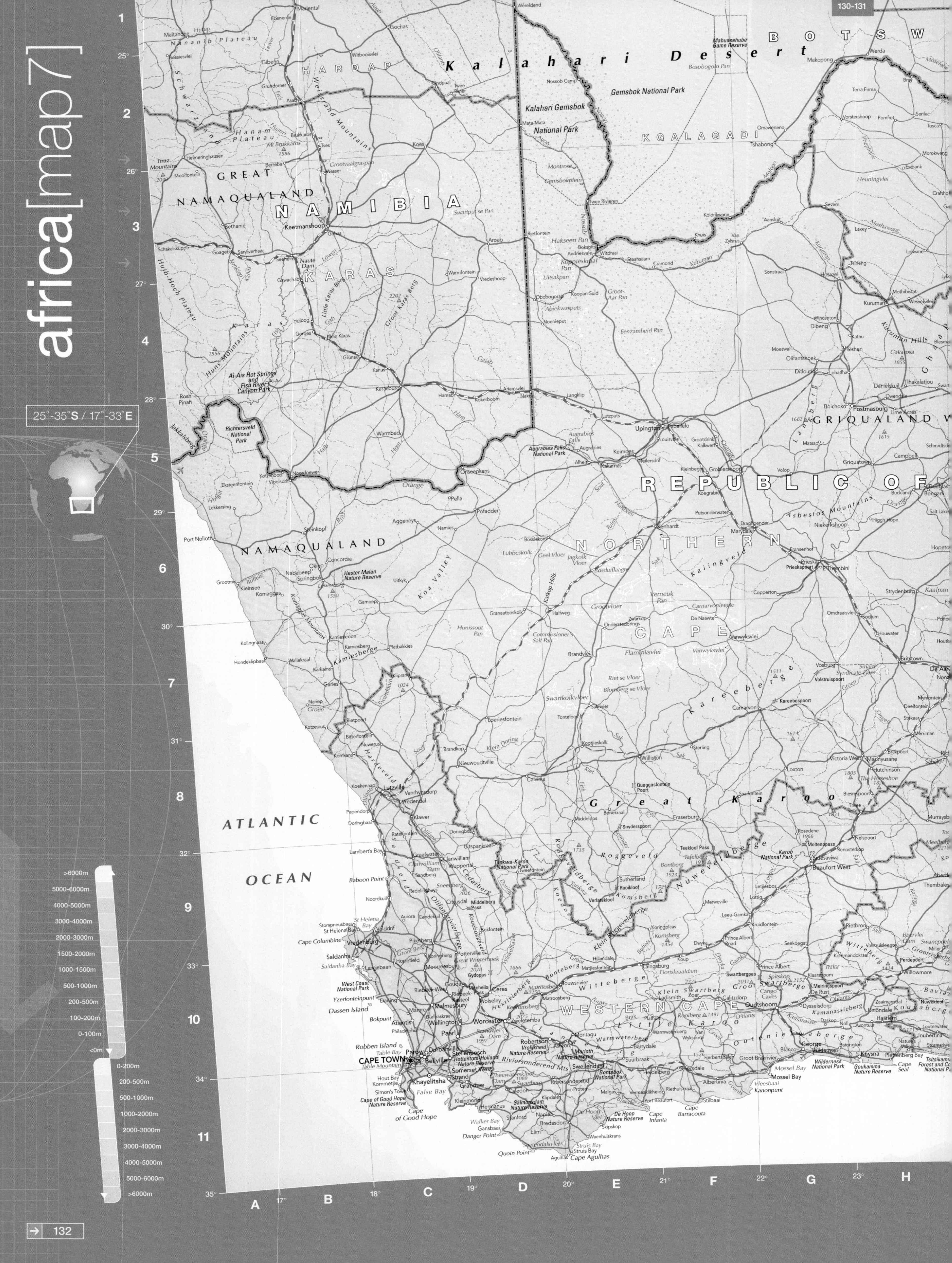

25°-35°S / 17°-33°E

>6000m
5000-6000m
4000-5000m
3000-4000m
2000-3000m
1500-2000m
1000-1500m
500-1000m
200-500m
100-200m
0-100m
<0m

0-200m
200-500m
500-1000m
1000-2000m
2000-3000m
3000-4000m
4000-5000m
5000-6000m
>6000m

ATLANTIC

OCEAN

Kalahari Desert

GREAT
NAMAQUALAND

NAMIBIA

HARDAP

KARAS

NAMAQUALAND

REPUBLIC OF

NORTHERN

CAPE

Great Karoo

WESTERN CAPE

Little Karoo

CAPE TOWN

BOTSW

KGALAGADI

GRIQUALAND

1
2
3
4
5
6
7
8
9
10
11

A B C D E F G H

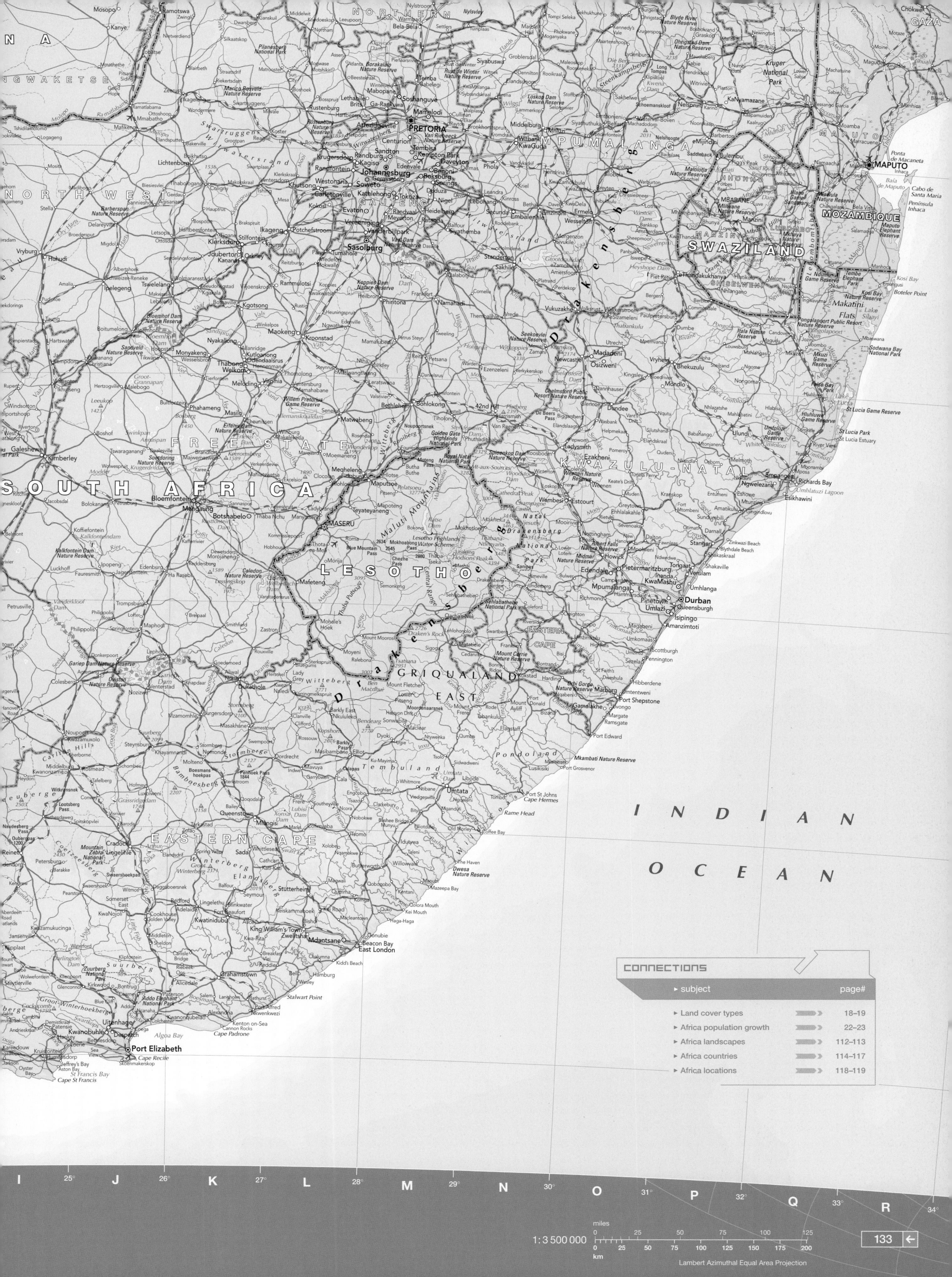

1 : 3 500 000

miles
0   25   50   75   100   125

km
0   25   50   75   100   125   150   175   200

Lambert Azimuthal Equal Area Projection

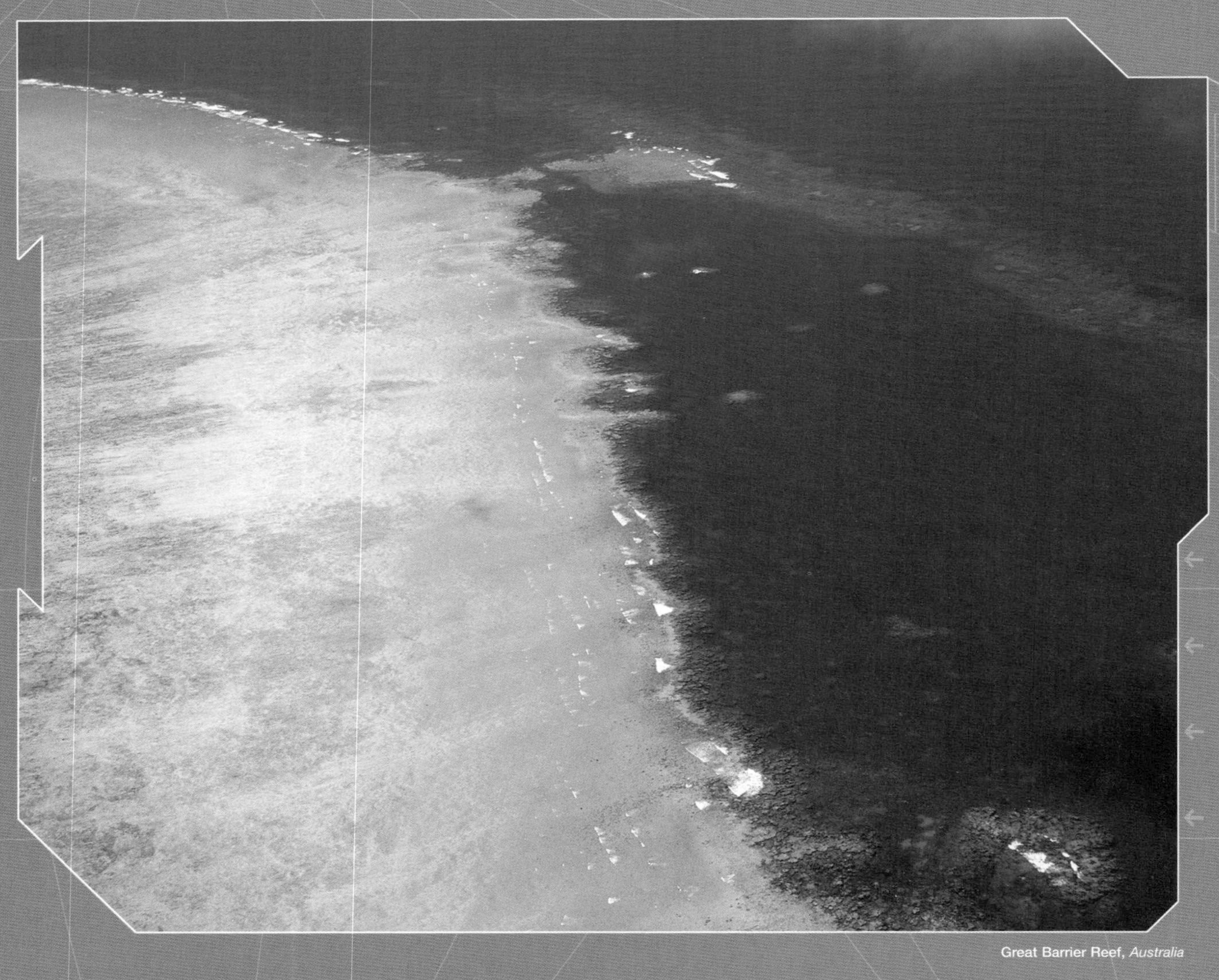

Great Barrier Reef, *Australia*

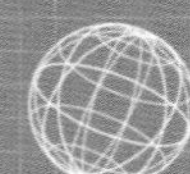

oceania

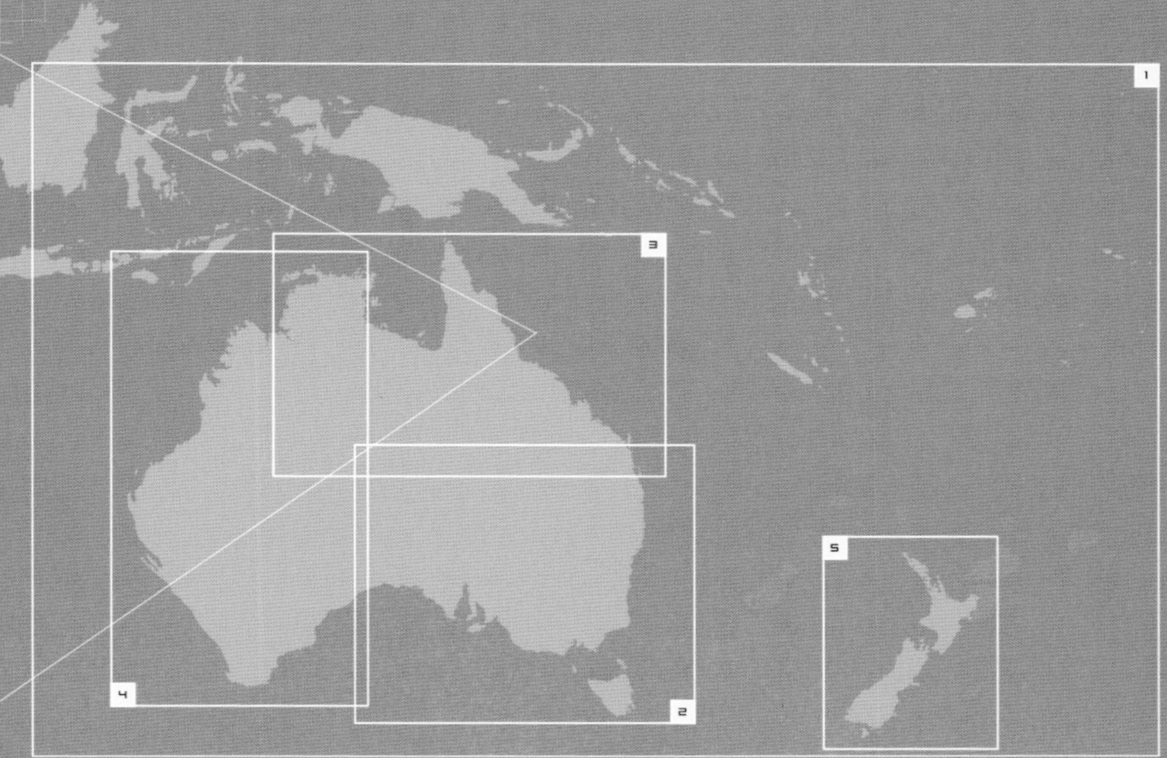

[contents]

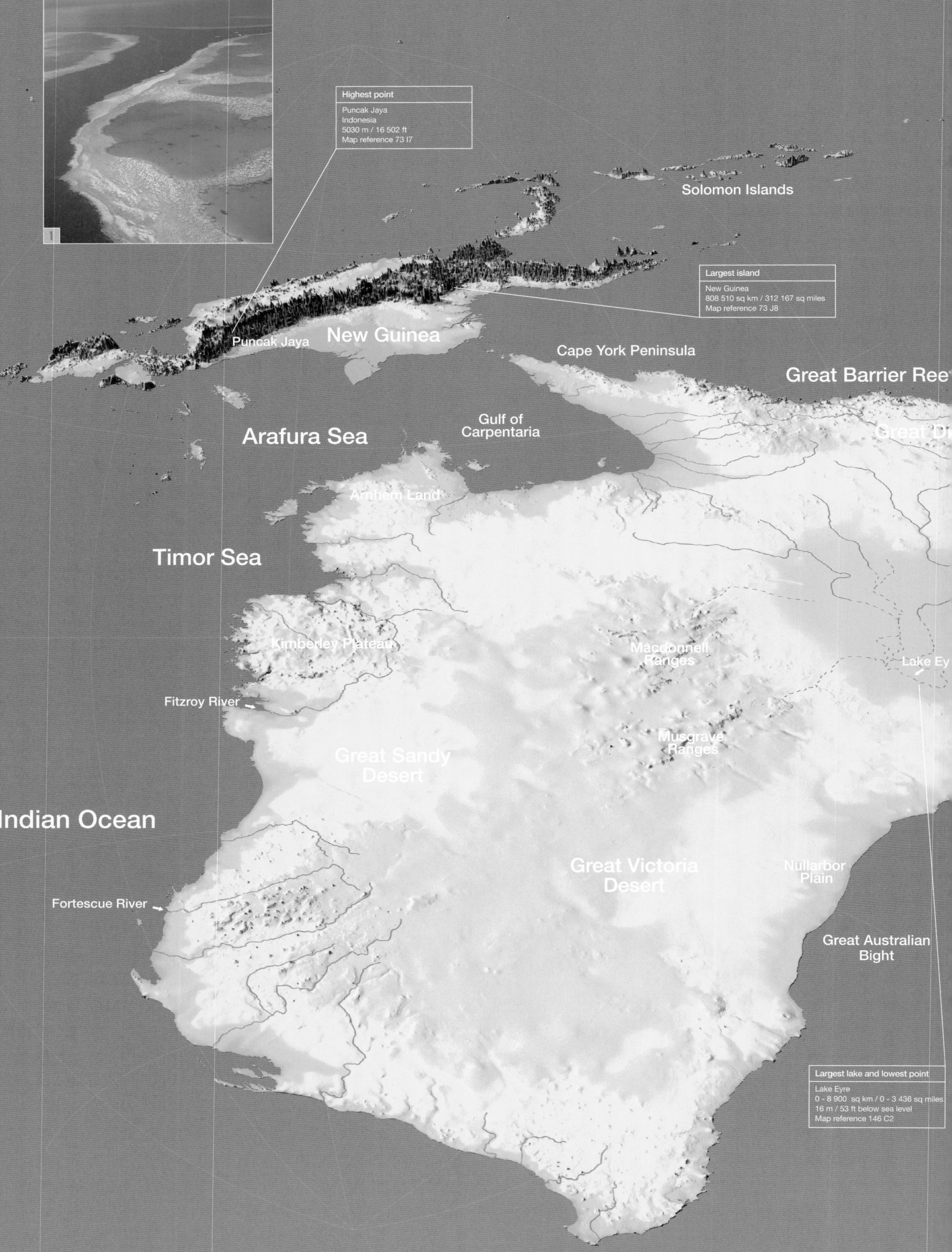

oceania[landscapes]

Solomon Islands

Puncak Jaya

New Guinea

Cape York Peninsula

Great Barrier Reef

Arafura Sea

Gulf of
Carpentaria

Great Di

Arnhem Land

Timor Sea

Kimberley Plateau

Macdonnell
Ranges

Lake Ey

Fitzroy River

Indian Ocean

Great Sandy
Desert

Musgrave
Ranges

Fortescue River

Great Victoria
Desert

Nullarbor
Plain

Great Australian
Bight

Fiji

New Caledonia

Coral Sea

Pacific Ocean

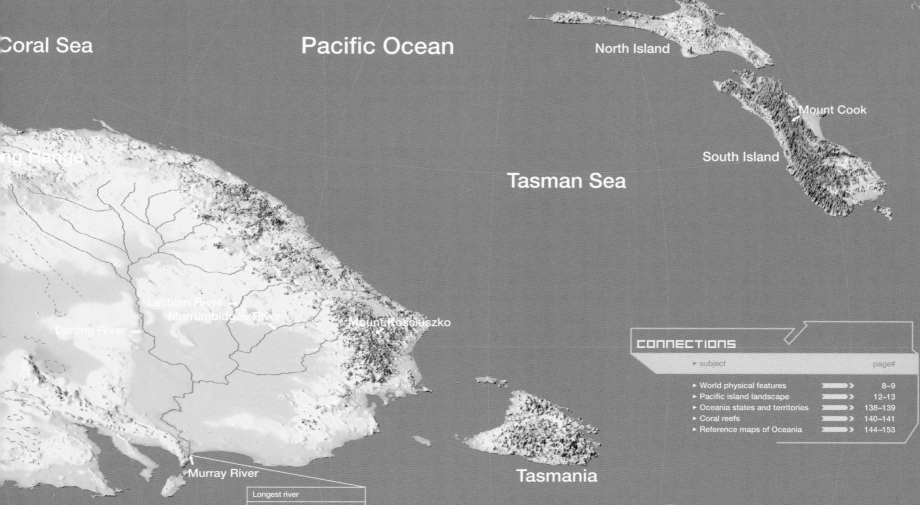

North Island

Mount Cook

South Island

Tasman Sea

ng Range

Lachlan River
Murrumbidgee River

Darling River

Mount Kosciuszko

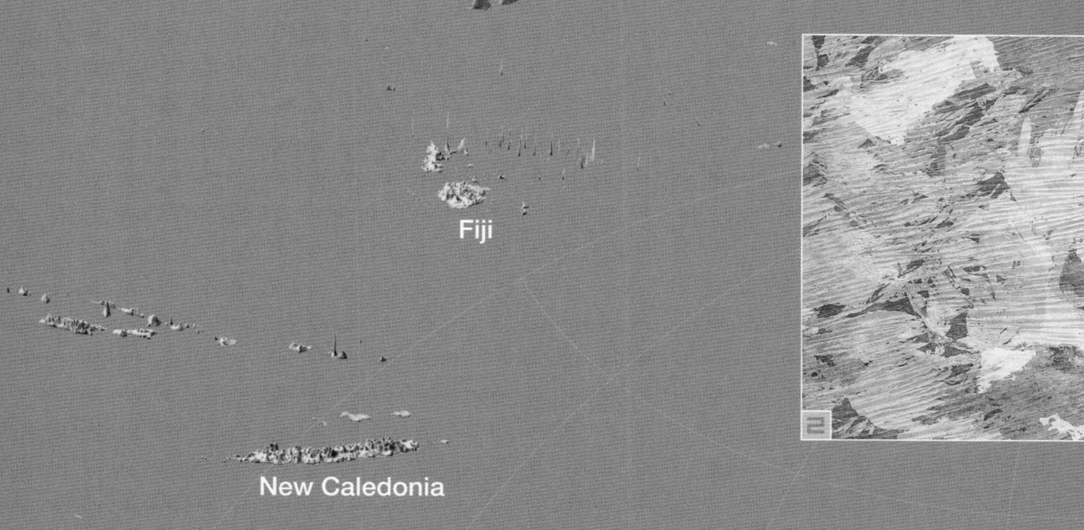

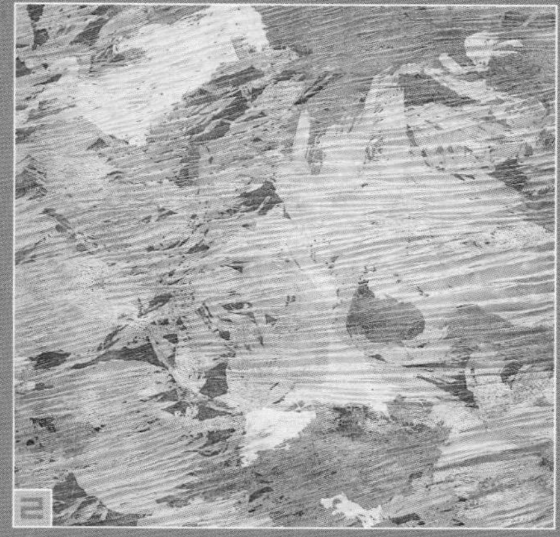

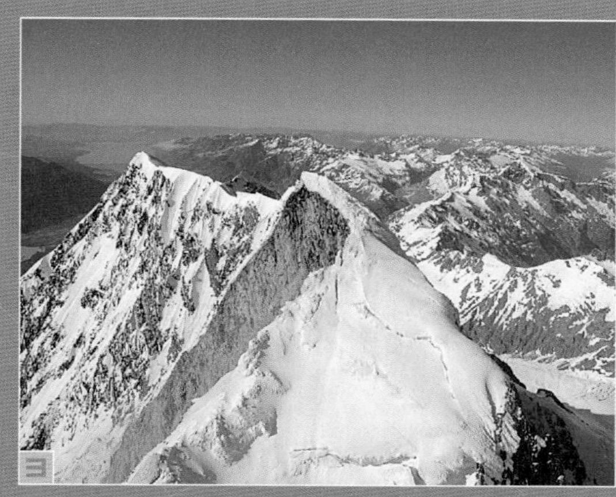

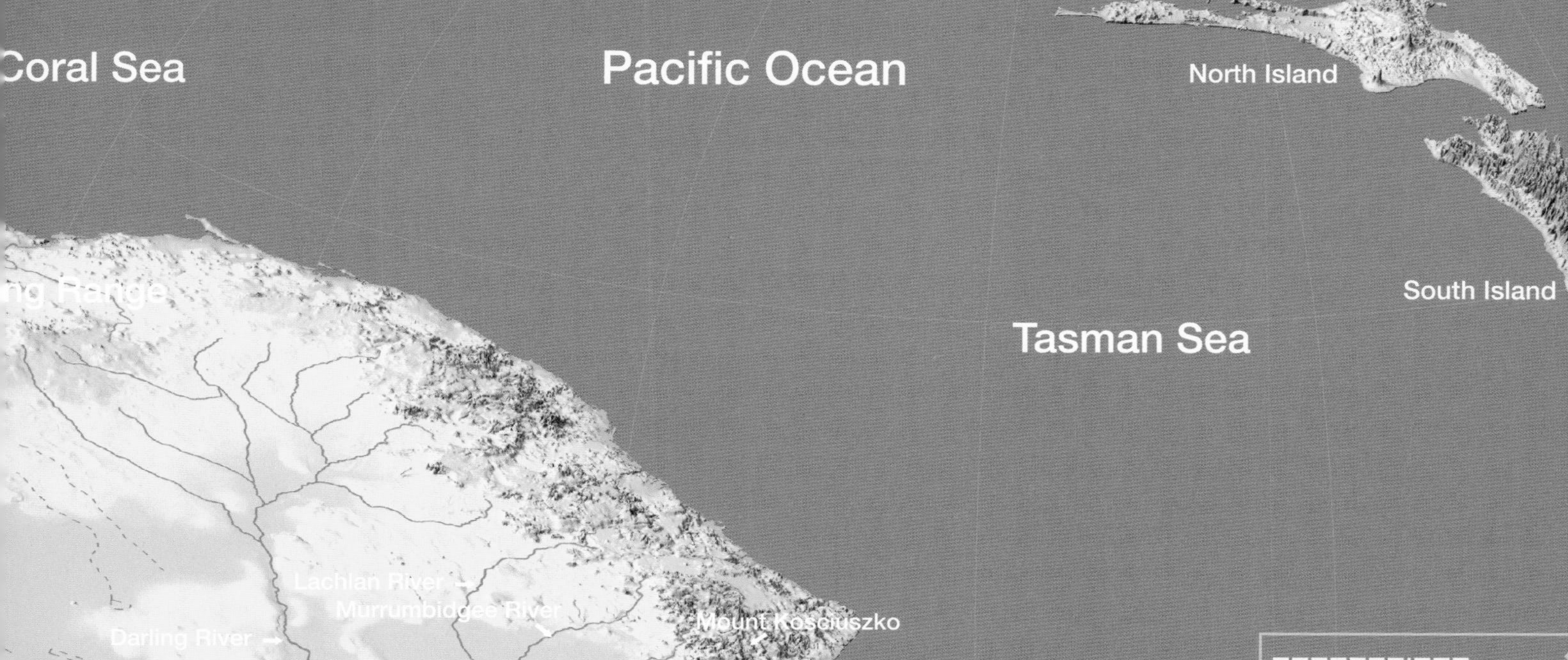

Murray River

Tasmania

Longest river
Murray-Darling
3 750 km / 2 330 miles
Map reference 146 C3

CONNECTIONS

▶ subject	page#
▶ World physical features	8–9
▶ Pacific island landscape	12–13
▶ Oceania states and territories	138–139
▶ Coral reefs	140–141
▶ Reference maps of Oceania	144–153

The continent of Oceania comprises Australia, the islands of New Zealand, New Guinea and numerous small islands and island groups in the Pacific Ocean, including Micronesia, Melanesia and Polynesia. The main landmass of Australia is largely desert, with many salt lakes and a low artesian basin in the east central area. The mountains of the Great Dividing Range run parallel to the east coast and are the source of the main river system, the Murray-Darling. The Great Barrier Reef, which stretches off the coast of Queensland, Australia, is the world's largest deposit of coral.

New Guinea is a mountainous island, most of which is covered with tropical forest. New Zealand has a great variety of landscape types, from tropical environments in the north of North Island to sub-Antarctic conditions in the south of South Island. North Island has extensive volcanic areas and South Island is mountainous, being dominated by the Southern Alps range.

1 Great Barrier Reef, *Australia*

This photograph shows the Great Barrier Reef which stretches for over 2 000 km off the coast of Queensland, Australia. This is the largest area of coral reefs in the world, and consists of a mixture of small islands, reefs and atolls. Whitsunday Island, shown here, is typical of the landscape. Beyond the reef is the Coral Sea.

2 Gibson Desert, *Australia*

The Gibson Desert in Western Australia has distinctive long, thin dune-like ridges which are covered with resilient desert grasses. The different coloured patches are due to a combination of seasonal new growth and fire damage. The dark areas on this image indicate the most recent summer fire outbreaks. The darkness fades as new growth appears.

Satellite/Sensor : SPOT

3 Mount Cook, *New Zealand*

Mount Cook on South Island, New Zealand is the highest peak in the country at 3 754 m. This photograph looks southeast towards Lake Pukaki, close to the horizon on the left. The peak is part of the Southern Alps mountain range and the National Park surrounding Mount Cook is designated a World Heritage area. The bare rock face below the summit resulted from a major avalanche in 1991 which reduced the height of the mountain by 20 m.

OCEANIA

HIGHEST MOUNTAINS

	m	ft	location	map
Puncak Jaya	5 030	16 502	Indonesia	73 I7
Puncak Trikora	4 730	15 518	Indonesia	73 I7
Puncak Mandala	4 700	15 420	Indonesia	73 J7
Puncak Yamin	4 595	15 075	Indonesia	73 I7
Mt Wilhelm	4 509	14 793	Papua New Guinea	73 J8
Mt Kubor	4 359	14 301	Papua New Guinea	73 J8

LARGEST ISLANDS

	sq km	sq miles	map
New Guinea	808 510	312 167	73 J8
South Island, New Zealand	151 215	58 384	153 F11
North Island, New Zealand	115 777	44 702	152 J6
Tasmania	67 800	26 178	147 E5

LONGEST RIVERS

	km	miles	map
Murray-Darling	3 750	2 330	146 C3
Darling	2 739	1 702	146 D3
Murray	2 589	1 608	146 C3
Murrumbidgee	1 690	1 050	147 E3
Lachlan	1 480	919	147 D3
Macquarie	950	590	147 E2

LAKES

	sq km	sq miles	map
Lake Eyre	0-8 900	0-3 436	146 C2
Lake Torrens	0-5 780	0-2 232	146 C2

LAND AREA

		map
Most northerly point	Eastern Island, North Pacific Ocean	220 H4
Most southerly point	Macquarie Island, South Pacific Ocean	220 F9
Most westerly point	Cape Inscription, Australia	151 A5
Most easterly point	Ile Clipperton, North Pacific Ocean	221 L5
Total land area: 8 844 516 sq km / 3 414 887 sq miles (includes New Guinea and Pacific Island nations)		

OCEANIA
COUNTRIES

		area sq km	area sq miles	population	capital	languages	religions	currency	map
AUSTRALIA		7 682 395	2 966 189	19 138 000	Canberra	English, Italian, Greek	Protestant, Roman Catholic, Orthodox	Dollar	144-145
FIJI		18 330	7 077	814 000	Suva	English, Fijian, Hindi	Christian, Hindu, Sunni Muslim	Dollar	145
KIRIBATI		717	277	83 000	Bairiki	Gilbertese, English	Roman Catholic, Protestant	Australian dollar	145
MARSHALL ISLANDS		181	70	51 000	Delap-Uliga-Djarrit	English, Marshallese	Protestant, Roman Catholic	US dollar	220
MICRONESIA, FEDERATED STATES OF		701	271	123 000	Palikir	English, Chuukese, Pohnpeian, local languages	Roman Catholic, Protestant	US dollar	220
NAURU		21	8	12 000	Yaren	Nauruan, English	Protestant, Roman Catholic	Australian dollar	145
NEW ZEALAND		270 534	104 454	3 778 000	Wellington	English, Maori	Protestant, Roman Catholic	Dollar	152-153
PAPUA NEW GUINEA		462 840	178 704	4 809 000	Port Moresby	English, Tok Pisin (creole), local languages	Protestant, Roman Catholic, traditional beliefs	Kina	144-145
SAMOA		2 831	1 093	159 000	Apia	Samoan, English	Protestant, Roman Catholic	Tala	145
SOLOMON ISLANDS		28 370	10 954	447 000	Honiara	English, creole, local languages	Protestant, Roman Catholic	Dollar	145
TONGA		748	289	99 000	Nuku'alofa	Tongan, English	Protestant, Roman Catholic	Pa'anga	145
TUVALU		25	10	11 000	Vaiaku	Tuvaluan, English	Protestant	Dollar	145
VANUATU		12 190	4 707	197 000	Port Vila	English, Bislama (creole), French	Protestant, Roman Catholic, traditional beliefs	Vatu	145

DEPENDENT TERRITORIES

		territorial status	area sq km	area sq miles	population	capital	languages	religions	currency	map
American Samoa		United States Unincorporated Territory	197	76	68 000	Fagatoga	Samoan, English	Protestant, Roman Catholic	US dollar	145
Ashmore and Cartier Islands		Australian External Territory	5	2	uninhabited					150
Baker Island		United States Unincorporated Territory	1	0.4	uninhabited					145
Cook Islands		Self-governing New Zealand Territory	293	113	20 000	Avarua	English, Maori	Protestant, Roman Catholic	Dollar	221
Coral Sea Islands Territory		Australian External Territory	22	8	uninhabited					145
French Polynesia		French Overseas Territory	3 265	1 261	233 000	Papeete	French, Tahitian, Polynesian languages	Protestant, Roman Catholic	Pacific franc	221
Guam		United States Unincorporated Territory	541	209	155 000	Agana	Chamorro, English, Tapalog	Roman Catholic	US dollar	73
Howland Island		United States Unincorporated Territory	2	1	uninhabited					145
Jarvis Island		United States Unincorporated Territory	5	2	uninhabited					221
Johnston Atoll		United States Unincorporated Territory	3	1	uninhabited					221
Kingman Reef		United States Unincorporated Territory	1	0.4	uninhabited					221
Midway Islands		United States Unincorporated Territory	6	2	uninhabited					220
New Caledonia		French Overseas Territory	19 058	7 358	215 000	Nouméa	French, local	Roman Catholic, Protestant, Sunni Muslim	Pacific franc	145
Niue		Self-governing New Zealand Overseas Territory	258	100	2 000	Alofi	English, Polynesian	Christian	NZ dollar	145
Norfolk Island		Australian External Territory	35	14	2 000	Kingston	English	Protestant, Roman Catholic	Australian Dollar	145
Northern Mariana Islands		United States Commonwealth	477	184	73 000	Capitol Hill	English, Chamorro, local languages	Roman Catholic	US dollar	73
Palmyra Atoll		United States Unincorporated Territory	12	5	uninhabited					221
Pitcairn Islands		United Kingdom Overseas Territory	45	17	68	Adamstown	English	Protestant	NZ dollar	221
Tokelau		New Zealand Overseas Territory	10	4	1 000		English, Tokelauan	Christian	NZ dollar	145
Wake Island		United States Unincorporated Territory	7	3	uninhabited					220
Wallis and Futuna Islands		French Overseas Territory	274	106	14 000	Matā'utu	French, Wallisian, Futunian	Roman Catholic	Pacific franc	145

Equator

Timor Sea

Barrow I.

North West Cape

Tropic of Capricorn

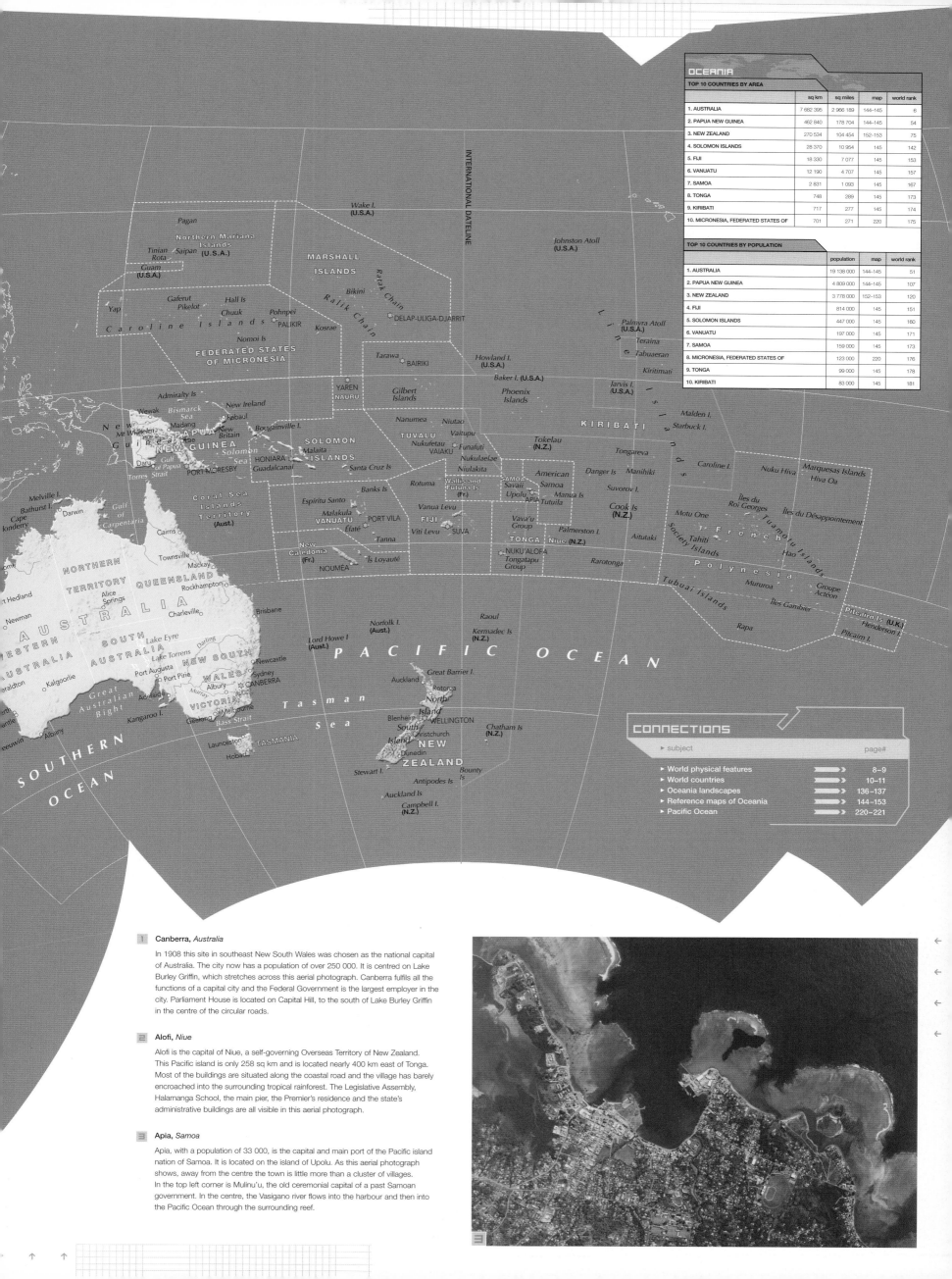

► World physical features   8–9
► World countries   10–11
► Oceania landscapes   136–137
► Reference maps of Oceania   144–153
► Pacific Ocean   220–221

OCEANIA

TOP 10 COUNTRIES BY AREA

	sq km	sq miles	map	world rank
1. AUSTRALIA	7 682 395	2 966 189	144–145	6
2. PAPUA NEW GUINEA	462 840	178 704	144–145	54
3. NEW ZEALAND	270 534	104 454	152–153	75
4. SOLOMON ISLANDS	28 370	10 954	145	142
5. FIJI	18 330	7 077	145	153
6. VANUATU	12 190	4 707	145	157
7. SAMOA	2 831	1 093	145	167
8. TONGA	748	289	145	173
9. KIRIBATI	717	277	145	174
10. MICRONESIA, FEDERATED STATES OF	701	271	220	175

TOP 10 COUNTRIES BY POPULATION

	population	map	world rank
1. AUSTRALIA	19 138 000	144–145	51
2. PAPUA NEW GUINEA	4 809 000	144–145	107
3. NEW ZEALAND	3 778 000	152–153	120
4. FIJI	814 000	145	151
5. SOLOMON ISLANDS	447 000	145	160
6. VANUATU	197 000	145	171
7. SAMOA	159 000	145	173
8. MICRONESIA, FEDERATED STATES OF	123 000	220	176
9. TONGA	99 000	145	178
10. KIRIBATI	83 000	145	181

CONNECTIONS

1   Canberra, *Australia*

In 1908 this site in southeast New South Wales was chosen as the national capital of Australia. The city now has a population of over 250 000. It is centred on Lake Burley Griffin, which stretches across this aerial photograph. Canberra fulfils all the functions of a capital city and the Federal Government is the largest employer in the city. Parliament House is located on Capital Hill, to the south of Lake Burley Griffin in the centre of the circular roads.

2   Alofi, *Niue*

Alofi is the capital of Niue, a self-governing Overseas Territory of New Zealand. This Pacific island is only 258 sq km and is located nearly 400 km east of Tonga. Most of the buildings are situated along the coastal road and the village has barely encroached into the surrounding tropical rainforest. The Legislative Assembly, Halamanga School, the main pier, the Premier's residence and the state's administrative buildings are all visible in this aerial photograph.

3   Apia, *Samoa*

Apia, with a population of 33 000, is the capital and main port of the Pacific island nation of Samoa. It is located on the island of Upolu. As this aerial photograph shows, away from the centre the town is little more than a cluster of villages. In the top left corner is Mulinu'u, the old ceremonial capital of a past Samoan government. In the centre, the Vasigano river flows into the harbour and then into the Pacific Ocean through the surrounding reef.

oceania[threats]

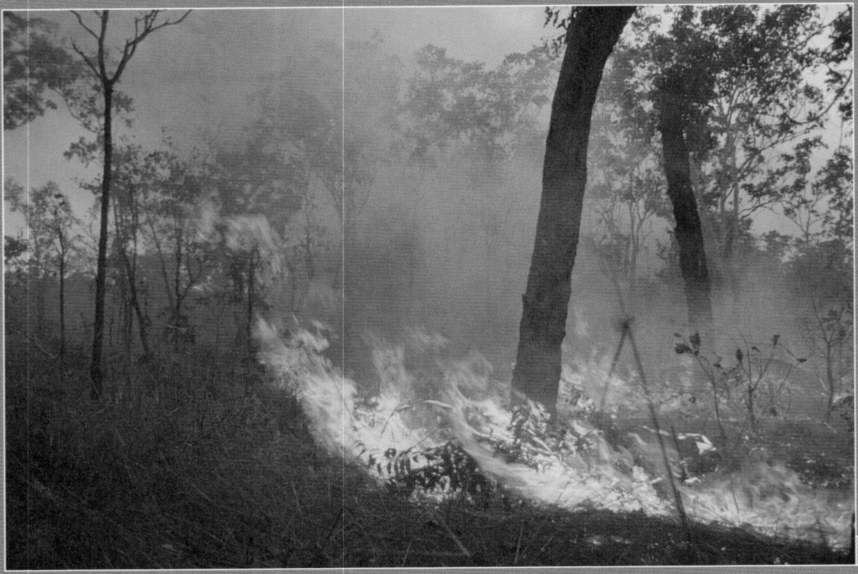

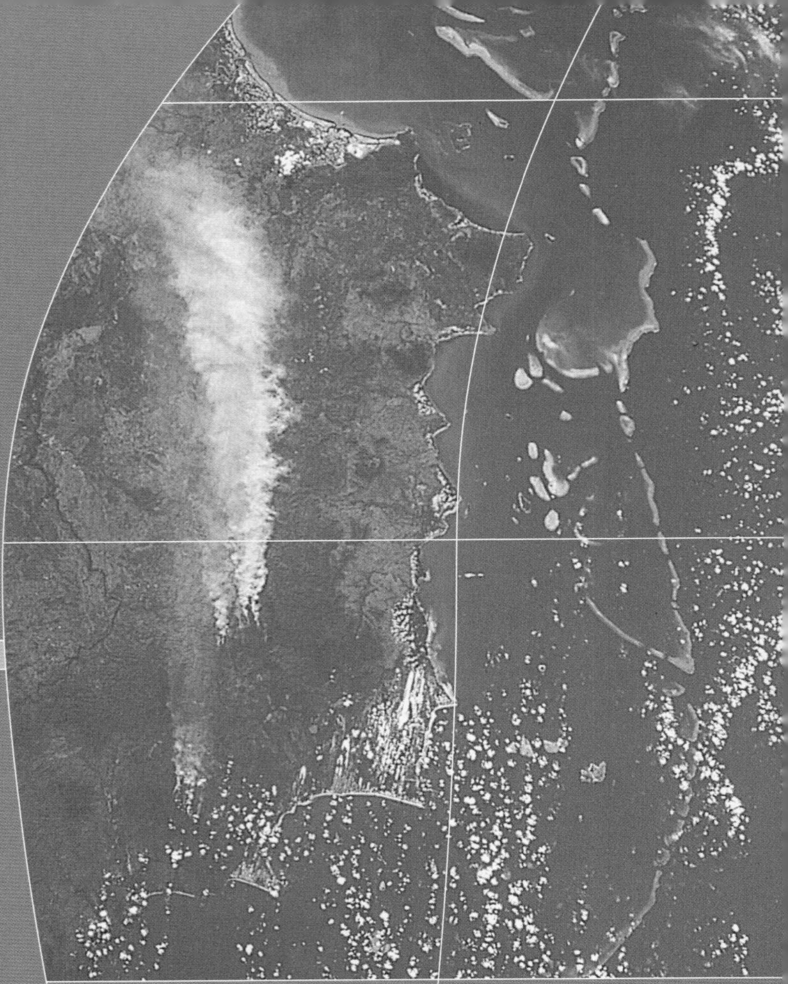

1 **Australian Bushfires**

Bushfires are an annual threat in the arid and savanna regions of Australia. Although fire can be of great benefit environmentally and ecologically, if it is not managed and controlled effectively it can have dramatic effects and can directly threaten settlements. In 1994 the suburbs of Sydney were affected by bushfires which destroyed 4 000 sq km of bush and grassland and in northern Australia over 300 000 sq km are affected each year. Satellite imagery, such as this image of a fire in northern Queensland, is an important tool in monitoring and managing bushfires. Imagery can be used to detect and map areas at risk, to map fire occurrences and to monitor post-fire recovery of the environment.

Satellite/Sensor : Apollo 7

CONNECTIONS

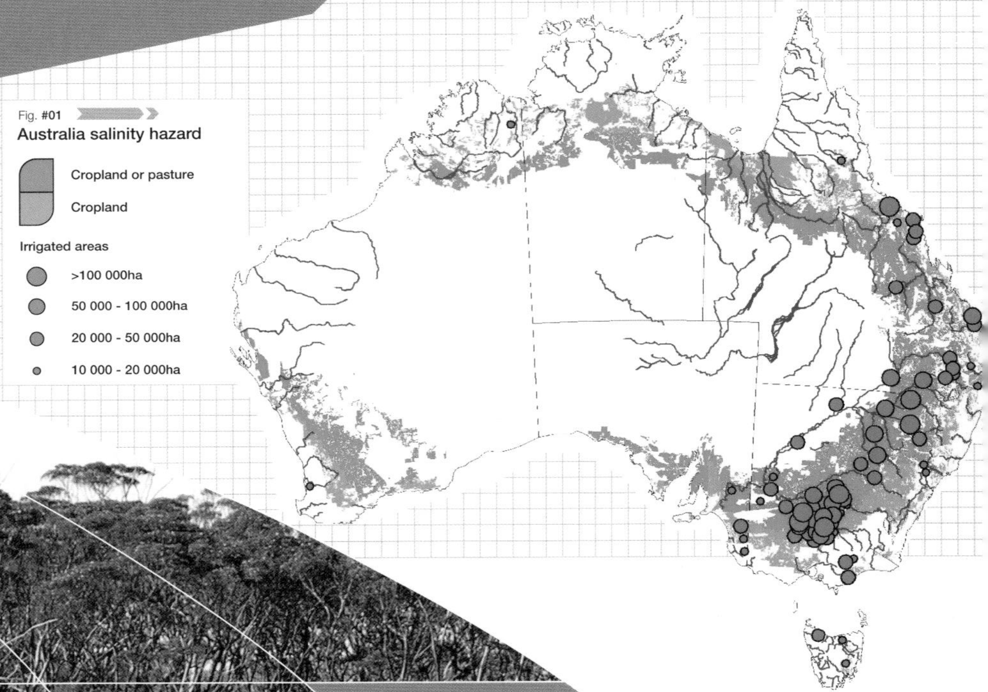

Fig. #01
Australia salinity hazard
Cropland or pasture
Cropland
Irrigated areas
>100 000ha
50 000 - 100 000ha
20 000 - 50 000ha
10 000 - 20 000ha

2

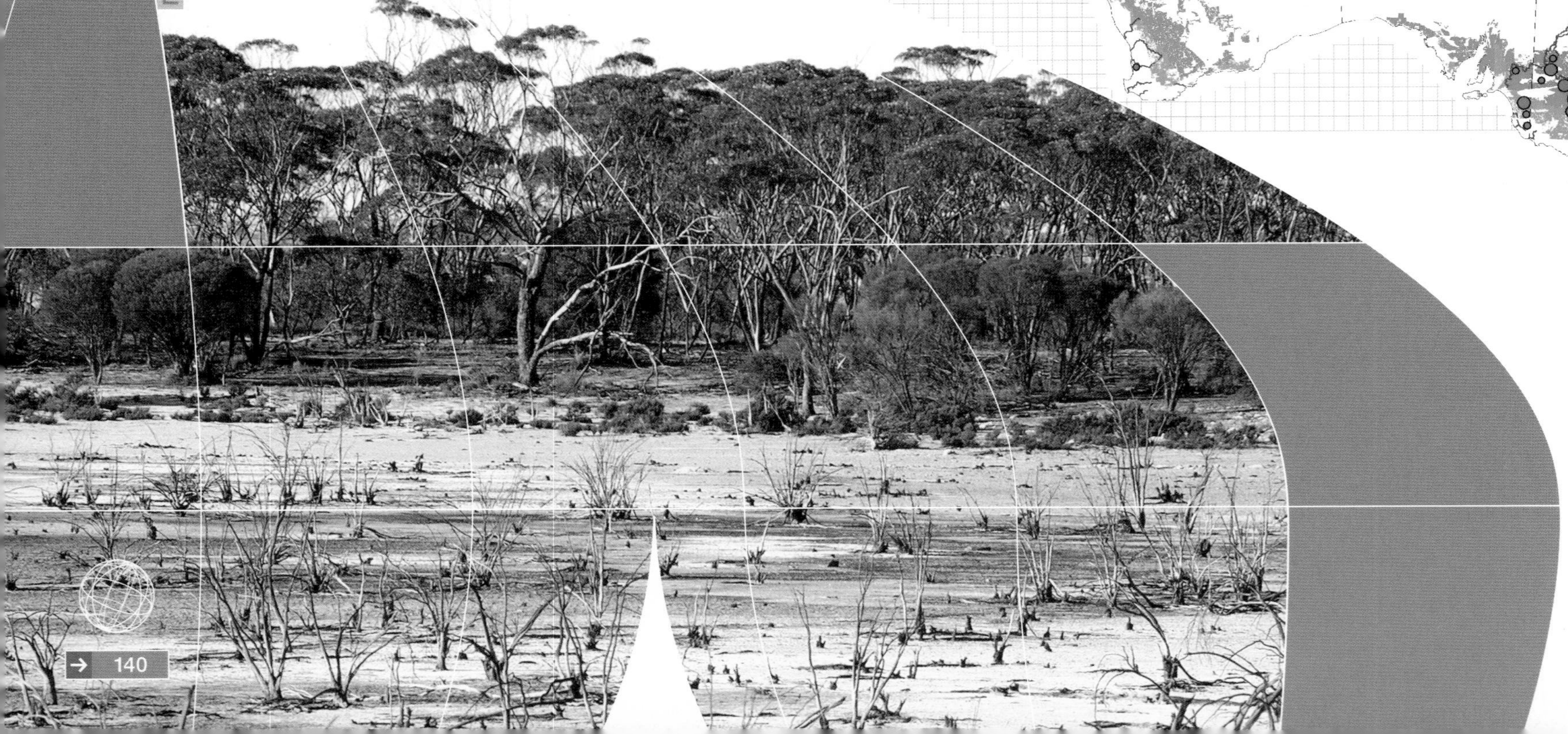

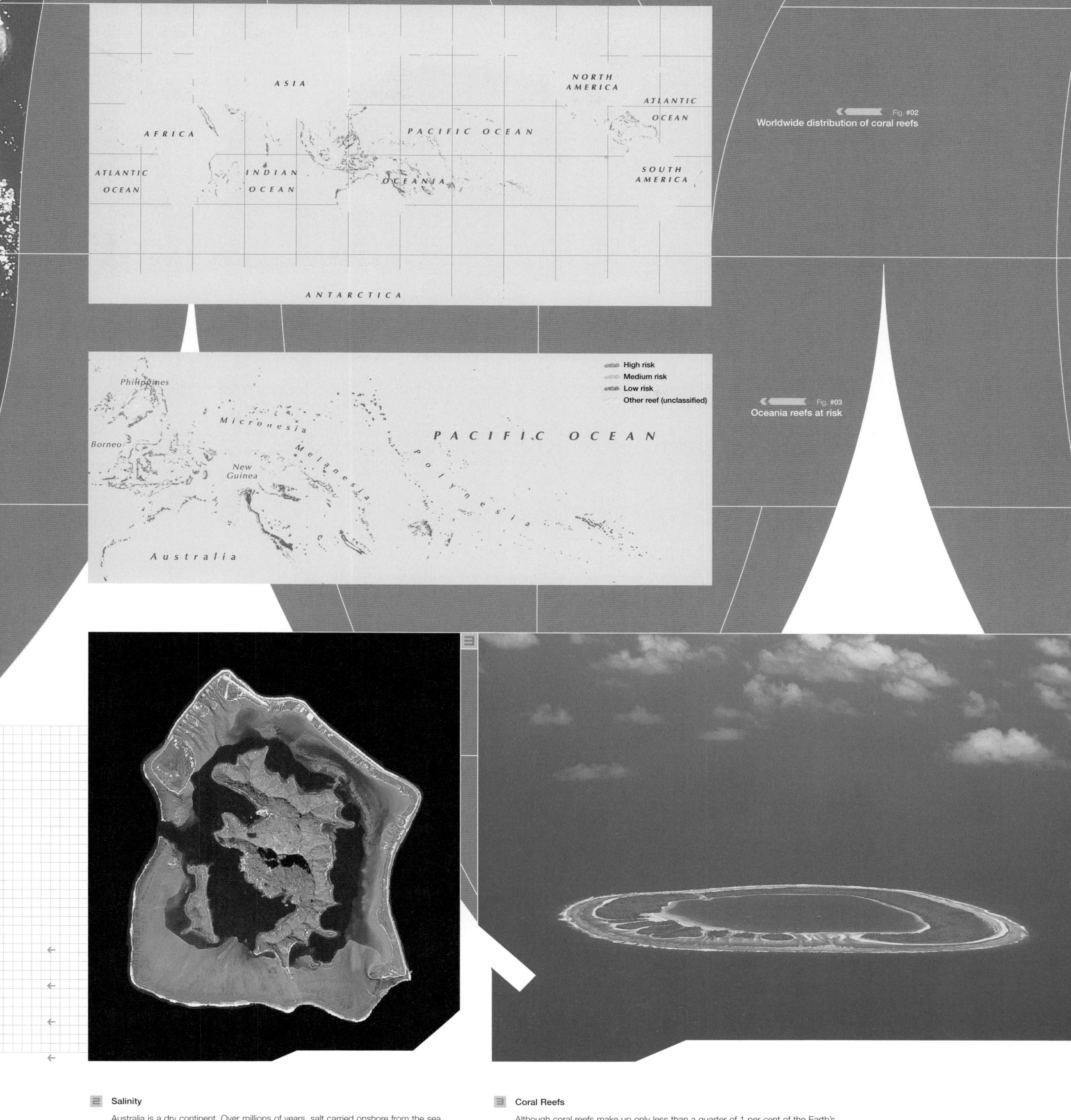

Fig. #02
Worldwide distribution of coral reefs

ASIA

NORTH
AMERICA

ATLANTIC
OCEAN

AFRICA

PACIFIC OCEAN

ATLANTIC
OCEAN

INDIAN
OCEAN

OCEANIA

SOUTH
AMERICA

ANTARCTICA

High risk
Medium risk
Low risk
Other reef (unclassified)

Fig. #03
Oceania reefs at risk

Philippines

Micronesia

PACIFIC OCEAN

Borneo

Melanesia

New
Guinea

Polynesia

Australia

2 Salinity

Australia is a dry continent. Over millions of years, salt carried onshore from the sea by winds and deposited by rain has accumulated in the soils. This salt becomes a problem when native vegetation is cleared, allowing excess water to percolate through the soil. This raises groundwater levels, bringing the salt to the surface and leaching salt into streams and rivers. Irrigation schemes add more water, making the problem worse. Salt kills crops and pastureland, damages roads and buildings, impairs water quality for both irrigation and human consumption and reduces biodiversity. The photograph shows an area badly affected by salinity near Kellerberrin, Western Australia. Approximately 5.7 million hectares of Australia's farmland is currently affected by salinity and it is predicted that, unless effective solutions are implemented, 17 million hectares of land and 20 000 km of streams could be salinized by 2050. The map shows areas where salt stored in the landscape is being mobilised by surplus water, creating the risk of salinity.

3 Coral Reefs

Although coral reefs make up only less than a quarter of 1 per cent of the Earth's marine environment, they are vitally important habitats, being home to over 25 per cent of all known marine fish species. They are also important sources of food and tourist income, and they provide physical protection for vulnerable coastlines. Reefs are widely distributed around the world (Fig. #02) with major concentrations in the Caribbean Sea, the Indian Ocean, southeast Asia and the Pacific Ocean.

Reefs are fragile environments, and many are under threat from coastal development, pollution and overexploitation of marine resources. The degree of risk varies, with the reefs of southeast Asia under the greatest threat. Over 25 per cent of the world's reefs are judged to be at high risk. In the Pacific Ocean over 40 per cent of reefs are at risk (Fig. #03). The beauty and fragility of these environments are suggested in the images above. The aerial photograph (right) shows the coral island of Mataiva and the SPOT satellite image (left) shows the island and reefs of Bora-Bora. Both are in the Pacific territory of French Polynesia.

1. Great Barrier Reef, *Queensland, Australia*

This Shuttle photograph of the northern end of the Great Barrier Reef shows two separate reef zones. The line of unbroken coral reefs, at the bottom right of the image contrasts to the randomly spaced reefs in the shallow waters off the coast of the Cape York Peninsula, at the left hand edge. The image captures only a tiny fraction of the whole reef which extends over 2 000 km along the northeast coast of Queensland.

Satellite/Sensor : Space Shuttle

2. Lake Eyre, *South Australia, Australia*

Lake Eyre, situated in one of the driest regions in South Australia, is the largest salt lake in Australia. The lake actually comprises two lakes, Lake Eyre North and the much smaller Lake Eyre South. Salt has been washed into the lake from underlying marine sediments and when dry, which is its usual state, the lake bed is a glistening sheet of white salt. In this photograph, the lake, viewed from the north, is in the process of drying out after being at a higher level.

Satellite/Sensor : Space Shuttle

3. Uluru (Ayers Rock), *Northern Territory, Australia*

Uluru (Ayers Rock), is a large single rock outcrop which rises 350 m above the vast plain of central Australia. This aerial photograph, looking west, shows how the steep, almost vertical walls of the rock rise from the flat surrounding land. The rock is composed of a collection of vertically bedded strata. In the far distance of the photograph, a similar rock formation, the Olgas, can be seen.

4. Banks Peninsula, *New Zealand*

The only recognizable volcanic feature on South Island, New Zealand is Banks Peninsula. It has been extensively eroded over the years yet it still possess the circular shape and radial drainage pattern typical of many volcanoes. The peninsula has been formed by two overlapping volcanic centres which are separated by a large harbour, Akaroa Harbour. In this aerial photograph, the peninsula is viewed from the east and at the top the Canterbury Plains are just visible.

5 Palm Valley, *Northern Territory, Australia*

The dark brown and blue area of this radar image, is a broad valley located in the arid landscape of central Australia, approximately 50 km south west of Alice Springs. Palm Valley, the oval shaped feature at the top left of the image, contains many rare species of palms. The mountains of the Macdonnell Ranges are seen as curving bands of folded sedimentary outcrops. In the top right of the image, the river Finke cuts across the mountain ridge and continues in a deep canyon to the lower centre of the image.

Satellite/Sensor : Space Shuttle/SIR-C/X-SAR

6 Sydney, *Australia*

Sydney, the largest city in Australia and capital of New South Wales state, has one of the world's finest natural harbours. It is Australia's chief port, and its main cultural and industrial centre. This satellite image of the city, in which north is at the bottom, was captured by the IKONOS satellite in late 1999. The image highlights the renowned Sydney Opera house, located on Bennelong Point. Also clearly visible are the Royal Botanical Gardens and west of these the main urban area of the city centre.

Satellite/Sensor : IKONOS

7 New Caledonia and Vanuatu, *Pacific Ocean*

The long narrow island of New Caledonia lies in the southern Pacific Ocean approximately 1 500 km east of Queensland, Australia. The territory comprises one large island and several smaller ones. This SeaWiFS satellite image clearly shows the extensive reef formations which extend far out into the ocean. The island has a landscape of rugged mountains with little flat land. Almost obscured by clouds, at the top right of this image, is a group of islands which collectively make up the small republic of Vanuatu.

Satellite/Sensor : OrbView2/SeaWiFS

CONNECTIONS

subject	page#
Uluru (Ayers Rock)	18–19
Oceania landscapes	136–137
Oceania countries	138–139
Coral reefs	140–141
Southwest Pacific Ocean	144–145
Pacific Ocean	220–221

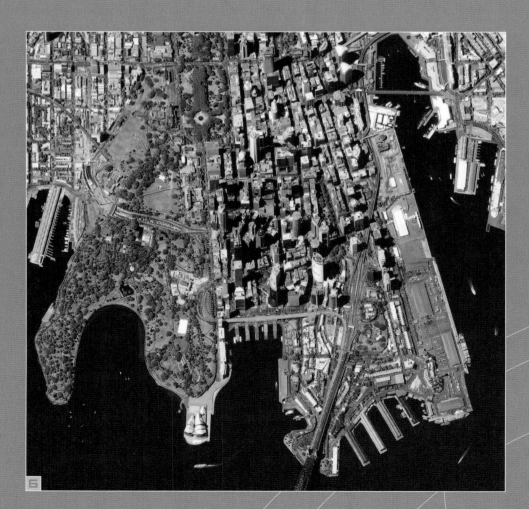

6

7

oceania[map1]
0°-50°S / 112°E-170°W
072-073
>6000m
5000-6000m
4000-5000m
3000-4000m
2000-3000m
1000-2000m
500-1000m
200-500m
0-200m
<0m
0-200m
200-500m
500-1000m
1000-2000m
2000-3000m
3000-4000m
4000-5000m
5000-6000m
>6000m
CONNECTIONS
subject page#
World physical features 8-9
Gibson Desert 136-137
Oceania countries 138-139
Oceania features 142-143
Coral reefs 140-141
Pacific Ocean 220-221
144
1:18 000 000
miles
km
Lambert Azimuthal Equal Area Projection
INDIAN OCEAN
SOUTHERN OCEAN
INDONESIA
AUSTRALIA
WESTERN AUSTRALIA
NORTHERN TERRITORY
SOUTH AUSTRALIA
QUEENSLAND
NEW SOUTH
VICTORIA
MALAYSIA
EAST TIMOR
Borneo
Celebes (Sulawesi)
New Guinea
Java Sea
Flores Sea
Banda Sea
Arafura Sea
Timor Sea
Seram Sea
Molucca Sea
Makassar Strait
Gulf of Carpentaria
Great Australian Bight
Torres Strait
Bass Strait
Great Sandy Desert
Gibson Desert
Great Victoria Desert
Simpson Desert
Tanami Desert
Sturt Stony Desert
Nullarbor Plain
Kimberley Plateau
Barkly Tableland
Arnhem Land
Cape York Peninsula
Macdonnell Ranges
Musgrave Ranges
Hamersley Range
Flinders Ranges
Great Dividing Range
Lake Eyre (North)
Lake Eyre (South)
Lake Torrens
Lake Gairdner
Lake Mackay
Lake Amadeus
Lake Carnegie
Uluru (Ayers Rock)
Timor
Halmahera
Seram
Flores
Sumba
Darwin
Alice Springs
Perth
Adelaide
Kalgoorlie
Port Hedland
Broome
Geraldton
Albany
Esperance
Cairns
Mount Isa
Tennant Creek
Katherine
Port Augusta
Whyalla
Port Lincoln
Broken Hill
Mildura
Bendigo
Ballarat
Geelong
Melbourne
Kupang
Dili
Jayapura
Port Moresby
Surabaya
Ujung Pandang (Makassar)
Denpasar
Merauke
Ashmore and Cartier Islands (Australia)
Tropic of Capricorn
Equator

Kapingamarangi
(Micronesia)

Abaiang Tarakei
BAIRIKI
Maiana

Howland I.
(U.S.A.)

Baker I.
(U.S.A.)

NAURU

Nauru
YAREN

Banaba
(Ocean I.)

Kuria Abemama
Aranuka

Nonouti

K I R I B A T I

Matthias
Group

New
Hanover

Lyra Reef

Tabat Is

Kavieng
Lihir Group
Tanga Is

Nuguria Is

Nukumanu Is

Tabiteuea
Onotoa

Beru Nikunau

Kingsmill Group

Tamana

Arorae

Nanumea

Nanumanga

Niutao

Nui

Phoenix
Islands

Kanton

Enderbury
McKean Birnie

Rawaki

Nikumaroro

Orona

Manra

PUA

New Britain

Rabaul
Pomio

Feni Is
Green Is

Buka I.

Arawa

Bougainville
Island

Choiseul

Vella Lavella
Kolombangara
Ranongga
Munda

New
Georgia

Santa
Isabel
Buala

Malu'u

S O L O M O N
I S L A N D S

TUVALU

Vaitupu

Nukufetau

Nanumea FUNAFUTI VAIAKU

Nukulaelae

Atafu

Tokelau
(New Zealand)

Nukunonu

Fakaofo

Swains I.

GUINEA

Lusancay
Islands
and Reefs

Trobriand Is

Goodenough I.

Fergusson I.

Normanby I.

D'Entrecasteaux Is

Woodlark I.

Louisiade Archipelago

Conflict Group

Tagula I.

HONIARA

Guadalcanal

New Georgia
Islands

Stewart
Islands

Yandina

Maramasike

Malaita

Apio

Kirakira

San Cristobal
(Makira)

Rennell

Duff Islands

Nupani,
Lata

Swallow Islands

Santa Cruz Islands

Utupua

Vanikoro Is

Ndeni

Cherry I.

Mitre I.

Niulakita

Rotuma
(Fiji)

Wallis and
Futuna Islands
(France)

Île Futuna
Îles de Hoorn

Sigave
Île Alofi

MATA'UTU
Îles Wallis

SAMOA

Mt Silisili
Falelima
Savai'i

APIA
Upolu

Safotu

Manua
Maia
Tau

American
Samoa
(U.S.A.)

Niuato'ou

Tafahi
Niuatoputapu

Coral
Sea

Coral Sea
Islands
Territory
(Australia)

Marion Reef

Flinders
Reefs

Îles Chesterfield

Torres Is

Uréparapara
Mota Lava

Vanua Lava
Banks Islands
797 Santa María I.

Espíritu Santo

Aoba Maéwo

Luganville Pentecost I.

V A N U A T U

Norsup Mt Marum
Malakula Milo

Ambrym
Ulei

Lamen
Shepherd Is

Cikobia

Great Sea Reef

Vetauua
Qelelevu

Vanua Levu

Yasawa
Group
Lautoka
Nadi
Viti Levu
Vatulele

Water
Rakiraki
Koro
Levuka
Ovalau

SUVA

Kadavu

Sigatoka
Kadavu Passage

Northern
Lau Group

Taveuni

Vanua Balavu

Vetauua

Koro
Sea

Moala
Matuku

Southern
Lau Group

Tubou
Lakeba
Oneata

Totoya

Fonualei
100
110

Vava'u
Group
150

Neiafu
Vava'u

Late

Kao 500
Tofua

Fonualei o'o
(Falcon I.)

Nomuka

Ha'apai Group

ALOFI

Niue
(New Zealand)

F I J I

Yatoa

Vatoa

Ono-i-Lau

Tuvana-i-Tholo
Tuvana-i-Colo

T O N G A

Récifs
d'Entrecasteaux

Grand Passage

Grand
Récif
de Cook

Récifs de
l'Astrolabe

Récif
des
Français

Ouvéa
Fayaoué

Îles Loyauté
Lifou

Maré

Koumac

Poindimié

Houaïlou

Mont
Humboldt
1618

WÉ

Tanna Yasur
Lénakel 361

Erromango

Potnarivin

Anatom
(Aneityum)

Hunter I.
100

Ceva-i-Ra

Ata

Tongatapu
Group
Tongatapu
'Eua

NUKU'ALOFA

Fonuafo'ou'o
Nomuka

Onoua

Nouvelle Calédonie

New Caledonia
(France)

Boulari
Dumbéa
NOUMÉA
Le Mont-Dore

Îdenhout

Grand Récif
du Sud

Île des Pins

Île Walpole

Minerva
Reefs

Great Barrier Reef

Mackay
Sarina

Swain Reefs

Saumarez
Reef

Capricorn Channel

Rockhampton
Gladstone

Yeppoon

P A C I F I C   O C E A N

Bundaberg

Maryborough

Fraser Island

Gympie
Maroochydore
Nambour
Caboolture

Brisbane
Beenleigh
Toowoomba
Gold Coast
Murwillumbah
Beaudesert
Lismore
Stanthorpe
Ballina
Casino

Grafton

Coffs Harbour

Middleton Reef

Elizabeth Reef

Norfolk Island
(Australia)

Armidale
Tamworth

Kempsey
Port Macquarie

Lord Howe I.
(Australia)

Kermadec Islands
(New Zealand)

Raoul I.

Macauley I.
Curtis I.

Havre Rock

L'Espérance Rock

Mount

Taree
Forster

Newcastle
Maitland
The Entrance
Gosford

Sydney
Wollongong

CANBERRA
Nowra

Goulburn

JERVIS BAY TERRITORY

Ulladulla
Batemans Bay
Moruya
Narooma

Bega

Eden

Cape Howe

Great Dividing Range

T a s m a n   S e a

Three Kings
Islands
Cape Maria van Diemen

North Cape

Awanui

Kaitaia

Whangarei

Dargaville

Great Barrier I.

North Island

Takapuna
Auckland
Manukau
Hamilton
Te Awamutu

Thames

Tauranga
Whakatane

Whakaari

East Cape

New Plymouth

Mt Taranaki
(Mt Egmont)
2518

Hawera

Te Kuiti
Tokoroa
Taupo

Gisborne

Hawke Bay

Wanganui

Napier
Hastings

Furneaux
Group
Flinders I.

Cape Farewell

Riwaka
Tasman
Bay

Richmond
Nelson

Levin
Feilding
Palmerston North
Masterton

NEW
ZEALAND

Launceston

Westport

Greymouth
Hokitika

Blenheim
Lower Hutt
WELLINGTON

C. Palliser

Port Arthur

South Island

Mt Cook
(Aoraki)
3754

Mt Aspiring
3033

Arthur's Pass

Kaikoura

Christchurch

Banks Peninsula

Ashburton

Chatham Islands
(New Zealand)

Chatham I.

Waitangi

Pitt I.

Cape Providence

Queenstown
Alexandra

Invercargill
Gore

Timaru
Waimate
Oamaru
Port Chalmers
Dunedin

Milton
Balclutha
Chaslands
Mistake

Stewart I.

Bluff

South West
Cape

Snares
Islands

Bounty Islands
(New Zealand)

Antipodes Islands
(New Zealand)

28°-44°S / 128°-158°E

148-149

150-151

Elevation scale (left):
>6000m
5000-6000m
4000-5000m
3000-4000m
2000-3000m
1000-2000m
500-1000m
200-500m
0-200m
<0m
0m

0-200m
200-500m
500-1000m
1000-2000m
2000-3000m
3000-4000m
4000-5000m
5000-6000m
>6000m

Map labels:

WESTERN AUSTRALIA

SOUTH AUSTRALIA

Tomkinson Ranges
Mt Davies 1058
Mount Kintore 1071
Mt Woodroffe 1440
Mt Harriet
Hamilton
Wintiri National Park
Sturt Stony Desert
Clifton Hills
Innamincka Regional Reserve
Cooper Creek

Mt Agnes 640
Blyth Range
Birksgate Range
Mt Sir Thomas 805
Anangu Pitjantjatjara Aboriginal Lands
Fregon
Mimili
Tarcoonyinna
Alberga
Lambina
Macumba
Macumba
Lake Lake Omaroona
Lake Howitt

Warakurna-Wingellina-Irrunytju Aboriginal Reserve
Everard Range
Mt Illbillee 917
Indulkana
Marla
Oodnadatta
Noolyeanna Lake
Kallakoopah Creek
Lake Hope
Lake Koolootoona

Purdu Saltpan
The Officer's Creek
Welbourn Hill
Woodmurra Creek
Lake Etamunbanie

Great Victoria Desert Conservation Park
Mount Willoughby
Peake
Lake Cadibarrawirracanna
Lake Eyre (North)
16 Lake Eyre National Park
Tirari Desert
Lake Hope
Lake Wangalanna

L. Meramangye
Observatory Hill
Coober Pedy
Lake Conway
Etadunna
Mungeranie
Lake Gregory

Great Victoria Desert
Tallaringa Conservation Park
Douglas Creek
Elliot Price Conservation Park
Marree
Strzelecki Regional Reserve
Lake Blanche

Serpentine Lakes
Wyola Lake
Dey-Dey Lake
Mabel Creek
William Creek
Finniss Springs Aboriginal Land
Moolawatana
Lake Frome

AUSTRALIA
Great Victoria Desert Nature Reserve
Nurral Lakes
Halinor Lake
Leisler Hills
Lake Maurice
Wilkinson Lakes
Woomera Prohibited Area
L. Anthony
L. Warida
Ingomar
Strzelecki Desert

Maralinga-Tjarutja Aboriginal Lands
Forrest Lakes
Mt Finke 361
Hall Moon Lake
Mulgathing
Carnes
Bon Bon
Parakylia
Roxby Downs
Andamooka
Freeling Heights 1058
Wooltana
Balcanoona
Lake Frome Regional Reserve

Ooldea Range
Maralinga
Ooldea
Wynbring
Lyons
Tarcoola
Kingoonya
Coondambo
Mount Eba
Lake Torrens National Park
Leigh Copley
Mt Hack 1128
Nantawarrina Aboriginal Land
Gammon Ranges Nat. Park

Nullarbor Plain
Cook
Fisher
Lake Labyrinth
L. Younghusband
Lake Torrens
Beltana
Mt Arden
Blinman
Flinders Ranges National Park

Reid
Deakin
Hughes
Ibould Lake
Yellabina Regional Reserve
Lake Harris
Noomera
L. Windabout
Parachilna
Wilpena

Forrest
Nullarbor Regional Reserve
Lake Tallacootra
Pureba Conservation Park
Lake Everard
Lake Gairdner National Park
Island Lagoon
Pernatty Lagoon
St Mary
Cradock
Merchant Hill
Mannahill
Olary

Well
Yalata Aboriginal Lands
Colona
Yumbarra Conservation Park
Koonibba
Lake Gairdner
Lake Woocalla
Carrieton
Baratta
Cockburn

Nullarbor National Park
Nullarbor
Head of Bight
Bookabie
Penong
Ceduna
Lake Macfarlane
Port Augusta
Wilmington
Orroroo
Yunta
Coombah
Popili Lake

Eucla
Fowlers Bay
Pt Bell
Denial
Smoky Bay
Wirrulla
Gawler Ranges
Iron Knob
Mt Remarkable National Park
Peterborough
Oakbank
Danggali Conservation Park

Great Australian Bight
Pt Brown
Streaky Bay
Poochera
Wudinna
Iron Baron
Whyalla
Port Pirie
Gladstone
Mt Bryan 934
Robertstown
Morgan
Chowilla Regional Reserve

St Francis Isles
Nuyts Archipelago
Scaele Bay
Point Kenny
Lake Yaninee
Kyancutta
Kimba
Lake Gilles Conservation Park
Crystal Brook
Snowtown
Balaklava
Eudunda
Barmera
Berri
Lake Victoria

Nuyts Archipelago Conservation Park
Cape Radstock
Anxious Bay
Minnipa
Pinkawillinie Conservation Park
Balumbah
Carappee Hill 496
Brinkworth
Kapunda
Waikerie
Loxton
Werri

C. Finniss
Flinders Island
Investigator Group
Pearson Isles
Cleve
Cowell
Aino Bay
Maitland
Gawler
Angaston
Swan Reach
Murray Sunset National Park

Eyre Peninsula
Darke Peak Conservation Park
Wallaroo
Moonta
Balaklava
Blanchetown
Cambrai
Wanbi
Big Desert Wilderness Park

Coffin Bay
Elliston
Cummins
Tumby Bay
Sir Joseph Banks Group
Port Victoria
Ardrossan
Gulf St Vincent
Murray Bridge
Billiat Conservation Park
Pinnaroo

Coffin Bay Peninsula
Mount Hope
Cockaleechie
Wardang Island
Minlaton
Adelaide
Strathalbyn
Tailem Bend
Lameroo
Ngarkat Conservation Park

Greenly I.
Coffin Bay National Park
Port Lincoln
Lincoln Nat. Park
Hardwicke Bay
Yorke Peninsula
Mount Barker
Goolwa
Lake Alexandrina
Coonalpyn
Wyper Nat

Sleaford Bay
Corny Pt
Willunga
Milang
Lake Albert
Tintinara
Little Desert National

C. Catastrophe
Thistle I.
Gambier Is
C. Spencer
Marion Bay
Sturt Bay
Rapid Bay
Victor Harbor
Encounter Bay
Meningie
Keith
Frances
Mt Arapiles State Park

Investigator Strait
Cape Borda
Pandana
Kingscote
D'Estrees Bay
Coorong National Park
Naracoorte
Bordertown
Wolseley
Dergholm State Park

Kangaroo Island
Flinders Chase Nat. Park
Cape Gantheaume Conservation Park
Younghusband Peninsula
Lacepede Bay
Lake Hindr
Nhi

C. de Couedic
Kingston S.E.
Cape Jaffa
Beachport
Millicent
Penola
Casterton

Lake Bonney
Canunda Nat. Park
Mount Gambier
Port MacDonnell Nat. Park
Discovery Bay Coastal Park
Portland
Cape Nelson

GREAT AUSTRALIAN BIGHT

SOUTHERN OCEAN

28° 32° 36° 40° 44°
128° 132° 136° 140°

148-149
QUEENSLAND
NEW SOUTH WALES
VICTORIA
TASMANIA
AUSTRALIAN CAPITAL TERRITORY
JERVIS BAY TERRITORY
Great Dividing Range
Tasman Sea
Bass Strait
Brisbane
Sydney
CANBERRA
Melbourne
Hobart
Newcastle
Wollongong
Gold Coast
Launceston
Furneaux Group
King Island
Flinders Island
144°
148°
152°
156°
160°
E
F
G
H
CONNECTIONS
subject
page#
World physical features 8-9
Oceania landscapes 136-137
Oceania countries 138-139
Oceania issues 140-141
Lake Eyre 142-143
1:6 000 000
miles
0 50 100 150 200 250
0 50 100 150 200 250 300 350 400
km
Lambert Azimuthal Equal Area Projection

11°-28°S / 128°-154°E

150-151

◄ 146-147 ▼

1 : 6 000 000

miles
0   50   100   150   200   250

km
0   50   100   150   200   250   300   350   400

Lambert Azimuthal Equal Area Projection

Elevation legend:
>6000m
5000-6000m
4000-5000m
3000-4000m
2000-3000m
1000-2000m
500-1000m
200-500m
0-200m
<0m

0-200m
200-500m
500-1000m
1000-2000m
2000-3000m
3000-4000m
4000-5000m
5000-6000m
>6000m

Grid references: 1, 2, 3, 4, 5 (rows); A, 132°, B, 136°, C (columns)

Latitude lines: 12°, 16°, 20°, 24°, 28°
Longitude: 128°, 132°, 136°

Seas and Gulfs:
Timor Sea
Joseph Bonaparte Gulf
Beagle Gulf
Van Diemen Gulf
Gulf of Carpent[aria]

Major regions:
NORTHERN TERRITORY
AUSTRALIA
SOUTH AUSTRALIA
Arnhem Land
Arnhem Land Aboriginal Land
Kakadu National Park
Tanami Desert
Central Desert
Simpson Desert
Barkly Tableland
Sturt Plain
Musgrave Ranges
Macdonnell Ranges
Tropic of Capricorn

Islands:
Bathurst Island
Melville Island
Tiwi Aboriginal Land
Groote Eylandt
Wessel Islands
Mornington I.
Wellesley Islands Aboriginal Reserve
Sir Edward Pellew Group
Vanderlin I.
The English Company's Is
Elcho I.

Places and features:
Darwin
Palmerston
Howard Springs
Humpty Doo
Katherine
Pine Creek
Hayes Creek
Daly River
Adelaide River
Batchelor
Alice Springs
Tennant Creek
Daly Waters
Elliot
Renner Springs
Barrow Creek
Ti Tree
Aileron
Yulara
Uluru National Park
Kings Canyon
Watarrka Nat. Park
Finke Gorge Nat. Park
West MacDonnell Nat. Park
Gregory National Park
Purnululu National Park
Lawn Hill National Park
Lake Argyle
Lake Woods
Lake Mackay
Lake Amadeus
Lake White
Lake Wills
Lake Hazlett
Lake Neale
Lake Hopkins
Lake MacDonald

Aboriginal Lands (selected):
Kakadu National Park
Jabiluka Aboriginal Land
Nitmiluk Nat. Park
Beswick Aboriginal Land
Hodgson Downs
Alawa Aboriginal Land
Garawa Aboriginal Land
Wakaya Aboriginal Land
Karlantijpa North Aboriginal Land
South Aboriginal Land
Warumungu Aboriginal Land
Central Australia Aboriginal Reserve
Western Desert Aboriginal Land
Tanami Downs Aboriginal Land
Mala Aboriginal Land
Haasts Bluff Aboriginal Land
Petermann Aboriginal Land
Katiti Aboriginal Land
Anangu Pitjantjatjara Aboriginal Lands
Balgo Aboriginal Reserve
Atnetye Aboriginal Land
Simpson Desert Regional Reserve
Witjira National Park

Mountains / Ranges:
Wingate Mountains
Pinkerton Range
Stokes Range
Ashburton Range
Davenport Range
Reynolds Range
Hann Range
Harts Range
Ehrenberg Range
Petermann Ranges
Olia Chain
Mann Ranges
Tomkinson Ranges
James Ranges
Krichauff Range

Cape Wessel
Cape Arnhem
Cape Wilberforce
Cape Croker
Mount Isa
Camooweal
Camooweal Caves National Park
Poeppel Corner

Coral Sea

PAPUA
NEW GUINEA

Louisiade Archipelago

Cape

York

Peninsula

Gulf

of

Carpentaria

Great Barrier Reef
Marine Park
(Far North Section)

Great
Barrier Reef
Marine Park
(Cairns Section)

Great Barrier Reef
Marine Park
(Central Section)

Coral Sea Islands
Territory
(Australia)

Great Barrier Reef
Marine Park
(Capricorn Section)

AUSTRALIA

QUEENSLAND

Great Dividing Range

Fraser Island
Fraser Island
National Park

Brisbane

CONNECTIONS

▶ subject   page#

▶ Land cover types   ⟹   18-19
▶ Great Barrier Reef   ⟹   136-137
▶ Oceania countries   ⟹   138-139
▶ Coral reefs   ⟹   140-141
▶ Oceania features   ⟹   142-143

148-149

NORTHERN TERRITORY

Beagle Gulf

Joseph Bonaparte Gulf

Timor Sea

INDONESIA

INDIAN OCEAN

Kimberley Plateau

King Leopold Ranges

Hamersley Range

Great Sandy Desert

Gibson Desert

Little Sandy Desert

Ashmore and Cartier Islands (Australia)

Lake Mackay Aboriginal Land

Central Australia Aboriginal Reserve

North Central Aboriginal Reserve

Eighty Mile Beach

Tropic of Capricorn

Ningaloo Marine Park

A U S T R A L I A
S O U T H A U S T R A L I A
Great Victoria Desert
Nullarbor Plain
Great Australian Bight
Shark Bay
Houtman Abrolhos
Geraldton
Perth
Fremantle
Rockingham
Mandurah
Bunbury
Albany
Esperance
Kalgoorlie
Boulder
Coolgardie
Norseman
Leonora
Laverton
Meekatharra
Wiluna
Carnarvon
Eucla
Darling Range
Stirling Range
Robinson Range
Carnarvon Range
Kimberley Range
Nicholson Range
Weld Range
Lake Barlee
Lake Moore
Lake Carnegie
Hampton Tableland
Roe Plains
Archipelago of the Recherche
Nuytsland Nature Reserve
Nullarbor National Park
Nullarbor Regional Reserve
Great Victoria Desert Nature Reserve
Maralinga-Tjarutja Aboriginal Lands
Anangu Pitjantjatjara Aboriginal Lands
Dundas Nature Reserve
Great Victoria Desert Conservation Park
C. Leeuwin
C. Naturaliste
Rottnest I.
Dirk Hartog Island
Pt Culver
Pt Dover
Pt Malcolm
146-147
28°
32°
36°
112°
116°
120°
124°
128°
A
B
C
D
E
5
6
7
>6000m
5000-6000m
4000-5000m
3000-4000m
2000-3000m
1000-2000m
500-1000m
200-500m
0-200m
<0m
0-200m
200-500m
500-1000m
1000-2000m
2000-3000m
3000-4000m
4000-5000m
5000-6000m
>6000m
10°-36°S / 112°-130°E
1:6 000 000
miles
km
0
50
100
150
200
250
300
350
400
Lambert Azimuthal Equal Area Projection
oceania[map4]

NORTH ISLAND

NEW ZEALAND

Tasman Sea

Bay of Plenty

Hawke Bay

connections

▶ subject	page#
▲ World volcanoes	14–15
▲ Mount Cook (Aoraki)	136–137
▲ Oceania countries	138–139
▲ Banks Peninsula	142–143
▲ Pacific Ocean	220–221

>6000m
5000–6000m
4000–5000m
3000–4000m
2000–3000m
1500–2000m
1000–1500m
500–1000m
200–500m
100–200m
0–100m
<0m

0–200m
200–500m
500–1000m
1000–2000m
2000–3000m
3000–4000m
4000–5000m
5000–6000m
>6000m

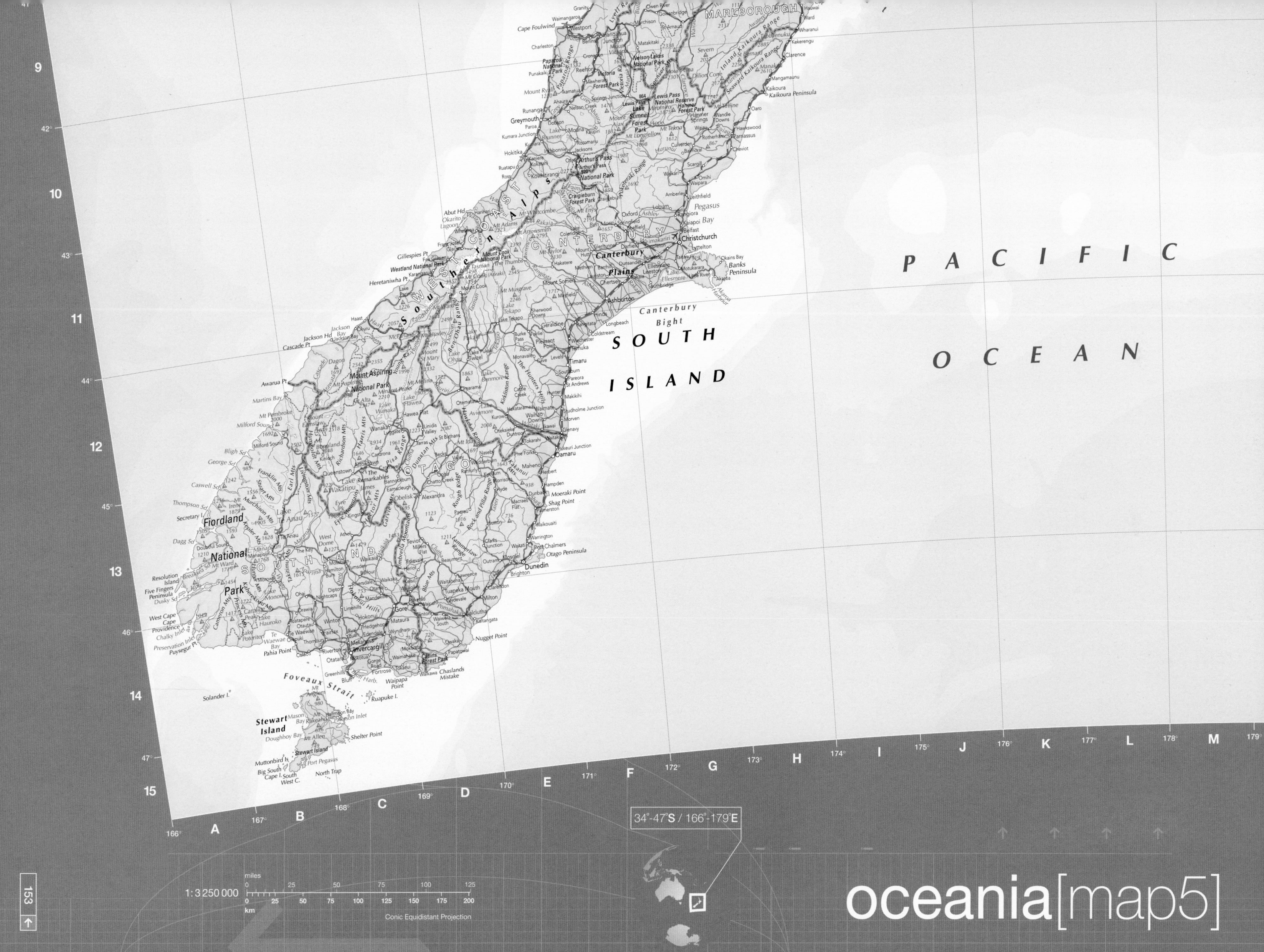

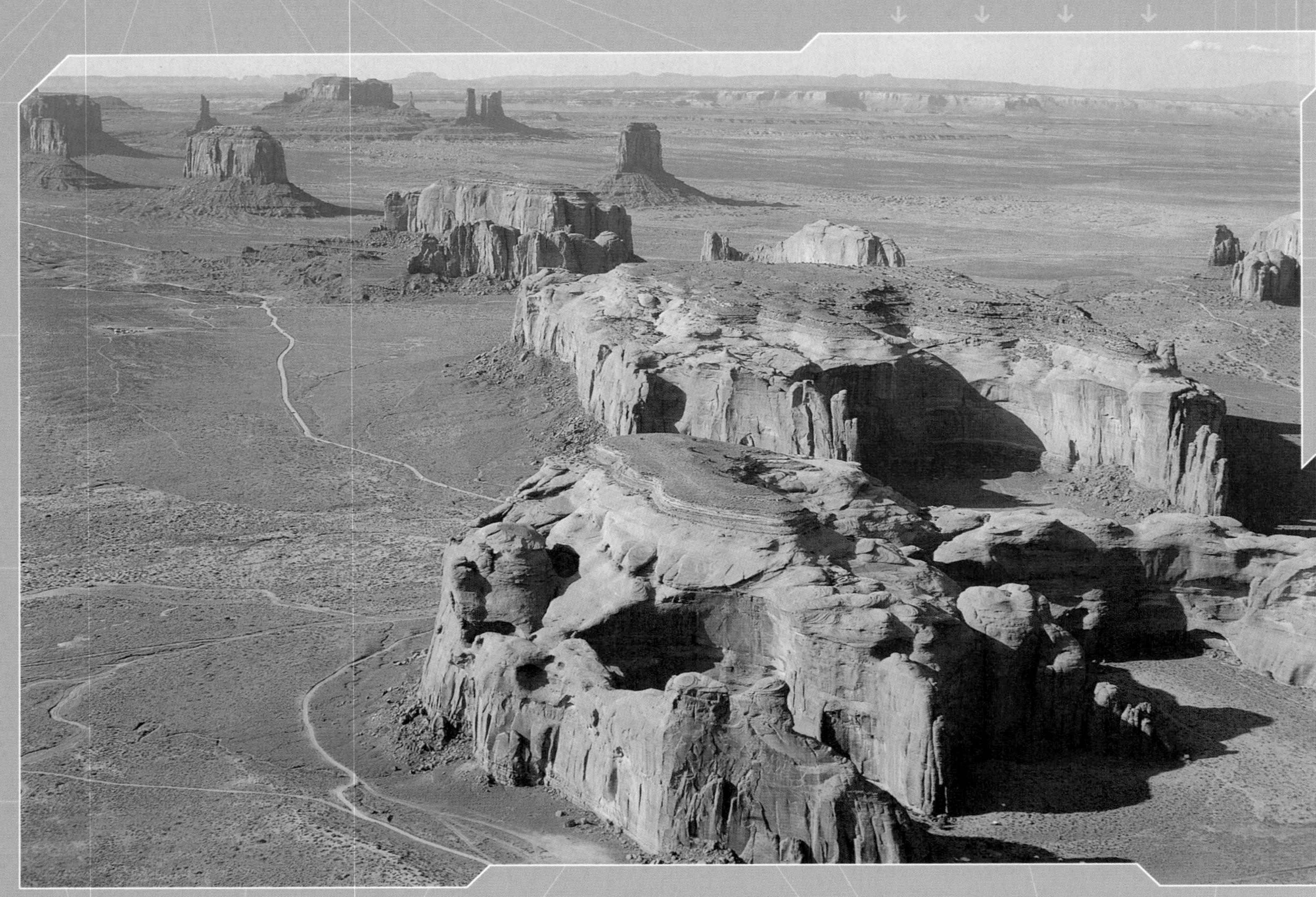

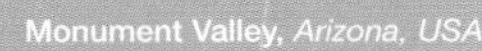

Monument Valley, *Arizona, USA*

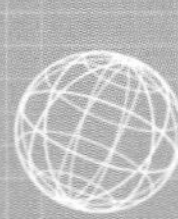

north**america**

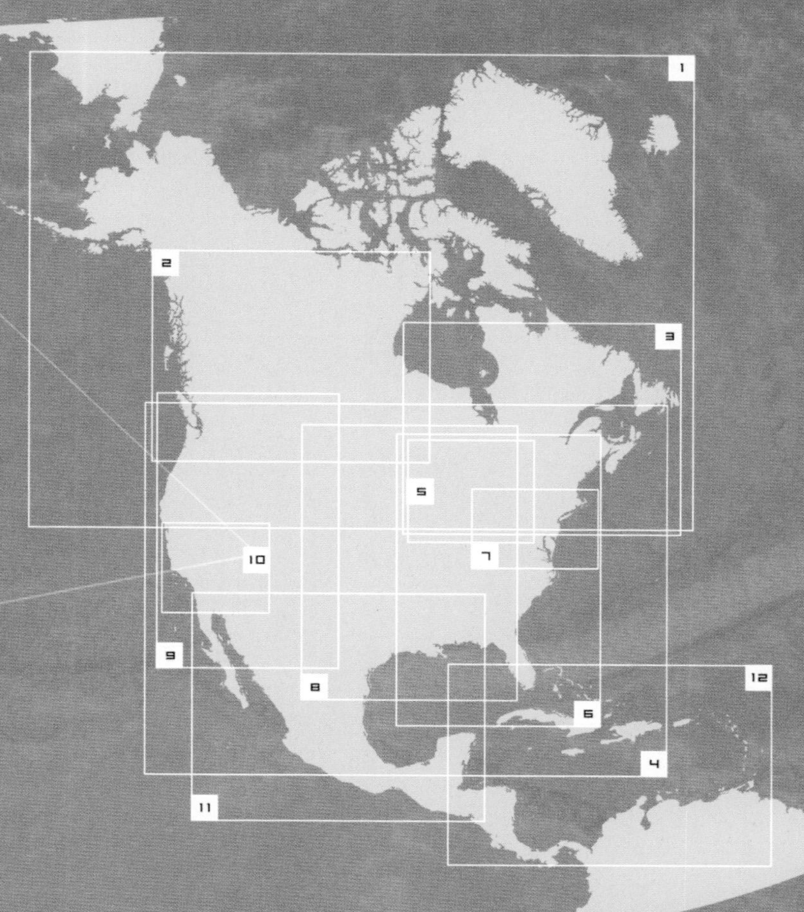

[contents]

Arctic Ocean

Mount McKinley

Mackenzie River

Victoria Island

Great Bear Lake

Great Slave Lake

Gulf of Alaska

Highest point

Mt McKinley
United States of America
6 194 m / 20 321 ft
Map reference 164 D3

Coast Mountains

Peace River

Pacific Ocean

Rocky Mountains

Lake Winnipeg

Snake River

Great Basin

Platte Riv

Grand Canyon

Death Valley

Great Plains

Lowest point

Death Valley
86 m / 282 ft below sea level
Map reference 181 C5

Colorado River

Baja California

Gulf of California

Sierra Madre Occidental

North America is the largest continent in the western hemisphere. This view illustrates how the west coast is dominated by the Rocky Mountains which stretch from Alaska in the north through Canada, USA, Mexico and Central America. The Great Plains stretch gradually east of the Rockies, and extend from the Arctic Ocean to the Gulf of Mexico. The Appalachian Mountains dominate the east of the USA, with lowlands skirting the east coast of the continent and the Gulf of Mexico.

Major water bodies are the Great Lakes, and Great Slave Lake and Great Bear Lake in the Arctic regions of Canada. In the northeast, Hudson Bay is a huge inland sea connected to the Atlantic Ocean by the Hudson Strait. The large purple feature at the centre top of the image is the high, snow-covered plateau in Greenland. The Caribbean Sea contains numerous islands, stretching from the Bahamas to the north coast of South America. In the south the Isthmus of Panama forms the link between Central and South America.

1 Grand Canyon, Arizona, *USA*

The Grand Canyon in northern Arizona, USA, is the largest canyon in the world and one of the most famous World Heritage Sites. It has been established as a National Park since 1919. This aerial view shows how the canyon has been carved out by the Colorado river, exposing many layers of sedimentary rock. The canyon reaches depths of over 1.5 km and there are many peaks and smaller canyons within the main gorge.

2 Mackenzie River Delta, *Canada*

This photograph looks west across the delta of the Mackenzie river towards the Richardson Mountains in the Northwest Territories of Canada. The isolated village of Alavik is located inside the tight bend in the river. The severe climate means that the river is only navigable here between June and October. The Mackenzie, including the Peace and Finlay rivers to the east of the Great Slave Lake, is the second longest river system in North America.

3 Appalachian Mountains, *USA*

This photograph from the Space Shuttle shows the heavily wooded ridges of the Appalachian Mountains in southwest Virginia. This narrow range, which is only approximately 160 km wide, forms the principal mountains in the eastern United States and runs parallel to the Atlantic coast. In the area shown in this image, some peaks exceed 1 200 m in height. The valleys between the mountain ridges have rich agricultural soils.

Satellite/Sensor: Space Shuttle

1

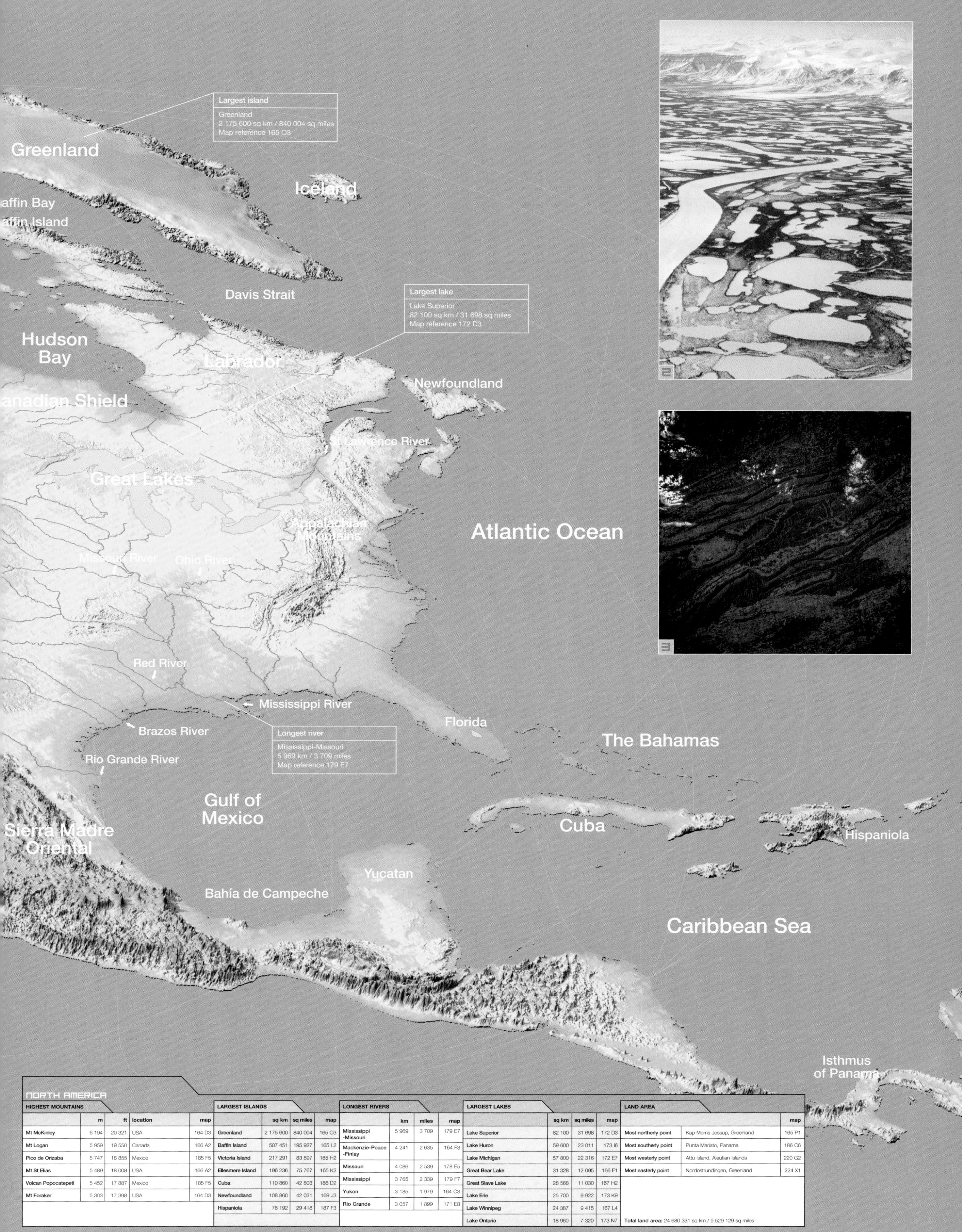

Greenland

Iceland

Baffin Bay

Baffin Island

Davis Strait

Hudson Bay

Labrador

Newfoundland

Canadian Shield

Great Lakes

St Lawrence River

Appalachian Mountains

Atlantic Ocean

Missouri River

Ohio River

Red River

Mississippi River

Brazos River

Florida

The Bahamas

Rio Grande River

Gulf of Mexico

Cuba

Hispaniola

Sierra Madre Oriental

Yucatan

Bahía de Campeche

Caribbean Sea

Isthmus of Panama

Largest island

Greenland
2 175 600 sq km / 840 004 sq miles
Map reference 165 O3

Largest lake

Lake Superior
82 100 sq km / 31 698 sq miles
Map reference 172 D3

Longest river

Mississippi-Missouri
5 969 km / 3 709 miles
Map reference 179 E7

NORTH AMERICA

HIGHEST MOUNTAINS

	m	ft	location	map
Mt McKinley	6 194	20 321	USA	164 D3
Mt Logan	5 959	19 550	Canada	166 A2
Pico de Orizaba	5 747	18 855	Mexico	185 F5
Mt St Elias	5 489	18 008	USA	166 A2
Volcán Popocatepetl	5 452	17 887	Mexico	185 F5
Mt Foraker	5 303	17 398	USA	164 D3

LARGEST ISLANDS

	sq km	sq miles	map
Greenland	2 175 600	840 004	165 O3
Baffin Island	507 451	195 927	165 L2
Victoria Island	217 291	83 897	165 H2
Ellesmere Island	196 236	75 767	165 K2
Cuba	110 860	42 803	186 D2
Newfoundland	108 860	42 031	169 J3
Hispaniola	76 192	29 418	187 F3

LONGEST RIVERS

	km	miles	map
Mississippi-Missouri	5 969	3 709	179 E7
Mackenzie-Peace-Finlay	4 241	2 635	164 F3
Missouri	4 086	2 539	178 E5
Mississippi	3 765	2 339	179 F7
Yukon	3 185	1 979	164 C3
Rio Grande	3 057	1 899	171 E8

LARGEST LAKES

	sq km	sq miles	map
Lake Superior	82 100	31 698	172 D3
Lake Huron	59 600	23 011	173 I6
Lake Michigan	57 800	22 318	172 E7
Great Bear Lake	31 328	12 095	166 F1
Great Slave Lake	28 568	11 030	167 H2
Lake Erie	25 700	9 922	173 K9
Lake Winnipeg	24 387	9 415	167 L4
Lake Ontario	18 960	7 320	173 N7

LAND AREA

		map
Most northerly point	Kap Morris Jessup, Greenland	165 P1
Most southerly point	Punta Mariato, Panama	186 C6
Most westerly point	Attu Island, Aleutian Islands	220 G2
Most easterly point	Nordostrundingen, Greenland	224 X1
Total land area: 24 680 331 sq km / 9 529 129 sq miles		

north**america**[countries]

NORTH AMERICA

COUNTRIES

	area sq km	area sq miles	population	capital	languages	religions	currency	map
ANTIGUA AND BARBUDA	442	171	65 000	St John's	English, creole	Protestant, Roman Catholic	E. Carib. dollar	187
THE BAHAMAS	13 939	5 382	304 000	Nassau	English, creole	Protestant, Roman Catholic	Dollar	186–187
BARBADOS	430	166	267 000	Bridgetown	English, creole	Protestant, Roman Catholic	Dollar	187
BELIZE	22 965	8 867	226 000	Belmopan	English, Spanish, Mayan, creole	Roman Catholic, Protestant	Dollar	185
CANADA	9 970 610	3 849 674	30 757 000	Ottawa	English, French	Roman Catholic, Protestant, Eastern Orthodox, Jewish	Dollar	164–165
COSTA RICA	51 100	19 730	4 024 000	San José	Spanish	Roman Catholic, Protestant	Colón	186
CUBA	110 860	42 803	11 199 000	Havana (La Habana)	Spanish	Roman Catholic, Protestant	Peso	186–187
DOMINICA	750	290	71 000	Roseau	English, creole	Roman Catholic, Protestant	E. Carib. dollar	187
DOMINICAN REPUBLIC	48 442	18 704	8 373 000	Santo Domingo	Spanish, creole	Roman Catholic, Protestant	Peso	187
EL SALVADOR	21 041	8 124	6 278 000	San Salvador	Spanish	Roman Catholic, Protestant	Colón	185
GRENADA	378	146	94 000	St George's	English, creole	Roman Catholic, Protestant	E. Carib. dollar	187
GUATEMALA	108 890	42 043	11 385 000	Guatemala City	Spanish, Mayan languages	Roman Catholic, Protestant	Quetzal	185
HAITI	27 750	10 714	8 142 000	Port-au-Prince	French, creole	Roman Catholic, Protestant, Voodoo	Gourde	186
HONDURAS	112 088	43 277	6 417 000	Tegucigalpa	Spanish, Amerindian languages	Roman Catholic, Protestant	Lempira	186
JAMAICA	10 991	4 244	2 576 000	Kingston	English, creole	Protestant, Roman Catholic	Dollar	186
MEXICO	1 972 545	761 604	98 872 000	Mexico City	Spanish, Amerindian languages	Roman Catholic, Protestant	Peso	184–185
NICARAGUA	130 000	50 193	5 071 000	Managua	Spanish, Amerindian languages	Roman Catholic, Protestant	Córdoba	186
PANAMA	77 082	29 762	2 856 000	Panama City	Spanish, English, Amerindian languages	Roman Catholic, Protestant, Sunni Muslim	Balboa	186
ST KITTS AND NEVIS	261	101	38 000	Basseterre	English, creole	Protestant, Roman Catholic	E. Carib. dollar	187
ST LUCIA	616	238	148 000	Castries	English, creole	Roman Catholic, Protestant	E. Carib. dollar	187
ST VINCENT AND THE GRENADINES	389	150	112 000	Kingstown	English, creole	Protestant, Roman Catholic	E. Carib. dollar	187
TRINIDAD AND TOBAGO	5 130	1 981	1 294 000	Port of Spain	English, creole, Hindi	Roman Catholic, Hindu, Protestant, Sunni Muslim	Dollar	187
UNITED STATES OF AMERICA	9 809 378	3 787 422	283 230 000	Washington	English, Spanish	Protestant, Roman Catholic, Sunni Muslim, Jewish	Dollar	170–171

DEPENDENT TERRITORIES

	territorial status	area sq km	area sq miles	population	capital	languages	religions	currency	map
Anguilla	United Kingdom Overseas Territory	155	60	11 000	The Valley	English	Protestant, Roman Catholic	E. Carib. Dollar	187
Aruba	Self-governing Netherlands Territory	193	75	101 000	Oranjestad	Papiamento, Dutch, English	Roman Catholic, Protestant	Florin	187
Bermuda	United Kingdom Overseas Territory	54	21	63 000	Hamilton	English	Protestant, Roman Catholic	Dollar	171
Cayman Islands	United Kingdom Overseas Territory	259	100	38 000	George Town	English	Protestant, Roman Catholic	Dollar	186
Clipperton, Île	French Overseas Territory	7	3	uninhabited					221
Greenland	Self-governing Danish Territory	2 175 600	840 004	56 000	Nuuk (Godthåb)	Greenlandic, Danish	Protestant	Danish krone	165
Guadeloupe	French Overseas Department	1 780	687	428 000	Basse-Terre	French, creole	Roman Catholic	French franc	187
Martinique	French Overseas Department	1 079	417	383 000	Fort-de-France	French, creole	Roman Catholic, traditional beliefs	French franc	187
Montserrat	United Kingdom Overseas Territory	100	39	4 000	Plymouth	English	Protestant, Roman Catholic	E. Carib. Dollar	187
Navassa Island	United States Unincorporated Territory	5	2	uninhabited					186
Netherlands Antilles	Self-governing Netherlands Territory	800	309	215 000	Willemstad	Dutch, Papiamento, English	Roman Catholic, Protestant	NA guilder	187
Puerto Rico	United States Commonwealth	9 104	3 515	3 915 000	San Juan	Spanish, English	Roman Catholic, Protestant	US dollar	187
St Pierre and Miquelon	French Territorial Collectivity	242	93	7 000	St-Pierre	French	Roman Catholic	French franc	169
Turks and Caicos Islands	United Kingdom Overseas Territory	430	166	17 000	Grand Turk	English	Protestant	US dollar	187
Virgin Islands (U.K.)	United Kingdom Overseas Territory	153	59	24 000	Road Town	English	Protestant, Roman Catholic	US dollar	187
Virgin Islands (U.S.A.)	United States Unincorporated Territory	352	136	121 000	Charlotte Amalie	English, Spanish	Protestant, Roman Catholic	US dollar	187

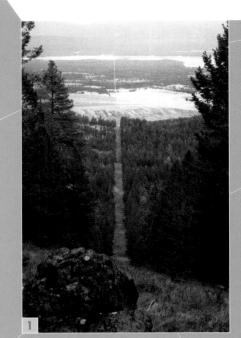

1

Tropic of Cancer

2

3

CONNECTIONS

▸ subject page#

▸ World physical features 8–9
▸ World countries 10–11
▸ North America landscapes 156–157
▸ North America environments 162–163
▸ Reference maps of North America 164–187

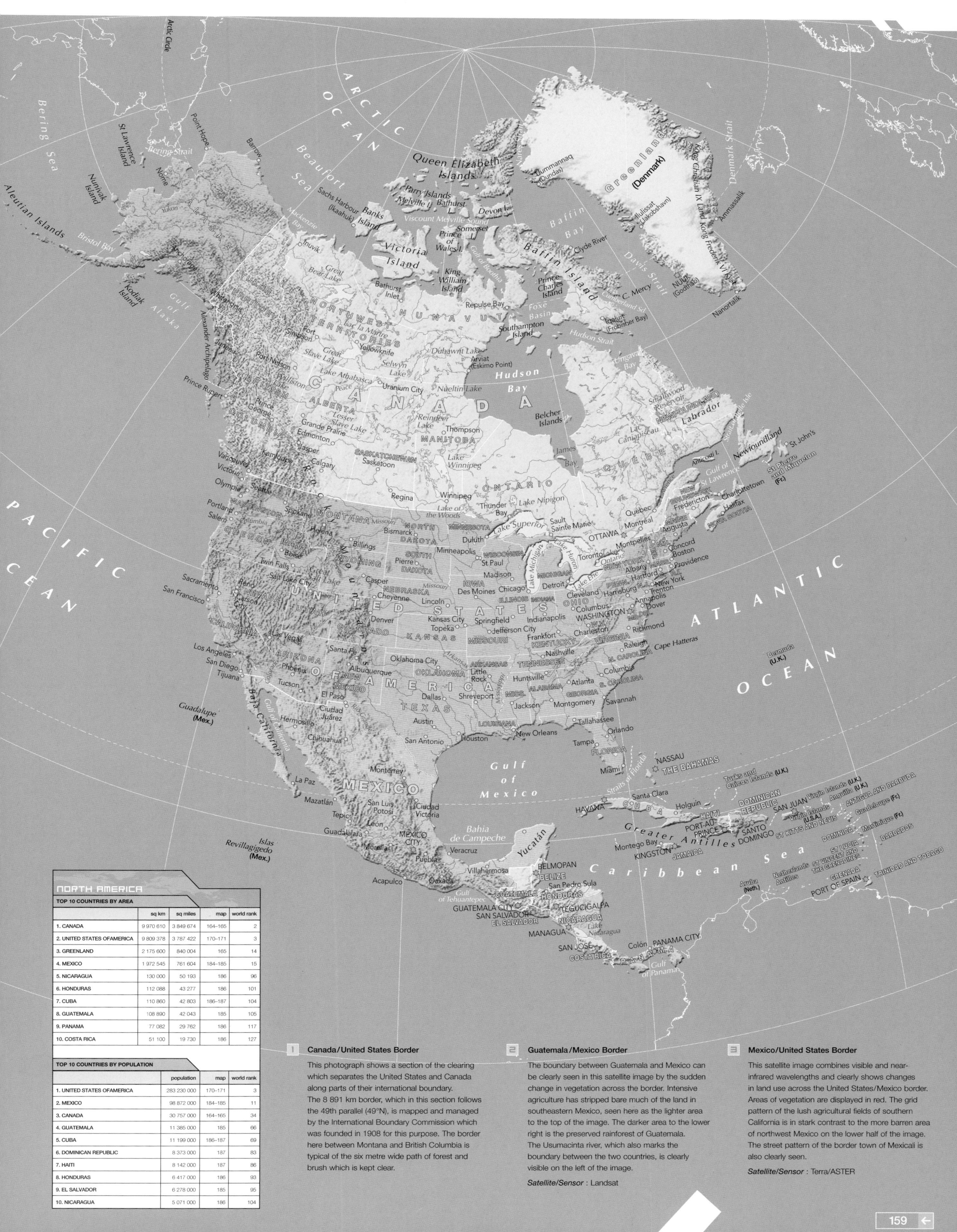

ARCTIC OCEAN

PACIFIC OCEAN

ATLANTIC OCEAN

NORTH AMERICA

TOP 10 COUNTRIES BY AREA

	sq km	sq miles	map	world rank
1. CANADA	9 970 610	3 849 674	164–165	2
2. UNITED STATES OF AMERICA	9 809 378	3 787 422	170–171	3
3. GREENLAND	2 175 600	840 004	165	14
4. MEXICO	1 972 545	761 604	184–185	15
5. NICARAGUA	130 000	50 193	186	96
6. HONDURAS	112 088	43 277	186	101
7. CUBA	110 860	42 803	186–187	104
8. GUATEMALA	108 890	42 043	185	105
9. PANAMA	77 082	29 762	186	117
10. COSTA RICA	51 100	19 730	186	127

TOP 10 COUNTRIES BY POPULATION

	population	map	world rank
1. UNITED STATES OF AMERICA	283 230 000	170–171	3
2. MEXICO	98 872 000	184–185	11
3. CANADA	30 757 000	164–165	34
4. GUATEMALA	11 385 000	185	66
5. CUBA	11 199 000	186–187	69
6. DOMINICAN REPUBLIC	8 373 000	187	83
7. HAITI	8 142 000	187	86
8. HONDURAS	6 417 000	186	93
9. EL SALVADOR	6 278 000	185	95
10. NICARAGUA	5 071 000	186	104

1 Canada/United States Border

This photograph shows a section of the clearing which separates the United States and Canada along parts of their international boundary.
The 8 891 km border, which in this section follows the 49th parallel (49°N), is mapped and managed by the International Boundary Commission which was founded in 1908 for this purpose. The border here between Montana and British Columbia is typical of the six metre wide path of forest and brush which is kept clear.

2 Guatemala/Mexico Border

The boundary between Guatemala and Mexico can be clearly seen in this satellite image by the sudden change in vegetation across the border. Intensive agriculture has stripped bare much of the land in southeastern Mexico, seen here as the lighter area to the top of the image. The darker area to the lower right is the preserved rainforest of Guatemala.
The Usumacinta river, which also marks the boundary between the two countries, is clearly visible on the left of the image.

Satellite/Sensor : Landsat

3 Mexico/United States Border

This satellite image combines visible and near-infrared wavelengths and clearly shows changes in land use across the United States/Mexico border. Areas of vegetation are displayed in red. The grid pattern of the lush agricultural fields of southern California is in stark contrast to the more barren area of northwest Mexico on the lower half of the image. The street pattern of the border town of Mexicali is also clearly seen.

Satellite/Sensor : Terra/ASTER

1 San Andreas Fault, *California, USA*

The San Andreas fault is a large break in the Earth's crust between the North American and Pacific plates. It runs for over 950 km from northwest California to the Gulf of California. Movement between the two plates causes earthquakes which present a serious threat to this part of the United States. The fault runs diagonally across this satellite image from left to right, with the supplementary Garlock fault stretching to the top of the image. The proximity of the faults to Los Angeles, the large grey area at the bottom of the image, is obvious.

Satellite/Sensor : Landsat

2 Mount St Helens, *Washington, USA*

After lying dormant since 1857, Mount St Helens in the Cascade mountain range in Washington state, USA erupted violently in May 1980. The eruption was one of the largest volcanic events in North American history and caused the loss of sixty lives. The explosion reduced the height of the mountain by 390 m and flattened trees and killed wildlife over an area of twenty five kilometres radius. The result was the new horseshoe-shaped crater seen in this aerial photograph.

3 Popocatépetl, *Mexico*

This false-colour satellite image shows the Mexican volcano Popocatépetl four days after its eruption in December 2000. The eruption sent molten rock high into the air and over 50 000 people were evacuated from the surrounding area. The bright green spot in the crater indicates that its temperature is still very high. The volcano lies only seventy kilometres southeast of Mexico City, and its name, which is the Aztec word for 'smoking mountain' is suggestive of the threat it presents.

Satellite/Sensor : SPOT

4 Atlantic Hurricanes

Tropical storms have different names in different parts of the world – typhoons in the northwest Pacific Ocean, cyclones in the Indian Ocean region and hurricanes in the Atlantic Ocean and east Pacific. The effects of their strong winds and heavy rain can be devastating.

The Atlantic hurricane season lasts from June to November, with the majority of storms occurring between August and October. The storms present a threat to the islands of the Caribbean and Bermuda and to the east coast of the United States of America. In both 1999 and 2000 there were eight tropical storms which reached hurricane force, as shown on the map Fig. #01. The most severe of these was Hurricane Floyd which developed during early September 1999. It achieved maximum sustained wind speeds of 249 km per hour and made landfall near Cape Fear, North Carolina, USA. Although wind speeds had dropped to around 166 km per hour, it had a devastating effect and fifty seven deaths were directly attributed to the hurricane, making it the deadliest US hurricane since 1972. The computer-generated images show Floyd just off the Florida coast and the inset image indicates wind directions and rainfall levels (yellow-orange over 10mm per hour) at the centre of the hurricane.

Fig. #01
Atlantic hurricane tracks
1999-2000

Hurricane Strength
1999
2000

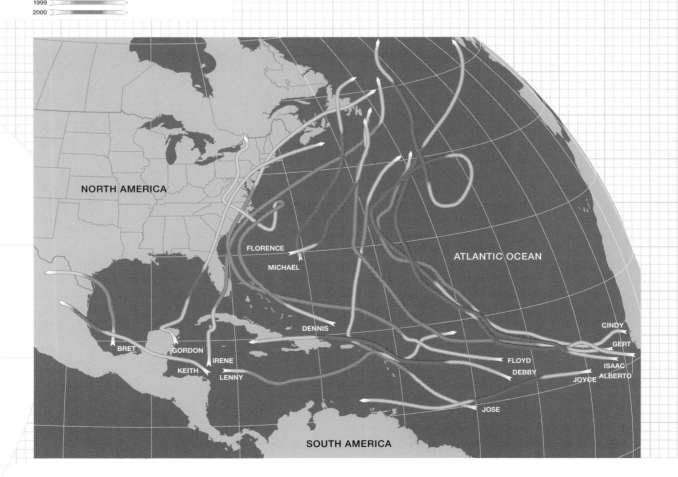

NORTH AMERICA

ATLANTIC OCEAN

FLORENCE
MICHAEL

DENNIS

CINDY

GERT

BRET
GORDON
KEITH
IRENE
LENNY

FLOYD
DEBBY

ISAAC
JOYCE ALBERTO

JOSE

SOUTH AMERICA

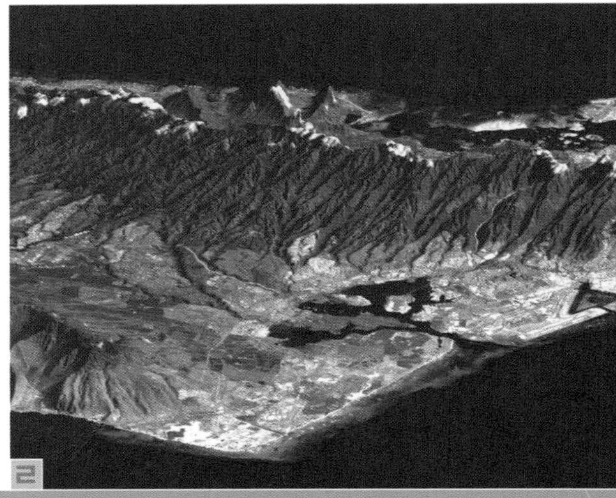

northamerica[environments]

1 Suburbia, California, *USA*

A new housing development west of Stockton, California is shown in this
vertical aerial photograph. Water-front properties are in great demand in this
area and each house on the finger-like promontories has its own berth, with
access via canals to the California Delta waterways of the Sacramento and
San Joaquin rivers. Development is continuing on the empty plots at the
lower right of the photograph.

2 Island Environment, Hawaii, *USA*

This image shows a perspective view of Honolulu and surrounding area on
the Hawaiian island of Oahu. The three-dimensional effect is a result of using
height data collected during the Shuttle Radar Topography Mission (SRTM)
of the Space Shuttle Endeavour. This height data has been combined with a
Landsat 7 satellite image which has been draped over the surface of the
elevation model. Honolulu, Pearl Harbour, the Koolau mountain range and
offshore reef patterns are all visible on the image.

Satellite/Sensor : Space Shuttle and Landsat

3 Great Plains, Montana, *USA*

A wheat farm on the Great Plains of Montana is shown in this aerial
photograph. The high grasses of the Great Plains once sustained large herds
of buffalo and the cattle and sheep of large ranches. Today the environment
is dominated by large farms using modern extensive farming techniques.

4 Arctic Coastline, *Greenland*

This Space Shuttle photograph gives a northeast view of the south-southeast
tip of Greenland. This is a typical scene of the glaciated coastline which
surrounds the world's largest island. The dark elongated fingers are inlets,
or fjords, which stretch from the North Atlantic Ocean towards the interior.
Large white areas to the top of the image mark the start of the permanent
ice cap which stretches north across the island to the Arctic Ocean.

Satellite/Sensor : Space Shuttle

5 Protected Environment, Yellowstone National Park, *USA*

The Lower Falls in the Grand Canyon of the Yellowstone River are one of many
spectacular features in Yellowstone National Park, Wyoming. The park mainly
lies within a volcanically active basin in the Rocky Mountains. It became the
world's first national park in 1872 with the purpose of preserving this area of
great natural beauty. As well as many geysers, hot springs, lakes and
waterfalls the park has a rich variety of flora and fauna.

6 Irrigation, Wyoming, *USA*

This aerial photograph shows fields watered by centre-pivot irrigation next to
the Bighorn river in northern Wyoming. This method of irrigation has created
circular patterns in the landscape. Each circle is fed from a rotating structure of
up to 300 m in length. The flow is carefully controlled so that the whole area is
supplied with an equal amount of water. The system makes it possible to grow
crops in otherwise infertile parts of the state.

Fig. #01
Land protected by the
US Federal Government

Kobuk Valley
N.P.   Gates of the
Arctic N.P.

A L A S K A

Denali
N.P.

Wrangell-
St Elias N.P.

Katmai
N.P.

Kenai Fjords N.P.

Glacier
Bay N.P.

Kauai

Oahu

Maui

Haleakala
N.P.

Hawaiian
Islands

Hawaii

Hawaii
Volcanoes
N.P.

North
Cascades
N.P.
Olympic N.P.   Colville
I.R.   Glacier
N.P.   Blackfeet
I.R.

Mount
Rainier N.P.   Yakima
I.R.   Flathead
I.R.

Fort Peck
I.R.

Voyageurs
N.P.

Isle Royale
N.P.

Crater
Lake N.P.   Yellowstone
N.P.

Grand Teton
N.P.

Northern
Cheyenne I.R.
Crow I.R.

Standing Rock
I.R.
Cheyenne River
I.R.

Lake Traverse
I.R.

Wind
River
I.R.

Badlands
N.P.
Pine Rosebud
Ridge I.R.

Yosemite
N.P.

Uintah &
Ouray I.R.

Rocky Mountain
N.P.

Kings Canyon
N.P.   Capitol
Reef N.P.

Canyonlands N.P.

Shenandoah
N.P.

Sequoia
N.P.   Death
Valley
N.P.   Bryce
Canyon N.P.

Navajo I.R.

Osage
I.R.

Channel Is.
N.P.   Mojave
N.P.   Grand
Canyon N.P.   Hopi I.R.

Great Smoky
Mts N.P.

Joshua Tree
N.P.   Fort Apache I.R.
San Carlos I.R.

Organ Pipe
Cactus N.P.   White Sands
Nat. Mon.

Big Bend
N.P.

Everglades
N.P.

National forest

National grassland

National wildlife refuge

National park

Indian reservation

Bureau of Land Management land

Military reservation

National wild and scenic river

163 ←

northamerica[map1]

40°-85°N / 10°-180°W

CONNECTIONS

► subject	page#
► World countries	10–11
► World changes	20–21
► North America landscapes	156–157
► North America countries	158–159
► Arctic features	214–215
► Arctic Ocean	224

>6000m
5000-6000m
4000-5000m
3000-4000m
2000-3000m
1000-2000m
500-1000m
200-500m
0-200m
<0m

0-200m
200-500m
500-1000m
1000-2000m
2000-3000m
3000-4000m
4000-5000m
5000-6000m
>6000m

RUSSIAN FEDERATION

U.S.A. ALASKA

CANADA

YUKON TERRITORY

NORTHWEST TERRITORIES

BRITISH COLUMBIA

ALBERTA

SASK

Brooks Range

Alaska Range

Aleutian Islands

Aleutian Range

Fox Islands

Bristol Bay

Kuskokwim Mountains

Philip Smith Mountains

Mackenzie Mountains

Rocky Mountains

Coast Mountains

Gulf of Alaska

Bering Strait

Chukchi Sea

Beaufort Sea

ARCTIC OCEAN

PACIFIC OCEAN

Great Bear Lake

Great Slave Lake

WASHINGTON

OREGON

IDAHO

MONTANA

WYOMING

NEVADA

CALIFORNIA

UTAH

COLORADO

Vancouver Island

Queen Charlotte Islands

Prince of Wales Island

Alexander Archipelago

Kodiak Island

miles
0   200   400   600

km
0   200   400   600   800   1000

1:15 000 000

Lambert Conformal Conic Projection

170-171

120°

130°

140°

150°

160°

170°

180°

110°

50°

40°

Arctic Circle

Greenland
(Kalaallit Nunaat)
(Denmark)
Nationalparken i Nord-og Østgrønland
Greenland Sea
Denmark Strait
ICELAND
REYKJAVÍK
Arctic Circle
Baffin Bay
Davis Strait
Labrador Sea
Hudson Bay
James Bay
Hudson Strait
Foxe Basin
Foxe Channel
Ungava Bay
Queen Elizabeth Islands
Parry Islands
Ellesmere Island
Axel Heiberg Island
Devon Island
Lancaster Sound
Baffin Island
Somerset Island
Prince of Wales Island
Victoria Island
Southampton Island
Coats Island
Belcher Islands
Péninsule d'Ungava
NUNAVUT
CANADA
MANITOBA
ONTARIO
QUÉBEC
Labrador
NEWFOUNDLAND
Newfoundland
Gulf of St Lawrence
Cabot Strait
NEW BRUNSWICK
NOVA SCOTIA
PRINCE EDWARD ISLAND
Sable Island
Gulf of Maine
ATLANTIC OCEAN
UNITED STATES OF AMERICA
NORTH DAKOTA
SOUTH DAKOTA
MINNESOTA
WISCONSIN
MICHIGAN
IOWA
NEBRASKA
ILLINOIS
INDIANA
OHIO
PENNSYLVANIA
NEW YORK
MAINE
Lake Superior
Lake Michigan
Lake Huron
Lake Erie
Lake Winnipeg
OTTAWA
Montréal
Québec
Toronto
Winnipeg
Thunder Bay
Minneapolis
St Paul
Milwaukee
Chicago
Detroit
Cleveland
Boston
New York
Halifax
St John's
Iqaluit
Nuuk (Godthåb)
North Magnetic Pole (2000)
North Geomagnetic Pole (2000)
Administrative divisions in the U.S.A. numbered on the map:
1. CONNECTICUT
2. MASSACHUSETTS
3. NEW HAMPSHIRE
4. RHODE ISLAND
170-171
100°
90°
80°
70°
60°
J
K
L
M
N

48°-65°N / 92°-142°W

1

2

3

4

5

A

B

C

D

E

F

G

64°

60°

56°
142°

52°

48°
136°

140°

132°

128°

124°

120°

>6000m
5000-6000m
4000-5000m
3000-4000m
2000-3000m
1000-2000m
500-1000m
200-500m
0-200m
<0m

0-200m
200-500m
500-1000m
1000-2000m
2000-3000m
3000-4000m
4000-5000m
5000-6000m
>6000m

PACIFIC

OCEAN

YUKON TERRITORY

ALASKA

U.S.A.

BRITISH

COLUMBIA

Whitehorse

Queen Charlotte Islands

Vancouver Island

Mackenzie Mountains

Coast Mountains

Rocky Mountains

Prince George

Prince Rupert

Kamloops

Vancouver

Victoria

WASHINGTON

Arctic Circle

180-181

1 : 6 500 000

miles
0 50 100 150 200 250 300

km
0 50 100 150 200 250 300 350 400 450 500

Conic Equidistant Projection

40°-57°N / 52°-95°W

>6000m
5000-6000m
4000-5000m
3000-4000m
2000-3000m
1000-2000m
500-1000m
200-500m
0-200m
<0m

0-200m
200-500m
500-1000m
1000-2000m
2000-3000m
3000-4000m
4000-5000m
5000-6000m
>6000m

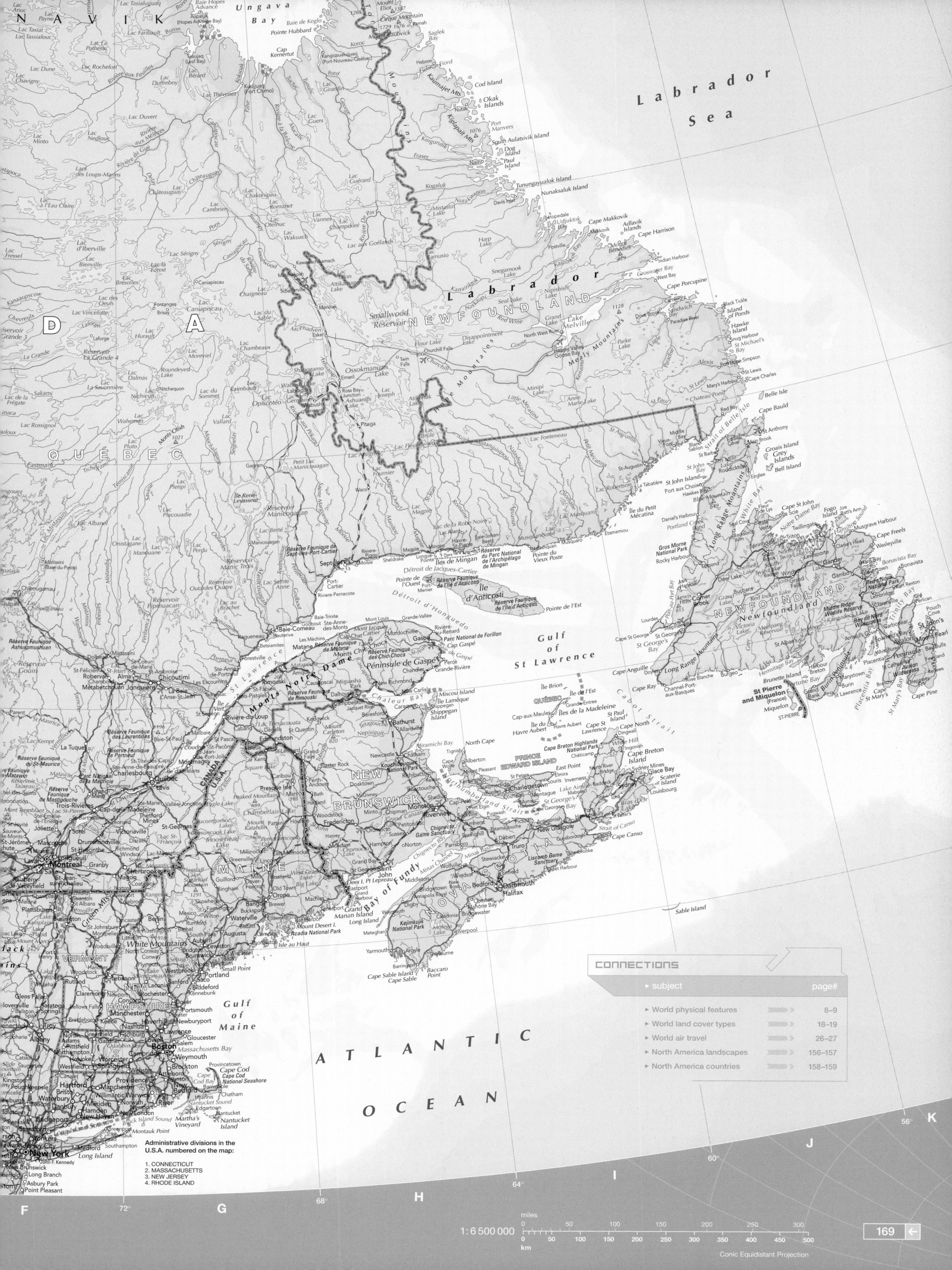
Ungava Bay
Labrador Sea
Labrador
NEWFOUNDLAND
QUEBEC
Smallwood Reservoir
Lake Melville
Mealy Mountains
Cape Harrison
Cape Porcupine
Nain
Hopedale
Goose Bay
Churchill Falls
Gulf of St Lawrence
Île d'Anticosti
Newfoundland
Strait of Belle Isle
Cabot Strait
Long Range Mountains
St John's
Avalon Peninsula
Gander
Corner Brook
St Pierre and Miquelon (France)
Cape Breton Island
Sydney
PRINCE EDWARD ISLAND
Charlottetown
NOVA SCOTIA
Halifax
Dartmouth
Sable Island
Bay of Fundy
NEW BRUNSWICK
Fredericton
Saint John
Moncton
Bathurst
Péninsule de Gaspé
Gaspé
Îles de la Madeleine
Chaleur Bay
St Lawrence
Monts Notre Dame
Rimouski
Sept-Îles
Baie-Comeau
Chicoutimi
Québec
Trois-Rivières
Montreal
Sherbrooke
MAINE
Augusta
Bangor
Portland
Gulf of Maine
VERMONT
NEW HAMPSHIRE
White Mountains
Green Mts
Boston
Providence
Hartford
New Haven
New York
Long Island
Cape Cod
Nantucket Island
Martha's Vineyard
ATLANTIC
OCEAN
Administrative divisions in the U.S.A. numbered on the map:
1. CONNECTICUT
2. MASSACHUSETTS
3. NEW JERSEY
4. RHODE ISLAND
CONNECTIONS
subject page#
World physical features 8–9
World land cover types 18–19
World air travel 26–27
North America landscapes 156–157
North America countries 158–159
1:6 500 000
miles 0 50 100 150 200 250 300
km 0 50 100 150 200 250 300 350 400 450 500
Conic Equidistant Projection
F G H I J K
72° 68° 64° 60° 56°

164-165

17°-50°N / 67°-125°W

UNITED STATES OF AMERICA

MEXICO

PACIFIC OCEAN

British Columbia · Alberta · Saskatchewan · Washington · Oregon · Idaho · Montana · North Dakota · South Dakota · Nebraska · Wyoming · Nevada · Utah · Colorado · California · Arizona · New Mexico · Texas

Vancouver Island · Vancouver · Victoria · Seattle · Everett · Bellevue · Tacoma · Olympia · Bremerton · Spokane · Calgary · Lethbridge · Medicine Hat · Regina · Saskatoon

Portland · Salem · Eugene · Roseburg · Medford · Coos Bay · Grants Pass · Klamath Falls

Sacramento · San Francisco · San Jose · Oakland · Berkeley · Santa Rosa · Vallejo · Stockton · Modesto · Fresno · Bakersfield · Santa Barbara · Los Angeles · Long Beach · Pasadena · Riverside · San Bernardino · Santa Ana · Anaheim · Oceanside · San Diego · Tijuana · Mexicali · Ensenada

Reno · Carson City · Las Vegas · Henderson · Boulder City · Lake Mead

Salt Lake City · Ogden · Provo · Boise · Billings · Great Falls · Helena · Missoula · Butte

Denver · Aurora · Boulder · Colorado Springs · Pueblo · Cheyenne · Casper · Rapid City · Sioux Falls

Phoenix · Mesa · Chandler · Glendale · Tucson · Flagstaff · Yuma · Nogales

Albuquerque · Santa Fe · Las Cruces · Roswell · El Paso · Ciudad Juárez

Lubbock · Amarillo · Midland · San Angelo · Del Rio · Laredo · Nuevo Laredo · Monterrey · Saltillo

Chihuahua · Ciudad Delicias · Hermosillo · Guaymas · Ciudad Obregón · Navojoa · Los Mochis · Culiacán · Mazatlán · Durango · Torreón · Gómez Palacio

Baja California · Gulf of California · Guadalupe (Mexico)

La Paz · Cabo San Lucas · San José del Cabo · Ciudad Constitución

Tropic of Cancer

Sierra Madre Occidental · Sierra Madre Oriental · Sierra Madre del Sur

Aguascalientes · Zacatecas · San Luis Potosí · Guadalajara · León · Guanajuato · Querétaro · Morelia · Toluca · MEXICO CITY · Puebla · Cuernavaca · Tlaxcala · Tepic · Puerto Vallarta · Colima

Islas Revillagigedo (Mexico) · Isla Socorro · Isla Clarión · Isla San Benedicto · Isla Roca Partida

Rocky Mountains · Great Basin · Mojave Desert · Death Valley · Colorado Plateau · Grand Canyon · Great Salt Lake Desert · High Desert · Columbia Plateau · Snake River · Colorado River · Edwards Plateau · Llano Estacado

Channel Islands · Santa Cruz Island · Santa Rosa Island · San Nicolas Island · San Clemente Island

Elevation legend:
>6000m · 5000-6000m · 4000-5000m · 3000-4000m · 2000-3000m · 1000-2000m · 500-1000m · 200-500m · 0-200m · <0m

Depth legend:
0-200m · 200-500m · 500-1000m · 1000-2000m · 2000-3000m · 3000-4000m · 4000-5000m · 5000-6000m · >6000m

1:12 000 000

miles 0 100 200 300 400 500
km 0 100 200 300 400 500 600 700 800

Lambert Conformal Conic Projection

Grid references: 2 · 3 · A · 4 · 5 · B · 6 · 7 · C · 8 · D · E · F

130° · 125° · 120° · 115° · 110° · 105° · 100°
45° · 40° · 35° · 30° · 25° · 20° · 17°

ATLANTIC

OCEAN

Bermuda
(U.K.)
HAMILTON

THE BAHAMAS

West

Indies

Turks and
Caicos Islands
(U.K.)

Hispaniola

Gulf of Mexico

HAVANA
(La Habana)

CUBA

Greater

Antilles

DOMINICAN
REPUBLIC
SANTO
DOMINGO

HAITI
PORT-AU-
PRINCE

Cayman Islands
(U.K.)

JAMAICA

KINGSTON

Caribbean Sea

GUATEMALA

BELIZE

41°-49°N / 76°-93°W

Elevation scale:
>6000m
5000-6000m
4000-5000m
3000-4000m
2000-3000m
1500-2000m
1000-1500m
500-1000m
200-500m
100-200m
0-100m
<0m

0-50m
50-100m
100-200m
200-500m
500-1000m
1000-2000m
2000-3000m
3000-4000m
4000-5000m
5000-6000m
>6000m

Lake Superior

Lake Michigan

MINNESOTA

WISCONSIN

MICHIGAN

IOWA

ILLINOIS

INDIANA

UNITED STATES OF AMERICA

Thunder Bay

Duluth
Superior

Eau Claire

La Crosse

Madison

Milwaukee

Green Bay

Oshkosh

Appleton

Chicago

Rockford

Cedar Rapids

Dubuque

Marquette

Escanaba

178-179

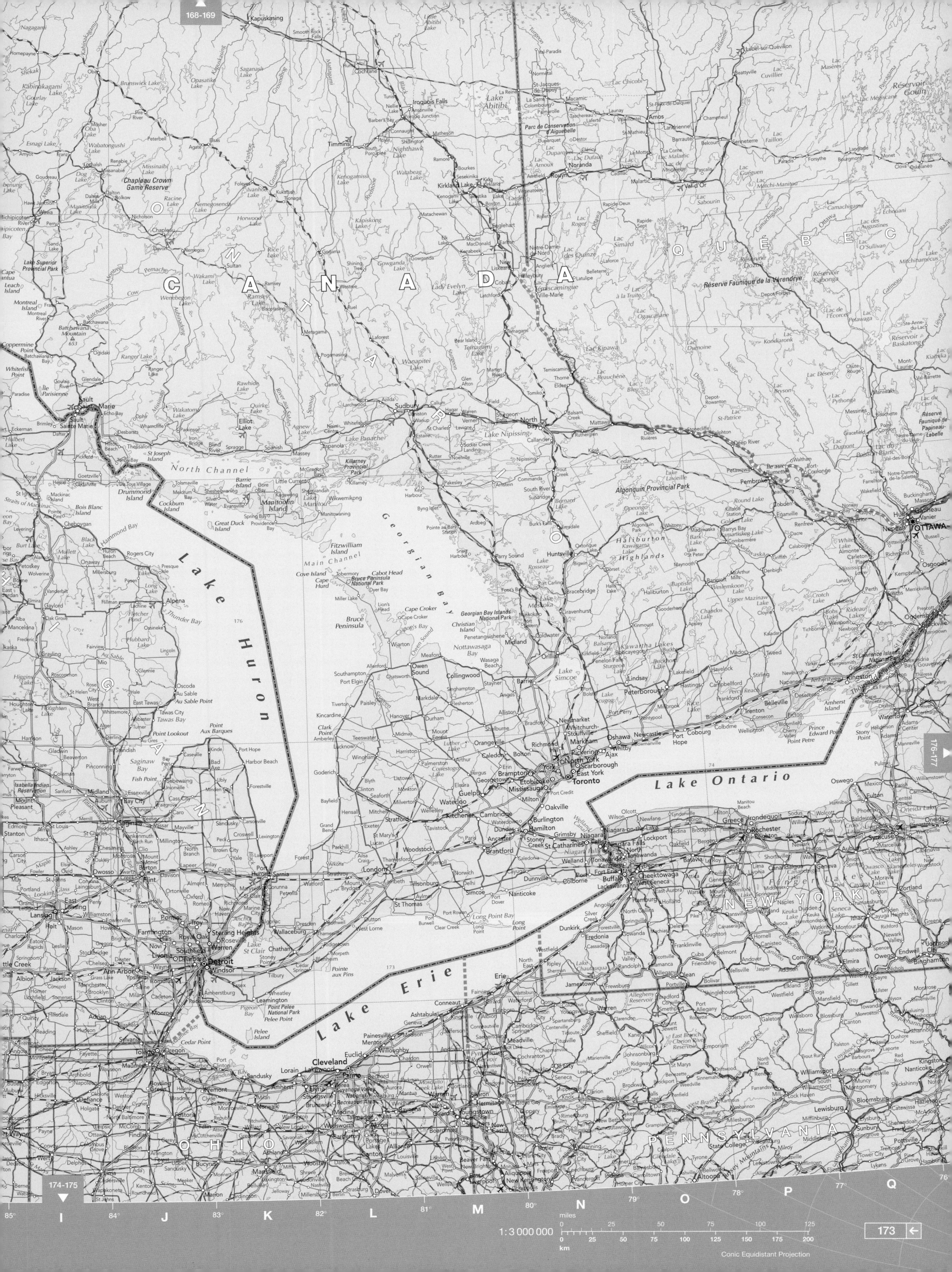

168-169
C A N A D A
O N T A R I O
Q U É B E C
M I C H I G A N
N E W Y O R K
P E N N S Y L V A N I A
O H I O
Lake Huron
Lake Ontario
Lake Erie
Georgian Bay
Lake St Clair
Lake Nipissing
Lake Simcoe
Lake Abitibi
North Channel
Main Channel
Saginaw Bay
Thunder Bay
Long Point Bay
Algonquin Provincial Park
Haliburton Highlands
Kawartha Lakes
Chapleau Crown Game Reserve
Lake Superior Provincial Park
Parc de Conservation d'Aiguebelle
Réserve Faunique de la Vérendrye
Bruce Peninsula National Park
Georgian Bay Islands National Park
Point Pelee National Park
Manitoulin Island
Bruce Peninsula
OTTAWA
Toronto
Detroit
Windsor
Cleveland
Buffalo
Rochester
Syracuse
Hamilton
London
Kitchener
Sudbury
North Bay
Sault Sainte Marie
Timmins
Kingston
Erie
Toledo
Akron
Flint
Lansing
Saginaw
Youngstown
Kapuskasing
Cochrane
Val-d'Or
Rouyn
Noranda
Pembroke
Barrie
Peterborough
Oshawa
Belleville
Niagara Falls
St Catharines
Sarnia
Port Huron
Owen Sound
Mississauga
Brampton
Scarborough
North York
Guelph
Cambridge
Brantford
Chatham
Jamestown
Elmira
Binghamton
Williamsport
State College
Altoona
Mansfield
Canton
Sandusky
Lorain
Ashtabula
174-175
176-177
85° 84° 83° 82° 81° 80° 79° 78° 77° 76°
I J K L M N O P Q
1:3 000 000
miles 0 25 50 75 100 125
km 0 25 50 75 100 125 150 175 200
Conic Equidistant Projection

Administrative divisions in the U.S.A.
numbered on map:

1. CONNECTICUT
2. MASSACHUSETTS
3. RHODE ISLAND
4. DELAWARE

northamerica[map6]

22°·48'N / 92°·70'W

1 : 6 500 000

Lambert Conformal Conic Projection

CONNECTIONS

	subject	page#
▲	World land cover types	18–19
▲	World cities	24–25
▲	North America landscapes	156–157
▲	North America countries	158–159
▲	North America threats	160–161
▲	Atlantic Ocean	216–217

7

186–187 ▶

ATLANTIC

OCEAN

THE BAHAMAS

Great Bahama Bank

Little Bahama Bank

Grand Bahama

Andros

Eleuthera

New Providence
NASSAU

San Salvador

Cat Island

Rum Cay

Long Island

Crooked Island

Acklins Island

Mayaguana

GEORGIA

SOUTH CAROLINA

FLORIDA

ALABAMA

MISSISSIPPI

LOUISIANA

Gulf

of

Mexico

CUBA

HAVANA
(La Habana)

Tropic of Cancer

Straits of Florida

New Orleans

Atlanta

Tampa

St Petersburg

Orlando

Miami

Fort Lauderdale

West Palm Beach

Everglades National Park

Key West

Jacksonville

Savannah

Charleston

Myrtle Beach

Mobile

Pensacola

Tallahassee

Birmingham

Columbus

Montgomery

miles
0   50   100   150   200   250   300

km
0   50   100   150 200 250 300 350 400 450 500

>6000m
5000-6000m
4000-5000m
3000-4000m
2000-3000m
1000-2000m
500-1000m
200-500m
0-200m

<0m
0-200m
200-500m
500-1000m
1000-2000m
2000-3000m
3000-4000m
4000-5000m
5000-6000m
>6000m

northamerica[map7]

36°-45°N / 68°-85°W

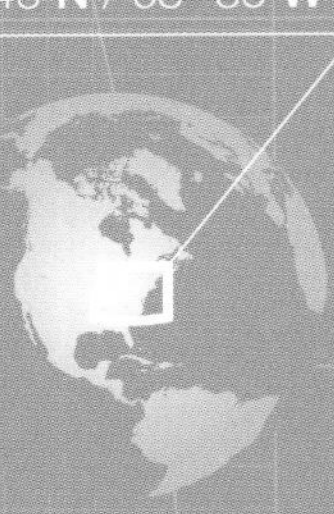

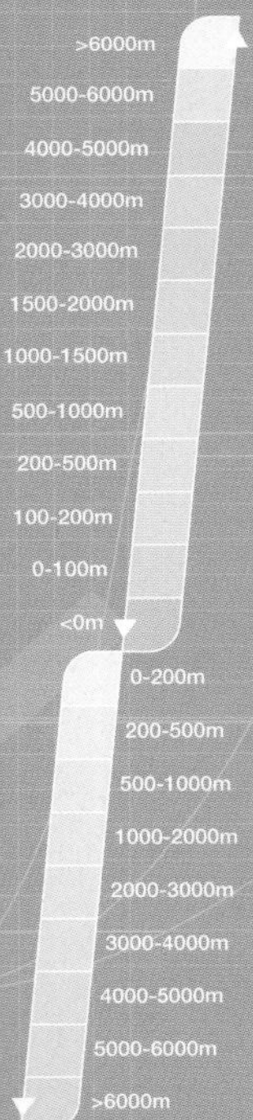

172-173

>6000m
5000-6000m
4000-5000m
3000-4000m
2000-3000m
1500-2000m
1000-1500m
500-1000m
200-500m
100-200m
0-100m
<0m
0-200m
200-500m
500-1000m
1000-2000m
2000-3000m
3000-4000m
4000-5000m
5000-6000m
>6000m

174-175

CONNECTIONS

Gulf of Maine

ATLANTIC OCEAN

1 : 3 000 000

miles

km

Lambert Conformal Conic Projection

CANADA
ONTARIO
QUÉBEC
MANITOBA
SASKATCHEWAN
UNITED STATES
MONTANA
WYOMING
COLORADO
NORTH DAKOTA
SOUTH DAKOTA
NEBRASKA
KANSAS
MINNESOTA
IOWA
MISSOURI
WISCONSIN
ILLINOIS
MICHIGAN
INDIANA
OHIO
KENTUCKY
WEST VIRGINIA
Lake Superior
Lake Michigan
Lake Huron
Lake Erie
Georgian Bay
Winnipeg
Regina
Thunder Bay
Duluth
Minneapolis
Milwaukee
Chicago
Detroit
Toronto
Cleveland
Columbus
Indianapolis
Cincinnati
St Louis
Kansas City
Omaha
Lincoln
Des Moines
Denver
Colorado Springs
Cheyenne
Bismarck
Sioux Falls
166-167
174-175
180-181
178
1
2
3
4
48°
44°
40°

CONNECTIONS

subject	page#
▲ World physical features	8–9
▲ World changes	20–21
▲ North America countries	158–159
▲ North America environments	162–163

25° 52'N / 82° 104'W

1:6 500 000

Lambert Conformal Conic Projection

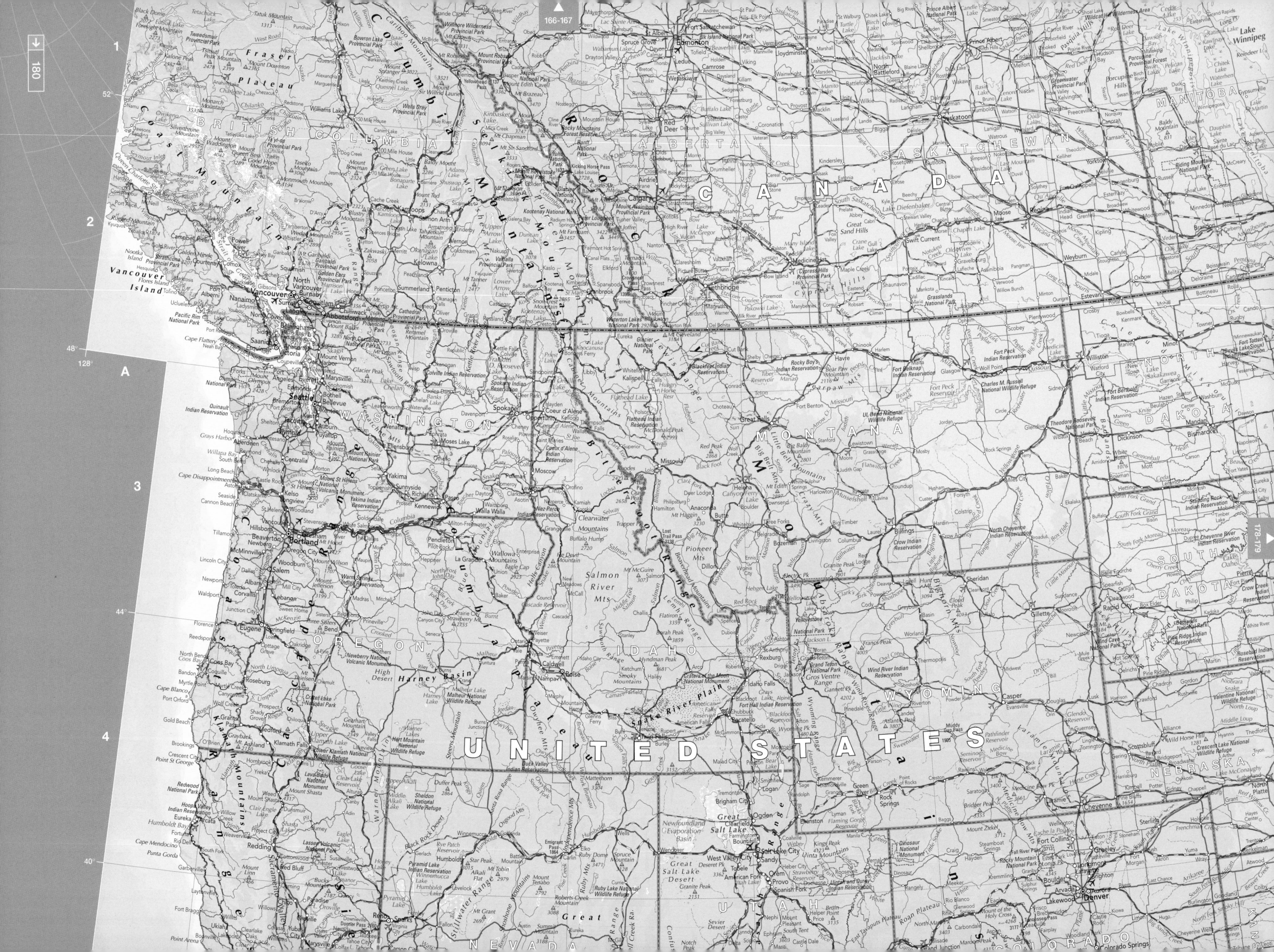

◄ 166-167

northamerica[map9]

CONNECTIONS

subject	page#
World land images	12–13
World earthquakes	14–15
North America countries	158–159
North America threats	160–161
North America environments	162–163

northamerica[map10]

32°-40°N / 109°-124°W

>6000m
5000-6000m
4000-5000m
3000-4000m
2000-3000m
1500-2000m
1000-1500m
500-1000m
200-500m
100-200m
0-100m
<0m
0-200m
200-500m
500-1000m
1000-2000m
2000-3000m
3000-4000m
4000-5000m
5000-6000m
>6000m

CONNECTIONS

subject	page#
World earthquakes	14–15
World cities	24–25
North America landscapes	156–157
North America countries	158–159
North America threats	160–161
North America environments	162–163

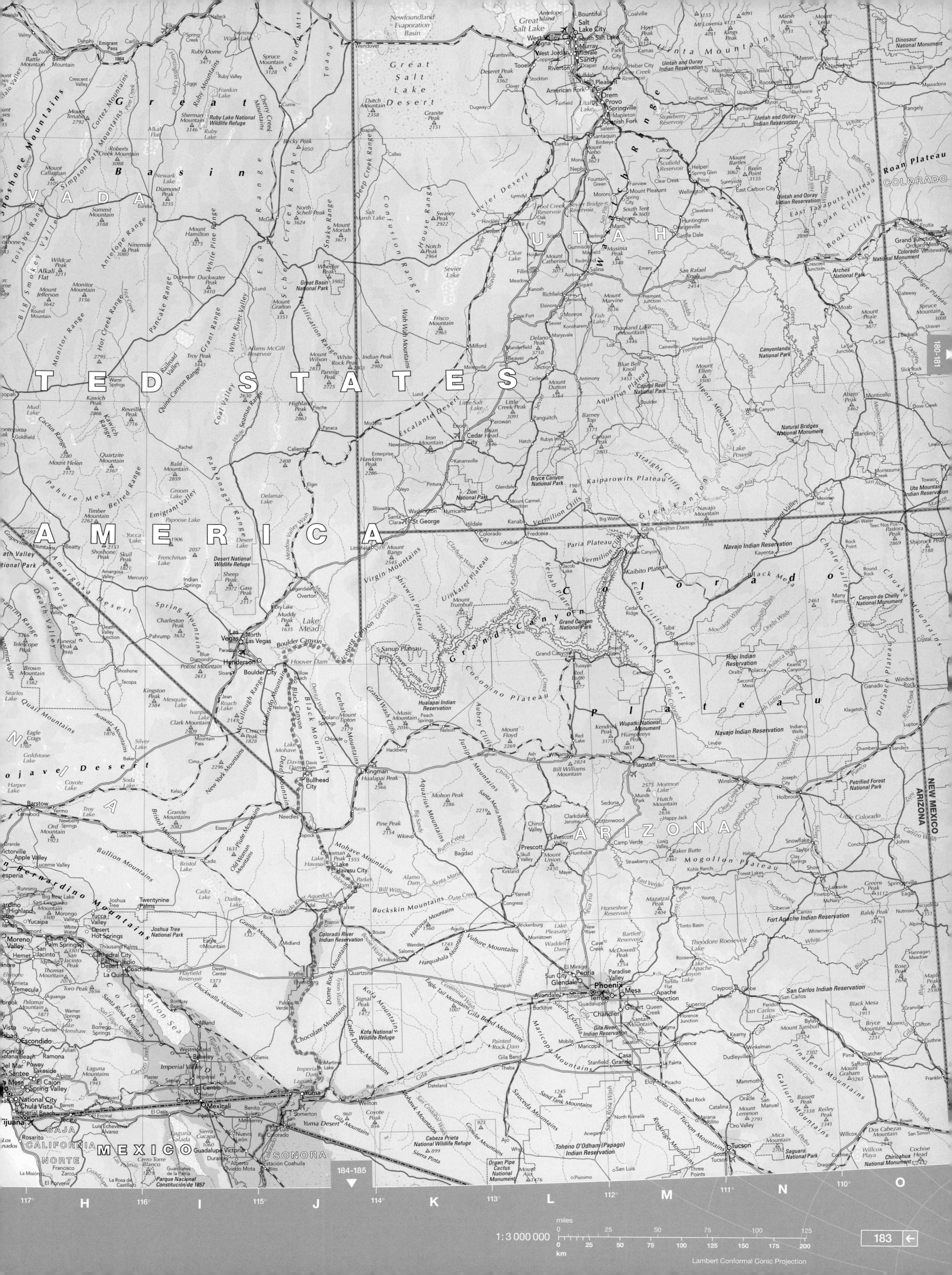

northamerica[map11]

13°-32°N / 88°-116°W

Elevation scale (left legend):
- >6000m
- 5000-6000m
- 4000-5000m
- 3000-4000m
- 2000-3000m
- 1000-2000m
- 500-1000m
- 200-500m
- 0-200m
- <0m

Depth scale:
- 0-200m
- 200-500m
- 500-1000m
- 1000-2000m
- 2000-3000m
- 3000-4000m
- 4000-5000m
- 5000-6000m
- >6000m

CONNECTIONS

PACIFIC OCEAN

ARIZONA · NEW MEXICO · SONORA · CHIHUAHUA · DURANGO · SINALOA · NAYARIT · JALISCO · COLIMA · BAJA CALIFORNIA NORTE · BAJA CALIFORNIA SUR

Tropic of Cancer

UNITED STATES OF AMERICA

ALABAMA
MISSISSIPPI
LOUISIANA
FLORIDA
TEXAS
Edwards Plateau
Stockton Plateau

New Orleans
Houston
San Antonio
Austin
Dallas
Fort Worth
Corpus Christi
Galveston
Beaumont
Baton Rouge
Mobile
Pensacola

COAHUILA
NUEVO LEÓN
TAMAULIPAS
ZACATECAS
SAN LUIS POTOSÍ
MÉXICO
GUANAJUATO
QUERÉTARO
HIDALGO
VERACRUZ
MICHOACÁN
GUERRERO
OAXACA
PUEBLA
CHIAPAS
TABASCO
CAMPECHE
YUCATÁN
QUINTANA ROO

Monterrey
Saltillo
Nuevo Laredo
Laredo
Matamoros
Reynosa
Ciudad Victoria
Tampico
Ciudad Madero
San Luis Potosí
Ciudad de Valles
León
Guadalajara
Querétaro
MEXICO CITY
Toluca
Puebla
Veracruz
Jalapa Enríquez
Orizaba
Poza Rica
Tuxpan
Acapulco
Chilpancingo
Oaxaca
Tehuacán
Coatzacoalcos
Minatitlán
Villahermosa
Tuxtla Gutiérrez
San Cristóbal de las Casas
Campeche
Mérida
Progreso
Valladolid
Chetumal
Cancún
Cozumel

Gulf of Mexico
Bahía de Campeche
Gulf of Tehuantepec
Istmo de Tehuantepec
Sierra Madre del Sur
Sierra Madre Oriental

Arrecife Alacrán
Cayo Nuevo
Cayos Arcas

BELIZE
BELMOPAN
BELIZE

GUATEMALA
GUATEMALA CITY

HONDURAS

EL SALVADOR
SAN SALVADOR

Gulf of Honduras

Administrative divisions in Mexico
numbered on the map:

1. AGUASCALIENTES
2. DISTRITO FEDERAL
3. MORELOS
4. TLAXCALA

E   F   G   H   I
100°   96°   92°   88°

miles
0   100   200
1:7 000 000
0   100   200   300   400
km

Lambert Conformal Conic Projection

6°-26°N / 60°-89°W

174-175

184-185

Elevation scale:
- >6000m
- 5000-6000m
- 4000-5000m
- 3000-4000m
- 2000-3000m
- 1000-2000m
- 500-1000m
- 200-500m
- 0-200m
- <0m

Bathymetry scale:
- 0-200m
- 200-500m
- 500-1000m
- 1000-2000m
- 2000-3000m
- 3000-4000m
- 4000-5000m
- 5000-6000m
- >6000m

1 : 7 000 000

miles
0 50 100 150 200 250 300

km
0 50 100 150 200 250 300 350 400 450 500

Lambert Conformal Conic Projection

Map labels

Gulf of Mexico

FLORIDA
U.S.A.
West Palm Beach
Fort Lauderdale
Miami
Miami Beach

THE BAHAMAS
NASSAU
Grand Bahama
Great Abaco
Andros
Eleuthera
Great Exuma

Tropic of Cancer

HAVANA (La Habana)
Matanzas
Pinar del Río
Cienfuegos
Santa Clara
CUBA
Camagüey
Holguín
Santiago de Cuba

Cayman Islands (U.K.)
GEORGE TOWN
Grand Cayman

JAMAICA
KINGSTON
Montego Bay

Yucatán Channel

MEXICO
YUCATAN
Mérida
Cancún
Cozumel
QUINTANA ROO
Chetumal

BELIZE
BELMOPAN

Gulf of Honduras

HONDURAS
San Pedro Sula
TEGUCIGALPA
MOSQUITIA

EL SALVADOR
SAN SALVADOR
San Miguel

NICARAGUA
MANAGUA
Lake Nicaragua

COSTA RICA
SAN JOSE
Península de Nicoya

PANAMA
PANAMA CITY
Gulf of Panama

Caribbean Sea

Islas de la Bahía
Roatán

Pedro Bank

Serranilla Bank

Isla de San Andrés (Colombia)

Isla de Providencia (Colombia)

West Indies

Leeward Islands

Windward Islands

Lesser Antilles

Greater Antilles

Caribbean Sea

Turks and Caicos Islands (U.K.)

San Salvador
Rum Cay
Long Island
Crooked Island
Acklins Island
Great Inagua
Little Inagua I.

North Caicos
Grand Caicos
East Caicos
South Caicos
GRAND TURK (Cockburn Town)
Grand Turk

HAITI
PORT-AU-PRINCE
Cap-Haïtien
Gonaïves
St Marc
Jérémie
Les Cayes
Jacmel

DOMINICAN REPUBLIC
SANTO DOMINGO
Santiago
San Francisco de Macorís
La Romana
San Pedro de Macorís
Puerto Plata
Barahona

Hispaniola

Puerto Rico (U.S.A.)
SAN JUAN
Bayamón
Ponce
Mayagüez
Arecibo
Aguadilla

Virgin Is (U.K.)
ROAD TOWN
Tortola
Virgin Gorda
Anegada

Virgin Is (U.S.A.)
CHARLOTTE AMALIE
St Thomas
St John
St Croix
Christiansted
Frederiksted

Anguilla (U.K.)
THE VALLEY

St Maarten (Neth.)
Saint Martin (Fr.)
St-Barthélemy (Fr.)

Barbuda

ANTIGUA AND BARBUDA
ST JOHN'S
Antigua

ST KITTS AND NEVIS
BASSETERRE
St Kitts
Nevis
Charlestown

Saba
St Eustatius (Neth.)
Oranjestad
Redonda

Montserrat
PLYMOUTH
Soufrière Hills

Guadeloupe (France)
BASSE-TERRE
Pointe-à-Pitre
Grande-Terre
Basse-Terre
Marie-Galante
Grand Bourg
Îles des Saintes
La Désirade

Aves (Venezuela)

DOMINICA
ROSEAU
Portsmouth
Scotts Head

Martinique (France)
FORT-DE-FRANCE

ST LUCIA
CASTRIES
Vieux Fort
Soufrière

ST VINCENT AND THE GRENADINES
KINGSTOWN
St Vincent
Bequia
Mustique
Canouan
The Grenadines
Carriacou

GRENADA
ST GEORGE'S
Grenville
Ronde

BARBADOS
BRIDGETOWN
Speightstown
Six Cross Roads

TRINIDAD AND TOBAGO
PORT OF SPAIN
Trinidad
Tobago
Scarborough
San Fernando

Aruba (Neth.)
ORANJESTAD

Netherlands Antilles
WILLEMSTAD
Curaçao
Bonaire

Isla de Margarita
La Asunción
Porlamar
Isla La Tortuga
Los Roques
Isla Orchila
Isla Blanquilla
Los Testigos

VENEZUELA
CARACAS
Maracaibo
Valencia
Maracay
Barcelona
Barquisimeto
Ciudad Guayana
Ciudad Bolívar
Maturín
Cumaná
Mérida
San Cristóbal
Cabimas
Coro
Puerto Cabello
Petare
Los Teques
Guarenas
Acarigua
San Fernando de Apure

Golfo de Venezuela
Lake Maracaibo

ZULIA
FALCON
LARA
ANZOATEGUI
MONAGAS
DELTA AMACURO
BOLIVAR
GUARICO
APURE
BARINAS
TACHIRA
SUCRE
MIRANDA
TRUJILLO
PORTUGUESA
COJEDES
ARAUCA
CASANARE

COLOMBIA
Santa Marta
Riohacha
Barranquilla
Valledupar
Cúcuta
Bucaramanga

GUYANA

Orinoco
Delta Amacuro

Cordillera Oriental
Sierra Nevada de Santa Marta

Parque Nacional Canaima

187 ←

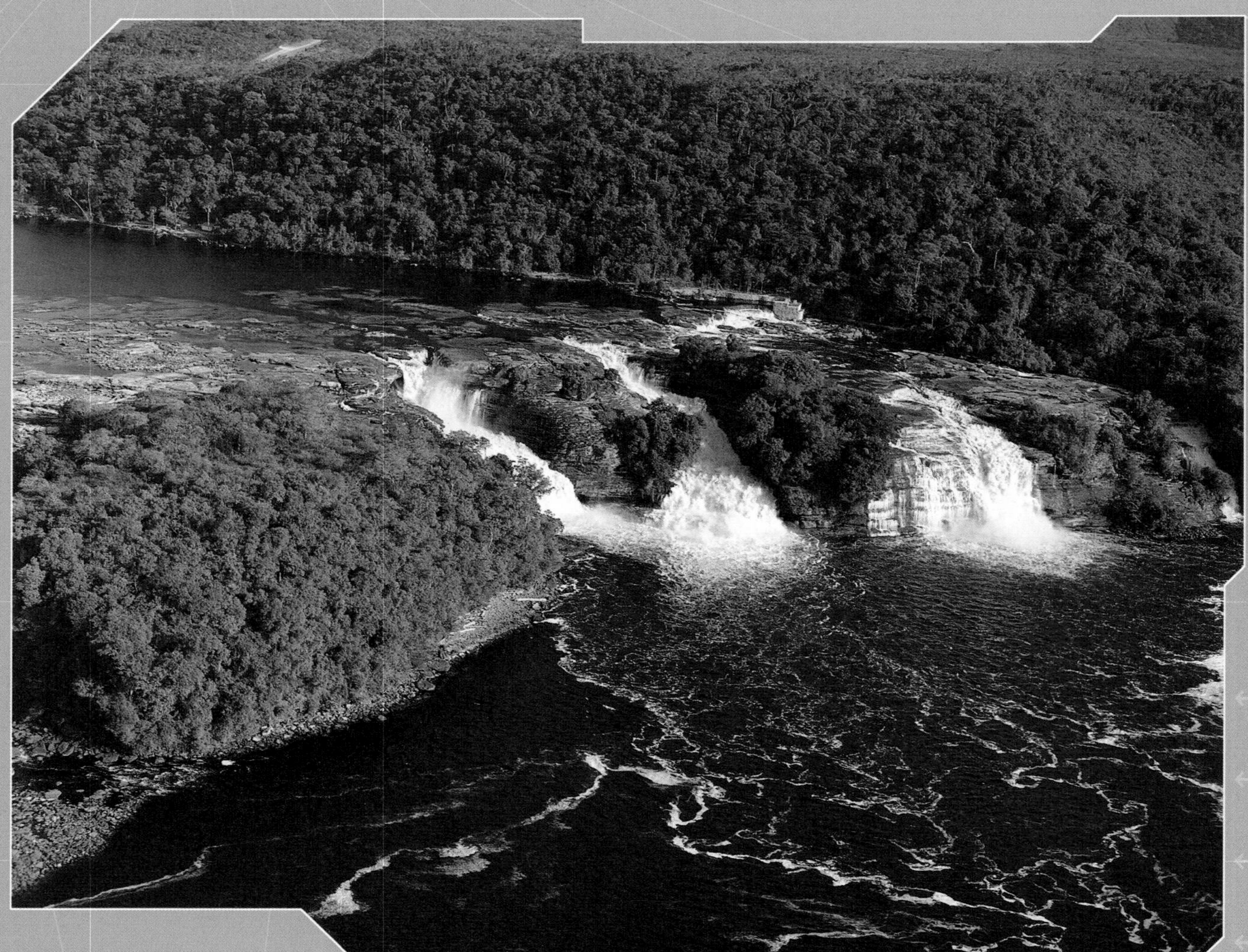

Canaima National Park, *Venezuela*

southamerica

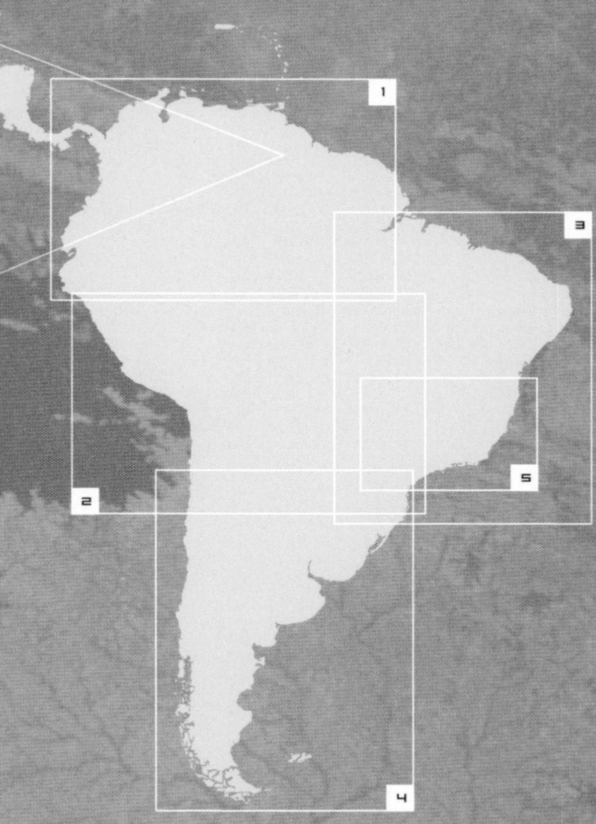

[contents]

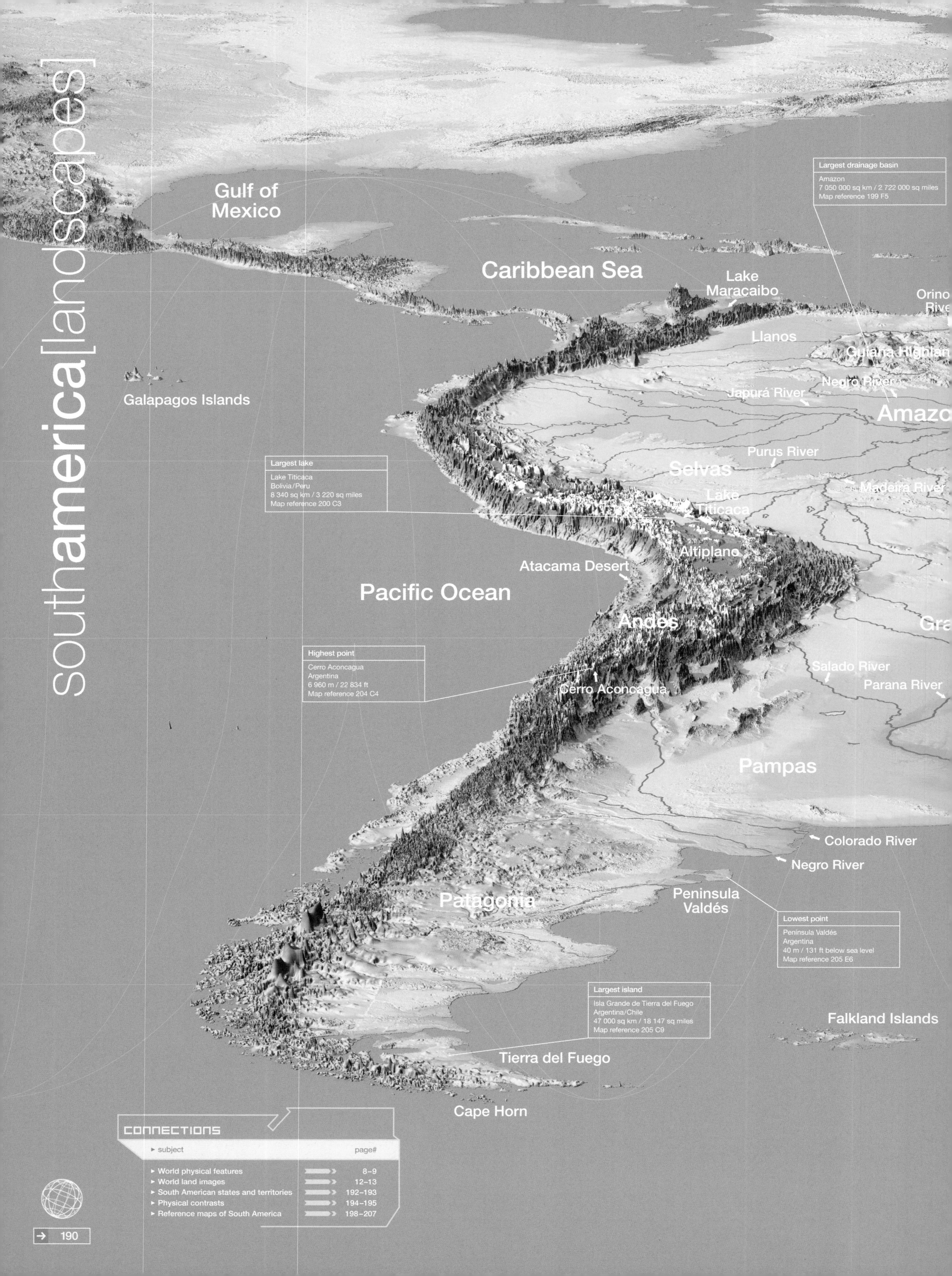

Gulf of
Mexico

Caribbean Sea

Lake
Maracaibo

Orino
Rive

Llanos

Guiana Highlan

Negro River

Galapagos Islands

Japurá River

Amazo

Purus River

Largest drainage basin

Amazon
7 050 000 sq km / 2 722 000 sq miles
Map reference 199 F5

Selvas

Madeira River

Largest lake

Lake Titicaca
Bolivia / Peru
8 340 sq km / 3 220 sq miles
Map reference 200 C3

Lake
Titicaca

Altiplano

Atacama Desert

Pacific Ocean

Andes

Gra

Highest point

Cerro Aconcagua
Argentina
6 960 m / 22 834 ft
Map reference 204 C4

Cerro Aconcagua

Salado River

Parana River

Pampas

Colorado River

Negro River

Peninsula
Valdés

Patagonia

Lowest point

Peninsula Valdés
Argentina
40 m / 131 ft below sea level
Map reference 205 E6

Largest island

Isla Grande de Tierra del Fuego
Argentina / Chile
47 000 sq km / 18 147 sq miles
Map reference 205 C9

Falkland Islands

Tierra del Fuego

Cape Horn

CONNECTIONS

← Orinoco River Delta
ngel Falls

Mouths of the Amazon ←

asin

Amazon River ←

Longest river

Amazon
6 516 km / 4 049 miles
Map reference 202 B1

Tocantins River

Sao Francisco River ←

Mato
Grosso

Brazilian
Highlands

haco

← Uruguay River

Atlantic Ocean

← Rio de la Plata

The spectacular Andes mountains dominate the western side of South America, bordering the Pacific for the entire length of the landmass. They stretch from Tierra del Fuego in the south, to Panama in the north. This huge mountain system has many volcanoes, is the source of many of the continent's large rivers, including the Amazon and Orinoco, and surrounds the Atacama Desert, the driest place on earth. The Altiplano is a high plateau within the Andes between the main west and east mountain ranges. Other upland areas include the Brazilian Highlands in the northeast and Patagonia, where the land rises steadily from the Atlantic coast to the Andes.

The Amazon Basin is a large lowland area, lying just south of the equator, through which the Amazon river and its many tributaries flow towards the huge delta on the Atlantic coast. The region contains vast areas of tropical rain forest. Huge, sparsely populated plains known as Llanos in the north and Pampas in the south provide further contrasts in the landscapes of the continent.

1 Amazon River, *Brazil*

The grey area on this satellite image is the isolated city of Manaus in northern Brazil. It sits at the confluence of the Amazon and Negro rivers. The Amazon, flowing from west to east, originates in the Andes mountains in Peru and carries a thick solution of silt and sand giving it a brown colour. The Negro river flows over hard base rock giving little sediment so the water is clearer, appearing dark in this image. The waters do not combine immediately but flow side by side for some distance before merging.

Satellite/Sensor : Terra, MISR

2 Pampas, *Argentina*

The Pampas grassland plains of Argentina stretch from the foothills of the Andes mountains to the east coast.
This photograph shows the Pampas in Neuquén Province. Eastern areas tend to be better irrigated but the whole area supports a major livestock industry.

3 Lake Viedma, *Argentina*

Lake Viedma in the centre of this image, Lake Argentino to the left, and Lake San Martin to the right are situated in southern Argentina. This image looks southwest and shows the lakes being fed by meltwater from the glaciers of the Andes Mountains. Lake Viedma is over 300 m above sea level. Waters from it flow into Lake Argentino then into the Santa Cruz river, across the Patagonia plateau to the Atlantic Ocean. The snow-capped ridge behind the lakes forms the boundary between Argentina and Chile.

Satellite/Sensor : Space Shuttle

SOUTH AMERICA

HIGHEST MOUNTAINS

	m	ft	location	map
Cerro Aconcagua	6 960	22 834	Argentina	204 C4
Nevado Ojos del Salado	6 908	22 664	Argentina/Chile	204 C2
Cerro Bonete	6 872	22 546	Argentina	204 C2
Cerro Pissis	6 858	22 500	Argentina	204 C2
Cerro Tupungato	6 800	22 309	Argentina/Chile	204 C4
Cerro Meredario	6 770	22 211	Argentina	204 B3

LARGEST ISLANDS

	sq km	sq miles	map
Isla Grande de Tierra del Fuego	47 000	18 147	205 C9
Isla de Chiloe	8 394	3 240	205 B6
East Falkland	6 760	2 610	205 F8
West Falkland	5 413	2 090	205 E8

LONGEST RIVERS

	km	miles	map
Amazon	6 516	4 049	202 B1
Rio de la Plata-Parana	4 500	2 796	204 F4
Purus	3 218	1 999	199 F5
Madeira	3 200	1 988	199 G5
Sao Francisco	2 900	1 802	202 E4
Tocantins	2 750	1 708	202 B2

LAKES

	sq km	sq miles	map
Lake Titicaca	8 340	3 220	200 C3

LAND AREA

		map
Most northerly point	Punta Gallinas, Colombia	198 D1
Most southerly point	Cape Horn, Chile	205 D9
Most westerly point	Galapagos Islands, Ecuador	216 H6
Most easterly point	Ilhas Martin Vas, Atlantic Ocean	216 M7
Total land area: 17 815 420 sq km / 6 878 572 sq miles		

southamerica[countries]

CONNECTIONS

subject	page#
World physical features	8–9
World countries	10–11
South America landscapes	190–191
South America contrasts	194–195
Reference maps of South America	198–207

SOUTH AMERICA

COUNTRIES

	area sq km	area sq miles	population	capital	languages	religions	currency	map
ARGENTINA	2 766 889	1 068 302	37 032 000	Buenos Aires	Spanish, Italian, Amerindian languages	Roman Catholic, Protestant	Peso	204–205
BOLIVIA	1 098 581	424 164	8 329 000	La Paz/Sucre	Spanish, Quechua, Aymara	Roman Catholic, Protestant, Bahaî	Boliviano	200–201
BRAZIL	8 547 379	3 300 161	170 406 000	Brasília	Portuguese	Roman Catholic, Protestant	Real	202–203
CHILE	756 945	292 258	15 211 000	Santiago	Spanish, Amerindian languages	Roman Catholic, Protestant	Peso	204–205
COLOMBIA	1 141 748	440 831	42 105 000	Bogotá	Spanish, Amerindian languages	Roman Catholic, Protestant	Peso	198
ECUADOR	272 045	105 037	12 646 000	Quito	Spanish, Quechua, other Amerindian languages	Roman Catholic	Sucre	198
GUYANA	214 969	83 000	761 000	Georgetown	English, creole, Amerindian languages	Protestant, Hindu, Roman Catholic, Sunni Muslim	Dollar	199
PARAGUAY	406 752	157 048	5 496 000	Asunción	Spanish, Guaraní	Roman Catholic, Protestant	Guaraní	201
PERU	1 285 216	496 225	25 662 000	Lima	Spanish, Quechua, Aymara	Roman Catholic, Protestant	Sol	200
SURINAME	163 820	63 251	417 000	Paramaribo	Dutch, Surinamese, English, Hindi	Hindu, Roman Catholic, Protestant, Sunni Muslim	Guilder	199
URUGUAY	176 215	68 037	3 337 000	Montevideo	Spanish	Roman Catholic, Protestant, Jewish	Peso	204
VENEZUELA	912 050	352 144	24 170 000	Caracas	Spanish, Amerindian languages	Roman Catholic, Protestant	Bolívar	198–199

DEPENDENT TERRITORIES

	territorial status	sq km	sq miles	population	capital	languages	religions	currency	map
Falkland Islands	United Kingdom Overseas Territory	12 170	4 699	2 000	Stanley	English	Protestant, Roman Catholic	Pound	205
French Guiana	French Overseas Department	90 000	34 749	165 000	Cayenne	French, creole	Roman Catholic	French franc	199
South Georgia and South Sandwich Islands	United Kingdom Overseas Territory	4 066	1 570	uninhabited					217

1 **Santiago**, *Chile*

In this Landsat satellite image, Santiago, capital city and main industrial centre of Chile, can be seen to the left of the snow-capped Andes mountains which form a natural boundary between Chile and its easterly neighbour, Argentina. The city, which has suffered many earthquakes and floods, was established as Chile's capital when the country became independent in 1818.

Satellite/Sensor : Landsat

2 **Brasília**, *Brazil*

Construction of Brasília as the administrative and political centre of Brazil began in 1956 and four years later it replaced Rio de Janeiro as the capital city of Brazil, South America's largest country. It is located on the Paraná, a headstream of the Tocantins river. In this infrared satellite image the city is in the centre, where buildings appear as light blue-grey. Lakes to the north and east of the city are blue-black, and vegetation along the small tributaries shows as red.

Satellite/Sensor : SPOT

3 **Lake Titicaca**, *Bolivia/Peru*

Lake Titicaca, located in a depression within the high plains (Altiplano) of South America, is the largest freshwater lake on the continent. The international boundary between Bolivia and Peru passes through the lake. In this oblique Shuttle photograph, the Andes mountains can be seen in the top right and bottom left. Persistent drought in the area has caused water levels to drop and expose the bottom of the lake, shown as white patches on the lake shore.

Satellite/Sensor : Space Shuttle

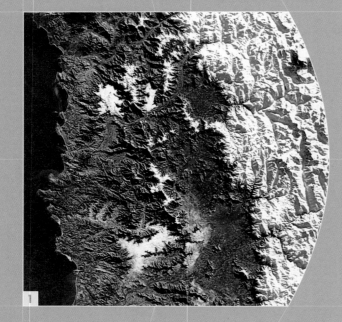

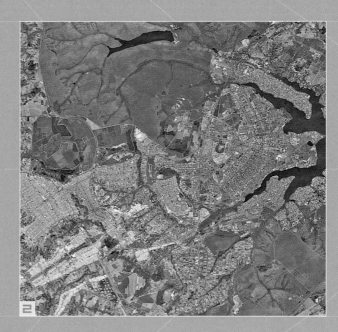

Caribbean Sea

ATLANTIC OCEAN

PACIFIC OCEAN

ATLANTIC OCEAN

Barranquilla
CARACAS
Maracay
Cumaná
Cartagena
Barquisimeto
Ciudad Bolívar
Montería
San Cristóbal
Golfo del Darién
Gulf of Panama
Orinoco
GEORGETOWN
PARAMARIBO
CAYENNE
VENEZUELA
GUYANA
SURINAME
French Guiana (Fr.)
Medellín
Tunja
BOGOTÁ
Puerto Ayacucho
Boa Vista
Isla de Coco
Isla de Malpelo (Colombia)
Ibagué
COLOMBIA
Cali
Neiva
Orinoco
Branco
Pasto
QUITO
Manta
ECUADOR
Cuenca
Guayaquil
Golfo de Guayaquil
Galapagos Islands (Ecuador)
Putumayo
Japurá
Tonantins
Santarém
Amazon
Belém
São Luís
Parnaíba
Iquitos
Amazon
Manaus
Negro
Tocantins
Xingu
Iriri
Maraba
Teresina
Fortaleza
Marañón
Yavari
Carauari
Juruá
Purus
Madeira
Tapajós
Chiclayo
Cruzeiro do Sul
PERU
Pucallpa
Trujillo
Porto Velho
Rio Branco
BRAZIL
Natal
João Pessoa
Floresta
Recife
Juàzeiro
São Francisco
Maceió
Huancayo
Guaporé
Aracaju
Cuzco
Trinidad
Salvador
LIMA
Ica
Mamoré
Juliaca
LA PAZ
BOLIVIA
Cuiabá
BRASÍLIA
Arequipa
Cochabamba
SUCRE
Santa Cruz
Goiânia
Patos de Minas
Teófilo Otôni
Arica
Potosí
Paraguay
Campo Grande
Uberaba
Belo Horizonte
Iquique
Tarija
PARAGUAY
Araçatuba
Campinas
Vitória
Antofagasta
San Salvador de Jujuy
Teuco
Pedro Juan Caballero
Maringá
Rio de Janeiro
Ilha da Trindade (Brazil)
Ilhas Martín Vas (Brazil)
Islas de los Desventurados (Chile)
San Miguel de Tucumán
ASUNCIÓN
Paraná
Iguaçu
São Paulo
Catamarca
Corrientes
Posadas
Curitiba
La Rioja
Salado
Santa Maria
Florianópolis
Archipiélago Juan Fernández (Chile)
San Juan
Santa Fé
Paraná
Concordia
Porto Alegre
Aconcagua
Mendoza
Rosario
Rio Grande
Valparaíso
SANTIAGO
Salado
Córdoba
Paraná
URUGUAY
BUENOS AIRES
MONTEVIDEO
Río de la Plata
Concepción
Santa Rosa
ARGENTINA
Colorado
Bahía Blanca
Mar del Plata
Neuquén
Negro
Viedma
Golfo San Matías
Isla de Chiloé
Trelew
Archipiélago de los Chonos
Golfo de San Jorge
Comodoro Rivadavia
Bahía Grande
STANLEY
Falkland Islands (U.K.)
Puerto Natales
Punta Arenas
Isla Grande de Tierra del Fuego
Ushuaia
Cape Horn
South Georgia and South Sandwich Islands (U.K.)

Tropic of Capricorn
Antarctic Circle

---

southamerica[contrasts]

1

2

1 La Paz, *Bolivia*

The Bolivian city of La Paz is the highest capital city in the world. It lies just southeast of Lake Titicaca, in a valley between the Cordillera Oriental and the Andes, sheltered from the severe winds and weather of the Altiplano. It has a population of over 1 million. The city was established by the Spanish conquistadors in the mid 1500's.

2 Farmland, *Ecuador*

On the western slopes of the Andes, erosion of the high volcanic peaks has created rich soils for farming, as seen here in Ecuador. The scattered farms are worked by indigenous Indian people who gather to sell, buy and barter at local weekly markets. Over 30 per cent of Ecuador's population is employed in agriculture and agricultural products account for almost half of the country's exports.

3 Glacier, *Patagonia*

Glaciers such as this, in the region of Patagonia, which straddles the Chile/Argentina border, are a great influence on the landscape. The surface of the glacier is deeply scarred by crevasses and patterns of debris within the ice indicate its current flow. Braided streams carry fine sediment away from the glacier.

Satellite/Sensor : Terra/ASTER

4 Galapagos Islands, *Ecuador*

This satellite image shows part of the Galapagos Islands, a group of islands created by volcanic activity. The craters of volcanoes on the main island of Isla Isabela and on Isla Fernandina to the west, can be clearly seen. Vegetation, which appears red, is limited as the landscape is dominated by lava flows. The Galapagos Islands are a group of isolated islands lying over 1 000 km west of the coast of Ecuador. They are renowned for their rich and unique wildlife.

Satellite/Sensor : SPOT

3

5

5 Andes Mountains

The Andes mountain range forms a formidable barrier down the whole length of the western side of the South American continent. This is clearly seen in this dramatic visualization created from digital terrain data. The western edge of the Andes descends steeply towards the Pacific Ocean with very little coastal lowland. Likewise to the east, the transition from high ground to low, flatter areas is also sudden, emphasizing the barrier of the mountains. To the south, the lowland areas form the grassy plains of the Pampas and to the north, the Amazon basin.

→ 194

CONNECTIONS

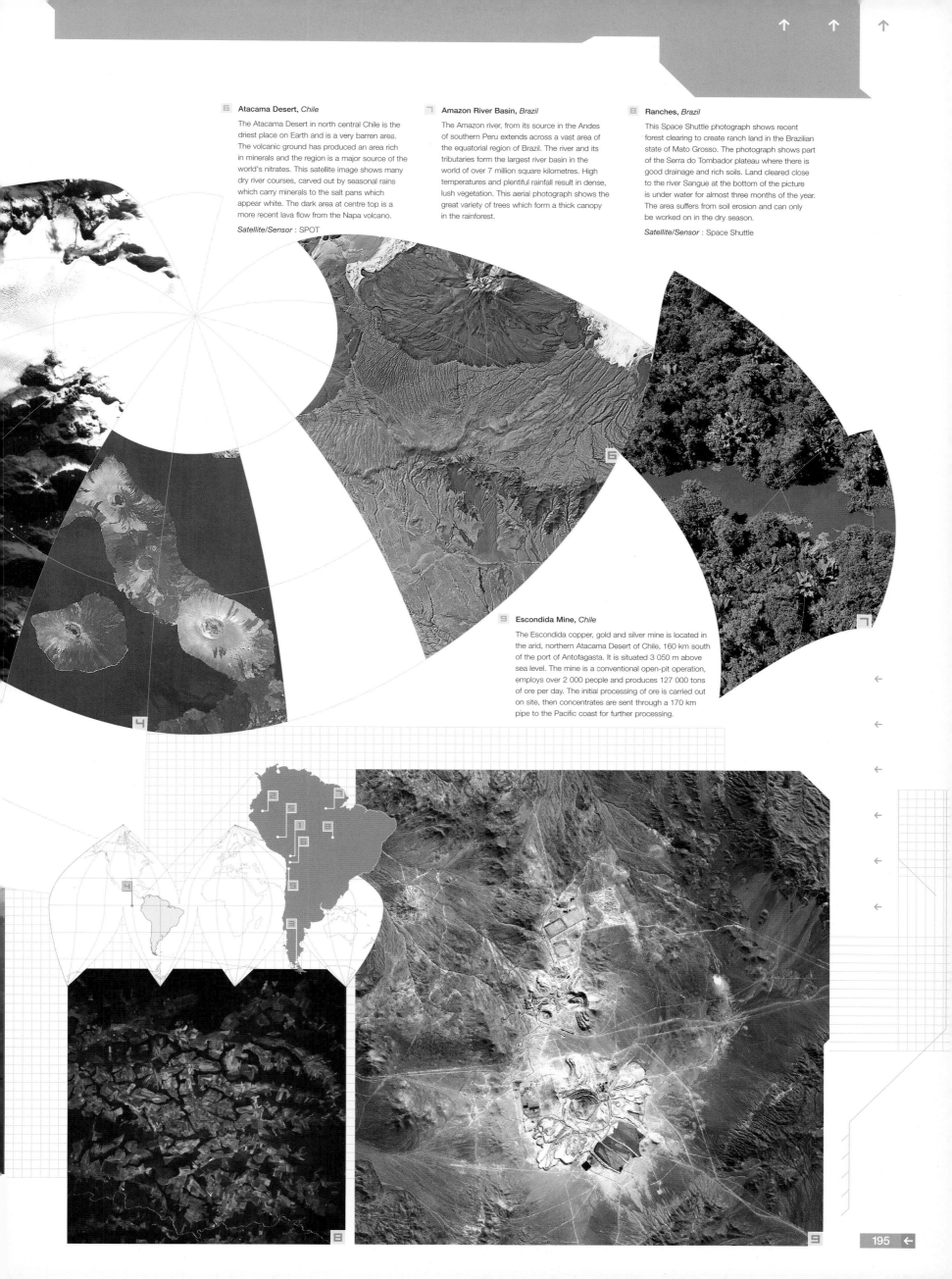

6 Atacama Desert, *Chile*

The Atacama Desert in north central Chile is the driest place on Earth and is a very barren area. The volcanic ground has produced an area rich in minerals and the region is a major source of the world's nitrates. This satellite image shows many dry river courses, carved out by seasonal rains which carry minerals to the salt pans which appear white. The dark area at centre top is a more recent lava flow from the Napa volcano.

Satellite/Sensor : SPOT

7 Amazon River Basin, *Brazil*

The Amazon river, from its source in the Andes of southern Peru extends across a vast area of the equatorial region of Brazil. The river and its tributaries form the largest river basin in the world of over 7 million square kilometres. High temperatures and plentiful rainfall result in dense, lush vegetation. This aerial photograph shows the great variety of trees which form a thick canopy in the rainforest.

8 Ranches, *Brazil*

This Space Shuttle photograph shows recent forest clearing to create ranch land in the Brazilian state of Mato Grosso. The photograph shows part of the Serra do Tombador plateau where there is good drainage and rich soils. Land cleared close to the river Sangue at the bottom of the picture is under water for almost three months of the year. The area suffers from soil erosion and can only be worked on in the dry season.

Satellite/Sensor : Space Shuttle

9 Escondida Mine, *Chile*

The Escondida copper, gold and silver mine is located in the arid, northern Atacama Desert of Chile, 160 km south of the port of Antofagasta. It is situated 3 050 m above sea level. The mine is a conventional open-pit operation, employs over 2 000 people and produces 127 000 tons of ore per day. The initial processing of ore is carried out on site, then concentrates are sent through a 170 km pipe to the Pacific coast for further processing.

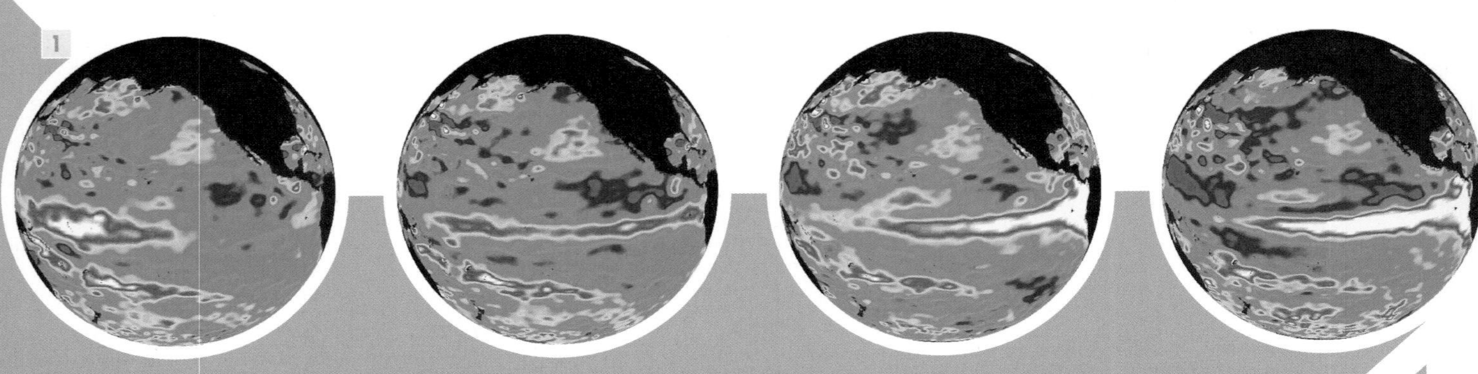

1 El Niño, *South America*

Periodically, atmospheric pressure becomes abnormally low in the middle of the Pacific Ocean and abnormally high over northern Australia. This results in the prevailing easterly winds weakening and changing direction. As a result, water off the west coast of South America becomes warmer by 4°–5°C. This phenomenon, known as El Niño, can have a dramatic effect on the world's climate, including higher rainfall in east Africa, and much lower rainfall and higher temperatures than normal in Australia.

The satellite images of the Earth show the development of El Niño during 1997. The red/white areas represent El Niño moving eastwards across the Pacific Ocean. The impacts of this on South America were drier conditions along the north coast, higher temperatures on the east and more rain in the northwest and southeast. The area most severely affected was the northwest coast. High river levels and flash floods were frequent and mudslides destroyed villages. Over 30 000 homes were lost in Peru during the course of the 1997–1998 El Niño event.

Satellite/Sensor : TOPEX/Poseidon

2 Mining, *South America*

The mineral distribution map of South America (Fig. #01) shows the great concentration of copper mining along the Andes mountain range. Large quantities of bauxite, the main ore for the production of aluminium, are mined in those areas with a tropical humid climate in the north of the continent. Symbol sizes on the map are proportional to mineral production as a percentage of world production, the largest representing over five per cent. While mining contributes enormously to the overall economy of South America, it also depletes natural resources and damages the environment. The photograph of the Bon Futuro tin mine in the Rondônia region of Brazil (number 7 on the map) shows how landscapes can be scarred by mining activities. Additional impacts can be the displacement of communities and the pollution of rivers and lakes.

Fig. #01
South America minerals

Metallic minerals

- Iron **Fe**
- Copper **Cu**
- Gold **Au**
- Aluminium **Al**
- Manganese **Mn**
- Lead **Pb**, Zinc **Zn**, Silver **Ag**
- Tin **Sn**, Antimony **Sb**
- Nickel **Ni**, Molybdenum **Mo**, Niobium **Nb**, Chromium **Cr**, Tungsten **W**

Industrial (non metallic) minerals

- Phosphate **P**, Borates **B**,
- Fluorspar **F**
- ◆ Diamonds **Diam.**

Symbol sizes reflect level of production from less than 1% to over 5% of world production.

Argentina
1 Aguilar, **Pb, Zn, Ag**
2 Bajo de la Alumbrera, **Cu, Mo, Au**
3 El Pachon, **Cu, Mo, Au**
4 Northern Provinces, **B**

Bolivia
5 Potosí, Oruro, **Sn, Sb, Pb, Zn, Ag, W**

Brazil
6 Trombetas, **Al**
7 Rondônia, **Sn**
8 Carajás, **Fe**
9 Igarape Azul, Carajás, **Mn**
10 Caraiba, **Cu**
11 Campo Formoso, **Cr**
12 Cana Brava, **Cr**
13 Niquelândia, **Ni**
14 Morro do Niquel, **Ni**
15 Tocantins, **Ni**
16 Urucum, **Mn, Fe**
17 Vazante, **Pb, Zn**
18 Boquira, **Pb, Zn**
19 Jequitinhonha, **Diam.**
20 Araxá, **Nb, P**
21 Morro Velho, **Au**
22 Iron Quadrilateral, **Fe**
23 Morro da Fumaça, **F**
24 Roraima, **Diam.**

Chile
25 Chuquicamata, **Abra, Cu, Mo**
26 Escondida, El Salvador, **Cu, Mo, Au**
27 Disputada, Andina, Pelambres, **Cu, Mo**
28 El Teniente, **Cu, Mo**
29 Cerro Colorado, Quebrada Blanca, **Cu, Mo**
30 La Candelaria, **Cu, Mo, Au**
31 Atacama, **Fe**

Colombia
32 Titiribi, **Au**
33 Cerro Matoso, **Ni**

Ecuador
34 Portovelo, **Au**

Guyana
35 Guyana, **Al**
36 Omai, **Au**

Peru
37 Northern Peru, **Pb, Zn, Ag, Cu, Mo**
38 Cerro de Pasco, central Peru, **Pb, Zn, Ag, Cu, Mo**
39 Cuajone, Toquepala, **Cu, Mo**
40 Tintaya, **Cu, Mo**
41 Cerro Verde, **Cu, Mo**
42 Marcona, **Fe**
43 Yanacocha, **Au**

Suriname
44 Suriname, **Al**

Venezuela
45 Cedeno, **Al**
46 Cerro Bolivar, San Isidro, **Fe**
47 Cristinas, **Au, Cu**

Deforestation, *Bolivia*

The two Landsat satellite images below were produced fifteen years apart. The upper image shows an area of tropical rainforest near the Bolivian city of Santa Cruz in 1984. The Piray river is the dark blue line in the bottom left of the image. Forest and natural vegetation appears as green, bare ground as red. The lower image, dated 1998, demonstrates the impact of deforestation in the region. Huge areas of the forest east of the river have been completely cleared for agriculture, in a similar way to that shown in the aerial photograph. Destruction of the rainforest is a major environmental issue and interrupting the forest canopy in this way causes humidity to drop rapidly and huge areas of forest become vulnerable to fire.

Satellite/Sensor : Landsat

CONNECTIONS

▸ subject	page#
▸ World climate and weather	16–17
▸ World land cover types	18–19
▸ World changes	20–21
▸ South America landscapes	190–191
▸ South America countries	192–193
▸ South America contrasts	194–195

8°S-14°N / 51°-82°W

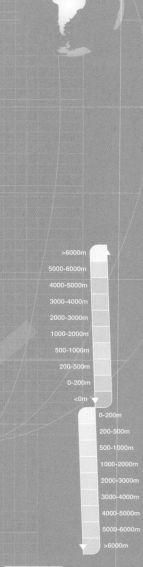

>6000m
5000-6000m
4000-5000m
3000-4000m
2000-3000m
1000-2000m
500-1000m
200-500m
0-200m
<0m

0-200m
200-500m
500-1000m
1000-2000m
2000-3000m
3000-4000m
4000-5000m
5000-6000m
>6000m

186-187
Martinique (France)
CASTRIES
ST LUCIA
St Vincent Passage
ST VINCENT AND THE GRENADINES
KINGSTOWN
BARBADOS
BRIDGETOWN
The Grenadines
ST GEORGE'S
GRENADA
Sea
Antilles
Isla Blanquilla
Isla Orchila
Los Roques
Isla de Margarita
NUEVA ESPARTA
DISTRITO FEDERAL
CARACAS
Maracay
MIRANDA
SUCRE
Cumaná
Barcelona
PORT OF SPAIN
Trinidad
TRINIDAD AND TOBAGO
Tobago
Gulf of Paria
Dragon's Mouths
Serpent's Mouth
MONAGAS
Maturín
GUÁRICO
ANZOÁTEGUI
DELTA AMACURO
Orinoco Delta
Ciudad Guayana
Ciudad Bolívar
San Fernando de Apure
VENEZUELA
BOLÍVAR
Puerto Páez
Puerto Ayacucho
Guiana Highlands
La Gran Sabana
Angel Falls
Pakaraima Mountains
Kaieteur Falls
GUYANA
GEORGETOWN
New Amsterdam
Linden
Lethem
Kanuku Mountains
PARAMARIBO
SURINAME
French Guiana
CAYENNE
St-Laurent-du-Maroni
Serra Tumucumaque
AMAPÁ
Macapá
ATLANTIC OCEAN
AMAZONAS
RORAIMA
Boa Vista
Parque Nacional do Pico da Neblina
Manaus
LITIGATED AREA
Parintins
Óbidos
Santarém
Monte Alegre
Almeirim
Altamira
Itaituba
BRAZIL
PARÁ
Amazon
CONNECTIONS
subject page#
World physical features 8–9
World volcanoes 14–15
World land cover types 18–19
South America landscapes 190–191
South America countries 192–193
South America contrasts 194–195
200-201
202-203
E
F
G
H
I
64°
60°
56°
52°
1:8 000 000
miles
0 100 200 300
km
0 100 200 300 400 500
Lambert Azimuthal Equal Area Projection
199

6°-28°S / 48°-80°W

>6000m
5000-6000m
4000-5000m
3000-4000m
2000-3000m
1000-2000m
500-1000m
200-500m
0-200m
<0m

0-200m
200-500m
500-1000m
1000-2000m
2000-3000m
3000-4000m
4000-5000m
5000-6000m
>6000m

PACIFIC

OCEAN

Tropic of Capricorn

PERU

CHILE

LIMA

LA PAZ

CONNECTIONS

▸ subject   page#

▸ World cities   ➔ 24–25
▸ South America landscapes   ➔ 190–191
▸ South America countries   ➔ 192–193
▸ South America contrasts   ➔ 194–195
▸ South America impacts   ➔ 196–197

202-203

204-205

1 : 8 000 000

miles
0   100   200   300
km
0   100   200   300   400   500

Lambert Azimuthal Equal Area Projection

ATLANTIC
OCEAN
Mouths of the Amazon
B R A Z I L
MARANHÃO
PIAUÍ
CEARÁ
BAHIA
TOCANTINS
PARÁ
GOIÁS
MATO GROSSO
PERNAMBUCO
SERGIPE
ALAGOAS
PARAÍBA
RIO GRANDE DO NORTE
AMAPÁ
DISTRITO FEDERAL
BRASÍLIA
Belém
Fortaleza (Ceará)
Recife (Pernambuco)
Salvador (Bahia)
Natal
João Pessoa
Maceió
Aracaju
Teresina
São Luís
Palmas
Goiânia
Macapá
Santarém
Ilha de Marajó
Serra da Ibiapaba
LITIGATED AREA
Chapada Diamantina
Serra Geral de Goiás
Serra do Roncador
Serra do Cachimbo
Serra Formosa
Planalto do Mato Grosso
Equator
Atol das Rocas

198-199
202

ATLANTIC
OCEAN
MINAS GERAIS
SÃO PAULO
RIO DE JANEIRO
PARANÁ
SANTA CATARINA
RIO GRANDE DO SUL
MATO GROSSO DO SUL
ESPÍRITO SANTO
PARAGUAY
ARGENTINA
MISIONES
Belo Horizonte
São Paulo
Rio de Janeiro
Curitiba
Florianópolis
Porto Alegre
Campinas
Santos
Campo Grande
Vitória
Tropic of Capricorn
Serra da Mantiqueira
Planalto do Brasil
200-201
204-205
20°
24°
28°
31°
56°
52°
48°
44°
40°
36°
32°
A
B
C
D
E
F
G
6
7
8
9
>6000m
5000-6000m
4000-5000m
3000-4000m
2000-3000m
1000-2000m
500-1000m
200-500m
0-200m
<0m
0-200m
200-500m
500-1000m
1000-2000m
2000-3000m
3000-4000m
4000-5000m
5000-6000m
>6000m
CONNECTIONS
subject page#
World countries 10–11
World population distribution 22–23
World cities 24–25
South America countries 192–193
Atlantic Ocean 216–217
0°-31°S / 32°-56°W
1:8 000 000
miles 0 100 200 300
km 0 100 200 300 400 500
Lambert Azimuthal Equal Area Projection
southamerica[map3]

Tropic of Capricorn
PACIFIC OCEAN
PARAGUAY
ARGENTINA
BRAZIL
URUGUAY
ASUNCIÓN
BUENOS AIRES
MONTEVIDEO
SANTIAGO
Atacama Desert
FORMOSA
CHACO
SALTA
TUCUMÁN
CATAMARCA
SANTIAGO DEL ESTERO
CORRIENTES
MISIONES
SANTA FE
ENTRE RÍOS
CÓRDOBA
LA RIOJA
SAN JUAN
SAN LUIS
MENDOZA
LA PAMPA
BUENOS AIRES
NEUQUÉN
RÍO NEGRO
ANTOFAGASTA
ATACAMA
COQUIMBO
VALPARAÍSO
O'HIGGINS
MAULE
BÍOBÍO
LA ARAUCANÍA
RIO GRANDE DO SUL
SANTA CATARINA
PARANÁ
Río de la Plata
Sierras de Córdoba
Bahía Blanca
Bahía Samborombón
Península Verde
Córdoba
Rosario
Santa Fe
Paraná
Mendoza
San Juan
San Luis
La Rioja
Catamarca
San Miguel de Tucumán
San Salvador de Jujuy
Resistencia
Corrientes
Posadas
Formosa
Santa Rosa
Neuquén
Viedma
Mar del Plata
La Plata
Porto Alegre
Valparaíso
Viña del Mar
Concepción
Talcahuano
La Serena
Coquimbo
Copiapó
Temuco
Valdivia
Osorno
200-201
202-203
204

24°56'S / 48-80°W

CONNECTIONS

South Georgia (U.K.)

1:8 000 000

1:8 000 000

Lambert Azimuthal Equal Area Projection

ATLANTIC OCEAN

Falkland Islands (U.K.)

15°-24°S / 38°-53°W

>6000m
5000-6000m
4000-5000m
3000-4000m
2000-3000m
1500-2000m
1000-1500m
500-1000m
200-500m
100-200m
0-100m
<0m

0-200m
200-500m
500-1000m
1000-2000m
2000-3000m
3000-4000m
4000-5000m
5000-6000m
>6000m

202-203

202-203

202-203
ATLANTIC
OCEAN
BAHIA
ESPÍRITO SANTO
RIO DE JANEIRO
Serra do Espinhaço
Planalto do Brasil
Serra da Mantiqueira
Serra do Mar
Serra dos Aimorés
Serra do Chifre
Serra do Cabral
Serra dos Tropeiros
Chapadão de Santa Maria
Represa Três Marias
Belo Horizonte
Rio de Janeiro
Vitória
Montes Claros
Governador Valadares
Juiz de Fora
Teófilo Otôni
Campos
Niterói
Ilhéus
Porto Seguro
Arquipélago dos Abrolhos
Cabo Frio
Cabo de São Tomé
Ilha Grande
Ilha do São Sebastião
H
I
J
K
L
M
N
O
46°
45°
44°
43°
42°
41°
40°
39°
38°
CONNECTIONS
subject
page#
World countries 10–11
World cities 24–25
South America landscapes 190–191
South America countries 192–193
Atlantic Ocean 216–217
1:3 300 000
miles
0 25 50 75 100 125
km
0 25 50 75 100 125 150 175 200
Conic Equidistant Projection

Paradise Bay, *Antarctica*

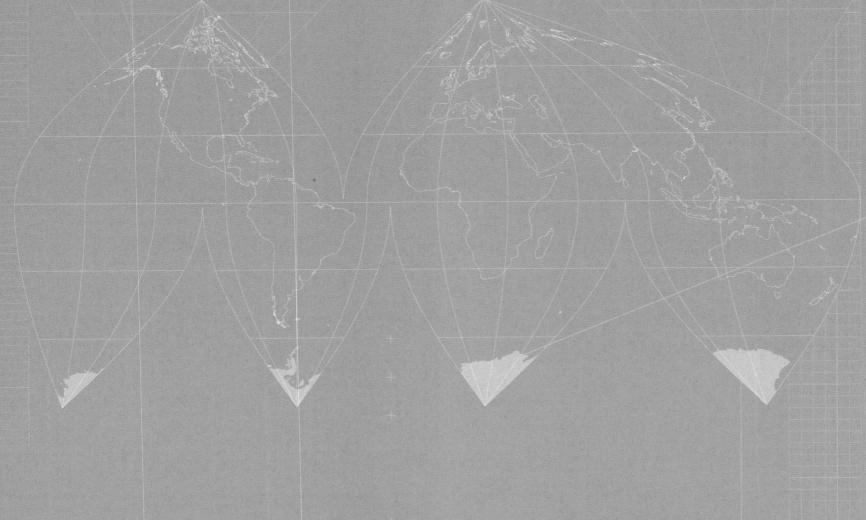

oceansandpoles

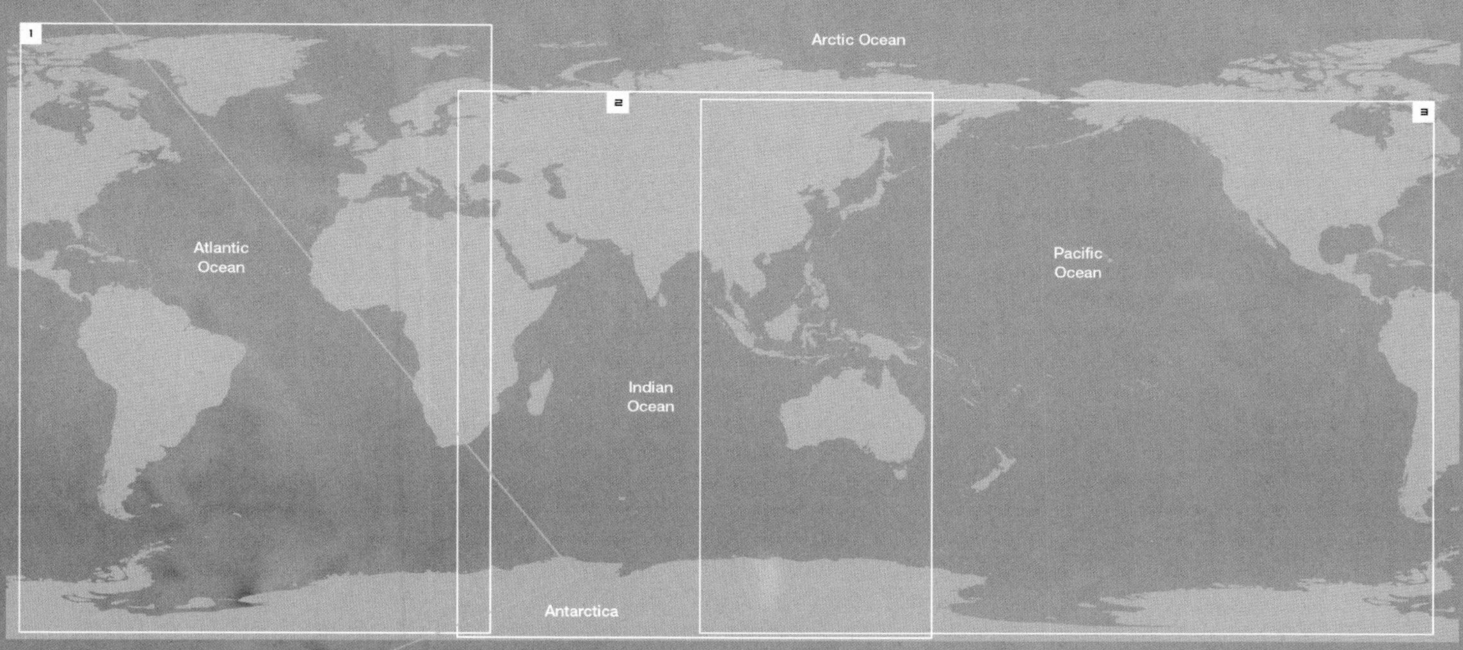

1
2
3
Arctic Ocean
Atlantic Ocean
Indian Ocean
Pacific Ocean
Antarctica

[contents]

oceans [features]

1

CONNECTIONS

▸ subject	page#
▸ World climate and weather	16–17
▸ South America impacts	196–197
▸ Atlantic Ocean	216–217
▸ Indian Ocean	218–219
▸ Pacific Ocean	220–221

Fig. #01
Ocean surface currents

→ Warm current
→ Cold current
→ Seasonal drift during northern winter

Fig. #02
Sea surface height

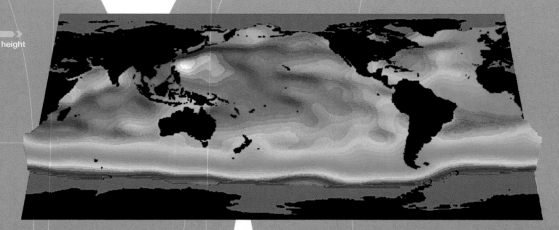

Fig. **#01–#02 Sea surface currents and height**

Most of the Earth's incoming solar radiation is absorbed by the surface waters of the oceans. The resultant warming is greatest around the equator and ocean surface currents, as shown on the map above (Fig. #01), redistribute the heat around the globe. They are influenced by winds, by density gradients caused by variations in temperature and salinity, and by the Earth's rotation which tends to deflect currents to the right in the northern hemisphere and to the left in the southern hemisphere. The circulation of ocean currents is a major influence on the world's climate. Sea surface circulation is reflected in variations in sea surface height (Fig. #02) which can vary greatly across currents. Currents flow along the slopes and are strongest where the slopes are steepest.

Satellite/Sensor : TOPEX/POSEIDON

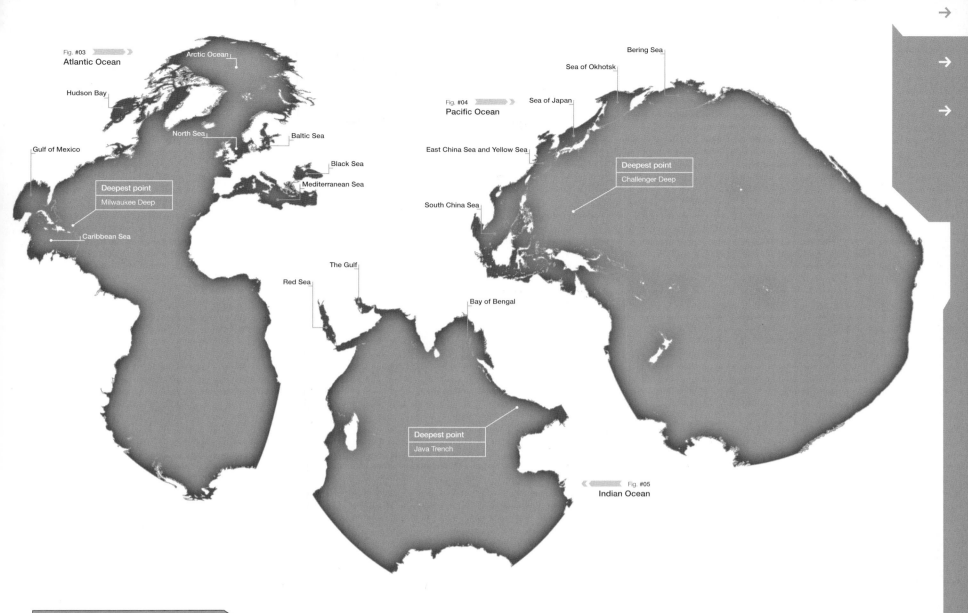

Fig. #03 Atlantic Ocean

Arctic Ocean

Hudson Bay

North Sea

Baltic Sea

Gulf of Mexico

Black Sea

Mediterranean Sea

Deepest point
Milwaukee Deep

Caribbean Sea

Bering Sea

Sea of Okhotsk

Fig. #04 Pacific Ocean

Sea of Japan

East China Sea and Yellow Sea

Deepest point
Challenger Deep

South China Sea

The Gulf

Red Sea

Bay of Bengal

Deepest point
Java Trench

Fig. #05 Indian Ocean

OCEANS

ATLANTIC OCEAN	area sq km	area sq miles	maximum depth metres	maximum depth feet	INDIAN OCEAN	area sq km	area sq miles	maximum depth metres	maximum depth feet	PACIFIC OCEAN	area sq km	area sq miles	maximum depth metres	maximum depth feet
Atlantic Ocean	86 557 000	33 420 000	8 605	28 231	Indian Ocean	73 427 000	28 350 000	7 125	23 376	Pacific Ocean	166 241 000	64 186 000	10 920	35 826
Arctic Ocean	9 485 000	3 662 000	5 450	17 880	Bay of Bengal	2 172 000	839 000	4 500	14 763	South China Sea	2 590 000	1 000 000	5 514	18 090
Caribbean Sea	2 512 000	970 000	7 680	25 196	Red Sea	453 000	175 000	3 040	9 973	Bering Sea	2 261 000	873 000	4 150	13 615
Mediterranean Sea	2 510 000	969 000	5 121	16 800	The Gulf	238 000	92 000	73	239	Sea of Okhotsk (Okhotskoye More)	1 392 000	537 000	3 363	11 033
Gulf of Mexico	1 544 000	596 000	3 504	11 495						East China Sea (Dong Hai) and Yellow Sea (Huang Hai)	1 202 000	464 000	2 717	8 913
Hudson Bay	1 233 000	476 000	259	849						Sea of Japan (East Sea)	1 013 000	391 000	3 743	12 280
North Sea	575 000	222 000	661	2 168										
Black Sea	508 000	196 000	2 245	7 365										
Baltic Sea	382 000	147 000	460	1 509										

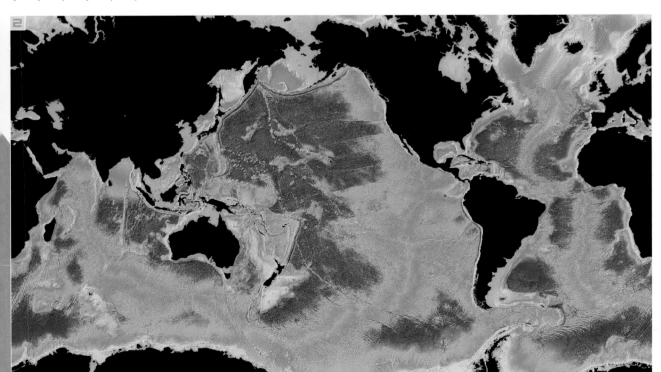

1 Perspective View, *Pacific Ocean*

This 3-D perspective view shows the sea trenches, ridges and basins of the western side of the Pacific Ocean. The image has been generated using sea depth values and extends from Australia and Melanesia at the bottom to Japan and the Kamchatka Peninsula at the top. Severe variations in depth of the sea bed are clearly seen. Deep trenches are shown by the darker areas. The New Hebrides, South Solomon and New Britain Trenches are visible at the bottom of the image and the Mariana Trench, the world's deepest, in the upper centre.

2 Global Seafloor Topography

This image has been produced from a combination of shipboard depth soundings and gravity data derived from satellite altimetry from the ERS-1 and Geosat satellites. The range of colours represents different depths of the ocean – from orange and yellow on the shallow continental shelves to dark blues in the deepest ocean trenches. The heavily fractured mid-ocean ridges (ranging from green to yellow) are particularly prominent.

ANTARCTICA

HIGHEST MOUNTAINS

	m	ft
Vinson Massif	4 897	16 066
Mt Tyree	4 852	15 918
Mt Kirkpatrick	4 528	14 855
Mt Markham	4 351	14 275
Mt Jackson	4 190	13 747
Mt Sidley	4 181	13 717

AREA

	sq km	sq miles
Total land area (excluding ice shelves)	12 093 000	4 669 292
Ice shelves	1 559 000	601 954
Exposed rock	49 000	18 920

HEIGHTS

	m	ft
Lowest bedrock elevation (Bentley Subglacial Trench)	-2 496	-8 189
Maximum ice thickness (Astrolabe Subglacial Basin)	4 776	15 669
Mean ice thickness (including ice shelves)	1 859	6 099

VOLUME

	cubic km	cubic miles
Ice sheet (including ice shelves)	25 400 000	10 160 000

CLIMATE

	°C	°F
Lowest screen temperature (Vostok Station, 21st July 1983)	-89.2	-128.6
Coldest place – Annual mean (Plateau Station)	-56.6	-69.9

1 Ozone Depletion

Since the 1970s, measurements have shown a thinning of the protective ozone layer in the Earth's atmosphere and the appearance of an ozone 'hole' over Antarctica. A major cause of this appears to be emissions of CFCs chlorofluorocarbons (CFCs) and halon gasses. This image from the Total Ozone Mapping Spectrometer (TOMS) sensor shows the ozone hole (blue) at its maximum extent of 11 million square miles in 2000. The unit of measurement for Ozone is the Dobson Unit (DU) with 300 being an average figure. In the image, yellow and orange represent high levels of 300–340DU, and dark blue low levels of 100–200 DU.

Satellite/Sensor : TOMS

2 Sea Ice Concentration

These images have been derived from data collected by the Special Sensor Microwave Imager (SSM/I) carried on US Department of Defense meteorological satellites. The colours represent ice concentration, ranging from the purple and red areas with a concentration of over 80 per cent, through to the green and yellow areas with concentrations between 20 and 40 per cent. The top image shows the ice at its lowest 2000 level in February, towards the end of the Antarctic summer. Ice builds up through the winter and by September (bottom), the ice is at its most extensive. In places the sea is frozen to a distance of over 1 000 km from the land.

Satellite/Sensor : SSM/I

3 Larsen Ice Shelf

This satellite image shows the edge of the Larsen Ice Shelf on the eastern side of the Antarctic Peninsula, and icebergs which have split, or 'calved' from the shelf. Ice shelves, which account for about 2 per cent of all Antarctic ice, typically undergo cycles of advance and retreat over many decades. Warmer surface temperatures over just a few months can cause an ice shelf to splinter and may prime it for a major collapse. This process can be expected to become more widespread if global, and particularly Antarctic summer, temperatures increase.

Satellite/Sensor : Landsat

4 Ice Sheet Thickness

Antarctica is covered by a permanent ice sheet that is in places more that 4 500 m thick. This map shows the thickness of ice, with the orange/red areas representing ice over 3 000 m thick. The thinnest ice is around the coast and on the high mountains, represented by the blue areas. The cross-section shows the ice cap (pale blue) in relation to the bedrock of Antarctica. This clearly shows that the thickest ice occurs above the deep glacial trenches, where the bedrock lies well below sea level.

5 Radar Image of Antarctica

This image of the whole of Antarctica is derived from data gathered by the Canadian RADARSAT satellite. In the image, light and dark areas represent relative measurements of radar reflectivity. Areas of finely powdered snow and smooth ice with few imperfections tend not to scatter radar waves projected against it, hence they appear dark. Irregular surfaces such as old, pitted ice, rock slides, and crevasses scatter the radar beam, giving a strong radar signal and thus appearing bright. Images such as this are valuable tools in the study of ice flow and stability on the continent.

Satellite/Sensor : RADARSAT

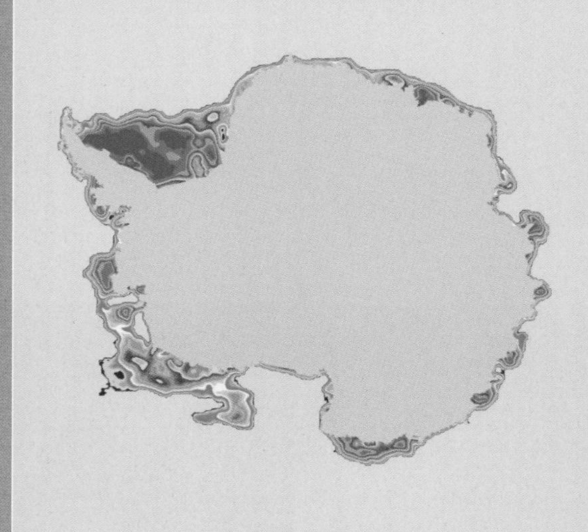

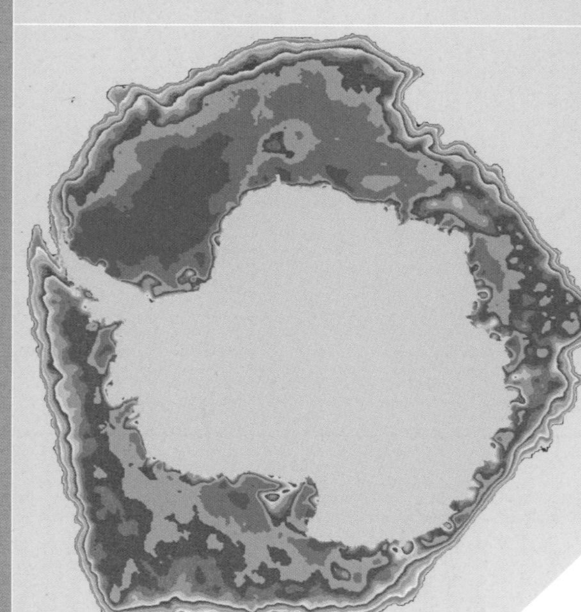

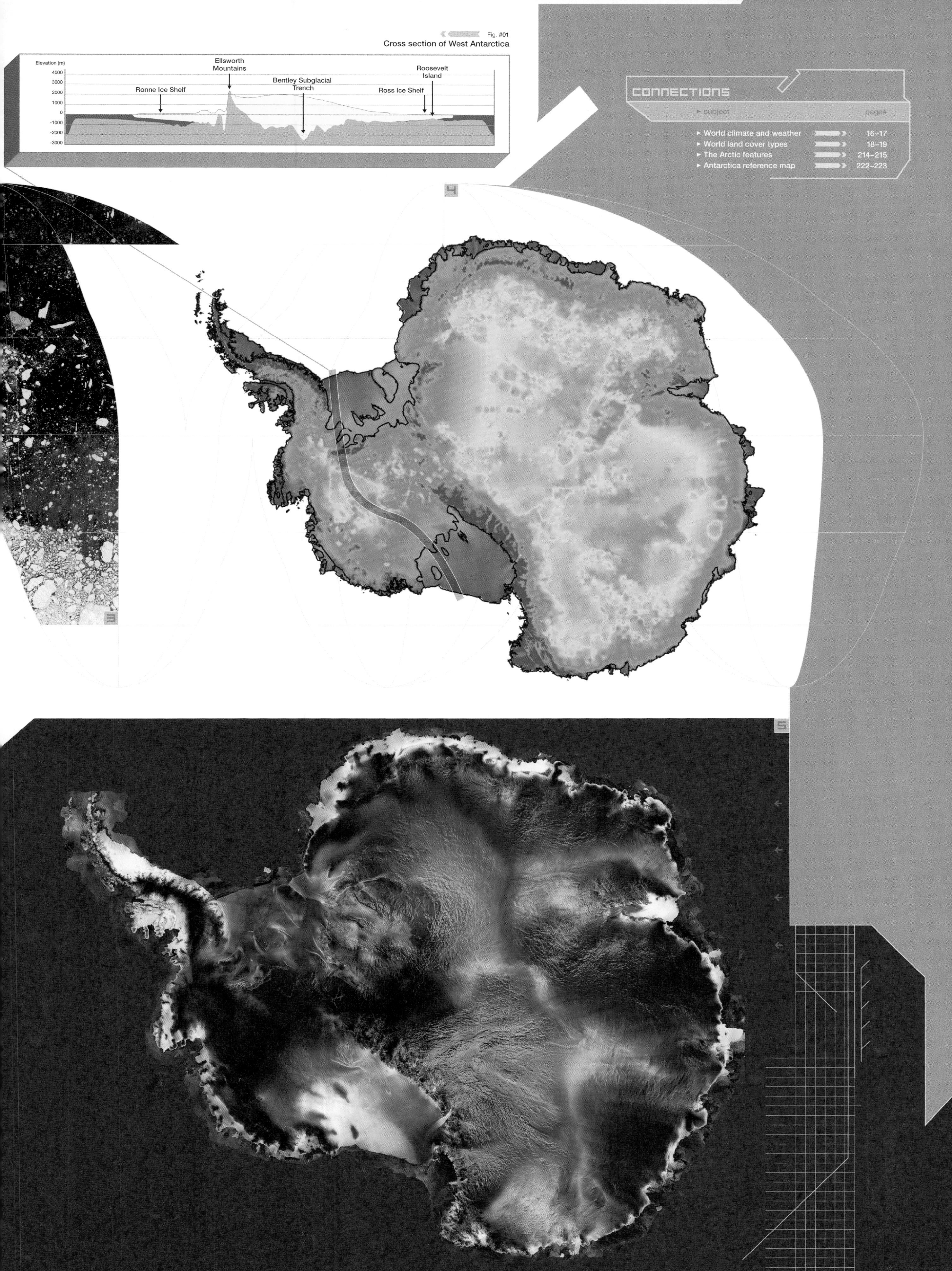

Elevation (m)
4000
3000
2000
1000
0
-1000
-2000
-3000

Fig. #01
Cross section of West Antarctica

Ellsworth
Mountains

Bentley Subglacial
Trench

Roosevelt
Island

Ronne Ice Shelf

Ross Ice Shelf

thearctic[features]

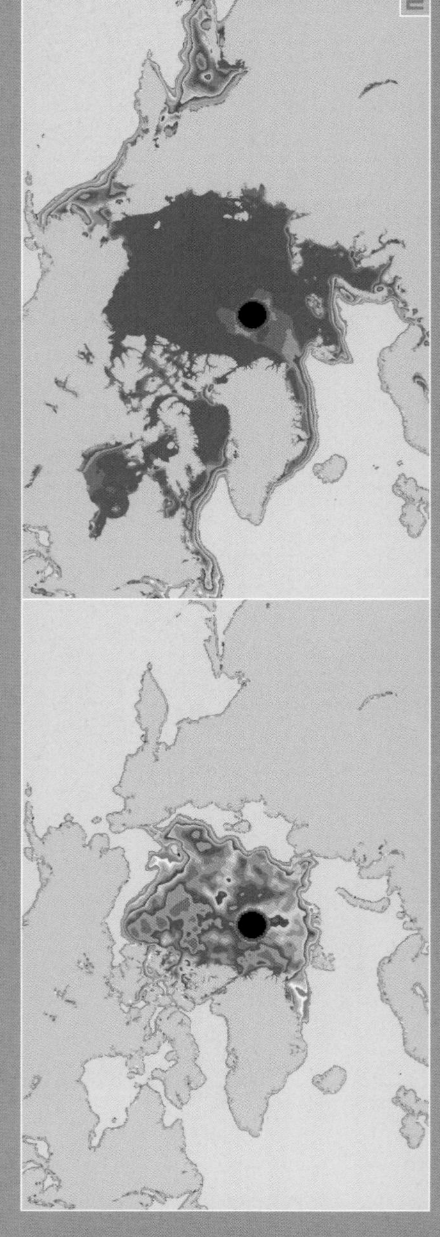

1 Tundra Landscape

Lakes and meandering rivers in a tundra landscape are shown in this photograph, taken in the short Arctic summer. Tundra is a cold-climate landscape type characterized by very low winter temperatures and short, cool summers. It is found in the region between 60°N and the Arctic ice cap and also at high altitudes beyond the climatic limits of tree growth. Tundra vegetation consists of dwarf shrubs, low herbaceous plants, lichens and mosses, on a permanently frozen subsoil.

2 Sea Ice Concentration

Although much of the Arctic Ocean is constantly frozen, there are wide variations in the amount of sea ice throughout the year, as shown by these images from the Special Sensor Microwave Imager (SSM/I). The purple areas show almost completely frozen sea (over ninety six per cent concentration) which extends as far south as Hudson Bay, Canada in February (top). By the end of the summer most of this ice has melted, as seen in the September image (bottom). The remaining sea ice at this time is thinner and more fragmented, even near the North Pole. Pink and brown areas represent concentrations of between sixty and eighty per cent.

Satellite/Sensor : SSM/I

Fig. #01
Peoples of the Arctic

The Arctic regions of Alaska, northern Canada, Greenland, and northern Scandinavia and Russian Federation contain the homelands of a diverse range of indigenous peoples. The main groups are shown on this map. These native peoples have subsisted for thousands of years on the resources of land and sea, as hunters, fishermen and reindeer herders. More recently, conflicts have arisen with governments eager to exploit the rich natural resources of the Arctic. There have also been moves towards greater autonomy for such groups. Most notably, in 1992 the Tungavik Federation of Nunavut and the government of Canada signed an agreement which addressed Inuit land claims and harvesting rights and established the new territory of Nunavut.

ALEUT
DENE TANANA
INUVIALUIT KOYUKON YUPIK
INUPIAQ
CHUKCHI
YUKAGHIR
YAKUT
DOLGAN
NENETS
KHANTY
CANADIAN INUIT
Arctic Ocean
CREE
LABRADOR INUIT
GREENLAND INUIT
SAAMI
Arctic Circle
Atlantic Ocean

CONNECTIONS

▸ subject	page#
▸ World climate and weather	16–17
▸ World land cover types	18–19
▸ North America landscapes	156–157
▸ Oceans features	210–211
▸ Antarctica features	212–213
▸ Arctic Ocean	224

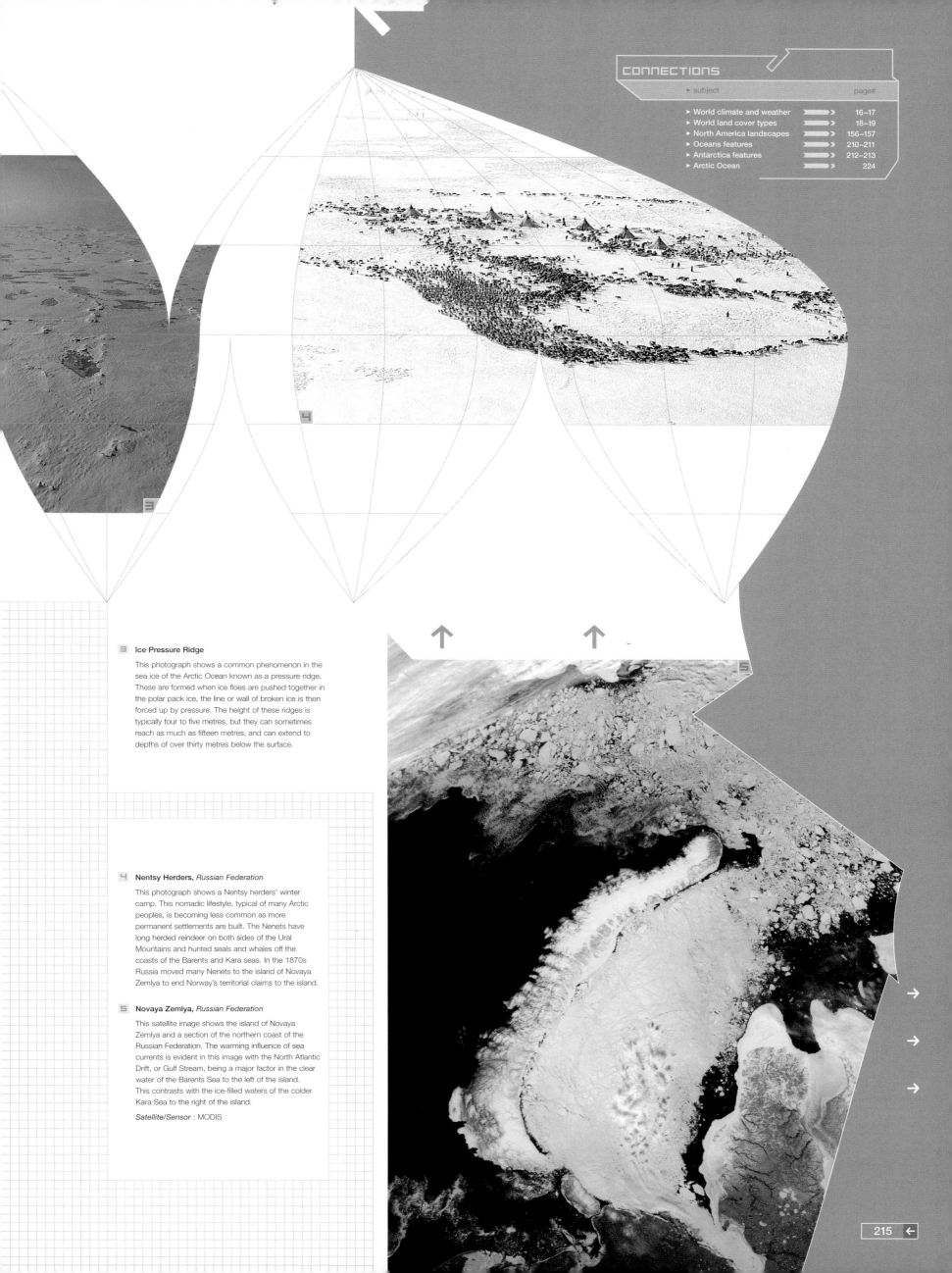

3 Ice Pressure Ridge

This photograph shows a common phenomenon in the sea ice of the Arctic Ocean known as a pressure ridge. These are formed when ice floes are pushed together in the polar pack ice, the line or wall of broken ice is then forced up by pressure. The height of these ridges is typically four to five metres, but they can sometimes reach as much as fifteen metres, and can extend to depths of over thirty metres below the surface.

4 Nentsy Herders, *Russian Federation*

This photograph shows a Nentsy herders' winter camp. This nomadic lifestyle, typical of many Arctic peoples, is becoming less common as more permanent settlements are built. The Nenets have long herded reindeer on both sides of the Ural Mountains and hunted seals and whales off the coasts of the Barents and Kara seas. In the 1870s Russia moved many Nenets to the island of Novaya Zemlya to end Norway's territorial claims to the island.

5 Novaya Zemlya, *Russian Federation*

This satellite image shows the island of Novaya Zemlya and a section of the northern coast of the Russian Federation. The warming influence of sea currents is evident in this image with the North Atlantic Drift, or Gulf Stream, being a major factor in the clear water of the Barents Sea to the left of the island. This contrasts with the ice-filled waters of the colder Kara Sea to the right of the island.

Satellite/Sensor : MODIS

→ 216

ATLANTIC
OCEAN
PACIFIC
OCEAN
Mid-Atlantic Ridge
CANADA
UNITED STATES OF AMERICA
MEXICO
GREENLAND (Denmark)
ICELAND
REYKJAVÍK
NORWAY
SWEDEN
FINLAND
RUSSIAN FEDERATION
MOSCOW
St Petersburg
HELSINKI
STOCKHOLM
OSLO
COPENHAGEN
DENMARK
REPUBLIC OF IRELAND
DUBLIN
UNITED KINGDOM
LONDON
AMSTERDAM
BRUSSELS
BERLIN
POLAND
WARSAW
MINSK
BELARUS
UKRAINE
KIEV
PRAGUE
VIENNA
BUDAPEST
ROMANIA
BUCHAREST
BELGRADE
SOFIA
BULGARIA
ZAGREB
PARIS
FRANCE
SWITZERLAND
MONACO
ITALY
ROME
Naples
GREECE
ATHENS
TURKEY
ANKARA
İstanbul
Black Sea
Baltic Sea
North Sea
Norwegian Sea
Mediterranean Sea
SPAIN
MADRID
PORTUGAL
LISBON
Oporto
Barcelona
Marseille
MOROCCO
RABAT
Casablanca
ALGERIA
ALGIERS
TUNISIA
TUNIS
LIBYA
TRIPOLI
WESTERN SAHARA
LAÂYOUNE
MAURITANIA
NOUAKCHOTT
MALI
NIGER
CHAD
NDJAMENA
Sahara
Hoggar
SENEGAL
DAKAR
THE GAMBIA
GUINEA-BISSAU
GUINEA
CONAKRY
SIERRA LEONE
FREETOWN
LIBERIA
MONROVIA
CÔTE D'IVOIRE
YAMOUSSOUKRO
Abidjan
BURKINA
OUAGADOUGOU
GHANA
ACCRA
TOGO
LOMÉ
BENIN
PORTO NOVO
NIGERIA
ABUJA
Lagos
CAMEROON
YAOUNDE
CENTRAL AFRICAN REPUBLIC
BANGUI
GABON
LIBREVILLE
SÃO TOMÉ AND PRÍNCIPE
CONGO
BRAZZAVILLE
DEM. REP. OF CONGO
KINSHASA
ANGOLA
LUANDA
Gulf of Guinea
Guinea Basin
Ascension (U.K.)
St Helena (U.K.)
JAMESTOWN
CAPE VERDE
PRAIA
Canary Islands (Spain)
Las Palmas de Gran Canaria
Madeira (Portugal)
FUNCHAL
Azores (Portugal)
PONTA DELGADA
Cape Verde Basin
Cape Verde Plateau
Sierra Leone Basin
Sierra Leone Rise
Monaco Basin
Canary Basin
Porcupine Abyssal Plain
Biscay Abyssal Plain
Azores-Biscay Rise
Horseshoe Seamounts
Iceland Basin
Reykjanes Ridge
Irminger Basin
Northwest Atlantic Mid-Ocean Channel
Labrador Sea
Baffin Bay
Baffin Island
Davis Strait
Denmark Strait
Hudson Bay
NUUK
Rockall Bank
Faroe Islands (Denmark)
TÓRSHAVN
Newfoundland
Grand Banks of Newfoundland
Flemish Cap
St Pierre and Miquelon (France)
Corner Seamounts
New England Seamounts
Bermuda (U.K.)
Bermuda Rise
Hatteras Abyssal Plain
Nares Deep
Nares Abyssal Plain
Sargasso Sea
Gulf of Mexico
Caribbean Sea
Guiana Basin
Demerara Abyssal Plain
Ceara Abyssal Plain
Amazon Cone
Pernambuco Abyssal Plain
OTTAWA
Montréal
Québec
Toronto
Boston
New York
Philadelphia
WASHINGTON
Chicago
Detroit
Minneapolis
St Louis
Atlanta
Miami
Orlando
Tampa
Houston
New Orleans
Dallas
San Antonio
Phoenix
Los Angeles
San Diego
Denver
Salt Lake City
Las Vegas
Edmonton
Calgary
Winnipeg
Rocky Mountains
Appalachian Mountains
Monterrey
MEXICO CITY
Guadalajara
Puebla
HAVANA
CUBA
NASSAU
THE BAHAMAS
JAMAICA
KINGSTON
HAITI
PORT-AU-PRINCE
DOMINICAN REPUBLIC
SANTO DOMINGO
Puerto Rico (U.S.A.)
BELIZE
GUATEMALA
GUATEMALA CITY
HONDURAS
TEGUCIGALPA
EL SALVADOR
SAN SALVADOR
NICARAGUA
MANAGUA
COSTA RICA
SAN JOSÉ
PANAMA
PANAMA CITY
VENEZUELA
CARACAS
COLOMBIA
BOGOTÁ
ECUADOR
QUITO
Guayaquil
PERU
LIMA
BOLIVIA
LA PAZ
SUCRE
GUYANA
GEORGETOWN
SURINAME
PARAMARIBO
French Guiana
CAYENNE
BRAZIL
BRASÍLIA
Manaus
Belém
Fortaleza
Recife
Salvador
Belo Horizonte
Galapagos Islands (Ecuador)
Cocos Ridge
Middle America Trench
Nazca Ridge
Cayman Trench
Puerto Rico Trench
Equator

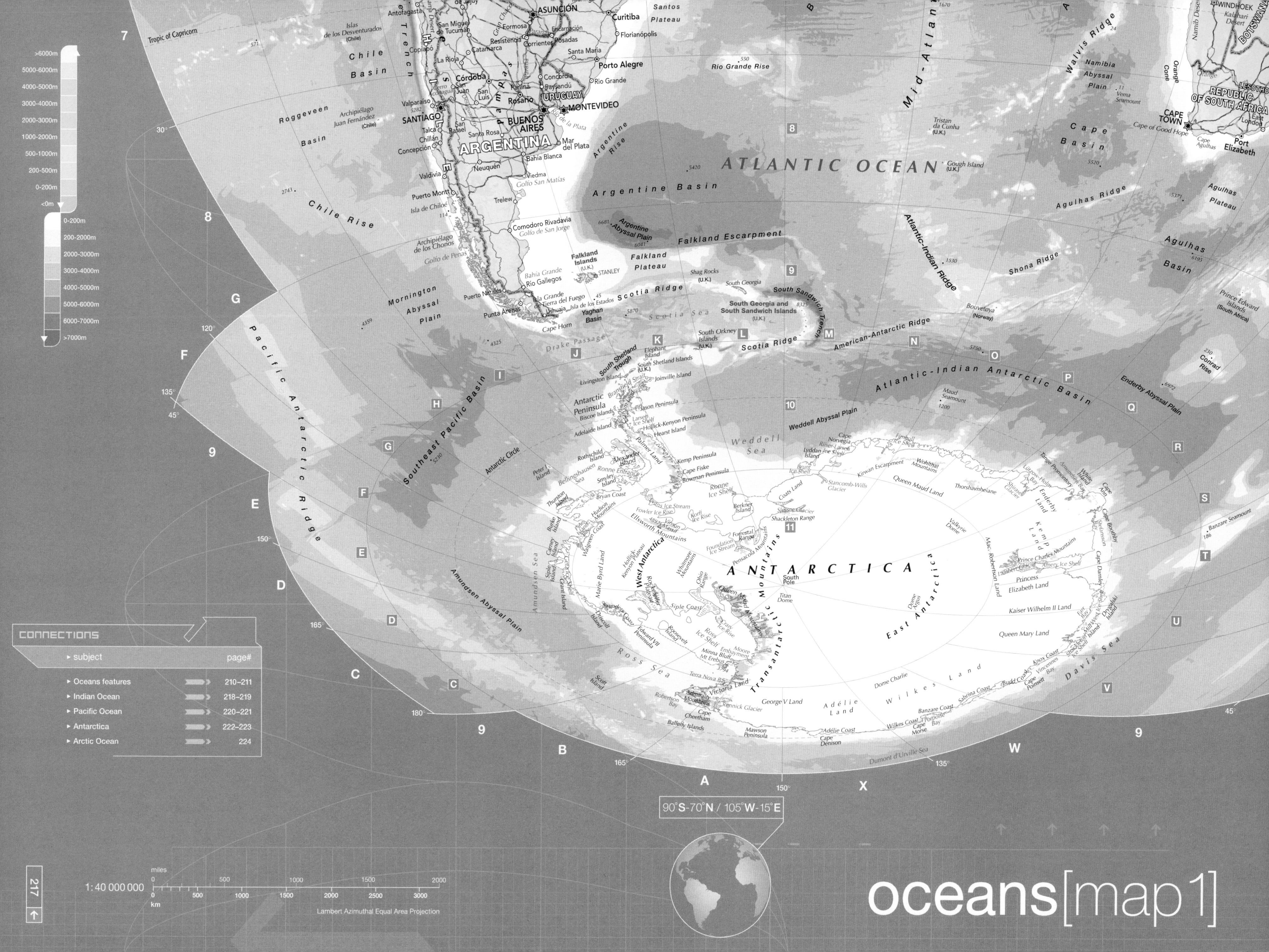
oceans[map 1]
90°S-70°N / 105°W-15°E
1:40 000 000
miles 0 500 1000 1500 2000
km 0 500 1000 1500 2000 2500 3000
Lambert Azimuthal Equal Area Projection
CONNECTIONS
subject page#
Oceans features 210–211
Indian Ocean 218–219
Pacific Ocean 220–221
Antarctica 222–223
Arctic Ocean 224
>6000m
5000-6000m
4000-5000m
3000-4000m
2000-3000m
1000-2000m
500-1000m
200-500m
0-200m
<0m
0-200m
200-2000m
2000-3000m
3000-4000m
4000-5000m
5000-6000m
6000-7000m
>7000m
ATLANTIC OCEAN
ANTARCTICA
West Antarctica
East Antarctica
Transantarctic Mountains
South Pole
Weddell Sea
Ross Sea
Amundsen Sea
Davis Sea
Scotia Sea
Drake Passage
Argentine Basin
Argentine Abyssal Plain
Falkland Escarpment
Falkland Plateau
Scotia Ridge
South Sandwich Trench
American-Antarctic Ridge
Atlantic-Indian Ridge
Atlantic-Indian Antarctic Basin
Weddell Abyssal Plain
Enderby Abyssal Plain
Mid-Atlantic Ridge
Walvis Ridge
Cape Basin
Agulhas Basin
Agulhas Ridge
Agulhas Plateau
Shona Ridge
Rio Grande Rise
Chile Basin
Chile Rise
Roggeveen Basin
Mornington Abyssal Plain
Southeast Pacific Basin
Pacific Antarctic Ridge
Amundsen Abyssal Plain
Antarctic Circle
Tropic of Capricorn
ARGENTINA
URUGUAY
REPUBLIC OF SOUTH AFRICA
BUENOS AIRES
MONTEVIDEO
SANTIAGO
ASUNCIÓN
CAPE TOWN
Falkland Islands (U.K.)
South Georgia and South Sandwich Islands (U.K.)
South Orkney Islands (U.K.)
South Shetland Islands (U.K.)
Bouvetøya (Norway)
Gough Island (U.K.)
Tristan da Cunha (U.K.)
Prince Edward Islands (South Africa)
Antarctic Peninsula
Queen Maud Land
Enderby Land
Kemp Land
Mac. Robertson Land
Princess Elizabeth Land
Kaiser Wilhelm II Land
Queen Mary Land
Wilkes Land
Adélie Land
George V Land
Victoria Land
Marie Byrd Land
Ellsworth Mountains
Ronne Ice Shelf
Ross Ice Shelf

RUSSIAN FEDERATION
KAZAKHSTAN
MONGOLIA
CHINA
INDIA
IRAN
SAUDI ARABIA
AFGHANISTAN
PAKISTAN
TURKEY
UKRAINE
EGYPT
SUDAN
ETHIOPIA
SOMALIA
KENYA
TANZANIA
LIBYA
CHAD
ANGOLA
ZAMBIA
MOZAMBIQUE
MADAGASCAR
MYANMAR
THAILAND
INDONESIA
AUSTRALIA
JAPAN
PHILIPPINES
INDIAN OCEAN
Arabian Sea
Bay of Bengal
South China Sea
Sea of Okhotsk
Caspian Sea
Black Sea
Mediterranean Sea
Red Sea
Gobi
Arabian Basin
Somali Basin
Mid-Indian Basin
West Australian Basin
Mascarene Basin
Madagascar Basin
Ninetyeast Ridge
Carlsberg Ridge
Mid-Indian Ridge
Chagos-Lacadive Ridge
Kyushu - Palau Ridge
South Honshu Ridge
1
2
3
4
5
6
7
→ 218

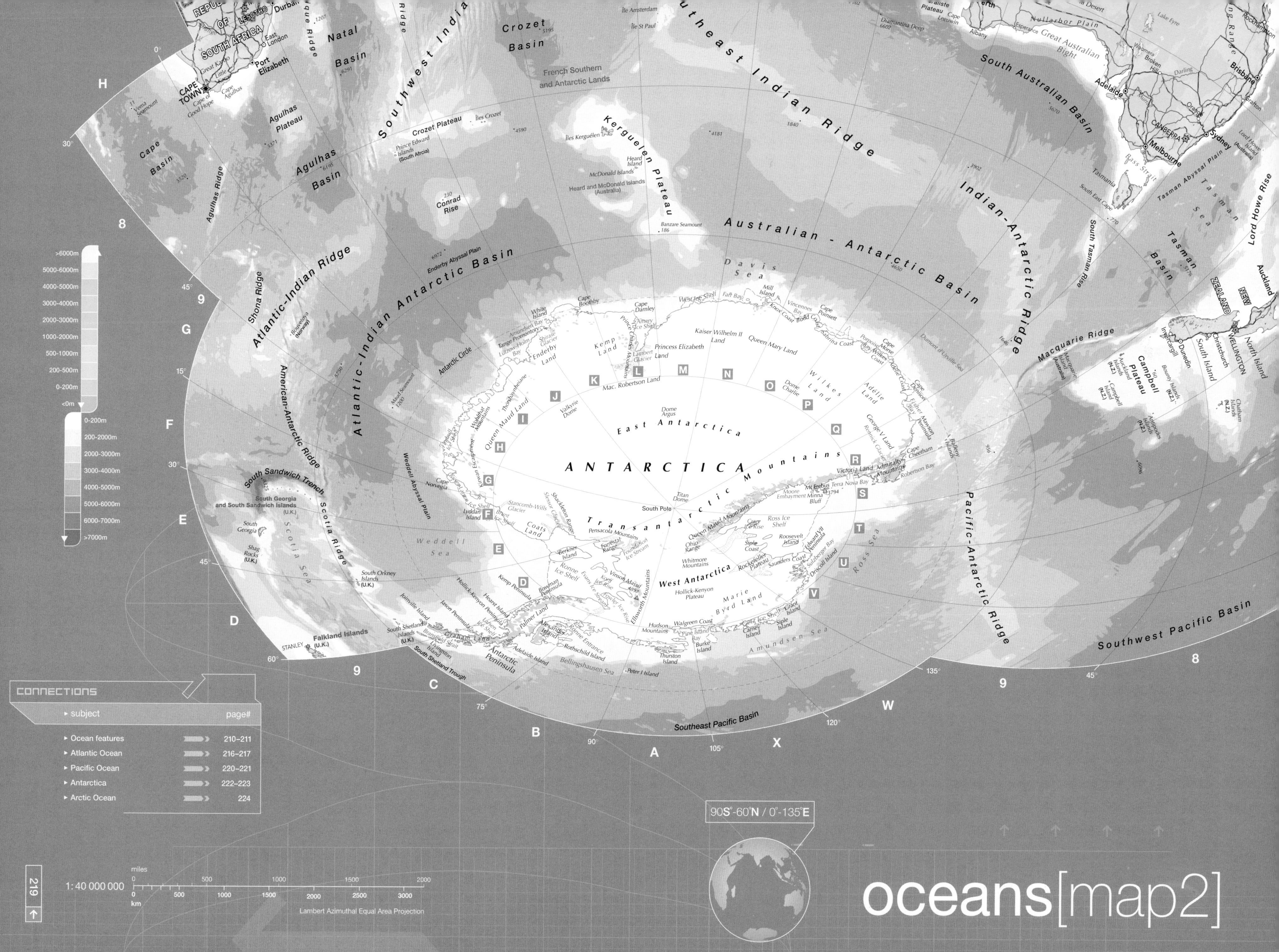

90S°·60'N / 0'·135'E

Map labels and features

New Zealand / Tasman region
Auckland
North Island
NEW
ZEALAND
WELLINGTON
Christchurch
South Island
Dunedin
Invercargill
Chatham Islands (N.Z.)
Bounty Islands (N.Z.)
Antipodes Islands (N.Z.)
Campbell Plateau
Auckland Islands (N.Z.)
Campbell Island (N.Z.)
Macquarie Ridge
Macquarie Island (Australia)
South Tasman Rise
Tasman Basin
Tasman Sea
Tasmania
South East Cape
Bass Strait
Melbourne
CANBERRA
Adelaide
Sydney
Brisbane
Lord Howe Island (Australia)
Lord Howe Rise
Tasman Abyssal Plain

Australia / Indian Ocean region
Great Australian Bight
South Australian Basin
Southeast Indian Ridge
Indian-Antarctic Ridge
Australian–Antarctic Basin
Kerguelen Plateau
Heard Island
McDonald Islands
Heard and McDonald Islands (Australia)
Îles Kerguelen
French Southern and Antarctic Lands
Crozet Basin
Crozet Plateau
Îles Crozet
Prince Edward Islands (South Africa)
Conrad Rise
Enderby Abyssal Plain
Atlantic-Indian Antarctic Basin
Southwest Indian Ridge
Atlantic-Indian Ridge

Africa region
SOUTH AFRICA
Durban
Port Elizabeth
CAPE TOWN
Cape of Good Hope
Natal Basin
Agulhas Basin
Agulhas Plateau
Snona Ridge
Cape Basin

Pacific / Antarctic region
Southwest Pacific Basin
Pacific-Antarctic Ridge
Ross Sea
Ross Ice Shelf
Roosevelt Island
Amundsen Sea
Marie Byrd Land
West Antarctica
Southeast Pacific Basin
Bellingshausen Sea
Antarctic Peninsula
Peter I Island
Thurston Island

Antarctica
ANTARCTICA
East Antarctica
West Antarctica
Transantarctic Mountains
Antarctica Mountains
South Pole
Wilkes Land
Adélie Land
George V Land
Victoria Land
Queen Mary Land
Kaiser Wilhelm II Land
Princess Elizabeth Land
Mac. Robertson Land
Kemp Land
Enderby Land
Queen Maud Land
Coats Land
Ellsworth Mountains
Whitmore Mountains
Hollick-Kenyon Plateau
Pensacola Mountains
Shackleton Range
Dome Argus
Dome Charlie
Davis Sea

Weddell / Scotia region
Weddell Sea
Weddell Abyssal Plain
Ronne Ice Shelf
Filchner Ice Shelf
Berkner Island
American-Antarctic Ridge
Scotia Ridge
Scotia Sea
South Sandwich Trench
South Georgia and South Sandwich Islands (U.K.)
South Georgia (U.K.)
Shag Rocks (U.K.)
South Orkney Islands (U.K.)
South Shetland Islands (U.K.)
South Shetland Trough
Falkland Islands (U.K.)
STANLEY

Lambert Azimuthal Equal Area Projection
1:40 000 000

Depth scale

>6000m
5000-6000m
4000-5000m
3000-4000m
2000-3000m
1000-2000m
500-1000m
200-500m
0-200m

0-200m
200-2000m
2000-3000m
3000-4000m
4000-5000m
5000-6000m
6000-7000m
>7000m
<0m

miles
km
0   500   1000   1500   2000   3000

90°S-60°N / 90°E-60°W

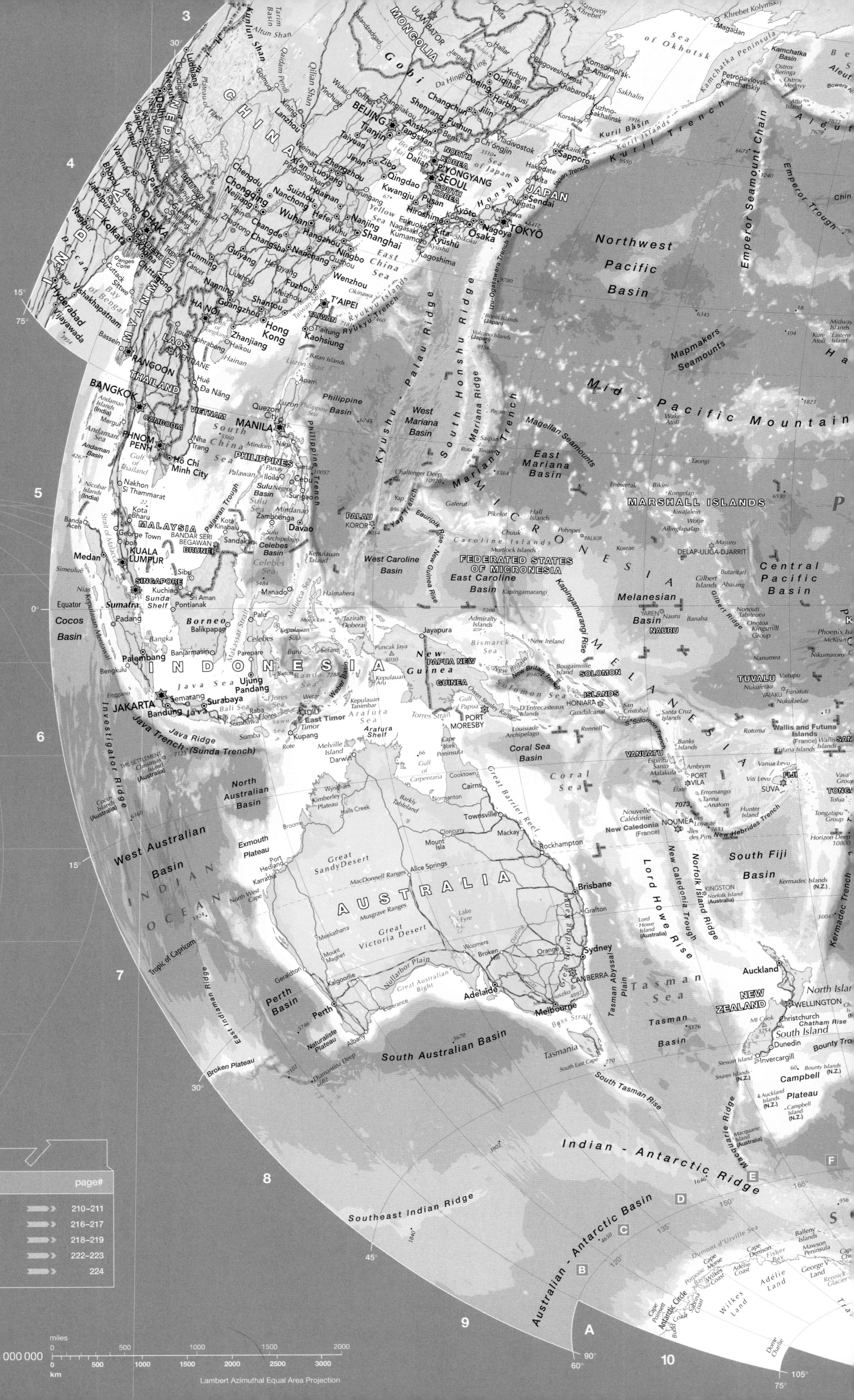

Depth scale

>6000m
5000-6000m
4000-5000m
3000-4000m
2000-3000m
1000-2000m
500-1000m
200-500m
0-200m
<0m

0-200m
200-2000m
2000-3000m
3000-4000m
4000-5000m
5000-6000m
6000-7000m
>7000m

1:45 000 000

miles 0 500 1000 1500 2000
km 0 500 1000 1500 2000 2500 3000

Lambert Azimuthal Equal Area Projection

CANADA
UNITED STATES OF AMERICA
MEXICO
MEXICO CITY
WASHINGTON
OTTAWA
New York
Boston
Philadelphia
Baltimore
Chicago
Detroit
Toronto
Montreal
Cleveland
Pittsburgh
Columbus
Indianapolis
Cincinnati
St Louis
Atlanta
Charlotte
Jacksonville
Orlando
Tampa
Miami
Houston
Dallas
Fort Worth
San Antonio
Austin
New Orleans
Memphis
Nashville
Denver
Phoenix
Las Vegas
Salt Lake City
Los Angeles
San Diego
San Francisco
San Jose
Sacramento
Portland
Seattle
Vancouver
Calgary
Edmonton
Winnipeg
Minneapolis
Milwaukee
Anchorage
Monterrey
Guadalajara
Puebla
Ciudad Juárez
Gulf of Alaska
Gulf of Mexico
Caribbean Sea
Sargasso Sea
Rocky Mountains
Appalachian Mountains
HAVANA
CUBA
THE BAHAMAS
NASSAU
PORT-AU-PRINCE
SANTO DOMINGO
DOMINICAN REPUBLIC
SAN JUAN
Puerto Rico
KINGSTON
JAMAICA
BELIZE
GUATEMALA
GUATEMALA CITY
HONDURAS
TEGUCIGALPA
EL SALVADOR
SAN SALVADOR
NICARAGUA
MANAGUA
SAN JOSÉ
COSTA RICA
PANAMA
PANAMA CITY
CARACAS
VENEZUELA
COLOMBIA
BOGOTA
Medellín
Cali
Barranquilla
ECUADOR
QUITO
Guayaquil
PERU
LIMA
BOLIVIA
LA PAZ
SUCRE
GUYANA
SURINAME
GEORGETOWN
PARAMARIBO
BRAZIL
BRASÍLIA
Manaus
São Paulo
Rio de Janeiro
PARAGUAY
ASUNCIÓN
URUGUAY
MONTEVIDEO
BUENOS AIRES
ARGENTINA
SANTIAGO
CHILE
Córdoba
Rosario
Falkland Islands (U.K.)
STANLEY
NORTHEAST PACIFIC BASIN
PACIFIC OCEAN
ATLANTIC OCEAN
Mid - Atlantic Ridge
Hawaiian Islands
Honolulu
French Polynesia
PAPEETE
Cook Islands (N.Z.)
Samoa
American Samoa (U.S.A.)
Niue (N.Z.)
Pitcairn Islands (U.K.)
ADAMSTOWN
Marquesas Islands
Tuamotu Islands
Galapagos Islands (Ecuador)
Easter Island (Isla de Pascua) (Chile)
East Pacific Rise
Gallego Rise
Galapagos Rise
Tiki Basin
Penrhyn Basin
Samoa Basin
Southwest Pacific Basin
Roggeveen Basin
Chile Basin
Chile Rise
Nazca Ridge (Southwest Peru Ridge)
Cocos Ridge
Middle America Trench
Peru-Chile Trench
Pacific - Antarctic Ridge
Mornington Abyssal Plain
Southeast Pacific Basin
Amundsen Abyssal Plain
Amundsen Ridges
Amundsen Sea
Ross Sea
SOUTHERN OCEAN
Marie Byrd Land
West Antarctica
Antarctic Peninsula
Argentine Basin
Argentine Rise
Falkland Plateau
Scotia Ridge
Drake Passage
Hatteras Abyssal Plain
Nares Abyssal Plain
Venezuelan Basin
Colombian Basin
Demerara Abyssal Plain
Tufts Abyssal Plain
New England Seamounts

antarctica[map1]

50°-90°S / 0°-180°-0°

ARGENTINE CLAIM

BRITISH ANTARCTIC TERRITORY

BRITISH ANTARCTIC TERRITORY

Scotia Ridge

Scotia Ridge

Scotia Ridge

Scotia Sea

Orcadas
(Arg.)
Coronation Island · Laurie Island
South Orkney
Islands (U.K.)

Weddell Abyss

CHILEAN CLAIM

Mount Usborne
·STANLEY
West Falkland · East Falkland
Falkland Islands (U.K.)
Beauchene Island

60°

Mount Adam

Weddell Sea

W e d d e l l   S e a

A
r
g
e
n
t
i
n
e
 Coast

Esperanza
(Argentina)
Marambio
(Argentina)

Halley
(U.K.)

Belgrano II
(Argentina)

Lyddan Island

Filchner Ice Shelf

Berkner Island

ARGENTINA

CHILE

Río Gallegos
Río Grande
Ushuaia

Isla de los Estados
Estrecho de Le Maire

Drake Passage

South Shetland Trough

South Shetland Islands
Livingston Island
King George Island
Elephant Island
Clarence Island

Bransfield Strait

Antarctic Peninsula

75°

Isla Contreras
Archipiélago
de la Reina Adelaida
Isla Desolación

Cape Horn
Islas Wollaston
Islas Hermite

Smith Island
Snow Island

Palmer (U.S.A.)
Vernadsky (Ukraine)

San Martín
(Argentina)
Rothera (U.K.)

Palmer Land

George VI
Sound

ARGENTINE CLAIM

Adelaide Island

Alexander Island

BRITISH ANTARCTIC TERRITORY

Rothschild Island
Charcot Island

English Coast

Ronne Ice Shelf

Fowler Ice Rise
Korff Ice Rise
Henry Ice Rise

Evans Ice Stream

Foundation Ice Stream

Bellingshausen Sea

Fletcher Peninsula
Bryan Coast

Sentinel Range

Heritage Range

Ellsworth Mountains

CHILEAN CLAIM

Peter I Island

Ellsworth Land

Mount Woollard
2677

West Antarctica

Hollick-Kenyon
Plateau

Mount
Murphy
2749

Abbot Ice Shelf

Eights Coast
Walgreen Coast

Thurston Island

Thwaites Glacier Tongue

Amundsen Sea

Amundsen Ridges

Southeast Pacific Basin

S O U T H E A S T   P A C I F I C   B A S I N

S
O
U
T
H
E
R
N

O
C
E
A
N

Kohler Range

M a r i e   B y r d   L a n d

Mount Sidley
4181

Executive
Committee
Range

Rockefeller Plateau

Ford Range

Ruppert Coast

Shirase Coast

Amundsen Abyssal Plain

Pacific-Antarctic Ridge

90°

105°

120°

135°

150°

165°

60°

Antarctic Circle

R O S

N

O

P

Q

R

S

T

U

V

1

2

3

>6000m
5000-6000m
4000-5000m
3000-4000m
2000-3000m
1000-2000m
500-1000m
200-500m
0-200m
<0m

0-200m
200-2000m
2000-3000m
3000-4000m
4000-5000m
5000-6000m
6000-7000m
>7000m

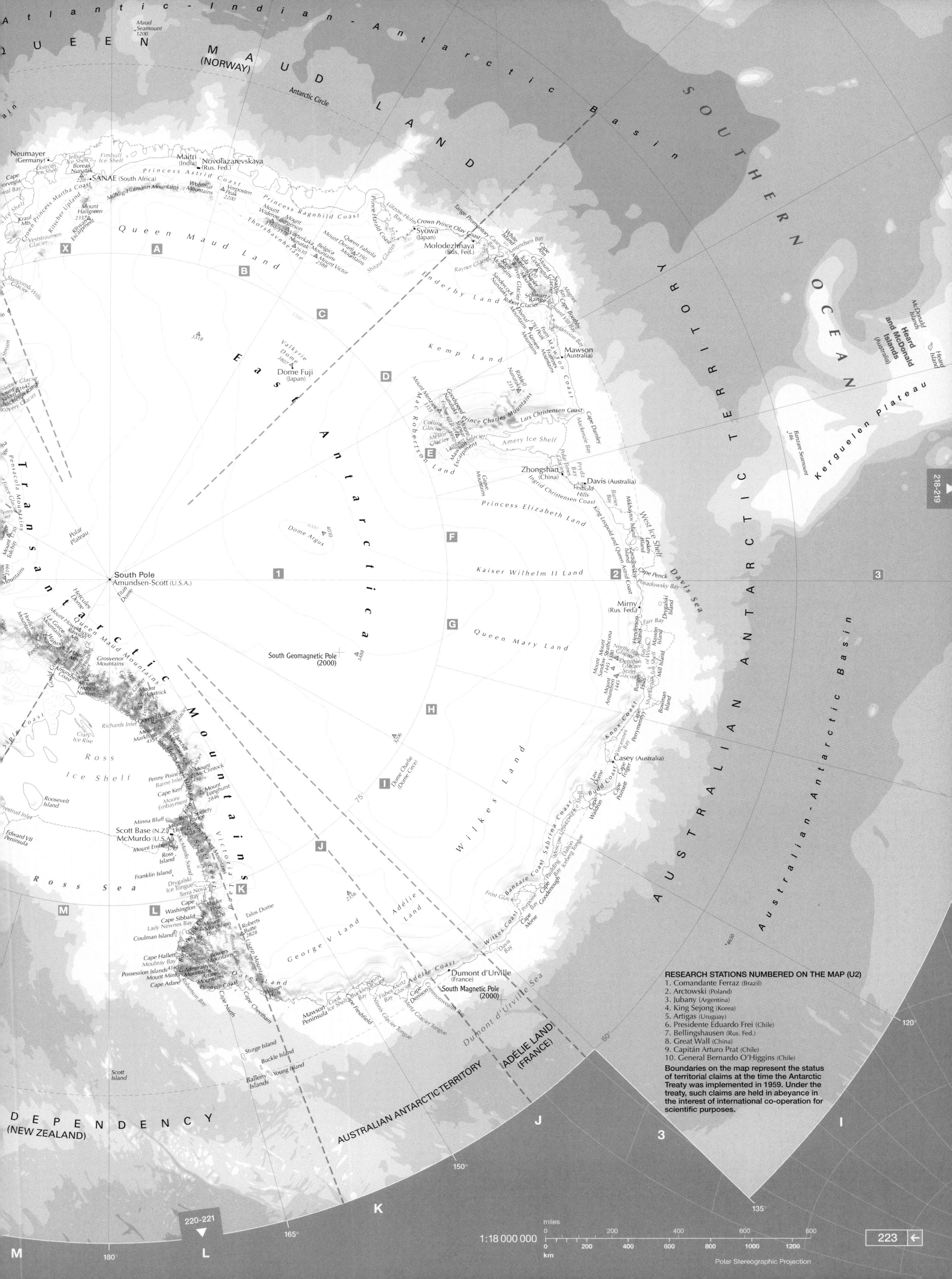

RESEARCH STATIONS NUMBERED ON THE MAP (U2)

1. Comandante Ferraz (Brazil)
2. Arctowski (Poland)
3. Jubany (Argentina)
4. King Sejong (Korea)
5. Artigas (Uruguay)
6. Presidente Eduardo Frei (Chile)
7. Bellingshausen (Rus. Fed.)
8. Great Wall (China)
9. Capitán Arturo Prat (Chile)
10. General Bernardo O'Higgins (Chile)

Boundaries on the map represent the status of territorial claims at the time the Antarctic Treaty was implemented in 1959. Under the treaty, such claims are held in abeyance in the interest of international co-operation for scientific purposes.

1:18 000 000

miles
0   200   400   600   800
0   200   400   600   800   1000   1200
km

Polar Stereographic Projection

218-219
220-221

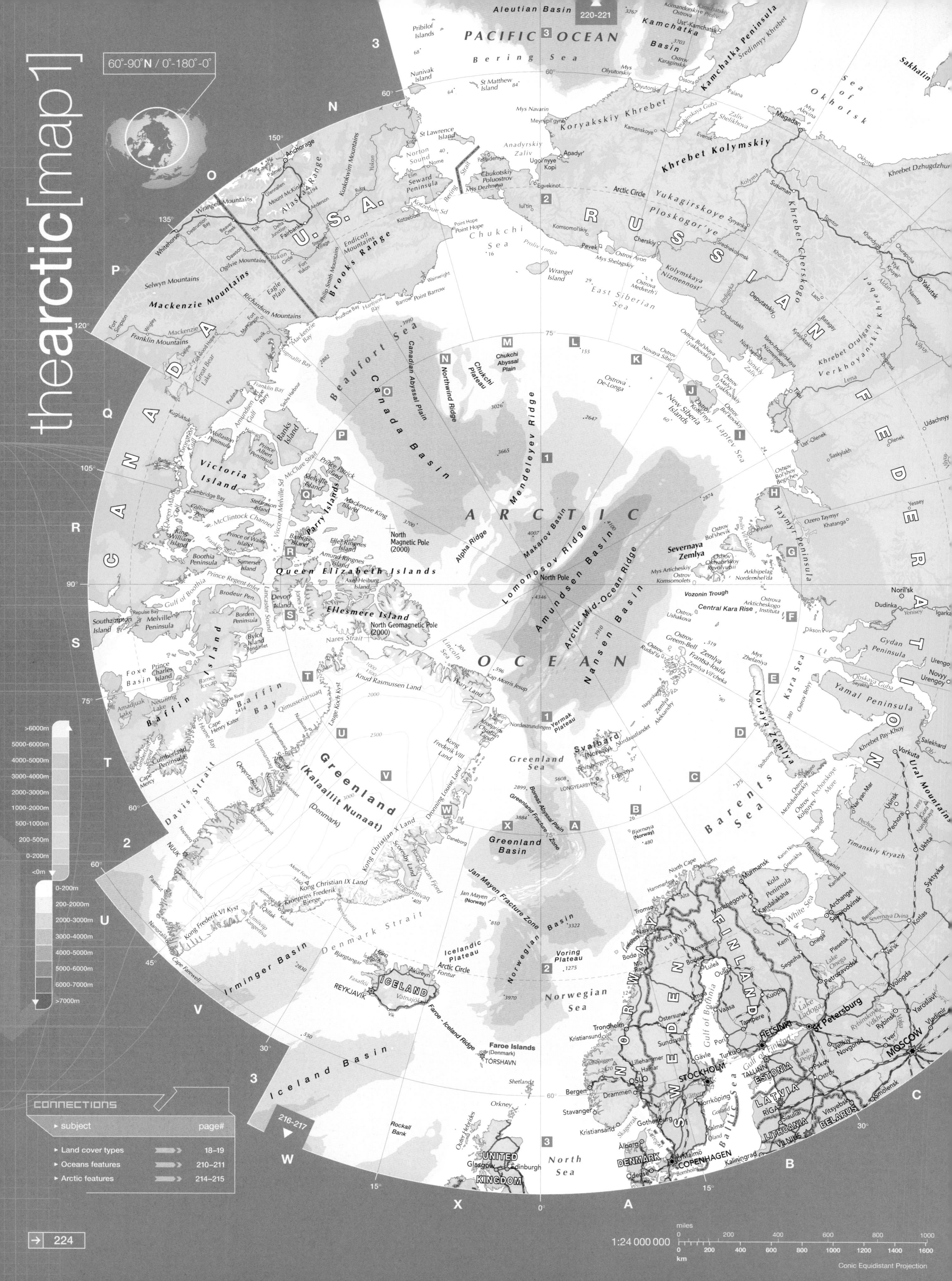

the arctic [map 1]
60°-90°N / 0°-180°-0°
>6000m
5000-6000m
4000-5000m
3000-4000m
2000-3000m
1000-2000m
500-1000m
200-500m
0-200m
<0m
0-200m
200-2000m
2000-3000m
3000-4000m
4000-5000m
5000-6000m
6000-7000m
>7000m
220-221
216-217
PACIFIC OCEAN
Aleutian Basin
Bering Sea
Kamchatka Basin
Kamchatka Peninsula
Sea of Okhotsk
Sakhalin
Magadan
Khrebet Kolymskiy
Koryakskiy Khrebet
Anadyrskiy Zaliv
Chukotskiy Poluostrov
Bering Strait
Arctic Circle
Yukagirskoye Ploskogor'ye
RUSSIAN FEDERATION
U.S.A.
CANADA
Anchorage
Alaska Range
Mount McKinley
Brooks Range
Wrangell Mountains
Mackenzie Mountains
Richardson Mountains
Chukchi Sea
Wrangel Island
East Siberian Sea
Beaufort Sea
Canada Basin
Canadian Abyssal Plain
Northwind Ridge
Chukchi Plateau
Chukchi Abyssal Plain
Mendeleyev Ridge
Alpha Ridge
Makarov Basin
Lomonosov Ridge
North Pole
Amundsen Basin
Arctic Mid-Ocean Ridge
Nansen Basin
ARCTIC OCEAN
Laptev Sea
New Siberia Islands
Severnaya Zemlya
Taymyr Peninsula
Kara Sea
Novaya Zemlya
Zemlya Frantsa-Iosifa
Yamal Peninsula
Barents Sea
Svalbard (Norway)
Greenland Sea
Yermak Plateau
Queen Elizabeth Islands
Ellesmere Island
Victoria Island
Banks Island
Parry Islands
North Magnetic Pole (2000)
North Geomagnetic Pole (2000)
Baffin Island
Baffin Bay
Davis Strait
Greenland (Kalaallit Nunaat) (Denmark)
Denmark Strait
Greenland Basin
Jan Mayen Fracture Zone
Norwegian Basin
Norwegian Sea
Voring Plateau
Icelandic Plateau
ICELAND
REYKJAVIK
Irminger Basin
Iceland Basin
Faroe - Iceland Ridge
Faroe Islands (Denmark)
TÓRSHAVN
Rockall Bank
UNITED KINGDOM
North Sea
NORWAY
SWEDEN
FINLAND
OSLO
STOCKHOLM
HELSINKI
TALLINN
ESTONIA
LATVIA
RIGA
LITHUANIA
VILNIUS
BELARUS
DENMARK
COPENHAGEN
St Petersburg
MOSCOW
Murmansk
Kola Peninsula
White Sea
Ural Mountains
1:24 000 000
miles
km
Conic Equidistant Projection

INTRODUCTION TO THE INDEX

The index includes all names shown on the reference maps in the atlas. Each entry includes the country or geographical area in which the feature is located, a page number and an alphanumeric reference. Additional entry details and aspects of the index are explained below.

Referencing

Names are referenced by page number and by grid reference. The grid reference relates to the alphanumeric values which appear in the margin of each map. These reflect the graticule on the map – the letter relates to longitude divisions, the number to latitude divisions.

Names are generally referenced to the largest scale map page on which they appear. For large geographical features, including countries, the reference is to the largest scale map on which the feature appears in its entirety, or on which the majority of it appears.

Rivers are referenced to their lowest downstream point – either their mouth or their confluence with another river. The river name will generally be positioned as close to this point as possible.

Alternative names

Alternative names appear as cross-references and refer the user to the index entry for the form of the name used on the map. Details of alternative names and their types also appear within the main entry. The different types of name form included are: alternative forms or spellings currently in common use; English conventional name forms normally used in English-language contexts; historical and former names; and long and short name forms.

For rivers with multiple names – for example those which flow through several countries – all alternative name forms are included within the main index entries, with details of the countries in which each form applies.

Administrative qualifiers

Administrative divisions are included in an entry to differentiate duplicate names – entries of exactly the same name and feature type within the one country – where these division names are shown on the maps. In such cases, duplicate names are alphabetized in the order of the administrative division names.

Additional qualifiers are included for names within selected geographical areas, to indicate more clearly their location.

Descriptors

Entries, other than those for towns and cities, include a descriptor indicating the type of geographical feature. Descriptors are not included where the type of feature is implicit in the name itself, unless there is a town or city of exactly the same name.

Insets

Where relevant, the index clearly indicates [inset] if a feature appears on an inset map.

Name forms and alphabetical order

Name forms are as they appear on the maps, with additional alternative forms included as cross-references. Names appear in full in the index, although they may appear in abbreviated form on the maps.

The Icelandic characters Ð and þ are transliterated and alphabetized as 'Th' and 'th'. The German character ß is alphabetized as 'ss'. Names beginning with Mac or Mc are alphabetized exactly as they appear. The terms Saint, Sainte, etc, are abbreviated to St, Ste, etc, but alphabetized as if in the full form.

Name form policies are explained in the Introduction to the Atlas (pp 4–5).

Numerical entries

Entries beginning with numerals appear at the beginning of the index, in numerical order. Elsewhere, numerals are alphabetized before 'a'.

Permuted terms

Names beginning with generic, geographical terms are permuted – the descriptive term is placed after, and the index alphabetized by, the main part of the name. For example, Mount Everest is indexed as Everest, Mount; Lake Superior as Superior, Lake. This policy is applied to all languages. Permuting has not been applied to names of towns, cities or administrative divisions beginning with such geographical terms. These remain in their full form, for example, Lake Isabella, USA.

Gazetteer entries and connections

Selected entries have been extended to include gazetteer-style information. Important geographical facts which relate specifically to the entry are included within the entry in coloured type.

Entries for features which also appear on, or which have a topical link to, the thematic pages of the atlas include a connection to those pages indicated by the symbol ➡➤.

Tables

Several tables, ranking geographical features by size, are included within the main index listing. Where possible these have been placed directly below the index entry for the feature ranked 1 in the table.

ABBREVIATIONS

admin. dist.	administrative district	imp. l.	impermanent lake	pref.	prefecture
admin. div.	administrative division	IN	Indiana	prov.	province
admin. reg.	administrative region	Indon.	Indonesia	pt	point
Afgh.	Afghanistan	Kazakh.	Kazakhstan	Qld	Queensland
AK	Alaska	KS	Kansas	Que.	Québec
AL	Alabama	KY	Kentucky	r.	river
Alg.	Algeria	Kyrg.	Kyrgyzstan	r. mouth	river mouth
AR	Arkansas	l.	lake	r. source	river source
Arg.	Argentina	LA	Louisiana	reg.	region
aut. comm.	autonomous community	lag.	lagoon	res.	reserve
aut. div.	autonomous division	Lith.	Lithuania	resr	reservoir
aut. reg.	autonomous region	Lux.	Luxembourg	RI	Rhode Island
aut. rep.	autonomous republic	MA	Massachusetts	Rus. Fed.	Russian Federation
AZ	Arizona	Madag.	Madagascar	S.	South
Azer.	Azerbaijan	Man.	Manitoba	S.A.	South Australia
b.	bay	MD	Maryland	salt l.	salt lake
B.C.	British Columbia	ME	Maine	Sask.	Saskatchewan
Bangl.	Bangladesh	Mex.	Mexico	SC	South Carolina
Bol.	Bolivia	MI	Michigan	SD	South Dakota
Bos.-Herz.	Bosnia-Herzegovina	MN	Minnesota	sea chan.	sea channel
Bulg.	Bulgaria	MO	Missouri	Sing.	Singapore
c.	cape	Moz.	Mozambique	Switz.	Switzerland
CA	California	MS	Mississippi	Tajik.	Tajikistan
Cent. Afr. Rep.	Central African Republic	MT	Montana	Tanz.	Tanzania
CO	Colorado	mt.	mountain	Tas.	Tasmania
Col.	Colombia	mt s	mountains	terr.	territory
CT	Connecticut	N.	North	Thai.	Thailand
Czech Rep.	Czech Republic	N.B.	New Brunswick	TN	Tennessee
DC	District of Columbia	N.S.	Nova Scotia	Trin. and Tob.	Trinidad and Tobago
DE	Delaware	N.S.W.	New South Wales	Turkm.	Turkmenistan
Dem. Rep. Congo	Democratic Republic of Congo	N.T.	Northern Territory	TX	Texas
depr.	depression	N.W.T.	Northwest Territories	U.A.E.	United Arab Emirates
des.	desert	N.Z.	New Zealand	U.K.	United Kingdom
Dom. Rep.	Dominican Republic	nat. park	national park	U.S.A.	United States of America
E.	East, Eastern	nature res.	nature reserve	Ukr.	Ukraine
Equat. Guinea	Equatorial Guinea	NC	North Carolina	union terr.	union territory
esc.	escarpment	ND	North Dakota	UT	Utah
est.	estuary	NE	Nebraska	Uzbek.	Uzbekistan
Eth.	Ethiopia	Neth.	Netherlands	VA	Virginia
Fin.	Finland	NH	New Hampshire	Venez.	Venezuela
FL	Florida	NJ	New Jersey	Vic.	Victoria
for.	forest	NM	New Mexico	vol.	volcano
Fr. Guiana	French Guiana	NV	Nevada	vol. crater	volcanic crater
g.	gulf	NY	New York	VT	Vermont
GA	Georgia	OH	Ohio	W.	West, Western
Guat.	Guatemala	OK	Oklahoma	W.A.	Western Australia
H.K.	Hong Kong	OR	Oregon	WA	Washington
HI	Hawaii	P.E.I.	Prince Edward Island	WI	Wisconsin
Hond.	Honduras	P.N.G.	Papua New Guinea	WV	West Virginia
i.	island	PA	Pennsylvania	WY	Wyoming
IA	Iowa	pen.	peninsula	Y.T.	Yukon Territory
ID	Idaho	plat.	plateau	Yugo.	Yugoslavia
IL	Illinois	Port.	Portugal		

index

1

1st Cataract rapids Egypt 121 G3
2nd Cataract rapids Sudan 121 F4
3rd Cataract rapids Sudan 121 F5
4th Cataract rapids Sudan 121 G5
5th Cataract rapids Sudan 121 G5
9 de Julio Arg. 204 E4
long form Nueve de Julio
15th of May City Egypt see **Medinet 15 Mayo**
25 de Mayo Buenos Aires Arg. 204 E4
long form Veinticinco de Mayo
25 de Mayo La Pampa Arg. 204 D5
long form Veinticinco de Mayo
25 de Mayo Mendoza Arg. 204 C4
long form Veinticinco de Mayo
26 Bakı Komissarı Azer. 107 G3
also known as imeni 26 Bakinskikh Komissarov; formerly known as Neftechala; long form İyirmi Altı Bakı Komissarı
42nd Hill S. Africa 133 N5
70 Mile House Canada 166 F5
100 Mile House Canada 166 F5
150 Mile House Canada 166 F4

A

Aabenraa Denmark see **Åbenrå**
Aachen Germany 48 D5
formerly known as Aix-la-Chapelle; historically known as Aquae Grani or Aquisgranum
Aadan Yabaal Somalia 128 E4
Aalborg Denmark see **Ålborg**
Aalen Germany 48 H7
Aalesund Norway see **Ålesund**
Aaley Lebanon see **'Āley**
Aalst Belgium 51 K2
also spelt Alost
Aanaar Fin. see **Inari**
Äänekoski Fin. 44 N3
Aansluit S. Africa 132 G3
Aarau Switz. 51 O5
Aarberg Switz. 51 N5
Aareavaara Sweden 44 M2
Aarhus Denmark see **Århus**
Aarlen Belgium see **Arlon**
Aarschot Belgium 51 K2
Aasiaat Greenland 165 N3
also known as Egedesminde
Aath Belgium see **Ath**
Aavasaksa Fin. 44 M2
Aba China 86 B1
also known as Ngawa
Aba Dem. Rep. Congo 126 F4
Aba Nigeria 125 G5
Abā ad Dūd Saudi Arabia 104 D2
Abā al Afan oasis Saudi Arabia 105 E4
Abā al Qūr, Sha'īb watercourse Saudi Arabia 109 M6
Abā ar Ruwāth, Wādī watercourse Saudi Arabia 109 N7
Abacaxis r. Brazil 199 G6
Ābādān Iran 100 B4
English form Abadan
Abadan Iran see **Ābādān**
Ābādān, Jazīrah i. Iran/Iraq 105 E1
Ābādeh Iran 100 C4
Ābādeh Ţashk Iran 100 C4
Abadia dos Dourados Brazil 206 F5
Abadiânia Brazil 206 E3
Abadla Alg. 123 E3
Abádszalók Hungary 49 R8
Abaeté Brazil 207 H6
Abaeté r. Brazil 207 H5
Abaetetuba Brazil 202 B2
Abagnar Qi China see **Xilinhot**
Abag Qi China see **Xin Hot**
Abaí Para. 201 G6
Abaiang atoll Kiribati 145 G1
also spelt Apaiang; formerly known as Apia
A Baiuca Spain 54 C1
Abaji Nigeria 125 G4
Abajo Peak U.S.A. 183 O4
Abakaliki Nigeria 125 H5
Abakan Rus. Fed. 80 E2
formerly known as Ust'-Abakanskoye
Abala Congo 126 B5
Abala Niger 125 F3
Abalak Niger 125 G3
Abalyanka r. Belarus 43 L7
Abana Turkey 106 C2
Abancay Peru 200 B3
Abanga r. Gabon 126 A5
Abapó Bol. 201 E4
Abariringa i. Kiribati see **Kanton**
Abarqū Iran 100 C4
A Barrela Spain 54 D2
Abarshahr Iran see **Neyshābūr**
Ābār 'Uwayrid Ţahtānī well Syria 109 K3
Abashiri Japan 90 I2
Abashiri-wan b. Japan 90 I2
Abasolo Mex. 185 F3
Abasula waterhole Kenya 128 C5
Abau P.N.G. 145 D3
Abava r. Latvia 42 C4
Abay Kazakh. 103 H2
also known as Churubay Nura; formerly known as Abay Bazar
Abay Kazakh. see **Karaul**
Abaya, Lake Eth. 128 C3
also known as Ābaya Hāyk'; formerly known as Margherita, Lake
Ābaya Hāyk' l. Eth. see **Abaya, Lake**
Abay Bazar Kazakh. see **Abay**
Ābay Wenz r. Eth./Sudan 128 C2 see **Blue Nile**
Abaza Rus. Fed. 80 E2
Abba Cent. Afr. Rep. 126 B3
Abbadia San Salvatore Italy 56 D6
Abbāsābād Iran 100 D3
Abbasanta Sardegna Italy 57 A8
Abbatis Villa France see **Abbeville**
Abbaye, Point U.S.A. 172 E4
Abbe, Lake Djibouti/Eth. 128 D2
Abbeville France 51 H2
historically known as Abbatis Villa
Abbeville GA U.S.A. 175 D6
Abbeville LA U.S.A. 179 D6
Abbeville SC U.S.A. 175 D5
Abbey Canada 167 I5
Abbeyfeale Rep. of Ireland 47 C11
Abbiategrasso Italy 56 A3
Abborrträsk Sweden 44 L2
Abbot, Mount Australia 149 E4
Abbot Bay Australia 149 E3
Abbotsford Canada 166 F5
Abbotsford U.S.A. 172 C6
Abbott NM U.S.A. 181 F5
Abbott VA U.S.A. 176 E8
Abbott WV U.S.A. 176 E7
Abbottabad Pak. 101 H3
Abbott Ice Shelf Antarctica 222 R2
Abchuha Belarus 43 K7
Abd, Oued el watercourse Alg. 55 L9
'Abd al 'Azīz, Jabal hill Syria 109 L1
'Abd al 'Azīz, Jabal plat. Syria 109 K1
'Abd al Kūrī i. Yemen 105 F5
'Abd Allah, Khawr sea chan. Iraq/Kuwait 107 G5
Abd al Ma'asīr well Saudi Arabia 109 J7
Ābdānān Iran 100 A3
Abdollāhābād Iran 100 D2
Abdulino Rus. Fed. 41 J5
Abéché Chad 120 D6
also known as Abeshr
Abejukolo Nigeria 125 G5
Abelbod well Mali 125 E2
Abellinum Italy see **Avellino**
Abel Tasman National Park N.Z. 152 H8
Abemama atoll Kiribati 145 G1
also spelt Apamama
Abenab Namibia 130 C3
Abengourou Côte d'Ivoire 124 E5
Abenójar Spain 54 G6
Åbenrå Denmark 45 J5
also spelt Aabenraa
Abensberg Germany 48 I7
Abeokuta Nigeria 125 F5
Abera Eth. 128 B3
Aberaeron U.K. 47 H11
Aberchirder U.K. 46 J6
Abercorn Zambia see **Mbala**
Abercrombie r. Australia 147 F3
Aberdare U.K. 47 I12
Aberdare National Park Kenya 128 C5
Aberdaron U.K. 47 H11
Aberdaugleddau U.K. see **Milford Haven**
Aberdeen Australia 147 F3
Aberdeen Hong Kong China 87 [inset]
also known as Heung Kong Tsai
Aberdeen S. Africa 132 I9
Aberdeen U.K. 46 J6
historically known as Devana
Aberdeen MD U.S.A. 177 I6
Aberdeen MS U.S.A. 175 B5
Aberdeen OH U.S.A. 176 B7
Aberdeen SD U.S.A. 178 C2
Aberdeen WA U.S.A. 180 B3
Aberdeen Island Hong Kong China 87 [inset]
also known as Ap Lei Chau
Aberdeen Lake Canada 167 L1
Aberdeen Road S. Africa 133 I9
Aberfeldy U.K. 46 I7
Aberfoyle U.K. 46 H7
Abergavenny U.K. 47 I12
also known as Y Fenni; historically known as Gobannium
Ābergelē Eth. 104 B5
Abergwaun U.K. see **Fishguard**
Aberhonddu U.K. see **Brecon**
Abermaw U.K. see **Barmouth**
Abernathy U.S.A. 179 B5
Abertawe U.K. see **Swansea**
Aberteifi U.K. see **Cardigan**
Aberystwyth U.K. 47 H11
Abeshr Chad see **Abéché**
Abez' Rus. Fed. 40 L2
Abhā Saudi Arabia 104 C4
Abhā, Jabal hill Saudi Arabia 104 C2
Abhanpur India 97 D5
Abhar Iran 100 B2
Abhar Rūd r. Iran 100 B3
Abia state Nigeria 125 G5
Abiad, Bahr el r. Sudan/Uganda 128 B2 see **White Nile**
Ābīata Hāyk' l. Eth. 128 C3
Ab-i Bazuft r. Iran 100 B4
Abibe, Serranía de mts Col. 198 B2

▶**Abidjan** Côte d'Ivoire 124 D5
Former capital of Côte d'Ivoire.

Abiekwasputs salt pan S. Africa 132 E4
Ab-i-Istada l. Afgh. 101 G3
Abijatta-Shalla National Park Eth. 128 C3
also known as Rift Valley Lakes National Park
Ab-i-Kavīr salt flat Iran 100 D3
Abiko Japan 91 G7
Abilene KS U.S.A. 178 C4
Abilene TX U.S.A. 179 C5
Abingdon U.K. 47 K12
Abingdon IL U.S.A. 172 C10
Abingdon VA U.S.A. 176 C9
Abington U.S.A. 177 O3
Abington Reef Australia 149 F3
Abinsk Rus. Fed. 41 F7
Ab-i-Panja r. Afgh./Tajik. see **Pyandzh**
Ab-i-Safed r. Afgh. 101 F2
Abiseo, Parque Nacional nat. park Peru 200 A1
Abisko nationalpark nat. park Sweden 44 L1
Abitibi r. Canada 168 D3
Abitibi, Lake Canada 168 D3
Āb Nafţ r. Iraq 107 F4
also known as Naft
Abnûb Egypt 121 F3
Åbo Fin. see **Turku**
Abohar India 96 B3
Aboisso Côte d'Ivoire 124 E5
Aboke Sudan 128 B2
Abomey Benin 125 F5
Abongabong, Gunung mt. Indon. 76 B1
Abong Mbang Cameroon 125 I6
Aboot Oman 105 F4
Aborlan Phil. 74 A4
Abou Déia Chad 126 C2
Abou Goulem Chad 120 D6
Aboumi Gabon 126 B5
Abqaiq Saudi Arabia 105 E2
also known as Buqayq
Abra, Lago del l. Arg. 204 E6
Abrād, Wādī watercourse Yemen 105 D5
Abraham's Bay Bahamas 187 E2
Abraka Nigeria 125 G5
Abrams U.S.A. 172 E6
Abra Pampa Arg. 200 D5
Abre Campo Brazil 207 K7
Abreojos, Punta pt Mex. 184 B3
'Abri Sudan 121 F4
Abrolhos, Arquipélago dos is Brazil 207 O5
Abrosovo Rus. Fed. 43 Q3
Abrud Romania 58 E2
Abruka i. Estonia 42 D3
Abruzzi admin. reg. Italy see **Abruzzo**
Abruzzo admin. reg. Italy 56 F6
also spelt Abruzzi
Abruzzo, Parco Nazionale d' nat. park Italy 56 F7
'Abs Yemen 104 C4
Absalom, Mount Antarctica 223 W1
Absaroka Range mts U.S.A. 180 E3
Absecon U.S.A. 177 K6
Abşeron Yarımadası pen. Azer. 107 G2
also known as Apsheronskiy Poluostrov
Absterna, Vozyera l. Belarus 42 I6
Abtar, Jabal al hills Syria 109 I3
Abū aḑ Ḑuhūr Syria 109 I2
Abū al Ḩusayn, Qā' imp. l. Jordan 109 J5
Abū'Alī i. Saudi Arabia 105 E2
Abu al Jirab i. U.A.E. 105 F2
Abū al Kūfah waterhole Iraq 109 N3
Abū 'Āmūd, Wādī watercourse Jordan 108 H7
Abū 'Arīsh Saudi Arabia 104 C4
Abu 'Aweigîla well Egypt 108 F7
Abu Ballûs hill Egypt 121 E3
Abū Dā'ir des. Yemen 105 D4
Abu Deleiq Sudan 121 G6

▶**Abu Dhabi** U.A.E. 105 F2
Capital of the United Arab Emirates. Also spelt Abū Ẓabī.
asia [changes] ➡ 68–69

Abū Ḑībā' waterhole Saudi Arabia 104 B3
Abu Durba Egypt 108 E9
Abu el Matâmîr Egypt 108 B7
Abufari Brazil 199 F6
Abū Farrūkh, Wādī watercourse Iraq 109 O4
Abu Gabra Sudan 126 E2
Abu Gamel Sudan 104 B5
Abū Ghar, Wādī watercourse Iraq 109 M5
Abū Ghizlān waterhole Iraq 109 O3
Abū Ghurayb Iraq 109 P4
Abu Gubeiha Sudan 128 A2
Abu Hâd, Wâdi watercourse Egypt 108 E9
Abū Ḩafnah, Wādī watercourse Jordan 109 J5
Abu Haggag Egypt 121 E2
Abū Ḩallūfah, Jabal hill Jordan 109 H6
Abu Hamed Sudan 121 G5
Abu Hammâd Egypt 108 C7
Abu Haraz Sudan 121 G5
Abu Hashim Sudan 121 G5
Abu Higar Sudan 121 G6
Abu Hummus Egypt 108 B6
Abu Huswa, Gebel hill Egypt 108 E9

▶**Abuja** Nigeria 125 G4
Capital of Nigeria.

Abū Jaḩaf, Wādī watercourse Iraq 109 O5
Abū Kamāl Syria 109 L3
Abū Kammāsh Libya 120 A1
Abu Kebîr Egypt 108 C7
Abū Khamsāt, Sha'īb watercourse Iraq 109 O6
Abukuma-kōchi plat. Japan 90 G6
Abu La'ot watercourse Sudan 121 F6
Abū Latt Island Saudi Arabia 104 C4
Abū Madd, Ra's hd Saudi Arabia 104 B2
Abu Matariq Sudan 126 E2
Abu Mena tourist site Egypt 121 F2
Abû Mînâ tourist site Egypt 108 A7
Abumombazi Dem. Rep. Congo 126 D4
Abu Musa i. The Gulf 105 F2
also known as Abū Mūsá, Jazīreh-ye
Abū Mūsá, Jazīreh-ye i. The Gulf see **Abu Musa**
Abunã r. Bol. 200 D2
Abunã Brazil 200 D2
Abunai Brazil 199 E5
Abū Nā'im well Libya 120 C2
Ābune Yosēf mt. Eth. 128 C1
Abū Nujaym Libya 120 B2
Abu Qîr, Khalîg b. Egypt 108 B6
Abū Qurīn Libya 120 B2
Abū Rāqah well Saudi Arabia 104 B2
Aburo mt. Dem. Rep. Congo 126 F4
Abu Road India 96 B4
also known as Kharari
Abū Rubayq Saudi Arabia 104 B3
Abū Rujmayn, Jabal mts Syria 109 J3
Abu Rûtha, Gebel mt. Egypt 108 F8
Abu Sallah watercourse Saudi Arabia 109 I9
Abū Sawādah well Saudi Arabia 105 E2
Abu Shagara, Ras pt Sudan 121 H4
Abu Simbel Egypt 121 F4
Abu Simbel Temple tourist site Egypt 121 F4
Abū Şukhayr Iraq 107 F5
Abu Sultân Egypt 108 D7
Abuta Japan 90 G3
Abu Tabaq well Sudan 121 G4
Abu Tarfa, Wâdi watercourse Egypt 108 E8
Abut Head N.Z. 153 E11
Abu Tig Egypt 106 B6
Abû Tiyûr, Gebel mt. Egypt 121 G3
Abū Ujayyijāt well Saudi Arabia 109 H9
Abuye Meda mt. Eth. 128 C2
Abuyog Phil. 74 C4
Abu Zabad Sudan 121 F6
Abū Ẓabī U.A.E. see **Abu Dhabi**
Abu Zenîma Egypt 121 G2
Abwong Sudan 128 B2
Åby Sweden 45 L4
Abyad Sudan 121 E6
Abyaḑ, Jabal al hill Saudi Arabia 108 G9
Abyaḑ, Jabal al mts Syria 109 I3
Abyān governorate Yemen 105 D5
Abyār al Hakīm well Libya 120 D2
Abyār an Nakhīlan well Libya 120 D2
Abyār Banī Murr well Saudi Arabia 108 G9
Abydos Australia 150 B4
Abyei Sudan 126 F2
Åbyn Sweden 44 M2
Abyssinia country Africa see **Ethiopia**
Abzakovo Rus. Fed. 102 D1
Abzanovo Rus. Fed. 102 D2
Acacias Col. 198 C4
Academician Vernadskiy research station Antarctica see **Vernadsky**
Academy Bay Rus. Fed. see **Akademii, Zaliv**
Academy Glacier Antarctica 223 T1
Acadia prov. Canada see **Nova Scotia**
Acadia National Park U.S.A. 177 Q1
Açailândia Brazil 202 C3
Acajutiba Brazil 202 E4
Acajutla El Salvador 185 H6
Acala Mex. 185 G5
Acamarachi mt. Chile see **Pili, Cerro**
Acambaro Mex. 185 E4
Acampamento de Caça do Mucusso Angola 127 D9
Acancéh Mex. 185 H4
Acandí Col. 198 B2
Acaponeta Mex. 184 D4
Acapulco Mex. 185 F5
long form Acapulco de Juárez
Acapulco de Juárez Mex. see **Acapulco**
Acará Brazil 202 B2
Acará r. Brazil 202 B2
Acará Miri r. Brazil 202 B2
Acaraú Brazil 202 D2
Acaraú r. Brazil 202 D2
Acaray, Represa de resr Para. 201 G6
Acarí Brazil 202 E3
Acari r. Brazil 207 H2
Acarí Peru 200 B3
Acarí r. Peru 200 B3
Acari, Serra hills Brazil/Guyana 199 G4
Acarigua Venez. 198 D2
Acatlan Mex. 185 F5
Acatzingo Mex. 185 F5
Acay, Nevado de mt. Arg. 200 D6
Acayucán Mex. 185 G5
Accho Israel see **'Akko**
Accomac U.S.A. 177 J8
also spelt Accomack
Accomack U.S.A. see **Accomac**

▶**Accra** Ghana 125 E5
Capital of Ghana.

Aceguá Brazil 204 G3
Aceh admin. dist. Indon. 76 B1
formerly spelt Acheh or Atjeh; historically known as Achin
Aceuchal Spain 54 E6
Achacachi Bol. 200 C4
Achaguas Venez. 199 D3
Achalpur India 96 C5
formerly known as Dadra or Elichpur
Achampet India 94 C2
Achan Rus. Fed. 82 E2
formerly known as Bolon'
Achanta India 94 D2
Achayvayam Rus. Fed. 39 R3
Acheh admin. dist. Indon. see **Aceh**
Achemelmel well Mali 123 F5
Achemmîm well Mauritania 124 D2
Acheng China 82 B3
Achern Germany 48 F7
Achhota India 94 D1
Achikulak Rus. Fed. 107 F1
Achill Island Rep. of Ireland 47 B10
Achim Germany 48 G2
Achin admin. dist. Indon. see **Aceh**
Achinsk Rus. Fed. 80 E1
Achisay Kazakh. 103 G4
also spelt Ashchysay
Achit Rus. Fed. 40 K4
Achit Nuur l. Mongolia 84 A1
Achkhoy-Martan Rus. Fed. 107 F2
formerly known as Novoselskoye
Achlades, Akra pt Greece 59 G12
Achnasheen U.K. 46 G6
Achosa-Rudnya Belarus 43 M9
Aci Castello Sicilia Italy 57 H11
Aci Catena Sicilia Italy 57 H11
Acıgöl l. Turkey 106 B3
Acıpayam Turkey 106 B3
Acireale Sicilia Italy 57 H11
Ackerman U.S.A. 175 B5
Ackley U.S.A. 174 A3
Acklins Island Bahamas 187 E2
Acobamba Huancavelica Peru 200 B3
Acobamba Junín Peru 200 B2
Acomayo Cusco Peru 200 C3
Acomayo Huánuco Peru 200 A2

▶**Aconcagua, Cerro** mt. Arg. 204 C4
Highest mountain in South America.
southamerica [landscapes] ➡ 190–191

Acopiara Brazil 202 E3
Acora Peru 200 C3
A Coruña Spain 54 C1
English form Corunna; also spelt La Coruña
Acostambo Peru 200 B3
Acoyapa Nicaragua 186 B5
Acquapendente Italy 56 D6
Acqui Terme Italy 56 A4
historically known as Aquae Statiellae
Acra U.S.A. 177 K3
Acragas Sicilia Italy see **Agrigento**
Acraman, Lake salt flat Australia 146 B3
Acre r. Brazil 200 D2
formerly known as Aquiry
Acre state Brazil 200 C2
Acre Israel see **'Akko**
Acreúna Brazil 206 C4
Acri Italy 57 I9
Ács Hungary 49 P8
Actaeon Group is Fr. Polynesia see **Actéon, Groupe**
Actéon, Groupe is Fr. Polynesia 221 I7
English form Actaeon Group
Acton Canada 173 M7
Acton U.S.A. 182 F7
Actopán Mex. 185 F4
Açuã r. Brazil 201 D1
Açuçena Brazil 207 K6
Acunum Acusio France see **Montélimar**
Acurenam Equat. Guinea 125 H6
Açurizal Brazil 201 F3
Ada Ghana 125 F5
Ada MN U.S.A. 178 C2
Ada OH U.S.A. 176 B5
Ada OK U.S.A. 179 C5
Ada Vojvodina, Srbija Yugo. 58 B3
Ādaba Eth. 128 C3
Adabazar Turkey see **Sakarya**
Adabîya Egypt 108 D8
Adaf, Djebel mts Alg. 123 H5
Adaja r. Spain 54 G3
Adak Sweden 44 L2
Adalia Turkey see **Antalya**
Adam Oman 105 G3
Adam, Mount hill Falkland Is 205 F8
Adamantina Brazil 206 B8
Adamaoua prov. Cameroon 125 I5
Adamas Greece 59 F12
also spelt Adhámas
Adamawa state Nigeria 125 H4
Adamclisi Romania 58 I4
Adamello mt. Italy 56 C2
Adamello-Brenta, Parco Naturale nature res. Italy 56 C2
Adaminaby Australia 147 F4
Adamovka Rus. Fed. 102 D2
Adams KY U.S.A. 176 C7
Adams MA U.S.A. 177 L3
Adams NY U.S.A. 177 I2
Adams WI U.S.A. 172 D7
Adams, Cape Antarctica 222 T2
Adams, Mount N.Z. 153 E11
Adam's Bridge sea feature India/Sri Lanka 94 C4
Adams Center U.S.A. 177 I2
Adams Lake Canada 166 G5
Adams McGill Reservoir U.S.A. 183 I3
Adams Mountain U.S.A. 166 D4
Adam's Peak Sri Lanka 94 D5
also known as Samanala or Sri Pada
Adams Peak U.S.A. 182 D2

▶**Adamstown** Pitcairn Is 221 J7
Capital of the Pitcairn Islands.

Adamstown U.S.A. 177 I5
'Adan Yemen see **Aden**
Adana Turkey 106 C3
also known as Seyhan; historically known as Ataniya
Adana prov. Turkey 108 G1
Adana Yemen see **Aden**
'Adan as Sughra Yemen 104 D5
English form Little Aden
Adang, Teluk b. Indon. 77 G3
Adani Nigeria 125 G5
Adapazari Turkey see **Sakarya**
Adaran, Jabal mt. Yemen 105 D5
Adare Rep. of Ireland 47 D11
Adare, Cape Antarctica 223 L2
Adarmo, Khawr watercourse Sudan 104 A3
Adatara-san vol. Japan 90 G6
Adavale Australia 149 E5
Ādaži Latvia 42 F4
Adban Afgh. 101 G2
Adda r. Italy 56 B3
Ad Dabbah Sudan see **Ed Debba**
Ad Dafīnah Saudi Arabia 104 C3
Ad Daghghārah Iraq 107 F4
Ad Dahnā' des. Saudi Arabia 105 D3
also spelt Dahana
Ad Dākhilīyah admin. reg. Oman 105 G3
Ad Dakhla W. Sahara 122 B5
also spelt Dakhla; formerly known as Villa Cisneros
Aḑ Ḑāli' Yemen 104 D5
Ad Damir Sudan see **Ed Damer**
Ad Dammām Saudi Arabia see **Dammam**
Addanki India 94 C3
Ad Dār al Ḩamrā' Saudi Arabia 104 B2
Ad Darb Saudi Arabia 104 C4
Adda Sud, Parco dell' park Italy 56 B3
Addatigala India 94 D2
Ad Dawādimī Saudi Arabia 104 D2
Ad Dawḩah Qatar see **Doha**
Ad Daww plain Syria 109 I3
Addax, Réserve Naturelle Intégrale dite Sanctuaire des nature res. Niger 125 H2
Ad Dibdibah plain Saudi Arabia 105 D2
Ad Dibīn Yemen 105 E4
Ad Dikākah des. Saudi Arabia 105 E4
Ad Dilam Saudi Arabia 105 D3
Ad Dir'īyah Saudi Arabia 105 D2

▶**Addis Ababa** Eth. 128 C2
Capital of Ethiopia. Also spelt Ādīs Ābeba.

Addison U.S.A. 177 H3
Ad Dīwānīyah Iraq 107 F5
also spelt Diwaniyah
Ad Dīwānīyah governorate Iraq see **Al Qādisīyah**
Addo S. Africa 133 J10
Addo Elephant National Park S. Africa 133 J10
Addoo Atoll Maldives see **Addu Atoll**
Addu Atoll Maldives 93 D11
also known as Seenu Atoll; also spelt Addoo Atoll
Aḑ Ḑulū'īyah Iraq 109 P3
Ad Duwayd well Saudi Arabia 107 E5
Ad Duwayḩirah Saudi Arabia 104 D2
Ad Duwaym Sudan see **Ed Dueim**
Ad Duwayris well Saudi Arabia 105 E3
Adel GA U.S.A. 175 D6
Adel IA U.S.A. 178 D3

▶**Adelaide** Australia 146 C3
State capital of South Australia.

Adelaide Bahamas 175 E7
Adelaide S. Africa 133 K9
Adelaide Island Antarctica 222 T2
Adelaide River Australia 148 A2
Adelebsen Germany 48 G4
Adele Island Australia 150 C2
Adelfoi i. Greece 59 H12
Adélie Coast Antarctica 223 J2
Adélie Coast reg. Antarctica see **Adélie Land**
Adélie Land reg. Antarctica 223 J2
also known as Adélie Coast or Terre Adélie
Adelong Aboriginal Reserve Australia 151 C6
Adelsheim Germany 48 G6
Adelunga Uzbek. 103 G4
Aden Yemen 104 D5
also spelt 'Adan; historically known as Adana
Aden, Gulf of Somalia/Yemen 128 E2
Adena U.S.A. 176 E5
Adenau Germany 48 D5
Adendorp S. Africa 133 I9
Aderbissinat Niger 125 G3
Aderno Sicilia Italy see **Adrano**
Adesar India 96 A5
Adhaman az Zaur, Wādī watercourse Iraq 109 N5
Adhámas Greece see **Adamas**
Adhan, Jabal mt. U.A.E. 105 G2
Adhanah, Wādī watercourse Yemen 104 D5
Adh Dhayd U.A.E. 105 F2
Adh Dhāyūf well Saudi Arabia 104 D2
'Adhfā' well Saudi Arabia 107 E5
'Ādhirīyāt, Jibāl al mts Jordan 109 H7
Adhoi India 96 A5
Adi i. Indon. 73 H7
Ādī Ārk'ay Eth. 128 C1
Adícora Venez. 198 D2
Ādī Da'iro Eth. 104 B5
'Adid Umm Inderab well Sudan 121 F6
Adige r. Italy 56 E3
Adigey Autonomous Oblast aut. rep. Rus. Fed. see **Adygeya, Respublika**
Ādīgrat Eth. 128 C1
Adıgüzel Barajı resr Turkey 106 B3
Adi Keyih Eritrea 121 H6
Adi Kwala Eritrea 121 H6
Adilabad India 94 C2
Adilanga Uganda 128 B4
Adilcevaz Turkey 107 E3
Adin U.S.A. 180 B4
Adīrī Libya 120 B3
Adirondack Mountains U.S.A. 177 K1
Ādīs Ābeba Eth. see **Addis Ababa**
Ādīs Zemen Eth. 128 C1
Adi Ugri Eritrea see **Mendefera**
Adıyaman Turkey 107 D3
Adjoantali reg. Alg. 123 G5
Adjud Romania 58 I2
Adjumani Uganda 128 A4
Adlavik Islands Canada 169 J2
Admiralty Gulf Australia 150 D2
Admiralty Gulf Aboriginal Reserve Australia 150 D2
Admiralty Inlet Canada 165 K2
Admiralty Island Canada 165 I3
Admiralty Island U.S.A. 164 F4
Admiralty Island National Monument - Kootznoowoo Wilderness nat. park U.S.A. 164 F4
Admiralty Islands P.N.G. 73 K7
Admiralty Mountains Antarctica 223 L2
Ādo Eth. 128 E3
Ado-Ekiti Nigeria 125 G5
Adok Sudan 128 A2
Adolfo Gonzáles Chaves Arg. 204 E5
Adolfsström Sweden 44 L2
Adolphus Island Australia 150 E2
Adonara i. Indon. 75 B5
also spelt Adunara
Adoni India 94 C3
Adour r. France 50 E9
Adra India 97 E5
Adra Spain 55 H8
Adra r. Spain 55 I8
Adramyttium Turkey see **Edremit**
Adramyttium, Gulf of Turkey see **Edremit Körfezi**
Adrano Sicilia Italy 57 G11
also spelt Aderno; historically known as Hadranum
Adrar Alg. 123 E4
Adrar mts Alg. 123 G4
Adrar hills Mali see **Ifôghas, Adrar des**
Adrar admin. reg. Mauritania 122 C5
Adraskand r. Afgh. 101 E3
Adrasmon Tajik. 101 G1
Adré Chad 120 D6
Adrian MI U.S.A. 173 I9
Adrian TX U.S.A. 179 B5
Adrianople Turkey see **Edirne**
Adrianopolis Turkey see **Edirne**
Adriatic Sea Europe 56 F4
Adua Eth. see **Ādwa**
Adunara i. Indon. see **Adonara**
Adur India 94 C4
Adusa Dem. Rep. Congo 126 F4
Adutiškis Lith. 42 H6
Aduwa Eth. see **Ādwa**
Adverse Well Australia 150 C4
Ādwa Eth. 128 C1
also spelt Aduwa; formerly spelt Adua
Adwufia Ghana 124 E5
Adycha r. Rus. Fed. 39 N3
Adygeya aut. rep. Rus. Fed. see **Adygeya, Respublika**
Adygeya, Respublika aut. rep. Rus. Fed. 41 F7
formerly known as Adigey Autonomous Oblast or Adygeyskaya Avtonomnaya Oblast'; short form Adygeya
Adygeysk Rus. Fed. 41 F7
formerly known as Teuchezhsk
Adygeyskaya Avtonomnaya Oblast' aut. rep. Rus. Fed. see **Adygeya, Respublika**
Adyk Rus. Fed. 41 H7
formerly known as Yuzhnyy
Adzhiyan Turkm. 102 C5
Adzopé Côte d'Ivoire 124 E5
Adz'va r. Rus. Fed. 40 L2
Adz'vavom Rus. Fed. 40 K2
Aegean Sea Greece/Turkey 59 F10
Aegina i. Greece see **Aigina**
Aegna i. Estonia 42 F2
Aegviidu Estonia 42 G2
Aegyptus country Africa see **Egypt**
Aela Jordan see **Al 'Aqabah**
Aelana Jordan see **Al 'Aqabah**
Aelia Capitolina Israel/West Bank see **Jerusalem**
Aelōnlaplap atoll Marshall Is see **Ailinglapalap**
Aenus Turkey see **Enez**
Ærø i. Denmark 48 H1
Aerzen Germany 48 G3
Aesernia Italy see **Isernia**
A Estrada Spain 54 C2
Äetsä Fin. 45 M3
Afabet Eritrea 121 H5
Afal watercourse Saudi Arabia see **'Ifāl, Wādī**
Afanas'yevo Rus. Fed. 40 J4
Afándou Greece see **Afantou**
Afantou Greece 59 J12
also spelt Afándou

Afar admin. reg. Eth. 128 D1
Afar Oman 105 G3
Afar Depression Eritrea/Eth. 121 I6
Āfdem Eth. 128 D2
Afféri Côte d'Ivoire 124 E5
Affreville Alg. see Khemis Miliana
Afghānestān country Asia see Afghanistan
▶Afghanistan country Asia 101 E3
spelt Afghānestān in Dari and Pushtu
asia [countries] ▶ 64–67
Afgooye Somalia 128 E4
'Afif Saudi Arabia 104 C3
Afikpo Nigeria 125 G5
Afim'ino Rus. Fed. 43 P4
Afiun Karahissar Turkey see Afyon
Åfjord Norway 44 J3
Aflou Alg. 123 F2
Afmadow Somalia 128 D4
Afognak Island U.S.A. 164 D4
Afojjar well Mauritania 124 B2
A Fonsagrada Spain 54 D1
also known as Fonsagrada
Afonso Cláudio Brazil 207 L7
Afragola Italy 56 G8
Afrânio Brazil 202 D4
Āfrēra Terara vol. Eth. 128 D1
Āfrēra YeChe'ew Hāyk' l. Eth. 128 D1
Africa Nova country Africa see Tunisia
'Afrīn Syria 109 H1
'Afrīn, Nahr r. Syria/Turkey 109 H1
Afşar Barajı resr Turkey 59 J10
Afşin Turkey 107 D3
also known as Efsus
Afsluitdijk barrage Neth. 48 C3
Aftol well Eth. 128 E3
Afton NY U.S.A. 177 J3
Afton WY U.S.A. 180 E4
Aftoût Faï depr. Mauritania 124 B2
Afuá Brazil 202 B2
'Afula Israel 108 G5
Afyon Turkey 106 B3
also known as Afyonkarahisar; historically known as Afiun Karahissar
Afyonkarahisar Turkey see Afyon
Aga Egypt 108 C7
Aga r. Rus. Fed. 85 G1
Aga-Buryat Autonomous Okrug admin. div. Rus. Fed. see Aginskiy Buryatskiy Avtonomnyy Okrug
Agadem well Niger 125 I2
Agadès Niger see Agadez
Agadez Niger 125 G2
also spelt Agadès
Agadez dept Niger 125 H2
Agadir Morocco 122 C3
Agadyr' Kazakh. 103 H2
also spelt Aqadyr
Agaie Nigeria 125 G4
Agalega Islands Mauritius 218 K6
Agalta nat. park Hond. 186 B4
Agana Guam see Hagåtña
Agapovka Rus. Fed. 102 D1
Agar India 96 C5
Agārak well Niger 125 G2
Agâraktem well Mali 122 D5
Āgaro Eth. 128 C3
Agartala India 97 F5
Agashi India 94 B2
Agassiz National Wildlife Refuge nature res. U.S.A. 178 D1
Agate Canada 168 D3
Agathe France see Agde
Agathonisi i. Greece 59 H11
Agatti i. India 94 B4
Agawa r. Canada 173 I3
Agbor Bojiboji Nigeria 125 G5
Agboville Côte d'Ivoire 124 D5
Ağcabädi Azer. 107 F2
also spelt Agdzhabedi
Ağdam Azer. 107 F3
Ağdaş Azer. 107 F2
also spelt Agdash
Agdash Azer. see Ağdaş
Agde France 51 J9
historically known as Agathe
Agdzhabedi Azer. see Ağcabädi
Agedabia Libya see Ajdābiyā
Agen France 50 G8
historically known as Aginnum
Agenebode Nigeria 125 G5
Āgere Maryam Eth. 128 C3
Ageyevo Rus. Fed. 43 R7
Aggeneys S. Africa 132 C6
Aggershus county Norway see Akershus
Aggteleki nat. park Hungary 49 R7
Agharri, Sha'ib al watercourse Iraq 109 L4
Aghezzaf well Mali 125 E2
also spelt Arezzaf
Aghil Pass China/Jammu and Kashmir 89 B4
Aghireşu Romania 58 E2
Aghouavil des. Mauritania 124 D2
Aghrîjît well Mauritania 124 C2
Aghzoumal, Sabkhat salt pan W. Sahara 122 B4
Agia Greece 59 D9
also spelt Ayiá
Agiabampo Mex. 184 C3
Agia Eirinis, Akra pt Greece 59 G9
Agia Marina Greece 59 H11
Agiasos Greece 59 H9
also spelt Ayiásos
Agia Vervara Greece 59 G13
Agigea Romania 58 J4
Agighiol Romania 58 J3
Agiguan i. N. Mariana Is see Aguijan
Ağın Turkey 107 D3
Aginskiy Buryatskiy Avtonomnyy Okrug admin. div. Rus. Fed. 85 G1
English form Aga-Buryat Autonomous Okrug
Aginskoye Rus. Fed. 85 G1
Aginnum France see Agen
Agioi Apostoloi Greece 59 E10
Agios Dimitrios Greece 59 E11
also spelt Áyios Dhimítrios
Agios Dimitrios, Akra pt Greece 59 F11
also spelt Áyios Dhimítrios, Ákra
Agios Efstratios Greece 59 F9
Agios Efstratios i. Greece 59 G9
also spelt Áyios Evstrátios
Agios Fokas, Akra pt Greece 59 H9
Agios Georgios i. Greece 59 E11
also spelt Áyios Yeóryios
Agios Ioannis, Akra pt Greece 59 G13
Agios Kirykos Greece 59 H11
Agios Konstantinos Greece 59 D10
Agios Nikolaos Greece 59 G13
also spelt Áyios Nikólaos
Agios Paraskevi Greece 59 H9
Agios Petros Greece 59 D11
Agiou Orous, Kolpos b. Greece 59 E8
Agirwat Hills Sudan 121 G5
Agisanang S. Africa 133 J3
Agly r. France 51 J10
Agnantero Greece 59 C9
Agnes, Mount hill Australia 146 A1
Agnew Australia 151 C6
Agnew Lake Canada 173 L4
Agnibilékrou Côte d'Ivoire 124 E5
Agnita Romania 58 F3
Agniye-Afanas'yevsk Rus. Fed. 82 E2
Agno r. Italy 56 D3
Agnone Italy 56 G7
Ago-Are Nigeria 125 F4
Agogo Ghana 125 E5
Agona Junction Ghana 125 E5
Agong China 84 D4
Agounni Jefal well Mali 124 E2
Agoura U.S.A. 182 F7
Agous-n-Ehsel well Mali 125 F2
also known as Ehcel
Agout r. France 51 H9
Agra India 96 C4
Agrakhanskiy Poluostrov pen. Rus. Fed. 102 A4
Agram Croatia see Zagreb
Agreda Spain 55 J3
Agri r. Italy 57 I8
Ağrı Turkey 107 E3
also known as Karaköse
Agria Gramvousa i. Greece 59 E13
Ağrı Dağı mt. Turkey see Ararat, Mount
Agrigan i. N. Mariana Is see Agrihan
Agrigento Sicilia Italy 57 F11
formerly known as Girgenti; historically known as Acragas or Agrigentum
Agrigentum Sicilia Italy see Agrigento
Agrihan i. N. Mariana Is 73 K3
also spelt Agrigan; formerly spelt Grigan
Agrij r. Romania 58 E1
Agrinio Greece 59 C10
Agropoli Italy 57 G8
Agryz Rus. Fed. 40 J4
Ågskaret Norway 44 K2
Ağstafa Azer. 107 F2
Ağsu Azer. 107 G2
also spelt Akhsu
Agtertang S. Africa 133 J7
Agua Blanca Arg. 204 D5
Água Boa Brazil 207 K4
Agua Brava, Laguna lag. Mex. 184 D4
Agua Clara Bol. 200 D3
Água Clara Brazil 206 A7
Aguaclara Col. 198 C3
Aguada Mex. 185 H5
Aguadilla Puerto Rico 187 G3
Aguado Cecilio Arg. 204 D6
Agua Doce do Norte Brazil 207 L5
Aguados, Serra dos mts Brazil 206 D9
Agua Dulce Bol. 200 D2
Aguadulce Panama 186 C5
Agua Escondida Arg. 204 C5
Agua Fria r. U.S.A. 183 L8
Aguanaval r. Mex. 185 E3
Aguanga U.S.A. 183 H8
Aguanqueterique Hond. 186 B4
Aguanus r. Canada 169 I3
Aguapeí Brazil 201 F4
Aguapeí r. Mato Grosso do Sul Brazil 206 B8
also known as Feio
Aguapeí r. Brazil 201 F3
Aguapeí, Serra hills Brazil 201 F4
Agua Prieta Mex. 184 C2
Aguaragüe, Cordillera de mts Bol. 201 E5
Aguaray Arg. 201 E5
A Guardia Spain 54 C3
also spelt La Guardia
Aguaro-Guariquito, Parque Nacional nat. park Venez. 199 E2
Aguaruto Mex. 184 D3
Aguas r. Spain 55 J7
Águas Belas Brazil 202 E4
Aguascalientes Mex. 185 E4
Aguascalientes state Mex. 185 E4
Águas Formosas Brazil 203 D6
Águas Vermelhas Brazil 207 L2
Aguasvivas r. Spain 55 K3
Água Verde r. Brazil 201 F3
Água Vermelha, Represa resr Brazil 206 C6
Aguaytia Peru 200 B2
Agudo Spain 54 G6
Agudos Brazil 206 E9
Águeda Port. 54 C4
Águeda r. Port./Spain 54 E3
Aguelal Niger 125 H2
Aguelhok Mali 125 F2
Aguemour, Oued watercourse Alg. 123 F4
Aguessis well Niger 123 H6
Aguié Niger 125 G3
Aguijan i. N. Mariana Is 73 K4
also spelt Agiguan
Águila mt. Spain 55 J4
Aguila U.S.A. 183 K8
Aguilar de Campóo Spain 54 G2
Águilas Spain 55 J7
Aguililla Mex. 185 E5
Aguisan Phil. 74 B4
Agula'i Eth. 104 B5
Agulhas S. Africa 132 E11

▶Agulhas, Cape S. Africa 132 E11
Most southerly point of Africa.

Agulhas Negras mt. Brazil 203 C7
Aguntum Italy see San Candido
Agusan r. Phil. 74 C4
Agutaya i. Phil. 74 B4
Ağva Turkey 106 B2
Agvali Rus. Fed. 102 A4
Agwarra Nigeria 125 G4
Agwei r. Sudan 128 B3
Ahaggar plat. Alg. see Hoggar
Ahakeye Aboriginal Land res. Australia 148 B4
Ahar Iran 100 A2
Ahaura N.Z. 153 F10
Ahaura r. N.Z. 153 F10
Ahaus Germany 48 E3
Ahigal Spain 54 E4
Ahillo mt. Spain 54 G7
Ahimanawa Range mts N.Z. 152 K6
Ahioma P.N.G. 149 F1
Ahipara N.Z. 152 H3
Ahipara Bay N.Z. 152 H3
Ahiri India 94 D2
Ahititi N.Z. 152 I6
Ahja r. Estonia 42 I3
Ahklun Mountains U.S.A. 164 C4
Ahlat Turkey 107 E3
Ahlen Germany 48 E4
Ahmadabad India 96 B5
formerly spelt Ahmedabad
Aḥmadābād Iran 101 E3
Aḥmad al Bāqir, Jabal mt. Jordan 108 G8
Ahmadnagar India 94 B2
formerly spelt Ahmednagar
Ahmadpur India 94 C2
also known as Rajura
Ahmadpur East Pak. 101 G4
Ahmadpur Sial Pak. 101 G4
Ahmar Mountains Eth. 128 D2
Ahmedabad India see Ahmadabad
Ahmednagar India see Ahmadnagar
Ahmetli Turkey 59 I10
Ahoada Nigeria 125 G5
Ahome Mex. 184 C3
Ahore India 96 B4
Ahoskie U.S.A. 177 I9
Ahram Iran 100 B4
Ahrâmât el Jîzah tourist site Egypt see Giza Pyramids
Ahraura India 97 D4
Ahrensburg Germany 48 H2
Ähtäri Fin. 40 C3
Ahtme Estonia 42 I2
Āhū Iran 100 B4
Ahuacatlán Mex. 184 D4
Ahuachapán El Salvador 185 H6
Ahualulco Jalisco Mex. 184 E4
Ahualulco San Luis Potosí Mex. 185 E4
Ahun France 51 I6
Ahunapalu Estonia 42 I3
Ahuriri r. N.Z. 153 E12
Ahväz Iran 100 B4
also spelt Ahwāz
Ahvenanmaa is Fin. see Åland Islands
Ahwa India 94 B1
Aḥwar Yemen 105 D5
Ahwāz Iran see Ahväz
Ai r. China 83 B4
Ai-Ais Namibia 130 C5
Ai-Ais Hot Springs and Fish River Canyon Park nature res. Namibia 130 C5
Aibag Gol r. China 85 F3
Aibetsu Japan 90 H3
Aichach Germany 48 I7
Aichi pref. Japan 91 E7
Aid U.S.A. 176 C7
Aida Japan 91 D7
Aidin Turkm. 102 C5
Aigiali Greece 59 G12
also spelt Aiyiáli
Aigialousa Cyprus 108 F2
also known as Yialousa
Aigina Greece 59 E11
Aigina i. Greece 59 E11
English form Aegina; also spelt Aíyina
Aiginio Greece 58 D8
also known as Aiyinion
Aigio Greece 59 D10
also known as Aiyion
Aigle Switz. 51 M6
Aigle de Chambeyron mt. France 51 M8
Aigoual, Mont mt. France 51 J8
Aiguá Uruguay 204 G4
Aiguebelle, Parc de Conservation d' nature res. Canada 173 O2
Aigües Tortes i Estany de St Maurici, Parque Nacional d' nat. park Spain 55 L2
Aiguille de Scolette mt. France/Italy 51 M7
Aiguilles d'Arves mts France 51 M7
Aiguille Verte mt. France 51 M7
Aigurande France 50 H6
Aihua China see Yunxian
Aihui China see Heihe
Aija Peru 200 A2
Aijal India see Aizawl
Aiken U.S.A. 175 D5
Ailao Shan mts China 86 B3
Aileron Australia 148 B4
Aileu East Timor 75 C5
Ailigandí Panama 186 D5
Ailing China 87 D3
Ailinglabelab atoll Marshall Is see Ailinglapalap
Ailinglapalap atoll Marshall Is 220 F6
also spelt Aelōnlaplap or Ailinglabelab; formerly known as Lambert
Ailly-sur-Noye France 51 I3
Ailsa Craig Canada 173 L7
Ailsa Craig i. U.K. 47 G8
Aimogasta Arg. 204 D3
Aimorés Brazil 203 D6
Aimorés, Serra dos hills Brazil 203 D6
Ain r. France 51 L7
'Aïn 'Amûr spring Egypt 121 F3
Ainaži Latvia 42 F4
Aïn Beïda Alg. 123 G2
formerly known as Daoud
Aïn Beni Mathar Morocco 123 E2
'Aïn Ben Tili Mauritania 122 C4
Aïn Bessem Alg. 55 O8
Aïn Biré well Mauritania 124 C2
Aïn Boucif Alg. 55 O9
'Aïn Dalla spring Egypt 121 E3
Aïn Defla Alg. 123 F1
formerly known as Duperré
Aïn Deheb Alg. 123 F2
Aïn Draham Tunisia 57 A12
Aïn el Bâgha well Egypt 108 E8
'Aïn el Furtâga well Egypt 108 F8
Aïn el Hadjadj well Alg. 123 F3
'Aïn el Hadjadj well Alg. 123 G4
Aïn el Hadjel Alg. 123 F2
Aïn el Maqfi spring Egypt 121 F3
Aïn Galakka spring Chad 120 C5
Aïn Mdila well Alg. 123 G2
Aïn-M'Lila Alg. 123 G1
Ainos nat. park Greece 59 B10
Aïn Oussera Alg. 123 F2
Aïn Salah Alg. see In Salah
Aïn Sefra Alg. 123 E2
Ainslie, Lake Canada 169 I4
Ainsworth IA U.S.A. 172 B9
Ainsworth NE U.S.A. 178 C3
Aintab Turkey see Gaziantep
Aïn Taya Alg. 55 O8
Aïn Tédélès Alg. 55 L9
Aïn Temouchent Alg. 123 E2
'Aïn Tibaghbagh spring Egypt 121 E2
'Aïn Timeira spring Egypt 121 E2
Aïn Tî-m Misaou well Alg. 123 F5
'Aïn Zeitûn Egypt 106 A5
Aipe Col. 198 C4
Aiquile Bol. 200 D4
Air i. Indon. 77 D2
also known as Raibu
Airão Brazil 199 F5
Airbangis Indon. 76 B2
Airdrie Canada 167 H5
Aire r. France 51 K3
Aire-sur-l'Adour France 50 F9
Air Force Island Canada 165 L3
Airgin Sum China 85 F3
Airhitam r. Indon. 77 E3
Airhitam, Teluk b. Indon. 77 E3
Airlie Beach Australia 149 F4
Airlie Island Australia 150 A4
Airolo Switz. 51 O6
Airpanas Indon. 75 C4
Air Ronge Canada 167 J4
Airvault France 50 F6
Aisatung Mountain Myanmar 78 A3
Aisch r. Germany 48 I6
Aisén admin. reg. Chile 205 B7
Aishalton Guyana 199 G4
Ai Shan hill China 85 I4
Aishihik Canada 166 B2
Aishihik Lake Canada 166 B2
Aisimi Greece see Aisymi
Aisne r. France 51 I3
Aïssa, Djebel mt. Alg. 123 E2
Aisymi Greece 58 G7
also spelt Aisími
Aitamännikkö Fin. 44 N2
Aitana mt. Spain 55 K6
Aitape P.N.G. 73 J7
also spelt Eitape
Aït Benhaddou tourist site Morocco 122 D3
Aitkin U.S.A. 174 A2
Aitoliko Greece 59 C10
Aitova Rus. Fed. 41 J5
Aiud Romania 58 E2
also known as Nagyenyed
Aivadzh Tajik. 101 G2
also spelt Ayvadzh
Aiviekste r. Latvia 42 G5
Aix France see Aix-en-Provence
Aix r. France 51 K7
Aix-en-Othe France 51 J4
Aix-en-Provence France 51 L9
historically known as Aquae Sextiae; short form Aix
Aixe-sur-Vienne France 50 H7
Aix-la-Chapelle Germany see Aachen
Aix-les-Bains France 51 L7
historically known as Aquae Gratianae
Āīy Ādī Eth. 128 C1
Aiyiáli Greece see Aigiali
Aíyina i. Greece see Aigina
Aiyinion Greece see Aiginio
Aíyion Greece see Aigio
Aizawl India 97 G5
formerly spelt Aijal
Aizenay France 50 E6
Aizkraukle Latvia 42 G5
formerly known as Stučka or Stuchka or imeni Petra Stuchki
Aizpute Latvia 42 C5
Aizu-wakamatsu Japan 90 F6
Ajā, Jibāl mts Saudi Arabia 104 C2
Ajaccio Corse France 52 D3
Ajaccio, Golfe d' b. Corse France 56 A7
Ajaigarh India 96 D4
Ajajú r. Col. 198 C4
Ajalpán Mex. 185 F5
Ajanta India 94 B1
Ajanta Range hills India see Sahyadriparvat Range
Ajasse Nigeria 125 G4
Ajax Canada 173 N7
Ajax, Mount N.Z. 153 G10
Ajayameru India see Ajmer
Ajban U.A.E. 105 F2
Aj Bogd Uul mts Mongolia 84 B2
Ajdābiyā Libya 120 D2
formerly spelt Agedabia
Ajdovščina Slovenia 56 F3
a-Jiddét des. Oman see Ḥarāsīs, Jiddat al
Ajigasawa Japan 90 G4
'Ajīj, Wādī al watercourse Iraq 109 M2
Ajimganj India 97 F4
Ajka Hungary 49 O8
'Ajlūn Jordan 108 G5
Ajman U.A.E. 105 F2
Ajmer India 96 B4
formerly known as Ajayameru or Ajmer-Merwara
Ajmer-Merwara India see Ajmer
Ajo U.S.A. 183 L9
Ajo, Mount U.S.A. 183 L9
Ajra India 94 B2
Ajuy Phil. 74 B4
Akāashat Iraq 107 D4
Akabira Japan 90 H3
Akabli Alg. 123 F4
Akaboun well Mali 125 F2
Akademii, Zaliv b. Rus. Fed. 82 E1
English form Academy Bay
Akademii Nauk, Khrebet mt. Tajik. see Akademiyai Fanho, Qatorkŭhi
Akademiyai Fanho, Qatorkŭhi mt. Tajik. 101 G2
also known as Akademii Nauk, Khrebet
Akagera National Park Rwanda 126 F5
also known as Kagera, Parc National de la or L'Akagera, Parc National de
Akagi Japan 91 C7
Akaishi-dake mt. Japan 91 F7
Āk'ak'i Beseka Eth. 128 C2
Akalkot India 94 C2
Akama, Akra c. Cyprus see Arnauti, Cape
Akamagaseki Japan see Shimonoseki
Akamkpa Nigeria 125 H5
Akan Japan 90 I3
Akan-ko l. Japan 90 H3
Akan National Park Japan 90 I3
Akarkar well Niger 125 G3
Akarnanika mts Greece 59 B10
Akaroa N.Z. 153 G11
Akaroa Harbour N.Z. 153 G11
Akas reg. India 97 G4
'Akāsh, Wādī watercourse Iraq 109 L3
Akasha Sudan 121 F4
'Akāshāt Iraq 109 K4
Akashi Japan 91 D7
Äkäsjokisuu Fin. 44 M2
Akbakay Kazakh. 103 H3
Akbalyk Kazakh. 103 I3
also spelt Aqbalyq
Akbarābād Iran 100 C4
Akbarpur Uttar Pradesh India 96 D4
Akbarpur Uttar Pradesh India 97 D4
Akbasty Kazakh. 102 E3
Akbaytal Tajik. 101 H2
also known as Rabatakbaytal or Rabotoqbaytal
Akbaytal Pass Tajik. 101 H2
Akbeit Kazakh. 103 G2
also spelt Aqbeyit
Akbou Alg. 55 P8
Akbulak Rus. Fed. 102 C2
Akçadağ Turkey 107 D3
Akçakale Turkey 107 D3
Akçakertikbeli Geçidi pass Turkey 59 J9
Akçakoca Turkey 106 B2
Akçalı Dağları mt. Turkey 106 C3
Akçalı Dağları mts Turkey 108 D1
Akçaova Turkey 59 I11
Akçay r. Turkey 59 J11
Akchakaya, Vpadina depr. Turkm. 102 D4
Akchâr reg. Mauritania 124 B2
Akchatau Kazakh. 103 H3
also known as Aqshatau
Akchi Kazakh. see Akshiy
Akdağ mt. Turkey 59 J9
Akdağlar mts Turkey 106 B3
Akdağmadeni Turkey 106 C3
Akdepe Turkm. 102 D4
formerly known as Leninsk
Akdere Turkey 108 E1
Ak Dovurak Rus. Fed. 84 A1
Akelamo Indon. 75 D2
Akele Guzai prov. Eritrea 104 B5
Akelo Sudan 128 B3
Åkersberga Sweden 45 L4
Akershus county Norway 45 J3
also spelt Aggershus
Åkerstrømmen Norway 45 J3
Akespe Kazakh. 103 E3
Aketi Dem. Rep. Congo 126 D4
Akgyr Erezi hills Turkm. see Akkyr, Gory
Akhalgori Georgia 107 F2
formerly known as Leningori
Akhal Oblast admin. div. Turkm. see Akhal'skaya Oblast'
Akhal'skaya Oblast' admin. div. Turkm. 102 D5
English form Akhal Oblast; formerly known as Ashkhabadskaya Oblast'
Akhalts'ikhe Georgia 107 E2
Akhdar, Al Jabal al mts Libya 120 D2
Akhḍar, Jabal mts Oman 105 G3
Akhḍar, Wādī al watercourse Saudi Arabia 109 H9
Akheloy Bulg. 58 I6
Akhisar Turkey 106 A3
historically known as Thyatira
Akhmīm Egypt 121 F3
also spelt Ekhmîm; historically known as Chemmis or Panoplis
Akhnoor Jammu and Kashmir 96 B2
Akhsu Azer. see Ağsu
Akhta Armenia see Hrazdan
Akhtarīn Syria 109 I1
Akhtubinsk Rus. Fed. 102 A2
Akhty Rus. Fed. 102 A4
Akhtyrka Ukr. see Okhtyrka
Aki Japan 91 C8
Akiéni Gabon 126 B5
Akimiski Island Canada 168 D2
Akıncılar Turkey 107 D2
Akıncılar Turkey see Selçuk
Åkirkeby Denmark 45 K5
Akishma r. Rus. Fed. 82 D1
Akita Japan 90 G5
Akita pref. Japan 90 G5
Akitio N.Z. 152 K8
Akjoujt Mauritania 124 B2
Akka Morocco 122 C3
Akkajaure l. Sweden 44 L2
Akkala Uzbek. 102 D4
also spelt Oqqal'a
Akkem Rus. Fed. 88 D1
Akkerman Ukr. see Bilhorod-Dnistrovs'kyy
Akkermanovka Rus. Fed. 102 D2
Akkeshi Japan 90 I3
Akkeshi-wan b. Japan 90 I3
'Akko Israel 108 G5
historically known as Accho or Acre or St-Jean-d'Acre or Ptolemais
Akkol' Akmolinskaya Oblast' Kazakh. 103 G1
also spelt Aqköl; formerly known as Alekseyevka
Akkol' Almatinskaya Oblast' Kazakh. 103 H3
Akkol' Atyrauskaya Oblast' Kazakh. 41 I7
also spelt Aqköl
Akkol' Zhambylskaya Oblast' Kazakh. 103 G4
Akköy Turkey 106 A3
Akköy Turkey 59 K11
Akku Kazakh. 103 I2
formerly known as Lebyazh'ye
Akkul' Kazakh. see Akkol'
Akkum Kazakh. 103 F3
Akkuş Turkey 107 D2
Akkyr, Gory hills Turkm. 102 C4
also known as Akgyr Erezi
Akkystau Kazakh. 102 B3
also known as Aqqystaū
Aklavik Canada 164 F3
Aklera India 96 C4
Aklub reg. Saudi Arabia 104 D4
Ak-Mechet Kazakh. see Kyzylorda
Akmena r. Lith. 42 D6
Akmenė Lith. 42 D5
Akmenrags pt Latvia 42 C5
Akmeqit China 89 B4
Akmola Kazakh. see Astana
Akmola Oblast admin. div. Kazakh. see Akmolinskaya Oblast'
Akmolinsk Kazakh. see Astana
Akmolinskaya Oblast' admin. div. Kazakh. 103 G2
English form Aqmola Oblast; also known as Aqmola Oblysy; formerly known as Akmola Oblast or Tselinogradskaya Oblast'
Akniste Latvia 42 G5
Aknoul Morocco 122 E2
Akō Japan 91 D7
Akobo Sudan 128 B3
Akobo Wenz r. Eth./Sudan 128 B3
Akodia India 96 C5
Akola Maharashtra India 94 B2
Akola Maharashtra India 94 C1
Akom II Cameroon 125 H6
Akonolinga Cameroon 125 I6
Akop Sudan 126 F2
Akordat Eritrea 121 H6
Akören Turkey 106 C3
Akot India 96 C5
Akouménaye Fr. Guiana 199 H4
Akoupé Côte d'Ivoire 124 E5
Ak-Oyuk, Gora mt. Rus. Fed. 84 A1
Akpatok Island Canada 165 M3
Akqi China 88 B3
Akraifnio Greece 59 E10
Akranes Iceland 44 [inset] B2
Akrathos, Akra pt Greece 59 F8
Åkrē Iraq 109 O1
Akréréb Niger 125 H2
Akritas, Akra pt Greece 59 C12
Akron CO U.S.A. 178 B3
Akron IN U.S.A. 172 G9
Akron OH U.S.A. 176 D4
Akrotiri Bay Cyprus 108 E3
also known as Akrotirion Bay or Akrotiriou, Kolpos
Akrotirion Bay Cyprus see Akrotiri Bay
Akrotiriou, Kolpos b. Cyprus see Akrotiri Bay
Akrotiri Sovereign Base Area military base Cyprus 108 D3

▶Aksai Chin terr. Asia 89 B5
Disputed territory (China/India). Also known as Aqsayqin Hit.

Aksakal Turkey 59 J8
Aksakovo Bulg. 58 I5
Aksakovo Rus. Fed. 40 J5
Aksaray Turkey 106 C3
Aksarka Rus. Fed. 38 G3
Aksay China 84 B4
also known as Hongliuwan
Aksay Kazakh. 102 C2
also spelt Aqsay; formerly known as Kazakhstan
Ak-Say r. Kyrg. 103 H4
Aksay Rus. Fed. 41 F7
Akşehir Turkey 106 B3
historically known as Philomelium
Akşehir Gölü l. Turkey 106 B3
Akseki Turkey 106 B3
Aksenovo Rus. Fed. 41 J5
Aks-e Rostam r. Iran 100 C4
Aksha Rus. Fed. 85 G1
Akshatau Kazakh. 102 D2
Akshiganak Kazakh. 103 E2
Akshiy Kazakh. 103 I4
also spelt Aqshi; formerly spelt Akchi
Akshukur Kazakh. 102 B4
also spelt Aqshuqyr
Aksu Xinjiang China 88 C3
Aksu Xinjiang China 88 C3
Aksu Almatinskaya Oblast' Kazakh. 103 I3
also spelt Aqsū
Aksu Pavlodarskaya Oblast' Kazakh. 103 I1
also spelt Aqsū; formerly known as Ermak or Yermak
Aksu Severnyy Kazakhstan Kazakh. 103 G1
also spelt Aqsū
Aksu Zapadnyy Kazakhstan Kazakh. 102 C2
also spelt Aqsū
Aksu r. Kazakh. 103 I3
Aksu r. Tajik. see Oksu
Aksu Turkey 108 B1
Aksu r. Turkey 107 B3
Aksuat Kustanayskaya Oblast' Kazakh. 103 F2
Aksuat Vostochnyy Kazakhstan Kazakh. 88 C2
also spelt Aqsūat
Aksuat, Ozero salt l. Kazakh. see Bol'shoy Aksuat, Ozero
Aksu-Ayuly Kazakh. 103 H2
also spelt Aqsū-Ayuly
Aksuek Kazakh. 103 H3
Aksu He r. China 88 C3
Āksum Eth. 128 C1
historically known as Axum
Aksüme China 88 C2
Aksu-Zhabaglinskiy Zapovednik nature res. Kazakh. 103 G4
Aktag mt. China 89 D4
Ak-Tal Rus. Fed. 88 F1
Aktash Uzbek. 103 F5
also spelt Oqtosh
Aktau Karagandinskaya Oblast' Kazakh. 103 G3
Aktau Karagandinskaya Oblast' Kazakh. 103 H2
Aktau Mangistauskaya Oblast' Kazakh. 102 B4
also spelt Aqtaū; formerly known as Shevchenko
Aktepe Turkey 109 H1
Aktobe China 88 B4
Aktogay Karagandinskaya Oblast' Kazakh. 103 H2
also spelt Aqtoghay
Aktogay Pavlodarskaya Oblast' Kazakh. 103 H1
also spelt Aqtoghay; formerly known as Krasnokutsk or Krasnokutskoye
Aktogay Vostochnyy Kazakhstan Kazakh. 103 I3
Aktsyabrski Belarus 43 L6
also spelt Oktyabr'skaya
Aktsyabrski Belarus 43 J9
also spelt Oktyabr'skiy; formerly known as Karpilovka
Aktsyabrski Belarus 43 K7
also spelt Oktyabr'skiy
Aktumsyk Kazakh. 102 D3
Aktumsyk, Mys pt Uzbek. 102 D3
Ak-Tüz Kyrg. 103 H4
also spelt Aktyuz
Aktyubinsk Kazakh. 102 D2
also spelt Aqtöbe
Aktyubinskaya Oblast' admin. div. Kazakh. 102 D2
English form Aktyubinsk Oblast; also known as Aqtöbe Oblysy
Aktyubinsk Oblast admin. div. Kazakh. see Aktyubinskaya Oblast'
Aktyuz Kyrg. see Ak-Tüz
Akujärvi Fin. 44 N1
Akula Dem. Rep. Congo 126 D4
Akulichi Rus. Fed. 43 O8
Akulivik Canada 165 L3
Akumadan Ghana 125 E5
Akune Japan 91 B8
Akur mt. Uganda 128 B4
Akure Nigeria 125 G5
Akureyri Iceland 44 [inset] C2
Akuroa N.Z. 152 I4
Akwa Ibom state Nigeria 125 G5
Akwanga Nigeria 125 H4
Akyab Myanmar see Sittwe
Ak"yar Rus. Fed. 102 D2
Akyatan Gölü salt l. Turkey 108 G1
Akzhal Karagandinskaya Oblast' Kazakh. 103 H3
Akzhal Vostochnyy Kazakhstan Kazakh. 103 J2
also spelt Aqzhal
Akzhar Kzyl-Ordinskaya Oblast' Kazakh. 103 F3
Akzhar Vostochnyy Kazakhstan Kazakh. 88 C2
also spelt Aqzhar
Akzhar Zhambylskaya Oblast' Kazakh. 103 G4
Akzhaykyn, Ozero salt l. Kazakh. 103 F3
also known as Aqzhayqyn Köli
Ål Norway 45 J3
Ala r. Belarus 43 K9
Ala Italy 56 D3
'Alā, Jabal al hills Syria 109 H2
Alabama r. U.S.A. 175 C6
Alabama state U.S.A. 175 C5
Alabaster AL U.S.A. 175 C5
Alabaster MI U.S.A. 173 J6
Al 'Abṭīyah well Iraq 107 F5
Ala-Buka Kyrg. 103 G4
Al Abyaḍ Libya 120 B3
Al Abyār Libya 120 D1
Alaca Turkey 106 C2
also known as Huseyinabat
Alacahan Turkey 107 D3
Alaçam Turkey 106 C2
Alaçam Dağları mts Turkey 59 J9
Alacant Spain see Alicante
Alaçatı Turkey 59 H10
Alacrán, Arrecife reef Mex. 185 H4
Aladag mt. Bulg. 58 G7
Aladağ Turkey 106 C3
also known as Bademli
Ala Dag mt. Turkey 107 E3
Ala Dağlar mts Turkey 107 E3
Ala Dağları mts Turkey 106 C3
Al 'Adam Libya 120 D2
Alaejos Spain 54 F3
Al Aflāj reg. Saudi Arabia 105 D3
Alagadiço Brazil 199 F4
Alagapuram India 94 C4
Alag Hayrhan Uul mt. Mongolia 84 B2
Alagir Rus. Fed. 41 H8
Alagoas state Brazil 202 E4
Alagoinhas Brazil 202 E5
Alagón Spain 55 J3
Alagón r. Spain 54 E5
Alah r. Phil. 74 C5
Alahanpanjang Indon. 76 C3
Alahärmä Fin. 44 M3
Al Aḥmadī Kuwait 107 G5
Alaid, Ostrov i. Rus. Fed. see Atlasova, Ostrov
Alaior Spain 55 P5
Alai Range mts Asia 99 I2
also known as Alay Kyrka Toosu or Alayskiy Khrebet or Oloy, Qatorkŭhi
Ālaivān Iran 100 C3
Al Ajā'is hills Saudi Arabia 109 K8
Al 'Ajā'iz well Oman 105 G4
Al Ajām Saudi Arabia 105 E2
Alajärvi Fin. 44 M3
Alajaure naturreservat nature res. Sweden 44 M1
Al Ajfar Saudi Arabia 104 C2
Alajõgi r. Estonia 42 I2
Alajuela Costa Rica 186 B5
Alakanuk U.S.A. 164 C3
Alaknanda r. India 96 C3
Alakol', Ozero salt l. Kazakh. 88 C2
also known as Ala Kul
Ala Kul salt l. Kazakh. see Alakol', Ozero
Alakurtti Rus. Fed. 44 O2
Al 'Alamayn Egypt see El 'Alamein
Alalaú r. Brazil 199 F5
Al 'Alayyah Saudi Arabia 104 C4
Alama Somalia 128 D3
Al 'Amādīyah Iraq 107 E3
Alamagan i. N. Mariana Is 73 K3
also spelt Alamaguan
Alamaguan i. N. Mariana Is see Alamagan
Al 'Amār Saudi Arabia 104 D2
Al 'Amārah Iraq 107 F5
'Alāmarvdasht watercourse Iran 100 C4
Ālamat'ā Eth. 104 B5
'Alam el Rûm, Râs pt Egypt 121 E2
Al Amghar waterhole Iraq 107 F5
Al Amghar waterhole Saudi Arabia 109 N7
Alamicamba Nicaragua 186 B4
Alaminos Phil. 74 A2
Alamito Creek r. U.S.A. 181 F7
Al Amlah Saudi Arabia 104 C3
'Alam Nafāza hill Egypt 108 A7
Alamo U.S.A. 174 B5
Alamo Dam U.S.A. 183 K7
Alamogordo U.S.A. 181 F6
Alamo Heights U.S.A. 179 C6
Alamos Sonora Mex. 184 C2
Alamos Sonora Mex. 184 C3
Alamos r. Mex. 185 E3
Alamos, Sierra mts Mex. 184 C3
Alamosa U.S.A. 181 F5
Alamosa Creek r. U.S.A. 181 F6
Álamos de Peña Mex. 184 D2
Alampur India 94 C3
Al 'Anad Yemen 104 D5
Alanäs Sweden 44 K2
Al Anbār governorate Iraq 107 E4
Åland is Fin. see Åland Islands
Aland r. Germany 48 I2
Aland India 94 C2
Aland r. Iran 107 F3
Åland Islands Fin. 45 L3
also known as Ahvenanmaa; short form Åland
Ålands Hav sea chan. Fin./Sweden 45 L4
Alandur India 94 D3
Alangalang, Tanjung pt Indon. 77 G3
Alang Besar i. Indon. 76 C2
Alange, Embalse de resr Spain 54 E6
Alanggantang i. Indon. 76 D3
Alanson U.S.A. 173 I5
Alanya Turkey 106 C3
historically known as Coracesium
'Alā' od Dīn Iran 100 C4
Alapaha r. U.S.A. 175 D6
Alapakam India 94 C4
Alapli Turkey 41 D8
Alappuzha India see Alleppey
Alapur India 96 C4
Al 'Aqabah Jordan 108 G8
also spelt 'Aqaba; historically known as Aela or Aelana
Al 'Aqīq Saudi Arabia 104 C3
Al 'Aqūlah well Saudi Arabia 105 E3
Al 'Arabiyah i. Saudi Arabia 107 G6
Al 'Arabīyah as Sa'ūdīyah country Asia see Saudi Arabia
Alarcón, Embalse de resr Spain 55 I5
Al 'Arīdah Saudi Arabia 104 C4
Al Arīn Saudi Arabia 104 C4
Al Arṭāwīyah Saudi Arabia 105 D2
Alas Indon. 77 G5
Alas, Selat sea chan. Indon. 77 G5

Almora India 96 C3
Almoradí Spain 55 K6
Almorox Spain 54 G4
Al Mota well Niger 125 G3
Almoustarat Mali 125 F2
Al Mu'ayzilah hill Saudi Arabia 109 J8
Al Mubarrez Saudi Arabia 105 E2
Al Mudairib Oman 105 G3
Al Mudawwarah Jordan 108 H8
Al Muharraq Bahrain 105 E2
Al Muḩtaţab depr. Saudi Arabia 109 H9
Al Mukallā Yemen see Mukalla
Al Mukhā Yemen see Mocha
Al Mukhaylī Libya 120 D1
Al Munbaţiḩ des. Saudi Arabia 105 E3
Al Mundafan pass Saudi Arabia 105 D4
Almuñécar Spain 54 H8
historically known as Sexi
Al Muqdādīyah Iraq 107 F4
Al Murayr well Saudi Arabia 109 K7
Al Mūrītānīyah country Africa see Mauritania
Al Murūt well Saudi Arabia 107 D5
Almus Turkey 107 D2
also known as Tozanlı
Al Musannāh ridge Saudi Arabia 105 D1
Al Musayjīd Saudi Arabia 104 B2
Al Musayyib Iraq 109 P5
Al Muthannā governorate Iraq 107 F5
Al Muwayh Saudi Arabia 104 C3
Al Muwayliḩ Saudi Arabia 104 A2
Almyropotamos Greece 59 F10
Almyros Greece 59 D9
also spelt Almirós
Almyrou, Ormos b. Greece 59 F13
Alness U.K. 46 H6
Alnwick U.K. 46 K8

▶Alofi Niue 145 I3
Capital of Niue.
oceania [countries] ▶▶ 138–139

Alofi, Île i. Wallis and Futuna Is 145 H3
Aloi Uganda 128 B4
Aloja Latvia 42 F4
Alol' Rus. Fed. 43 K5
Alolya r. Rus. Fed. 43 J5
Along India 97 G3
Alonnisos i. Greece 59 E9
Alonso r. Brazil 206 B11
Alor i. Indon. 75 C5
Alor, Kepulauan is Indon. 75 C5
Alor, Selat sea chan. Indon. 75 B5
Álora Spain 54 G8
Alor Setar Malaysia 76 C1
also spelt Alur Setar; formerly spelt Alor Star
Alor Star Malaysia see Alor Setar
Alosno Spain 54 D7
Alost Belgium see Aalst
Alot India 96 B5
Alota Bol. 200 D5
Alotau P.N.G. 149 F1
Aloysius, Mount Australia 151 E5
Alpachiri Arg. 204 E5
Alpagut Turkey 59 J9
Alpaugh U.S.A. 182 E6
Alpena U.S.A. 173 J5
Alpercatas, Serra das hills Brazil 202 C3
Alpha Australia 149 E4
Alpha S. Africa 133 P4
Alpha U.S.A. 172 C9
Alpi Apuane, Parco Naturale delle nature res. Italy 56 C4
Alpine AZ U.S.A. 183 O8
Alpine CA U.S.A. 183 H9
Alpine NY U.S.A. 177 I3
Alpine TX U.S.A. 179 B6
Alpine WY U.S.A. 180 E4
Alpine National Park Australia 147 E4
Alpinópolis Brazil 206 G7
▶Alps mts Europe 51 M7
europe [landscapes] ▶▶ 30–31
Al Qā' Saudi Arabia 104 C3
Al Qa'āmīyāt reg. Saudi Arabia 105 D4
Al Qaddāḩīyah Libya 120 B2
Al Qādisīyah governorate Iraq 107 F5
formerly known as Ad Dīwānīyah
Al Qadmūs Syria 108 H2
Al Qaffāy i. U.A.E. 105 F2
Al Qafrah Yemen 105 D5
Al Qāhirah Egypt see Cairo
Al Qahmah Saudi Arabia 104 C4
Al Qā'im Iraq 109 L3
Al Qā'iyah Saudi Arabia 104 C2
Al Qā'iyah well Saudi Arabia 105 D2
Al Qal'a Beni Hammad tourist site Alg. 123 G2
Al Qalībah Saudi Arabia 104 B1
Al Qāmishlī Syria 107 E3
Al Qar'ah well Saudi Arabia 105 D2
Al Qar'ah lava field Syria 108 H5
Al Qarn Yemen 105 D5
Al Qaryatayn Syria 109 I3
Al Qaşīm prov. Saudi Arabia 104 C2
Al Qaşr Saudi Arabia 104 C2
Al Qaţīf Saudi Arabia 105 E2
Al Qaţn Yemen 105 E5
Al Qaţrānah Jordan 108 H6
Al Qaţrūn Libya 120 B3
Al Qawnas reg. Saudi Arabia 105 D3
Al Qayşūmah Saudi Arabia 105 D1
Al Qayşūmah well Saudi Arabia 107 E5
Al Qiblīyah i. Oman 105 G4
Al Qulayyibah waterhole Saudi Arabia 109 N9
Al Qumur country Africa see Comoros
Al Qunayţirah Syria 108 G4
Al Qunayţirah governorate Syria 108 G4
Al Qunfidhah Saudi Arabia 104 C4
Al Qurayn Saudi Arabia 104 C2
Al Qurayni oasis Saudi Arabia 105 F3
Al Qurayyah Saudi Arabia 104 C2
Al Qurayyah U.A.E. 105 G2
Al Qurayyāt Saudi Arabia 107 D5
Al Qurnah Iraq 107 F5
Al Quwārah Saudi Arabia 104 C2
Al Quwayī' Saudi Arabia 105 D3
Al Quwayīyah Saudi Arabia 105 D2
Al Quwayrah Jordan 108 G8
Al Quzah Yemen 105 E5
Al Rabbād reg. U.A.E. 105 F3
Alrar Est Alg. 123 H3
Alroy Downs Australia 148 C3
Alsace admin. reg. France 51 N4
Alsace, Plaine d' valley France 51 N5
Al Samha U.A.E. 100 C5
Al Samit well Iraq 107 E5
Alsask Canada 167 I5
Alsek r. U.S.A. 164 F4
Alsfeld Germany 48 G5
Al'skiy Khrebet mt. Rus. Fed. 82 E1
Alston U.K. 47 J9
Alstonville Australia 147 G2
Alsuku Nigeria 125 H5
Alsunga Latvia 42 C5
Alsviķi Latvia 42 H4
Alta Norway 44 M1
Alta, Mount N.Z. 153 C12
Altadena U.S.A. 182 F7
Altaelva r. Norway 44 M1
Altafjorden sea chan. Norway 44 M1
Alta Floresta Brazil 201 F2
Alta Gracia Arg. 204 D3
Alta Gracia Nicaragua 186 B5
Altai Mountains Asia 88 D1
also known as Altayskiy Khrebet
Altamaha r. U.S.A. 175 D6
Altamira Amazonas Brazil 199 E4
Altamira Pará Brazil 199 H5
Altamira Chile 204 C2
Altamira Col. 198 C4
Altamira Costa Rica 186 B5
Altamira Mex. 185 F4
Altamira, Cuevas de tourist site Spain 54 G1
Altamira, Sierra de mts Spain 54 F5
Altamonte Springs City U.S.A. 175 D6
Altamura Italy 57 I8
Altan Rus. Fed. 85 F1
Altanbulag Mongolia 85 E2
Altan Emel China 85 H1
also known as Xin Barag Youqi
Altan Ovoo mt. China/Mongolia 84 A2
Altan Shiret China 85 F4
also known as Ejin Horo Qi; also spelt Altan Xiret
Altan Xiret China see Altan Shiret
Alta Paraiso de Goiás Brazil 202 C5
Altapirire Venez. 199 E2
Altar Mex. 184 C2
Altar r. Mex. 181 E7
Altar, Desierto de des. Mex. 184 B1
Altata Mex. 184 D3
Altavista U.S.A. 176 F8
Altay China 84 A2
Altay Mongolia 84 C2
Altay, Respublika aut. rep. Rus. Fed. 84 A1
English form Altay Republic; formerly known as Gorno-Altayskaya Avtonomnaya Oblast' or Gornyy Altay
Altay Kray admin. div. Rus. Fed. see Altayskiy Kray
Altay Republic aut. rep. Rus. Fed. see Altay, Respublika
Altayskiy Khrebet mts Asia see Altai Mountains
Altayskiy Kray admin. div. Rus. Fed. 88 C1
English form Altay Kray
Altayskiy Zapovednik nature res. Rus. Fed. 84 A1
Altdorf Switz. 51 O6
Altea Spain 55 K6
Alteidet Norway 44 M1
Altenburg Germany 49 J5
Altenkirchen (Westerwald) Germany 48 E5
Altenqoke China 84 B4
Alter do Chão Brazil 199 H5
Alter do Chão Port. 54 D5
Altevatnet l. Norway 44 L1
Altin Köprü Iraq 107 F4
Altınoluk Turkey 59 H9
Altinópolis Brazil 206 F8
Altınova Turkey 59 H9
Altınözü Turkey 108 H1
Altıntaş Turkey 59 K9
Altınyaka Turkey 108 B1
Altiplano plain Bol. 200 C4
Altmühltal park Germany 48 I7
Altnaharra U.K. 46 H5
Alto U.S.A. 172 H8
Alto Araguaia Brazil 203 A6
Alto Cedro Cuba 186 E2
Alto Chicapa Angola 127 C7
Alto Cruz mt. Spain 55 I3
Alto Cuchumatanes mts Guat. 185 H6
Alto de Cabezas mt. Spain 55 H2
Alto de Covelo pass Spain 54 D2
Alto del Moncayo mt. Spain 55 J3
Alto de Pencoso hills Arg. 204 D4
Alto do Trevim mt. Port. 54 C4
Alto Garças Brazil 202 A6
Alto Ligonha Moz. 131 H2
Alto Madidi, Parque Nacional nat. park Bol. 200 C3
Alto Molócuè Moz. 131 H2
Alton U.K. 47 L12
Alton IL U.S.A. 174 B4
Alton KY U.S.A. 176 A7
Alton MO U.S.A. 174 B4
Alton NH U.S.A. 177 N2
Altona B.C. Canada 166 F3
Altona Man. Canada 167 L5
Alto Nevado mt. Chile 205 B7
Altoona PA U.S.A. 176 G5
Altoona WI U.S.A. 172 B6
Alto Pacajá r. Brazil 202 B2
Alto Parnaíba Brazil 202 C4
Alto Purús r. Peru 200 C2
Alto Rio Doce Brazil 207 J8
Alto Río Senguerr Arg. 205 C7
Altos Brazil 202 D3
Altos de Chacaya Chile 200 C4
Altos de Chinchilla mts Spain 55 J6
Alto Sucuriú Brazil 206 A6
Altotero mt. Spain 55 H2
Altotonga Mex. 185 F5
Altötting Germany 49 J7
Alto Uruguai Brazil 203 A8
Altukhovo Rus. Fed. 43 P9
Altun Ha tourist site Belize 185 H5
Altun Shan mt. China 84 B4
Altun Shan mts China 84 B4
also known as Astin Tag
Alturas U.S.A. 180 B4
Altus U.S.A. 179 C5
Altynkul' Uzbek. 102 D4
also spelt Oltinkŭl
Altyn-Topkan Tajik. see Oltintopkan
Alu Estonia 42 F2
Alua Moz. 131 H2
Al 'Ubaydī Iraq 109 M3
Al Ubaylah Saudi Arabia 105 E3
Alucra Turkey 107 D2
Al 'Udaylīyah Saudi Arabia 105 E2
Al Udayn Yemen 104 C5
Alūksne Latvia 42 I4
Alūksnes l. Latvia 42 I4
Al 'Ulā Saudi Arabia 104 B2
Al'ulah reg. Yemen 105 D5
Alūm Iran 100 B3
Alum Bridge U.S.A. 176 E6
Alum Creek Lake U.S.A. 176 C5
Alunda Sweden 45 L3
Aluniş Romania 58 F2
Alupka Ukr. 106 C1
Al 'Uqaylah Libya 120 C2
Al 'Uqaylah Saudi Arabia see An Nabk
Al 'Uqayr Saudi Arabia 105 E2
Al Uqşur Egypt see Luxor
Alur India 94 C3
Al Urayq des. Saudi Arabia 107 D5
Al 'Urdun country Asia see Jordan
Alur Setar Malaysia see Alor Setar
Alushta Ukr. 41 E7
Al Uthaylī Saudi Arabia 104 B1
Aluva India see Alwaye
Al 'Uwayjā' well Saudi Arabia 105 D3
Al 'Uwayjā' well Saudi Arabia 105 E3
Al 'Uwaynah well Saudi Arabia 105 E2
Al 'Uwaynāt Libya 120 E4
Al 'Uwaynāt Libya 120 A3
Al 'Uwaynidhīyah i. Saudi Arabia 104 B2
Al 'Uwayqīlah Saudi Arabia 107 E5
Al Uyainah Saudi Arabia 105 D2
Al 'Uyaynah well Saudi Arabia 108 H9
Al 'Uzaym Saudi Arabia 104 C2
Al 'Uzayr Iraq 107 F5
Alva r. Port. 54 C4
Alva U.S.A. 178 C4
Alvand, Kūh-e mt. Iran 100 B3
Alvão, Parque Natural do nature res. Port. 54 D3
Alvarado Mex. 185 G5
Alvarado U.S.A. 179 C5
Alvarães Brazil 199 E5
Álvares Machado Brazil 206 B9
Älvdalen Sweden 45 K3
Älvdalen valley Sweden 45 K3
Alvedro airport Spain 54 C1
Alverca Port. 54 B6
Alvesta Sweden 45 K4
Alvin TX U.S.A. 179 D6
Alvin WI U.S.A. 172 E5
Alvinópolis Brazil 207 J7
Älvkarleby Sweden 45 L3
Älvsbyn Sweden 44 M2
Al Wafrah Kuwait 107 F5
also spelt Wafra
Al Wajh Saudi Arabia 104 B2
Al Wakrah Qatar 105 E2
Al Wannān Saudi Arabia 105 E2
Al Waqbá well Saudi Arabia 105 D1
Alwar India 96 C4
Al Wari'ah Saudi Arabia 105 D2
Al Waţīyah Libya 120 A1
Alwaye India 94 C4
also known as Aluva
Al Widyān plat. Iraq/Saudi Arabia 107 E4
Al Wigh Libya 120 B3
Al Wigh, Ramlat des. Libya 120 C3
Al Wusayl Qatar 105 E2
Al Wusayţ well Saudi Arabia 104 D1
Al Wusţá admin. reg. Oman 105 G3
Alxa Youqi China see Ehen Hudag
Alxa Zuoqi China see Bayan Hot
Al Yamāmah Saudi Arabia 105 D2
Alyangula Australia 148 C2
Al Yāsāt i. U.A.E. 105 E2
Alyawarra Aboriginal Land res. Australia 148 B4
Alytus Lith. 42 F7
Al Yūsufiyah Iraq 109 P4
Alzada U.S.A. 178 A2
Alzey Germany 48 F6
Alzira Spain 55 K5
also spelt Alcira
Amacayacu, Parque Nacional nat. park Col. 198 D5
Åmådalen Sweden 45 K3
Amadeus, Lake salt flat Australia 148 A5
Amadi Sudan 128 A3
Amadjuak Lake Canada 165 L3
Amadora Port. 54 B6
Amadror plain Alg. 123 G4
Amaga Col. 198 C3
Amagi Japan 91 B8
Amahai Indon. 75 D3
Amakusa-Kami-shima i. Japan 91 B8
Amakusa-nada b. Japan 91 A8
Amakusa-Shimo-shima i. Japan 91 B8
Amal Oman 105 F4
Åmål Sweden 45 K4
Amalaoulaou well Mali 125 F3
Amalapuram India 94 D2
Amalat r. Rus. Fed. 81 J2
Amalia S. Africa 133 J4
Amaliada Greece 59 C11
Amalner India 96 B5
Amamapare Indon. 73 I7
Amambaí Brazil 201 G5
Amambaí, Serra de hills Brazil/Para. 201 G5
Amami-Ō-shima i. Japan 81 L7
Amami-shotō is Japan 81 L7
Amamula Dem. Rep. Congo 126 E5
Amån r. Sweden 45 K3
Amanã, Lago l. Brazil 199 E5
Amanbidji Aboriginal Land res. Australia 148 A3
Amanda U.S.A. 176 C6
Amandola Italy 56 F6
Amangel'dy Aktyubinskaya Oblast' Kazakh. 102 D2
also spelt Amankeldi
Amangel'dy Kustanayskaya Oblast' Kazakh. 103 F2
also spelt Amankeldi
Amankaragay Kazakh. 103 F1
also spelt Amanqaraghay
Amankeldi Kazakh. see Amangel'dy
Amankeldi Kazakh. see Amangel'dy
Amanotkel' Kazakh. 103 E3
Amanqaraghay Kazakh. see Amankaragay
Amantea Italy 57 I9
Amanzimtoti S. Africa 133 O7
Amapá Brazil 200 C2
Amapá state Brazil 199 I4
Amapala Hond. 186 B4
Amapari r. Brazil 199 I4
Amara Abu Sin Sudan 121 G6
Amaradia r. Romania 58 E4
Amaral Ferrador Brazil 203 A9
Amarante Brazil 202 D3
Amarante do Maranhão Brazil 202 C3
Amarapura Myanmar 78 B3
Amaravati r. India 94 C4
Amardalay Mongolia 85 E2
Amargosa Brazil 202 E5
Amargosa watercourse U.S.A. 181 C5
Amargosa Desert U.S.A. 183 H5
Amargosa Range mts U.S.A. 183 H5
Amargosa Valley U.S.A. 183 H5
Amargura Island Tonga see Fonualei
Amarillo U.S.A. 179 B5
Amarkantak India 97 D5
Amaro, Monte mt. Italy 56 G6
Amarpur India 97 F5
Amarwara India 96 C5
Amasa U.S.A. 172 E4
Amasia Turkey see Amasya
Amasine W. Sahara 122 B4
Amasra Turkey 106 C2
Amâssine well Mali 125 F2
Amasya Turkey 106 C2
historically known as Amasia
Amata Australia 151 E5
Amataurá Brazil 199 D5
Amatenango Mex. 185 G5
Amatikulu S. Africa 133 P6
Amatique, Bahía de b. Guat. 185 H6
Amatlán de Cañas Mex. 184 D4

▶Amazon r. S. America 202 B1
Longest river in South America and 2nd in the world. Also spelt Amazonas.
southamerica [landscapes] ▶▶ 190–191
southamerica [contrasts] ▶▶ 194–195

Amazon, Mouths of the Brazil 202 B1
Amazon, Source of the Peru 200 C3
Amazonas state Brazil 199 E6
Amazonas dept Col. 198 D5
Amazonas dept Peru 198 B6
Amazonas r. S. America see Amazon
Amazonas state Venez. 199 E4
Amazônia, Parque Nacional nat. park Brazil 199 G6
Amba Ālagē mt. Eth. 128 C1
Ambad India 94 B2
Amba Farit mt. Eth. 128 C2
Ambahikily Madag. 131 [inset] I4
Ambajogai India 94 C2
also spelt Ambejogai
Ambala India 96 C3
Ambalajanakomby Madag. 131 [inset] J3
Ambalakirajy Madag. 131 [inset] J3
Ambalangoda Sri Lanka 94 D5
Ambalatany Madag. 131 [inset] J4
Ambalavao Madag. 131 [inset] J4
Ambam Cameroon 125 H6
Ambanja Madag. 131 [inset] K2
Ambar Iran 100 D4
Ambarchik Rus. Fed. 39 Q3
Ambarès-et-Lagarve France 50 F8
Ambargasta, Salinas de salt pan Arg. 204 D3
Ambarnyy Rus. Fed. 40 E2
Ambasa India 97 F5
Ambasamudram India 94 C4
Ambathala Australia 149 E5
Ambato Ecuador 198 B5
Ambato, Sierra mts Arg. 204 D3
Ambato Boeny Madag. 131 [inset] J3
Ambato Finandrahana Madag. 131 [inset] J4
Ambatolahy Madag. 131 [inset] J4
Ambatolampy Madag. 131 [inset] J3
Ambatomainty Madag. 131 [inset] J3
Ambatondrazaka Madag. 131 [inset] K3
Ambatosia Madag. 131 [inset] K2
Ambazac France 50 H7
Ambejogai India see Ambajogai
Ambelau i. Indon. 75 C3
Ambelón Greece see Ampelonas
Amberg Germany 48 I6
Amberg U.S.A. 172 F5
Ambergris Cay i. Belize 185 I5
Ambergris Cays is Turks and Caicos Is 187 F2
Ambérieu-en-Bugey France 51 L7
Amberley Canada 173 L6
Amberley N.Z. 153 G11
Ambert France 51 J7
Ambgaon India 94 D1
Ambianum France see Amiens
Ambidédi Mali 124 C3
Ambika r. India 94 B1
Ambikapur India 97 D5
Ambilobe Madag. 131 [inset] K2
Ambition, Mount Canada 166 D3
Amble U.K. 46 K8
Ambleside U.K. 47 J9
Amblève r. Belgium 51 L2
Ambo India 97 E5
Ambo Peru 200 A2
Amboasary Madag. 131 [inset] J5
Amboasary Gara Madag. 131 [inset] K3
Amboavory Madag. 131 [inset] K3
Ambodifotatra Madag. 131 [inset] K3
Ambodiharina Madag. 131 [inset] K4
Ambodiratrimo Madag. 131 [inset] J3
Ambohijanahary Madag. 131 [inset] J3
Ambohimahasoa Madag. 131 [inset] J4
Ambohipaky Madag. 131 [inset] J3
Ambohitra mt. Madag. 131 [inset] K2
Ambohitralanana Madag. 131 [inset] L2
Amboina Indon. see Ambon
Amboise France 50 G5
Ambon Indon. 75 D3
formerly known as Amboina
Ambon i. Indon. 75 C3
Amboró, Parque Nacional nat. park Bol. 201 D4
Amboseli National Park Kenya 128 C5
Ambositra Madag. 131 [inset] J4
Ambovombe Madag. 131 [inset] J5
Amboy CA U.S.A. 183 I7
Amboy IL U.S.A. 172 D9
Ambre, Cap d' c. Madag. see Bobaomby, Tanjona
Ambrim i. Vanuatu see Ambrym
Ambriz Angola 127 B6
Ambriz, Coutada do nature res. Angola 127 B6
Ambrizete Angola see N'zeto
Ambrosio Brazil 198 D5
Ambrym i. Vanuatu 145 F3
also spelt Ambrim
Ambunten Indon. 77 F4
Ambur India 94 C3
Am-Dam Chad 120 D6
Amdals Verk Norway 45 J4
Amded, Oued watercourse Alg. 123 F5
Amderma Rus. Fed. 40 L1
Amdillis well Mali 125 E2
Am Djéména Chad 120 C6
Amdo China 89 E5
also known as Lharigarbo
Amealco Mex. 185 E4
Ameca Mex. 184 D4
Amecameca Mex. 185 F5
Amedamit mt. Eth. 128 C2
Ameghino Arg. 204 E4
Ameland i. Neth. 48 C2
Amelia Italy 56 E6
Amelia Court House U.S.A. 176 H8
Amellu India 96 D4
Amendolara Italy 57 I9
Amenia U.S.A. 177 L4
American, North Fork r. U.S.A. 182 C3
Americana Brazil 206 F9
American Falls U.S.A. 180 D4
American Falls Reservoir U.S.A. 180 D4
American Fork U.S.A. 183 M1

▶American Samoa terr. S. Pacific Ocean 145 I3
United States Unincorporated Territory. Formerly known as Eastern Samoa.
oceania [countries] ▶▶ 138–139

Americus U.S.A. 175 C5
Ameringkogel mt. Austria 49 L8
Amersfoort Neth. 48 C3
Amersfoort S. Africa 133 N4
Amery Canada 167 M3
Amery Ice Shelf Antarctica 223 E2
Ames U.S.A. 174 A3
Amesbury U.S.A. 177 O3
Amet India 96 B4
Amethi India 97 D4
Amfilochia Greece 59 C10
Amfissa Greece 59 D10
Amga Rus. Fed. 39 N3
Amgalang China 85 H1
also known as Xin Barag Zuoqi
Amgu Rus. Fed. 82 E3
Amguema Rus. Fed. 39 S3
Amguid Alg. 123 G4
Amgun' r. Rus. Fed. 82 E1
Amhara admin. reg. Eth. 128 C2
Amherst Canada 169 H4
Amherst MA U.S.A. 177 M3
Amherst OH U.S.A. 176 C4
Amherst VA U.S.A. 176 F8
Amherst, Mount hill Australia 150 D3
Amherstburg Canada 173 J8
Amherstdale U.S.A. 176 D8
Amherst Island Canada 173 Q6
Amherstview Canada 173 Q6
Amida Turkey see Diyarbakır
Amidon U.S.A. 178 B2
Amiens France 51 I3
historically known as Ambianum or Samarobriva
'Amīj, Wādī watercourse Iraq 107 E4
Amik Ovası marsh Turkey 107 D3
Amilhayt, Wādī al r. Oman 105 F4
Amilly France 51 I5
'Amīnābād Iran 100 C4
Amindhaion Greece see Amyntaio
Amindivi i. India see Amini
Amindivi Islands India 94 B4
Amini i. India 94 B4
also known as Amindivi
Amino Japan 91 D7
Aminuis Namibia 130 C4
Amioun Lebanon 108 G3
Amipshahr India 96 C3
Amīrābād Eşfahān Iran 100 B3
Amīrābād Īlām Iran 100 A3
Amirabad Iran see Fūlād Maḩalleh
Amirante Islands Seychelles 218 K6
Amirli Iraq 109 P3
Amisk Lake Canada 167 K4
Amistad, Represa de resr Mex./U.S.A. see Amistad Reservoir
Amistad Reservoir Mex./U.S.A. 185 E2
also known as Amistad, Represa de
Amisus Turkey see Samsun
Amite U.S.A. 175 B6
Amite Creek r. U.S.A. 175 B6
Amla India 96 C5
also known as Sarni
Amlaḩ, Jabal al hill Saudi Arabia 104 C4
Amlamé Togo 125 F5
Amlekhganj Nepal 97 E4
Åmli Norway 45 J4
Amlwch U.K. 47 H10
'Amm Adam Sudan 121 H5
Amman Jordan see 'Ammān

▶'Ammān Jordan 108 G6
Capital of Jordan. English form Amman; historically known as Philadelphia or Rabbath Ammon.

Ammanazar Turkm. 102 C5
Ämmänsaari Fin. 44 O2
'Ammār reg. Yemen 105 D5
'Ammār, Tall hill Syria 109 H5
Ammarnäs Sweden 44 L2
Ammaroodinna watercourse Australia 146 B1
Ammassalik Greenland 165 P3
also known as Tasiilaq; also spelt Angmagssalik
Ammer r. Germany 48 I8
Ammerån r. Sweden 44 L3
Ammersee l. Germany 48 I8
Ammochostos Cyprus see Famagusta
Ammochostos Bay Cyprus 108 F2
also known as Famagusta Bay
Am Nābiyah Yemen 104 C5
Amne Machin Range mts China see A'nyêmaqên Shan
Amnok-kang r. China/N. Korea see Yalu Jiang
Amod India 96 B5
Amo Jiang r. China 86 B4
Amol Iran 100 C2
Amolar Brazil 201 F4
Amoliani i. Greece 59 E8
Amontada Brazil 202 E2
Amor mt. Spain 54 G5
Amorebieta Spain 55 I1
Amores r. Arg. 204 F3
Amorgos i. Greece 59 G12
Amorinópolis Brazil 206 B3
Amory U.S.A. 175 B5
Amos Canada 168 E3
Åmot Buskerud Norway 45 J4
Åmot Telemark Norway 45 I4
also known as Ytre Vinje
Amotape, Cerros de mts Peru 198 A6
Åmotfors Sweden 45 K4
Amourj Mauritania 124 D2
Amoy China see Xiamen
Ampah Indon. 77 F3
Ampanefena Madag. 131 [inset] K2
Ampani India 95 D2
Ampanihy Madag. 131 [inset] J5
Ampanotoamaizina Madag. 131 [inset] K3
Amparafaka, Tanjona pt Madag. 131 [inset] J2
Amparafaravola Madag. 131 [inset] K3
Amparai Sri Lanka 94 D5
Amparo Brazil 206 G9
Ampasimanolotra Madag. 131 [inset] K3
formerly known as Vohibinany
Ampelonas Greece 59 D9
also known as Ambelón
Ampenan Indon. 77 G5
Amper r. Germany 48 I7
Amper Nigeria 125 H4
Amphitrite Group is Paracel Is 72 D3
Ampibaku Indon. 75 B3
Ampisikinana Madag. 131 [inset] K2
formerly spelt Ampitsikinana
Ampitsikinana Madag. see Ampisikinana
Ampoa Indon. 75 B3
Amposta Spain 55 L4
Amqui Canada 169 H3
Amrabad India 94 C2
'Amrah, Jabal hill Saudi Arabia 104 C2
Amrān Yemen 104 C5
Amraoti India see Amravati
Amravati India 94 C1
formerly spelt Amraoti
Amreli India 96 A5
Am Rijā' Yemen 121 J6
Amritsar India 96 B3
Amroha India 96 C3
Amrum i. Germany 48 F1
Åmsele Sweden 44 L2
Amstelveen Neth. 48 B3

▶Amsterdam Neth. 48 B3
Official capital of the Netherlands.
world [countries] ▶▶ 10–11

Amsterdam S. Africa 133 O3
Amsterdam NY U.S.A. 177 K3
Amsterdam OH U.S.A. 176 E5
Amsterdam, Île i. Indian Ocean 219 M8
English form Amsterdam Island
Amsterdam Island Indian Ocean see Amsterdam, Île
Amstetten Austria 49 L7
Am Timan Chad 126 D2
Amú r. Col. 198 C4
Amu Co l. China 89 E5
'Amūd, Jabal al mt. Saudi Arabia 109 K7
Amudar'ya r. Asia 99 F1
English form Amu Darya; also known as Dar"yoi Amu; also spelt Amudaryo, Amyderya; historically known as Oxus
Amu Darya r. Asia see Amudar'ya
Amudaryo r. Asia see Amudar'ya
Amund Ringnes Island Canada 165 J2
Amundsen, Mount Antarctica 223 G2
Amundsen Bay Antarctica 223 D2
Amundsen Coast Antarctica 223 O1
Amundsen Glacier Antarctica 223 N1
Amundsen Gulf Canada 164 G2
Amundsen-Scott research station Antarctica 223 A1
Amundsen Sea Antarctica 222 Q2
Amuntai Indon. 77 F3
Amur r. Rus. Fed. 82 F1
also known as Heilong Jiang
'Amur, Wadi watercourse Sudan 121 G5
Amurang Indon. 75 C2
Amur Oblast admin. div. Rus. Fed. see Amurskaya Oblast'
Amursk Rus. Fed. 82 E2
formerly known as Padali
Amurskaya Oblast' admin. div. Rus. Fed. 82 C1
English form Amur Oblast
Amurskiy Rus. Fed. 102 D1
Amurskiy liman strait Rus. Fed. 82 F1
Amurzet Rus. Fed. 82 C3
Amvrakikos Kolpos b. Greece 59 B10
Amyderya r. Asia see Amudar'ya
Amyntaio Greece 58 C8
also known as Amindhaion
Amyot Canada 173 I2
Amzacea Romania 58 J5
Amzérakad well Mali 125 F2
Am-Zoer Chad 120 D6
Ana r. Turkey 58 I7
Anaa atoll Fr. Polynesia 221 I7
Anabanua Indon. 75 B3
Anabar r. Rus. Fed. 39 L2
Ana Branch r. Australia 146 D3
Anabtā West Bank 108 G5
Anacapa Islands U.S.A. 182 E7
Anaco Venez. 199 E2
Anaconda U.S.A. 180 D3
Anacortes U.S.A. 180 B2
Anadarko U.S.A. 179 C5
Anadolu Dağları mts Turkey 107 D2
Anadyr' Rus. Fed. 39 R3
Anadyr' r. Rus. Fed. 39 R3
Anadyr, Gulf of Rus. Fed. see Anadyrskiy Zaliv
Anadyrskiy Zaliv b. Rus. Fed. 39 S3
English form Anadyr, Gulf of
Anafi Greece 59 G12
Anafi i. Greece 59 G12
Anagé Brazil 202 D5
Anagni Italy 56 F7
historically known as Anagnia
Anagnia Italy see Anagni
'Ānah Iraq 107 E4
Anaheim U.S.A. 182 G8
Anahim Lake Canada 166 E4
Anáhuac Nuevo León Mex. 185 E3
Anáhuac Veracruz Mex. 185 F4
Anahuac U.S.A. 179 D6
Anaimalai Hills India 94 C4
Anai Mudi Peak India 94 C4
Anaiteum i. Vanuatu see Anatom
Anajás Brazil 202 B2
Anajás, Ilha i. Brazil 202 B2
Anajatuba Brazil 202 C2
Anakao Madag. 131 [inset] I4
Anakapalle India 95 D2
Anakie Australia 149 E4
Analalava Madag. 131 [inset] J2
Analavelona mts Madag. 131 [inset] I4
Anamã Brazil 199 F5
Ana María, Golfo de b. Cuba 186 D2
Anambas, Kepulauan is Indon. 77 D2
Anambra state Nigeria 125 G5
Anamosa U.S.A. 174 B3
Anamu r. Brazil 199 G4
Anamur Turkey 106 C3
Anan Japan 91 D8
Anand India 96 B5
Anandapur India 97 E5
Anandpur India 96 C3
Anandpur r. India 97 E5
Ananes i. Greece 59 F12
Anan'ev Kyrg. 103 I4
also known as Anan'yevo
Anangu Pitjantjatjara Aboriginal Lands res. Australia 146 A1
Anantapur India 94 C3
Anantnag Jammu and Kashmir 96 B2
also known as Islamabad
Anant Peth India 96 C4
Ananyev Ukr. see Anan'yiv
Anan'yevo Kyrg. see Anan'ev
Anan'yiv Ukr. 41 D7
also spelt Ananyev
Anapa Rus. Fed. 41 F7
Anápolis Brazil 206 E3
Anapú r. Brazil 199 I5
Anār Fin. see Inari
Anār Iran 100 C4
Anārak Iran 100 C3
Anarbar r. Iran 100 B3
Anardara Afgh. 101 E3
Anare Mountains Antarctica 223 L2
Añasco Puerto Rico 187 G3
Ånäset Sweden 44 M2
Anatahan i. N. Mariana Is 73 K3
also spelt Anatajan
Anatajan i. N. Mariana Is see Anatahan
Anatolia reg. Turkey 106 B3
Anatoliki Makedonia kai Thraki admin. reg. Greece 58 G7
Anatom i. Vanuatu 145 F4
also known as Anetchom, Île or Aneytioum, Île or Kéamu; also spelt Aneityum or Anaiteum
Añatuya Arg. 204 E3
Anatye Aboriginal Land res. Australia 148 C4
Anauá r. Brazil 199 F4
Anaurilândia Brazil 206 A9
Anavilhanas, Arquipélago das is Brazil 199 F5
Anaypazari Turkey see Gülnar
Anaz mts Saudi Arabia 109 H9
Anbei China 84 C3
Anbyon N. Korea 83 B5
Ancares, Serra dos mts Spain 54 D2
Ancash dept Peru 200 A2
Ancaster Canada 173 N7
Ancasti, Sierra mts Arg. 204 D3
Ancenis France 50 E5
Anchán Arg. 205 D6
Anchang China see Anxian
Anchau Nigeria 125 H4
Anchieta Brazil 207 M7
Anchodaya Bol. 200 C3
Anchorage U.S.A. 164 E3
Anchorage Island atoll Cook Is see Suwarrow
Anchorage Reefs P.N.G. 149 F1
Anchor Bay U.S.A. 173 K8
Anchuthengu India see Anjengo
Anci China see Langfang
Ančia r. Lith. 42 D6
Anclitas, Cayo i. Cuba 186 D2
An Cóbh Rep. of Ireland see Cóbh
Ancón Peru 200 A2
Ancona Italy 56 F5
Ancuabe Moz. 129 C8
Ancud Chile 205 B6
Ancud, Golfo de g. Chile 205 B6
Ancyra Turkey see Ankara
Anda China see Daqing
Anda China 82 B3
Anda i. Indon. 75 C1
Andacollo Chile 204 C3
Andahuaylas Peru 200 B3
Andal India 97 E5
also spelt Ondal
Andalgalá Arg. 204 D2
Åndalsnes Norway 44 I3
Andalucía aut. comm. Spain 54 G7
English form Andalusia
Andalusia S. Africa see Jan Kempdorp
Andalusia aut. comm. Spain see Andalucía
Andalusia AL U.S.A. 175 C6
Andalusia IL U.S.A. 172 C9
Andām, Wādī r. Oman 105 G3
Andaman and Nicobar Islands union terr. Andaman & Nicobar Is India 95 G4
Andaman and Nicobar Islands union terr. India 93 H9
Andaman Islands India 95 G3
Andaman Sea Indian Ocean 79 A6
Andaman Strait India 95 G3
also known as Middle Strait
Andamooka Australia 146 C2
Andapa Madag. 131 [inset] K2
Andarāb Afgh. 101 G3
also known as Banow
Andarob Tajik. 101 G2
also spelt Anderob
Andeba Ye Midir Zerf Chaf pt Eritrea 104 C5
Andeg Rus. Fed. 40 J2
Andegavum France see Angers
Andelle r. France 50 H3
Andenes Norway 44 L1
Andenne Belgium 51 L2
Andéramboukane Mali 125 F3
Anderdalen Nasjonalpark nat. park Norway 44 L1
Andermatt Switz. 51 O6
Andernos-les-Bains France 50 E8
Anderob Tajik. see Andarob
Anderson r. Canada 164 G3
Anderson AK U.S.A. 164 E3
Anderson CA U.S.A. 182 B1
Anderson IN U.S.A. 174 C3
Anderson MO U.S.A. 178 D4
Anderson SC U.S.A. 174 D5
Anderson TX U.S.A. 179 D6
Anderson Bay Australia 147 E5
Anderson Reservoir U.S.A. 182 C4
Andes Col. 198 C3
▶Andes mts S. America 200 A2
southamerica [contrasts] ▶▶ 194–195
Andévalo, Sierra de hills Spain 54 D7
Andfjorden sea chan. Norway 44 L1
Andhiparos i. Greece see Antiparos
Andhra Pradesh state India 94 C2
Andía, Sierra de mts Spain 55 J2
Andijon Uzbek. see Andizhan

index

A

Andijon Wiloyati *admin. div.* Uzbek. *see* **Andizhanskaya Oblast'**
Andikira Greece *see* **Antikyra**
Andikithira *i.* Greece *see* **Antikythira**
Andilamena Madag. **131** [inset] K3
Andilanatoby Madag. **131** [inset] K3
Andimeshk Iran **100** B3
Andímilos *i.* Greece *see* **Antimilos**
Andípaxoi *i.* Greece *see* **Antipaxoi**
Andípsara *i.* Greece *see* **Antipsara**
Andirá Brazil **206** C10
Andir He *r.* China **89** C4
Andırın Turkey **107** D3
Andirlangar China **89** C4
Andiyskoye Koysu *r.* Rus. Fed. **102** A4
Andiyur India **94** C4
Andizhan Uzbek. **103** H4
also spelt Andijon
Andizhan Oblast *admin. div.* Uzbek. *see* **Andizhanskaya Oblast'**
Andizhanskaya Oblast' *admin. div.* Uzbek. **103** H4
English form Andizhan Oblast; also known as Andijon Wiloyati
Andkhui *r.* Afgh. **101** F2
Andkhvoy Afgh. **101** F2
Andoany Madag. **131** [inset] K2
formerly known as Hell-Ville
Andoas Peru **198** B5
Andoas Nuevo Ecuador **198** B5
Andoga *r.* Rus. Fed. **43** S2
Andogskaya Gryada *hills* Rus. Fed. **43** S2
Andohahela, Réserve d' *nature res.* Madag. **131** [inset] J5
Andohajango Madag. **131** [inset] K2
Andol India **94** C2
Andola India **94** C2
Andong China *see* **Dandong**
Andong S. Korea **83** C5
Andongwei *Shandong* China **85** H5
Andoom Australia **149** D2
▶**Andorra** *country* Europe **55** M2
europe [countries] ➡ 32–35
Andorra Spain **55** K4

▶**Andorra la Vella** Andorra **55** M2
Capital of Andorra. Also spelt Andorra la Vieja.

Andorra la Vieja Andorra *see* **Andorra la Vella**
Andover U.K. **47** K12
Andover *MA* U.S.A. **177** N3
Andover *NH* U.S.A. **177** N2
Andover *NY* U.S.A. **176** H3
Andover *OH* U.S.A. **176** E4
Andøya *i.* Norway **44** K1
Andozero, Ozero *l.* Rus. Fed. **43** S2
Andradas Brazil **206** G9
Andrade U.S.A. **183** J9
Andradina Brazil **206** B7
Andramasina Madag. **131** [inset] J3
Andramy Madag. **131** [inset] J3
Andranomavo Madag. **131** [inset] J3
Andranomena Madag. **131** [inset] K3
Andranopasy Madag. **131** [inset] I4
Andranovondronina Madag. **131** [inset] K2
Andranovory Madag. **131** [inset] J4
Andreanof Islands U.S.A. **221** G2
Andreapol' Rus. Fed. **43** N5
André Félix, Parc National de *nat. park* Cent. Afr. Rep. **126** D2
André Fernandes Brazil **207** L2
Andrelândia Brazil **203** C7
Andrequicé Brazil **207** I5
Andrew Canada **167** H4
Andrew Bay Myanmar **78** A4
Andrews *SC* U.S.A. **175** E5
Andrews *TX* U.S.A. **179** B5
Andreyevka *Almatinskaya Oblast'* Kazakh. **103** J3
Andreyevka *Severnyy Kazakhstan* Kazakh. **103** F1
Andreyevka Rus. Fed. **102** B1
Andreyevskoye Rus. Fed. *see* **Dneprovskoye**
Andreykovichi Rus. Fed. **43** O9
Andreykovo Rus. Fed. **43** P6
Andria Italy **56** I7
Andriba Madag. **131** [inset] J3
Andrieskraal S. Africa **133** I10
Andriesvale S. Africa **132** E3
Andringitra *mts* Madag. **131** [inset] J4
Androka Madag. **131** [inset] J5
Androna *reg.* Madag. **131** [inset] K2
Androniki Rus. Fed. **43** U4
Andropov Rus. Fed. *see* **Rybinsk**
Andros *i.* Bahamas **186** D1
Andros Greece **59** F11
Andros *i.* Greece **59** F11
Androscoggin *r.* U.S.A. **177** P2
Androsovka Rus. Fed. **102** B1
Andros Town Bahamas **186** D1
Andrott *i.* India **94** B4
Andrushevka Ukr. *see* **Andrushivka**
Andrushivka Ukr. **41** D6
also spelt Andrushevka
Andrychów Poland **49** Q6
Andselv Norway **44** L1
Andsnes Norway **44** M1
Andújar Spain **54** G6
Andulo Angola **127** C7
Anec, Lake *salt flat* Australia **150** E4
Anecón Grande *mt.* Arg. **205** C6
Aneen-Kio *terr.* N. Pacific Ocean *see* **Wake Atoll**
Anéfis Mali **125** F2
Anéfis *well* Mali **125** E2
Anegada *i.* Virgin Is (U.K.) **187** G3
Anegada, Bahía *b.* Arg. **204** E6
Anegada Passage Virgin Is (U.K.) **187** H3
Anegam U.S.A. **183** L9
Aného Togo **125** F5
Aneityum *i.* Vanuatu *see* **Anatom**
'Aneiza, Jabal *hill* Iraq *see* **'Unayzah, Jabal**
Anekal India **94** C3
Añelo Arg. **204** C5
Anemourion *tourist site* Turkey **108** D1
Anesbaraka *well* Alg. **123** G6
Anet France **50** H4
Anetchom, Île *i.* Vanuatu *see* **Anatom**
Aneto *mt.* Spain **55** L2
Aney Niger **125** I2
Aneytioum, Île *i.* Vanuatu *see* **Anatom**
Anfile Bay Eritrea **121** I6
Anfu China **87** E3
also known as Pingdu
Angadippuram India **94** C4
Angadoka, Lohatanjona *hd* Madag. **131** [inset] J2
Angahook Lorne State Park *nature res.* Australia **147** D4
Angalarri *r.* Australia **148** A2
Angamma, Falaise d' *esc.* Chad **120** C5
Angamos, Isla *i.* Chile **205** B8
Angamos, Punta *pt* Chile **200** C5
Ang'angxi China **85** I2

▶**Angara** *r.* Rus. Fed. **84** E1
Part of the Yenisey-Angara-Selenga, 3rd longest river in Asia. English form Upper Tunguska; also known as Verkhnyaya Tunguska.
asia [landscapes] ➡ 62–63

Angaradébou Benin **125** F4
Angarapa Aboriginal Land *res.* Australia **148** B4
Angarsk Rus. Fed. **80** G2
Angas Downs Australia **148** B5
Angas Range *hills* Australia **150** E4
Angaston Australia **146** C3
Angat Phil. **74** B3
Angatuba Brazil **206** E10
Angaur *i.* Palau **73** H5
also spelt Ngeaur *or* Niaur
Ånge Sweden **44** K3
Ángel, Salto del *waterfall* Venez. *see* **Angel Falls**
Ángel de la Guarda, Isla *i.* Mex. **184** B2
Angeles Phil. **74** B3

▶**Angel Falls** Venez. **199** F3
Highest waterfall in the world. Also known as Ángel, Salto del.

Ängelholm Sweden **45** K4
Angelina *r.* U.S.A. **179** D6
Angellala Creek *r.* Australia **149** E5
Angelo *r.* Australia **150** B4
Angels Camp U.S.A. **182** D3
Ängereb Eth. **104** B5
Ängereb Wenz *r.* Eth. **128** C1
Ångermanälven *r.* Sweden **44** L3
Angermünde Germany **49** L2
Angers France **50** F5
historically known as Andegavum *or* Juliomagus
Anggana Indon. **77** G3
Angical Brazil **202** C4
Angicos Brazil **202** E3
Angikuni Lake Canada **167** L2
Angiola U.S.A. **182** E6
Angkor *tourist site* Cambodia **79** C5
Anglem, Mount *hill* N.Z. **153** B14
also known as Hananui
Anglesey *i.* U.K. **47** H10
also known as Ynys Môn
Angleton U.S.A. **179** D6
Angliers Canada **173** N3
Anglin *r.* France **50** G6
Anglo-Egyptian Sudan *country* Africa *see* **Sudan**
Angmagssalik Greenland *see* **Ammassalik**
Ang Mo Kio Sing. **76** [inset]
Ango Dem. Rep. Congo **126** E3
Angoche Moz. **131** H3
formerly known as António Enes
Angohrān Iran **100** D5
Angol Chile **204** B5
▶**Angola** *country* Africa **127** C7
formerly known as Portuguese West Africa
africa [countries] ➡ 114–117
Angola *IN* U.S.A. **174** C3
Angola *NY* U.S.A. **176** F3
Angola, Planalto de *plat.* Moz. **131** G2
Angoon U.S.A. **164** F4
Angora Turkey *see* **Ankara**
Angostura Mex. **184** C3
Angoulême France **50** G7
historically known as Iculisma
Angra dos Reis Brazil **207** I10
Angren Uzbek. **103** G4
Ångsö naturreservat *nature res.* Sweden **45** L4
Ang Thong Thai. **79** C5
Angu Dem. Rep. Congo **126** E4
Angualasto Arg. **204** C3
Anguang China **85** I2

▶**Anguilla** *terr.* West Indies **187** H3
United Kingdom Overseas Territory.
oceania [countries] ➡ 138–139

Anguilla Cays *is* Bahamas **186** D2
Anguille, Cape Canada **169** J4
Anguli Nur *l.* China **85** G3
Anguo China **85** G4
Angurugu Australia **148** C2
Angus Canada **173** N6
Angustura Brazil **201** E2
Angwin U.S.A. **182** B3
Anhanguera Brazil **206** E5
Anholt *i.* Denmark **45** J4
Anhua China **87** D2
also known as Dongping
Anhui *prov.* China **87** F1
English form Anhwei
Anhumas Brazil **202** A6
Anhwei *prov.* China *see* **Anhui**
Aniak U.S.A. **164** D3
Aniakchak National Monument and Preserve *nat. park* U.S.A. **164** D4
Anicuns Brazil **206** D3
Ánidhros *i.* Greece *see* **Anydro**
Anié Togo **125** F5
Anie, Pic d' *mt.* France **50** F10
Aniene *r.* Italy **56** E7
Anikhovka Rus. Fed. **103** E2
Anikovo Rus. Fed. **40** G4
Animas *r.* U.S.A. **181** E5
Anina Romania **58** C3
Anishino Rus. Fed. **43** S7
Anisoc Equat. Guinea **125** H6
Anitaguipan Point Phil. **74** C4
Anıtlı Turkey **108** D1
Aniva Rus. Fed. **82** F3
Aniva, Mys *c.* Rus. Fed. **82** F3
Aniva, Zaliv *b.* Rus. Fed. **82** F3
Anivorano Madag. **131** [inset] K3
Anivorano Avaratra Madag. **131** [inset] K2
Aniwa U.S.A. **172** D5
Anjad India **96** B5
Anjafy *mt.* Madag. **131** [inset] J3
Anjalankoski Fin. **45** N3
Anjangaon India **96** C5
Anjar India **96** A5
Anjengo India **94** C4
also known as Anchuthengu
Anji China **87** F2
also known as Dipu
Anji India **94** C1
Anjiang China *see* **Qianyang**
Anjihai China **88** D2
Anjir Avand Iran **100** C3
Anjō Japan **91** E7
Anjoman Iran **100** D3
Anjou *reg.* France **50** F5
Anjou, Val d' *valley* France **50** F5
Anjouan *i.* Comoros *see* **Nzwani**
Anjozorobe Madag. **131** [inset] J3
Anjŭ N. Korea **83** B5
Anjuman *reg.* Afgh. **101** G3
Anka Nigeria **125** G3
Ankaboa, Tanjona *pt* Madag. **131** [inset] I4
formerly known as St-Vincent, Cap
Ankang China **87** D1

▶**Ankara** Turkey **106** C3
Capital of Turkey. Historically known as Ancyra or Angora.

Ankaratra *mts* Madag. **131** [inset] J3
Ankarsrum Sweden **45** L4
Ankatafa Madag. **131** [inset] K2
Ankavandra Madag. **131** [inset] J3
Ankazoabo Madag. **131** [inset] J4
Ankazobe Madag. **131** [inset] J3
Ankeny U.S.A. **174** A3
Ankerika Madag. **131** [inset] J2
An Khê Vietnam **79** E5
formerly known as An Tuc
Ankiliabo Madag. **131** [inset] I4
Anklam Germany **49** K2
Ankleshwar India **96** B5
formerly spelt Anklesvar
Anklesvar India *see* **Ankleshwar**
Ankofa *mt.* Madag. **131** [inset] K3
Ankogel *mt.* Austria **49** K8
Ankola India **94** B3
Ankouzhen China **85** E5
An'kovo Rus. Fed. **43** U5
Ankpa Nigeria **125** G5
Anling China *see* **Yanling**
Anloga Ghana **125** F5
Anlong China **86** C3
Ânlong Vêng Cambodia **79** D5
Anlu China **87** E2
Anmoore U.S.A. **176** E6
An Muileann gCearr Rep. of Ireland *see* **Mullingar**
Anmyŏn-do *i.* S. Korea **83** B5
Ann, Cape Antarctica **223** D2
Ann, Cape U.S.A. **177** O3
Anna Rus. Fed. **41** G6
Anna U.S.A. **176** A5
Anna, Lake U.S.A. **176** H7
Annaba Alg. **123** G1
formerly known as Bône; *historically known as* Bona *or* Hippo Regius
Annaberg-Buchholtz Germany **49** K5
An Nabk Saudi Arabia **109** I6
also known as Al 'Uqaylah
An Nabk Syria **109** H3
An Nafūd *des.* Saudi Arabia **104** C1
Annai Guyana **199** G4
An Nā'ikah, Qarārat *depr.* Libya **120** C3
An Najaf Iraq **107** F5
An Najaf *governorate* Iraq **107** E5
An Najaf, Baḥr *l.* Iraq **109** P6
Annalee *r.* Rep. of Ireland **47** E9
Annam *reg.* Vietnam **78** D4
Annam Highlands *mts* Laos/Vietnam **78** D4
Annan U.K. **47** I9
Annan *r.* U.K. **47** I9
'Annān, Wādī al *watercourse* Syria **109** J3
Annandale U.S.A. **177** H7
Anna Plains Australia **150** C3

▶**Annapolis** U.S.A. **177** I7
State capital of Maryland. Historically known as Anne Arundel Town or Providence.

Annapolis Royal Canada **169** H4
Annapurna Conservation Area *nature res.* Nepal **97** E3

▶**Annapurna I** *mt.* Nepal **97** D3
10th highest mountain in the world and in Asia.
world [physical features] ➡ 8–9

Annapurna II *mt.* Nepal **97** E3
Ann Arbor U.S.A. **173** J8
Anna Regina Guyana **199** G3
An Nás Rep. of Ireland *see* **Naas**
An Nashū, Wādī *watercourse* Libya **120** B3
An Nāṣirīyah Iraq **107** F5
Annaspan *imp. l.* S. Africa **133** J5
An Nawfalīyah Libya **120** C2
Annean, Lake *salt flat* Australia **151** B5
Anne Arundel Town U.S.A. *see* **Annapolis**
Annecy France **51** M7
Annecy, Lac d' *l.* France **51** M7
Annecy-le-Vieux France **51** M7
Anne Marie Lake Canada **169** I2
Annemasse France **51** M6
Annette Island U.S.A. **166** D4
Annie *r.* Australia **149** D2
Annikvere Estonia **42** H2
An Nimārah Syria **109** I5
An Nimāṣ Saudi Arabia **104** C4
Anning China **86** B3
formerly known as Lianran
Anning He *r.* China **86** B3
Anino Rus. Fed. **43** S2
Anniston U.S.A. **175** C5
Annobón *i.* Equat. Guinea **125** G7
formerly known as Pagalu
Annonay France **51** K7
Annotto Bay Jamaica **186** D3
An Nu'ayrīyah Saudi Arabia **105** E2
An Nukhaylah *waterhole* Iraq **109** P4
An Nu'mānīyah Iraq **107** F4
An Nuşayʻah Qatar **105** E2
An Nuşayrīyah, Jabal *mts* Syria **108** H2
Annville U.S.A. **176** B8
Anogeia Greece **59** F13
also spelt Anóyia
Anoka U.S.A. **174** A2
Anori Brazil **199** F5
Anorontany, Tanjona *hd* Madag. **131** [inset] I2
Anosibe An'Ala Madag. **131** [inset] K3
Anou I-n-Atei *well* Alg. **123** G5
Ânou Mellene *well* Mali **125** F2
Anou-n-Bidek *well* Alg. **123** G6
Ano Viannos Greece **59** G13
Anóyia Greece *see* **Anogeia**
Anpu China **87** D4
Anpu Gang *b.* China **87** D4
Anqing China **87** F2
Anqiu China **85** H4
Anren China **87** E3
Anruth China **85** F4
also known as Zhenwudong
Anse-à-Galets Haiti **187** E3
Anse-à-Pitre Haiti **187** F3
Anse-à-Veau Haiti **187** E3
Anseba Shet *watercourse* Eritrea **104** B4
Anse d'Hainault Haiti **187** E3
Anser Group *is* Australia **147** E4
Anserma Col. **198** C3
Anshan China **85** I3
Anshun China **86** C3
Anshunchang China **86** B2
Ansina Uruguay **204** G3
An Sirḥān, Wādī *watercourse* Saudi Arabia **107** D5
Ansjö Sweden **44** L3
Anson U.S.A. **179** C5
Anson Bay Australia **148** A2
Ansongo Mali **125** F3
Ansongo-Ménaka, Réserve Partielle de Faune d' *nature res.* Mali **125** F3
Ansonia U.S.A. **176** A5
Ansonville Canada **173** M2
Ansted U.S.A. **176** D7
Anstruther U.K. **46** J7
Ansu China *see* **Xushui**
Anta India **96** C4
Anta Peru **200** B3
Antabamba Peru **200** B3
Antakya Turkey **106** D3
also known as Hatay; *historically known as* Antioch *or* Antiochia
Antalaha Madag. **131** [inset] K2
Antalya Turkey **106** B3
also spelt Adalia; *historically known as* Attalea *or* Attalia
Antalya *prov.* Turkey **108** B1
Antalya Körfezi *g.* Turkey **106** B3
Antanambao Manampotsy Madag. **131** [inset] K3
Antanambe Madag. **131** [inset] K3

▶**Antananarivo** Madag. **131** [inset] J3
Capital of Madagascar. Formerly spelt Tananarive; short form Tana.

Antananarivo *prov.* Madag. **131** [inset] J3
Antanifotsy Madag. **131** [inset] J3
Antanimora Atsimo Madag. **131** [inset] J5
Antanṭûr, Râs *pt* Egypt **108** F9
An tAonach Rep. of Ireland *see* **Nenagh**

▶**Antarctica 222**
Most southerly and coldest continent, and the continent with the highest average elevation.
world [land cover] ➡ 18–19
antarctica [features] ➡ 212–213

Antarctic Peninsula Antarctica **222** T2
Antaritarika Madag. **131** [inset] J5
Antelope Island U.S.A. **183** L1
Antelope Range *mts* U.S.A. **183** H2
Antequera Spain **54** G7
Anthony *KS* U.S.A. **178** C4
Anthony *NM* U.S.A. **181** F6
Anthony, Lake *salt flat* Australia **146** B2
Anthony Lagoon Australia **148** B3
Anti Atlas *mts* Morocco **122** C3
also known as Petit Atlas
Antibes France **51** N9
Anticosti, Île d' *i.* Canada **169** I3
English form Anticosti Island
Anticosti Island Canada *see* **Anticosti, Île d'**
Antifer, Cap d' *c.* France **50** G3
Antigo U.S.A. **172** D5
Antigonish Canada **169** I4
Antigua *i.* Antigua and Barbuda **187** H3
Antigua Guat. **185** H6
long form Antigua Guatemala
Antigua *country* West Indies *see* **Antigua and Barbuda**
▶**Antigua and Barbuda** *country* West Indies **187** H3
short form Antigua
northamerica [countries] ➡ 158–159
Antigua Guatemala Guat. *see* **Antigua**
Antiguo-Morelos Mex. **185** F4
Antikyra Greece **59** D10
also spelt Andikira
Antikythira *i.* Greece **59** E13
also spelt Andikithira
Antikythiro, Steno *sea chan.* Greece **59** E13
Anti Lebanon *mts* Lebanon/Syria *see* **Sharqī, Jabal ash**
Antilla Arg. **204** D2
Antilla Cuba **186** E2
Antimilos *i.* Greece **59** F12
also spelt Andímilos
Antimony U.S.A. **183** M3
An tInbhear Mór Rep. of Ireland *see* **Arklow**
Antioch Turkey *see* **Antakya**
Antioch *CA* U.S.A. **182** C3
Antioch *IL* U.S.A. **172** E8
Antiocheia ad Cragum *tourist site* Turkey **108** D1
Antiochia Turkey *see* **Antakya**
Antioquia Col. **198** C3
Antioquia *dept* Col. **198** C3
Antiparos *i.* Greece **59** G11
also spelt Andhíparos
Antipaxoi *i.* Greece **59** B9
also spelt Andípaxoi
Antipino Rus. Fed. **43** O6
Antipodes Islands N.Z. **145** G6
Antipsara *i.* Greece **59** G10
also spelt Andípsara
Antitilos *i.* Greece **59** I12
Antium Italy *see* **Anzio**
Antlers U.S.A. **179** D5
An t-Ob U.K. *see* **Leverburgh**
Antofagasta Chile **200** C5
Antofagasta *admin. reg.* Chile **200** C5
Antofagasta de la Sierra Arg. **204** D2
Antonibe Madag. **131** [inset] J2
Antônio Carlos Brazil **207** J8
Antônio de Biedma Arg. **205** D7
Antônio Dias Brazil **207** K6
António Enes Moz. *see* **Angoche**
Antônio Lemos Brazil **202** B2
Antón Recio Cuba **186** C2
Antopal' Belarus **42** F9
Antrim U.K. **47** F9
Antrim Hills U.K. **47** F8
Antrim Plateau Australia **150** E3
Antrodoco Italy **56** F6
Antropovo Rus. Fed. **40** G4
Antsahabe Madag. **131** [inset] K2
Antsalova Madag. **131** [inset] J3
Antsambalahy Madag. **131** [inset] K2
Antseranana Madag. *see* **Antsirañana**
Antsiferovo Rus. Fed. **43** O3
Antsirabe Madag. **131** [inset] J3
Antsirabe Avaratra Madag. **131** [inset] K2
Antsirañana Madag. **131** [inset] K2
formerly known as Diégo Suarez; *formerly spelt* Antseranana
Antsirañana *prov.* Madag. **131** [inset] K2
Antsla Estonia **42** H4
Antsohihy Madag. **131** [inset] J2
Antsohimbondrona Madag. **131** [inset] K2
formerly known as Port St-Louis
Antsondrodava Madag. **131** [inset] J3
Anttis Sweden **44** M2
Anttola Fin. **45** N3
Antu China *see* **Songjiang**
An Tuc Vietnam *see* **An Khê**
Antuco Chile **204** C5
Antuco, Volcán *vol.* Chile **204** C5
Antufash, Jazirat *i.* Yemen **104** C5
English form Antufush Island
Antufush Island Yemen *see* **Antufash, Jazirat**
Antwerp Belgium **51** K1
also known as Anvers; *also spelt* Antwerpen
Antwerp U.S.A. **177** J1
Antwerpen Belgium *see* **Antwerp**
An Uaimh Rep. of Ireland *see* **Navan**
Anuc, Lac *l.* Canada **169** F1
Anuchino Rus. Fed. **82** D4
Anueque, Sierra *mts* Arg. **205** C6
Anugul India **95** E1
Anupgarh India **96** B3
Anuradhapura Sri Lanka **94** D4
Anurrete Aboriginal Land *res.* Australia **148** B4
Anvers Belgium *see* **Antwerp**
Anvers Island Antarctica **222** T2
Anvil Range *mts* Canada **166** C2
Anxi *Fujian* China **87** F3
also known as Fengcheng
Anxi *Gansu* China **84** B3
also known as Yuanquan
Anxian China **86** C2
also known as Anchang
Anxiang China **87** E2
Anxin China **85** G4
also known as Xin'an
Anxious Bay Australia **146** B3
Anxur Italy *see* **Terracina**
Anyang China *see* **Du'an**
Anyang China **85** G4
also known as Zhangde
Anyang S. Korea **83** B5
Anyar Indon. **77** D4
Anydro *i.* Greece **59** G12
also known as Ánidhros
A'nyêmaqên Shan *mts* China **86** A1
English form Amne Machin Range
Anyi China **87** E2
also known as Longjin
Anykščiai Lith. **42** G6
Anyuan *Jiangxi* China **87** E3
also known as Xinshan
Anyuan *Jiangxi* China **87** E3
Anyue China **86** C2
also known as Yueyang
Anyuy *r.* Rus. Fed. **82** E2
Anyuysk Rus. Fed. **39** Q3
Anzac *Alta* Canada **167** I3
Anzac *B.C.* Canada **166** F4
Anze China **85** G4
Anzhero-Sudzhensk Rus. Fed. **80** D1
Anzi Dem. Rep. Congo **126** D5
Anzio Italy **56** E7
historically known as Antium
Anzoátegui *state* Venez. **199** E2
Aoba *i.* Vanuatu **145** F3
also known as Omba; *also spelt* Oba
Ao Luang National Park Thai. **78** B4
Aoga-shima *i.* Japan **91** F8
Aohan Qi China *see* **Xinhui**
Aomen China *see* **Macau**
Aomori Japan **90** G4
Aomori *pref.* Japan **90** G4
Aoos *r.* Greece **59** B8
Ao Phang Nga National Park Thai. **79** B6
Aoraki N.Z. *see* **Mount Cook**
Aoraki *mt.* N.Z. *see* **Cook, Mount**
Aôral, Phnum *mt.* Cambodia **79** D5
Aorangi *mt.* N.Z. *see* **Cook, Mount**
Aorere *r.* N.Z. **152** G8
Aosta Italy **51** N7
Aotearoa *country* Oceania *see* **New Zealand**
Aouderas Niger **125** H2
Aoufist W. Sahara **122** B4
Aouhinet bel Egra *well* Alg. **122** D4
Aouk, Bahr *r.* Cent. Afr. Rep./Chad **126** C2
Aoukalé *r.* Cent. Afr. Rep./Chad **126** D2
Aoukâr *reg.* Mali/Mauritania **122** D5
Aoukenek *well* Mali **125** F2
Aoulef Alg. **123** F4
Aoulime, Jbel *mt.* Morocco **122** C3
Aourou Mali **124** C3
Aoxi China *see* **Le'an**
Aoya Japan **91** D7
Aoyang China *see* **Shanggao**
Aozou Chad **120** C4
Apa *r.* Brazil **201** F5
Apac Uganda **128** B4
Apache U.S.A. **179** C5
Apache, Lake U.S.A. **183** M8
Apache Junction U.S.A. **183** M8
Apagado, Volcán *vol.* Bol. **200** D5
Apahida Romania **58** E2
Apaiai *r.* Brazil **206** E10
Apaiang *atoll* Kiribati *see* **Abaiang**
Apalachee Bay U.S.A. **175** C6
Apalachicola U.S.A. **175** C6
Apalachicola *r.* U.S.A. **175** C6
Apalachicola Bay U.S.A. **175** C6
Apam Ghana **125** E5
Apamama *atoll* Kiribati *see* **Abemama**
Apamea Turkey *see* **Dinar**
Apan Mex. **185** F5
Apaporis *r.* Col. **198** D5
Apar, Teluk *b.* Indon. **77** G3
Aparecida do Rio Doce Brazil **206** B5
Aparecida do Tabuado Brazil **206** B7
Aparima N.Z. *see* **Riverton**
Aparima *r.* N.Z. **153** C14
Aparri Phil. **74** B2
Aparurén Venez. **199** F3
Apas, Sierra *hills* Arg. **205** D6
Apaščia *r.* Lith. **42** F5
Apatin *Vojvodina, Srbija* Yugo. **56** K3
Apatity Rus. Fed. **44** P2
Apatou Fr. Guiana **199** H3
Apatzingán Mex. **185** E5
Ape Latvia **42** H4
Apediá *r.* Brazil **201** E2
Apeldoorn Neth. **48** C3
Apennines *mts* Italy **53** D3
also known as Appennino
Apere *r.* Bol. **200** D3
Apex Mountain Canada **166** B2
Aphrodite's Birthplace *tourist site* Cyprus **108** D3
also known as Petra tou Romiou
Api Dem. Rep. Congo **126** E4
Api *mt.* Nepal **96** D3
Api, Tanjung *pt* Indon. **75** B3
Apia Col. **198** C3
Apia *atoll* Kiribati *see* **Abaiang**

▶**Apia** Samoa **145** H3
Capital of Samoa.
oceania [countries] ➡ 138–139

Apiacas, Serra dos *hills* Brazil **201** F2
Apiaí Brazil **203** B8
Apiaú, Serra do *mts* Brazil **199** F4
Apio Solomon Is **145** F2
Apipilulco Mex. **185** F5
Apishapa *r.* U.S.A. **178** B4
Apiti N.Z. **152** J7
Apizaco Mex. **185** F5
Apizolaya Mex. **179** B7
Aplao Peru **200** B4
Ap Lei Chau *i. Hong Kong* China *see* **Aberdeen Island**
Apo, Mount *vol.* Phil. **74** C5
Apodi Brazil **202** E3
Apodi, Chapada do *hills* Brazil **202** E3
Apo East Passage Phil. **74** B3
Apoera Suriname **199** G3
Apolda Germany **48** I4
Apollinopolis Magna Egypt *see* **Idfu**
Apollo Bay Australia **147** D4
Apollonia Bulg. *see* **Sozopol**
Apollonia Greece **59** F12
Apolo Bol. **200** C3
Apopka U.S.A. **175** D6
Aporé *r.* Brazil **206** C6
Apostle Islands U.S.A. **172** C4
Apostle Islands National Lakeshore *nature res.* U.S.A. **172** C3
Apostolens Tommelfinger *mt.* Greenland **165** O3
Apóstoles Arg. **204** G2
Apostolos Andreas, Cape Cyprus **108** F2
also known as Zafer Burnu
Apoteri Guyana **199** G3
Apo West Passage Phil. **74** B3
Appalachia U.S.A. **176** C9
▶**Appalachian Mountains** U.S.A. **176** B9
northamerica [landscapes] ➡ 156–157
Appalla *i.* Fiji *see* **Kabara**
Appennino *mts* Italy *see* **Apennines**
Appennino Abruzzese *mts* Italy **56** F6
Appennino Lucano *mts* Italy **57** H8
Appennino Napoletano *mts* Italy **56** H7
Appennino Tosco-Emiliano *mts* Italy **56** C5
Appiano sulla Strada del Vino Italy **56** D2
Applecross U.K. **46** G6
Appleton *MN* U.S.A. **178** C2
Appleton *WI* U.S.A. **172** E6
Apple Valley U.S.A. **183** G7
Appomattox U.S.A. **176** G8
Aprelevka Rus. Fed. **43** S6
Aprilia Italy **56** E7
Apsheronsk Rus. Fed. **41** F7
formerly known as Apsheronskaya
Apsheronskaya Rus. Fed. *see* **Apsheronsk**
Apsheronskiy Poluostrov *pen.* Azer. *see* **Abşeron Yarımadası**
Apsley Canada **173** O6
Apsley Strait Australia **148** A1
Apt France **51** L9
Apucarana Brazil **206** B10
Apucarana, Serra da *hills* Brazil **206** B10
Apulum Romania *see* **Alba Iulia**
Apurahuan Phil. **74** A4
Apure *r.* Venez. **198** E3
Apure *state* Venez. **198** D3
Apurímac *dept* Peru **200** B3
Apurímac *r.* Peru **200** B3
Apurito Venez. **198** D3
Aq"a Georgia *see* **Sokhumi**
'Aqaba Jordan *see* **Al 'Aqabah**
'Aqaba, Gulf of Asia **104** A1
'Aqaba, Wādī el *watercourse* Egypt **108** E7
Aqadyr Kazakh. *see* **Agadyr'**
Aqal China **88** B3
Aqbalyq Kazakh. *see* **Akbalyk**
Aqbeyit Kazakh. *see* **Akbeit**
Āqchah Afgh. **101** F2
Aq Chai *r.* Iran **107** F3
Āqdā Iran **100** C3
Aqdoghmish *r.* Iran **100** A2
Aqiq Sudan **121** H5
Aqiq, Khalīg *b.* Sudan **104** B4
Aqiq, Wādī al *watercourse* Saudi Arabia **104** C2
Aqitag *mt.* China **88** E3
Aqköl Kazakh. *see* **Akkol'**
Aqköl Kazakh. *see* **Akkol'**
Aqla *well* Saudi Arabia **104** B2
Aqmola Kazakh. *see* **Astana**
Aqmola Oblast *admin. div.* Kazakh. *see* **Akmolinskaya Oblast'**
Aqmola Oblysy *admin. div.* Kazakh. *see* **Akmolinskaya Oblast'**
Āq Qal'eh Iran **100** C2
formerly known as Pahlavi Dezh
Aqqan China **89** D4
formerly known as Atqan
Aqqikkol Hu *salt l.* China **89** E4
Aqqystaū Kazakh. *see* **Akkystau**
Aqra', Wādī al *watercourse* Saudi Arabia **109** L7
'Aqraba West Bank **108** G5
'Aqrah Iraq **107** E3
'Aqran *hill* Saudi Arabia **109** J6
Aqsay Kazakh. *see* **Aksay**
Aqsayqin Hit *terr.* Asia *see* **Aksai Chin**
Aqshataū Kazakh. *see* **Akchatau**
Aqshi Kazakh. *see* **Akshiy**
Aqshuqyr Kazakh. *see* **Akshukur**
Aqsū Kazakh. *see* **Aksu**
Aqsū Kazakh. *see* **Aksu**
Aqsū Kazakh. *see* **Aksu**
Aqsū Kazakh. *see* **Aksu**
Aqsūat Kazakh. *see* **Aksuat**
Aqsū-Ayuly Kazakh. *see* **Aksu-Ayuly**
Aqtaū Kazakh. *see* **Aktau**
Aqtöbe Kazakh. *see* **Aktyubinsk**
Aqtöbe Oblysy *admin. div.* Kazakh. *see* **Aktyubinskaya Oblast'**
Aqtoghay Kazakh. *see* **Aktogay**
Aqtoghay Kazakh. *see* **Aktogay**
Aquae Grani Germany *see* **Aachen**
Aquae Gratianae France *see* **Aix-les-Bains**
Aquae Sextiae France *see* **Aix-en-Provence**
Aquae Statiellae Italy *see* **Acqui Terme**
Aquarius Mountains U.S.A. **183** K7
Aquarius Plateau U.S.A. **183** M4
Aquaviva delle Fonti Italy **56** I8
Aquidabánmí *r.* Para. **201** F5
Aquidauana Brazil **201** G5
Aquidauana *r.* Brazil **201** F4
Aquila Mex. **184** E5
Aquiles Mex. **184** D2
Aquin Haiti **187** E3
Aquincum Hungary *see* **Budapest**
Aquiry *r.* Brazil *see* **Acre**
Aquisgranum Germany *see* **Aachen**
Aquitaine *admin. reg.* France **50** F8
Aqzhal Kazakh. *see* **Akzhal**
Aqzhar Kazakh. *see* **Akzhar**
Aqzhayqyn Kōli *salt l.* Kazakh. *see* **Akzhaykyn, Ozero**
Ara India **97** E4
formerly spelt Arrah
Ara *r.* Spain **55** L2
Āra Ārba Eth. **128** D3
Arab U.S.A. **174** C5
Arab, Bahr el *watercourse* Sudan **126** F2
'Arab, Khalīg el *b.* Egypt **121** F2
'Arabah, Wādī *watercourse* Egypt **108** D8
'Arabābād Iran **100** D3
Ara Bacalle *well* Eth. **128** D3
'Arabah, Wādī *r.* Yemen **105** E4
'Arabah, Wādī al *watercourse* Israel/Jordan **108** G8
also known as Ha 'Arava
Arabelo Venez. **199** E3
Arabian Gulf Asia *see* **The Gulf**
Arabian Oryx Sanctuary *tourist site* Saudi Arabia **105** G4
Arabian Sea Indian Ocean **99** H6
Ara Bonel Eth. **128** D3
Arabopó Venez. **199** F3
Araç Turkey **106** C2
Araca *r.* Brazil **199** F5
Aracaju Brazil **202** E4
Aracanguy, Montes de *hills* Para. **201** G6
Aracar, Volcán *vol.* Arg. **200** D6
Aracati Brazil **202** E3
Aracatu Brazil **202** D5
Araçatuba Brazil **206** C8
Aracena Spain **54** E7
Aracena, Isla *i.* Chile **205** C9
Aracena, Sierra de *hills* Spain **54** D7
Arachthos *r.* Greece **59** C9
also spelt Arakhthos
Aračinovo Macedonia **58** C6
Aracoiaba Brazil **202** E3
Aracruz Brazil **203** D6
Araçuaí Brazil **203** D6
Araçuaí *r.* Brazil **203** D6
'Arad Israel **108** G6
Arad Romania **58** C2
Arada Chad **120** D6
'Arādah U.A.E. **105** F3
Arādān Iran **100** C3
Aradeib, Wadi *watercourse* Sudan **120** D6
Arafura Sea Australia/Indon. **144** C2
Aragarças Brazil **206** A2
Aragón *aut. comm.* Spain **55** K3
Aragón *r.* Spain **55** J2
Aragoncillo *mt.* Spain **55** I4
Aragua *state* Venez. **199** E2
Araguacema Brazil **202** B4
Araguaçu Brazil **202** B5
Aragua de Barcelona Venez. **199** E2
Aragua de Maturín Venez. **199** F2
Araguaia *r.* Brazil **206** A3
Araguaia, Parque Nacional de *nat. park* Brazil **202** B4
Araguaiana Brazil **206** B2
Araguaína Brazil **202** B3
Araguana Brazil **202** B3
Araguao, Boca *r. mouth* Venez. **199** F2
Araguapiche, Punta *pt* Venez. **199** F2
Araguari Brazil **206** E5
Araguari *r. Amapá* Brazil **199** I4
Araguari *r. Minas Gerais* Brazil **206** E5
Araguatins Brazil **202** B3
Aragvi *r.* Georgia **107** F2
'Ārah, Ra's *pt* Yemen **104** C5

Axioma Brazil 199 E6
Axios r. Greece 58 D8
Axmars naturreservat nature res. Sweden 45 L3
Axum Eth. see Āksum
Ay Kazakh. 103 J3
Ayabe Japan 91 D7
Ayachi, Jbel mt. Morocco 122 D2
Ayacucho Arg. 204 F5
Ayacucho Peru 200 B3
Ayacucho dept Peru 200 B3
Ayadaw Myanmar 78 A3
Ayagoz Kazakh. 103 J3
also spelt Ayaköz; formerly spelt Ayaguz
Ayagoz watercourse Kazakh. 103 J3
Ayaguz Kazakh. see Ayagoz
Ayakagytma, Vpadina depr. Uzbek. 103 F4
Ayakkuduk Uzbek. 103 F4
also spelt Oyoqquduq
Ayakkum Hu salt l. China 89 E4
Ayaköz Kazakh. see Ayagoz
Ayamé Côte d'Ivoire 124 E5
Ayamiken Equat. Guinea 125 H6
Ayamonte Spain 54 D7
Ayan Rus. Fed. 39 N4
Ayancık Turkey 106 C2
Ayang N. Korea 83 B5
Ayangba Nigeria 125 G5
Ayanka Rus. Fed. 39 Q3
Ayapel, Serranía de mts Col. 198 C3
Ayaş Turkey 106 C2
Ayaviri Peru 200 C3
Ayayei Eth. 128 C1
Āybak Afgh. 101 G2
Aydabul Kazakh. 103 G1
Aydar r. Ukr. 41 F6
Aydarkul', Ozero l. Uzbek. 103 F4
Aydarly Kazakh. 103 F3
'Aydim, Wādī r. Oman 105 F4
Aydın Turkey 106 A3
Aydın prov. Turkey 59 J11
Aydıncık Turkey 108 E1
also known as Gilindire
Aydın Dağları mts Turkey 106 A3
Aydingkol Hu marsh China 88 E3
Ayeat, Gora hill Kazakh. 103 G3
Ayedo mt. Spain 55 I2
Āyelu Terara vol. Eth. 128 D2
Ayem Gabon 126 A5
Ayer U.S.A. 177 N3
Ayers Rock hill Australia see Uluru
Ayeyarwady r. Myanmar see Irrawaddy
Aygyrzhal Kazakh. 103 J2
Ayiá Greece see Agia
Ayiásos Greece see Agiasos
Ayila Ri'gyü mts China 89 B5
Áyios Dhimítrios Greece see Agios Dimitrios
Áyios Dhimítrios, Ákra pt Greece see Agios Dimitrios, Akra
Áyios Evstrátios i. Greece see Agios Efstratios
Áyios Nikólaos Greece see Agios Nikolaos
Áyios Yeóryios i. Greece see Agios Georgios
Ayke, Ozero l. Kazakh. 103 E2
Āykel Eth. 128 C1
Aykhal Rus. Fed. 39 L3
Aykino Rus. Fed. 40 I3
Aykol China 88 C3
Aylesbury U.K. 47 L12
Aylett U.S.A. 177 H8
Ayllón, Sierra de mts Spain 55 H3
Aylmer Canada 173 M8
Aylmer Lake Canada 167 I1
Aymagambetov Kazakh. 103 E2
'Ayn, Ra's al c. Oman 105 G4
'Ayn, Wādī al watercourse Oman 105 F3
Ayna Peru 200 B3
Aynabulak Kazakh. 103 I3
'Ayn al 'Abd Libya 120 C2
'Ayn al 'Abd well Saudi Arabia 105 E1
'Ayn al Bayḍā' well Syria 109 I3
'Ayn al Ghazāl spring Libya 120 E4
'Ayn al Mazr'ah well Saudi Arabia 104 B2
'Ayn Ba Ma'bad Yemen 105 D5
'Ayn Dibis Iraq 109 O2
'Ayn Hindī oasis Oman 105 G4
Ayní Tajik. 101 G2
'Aynin well Saudi Arabia 104 C3
'Ayn Sifnī Iraq 109 O1
'Ayn Umm al Banāt waterhole Iraq 109 N3
'Ayn Zuwayyah spring Libya 120 E4
Ayon, Ostrov i. Rus. Fed. 39 Q3
Ayoquezco Mex. 185 F5
Ayora Spain 55 J5
Ayorou Niger 125 F3
Ayos Cameroon 125 I6
'Ayoûn 'Abd el Mâlek well Mauritania 122 D4
'Ayoûn el 'Atroûs Mauritania 124 C2
Ayr Australia 149 E3
Ayr U.K. 46 H8
Ayr r. U.K. 46 H8
Ayrag Nuur salt l. Mongolia 84 B1
Ayrancı Turkey 106 C3
Ayrancılar Turkey 59 I10
Ayre, Point of Isle of Man 47 H9
Aysarinskoye Kazakh. see Zaozernyy
Aysary Kazakh. see Zaozernyy
Āysha Eth. 128 D2
Ayteke Bi Kazakh. 103 E3
formerly known as Novokazalinsk or Zhangaqazaly
Aytos Bulg. 58 I6
Aytoska Reka r. Bulg. 58 I6
Aytré France 50 E6
Ayun Oman 105 F4
Ayuthia Thai. see Ayutthaya
Ayutla Guerrero Mex. 185 F5
Ayutla Jalisco Mex. 184 D4
Ayutthaya Thai. 79 C5
also known as Krungkao; also spelt Ayuthia; long form Phra Nakhon Si Ayutthaya
Ayvacık Turkey 106 A3
Ayvadzh Tajik. see Aivadzh
Ayvalı Turkey 107 D3
Ayvalık Turkey 106 A3
Aywat al Manāhil, Wādī r. Yemen 105 E4
Aywat aş Şay'ar, Wādī r. Yemen 105 E4
Azacualpa Hond. 186 B4
Azak Rus. Fed. see Azov
Azambuja Port. 54 C5
Azamgarh India 97 D4
Azangaro Peru 200 C3
Azanja Srbija Yugo. 58 B4
Azaouâd reg. Mali 124 E2
Azaouagh, Vallée de watercourse Mali/Niger 125 F2
Azapa Chile 200 C4
Azar watercourse Niger 125 G2
Azaran Iran see Hashtrud
Āzārbayjan country Asia see Azerbaijan
Āzārbāyjān-e Gharbī prov. Iran 100 A2
Āzārbāyjān-e Sharqī prov. Iran 100 A2
Azare Nigeria 125 H4
Azarychy Belarus 43 K9
Azatskoye, Ozero l. Rus. Fed. 43 S2
A'zāz Syria 109 I1
Azazga Alg. 55 P8
Azbine mts Niger see L'Aïr, Massif de
Azdavay Turkey 106 C2
Azélik well Niger 125 H2
Azemmour Morocco 122 C2
▶Azerbaijan country Asia 107 F2
spelt Azārbayjan in Azeri; formerly known as Azerbaydzhanskaya S.S.R.; historically known as Atropatene
asia [countries] ▶▶▶ 64–67
Azerbaydzhanskaya S.S.R. country Asia see Azerbaijan
Azergues r. France 51 K7
Āzezo Eth. 128 C1
Azhu-Tayga, Gora mt. Rus. Fed. 88 E1
Azilal Morocco 122 D2
Azilda Canada 173 L4
Azingo Gabon 126 A5
'Azīzābād Iran 100 D4
Azizbekov Armenia see Vayk'
Aziziye Turkey see Pınarbaşı
Azlam, Wādī watercourse Saudi Arabia 104 A2
Aznakayevo Rus. Fed. 40 J5
Aznalcóllar Spain 54 E7
Azogues Ecuador 198 B5
Azopol'ye Rus. Fed. 40 H2
▶Azores terr. N. Atlantic Ocean 216 M3
Autonomous Region of Portugal. Long form Arquipélago dos Açores.
europe [countries] ▶▶▶ 32–35
Azotus Israel see Ashdod
Azov Rus. Fed. 41 F7
historically known as Azak
Azov, Sea of Rus. Fed./Ukr. 41 F7
also known as Azovs'ke More or Azovskoye More
Azovo-Sivashskiy Zapovidnyk nature res. Ukr. 41 E7
Azovs'ke More sea Rus. Fed./Ukr. see Azov, Sea of
Azovskoye More sea Rus. Fed./Ukr. see Azov, Sea of
Azpeitia Spain 55 I1
Azraq, Bahr el r. Eth./Sudan 104 A5 see Blue Nile
Azrou Morocco 122 D2
Azrou, Oued watercourse Alg. 123 G5
Aztec U.S.A. 181 E5
Azua Dom. Rep. 187 F3
Azuaga Spain 54 F6
Azuay prov. Ecuador 198 B5
Azúcar r. Chile 204 C2
Azuchi-Ō-shima i. Japan 91 A8
Azuer r. Spain 55 H5
Azuero, Península de pen. Panama 186 C6
Azufre, Cerro del mt. Chile 204 C2
Azul Arg. 204 F5
Azul r. Mex. 185 H5
also known as Blue Creek
Azul, Cordillera mts Peru 200 B2
Azul, Serra hills Brazil 201 G3
Azum, Wadi watercourse Sudan 120 D6
Azuma-san vol. Japan 90 G6
Azurduy Bol. 201 D5
Azyory Belarus 42 F8
'Azza Gaza see Gaza
Az Zabadānī Syria 108 H4
Az Zabīrah well Saudi Arabia 104 C2
Az Zafīrī reg. Iraq 107 E5
Az Zāhirah admin. reg. Oman 105 G3
Az Zahrān Saudi Arabia see Dhahran
Az Zallāf, Wādī watercourse Libya 120 B3
Az Zallāq Bahrain 105 E2
Azzano Decimo Italy 56 E3
Az Zaqāzīq Egypt see Zagazig
Az Zarbah Syria 109 H1
Az Zarqā' Jordan 108 H5
also spelt Zarqā'
Az Zāwiyah Libya 120 B1
Az Zaydīyah Yemen 104 C5
Azzeffāl hills Mauritania/W. Sahara 122 B5
Azzel Matti, Sebkha salt pan Alg. 123 F4
Az Zilfī Saudi Arabia 104 D2
Az Zintān Libya 120 B2
Az Zubayr Iraq 107 F5
Az Zuhrah Yemen 104 C5
Az Zuqur i. Yemen 104 C5
English form Az Zuqur Island
Az Zuqurt oasis Saudi Arabia 105 E4
Az Zuwaytīnah Libya 120 D2

↓ B

Baa Indon. 75 B5
Baai r. Indon. 77 G2
Ba'albek Lebanon 108 H3
Ba'al Hazor mt. West Bank 108 G6
Baardheere Somalia 128 D4
formerly spelt Bardera
Bab India 96 C4
Baba mt. Bulg. 58 E6
Bābā, Kūh-e mts Afgh. 101 G3
Baba Burnu pt Turkey 59 H9
Babaçulândia Brazil 202 C3
Babadağ mt. Azer. 107 G2
Babadag Romania 58 J4
Babadağ Turkey 59 J11
Baba Dağ mt. Turkey 59 K12
Babadag, Podişul plat. Romania 58 J4
Babadaykhan Akhal'skaya Oblast' Turkm. 102 E5
formerly known as Kirovsk
Babadaykhan Akhal'skaya Oblast' Turkm. 102 E5
formerly known as Kommuna
Babadurmaz Turkm. 102 D5
Babaeski Turkey 106 A2
Babahoyo Ecuador 198 B5
Babai r. Nepal 97 D3
Babai Gaxun China 84 E3
Babak Phil. 74 C5
Bābā Kalān Iran 100 B4
Babakourimigana well Niger 125 H3
Bāb al Mandab strait Africa/Asia 121 I6
Bab al Mandab, Cape Yemen see Bāb al Mandab, Ra's
Bāb al Mandab, Ra's c. Yemen 104 C5
English form Bab al Mandab, Cape
Babana Indon. 75 A3
Babanango S. Africa 133 P5
Babanki Cameroon 125 H5
Babanusa Sudan 126 E2
Babao China see Qilian
Babao China 86 C4
Babar i. Indon. 75 D4
Babar, Kepulauan is Indon. 75 D4
Babat Indon. 77 F4
Babati Tanz. 129 B6
Babau Indon. 75 B5
Babayevo Rus. Fed. 43 Q2
Babayurt Rus. Fed. 102 A4
Babeldaob i. Palau 73 H5
also spelt Babelthuap
Babelegi S. Africa 133 M2
Babelthuap i. Palau see Babeldaob
Băbeni Romania 58 F4
Baberu India 96 D4
Bab Ezzouar Alg. 55 O8
Babi, Pulau i. Indon. 76 B2
Babia Góra mt. Poland 49 Q6
Babian Jiang r. China 86 B4
Bābil Egypt 108 C7
Bābil governorate Iraq 107 F4
formerly known as Al Ḥillah
Babilē Eth. 128 D2
Babimost Poland 49 M3
Babinavichy Belarus 43 L7
Babinda Australia 149 E3
Babine r. Canada 166 E4
Babine Lake Canada 166 E4
Babine Range mts Canada 166 E4
Babinga Dem. Rep. Congo 126 C5
Babītes ezers l. Latvia 42 E5
Babo Indon. 73 H7
Bābol Iran 100 C2
Bābol Sar Iran 100 C2
Babonā r. Brazil 199 E6
Babongo Cameroon 125 I5
Baboon Point S. Africa 132 C9
Baboua Cent. Afr. Rep. 126 B3
Babruysk Belarus 43 K8
also spelt Bobruysk
Babstovo Rus. Fed. 82 D2
Babtai Lith. 42 E6
Bab Taza Morocco 54 F9
Babu China see Hezhou
Babuna Planina mts Macedonia 58 C7
Babusar Pass Pak. 101 H3
Babushkin Rus. Fed. 85 E1
formerly known as Mysovsk
Babušnica Srbija Yugo. 58 D5
Babuyan Phil. 74 A4
Babuyan i. Phil. 74 B2
Babuyan Channel Phil. 74 B2
Babuyan Islands Phil. 74 B2
Babylon tourist site Iraq 107 F4
Babynino Rus. Fed. 43 Q7
Bač Vojvodina, Srbija Yugo. 58 A3
Bacaadweyn Somalia 128 E3
Bacaba r. Brazil 198 D5
Bacabáchi Mex. 184 C3
Bacabal Maranhão Brazil 202 C3
Bacabal Pará Brazil 199 G6
Bacajá r. Brazil 199 I5
Bacakliyayla Tepesi mt. Turkey 106 B2
Bacalar Mex. 185 H5
Bacalar Chico, Boca sea chan. Mex. 185 I5
Bacan i. Indon. 75 C3
Bacanora Mex. 184 C2
Bacarra Phil. 74 B2
Bacău Romania 58 H2
Baccarat France 51 M4
Baccaro Point Canada 169 H5
Bacchiglione r. Italy 56 E3
Bắc Giang Vietnam 78 D3
Bachaquero Venez. 198 D2
Bacheykava Belarus 43 K6
Bach Ice Shelf Antarctica 222 T2
Bachiniva Mex. 181 F7
Bạch Long Vi, Đao i. Vietnam 78 D3
Bachu China 88 B4
formerly known as Maralbashi or Maralwexi
Bachuma Eth. 128 B3
Back r. Australia 149 D3
Back r. Canada 167 M1
Bačka reg. Hungary/Yugo. 58 A2
Bačka Palanka Vojvodina, Srbija Yugo. 58 A3
Bačka Topola Vojvodina, Srbija Yugo. 58 A3
Backbone Mountain U.S.A. 176 F6
Backbone Ranges mts Canada 166 D2
Backe Sweden 44 L3
Bäckefors Sweden 45 K4
Bäckhammar Sweden 45 K4
Bački Petrovac Vojvodina, Srbija Yugo. 58 A3
Backnang Germany 48 G7
Bačko Gradište Vojvodina, Srbija Yugo. 58 B3
Backstairs Passage Australia 146 C3
Bac Lac Vietnam 78 D3
Bac Liêu Vietnam 79 D6
Bắc Ninh Vietnam 78 D3
Bacnotan Phil. 74 B2
Baco, Mount Phil. 74 B3
Bacoachi Mex. 184 C2
Bacoachi watercourse Mex. 181 E7
Bacobampo Mex. 184 C3
Bacolod Phil. 74 B4
Bắc Quang Vietnam 78 D3
Bacqueville-en-Caux France 50 G3
Bácsalmás Hungary 49 Q9
Bactra Afgh. see Balkh
Bacubirito Mex. 184 D3
Baculin Bay Phil. 74 C5
Baculin Point Phil. 74 C4
Bacuri Brazil 202 C2
Bad r. U.S.A. 178 B2
Bada China see Xilin
Bada mt. Eth. 128 C3
Bada i. Myanmar 79 B6
Badagara India 94 B4
Badain Jaran Shamo des. China 84 D3
Badajós Amazonas Brazil 199 F5
Badajós Pará Brazil 202 C2
Badajós, Lago l. Brazil 199 F5
Badajoz Spain 54 E6
Badakhshān prov. Afgh. 101 G2
Badakhshan aut. rep. Tajik. see Kŭhistoni Badakhshon
Badakhshoni Kŭhī aut. rep. Tajik. see Kŭhistoni Badakhshon
Badami India 94 B3
Badanah Saudi Arabia 107 E5
Badaojiang China see Baishan
Badarinath mts India see Badrinath Peaks
Badarīyāt, Ḥazm al plat. Saudi Arabia 109 L7
Badarpur India 97 G4
Badas, Kepulauan is Indon. 77 D2
Bad Aussee Austria 49 K8
Bad Axe U.S.A. 173 K7
Bad Bergzabern Germany 48 E6
Bad Berka Germany 48 I5
Bad Berleburg Germany 48 F4
Bad Bevensen Germany 48 H2
Badbeck Canada 169 I4
Badderen Norway 44 M1
Baddo r. Pak. 101 F4
Bad Doberan Germany 48 I1
Badéguichéri Niger 125 G3
Bademli Turkey see Aladağ
Bademli Geçidi pass Turkey 106 B3
Bad Ems Germany 48 E5
Baden Austria 49 N7
Baden Switz. 51 O5
Baden-Baden Germany 48 F7
Baden-Württemberg land Germany 48 F7
Badér Niger 125 G3
Bad Freienwalde Germany 49 L3
Badgastein Austria 49 K8
Badger Canada 169 K3
Bādghīs prov. Afgh. 101 E3
Bad Harzburg Germany 48 H4
Bad Hersfeld Germany 48 G5
Bad Hofgastein Austria 49 K8
Bad Homburg vor der Höhe Germany 48 F5
Badi r. Guinea 124 B4
Badia Polesine Italy 56 D3
Badigeru Swamp Sudan 128 B3
Badin Pak. 101 G5
Badinko, Réserve du nature res. Mali 124 C3
Badiraguato Mex. 184 D3
Bad Ischl Austria 49 K8
Bādiyat ash Shām des. Asia see Syrian Desert
Badje-Sohppar Sweden see Övre Soppero
Badkhyzskiy Zapovednik nature res. Turkm. 101 E3
Bad Kissingen Germany 48 H5
Bad Königsdorff Poland see Jastrzębie-Zdrój
Bad Kreuznach Germany 48 E6
Bad Krozingen Germany 48 E8
Badlands reg. ND U.S.A. 178 B2
Badlands reg. SD U.S.A. 178 B3
Badlands National Park U.S.A. 178 B3
Bad Langensalza Germany 48 H4
Bad Lauterberg im Harz Germany 48 H4
Bad Liebenwerda Germany 49 K4
Bad Lippspringe Germany 48 F4
Bad Mergentheim Germany 48 G6
Bad Nauheim Germany 48 F5
Badnawar India 96 B5
Bad Neuenahr-Ahrweiler Germany 48 E5
Bad Neustadt an der Saale Germany 48 H5
Bad Oldesloe Germany 48 H2
Badong China 87 D2
also known as Xinling
Ba Đồng Vietnam 79 D6
Badou Togo 125 F5
Badplaas S. Africa 133 O2
Bad Pyrmont Germany 48 G4
Bad Ragaz Switz. 51 P5
Badr City Egypt 108 C7
Bad Reichenhall Germany 49 J8
Badr Ḥunayn Saudi Arabia 104 B3
Badrinath Peaks India 96 C3
also known as Badarinath or Chaukhamba
Bad River Indian Reservation res. U.S.A. 172 C4
Bad Säckingen Germany 48 E8
Bad Salzuflen Germany 48 F3
Bad Salzungen Germany 48 H5
Bad Schwartau Germany 48 H2
Bad Segeberg Germany 48 H2
Badu China 87 F3
Badu Island Australia 73 J9
Badulla Sri Lanka 94 D5
Badvel India 94 C3
Bad Waldsee Germany 48 G8
Bad Windsheim Germany 48 H6
Badzhal'skiy Khrebet mts Rus. Fed. 82 D2
Bad Zwischenahn Germany 48 F2
Bae Colwyn U.K. see Colwyn Bay
Bæir Iceland 44 [inset] B2
Baena Spain 54 G7
Baeza Ecuador 198 B5
Baeza Spain 55 H7
Bafang Cameroon 125 H5
Bafatá Guinea-Bissau 124 B3
Baffa Pak. 101 H3
Baffin Bay sea Canada/Greenland 165 M2
▶Baffin Island Canada 165 L2
2nd largest island in North America and 5th in the world.
northamerica [landscapes] ▶▶▶ 156–157
Bafia Cameroon 125 H5
Bafilo Togo 125 F4
Bafing r. Guinea/Mali 124 C3
Bafing, Réserve du nature res. Mali 124 C3
Bafing Makana Mali 124 C3
Bafoulabé Mali 124 C3
Bafoussam Cameroon 125 H5
Bāfq Iran 100 C4
Bafra Turkey 106 C2
Bafra Burnu pt Turkey 106 C2
Bāft Iran 100 D4
Bafwasende Dem. Rep. Congo 126 E4
Baga Nigeria 125 I3
Baga Spain 55 M2
Baga Bogd Uul mts Mongolia 84 D2
Bagac Bay Phil. 74 B3
Bagaha India 97 E4
Bagahak hill Sabah Malaysia 77 G1
Bagalkot India 94 B2
Bagamoyo Tanz. 129 C6
Bagan China 86 A1
Bagan Datoh Malaysia see Bagan Datuk
Bagan Datuk Malaysia 76 C2
formerly known as Bagan Datoh
Baganga Phil. 74 C5
Bagani Namibia 130 D3
Bagan Peninsula Phil. 74 B5
Bagansiapiapi Indon. 76 C2
Bagar watercourse Kazakh. 88 C1
Bagarası Turkey 59 I11
Bagaré well Niger 125 G3
Bagaroua Niger 125 G3
Bagata Dem. Rep. Congo 126 C5
Bagazán Peru 198 C6
Bagbag Sudan 121 F6
Bagdad U.S.A. 183 K7
Bagé Brazil 204 G3
Bagepalli India 94 C3
Bagerhat Bangl. see Bagherhat
Bages et de Sigean, Étang de lag. France 51 I9
Bageshwar India 96 C3
Bagevadi India 94 C2
Baggå Sweden 45 K4
Baggs U.S.A. 180 F4
Bagh India 96 B5
Baghak Pak. 101 F4
Baghbaghū Iran 101 E2
▶Baghdād Iraq 107 F4
Capital of Iraq. English form Baghdad.
Baghdad Iraq see Baghdād
Bāgh-e Bābū'īyeh Iran 100 D4
Bagherhat Bangl. 97 F5
also spelt Bagerhat
Bagheria Sicilia Italy 57 F10
Bāghīn Iran 100 D4
Baghlān Afgh. 101 G2
Baghlān prov. Afgh. 101 G3
Baghlī Da hill Iran 100 A2
Baginda, Tanjung pt Indon. 77 D3
Bağırsak Deresi r. Syria/Turkey see Sājūr, Nahr
Bagley U.S.A. 178 D2
Baglung Nepal 97 D3
Bagn Norway 45 J3
Bagnara Calabra Italy 57 H10
Bagnères-de-Bigorre France 50 G9
Bagnères-de-Luchon France 50 G10
Bagno di Romagna Italy 56 D5
Bagnolo Mella Italy 56 C3
Bagnols-sur-Cèze France 51 K8
Bagnuiti r. Nepal 97 E4
Bago Myanmar see Pegu
Bago admin. div. Myanmar see Pegu
Bago Phil. 74 B4
Bagoé r. Côte d'Ivoire/Mali 124 D3
Bagong China see Sansui
Bagrationovsk Rus. Fed. 42 B7
historically known as Eylau or Preussisch-Eylau
Bagrax China see Bohu
Bagrax Hu l. China see Bosten Hu
Bagre Brazil 202 B2
Bagua Peru 198 B6
Baguio Phil. 74 B2
Baguio Point Phil. 74 B2
Bağyurdu Turkey 59 I10
Bagzane, Monts mts Niger 125 H2
Bahadurganj Nepal 89 C7
Bahadurgarh India 96 C3
Bahābād Iran see Rafsanjān
▶Bahamas country West Indies 186 D1
northamerica [countries] ▶▶▶ 158–159
Baharampur India 97 F4
formerly spelt Berhampur
Bahardipur Pak. 101 G5
Bahariya Oasis Egypt 121 F3
Bahau r. Indon. 77 G2
Bahau Malaysia 76 C2
Bahaur Indon. 77 F3
Bahawalnagar Pak. 101 H4
Bahawalpur Pak. 101 G4
Bahçe Adana Turkey 108 G1
Bahçe Osmaniye Turkey 107 D3
Ba He r. China 86 C2
Bäherden Turkm. see Bakherden
Baheri India 96 C3
Bahi Tanz. 129 B6
Bahia Brazil see Salvador
Bahia state Brazil 202 D5
Bahía Asunción Mex. 181 D8
Bahía Blanca Arg. 204 E5
Bahía Bustamante Arg. 205 D7
Bahía Kino Mex. 184 C2
Bahía Laura Arg. 205 D8
Bahía Negra Para. 201 F5
Bahía San Blas Arg. 204 E6
Bahía Tortugas Mex. 184 B3
Bahīg Egypt 108 A7
Bahir Dar Eth. 128 C2
Bahlā Oman 105 G3
Bahlui r. Romania 58 I1
Bahmanshīr, Khowr-e r. Iran 100 B4
Bahomonte Indon. 75 B3
Bahr Saudi Arabia 104 C4
Bahraich India 97 D4
▶Bahrain country Asia 105 E2
spelt Al Baḥrayn in Arabic
asia [countries] ▶▶▶ 64–67
Bahrain, Gulf of Asia 105 E2
Bahrāmābād Iran 100 B2
Bahrāmjerd Iran 100 D4
Bahr el Jebel state Sudan 128 A3
Bahror India 96 C4
Bāhū Kālāt Iran 101 E5
Bahushewsk Belarus 43 L7
Bahuaja-Sonene, Parque Nacional nat. park Peru 200 C3
Baia Romania 58 H1
Baia Romania 58 J4
Baia de Aramă Romania 58 D4
Baia de Arieş Romania 58 E2
Baía dos Tigres Angola 127 A9
Baía Farta Angola 127 B8
Baia Mare Romania 53 G2
Baião Brazil 202 B2
Baiazeh Iran 100 C3
Baibeli well Chad 120 D5
Baibokoum Chad 126 B3
Baicheng China see Xiping
Baicheng Jilin China 85 I2
Baicheng Xinjiang China 88 C3
also known as Bay
Băicoi Romania 58 G3
Baidoa Somalia see Baydhabo
Baidoi Co l. China 89 D5
Baidu China 87 F3
Baidunzi China 84 B3
Baie-aux-Feuilles Canada see Tasiujaq
Baie-Comeau Canada 169 G3
Baie de Henne Haiti 187 E3
Baie-du-Poste Canada see Mistissini
Baie-Johan-Beetz Canada 169 I3
Baie-St-Paul Canada 169 G4
Baie-Trinite Canada 169 H3
Baie Verte Canada 169 J3
Baigou r. China 85 H4
Baiguan China see Shangyu
Baiguo China 87 E2
Baigura mt. Spain 55 J2
Baihanchang China 86 A3
Baihar India 96 D5
Baihe Jilin China 82 C4
formerly known as Erdaobaihe
Baihe Shaanxi China 87 D1
Bai He r. China 87 E1
Baiji Iraq see Bayjī
Baijiantan China 88 D2
Baijnath Himachal Pradesh India 96 C2
Baijnath Uttaranchal India 96 C3
▶Baikal, Lake Rus. Fed. 81 H2
Deepest lake in the world and in Asia. 3rd largest lake in Asia and 9th in the world. Also known as Baykal, Ozero.
world [physical features] ▶▶▶ 8–9
Baikanthpur India 97 D4
Baikouquan China 88 D2
Baikunthpur India 97 D5
Bailang China 85 I2
Bailanhe Shuiku resr China 87 E2
Baile Átha Cliath Rep. of Ireland see Dublin
Baile Átha Luain Rep. of Ireland see Athlone
Băile Govora Romania 58 F3
Băile Herculane Romania 58 D4
Bailén Spain 54 H6
Băile Olăneşti Romania 58 F3
Băileşti Romania 58 E4
Băileştilor, Câmpia plain Romania 58 E4
Băile Tuşnad Romania 58 G2
Bailey S. Africa 133 K8
Bailey Ice Stream Antarctica 223 W1
Bailey Range hills Australia 151 C6
Baileyton U.S.A. 176 C9
Bailicun China 87 D3
Bailingmiao China 85 F3
also known as Darhan Muminggan Lianheqi
Baillie r. Canada 167 J1
Bailong Jiang r. China 86 C1
Bailundo Angola 127 B8
formerly known as Teixeira da Silva
Baima China 86 B1
also known as Sêraitang
Baima China see Baxoi
Bainang China 89 E6
also known as Norkyung
Bainbridge GA U.S.A. 175 C6
Bainbridge IN U.S.A. 177 J3
Bainbridge OH U.S.A. 176 B6
Bain-de-Bretagne France 50 E5
Bainduru India 94 B3
Bainet Haiti 187 E3
Baingoin China 89 E6
also known as Porong
Baini China see Yuqing
Baiona Spain 54 C2
also spelt Bayona
Baiqên China 86 B1
Baiquan China 82 B3
Bā'ir Jordan 109 H7
Bā'ir, Wādī watercourse Jordan/Saudi Arabia 109 I6
Bairab Co l. China 89 C5
Bairagnia India 97 E4
Baird U.S.A. 179 C5
Baird, Mount Canada 166 C1
Baird Mountains U.S.A. 164 D3
▶Bairiki Kiribati 145 G1
Capital of Kiribati, on Tarawa atoll.
Bairin Qiao China 85 H3
formerly known as Balinqiao
Bairin Youqi China see Daban
Bairin Zuoqi China see Lindong
Bairkum Kazakh. 103 G4
also spelt Bayyrqum
Bairnsdale Australia 147 E4
Bais France 50 F4
Bais Phil. 74 B4
Baïse r. France 50 G8
Baisha Chongqing China 86 C2
Baisha Hainan China 87 D5
also known as Yacha
Baisha Jiangxi China 87 E3
Baisha Sichuan China 87 D2
Baishan China see Mashan
Baishan Jilin China 82 B4
formerly known as Badaojiang or Hunjiang
Baishan Jilin China 82 B4
Baishui China 85 F5
Baishui Jiang r. China 86 C1
Băişoara Romania 58 E2
Baisogala Lith. 42 E6
Baitadi Nepal 96 D3
Baitang China 86 A1
Bai Thuong Vietnam 78 D4
Baitle r. China 85 H3
Baixa da Banheira Port. 54 B6
Baixi China see Yibin
Baixiang China 85 G4
Baixingt China 85 I3
Baixo Guandu Brazil 207 M6
Baixo-Longa Angola 127 B9
Baiyang Dian resr China 85 H4
Baiyanghe China 88 E3
Baiyashi China see Dong'an
Baiyin China 84 E4
Baiyü China 86 A2
also known as Jianshe
Baiyuda Desert Sudan 121 G5
Baiyu Shan mts China 85 E4
Baja Hungary 49 P9
Baja, Punta pt Mex. 184 B2
Baja California pen. Mex. 184 B2
English form Lower California
Baja California Norte state Mex. 184 B2
Baja California Sur state Mex. 184 B3
Bajan Mex. 185 E3
Bajang Nepal 96 D3
Bajau i. Indon. 77 D2
Bajaur reg. Pak. 101 G3
Bajawa Indon. 75 B5
Baj Baj India 97 F5
Bājgīrān Iran 100 D2
Bājil Yemen 104 C5
Bajina Bašta Srbija Yugo. 58 A5
Bajitpur Bangl. 97 F4
Bajmok Vojvodina, Srbija Yugo. 58 A3
Bajna India 96 C4
Bajo Baudó Col. 198 B3
Bajo Boquete Panama 186 C5
Bajo Caracoles Arg. 205 C7
Bajoga Nigeria 125 H4
Bajo Grande Arg. 205 C7
Bajo Hondo Arg. 204 D3
Bajrakot India 97 E5
Bajram Curri Albania 58 B6
Baka, Bukit mt. Indon. 77 F3
Bakaba Chad 126 C3
Bakala Cent. Afr. Rep. 126 D3
Bakaly Rus. Fed. 40 J5
Bakanas Kazakh. 103 I3
Bakanas watercourse Kazakh. 103 I3
Bakau Gambia 124 A3
Bakayan, Gunung mt. Indon. 77 G2
Bakel Senegal 124 B3
Baker CA U.S.A. 183 H6
Baker LA U.S.A. 175 B6
Baker MT U.S.A. 180 F3
Baker OR U.S.A. 180 C3
Baker WV U.S.A. 176 G6
Baker, Mount vol. U.S.A. 180 B2
Baker Butte mt. U.S.A. 183 M7
▶Baker Island N. Pacific Ocean 145 H1
United States Unincorporated Territory.
oceania [countries] ▶▶▶ 138–139
Baker Island U.S.A. 166 C4
Baker Lake salt flat Australia 151 D5
Baker Lake Canada 167 M1
also known as Qamanittuaq
Baker Lake l. Canada 167 M1
Baker's Dozen Islands Canada 168 E1
Bakersfield U.S.A. 182 F6
Bakerville S. Africa 133 K2
Bakhā Oman 105 G2
Bakharden Turkm. see Bakherden
Bakhardok Turkm. 102 D5
also spelt Bokurdak
Bākharz mts Iran 101 E3
Bakhchisaray Ukr. see Bakhchysaray
Bakhchysaray Ukr. 41 E7
also spelt Bakhchisaray
Bakherden Turkm. 102 D5
also spelt Bäherden; formerly spelt Bakharden
Bakhirevo Rus. Fed. 82 C2
Bakhmach Ukr. 41 E6
Bakhmut Ukr. see Artemivs'k
Bakhmutovo Rus. Fed. 43 P5
Bakhta Rus. Fed. 39 I3
Bākhtarān Iran see Kermānshāh
Bākhtarān prov. Iran see Kermānshāh
Bakhtegan, Daryācheh-ye l. Iran 100 C4
Bakhtiari Country reg. Iran 100 B3
Bakhtiyarpur India 97 E4
Bakhty Kazakh. 88 C2
also spelt Baqty
Bakhuis Gebergte mts Suriname 199 G3
Baki Azer. see Baku
Baki well Chad 120 D5
Bakin Birji Niger 125 H3
Bakır r. Turkey 59 I10
Bakırköy Turkey 106 B2
Bakkaflói b. Iceland 44 [inset] D2
Baklan Turkey 59 K11
Baklanka Rus. Fed. 43 V3
Baklanovo Rus. Fed. 43 M6
Bakloh India 96 B2
Bako Côte d'Ivoire 124 D4
Bako Eth. 128 C2
Bako National Park Sarawak Malaysia 77 E2
Bakool admin. reg. Somalia 128 D4
Bakota Dem. Rep. Congo 126 D5
Bakouma Cent. Afr. Rep. 126 D3
Bakoumba Gabon 126 B5
Bakoy r. Mali 124 C3
Baksan Rus. Fed. 41 G8
Baktalórántháza Hungary 49 T8
▶Baku Azer. 107 G2
Capital of Azerbaijan. Also spelt Bakı or Baky.
Bakung i. Indon. 76 D2
Bakuny Belarus 42 F9
Bakuriani Georgia 107 E2
Bakutis Coast Antarctica 222 P2
Baky Azer. see Baku
Bakyy Uyandino r. Rus. Fed. 39 O3
Balā Turkey 106 C3
Bala U.K. 47 I11
also known as Y Bala
Bala, Cerros de mts Bol. 200 C3
Balabac i. Phil. 74 A5
Balabac Strait Malaysia/Phil. 77 G1
Balābād, Gardaneh-ye pass Iran 100 C3
Balabalangan, Kepulauan atolls Indon. 77 G3
Balabanovo Rus. Fed. 43 R6
Bălăceanu Romania 58 I3
Bălăciţa Romania 58 E4
Balad Iraq 107 F4
Bālā Deh Iran 100 B4
Baladeh Māzandarān Iran 100 B2
Baladeh Māzandarān Iran 100 B2
Balaghat India 96 D5
Balaghat Range hills India 94 B2
Balaguer Spain 55 L3
Bālā Ḥowz Iran 100 D4
Balaiberkuak Indon. 77 E3
Balaikarangan Indon. 77 E2
Balaipungut Indon. 76 C2
Balairiam Indon. 77 E3
Balaisepuac Indon. 77 E3
Balaitous mt. France 50 F10
Balaka Malawi 129 B8
Balakān Azer. 107 F2
Balakhna Rus. Fed. 40 G4
Balakirevo Rus. Fed. 43 T5
Balaklava Australia 146 C3
Balaklava Ukr. 41 E7
Balakleya Ukr. see Balakliya
Balakliya Ukr. 41 F6
also spelt Balakleya
Balakovo Rus. Fed. 102 A1
Balama Moz. 131 H2
Balambangan i. Sabah Malaysia 77 G1
Bālā Morghāb Afgh. 101 E3
Balan India 96 A4
Bălan Romania 58 E2
Balancán Mex. 185 H5
Balanda Rus. Fed. see Kalininsk
Balan Dağı hill Turkey 59 J12
Balanga Phil. 74 B3
Balangala Dem. Rep. Congo 126 C4
Balangir India 95 D1
Balangoda Sri Lanka 94 D5
Balapur India 94 C1
Balarampur India 97 E5
Balase r. Indon. 75 B3
Bălăşeşti Romania 58 I2
Balashi Rus. Fed. 102 B2
Balashikha Rus. Fed. 43 S6
Balashov Rus. Fed. 41 G6
Balasinor India 96 B5
Balassagyarmat Hungary 49 Q7
Balaton l. Hungary see Balaton, Lake

Barjaude, Montagne de *mt.* France **51** M9
Barjols France **51** M9
Barjora India **97** E5
Barjūj, Wādī *watercourse* Libya **120** B3
Barka *prov.* Eritrea **104** B4
Barkā Oman **105** G3
Barkam China **86** B2
Barkan, Ra's-e *pt* Iran **100** B4
Barkava Latvia **42** H5
Barker, Lake *salt flat* Australia **151** C6
Barkerville Canada **166** F4
Barkéwol el Abiod Mauritania **124** B2
Barkhan Pak. **101** G4
Barki Saraiya India **97** E4
Bark Lake Canada **173** P5
Barkley, Lake U.S.A. **174** C4
Barkley Sound *inlet* Canada **166** E5
Barkly East S. Africa **133** L7
Barkly Pass S. Africa **133** L8
Barkly Tableland *reg.* Australia **148** B3
Barkly West S. Africa **133** I5
Barkol China **84** B3
Barkol Hu *salt l.* China **84** B3
Barkot India **96** C3
Bârlad Romania **58** I2
formerly spelt Bîrlad
Bârladului, Podișul *plat.* Romania **58** I2
Barlag Gol *watercourse* Mongolia **84** B2
Bar-le-Duc France **51** L4
Barlee, Lake *salt flat* Australia **151** B6
Barlee Range *hills* Australia **150** A4
Barlee Range Nature Reserve Australia **150** A4
Barletta Italy **56** I7
historically known as Barduli
Barlinek Poland **49** M3
Barlow Canada **166** B2
Barlow Lake Canada **167** K2
Barmedman Australia **147** E3
Barmen-Elberfeld Germany *see* **Wuppertal**
Barmer India **96** A4
also spelt Balmer
Barmera Australia **146** D3
Barm Fīrūz, Kūh-e *mt.* Iran **107** G5
Barmouth U.K. **47** H11
also known as Abermaw
Barmstedt Germany **48** G2
Barnagar India **96** B5
Barnala India **96** B3
Barnard, Mount Canada/U.S.A. **166** B3
Barnard Castle U.K. **47** K9
Barnato Australia **147** E2
Barnaul Rus. Fed. **80** C2
Barnegat U.S.A. **177** K6
Barnegat Bay U.S.A. **177** K6
Barne Inlet Antarctica **223** K1
Barnesboro U.S.A. **176** G5
Barnes Icecap Canada **165** L2
Barnesville *GA* U.S.A. **175** D5
Barnesville *MN* U.S.A. **178** C2
Barnet U.S.A. **177** M1
Barneveld Neth. **48** C3
Barneville-Carteret France **50** E3
Barney Top *mt.* U.S.A. **183** M4
Barnhart U.S.A. **179** B6
Barnjarn Aboriginal Land *res.* Australia **148** B2
Bârnova, Dealul *hill* Romania **58** I1
Barnsdall U.S.A. **178** C4
Barnsley U.K. **47** K10
Barnstable U.S.A. **177** O4
Barnstaple U.K. **47** H12
Barnstaple Bay U.K. *see* **Bideford Bay**
Barnwell U.S.A. **175** D5
Baro Nigeria **125** G4
Baroda India *see* **Vadodara**
Baroda India **96** C4
Baroda S. Africa **133** J8
Baroe S. Africa **133** I10
Baroghil Pass Afgh. **101** H2
Barong China **86** A2
Baron'ki Belarus **43** N8
Barons Range *hills* Australia **150** D5
Baroua Cent. Afr. Rep. **126** E3
Baro Wenz *r.* Eth. **128** B2
Barowka Belarus **42** I6
Barpeta India **97** F4
Bar Pla Soi Thai. *see* **Chon Buri**
Barqa, Gebel *mt.* Egypt **108** F9
Barqā al Ashqar *reg.* Yemen **105** D4
Barqā 'Damaj *well* Saudi Arabia **109** H9
Barques, Point Aux U.S.A. **173** K6
Barquisimeto Venez. **198** D2
Barr, Râs el *pt* Egypt **108** C6
Barra Brazil **202** D4
Barra *i.* U.K. **46** E7
also spelt Barraigh
Barraba Australia **147** F2
Barra Bonita Brazil **206** E9
Barra Bonita, Represa *resr* Brazil **206** E9
Barracão do Barreto Brazil **201** F2
Barrackville U.S.A. **176** E6
Barracouta, Cape S. Africa **132** F11
Barra da Estiva Brazil **202** D5
Barra de Navidad Mex. **184** D5
Barra de Santos *inlet* Brazil **206** G11
Barra de São Francisco Brazil **207** M5
Barra de São João Brazil **207** L9
Barra do Bugres Brazil **201** F3
Barra do Corda Brazil **202** C3
Barra do Cuanza Angola **127** B7
Barra do Cuieté Brazil **207** L6
Barra do Garças Brazil **206** A2
Barrado Mendes Brazil **202** D4
Barra do Piraí Brazil **207** J9
Barra do Rocha Brazil **207** M1
Barra do São Manuel Brazil **201** F1
Barra do Una Brazil **206** F11
Barra Falsa, Ponta da *pt* Moz. **131** G4
Barraigh *i.* U.K. *see* **Barra**
Barra Kruta Hond. **186** C4
Barra Longa Brazil **207** J7
Barra Mansa Brazil **207** I9
Barrâmîya Egypt **121** G3
Barranca Peru **200** A2
Barranca Venez. **198** C2
Barrancabermeja Col. **198** C3
Barranca del Cobre, Parque Natural *nature res.* Mex. **184** D3
Barrancas *r.* Arg. **204** C5
Barrancas *Barinas* Venez. **198** D2
Barrancas *Monagas* Venez. **199** F2
Barranco de Loba Col. **198** C2
Barranquilla *Atlántico* Col. **198** C2
Barranquilla *Guaviare* Col. **198** C4
Barranquita Peru **198** B6
Barras Brazil **202** D3
Barraute Canada **173** P2
Barrax Spain **55** I5
Barre *MA* U.S.A. **177** M3
Barre *VT* U.S.A. **177** M1
Barreal Arg. **204** C3
Barre des Ecrins *mt.* France **51** M8
Barreiras Brazil **202** C5
Barreirinha Brazil **199** G5
Barreirinhas Brazil **202** D2
Barreiro *r.* Brazil **206** A2
Barreiro do Nascimento Brazil **202** B4
Barreiros Brazil **202** F4
Barren Island India **95** G3
Barren Island Kiribati *see* **Starbuck Island**
Barren Islands U.S.A. **164** D4
Barretos Brazil **206** E7
Barrett U.S.A. **183** H9
Barrett, Mount *hill* Australia **150** D3
Barrhead Canada **167** H4
Barrhill N.Z. **153** F11
Barrī *i.* Saudi Arabia **104** C4
Barrie Canada **168** E4
Barrie Island Canada **173** K5
Barrier, Cape N.Z. **152** J4
Barrier Bay Antarctica **223** F2
Barrière Canada **166** F5
Barrier Range *hills* Australia **146** D2
Barrier Reef Belize **185** I5
Barrington Canada **169** H5
Barrington S. Africa **132** G10
Barrington, Mount Australia **147** F3
Barrington Lake Canada **167** K3
Barrington Tops National Park Australia **147** F3
Barro Alto Brazil **206** E2
Barrocão Brazil **207** J3
Barrolândia Brazil **207** N3
Barron U.S.A. **172** B5
Barronett U.S.A. **172** B5
Barroso Brazil **207** J8
Barrow Arg. **204** E5
Barrow *r.* Rep. of Ireland **47** F11
Barrow U.S.A. **164** D2
Barrow, Point U.S.A. **164** D2
Barrow Creek Australia **148** B4
Barrow-in-Furness U.K. **47** I9
Barrow Island Australia **150** A4
Barrow Island Nature Reserve Australia **150** A4
Barrow Range *hills* Australia **151** D5
Barrow Strait Canada **165** J2
Barr Smith Range *hills* Australia **151** C5
Barry U.K. **47** I12
Barrydale S. Africa **132** E10
Barry Islands Canada **167** I1
Barry Mountains Australia **147** E4
Barrys Bay Canada **168** E4
Barryton U.S.A. **173** H7
Barryville N.Z. **152** J6
Barryville U.S.A. **177** K4
Barsakel'mes, Ostrov *i.* Kazakh. **102** D3
Barsakel'messkiy Zapovednik *nature res.* Kazakh. **102** E3
Barsalogo Burkina **125** E3
Barsalpur India **96** B3
Barshatas Kazakh. **103** I2
formerly known as Chubartau
Barshi India *see* **Barsi**
Barsi India **94** B2
formerly spelt Barshi
Barstow U.S.A. **183** G7
Barstyčiai Lith. **42** C5
Barsuki Rus. Fed. **43** S7
Barsur India **94** D2
Bar-sur-Aube France **51** K4
Bar-sur-Seine France **51** K4
Bārta Latvia **42** C5
Bārta *r.* Latvia **42** C5
Bartang *r.* Tajik. **101** G2
Barth Germany **49** J1
Bartholomew, Bayou *r.* U.S.A. **175** A5
Bartica Guyana **199** G3
Bartın Turkey **106** C2
Bartle Frere, Mount Australia **149** E3
Bartles U.S.A. **176** C7
Bartles, Mount U.S.A. **183** N2
Bartlesville U.S.A. **178** C4
Bartlett *NE* U.S.A. **178** C3
Bartlett *NH* U.S.A. **177** N1
Bartlett Lake Canada **167** G2
Bartlett Reservoir U.S.A. **183** M8
Bartletts N.Z. **152** L6
Barton U.S.A. **177** M1
Bartonville U.S.A. **172** D10
Bartoszyce Poland **49** R1
Bartow U.S.A. **175** D7
Bartuva *r.* Lith. **42** C5
Baru, Isla de *i.* Col. **198** C2
Baruipur India **97** F5
Barūm Yemen **105** E5
Barumun *r.* Indon. **76** C2
Barung *i.* Indon. **77** F5
Barunga Australia *see* **Bamyili**
Barun-Torey, Ozero *l.* Rus. Fed. **85** G1
Barus Indon. **76** B2
Baruunharaa Mongolia **85** E1
Baruunsuu Mongolia **85** E3
Baruunturuun Mongolia **84** B1
Baruun Urt Mongolia **85** G2
Baruva India **95** E2
Barwa India **97** E5
Barwah India **96** C5
Barwala *Gujarat* India **96** A5
Barwala *Haryana* India **96** B3
Barwānah Iraq **109** N3
Barwani India **96** B5
Barwa Sagar India **96** C4
Barwice Poland **49** N2
Barwon *r.* Australia **147** E2
Baryatino Rus. Fed. **43** P7
Barybino Rus. Fed. **43** S6
Barycz *r.* Poland **49** N4
Barygaza India *see* **Bharuch**
Barysaw Belarus **43** J7
also spelt Borisov
Barysh Rus. Fed. **41** H5
Basaga Turkm. **101** F2
formerly spelt Bossaga
Bāsa'īdū Iran **100** C5
Basail Arg. **204** F2
Basăk, Tônlé *r.* Cambodia **79** D6
Basalt *r.* Australia **149** E3
Basalt Island *Hong Kong* China **87** [inset]
also known as Fo Shek Chau
Basanga Dem. Rep. Congo **127** E6
Basankusu Dem. Rep. Congo **126** C4
Basantpur India **97** E4
Basarabeasca Moldova **58** J2
formerly known as Romanovka; *formerly spelt* Bessarabka
Basarabi Romania **58** J4
Basargechar Armenia *see* **Vardenis**
Basavilbaso Arg. **204** F4
Basay Phil. **74** B4
Basco Phil. **74** B1
Bascombe Well Conservation Park *nature res.* Australia **146** B3
Bas-Congo *prov.* Dem. Rep. Congo **127** B6
formerly known as Bas-Zaïre
Bascuñán, Cabo *c.* Chile **204** C3
Bascuñana, Sierra de *mts* Spain **55** I4
Basedow Range *hills* Australia **148** B5
Basel Switz. **51** N5
English form Basle; *also spelt* Bâle
Basel-Mulhouse *airport* France **51** N5
Basentello *r.* Italy **56** I8
Basento *r.* Italy **57** I8
Basey Phil. **74** C4
Bashākerd, Kūhhā-ye *mts* Iran **100** D5
Bashan China *see* **Chongren**
Bashanta Rus. Fed. *see* **Gorodovikovsk**
Bashaw Canada **167** H4
Bashee *r.* S. Africa **133** M9
Bashee Bridge S. Africa **133** M8
Bashgul *r.* Afgh. **101** G3
Bāshī Iran **100** B4
Bashi Channel Taiwan **73** F2
Bashimuke Dem. Rep. Congo **127** E6
Ba'shīqah, Jabal *mt.* Iraq **109** O1
Bashkaus *r.* Rus. Fed. **88** D1
Bashkiria *aut. rep.* Rus. Fed. *see* Bashkortostan, Respublika
Bashkirskaya A.S.S.R. *aut. rep.* Rus. Fed. *see* Bashkortostan, Respublika
Bashkirskiy Zapovednik *nature res.* Rus. Fed. **102** D1
Bashkortostan, Respublika *aut. rep.* Rus. Fed. **102** D1
formerly known as Bashkiria *or* Bashkirskaya A.S.S.R.
Bashmakovo Rus. Fed. **41** G5
Bāsht Iran **100** B4
Bashtanka Ukr. **41** E7
Bashūri, Ra's *pt* Yemen **105** F5
Basi India **96** C4
Basia India **97** E5
Basilaki Island P.N.G. **149** F1
Basilan *i.* Phil. **74** B5
Basilan Strait Phil. **74** B5
Basildon U.K. **47** M12
Basile U.S.A. **179** D6
Basile, Pico *mt.* Equat. Guinea **125** H6
Basilicata *admin. reg.* Italy **57** H8
Basin U.S.A. **180** E3
Basingstoke U.K. **47** K12
Basin Lake Canada **167** J4
Bāsīra *r.* Iraq **107** F4
Basirhat India **97** F5
Basīț, Ra's al *pt* Syria **108** G2
Baskakovka Rus. Fed. **43** P7
Başkale Turkey **107** F3
Baskatong, Réservoir Canada **168** F4
Baskerville, Cape Australia **150** C3
Başkomutan Milli Parkı *nat. park* Turkey **106** B3
Baskunchak, Ozero *l.* Rus. Fed. **102** A2
Basle Switz. *see* **Basel**
Basmat India **94** C2
Baso *i.* Indon. **76** C3
Basoda India **96** C5
Basoko Dem. Rep. Congo **126** D4
Basongo Dem. Rep. Congo **126** D6
Basotu Tanz. **129** B6
Basque Country *aut. comm.* Spain *see* **País Vasco**
Basra Iraq **107** F5
also spelt Al Başrah
Bassano Canada **167** H5
Bassano del Grappa Italy **56** D3
Bassar Togo **125** F4
Bassas da India *reef* Indian Ocean **131** H4
Bassas de Pedro Padua Bank *sea feature* India **94** B3
also known as Munyal-Par
Bassawa Côte d'Ivoire **124** D4
Bassein Myanmar **78** A4
also spelt Puthein; *formerly spelt* Pathein
Bassein *r.* Myanmar **78** A4
Basse-Kotto *pref.* Cent. Afr. Rep. **126** D3
Basse-Normandie *admin. reg.* France **50** F4
Basse Santa Su Gambia **124** B3

▶**Basse-Terre** Guadeloupe **187** H3
Capital of Guadeloupe.

Basse-Terre *i.* Guadeloupe **187** H3

▶**Basseterre** St Kitts and Nevis **187** H3
Capital of St Kitts and Nevis.

Bassett *NE* U.S.A. **178** C3
Bassett *VA* U.S.A. **176** F9
Bassett Peak U.S.A. **183** N9
Bassikounou Mauritania **124** D3
Bassila Benin **125** F4
Basso, Plateau de Chad **120** D5
Bass Strait Australia **147** E4
Basswood Lake Canada **168** B3
Basswood Lake U.S.A. **172** B2
Båstad Sweden **45** K4
Bastak Iran **100** C5
Bastānābād Iran **100** A2
Basti India **97** D4
Bastia *Corse* France **51** P10
Bastia Italy **56** E5
Bastian U.S.A. **176** D8
Bastogne Belgium **51** L2
Bastos Brazil **206** C8
Bastrop *LA* U.S.A. **175** B5
Bastrop *TX* U.S.A. **179** C6
Bastuträsk Sweden **44** M2
Basu, Tanjung *pt* Indon. **76** C3
Basul *r.* Pak. **101** F5
Basuo China *see* **Dongfang**
Basutoland *country* Africa *see* **Lesotho**
Basya *r.* Belarus **43** M8
Bas-Zaïre *prov.* Dem. Rep. Congo *see* **Bas-Congo**
Bat *mt.* Croatia **56** I5
Bat, Al-Khutm and Al-Ayn *tourist site* Oman **105** G3
Bata Equat. Guinea **125** H6
Bataan Peninsula Phil. **74** B3
Batabanó, Golfo de *b.* Cuba **186** C2
Batac Phil. **74** B2
Batagay Rus. Fed. **39** N3
Batagay-Alyta Rus. Fed. **39** N3
Bataguaçu Brazil **206** A8
Batak Bulg. **58** F7
Batakan Indon. **77** F4
Batala India **96** B3
Batalha Brazil **202** D3
formerly known as Belo Monte
Batalha Port. **54** C5
Batam *i.* Indon. **76** D2
Batama Dem. Rep. Congo **126** E4
Batamay Rus. Fed. **39** M3
Batamshinskiy Kazakh. **102** D2
also known as Batamshy
Batamshy Kazakh. *see* **Batamshinskiy**
Batan *i.* Phil. **74** B1
Batan *i.* Phil. **74** C3
Batang China **86** A2
also known as Xiaqiong
Batang Indon. **77** E4
Batangafo Cent. Afr. Rep. **126** C3
Batang Ali National Park *Sarawak* Malaysia **77** F2
Batangas Phil. **74** B3
Batanghari *r.* Indon. **76** D3
Batangpele *i.* Indon. **75** D3
Batangtoru Indon. **76** B2
Batan Islands Phil. **74** B1
Bátaszék Hungary **49** P9
Batatais Brazil **206** F7
Batavia Indon. *see* **Jakarta**
Batavia *NY* U.S.A. **176** G3
Batavia *OH* U.S.A. **176** A6
Bataysk Rus. Fed. **41** F7
Batbatan *i.* Phil. **74** B4
Batchawana Canada **173** I3
Batchawana *r.* Canada **173** I4
Batchawana Bay Canada **173** I4
Batchawana Mountain *hill* Canada **168** C4
Batchelor Australia **148** A2
Bătdâmbâng Cambodia **79** C5
also spelt Battambang
Bateemeucica, Gunung *mt.* Indon. **76** A1
Batéké, Plateaux Congo **126** B5
Batemans Bay Australia **147** F3
Båteng Norway **44** N1
Batesburg U.S.A. **175** D5
Bates Range *hills* Australia **151** C5
Batesville *AR* U.S.A. **174** B5
Batesville *MS* U.S.A. **174** B5
Batetskiy Rus. Fed. **43** L3
Bath *N.B.* Canada **169** H4
Bath *Ont.* Canada **173** Q6
Bath U.K. **47** J12
Bath *ME* U.S.A. **177** P2
Bath *NY* U.S.A. **177** H3
Bath *PA* U.S.A. **177** J5
Batha *pref.* Chad **120** C6
Batha *watercourse* Chad **120** C6
Bathinda India **96** B3
also spelt Bhatinda
Bathurst Australia **147** F3
Bathurst Canada **169** H4
Bathurst Gambia *see* **Banjul**
Bathurst S. Africa **133** K10
Bathurst, Cape Canada **164** G2
Bathurst Bay Australia **149** E2
Bathurst Inlet Canada **167** I1
Bathurst Inlet *inlet* Canada **167** I1
Bathurst Island Australia **148** A1
Bathurst Island Canada **165** J2
Batī Eth. **128** D2
Batia Benin **125** F4
Batié Burkina **124** E4
Batikala, Tanjung *pt* Indon. **75** B3
Batı Menteşe Dağları *mts* Turkey **59** I11
Bāţin, Wādī al *watercourse* Asia **105** D1
Batista, Serra da *hills* Brazil **202** D4
Batı Toroslar *mts* Turkey **106** B3
Batken Kyrg. **103** G5
Batken *admin. div.* Kyrg. **103** G5
Bāţlāq-e Gavkhūnī *marsh* Iran **100** C3
Batman Turkey **107** E3
Batna Alg. **123** G2
Baţn aţ Ţarfā' *depr.* Saudi Arabia **105** E3
Batočina *Srbija* Yugo. **58** C4
Batok, Bukit Sing. **76** [inset]
Batok, Bukit *hill* Sing. **76** [inset]

▶**Baton Rouge** U.S.A. **175** B6
State capital of Louisiana.

Batopilas Mex. **184** D3
Batote Jammu and Kashmir **96** B2
Batouri Cameroon **125** I5
Batrā' *tourist site* Jordan *see* **Petra**
Batrā, Jabal *mt.* Saudi Arabia **104** B2
Batrā', Jabal al *mt.* Jordan **108** G8
Ba Tri Vietnam **79** D6
Batroûn Lebanon **108** G3
Båtsfjord Norway **44** O1
Bat-Sot Rus. Fed. **84** B1
Battambang Cambodia *see* **Bătdâmbâng**
Batti India **96** B3
Batticaloa Sri Lanka **94** D5
Batti Malv *i.* India **95** G4
Battipaglia Italy **57** G8
Battle *r.* Canada **167** I4
Battle Creek *r.* Australia **148** A2
Battle Creek *r.* Canada/U.S.A. **167** I5
Battle Creek U.S.A. **173** H8
Battlefields Zimbabwe **131** F3
Battleford Canada **167** I4
Battle Mountain U.S.A. **183** H1
Battle Mountain *mt.* U.S.A. **183** G1
Battura Glacier Jammu and Kashmir **96** B1
Batu *mt.* Eth. **128** C3
Batu, Bukit *mt.* *Sarawak* Malaysia **77** F2
Batu, Pulau-pulau *is* Indon. **76** B3
Batu, Tanjung *pt* Indon. **77** G2
Batuata *i.* Indon. **75** B4
Batuayau, Bukit *mt.* Indon. **77** F2
Batubetumbang Indon. **77** D3
Batu Bora, Bukit *mt.* *Sarawak* Malaysia **77** F2
Batudaka *i.* Indon. **75** B3
Batu Gajah Malaysia **76** C1
Batuhitam, Tanjung *pt* Indon. **75** B3
Batui Indon. **75** B3
Batulaki Phil. **74** C5
Batulicin Indon. **77** G3
Batulilangmebang, Gunung *mt.* Indon. **77** F2
Batum Georgia *see* **Bat'umi**
Bat'umi Georgia **107** E2
English form Batum
Batumonga Indon. **76** C3
Batu Pahat Malaysia **76** C2
Batu Puteh, Gunung *mt.* Malaysia **76** C1
Baturaja Indon. **76** D4
Baturetno Indon. **77** E5
Baturino Rus. Fed. **43** N6
Batusangkar Indon. **76** C3
Batyrevo Rus. Fed. **40** H5
Batys Qazaqstan Oblysy *admin. div.* Kazakh. *see* **Zapadnyy Kazakhstan**
Batz, Île de *i.* France **50** B4
Bau *r.* Brazil **201** G1
Bau *Sarawak* Malaysia **77** E2
Baubau Indon. **75** B4
Baucau East Timor *see* **Baukau**
Bauchi Nigeria **125** H4
Bauchi *state* Nigeria **125** H4
Bauda India **95** E1
Baudette U.S.A. **178** D1
Baudo, Serranía de *mts* Col. **198** B3
Baudouinville Dem. Rep. Congo *see* **Moba**
Bauet *well* Eth. **128** E3
Baugé France **50** F5
Bauges *mts* France **51** M7
Baukau East Timor **75** C5
also known as Baucau
Bauld, Cape Canada **169** K3
Baumann Fiord *inlet* Canada **165** K2
Baume-les-Dames France **51** M5
Baunei *Sardegna* Italy **57** B8
Bauru Brazil **206** D9
Baús Brazil **206** A5
Baushar Oman **105** G3
Bauska Latvia **42** F5
Bautino Kazakh. **102** B3
Bautzen Germany **49** L4
Bauyrzhan Momysh-Uly Kazakh. **103** G4
formerly known as Burnoye
Bavaria *land* Germany *see* **Bayern**
Bavaria *reg.* Germany **48** I7
also known as Bayern
Bavda India **94** B2
Båven *l.* Sweden **45** L4
Baviaanskloofberge *mts* S. Africa **132** H10
Bavispe Mex. **184** C2
Bavispe *r.* Mex. **184** C2
Bavla India **96** B5
Bavleny Rus. Fed. **43** U5
Bavly Rus. Fed. **40** J5
Baw Myanmar **78** A3
Bawal India **96** C3
Bawal *i.* Indon. **77** E3
Bawan Indon. **77** F3
Bawang, Tanjung *pt* Indon. **77** E3
Baw Baw National Park Australia **147** E4
Bawdwin Myanmar **78** B3
Bawean *i.* Indon. **77** F4
Bawiti Egypt **121** F2
Bawku Ghana **125** E4
Bawlake Myanmar **78** B4
Bawolung China **86** B2
Baxi China **86** B1
Baxian China *see* **Banan**
Baxian China *see* **Bazhou**
Baxkorgan China **88** E4
Baxley U.S.A. **175** D6
Baxoi China **86** A2
also known as Baima
Bay China *see* **Baicheng**
Bay *admin. reg.* Somalia **128** D4
Bay, Laguna de *lag.* Phil. **74** B3
Bay, Réserve de *nature res.* Mali **124** E3
Baya *r.* Côte d'Ivoire **124** E5
Bayad Alg. **57** A13
Bayamo Cuba **186** D2
Bayamón Puerto Rico **187** G3
Bayan China **82** B3
Bayan China *see* **Hualong**
Bayan Indon. **77** G5
Bayan *Arhangay* Mongolia **84** D2
Bayan *Govĭ-Altay* Mongolia **84** B2
Bayan *Hentiy* Mongolia **85** F1
Bayana India **96** C4
Bayanaul Kazakh. **103** H2
Bayanbulag *Bayanhongor* Mongolia **84** C2
Bayanbulag *Bayanhongor* Mongolia **84** C2
Bayanbulag *Hentiy* Mongolia **85** F2
Bayanbulak China **88** D2
Bayandelger Mongolia **85** F2
Bayang, Pegunungan *mts* Indon. **77** E2
Bayanga-Didi Cent. Afr. Rep. **126** B3
Bayan Gol China *see* **Dengkou**
Bayangol Mongolia **84** B2
Bayangol Rus. Fed. **84** D1
Bayan Har Shan *mts* China **84** B5
Bayan Har Shankou *pass* China **86** A1
Bayanhongor Mongolia **84** D2
Bayanhongor *prov.* Mongolia **84** C2
Bayan Hot China **85** E4
also known as Alxa Zuoqi
Bayanhushuu Mongolia **84** D2
Bayan-Kol *Respublika Tyva* Rus. Fed. **84** B1
Bayan-Kol Rus. Fed. **88** G1
Bayan Mod China **84** E3
Bayan Nuru China **84** E3
also known as Xar Burd
Bayano, Lago *l.* Panama **186** D5
Bayan Obo Kuangqu China **85** F3
Bayan-Ölgiy *prov.* Mongolia **84** A1
Bayan-Ovoo *Govĭ-Altay* Mongolia **84** B2
Bayan-Ovoo *Hentiy* Mongolia **85** F1
Bayan-Ovoo *Hentiy* Mongolia **85** G2
Bayan Qagan China **85** G3
also known as Qahar Youyi Houqi
Bayansayr Mongolia **84** C2
Bayan Shan *mt.* China **84** C4
Bayanteeg Mongolia **84** D2
Bayan Tohoi China **85** H1
also known as Ewenkizu Zizhiqi
Bayantöhöm Mongolia **85** E2
Bayan Ul Hot China **85** H2
also known as Xi Ujimqin Qi
Bayan Uul *mts* Mongolia **84** A1
Bayard *NE* U.S.A. **178** B3
Bayard *WV* U.S.A. **176** F6
Bayasgalant Mongolia **85** G2
Bayat Turkey **106** B3
Bayawan Phil. **74** B4
Bayāẓ Iran **100** C4
Baybay Phil. **74** C4
Bay Bulls Canada **169** K4
Bayburt Turkey **107** E2
Baychunas Kazakh. **102** C3
also spelt Bayshonas
Bay City *MI* U.S.A. **173** J7
Bay City *TX* U.S.A. **179** C6
Baydā, Jabal al *hill* Saudi Arabia **104** B2
Baydaratskaya Guba Rus. Fed. **40** M1
Baydhabo Somalia **128** D4
formerly known as Baidoa
Baydrag Mongolia **84** C2
Baydrag Gol *r.* Mongolia **84** C2
Bay du Nord Wilderness *nature res.* Canada **169** K3
Baydzhansay Kazakh. *see* **Bayzhansay**
Bayelsa *state* Nigeria **125** G5
Bayerische Rhön *park* Germany **48** G5
Bayerischer Wald *mts* Germany **49** J6
Bayerischer Wald *nat. park* Germany **49** J6
Bayern *land* Germany **51** R3
English form Bavaria
Bayern *reg.* Germany *see* **Bavaria**
Bayer Wald, Nationalpark *nat. park* Germany **49** K7
Bayeux France **50** F3
Bayeva Belarus **43** M7
Bayevo Rus. Fed. **103** J1
Bayfield Canada **173** L7
Baygakum Kazakh. **103** F3
Bayganin Kazakh. **102** C2
formerly known as Karaulkel'dy
Baygora Kazakh. **103** E1
Bayḩan al Qişab Yemen **105** D5
Bayındır Turkey **106** A3
Bay Islands *is* Hond. *see* **La Bahía, Islas de**
Bayizhen China **89** F6
Bayjī Iraq **107** E4
also spelt Baiji
Baykadam Kazakh. *see* **Saudakent**
Baykal, Ozero *l.* Rus. Fed. *see* **Baikal, Lake**
Baykal-Amur Magistral Rus. Fed. **82** C1
Baykal Range *mts* Rus. Fed. *see* **Baykal'skiy Khrebet**
Baykal'sk Rus. Fed. **84** E1
Baykal'skiy Khrebet *mts* Rus. Fed. **81** H2
English form Baykal Range
Baykal'skiy Zapovednik *nature res.* Rus. Fed. **85** E1
Baykan Turkey **107** E3
Bay-Khaak Rus. Fed. **84** B1
Bay-Khozha Kazakh. **103** E3
Baykibashevo Rus. Fed. **40** K5
Baykit Rus. Fed. **39** J3
Baykonur *Karagandinskaya Oblast'* Kazakh. **103** F3
Baykonur *Kzyl-Ordinskaya Oblast'* Kazakh. **103** E3
also spelt Baykonyr *or* Bayqongyr; *formerly known as* Leninsk *or* Toretam *or* Tyuratam
Baykonyr Kazakh. *see* **Baykonur**
Bayley Point Aboriginal Reserve Australia **148** C3
Baymak Rus. Fed. **102** D1
Bay Minette U.S.A. **175** C6
Baynūna'h *reg.* U.A.E. **105** F3
Bay of Islands Maritime and Historic Park *nature res.* N.Z. **152** I3
Bay of Plenty *admin. reg.* N.Z. **152** K5
Bayombong Phil. **74** B2
Bayona Spain *see* **Baiona**
Bayonne France **50** E9
historically known as Lapurdum
Bayo Point Phil. **74** B4
Bayóvar Peru **198** A6
Bay Point Phil. **74** A4
Bay Port U.S.A. **173** J7
Bayqadam Kazakh. *see* **Saudakent**
Bayqongyr Kazakh. *see* **Baykonur**
Bayramaly Turkm. **103** E5
Bayramiç Turkey **106** A3
Bayreuth Germany **48** I6
Bayrūt Lebanon *see* **Beirut**
Bay St Louis U.S.A. **175** B6
Baysh *watercourse* Saudi Arabia **104** C4
Bayshonas Kazakh. *see* **Baychunas**
Bay Springs U.S.A. **175** B6
Baysun Uzbek. **103** F5
also spelt Boysun
Baysuntau, Gory *mts* Uzbek. **103** F5
Bayt al Faqīh Yemen **104** C5
Baytik-Shan *mts* China **84** A2
Bayt Lahm West Bank *see* **Bethlehem**
Baytown U.S.A. **179** D6
Bayu Indon. **75** B3
Bayunglincir Indon. **76** C3
Bay View N.Z. **152** K7
Bayy al Kabīr, Wādī *watercourse* Libya **120** B2
Bayyrqum Kazakh. *see* **Bairkum**
Bayzhansay Kazakh. **103** G4
also spelt Baydzhansay
Baza Spain **55** I7
Baza, Sierra de *mts* Spain **55** I7
Bazarchulan Kazakh. **102** B2
formerly spelt Bazarshulan
Bazardyuzi, Gora *mt.* Azer./Rus. Fed. **107** F2
Bāzār-e Māsāl Iran **100** B2
Bazarkhanym, Gora *mt.* Uzbek. **103** G5
Bazar-Korgon Kyrg. **103** H4
also spelt Bazar Kurgan
Bazar Kurgan Kyrg. *see* **Bazar-Korgon**
Bazarnyy Karabulak Rus. Fed. **41** H5
Bazarnyy Syzgan Rus. Fed. **41** H5
Bazarshulan Kazakh. *see* **Bazarchulan**
Bazartobe Kazakh. **102** B2
Bazaruto, Ilha do *i.* Moz. **131** G4
Bazas France **50** F8
Bazdar Pak. **101** F5
Bazhong China **86** C2
Bazhou China **85** H4
formerly known as Baxian
Bazin *r.* Canada **169** F4
Baziwehn Liberia **124** C4
Bazmān Iran **101** E5
Bazmān, Kūh-e *mt.* Iran **101** E4
Bcharre Lebanon **108** H3
Be *r.* Vietnam **79** D6
Bé, Nossi *i.* Madag. *see* **Bé, Nosy**
Bé, Nosy *i.* Madag. **131** [inset] K2
formerly spelt Bé, Nossi
Beach U.S.A. **178** B2
Beachburg Canada **173** Q5
Beach City U.S.A. **176** D5
Beach Haven U.S.A. **177** K6
Beachport Australia **146** D4
Beachy Head U.K. **47** M13
Beacon Australia **151** B6
Beacon U.S.A. **177** L4
Beacon Bay S. Africa **133** L9
Beaconsfield Australia **147** E5
Beagle, Canal *sea chan.* Arg. **205** C9
Beagle Bank *reef* Australia **150** C2
Beagle Bay Australia **150** C3
Beagle Bay Aboriginal Reserve Australia **150** C3
Beagle Gulf Australia **148** A2
Beagle Island Australia **151** A6
Bealanana Madag. **131** [inset] K2
Béal an Átha Rep. of Ireland *see* **Ballina**
Béal Átha na Sluaighe Rep. of Ireland *see* **Ballinasloe**
Beampingaratra *mts* Madag. **131** [inset] J5
Beandrarezona Madag. **131** [inset] K2
Bear *r.* U.S.A. **180** D4
Bearalváhki Norway *see* **Berlevåg**
Bear Creek Canada **166** B1
Bear Creek *r.* U.S.A. **178** B4
Beardmore Glacier Antarctica **223** L1
Beardmore Reservoir Australia **147** F1
Beardstown U.S.A. **174** B3
Bear Island *i.* Arctic Ocean *see* **Bjørnøya**
Bear Island Canada **173** M4
Bear Island *i.* Canada **168** D2
Bear Island *i.* Rep. of Ireland **47** C12
Bear Lake *l.* Canada **167** L4
Bear Lake U.S.A. **172** G6
Bear Lake *l.* U.S.A. **180** E4
Bearma *r.* India **96** C4
Bear Mountain U.S.A. **178** B3
Bearnaraigh *i.* U.K. *see* **Berneray**
Bear Paw Mountain U.S.A. **180** E2
Bearpaw Mountains U.S.A. **180** E2
Bear Peninsula Antarctica **222** Q2
Bearskin Lake Canada **168** B2
Beas *r.* India **96** B3
Beasain Spain **55** I1
Beata, Cabo *c.* Dom. Rep. **187** F3
Beata, Isla *i.* Dom. Rep. **187** F3
Beatrice U.S.A. **178** C3
Beatrice Zimbabwe **131** F3
Beatrice, Cape Australia **148** C2
Beatton *r.* Canada **166** F3
Beatty U.S.A. **183** H5
Beattyville Canada **168** E3
Beattyville U.S.A. **176** B8
Beaucaire France **51** K9
Beauchêne, Lac *l.* Canada **173** O4
Beauchene Island Falkland Is **205** F9
Beaudesert Australia **147** G1
Beaufort Australia **147** D4
Beaufort *Sabah* Malaysia **77** F1
Beaufort *NC* U.S.A. **174** E5
Beaufort *SC* U.S.A. **175** D5
Beaufort Castle *tourist site* Lebanon **108** G4
Beaufort-en-Vallée France **50** F5
Beaufort Island *Hong Kong* China **87** [inset]
also known as Lo Chau
Beaufort Sea Canada/U.S.A. **164** G2
Beaufort West S. Africa **132** G9
Beaugency France **50** H5
Beaulieu-sur-Dordogne France **50** H8
Beauly U.K. **46** H6
Beauly *r.* U.K. **46** H6
Beaumont Belgium **51** K2
Beaumont N.Z. **153** D13
Beaumont *CA* U.S.A. **183** H8
Beaumont *MS* U.S.A. **175** B6
Beaumont *TX* U.S.A. **179** D6
Beaumont-de-Lomagne France **50** G9
Beaumont-le-Roger France **50** G3
Beaune France **51** K5
Beaune-La Rolande France **51** I4
Beauraing Belgium **51** K2
Beauséjour Canada **167** L5
Beauvais France **51** I3
Beauval Canada **167** J4
Beauvoir-sur-Mer France **50** D6
Beaver *r.* *Alta/Sask.* Canada **167** J4
Beaver *r.* *Ont.* Canada **168** C2
Beaver *r.* *Y.T.* Canada **166** C2
Beaver *r.* *Y.T.* Canada **166** E3
Beaver *OK* U.S.A. **178** B4
Beaver *UT* U.S.A. **183** L3
Beaver *r.* *OK* U.S.A. **178** B4
Beaver *r.* *UT* U.S.A. **183** L2
Beaver City U.S.A. **178** C3
Beaver Creek Canada **166** A2
Beaver Creek *r.* *MO* U.S.A. **178** D4
Beaver Creek *r.* *MT* U.S.A. **180** F2
Beaver Creek *r.* *ND* U.S.A. **178** B2
Beaver Creek *r.* *NE* U.S.A. **178** C3
Beaver Dam *KY* U.S.A. **174** C4
Beaver Dam *WI* U.S.A. **172** E7
Beaver Dam Lake U.S.A. **172** E7
Beaver Falls U.S.A. **176** E5
Beaver Glacier Antarctica **223** D2
Beaverhead *r.* U.S.A. **180** D3
Beaverhead Mountains U.S.A. **180** D3
Beaverhill Lake Canada **167** H4
Beaver Hill Lake Canada **167** M4
Beaver Island U.S.A. **172** H5
Beaverlodge Canada **166** G4
Beaver Run Reservoir U.S.A. **176** F5
Beaverton *MI* U.S.A. **173** I7
Beaverton *OR* U.S.A. **180** B3
Beawar India **96** B4
Beazley Arg. **204** D4
Bebedero, Salina del *salt pan* Arg. **204** D4
Bébédjia Chad **126** C2
Bebedouro Brazil **206** E7
Beberibe Brazil **202** E3
Bebra Germany **48** G5
Bêca China **86** A2
Beccles U.K. **47** N11
Bečej *Vojvodina, Srbija* Yugo. **58** B3
also known as Óbecse
Becerreá Spain **54** D2
Becerrero *hill* Spain **54** G7
Becerro, Cayos *is* Hond. **186** C4
Béchar Alg. **123** E3
formerly known as Colomb-Béchar
Becharof Lake U.S.A. **164** D4
Bechevinka Rus. Fed. **43** S2
Bechuanaland *country* Africa *see* **Botswana**
Beçin Turkey **59** I11
Becker, Mount Antarctica **222** T1
Beckley U.S.A. **176** D8
Becks N.Z. **153** D12
Becky Peak U.S.A. **183** J2
Beclean Romania **58** F1
Bečva *r.* Czech Rep. **49** O6
Beda Häyk' *l.* Eth. **128** D2
Bédarieux France **51** J9
Bedeau Alg. *see* **Ras el Ma**
Bedel', Pereval *pass* China/Kyrg. *see* **Bedel Pass**
Bedelē Eth. **128** C2
Bedel Pass China/Kyrg. **88** B3
also known as Bedel', Pereval
Bedford Canada **169** I4
Bedford S. Africa **133** K9
Bedford U.K. **47** L11
Bedford *IA* U.S.A. **178** D3
Bedford *IN* U.S.A. **174** C4
Bedford *KY* U.S.A. **174** C4
Bedford *NY* U.S.A. **177** L4
Bedford *PA* U.S.A. **176** G5
Bedford *VA* U.S.A. **176** F8
Bedford, Cape Australia **149** E2
Bedford Downs Australia **150** D3
Bedford Heights U.S.A. **176** D4
Bedi India **96** A5
Bedinggong Indon. **77** D3
Bednja *r.* Croatia **56** I2
Bednodem'yanovsk Rus. Fed. **41** G5

index

B

Beshir Turkm. 103 F5
Beshkent Uzbek. 103 F5
Beshneh Iran 100 C4
Besh-Ter, Gora mt. Kyrg./Uzbek. 103 G4
also known as Besh-Ter Toosu or Beshtor Toghi
Besh-Ter Toosu mt. Kyrg./Uzbek. see Besh-Ter, Gora
Beshtor Toghi mt. Kyrg./Uzbek. see Besh-Ter, Gora
Besikama Indon. 75 C5
Beşiri Turkey 107 E3
Besitang Indon. 76 B1
Beskid Niski hills Poland 49 S6
Beskid Sądecki mts Poland 49 R6
Beskra Alg. see Biskra
Beslan Rus. Fed. 41 H8
Beslet mt. Bulg. 58 E7
Besna Kobila mt. Yugo. 58 D6
Besnard Lake Canada 167 J4
Besni Turkey 107 D3
Besor watercourse Israel 108 F6
Beşparmak Dağları mts Cyprus see Pentadaktylos Range
Béssao Chad 126 B3
Bessarabka Moldova see Basarabeasca
Bessaye, Gora mt. Kazakh. 103 G4
Bessemer AL U.S.A. 175 C5
Bessemer MI U.S.A. 172 C4
Besshoky, Gora hill Kazakh. 102 C3
Bessines-sur-Gartempe France 50 H6
Bessonovka Rus. Fed. 41 H5
Bessou, Mont de hill France 51 I7
Bestamak Aktyubinskaya Oblast' Kazakh. 102 C2
Bestamak Vostochnyy Kazakhstan Kazakh. 103 I2
Bestobe Kazakh. 103 H1
Beswick Australia 148 B2
Beswick Aboriginal Land res. Australia 148 B2
Betafo Madag. 131 [inset] J3
Betanzos Bol. 200 D4
Betanzos Spain 54 C1
Bétaré Oya Cameroon 125 I5
Bete Grise U.S.A. 172 F3
Bete Hor Eth. 128 C2
Bétérou Benin 125 F4
Betet i. Indon. 76 D3
Beth, Oued r. Morocco 122 D2
Bethal S. Africa 133 N3
Bethanie Namibia 130 C5
Bethany MO U.S.A. 178 D3
Bethany OK U.S.A. 179 C5
Bethari Nepal 97 D4
Bethel AK U.S.A. 164 C3
Bethel ME U.S.A. 177 O1
Bethel OH U.S.A. 176 A7
Bethesda MD U.S.A. 177 H6
Bethesda OH U.S.A. 176 D5
Bethesdaweg S. Africa 133 I8
Bethlehem S. Africa 133 M5
Bethlehem U.S.A. 177 J5
Bethlehem West Bank 108 G6
also spelt Bayt Lahm or Bet Lehem
Bethlesdorp S. Africa 133 J10
Bethulie S. Africa 133 J7
Béthune France 51 I2
Betijoque Venez. 198 D2
Betim Brazil 207 I6
Betioky Madag. 131 [inset] J4
Betiri, Gunung mt. Indon. 77 F5
Bet Lehem West Bank see Bethlehem
Betlitsa Rus. Fed. 43 O7
Betma India 96 B5
Betong Thai. 79 C7
Betoota Australia 149 D5
Bétou Congo 126 C4
Betpak-Dala plain Kazakh. 103 G3
Betrandraka Madag. 131 [inset] J3
Betroka Madag. 131 [inset] J4
Bet She'an Israel 108 G5
Betsiamites Canada 169 G3
Betsiamites r. Canada 169 G3
Betsiboka r. Madag. 131 [inset] J2
Betsie, Point U.S.A. 172 G6
Betsy Bay Bahamas 187 E2
Betsy Lake U.S.A. 173 H4
Bettendorf U.S.A. 172 C9
Bettiah India 97 E4
Betul India 96 C5
Betwa r. India 96 C4
Betws-y-coed U.K. 47 I10
Betygala Lith. 42 E6
Béu Angola 127 B6
Beulah U.S.A. 178 B2
Beurfou well Chad 120 B6
Beuthen Poland see Bytom
Beuvron r. France 50 H5
Beverley U.K. 47 L10
Beverly MA U.S.A. 177 O3
Beverly OH U.S.A. 176 D6
Beverly Hills U.S.A. 182 F7
Beverungen Germany 48 G4
Beverwijk Neth. 48 B3
Bex Switz. 51 N6
Bextograk China 88 D4
Beyağaç Turkey 59 J11
Beyazköy Turkey 58 I7
Beyce Turkey see Orhaneli
Beydağ Turkey 59 J10
Bey Dağları mts Turkey 106 B3
Beykonak Turkey 108 B1
Beykoz Turkey 106 B2
Beyla Guinea 124 C4
Beylagan Azer. see Beyläqan
Beyläqan Azer. 107 F3
also spelt Beylagan; formerly known as Zhdanovsk
Beylul Eritrea 121 I6
Beyneu Kazakh. 102 C3
Beyoneisu Retugan i. Japan 91 F9
Beypazarı Turkey 106 B2
Beypınarı Turkey 107 D3
Beypore India 94 B4
Beyra Somalia 128 E3
Beyram Iran 100 C5
Beyrouth Lebanon see Beirut
Beyşehir Turkey 106 B3
Beyşehir Gölü l. Turkey 106 B3
Beytüşşebap Turkey 107 E3
also known as Elki
Bezameh Iran 100 D3
Bezbozhnik Rus. Fed. 40 I4
Bezdan Vojvodina, Srbija Yugo. 56 K3
Bezenjān Iran 100 D4
Bezhanitskaya Vozvyshennost' hills Rus. Fed. 43 K5
Bezhanitsy Rus. Fed. 43 K5
Bezhanovo Bulg. 58 F5
Bezhetsk Rus. Fed. 43 R4
Bezhetskiy Verkh reg. Rus. Fed. 43 R4
Béziers France 51 J9
Bezmein Turkm. see Byuzmeyin
Bezwada India see Vijayawada
Bhabhar India 96 A4
Bhabra India 96 B5
Bhabua India 97 D4
Bhachau India 96 A5
Bhadar r. India 96 A5
Bhadarwah Jammu and Kashmir 96 B2
Bhadaur India 101 H4
Bhadgaon Nepal see Bhaktapur
Bhadohi India 97 D4
Bhadra India 96 B3
Bhadrachalam India 94 D2
Bhadrachalam Road Station India see Kottagudem
Bhadrakh India 97 E5
Bhadra Reservoir India 94 B3
Bhadravati India 94 B3
Bhag Pak. 101 F4
Bhagalpur India 97 E4
Bhagirathi r. India 97 F5
Bhainsa India 94 C2
Bhainsdehi India 96 C5
Bhairab Bazar Bangl. 97 F4
Bhairawa Nepal 97 D4
also known as Siddharthanagar; also spelt Bhairawaha
Bhairawaha Nepal see Bhairawa
Bhairi Hol mt. Pak. 101 F5
Bhakkar Pak. 101 G4
Bhaktapur Nepal 97 E4
also known as Bhadgaon
Bhalki India 94 C2
Bhalwal Pak. 101 H3
Bhamgarh India 96 C5
Bhamo Myanmar 78 B2
Bhandara India 96 C5
Bhander India 96 C4
Bhanjanagar India 95 E2
Bhanpura India 96 B4
Bhanrer Range hills India 96 C5
Bharat country Asia see India
Bharatpur India 96 C4
Bharatpur Nepal 97 E4
Bhareli r. India 97 G4
Bhari r. Pak. 101 E5
Bharthana India 96 C4
Bharuch India 96 B5
formerly known as Broach; historically known as Barygaza or Bhrigukaccha
Bhatapara India 97 D5
Bhatghar Lake India 94 B2
Bhatiapara Ghat Bangl. 97 F5
Bhatinda India see Bathinda
Bhatkal India 94 B3
Bhatnair India see Hanumangarh
Bhatpara India 97 F5
Bhaun Gharibwal Pak. 101 H3
Bhavani India 94 C4
Bhavani r. India 94 C4
Bhavani Sagar l. India 94 C4
Bhavnagar India 96 B5
Bhawana Pak. 101 H4
Bhawanipatna India 95 D2
Bhearnaraigh, Eilean i. U.K. see Berneray
Bheemavaram India see Bhimavaram
Bhekuzulu S. Africa 133 O4
Bhera Pak. 101 H3
Bheri r. Nepal 97 D3
Bhilai India 96 D5
Bhildi India 96 B4
Bhilwara India 96 B4
Bhima r. India 94 C2
Bhimavaram India 94 D2
formerly spelt Bheemavaram
Bhimbar Pak. 101 H3
Bhimnagar India 97 E4
Bhimphedi Nepal 97 E4
Bhind India 96 C4
Bhindar India 96 B4
Bhinga India 97 D4
Bhingar India 94 B2
Bhinmal India 96 B4
Bhiwandi India 94 B2
Bhiwani India 96 C3
Bhogat India 96 A5
Bhojpur Nepal 97 E4
Bhokardan India 94 B1
Bhola Bangl. 97 F5
Bhongaon India 96 C4
Bhongir India 94 C2
Bhongweni S. Africa 133 N7
Bhopal India 96 C5
Bhopalpatnam India 94 D2
Bhor India 94 B2
Bhrigukaccha India see Bharuch
Bhuban India 95 E1
Bhubaneshwar India 95 E1
formerly spelt Bhubaneswar
Bhubaneswar India see Bhubaneshwar
Bhuban Hills India 97 G4
Bhuj India 96 A5
Bhumiphol Dam Thai. 78 B4
Bhunya Swaziland 133 P3
Bhurgaon Bhutan 97 F4
Bhusawal India 96 B5
▶Bhutan country Asia 97 F4
known as Druk-Yul in Dzongkha
asia [countries] ▶▶ 64–67
Bhuttewala India 96 A4
Bhuvanagiri India 94 C4
Biá r. Brazil 199 E5
Bia, Monts mts Dem. Rep. Congo 127 E7
Bia, Phou mt. Laos 78 C4
Biābān mts Iran 100 D5
Biafra, Bight of g. Africa see Benin, Bight of
Biak Irian Jaya Indon. 73 I7
Biak i. Indon. 73 I7
Biak Sulawesi Tengah Indon. 75 B3
Biała r. Poland 49 R5
Biała Piska Poland 49 T2
Biała Podlaska Poland 49 U3
Białobrzegi Poland 49 R4
Białogard Poland 49 M2
Białowieski Park Narodowy nat. park Poland 42 E9
Biały Bór Poland 49 N2
Białystok Poland 49 U2
formerly spelt Belostok
Biancavilla Sicilia Italy 57 G11
Bianco Italy 57 I10
Bianco, Monte mt. France/Italy see Blanc, Mont
Bianga Cent. Afr. Rep. 126 D3
Biankouma Côte d'Ivoire 124 D5
Bianouan Côte d'Ivoire 124 E5
Bianzhuang China see Cangshan
Biaora India 96 C5
Bi'ār Ghabāghib well Syria 109 K2
Biārjmand Iran 100 C2
Biaro i. Indon. 75 C2
Biarritz France 50 E9
Bi'ār Tabrāk well Saudi Arabia 105 D2
Biasca Switz. 51 O6
Biba Egypt 121 F2
Bibai Japan 90 G3
Bibala Angola 127 B8
formerly known as Vila Arriaga
Bibas Gabon 126 A4
Bibbenluke Australia 147 F4
Bibbiena Italy 56 D5
Biberach an der Riß Germany 48 G7
Bibiani Ghana 124 E5
Bibirevo Rus. Fed. 43 N5
Bibiyana r. Bangl. 97 F4
Biblos Lebanon see Jbail
Bicas Brazil 207 J8
Bicaz Romania 58 H2
Bicheng China see Bishan
Bicheno Australia 147 F5
Bichevaya Rus. Fed. 82 D3
Bichi Nigeria 125 H3
Bichi r. Rus. Fed. 82 E1
Bicholim India 94 B3
Bichraltar Nepal 97 E4
Bichura Rus. Fed. 85 E1
Bichvint'a Georgia 107 E2
also known as Pitsunda
Bickerton Island Australia 148 C2
Bicuari, Parque Nacional do nat. park Angola 127 B8
Bid India 94 B2
also spelt Bir
Bida Nigeria 125 G4
Bidache France 50 E9
Bidadari, Tanjong pt Sabah Malaysia 77 G1
Bidar India 94 C2
Bidasar India 96 B4
Bidbid Oman 105 G3
Biddeford U.S.A. 177 O2
Bideford U.K. 47 H12
Bideford Bay U.K. 47 H12
also known as Barnstaple Bay
Bidente r. Italy 56 E4
Bidjovagge Norway 44 M1
Bidkhan, Kūh-e mt. Iran 100 D4
Bidokht Iran 100 D3
Bidon 5 tourist site Alg. 123 F5
Bidzhan Rus. Fed. 82 C3
Bidzhar r. Rus. Fed. 82 D3
Bié Angola see Kuito
Bié prov. Angola 127 C8
Biebrza r. Poland 49 T2
Biebrzański Park Narodowy nat. park Poland 49 T2
Biedenkopf Germany 48 F5
Biel Switz. 51 N5
also known as Bienne
Bielawa Poland 49 N5
Bielefeld Germany 48 F3
Bielitz Poland see Bielsko-Biała
Biella Italy 56 A3
Bielsko-Biała Poland 49 Q6
historically known as Bielitz
Bielsk Podlaski Poland 49 U3
Bielstein hill Germany 51 P1
Bienenbüttel Germany 48 H2
Biên Hoa Vietnam 79 D6
Bienne r. France 51 L6
Bienne Switz. see Biel
Bienvenida hill Spain 54 E6
Bienville, Lac l. Canada 169 F2
Bierbank Australia 149 E5
Bierutów Poland 49 O4
Biesiesvlei S. Africa 133 J3
Biesiespoort S. Africa 132 H8
Bieszczady mts Poland 49 T6
Bieszczadzki Park Narodowy nat. park Poland 49 T6
Bièvre Belgium 51 L3
Biferno r. Italy 56 H7
Bifoun Gabon 126 A5
Bifröst Iceland 44 [inset] B2
Bifuka Japan 90 H2
Big r. U.S.A. 182 A2
Biga Turkey 106 A2
Biga r. Turkey 59 I8
Bigadiç Turkey 106 B3
Biganos France 50 F8
Biga Yarımadası pen. Turkey 59 H9
Big Baldy Mountain U.S.A. 180 E3
Big Bay U.S.A. 172 F4
Big Bay de Noc U.S.A. 172 F5
Big Bear Lake U.S.A. 183 H7
Big Belt Mountains U.S.A. 180 E3
Big Bend Swaziland 133 P3
Big Bend National Park U.S.A. 179 B6
Big Black r. U.S.A. 175 B5
Big Blue r. U.S.A. 178 C4
Big Canyon watercourse U.S.A. 179 B6
Big Cypress National Preserve nature res. U.S.A. 175 D7
Big Desert Wilderness Park nature res. Australia 146 D3
Big Eau Pleine Reservoir U.S.A. 172 D6
Biger Nuur salt l. Mongolia 84 C2
Big Fork r. U.S.A. 174 A1
Biggar Canada 167 J4
Biggar U.K. 46 I8
Biggar, Lac l. Canada 168 F3
Biggarsberg S. Africa 133 N5
Bigge Island Australia 150 D2
Biggenden Australia 149 G5
Bigger, Mount Canada 166 B3
Biggleswade U.K. 47 L11
Biggs U.S.A. 182 C2
Big Hole r. U.S.A. 180 D3
Bighorn r. U.S.A. 180 F3
Bighorn Mountains U.S.A. 180 F3
Bigil'dino Rus. Fed. 43 U8
Big Island Nunavut Canada 165 L3
Big Island N.W.T. Canada 167 G2
Big Island U.S.A. 176 F8
Big Kalzas Lake Canada 166 C2
Big Lake U.S.A. 179 B6
Big Lake l. U.S.A. 174 H2
Big Muddy Creek r. U.S.A. 180 F2
Bignona Senegal 124 A3
Bigobo Dem. Rep. Congo 127 E6
Big Otter r. U.S.A. 176 F8
Big Pine U.S.A. 182 F4
Big Pine Peak U.S.A. 182 E7
Big Rapids U.S.A. 172 H7
Big Rib r. U.S.A. 172 D6
Big River Canada 167 J4
Big Sable Point U.S.A. 172 G6
Big Salmon Canada 166 C2
Big Salmon r. Canada 166 C2
Big Sand Lake Canada 167 L3
Big Sandy r. U.S.A. 180 E4
Big Sandy watercourse U.S.A. 183 K7
Big Sandy Creek r. U.S.A. 178 B4
Big Sandy Lake Canada 167 J4
Big Sioux r. U.S.A. 178 C3
Big Smokey Valley U.S.A. 183 G3
Big South Cape Island N.Z. 153 B15
Big South Fork National River and Recreation Area park U.S.A. 176 A9
Big Spring U.S.A. 179 B5
Big Stone Canada 167 I5
Big Sur U.S.A. 182 C5
Big Thicket National Preserve nature res. U.S.A. 179 D6
Big Timber U.S.A. 180 E3
Big Trout Lake Canada 168 B2
Big Trout Lake l. Canada 168 B2
Big Valley Canada 167 H4
Big Water U.S.A. 183 M4
Bigwin Canada 173 N5
Bihać Bos.-Herz. 56 H4
Bihar state India 97 E4
Bihariganj India 97 E4
Bihar Sharif India 97 E4
Bihor, Vârful mt. Romania 58 D2
Bihoro Japan 90 I3
Bihpuriagaon India 97 G4
Bijagós, Arquipélago dos is Guinea-Bissau 124 A4
Bijainagar India 96 B4
Bijaipur India 96 C4
Bijapur India 94 B2
Bījār Iran 100 A3
Bijarpur India 94 D2
Bijawar India 96 C4
Bijbehara Jammu and Kashmir 96 B2
Bijeljina Bos.-Herz. 56 L4
Bijelolasica mt. Croatia 56 H3
Bijelo Polje Crna Gora Yugo. 58 A5
Bijie China 86 C3
Bijni India 97 F4
Bijnor India 96 C3
Bijolia India 96 B4
Bijrān well Saudi Arabia 105 E2
Bijrān, Khashm hill Saudi Arabia 105 E2
Bikampur India 96 B4
Bikaner India 96 B3
Bikbauli Kazakh. 103 E3
Bikfaiya Lebanon 108 G4
Bikin Rus. Fed. 82 D3
Bikin r. Rus. Fed. 82 D3
Bikini atoll Marshall Is 220 F5
Bikita Zimbabwe 131 F4
Bikori Sudan 128 B2
Bikoro Dem. Rep. Congo 126 C5
Bikou China 86 C1
Bikramganj India 97 E4
Bilaa Point Phil. 74 C4
Bilād Banī Bū 'Alī Oman 105 G3
Bilād Banī Bū Ḥasan Oman 105 G3
Bilād Ghāmid reg. Saudi Arabia 104 C3
Bilād Zahrān reg. Saudi Arabia 104 C3
Bilanga Burkina 125 E3
Bilangbilangan i. Indon. 77 G2
Bilara India 96 B4
Bilari India 96 C3
Bilaspur Chhattisgarh India 97 D5
Bilaspur Himachal Pradesh India 96 C3
Biläsuvar Azer. 107 G3
formerly known as Pushkino
Bilatan i. Phil. 74 B5
Bila Tserkva Ukr. 41 D6
also spelt Belaya Tserkva
Bilauktaung Range mts Myanmar/Thai. 79 B5
Bilbao Spain 55 I1
also spelt Bilbo
Bilbeis Egypt 121 F2
Bilbo Spain see Bilbao
Bilbor Romania 58 G1
Bildudalur Iceland 44 [inset] B2
Bileća Bos.-Herz. 56 K6
Bilecik Turkey 106 B2
Biled Romania 58 B3
Bilesha Plain Kenya 128 D4
Biłgoraj Poland 49 T5
Bilharamulo Tanz. 128 A5
Bilhaur India 96 D4
Bilhorod-Dnistrovs'kyy Ukr. 41 D7
also spelt Belgorod-Dnestrovskyy; formerly known as Akkerman; historically known as Cetatea Albă or Tyras
Bili Chad 126 C2
Bili r. Dem. Rep. Congo 126 D3
Bilibino Rus. Fed. 39 Q3
Bilibiza Moz. 129 D8
Bilikōl l. Kazakh. see Biylikol', Ozero
Bilin Myanmar 78 B4
Biliran i. Phil. 74 C4
Bilisht Albania 58 B8
Bilis Qooqaani Somalia 128 D4
Biliu r. China 85 I4
Bill U.S.A. 180 F4
Billabalong Australia 151 A5
Billabong Creek r. Australia see Moulamein Creek
Billdal Sweden 45 J4
Billère France 50 F9
Billiat Conservation Park nature res. Australia 146 D3
Billiluna Australia 150 D3
Billiluna Aboriginal Reserve Australia 150 D3
Billings U.S.A. 180 E3
Billiton i. Indon. see Belitung
Bill of Portland hd U.K. 47 J13
also known as Portland Bill
Billund airport Denmark 45 J5
Bill Williams r. U.S.A. 183 J7
Bill Williams Mountain U.S.A. 183 L6
Bilma Niger 125 I2
Bilo Eth. 128 C2
Biloela Australia 149 F5
Bilohirs'k Ukr. 41 E7
also spelt Belogorsk; formerly known as Karasubazar
Bilohir"ya Ukr. 41 C6
Biloku Guyana 199 G4
Biloli India 94 C2
Biloluts'k Ukr. 41 F6
Bilovods'k Ukr. 41 F6
Biloxi U.S.A. 175 B6
Bilpa Morea Claypan salt flat Australia 148 C5
Bilqās Qism Auwal Egypt 108 C6
Bilshausen Germany 48 H4
Bilsi India 96 C3
Biltine Chad 120 D6
Biltine pref. Chad 120 D6
Bilugyun Island Myanmar 78 B4
Bilungala Indon. 75 B2
Bilwascarma Nicaragua 186 C4
Bilyayivka Ukr. 41 D7
also spelt Belyayevka
Bima r. Dem. Rep. Congo 126 E4
Bima Indon. 77 G5
Bima, Teluk b. Indon. 77 G5
Bimbe Angola 127 B7
Bimbila Ghana 125 F4
Bimini Islands Bahamas 186 D1
Bimlipatam India 95 D2
Bina-Etawa India 96 C4
Binaija, Gunung mt. Indon. 75 D3
Binalbagan Phil. 74 B4
Bīnālūd, Kūh-e mts Iran 100 D2
Binatang Sarawak Malaysia 77 E2
Binboğa Dağı mt. Turkey 107 D3
Bincheng China 85 H4
formerly known as Binxian
Binchuan China 86 B3
also known as Niujing
Binder Chad 126 B2
Bindki India 96 D4
Bindu Dem. Rep. Congo 127 C6
Bindura Zimbabwe 131 F3
Binefar Spain 55 L3
Binga Zimbabwe 131 E3
Binga, Monte mt. Moz. 131 G3
Bingara Australia 147 F2
Bingaram i. India 94 B4
Bing Bong Australia 148 C2
Bingcaowan China 84 D4
Bingen am Rhein Germany 48 E6
Bingham U.S.A. 174 G2
Binghamton U.S.A. 177 J3
Bin Ghanīmah, Jabal hills Libya 120 B3
Bin Ghashir Libya 120 B1
Bingmei China see Congjiang
Bingöl Turkey 107 E3
also known as Çapakçur
Bingöl Dağı mt. Turkey 107 E3
Bingxi China see Yushan
Bingzhongluo China 86 A2
Binh Son Vietnam 79 E5
Binicuil Phil. 74 B4
Bini Erda well Chad 120 C4
Binika India 97 D5
Binjai Indon. 76 B2
Bin Jawwād Libya 120 C2
Binna, Raas pt Somalia 128 F2
Binnaway Australia 147 F2
Binongko i. Indon. 75 C4
Binpur India 97 E5
Bintan i. Indon. 76 D2
Bintang, Bukit mts Malaysia 76 C1
Bintuan Phil. 74 B3
Bintuhan Indon. 76 C4
Bintulu Sarawak Malaysia 77 F2
Binubusan Phil. 74 B3
Binxian Heilong. China 82 B3
also known as Binzhou
Binxian Shaanxi China 87 D1
Binxian China see Bincheng
Binyang China 87 D4
also known as Binzhou
Bin-Yauri Nigeria 125 G4
Binzhou China see Binyang
Binzhou China see Binxian
Binzhou China 85 H4
Biobío admin. reg. Chile 204 B5
Biobío r. Chile 204 B5
Bioco i. Equat. Guinea 125 H6
also spelt Bioko; formerly known as Fernando Póo or Macias Nguema
Biograd na Moru Croatia 56 H5
Biogradska Gora nat. park Yugo. 58 A6
Bioko i. Equat. Guinea see Bioco
Biokovo park Croatia 56 J5
Biquinhas Brazil 207 H5
Bir India see Bid
Bir, Ras pt Djibouti 128 D2
Bira Rus. Fed. 82 D2
Bira r. Rus. Fed. 82 D2
Bi'r Abā al 'Ajjāj well Saudi Arabia 104 B2
Bîr Abraq well Egypt 121 G4
Bîr Abu Darag well Egypt 108 D8
Bîr Abu Garad well Sudan 121 F5
Bîr Abu Hashim well Egypt 121 G4
Bîr Abu Husein well Egypt 121 F4
Bi'r Abū Jady oasis Syria 109 J1
Bîr Abu Minqâr well Egypt 121 E3
Bi'r ad Damar well Libya 120 A3
Bi'r adh Dhakar well Libya 120 D3
Bir Aïdiat well Mauritania 122 C4
Birāk Libya 120 B3
Birakan Rus. Fed. 82 C2
Bi'r al Amīr well Saudi Arabia 104 B2
Bi'r al Aṭbaq well Saudi Arabia 104 B2
Bi'r al 'Awādī well Saudi Arabia 104 B3
Bi'r al Fātiyah well Libya 120 B2
Bi'r al Ghanam Libya 120 B1
Bi'r al Ḥalbā well Syria 109 J3
Bi'r al Ḥisw well Saudi Arabia 104 C2
Bi'r al Ikhwān well Libya 120 D3
Bi'r al Jadīd well Libya 120 B3
Bi'r al Jāhilīyah well Saudi Arabia 104 C3
Bi'r al Marba'ah well Syria 109 K3
Bi'r al Mashī well Saudi Arabia 104 B2
Bi'r al Mastūtah well Libya 120 B3
Bi'r al Mulūsi Iraq 107 E4
Bi'r al Mulūṣi waterhole Iraq 109 L4
Bi'r al Munbaṭiḥ well Syria 109 J3
Bi'r al Mushayqiq well Libya 120 A2
Bi'r al Muwayliḥ well Libya 120 C2
Bi'r al Qurr well Saudi Arabia 104 B2
Bîr 'Amrâne well Mauritania 122 C5
Birandozero Rus. Fed. 40 F3
Bi'r an Nakhīlī waterhole Iraq 109 N3
Bir Anzarane W. Sahara 122 B5
Birao Cent. Afr. Rep. 126 D2
Bir Aouine well Tunisia 123 H2
Bi'r ar 'Alaqah well Libya 120 B2
Bi'r 'Arja well Saudi Arabia 104 C2
Bi'r as Sakhā well Saudi Arabia 104 C3
Biratar Bulak spring China 88 E3
Biratnagar Nepal 97 E4
also known as Morang
Biratori Japan 90 H3
Bi'r aṭ Ṭarfāwī well Libya 120 E2
Bi'r at Tayyārīyah well Syria 109 K3
Bi'r aṭ Ṭuwaylah waterhole Iraq 109 L4
Bi'r 'Azīz well Saudi Arabia 105 E3
Bi'raz Zurq well Saudi Arabia 104 C4
Bi'r Başīrī well Syria 109 I3
Bi'r Baydā well Saudi Arabia 104 B2
Bîr Bayly well Egypt 120 E2
Bîr Beida well Egypt 108 F7
Bir Bel Guerdâne well Mauritania 122 C4
Bir Ben Takoul well Alg. 123 E4
Bîr Bidi well Sudan 121 E5
Bi'r Bū Athlah well Libya 120 D3
Bi'r Budayy well Saudi Arabia 104 B2
Bîr Buerât well Egypt 108 D8
Bi'r Bū Rāḥah well Libya 120 A3
Bi'r Buraym well Saudi Arabia 104 C3
Birch r. Canada 167 H3
Bir Chali well Mali 122 D5
Birch Hills Canada 167 J4
Birchip Australia 147 D3
Birch Lake N.W.T. Canada 167 G2
Birch Lake Sask. Canada 167 I4
Birch Lake U.S.A. 172 B3
Birch Mountains Canada 167 H3
Birch River Canada 167 K4
Birch River U.S.A. 176 E7
Birch Run U.S.A. 173 J7
Birchwood U.S.A. 172 B5
Bircot Eth. 128 D3
Bir Di Sudan 126 F3
Bîr Dibis well Egypt 121 F4
Bîr Dignâsh well Egypt 120 E2
Bird Island N. Mariana Is see Farallon de Medinilla
Bîr Dolmane well Alg. 123 H3
Birdsboro U.S.A. 177 J5
Birdseye U.S.A. 183 M2
Birdsville Australia 148 C5
Birdum r. Australia 148 B2
Birecik Turkey 107 D3
Bir ed Deheb well Alg. 123 E4
Bîr el 'Adeid well Egypt 108 F9
Bîr el 'Agramîya well Egypt 108 C8
Bîr el Duweidar well Egypt 108 D7
Bîr el Fakâma well Sudan 104 A4
Bir el Gheralia well Tunisia 123 H2
Bir El Hadjaj well Alg. 123 F4
Bîr el Haimur well Egypt 121 G4
Bîr el Istabl well Egypt 121 E2
Bîr el Khamsa well Egypt 106 A5
Bîr el Malha well Egypt 108 E8
Bîr el Nuss well Egypt 121 E2
Bîr el-Obeiyid well Egypt 121 E3
Bîr el Qatrâni well Egypt 121 E2
Bîr el Râbia well Egypt 106 A5
Birendranagar Nepal see Surkhet
Bîr en Natrûn well Sudan 121 E5
Bîr en Nugeim well Sudan 121 G5
Bir es Smeha well Alg. 123 G2
Bireun Indon. 76 B1
Bi'r Fāḍil well Saudi Arabia 105 D3
Bi'r Fajr well Saudi Arabia 104 B1
Bîr Fanoidig well Sudan 104 A4
Bi'r Fardān well Saudi Arabia 105 E3
Bîr Fuâd well Egypt 121 E2
Bîr Furawiya well Sudan 120 D6
Bir Gandouz W. Sahara 122 A5
Bi'r Ghawdah well Saudi Arabia 104 D3
Bîr Gifgâfa well Egypt 108 E7
Bîr Gindali well Egypt 108 C8
Bi'r Ḥādī oasis Saudi Arabia 105 E4
Bi'r Ḥajal well Syria 109 K3
Birhan mt. Eth. 128 C2
Bi'r Ḥarāqī well Saudi Arabia 104 C3
Bîr Hasana well Egypt 108 E7
Bir Hatab well Sudan 121 G4
Bi'r Ḥaymir well Saudi Arabia 104 B2
Bi'r Ḥayzān well Saudi Arabia 104 B2
Bîr Hismet 'Umar well Sudan 121 G4
Bi'r Ḥudūf well Saudi Arabia 104 C3
Bi'r Ḥumaymah well Syria 109 K3
Bîr Huwait well Sudan 121 G4
Bi'r Ḥuwaymiḍah well Saudi Arabia 104 C2
Bi'r Ibn Ghunayn well Saudi Arabia 104 B2
Bi'r Ibn Hirmās Saudi Arabia see Al Bi'r
Bi'r Ibn Sarrār well Saudi Arabia 104 C4
Bi'r Idimah well Saudi Arabia 104 D4
Biriguí Brazil 206 C8
Birin, Col de pass Alg. 55 N9
Birini Cent. Afr. Rep. 126 D3
Birjand Iran 101 D3
Bi'r Jaydah well Saudi Arabia 104 B2
Bi'r Jifah well Yemen 105 D5
Bi'r Jubnī well Libya 120 E2
Bi'r Jugjug well Saudi Arabia 104 C3
Birkat Abū Salīm waterhole Saudi Arabia 104 C2
Birkat al 'Aṣāfīr waterhole Saudi Arabia 109 O8
Birkat al Ḥamrā well Saudi Arabia 104 C1
Birkat al Hatyan waterhole Saudi Arabia 109 O8
Birkat ash Shiḥīyāt waterhole Saudi Arabia 109 O8
Birkat aẓ Ẓafīrī waterhole Saudi Arabia 109 O8
Birkat Zubālah waterhole Saudi Arabia 107 E5
Birkeland Norway 45 J4
Birkenhead U.K. 47 I10
Birket Qârûn l. Egypt 121 F2
Bi'r Khamrān waterhole Iraq 109 O3
Bi'r Khurbah well Saudi Arabia 104 B2
Bi'r Khuwārah well Saudi Arabia 104 C3
Bîr Kiau well Sudan 121 G4
Birkim Iraq 107 F3
Birkirkara Malta 57 G13
Birksgate Range hills Australia 146 A1
Bîr Labasoi well Sudan 121 G4
Bîrlad Romania see Bârlad
Bîr Lahfân well Egypt 108 E6
Bir Lahmar W. Sahara 122 C4
Birlik Kazakh. 103 H3
formerly spelt Brlik
Birlik Kazakh. see Brlik
Bîr Likeit el Fauqani well Sudan 104 A3
Bîr Liseila well Sudan 121 G4
Bîr Majal well Egypt 121 G4
Birmal reg. Afgh. 101 G3
Bi'r Malīyah well Saudi Arabia 104 C3
Birmingham U.K. 47 K11
Birmingham U.S.A. 175 C5
Bîr Misâha well Egypt 121 E4
Birmitrapur India 97 E5
Bîr Mogreïn Mauritania 122 C4
formerly known as Fort Trinquet
Bi'r Muḥaymid al Wazwaz well Syria 109 J3
Bi'r Mujayfil well Saudi Arabia 108 G8
Bîr Murra well Egypt 121 G4
Bi'r Muwayliḥ well Syria 109 K3
Bi'r Nabṭ well Saudi Arabia 104 B2
Bîr Nagib well Egypt 121 G4
Bîr Nâhid oasis Egypt 121 F2
Bi'r Najib well Syria 109 K3
Bi'r Nasīf Saudi Arabia 104 B2
Bîr Nawari well Sudan 121 G4
Birni Benin 125 F4
Birnie i. Kiribati 145 H2
Birnin-Gaouré Niger 125 F3
Birnin-Gwari Nigeria 125 G4
Birnin-Kebbi Nigeria 125 G3
Birnin Konni Niger 125 G3
Birnin Kudu Nigeria 125 H4
Birniwa Nigeria 125 H3
Bîr Nukheila well Sudan 121 E5
Birobidzhan Rus. Fed. 82 D2
Birofel'd Rus. Fed. 82 D2
Bîr Ounâne well Mali 122 E5
Birpur India 97 E4
Bîr Qaṣr el Sirr well Egypt 106 A5
Bîr Quleib well Egypt 121 G3
Birr Rep. of Ireland 47 E10
Birrie r. Australia 147 E2
Birrindudu Australia 148 A3
Birriyet el Aşeifar Egypt 108 E6
Bîr Rôd Sâlim well Egypt 108 E7
Bîr Rouni well Alg. 123 G2
Bi'r Sābil Iraq 107 E4
Bîr Sahara well Egypt 121 F4
Bîr Salala well Sudan 121 G4
Birsay U.K. 46 I4
Bîr Shalatein Egypt 121 G4
Bi'r Shamandūr well Syria 109 K1
Birshoghyr Kazakh. see Berchogur
Bi'r Simād waterhole Iraq 109 O3
Birsk Rus. Fed. 40 J5
Bir Sohanit well Sudan 104 A3
Birštonas Lith. 42 F7
Bîr Tâba Egypt 108 F8
Bi'r Ṭalḥah well Saudi Arabia 105 D3
Bir Tanguer well Alg. 123 G3
Bi'r Ṭānjidar well Libya 120 D2
Bîr Tarfâwi well Egypt 121 F4
Bi'r Ṭarūfāwī waterhole Iraq 109 O4
Bîr Thâl well Egypt 108 E8
Birthday Mountain hill Australia 149 D2
Birtle Canada 167 K5
Biru China 89 F6
also known as Biruxiong
Bîr Udeib well Egypt 108 D8
Biruintsa Moldova see Ştefan Vodă
Bi'r Umm el Gharāniq Libya 120 C2
Bîr Umm Fawâkhir well Egypt 104 A2
Bi'r Umm Missā well Saudi Arabia 104 B2
Bîr Ungât well Egypt 121 G4
Biruni Uzbek. see Beruni
Birur India 94 B3
Bi'r Usaylīlah well Saudi Arabia 105 D3
Biruxiong China see Biru
Bîr Wario well Sudan 121 G5
Bi'r Wedeb well Libya 120 B3
Bi'r Wurshah well Saudi Arabia 104 C3
Biryakovo Rus. Fed. 43 V2
Biržai Lith. 42 F5
Bir Zar well Tunisia 123 H3
Bisa i. Indon. 75 C3
Bisalpur India 96 C3
Bisau India 96 B3
Bisbee U.S.A. 181 E7
Biscarrosse France 50 E8
Biscarrosse et de Parentis, Étang de l. France 50 E8
Biscay, Bay of sea France/Spain 50 A7
Biscayne Bay U.S.A. 175 D7
Biscayne National Park U.S.A. 175 D7
Bischofshofen Austria 49 K8
Bischofswerda Germany 49 L4
Biscoe Islands Antarctica 222 T2
Biscotasing Canada 168 D4
Bisert' r. Rus. Fed. 40 K4
Bisertsi Bulg. 58 H5
Biševo i. Croatia 56 H6
Bisezhai China 86 B4
Bisha Eritrea 121 H6
Bishah reg. Saudi Arabia 104 C4
Bishah, Wādī watercourse Saudi Arabia 104 D3
Bishan China 86 C2
also known as Bicheng
Bishbek Kyrg. see Bishkek

▶Bishkek Kyrg. 103 H4
Capital of Kyrgyzstan. Also spelt Bishbek or Pishpek; formerly known as Frunze.

Bishnupur India 97 E5
Bisho S. Africa 133 L9
Bishop U.S.A. 182 F4
Bishop Auckland U.K. 47 K9
Bishop Lake Canada 167 G1
Bishop's Stortford U.K. 47 M12
Bishopville U.S.A. 175 D5
Bishri, Jabal hills Syria 109 K2
Bishti i Pallës pt Albania 58 A7
Bishui China 82 A1
Bishui China see Biyang
Bisi S. Africa 133 N7
Bisinaca Col. 198 D3
Biskra Alg. 123 G2
also spelt Beskra
Biskupiec Poland 49 R2
Bislig Phil. 74 C4
Bislig Bay Phil. 74 C4

▶Bismarck U.S.A. 178 B2
State capital of North Dakota.

Bismarck Archipelago is P.N.G. 73 K7
Bismarck Sea P.N.G. 73 K7
Bismil Turkey 107 E3
Bismo Norway 45 J3
Bison U.S.A. 178 B2
Bīsotūn Iran 100 A3
Bispgården Sweden 44 L3
Bissa, Djebel mt. Alg. 55 M8
Bissamcuttak India 95 D2

▶Bissau Guinea-Bissau 124 B4
Capital of Guinea-Bissau.

Bissaula Nigeria 125 H5
Bissett Canada 167 M5
Bissikrima Guinea 124 C4
Bissorã Guinea-Bissau 124 B3
Bistcho Lake Canada 166 G3
Bistra mt. Macedonia 58 B7
Bistra r. Romania 58 D3
Bistra mt. Yugo. 58 B6
Bistret Romania 58 E5
Bistreţ, Lacul l. Romania 58 E5

index

B

Carwell Australia 149 E5
Cary U.S.A. 174 E5
Caryapundy Swamp Australia 147 D2
Caryville TN U.S.A. 176 A9
Caryville WI U.S.A. 172 B6
Casabindo, Cerro de mt. Arg. 200 D5
Casablanca Chile 204 C4

▶Casablanca Morocco 122 D2
5th most populous city in Africa. Also known as Dar el Beida.
world [cities] 24–25

Casa Branca Brazil 206 F8
Casa de Janos Mex. 184 C2
Casa de Piedra, Embalse resr Arg. 204 D5
Casa Grande U.S.A. 183 M9
Casale Monferrato Italy 56 A3
Casalins Arg. 204 F5
Casalmaggiore Italy 56 C4
Casalpusterlengo Italy 56 B3
Casalvasco Brazil 201 E3
Casamance r. Senegal 124 A3
Casanare dept Col. 198 D3
Casanare r. Col. 198 D3
Casares Nicaragua 186 B5
Casas Grandes Mex. 184 D2
Casas Grandes r. Mex. 184 D2
Casas-Ibáñez Spain 55 J5
Casbas Arg. 204 E5
Casca Brazil 203 A9
Cascada de Bassaseachic, Parque Nacional nat. park Mex. 184 C2
Cascade Australia 151 C7
Cascade r. N.Z. 153 C12
Cascade IA U.S.A. 174 B3
Cascade ID U.S.A. 180 C3
Cascade Point N.Z. 153 C12
Cascade Range mts Canada/U.S.A. 164 G5
Cascade Reservoir U.S.A. 180 C3
Cascais Port. 54 B6
Cascal, Paso del pass Nicaragua 186 B5
Cascapédia r. Canada 169 H3
Cascavel Ceará Brazil 202 E3
Cascavel Paraná Brazil 203 A8
Căscioarele Romania 58 H4
Casco U.S.A. 172 F6
Casco Bay U.S.A. 177 P2
Caserta Italy 56 G7
Caseville U.S.A. 173 J7
Casey research station Antarctica 223 H2
Casey Bay Antarctica 223 D2
Caseyr, Raas c. Somalia 128 F2
English form Guardafui, Cape
Cashel Rep. of Ireland 47 E11
Cashmere Australia 147 F1
Cashton U.S.A. 172 C7
Casigua Falcón Venez. 198 D2
Casigua Zulia Venez. 198 C2
Casiguran Phil. 74 B2
Casiguran Sound sea chan. Phil. 74 B2
Casilda Arg. 204 E4
Casimcea Romania 58 J4
Casimcea r. Romania 58 J4
Casimiro de Abreu Brazil 207 K9
Casino Australia 147 G2
Casinos Spain 55 K5
Casita Mex. 181 E7
Čáslav Czech Rep. 49 M6
Casma Peru 200 A2
Casnewydd U.K. see Newport
Casnovia U.S.A. 172 H7
Casogoran Bay Phil. 74 C4
Casoli Italy 56 G6
Caspe Spain 55 K3
Casper U.S.A. 180 F4
Caspian U.S.A. 172 E4
Caspian Lowland Kazakh./Rus. Fed. 102 A3
also known as Kaspiy Mangy Oypaty or Prikaspiyskaya Nizmennost'

▶Caspian Sea Asia/Europe 102 B4
Largest lake in the world and in Asia/Europe. Lowest point in Europe. Also known as Kaspiyskoye More.
world [physical features] 8–9

	lake	area sq km	area sq miles	location		page#
largest lakes	1▶ Caspian Sea	371 000	143 243	Asia/Europe	➡	102 B4
	2▶ Lake Superior	82 100	31 698	North America	➡	172 F3
	3▶ Lake Victoria	68 800	26 563	Africa	➡	128 B5
	4▶ Lake Huron	59 600	23 011	North America	➡	173 J5
	5▶ Lake Michigan	57 800	22 316	North America	➡	172 F7
	6▶ Aral Sea	33 640	12 988	Asia	➡	102 D3
	7▶ Lake Tanganyika	32 900	12 702	Africa	➡	127 F6
	8▶ Great Bear Lake	31 328	12 095	North America	➡	166 F1
	9▶ Lake Baikal	30 500	11 776	Asia	➡	81 H2
	10▶ Lake Nyasa	30 044	11 600	Africa	➡	129 B7

Cass r. U.S.A. 173 J7
Cassacatiza Moz. 131 G2
Cassadaga U.S.A. 176 F3
Cassai Angola 127 D7
Cassamba Angola 127 D8
Cassano allo Ionio Italy 57 I9
Cassara Brazil 201 E3
Cass City U.S.A. 173 J7
Casselman Canada 168 F4
Casselton U.S.A. 178 C2
Cássia Brazil 206 G7
Cassiar Mountains Canada 166 D3
Cassilândia Brazil 206 B6
Cassilis Australia 147 F3
Cassinga Angola 127 C8
also spelt Kassinga
Cassino Brazil 204 G4
Cassino Italy 56 F7
Cassis France 51 L9
Cassley r. U.K. 46 H6
Cassongue Angola 127 B7
Cassopolis U.S.A. 172 G9
Cassville MO U.S.A. 178 D4
Cassville WI U.S.A. 172 C8
Castalla Spain 55 K6
Castanhal Amazonas Brazil 199 F6
Castanhal Pará Brazil 202 C2
Castanheira de Pêra Port. 54 C4
Castanheiro Brazil 199 E5
Castanho Brazil 201 E1
Castaño Nuevo Arg. 204 C3
Castaños Mex. 185 E3
Castejón, Montes de mts Spain 55 J3
Castèl di Sangro Italy 56 G7
Castelfiorentino Italy 56 C5
Castelfranco Emilia Italy 56 D4
Castelfranco Veneto Italy 56 D3
Casteljaloux France 50 G8
Castellammare, Golfo di b. Sicilia Italy 57 E10
Castellammare di Stabia Italy 57 G8
Castellane France 51 M9
Castellaneta Italy 57 I8
Castellanos mt. Spain 55 I6
Castellar de la Frontera Spain 54 F8
Castelldefels Spain 55 M3
Castell de Ferro Spain 55 H8
Castelli Buenos Aires Arg. 204 F5
Castelli Chaco Arg. 204 E2
Castell-nedd U.K. see Neath
Castell Newydd Emlyn U.K. see Newcastle Emlyn
Castello de Ampurias Spain see Castelló d'Empúries
Castelló de la Plana Spain 55 K5
also spelt Castellón de la Plana
Castelló d'Empúries Spain 55 O2
also spelt Castello de Ampurias
Castellón de la Plana Spain see Castelló de la Plana
Castelnaudary France 51 H9
Castelnau-de-Médoc France 50 F7
Castelnovo ne'Monti Italy 56 C4
Castelo Brazil 207 L7
Castelo Branco Port. 54 D5
Castelo Branco admin. dist. Port. 54 D4
Castelo de Vide Port. 54 D5
Castelo do Piauí Brazil 202 D3
Castèl San Pietro Terme Italy 56 D4
Castelsardo Sardegna Italy 56 A8
Castelsarrasin France 50 H8
Casteltermini Sicilia Italy 57 F11
Castelvetrano Sicilia Italy 57 E11
Castèl Volturno Italy 56 F7
Casterton Australia 146 D4
Castets France 50 E9
Castiglione dei Pepoli Italy 56 D4
Castiglione del Lago Italy 56 E5
Castiglione della Pescaia Italy 56 C6
Castiglione delle Stiviere Italy 56 C3
Castiglion Fiorentino Italy 56 D5
Castile U.S.A. 176 G3
Castilho Brazil 206 B7
Castilla Chile 204 C2
Castilla Peru 198 A6
Castilla - La Mancha aut. comm. Spain 55 H5
Castilla y León aut. comm. Spain 55 G3
Castillejo Venez. 199 F3
Castilletes Col. 198 D2
Castillo, Canal del sea chan. Chile 205 B8
Castillo, Pampa del hills Arg. 205 C7
Castillos Uruguay 204 G4
Castillos, Lago de l. Uruguay 204 G4
Castlebar Rep. of Ireland 47 C10
also known as Caisleán an Bharraigh
Castleblayney Rep. of Ireland 47 F9
Castle Dale U.S.A. 183 M2
Castle Danger U.S.A. 172 B3
Castle Dome Mountains U.S.A. 183 J8
Castle Douglas U.K. 47 I9
Castlegar Canada 166 G5
Castle Island Bahamas 187 E2
Castleisland Rep. of Ireland 47 C11
Castlemaine Australia 147 E4
Castle Mountain Canada 166 H5
formerly known as Eisenhower, Mount
Castle Mountain U.S.A. 182 D6
Castle Peak hill Hong Kong China 87 [inset]
also known as Tsing Shan
Castle Peak Bay Hong Kong China 87 [inset]
also known as Tsing Shan Wan
Castlepoint N.Z. 152 K8
Castlepollard Rep. of Ireland 47 E10
Castlerea Rep. of Ireland 47 D10
Castlereagh r. Australia 147 E2
Castle Rock CO U.S.A. 180 F5
Castle Rock WA U.S.A. 180 B3
Castle Rock Lake U.S.A. 172 C7
Castor Canada 167 I4
Castor, Rivière du r. Canada 168 E2
Castor Creek r. U.S.A. 179 D6
Castra Regina Germany see Regensburg
Castres France 51 I9
Castricum Neth. 48 B3

▶Castries St Lucia 187 H4
Capital of St Lucia.

Castro Brazil 203 B8
Castro Chile 205 B6
Castro Alves Brazil 202 E5
Castrocaro Terme Italy 56 D4
Castro del Río Spain 54 G7
Castro de Rei Spain 54 D1
Castro Marim Port. 54 D7
Castro-Urdiales Spain 55 H1
Castro Verde Port. 54 C7
Castrovillari Italy 57 I9
Castroville U.S.A. 182 C5
Castrovirreyna Peru 200 B3
Castuera Spain 54 F6
Cast Uul mt. Mongolia 84 A1
Caswell Sound inlet N.Z. 153 B12
Çat Turkey 107 E3
Catabola Angola 127 C8
formerly known as Nova Sintra
Catacamas Hond. 186 B4
Catacaos Peru 198 A6
Catacocha Ecuador 198 B6
Cataguases Brazil 207 K8
Catahoula Lake U.S.A. 179 D6
Cataiñgan Phil. 74 B3
Çatak Turkey 107 E3
Catalão Brazil 206 F5
Çatalca Turkey 58 J7
Çatalca Yarımadası pen. Turkey 58 J7
Catalina U.S.A. 183 N9
Catalonia aut. comm. Spain see Cataluña
Cataluña aut. comm. Spain 55 M3
English form Catalonia; also spelt Catalunya
Catalunya aut. comm. Spain see Cataluña
Çatalzeytin Turkey 106 C2
Catamarca Arg. 204 D3
Catamarca prov. Arg. 204 D2
Catambia Moz. see Catandica
Catana Sicilia Italy see Catania
Catanauan Phil. 74 B3
Catandica Moz. 131 G3
formerly known as Catambia or Vila Gouveia
Catanduanes i. Phil. 74 C3
Catanduva Brazil 206 D8
Catanduvas Brazil 203 A8
Catania Sicilia Italy 57 H11
historically known as Catana
Catania, Golfo di g. Sicilia Italy 57 H11
Catán Lil Arg. 204 C5
Catanzaro Italy 57 I10
Cataquazeamã Brazil 201 E2
Cataract U.S.A. 172 C6
Cataract Creek watercourse U.S.A. 183 L5
Catarina Brazil 202 E3
Catarina U.S.A. 179 C6
Catarino Rodriguez Mex. 185 E3
Catarman Phil. 74 C3
Catarroja Spain 55 K5
Catastrophe, Cape Australia 146 B3
Catata Nova Angola 127 B8
Catatumbo Bari nat. park Col. 198 C2
Catavi Bol. 200 D4
Catawba U.S.A. 172 C5
Catawba r. U.S.A. 174 D5
Catawissa U.S.A. 177 I5
Cat Ba, Đao i. Vietnam 78 D3
Catbalogan Phil. 74 C4
Cateel Phil. 74 C5
Cateel Bay Phil. 74 C5
Catemaco Mex. 185 G5
Catembe Moz. 133 Q3
Catengue Angola 127 B8
Catete Angola 127 B7
Catete r. Brazil 199 H6
Cathcart S. Africa 133 L9
Cathedral City U.S.A. 183 H8
Cathedral Peak Lesotho 133 N5
Cathedral Provincial Park Canada 166 F5
Catherine, Mount U.S.A. 183 L3
Catheys Valley U.S.A. 182 D4
Cathlamet U.S.A. 180 B3
Catió Guinea-Bissau 124 B4
Catisimiña Venez. 199 F3
Cat Island Bahamas 187 E1
Catlins Forest Park nature res. N.Z. 153 D14
Catoche, Cabo c. Mex. 185 I4
Catolé do Rocha Brazil 202 E3
Catolé Grande r. Brazil 207 M2
Catolo Angola 127 C7
Catorce Mex. 185 E4
Catota Angola 127 C8
Catoute mt. Spain 54 E2
Catria, Monte mt. Italy 56 E5
Catriló Arg. 204 E5
Catrimani Brazil 199 F4
Catrimani r. Brazil 199 F4
Catskill U.S.A. 177 L3
Catskill Mountains U.S.A. 177 K3
Cattenom France 51 M3
Cattle Creek N.Z. 153 E12
Cattolica Italy 56 E5
Catúa Arg. 200 D5
Catuane Moz. 131 G5
Catur Moz. 129 B8
Catuxi r. Brazil 202 B2
Cauayan Phil. 74 B4
Caubvick, Mount Canada 169 I1
Cauca dept Col. 198 B4
Cauca r. Col. 198 C2
Caucaia Brazil 202 E2
Caucasia Col. 198 C3
▶Caucasus mts Asia/Europe 107 E2
also known as Bol'shoy Kavkaz
europe [countries] 32–33
Caucete Arg. 204 C3
Cauchari, Salar de salt flat Arg. 200 D5
Cauchon Lake Canada 167 L4
Caucomgomoc Lake U.S.A. 174 G2
Caudete Spain 55 K6
Caudry France 51 J2
Cauit Point Phil. 74 C4
Caulnes France 50 D4
Caulonia Italy 57 I10
Caungula Angola 127 C7
Caunao r. Cuba 186 D2
Cauquenes Chile 204 B4
Cauno Angola 127 C9
Caura r. Venez. 199 E3
Caurés r. Brazil 199 F5
Causapscal Canada 169 H3
Căuşeni Moldova 58 K2
formerly spelt Kaushany
Căuşeni prov. Moldova 53 H2
Caussade France 50 H8
Cautário r. Brazil 201 D3
Caution, Cape Canada 166 E5
Cauto r. Cuba 186 D2
Cava de'Tirreni Italy 57 G8
Cávado r. Port. 54 C3
Cavaglià Italy 56 A3
Cavaillon France 51 L9
Cavalcante Goiás Brazil 202 C5
Cavalcante Rondônia Brazil 201 E2
Cavalier U.S.A. 178 C1
Cavalleria, Cap de c. Spain 55 P4
Cavalli Islands N.Z. 152 H2
Cavally r. Côte d'Ivoire 124 D5
Cavan Rep. of Ireland 47 E10
Çavdarhisar Turkey 59 K9
Çavdır Turkey 106 B3
Cave N.Z. 153 E12
Cave City AR U.S.A. 174 B4
Cave City KY U.S.A. 174 C4
Cave Creek U.S.A. 183 M8
Caveira Brazil 207 J3
Cavenagh Range hills Australia 151 E5
Cavera, Serra do hills Brazil 203 A9
Cavernoso, Serra do mts Brazil 203 A8
Cave Run Lake U.S.A. 176 B7
Caviana, Ilha i. Brazil 202 B1
Cavili reef Phil. 74 B4
Cavite Phil. 74 B3
Cavo, Monte hill Italy 56 E7
Cavone r. Italy 57 I8
Cavongo Angola 127 C8
Çavuşçu Turkey 106 B3
Çavuşköy Turkey 108 B1
Cawndilla Lake imp. l. Australia 147 D3
Cawnpore India see Kanpur
Cawood U.S.A. 176 B9
Caxambu Brazil 207 I8
Caxias Amazonas Brazil 198 D6
Caxias Maranhão Brazil 202 D3
Caxias do Sul Brazil 203 B9
Caxito Angola 127 B7
Caxiuana, Baía de l. Brazil 199 I5
Çay Turkey 106 B3
Cayambe-Coca, Parque Nacional nat. park Ecuador 198 B5
Çaybaşı Turkey see Çayeli
Çayce U.S.A. 175 D5
Çaycuma Turkey 106 C2
Çayeli Turkey 107 E2
also known as Çaybaşı

▶Cayenne Fr. Guiana 199 H3
Capital of French Guiana.

Cayey Puerto Rico 187 G3
Çaygören Barajı resr Turkey 59 J9
Çayhan Turkey 106 C3
Çayhisar Turkey 59 J12
Çayırhan Turkey 106 B2
Caylus France 50 H8
Cayman Brac i. Cayman Is 186 D3

▶Cayman Islands terr. West Indies 186 C3
United Kingdom Overseas Territory.
oceania [countries] 138–139

Cay Sal i. Bahamas 186 C2
Cay Santo Domingo i. Bahamas 186 E2
Cayucos U.S.A. 182 D6
Cayuga Canada 173 N8
Cayuga Heights U.S.A. 177 I3
Cayuga Lake U.S.A. 177 I3
Cazage Angola 127 D7
also spelt Cazaje
Cazaje Angola see Cazage
Cazalla de la Sierra Spain 54 F7
Căzănești Romania 58 I4
Caza Pava Arg. 204 F3
Cazaux et de Sanguinet, Étang de l. France 50 E8
Cazê China 89 D6
Cazenovia U.S.A. 177 J3
Cazères France 50 H9
Čažma Croatia 56 I3
Cazombo Angola 127 D7
Cazorla Spain 55 I7
Cazula Moz. 131 G2
Cea r. Spain 54 F2
Ceadâr-Lunga Moldova see Ciadîr-Lunga
Ceanannus Mór Rep. of Ireland see Kells
Ceará Brazil see Fortaleza
Ceará state Brazil 202 E3
Ceatalchioi Romania 58 J3
Ceatharlach Rep. of Ireland see Carlow
Ceballos Mex. 184 D3
Cebireis Dağı mt. Turkey 108 D1
Cebollar Arg. 204 D3
Ceboruco, Volcán vol. Mex. 184 D4
Cebreros Spain 54 G4
Cebu Phil. 74 B4
Cebu i. Phil. 74 B4
Ceccano Italy 56 F7
Cecil U.S.A. 172 E6
Cecil Plains Australia 147 F1
Cecil Rhodes, Mount hill Australia 151 C5
Cecilton U.S.A. 177 J6
Cecina Italy 56 C5
Cecina r. Italy 56 C5
Ceclavín Spain 54 E5
Cedar r. MI U.S.A. 173 I7
Cedar r. ND U.S.A. 178 B2
Cedar r. NE U.S.A. 178 C3
Cedarberg mts S. Africa 132 C9
Cedar Bluff U.S.A. 176 D8
Cedar City U.S.A. 183 K4
Cedar Creek Reservoir U.S.A. 179 C5
Cedaredge U.S.A. 180 F5
Cedar Falls U.S.A. 174 A3
Cedar Grove CA U.S.A. 182 F5
Cedar Grove IN U.S.A. 176 A6
Cedar Grove WI U.S.A. 172 F7
Cedar Grove WV U.S.A. 176 D7
Cedar Island U.S.A. 177 J8
Cedar Lake Man. Canada 167 K4
Cedar Lake Ont. Canada 173 O4
Cedar Point U.S.A. 176 B4
Cedar Rapids U.S.A. 174 B3
Cedar Ridge U.S.A. 183 M5
Cedar River U.S.A. 172 F5
Cedar Run U.S.A. 177 K6
Cedar Springs Canada 173 K8
Cedar Springs U.S.A. 172 H7
Cedarville S. Africa 133 N7
Cedarville IL U.S.A. 172 D8
Cedarville MI U.S.A. 173 I5
Cedarville OH U.S.A. 176 B6
Cedegolo Italy 56 C2
Cedeira Spain 54 C1
Cedeño Hond. 186 B4
Cedral Quintana Roo Mex. 185 I4
Cedral San Luis Potosí Mex. 185 E4
Cedro Brazil 202 E3
Cedros Hond. 186 B4
Cedros Mex. 185 E3
Cedros, Cerro mt. Mex. 181 D7
Cedros, Isla i. Mex. 184 B2
Ceduna Australia 146 B3
Cée Spain 54 B2
Ceelayo Somalia 128 F2
Ceelbuur Somalia 128 E3
Ceel Dhaab Somalia 128 E2
Ceeldheere Somalia 128 E4
Ceel Gaal Bari Somalia 128 F2
Ceel Gaal Woqooyi Galbeed Somalia 128 D2
Ceel Huur Somalia 128 F3
Ceel Walaaq well Somalia 128 D4
Ceerigaabo Somalia 128 E2
Cefalù Sicilia Italy 57 G10
historically known as Cephaloedium
Cega r. Spain 54 G3
Cegléd Hungary 49 Q8
Čegrane Macedonia 58 B7
Ceheng China 86 C3
also known as Zhelou
Cehu Silvaniei Romania 58 E1
Ceira r. Port. 54 C4
Çekerek Turkey 106 C2
also known as Hacıköy
Celah, Gunung mt. Malaysia 76 C1
Celano Italy 56 F6
Celaque, Parque Nacional nat. park Hond. 186 A4
Celaya Mex. 185 E4
Celbridge Rep. of Ireland 47 F10
Célé r. France 50 H8

▶Celebes i. Indon. 75 B3
4th largest island in Asia. Also known as Sulawesi.
asia [landscapes] 62–63

Celebes Sea Indon./Phil. 75 B2
Celendín Peru 198 B6
Celina OH U.S.A. 176 A5
Celina TN U.S.A. 174 C4
Celje Slovenia 56 H2
Cella Spain 55 J4
Celldömölk Hungary 49 O8
Celle Germany 48 H3
Celles-sur-Belle France 50 F6
Cellina r. Italy 56 E2
Celone r. Italy 56 H7
Celovec Austria see Klagenfurt
Celtic Sea Rep. of Ireland/U.K. 47 F13
Cemaru, Gunung mt. Indon. 77 F2
Çemilbey Turkey 106 C2
Çemişgezek Turkey 107 D3
Cempi, Teluk b. Indon. 77 G5
Cenad Romania 58 B2
Cenajo, Embalse del resr Spain 55 J6
Cencenighe Agordino Italy 56 D2
Cenderawasih, Teluk b. Indon. 73 I7
also known as Irian, Teluk
Cenei Romania 58 B3
Cenis, Col du Mont pass France 51 M7
Ceno r. Italy 56 C4
Cenon France 50 F8
Čenta Vojvodina, Srbija Yugo. 58 B3
Centane S. Africa see Kentani
Centenário do Sul Brazil 206 B9
Centenary Zimbabwe 131 F3
Centennial Wash watercourse U.S.A. 183 L8
Center ND U.S.A. 178 B2
Center NE U.S.A. 178 C3
Center TX U.S.A. 179 D6
Centerburg U.S.A. 176 C5
Center City U.S.A. 178 D2
Centereach U.S.A. 177 L5
Center Hill Lake resr U.S.A. 174 C5
Center Point U.S.A. 175 C5
Centerville AL U.S.A. 175 C5
Centerville IA U.S.A. 174 A3
Centerville MO U.S.A. 174 B4
Centerville NC U.S.A. 176 G9
Centerville OH U.S.A. 176 C7
Centerville PA U.S.A. 176 F4
Centerville TN U.S.A. 174 C5
Centerville TX U.S.A. 179 D6
Centerville WV U.S.A. 176 E6
Cento Italy 56 D4
Centrafricaine, République country Africa see Central African Republic
Central admin. dist. Botswana 131 E4
Central Brazil 202 D4
Central Chile 200 C5
Central admin. reg. Ghana 125 E5
Central prov. Kenya 128 C5
Central admin. reg. Malawi 129 B8
Central U.S.A. 181 E6
Central prov. Zambia 127 F8
Central, Cordillera mts Bol. 200 D4
Central, Cordillera mts Col. 198 B4
Central, Cordillera mts Dom. Rep. 187 F3
Central, Cordillera mts Panama 186 C5
Central, Cordillera mts Peru 200 A2
Central, Cordillera mts Phil. 74 B2
Central African Empire country Africa see Central African Republic
▶Central African Republic country Africa 126 C3
known as Centrafricaine, République in French; formerly known as Central African Empire or Ubangi-Shari
africa [countries] 114–117
Central Australia Aboriginal Reserve Australia 150 E4
Central Brahui Range mts Pak. 101 F4
Central Butte Canada 167 J5
Central City IA U.S.A. 174 B3
Central City NE U.S.A. 178 C3
Central City PA U.S.A. 176 G5
Central de Minas Brazil 207 L5
Central Desert Aboriginal Land res. Australia 148 A4
Central Falls U.S.A. 177 N4
Centralia IL U.S.A. 174 B4
Centralia WA U.S.A. 180 B3
Central Islip U.S.A. 177 L5
Central Kalahari Game Reserve nature res. Botswana 131 D4
Central Makran Range mts Pak. 101 F5
Central Mount Wedge Australia 148 A4
Central'noolesnoy Zapovednik nature res. Rus. Fed. 43 N5
Central Plateau Conservation Area nature res. Australia 147 E5
Central Provinces state India see Madhya Pradesh
Central Range mts Lesotho 133 M6
Central Range mts P.N.G. 73 J7
Central Russian Upland hills Rus. Fed. 43 R7
also known as Sredne-Russkaya Vozvyshennost'
Central Siberian Plateau Rus. Fed. 39 L3
also known as Siberia or Sredne-Sibirskoye Ploskogor'ye
Central Square U.S.A. 177 I2
Central Valley U.S.A. 182 B1
Centre prov. Cameroon 125 H5
Centre admin. reg. France 50 H5
Centre U.S.A. 175 C5
Centreville MD U.S.A. 177 I6
Centreville VA U.S.A. 176 H7
Centurion S. Africa 133 M2
formerly known as Verwoerdburg
Cenxi China 87 D4
Ceos i. Greece see Kea
Céou r. France 50 H8
Cephaloedium Sicilia Italy see Cefalù
Cephalonia i. Greece 59 B10
also known as Kefallinia; also spelt Kefallonia
Čepin Croatia 56 K3
Čepkeliu nature res. Lith. 42 F8
Ceprano Italy 56 F7
Cepu Indon. 77 E4
Cer hills Yugo. 58 A4
Ceram i. Indon. see Seram
Ceram Sea Indon. see Seram Sea
Cerbat Mountains U.S.A. 183 J6
Cerbol r. Spain see Servol
Cercal hill Port. 54 C7
Čerchov mt. Czech Rep. 49 J6
Cère r. France 51 H8
Cerea Italy 56 D3
Cereal Canada 167 I5
Cereales Arg. 204 E5
Ceres Arg. 204 E3
Ceres Brazil 206 D2
Ceres S. Africa 132 D10
Ceres U.S.A. 182 D4
Céret France 51 I10
Cereté Col. 198 C2
Cerf, Lac du l. Canada 173 R4
Cerignola Italy 56 H7
Cerigo i. Greece see Kythira
Çerikli Turkey 106 C3
Cêringgolêb China see Dongco
Çerkeş Turkey 106 C2
Çerkezköy Turkey 58 J7
Cerknica Slovenia 56 G3
Cermei Romania 58 C2
Çermik Turkey 107 D3
Cerna Romania 58 J3
Cerna r. Romania 58 D3
Cerna r. Romania 58 D4
Cerna r. Romania 58 F4
Cernat Romania 58 H3
Cernăuţi Ukr. see Chernivtsi
Cernavodă Romania 58 J4
Cernay France 51 N5
Cerqueira César Brazil 206 D10
Cerralvo Mex. 185 F3
Cerralvo, Isla i. Mex. 184 C3
Cërrik Albania 58 A7
Cerrillos Arg. 200 D6
Cerritos Mex. 185 E4
Cerro Azul Brazil 203 B8
Cerro Azul Mex. 185 F4
Cerro de Pasco Peru 200 A2
Cerro Hoya, Parque Nacional nat. park Panama 186 C6
Cerro Manantiales Chile 205 C9
Cerrón mt. Spain 55 H8
Cerrón, Cerro mt. Venez. 198 D2
Cerro Negro Chile 200 C5
Cerros Colorados, Embalse resr Arg. 204 C5
Cerros de Amotape, Parque Nacional nat. park Peru 198 A5
Certaldo Italy 56 D5
Certeju de Sus Romania 58 D3
Cervantes Australia 151 A6
Cervantes, Cerro mt. Arg. 205 B8
Cervaro r. Italy 56 H7
Cervati, Monte mt. Italy 57 H8
Cervenia Romania 58 G5
Cervera Spain 55 M3
Cervera de Pisuerga Spain 54 G2
Cerveteri Italy 56 E7
historically known as Caere
Cervia Italy 56 E4
Cervialto, Monte mt. Italy 57 H8
Cervignano del Friuli Italy 56 F3
Cervina, Punta mt. Italy 56 D2
Cervione Corse France 51 P10
Cervo Spain 54 D1
César dept Col. 198 C2
César r. Col. 198 C2
Cesarò Sicilia Italy 57 G11
Cesena Italy 56 E4
Cesenatico Italy 56 E4
Cēsis Latvia 42 G4
historically known as Wenden
Česká Lípa Czech Rep. 49 L5
Česká Republika country Europe see Czech Republic
České Budějovice Czech Rep. 49 L7
formerly known as Budweis
České Středohoří hills Czech Rep. 49 K5
Českomoravská Vysočina hills Czech Rep. 49 L6
Český Krumlov Czech Rep. 49 L7
Český Les mts Czech Rep./Germany 49 J6
Český Těšín Czech Rep. 49 P6
Česma r. Croatia 56 I3
Çeşme Turkey 106 A3
Cessnock Australia 147 F3
Cesson-Sévigné France 50 E4
Cestas France 50 F8
Cestos r. Liberia 124 C5
Cesuras Spain 54 C1
Cesvaine Latvia 42 H5
Cêtar China 84 D4
formerly known as Qaidar
Cetate Romania 58 E4
Cetatea Albă Ukr. see Bilhorod-Dnistrovs'kyy
Cetina r. Croatia 56 I5
Cetinje Crna Gora Yugo. 56 K6
Cetraro Italy 57 H9

▶Ceuta N. Africa 54 F9
Spanish Territory.
africa [countries] 114–117

Ceva-i-Ra reef Fiji 145 G4
also spelt Theva-i-Ra
Cévennes mts France 51 J9
Cévennes, Parc National des nat. park France 51 J8
Čevetjävri Fin. see Sevettijärvi
Cevizli Turkey 109 I1
Cevizlik Turkey see Maçka
Ceyhan Turkey 106 C3
Ceyhan r. Turkey 107 C3
Ceyhan Boğazı r. mouth Turkey 108 G1
Ceylanpınar Turkey 107 E3
also known as Resülayn
Ceylon country Asia see Sri Lanka
Cézanne r. France 51 K8
Chaacha Turkm. 102 E5
also spelt Chäche
Chābahār Iran 101 E5
Chablais mts France 51 M6
Chablé Mex. 185 H5
Chablis France 51 J5
Chabre ridge France 51 L8
Chabrol i. New Caledonia see Lifou
Chabyêr Caka salt l. China 89 D6
Chaca Chile 200 C4
Chacabuco Arg. 204 E4
Chacarilla Bol. 200 C4
Chachahuén, Sierra mt. Arg. 204 C5
Chachapoyas Peru 198 B6
Chacharaura-Binaganj India 96 C4
Chäche Turkm. see Chaacha
Chachersk Belarus 43 L9
Chachevichy Belarus 43 K8
Chachoengsao Thai. 79 C5
Chaco prov. Arg. 204 E2
formerly known as Presidente Juan Perón
Chaco Boreal reg. Para. 201 F5
Chaco Culture National Historical Park nat. park U.S.A. 181 F5
Chacon, Cape U.S.A. 166 C4
Chacorão, Cachoeira da waterfall Brazil 199 G6
Chacra de Piros Peru 200 B2

▶Chad country Africa 120 C6
5th largest country in Africa. Also spelt Tchad or Tshad.
africa [countries] 114–117

▶Chad, Lake Africa 120 B6
4th largest lake in Africa.
africa [landscapes] 112–113

Chadaasan Mongolia 84 D2
Chadan Rus. Fed. 84 A1
Chadileo r. Arg. 204 D5
Chadron U.S.A. 178 B3
Chadyr-Lunga Moldova see Ciadîr-Lunga
Chae Hom Thai. 78 B4
Chaek Kyrg. 103 H4
also spelt Chayek
Chaeryŏng N. Korea 83 B5
Chae Son National Park Thai. 78 B4
Chaffee U.S.A. 174 B4
Chaffers, Isla i. Chile 205 B7
Chaffey U.S.A. 172 A4
Chafurray Col. 198 C4
Chagai Pak. 101 F4
Chagai Hills Afgh./Pak. 101 E4
Chagalamarri India 94 C3
Chagan Kzyl-Ordinskaya Oblast' Kazakh. 103 F3
Chagan Vostochnyy Kazakhstan Kazakh. 103 I2
also spelt Shaghan
Chaganuzun Rus. Fed. 84 A1
Chagdo Kangri reg. China 89 D5
Chagha Khūr mt. Iran 100 B4
Chaghcharān Afgh. 101 F3
Chaglinka r. Kazakh. 103 G1
Chagny France 51 K6
Chagoda Rus. Fed. 43 Q2
Chagoda r. Rus. Fed. 43 Q2
Chagodoshcha r. Rus. Fed. 43 R3
Chagos Archipelago is Indian Ocean 218 L6
Chagoyan Rus. Fed. 82 C1
Chagra r. Rus. Fed. 102 B1
Chagrayskoye Plato plat. Kazakh. see Shagyray, Plato
Chagres, Parque Nacional nat. park Panama 186 D5
Chaguanas Trin. and Tob. 187 H5
Chaguaramas Venez. 199 E2
Chagyl Turkm. 102 C4
Chagyllyshor, Vpadina depr. Turkm. 102 C4
Chaha r. Ukr. 58 K3
Chahah Burjal Afgh. 101 E4
Chāh Ākhvor Iran 101 D3
Chaharbagh Afgh. 101 G3
Chahār Maḥāll va Bakhtīārī prov. Iran 100 B3
Chah Baba well Iran 100 C3
Chāh Bahār, Khalīj-e b. Iran 101 E5
Chahbounia Alg. 55 N9
Chāh-e Āqalū well Iran 100 C4
Chāh-e Bābā well Iran 100 C3
Chāh-e Gonbad well Iran 100 D3
Chāh-e Kavīr well Iran 100 D3
Chāh-e Khorāsān well Iran 100 C3
Chāh-e Malek well Iran 100 C3
Chāh-e Malek Mīrzā well Iran 100 C4
Chāh-e Mīrzā well Iran 100 C3
Chāh-e Mūjān well Iran 100 C3
Chāh-e Nūklok well Iran 100 C3
Chāh-e Nūklok well Iran 101 D3
Chāh-e Pansu well Iran 100 C3
Chāh-e Qeyşar well Iran 100 C4
Chāh-e Qobād well Iran 100 C3
Chāh-e Raḥmān well Iran 101 D4
Chāh-e Shūr well Iran 100 C3
Chāh-e Ţāqestān well Iran 100 C4
Chāh-e Tūnī well Iran 100 D3
Chāh Haji Abdulla well Iran 100 C3
Chāh-i-Ab Afgh. 101 G2
Chāh Pās well Iran 100 C3
Chāh Ru'ī well Iran 101 D4
Chah Sandan Pak. 101 E4
Chahuites Mex. 185 G5
Chai r. China 82 A4
Chaibasa India 97 E5
Chaigneau, Lac l. Canada 169 H2
Chaigoubu China see Huai'an
Chaillu, Massif du mts Gabon 126 A5
Chainat Thai. 79 C5
Chainjoin Co l. China 89 D5
Chai Si r. Thai. 79 C5
Chaitén Chile 205 B6
Chai Wan Hong Kong China 87 [inset]
Chaiwopu China 88 D3
Chaiya Thai. 79 B6
Chaiyaphum Thai. 79 C5
Chajarí Arg. 204 F3
Chakai India 97 E4
Chakar r. Pak. 101 G4
Chakari Zimbabwe 131 F3
Chake Chake Tanz. 129 C6
Chakhānsūr Afgh. 101 E4
Chakia India 97 D4
Chak Jhumra Pak. 101 H4
Chakonipau, Lake Canada 169 G1
Chakradharpur India 97 E5
Chakulia India 97 E5
Chakwal Pak. 101 H3
Chala Peru 200 B3
Chala Tanz. 129 A6
Chalais France 50 G7
Chalap Dalan mts Afgh. 101 F3
Chalatenango El Salvador 185 H6
Chaláua Moz. 131 H3
Chalaxung China 86 A1
Chalbi Desert Kenya 128 C4
Chalcedon Turkey see Kadıköy
Chalengkou China 84 B4
Chaleur Bay inlet Canada 169 H3
also known as Chaleurs, Baie de

Cheyenne River Indian Reservation res. U.S.A. 178 B2
Cheyenne Wells U.S.A. 178 B4
Cheyne Bay Australia 151 B7
Cheyur India 94 D3
Cheyyar r. India 94 C3
Chezacut Canada 166 E4
Chhabra India 96 C4
Chhapar India 96 B4
Chhapra India 97 E4
formerly spelt Chapra
Chhata India 96 C4
Chhatak Bangl. 97 F4
Chhatarpur Jharkhand India 97 E4
Chhatarpur Madhya Pradesh India 96 C4
Chhatrapur India 95 E2
Chhattisgarh state India 97 D5
Chhay Arêng, Stœng r. Cambodia 79 C6
Chhibramau India 96 C4
Chhindwara India 96 C5
Chhipa Barod India 96 C4
Chhlong, Prêk r. Cambodia 79 D5
Chhota Chhindwara India 96 C5
Chhota Udepur India 96 B5
Chhuikhadan India 96 D5
Chhuk Cambodia see Phumĭ Chhuk
Chhukha Bhutan 97 F4
Chiai Taiwan 87 G4
also spelt Jiayi
Ch'iak-san National Park S. Korea 83 C5
Chiang Dao Thai. 78 B4
Chiange Angola 127 B8
formerly known as Vila de Almoster
Chiang Kham Thai. 78 C4
Chiang Khan Thai. 78 C4
Chiang Mai Thai. 78 B4
also spelt Chiengmai
Chiang Rai Thai. 78 B4
Chiani r. Italy 56 E6
Chiapa Mex. 185 G5
Chiapas state Mex. 185 G5
Chiat'ura Georgia 107 E2
Chiautla Mex. 185 F5
Chiavari Italy 56 B4
Chiavenno Italy 56 B2
Chiba Japan 91 G7
Chiba pref. Japan 90 G7
Chibemba Angola 127 B8
Chibi China 87 E2
Chibia Angola 127 B8
formerly known as João de Almeida
Chibit Rus. Fed. 88 D1
Chibizovka Rus. Fed. see Zherdevka
Chiboma Moz. 131 G4
Chibougamau Canada 169 F3
Chibougamau, Lac l. Canada 169 F3
Chibu-Sangaku National Park Japan 91 E6
English form Japan Alps National Park
Chibuto Moz. 131 G5
Chibuzhang Hu l. China 89 E5
Chibwe Zambia 127 F8
Chicacole India see Srikakulam

▶Chicago U.S.A. 174 C3
4th most populous city in North America.
world [cities] 24–25

Chicago Heights U.S.A. 172 F9
Chicala Angola 127 C7
Chicamba Moz. 131 G3
Chicapa r. Angola 127 D6
Chic-Chocs, Monts mts Canada 169 H3
Chic-Chocs, Réserve Faunique des nature res. Canada 169 H3
Chicera Hamba hill Romania 58 F3
Chicha well Chad 120 C5
Chichagof Island U.S.A. 164 F4
Chichak r. Pak. 101 F5
Chichaoua Morocco 122 C3
Chichas, Cordillera de mts Bol. 200 D5
Chicheng China 85 G3
Chicheng China see Pengxi
Chichén Itzá tourist site Mex. 185 H4
Chichester U.K. 47 L13
Chichester Range mts Australia 150 B4
Chichgarh India 94 D1
Chichibu Japan 83 E6
Chichibu-Tama National Park Japan 91 F7
Chichijima-rettō is Japan 73 J1
Chichiriviche Venez. 199 D2
Chicholi India 96 C5
Chickahominy r. U.S.A. 177 I8
Chickasawhay r. U.S.A. 175 B6
Chickasha U.S.A. 179 C5
Chiclana de la Frontera Spain 54 E8
Chiclayo Peru 198 B6
Chico r. Chubut Arg. 205 C6
Chico r. Chubut Arg. 205 D7
Chico r. Santa Cruz Arg. 205 C8
Chico U.S.A. 182 C2
Chicoa Moz. 131 G2
Chicobea i. Fiji see Cikobia
Chicobi, Lac l. Canada 173 O2
Chicomba Angola 127 B8
Chicomo Moz. 131 G5
Chicomucelo Mex. 185 G6
Chiconono Moz. 129 B8
Chicopee U.S.A. 177 M3
Chico Sapocoy, Mount Phil. 74 B2
Chicoutimi Canada 169 G3
Chicoutimi r. Canada 169 G3
Chicualacuala Moz. 131 F4
formerly known as Malvérnia
Chicuma Angola 127 B8
Chidambaram India 94 C4
Chido S. Korea 83 B6
Chiede Angola 127 C9
Chiefland U.S.A. 175 D6
Chiemsee l. Germany 48 J8
Chiengi Zambia 127 F7
Chiengmai Thai. see Chiang Mai
Chienti r. Italy 56 F5
Chieo Lan Reservoir Thai. 79 B6
Chieri Italy 51 N7
Chiers r. France 51 L3
Chiese r. Italy 56 C3
Chieti Italy 56 G6
historically known as Teate
Chifeng China 85 H3
also known as Ulanhad
Chifre, Serra do mts Brazil 203 D6
Chifunde Moz. 131 G2
formerly known as Tembué
Chiganak Kazakh. 103 H3
also spelt Shyghanaq
Chiginagak, Mount vol. U.S.A. 164 D4
Chignecto Bay Canada 169 H4
Chignecto Game Sanctuary nature res. Canada 169 H4
Chignik U.S.A. 164 D4
Chigorodó Col. 198 B3
Chigu China 89 E6
Chiguana Bol. 200 D5
Chigubo Moz. 131 G4
Chigu Co l. China 89 E6
Chihli, Gulf of China see Bo Hai
Chihuahua Mex. 184 D2
Chihuahua state Mex. 184 D2
Chiili Kazakh. 103 F3
also spelt Shieli
Chijinpu China 84 C3
Chikalda India 96 C5
Chikan China 87 D4
Chikaskia r. U.S.A. 178 C4
Chik Ballapur India 94 C3
Chikhachevo Rus. Fed. 43 K4
Chikhali Kalan Parasia India 96 C5
Chikhli India 94 C1
Chikmagalur India 94 B3
Chikodi India 94 B2
Chikodi Road India 94 B2
Chikoy Rus. Fed. 85 E1
Chikoy r. Rus. Fed. 85 E1
Chikugo Japan 91 B8
Chikuma-gawa r. Japan 90 F6
Chikushino Japan 91 B8
Chikwa Zambia 129 B7
Chikwawa Malawi 129 B9
Chikyū-misaki pt Japan 90 G3
Chila Angola 127 B8
Chilanko r. Canada 166 F4
Chilanko Forks Canada 166 E4
Chilapa Mex. 185 F5
Chilas Jammu and Kashmir 96 B2
Chilaw Sri Lanka 94 C5
Chilca Peru 200 A3
Chilcaya Chile 200 C4
Chilcotin r. Canada 166 F5
Chilcott Island Australia 149 F3
Childers Australia 149 G5
Childress U.S.A. 179 B5
▶Chile country S. America 205 B7
southamerica [countries] 192–193
Chile Chico Chile 205 C7
Chilecito Arg. 204 D3
Chilengue, Serra do mts Angola 127 B8
Chilete Peru 200 A1
Chilhowie U.S.A. 176 D9
Chilia-Nouă Ukr. see Kiliya
Chilia Veche Romania 58 K3
Chilik Kazakh. 103 I4
also spelt Shelek
Chilik r. Kazakh. 103 I4
Chilika Lake India 95 E2
Chililabombwe Zambia 127 E8
formerly known as Bancroft
Chiliomodi Greece 59 D11
also known as Khiliomódhion
Chilko r. Canada 166 F4
Chilko Lake Canada 166 E5
Chilkoot Trail National Historic Site nat. park U.S.A. 164 F4
Chillagoe Australia 149 E3
Chillán Chile 204 B5
Chillar Arg. 204 F5
Chillicothe IL U.S.A. 172 D10
Chillicothe MO U.S.A. 178 D4
Chillicothe OH U.S.A. 176 C6
Chilliculco Peru 200 C4
Chillinji Jammu and Kashmir 96 B1
Chilliwack Canada 166 F5
Chil'mamedkum, Peski des. Turkm. 102 C4
Chilmari Bangl. 97 F4
Chiloé, Isla de i. Chile 205 B6
long form Chiloé, Isla Grande de
Chiloé, Isla Grande de i. Chile see Chiloé, Isla de
Chilombo Angola 127 D8
Chilonga Zambia 127 F8
Chiloquin U.S.A. 180 B4
Chilpancingo Mex. 185 F5
Chiltern Australia 147 E4
Chiltern Hills U.K. 47 L12
Chilton U.S.A. 172 E6
Chiluage Angola 127 D7
Chilubi Zambia 127 F7
Chilumba Malawi 129 B7
Chilung Taiwan 87 G3
English form Keelung; also spelt Jilong
Chilung Pass Jammu and Kashmir 96 C2
Chilwa, Lake Malawi 129 B8
Chimala Tanz. 129 B7
Chimaltenango Guat. 185 H6
Chimán Panama 186 D5
Chimanimani Zimbabwe 131 G3
formerly known as Mandidzuzure or Melsetter
Chi Ma Wan Hong Kong China 87 [inset]
Chimba Zambia 127 F7
Chimbas Arg. 204 C3
Chimbay Uzbek. 102 D4
also spelt Chimboy
Chimborazo mt. Ecuador 198 B5
Chimborazo prov. Ecuador 198 B5
Chimbote Peru 200 A2
Chimboy Uzbek. see Chimbay
Chimian Pak. 101 H4
Chimichaguá Col. 187 E5
Chimion Uzbek. 103 G4
Chimishliya Moldova see Cimişlia
Chimkent Kazakh. see Shymkent
Chimkentskaya Oblast' admin. div. Kazakh. see Yuzhnyy Kazakhstan
Chimoio Moz. 131 G3
formerly known as Vila Pery
Chimorra hill Spain 54 G6
Chimpay Arg. 204 D5
Chimtargha, Qullai mt. Tajik. 101 G2
also known as Chimtorga, Gora
Chimtorga, Gora mt. Tajik. see Chimtargha, Qullai
Chin state Myanmar 78 A3

▶China country Asia 80 D5
Most populous country in the world and in Asia. 2nd largest country in Asia and 4th largest in the world. Known in Chinese as Zhongguo; long form Zhongguo Renmin Gongheguo or Chung-hua Jen-min Kung-ho-kuo.
world [countries] 10–11
world [population] 22–23
asia [countries] 64–67

largest populations

	country	population	location	page#
1 ▶	China	1 260 137 000	Asia	80 D5
2 ▶	India	1 008 937 000	Asia	93 E6
3 ▶	USA	283 230 000	North America	170 E3
4 ▶	Indonesia	212 092 000	Asia	72 D8
5 ▶	Brazil	170 406 000	South America	202 B4
6 ▶	Russian Federation	145 491 000	Asia/Europe	38 F3
7 ▶	Pakistan	141 256 000	Asia	101 F4
8 ▶	Bangladesh	137 439 000	Asia	97 F4
9 ▶	Japan	127 096 000	Asia	90 E5
10 ▶	Nigeria	113 862 000	Africa	125 G4

China Mex. 185 F3
China, Republic of country Asia see Taiwan
China Bakir r. Myanmar see To
Chinacates Mex. 184 D3
China Lake U.S.A. 177 P1
Chinandega Nicaragua 186 B4
China Point U.S.A. 182 F9
Chinati Peak U.S.A. 181 F7
Chinaz Uzbek. 103 G4
also spelt Chinoz
Chincha Alta Peru 200 A3
Chinchaga r. Canada 166 G3
Chinchāl, Nahr r. Iraq 109 P3
Chinchilla Australia 149 F5
Chincholi India 94 C2
Chinchorro, Banco sea feature Mex. 185 I5
Chincolco Chile 204 C4
Chincoteague U.S.A. 177 J8
Chincoteague Bay U.S.A. 177 J8
Chinde Moz. 131 H3
Chin-do i. S. Korea 83 B6
Chindu China 86 A1
also known as Chuqung
Chindwin r. Myanmar 78 A3
Chineni Jammu and Kashmir 96 B2
Chinese Turkestan aut. reg. China see Xinjiang Uygur Zizhiqu
Chingaza, Parque Nacional nat. park Col. 198 C3
Chinghai prov. China see Qinghai
Chinghwa N. Korea 83 B5
Chingirlau Kazakh. 102 C2
also spelt Shyngghyrlau
Chingiz-Tau, Khrebet mts Kazakh. 103 I2
Chingleput India see Chengalpattu
Chingola Zambia 127 E8
Chinguar Angola 127 C8
Chinguetti Mauritania 122 B5
Chinguil Chad 126 C2
Chinhae S. Korea 83 C6
Chinhanda Moz. 131 G2
Chinhoyi Zimbabwe 131 F3
formerly spelt Sinoia
Chini India see Kalpa
Chiñijo Bol. 200 C3
Chining China see Jining
Chiniot Pak. 101 H4
Chinipas Mex. 184 C3
Chinit, Stœng r. Cambodia 79 D5
Chinju S. Korea 83 C6
Chinko r. Cent. Afr. Rep. 126 D3
Chinle U.S.A. 183 O5
Chinle Valley U.S.A. 183 O5
Chinle Wash watercourse U.S.A. 183 O5
Chinmen Taiwan 87 F3
also spelt Jinmen or Kinmen
Chinmen Tao i. Taiwan 87 F3
English form Quemoy
Chinna Ganjam India 94 D3
Chinnamanur India 94 C4
Chinnamp'o N. Korea see Namp'o
Chinna Salem India 94 C4
Chinnur India 94 C2
Chino Japan 91 F7
Chino U.S.A. 182 G7
Chino Creek watercourse U.S.A. 183 L7
Chinocup, Lake salt flat Australia 151 B7
Chinocup Nature Reserve Australia 151 B7
Chinon France 50 G5
Chinook U.S.A. 180 E2
Chinook Valley U.S.A. 183 L7
Chinoz Uzbek. see Chinaz
Chinsali Zambia 129 B7
Chintalnar India 94 D2
Chintamani India 94 C3
Chinteni Romania 58 E2
Chinú Col. 198 C2
Chinyama Litapi Zambia 127 D8
Chin'yavoryk Rus. Fed. 40 J3
Chioco Moz. 131 G3
Chioggia Italy 56 E3
Chiona Tanz. 129 B6
Chios Greece 59 H10
Chios i. Greece 59 G10
also spelt Khios
Chios Strait Greece 59 H10
English form Khios Strait
Chipanga Moz. 131 G3
Chipata Zambia 129 B8
formerly known as Fort Jameson
Chipchihua, Sierra de mts Arg. 205 C6
Chipili Zambia 127 F7
Chipindo Angola 127 B8
Chiping China 85 H4
Chipinga Zimbabwe see Chipinge
Chipinge Zimbabwe 131 G4
formerly spelt Chipinga
Chipiona Spain 54 E8
Chipley U.S.A. 175 C6
Chiplun India 94 B2
Chipman Canada 169 H4
Chipoia Angola 127 C8
Chippenham U.K. 47 J12
Chipperone, Monte mt. Moz. 131 G3
Chippewa r. MN U.S.A. 178 D2
Chippewa r. WI U.S.A. 172 A6
Chippewa, Lake U.S.A. 172 B5
Chippewa Falls U.S.A. 172 B6
Chipping Norton U.K. 47 K12
Chiprovtsi Bulg. 58 D5
Chipundu Zambia 127 F8
Chipuriro Zimbabwe see Guruve
Chipurupalle Andhra Pradesh India 95 D2
Chipurupalle Andhra Pradesh India 95 D2
Chiquian Peru 200 A2
Chiquibul, Parque Nacional nat. park Belize 185 H5
Chiquilá Mex. 185 I4
Chiquimula Guat. 185 H6
Chiquinquira Col. 198 C3
Chiquitirca Peru 200 B3
Chiquita, Mar l. Arg. 204 E4
Chiquitos, Llanos de plain Bol. 201 E4
Chiquitos Jesuit Missions tourist site Brazil 201 E4
Chir r. Rus. Fed. 41 G6
Chirada India 94 D3
Chiradzulu Malawi 129 B8
Chirala India 94 D3
Chiramba Moz. 131 G3
Chirambirá, Punta pt Col. 198 B3
Chiras Afgh. 101 F3
Chirawa India 89 A6
Chirchik Uzbek. 103 G4
Chirchik r. Uzbek. 103 G4
Chiredzi Zimbabwe 131 F4
Chire Wildlife Reserve nature res. Eth. 128 C1
Chirfa Niger 125 I1
Chirgua r. Venez. 199 E2
Chiricahua National Monument nat. park U.S.A. 183 O9
Chiricahua Peak U.S.A. 181 E7
Chiriguaná Col. 198 C2
Chirikof Island U.S.A. 164 D4
Chiriquí, Golfo de b. Panama 186 C5
Chiriquí, Laguna de b. Panama 186 C5
Chiriquí Grande Panama 186 C5
Chiri-san mt. S. Korea 83 B6
Chiri-san National Park S. Korea 83 B6
Chirka-Kem' r. Rus. Fed. 44 P2
Chirnside U.K. 46 J8
Chirpan Bulg. 58 G6
Chirripó, Parque Nacional nat. park Costa Rica 186 C5
Chirundu Zimbabwe 131 F3
Chirūyeh Iran 100 C5
Chisamba Zambia 127 F8
Chisana r. U.S.A. 166 A2
Chisasa Zambia 127 E8
Chisasibi Canada 168 E2
Chisec Guat. 185 H6
Chisekesi Zambia 127 E9
Chiselet Romania 58 H4
Chisenga Malawi 129 B7
Chishima-retto is Rus. Fed. see Kuril Islands
Chishmy Rus. Fed. 40 J5
Chisholm Canada 167 H4
Chisholm ME U.S.A. 177 O1
Chisholm MN U.S.A. 178 D2
Chishtian Mandi Pak. 101 H4
Chishui China 86 C2
Chishuihe China 86 C3
Chishui He r. China 86 C2
Chisimaio Somalia see Kismaayo

▶Chişinău Moldova 58 J1
Capital of Moldova. Formerly spelt Kishinev.

Chişineu-Criş Romania 58 C2
Chisone r. Italy 51 N8
Chistopol' Rus. Fed. 40 I5
Chistopol'ye Kazakh. 103 F1
Chistyakovskoye Kazakh. 103 G1
Chita Bol. 200 D5
Chita Col. 198 C3
Chita Rus. Fed. 85 G1
Chita Tanz. 129 B7
Chitado Angola 127 B9
Chitaldrug India see Chitradurga
Chitalwana India 96 A4
Chita Oblast admin. div. Rus. Fed. see Chitinskaya Oblast'
Chitato Angola 127 D6
formerly known as Portugália
Chitayevo Rus. Fed. 40 I3
Chitek Lake Canada 167 J4
Chitek Lake l. Canada 167 L4
Chitembo Angola 127 C8
Chitinskaya Oblast' admin. div. Rus. Fed. 85 H1
English form Chita Oblast
Chitipa Malawi 129 B7
Chitobe Moz. 131 G4
formerly known as Machaze
Chitokoloki Zambia 127 D8
Chitongo Zambia 127 E9
Chitor India see Chittaurgarh
Chitose Japan 90 G3
Chitradurga India 94 C3
formerly known as Chitaldrug
Chitrakut India 96 D4
Chitral Pak. 101 G3
Chitral r. Pak. 101 G3
Chitravati r. India 94 C3
Chitré Panama 186 C6
Chitrod India 96 A5
Chittagong Bangl. 97 F5
also spelt Chattagam
Chittagong admin. div. Bangl. 97 F5
Chittaranjan India 97 E5
formerly known as Mihidjan
Chittaurgarh India 96 B4
formerly known as Chitor; formerly spelt Chittorgarh
Chittoor India 94 C3
Chittorgarh India see Chittaurgarh
Chittur India 94 C4
Chitungulu Zambia 129 B8
Chitungwiza Zimbabwe 131 F3
Chiu Lung Hong Kong China see Kowloon
Chiume Angola 127 D8
Chiúre Novo Moz. 131 H2
Chiusa Sclafani Sicilia Italy 57 F11
Chiúta Moz. 131 G2
Chiva Spain 55 K5
Chivasso Italy 56 A3
Chivato, Punta pt Mex. 184 C3
Chivay Peru 200 C3
Chive Bol. 200 C3
Chivela Mex. 185 G5
Chivhu Zimbabwe 131 F3
formerly known as Enkeldoorn
Chivilcoy Arg. 204 E4
Chiyirchik, Pereval pass Kyrg. see Ashusuu
Chizarira Hills Zimbabwe 131 E3
Chizarira National Park Zimbabwe 131 E3
Chizha Vtoraya Kazakh. 102 B2
Chizu Japan 91 D7
Chkalov Rus. Fed. see Orenburg
Chkalovo Kazakh. 103 G1
Chkalovsk Rus. Fed. 40 G4
Chkalovskaya Oblast' admin. div. Rus. Fed. see Orenburgskaya Oblast'
Chkalovskiy Rus. Fed. 44 P2
Chkalovskoye Rus. Fed. 82 D3
Chlef Alg. see Ech Chélif
Chloride U.S.A. 183 J6
Chlumec nad Cidlinou Czech Rep. 49 M5
Chlya, Ozero l. Rus. Fed. 82 F1
Chmielnik Poland 49 R5
Choa Chu Kang Sing. 76 [inset]
Choa Chu Kang hill Sing. 76 [inset]
Chŏâm Khsant Cambodia 79 D5
also spelt Cheom Ksan
Choapa r. Chile 204 C3
Chobe admin. dist. Botswana 131 E3
Chobe National Park Botswana 131 E3
Choch'iwŏn S. Korea 83 B5
Chocianów Poland 49 M4
Chociwel Poland 49 M2
Choco dept Col. 198 B3
Chocolate Mountains U.S.A. 183 I8
Chocontá Col. 198 C3
Choctawhatchee r. U.S.A. 175 C6
Chodavaram India 94 D2
Chodecz Poland 49 Q3
Chodelka r. Poland 49 S4
Cho-do i. N. Korea 83 B5
Chodro Rus. Fed. 84 A1
Choduralyg Rus. Fed. 84 C1
Chodzież Poland 49 N3
Choele Choel Arg. 204 D5
Chofombo Moz. 131 F2
Choghādak Iran 100 B4
Chogo Lungma Glacier Jammu and Kashmir 96 B2
Chograyskoye Vodokhranilishche resr Rus. Fed. 41 H7
Choiceland Canada 167 J4
Choique Arg. 204 E5
Choiseul i. Solomon Is 145 E2
formerly known as Lauru
Choiseul Sound sea chan. Falkland Is 205 F8
Choix Mex. 184 C3
Chojna Poland 49 L3
Chojnice Poland 49 O2
Chojnów Poland 49 M4
Chōkai-san vol. Japan 90 G5
Ch'ok'ē Mountains Eth. 128 C2
Chokpar Kazakh. 103 H4
also spelt Shokpar or Shoqpar
Choksum China 89 D6
Chokue Moz. see Chókwè
Chokurdakh Rus. Fed. 39 O2
Chókwè Moz. 131 G5
formerly known as Vila de Trego Morais; formerly spelt Chokue
Cho La pass China 86 A2
Cholame U.S.A. 182 D6
Cholame Creek r. U.S.A. 182 D6
Chola Shan mts China 86 A1
Cholet France 50 F5
Choloma Hond. 186 B4
Cholpon-Ata Kyrg. 103 I4
Cholula Mex. 185 F5
Choluteca Hond. 186 B4
Choma Zambia 127 E9
Chŏmch'ŏn S. Korea 83 C5
Chomo China see Yadong
Chomo Ganggar mt. China 89 E6
Chomo Lhari mt. Bhutan 97 F4
Chomo Yummo mt. China/India 97 F3
Chomun India 96 B4
Chomutov Czech Rep. 49 K5
Chona r. Rus. Fed. 39 K3
Ch'ŏnan S. Korea 83 B5
Chon Buri Thai. 79 C5
also known as Bar Pla Soi
Chonchi Chile 205 B6
Chone Ecuador 198 A5
Chong'an China see Wuyishan
Ch'ŏngch'ŏn-gang r. N. Korea 83 B5
Ch'ongdo S. Korea 83 C6
Chonggye China see Qonggyai
Chŏngja S. Korea 91 A7
Ch'ŏngjin N. Korea 82 C4
Chŏngju N. Korea 83 B5
Ch'ŏngju S. Korea 83 B5
Chongkü China 86 A2
Chongli China 85 G3
also known as Xiwanzi
Chonglong China see Zizhong
Chongming China 87 G2
also known as Chengqiao
Chongming Dao i. China 87 G2
Chongoroi Angola 127 B8
Chŏngp'yŏng N. Korea 83 B5
Chongqing China 86 C2
formerly spelt Chungking
Chongqing China see Chongzhou
Chongqing municipality China 87 C2
Chongren China 87 E3
also known as Bashan
Chŏngŭp S. Korea 83 B6
Chongwe Zambia 127 F8
Chongyang China 87 E2
also known as Tiancheng
Chongyang Xi r. China 87 F3
Chongyi China 87 E3
also known as Hengshui
Chonggy-Tayga, Gora mt. Rus. Fed. 84 B1
Chongzhou China 86 B2
formerly known as Chongqing
Chongzuo China 87 C4
also known as Taiping
Chŏnju S. Korea 83 B6
Chonogol Mongolia 85 G2
Chontalpa Mex. 185 G5
Chon Thanh Vietnam 79 D6

▶Cho Oyu mt. China/Nepal 97 E3
6th highest mountain in the world and in Asia.
world [physical features] 8–9

Chop Ukr. 49 T7
Chopan India 97 D4
Chopda India 96 B5
Cho Phuoc Hai Vietnam 79 D6
Chopimzinho Brazil 203 A8
Choptank r. U.S.A. 177 I7
Choquecamata Bol. 200 D4
Chor Pak. 101 G5
Chora Greece 59 C11
also spelt Khóra
Chorley U.K. 47 J10
Chornobyl' Ukr. 41 D6
also spelt Chernobyl'
Chornomors'ke Ukr. 41 E7
Chornomors'kyy Zapovidnyk nature res. Ukr. 41 D7
Choroszcz Poland 49 T2
Chorrochó Brazil 202 E4
Chortkiv Ukr. 41 C6
also spelt Chertkov
Chorwad India 94 A1
Ch'ŏrwŏn S. Korea 83 B5
Chorzele Poland 49 R2
Ch'osan N. Korea 83 B4
Chōsen-kaikyō sea chan. Japan/S. Korea see Nishi-suidō
Chōshi Japan 91 G7
Choshuenco, Volcán vol. Chile 204 B5
Chosica Peru 200 A2
Chos Malal Arg. 204 C5
Chosmes Arg. 204 D4
Choszczno Poland 49 M2
Chota Peru 198 B6
Chota Nagpur reg. India 97 D5
Choteau U.S.A. 180 D3
Chotila India 96 A5
Choûm Mauritania 122 B5
Chowan r. U.S.A. 177 I9
Chowchilla U.S.A. 182 D4
Chowghat India 94 B4
Chowilla Regional Reserve nature res. Australia 146 D3
Chown, Mount Canada 166 G4
Choya Arg. 204 D3
Choybalsan Mongolia 85 G2
Choyr Mongolia 85 F2
Chozi Zambia 129 B7
Chreïrik well Mauritania 122 B5
Chřiby hills Czech Rep. 49 O6
Chrisman U.S.A. 174 C4
Chrissiesmeer S. Africa 133 O3
Christchurch N.Z. 153 G11
Christiana S. Africa 133 J4
Christiania Norway see Oslo
Christian Island Canada 173 M6
Christiansburg U.S.A. 176 E8
Christianshåb Greenland see Qasigiannguit
Christian Sound sea chan. U.S.A. 166 C4
Christiansted Virgin Is (U.S.A.) 187 G3
Christie U.S.A. 172 C6
Christie Bay Canada 167 I2
Christina r. Canada 167 I3
Christmas Creek Australia 150 D3
Christmas Creek r. Australia 150 D3

▶Christmas Island terr. Indian Ocean 218 O6
Australian External Territory.
asia [countries] 64–67

Christopher, Lake salt flat Australia 151 D5
Christos Greece 59 H11
also spelt Hristós
Chrudim Czech Rep. 49 M6
Chrysi i. Greece 59 G14
Chrysochou Bay Cyprus 108 D2
also known as Chrysochous, Kolpos; also spelt Khrysokhou Bay
Chrysochous, Kolpos b. Cyprus see Chrysochou Bay
Chrysoupoli Greece 58 F8
also known as Khrisoúpolis
Chu Kazakh. see Shu
Chu r. Kazakh. 103 F3
Chuadanga Bangl. 97 F5
Chuali, Lago l. Moz. 133 Q1
Chuansha China 87 G2
Chubalung China 86 A2
Chubarovka Ukr. see Polohy
Chubarovo Rus. Fed. 43 R6
Chubartau Kazakh. see Barshatas
Chubbuck U.S.A. 180 D4
Chubut prov. Arg. 205 C6
Chubut r. Arg. 205 D6
Chuchkovo Rus. Fed. 41 G5
Chuckwalla Mountains U.S.A. 183 I8
Chucul Arg. 204 D4
Chucunaque r. Panama 186 D5
Chudniv Ukr. 41 D6
Chudovo Rus. Fed. 43 M2
Chudskoye, Ozero l. Estonia/Rus. Fed. see Peipus, Lake
Chudzin Belarus 42 H9
Chudz"yavr, Ozero l. Rus. Fed. 44 P1
Chugach Mountains U.S.A. 164 E3
Chūgoku-sanchi mts Japan 91 C7
Chuggqēnsumdo China see Jigzhi
Chuguchak China see Tacheng
Chuguyev Ukr. see Chuhuyiv
Chuguyevka Rus. Fed. 82 D3
Chuhai China see Zhuhai
Chuhuyiv Ukr. 41 F6
also spelt Chuguyev
Chu-Iliyskiye Gory mts Kazakh. 103 H3
Chuka China 86 A2
Chukai Malaysia see Cukai
Chukchagirskoye, Ozero l. Rus. Fed. 82 E1
Chukchi Peninsula Rus. Fed. see Chukotskiy Poluostrov
Chukchi Sea Rus. Fed./U.S.A. 164 B3
Chukhloma Rus. Fed. 40 G4
Chukotskiy, Mys c. Rus. Fed. 39 S3
Chukotskiy Poluostrov pen. Rus. Fed. 39 S3
English form Chukchi Peninsula
Chulakkurgan Kazakh. see Shollakorgan
Chulaktau Kazakh. see Karatau
Chulasa Rus. Fed. 40 H2
Chula Vista U.S.A. 183 G9
Chulkovo Rus. Fed. 43 R8
Chulucanas Peru 198 A6
Chulung Pass Pak. 96 C2
Chuluut Gol r. Mongolia 84 D1
Chulym Rus. Fed. 80 C1
Chulyshman r. Rus. Fed. 84 A1
Chulyshmanskoye Ploskogor'ye plat. Rus. Fed. 84 A1
Chum Rus. Fed. 40 L2
Chuma Bol. 200 C3
Chumba Eth. 128 C3
Chumbicha Arg. 204 D3
Chumda China 86 A1
Chumerna mt. Bulg. 58 G6
Chumikan Rus. Fed. 82 D1
Chum Phae Thai. 78 C4
Chumphon Thai. 79 B6
Chum Saeng Thai. 78 C5
Chuna r. Rus. Fed. 39 J4
Chuña Huasi Arg. 204 D3
Chun'an China 87 F2
also known as Pailing
Chuna-Tundra plain Rus. Fed. 44 P2
Ch'unch'ŏn S. Korea 83 B5
Chundzha Kazakh. 103 I4
also spelt Shonzha
Chunga Zambia 127 E8
Chung-hua Jen-min Kung-ho-kuo country Asia see China
Chung-hua Min-kuo country Asia see Taiwan
Ch'ungju S. Korea 83 B5
Chungking China see Chongqing
Ch'ungmu S. Korea see T'ongyŏng
Chŭngsan N. Korea 83 B5
Chungu Tanz. 129 C7
Chungyang Shanmo mts Taiwan 87 G4
also known as Taiwan Shan
Chunhua China 82 C4
Chunhuhux Mex. 185 H5
Chunxi China see Gaochun
Chunya r. Rus. Fed. 39 J3
Chunya Tanz. 129 B7
Chu Oblast admin. div. Kyrg. see Chüy
Chuŏr Phnum Dângrêk mts Cambodia/Thai. 79 D5
Chuosijia China see Guanyinqiao
Chupa Rus. Fed. 44 P2
Chūplū Iran 100 A2
Chuquicamata Chile 200 C5
Chuquisaca dept Bol. 201 D5
Chuqung China see Chindu
Chur Rus. Fed. 40 J4
Chur Switz. 51 P6
also spelt Coire; historically known as Curia
Churachandpur India 97 G4
Chūrān Iran 100 C4
Churapcha Rus. Fed. 39 N3
Churayevo Rus. Fed. 40 J5
Church Hill MD U.S.A. 177 J6
Church Hill TN U.S.A. 176 C9
Churchill Canada 167 M3
Churchill r. Man. Canada 167 M3
Churchill r. Nfld. Canada 169 I2
formerly known as Hamilton
Churchill, Cape Canada 167 M3
Churchill Falls Canada 169 I2
Churchill Lake Canada 167 I4
Churchill Mountains Antarctica 223 K1
Churchill Peak Canada 166 E3
Churchill Sound sea chan. Canada 168 E1
Churchville U.S.A. 176 F7
Chureg-Tag, Gora mt. Rus. Fed. 84 A1
Churia Ghati Hills Nepal 97 E4
Churilovo Rus. Fed. 43 L6
Churin Peru 200 A2
Churov Rus. Fed. 40 H4
Churovichi Rus. Fed. 43 N9
Churu India 96 B3
Churubay Nura Kazakh. see Abay
Churuguara Venez. 198 D2
Chūrui Japan 90 H3
Churumuco Mex. 185 E5
Chushul Jammu and Kashmir 96 C2
Chuska Mountains U.S.A. 183 O5
Chusovaya r. Rus. Fed. 40 K4
Chusovoy Rus. Fed. 40 K4
Chust Ukr. see Khust
Chust Uzbek. 103 G4
Chute-Rouge Canada 173 Q4
Chutung Taiwan 87 G3
also known as Zhudong
Chuuk i. Micronesia 220 E5
Chuvashia aut. rep. Rus. Fed. see Chuvashskaya Respublika
Chuvashskaya A.S.S.R. aut. rep. Rus. Fed. see Chuvashskaya Respublika
Chuvashskaya Respublika aut. rep. Rus. Fed. 40 H5
English form Chuvashia; formerly known as Chuvashskaya A.S.S.R.
Chuwang-san National Park S. Korea 83 C5
Chuxiong China 86 B3
Chüy admin. div. Kyrg. 103 H4
English form Chu Oblast; also known as Chuyskaya Oblast'
Chuy Uruguay 204 G4
Chu Yang Sin mt. Vietnam 79 E5
Chuyskaya Oblast' admin. div. Kyrg. see Chüy
Chuzhou China 87 F1
Chyganak Kazakh. 103 G3
Chyhirynskaye Vodaskhovishcha resr Belarus 43 K8
Chymyshliya Moldova see Cimişlia
Chyrvonaya Slabada Belarus 43 J9
Chyrvonaye, Vozyera l. Belarus 42 I9
Chyulu Range mts Kenya 128 C5
Ciacova Romania 58 C3
Ciadâr-Lunga Moldova see Ciadîr-Lunga
Ciadîr-Lunga Moldova 58 J2
formerly spelt Ceadâr-Lunga or Ciadâr-Lunga or Chadyr-Lunga
Ciamis Indon. 77 E4
Ciampino airport Italy 56 E7
Cianjur Indon. 77 D4
Cianorte Brazil 206 A10
Cibadak Indon. 77 D4
Cibatu Indon. 77 E4
Cibecue U.S.A. 183 N7
Cibinong Indon. 77 D4
Cibitoke Burundi 126 F5
Cibolo Creek r. U.S.A. 179 C6
Ci Buni r. Indon. 77 D4
Cibuta, Sierra mt. Mex. 184 C2
Čićarija mts Croatia 56 F3
Çiçekdağı Turkey 106 C3
also known as Boyalık
Çiçekli Turkey 108 G1
Çiçekli Turkey 59 J9
Cicero U.S.A. 172 F9
Cícero Dantas Brazil 202 E4
Ćićevac Srbija Yugo. 58 C5
Cidacos r. Spain 55 J2
Cide Turkey 106 C2
Cidlina r. Czech Rep. 49 M5
Ciechanów Poland 49 R3
Ciechanowiec Poland 49 T3
Ciechocinek Poland 49 P3
Ciego de Ávila Cuba 186 D2
Ciénaga Col. 198 C2

Comrat Moldova **58** J2
formerly spelt Komrat
Con, Sông *r.* Vietnam **78** D4
Cona China **89** E7
also spelt Tsona

▶**Conakry** Guinea **124** B4
Capital of Guinea.

Conambo Ecuador **198** B5
Conambo *r.* Ecuador **198** B5
Cona Niyeo Arg. **205** D6
Conay Chile **204** C3
Concarán Arg. **204** D4
Concarneau France **50** C5
Conceição *Amazonas* Brazil **199** F5
Conceição *Mato Grosso* Brazil **201** F1
Conceição *Paraíba* Brazil **202** E3
Conceição *Rondônia* Brazil **201** E2
Conceição *Roraima* Brazil **199** F4
Conceição *r.* Brazil **207** H3
Conceição da Barra Brazil **203** E6
Conceição das Alagoas Brazil **206** E6
Conceição de Macabu Brazil **207** L9
Conceição do Araguaia Brazil **202** B4
Conceição do Coité Brazil **202** E4
Conceição do Mato Dentro Brazil **203** D6
Conceição do Maú Brazil **199** G4
Concepción *Corrientes* Arg. **204** F3
Concepción *Tucumán* Arg. **204** D2
Concepción *Beni* Bol. **200** D2
Concepción *Santa Cruz* Bol. **201** E4
Concepción Chile **204** B5
Concepción Mex. **185** E3
Concepción *r.* Mex. **184** B2
Concepción Panama **186** C5
Concepción Para. **201** F5
Concepción, Canal *sea chan.* Chile **205** B8
Concepción, Punta *pt* Mex. **184** C3
Concepción del Uruguay Arg. **204** F4
Conception, Point U.S.A. **182** D7
Conception Bay Namibia **130** B4
Concesio Italy **56** C3
Concession Zimbabwe **131** F3
Concha Mex. **184** D4
Conchas Brazil **206** E9
Conchas Lake U.S.A. **181** F6
Conches-en-Ouche France **50** G4
Conchi Chile **200** C5
Concho Mex. **184** D3
Concho U.S.A. **183** O7
Concho *r.* U.S.A. **179** C6
Conchos *r. Chihuahua* Mex. **184** D2
Conchos *r. Nuevo León/Tamaulipas* Mex. **185** F3
Concord *CA* U.S.A. **182** B4
Concord *MI* U.S.A. **173** I8
Concord *NC* U.S.A. **174** D5

▶**Concord** *NH* U.S.A. **177** N2
State capital of New Hampshire.

Concord *PA* U.S.A. **176** H5
Concord *VA* U.S.A. **176** G8
Concord *VT* U.S.A. **177** N1
Concordia Arg. **204** F3
Concórdia *Amazonas* Brazil **199** E6
Concórdia *Santa Catarina* Brazil **203** A8
Concordia *Antioquia* Col. **198** C3
Concordia *Meta* Col. **198** C4
Concordia Mex. **184** D4
Concordia Peru **198** C6
Concordia S. Africa **132** B6
Concordia U.S.A. **178** C4
Concord Peak Afgh. **101** H2
Con Cuông Vietnam **78** D4
Conda Angola **127** B7
Condamine Australia **149** F5
Condamine *r.* Australia **147** F1
Conde Brazil **202** E4
Condega Nicaragua **186** B4
Condeixa Brazil **202** B2
Condé-sur-Noireau France **50** F4
Condeúba Brazil **202** D5
Condobolin Australia **147** E3
Condoe Moz. **131** G3
Condom France **50** G9
Condon U.S.A. **180** B3
Condor, Cordillera del *mts* Ecuador/Peru **198** B6
Conecuh *r.* U.S.A. **175** C6
Conejos Mex. **184** E3
Conejos U.S.A. **181** F5
Conejos *r.* U.S.A. **181** F5
Conemaugh *r.* U.S.A. **176** F5
Conero, Monte *hill* Italy **56** F5
Conestogo Lake Canada **173** M7
Conesus Lake U.S.A. **176** H3
Conesville *IA* U.S.A. **172** B9
Conesville *OH* U.S.A. **176** D5
Coney Island Sing. *see* **Serangoon, Pulau**
Coney Island U.S.A. **177** L5
Conflict Group *is* P.N.G. **149** F1
Confluence U.S.A. **176** F6
Confoederatio Helvetica *country* Europe *see* **Switzerland**
Confolens France **50** G6
Confusion Range *mts* U.S.A. **183** K3
Confuso *r.* Para. **201** F6
Congdü China *see* **Nyalam**
Conghua China **87** E4
Congjiang China **87** D3
also known as Bingmei
Congleton U.K. **47** J10
▶**Congo** *country* Africa **126** B5
formerly known as Congo (Brazzaville) *or* French Congo *or* Middle Congo *or* Moyen Congo; *long form* Congo, Republic of
africa [countries] ▶ 114–117

▶**Congo** *r.* Congo/Dem. Rep. Congo **127** B6
2nd longest river in Africa and 8th in the world. Formerly known as Zaïre.
africa [landscapes] ▶ 112–113

Congo (Brazzaville) *country* Africa *see* **Congo**
Congo (Kinshasa) *country* Africa *see* **Congo, Democratic Republic of**

▶**Congo, Democratic Republic of** *country* Africa **126** D5
3rd largest and 4th most populous country in Africa. Formerly known as Zaire or Belgian Congo or Congo (Kinshasa) or Congo Free State.
africa [countries] ▶ 114–117

Congo, Republic of *country* Africa *see* **Congo**
Congo Basin Dem. Rep. Congo **126** D5
Congo Free State *country* Africa *see* **Congo, Democratic Republic of**
Congonhas Brazil **207** J7
Congonhinhas Brazil **206** C10
Congress U.S.A. **183** L7
Conguillo, Parque Nacional *nat. park* Chile **204** C5
Conhuas Mex. **185** H5
Cónico, Cerro *mt.* Arg. **205** C6
Conil de la Frontera Spain **54** E8
Coniston Canada **173** M4
Coniston U.K. **47** I9
Conjuboy Australia **149** E3
Conkal Mex. **185** H4
Conklin Canada **167** I4
Conkouati, Réserve de Faune *nature res.* Congo **126** A5
Conlara *r.* Arg. **204** D4
Conn *r.* Canada **168** E2
Conn, Lough *l.* Rep. of Ireland **47** C9
Connacht *reg.* Rep. of Ireland *see* **Connaught**

Connaught Canada **173** M2
Connaught *reg.* Rep. of Ireland **47** C10
also spelt Connacht
Conneaut U.S.A. **176** E4
Conneaut Lake U.S.A. **176** E4
Conneautville U.S.A. **176** E4
Connecticut *r.* U.S.A. **177** M4
Connecticut *state* U.S.A. **177** M4
Connel U.K. **46** G7
Connells Lagoon Conservation Reserve *nature res.* Australia **148** C3
Connemara Australia **149** D5
Connemara *reg.* Rep. of Ireland **47** C10
Connemara National Park Rep. of Ireland **47** C10
Conner, Mount *hill* Australia **148** A5
Connersville U.S.A. **174** C4
Connolly, Mount Canada **166** C2
Connors Range *hills* Australia **149** F4
Cononaco Ecuador **198** C5
Cononaco *r.* Ecuador **198** C5
Conover U.S.A. **172** D4
Conquista Bol. **200** D2
Conquista Brazil **206** F6
Conrad U.S.A. **180** E2
Conroe U.S.A. **179** D6
Conroe, Lake U.S.A. **179** D6
Consecon Canada **173** P6
Consejo Belize **186** A3
Conselheiro Lafaiete Brazil **203** D7
Conselheiro Pena Brazil **203** D6
Conselice Italy **56** D4
Consett U.K. **47** K9
Consolación del Sur Cuba **186** C2
Côn Sơn *i.* Vietnam **79** D6
Consort Canada **167** I4
Constance Germany *see* **Konstanz**
Constance, Lake Germany/Switz. **51** P5
also known as Bodensee
Constância dos Baetas Brazil **199** F6
Constanța Romania **58** J4
also spelt Küstence; *historically known as* Tomi
Constanța *airport* Romania *see* **Kogălniceanu**
Constantia *tourist site* Cyprus *see* **Salamis**
Constantia Germany *see* **Konstanz**
Constantina Spain **54** F7
Constantine Alg. **123** G1
also known as Qacentina; *historically known as* Cirta
Constantine U.S.A. **172** H9
Constantine, Cape U.S.A. **164** D4
Constantinople Turkey *see* **İstanbul**
Constitución de 1857, Parque Nacional *nat. park* Mex. **184** B1
Consuelo Australia **149** F5
Consuelo Brazil **201** E3
Consul Canada **167** I5
Consul *r.* Canada **167** K1
Contagem Brazil **207** I6
Contamana Peru **200** B1
Contarina Italy **56** E3
Contas *r.* Brazil **202** E5
Conthey Switz. **51** N6
Contoocook *r.* U.S.A. **177** N2
Contoy, Isla *i.* Mex. **186** B2
Contratacion Col. **198** C3
Contreras, Embalse de *resr* Spain **55** J5
Contreras, Isla *i.* Chile **205** B8
Contres France **50** H5
Contria Brazil **207** I5
Contwoyto Lake Canada **167** I1
Convención Col. **198** C2
Convent U.S.A. **175** B6
Convoy U.S.A. **176** A5
Conway S. Africa **133** J8
Conway *AR* U.S.A. **179** D5
Conway *KY* U.S.A. **176** A8
Conway *NC* U.S.A. **177** H9
Conway *NH* U.S.A. **177** N2
Conway *SC* U.S.A. **175** E5
Conway, Cape Australia **149** F4
Conway, Lake *salt flat* Australia **146** B2
Conway National Park Australia **149** F4
Conway Springs U.S.A. **178** C4
Coober Pedy Australia **146** B2
Cooch Behar India *see* **Koch Bihar**
Coogoon *r.* Australia **147** F1
Cook Australia **146** A2
Cook U.S.A. **172** A3
Cook, Bahía de *b.* Chile **205** C9
Cook, Cape Canada **166** E5
▶**Cook, Mount** Canada/U.S.A. **166** B2
oceania [landscapes] ▶ 136–137

▶**Cook, Mount** N.Z. **153** E11
Highest mountain in New Zealand. Also known as Aoraki or Aorangi.

Cook Atoll Kiribati *see* **Tarawa**
Cookes Peak U.S.A. **181** F6
Cookeville U.S.A. **174** C4
Cookhouse S. Africa **133** J9
Cook Ice Shelf Antarctica **223** K2
Cook Inlet *sea chan.* U.S.A. **164** D3

▶**Cook Islands** S. Pacific Ocean **221** H7
Self-governing New Zealand Territory.
oceania [countries] ▶ 138–139

Cooksburg U.S.A. **177** K3
Cooks Passage Australia **149** E2
Cookstown U.K. **47** F9
Cook Strait N.Z. **152** I8
Cooktown Australia **149** E2
Coolabah Australia **147** E2
Cooladdi Australia **149** E5
Coolah Australia **147** F2
Coolamon Australia **147** E3
Coolgardie Australia **151** C6
Coolibah Australia **148** A2
Coolimba Australia **151** A6
Cooloola National Park Australia **149** G5
Coolum Beach Australia **149** G5
Cooma Australia **147** F4
Coombah Australia **146** D3
Coonabarabran Australia **147** F2
Coonalpyn Australia **146** C3
Coonamble Australia **147** F2
Coonana Aboriginal Reserve Australia **151** C6
Coondambo Australia **146** B2
Coondapoor India *see* **Kundapura**
Coongan *r.* Australia **150** B4
Coongan Aboriginal Reserve Australia **150** B4
Coongoola Australia **147** E1
Coon Rapids U.S.A. **174** A2
Cooper *r.* Australia **148** B2
Cooper U.S.A. **179** D5
Cooper Creek *watercourse* Australia **146** C2
also known as Barcoo Creek
Cooperdale U.S.A. **176** C5
Coopernook Australia **147** G2
Coopersburg U.S.A. **177** J5
Coopers Mills U.S.A. **177** P1
Cooper's Town Bahamas **186** D1
Cooperstown *ND* U.S.A. **178** C2
Cooperstown *NY* U.S.A. **177** K3
Coopracambra National Park Australia **147** F4
Coorabie Australia **146** A2
Coor-de-Wandy *hill* Australia **151** B5
Coorong National Park Australia **146** C4
Coorow Australia **151** B6
Cooroy Australia **149** G5
Coosa *r.* U.S.A. **175** C5
Coos Bay U.S.A. **180** A4
Coos Bay *b.* U.S.A. **180** A4
Cootamundra Australia **147** F3
Coqum *r.* India **94** D3
Copahue, Volcán *vol.* Chile **204** C5
Copainalá Mex. **185** G5

Copala Mex. **185** F5
Copal Urcu Peru **198** C5
Copán *tourist site* Hond. **186** A4
Cope, Cabo *c.* Spain **55** J7
Copemish U.S.A. **172** H6

▶**Copenhagen** Denmark **45** K5
Capital of Denmark. Also known as København.

Copere Bol. **201** E4
Copetonas Arg. **204** E5
Copeton Reservoir Australia **147** F2
Cô Pi, Phou *mt.* Laos/Vietnam **78** D4
Copiapó Chile **204** C2
Copiapo, Volcán *vol.* Chile **204** C2
Copley Australia **146** C2
Coporaque Peru **200** C3
Copparo Italy **56** D4
Coppename *r.* Suriname **199** G3
Copperbelt *prov.* Zambia **127** E8
formerly known as Western Province
Copperfield *r.* Australia **149** D3
Copper Harbor U.S.A. **172** F3
Coppermine Canada *see* **Kugluktuk**
Coppermine *r.* Canada **167** H1
Coppermine Point Canada **168** C4
Copperton S. Africa **132** G6
Copperton U.S.A. **183** L1
Copp Lake Canada **167** H2
Copşa Mică Romania **58** F2
Coqên China **89** D6
Coquilhatville Dem. Rep. Congo *see* **Mbandaka**
Coquille *i.* Micronesia *see* **Pikelot**
Coquille U.S.A. **180** A4
Coquimbo Chile **204** C3
Coquimbo *admin. reg.* Chile **204** C3
Coquitlam Canada **166** F5
Corabia Romania **58** F5
Coração de Jesus Brazil **202** C6
Coracesium Turkey *see* **Alanya**
Coracora Peru **200** B3
Coral Bay Australia **150** A4
Coral Harbour Canada **165** K3
Coral Sea S. Pacific Ocean **145** E3

▶**Coral Sea Islands Territory** *terr.* Australia **145** E3
Australian External Territory.
oceania [countries] ▶ 138–139

Coralville U.S.A. **172** B9
Corangamite, Lake Australia **147** D4
Coranzuli Arg. **200** D5
Coraopolis U.S.A. **176** E5
Corato Italy **56** I7
Corbett National Park India **96** C3
Corbie France **51** I3
Corbin U.S.A. **176** A9
Corbones *r.* Spain **54** F7
Corbu Romania **58** J4
Corby U.K. **47** L11
Corcaigh Rep. of Ireland *see* **Cork**
Córcoles *r.* Spain **55** H5
Corcoran U.S.A. **182** E5
Corcovado Arg. **205** C6
Corcovado, Golfo de *sea chan.* Chile **205** B6
Corcovado, Parque Nacional *nat. park* Costa Rica **186** C5
Corcyra *i.* Greece *see* **Corfu**
Cordeiro Brazil **207** K9
Cordele U.S.A. **175** D6
Cordelia U.S.A. **182** B3
Cordell U.S.A. **179** C5
Cordillera de los Picachos, Parque Nacional *nat. park* Col. **198** C4
Cordilleras Range *mts* Phil. **74** B4
Cordillo Downs Australia **149** D5
Cordisburgo Brazil **207** I6
Córdoba *Córdoba* Arg. **204** D3
Córdoba *Río Negro* Arg. **204** C6
Córdoba *prov.* Arg. **204** E4
Córdoba *dept* Col. **198** C2
Córdoba *Durango* Mex. **185** E3
Córdoba *Veracruz* Mex. **185** F5
Córdoba Spain **54** G7
historically known as Cordova *or* Corduba *or* Karmona
Córdoba, Sierras de *mts* Arg. **204** D4
Córdova Peru **200** B3
Cordova Spain *see* **Córdoba**
Cordova *AK* U.S.A. **164** E3
Cordova *IL* U.S.A. **172** C9
Cordova Bay U.S.A. **166** C4
Corduba Spain *see* **Córdoba**
Coreaú Brazil **202** D2
Corella *r.* Australia **149** D3
Corella Lake *salt flat* Australia **148** B3
Corfield Australia **149** D4
Corfu *i.* Greece **59** A9
also known as Kerkyra; *also spelt* Kérkira; *historically known as* Corcyra
Corguinho Brazil **203** A6
Coria Spain **54** E5
Coria del Río Spain **54** E7
Coribe Brazil **202** C5
Coricudgy *mt.* Australia **147** F3
Corigliano, Golfo di *b.* Italy **57** I9
Corigliano Calabro Italy **57** I9
Coringa Islands Australia **149** F3
Corinium U.K. *see* **Cirencester**
Corinne Canada **167** J5
Corinth Greece **59** D11
also spelt Korinthos; *historically known as* Corinthus
Corinth *MS* U.S.A. **174** B5
Corinth *NY* U.S.A. **177** L2
Corinth, Gulf of *sea chan.* Greece **59** D10
also known as Korinthiakos Kolpos
Corinthus Greece *see* **Corinth**
Corinto Brazil **203** C6
Corinto Nicaragua **186** B4
Corixa Grande *r.* Bol./Brazil **201** F4
Corixinha *r.* Brazil **201** F4
Cork Rep. of Ireland **47** D12
also spelt Corcaigh
Corlay France **50** C4
Corleone *Sicilia* Italy **57** F11
Çorlu Turkey **106** A2
Çorlu *r.* Turkey **58** I7
Cormeilles France **50** G3
Cormorant Canada **167** K4
Cormorant Lake Canada **167** K4
Cormorant Provincial Forest *nature res.* Canada **167** K4
Cornacchia, Monte *mt.* Italy **56** H7
Cornelia S. Africa **133** M4
Cornelia U.S.A. **179** G5
Cornélio Procópio Brazil **206** C10
Corneliskondre Suriname **199** G3
Cornell U.S.A. **172** B5
Cornellà de Llobregat Spain **55** N3
Corner Brook Canada **169** J3
Corneto Italy *see* **Tarquinia**
Cornetto *mt.* Italy **56** D3
Cornettsville U.S.A. **176** B8
Cornia *r.* Italy **56** C6
Corning *AR* U.S.A. **174** B4
Corning *CA* U.S.A. **182** B2
Corning *IA* U.S.A. **178** D3
Corning *NY* U.S.A. **177** H3
Corning *OH* U.S.A. **176** C6
Cornish *watercourse* Australia **149** E4
Cornish, Estrada *b.* Chile **205** B7
Corn Islands *is* Nicaragua *see* **Maíz, Islas del**
Corno, Monte *mt.* Italy **56** F6
Cornouaille *reg.* France **50** B4
Cornucopia U.S.A. **172** B4
Cornwall *Ont.* Canada **169** F4

Cornwall *P.E.I.* Canada **169** I4
Cornwall U.S.A. **177** I5
Cornwallis Island Canada **165** J2
Cornwall Island Canada **165** J2
Corny Point Australia **146** C3
Coro Venez. **198** D2
Coroaci Brazil **203** D6
Coroatá Brazil **202** C3
Corocoro Bol. **200** C4
Corocoro, Isla *i.* Venez. **199** F2
Coroglen N.Z. **152** J4
Coroico Bol. **200** D4
Corolla U.S.A. **177** J9
Coromandel Brazil **206** F5
Coromandel N.Z. **152** J4
Coromandel Coast India **94** D4
Coromandel Forest Park *nature res.* N.Z. **152** J5
Coromandel Peninsula N.Z. **152** J4
Coromandel Range *hills* N.Z. **152** J4
Coron Phil. **74** B3
Corona *CA* U.S.A. **182** G8
Corona *NM* U.S.A. **181** F6
Coronado U.S.A. **183** G9
Coronado, Bahía de *b.* Costa Rica **186** C5
Coronation Canada **167** I4
Coronation Gulf Canada **165** H3
Coronation Island S. Atlantic Ocean **222** U2
Coronation Islands Australia **150** D2
Coron Bay Phil. **74** B4
Coronda Arg. **204** E3
Coronel Brandsen Arg. **204** F4
Coronel Dorrego Arg. **204** E5
Coronel Fabriciano Brazil **203** D6
Coronel Francisco Sosa Arg. **204** D6
Coronel Moldes Arg. **204** D2
Coronel Murta Brazil **207** K3
Coronel Oviedo Para. **201** F6
Coronel Portillo Peru **198** B5
Coronel Pringles Arg. **204** E5
Coronel Sapucaia Brazil **201** G5
Coronel Suárez Arg. **204** E5
Coronel Vidal Arg. **204** F5
Çorovodë Albania **58** B8
Corowa Australia **147** E3
Corozal Belize **185** H5
Corozal Venez. **187** H5
Corozo Pando Venez. **199** E2
Corpen Aike Arg. **205** C8
Corpus Christi U.S.A. **179** C7
Corpus Christi, Lake U.S.A. **179** C6
Corque Bol. **200** D4
Corral Chile **204** B5
Corral de Almaguer Spain **55** H5
Corral de Cantos *mt.* Spain **54** G5
Corralilla Cuba **186** C2
Corralitos U.S.A. **182** C5
Corrandibby Range *hills* Australia **151** A5
Corrane Moz. **131** H2
Corrasi, Punta *mt. Sardegna* Italy **57** B8
Corraun Peninsula Rep. of Ireland **47** C10
Córrego do Ouro Brazil **206** C3
Córrego Novo Brazil **207** K6
Corrente Brazil **202** C4
Corrente *r. Bahia* Brazil **202** D5
Corrente *r. Minas Gerais* Brazil **206** C6
Corrente Grande *r.* Brazil **207** K6
Correntes Brazil **203** A6
Correntes *r.* Brazil **201** G4
Correnti, Isola delle *i. Sicilia* Italy **57** H12
Correntina Brazil **202** C5
Correntina *r.* Brazil *see* **Éguas**
Corrèze France **50** H7
Corrèze *r.* France **51** H7
Corrib, Lough *l.* Rep. of Ireland **47** C10
Corrientes Arg. **204** F2
Corrientes *prov.* Arg. **204** F3
Corrientes *r.* Arg. **204** F3
Corrientes *r.* Peru **198** C5
Corrientes, Cabo *c.* Arg. **204** F5
Corrientes, Cabo *c.* Col. **198** B3
Corrientes, Cabo *c.* Cuba **186** B2
Corrientes, Cabo *c.* Mex. **184** D4
Corrigan U.S.A. **179** D6
Corrigin Australia **151** B7
Corriverton Guyana **199** G3
Corrubedo, Cabo *c.* Spain **54** B2
Corry U.S.A. **176** F4
Corryong Australia **147** E4
Corsaglia *r.* Italy **51** N8
Corse *admin. reg.* France **56** B6
Corse *i.* France *see* **Corsica**
Corse, Cap *c. Corse* France **51** P9
▶**Corsica** *i.* France **51** O10
also known as Corse
europe [environments] ▶ 36–37
Corsicana U.S.A. **179** C5
Corsico, Baie de *b.* Gabon **126** A4
Cort Adelaer, Kap *c.* Greenland *see* **Kangeq**
Cortale Italy **57** I10
Corte *Corse* France **51** P10
Cortegana Spain **54** E7
Cortes Spain **55** J3
Cortes, Sea of *g.* Mex. *see* **California, Gulf of**
Cortes de la Frontera, Reserva Nacional de *nature res.* Spain **54** F8
Cortez U.S.A. **181** E5
Cortez Mountains U.S.A. **183** H1
Cortina d'Ampezzo Italy **56** E2
Cortland *NY* U.S.A. **177** I3
Cortland *OH* U.S.A. **176** E4
Cortona Italy **56** D5
Corubal *r.* Guinea-Bissau **124** B4
Coruche Port. **54** C6
Çoruh Turkey *see* **Artvin**
Çoruh *r.* Turkey **107** E2
Çorum Turkey **106** C2
Corumbá Brazil **201** F4
Corumbá *r.* Brazil **206** E5
Corumbá de Goiás Brazil **206** E2
Corumbaíba Brazil **206** E5
Corumbataí *r.* Brazil **206** B10
Corumbaú, Ponta *pt* Brazil **207** N3
Corund Romania **58** G2
Corunna Canada **173** K8
Corunna Spain *see* **A Coruña**
Corunna U.S.A. **173** I8
Coruripe Brazil **202** E4
Corvallis U.S.A. **180** B3
Corwen U.K. **47** I11
Corydon *IA* U.S.A. **174** A3
Corydon *IN* U.S.A. **174** C4
Coryville U.S.A. **176** G4
Cos *i.* Greece *see* **Kos**
Cosalá Mex. **184** D3
Cosamaloapan Mex. **185** G5
Coscaya Chile **200** C4
Cosenza Italy *see* **Cosenza**
Cosenza Italy **57** I9
historically known as Cosentia
Coșereni Romania **58** H4
Coshocton U.S.A. **176** D5
Cosmoledo Atoll Seychelles **129** E7
Cosmo Newbery Aboriginal Reserve Australia **151** C6
Cosmópolis Brazil **206** F9
Cosne-Cours-sur-Loire France **51** I5
Cosquín Arg. **204** D3
Cossato Italy **56** A3
Cossé-le-Vivien France **50** F5
Costa Brazil **202** D3
Costa Blanca *coastal area* Spain **55** K6
Costa Brava *coastal area* Spain **55** O3
Costache Negri Romania **58** I3
Costa de la Luz *coastal area* Spain **54** D7
Costa del Azahar *coastal area* Spain **55** K5
Costa del Sol *coastal area* Spain **54** F8
Costa Dorada *coastal area* Spain **55** N3
Costa Marques Brazil **201** D3
Costa Rica Brazil **203** A6

▶**Costa Rica** *country* Central America **186** B5
northamerica [countries] ▶ 158–159
Costa Rica Mex. **184** D3
Costa Verde *coastal area* Spain **54** E1
Costermansville Dem. Rep. Congo *see* **Bukavu**
Costești Romania **58** F4
Costești Romania **58** I2
Costigan Lake Canada **167** J3
Coșușțea *r.* Romania **58** E4
Cotabambas Peru **200** B3
Cotabato Phil. **74** C5
Cotacajes *r.* Bol. **200** D4
Cotagaita Bol. **200** D5
Cotahuasi Peru **200** B3
Cotaxé *r.* Brazil **203** D6
Cote, Mount U.S.A. **166** D3
Coteau des Prairies *slope* U.S.A. **178** C2
Coteau du Missouri *slope ND* U.S.A. **178** B1
Coteau du Missouri *slope SD* U.S.A. **178** B2
Coteaux Haiti **187** E3
Côte d'Azur *coastal area* France **51** N9
▶**Côte d'Ivoire** *country* Africa **124** D4
formerly known as Ivory Coast
africa [countries] ▶ 114–117
Côte Française de Somalis *country* Africa *see* **Djibouti**
Cotegipe Brazil **202** C4
Cotentin *pen.* France **50** E3
Côtes de Meuse *ridge* France **51** K3
Coti *r.* Brazil **200** D2
Cotiaeum Turkey *see* **Kütahya**
Cotiella *mt.* Spain **55** L2
Cotingo *r.* Brazil **199** F4
Cotmeana *r.* Romania **58** F4
Cotonou Benin **125** F5
Cotopaxi *prov.* Ecuador **198** B5
Cotopaxi, Volcán *vol.* Ecuador **198** B5
Cotovsc Moldova *see* **Hîncești**
Cotswold Hills U.K. **47** J12
Cottage Grove U.S.A. **180** B4
Cottbus Germany **49** L4
Cotteliar *r.* India **94** D3
Cottian Alps *mts* France/Italy **51** M8
also known as Cottiennes, Alpes *or* Cozie, Alpi
Cottica Suriname **199** H4
Cottiennes, Alpes *mts* France/Italy *see* **Cottian Alps**
Cotton U.S.A. **172** A3
Cottonbush Creek *watercourse* Australia **148** C4
Cottonwood *AZ* U.S.A. **183** L7
Cottonwood *CA* U.S.A. **182** B1
Cottonwood *r. KS* U.S.A. **178** C4
Cottonwood *r. MN* U.S.A. **178** D2
Cottonwood Creek *watercourse* U.S.A. **181** G7
Cottonwood Falls U.S.A. **178** C4
Cottonwood Wash *watercourse* U.S.A. **183** N7
Cotui Dom. Rep. **187** F3
Cotulla U.S.A. **179** C6
Couchman Range *hills* Australia **150** D2
Coudersport U.S.A. **176** G4
Coudres, Île aux *i.* Canada **169** G4
Couëdic, Cape de *c.* Australia **146** C4
Couëron France **50** E5
Couesnon *r.* France **50** E4
Couiza France **51** I10
Coulee Dam U.S.A. **180** C3
Coulman Island Antarctica **223** L2
Coulogne France **51** H2
Couloir 1 *well* Alg. **123** H4
Coulommiers France **51** J4
Coulonge *r.* Canada **168** E4
Coulterville U.S.A. **182** D4
Council U.S.A. **180** C3
Council Bluffs U.S.A. **178** D3
Council Grove U.S.A. **178** C4
Councillor Island Australia **147** E4
Coupeville U.S.A. **180** B2
Courageous Lake Canada **167** I1
Courantyne *r.* Guyana **199** G3
Courland Lagoon *b.* Lith./Rus. Fed. **42** C6
also known as Kurshskiy Zaliv *or* Kurskiy Zaliv *or* Kuršių marios
Cournon-d'Auvergne France **51** J7
Coursan France **51** J9
Courtenay Canada **166** E5
Courthézon France **51** K8
Courtland U.S.A. **177** H9
Courtrai Belgium *see* **Kortrijk**
Coushatta U.S.A. **179** D5
Coutances France **50** E3
Coutinho Moz. *see* **Ulongue**
Couto de Magalhães de Minas Brazil **207** J5
Coutras France **50** F7
Coutts Canada **167** I5
Couvin Belgium **51** K2
Couzeix France **50** H7
Covaleda Spain **55** I3
Covasna Romania **58** H3
Cove Fort U.S.A. **183** L3
Cove Island Canada **173** L5
Covelo U.S.A. **182** A2
Cove Mountains *hills* U.S.A. **176** G6
Covendo Bol. **200** D3
Coventry U.K. **47** K11
Covesville U.S.A. **176** G8
Covilhã Port. **54** D4
Covington *GA* U.S.A. **175** D5
Covington *IN* U.S.A. **174** C3
Covington *KY* U.S.A. **176** A6
Covington *LA* U.S.A. **175** B6
Covington *OH* U.S.A. **176** A5
Covington *TN* U.S.A. **174** B5
Covington *VA* U.S.A. **176** E8
Cowal, Lake *dry lake* Australia **147** E3
Cowan U.S.A. **176** B7
Cowan, Lake *salt flat* Australia **151** C6
Cowcowing Lakes *salt flat* Australia **151** B6
Cowdenbeath U.K. **46** I7
Cowell Australia **146** C3
Cowen U.S.A. **176** E7
Cowes Australia **147** E4
Cowley Australia **149** E5
Cowlitz *r.* U.S.A. **180** B3
Cowpasture *r.* U.S.A. **176** F8
Cowra Australia **147** F3
Cox *r.* Australia **148** B2
Coxá *r.* Brazil **207** I1
Coxen Hole Hond. *see* **Roatán**
Coxilha de Santana *hills* Brazil/Uruguay **204** G3
Coxilha Grande *hills* Brazil **203** A9
Coxim Brazil **203** A6
Coxim *r.* Brazil **203** A6
Coxsackie U.S.A. **177** L3
Cox's Bazar Bangl. **97** F5
Coyah Guinea **124** B4
Coy Aike Arg. **205** C8
Coyame Mex. **181** F7
Coyanosa Creek *watercourse* U.S.A. **179** B6
Coyote *r.* Mex. **181** D7
Coyote, Punta *pt* Mex. **184** C3
Coyote Lake U.S.A. **183** H6
Coyote Peak *hill* U.S.A. **183** J9
Coyote Peak U.S.A. **182** F5
Coyotitán Mex. **184** D4
Coyuca de Benítez Mex. **185** E5
Coyuca de Catalán Mex. **185** E5
Cozad U.S.A. **178** C3
Cozia, Vârful *mt.* Romania **58** F3
Cozie, Alpi *mts* France/Italy *see* **Cottian Alps**
Cozumel Mex. **185** I4
Cozumel, Isla de *i.* Mex. **185** I4
Cozzo del Pellegrino *mt.* Italy **57** I9
Crab Island Australia **149** D1

Crab Orchard U.S.A. **176** A8
Cracovia Poland *see* **Kraków**
Cracow Australia **149** F5
Cracow Poland *see* **Kraków**
Cradle Mountain Lake St Clair National Park Australia **147** E5
Cradock Australia **146** C2
Cradock S. Africa **133** J9
Crafthole S. Africa **132** I3
Craig *AK* U.S.A. **166** C4
Craig *CO* U.S.A. **180** F4
Craigavon U.K. **47** F9
Craigieburn Australia **147** E4
Craigieburn N.Z. **153** F11
Craigieburn Forest Park *nature res.* N.Z. **153** F11
Craignure U.K. **46** G7
Craigsville *VA* U.S.A. **176** F7
Craigsville *WV* U.S.A. **176** E7
Crail U.K. **46** J7
Crailsheim Germany **48** H6
Craiova Romania **58** E4
Cramlington U.K. **47** K8
Cramond S. Africa **132** F4
Cranberry Junction Canada **166** D4
Cranberry Lake U.S.A. **177** K1
Cranberry Portage Canada **167** K4
Cranbourne Australia **147** E4
Cranbrook Canada **167** H5
Crandon U.S.A. **172** E5
Crane *OR* U.S.A. **180** C4
Crane *TX* U.S.A. **179** B6
Crane Lake *l.* Canada **167** I5
Crane Lake U.S.A. **172** A2
Cranston *KY* U.S.A. **176** B7
Cranston *RI* U.S.A. **177** N4
Cranz Rus. Fed. *see* **Zelenogradsk**
Craolândia Brazil **202** C3
Craon France **50** F5
Crary Ice Rise Antarctica **223** M1
Crary Mountains Antarctica **222** P1
Crasna Romania **58** D1
Crasna *r.* Romania **58** D1
Crater Lake National Park U.S.A. **180** B4
Crater Peak U.S.A. **182** C1
Craters of the Moon National Monument *nat. park* U.S.A. **180** D4
Crateús Brazil **202** D3
Crato Brazil **202** E3
Crato Port. **54** D5
Cravari *r.* Brazil **201** F3
Cravinhos Brazil **206** F8
Cravo Norte Col. **198** D3
Crawford U.S.A. **178** B3
Crawford Point Phil. **74** A4
Crawford Range *hills* Australia **148** B4
Crawfordsville U.S.A. **174** C3
Crawfordville U.S.A. **175** C6
Crawley U.K. **47** L12
Crazy Mountains U.S.A. **180** E3
Crean Lake Canada **167** J4
Crécy-en-Ponthieu France **51** H2
Crediton U.K. **47** I13
Cree *r.* Canada **167** J3
Creede U.S.A. **181** F5
Creedmoor U.S.A. **176** G9
Creel Mex. **184** D3
Cree Lake Canada **167** J3
Creighton Canada **167** K4
Creighton S. Africa **133** N7
Creil France **51** I3
Crema Italy **56** B3
Cremona Canada **167** H5
Cremona Italy **56** C3
Crepori *r.* Brazil **199** G6
Crépy-en-Valois France **51** I3
Cres Croatia **56** G4
Cres *i.* Croatia **56** G4
Crescent City U.S.A. **180** A4
Crescent Group *is* Paracel Is **72** D3
Crescent Head Australia **147** G2
Crescent Junction U.S.A. **183** O3
Crescent Lake National Wildlife Refuge *nature res.* U.S.A. **178** B3
Crescent Peak U.S.A. **183** I6
Crescent Valley U.S.A. **183** H1
Cresco U.S.A. **174** A3
Crespo Arg. **204** E4
Cresswell *watercourse* Australia **148** B3
Cresswell Downs Australia **148** B3
Crest France **51** L8
Crest Hill *hill* Hong Kong China **87** [inset]
also known as Tai Shek Mo
Crestline U.S.A. **176** C5
Creston Canada **167** G5
Creston *IA* U.S.A. **178** D3
Creston *WY* U.S.A. **180** F4
Crestview U.S.A. **175** C6
Creta *i.* Greece *see* **Crete**
Crêt de la Neige *mt.* France **51** L6
Crete *i.* Greece **59** F13
also spelt Kriti; *historically known as* Creta
Crete U.S.A. **178** C3
Crêt Monniot *mt.* France **51** M5
Creus, Cap de *c.* Spain **55** O2
Creuse *r.* France **51** G5
Crevalcore Italy **56** D4
Crevasse Valley Glacier Antarctica **222** O1
Crevillente Spain **55** K6
Crewe U.K. **47** J10
Crewe U.S.A. **176** G8
Crianlarich U.K. **46** H7
Criccieth U.K. **47** H11
Criciúma Brazil **203** B9
Cricova Moldova **58** J1
formerly spelt Krikovo
Cricovu Sărat *r.* Romania **58** H4
Cridersville U.S.A. **176** A5
Crieff U.K. **46** I7
Criffell *hill* U.K. **47** I9
Crikvenica Croatia **56** G3
Crillon, Mount U.S.A. **166** B3
Crimea *pen.* Ukr. **41** E7
also known as Krymş'kyy Pivostriv; *short form* Krym'
Crimmitschau Germany **49** J5
Cripple Creek U.S.A. **180** F5
Crișan Romania **58** K3
Crisfield U.S.A. **177** J8
Cristais, Serra dos *mts* Brazil **206** F4
Cristal, Monts de *mts* Equat. Guinea/Gabon **125** H6
Cristalândia Brazil **202** B4
Cristalina Brazil **206** F3
Cristalino *r.* Brazil **201** G2
Cristalino *r.* Brazil *see* **Mariembero**
Cristianópolis Brazil **206** E4
Cristina Brazil **207** H9
Cristino Castro Brazil **202** C4
Cristuru Secuiesc Romania **58** G2
Crișul Alb *r.* Romania **58** C2
Crișul Negru *r.* Romania **58** C2
Crișul Repede *r.* Romania **58** C1
Crișurilor, Câmpia *plain* Romania **58** C2
Criterion *mt.* Peru **200** B3
Criuleni Moldova **58** K1
formerly spelt Kriulyany
Crivitz Germany **48** I2
Crivitz U.S.A. **172** E5
Crixás Brazil **202** B5
Crixás Açu *r.* Brazil **202** B5
Crixás Mirim *r.* Brazil **202** B5
Crna *r.* Macedonia **58** C7
Crna Gora *mt.* Yugo. **58** A6
Crna Gora *mts* Macedonia/Yugo. **58** C6
Crna Gora *aut. rep.* Yugo. **58** A6
English form Montenegro
Crna Trava *Srbija* Yugo. **58** D6
Crni Drim *r.* Macedonia **58** B7
Crni Timok *r.* Yugo. **58** D5
Črni vrh *mt.* Slovenia **56** H2
Črnomelj Slovenia **56** H3

Danbury CT U.S.A. 177 L4
Danbury NC U.S.A. 176 E9
Danbury NH U.S.A. 177 N2
Danbury WI U.S.A. 172 A4
Danby U.S.A. 177 M2
Danby Lake U.S.A. 183 I7
Dancheng China 87 E1
Dancheng China see Xiangshan
Dande r. Angola 127 B7
Dande Eth. 128 C3
Dandel'dhura Nepal 96 D3
Dandeli India 94 B3
Dando Angola 127 C7
Dandong China 83 B4
formerly known as Andong
Dandridge U.S.A. 174 D4
Danė r. Lith. 42 C6
Daneborg Greenland 165 Q2
Daneţi Romania 58 F5
Dänew Turkm. see Dyanev
Danfeng China 87 D1
also known as Longjuzhai
Danfeng China see Shizong
Dangan Liedao i. China 87 E4
Dangara Tajik. see Danghara
Dangbizhen Rus. Fed. 82 C3
Dangchang China 86 C1
Dangchengwan China see Subei
Dange Angola 127 B6
formerly known as Quitexe
Danger Islands atoll Cook Is see Pukapuka
Danger Point S. Africa 132 D11
Dangé-St-Romain France 50 G6
Danggali Conservation Park nature res. Australia 146 D3
Danghara Tajik. 101 G2
also spelt Dangara
Danghe Nanshan mts China 84 B4
Dangila Eth. 128 C2
Dangjin Shankou pass China 84 B4
Dangla Shan mts China see Tanggula Shan
Dan Gorayo Somalia 128 F2
Dangori India 97 G4
Dangqên China 89 E6
Dangriga Belize 185 H5
formerly known as Stann Creek
Dangshan China 87 F1
Dangtu China 87 F2
Dan-Gulbi Nigeria 125 G4
Dangur Eth. 128 B2
Dangur Mountains Eth. 128 B2
Dangyang China 87 D2
Daniel's Harbour Canada 169 J3
Daniëlskuil S. Africa 132 H5
Danielson U.S.A. 177 N4
Danielsrus S. Africa 133 M4
Danielsville U.S.A. 175 D5
Danilkovo Rus. Fed. 43 S2
Danilov Rus. Fed. 43 V3
Danilovgrad Crna Gora Yugo. 58 A6
Danilovka Kazakh. 103 G1
Danilovka Rus. Fed. 41 H6
Danilovskaya Vozvyshennost' hills Rus. Fed. 40 F4
Daning China 85 F4
Dänizkänarı Azer. 107 G2
Danjiang China see Leishan
Danjiangkou China 87 D1
formerly known as Junxian
Danjiangkou Shuiku resr China 87 D1
Danjo-guntō is Japan 91 A8
Dank Oman 105 G3
Dankalia prov. Eritrea 104 C5
Dankov Rus. Fed. 43 U8
Dankova, Pik mt. Kyrg. 103 I4
Danleng China 86 B2
Danlí Hond. 186 B4
Danmark Fjord inlet Greenland 165 Q1
English form Denmark Fjord
Dannebrog Ø i. Greenland see Qillak
Dannemora U.S.A. 177 L1
Dannenberg (Elbe) Germany 48 I2
Dannet well Niger 125 G2
Dannevirke N.Z. 152 K8
Dannhauser S. Africa 133 O5
Dan Sai Thai. 78 C4
Danshui Taiwan see Tanshui
Dansville U.S.A. 176 H3
Danta Gujarat India 96 B4
Danta Rajasthan India 89 A7
Dantewara India 94 D2
Dantu China 87 F1
also known as Zhenjiang

▶Danube r. Europe 58 J3
2nd longest river in Europe. Also spelt Donau (Austria/Germany) or Duna (Hungary) or Dunaj (Slovakia) or Dunărea (Romania) or Dunav (Bulgaria/Croatia/Yugoslavia) or Dunay (Ukraine).
europe [landscapes] ▶▶ 30–31

Danube Delta Romania 58 K3
also known as Dunării, Delta
Danubyu Myanmar 78 A4
Danumparai Indon. 77 F2
Danum Valley Conservation Area nature res. Sabah Malaysia 77 G1
Danville AR U.S.A. 179 D5
Danville IL U.S.A. 174 C3
Danville IN U.S.A. 174 C4
Danville KY U.S.A. 176 A8
Danville OH U.S.A. 176 C5
Danville VA U.S.A. 176 F9
Danville VT U.S.A. 177 M1
Danxian China see Danzhou
Danyang China 87 F2
Danzhai China 87 C3
also known as Longquan
Danzhou Guangxi China 87 D3
Danzhou Hainan China 87 D5
also known as Nada; formerly known as Danxian
Danzhou China see Yichuan
Danzig Poland see Gdańsk
Danzig, Gulf of Poland/Rus. Fed. see Gdańsk, Gulf of
Dao Phil. 74 B4
Dão r. Port. 54 C4
Daocheng China 86 B2
also known as Dabba or Jinzhu
Daojiang China see Daoxian
Daokou China see Huaxian
Daoshiping China 87 D2
Daotanghe China 84 D4
Dao Tay Sa is S. China Sea see Paracel Islands
Dao Timmi Niger 125 I1
Daoud Alg. see Aïn Beïda
Daoudi well Mauritania 124 D3
Daoukro Côte d'Ivoire 124 E5
Daoxian China 87 D3
also known as Daojiang
Daozhen China 87 C2
also known as Yuxi
Dapa Phil. 74 C4
Dapaong Togo 125 F4
Dapchi Nigeria 125 H3
Daphabum mt. India 97 H4
Daphnae tourist site Egypt 108 D7
also known as Kawm Dafanah
Daphne U.S.A. 175 C6
Dapiak, Mount Phil. 74 B4
Dapingdi China see Yanbian
Dapitan Phil. 74 B4
Daqahliya governorate Egypt 108 C6
Da Qaidam Zhen China 84 B4
Daqiao China 86 B3
Daqing China 82 B3
also known as Anda; formerly known as Sartu
Daqing Shan mts China 85 F3
Daqin Tal China 85 I3
also known as Naiman Qi
Daqiu China 87 F3
Daqq-e Patargān salt flat Iran 101 E3
Daqq-e Tundi, Dasht-e imp. l. Afgh. 101 E3
Daquan China 84 B3
Daquanwan China 84 B3
Dāqūq Iraq 107 F4
Daqu Shan i. China 87 G2
Dara Senegal 124 B3
formerly spelt Dahra
Dar'ā Syria 108 H5
Dar'ā governorate Syria 108 H5
Dāra, Gebel mt. Egypt 106 C6
Daraá r. Brazil 199 E5
Dārāb Iran 100 C4
Daraga Phil. 74 B3
Darahanava Belarus 43 J8
Daraim Afgh. 96 A1
Daraina Madag. 131 [inset] K2
Daraj Libya 120 A2
Daram i. Phil. 74 C4
Dārān Iran 100 B3
Đa Răng, Sông r. Vietnam 79 E5
Darasun Rus. Fed. 85 G1
Daraut-Kurgan Kyrg. see Daroot-Korgan
Đaravica mt. Yugo. 58 B6
Darazo Nigeria 125 H4
Darb Saudi Arabia 104 C4
Darband Iran 100 D4
Darband Uzbek. see Derbent
Darband, Kūh-e mt. Iran 100 D4
Darb-e Behesht Iran 100 D4
Darbėnai Lith. 42 C5
Dar Ben Karricha el Behri Morocco 54 F9
Darbhanga India 97 E4
Darcang China 86 A1
Dar Chabanne Tunisia 57 C12
Dar Chaoui Morocco 54 F9
D'Arcy Canada 166 F5
Darda Croatia 56 K3
Dardanelle AR U.S.A. 179 D5
Dardanelle CA U.S.A. 182 E3
Dardanelle, Lake U.S.A. 179 D5
Dardanelles strait Turkey 106 A2
also known as Çanakkale Boğazı; historically known as Hellespont
Dardo China see Kangding
Dar el Beida Morocco see Casablanca
Darende Turkey 107 D3

▶Dar es Salaam Tanz. 129 C6
Former capital of Tanzania.

Dārestān Iran 100 C4
Darfield N.Z. 153 G11
Darfo Boario Terme Italy 56 C3
Dargai Pak. 101 G3
Darganata Turkm. 103 E4
Dargaville N.Z. 152 H3
Dargin, Jezioro l. Poland 49 S1
Dargo Australia 147 E4
Darhan Mongolia 85 E1
Darhan Muminggan Lianheqi China see Bailingmiao
Darıca Turkey 58 K8
Darıcı Turkey 59 J9
Darien CT U.S.A. 177 L4
Darien GA U.S.A. 175 D6
Darién, Golfo del g. Col. 198 B2
Darién, Parque Nacional de nat. park Panama 186 D6
Darién, Serranía del mts Panama 186 D5
Dar'inskiy Kazakh. 103 H2
also known as Dariya
Dar'inskoye Kazakh. 102 B2
Dario Nicaragua 186 B4
Dariya Kazakh. see Dar'inskiy
Dariz Oman 105 G3
Darjeeling India 97 F4
also spelt Darjiling
Darjiling India see Darjeeling
Darkhovin Iran 100 B4
Darlag China 86 A1
also known as Gyümai

▶Darling r. Australia 147 D3
2nd longest river in Oceania. Part of the longest (Murray-Darling).
oceania [landscapes] ▶▶ 136–137

Darling S. Africa 132 C10
Darling Downs hills Australia 147 F1
Darling Range hills Australia 151 A7
Darlington U.K. 47 K9
Darlington SC U.S.A. 175 E5
Darlington WI U.S.A. 172 C8
Darlington Dam resr S. Africa 133 J10
Darlington Point Australia 147 E3
Darlot, Lake salt flat Australia 151 C5
Darłowo Poland 49 N1
Dărmănești Romania 58 H2
Darma Pass China/India 89 C6
Darmaraopet India 94 C2
Darmstadt Germany 48 F6
Darna r. India 94 B1
Darnah Libya 120 D1
also spelt Derna
Darnall S. Africa 133 P6
Darnick Australia 147 D3
Darnley, Cape Antarctica 223 E2
Darnley Bay Canada 164 G3
Daroca Spain 55 J3
Daroot-Korgan Kyrg. 103 H5
also spelt Daraut-Kurgan
Darovskoy Rus. Fed. 40 H4
Dar Pahn Iran 100 D5
Darr watercourse Australia 149 D4
Darregueira Arg. 204 E5
Darreh Bīd Iran 100 D3
Darreh Gaz Iran 101 D2
also known as Moḩammadābād
Darreh Gozaru r. Iran see Gīzeh Rūd
Darreh-ye Bāhābād Iran 100 C4
Darreh-ye Shahr Iran 100 A3
Darreh-ye Shekārī r. Afgh. 101 G3
Darreh-ye Shekārī r. Afgh. 101 G3
Darro watercourse Eth. 128 D3
Darsa i. Yemen 105 F5
Darsi India 94 C3
Darß pen. Germany 49 J1
Darßer Ort c. Germany 49 J1
Darta Turkm. 102 C4
formerly known as Kianly; formerly spelt Tarta
Dār Ta'izzah Syria 109 H1
Dartang China see Baqên
Dartford U.K. 47 M12
Dartmoor Australia 146 D4
Dartmoor hills U.K. 47 H13
Dartmoor National Park U.K. 47 I13
Dartmouth Canada 169 I4
Dartmouth U.K. 47 I13
Dartmouth, Lake salt flat Australia 149 E5
Dartmouth Reservoir Australia 147 E4
Daru P.N.G. 73 J8
Daru waterhole Sudan 121 G5
Daruba Indon. 75 D2
Daruvar Croatia 56 J3
Darvaza Turkm. 102 D4
also spelt Derweze
Darvi Mongolia 84 B2
Darvi Mongolia see Bulgan
Darvinskiy Gosudarstvennyy Zapovednik nature res. Rus. Fed. 43 S3
Darvoz, Qatorkūhi mts Tajik. 101 G2
Darwendale Zimbabwe 131 F3
Darwha India 94 C1

▶Darwin Australia 148 A2
Capital of Northern Territory. Historically known as Palmerston.

Darwin Falkland Is 205 F8
Darwin, Canal sea chan. Chile 205 B7
Darwin, Monte mt. Chile 205 C9
Darya Khan Pak. 101 G4
Dar'yalyktakyr, Ravnina plain Kazakh. 103 F3
Daryānah Libya 120 D1
Dar"yoi Amu r. Asia see Amudar'ya
Dar"yoi Sir r. Asia see Syrdar'ya
Dārzīn Iran 100 D4
Dās i. U.A.E. 105 F2
Dasada India 96 A5
Dasha r. China 85 G4
Dashbalbar Mongolia 85 G1
Dashhowuz Turkm. see Dashkhovuz
Dashiqiao China 85 I3
formerly known as Yingkou
Dashitou China 88 E3
Dashizhai China 85 I2
Dashkawka Belarus 43 L8
Dashkesan Azer. see Daşkäsän
Dashkhovuz Turkm. 102 D4
also known as Dashoguz; also spelt Dashhowuz; formerly known as Tashauz
Dashkhovuz Oblast admin. div. Turkm. see Dashkhovuzskaya Oblast'
Dashkhovuzskaya Oblast' admin. div. Turkm. 102 D4
English form Dashkhovuz Oblast; formerly known as Tashauzskaya Oblast'
Dashköpri Turkm. see Tashkepri
Dashoguz Turkm. see Dashkhovuz
Dasht Iran 100 D2
Dasht r. Pak. 101 E5
Dashtak Qaléhsi Iran 100 D2
formerly spelt Dashtak Qal'ehsi
Dashtak Qal'ehsi Iran see Dashtak Qaléhsi
Dasht-e Bar Iran 100 D4
Dasht-e Palang r. Iran 100 C4
Dashtiari Iran 101 E5
Dashuikeng China 85 E4
Dashuiqiao China 84 C4
Dashuitou China 84 E4
Daska Pak. 101 H3
Daşkäsän Azer. 107 F2
also spelt Dashkesan
Daskop S. Africa 132 G10
Dasongshu China 86 C3
Daspar mt. Pak. 101 H2
Dassa Benin 125 F5
Dassalan i. Phil. 74 B5
Dassen Island S. Africa 132 C10
Dastakān, Ra's-e pt Iran 100 C5
Da Suifen He r. China 82 C4
Dasuya India 96 B3
Dasville S. Africa 133 M3
Datadian Indon. 77 F2
Datça Turkey 106 A3
Date Japan 90 G3
Date Creek watercourse U.S.A. 183 K7
Dateland U.S.A. 183 K9
Datha India 96 B5
Datia India 96 C4
Datian China 87 F3
also known as Junxi
Datian Ding mt. China 87 D4
Datong China see Tong'an
Datong Heilong. China 82 B3
Datong Qinghai China 84 D4
also known as Qiaotou
Datong Shanxi China 85 G3
Datong He r. China 84 D4
Datong Shan mts China 84 C4
Datta Rus. Fed. 82 F2
Datu i. Indon. 77 F2
Datu, Tanjung c. Indon./Malaysia 77 E2
Datuk, Tanjung pt Indon. 76 C3
Datu Piang Phil. 74 C5
also known as Dulawan
Daudkandi Bangl. 97 F5
Daud Khel Pak. 101 G3
Daudnagar India 97 E4
Daudzeva Latvia 42 G5
Daugai Lith. 42 F7
Daugailiai Lith. 42 G6
Daugava r. Latvia 42 F4
Daugavpils Latvia 42 H6
also known as Dvinsk; formerly known as Dünaburg
Daugyvenė r. Lith. 42 E5
Daulatabad Afgh. 101 F2
Daulatabad Iran see Malāyer
Daulatpur Bangl. 97 F5
Daule Ecuador 198 B5
Daun Germany 48 D5
Daund India 94 B2
Daung Kyun i. Myanmar 79 B5
also known as Ross Island
Daungyu r. Myanmar 78 A3
Dauphin Canada 167 K5
Dauphiné reg. France 51 L7
Dauphiné, Alpes du mts France 51 L8
Dauphin Island U.S.A. 175 B6
Dauphin Lake Canada 167 L5
Daura Nigeria 125 H3
Daurie Creek r. Australia 151 A5
Dauriya Rus. Fed. 85 H1
Daurskiy Khrebet mts Rus. Fed. 85 F1
Dausa India 96 C4
Dâu Tiêng, Hô resr Vietnam 79 D6
Däväçi Azer. 107 G2
also spelt Divichi
Davangere India 94 B3
Davao Phil. 74 C5
Davao Gulf Phil. 74 C5
Dāvarān Iran 100 D4
Dāvar Panāh Iran 101 E5
also known as Dizak
Davel S. Africa 133 N3
Davenport IA U.S.A. 174 B3
Davenport NY U.S.A. 177 K3
Davenport WA U.S.A. 180 C3
Davenport Downs Australia 149 D5
Davenport Range hills Australia 148 B4
Daveyton S. Africa 133 M3
David Panama 186 C5
David City U.S.A. 178 C3
Davidson Canada 167 J5
Davidson, Mount hill Australia 148 A4
Davidson Lake Canada 167 L4
Davies, Mount Australia 146 A1
Davinópolis Brazil 206 F5
Davis research station Antarctica 223 F2
Davis r. Australia 150 C4
Davis i. Myanmar see Than Kyun
Davis CA U.S.A. 182 C3
Davis WV U.S.A. 176 F6
Davis, Mount hill U.S.A. 176 F6
Davis Bay Antarctica 223 I2
Davis Dam U.S.A. 183 J6
Davis Dam dam U.S.A. 183 J6
Davis Inlet Canada 169 I2
Davison U.S.A. 173 J7
Davis Sea Antarctica 223 G2
Davis Strait Canada/Greenland 165 N3
Davlekanovo Rus. Fed. 40 J5
Davlia Greece 59 D10
also spelt Dhávlia
Davos Switz. 51 P6
Davutlar Turkey 59 I11
Davy U.S.A. 176 D8
Davyd-Haradok Belarus 42 I9
Davydkovo Rus. Fed. see Tolbukhino
Davydovo Rus. Fed. 43 T4
Davy Lake Canada 167 I3
Dawa China 85 I3
Dawa Co l. China 89 D6
Dawāsir reg. Saudi Arabia 104 D3
Dawāsir, Wādī ad watercourse Saudi Arabia 104 D3
Dawa Wenz r. Eth. 128 D3
Dawaxung China 89 D6
Dawê China 86 B2
Dawei Myanmar see Tavoy
Dawei r. Myanmar see Tavoy
Dawen r. China 85 H5
Dawera i. Indon. 75 D4
Dawhat Bilbul b. Saudi Arabia 105 E2
Dawhinava Belarus 42 I7
Dawna Range mts Myanmar/Thai. 78 B4
Dawqah Oman 105 F4
Dawqah Saudi Arabia 104 C4
Dawran Yemen 104 D5
Dawson r. Australia 149 F4
Dawson Canada 166 B1
Dawson GA U.S.A. 175 C6
Dawson ND U.S.A. 180 H3
Dawson, Isla i. Chile 205 C9
Dawson, Mount Canada 167 G5
Dawson Bay Canada 167 K4
Dawson Creek Canada 166 F4
Dawson Inlet Canada 167 M2
Dawson Range mts Canada 166 A2
Dawsons Landing Canada 166 E5
Dawu Hubei China 87 E2
Dawu China see Maqên
Dawu Sichuan China 86 B2
also known as Xianshui
Dawu Taiwan see Tawu
Dawukou China see Shizuishan
Dawu Shan hill China 87 E2
Dawwah Oman 105 G3
Dax France 50 E9
Daxian China see Dazhou
Daxiang Ling mts China 86 B2
Daxihaizi Shuiku l. China 88 D3
Daxin China 87 C4
also known as Taocheng
Daxing China see Ninglang
Daxing China see Lüchun
Daxue China see Wencheng
Daxue Shan mts China 86 B2
Dayan China see Lijiang
Dayang r. China 85 I4
Dayangshu China 85 J1
Dayan Nuur l. Mongolia 84 A1
Dayao China 86 B3
also known as Jinbi
Dayao Shan mts China 87 D4
Dâyat en Nahârât well Mali 124 E2
Daye China 87 E2
Dayi China 86 B2
also known as Jinyuan
Daying Jiang r. China 86 A3
Dayishan China see Guanyun
Dayl Oman 105 G2
Daylesford Australia 147 E4
Dayong China 87 D2
formerly known as Zhangjiajie
Dayr Abū Sa'īd Jordan 108 G5
Dayr az Zawr Syria 109 L2
also spelt Deir-ez-Zor
Dayr az Zawr governorate Syria 109 L2
Dayr Ḥāfir Syria 109 I1
Daysland Canada 167 H4
Dayton OH U.S.A. 176 A6
Dayton TN U.S.A. 174 C5
Dayton TX U.S.A. 179 D6
Dayton VA U.S.A. 176 G7
Dayton WA U.S.A. 180 C3
Daytona Beach U.S.A. 175 D6
Dayu China 87 E3
also known as Nan'ao
Dayu Indon. 77 F3
Dayu Ling mts China 87 E3
Da Yunhe canal China 87 F1
English form Grand Canal
Dayyina i. U.A.E. 105 F2
Dazaifu Japan 91 B8
Dazhe China see Pingyuan
Dazhongji China see Dafeng
Dazhou China 87 C2
formerly known as Daxian
Dazhou Dao i. China 87 D5
Dazhu China 87 C2
also known as Zhuyang
Dazu China 86 C2
also known as Longgang
De Aar S. Africa 132 I7
Dead r. U.S.A. 172 F4
Deadman's Cay Bahamas 187 E2
Dead Mountains U.S.A. 183 J7

▶Dead Sea salt l. Asia 98 B3
Lowest point in the world and in Asia. Also known as Bahrat Lut or HaMelaḥ, Yam.

Deadwood U.S.A. 178 B2
Deakin Australia 151 E6
Deal U.K. 47 N12
Dealesville S. Africa 133 J5
Dean r. Canada 166 E4
De'an China 87 E2
also known as Puting
Dean Channel Canada 166 E4
Deán Funes Arg. 204 D3
Deanuvuotna inlet Norway see Tanafjorden
Dearborn U.S.A. 173 J8
Dease r. B.C. Canada 166 D3
Dease r. N.W.T. Canada 167 G1
Dease Arm b. Canada 166 F1
Dease Lake Canada 166 D3
Dease Lake l. Canada 166 D3
Dease Strait Canada 165 I3
Death Valley U.S.A. 183 H5

▶Death Valley depr. U.S.A. 183 G5
Lowest point in the Americas.
northamerica [landscapes] ▶▶ 156–157

Death Valley Junction U.S.A. 183 H5
Death Valley National Park U.S.A. 183 G5
Deauville France 50 G3
Deaver U.S.A. 180 E3
Debagram India 97 F5
Debak Sarawak Malaysia 77 E2
Debao China 86 C4
Debar Macedonia 58 B7
Debark Eth. 128 C1
Debay well Yemen 105 E4
Debden Canada 167 J4
De Beers Pass S. Africa 133 N5
Debert Canada 169 I4
Debesy Rus. Fed. 40 J4
Dębica Poland 49 S5
De Biesbosch, Nationaal Park nat. park Neth. 48 B4
Debila Alg. 123 G2
Debin Rus. Fed. 39 P3
Dęblin Poland 49 S4
Dębno Poland 49 L3
Débo, Lac l. Mali 124 D3
Deborah East, Lake salt flat Australia 151 B6
Deborah West, Lake salt flat Australia 151 B6
Deboyne Islands P.N.G. 149 G1
Debre Birhan Eth. 128 C2
Debrecen Hungary 49 S8
Debre Markos Eth. 128 C2
Debre Sina Eth. 128 C2
Debre Tabor Eth. 128 C2
Debre Werk' Eth. 128 C2
Debre Zeyit Eth. 128 C2
Debrzno Poland 49 O2
Deçan Kosovo, Srbija Yugo. see Dečani
Dečani Kosovo, Srbija Yugo. 58 B6
also spelt Deçan
Decatur AL U.S.A. 174 C5
Decatur GA U.S.A. 175 C5
Decatur IL U.S.A. 174 B4
Decatur IN U.S.A. 176 A5
Decatur MI U.S.A. 172 H8
Decatur MS U.S.A. 175 B5
Decatur TN U.S.A. 174 C5
Decatur TX U.S.A. 179 C5
Decazeville France 51 I8

▶Deccan plat. India 94 C2
Plateau making up most of southern and central India.

Deception watercourse Botswana 130 E4
Deception Bay Australia 147 G1
Dechang China 86 B3
also known as Dezhou
Decheng China see Deqing
Děčín Czech Rep. 49 L5
Decize France 51 J6
Decorah U.S.A. 174 B3
Dedap i. Indon. see Penasi, Pulau
Dedaye Myanmar 78 A4
Dedebağı Turkey 59 K11
Dedegöl Dağları mts Turkey 106 B3
Deder Eth. 128 D2
Dedinovo Rus. Fed. 43 U6
Dedo de Deus mt. Brazil 206 F11
Dedop'listsqaro Georgia 107 F2
formerly known as Tsiteli Tskaro
Dédougou Burkina 124 E3
Dedovichi Rus. Fed. 43 K4
Dedu China 82 B2
also known as Qingshan
Dedurovka Rus. Fed. 102 C2
Dedza Malawi 129 B8
Dedza Mountain Malawi 131 G2
Dee r. England/Wales U.K. 47 I10
Dee r. Scotland U.K. 46 J6
Deeg India 96 C4
Deelfontein S. Africa 132 H7
Deep Bay Hong Kong China 87 [inset]
also known as Shenzhen Wan
Deep Bight inlet Australia 150 D2
Deep Creek Lake U.S.A. 176 F6
Deep Creek Range mts U.S.A. 183 K2
Deep Gap U.S.A. 176 D9
Deep River Canada 168 E4
Deep River U.S.A. 177 M4
Deer Creek r. U.S.A. 182 B2
Deer Creek Reservoir U.S.A. 183 M1
Deeri Somalia 128 E3
Deering, Mount Australia 151 E5
Deer Island Canada 169 H4
Deer Island AK U.S.A. 164 C4
Deer Island ME U.S.A. 177 Q1
Deer Isle U.S.A. 177 Q1
Deer Lake Nfld. Canada 169 J3
Deer Lake Ont. Canada 167 M4
Deer Lake l. Canada 167 M4
Deer Lodge U.S.A. 180 D3
Deer Park U.S.A. 180 C3
Deerpass Bay Canada 166 F1
Deesa India see Disa
Defeng China see Liping
Defensores del Chaco, Parque Nacional nat. park Para. 201 E5
Defiance U.S.A. 176 A4
Defiance Plateau U.S.A. 183 O6
Défirou well Niger 125 I1
De Funiak Springs U.S.A. 175 C6
Degana India 96 B4
Degano r. Italy 56 E2
Dêgê China 86 A2
also known as Gengqing
Degebe r. Port. 54 D6
Degeberga Sweden 45 K5
Degeh Bur Eth. 128 D2
Dégelis Canada 169 G4
formerly known as Ste-Rose-du-Dégelé
Degema Nigeria 125 G5
Degerfors Sweden 45 K4
Deggendorf Germany 49 J7
Degh r. Pak. 101 H4
Değirmencik r. Turkey 59 J9
Değirmenlik Cyprus see Kythrea
Degodia reg. Eth. 128 D3
De Grey Australia 150 B4
De Grey r. Australia 150 B4
Degtevo Rus. Fed. 41 G6
Degtyarevka Rus. Fed. 43 N8
Dehaj Iran 100 C4
Dehak Iran 101 E5
Dehalak Deset i. Eritrea 121 I6
Deh Bakrī Iran 100 D4
Deh Barez Iran see Fāryāb
Deh Bīd Iran 100 C4
Deh-Dasht Iran 100 B4
Dehdez Iran 100 B4
Dehej India 96 B5
Deh-e Khalīfeh Iran 100 B4
Deh-e Kohneh Iran 100 B4
Dehel Island Eritrea 104 B5
Dehgāh Iran 100 B2
Deh Golān Iran 100 A3
Dehī Afgh. 101 F3
Deh Khvājeh Iran 100 C4
Dehkūyeh Iran 100 C5
Dehlorān Iran 100 A3
Deh Mollā Iran 100 B4
De Hoge Veluwe, Nationaal Park nat. park Neth. 48 C3
De Hoop Nature Reserve S. Africa 132 E11
De Hoop Vlei l. S. Africa 132 E11
Dehqonobod Uzbek. see Dekhkanabad
Dehra Dun India 96 C3
Dehri India 97 E4
Deh Shū Afgh. 101 E4
Dehua China 87 F3
also known as Longxun
Dehui China 82 B3
Deim Zubeir Sudan 126 E3
Deinze Belgium 51 J2
Deir el Qamar Lebanon 108 G4
Deir-ez-Zor Syria see Dayr az Zawr
Dej Romania 58 E1
Dejë, Mal mt. Albania 58 B7
Dejen Eth. 128 C2
Deji China see Rinbung
Dejiang China 87 D2
also known as Jiangsi
Deka Drum Zimbabwe 131 E3
De Kalb IL U.S.A. 174 B3
De Kalb MS U.S.A. 175 B5
De Kalb TX U.S.A. 179 D5
De Kalb Junction U.S.A. 177 J1
De-Kastri Rus. Fed. 81 O2
Dekemhare Eritrea 121 H6
Dekese Dem. Rep. Congo 126 D5
Dekhkanabad Uzbek. 103 F5
also spelt Dehqonobod
Dékoa Cent. Afr. Rep. 126 C3
Delaki Indon. 75 C5
Delamar Lake U.S.A. 183 J4
Delami Sudan 128 A2
De Land U.S.A. 175 D6
Delano U.S.A. 182 E6
Delano Peak U.S.A. 183 L3

▶Delap-Uliga-Djarrit Marshall Is 220 F5
Capital of the Marshall Islands, on Majuro atoll. Also spelt Dalap-Uliga-Darrit or Djarrit-Uliga-Dalap.

Delārām Afgh. 101 E3
Delareyville S. Africa 133 J3
Delaronde Lake Canada 167 J4
Delavan U.S.A. 172 E8
Delaware U.S.A. 176 B5
Delaware r. KS U.S.A. 178 D4
Delaware r. NJ/PA U.S.A. 177 J6
Delaware state U.S.A. 177 J7
Delaware, East Branch r. U.S.A. 177 J4
Delaware, West Branch r. U.S.A. 177 J4
Delaware Bay U.S.A. 177 J6
Delaware City U.S.A. 177 J6
Delaware Water Gap National Recreational Area park U.S.A. 177 K4
Delay r. Canada 169 G1
Delbarton U.S.A. 176 C8
Delbeng Sudan 126 F3
Del Bonita Canada 167 H5
Delburne Canada 167 H4
Delčevo Macedonia 58 D7
Delegate Australia 147 F4
Delémont Switz. 51 N5
Delevan CA U.S.A. 182 B2
Delevan NY U.S.A. 176 G3
Delfinópolis Brazil 206 G7
Delft Neth. 48 B3
Delft Island Sri Lanka 94 C4
Delfzijl Neth. 48 D2
Delgado, Cabo c. Moz. 129 D7
Delgermörön Mongolia 84 C2
Delger Mörön r. Mongolia 84 D1
Delgo Sudan 121 F4
Delhi Canada 173 M8
Delhi China 84 C4
formerly known as Delingha
▶Delhi India 96 C3
world [cities] ▶▶ 24–25
Delhi admin. div. India 89 B6
Delhi CA U.S.A. 182 D4
Delhi LA U.S.A. 175 B5
Delhi NY U.S.A. 177 K3
Deli i. Indon. 77 D4
Deli r. Turkey 107 E3
Delice Turkey 106 C3
Delice r. Turkey 106 C2
Délices Fr. Guiana 199 H3
Delījān Iran 100 B3
Deliktaş Turkey 59 H10
Déline Canada 166 F1
formerly known as Fort Franklin
Delingha China see Delhi
Delisle Canada 167 J5
Delitua Indon. 76 B2
Delitzsch Germany 49 J4
Dell Rapids U.S.A. 178 C3
Dellys Alg. 123 F1
Del Mar U.S.A. 183 G9
Delmar DE U.S.A. 177 J7
Delmar IA U.S.A. 172 C8
Delmas S. Africa 133 M3
Delmenhorst Germany 48 F2
Delmont U.S.A. 176 F5
Delmore Downs Australia 148 B4
Delnice Croatia 56 G3
Del Norte U.S.A. 181 F5
Delong China 86 C4
De-Longa, Ostrova is Rus. Fed. 39 P2
English form De Long Islands
De Long Islands Rus. Fed. see De-Longa, Ostrova
De Long Mountains U.S.A. 164 C3
De Long Strait Rus. Fed. see Longa, Proliv
Deloraine Australia 147 E5
Deloraine Canada 167 K5
Delphi tourist site Greece 59 D10
Delphi U.S.A. 174 C3
Delphos U.S.A. 176 A5
Delportshoop S. Africa 133 I5
Delray Beach U.S.A. 175 D7
Del Río Mex. 184 C2
Del Rio U.S.A. 179 B6
Delsbo Sweden 45 L3
Delta state Nigeria 125 G5
Delta CO U.S.A. 181 E5
Delta OH U.S.A. 176 A4
Delta UT U.S.A. 183 L2
Delta Amacuro state Venez. 199 F2
Delta du Saloum, Parc National du nat. park Senegal 124 A3
Delta Junction U.S.A. 164 E3
Delta National Wildlife Refuge nature res. U.S.A. 175 B6
Delta Reservoir U.S.A. 177 J2
Deltona U.S.A. 175 D6
Delungra Australia 147 F2
Delvada India 94 A1
Delvinë Albania 59 B9
Dema r. Rus. Fed. 102 C1
Demak Indon. 77 E4
Demavend mt. Iran see Damāvand, Qolleh-ye
Demba Dem. Rep. Congo 127 D6
Dembava Lith. 42 F6
Dembia Cent. Afr. Rep. 126 E3
Dembi Dolo Eth. 128 B2
Demerara Guyana see Georgetown
Demidov Rus. Fed. 43 M6
Deming U.S.A. 181 F6
Demini r. Brazil 199 F5
Demini, Serras do mts Brazil 199 F4
Demirci Turkey 106 B3
Demir Hisar Macedonia 58 C7
Demirköprü Barajı resr Turkey 106 B3
Demirköy Turkey 58 I7
Demirler r. Turkey 59 K10
Demistkraal S. Africa 133 I10
Demmin Germany 49 K2
Democracia Brazil 199 F6
Demopolis U.S.A. 175 C5
Dempo, Gunung vol. Indon. 76 C4
Dempster Highway Canada 166 B1
Dêmqog Jammu and Kashmir 96 C2
Demyakhi Rus. Fed. 43 N6
Dem'yanovo Rus. Fed. 40 H3
Demyansk Rus. Fed. 43 N4
De Naawte S. Africa 132 F7
Denair U.S.A. 182 D4
Denakil reg. Eritrea/Eth. 121 I6
also spelt Danakil
Denali National Park and Preserve U.S.A. 164 D3
formerly known as Mount McKinley National Park
Denan Eth. 128 D3
Denare Beach Canada 167 K4
Denau Uzbek. 103 F5
also spelt Denow
Denbigh Canada 168 E4
Denbigh U.K. 47 I10
Den Bosch Neth. see 's-Hertogenbosch
Den Burg Neth. 48 B2
Den Chai Thai. 78 C4
Dendang Indon. 77 D3
Dendâra Mauritania 124 D2
Dendermonde Belgium 51 K1
also known as Termonde
Đeneral Janković Kosovo, Srbija Yugo. 58 C6
also spelt Djeneral Janković
Denezhkin Kamen', Gora mt. Rus. Fed. 40 K3
Dengas Niger 125 H3
Denge Nigeria 125 G3
Dengfeng China 87 E1
Dênggar China 89 D6
Dengjiabu China see Yujiang
Dêngka China see Têwo
Dêngkagoin China see Têwo
Dengkou China 85 E3
also known as Bayan Gol
Dêngqên China 97 G3
also known as Gyamotang
Dengta China 87 E4
Denguiro Cent. Afr. Rep. 126 D3
Dengxian China see Dengzhou
Dengzhou China 87 E1
formerly known as Dengxian
Dengzhou China see Penglai
Den Haag Neth. see The Hague
Denham Australia 151 A5
Denham r. Australia 150 E2
Denham Range mts Australia 149 F4
Denham Sound sea chan. Australia 151 A5
Den Helder Neth. 48 B3
Denholm Canada 167 I4
Denia Spain 55 L6

index

D

Dnyapro *r.* Belarus **41** D5 *see* **Dnieper**
Dnyaprowska-Buhski, Kanal *canal* Belarus **42** F9
Doa Moz. **131** G3
Doabi Mekh-i-Zarin Afgh. **101** F3
Doaktown Canada **169** H4
Doangdoangan Besar *i.* Indon. **77** G4
Doangdoangan Kecil *i.* Indon. **77** G4
Doany Madag. **131** [inset] K2
Doba Chad **126** C2
Doba China *see* **Toiba**
Dobasna *r.* Belarus **43** L9
Dobbertiner Seenlandschaft *park* Germany **49** J2
Dobbs, Cape Canada **167** O1
Dobczyce Poland **49** R6
Dobele Latvia **42** E5
Döbeln Germany **49** K4
Doberai, Jazirah *pen.* Indon. **73** H7
English form Doberai Peninsula; *formerly known as* Vogelkop Peninsula
Doberai Peninsula Indon. *see* **Doberai, Jazirah**
Döbern Germany **49** L4
Dobiegniew Poland **49** M3
Doblas Arg. **204** D5
Dobo Indon. **73** H8
Doboj Bos.-Herz. **56** K4
Do Borji Iran **100** C4
Dobra Poland **49** P4
Dobre Miasto Poland **49** R2
Dobrești Romania **58** D2
Dobrich Bulg. **58** I5
formerly known as Tolbukhin
Dobrinka Rus. Fed. **41** G5
Dobříš Czech Rep. **49** L6
Dobromyl' Ukr. **49** T6
Dobrotești Romania **58** F4
Dobrovăț Romania **58** I2
Dobrovol'sk Rus. Fed. **42** D7
Dobroye Rus. Fed. **43** U9
Dobruchi Rus. Fed. **42** I3
Dobrudzhansko Plato *plat.* Bulg. **58** I5
Dobrun Romania **58** F4
Dobrush Belarus **43** M9
Dobryanka Rus. Fed. **40** K4
Dobryanka Ukr. **43** M9
Dobrynikha Rus. Fed. **43** S6
Dobskie, Jezioro *l.* Poland **49** S1
Dobson N.Z. **153** F10
Dobson *r.* N.Z. **153** D12
Dobzha China **89** E6
Doc Can *reef* Phil. **74** A5
Doce *r. Espírito Santo* Brazil **203** E6
Doce *r. Goiás* Brazil **206** B5
Do China Qala Afgh. **101** G4
Doctor Arroyo Mex. **185** E4
Doctor Belisario Domínguez Mex. **184** D2
Doctor Hicks Range *hills* Australia **151** D6
Doctor Petru Groza Romania *see* **Ștei**
Doda Tanz. **129** C6
Dod Ballapur India **94** C3
Dodecanese *is* Greece **59** I13
also spelt Dodekanisos *or* Dhodhekánisos
Dodekanisos *is* Greece *see* **Dodecanese**
Dodge Center U.S.A. **174** A2
Dodge City U.S.A. **178** B4
Dodgeville U.S.A. **172** C8
Dodman Point U.K. **47** H13
Dodola Eth. **128** C3

▶**Dodoma** Tanz. **129** B6
Capital of Tanzania.

Dodoma *admin. reg.* Tanz. **129** B6
Dodori National Reserve *nature res.* Kenya **128** D5
Dodsonville U.S.A. **176** B6
Doetinchem Neth. **48** D4
Dofa Indon. **75** C3
Dofteana *r.* Romania **58** G3
Dog *r.* Canada **168** B3
Dogai Coring *salt l.* China **89** E5
Dogaicoring Qangco *salt l.* China **89** E5
Doğanbey *Aydın* Turkey **59** I11
Doğanbey *İzmir* Turkey **59** H10
Doğanşehir Turkey **107** D3
Dog Creek Canada **166** F5
Doghārūn Iran **101** E3
Dog Island Canada **169** I1
Dog Lake *Man.* Canada **167** L5
Dog Lake *Ont.* Canada **168** B3
Dog Lake *Ont.* Canada **168** C3
Dognecea Romania **58** C3
Dōgo *i.* Japan **91** C6
Dogoble *well* Somalia **128** E2
Dogondoutchi Niger **125** G3
Dogoumbo Chad **126** C2
Dōgo-yama *mt.* Japan **91** C7
Dog Rocks *is* Bahamas **186** D1
Doğubeyazıt Turkey **107** F3
Doğu Menteşe Dağları *mts* Turkey **106** B3
Dogxung Zangbo *r.* China **89** D6
also known as Raka Zangbo

▶**Doha** Qatar **105** E2
Capital of Qatar. Also spelt Ad Dawḥah

Dohad India *see* **Dahod**
Dohazari Bangl. **78** A3
Dohrighat India **89** C7
Doi *i.* Fiji **145** H4
also spelt Ndoi
Doi Inthanon National Park Thai. **78** B4
Doi Luang National Park Thai. **78** B4
Doilungdêqên China **89** E6
also known as Namka
Doïranis, Limni *l.* Greece/Macedonia *see* **Dojran, Lake**
Doire U.K. *see* **Londonderry**
Doi Saket Thai. **78** B4
Doisanagar India **97** E5
Dois Córregos Brazil **206** E9
Dois Irmãos, Serra dos *hills* Brazil **202** D4
Dojran, Lake Greece/Macedonia **58** D7
also known as Doïranis, Limni *or* Dojransko, Ezero
Dojransko Ezero *l.* Greece/Macedonia *see* **Dojran, Lake**
Doka Sudan **121** G6
Dokali Iran **100** C3
Dokhara, Dunes de *des.* Alg. **123** G2
Dokkum Neth. **48** C2
Dokos *i.* Greece **59** E11
also spelt Dhokós
Dokri Pak. **101** G5
Dokshukino Rus. Fed. *see* **Nartkala**
Dokshytsy Belarus **42** I7
Doksy Czech Rep. **49** L5
Dokuchayeva, Mys *c.* Rus. Fed. **90** J2
Dokuchayevka Kazakh. **103** F2
Dokuchayevs'k Ukr. **41** F7
formerly known as Olenivs'ki Kar"yery *or* Yelenovskiye Kar'yery
Dolak, Pulau *i.* Indon. **73** I8
also known as Yos Sudarso
Dolan Springs U.S.A. **183** J6
Dolavón Arg. **205** D6
Dolbeau Canada **169** F3
Dol-de-Bretagne France **50** E4
Dole France **51** L5
Dolgellau U.K. **47** I11
Dolgeville U.S.A. **177** K2
Dolgiy, Ostrov *i.* Rus. Fed. **40** K1
Dolgorukovo Rus. Fed. **43** T9
Dolgoye *Lipetskaya Oblast'* Rus. Fed. **43** U8
Dolgoye *Orlovskaya Oblast'* Rus. Fed. **43** S9
Dolgusha Rus. Fed. **43** T9
Dolhasca Romania **58** H1
Dolianova *Sardegna* Italy **57** B9
Dolinsk Rus. Fed. **82** F3
Dolisie Congo *see* **Loubomo**
Dolit Indon. **75** C3
Doljevac *Srbija* Yugo. **58** C5
Dolleman Island Antarctica **222** T2
Dolna Lipnitska Bulg. **58** G5
Dolni Chiflik Bulg. **58** I6
formerly known as Georgi Traykov
Dolni Dŭbnik Bulg. **58** F5
Dolno Kamartsi Bulg. **58** E6
Dolno Levski Bulg. **58** F6
Dolný Kubín Slovakia **49** Q6
Dolo Indon. **75** A3
Dolomites *mts* Italy **56** D3
also known as Dolomiti *or* Dolomitiche, Alpi
Dolomiti *mts* Italy *see* **Dolomites**
Dolomiti Bellunesi, Parco Nazionale delle *nat. park* Italy **56** D2
Dolomitiche, Alpi *mts* Italy *see* **Dolomites**
Dolon, Pereval *pass* Kyrg. *see* **Dolon Ashuusu**
Dolon Ashuusu *pass* Kyrg. **103** H4
also known as Dolon, Pereval
Dolonnur China *see* **Duolun**
Dolo Odo Eth. **128** D3
Doloon Mongolia **85** E2
Dolores Arg. **204** F5
Dolores Guat. **185** H5
Dolores Mex. **184** C3
Dolores Uruguay **204** F4
Dolores *r.* U.S.A. **183** O3
Dolores Hidalgo Mex. **185** E4
Dolovo *Vojvodina, Srbija* Yugo. **58** B4
Dolphin, Cape Falkland Is **205** F8
Dolphin and Union Strait Canada **164** H3
Dolphin Head Namibia **130** B5
Dolphin Island Nature Reserve Australia **150** B4
Đô Lương Vietnam **78** D4
Dolzhitsy Rus. Fed. **43** K3
Dom, Gunung *mt.* Indon. **73** I7
Domaniç Turkey **106** B3
also known as Hisarköy
Domar Bangl. **97** F4
Domartang China *see* **Banbar**
Domažlice Czech Rep. **49** J6
Domba China **97** G2
Dombarovskiy Rus. Fed. **102** D2
Dombås Norway **45** J3
Dombe Moz. **131** G3
Dombe Grande Angola **127** B8
Dombegyház Hungary **49** S9
Dombóvár Hungary **49** P9
Dombra Angola **127** C8
Dombrau Poland *see* **Dąbrowa Górnicza**
Dombrovitsa Ukr. *see* **Dubrovytsya**
Dombrowa Poland *see* **Dąbrowa Górnicza**
Dom Cavati Brazil **207** K6
Domda China *see* **Qingshuihe**
Dome Argus *ice feature* Antarctica **223** F1
Dome Charlie *ice feature* Antarctica **223** H2
also known as Dome Circe
Dome Circe *ice feature* Antarctica *see* **Dome Charlie**
Dome Fuji *research station* Antarctica **223** C1
Domeikava Lith. **42** E7
Domel Island Myanmar *see* **Letsok-aw Kyun**
Dome Rock Mountains U.S.A. **183** J8
Domett, Cape Australia **150** E2
Domett, Mount N.Z. **152** G9
Domeyko Chile **204** C3
Dom Feliciano Brazil **203** A9
Domfront France **50** F4
Domingos Martins Brazil **207** M7
▶**Dominica** *country* West Indies **187** H4
northamerica [countries] ⟹ 158–159
Dominical Costa Rica **186** C5
Dominicana, República *country* West Indies *see* **Dominican Republic**
▶**Dominican Republic** *country* West Indies **187** F3
also known as Dominicana, República; *historically known as* Santo Domingo
northamerica [countries] ⟹ 158–159
Dominica Passage Dominica/Guadeloupe **187** H4
Dominion, Cape Canada **165** L3
Dominique *i.* Fr. Polynesia *see* **Hiva Oa**
Domiongo Dem. Rep. Congo **126** D6
Dom Joaquim Brazil **207** J5
Domka Bhutan **97** F4
Domnești Romania **58** F3
Domnești Romania **58** G4
Domo Eth. **128** E3
Domodedovo Rus. Fed. **43** S6
Domodossola Italy **56** A2
Domokos Greece **59** D9
also spelt Dhomokós
Domoni Comoros **129** E8
Domozhirovo Rus. Fed. **43** O1
Dom Pedrito Brazil **203** A9
Dom Pedro Brazil **202** C3
Dompu Indon. **77** G5
Domula China **89** C5
Domusnovas *Sardegna* Italy **57** A9
Domuyo, Volcán *vol.* Arg. **204** C5
Domville, Mount *hill* Australia **147** F2
Domžale Slovenia **56** G2
Don *r.* Australia **149** F3
Don *r.* India **94** C2
Don Mex. **184** C3

▶**Don** *r.* Rus. Fed. **43** U9
5th longest river in Europe.
europe [landscapes] ⟹ 30–31

Don *r.* U.K. **46** J6
Don, Xé *r.* Laos **79** D5
Donadeu Arg. **204** E2
Donald Australia **147** D4
Donaldsonville U.S.A. **175** B6
Donalnes, Cerro *mt.* Chile **204** C2
Donalsonville U.S.A. **175** C6
Doñana, Parque Nacional de *nat. park* Spain **54** E8
Donau *r.* Austria/Germany **49** L7 *see* **Danube**
Donaueschingen Germany **48** F8
Donauwörth Germany **48** H7
Don Benito Spain **54** F6
Doncaster U.K. **47** K10
Dondo Angola **127** B7
Dondo Moz. **131** G3
Dondo, Tanjung *pt* Indon. **75** B2
Dondo, Teluk *b.* Indon. **75** B2
Dondonay *i.* Phil. **74** B4
Dondra Head Sri Lanka **94** D5
Donegal Rep. of Ireland **47** D9
Donegal Bay Rep. of Ireland **47** D9
Dönenbay Kazakh. *see* **Dunenbay**
Donets'k Ukr. **41** F7
formerly known as Stalino *or* Yuzovka
Donets'kyy Kryazh *hills* Rus. Fed./Ukr. **41** F6
Dønfoss Norway **45** J3
Donga *r.* Cameroon/Nigeria **125** H4
Donga Nigeria **125** H5
Dong'an China **87** D3
also known as Baiyashi
Dongara Australia **151** A6
Dongargaon India **94** D1
Dongargarh India **96** D5
Dongbatu China **84** B3
Dongbo China *see* **Mêdog**
Dongchuan China **86** B3
formerly known as Xincun
Dongchuan China *see* **Yao'an**
Dongco China **89** D5
also known as Céringgolêb
Dong Co *l.* China **89** D5
Dongcun China *see* **Haiyang**
Dongcun China *see* **Lanxian**
Dong'e China **85** H4
also known as Tongcheng
Dongfang China **87** D5
also known as Basuo
Dongfanghong China **82** D3
Dongfeng China **82** B4
Donggala Indon. **75** A3
Donggang China **83** B5
formerly known as Dadong *or* Donggou
Donggi Cona *l.* China **84** C5
Donggou China *see* **Donggang**
Donggu China **87** E3
Dongguan China **87** E4
Đông Hà Vietnam **78** D4
Donghai China **87** F1
also known as Niushan
Dong Hai *sea* N. Pacific Ocean *see* **East China Sea**
Donghai Dao *i.* China **87** D4
Dong He *r.* China **86** C2
Dong He *watercourse* China **84** D3
Đông Hới Vietnam **78** D4
Dong Jiang *r.* China **87** E4
Dongjingcheng China **82** C3
Dongkait, Tanjung *pt* Indon. **75** A3
Dongkou China **87** D3
Donglan China **87** C3
Dongle China **84** D4
Dongliao *r.* China **85** I3
Donglük China **88** E4
Dongmen China *see* **Luocheng**
Dongming China **85** G5
Dongning China **82** C3
Dongo Angola **127** B8
Dongo Italy **56** B2
Dongobesh Tanz. **129** B6
Dongola Sudan **121** F5
Dongotona Mountains Sudan **128** B3
Dongou Congo **126** C4
Dong Phraya Fai *mts* Thai. **78** C4
Dong Phraya Yen *esc.* Thai. **79** C5
Dongping *Guangdong* China **87** E4
Dongping China *see* **Anhua**
Dongping *Shandong* China **85** H5
Dongping Hu *l.* China **85** H4
Dongpo China *see* **Meishan**
Dongqiao China **89** E6
Dongshan *Fujian* China **87** F4
also known as Xibu
Dongshan China *see* **Jiangning**
Dongshan *Jiangsu* China **87** G2
Dongshan China *see* **Shangyou**
Dongshao China **87** E3
Dongsha Qundao *is* China **81** J8
English form Pratas Islands
Dongsheng China **85** F4
Dongshuan China *see* **Tangdan**
Dongtai China **87** G1
Dongtai *r.* China **87** G1
Dong Taijnar Hu *l.* China **84** B4
Dongting Hu *l.* China **87** E2
Dongtou China **87** G3
also known as Bei'ao
Donguena Angola **127** B9
Donguila Gabon **126** A4
Dong Ujimqin Qi China *see* **Uliastai**
Dongxiang China *see* **Xuanhan**
Dongxiangzu China *see* **Xiaonan**
Dongxing China **82** B3
Dongyang China **87** G2
Dongying China **85** H4
Dongzhen China **84** D4
Dongzhi China **87** F2
also known as Yaodu
Doniphan U.S.A. **174** B4
Donja Dubnica *Kosovo, Srbija* Yugo. **58** C6
Donjek *r.* Canada **166** A2
Donji Miholjac Croatia **56** K3
Donji Milanovac *Srbija* Yugo. **58** D4
Donji Vakuf Bos.-Herz. **56** J4
also known as Srbobran
Donji Zemunik Croatia **56** H4
Donkerpoort S. Africa **133** J7
Donmanick Islands Bangl. **97** F5
Dønna *i.* Norway **44** K2
Donnacona Canada **169** G4
Donnelly Canada **167** G4
Donnellys Crossing N.Z. **152** H3
Donner Pass U.S.A. **182** D2
Donnersberg *hill* Germany **48** E6
Donnybrook Australia **151** A7
Donostia - San Sebastián Spain **55** J1
Donoussa Greece **59** G11
Donoussa *i.* Greece **59** G11
Donovan U.S.A. **172** F10
Donskoy Rus. Fed. **43** T8
Donskoye *Lipetskaya Oblast'* Rus. Fed. **43** T9
formerly known as Vodopyanovo
Donskoye *Stavropol'skiy Kray* Rus. Fed. **41** G7
Donsol Phil. **74** B3
Donthami *r.* Myanmar **78** B4
Donzenac France **50** H7
Doomadgee Australia **148** C3
Doomadgee Aboriginal Reserve Australia **148** C3
Doon Doon Aboriginal Reserve Australia **150** E3
Door Peninsula U.S.A. **172** F6
Dooxo Nugaaleed *valley* Somalia **128** F2
Do Qu *r.* China **86** B2
Dor *watercourse* Afgh. **101** E4
also known as Pudai
Dor Rus. Fed. **43** Q6
Dora, Lake *salt flat* Australia **150** C4
Dorado Mex. **184** D3
Do Rāhak Iran **100** B5
Dorah Pass Pak. **101** G2
Doramarkog China **86** A1
Doran Lake Canada **167** I2
Dora Riparia *r.* Italy **51** N7
D'Orbigny Bol. **201** E5
Dorbiljin China *see* **Emin**
Dorbod China *see* **Taikang**
Dorbod Qi China *see* **Ulan Hua**
Đorče Petrov Macedonia **58** C6
Dorchester U.K. **47** J13
Dordabis Namibia **130** C4
Dordogne *r.* France **51** F7
Dordrecht Neth. **48** B4
Dordrecht S. Africa **133** L8
Doré Lake Canada **167** J4
Doré Lake *l.* Canada **167** J4
Dores do Guanhães Brazil **207** K6
Dores do Indaiá Brazil **203** C6
Dorey Mali **125** E3
Dorfen Germany **48** J7
Dorfmark Germany **48** G3
Dorgali *Sardegna* Italy **57** B8
Dörgön Mongolia **84** B1
Dori *r.* Afgh. **101** F4
Dori Burkina **125** E3
Doring *r.* S. Africa **132** C8
Doring *r.* S. Africa **132** D9
Doringbaai S. Africa **132** C8
Doringbos S. Africa **132** D8
Dorisvale Australia **148** A2
Dormaa-Ahenkro Ghana **124** E5
Dormans France **51** J3
Dormidontovka Rus. Fed. **82** D3
Dornakal India **94** D2
Dornbirn Austria **48** G8
Dornoch U.K. **46** H6
Dornoch Firth *est.* U.K. **46** H6
Dornod *prov.* Mongolia **85** G1
Dornogovĭ *prov.* Mongolia **85** F2
Doro Mali **125** E2
Dorobanţu Romania **58** H4
Dorobino Rus. Fed. **43** S8
Dorog Hungary **49** P8
Dorogobuzh Rus. Fed. **43** O7
Dorohoi Romania **53** H2
Dorokhovo Rus. Fed. **43** R6
Dorokhsh Iran **101** D3
Döröö Nuur *salt l.* Mongolia **84** B2
Dorostol Bulg. *see* **Silistra**
Dorotea Sweden **44** L2
Dorowa Zimbabwe **131** F3
Dorpat Estonia *see* **Tartu**
Dorre Island Australia **151** A5
Dorrigo Australia **147** G2
Dorris U.S.A. **180** B4
Dorsale Camerounaise *slope* Cameroon/Nigeria **125** H5
Dorset Canada **173** O5
Dorsoidong Co *l.* China **89** E5
Dortmund Germany **48** E4
Dorton U.S.A. **176** C8
Dörtyol Turkey **106** D3
Doruma Dem. Rep. Congo **126** E3
Dorūneh Iran **100** D3
Dorylaeum Turkey *see* **Eskişehir**
Do Sārī Iran **100** D4
Dos Bahías, Cabo *c.* Arg. **205** D7
Dos Cabezas Mountains U.S.A. **183** O9
Dos de Mayo Peru **198** C6
Doshakh, Koh-i- *mt.* Afgh. **101** E3
Dos Hermanas Spain **54** F7
Dos Lagunos Guat. **185** H5
Đo Son Vietnam **78** D3
Dos Palos U.S.A. **182** D5
Dospat Bulg. **58** F7
Dospat *r.* Bulg. **58** F7
Dos Pozos Arg. **205** D6
Dosse *r.* Germany **49** J3
Dosso Niger **125** F3
Dosso *dept* Niger **125** F3
Dosso, Réserve Partielle de *nature res.* Niger **125** F3
Dossor Kazakh. **102** C3
Dostyk Kazakh. **88** C2
also spelt Dostyq; *formerly known as* Druzhba
Dostyq Kazakh. *see* **Dostyk**
Dothan U.S.A. **175** C6
Dötlingen Germany **48** F3
Douai France **51** J2
Douako Guinea **124** C4
Douala Cameroon **125** H5
Douala-Edéa, Réserve *nature res.* Cameroon **125** H6
Douarnenez France **50** B4
Douarnenez, Baie de *b.* France **50** B4
Double Headed Shot Cays *is* Bahamas **186** C2
Double Island *Hong Kong* China **87** [inset]
also known as Wong Wan Chau
Double Island Point Australia **149** G5
Double Mountain Fork *r.* U.S.A. **179** B5
Double Peak U.S.A. **182** F6
Double Point Australia **149** E3
Double Springs U.S.A. **174** C5
Doubs *r.* France/Switz. **51** L6
Doubtful Bay Australia **150** D2
Doubtful Island Bay Australia **151** B7
Doubtful Sound N.Z. **153** B13
Doué-la-Fontaine France **50** F5
Douentza Mali **124** E3
Dougga *tourist site* Tunisia **123** H1
Doughboy Bay N.Z. **153** B15

▶**Douglas** Isle of Man **47** H9
Capital of the Isle of Man.

Douglas N.Z. **152** I7
Douglas S. Africa **132** H6
Douglas *AZ* U.S.A. **181** E7
Douglas *GA* U.S.A. **175** D6
Douglas *WY* U.S.A. **180** F4
Douglas Apsley National Park Australia **147** F5
Douglas Channel Canada **166** D4
Douglas City U.S.A. **182** B1
Douglas Creek *watercourse* Australia **146** C2
Douglas Creek *r.* U.S.A. **183** P1
Douglas Range *mts* Antarctica **222** T2
Douglas Reef *i.* Japan *see* **Okino-Tori-shima**
Douglasville U.S.A. **175** C5
Dougoulé *well* Niger **125** H3
Douhi Chad **120** C5
Douhudi China *see* **Gong'an**
Doukato, Akra *pt* Greece **59** B10
Doulaincourt-Saucourt France **51** L4
Douliu Taiwan *see* **Touliu**
Doullens France **51** I2
Doumè Benin **125** F4
Doumé Cameroon **125** I5
Doumé *r.* Cameroon **125** I5
Doumen China **87** E4
also known as Jing'an
Douna Mali **125** E3
Dounkassa Benin **125** F4
Doupovské Hory *mts* Czech Rep. **49** K5
Dourada, Cachoeira *waterfall* Brazil **206** D5
Dourada, Serra *hills* Brazil **206** C3
Dourada, Serra *mts* Brazil **202** B5
Dourados Brazil **203** A7
Dourados *r.* Brazil **203** A7
Dourados, Serra dos *hills* Brazil **203** A7
Dourbali Chad **126** B2
Dourdou *r.* France **51** I8
Dourdoura Chad **126** D2
Douro *r.* Port. **54** C3
also spelt Duero (Spain)
Doushi China *see* **Gong'an**
Doushui Shuiku *resr* China **87** E3
Doutor Camargo Brazil **206** A10
Douve *r.* France **50** E3
Douz Tunisia **123** H2
Douze *r.* France **50** F9
Douziat Chad **120** C6
Dove *r.* U.K. **47** K11
Dove Brook Canada **169** J2
Dove Bugt *b.* Greenland **165** Q2
Dove Creek U.S.A. **183** P4
Dover U.K. **47** N12
historically known as Dubris

▶**Dover** *DE* U.S.A. **177** J6
State capital of Delaware.

Dover *NH* U.S.A. **177** O2
Dover *NJ* U.S.A. **177** K5
Dover *OH* U.S.A. **176** D5
Dover *TN* U.S.A. **174** C4
Dover, Point Australia **151** D7
Dover, Strait of France/U.K. **50** H2
also known as Pas de Calais
Dover-Foxcroft U.S.A. **174** G2
Dover Plains U.S.A. **177** L4
Dovey *r.* U.K. *see* **Dyfi**
Doveyrich, Rūd-e *r.* Iran/Iraq **107** G5
Dovnsklint *cliff* Denmark **48** H1
Dovrefjell *mts* Norway **44** J3
Dovrefjell Nasjonalpark *nat. park* Norway **44** J3
Dow, Lake Botswana *see* **Xau, Lake**
Dowa Malawi **129** B8
Dowagiac U.S.A. **172** G9
Dowgha'i Iran **100** D2
Dowi, Tanjung *pt* Indon. **76** B2
Dowlatābād Afgh. **101** F2
Dowlatābād *Fārs* Iran **100** B4
Dowlatābād *Fārs* Iran **100** C4
Dowlatābād *Khorāsan* Iran **100** D2
Dowlatābād *Khorāsan* Iran **101** D3
Dowlatābād *Khorāsan* Iran **101** E2
Dowl at Yār Afgh. **101** F3
Downey *CA* U.S.A. **182** F8
Downey *ID* U.S.A. **172** B9
Downham Market U.K. **47** M11
Downieville U.S.A. **182** D2
Downpatrick U.K. **47** G9
Downs U.S.A. **178** C4
Downsville *NY* U.S.A. **177** K3
Downsville *WI* U.S.A. **172** B6
Downton, Mount Canada **166** E4
Dow Rūd Iran **100** B3
Dow Sar Iran **100** A3
Dowshī Afgh. **101** G3
Dowsk Belarus **43** L8
Dowzha Belarus **43** L6
Doyle U.S.A. **182** D1
Doyles Canada **169** J4
Doyrentsi Bulg. **58** F5
Dozdān *r.* Iran **100** D5
Dōzen *is* Japan **91** C6
Dozois, Réservoir Canada **168** E4
Dozulé France **50** F3
Drâa, Oued *watercourse* Morocco **122** C3
Dracena Brazil **206** B8
Drachkava Belarus **42** J8
Drachten Neth. **48** D2
Dragalina Romania **58** I4
Dragan *l.* Sweden **44** K2
Drăgănești-Olt Romania **58** F4
Drăgănești-Vlașca Romania **58** G4
Drăgășani Romania **58** F4
Draghoender S. Africa **132** G6
Dragoman Bulg. **58** D6
Dragonada *i.* Greece **59** H13
also spelt Dhragonádha
Dragonera, Isla *i.* Spain *see* **Sa Dragonera**
Dragones Arg. **201** E5
Dragonisi *i.* Greece **59** G11
also known as Dhragónisos
Dragon Rocks Nature Reserve Australia **151** B7
Dragon's Mouths *strait* Trin. and Tob./Venez. **187** H5
Dragoon U.S.A. **183** N9
Dragør Denmark **45** K5
Dragoș Vodă Romania **58** I4
Dragsfjärd Fin. **45** M3
Draguignan France **51** M9
Drăgușeni Romania **58** I3
Drahichyn Belarus **42** G9
also spelt Drogichin
Drakensberg *mts* Lesotho/S. Africa **133** M6
Drakensberg *mts* S. Africa **131** F5
Drakensberg Garden S. Africa **133** N6
Draken's Rock *mt.* S. Africa **133** M7
Drakes Bay U.S.A. **182** A4
Drakulya *r.* Ukr. **58** K3
Drama Greece **58** F7
Drammen Norway **45** J4
Drang, Prêk *r.* Cambodia **79** D5
Drangajökull *ice cap* Iceland **44** [inset] B2
Drangedal Norway **45** J4
Drangme Chhu *r.* Bhutan **97** F4
Dranov, Lacul *l.* Romania **58** K4
Dranske Germany **49** K1
Draper U.S.A. **183** M1
Draper, Mount U.S.A. **166** B3
Drapsaca Afgh. *see* **Kondūz**
Dras Jammu and Kashmir **96** B2
Drau *r.* Austria **49** L9
also spelt Drava *or* Dráva
Drava *r.* Croatia/Slovenia **49** N9
also spelt Drau *or* Dráva
Dráva *r.* Hungary **56** K3
also spelt Drau *or* Drava
Dravinja *r.* Slovenia **56** H2
Dravograd Slovenia **56** H2
Drawa *r.* Poland **49** M3
Drawieński Park Narodowy *nat. park* Poland **49** M2
Drawno Poland **49** M2
Drawsko, Jezioro *l.* Poland **49** N2
Drawsko Pomorskie Poland **49** M2
Drayton Valley Canada **167** H4
Drebber Germany **48** F3
Dreieich Germany **48** F5
Dreistelzberge *hill* Germany **48** G5
Drenovci Croatia **56** K4
Drenovets Bulg. **58** D5
Drepano, Akra *pt* Greece **59** E9
Dresden Canada **173** K8
Dresden Germany **49** K4
Dresden U.S.A. **174** B4
Dretun' Belarus **43** K6
Dreux France **50** H4
Drevsjø Norway **45** K3
Drewryville U.S.A. **177** H9
Drezdenko Poland **49** M3
Dričeni Latvia **42** I5
Dridža *l.* Latvia **42** I6
Driftwood U.S.A. **176** G4
Driggs U.S.A. **180** E4
Drillham Australia **149** F5
Drin *r.* Albania **58** A6
Drina *r.* Bos.-Herz./Yugo. **56** L4
Drincea *r.* Romania **58** D4
Drini i Zi *r.* Albania **58** B6
Drinit, Gjiri i *b.* Albania **58** A7
Drino *r.* Albania **59** B8
Driscoll Island Antarctica **222** O1
Drissa Belarus *see* **Vyerkhnyadzvinsk**
Drniš Croatia **56** I5
Drobeta - Turnu Severin Romania **58** D4
also known as Turnu Severin
Drochtersen Germany **48** G2
Drogheda Rep. of Ireland **47** F10
also spelt Droichead Átha
Drogichin Belarus *see* **Drahichyn**
Drogobych Ukr. *see* **Drohobych**
Drohiczyn Poland **49** T3
Drohobych Ukr. **53** G2
also spelt Drogobych
Droichead Átha Rep. of Ireland *see* **Drogheda**
Droitwich U.K. **47** J11
Dronne *r.* France **50** F7
Dronning Ingrid Land *reg.* Greenland **165** O3
Dronning Louise Land *reg.* Greenland **165** Q2
Dronning Maud Land *reg.* Antarctica *see* **Queen Maud Land**
Droogmakerij de Beemster *tourist site* Neth. **48** B3
Dropt *r.* France **50** F8
Drosh Pak. **101** G3
Drosia Greece **59** E10
also spelt Dhrosiá
Droskovo Rus. Fed. **43** S9
Drovyanaya Rus. Fed. **85** G1
Drowning *r.* Canada **168** C3
Drūkšių ežeras *l.* Belarus/Lith. **42** H6
also known as Drysyvaty Vozyera
Druk-Yul *country* Asia *see* **Bhutan**
Drumheller Canada **167** H5
Drummond *atoll* Kiribati *see* **Tabiteuea**
Drummond, Lake U.S.A. **177** I9
Drummond Island Kiribati *see* **McKean**
Drummond Island U.S.A. **173** J5
Drummond Range *hills* Australia **149** E5
Drummondville Canada **169** F4
Drummore U.K. **47** H9
Drumnadrochit U.K. **46** H6
Drury Lake Canada **166** C2
Druskieniki Lith. *see* **Druskininkai**
Druskininkai Lith. **42** F8
formerly known as Druskieniki
Drusti Latvia **42** G4
Druts' *r.* Belarus **43** L8
Druya Belarus **42** I6
Druzhba Kazakh. *see* **Dostyk**
Druzhba Ukr. **43** O9
Druzhina Rus. Fed. **39** O3
Druzhinnoye, Ozero *l.* Rus. Fed. **43** S1
Druzhnaya Gorka Rus. Fed. **43** L2
Druzhylavichy Belarus **42** G9
Drwęca *r.* Poland **49** P2
Dry *r.* Australia **148** B2
Dryanovo Bulg. **58** G6
Dryazhno Rus. Fed. **43** J3
Dry Bay U.S.A. **166** B3
Dryberry Lake Canada **168** A3
Drybin Belarus **43** M7
Dry Cimarron *r.* U.S.A. **178** B4
Dryden Canada **168** A3
Dryden *NY* U.S.A. **177** I3
Dryden *VA* U.S.A. **176** C9
Dry Fork *r.* U.S.A. **180** F4
Drygalski Fjord *inlet* S. Georgia **205** [inset]
Drygalski Ice Tongue Antarctica **223** L1
Drygalski Island Antarctica **223** G2
Drygarn Fawr *hill* U.K. **47** I11
Dry Harts *r.* S. Africa **133** I4
Dry Lake U.S.A. **183** J5
Dry Lake *l.* U.S.A. **182** G2
Dry Ridge U.S.A. **176** A7
Drysa *r.* Belarus **43** I6
Drysdale *r.* Australia **150** D2
Drysdale Island Australia **148** B1
Drysdale River National Park Australia **150** D2
Drysyvaty Vozyera *l.* Belarus/Lith. *see* **Drūkšių ežeras**
Dry Tortugas *is* U.S.A. **175** D7
Drzewica Poland **49** R4
Dschang Cameroon **125** H5
Dua *r.* Dem. Rep. Congo **126** D4
Dūāb *r.* Iran **100** B3
Du'an China **87** D4
also known as Anyang
Duancun China *see* **Wuxiang**
Duaringa Australia **149** F4
Duars *reg.* India **97** F4
Duarte, Pico *mt.* Dom. Rep. **187** F3
formerly known as Trujillo, Monte
Dubā Saudi Arabia **104** A2
Dubai U.A.E. **105** F2
also spelt Dubayy
Dubakella Mountain U.S.A. **182** A1
Dubăsari Moldova **58** K1
formerly spelt Dubesar' *or* Dubossary
Dubăsari *prov.* Moldova **53** H2
Dubawnt *r.* Canada **167** L2
Dubawnt Lake Canada **167** K2
Dubayy U.A.E. *see* **Dubai**
Dubbagh, Jabal ad *mt.* Saudi Arabia **104** A2
Dubbo Australia **147** F3
Dube *r.* Liberia **124** D5
Dübendorf Switz. **51** O5
Dübener Heide *park* Germany **49** J4
Dubesar' Moldova *see* **Dubăsari**
Dubets Rus. Fed. **43** T3
Dubičiai Lith. **42** F7
Dubinës, Maja e *mt.* Albania **58** A6
Dubingiai Lith. **42** G6
Dublán Mex. **184** D2
Dublin Canada **172** F2

▶**Dublin** Rep. of Ireland **47** F10
Capital of the Republic of Ireland. Also known as Baile Átha Cliath.

Dublin *GA* U.S.A. **175** D5
Dublin *VA* U.S.A. **176** E8
Dubna *r.* Latvia **42** H5
Dubna *Moskovskaya Oblast'* Rus. Fed. **43** S5
Dubna *Tul'skaya Oblast'* Rus. Fed. **43** R7
Dubnica nad Váhom Slovakia **49** P7
Dubno Ukr. **41** C6
Dubois U.S.A. **180** D3
Du Bois U.S.A. **176** G4
Dubossary Moldova *see* **Dubăsari**
Dubovaya Roshcha Rus. Fed. **43** R8
Dubovka *Tul'skaya Oblast'* Rus. Fed. **43** T8
Dubovka *Volgogradskaya Oblast'* Rus. Fed. **41** H6
Dubovoye, Ozero *l.* Rus. Fed. **43** V6
Dubovskoye Rus. Fed. **41** G7
Dubrar Pass Azer. **107** G2
Dubréka Guinea **124** B4
Dubris U.K. *see* **Dover**
Dubrovichi Rus. Fed. **43** U7
Dubrovka *Bryanskaya Oblast'* Rus. Fed. **43** O8
Dubrovka *Pskovskaya Oblast'* Rus. Fed. **43** J5
Dubrovka *Pskovskaya Oblast'* Rus. Fed. **43** K4
Dubrovnik Croatia **56** K6
historically known as Ragusa
Dubrovytsya Ukr. **41** C6
formerly known as Dombrovitsa
Dubrowna Belarus **43** L7
Dubun Kazakh. **103** J4
Dubuque U.S.A. **174** B3
Dubysa *r.* Lith. **42** E6
Duc de Gloucester, Îles du *is* Fr. Polynesia **221** I7
English form Duke of Gloucester Islands
Ducey France **50** E4
Duchang China **87** F2
Duchateau Entrance *sea chan.* P.N.G. **149** G1
Ducherow Germany **49** K2
Duchesne U.S.A. **183** N1
Duchesne *r.* U.S.A. **183** O1
Duchess Australia **148** C4
Duchess Canada **167** I5
Ducie Island Pitcairn Is **221** J7
Duck *r.* U.S.A. **174** C4
Duck Bay Canada **167** K4
Duck Creek *r.* Australia **150** B4
Duck Lake Canada **167** J4
Duck Valley Indian Reservation *res.* U.S.A. **180** C4
Duckwater U.S.A. **183** I3
Duckwater Peak U.S.A. **183** I3
Đưc Trọng Vietnam **79** E6
Duda *r.* Col. **198** C4
Duderstadt Germany **48** H4
Dudestii Vechi Romania **58** B2
Dudhi India **97** D4
Dudinka Rus. Fed. **39** I3
Dudley U.K. **47** J11
Dudleyville U.S.A. **183** N9
Dudna *r.* India **94** C2
Dudorovskiy Rus. Fed. **43** Q8
Duduza S. Africa **133** M3
Duékoué Côte d'Ivoire **124** D5
Duen, Bukit *vol.* Indon. **76** C3
Dueré Brazil **202** B4
Duerna *r.* Spain **54** F2
Duero *r.* Spain **55** I3
also spelt Douro (Portugal)
Dufault, Lac *l.* Canada **173** O2
Dufferin, Cape Canada **168** E1
Duffer Peak U.S.A. **180** C4
Duffield U.S.A. **176** C9
Duff Islands Solomon Is **145** F2
Duffreboy, Lac *l.* Canada **169** G1
Dufftown U.K. **46** I6
Dufourspitze *mt.* Italy/Switz. **56** A3
Dufrost Canada **167** L5
Dugab Uzbek. **103** F5
also spelt Dughoba
Dugald *r.* Australia **149** D3
Duga Resa Croatia **56** H3
Duga-Zapadnaya, Mys *c.* Rus. Fed. **39** O4
Dughdash *mts* Saudi Arabia **109** H8
Dughoba Uzbek. *see* **Dugab**
Dugi Otok *i.* Croatia **56** H4
Dugi Rat Croatia **56** I5
Dugna Rus. Fed. **43** R7
Dugopolje Croatia **56** I5
Dugo Selo Croatia **56** I3
Dugui Qarag China **85** F4
Düğüncübaşı Turkey **58** I7
Dugway U.S.A. **183** L1
Du He *r.* China **87** D1

Edsbyn Sweden 45 K3
Edsele Sweden 44 L3
Edson Canada 167 G4
Eduardo Castex Arg. 204 D4
Eduni, Mount Canada 166 D1
Edward r. N.S.W. Australia 147 E3
Edward r. Qld Australia 149 D2
Edward, Lake Dem. Rep. Congo/Uganda 126 F5
also known as Rutanzige, Lake; formerly known as Idi Amin Dada, Lake
Edward, Mount Antarctica 222 T1
Edwardesabad Pak. see Bannu
Edward Island Australia 148 B2
Edward Island Canada 172 E2
Edward River Aboriginal Reserve Australia 149 D2
Edwards U.S.A. 177 J1
Edwards Plateau U.S.A. 179 B6
Edwardsville U.S.A. 174 B4
Edward VIII Bay Antarctica 223 D2
Edward VII Peninsula Antarctica 223 N1
Edwin B. Forsythe National Wildlife Refuge nature res. U.S.A. 177 K6
Edziza, Mount Canada 166 D3
Edzo Canada see Rae-Edzo
Eel r. U.S.A. 182 A1
Eel, South Fork r. U.S.A. 182 A1
Eendekuil S. Africa 132 C9
Eenzamheid Pan salt pan S. Africa 132 E4
Eesti country Europe see Estonia
Éfaté i. Vanuatu 145 F3
also spelt Vaté; formerly known as Sandwich Island
Efes tourist site Turkey see Ephesus
Effingham U.S.A. 174 B4
Eflâni Turkey 106 C2
Efsus Turkey see Afşin
Eftimie Murgu Romania 58 D4
Eg Mongolia 85 F1
Ega r. Spain 55 J2
Egadi, Isole is Sicilia Italy 57 D10
English form Egadi Islands
Egadi Islands is Sicilia Italy see Egadi, Isole
Egan Range mts U.S.A. 183 J3
Eganville Canada 173 P5
Egbe Nigeria 125 G4
Egedesminde Greenland see Aasiaat
Egentliga Finland reg. Fin. see Varsinais-Suomi
Eger r. Germany 49 J5
Eger Hungary 49 R8
Egersund Norway 45 I4
Egerton, Mount hill Australia 151 B5
Eggenfelden Germany 49 J7
Egg Harbor U.S.A. 172 F5
Egg Harbor City U.S.A. 177 K6
Egg Lake Canada 167 J4
Eggum Norway 44 K1
Egilsstaðir Iceland 44 [inset] D2
Eğin Turkey see Kemaliye
Eginbah Australia 150 B4
Egindibulaq Kazakh. see Yegindybulak
Egindy Kazakh. 103 H2
Eğirdir Turkey 106 B3
Eğirdir Gölü l. Turkey 106 B3
Egiyn Gol r. Mongolia 84 D1
Égletons France 51 I7
Eglinton Island Canada 165 H2
Eglisau Switz. 51 O5
Egmont, Cape N.Z. 152 H7
Egmont, Mount vol. N.Z. see Taranaki, Mount
Egmont National Park N.Z. 152 I7
Egmont Village N.Z. 152 I7
Egua Col. 199 E3
Éguas r. Brazil 202 C5
also known as Correntina
Egvekinot Rus. Fed. 39 S3

▶Egypt country Africa 121 F3
2nd most populous country in Africa. Known as Misr or Mudraya in Arabic; formerly known as United Arab Republic; historically known as Aegyptus.
africa [countries] ⟹ 114–117

Ehcel well Mali see Agous-n-Ehsel
Ehen Hudag China 84 D4
also known as Alxa Youqi
Ehime pref. Japan 91 C8
Ehingen (Donau) Germany 48 G7
Ehrenberg U.S.A. 183 J8
Ehrenberg Range hills Australia 148 A4
Eibar Spain 55 I1
Eibergen Neth. 48 D3
Eichstätt Germany 48 I7
Eide Norway 44 I3
Eider r. Germany 48 F1
Eidfjord Norway 45 I3
Eiði Faroe Is 46 E1
Eidsvåg Norway 44 J3
Eidsvold Australia 149 F5
Eidsvoll Norway 45 J3
Eifel hills Germany 48 D5
Eigg i. U.K. 46 F7
Eight Degree Channel India/Maldives 94 B5
Eights Coast Antarctica 222 R2
Eighty Mile Beach Australia 150 C3
Eilat Israel 108 F8
also spelt Elat
Eildon, Lake Australia 147 E4
Eildon State Park nature res. Australia 147 E4
Eileen Lake Canada 167 J2
Eilenburg Germany 49 J4
Eilerts de Haan, Natuurreservaat nature res. Suriname 199 G4
Eilerts de Haan Gebergte mts Suriname 199 G4
Eil Malk i. Palau 73 H5
also known as Mecherchar
Einasleigh Australia 149 E3
Einasleigh r. Australia 149 D3
Einbeck Germany 48 G4
Eindhoven Neth. 48 C4
Eindpaal Namibia 132 D2
Einme Myanmar 78 A4
Einsiedeln Switz. 51 O5
Éire country Europe see Ireland, Republic of
Eiriosgaigh i. U.K. see Eriskay
Eirú r. Brazil 198 D6
Eirunepé Brazil 198 D6
Eisberg hill Germany 48 G4
Eiseb watercourse Namibia 130 D3
Eisenach Germany 48 H5
Eisenerz Austria 49 L8
Eisenerzer Alpen mts Austria 49 L8
Eisenhower, Mount Canada see Castle Mountain
Eisenhüttenstadt Germany 49 L3
Eisenstadt Austria 49 N8
Eišiškės Lith. 42 F7
Eisleben Lutherstadt Germany 48 I4
Eistow N.Z. 152 J5
Eitape P.N.G. see Aitape
Eivinvik Norway 45 I3
Eivissa Spain see Ibiza
Eivissa i. Spain see Ibiza
Ejea de los Caballeros Spain 55 J2
Ejeda Madag. 131 [inset] J5
Ejin Horo Qi China see Altan Shiret
Ejin Qi China see Dalain Hob
Ej Jill, Sebkhet salt flat Mauritania 122 B5
Ejmiadzin Armenia see Ejmiatsin
Ejmiatsin Armenia 107 F2
formerly spelt Echmiadzin or Ejmiadzin
Ejura Ghana 125 E5
Ekalaka U.S.A. 180 F3
Ekang Nigeria 125 H5
Ekangala S. Africa 133 M2
Ékata Gabon 126 B4
Ekawasaki Japan 91 C8
Ekenäs Fin. 45 M4
also known as Tammisaari
Ekenäs Sweden 45 K4
Ekenäs skärgårds Nationalpark nat. park Fin. 45 M4
also known as Tammisaaren Saariston Kansallispuisto
Ekerem Turkm. see Okarem
Eket Nigeria 125 G5
Eketahuna N.Z. 152 J8
Ekhinos Greece see Echinos
Ekhmîm Egypt see Akhmim
Ekibastuz Kazakh. 103 H2
Ekimchan Rus. Fed. 82 D1
Ekinyazı Turkey 109 K1
Ekiti state Nigeria 125 G5
Ekka Island Canada 166 F1
Ekoli Dem. Rep. Congo 126 E5
Ekonda Rus. Fed. 39 K3
Ekondo Titi Cameroon 125 H5
Ekostrovskaya Imandra, Ozero l. Rus. Fed. 44 P2
Ekouamou Congo 126 C4
Ekpoma Nigeria 125 G5
Eksere Turkey see Gündoğmuş
Ekshärad Sweden 45 K3
Eksjö Sweden 45 K4
Ekskavatornyy Rus. Fed. 82 A1
Eksteenfontein S. Africa 132 B5
Ekström Ice Shelf Antarctica 223 X2
Ekträsk Sweden 44 L2
Ekwan r. Canada 168 D2
Ekwan Point Canada 168 D2
Ela Myanmar 78 B4
El Aaiún W. Sahara see Laâyoune
El Abbasiya Sudan 121 F6
Elafonisos i. Greece 59 D12
Elafonisou, Steno sea chan. Greece 59 D12
El 'Agrûd well Egypt 108 F7
Elaia, Cape Cyprus 108 F2
also known as Zeytin Burnu; also spelt Elea, Cape
El Aïadia well Sudan 121 G5
El 'Aiyat Egypt 108 C8
El 'Alamein Egypt 121 F2
also spelt Al 'Alamayn
El Alamo Mex. 184 A2
El Alia Alg. 123 G2
El Alia Tunisia 57 B11
El Alto Peru 198 A6
El 'Âmirîya Egypt 108 A6
El Amria Alg. 55 J9
Elands r. S. Africa 133 N1
Elands r. S. Africa 133 O2
Elandsberg mt. S. Africa 133 K9
Elandsdoorn S. Africa 133 N2
Elandsdrif S. Africa 133 J9
Elandskraal S. Africa 133 O5
Elandslaagte S. Africa 133 N5
Elandsputte S. Africa 133 K2
El Aouinet Alg. 57 A13
El Arahal Spain 54 F7
El Araïche Morocco see Larache
El Arco Mex. 184 B2
El Aricha Alg. 123 E2
El 'Arîsh Egypt 121 G2
Elasa i. Greece 59 H13
El Ashmûnein Egypt 121 F3
historically known as Hermopolis Magna
El Asnam Alg. see Ech Chélif
Elassona Greece 59 D9
El Astillero Spain 54 H1
Elat Israel see Eilat
El 'Atf reg. W. Sahara 122 B5
Elati mt. Greece 59 B10
Elato atoll Micronesia 73 K5
Elazığ Turkey 107 D3
Elba U.S.A. 175 C6
Elba, Isola d' i. Italy 56 C6
historically known as Ilva
El Bahr El Ahmar governorate Egypt 108 C9
El'ban Rus. Fed. 82 E2
El Banco Col. 198 C2
El Bânoûn well Mauritania 124 D2
El Barco de Ávila Spain 54 F4
El Barco de Valdeorras Spain see O Barco
El Barreal salt l. Mex. 184 D2
El Barun Sudan 128 B2
Elbasan Albania 58 B7
Elbaşı Turkey 106 C3
El Bauga Sudan 121 G5
El Baúl Venez. 199 D2
El Bayadh Alg. 123 F2
formerly known as Géryville
Elbe r. Germany 48 G2
also known as Labe (Czech Republic)
'Elb el Fçâl des. Mauritania 124 C2
El Beqa'a valley Lebanon 109 H3
El Berié well Mauritania 124 C2
Elberta U.S.A. 183 M2
Elberton U.S.A. 175 D5
El Beru Hagia Somalia 128 D4
Elbeuf France 50 H3
Elbeyli Turkey 109 I1
El Beyyed well Mauritania 122 C5
El Beyyed well Mauritania 124 C2
El Billete, Cerro mt. Mex. 185 E5
Elbing Poland see Elbląg
Elbistan Turkey 107 D3
Elbląg Poland 49 Q1
historically known as Elbing
Elbląski, Kanał canal Poland 49 Q1
El Bluff Nicaragua 186 C4
El Bolsón Arg. 205 C6
El Bordj Alg. 55 L9
El Borma Tunisia 123 H3
El Boulaida Alg. see Blida
Elbow Canada 167 J5
Elbow Lake U.S.A. 178 C2
El Bozal Mex. 185 E4

▶Elbrus mt. Rus. Fed. 41 G8
Highest mountain in Europe.
europe [landscapes] ⟹ 30–31

El Buheyrat state Sudan 126 F3
El Buitre mt. Spain 55 J6
El Burg Egypt 108 C6
El Burgo de Osma Spain 55 H3
El Burumbul Egypt 108 C8
Elburz Mountains Iran 100 B2
also known as Alborz, Reshteh-ye
El Cain Arg. 205 C6
El Cajon U.S.A. 183 H9
El Callao Venez. 199 F3
El Campo U.S.A. 179 C6
El Canton Venez. 198 D3
El Capulín r. Mex. 179 B7
El Carmelo Venez. 198 D2
El Carmen Arg. 200 D6
El Carmen Beni Bol. 201 E3
El Carmen Santa Cruz Bol. 201 F4
El Carmen Ecuador 198 B5
El Carmen Venez. 199 E4
El Caroche mt. Spain 55 K5
also spelt Caroch
El Casco Mex. 184 D3
El Cebú, Cerro mt. Mex. 185 G6
El Centro U.S.A. 183 I9
El Cerro Bol. 201 E4
El Chaparro Venez. 199 E2
Elche Spain 55 K6
historically known as Ilici
El Chichónal vol. Mex. 185 G5
El Chilicote Mex. 184 D2
Elcho U.S.A. 172 D5
Elcho Island Australia 148 B1
El Coca Ecuador see Puerto Francisco de Orellana
El Cocuy, Parque Nacional nat. park Col. 198 C3
El Collado hill Spain 54 G6
El Contador, Puerto de pass Spain 55 I7
El Cotorro Cuba 186 C2
El Cuy Arg. 204 C5
El Cuyo Mex. 185 I4
Elda Spain 55 K6
El Dab'a Egypt 53 H5
El Dalgamûn Egypt 108 B7
Eldama Ravine Kenya 128 B4
Elde r. Germany 48 I2
El Debb well Eth. 128 D3
Eldee Canada 173 N4
El Deir Egypt 108 C7
Eldena U.S.A. 172 D9
Elderon U.S.A. 172 D6
El Desemboque Mex. 181 D7
Eldhraun lava field Iceland 44 [inset] C3
El Diamante Mex. 184 E2
El Difícil Col. 198 C2
El'dikan Rus. Fed. 39 N3
El Diviso Col. 198 B4
El Djezair Alg. see Algiers
El Doctor Mex. 184 B2
Eldon U.S.A. 178 D4
Eldorado Arg. 204 G2
Eldorado Brazil 203 B8
El Dorado Col. 198 D4
El Dorado Mex. 184 D3
El Dorado AR U.S.A. 179 D5
El Dorado KS U.S.A. 178 C4
Eldorado U.S.A. 179 B6
El Dorado Venez. 199 F3
Eldorado Mountains U.S.A. 183 J6
Eldoret Kenya 128 B4
Eldridge U.S.A. 172 C9
Eldridge, Mount U.S.A. 166 A2
Elea, Cape Cyprus see Elaia, Cape
Eleanor U.S.A. 176 D7
Electric Peak U.S.A. 180 E3
El Eglab plat. Alg. 122 D4
El 'Ein well Sudan 121 F5
Eleja Latvia 42 E5
El Ejido Spain 55 I8
Elek Hungary 49 S9
Elek r. Rus. Fed. see Ilek
Elekmonar Rus. Fed. 88 D1
Elektrėnai Lith. 42 F7
Elektrogorsk Rus. Fed. 43 T6
Elektrostal' Rus. Fed. 43 T6
Elektrougli Rus. Fed. 43 T6
Elele Nigeria 125 G5

▶Elemi Triangle terr. Africa 128 B3
Disputed territory (Ethiopia/Kenya/Sudan) administered by Kenya.

Elena Bulg. 58 G6
El Encanto Col. 198 C5
El Encinal Mex. 183 H9
Elephanta Caves tourist site India 94 B2
Elephant Butte Reservoir U.S.A. 181 F6
Elephant Island Antarctica 222 U2
Éléphants de Kaniama, Réserve des nature res. Dem. Rep. Congo 127 E6
Éléphants de Sakania, Réserve Partielle aux nature res. Dem. Rep. Congo 127 F7
Eleshnitsa Bulg. 58 E7
Eleşkirt Turkey 107 E3
also known as Aleşkirt
El Espinar Spain 54 G4
El Estor Guat. 185 H6
Eleuthera i. Bahamas 186 D1
Eleva U.S.A. 172 B6
Eleven Point r. U.S.A. 178 E4
El Fahs Tunisia 57 B12
El Faiyûm Egypt 121 F2
also spelt Al Fayyūm
El Faiyûm governorate Egypt 108 B8
El Faouar Tunisia 123 H2
El Fasher Sudan 120 E6
El Fashn Egypt 106 B5
El Fendek Morocco 54 F9
El Ferrol Spain see Ferrol
El Ferrol del Caudillo Spain see Ferrol
El Fud Eth. 128 D3
El Fuerte Mex. 184 C3
El Fula Sudan 126 F2
Elgå Norway 45 J3
Elgal waterhole Kenya 128 C4
El Gamâlîya Egypt 108 C6
El Gçaib well Mali 122 D5
formerly known as El Ksaib Ounane
El Geili Sudan 121 G6
El Geneina Sudan 120 D6
El Geteina Sudan 121 G6
El Gezira state Sudan 121 G6
El Ghaba Sudan 121 F5
El Ghalla, Wadi watercourse Sudan 126 E2
El Ghallâouîya well Mauritania 122 C5
El Gheddiya Mauritania 124 C2
El Ghor plain Jordan/West Bank see Al Ghawr
Elgin U.K. 46 I6
Elgin IL U.S.A. 178 E3
Elgin NV U.S.A. 183 J4
Elgin OR U.S.A. 180 C3
Elgin TX U.S.A. 179 C6
Elgin Down Australia 149 E4
El'ginskiy Rus. Fed. 39 O3
El Gir well Sudan 121 F5
El Giza Egypt see Giza
El Giza governorate Egypt 108 A9
El Gogorrón, Parque Nacional nat. park Mex. 185 E4
El Goléa Alg. 123 F3
El Golfo de Santa Clara Mex. 184 B2
Elgon, Mount Uganda 128 B4
Elgoras, Gora hill Rus. Fed. 44 O1
El Guante Mex. 184 D2
El Guetar Tunisia 123 H2
El Guettâra well Mali 123 E5
El'gyay Rus. Fed. 39 L3
El Haddâdi Egypt 108 B6
El Hamma Tunisia 123 H2
El Hammâm Egypt 121 F2
El Ḥammâmi reg. Mauritania 122 C5
El Hâmûl Egypt 108 C6
El Hank reg. Alg. 122 D4
El Ḥank esc. Mali/Mauritania 122 C5
El Haouaria Tunisia 57 D11
El Harra Egypt 121 F2
El Hasira Sudan 104 A5
El Hato del Volcán Panama 186 C5
El Hawata Sudan 121 G6
El Heiz Egypt 106 B5
El Hierro i. Canary Is 122 A4
El Higo Mex. 185 F4
El Hilla Sudan 121 E6
El Homr Alg. 123 F3
El Homra Sudan 121 F6
El Houeïtat well Mauritania 124 C2
El Huecu Arg. 204 C5
El Huseiniya Egypt 108 C7
Eli well Niger 125 H3
Elias Garcia Angola 127 D7
Elías Piña Dom. Rep. 187 F3
Elichpur India see Achalpur
Elihu U.S.A. 176 A8
Elila Dem. Rep. Congo 126 E5
Elila r. Dem. Rep. Congo 126 E5
El 'Ilw el Ahmar el Qibli hill Egypt 108 B9
Elim S. Africa 132 D11
Elim U.S.A. 164 C3
Elimäki Fin. 42 H1
Elimberrum France see Auch
Elin Pelin Bulg. 58 E6
Eliot, Mount Canada 169 I1
Elizondo Spain 55 J1
Elipa Dem. Rep. Congo 126 E5
Elisabetha Dem. Rep. Congo 126 D4
also known as Lokutu
Élisabethville Dem. Rep. Congo see Lubumbashi
Eliseu Martins Brazil 202 D4
El Iskandarîya Egypt see Alexandria
El Iskandarîya governorate Egypt 108 A6
Elista Rus. Fed. 41 H7
formerly known as Stepnoy
Elizabeth U.S.A. 177 K5
Elizabeth, Mount hill Australia 150 D3
Elizabeth City U.S.A. 177 I9
Elizabeth Creek r. Australia 148 C3
Elizabeth Island Pitcairn Is see Henderson Island
Elizabeth Islands U.S.A. 177 O4
Elizabeth Point Namibia 130 B5
Elizabeth Reef Australia 145 E4
Elizabethton U.S.A. 176 C9
Elizabethtown KY U.S.A. 174 C4
Elizabethtown NC U.S.A. 174 E5
Elizabethtown NY U.S.A. 177 L1
Elizabethville U.S.A. 177 I5
Elizavety, Mys c. Rus. Fed. 39 O4
El Jadida Morocco 122 C2
formerly known as Mazagan
El Jaralito Mex. 184 D3
El Jebelein Sudan 121 G6
El Jem Tunisia 123 H2
El Jicaro Nicaragua 186 B4
El Juile Mex. 185 G5
Elk r. Canada 167 H5
Ełk Poland 49 T2
historically known as Lyck
Ełk r. Poland 49 T2
Elk r. MD U.S.A. 177 J6
Elk r. TN U.S.A. 174 C5
El Kaa Lebanon see Qaa
El Kab Sudan 121 G5
Elkader U.S.A. 174 B3
El Kala Alg. 123 H1
formerly spelt La Calle
El Kamlin Sudan 121 G6
El Karabi Sudan 121 G5
Elkas kalns hill Latvia 42 G4
Elk City U.S.A. 179 C5
Elk Creek U.S.A. 182 B2
Elkedra Australia 148 B4
Elkedra watercourse Australia 148 C4
El Kelaâ des Srarhna Morocco 122 D2
El Kerē Eth. 128 D3
Elkford Canada 167 H5
Elk Grove U.S.A. 182 C3
El Khalil West Bank see Hebron
El Khandaq Sudan 121 F5
El Khârga Egypt 121 F3
also spelt Al Khārijah
Elkhart IN U.S.A. 174 C3
Elkhart KS U.S.A. 178 B4
El Khartûm Sudan see Khartoum
El Khatatba Egypt 108 B7
El Khenachich esc. Mali see El Khnâchîch
El Khnâchîch esc. Mali 122 D5
also spelt El Khenachich
Elkhorn U.S.A. 172 E8
Elkhorn r. U.S.A. 178 C3
Elkhorn City U.S.A. 176 C8
Elkhovo Bulg. 58 H6
Elki Turkey see Beytüşşebap
Elkin U.S.A. 176 E9
Elkins U.S.A. 176 F7
Elk Island National Park Canada 167 H4
Elk Lake Canada 168 D4
Elk Lake l. U.S.A. 172 H6
Elkland U.S.A. 177 H4
Elk Mountain U.S.A. 180 F4
Elko Canada 167 H5
Elko U.S.A. 183 I1
El K'oran Eth. 128 E3
Elk Park U.S.A. 176 D9
Elk Point Canada 167 I4
Elk Point U.S.A. 178 C3
Elk River U.S.A. 174 A2
El Ksaib Ounane well Mali see El Gçaib
El Ksour Tunisia 57 A13
Elk Springs U.S.A. 183 P1
Elkton KY U.S.A. 174 C4
Elkton MD U.S.A. 177 J6
Elkton VA U.S.A. 176 G7
Elkview U.S.A. 176 D7
El Lagowa Sudan 126 F2
Ellas country Europe see Greece
Ellavalla Australia 151 A5
Ellaville U.S.A. 175 C5
Ell Bay Canada 167 O1
Ellef Ringnes Island Canada 165 I2
Ēl Lēh Eth. 128 C4
El Lein well Kenya 128 D5
Elleker Australia 151 B7
Elléloyé well Chad 120 C5
Ellen, Mount U.S.A. 183 N3
Ellenabad India 96 B3
Ellenboro U.S.A. 176 D6
Ellenburg Depot U.S.A. 177 L1
Ellendale DE U.S.A. 177 J7
Ellendale ND U.S.A. 178 C2
Ellensburg U.S.A. 180 B3
Ellenville U.S.A. 177 K4
El León, Cerro mt. Mex. 184 D3
Ellesmere N.Z. 153 G11
Ellesmere, Lake N.Z. 153 G11

▶Ellesmere Island Canada 165 K2
4th largest island in North America and 10th in the world.
northamerica [landscapes] ⟹ 156–157

Ellesmere Island National Park Reserve Canada 165 L1
Ellesmere Port U.K. 47 J10
Ellice r. Canada 167 K1
Ellice Island atoll Tuvalu see Funafuti
Ellice Islands country S. Pacific Ocean see Tuvalu
Ellicott City U.S.A. 177 I6
Ellicottville U.S.A. 176 G3
Ellijay U.S.A. 174 C5
El Limón Mex. 185 F4
Elliot Australia 148 B3
Elliot S. Africa 133 L8
Elliot, Mount Australia 149 E3
Elliotdale S. Africa 133 M8
also known as Xhora
Elliot Knob mt. U.S.A. 176 F7
Elliot Lake Canada 168 D4
Elliot Price Conservation Park nature res. Australia 146 C2
Ellis U.S.A. 178 C4
Ellisras S. Africa 131 E4
Elliston Australia 146 B3
Elliston U.S.A. 176 E8
Ellisville U.S.A. 175 B6
Ellon U.K. 46 J6
Ellora Caves tourist site India 94 B1
Ellsworth KS U.S.A. 178 C4
Ellsworth ME U.S.A. 177 Q1
Ellsworth WI U.S.A. 174 A2
Ellsworth Land reg. Antarctica 222 R1
Ellsworth Mountains Antarctica 222 S1
Ellwangen (Jagst) Germany 48 H7
El Macao Dom. Rep. 187 F3
El Mahalla el Kubra Egypt 108 C7
El Mahârîq Egypt 121 F3
El Maharraqa Egypt 108 C8
El Mahia reg. Mali 123 E5
El Maitén Arg. 205 C6
El Maks el Bahari Egypt 121 F3
Elmakuz Dağı mt. Turkey 108 E1
Elmalı Turkey 106 B3
El Mallâha marsh Egypt 108 E9
El Malpais National Monument nat. park U.S.A. 181 F6
El Ma'mûra Egypt 108 B6
El Manaqil Sudan 121 G6
El Mango Venez. 199 E4
El Mansûra Egypt 121 F2
also spelt Al Manşūrah
El Mansûrîya Egypt 108 C7
El Manteco Venez. 199 F3
El Manzla Morocco 54 F9
El Marsa Tunisia 57 C12
El Matarîya Egypt 108 D6
El Medo Eth. 128 D3
El Meghaïer Alg. 123 G2
El Melemm Sudan 126 F2
El Melhes well Mauritania 124 B2
El Mesellemiya Sudan 121 G6
El Messir well Chad 120 C6
El Mex Egypt 108 A6
El Miamo Venez. 199 F3
Elmina Ghana 125 E5
also known as São Jorge da Mina
El Mîna Lebanon 108 G3
El Minya Egypt 108 C8
El Minya Egypt 121 F2
El Minya governorate Egypt 108 B9
Elmira Ont. Canada 173 M7
Elmira P.E.I. Canada 169 I4
Elmira MI U.S.A. 173 I5
Elmira NY U.S.A. 177 I3
El Mirage U.S.A. 183 L8
El Moïnane well Mauritania 124 C2
Elmore Australia 147 E4
El Morro mt. Arg. 204 D4
El Mraïfig well Mauritania 124 C3
El Mraïti well Mali 125 E2
El Mreyyé reg. Mauritania 124 D2
Elmshorn Germany 48 G2
El Muglad Sudan 126 E2
El Mugrón mt. Spain 55 J6
Elmwood U.S.A. 172 D10
El Mzereb well Mali 122 D4
Elne France 51 I10
Elnesvågen Norway 44 I3
El Nido Phil. 74 A4
El Oasis Mex. 183 I9
El Obeid Sudan 121 F6
El Ocote, Parque Natural nature res. Mex. 185 G5
El Odaiya Sudan 121 F6
El Oro Ecuador 198 B5
El Oro Mex. 184 E3
Elos Greece 59 E13
El Oued Alg. 123 G2
Eloy U.S.A. 183 M9
El Palmar Venez. 199 F3
El Palmito Mex. 184 D3
El Pao Bolívar Venez. 199 F2
El Pao Cojedes Venez. 199 D2
Elpaputih, Teluk b. Indon. 75 D3
El Paraíso Hond. 186 B4
El Paso IL U.S.A. 174 B3
El Paso U.S.A. see Derby
El Paso TX U.S.A. 181 F7
El Peñón Arg. 204 D2
El Perelló Spain 55 L4
Elphinstone i. Myanmar see Thayawthadangyi Kyun
El Pilar Venez. 199 F2
El Pino, Sierra mts Mex. 185 E2
El Pintado Arg. 201 E6
El Pluma Arg. 205 C7
El Pocito Bol. 201 E3
El Portele b. Col. 198 C1
El Porvenír Col. 198 D3
El Porvenir Mex. 183 H9
El Porvenír Mex. 184 D2
El Porvenír Panama 186 D5
El Prat de Llobregat Spain 55 N3
also known as Prat de Llobregat
El Progreso Guat. 185 H6
also known as Guastatoya
El Puente Bol. 200 D5
El Puente Nicaragua 186 B4
El Puerto de Santa María Spain 54 E8
El Qâ' valley Egypt 108 E9
El Qâhira Egypt see Cairo
El Qâhira governorate Egypt 108 C8
El Qanâtir el Qahirîya Egypt 108 C7
El Qantara Egypt 106 C5
El Qantara el Sharqîya Egypt 108 D7
El Qasimiye r. Lebanon 108 G4
El Qasr Egypt 121 F3
El Quds Israel/West Bank see Jerusalem
El Quebrachal Arg. 204 D2
El Quss Abû Saîd plat. Egypt 121 E3
El Real Panama 186 D5
El Regocijo Mex. 184 D4
El Reno U.S.A. 179 C5
El Retorno Mex. 185 E4
El Rey, Parque Nacional nat. park Arg. 201 D6
El Ridisîya Bahari Egypt 121 G3
El Rio U.S.A. 182 E7
El Roda Egypt 108 B8
El Rosario watercourse Mex. 181 D7
Elrose Canada 167 I5
Elroy U.S.A. 172 C7
El Rucio Mex. 185 E4
Elsa Canada 166 C2
Elsa r. Italy 56 C5
El Saff Egypt 121 F2
El Sahuaro Mex. 184 B2
El Salado Arg. 205 D8
El Salado Mex. 185 E3
El Sâlhîya Egypt 108 D7
El Salto Mex. 184 D4

▶El Salvador country Central America 185 H6
also known as Salvador
northamerica [countries] ⟹ 158–159

El Salvador Chile 204 C2
El Salvador Mex. 185 E3
El Salvador Phil. 74 C4
El Samán de Apure Venez. 199 D3
Elsas Canada 173 K2
El Sauz Mex. 184 D2
El Seibo Dom. Rep. 187 F3
Elsen Nur l. China 84 B5
El Serrat Andorra 55 M2
El Shab well Egypt 121 F4
El Shâyib hill Egypt 108 B8
El Shuhada Egypt 108 C7
Elsie U.S.A. 173 I7
Elsinore Denmark see Helsingør
Elsinore CA U.S.A. 183 G8
Elsinore UT U.S.A. 183 L3
Elsinore Lake U.S.A. 183 G8
Elsnes Norway 44 M1
El Sosneado Arg. 204 C4
Elsterniederung und Westliche Oberlausitzer Heide park Germany 49 K4
Elsterwerda Germany 49 K4
El Sueco Mex. 184 D2
El Suweis Egypt see Suez
El Suweis governorate Egypt 108 C8
El Tajin tourist site Mex. 185 F4
El Tama, Parque Nacional nat. park Venez. 198 C3
El Tarabil hill Egypt 108 D8
El Tarf Alg. 123 H1
El Teleno mt. Spain 54 E2
El Temascal Mex. 185 F3
Eltham N.Z. 152 I7
El Thamad Egypt 121 G2
El Tigre Venez. 199 E2
El Tigre, Parque Nacional nat. park Guat. 185 H5
El Tocuyo Venez. 198 D2
El'ton Rus. Fed. 102 A2
El'ton, Ozero l. Rus. Fed. 102 A2
El Toro Chile 204 C3
El Totumo Venez. 198 C2
El Trébol Arg. 204 E4
El Tren Mex. 184 B2
El Triunfo Mex. 184 C4
El Tunal Arg. 204 D2
El Tuparro, Parque Nacional nat. park Col. 198 D3
El Tûr Egypt 121 G2
El Turbio Chile 205 B8
El Turbón mt. Spain 55 L2
El Uqsur Egypt see Luxor
Eluru India 94 D2
El 'Uteishan well Sudan 121 G5
Elva Estonia 42 H3
El Vallecillo Mex. 184 C2
Elvanlı Turkey see Tömük
Elvas Port. 54 D6
Elvebakken Norway 44 M1
Elven France 50 D5
El Vendrell Spain 55 M3
also spelt Vendrell
Elvenes Norway 44 O1
Elverum Norway 45 J3
El Viejo mt. Col. 198 C3
El Viejo Nicaragua 186 B4
El Vigía, Cerro mt. Mex. 184 D4
Elvira Brazil 198 C6
Elvire r. Australia 150 E3
Elvire Aboriginal Reserve Australia 150 D3
Elvo r. Italy 56 A3
El Wâdi El Jadîd governorate Egypt 106 A6
El Wak Kenya 128 D4
El Wasta Egypt 108 C8
El Watya well Egypt 121 E2
Elwood IN U.S.A. 174 C3
Elwood NE U.S.A. 178 C3
Elwood NJ U.S.A. 177 K6
El Wuz Sudan 121 F6
Ely U.K. 47 M11
Ely MN U.S.A. 174 B2
Ely NV U.S.A. 183 J2
El Yagual Venez. 198 D3
El Yibo well Kenya 128 C3
Elyria U.S.A. 176 C4
Elysburg U.S.A. 177 I5
El Zacatón, Cerro mt. Mex. 185 F5
El Zape Mex. 184 D3
El Zawâmil Egypt 108 C7
Emajõgi r. Estonia 42 I3
Emām Qolī Iran 100 D2
Emāmrūd Iran 100 C2
formerly known as Shāhrūd
Emām Şaḩeb Afgh. 101 G2
Emām Taqī Iran 101 D2
formerly known as Shāh Taqī
Emangusi S. Africa 133 Q3
E. Martínez Mex. see Emiliano Martínez
Emas, Parque Nacional das nat. park Brazil 206 A5
Emazar Kazakh. 88 C2
Emba Kazakh. 102 D2
also known as Embi or Zhem
Emba r. Kazakh. 102 C3
Embalenhle S. Africa 133 N3
Embarcación Arg. 201 D5
Embarras Portage Canada 167 I3
Embarrass U.S.A. 172 A3
Embetsu Japan see Enbetsu
Embi Kazakh. see Emba
Embiah, Mount hill Sing. 76 [inset]
Embira r. Brazil see Envira
Émbonas Greece see Emponas
Emborcação, Represa de resr Brazil 206 F5
Emborion Greece see Emporeio
Embu Brazil 206 G10
Embu Kenya 128 C5
Embundo Angola 127 C9
Emden Germany 48 E2
Emecik Turkey 59 I12
Emei China see Emeishan
Emeishan China 86 B2
formerly known as Emei
Emei Shan mt. China 86 B2
Emel' r. Kazakh. 88 C2
Emerald Australia 149 F4
Emeril Canada 169 H2
Emerita Augusta Spain see Mérida
Emerson Canada 167 L5
Emerson U.S.A. 176 B7
Emery U.S.A. 183 M3
Emesa Syria see Homs
Emet Turkey 106 B3
Emigrant Gap U.S.A. 182 D2
Emigrant Pass U.S.A. 183 H1
Emigrant Valley U.S.A. 183 I4
eMijindini S. Africa 133 P2
Emi Koussi mt. Chad 120 C5
Emile r. Canada 167 G2
Emiliano Martínez Mex. 184 D3
short form E. Martínez
Emiliano Zapata Mex. 185 H5
Emilia-Romagna admin. reg. Italy 56 D4
Emin China 88 C2
also known as Dorbiljin
Emine, Nos pt Bulg. 58 I6
Eminence U.S.A. 174 B4
Emin He r. China 88 C2
Eminska Planina hills Bulg. 58 I6
Emirdağ Turkey 106 B3
Emir Dağı mt. Turkey 106 B3
Emlenton U.S.A. 176 F4
Emmaboda Sweden 45 K4
Emmahaven Indon. see Telukbayur
Emmaste Estonia 42 D3
Emmaus Rus. Fed. 43 R5
Emmaus U.S.A. 177 J5
Emmeloord Neth. 48 C3
Emmelshausen Germany 48 E5
Emmen Neth. 48 D3
Emmen Switz. 51 O5
Emmendingen Germany 48 E7
Emmerich Germany 48 D4
Emmet Australia 149 E5
Emmetsburg U.S.A. 178 D3
Emmett U.S.A. 180 C4
Emmiganuru India 94 C3
formerly spelt Yemmiganur
Emmitsburg U.S.A. 177 H6
Emo Canada 168 A3
Emőd Hungary 49 R8
Emona Slovenia see Ljubljana
Emory U.S.A. 179 D5
Emory Peak U.S.A. 179 B6
Empada Guinea-Bissau 124 B4
Empalme Mex. 184 C3
Empanadas mt. Spain 55 I7
Empangeni S. Africa 133 P5
Empedrado Arg. 204 F2
Empexa, Salar de salt flat Bol. 200 C5
Empire U.S.A. 172 G6
Empoli Italy 56 C5
Emponas Greece 59 I12
also spelt Émbonas
Emporeio Greece 59 G12
also known as Emborion
Emporia KS U.S.A. 178 C4
Emporia VA U.S.A. 176 H9
Emporium U.S.A. 176 G4
Empress Canada 167 I5
Empress Mine Zimbabwe 131 F3
Empty Quarter des. Saudi Arabia see Rub' al Khālī
'Emrānī Iran 100 D3
Ems r. Germany 48 E2
Emsdale Canada 173 N5
Emsdetten Germany 48 E3
Ems-Jade-Kanal canal Germany 48 E2
Emthonjeni S. Africa 133 O2
Emu Creek r. Australia 149 D3
Emumägi hill Estonia 42 H3
Emu Park Australia 149 F4
Emur r. China 82 A1
Emur Shan mts China 82 A1
eMzinoni S. Africa 133 N3
Ena Japan 91 E7
Enafors Sweden 44 K3
Enambú Col. 198 D4

highest mountains	mountain	height	location	page#
1 ►	Mount Everest	8 848m / 29 028ft	China/Nepal Asia	>>> 97 E4
2 ►	K2	8 611m / 28 251ft	China/Jammu and Kashmir Asia	>>> 96 C2
3 ►	Kangchenjunga	8 586m / 28 169ft	India/Nepal Asia	>>> 97 E3
4 ►	Lhotse	8 516m / 27 939ft	China/Nepal Asia	>>> 97 E4
5 ►	Makalu	8 463m / 27 765ft	China/Nepal Asia	>>> 97 E4
6 ►	Cho Oyu	8 201m / 26 906ft	China/Nepal Asia	>>> 97 E3
7 ►	Dhaulagiri	8 167m / 26 794ft	Nepal Asia	>>> 97 D3
8 ►	Manaslu	8 163m / 26 781ft	Nepal Asia	>>> 97 E3
9 ►	Nanga Parbat	8 126m / 26 660ft	Jammu and Kashmir Asia	>>> 96 B2
10 ►	Annapurna I	8 091m / 25 545ft	Nepal Asia	>>> 97 D3

Friesack Germany 49 J3
Friesoythe Germany 48 E2
Friggesund Sweden 45 L3
Frio r. TX U.S.A. 179 C6
Frio watercourse U.S.A. 179 B5
Friol Spain 54 D1
Frisco U.S.A. 180 F5
Frisco Mountain U.S.A. 183 K3
Frissell, Mount hill U.S.A. 177 L3
Friuli - Venezia Giulia admin. reg. Italy 56 F2
Friza, Proliv strait Rus. Fed. 81 P3
Froan nature res. Norway 44 J2
Frobisher Bay Canada see Iqaluit
Frobisher Bay b. Canada 165 M3
Frobisher Lake Canada 167 I3
Frohavet b. Norway 44 J3
Frohburg Germany 49 J4
Frohnleiten Austria 49 M8
Frolovo Rus. Fed. 41 G6
Frombork Poland 49 Q1
Frome watercourse Australia 146 C2
Frome U.K. 47 J12
Frome, Lake salt flat Australia 146 C2
Fromveur, Passage du strait France 50 A4
Fronteira Port. 54 D5
Fronteiras Brazil 202 D3
Frontera Coahuila Mex. 185 E3
Frontera Tabasco Mex. 185 G5
Frontera, Punta pt Mex. 185 G5
Fronteras Mex. 184 C2
Frontignan France 51 J9
Front Royal U.S.A. 176 G7
Frosinone Italy 56 F7
historically known as Frusino
Frosta Norway 44 J3
Frostburg U.S.A. 176 G6
Frost Glacier Antarctica 223 I2
Frøya i. Norway 44 J3
Fruges France 51 I2
Fruita U.S.A. 183 P2
Fruitland IA U.S.A. 172 B9
Fruitland MD U.S.A. 177 J7
Fruitland UT U.S.A. 183 N1
Fruitport U.S.A. 172 G7
Fruitvale U.S.A. 183 P2
Fruktovaya Rus. Fed. 43 U7
Frunze Kyrg. 103 G4
also known as Frunzenskoye
Frunze Kyrg. see Bishkek
Frunzenskoye Kyrg. see Frunze
Frunzivka Ukr. 58 K1
Frusino Italy see Frosinone
Fruška Gora nat. park Yugo. 58 A3
Frutigen Switz. 51 N6
Frutillar Chile 205 B6
Frutuoso Brazil 201 E3
Fryanovo Rus. Fed. 43 T5
Fryazino Rus. Fed. 43 T6
Frýdek-Místek Czech Rep. 49 P6
Fryeburg U.S.A. 177 O1
Fu'an China 87 F3
Fucheng China see Fengyang
Fucheng China see Fuxian
Fuchū Japan 91 C7
Fuchuan China 87 D3
also known as Fuyang
Fuchun Jiang r. China 87 G2
Fudai Japan 90 G4
Fude China 87 F3
Fuding China 87 G3
Fudua waterhole Kenya 128 C5
Fudul reg. Saudi Arabia 105 D3
Fuengirola Spain 54 G8
Fuenlabrada Spain 54 H4
Fuente-Álamo Spain 55 J6
Fuente Álamo Spain 55 J7
Fuente Albilla, Cerro de mt. Spain 55 J6
Fuente de Cantos Spain 54 E6
Fuente Obejuna Spain 54 F6
Fuentesaúco Spain 54 F3
Fuentes de Ebro Spain 55 K3
Fuerte Olimpo Para. 201 F5
Fuerteventura i. Canary Is 122 B3
Fuga i. Phil. 74 B2
Fugloy i. Faroe Is 46 F1
Fuglstad Norway 44 K2
Fugou China 87 E1
Fugu China 85 F4
Fuguo China see Zhanhua
Fuhai China 88 D2
also known as Burultokay
Fuhaymī Iraq 109 N3
Fujairah U.A.E. 105 G2
also spelt Al Fujayrah or Fujeira
Fujeira U.A.E. see Fujairah
Fuji China see Luxian
Fuji Japan 91 F7
Fujian prov. China 87 F3
English form Fukien
Fu Jiang r. China 86 C2
Fujieda Japan 91 F7
Fuji-Hakone-Izu National Park Japan 91 F7
Fujiidera Japan 91 D7
Fujin China 82 C3
Fujinomiya Japan 91 F7
Fujioka Japan 91 F6
Fuji-san vol. Japan 91 F7
Fujiyoshida Japan 91 F7
Fūka Egypt 106 A5
Fukagawa Japan 90 H3
Fukang China 88 D2
Fukaura Japan 90 F4
Fukaya Japan 91 F6
Fukien prov. China see Fujian
Fukuchiyama Japan 91 D7
Fukue Japan 91 A8
Fukue-jima i. Japan 91 A8
Fukui Japan 91 E6
Fukui pref. Japan 91 E7
Fukuno Japan 91 E6
Fukuoka Japan 91 B8
Fukuoka pref. Japan 91 B8
Fukushima Fukushima Japan 90 G6
Fukushima Hokkaidō Japan 90 G4
Fukushima pref. Japan 90 G6
Fukuyama Japan 91 B9
Fūl, Gebel hill Egypt 108 D8
Fulacunda Guinea-Bissau 124 B4
Fūlād Maïalleh Iran 100 C2
also known as Amirabad
Fulayj Oman 105 G3
Fulchhari Bangl. 97 F4
Fulda Germany 48 G5
Fulda r. Germany 48 G4
Fule China 86 C3
Fuli China see Jixian
Fuliji China 87 F1
Fulin China see Hanyuan
Fuling China 87 C2
Fulitun China see Jixian
Fullerton CA U.S.A. 182 G8
Fullerton NE U.S.A. 178 C3
Fullerton, Cape Canada 167 N2
Fulnek Czech Rep. 49 O6
Fulton KY U.S.A. 174 B4
Fulton MO U.S.A. 174 B4
Fulton MS U.S.A. 174 B5
Fulton NY U.S.A. 177 I2
Fulufjället naturreservat nature res. Sweden 45 K3
Fulunäs Sweden 45 K3
Fumay France 51 K3
Fumel France 50 G8
Fumin China 86 B3
also known as Yongding
Funabashi Japan 91 F7
Funafuti atoll Tuvalu 145 G2
formerly known as Ellice Island
Funan China 87 E1
Funan China see Fusui
Funäsdalen Sweden 44 K3

▶Funchal Madeira 122 A2
Capital of Madeira.

Fundación Col. 198 C2
Fundão Brazil 203 D6
Fundão Port. 54 D4
Fundi Italy see Fondi
Fundición Mex. 184 C3
Fundo das Figuerias Cape Verde 124 [inset]
Fundulea Romania 58 H4
Fundy, Bay of g. Canada 169 H4
Fünen i. Denmark see Fyn
Funeral Peak U.S.A. 183 H5
Fünfkirchen Hungary see Pécs
Fung Wong Shan hill Hong Kong China see Lantau Peak
Funhalouro Moz. 131 G4
Funing Jiangsu China 87 F1
Funing Yunnan China 86 C4
also known as Xinhua
Funiu Shan mts China 87 D1
Funnel Creek r. Australia 149 F4
Funsi Ghana 125 E4
Funtua Nigeria 125 G4
Funzie U.K. 46 L3
Fuping China 85 G4
Fuqing China 87 F3
Fuquan China 87 C3
also known as Chengxian
Furancungo Moz. 131 G2
Furano Japan 90 H3
Fürgun, Küh-e mt. Iran 100 D5
Furmanov Rus. Fed. 40 G4
Furmanovka Kazakh. see Moyynkum
Furmanovo Kazakh. see Zhalpaktal
Furmanovo Rus. Fed. 90 D3
Furnas, Represa resr Brazil 207 G8
Furneaux Group is Australia 147 F5
Furnes Belgium see Veurne
Furong China see Wan'an
Fürstenau Germany 48 E3
Fürstenberg Germany 49 K2
Fürstenfeld Austria 49 N8
Fürstenfeldbruck Germany 48 I7
Fürstenwalde Germany 49 L3
Fürth Germany 48 H6
Furth im Wald Germany 49 J6
Furubira Japan 90 G3
Furudal Sweden 45 K3
Furukawa Japan 90 G5
Fury and Hecla Strait Canada 165 K3
Fusagasugá Col. 198 C3
Fusan S. Korea see Pusan
Fushan Shandong China 85 I4
Fushan Shanxi China 85 F5
Fushë-Krujë Albania 58 A7
Fushun Liaoning China 82 A4
Fushun Sichuan China 86 C2
Fusong China 82 B4
Fusui China 87 C4
also known as Xinning; formerly known as Funan
Futago-san vol. Japan 91 B8
Futaleufú Chile 205 C6
Fu Tau Pun Chau i. Hong Kong China 87 [inset]
Futog Vojvodina, Srbija Yugo. 58 A3
Futtsu Japan 91 F7
Futuna i. Vanuatu 145 G3
also spelt Fotuna; formerly known as Erronan
Futuna, Île i. Wallis and Futuna Is 145 H3
Futuna Islands Wallis and Futuna Is 145 H3
English form Hoorn Islands; also known as Hoorn, Îles de or Horne, Îles de.
Futun Xi r. China 87 F3
Fuwa Egypt 108 B6
Fuwayrit Qatar 105 E2
Fuxian China see Wafangdian
Fuxian China 85 F5
also known as Fucheng
Fuxin Liaoning China 85 I3
also known as Fuxinzhen
Fuxin Liaoning China 85 I3
Fuxing China see Wangmo
Fuxinzhen China see Fuxin
Fuyang Anhui China 87 E1
Fuyang China see Fuchuan
Fuyang Zhejiang China 87 F2
Fuyang r. China 85 H4
Fuying Dao i. China 87 G3
Fuyu Heilong. China 85 J2
Fuyu China see Songyuan
Fuyu Jilin China 82 B3
formerly known as Sanchahe
Fuyuan Heilong. China 82 D2
Fuyuan Yunnan China 86 C3
also known as Zhong'an
Fuyun China 84 A2
also known as Koktokay
Füzesabony Hungary 49 R8
Füzesgyarmat Hungary 49 S8
Fuzhou China 87 F3
formerly spelt Foochow
Fuzhou China see Linchuan
Füzuli Azer. 107 F3
also spelt Fizuli; formerly known as Karyagino
Fwamba Dem. Rep. Congo 127 D6
Fyn county Denmark 45 J5
Fyn i. Denmark 38 B4
also known as Fünen
Fyne, Loch inlet U.K. 46 G8
Fyresvatn l. Norway 45 J4
F.Y.R.O.M. country Europe see Macedonia
Fyteies Greece 59 C10
also known as Fitíai

↓ G

Gaâfour Tunisia 57 B12
Gaalkacyo Somalia 128 E3
Ga'âr, Birket el salt l. Egypt 108 B7
Gaat r. Sarawak Malaysia 77 F2
Gab watercourse Namibia 132 B4
Gabakly Turkm. see Kabakly
Gabangab well Eth. 128 E3
Gabas r. France 50 F9
Gabasumdo China see Tongde
Gabbac, Raas pt Somalia 128 F2
Gabbs Valley Range mts U.S.A. 182 F3
Gabd Pak. 101 E5
Gabela Angola 127 B7
Gaberones Botswana see Gaborone
Gabès Tunisia 123 H2
Gabès, Golfe de g. Tunisia 123 H2
English form Gabès, Gulf of
Gabès, Gulf of Tunisia see Gabès, Golfe de
Gabgaba, Wadi watercourse Sudan 121 G4
Gable End Foreland hd N.Z. 152 M6
▶Gabon country Africa 126 A5
africa [countries] ⟹ 114–117
Gabon, Estuaire du est. Gabon 126 A4

▶Gaborone Botswana 131 E5
Capital of Botswana. Formerly spelt Gaberones.

Gabou Senegal 124 B3
Gabriel Vera Bol. 200 D4
Gabriel y Galán, Embalse de resr Spain 54 E4
Gābrik Iran 100 D5
Gābrik watercourse Iran 100 D5
Gabrovnitsa Bulg. 58 E5
Gabrovo Bulg. 58 G6
Gabú Guiné-Bissau 124 B3
Gabuli vol. Eth. 128 D1
Gacé France 50 G4
Gacko Bos.-Herz. 56 K5
Gädäbäy Azer. 107 F2
Gadabedji, Réserve Totale de Faune de nature res. Niger 125 G3
Gadag India 94 B3
Gadaisu P.N.G. 149 F1
Gäddede Sweden 44 K2
Gadê China 86 A1
also known as Pagqên
Gadebusch Germany 48 I2
Gades Spain see Cádiz
Gadhada India 96 A5
Gadhra India 94 A1
Gadsden U.S.A. 175 C5
Gadwal India 94 C2
Gadyach Ukr. see Hadyach
Gadyn Turkm. 103 E5
Gadzi Cent. Afr. Rep. 126 C3
Gadžin Han Srbija Yugo. 58 D5
Gael'dnuvuop'pi Norway 44 M1
Gael Hamke Bugt b. Greenland 165 Q2
Găeşti Romania 58 G4
Gaeta Italy 56 F7
Gaeta, Golfo di g. Italy 56 F7
Gafanha da Nazaré Port. 54 C4
Gaferut i. Micronesia 73 K5
Gaffney U.S.A. 174 D5
Gafra, Wâdi el watercourse Egypt 108 C7
Gafsa Tunisia 123 H2
historically known as Capsa
Gag i. Indon. 75 D3
Gagal Chad 126 B2
Gagaon India 96 B5
Gagarin Rus. Fed. 43 Q6
formerly known as Gzhatsk
Gagarin Uzbek. 103 G4
formerly known as Yerzhar
Gagere watercourse Nigeria 125 G3
Gagliano del Capo Italy 57 K9
Gagnoa Côte d'Ivoire 124 D5
Gagnon Canada 169 G3
Gago Coutinho Angola see Lumbala N'guimbo
Gagra Georgia 107 E2
Gaiá r. Spain 55 M3
also spelt Gayá
Gaiab watercourse Namibia 130 C6
Gaibandha Bangl. 97 F4
Găiceana Romania 58 I2
Gaifi, Wâdi el watercourse Egypt 108 F7
Gail r. Austria 49 K9
Gail U.S.A. 179 B5
Gaillac France 50 H9
Gaillimh Rep. of Ireland see Galway
Gaillon France 50 H3
Gaindaingoinkor China see Lhünzhub
Gainesboro U.S.A. 178 F4
Gainesville FL U.S.A. 175 D6
Gainesville GA U.S.A. 174 D5
Gainesville MO U.S.A. 178 D4
Gainesville TX U.S.A. 179 C5
Gainsborough U.K. 47 L10
Gairdner r. Australia 151 B7
Gairdner, Lake salt flat Australia 146 B2
Gairloch U.K. 46 G6
Gairo Tanz. 129 C6
Gaixian China see Gaizhou
Gaizhou China 85 I3
formerly known as Gaixian
Gaizinkalns hill Latvia 42 G5
Gaja r. Hungary 49 P8
Gajah Hutan, Bukit hill Malaysia 76 C1
Gajapatinagaram India 95 D2
Gaji r. Nigeria 125 H4
Gajiram Nigeria 125 I3
Gajol India 97 F4
Gajos well Kenya 128 C4
Gakarosa mt. S. Africa 132 H4
Gakem Nigeria 125 H5
Gakuch Jammu and Kashmir 96 B1
Gala China 89 E6
Galaasiya Uzbek. 103 F5
also spelt Galaosiyo
Galâla el Bahariya, Gebel el plat. Egypt 108 C8
Galán, Cerro mt. Arg. 204 D2
Galana r. Kenya 128 D5
Galand Iran 100 C2
Galang Besar i. Indon. 76 D2
Galangue Angola 127 C8
Galanta Slovakia 49 O7
Galaosiyo Uzbek. see Galaasiya
Galápagos, Islas is Pacific Ocean see Galapagos Islands

▶Galapagos Islands is Pacific Ocean 221 M6
Part of Ecuador. Most westerly point of South America. Also known as Galápagos, Islas or Colón, Archipiélago de.
southamerica [contrasts] ⟹ 194–195

Galashiels U.K. 46 J8
Galata Bulg. 58 I5
Galatea N.Z. 152 K6
Galați Romania 58 J3
Galatina Italy 57 K8
Galatini Greece 59 C8
Galatista Greece 59 E8
Galatone Italy 57 K8
Galax U.S.A. 176 E9
Galaymor Turkm. see Kala-I-Mor
Galdhøpiggen mt. Norway 45 J3
Galeana Chihuahua Mex. 184 D2
Galeana Nuevo León Mex. 185 E3
Galegu Sudan 121 G6
Galela Indon. 75 C2
Galena AK U.S.A. 164 D3
Galena IL U.S.A. 174 B3
Galena KS U.S.A. 178 D4
Galena MD U.S.A. 177 J6
Galena MO U.S.A. 178 D4
Galena Bay Canada 166 G5
Galera, Punta pt Chile 204 B6
Galera, Punta pt Ecuador 198 A4
Galera, Punta pt Mex. 185 F6
Galera Point Trin. and Tob. 187 H5
Galeras vol. Col. 198 B4
Galesburg IL U.S.A. 174 B3
Galesburg MI U.S.A. 172 H8
Galeshewe S. Africa 133 I5
Galesville U.S.A. 172 B6
Galeton U.S.A. 176 H4
Galga r. Hungary 49 Q8
Galguduud admin. reg. Somalia 128 E3
Gal Hareeri Somalia 128 E3
Gália Brazil 206 D9
Galicea Mare Romania 58 E4
Galich Rus. Fed. 40 G4
Galichskaya Vozvyshennost' hills Rus. Fed. 40 G4
Galicia aut. comm. Spain 54 D2
Galičica nat. park Macedonia 58 B7
Galilee, Sea of l. Israel 108 G5
also known as Tiberias, Lake or Kinneret, Yam
Galiléia Brazil 207 L6
Galissas Greece 59 F11
Galitsa Rus. Fed. 43 S8
Galiuro Mountains U.S.A. 183 N9
Galiwinku Australia 148 B2
Gallabat Sudan 121 H6
Gallarate Italy 56 A3
Gallatin MO U.S.A. 178 D4
Gallatin TN U.S.A. 174 C4
Gallatin r. U.S.A. 180 E3
Galle Sri Lanka 94 D5
Gállego r. Spain 55 K3
Gallegos r. Arg. 205 C8
Gallegos, Cabo c. Chile 205 B7
Gallia country Europe see France

▶Gallinas, Punta pt Col. 198 D1
Most northerly point of South America.

Gallipoli Italy 57 K8
Gallipoli Turkey 106 A2
also spelt Gelibolu; historically known as Callipolis
Gallipolis U.S.A. 176 C7
Gällivare Sweden 44 M2
Gallneukirchen Austria 49 L7
Gallo r. Spain 55 I4
Gällö Sweden 44 K3
Gallo, Capo c. Sicilia Italy 57 F10
Gallup KY U.S.A. 176 C7
Gallup NM U.S.A. 181 E6
Gallur Spain 55 J3
Gallura reg. Sardegna Italy 56 A8
Gallyaaral Uzbek. 103 F4
also spelt Ghallaorol
Galma watercourse Nigeria 125 G4
Galoya Sri Lanka 94 D4
Gal Oya National Park Sri Lanka 94 D5
Gal Shiikh Somalia 128 E2
Galt U.S.A. 182 C3
Gal Tardo Somalia 128 E4
Galtat Zemmour W. Sahara 122 B4
Galtee Mountains hills Rep. of Ireland 47 D11
Galtymore hill Rep. of Ireland 47 D11
Galūgāh, Kūh-e mts Iran 100 C4
Galūgāh-e Āsiyeh Iran 101 D3
Galunggung, Gunung vol. Indon. 77 E4
Galva U.S.A. 172 C9
Galveias Port. 54 D5
Galveston IN U.S.A. 172 G10
Galveston TX U.S.A. 179 D6
Galveston Bay U.S.A. 179 D6
Gálvez Arg. 204 E4
Galwa Nepal 97 D3
Galway Rep. of Ireland 47 C10
also spelt Gaillimh
Galway Bay Rep. of Ireland 47 C10
Gâm r. Vietnam 78 D3
Gamá Brazil 206 E3
Gama, Isla i. Arg. 204 E6
Gamaches France 50 H3
Gamagōri Japan 91 E7
Gamalakhe S. Africa 133 O7
Gamalama vol. Indon. 75 C2
Gamarra Col. 198 C2
Gämäs Fin. see Kaamanen
Gamawa Nigeria 125 H3
Gamay Bay Phil. 74 C3
Gamba China 89 E6
also known as Gongbalou
Gamba Gabon 126 A5
Gambēla Eth. 128 B2
Gambēla admin. reg. Eth. 128 B3
Gambēla National Park Eth. 128 B3
Gambell U.S.A. 164 B3
▶Gambia country Africa 124 A3
africa [countries] ⟹ 114–117
Gambia r. Gambia 124 A3
Gambie r. Senegal 124 B3
Gambier, Îles is Fr. Polynesia 221 J7
English form Gambier Islands; also known as Mangareva Islands
Gambier Islands Australia 146 C3
Gambier Islands Fr. Polynesia see Gambier, Îles
Gambo Canada 169 K3
Gamboma Congo 126 B5
Gamboola Australia 149 D3
Gamboula Cent. Afr. Rep. 126 B3
Gamda China see Zamtang
Gamka r. S. Africa 132 F10
Gamkunoro, Gunung vol. Indon. 75 C2
Gamlakarleby Fin. see Kokkola
Gamleby Sweden 45 L4
Gammams well Sudan 121 G5
Gammelstaden Sweden 44 M2
Gammon Ranges National Park Australia 146 C2
Gamoep S. Africa 132 C6
Gamova, Mys pt Rus. Fed. 82 C4
Gampaha Sri Lanka 94 D5
Gampola Sri Lanka 94 D5
Gams Switz. 51 P5
Gamshadzai Kūh mts Iran 101 E4
Gamtog China 86 A2
Gamtoos r. S. Africa 133 J10
Gamud mt. Eth. 128 C3
Gamvik Norway 44 O1
Gan r. China 85 J1
Gana China see Gengda
Ganado U.S.A. 183 O6
Ganāh Egypt 108 B7
Gananoque Canada 168 E4
Ganāveh Iran 100 B4
Gäncä Azer. 107 F2
also spelt Gandzha; formerly known as Kirovabad; formerly spelt Gyandzha
Gand Belgium see Ghent
Ganda Angola 127 B8
formerly known as Mariano Machado
Gandadiwata, Bukit mt. Indon. 75 A3
Gandai India 96 D5
Gandajika Dem. Rep. Congo 127 D6
Gandara Spain 54 C1
Gandarbal Jammu and Kashmir 96 B2
Gandari Mountain Pak. 101 G4
Gandava Pak. 101 F4
Gander Canada 169 K3
Gander r. Nfld. Canada 169 K3
Ganderkesee Germany 48 F2
Gander Lake Canada 169 K3
Gandesa Spain 55 L3
Gandevi India 94 B1
Gandhidham India 96 A5
Gandhinagar India 96 B5
Gandhi Sagar resr India 96 B4
Gandi, Wadi watercourse Sudan 126 E2
Gandia Spain 55 K6
Gand-i-Zureh plain Afgh. 101 E4
Gandomān Iran 100 B4
Gandu Brazil 202 E5
Gandvik Norway 44 O1
Gandzha Azer. see Gäncä
Ganeb well Mauritania 124 C2
Ganga r. Bangl./India see Ganges
Ganga Nigeria 125 G4
Ganga r. Sri Lanka 94 D5
Gangakher India 94 C2
Gangán Arg. 205 C6
Gangán, Pampa de plain Arg. 205 C6
Ganganagar India 96 B3
Gangapur Maharashtra India 94 B2
Gangapur Rajasthan India 96 B4
Gangapur Rajasthan India 96 C4
Gangara Niger 125 H3
Gangavali r. India 94 B3
Gangaw Myanmar 78 A3
Gangawati India 94 C3
Gangaw Range mts Myanmar 78 B3
Gangca China 84 D4
also known as Shaliuhe
Gangdhar India 96 B5
Gangdisê Shan mts China 89 C6
English form Kailas Range
Ganges r. Bangl./India 96 F5
also known as Ganga or Padma (Bangl.)
Ganges France 51 J9
▶Ganges, Mouths of the Bangl./India 97 F5
asia [landscapes] ⟹ 62–63
Gangi Sicilia Italy 57 G11
Ganglota Liberia 124 C5
Gangouyi China 84 E5
Gangra Turkey see Çankırı
Gangrar India 96 B4
Gangtok India 97 F4
Gangu China 86 C1
Gangziyao China 85 G4
Ganhezi China 88 E2
Gani Indon. 75 D3
Ganiakali Guinea 124 C4
Ganjam India 95 E2
Gan Jiang r. China 87 F2
Ganjig China 85 I3
also known as Horqin Zuoyi Houqi
Gankovo Rus. Fed. 43 O2
Ganluo China 86 B2
also known as Xinshiba
Gannan China 85 I2
Gannat France 51 J6
Gannett Peak U.S.A. 180 E4
Ganq China 84 B4
Ganquan China 85 F4
Gansbaai S. Africa 132 D11
Gänserndorf Austria 49 N7
Ganshui China 86 C2
Ganskuil S. Africa 133 K1
Gansu prov. China 84 C3
English form Kansu
Gantamaa Somalia 128 D4
Gantapara India 95 D1
Gantheaume Point Australia 150 C3
Gant'iadi Georgia 107 E2
formerly known as Pilenkovo
Ganting China see Huxian
Gantsevichi Belarus see Hantsavichy
Ganxian China 87 E3
also known as Meilin
Ganyal r. India 94 C1
Ganye Nigeria 125 I4
Ganyesa S. Africa 132 I3
Ganyu China 87 F1
also known as Qingkou
Ganyushkino Kazakh. 102 B3
Ganzhe China see Minhou
Ganzhou China 87 E3
Ganzi Sudan 128 A3
Ganzurino Rus. Fed. 85 E1
Gao Mali 125 E2
Gao admin. reg. Mali 125 F2
Gao'an China 87 E2
Gaocheng China 85 G4
Gaocheng China see Litang
Gaochun China 87 F2
also known as Chunxi
Gaocun China see Mayang
Gaohebu China 87 F2
Gaojian China 87 G2
Gaolan China 84 D4
formerly known as Shidongsi
Gaoleshan China see Xianfeng
Gaoliangjian China see Hongze
Gaoligong Shan mts China 86 A3
Gaoling China 87 D1
also known as Luyuan
Gaomi China 85 H4
Gaomutang China 87 D3
Gaoping China 85 G5
Gaoqing China 85 H4
also known as Tianzhen
Gaotai China 84 C4
Gaotang China 85 H4
Gaotangling China see Wangcheng
Gaotingzhen China see Daishan
Gaotouyao China 85 F4
Gaoua Burkina 124 E4
Gaoual Guinea 124 B4
Gaoxian China 86 C2
also known as Wenjiang
Gaoxiong Taiwan see Kaohsiung
Gaoyang China 85 G4
Gaoyi China 85 G4
Gaoyou China 87 F1
Gaoyou Hu l. China 87 F1
Gaozhou China 87 D4
Gap France 51 M8
Gapan Phil. 74 B3
Gapuwiyak Australia 148 B2
Gaqoi China 89 C6
Gar China 99 K3
also known as Gargunsa or Shiquanhe
Gar Pak. 101 E5
Gar' r. Rus. Fed. 82 C1
Garaa Tebourt well Tunisia 123 H3
Garabekevyul Turkm. 103 F5
formerly spelt Karabekaul
Garabil Belentligi hills Turkm. see Karabil', Vozvyshennost'
Garabinzam Congo 126 B4
Garabogazköl Aylagy b. Turkm. see Kara-Bogaz-Gol, Zaliv
Garabogazköl Bogazy sea chan. Turkm. see Kara-Bogaz-Gol, Proliv
Garacad Somalia 128 F3
Garachiné Panama 186 D5
Garachiné, Punta pt Panama 186 D5
Garadag Somalia 128 E2
Gara Ekar hill Alg. 123 G6
Garagoa Col. 198 C3
Garagum des. Kazakh. see Karakum Desert
Garagum des. Turkm. see Karakum Desert
Garah Australia 147 F2
Garalo Mali 124 D4
Garamätnyyaz Turkm. see Karamet-Niyaz
Garamba r. Dem. Rep. Congo 126 F4
Garanhuns Brazil 202 E4
Ga-Rankuwa S. Africa 133 L2
Garapu Brazil 202 A5
Garapuava Brazil 206 G3
Garar, Plaine de plain Chad 126 D2
Garawa Aboriginal Land res. Australia 148 C3
Garba Cent. Afr. Rep. 126 D2
Garbahaarey Somalia 128 D4
Garba Tula Kenya 128 C4
Garberville U.S.A. 182 A1
Garbo China see Lhozhag
Garbosh, Kūh-e mt. Iran 100 B3
Gârbova, Vârful hill Romania 58 H3
Garbsen Germany 48 G3
Garça Brazil 206 D9
Garças, Rio das r. Brazil 206 A2
Gârceni Romania 58 I2
Garcias Brazil 206 A7
Garcia Sola, Embalse de resr Spain 54 F5
Gârcina Romania 58 H2
Gard r. France 51 K9
Garda Italy 56 C3
Garda, Lago di l. Italy see Garda, Lake
Garda, Lake Italy 56 C3
also known as Garda, Lago di
Gardabani Georgia 107 F2
Gârda de Sus Romania 58 D2
Garde Lake Canada 167 J2
Gardelegen Germany 48 I3
Garden City U.S.A. 178 B4
Garden Corners U.S.A. 172 G5
Garden Grove U.S.A. 182 G8
Garden Hill Canada 167 M4
Garden Island U.S.A. 172 H5
Garden Mountain U.S.A. 176 D8
Gardermoen airport Norway 45 J3
also known as Oslo
Gardez Afgh. 101 G3
Gardinas Belarus see Hrodna
Gardiner U.S.A. 177 P1
Gardiner, Mount Australia 148 B4
Gardiner Range hills Australia 148 A3
Gardiners Island U.S.A. 177 M4
Gardiner's Range mts Australia 148 B4
Gardner atoll Micronesia see Faraulep
Gardner IL U.S.A. 172 E9
Gardner MA U.S.A. 177 N3
Gardner Inlet Antarctica 222 T1
Gardner Island Kiribati see Nikumaroro
Gardner Pinnacles is U.S.A. 221 G4
formerly known as Man-of-War Rocks or Pollard Islands
Gardnerville U.S.A. 182 E3
Gardno, Jezioro lag. Poland 49 O1
Gárdony Hungary 49 P8
Gardsjönås Sweden 44 L2
Gärdslösa Sweden 45 L4
Gáregasnjárga Fin. see Karigasniemi
Gares Spain see Puente la Reina
Garešnica Croatia 56 I3
Garet El Djenoun mt. Alg. 123 G4
Gare Tigre Fr. Guiana 199 H3
Garfield U.S.A. 181 F5
Garforth U.K. 47 K10
Gargalianoi Greece 59 C11
Gargáligas r. Spain 54 F5
Gargano, Parco Nazionale del nat. park Italy 56 H7
Gargantua, Cape Canada 168 C4
Gargunsa China see Gar
Gargždai Lith. 42 C6
Garhakota India 96 C5
Garhbeta India 97 E5
Garhchiroli India 94 D1
Garhi India 96 B5
Garhi Khairo Pak. 101 F4
Garhi Malehra India 96 C4
Garhmuktesar India 96 C3
Garhshankar India 96 C3
Garibaldi Brazil 203 B9
Garibaldi Canada 166 F5
Garibaldi, Mount Canada 166 F5
Garibaldi Provincial Park Canada 166 F5
Gariep Dam resr S. Africa 133 J7
Gariep Dam Nature Reserve S. Africa 133 J7
Garies S. Africa 132 B7
Garissa Kenya 128 C5
Garkalne Latvia 42 F4
Garkung Caka l. China 89 D5
Garland U.S.A. 179 C5
Garliava Lith. 42 E7
Gârliciu Romania 58 J4
Garlin France 50 F9
Garm Tajik. see Gharm
Garmab Afgh. 101 F3
Garmdasht Iran 100 B4
Garmeh Iran 100 D2
Garmi Iran 100 B2
Garmisch-Partenkirchen Germany 48 I8
Garmo, Qullai mt. Tajik. 101 G2
also known as Kommunizma, Pik or Kommunizm, Qullai
Garmsar Iran 100 C3
Garmsel reg. Afgh. 101 E4
Garner IA U.S.A. 174 A3
Garner KY U.S.A. 176 C8
Garnett U.S.A. 178 D4
Garnpung Lake imp. l. Australia 147 D3
Garo Hills India 97 F4
Garonne r. France 50 F8
Garoowe Somalia 128 F2
Garoth India 96 B4
Garou, Lac l. Mali 124 E2
Garoua Cameroon 125 I4
Garoua Boulai Cameroon 125 I5
Garqêntang China see Sog
Garrett U.S.A. 173 H9
Garrison KY U.S.A. 176 B7
Garrison ND U.S.A. 178 B2
Garrucha Spain 55 J7
Garrygala Turkm. 102 D5
formerly spelt Kara-Kala
Garry Lake Canada 167 K1
Garryowen S. Africa 133 L8
Garsen Kenya 128 D5
Garshy Turkm. see Karshi
Garsila Sudan 120 D6
Gartar China see Qianning
Gartempe r. France 50 G6
Gartog China see Markam
Gartok China see Garyarsa
Garut Indon. 77 D4
Garvie Mountains N.Z. 153 C13
Garwa India 97 D4
Garwolin Poland 49 S4
Gar Xincun China 89 C5
Gary IN U.S.A. 174 C3
Gary WV U.S.A. 176 D8
Garyarsa China 89 C6
also known as Gartok
Garyi China 86 A2
Garyū-zan mt. Japan 91 C7
Garza Arg. 204 E3
Gar Zangbo r. China 89 B5
Garzê China 86 A2
Garzón Col. 198 C4
Gasan-Kuli Turkm. see Esenguly
Gasan-Kuliyskiy Zapovednik nature res. Turkm. 102 C5
Gascogne reg. France see Gascony
Gascogne, Golfe de g. France/Spain see Gascony, Gulf of
Gasconade r. U.S.A. 174 B4
Gascony reg. France 50 F9
also spelt Gascogne
Gascony, Gulf of France/Spain 50 D9
also known as Gascogne, Golfe de or Gascuña, Golfo de
Gascoyne r. Australia 151 A5
Gascoyne, Mount hill Australia 151 B5
Gascoyne Junction Australia 151 A5
Gascuña, Golfo de g. France/Spain see Gascony, Gulf of
Gash and Setit prov. Eritrea 104 B5
Gasherbrum mt. Jammu and Kashmir 96 C2
Gash Setit Wildlife Reserve nature res. Eritrea 121 H6
Gasht Iran 101 E5
Gas Hu salt l. China 88 E4
Gashua Nigeria 125 H3
Gaspar Cuba 186 D2
Gaspar, Selat sea chan. Indon. 77 D3
Gaspé Canada 169 H3
Gaspé, Baie de b. Canada 169 H3
Gaspé, Cap c. Canada 169 H3
Gaspé, Péninsule de pen. Canada 169 H3
Gassan Burkina 124 E3
Gassan vol. Japan 90 G5
Gassane Senegal 124 B3
Gassaway U.S.A. 176 E7
Gassol Nigeria 125 H4
Gass Peak U.S.A. 183 I5
Gasteiz Spain see Vitoria-Gasteiz
Gastello Rus. Fed. 82 F2
Gaston U.S.A. 176 H9
Gaston, Lake U.S.A. 176 H9
Gastonia U.S.A. 174 D5
Gastouni Greece 59 C11
Gastre Arg. 205 C6
Gata, Cabo de c. Spain 55 I8
Gata, Cape Cyprus 108 E3
also known as Gatas, Akra
Gata, Sierra de mts Spain 54 E4
Gataga r. Canada 166 E3
Gătaia Romania 58 C3
Gatas, Akra c. Cyprus see Gata, Cape
Gatchina Rus. Fed. 43 L2
Gateshead U.K. 47 K9
Gates of the Arctic National Park and Preserve U.S.A. 164 D3
Gatesville U.S.A. 179 C6
Gateway U.S.A. 183 P3
Gatico Chile 200 C5
Gatineau Canada 168 F4
Gatineau r. Canada 168 F4
Gatlinburg U.S.A. 179 G5
Gatong China see Jomda
Gatooma Zimbabwe see Kadoma
Gatton Australia 147 G1
Gatún Panama 186 D5
Gatún, Lago l. Panama 186 C5
Gatvand Iran 100 B3
Gatwick airport U.K. 47 L12
Gaúcha do Norte Brazil 202 A5
Gaud-i-Zirreh depr. Afgh. 101 E4
Gauer Lake Canada 167 L3
Gauhati India see Guwahati
Gauja r. Latvia 42 F4
Gaujas nacionālais parks nat. park Latvia 42 G4
Gaul country Europe see France
Gaula r. Norway 44 J3
Gauley Bridge U.S.A. 176 D7
Gaupne Norway 45 I3
Gaurdak Turkm. see Govurdak

Glevum U.K. see Gloucester
Glina r. Bos.-Herz./Croatia 56 I3
Glina Croatia 56 I3
Glinka Rus. Fed. 43 N7
Glittertinden mt. Norway 45 J3
Gliwice Poland 49 P5
historically known as Gleiwitz
Globe U.S.A. 183 N8
Glodeanu-Sărat Romania 58 H4
Glodeni Romania 58 F2
Glogau Poland see Głogów
Gloggnitz Austria 49 M8
Glogovac Kosovo, Srbija Yugo. 58 B6
Głogów Poland 49 N4
historically known as Glogau
Głogówek Poland 49 O5
Głogów Małopolski Poland 49 S5
Glomfjord Norway 44 K2
Glomma r. Norway 45 J4
Glommersträsk Sweden 44 L2
Glória Brazil 202 E4
Glorieuses, Îles is Indian Ocean 129 E7
English form Glorioso Islands
Glorioso Islands Indian Ocean see Glorieuses, Îles
Gloucester Australia 147 F2
Gloucester P.N.G. 145 D2
Gloucester U.K. 47 J12
historically known as Glevum
Gloucester MA U.S.A. 177 O3
Gloucester VA U.S.A. 177 I8
Gloucester Island Australia 149 F4
Gloucester Point U.S.A. 177 I8
Glover Reef Belize 185 I5
Gloversville U.S.A. 177 K2
Glovertown Canada 169 K3
Glöwen Germany 48 J3
Głowno Poland 49 Q4
Głubczyce Poland 49 O5
Glubinnoye Rus. Fed. 82 D3
Glubokiy Rus. Fed. 41 G6
Glubokoye Belarus see Hlybokaye
Glubokoye Kazakh. 88 C1
Glubokoye, Ozero l. Rus. Fed. 43 K1
Glücksburg (Ostsee) Germany 48 G1
Glückstadt Germany 48 G2
Gluggarnir hill Faroe Is 46 F2
Glukhov Ukr. see Hlukhiv
Gmelinka Rus. Fed. 102 A2
Gmünd Austria 49 L7
Gmunden Austria 49 K8
Gnadenhutten U.S.A. 176 D5
Gnarp Sweden 45 L3
Gnarrenburg Germany 48 G2
Gnesen Poland see Gniezno
Gniew Poland 49 P2
Gniewkowo Poland 49 P3
Gniezno Poland 49 O3
historically known as Gnesen
Gnisvärd Sweden 45 L4
Gnjilane Kosovo, Srbija Yugo. 58 C6
Gnoien Germany 49 J2
Gnowangerup Australia 151 B7
Gnows Nest Range hills Australia 151 B6
Goa state India 94 B3
Goageb Namibia 130 C5
Goalpara India 97 F4
Goang Indon. 75 A5
Goaso Ghana 124 E5
Goat Fell hill U.K. 46 G8
Goba Eth. 128 D3
Gobabis Namibia 130 C4
Gobannium U.K. see Abergavenny
Gobas Namibia 130 C5
Gobernador Crespo Arg. 204 E3
Gobernador Duval Arg. 204 D5
Gobernador Gregores Arg. 205 C8
Gobernador Mayer Arg. 205 C8
Gobernador Virasoro Arg. 204 F3
Gobi des. China/Mongolia 85 E2
English form Gobi Desert
Gobi Desert China/Mongolia see Gobi
Gobiki Rus. Fed. 43 O8
Göblberg hill Austria 49 K7
Gobō Japan 91 D8
Goch Germany 48 D4
Gochas Namibia 130 C5
Go Công Vietnam 79 D6
Godagari Bangl. 97 F4
Godavari r. India 94 D2
Godbout Canada 169 H3
Godbout r. Canada 169 H3
Godda India 97 E4
Goddard, Mount U.S.A. 182 F4
Godē Eth. 128 D3
Godeal hill Port. 54 C6
Godech Bulg. 58 E5
Goderich Canada 168 D5
Goderville France 50 G3
Godhavn Greenland see Qeqertarsuaq
Godhra India 96 B5
Godinlabe Somalia 128 E3
Godo, Gunung mt. Indon. 75 C3
Gödöllő Hungary 49 Q8
Gods r. Canada 167 M3
Gods Lake Canada 167 M4
God's Mercy, Bay of Canada 167 O2
Godthåb Greenland see Nuuk
Godučohkka mt. Sweden 44 L1
also spelt Kåtotjåkka
Godwin-Austen, Mount China/Jammu and Kashmir see K2
Goedemoed S. Africa 133 K7
Goedgegun Swaziland see Nhlangano
Goéland, Lac au l. Canada 168 E3
Goélands, Lac aux l. Canada 169 I2
Goes Neth. 48 A4
Goetzville U.S.A. 173 I4
Goffstown U.S.A. 177 N2
Gogama Canada 168 D4
Gogebic, Lake U.S.A. 172 D4
Gogebic Range hills U.S.A. 172 D4
Gogeç Turkey 109 K1
Gogland, Ostrov i. Rus. Fed. 42 H1
Gogoi Moz. 131 G4
Gogolevka Rus. Fed. 43 M7
Gogoşu Romania 58 D4
Gogounou Benin 125 F4
Gogra India see Ghaghra
Gogra r. India see Ghaghara
Gogrial Sudan 126 F2
Gogunda India 96 B4
Gohad India 96 C4
Gohana India 96 C3
Goharganj India 96 C5
Goiana Brazil 202 F3
Goianésia Brazil 206 D2
Goiânia Brazil 206 D3
Goianinha Brazil 202 F3
Goianira Brazil 206 D3
Goiás Brazil 206 C2
Goiás state Brazil 206 C3
Goiatuba Brazil 206 D5
Goincang China 86 B1
Goio-Erê Brazil 203 A8
Goi-Pula Dem. Rep. Congo 127 E6
Goito Italy 56 C3
Gojeb Wenz r. Eth. 128 C3
Gojra Pak. 101 H4
Gokak India 94 B2
Gokarn India 94 B3
Gök Çay r. Turkey 108 D1
Gökçeada i. Turkey 106 A2
also known as İmroz
Gökçedağ Turkey 106 B3
Gökçen Turkey 59 I10
Gökçeören Turkey 59 J10
Gökdepe Turkm. see Gekdepe
Gökdere r. Turkey 108 D1
Gökirmak r. Turkey 106 C2
Goklenkuy, Solonchak salt l. Turkm. 102 D4
Gökova Turkey see Ula
Gökova Körfezi b. Turkey 106 A3
Gokprosh Hills Pak. 101 E5
Göksun Turkey 107 D3
Göksu Nehri r. Turkey 106 C3
Goksu Parkı Turkey 108 E1
Gokteik Myanmar 78 B3
Göktepe Turkey 108 D1
Gokwe Zimbabwe 131 F3
Gol Norway 45 J3
Gola India 96 D3
Golaghat India 97 G4
Golakganj India 97 F4
Golan hills Syria 108 G4
also spelt Al Jawlān or HaGolan
Gołańcz Poland 49 O3
Golbāf Iran 100 D4
Golbahār Afgh. 101 G3
Gölbaşı Turkey 107 D3
Golconda India 94 C2
Golconda IL U.S.A. 174 B4
Golconda NV U.S.A. 183 G1
Gölcük Turkey 59 I9
Gölcük Turkey 106 B2
Gölçük Turkey see Etili
Gölcük r. Turkey 59 J9
Golczewo Poland 49 L2
Gold U.S.A. 176 H4
Gołdap Poland 49 T1
Gołdapa r. Poland 49 S1
Gold Beach U.S.A. 180 A4
Goldberg Germany 49 J2
Gold Coast country Africa see Ghana
Gold Coast Australia 147 G2
formerly known as South Coast Town
Gold Coast coastal area Ghana 125 E5
Golden Canada 167 G5
Golden Bay N.Z. 152 G8
Goldendale U.S.A. 180 B3
Golden Downs N.Z. 153 G9
Golden Ears Provincial Park Canada 166 F5
Golden Gate Highlands National Park S. Africa 133 M5
Golden Hinde mt. Canada 166 E5
Golden Lake Canada 168 E4
Golden Meadow U.S.A. 175 B6
Golden Valley S. Africa 133 J9
Golden Valley Zimbabwe 131 F3
Goldfield U.S.A. 183 G4
Gold River Canada 166 E5
Goldsand Lake Canada 167 K3
Goldsboro U.S.A. 174 E5
Goldstone Lake U.S.A. 183 H6
Goldsworthy Australia 150 B4
Goldthwaite U.S.A. 179 C6
Goldvein U.S.A. 176 H7
Göle Turkey 107 E2
also known as Merdenik
Goleniów Poland 49 L2
Golestān Afgh. 101 E3
Golestān prov. Iran 100 C2
Goleta U.S.A. 182 E7
Golfito Costa Rica 186 C5
Golfo de Tehuantepec g. Mex. see Tehuantepec, Gulf of
Golfo di Orosei Gennargentu e Asinara, Parco Nazionale del nat. park Sardegna Italy 57 B8
Gölgeli Dağları mts Turkey 106 B3
Gölhisar Turkey 59 K11
Goliad U.S.A. 179 C6
Golija nat. park Yugo. 58 B5
Golija Planina mts Yugo. 58 B5
Golingka China see Gongbo'gyamda
Golitsyno Rus. Fed. 43 S6
Gölköy Turkey 107 D2
also known as Kuşluyan
Gollel Swaziland see Lavumisa
Gölmarmara Turkey 59 I10
Golmberg hill Germany 49 K3
Golmud China 84 B4
Golmud He r. China 84 B4
Golo i. Phil. 74 B3
Golobino Rus. Fed. 43 V6
Golodnaya Step' plain Uzbek. 103 F4
Golondrina Arg. 204 E3
Gölovası Turkey 108 G1
Golovnino Rus. Fed. 90 I3
Golpāyegān Iran 100 B3
Gölpazarı Turkey 106 B2
Golspie U.K. 46 I6
Golub-Dobrzyń Poland 49 Q2
Golubovka Kazakh. 103 H1
Golungo Alto Angola 127 B7
Goluzino Rus. Fed. 43 V2
Gol Vardeh Iran 101 E3
Golweyn Somalia 128 E4
Golyama Syutkya mt. Bulg. 58 F7
Golyama Zhelyazna Bulg. 58 F6
Golyam Perelik mt. Bulg. 58 F7
Golyam Persenk mt. Bulg. 58 F7
Golyashi Belarus see Sasnovy Bor
Gölyazı Turkey 59 J8
Golynki Rus. Fed. 43 M7
Golyshi Rus. Fed. see Vetluzhskiy
Goma Dem. Rep. Congo 126 F5
Goma Uganda 128 A5
Gomang Co salt l. China 89 E6
Gomati r. India 96 D4
Gombak, Bukit hill Sing. 76 [inset]
Gombari Dem. Rep. Congo 126 F4
Gombe Nigeria 125 H4
Gombe state Nigeria 125 H4
Gombe r. Tanz. 129 A6
Gombi Nigeria 125 I4
Gombroon Iran see Bandar-e 'Abbās
Gömeç Turkey 59 H9
also known as Armutova
Gomel' Belarus see Homyel'
Gomel Oblast admin. div. Belarus see Homyel'skaya Voblasts'
Gomel'skaya Oblast' admin. div. Belarus see Homyel'skaya Voblasts'
Gómez Palacio Mex. 184 E3
Gómez Rendón Ecuador 198 A5
Gomīl, Rūbār-e r. Iraq 109 O1
Gomīshān Iran 100 C2
Gommern Germany 48 I3
Gomo China 89 D5
Gomo Co salt l. China 89 D5
Gomorovichi Rus. Fed. 43 P1
Gomumu i. Indon. 75 C3
Gonabad Iran see Jūymand
Gonaïves Haiti 187 E3
Gonarezhou National Park Zimbabwe 131 F4
Gonbad-e Kavus Iran 100 C2
Gonda India 97 D4
Gondal India 96 A5
Gonda Libah well Eth. 128 E2
Gondar Col. 198 C5
Gondar Eth. see Gonder
Gonder Eth. 128 C1
formerly spelt Gondar
Gondey Chad 126 C2
Gondia India 96 D5
Gondomar Spain 54 C2
Gönen Turkey 106 A2
Gönen r. Turkey 59 I8
Gonfreville-l'Orcher France 50 G3
Gong'an China 87 E2
also known as Douhudi; formerly known as Doushi
Gongbalou China see Gamba
Gongbo'gyamda China 89 F6
also known as Golingka
Gongcheng China 87 D3
Gonggar China 89 E6
also known as Gyixong
Gongga Shan mt. China 86 B2
also known as Minya Konka
Gonghe China 84 D4
also known as Qabqa
Gonghe China see Mouding
Gonghui China 85 G3
Gongjiang China see Yudu
Gongliu China 88 C3
also known as Tokkuztara
Gongola r. Nigeria 125 I4
Gongolgon Australia 147 E2
Gongoué Gabon 126 A5
Gongpoquan China 84 C3
Gongquan China see Gongxian
Gongshan China 86 A3
also known as Cikai
Gongtang China see Damxung
Gongwang Shan mts China 86 B3
Gongxian China see Gongyi
Gongxian China 86 C2
also known as Gongquan
Gongyi China 87 E1
formerly known as Gongxian or Xiaoyi
Gongzhuling China 82 B4
formerly known as Huaide
Goniądz Poland 49 T2
Goniri Nigeria 125 I4
Gonjo China 86 A2
also known as Kasha
Gonjog China 89 D6
Gonnesa Sardegna Italy 57 A9
Gonnoi Greece 59 D9
Gonnosfanadiga Sardegna Italy 57 A9
Gōnoura Japan 91 A8
Gonubie S. Africa 133 M9
Gonzáles Mex. 185 F4
Gonzales CA U.S.A. 182 C5
Gonzales TX U.S.A. 179 C6
González Moreno Arg. 204 E4
Gonzalo Vásquez Panama 186 D5
Goochland U.S.A. 176 H8
Goode U.S.A. 176 F8
Goodenough, Cape Antarctica 223 I2
Goodenough Island P.N.G. 145 E2
Gooderham Canada 173 O6
Good Harbor Bay U.S.A. 172 H5
Good Hart U.S.A. 173 H5
Good Hope Botswana 133 J2
Good Hope U.S.A. 172 C10
Good Hope, Cape of S. Africa 132 C11
Good Hope Mountain Canada 166 E5
Goodland U.S.A. 178 B4
Goodman U.S.A. 172 E5
Goodooga Australia 147 E2
Goodparla Australia 148 B2
Goodrich U.S.A. 172 C5
Goodspeed Nunataks Antarctica 223 E2
Goodwood r. Canada 169 G2
Goole U.K. 47 L10
Goolgowi Australia 147 E3
Goolwa Australia 146 C3
Goomadeer r. Australia 148 B1
Goomalling Australia 151 B6
Goombalie Australia 147 E2
Goomeri Australia 149 G5
Goonda Moz. 131 G3
Goondiwindi Australia 147 F2
Goongarrie, Lake salt flat Australia 151 C6
Goongarrie National Park Australia 151 C6
Goonyella Australia 149 E4
Goorly, Lake salt flat Australia 151 B6
Goose r. Canada 169 I2
Goose r. U.S.A. 178 C2
Goose Bay Canada see Happy Valley - Goose Bay
Goose Creek U.S.A. 175 D5
Goose Creek r. U.S.A. 180 D4
Goose Green Falkland Is 205 F8
Goose Lake U.S.A. 180 B4
Goose Lake Canal r. U.S.A. 182 E6
Gooty India 94 C3
Gop India 95 E2
Gopalganj Bangl. 97 F5
Gopalganj India 97 E4
Gopeshwar India 96 C3
formerly known as Chamoli
Gopichettipalayam India 94 C4
Gopiganj India 97 D4
Göppingen Germany 48 G7
Góra Poland 49 N4
Goradiz Azer. see Horadiz
Goragorskiy Rus. Fed. 41 H8
Góra Kalwaria Poland 49 S4
Gorakhpur India 97 D4
Goražde Bos.-Herz. 56 K5
Gorbachevo Rus. Fed. 43 S8
Gorchukha Rus. Fed. 40 G4
Gorczański Park Narodowy nat. park Poland 49 R6
Gorda, Banco sea feature Hond. 186 C4
Gorda, Punta pt Nicaragua 186 C4
Gorda, Punta pt U.S.A. 180 A4
Gorda, Sierra mts Spain 54 G7
Gördalen Sweden 45 K3
Gördes Turkey 106 B3
Gordeyevka Rus. Fed. 43 M9
Gordon r. Canada 167 O1
Gordon NE U.S.A. 178 B3
Gordon WI U.S.A. 172 B4
Gordon, Isla i. Chile 205 C9
Gordon, Lake Australia 147 E5
Gordon Bay Australia 148 A1
Gordon Downs Australia 150 E3
Gordon Lake Canada 167 H2
Gordonsville U.S.A. 176 G7
Gordonvale Australia 149 E3
Goré Chad 126 C3
Gorē Eth. 128 B2
Gore N.Z. 153 C14
Gore U.S.A. 176 G6
Gore Bay Canada 173 K5
Gorelki Rus. Fed. 43 S7
Goreloye Rus. Fed. 41 G5
Gore Point U.S.A. 164 D4
Goretovo Rus. Fed. 43 Q6
Gorey Rep. of Ireland 47 F11
Gorg Iran 101 D4
Gorgān Iran 100 C2
also spelt Gurgan; formerly known as Asterabad or Astrabad; historically known as Hyrcania or Varkana
Gorgan Bay Iran 100 C2
Gorge Range hills Australia 150 B4
Gorge Range mts Australia 149 E3
Gorge Road N.Z. 153 C14
Gorges Namibia 132 B4
Gorgol admin. reg. Mauritania 124 B2
Gorgona, Isola di i. Italy 56 B5
Gorgora Eth. 128 C1
Gorgoram Nigeria 125 H3
Gorgova, Lacul l. Romania 58 K3
Gorham U.S.A. 177 N1
Gori Georgia 107 F2
Gorinchem Neth. 48 B4
Goris Armenia 107 F3
Goritsa Bulg. 58 I6
Goritsy Rus. Fed. 43 R4
Gorizia Italy 56 F3
Gorka Rus. Fed. 43 T5
Gorkhā Nepal 97 E4
Gorki Belarus see Horki
Gor'kiy Rus. Fed. see Nizhniy Novgorod
Gor'kovskaya Oblast' admin. div. Rus. Fed. see Nizhegorodskaya Oblast'
Gor'kovskoye Vodokhranilishche resr Rus. Fed. 43 V4
Gor'koye, Ozero salt l. Rus. Fed. 103 J1
Gor'koye, Ozero salt l. Rus. Fed. 103 J1
Gorlice Poland 49 S6
Görlitz Germany 49 L4
Gorlovka Ukr. see Horlivka
Gorlovo Rus. Fed. 43 U8
Gormi India 96 C4
Gorna Dzhumaya Bulg. see Blagoevgrad
Gorna Oryakhovitsa Bulg. 58 G5
Gorni Dŭbnik Bulg. 58 F5
Gornja Radgona Slovenia 56 H2
Gornja Toponica Srbija Yugo. 58 C5
Gornji Matejevac Srbija Yugo. 58 C5
Gornji Milanovac Srbija Yugo. 58 B4
Gornji Vakuf Bos.-Herz. 56 J5
also known as Uskoplje
Gorno Ablanovo Bulg. 58 G5
Gorno-Altaysk Rus. Fed. 80 D2
Gorno-Altayskaya Avtonomnaya Oblast' aut. rep. Rus. Fed. see Altay, Respublika
Gorno-Badakhshan aut. rep. Tajik. see Kŭhistoni Badakhshon
Gornopravdinsk Rus. Fed. 38 G3
Gornotrakiyska Nizina lowland Bulg. 58 G6
Gornozavodsk Rus. Fed. 40 K4
formerly known as Novopashiyskiy
Gornozavodsk Rus. Fed. 82 F3
Gornyak Rus. Fed. 88 C1
Gornyak Rus. Fed. 43 U8
Gornye Klyuchi Rus. Fed. 82 D3
Gornyy Khabarovskiy Kray Rus. Fed. 82 E2
formerly known as Solnechnyy
Gornyy Primorskiy Kray Rus. Fed. 90 C2
Gornyy Saratovskaya Oblast' Rus. Fed. 102 B2
Gornyy Altay aut. rep. Rus. Fed. see Altay, Respublika
Gornyy Badakhshan aut. rep. Tajik. see Kŭhistoni Badakhshon
Gornyy Balykley Rus. Fed. 41 H6
Goro Eth. 128 D3
Goro i. Fiji see Koro
Goroch'an mt. Eth. 128 C2
Gorodenka Ukr. see Horodenka
Gorodets Rus. Fed. 40 G4
Gorodishche Penzenskaya Oblast' Rus. Fed. 41 H5
Gorodishche Volgogradskaya Oblast' Rus. Fed. 41 H6
Gorodok Belarus see Haradok
Gorodok Belarus see Haradok
Gorodok Rus. Fed. see Zakamensk
Gorodok Ukr. see Horodok
Gorodovikovsk Rus. Fed. 41 G7
formerly known as Bashanta
Goroka P.N.G. 73 K8
Goroke Australia 146 D4
Gorokhovets Rus. Fed. 40 G4
Gorom Gorom Burkina 125 E3
Gorong, Kepulauan is Indon. 73 H7
Gorongosa Moz. 131 G3
formerly known as Vila Paiva de Andrada
Gorongosa mt. Moz. 131 G3
Gorongosa, Parque Nacional de nat. park Moz. 131 G3
Gorontalo Indon. 75 B2
Goronyo Nigeria 125 G3
Goroubi watercourse Niger 125 F3
Gorouol r. Burkina/Niger 125 F3
Górowo Iławeckie Poland 49 R1
Gorshechnoye Rus. Fed. 41 F6
Gór Stołowych, Park Narodowy nat. park Poland 49 N5
Goru, Vârful mt. Romania 58 H3
Görükle Turkey 59 J8
Gorumna Island Rep. of Ireland 47 C10
Gorutuba r. Brazil 207 J2
Goryachiy Klyuch Rus. Fed. 41 F7
Górzno Poland 49 Q2
Gorzów Wielkopolski Poland 49 M3
historically known as Landsberg
Gosainthan mt. China see Xixabangma Feng
Goschen Strait P.N.G. 149 F1
Gosford Australia 147 F3
Goshen CA U.S.A. 182 E5
Goshen IN U.S.A. 174 C3
Goshen NH U.S.A. 177 M2
Goshen VA U.S.A. 176 F8
Goshoba Turkm. see Koshoba
Goshogawara Japan 90 G4
Goslar Germany 48 H4
Gospić Croatia 56 H4
Gossas Senegal 124 A3
Gosse watercourse Australia 148 B3
Gossi Mali 125 E3
Gossinga Sudan 126 E2
Gostivar Macedonia 58 B7
Gostyń Poland 49 O4
Gostynin Poland 49 Q3
Gosu China 86 A1
Gota Eth. 128 D2
Götaälven r. Sweden 45 J4
Göteborg Sweden see Gothenburg
Gotel Mountains Cameroon/Nigeria 125 H5
Gotemba Japan see Gotenba
Gotenba Japan 91 F7
also spelt Gotemba
Götene Sweden 45 K4
Gotenhafen Poland see Gdynia
Gotha Germany 48 H5
Gothem Sweden 45 L4
Gothenburg Sweden 45 J4
also spelt Göteborg
Gothenburg U.S.A. 178 B3
Gothèye Niger 125 F3
Gotland i. Sweden 45 L4
Gotō-rettō is Japan 91 A8
Gotse Delchev Bulg. 58 E7
Gotska Sandön i. Sweden 45 L4
Gotska Sandön i. Sweden 45 L4
Gōtsu Japan 91 C7
Gottero, Monte mt. Italy 56 B4
Göttingen Germany 48 G4
Gottne Sweden 44 L3
Gott Peak Canada 166 F5
Gottwaldow Czech Rep. see Zlín
Gotval'd Ukr. see Zmiyiv
Gouako Cent. Afr. Rep. 126 D3
Gouda Neth. 48 B3
Gouda S. Africa 132 D10
Goudiri Senegal 124 B3
Goudoumaria Niger 125 H3
Goudreau Canada 173 I2
Gouéké Guinea 124 C4
Gougaram Niger 125 G2

▶Gough Island S. Atlantic Ocean 217 N8
Dependency of St Helena.

Gouin, Réservoir Canada 169 F3
Goukamma Nature Reserve S. Africa 132 G11
Goulais River Canada 173 I4
Goulburn Australia 147 F3
Goulburn r. Australia 147 E4
Goulburn Islands Australia 148 B1
Goulburn River National Park Australia 147 F3
Gould, Mount hill Australia 151 B5
Gould City U.S.A. 172 H4
Gould Coast Antarctica 223 O1
Goulféy Cameroon 125 I3
Goulia Côte d'Ivoire 124 D4
Goulou atoll Micronesia see Ngulu
Goumbou Mali 124 D3
Goumenissa Greece 58 D8
Goundam Mali 124 E2
Goundi Chad 126 C2
Gounou-Gaya Chad 126 B2
Gouraya Alg. 55 M8
Gouraye Mauritania 124 B3
Gourcy Burkina 124 E3
Gourdon France 50 H8
Gouré Niger 125 H3
Gourin France 50 C4
Gouripur Bangl. 97 F4
Gourits r. S. Africa 132 F11
Gourlay Lake Canada 173 I2
Gourma-Rharous Mali 125 E2
Goûrmél well Mauritania 124 C2
Gourmeur well Chad 120 D5
Gournay-en-Bray France 50 H3
Gouro Chad 120 C5
Goûr Oulad Ahmed reg. Mali 122 D5
Gourouro well Chad 120 D5
Goussainville France 51 I3
Gouvêa Brazil 207 J5
Gouveia Port. 54 D4
Gouverneur U.S.A. 177 J1
Gove U.S.A. 178 B4
Gove, Barragem do resr Angola 127 B8
Govedartsi Bulg. 58 E6
Govena, Mys hd Rus. Fed. 39 Q4
Gove Peninsula Australia 148 C2
Governador Valadares Brazil 203 D6
Governor Generoso Phil. 74 C5
Governor's Harbour Bahamas 186 D1
Govĭ-Altay prov. Mongolia 84 B2
Govĭ Altayn Nuruu mts Mongolia 84 C2
Govind Ballash Pant Sagar resr India 97 D4
Govindgarh India 97 D4
Govind Sagar resr India 96 C3
Govurdak Turkm. 103 F5
also spelt Gowurdak; formerly spelt Gaurdak
Gowanbridge N.Z. 153 G9
Gowanda U.S.A. 176 G3
Gowan Range hills Australia 149 E5
Gowd-e Ahmar Iran 100 C4
Gowdeh, Rūd-e watercourse Iran 100 C5
Gowd-e Hasht Tekkeh waterhole Iran 100 D3
Gowganda Canada 173 M3
Gowganda Lake Canada 173 M3
Gowmal Kalay Afgh. 101 G3
Gowurdak Turkm. see Govurdak
Goya Arg. 204 F3
Göyçay Azer. 107 F2
Goyder r. Australia 148 B2
Goyder watercourse Australia 148 B5
Goyder Lagoon salt flat Australia 146 C1
Goymatdag hills Turkm. see Koymatdag, Gory
Göynük Antalya Turkey 108 B1
Göynük Bingöl Turkey 107 E3
also known as Oğnut
Göynük Bolu Turkey 106 B2
Göynükbelen Turkey 59 K9
Goyō-zan mt. Japan 90 G5
Göytäpä Azer. 107 G3
Gözareh Afgh. 101 E3
Goz-Beïda Chad 120 D6
Gözcüler Turkey 108 G1
Gözene Turkey 107 D3
Gozha Co salt l. China 89 C5
Gözne Turkey 108 F1
Gozo i. Malta 57 G12
also known as Ghawdex
Goz Regeb Sudan 121 G5
Graaf-Reinet S. Africa 133 I9
Graafwater S. Africa 132 C9
Grabia r. Poland 49 P4
Grabo Côte d'Ivoire 124 D5
Grabouw S. Africa 132 D11
Grabovica Srbija Yugo. 58 D4
Grabovo Kazakh. 103 H1
Grabow Germany 48 I2
Grabowa r. Poland 49 N1
Grabów nad Prosną Poland 49 P4
Gračac Croatia 56 H4
Gračanica Bos.-Herz. 56 K4
Gračanica Jezero l. Yugo. 58 A6
Graçay France 50 H5
Grace, Lake salt flat Australia 151 B7
Gracefield Canada 168 E4
Gracemere Australia 149 F4
Grachevka Rus. Fed. 102 C1
Grachi Kazakh. 103 I2
Gracias Hond. 186 A4
Gradačac Bos.-Herz. 56 K4
Gradaús Brazil 202 B3
Gradaús, Serra dos hills Brazil 202 B4
Gradets Bulg. 58 H6
Gradignan France 50 F8
Gradishte hill Bulg. 58 H6
Gradiška Bos.-Herz. see Bosanska Gradiška
Gradište Croatia 56 K3
Gradiştea Romania 58 H4
Grado Italy 56 F3
Grado Spain 54 E1
Grady U.S.A. 179 B5
Gräfenhainichen Germany 49 J4
Gräftåvallen Sweden 44 K3
Grafton Australia 147 G2
Grafton ND U.S.A. 178 C1
Grafton WI U.S.A. 172 F7
Grafton WV U.S.A. 176 E6
Grafton, Cape Australia 149 E3
Grafton, Mount U.S.A. 183 J3
Grafton Passage Australia 149 E3
Graham NC U.S.A. 176 F9
Graham TX U.S.A. 179 C5
Graham, Mount U.S.A. 183 O9
Graham Bell Island Rus. Fed. see Greem-Bell, Ostrov
Graham Island B.C. Canada 166 C4
Graham Island Nunavut Canada 165 J2
Graham Lake U.S.A. 177 Q1
Graham Land reg. Antarctica 222 T2
Graham Moore, Cape Canada 165 L2
Grahamstown S. Africa 133 K10
Graiguenamanagh Rep. of Ireland 47 F11
Grajagan Indon. 77 F5
Grajaú Brazil 202 C3
Grajaú r. Brazil 202 C2
Grajewo Poland 49 T2
Gram Denmark 45 J5
Gramada mt. Yugo. 58 D6
Gramat France 50 H8
Gramatikovo Bulg. 58 I6
Grammichele Sicilia Italy 57 G11
Grámmos mt. Greece 59 B8
Gramoz, Mal mt. Albania/Greece 59 B8
Grampian U.S.A. 176 G5
Grampian Mountains U.K. 46 H7
Grampians, The mts Australia 147 D4
Grampians National Park Australia 147 D4
Gramsh Albania 58 B8
Gran Hungary see Esztergom
Granaatboskolk S. Africa 132 D7
Granada Col. 198 C4
Granada Nicaragua 186 B5
Granada Spain 55 H7
Granado hill Spain 54 D7
Gran Altiplanicie Central plain Arg. 205 C8
Granard Rep. of Ireland 47 E10
Gran Baja San Julián valley Arg. 205 C8
Gran Bajo depr. Arg. 205 D7
Gran Bajo Salitroso salt flat Arg. 204 D5
Granbury U.S.A. 179 C5
Granby Canada 169 F4
Granby U.S.A. 180 F4
Gran Canaria i. Canary Is 122 B4
English form Grand Canary
Gran Chaco reg. Arg./Para. 201 E6
Grand r. MO U.S.A. 174 C3
Grand r. SD U.S.A. 178 B2
Grand, North Fork r. U.S.A. 178 B2
Grand, South Fork r. U.S.A. 178 B2
Grandas Spain 54 E1
Grand Atlas mts Morocco see Haut Atlas
Grand Bahama i. Bahamas 186 D1
Grand Bank Canada 169 K4
Grand-Bassam Côte d'Ivoire 124 E5
Grand Bay Canada 169 H4
Grand Bay U.S.A. 175 B6
Grand Bend Canada 168 D5
Grand Bérard mt. France 51 M8
Grand Bourg Guadeloupe 187 H4
Grand Caicos i. Turks and Caicos Is 187 F2
Grand Canal China see Da Yunhe
Grand Canal Rep. of Ireland 47 E10
Grand Canary i. Canary Is see Gran Canaria
Grand Canyon U.S.A. 183 L5
▶Grand Canyon gorge U.S.A. 183 L5
world [land images] ➡ 12–13
northamerica [landscapes] ➡ 156–157
Grand Canyon National Park U.S.A. 183 L5
Grand Cayman i. Cayman Is 186 C3
Grand Centre Canada 167 I4
Grand Combin mt. Switz. 51 N7
Grand Detour U.S.A. 172 D9
Grande r. Arg. 204 C5
Grande r. Santa Cruz Bol. 201 E4
Grande r. Santa Cruz Bol. 201 E4
also known as Guapay
Grande r. Bahia Brazil 202 D4
Grande r. São Paulo Brazil 206 C7
Grande r. Peru 200 B3
Grande, Bahía b. Arg. 205 C8
Grande, Cayo i. Cuba 186 D2
Grande, Cerro mt. Mex. 185 F5
Grande, Ciénaga lag. Col. 198 C2
Grande, Ilha i. Brazil 203 C7
Grande, Serra hills Brazil 201 E2
Grande, Serra mt. Brazil 199 F4
also known as Carauná
Grande Cache Canada 166 G4
Grande Comore i. Comoros see Njazidja
Grande de Manacapuru, Lago l. Brazil 199 F5
Grande-Entree Canada 169 I4
Grande Leyre r. France 50 F8
Grande Prairie Canada 166 G4
Grand Erg de Bilma des. Niger 125 I2
Grand Erg Occidental des. Alg. 123 E3
English form Great Western Erg
Grand Erg Oriental des. Alg. 123 G3
English form Great Eastern Erg
Grande-Rivière Canada 169 H3
Grande Ronde r. U.S.A. 180 C3
Grandes, Salinas salt marsh Arg. 200 D5
Grandes, Salinas salt marsh Arg. 204 D3
Gran Desierto del Pinacate, Parque Natural del nature res. Mex. 184 B2
Grande-Terre i. Guadeloupe 187 H3
Grande Terre i. Mayotte 129 E8
Grande Tête de l'Obiou mt. France 51 L8
Grande-Vallée Canada 169 H3
Grand Falls N.B. Canada 169 H4
Grand Falls Nfld. Canada 169 K3
Grandfather Mountain U.S.A. 176 D9
Grand Forks Canada 166 G5
Grand Forks U.S.A. 178 C2
Grand-Fougeray France 50 E5
Grand Gorge U.S.A. 177 K3
Grand Gosier Haiti 187 F3
Grand Harbour Canada 169 H4
Grand Haven U.S.A. 172 G7
Grandin, Lac l. Canada 167 G1
Grand Island U.S.A. 178 C3
Grand Island i. U.S.A. 172 G4
Grand Isle U.S.A. 175 B6
Grand Junction CO U.S.A. 183 P2
Grand Junction MI U.S.A. 172 G8
Grand-Lahou Côte d'Ivoire 124 D5
Grand Lake N.B. Canada 169 H4
Grand Lake Nfld. Canada 169 I2
Grand Lake Nfld. Canada 169 J3
Grand Lake LA U.S.A. 179 D6
Grand Lake LA U.S.A. 179 E6
Grand Lake MI U.S.A. 173 J5
Grand Lake St Marys U.S.A. 176 A5
Grand Ledge U.S.A. 173 I8
Grand Manan Island Canada 169 H4
Grand Marais MI U.S.A. 172 H4
Grand Marais MN U.S.A. 174 B2
Grand Marsh U.S.A. 172 D7
Grândola Port. 54 C6
Grândola, Serra de mts Port. 54 C6
Grand Pacific Glacier Canada 166 B3
Grand Passage New Caledonia 145 F3
Grand Rapids Canada 167 L4
Grand Rapids MI U.S.A. 172 H8
Grand Rapids MN U.S.A. 174 A2
Grand Récif de Cook reef New Caledonia 145 F3
Grand Récif du Sud reef New Caledonia 145 F4
Grand St Bernard, Col du pass Italy/Switz. see Great St Bernard Pass
Grand Santi Fr. Guiana 199 H3
Grand Teton mt. U.S.A. 180 E4
Grand Teton National Park U.S.A. 180 E4
Grand Traverse Bay U.S.A. 172 H6

▶Grand Turk Turks and Caicos Is 187 F2
Capital of the Turks and Caicos Islands. Also known as Cockburn Town.

Grand Turk i. Turks and Caicos Is 187 F2
Grand Valley Swaziland 133 P3
Grand View U.S.A. 172 B4
Grandville U.S.A. 172 H8
Grandvilliers France 51 H3
Grand Wash watercourse U.S.A. 183 J5
Grand Wash Cliffs mts U.S.A. 183 J6
Grañén Spain 55 K3
Graneros Chile 204 C4
Granger U.S.A. 180 E4
Grängesberg Sweden 45 K3
Grangeville U.S.A. 180 C3
Granhult Sweden 44 M2
Granisle Canada 166 E4
Granite City U.S.A. 174 B4
Granite Falls U.S.A. 178 D2
Granite Mountain U.S.A. 182 G1
Granite Mountains CA U.S.A. 183 I7
Granite Mountains CA U.S.A. 183 I8
Granite Peak MT U.S.A. 180 E3
Granite Peak UT U.S.A. 183 K1
Granite Range mts U.S.A. 182 E1
Granitogorsk Kazakh. 103 H4
Granitola, Capo c. Sicilia Italy 57 E11
Granity N.Z. 153 F9
Granja Brazil 202 D2
Gran Laguna Salada l. Arg. 205 D7
Gran Morelos Mex. 181 F7
Granollers Spain 55 N3
Gran Pajonal plain Peru 200 B2
Gran Paradiso mt. Italy 51 N7
Gran Paradiso, Parco Nazionale del nat. park Italy 51 N7
Gran Pilastro mt. Austria/Italy 48 I9
also known as Hochfeiler
Gran San Bernardo, Colle del pass Italy/Switz. see Great St Bernard Pass
Gran Sasso d'Italia mts Italy 56 F6
Gran Sasso e Monti della Laga, Parco Nazionale del nat. park Italy 56 F6
Gransee Germany 49 K2
Grant U.S.A. 178 B3
Grant, Mount NV U.S.A. 182 F3
Grant, Mount NV U.S.A. 182 G2
Grant City U.S.A. 178 D3
Grantham U.K. 47 L11
Grant Island Antarctica 222 P2
Grant Lake Canada 167 G1
Granton U.S.A. 172 C6
Grantown-on-Spey U.K. 46 I6
Grant Park U.S.A. 172 F9
Grant Range mts U.S.A. 183 I3
Grants U.S.A. 181 F6
Grantsburg U.S.A. 172 A5
Grants Pass U.S.A. 180 B4
Grantsville U.S.A. 183 L1
Granville Canada 166 B2
Granville France 50 E4
Granville AZ U.S.A. 183 O8
Granville IL U.S.A. 172 D9
Granville NY U.S.A. 177 L2
Granville OH U.S.A. 176 C5
Granville Lake Canada 167 K3

	island	area sq km	area sq miles	location	page#
1 ▶	Greenland	2 175 600	840 004	North America ⟶	165 O2
2 ▶	New Guinea	808 510	312 167	Oceania ⟶	73 J8
3 ▶	Borneo	745 561	287 863	Asia ⟶	77 F2
4 ▶	Madagascar	587 040	266 657	Africa ⟶	131 J4
5 ▶	Baffin Island	507 451	195 927	North America ⟶	165 L2
6 ▶	Sumatra	473 606	182 860	Asia ⟶	76 B2
7 ▶	Honshū	227 414	87 805	Asia ⟶	91 F6
8 ▶	Great Britain	218 476	84 354	Europe ⟶	47 J9
9 ▶	Victoria Island	217 291	83 897	North America ⟶	165 H2
10 ▶	Ellesmere Island	196 236	75 767	North America ⟶	165 K2

largest islands

↓ H

Hearst Island Antarctica 222 T2
Heart r. U.S.A. 178 B2
Heath r. Bol./Peru 200 C3
Heathcote Australia 147 E4
Heathfield U.K. 47 M13
Heathrow airport U.K. 47 L12
Heathsville U.S.A. 177 I8
Heavener U.S.A. 179 D5
Hebbronville U.S.A. 179 C7
Hebei prov. China 85 G4
English form Hopei
Hebel Australia 147 E2
Heber AZ U.S.A. 183 N7
Heber CA U.S.A. 183 I9
Heber City U.S.A. 183 M1
Heber Springs U.S.A. 179 D5
Hebgen Lake U.S.A. 180 E3
Hebi China 85 G5
Hebian China 85 G4
Hebron Canada 169 I1
Hebron IN U.S.A. 172 F9
Hebron MD U.S.A. 177 J7
Hebron NE U.S.A. 178 C3
Hebron West Bank 108 G6
also known as Al Khalil or El Khalil; also spelt Hevron
Hebron Fiord inlet Canada 169 I1
Hebros r. Greece/Turkey see Evros
Heby Sweden 45 L4
Hecate Strait Canada 166 D4
Hecelchakán Mex. 185 H4
Hecheng China see Zixi
Hecheng China see Qingtian
Hechi China 87 D3
also known as Jinchengjiang
Hechingen Germany 48 F7
Hechuan China 86 C2
Hechuan China see Yongxing
Hecla Island Canada 167 L5
Hector U.S.A. 178 D2
Hector Mountain mts N.Z. 153 C13
Hedberg Sweden 44 L2
Hede China see Sheyang
Hédé France 50 E4
Hede Sweden 44 K3
Hedemora Sweden 45 K3
Hedenäset Sweden 44 M2
Hede Shuiku resr China 87 D4
Hedesunda Sweden 45 L3
He Devil Mountain U.S.A. 180 C3
Hedgehope N.Z. 153 C14
Hedmark county Norway 45 J3
Heerenveen Neth. 48 C3
Heerhugowaard Neth. 48 B3
Heerlen Neth. 48 C5
Hefa Israel see Haifa
Hefa, Mifraz b. Israel see Haifa, Bay of
Hefei China 87 F2
Hefeng China 87 D2
also known as Rongmei
Heflin U.S.A. 175 C5
Hegang China 82 C3
Heggadadevankote India 94 C3
Heggenes Norway 45 J3
Hegura-jima i. Japan 90 E6
Heguri-jima i. Japan 91 C8
Heho Myanmar 78 B3
Heiban Sudan 128 A2
Heidan r. Jordan see Haydān, Wādī al
Heide Germany 48 G1
Heidelberg Germany 48 F6
Heidelberg Gauteng S. Africa 133 M3
Heidelberg W. Cape S. Africa 132 E11
Heidenheim an der Brenz Germany 48 H7
Heihe China 82 B2
formerly known as Aihui
Heilbron S. Africa 133 L4
Heilbronn Germany 48 G6
Heiligenbeil Rus. Fed. see Mamonovo
Heiligenhafen Germany 48 H1
Hei Ling Chau i. Hong Kong China 87 [inset]
Heilongjiang prov. China 85 I2
English form Heilungkiang
Heilong Jiang r. China 82 D2
also known as Amur
Heilungkiang prov. China see Heilongjiang
Heimaey i. Iceland 44 [inset] B3
Heinävesi Fin. 44 O3
Heinola Fin. 45 N3
Heinrichswalde Rus. Fed. see Slavsk
Heinze Bay Myanmar 79 B5
Heinze Islands Myanmar 79 B5
Heishan China 85 I3
Heishantou China 85 H1
Heishi Beihu l. China 89 C5
Heishui China 86 B1
also known as Luhua
Heisker Islands U.K. see Monach Islands
Heitān, Gebel hill Egypt 108 E7
Heituo Shan mt. China 85 G4
Hejaz reg. Saudi Arabia see Hijaz
Hejian China 85 H4
Hejiang China 86 C2
He Jiang r. China 87 D4
Hejin China 85 F5
Hejing China 88 D3
Heka China 84 C5
Hekimhan Turkey 107 D3
Hekla vol. Iceland 44 [inset] C3
Hekou Gansu China 84 D4
Hekou Hubei China 87 E2
Hekou China see Yanshan
Hekou China see Yajiang
Hekou Yunnan China 86 B4
Hekpoort S. Africa 133 L2
Hel Poland 49 P1
Helagsfjället mt. Sweden 44 K3
Helan Shan mts China 85 E4
Helegiu Romania 58 H2
Helem India 97 G4
Helen i. Palau 73 H6
Helen, Mount U.S.A. 183 H4
Helena AR U.S.A. 174 B5

▶Helena MT U.S.A. 180 D3
State capital of Montana.

Helena OH U.S.A. 176 B4
Helen Reef Palau 73 H6
Helensburgh U.K. 46 H7
Helensville N.Z. 152 I4
Helenwood U.S.A. 176 A9
Helgoland i. Germany 48 E1
English form Heligoland
Helgoländer Bucht b. Germany 48 F1
English form Heligoland Bight
Helgum Sweden 44 L3
Heligoland i. Germany see Helgoland
Heligoland Bight b. Germany see Helgoländer Bucht
Helixi China see Ningguo
Hella Iceland 44 [inset] B3
Hellas country Europe see Greece
Helleh r. Iran 100 B4
Hellertown U.S.A. 177 J5
Hellespont strait Turkey see Dardanelles
Hellevoetsluis Neth. 48 B4
Hellhole Gorge National Park Australia 149 E5
Helligskogen Norway 44 M1
Hellín Spain 55 J6
Hells Canyon gorge U.S.A. 180 C3
Hell-Ville Madag. see Andoany
Helm U.S.A. 182 D5
Helmand prov. Afgh. 101 E4
Helmand r. Afgh. 101 E4
Helmantica Spain see Salamanca
Helmbrechts Germany 48 I5
Helme r. Germany 48 I4
Helmeringhausen Namibia 130 C5
Helmond Neth. 48 C4
Helmsdale U.K. 46 I5
Helmsdale r. U.K. 46 I5
Helmsley U.K. 47 K9
Helmsley Aboriginal Holding res. Australia 149 D2
Helmstedt Germany 48 I3
Helodrano Antongila b. Madag. 131 [inset] K2
Helong China 82 C4
Helper U.S.A. 183 N2
Helpmekaar S. Africa 133 O5
Helsingborg Sweden 45 K4
formerly spelt Hälsingborg
Helsingfors Fin. see Helsinki
Helsingør Denmark 45 K4
historically known as Elsinore

▶Helsinki Fin. 45 N3
Capital of Finland. Also known as Helsingfors.

Helston U.K. 47 G13
Heltermaa Estonia 42 E3
Helvacı Turkey 59 I10
Helvécia Brazil 203 E6
Helvetic Republic country Europe see Switzerland
Helvetinjärven kansallispuisto nat. park Fin. 45 M3
Helwân Egypt 121 F2
also spelt Hulwān
Hemel Hempstead U.K. 47 L12
Hemet U.S.A. 183 H8
Hemlo Canada 172 H2
Hemlock Lake U.S.A. 176 H3
Hemmoor Germany 48 G2
Hemnesberget Norway 44 K2
Hemphill U.S.A. 179 D6
Hempstead U.S.A. 179 C6
Hemse Sweden 45 L4
Hemsedal Norway 45 J3
Hemsedal valley Norway 45 J3
Henan China 86 B1
also known as Yêgainnyin
Henan prov. China 87 E1
English form Honan
Hen and Chickens Islands N.Z. 152 I3
Henares r. Spain 55 H4
Henashi-zaki pt Japan 90 F4
Henbury Australia 148 B5
Hendawashi Tanz. 129 B5
Henderson KY U.S.A. 174 C4
Henderson LA U.S.A. 179 E6
Henderson NC U.S.A. 176 G9
Henderson NV U.S.A. 183 J5
Henderson NY U.S.A. 177 I2
Henderson TN U.S.A. 174 B5
Henderson TX U.S.A. 179 D5
Henderson Island Antarctica 223 G2
Henderson Island Pitcairn Is 221 J7
historically known as Elizabeth Island
Hendersonville NC U.S.A. 174 D5
Hendersonville TN U.S.A. 174 C4
Henderville atoll Kiribati see Aranuka
Hendījān Iran 100 B4
Hendorābī i. Iran 100 C5
Hendriksdal S. Africa 133 O2
Hendrina S. Africa 133 N3
Hengām, Jazīreh-ye i. Iran 100 C5
Hengch'un Taiwan 87 G4
Hengdong China 87 E3
Hengduan Shan mts China 86 A2
Hengelo Neth. 48 D3
Hengnan China see Hengyang
Hengshan Heilong. China 82 C3
Hengshan Hunan China 87 E3
Hengshan Shaanxi China 85 F4
Heng Shan mt. China 87 E3
Heng Shan mts China 85 G4
Hengshui China 85 G4
Hengshui China see Chongyi
Hengxian China 87 D4
also known as Hengzhou
Hengyang Hunan China 87 E3
also known as Hengnan
Hengyang Hunan China 87 E3
also known as Xidu
Hengzhou China see Hengxian
Henlopen, Cape U.S.A. 177 J7
Hennebont France 50 C5
Hennef (Sieg) Germany 48 E5
Hennenman S. Africa 133 L4
Hennessey U.S.A. 179 C4
Hennigsdorf Berlin Germany 49 K3
Henniker U.S.A. 177 N2
Henrichemont France 51 I5
Henrietta U.S.A. 179 C5
Henrietta Maria, Cape Canada 168 D2
Henrique de Carvalho Angola see Saurimo
Henry r. Australia 150 A4
Henry U.S.A. 172 D9
Henry, Cape U.S.A. 177 I9
Henryetta U.S.A. 179 D5
Henry Ice Rise Antarctica 222 T1
Henryk Arctowski research station Antarctica see Arctowski
Henry Kater, Cape Canada 165 M3
Henry Mountains U.S.A. 183 N3
Henrys Fork r. U.S.A. 180 E4
Hensall Canada 173 L7
Henshaw, Lake U.S.A. 183 H8
Henstedt-Ulzburg Germany 48 G2
Hentiesbaai Namibia 130 B4
Hentiy prov. Mongolia 85 F2
Henzada Myanmar 78 A4
also spelt Hinthada
Heping China see Huishui
Heping China see Yanhe
Hepo China see Jiexi
Heppner U.S.A. 180 C3
Hepu China 87 D4
also known as Lianzhou
Heqiaoyi China 84 D4
Heqing Guangdong China 87 E4
Heqing Yunnan China 86 B3
also known as Yunhe
Hequ China 85 F4
Heraclea Turkey see Ereğli
Heraclea Pontica Turkey see Ereğli
Heraklion Greece see Iraklion
Herald Cays atolls Australia 149 F3
Herāt Afgh. 101 E3
historically known as Alexandria Areion
Herāt prov. Afgh. 101 E3
Hérault r. France 51 J9
Herbagat Sudan 104 B4
Herbert r. Australia 149 E3
Herbert watercourse Australia 148 C3
Herbert Canada 167 J5
Herbert N.Z. 153 E13
Herbert Downs Australia 148 C4
Herberton Australia 149 E3
Herbert River Falls National Park Australia 149 E3
Herbertsdale S. Africa 132 F11
Herbertville N.Z. 152 K8
Herbert Wash salt flat Australia 151 D5
Herbignac France 50 D5
Herbstein Germany 48 G5
Herceg-Novi Crna Gora Yugo. 56 K6
Herculândia Brazil 206 C8
Hercules Dome ice feature Antarctica 223 Q1
Heredia Costa Rica 186 B5
Hereford U.K. 47 J11
Hereford U.S.A. 179 B5
Herekino N.Z. 152 H3
Heretaniwha Point N.Z. 153 D11
Herford Germany 48 F3
Héricourt France 51 M5
Herington U.S.A. 178 C4
Heriot N.Z. 153 D13
Herisau Switz. 51 P5
Heritage Range mts Antarctica 222 S1
Herkimer U.S.A. 177 K2
Herlen Mongolia 85 F2
Herlen Gol r. China/Mongolia see Kerulen
Herlen He r. China/Mongolia see Kerulen
Herlong U.S.A. 182 D1
Hermagor Austria 49 K9
Herma Ness hd U.K. 46 L3
Hermann U.S.A. 174 B4
Hermannsburg Australia 148 B4
Hermanus S. Africa 132 D11
Hermel Lebanon 109 H3
Hermes, Cape S. Africa 133 N8
Hermidale Australia 147 E2
Hermitage MO U.S.A. 178 D4
Hermitage PA U.S.A. 176 E4
Hermitage Bay Canada 169 J4
Hermite, Islas is Chile 205 D9
Hermit Islands P.N.G. 73 K7
Hermon, Mount Lebanon/Syria 108 G4
also known as Sheikh, Jebel esh
Hermonthis Egypt see Armant
Hermopolis Magna Egypt see El Ashmûnein
Hermosa, Valle valley Arg. 205 C7
Hermosillo Mex. 184 C2
Hernád r. Hungary 49 R8
also spelt Hornád (Slovakia)
Hernandarias Para. 201 G6
Hernando U.S.A. 174 B5
Hernani Spain 55 J1
Herndon CA U.S.A. 182 E5
Herndon WV U.S.A. 176 D8
Herne Germany 48 E4
Herning Denmark 45 J4
Heroica Nogales Mex. see Nogales
Heron Bay Canada 172 G2
Herong China 87 E2
Hérouville-St-Clair France 50 F3
Herowābād Iran see Khalkhāl
Herradura Mex. 185 E4
Herrenberg Germany 48 F7
Herrera Arg. 204 E3
Herrera del Duque Spain 54 F5
Herrero, Punta pt Mex. 185 I5
Herrieden Germany 48 H6
Herrin U.S.A. 174 B4
Herrljunga Sweden 45 K4
Herrvik Sweden 45 L4
Hers r. France 50 H9
Herschel S. Africa 133 L7
Herschel Island Canada 164 F3
Hershey U.S.A. 177 I5
Hertel U.S.A. 172 A5
Hertford U.K. 47 L12
Hertford U.S.A. 177 I9
Hertzogville S. Africa 133 J5
Hervey Bay Australia 149 G5
Hervey Islands Cook Is 221 H7
Herzberg Germany 49 K4
Herzliyya Israel 108 F5
Herzogenaurach Germany 48 H6
Herzogenburg Austria 49 M7
Hesar Iran 100 B4
Heşar Iran 100 B3
Hesdin France 51 I2
Heshan China 87 D4
Heshengqiao China 87 E2
Heshui China 85 F5
also known as Xihuachi
Heshun China 85 G4
Hesperia CA U.S.A. 183 G7
Hesperia MI U.S.A. 172 G7
Hesquiat Canada 166 E5
Hess r. Canada 166 C2
Hesse land Germany see Hessen
Hessel U.S.A. 173 I4
Hesselberg hill Germany 48 H6
Hessen land Germany 48 G5
English form Hesse
Hessischer Spessart, Naturpark nature res. Germany 48 G5
Hessisch Lichtenau Germany 48 G4
Hess Mountains Canada 166 C2
Hester Malan Nature Reserve S. Africa 132 C6
Hestvika Norway 44 J3
Het r. Laos 78 D3
Hetch Hetchy Aqueduct canal U.S.A. 182 B4
Hettinger U.S.A. 178 B2
Hettstedt Germany 48 I4
Heung Kong Tsai Hong Kong China see Aberdeen
Heuningneskloof S. Africa 133 I6
Heuningspruit S. Africa 133 L4
Heuningvlei salt pan S. Africa 132 H3
Heuvelton U.S.A. 177 J1
Heves Hungary 49 R8
Hevron West Bank see Hebron
Hewlett U.S.A. 176 H8
Hexenkopf mt. Austria 48 H8
Hexham U.K. 47 J9
Hexian China 87 F2
Hexigten Qi China see Jingpeng
Hexipu China 84 D4
Hexrivierberg mts S. Africa 132 D10
Heyang China see Nanhe
Heyang China 85 F5
Heydebreck Poland see Kędzierzyn-Koźle
Heydon S. Africa 133 I8
Heygali well Eth. 128 E3
Heyin China see Guide
Heyshope Dam S. Africa 133 O3
Heyuan China 87 E4
Heywood Australia 146 D4
Heze China 85 G5
also known as Caozhou
Hezhang China 86 C3
Hezheng China 84 D5
Hezhou China 87 D3
also known as Babu
Hezuozhen China 84 D5
Hhohho reg. Swaziland 133 P3
Hialeah U.S.A. 175 D7
Hiawassee U.S.A. 174 D5
Hiawatha U.S.A. 178 D4
Hibata reg. Saudi Arabia 104 C4
Hibberdene S. Africa 133 O7
Hibbing U.S.A. 174 A2
Hibbs, Point Australia 147 E5
Hibernia Reef Australia 150 C2
Hibiki-nada b. Japan 91 B7
Hichān Iran 101 E5
Hickman U.S.A. 174 B4
Hickory U.S.A. 174 D5
Hicks Bay N.Z. 152 M5
Hicks Cays is Belize 185 H5
Hicksville NY U.S.A. 177 L5
Hicksville OH U.S.A. 176 A4
Hico U.S.A. 179 C5
Hidaka Japan 90 H3
Hidaka-sanmyaku mts Japan 90 H3
Hidalgo Coahuila Mex. 185 F3
Hidalgo Tamaulipas Mex. 185 F3
Hidalgo state Mex. 185 F4
Hidalgo del Parral Mex. 184 D3
Hidalgo Yalalag Mex. 185 F5
Hidasnémeti Hungary 49 S7
Hiddensee i. Germany 49 K1
Hidişelu de Sus Romania 58 D2
Hidrolândia Brazil 206 D3
Hierosolyma Israel/West Bank see Jerusalem
Hietaniemi Fin. 44 O2
Higashi-Hiroshima Japan 91 C7
Higashi-matsuyama Japan 91 F6
Higashine Japan 90 G5
Higashi-ōsaka Japan 91 D7
Higashi-suidō sea chan. Japan 91 A8
Higgins Bay U.S.A. 177 K2
Higgins Lake U.S.A. 173 I6
Higg's Hope S. Africa 132 H6
High Atlas mts Morocco see Haut Atlas
High Desert U.S.A. 180 B4
High Falls Reservoir U.S.A. 172 E5
Highflats S. Africa 133 O7
High Island i. Hong Kong China 87 [inset]
also known as Leung Shuen Wan Chau
High Island U.S.A. 179 D6
High Island i. U.S.A. 172 H5
High Island Reservoir Hong Kong China 87 [inset]
Highland CA U.S.A. 183 G7
Highland MN U.S.A. 172 B3
Highland NY U.S.A. 177 L4
Highland WI U.S.A. 172 C7
Highland Beach U.S.A. 177 I7
Highland Peak CA U.S.A. 182 E3
Highland Peak NV U.S.A. 183 J4
Highlands U.S.A. 177 L5
Highland Springs U.S.A. 177 H8
High Level Canada 167 G3
High Level Canal India 95 E1
Highline Canal U.S.A. 183 I9
Highmore U.S.A. 178 C2
High Point U.S.A. 174 E5
High Point hill U.S.A. 177 K4
High Prairie Canada 167 G4
High River Canada 167 H5
High Rock Bahamas 186 D1
Highrock Lake Canada 167 K4
High Rocky Point Australia 147 E5
High Springs U.S.A. 175 D6
High Tatras mts Poland/Slovakia see Tatra Mountains
Hightstown U.S.A. 177 K5
High Wycombe U.K. 47 L12
Higlale well Eth. 128 E3
Higuera de Abuya Mex. 184 D3
Higuera de Zaragoza Mex. 184 C3
Higüey Dom. Rep. 187 F3
Hihifo Tonga 145 H3
Hihnavaara Fin. 44 O2
Hiidenportin kansallispuisto nat. park Fin. 44 O3
Hiidenvesi l. Fin. 42 F1
Hiiraan Somalia 128 E3
Hiiraan admin. reg. Somalia 128 E3
Hiiumaa i. Estonia 42 D3
also known as Dagö; historically known as Oesel or Ösel
Hijānah, Buḩayrat al imp. l. Syria 109 H4
Hijānah, Wādī watercourse Syria 109 K3
Hijau, Gunung mt. Indon. 76 C3
Hijaz reg. Saudi Arabia 104 B2
English form Hejaz
Hiji Japan 91 B8
Hijo Phil. 74 C5
Hikari Japan 91 B8
Hiketa Japan 91 D7
Hikone Japan 91 E7
Hikurangi mt. N.Z. 152 M5
Hila Indon. 75 C4
Hilahila Indon. 75 B4
Hilaricos Chile 200 C5
Hilary Coast Antarctica 223 K1
Hildale U.S.A. 183 K4
Hildburghausen Germany 48 H5
Hilders Germany 48 H5
Hildesheim Germany 48 G3
Hilf, Ra's c. Oman 105 G3
Hili Bangl. 97 F4
Hillah Iraq 107 F4
also spelt Al Ḩillah
Hillandale S. Africa 132 E10
Hillard U.S.A. 176 B5
Hill City U.S.A. 178 C4
Hill Creek r. U.S.A. 183 O2
Hillerød Denmark 45 K5
Hillersden N.Z. 153 H9
Hillerse Germany 48 H3
Hillerstorp Sweden 45 K4
Hillesheim Germany 48 D5
Hillgrove Australia 149 E3
Hill Island Lake Canada 167 I2
Hillman U.S.A. 173 J5
Hillman, Lake salt flat Australia 151 B6
Hillsboro IL U.S.A. 174 B4
Hillsboro MO U.S.A. 174 B4
Hillsboro ND U.S.A. 178 C2
Hillsboro NH U.S.A. 177 N2
Hillsboro OH U.S.A. 176 B6
Hillsboro OR U.S.A. 180 B3
Hillsboro TX U.S.A. 179 C5
Hillsboro WI U.S.A. 172 C7
Hillsboro Canal U.S.A. 175 D7
Hillsborough Grenada 187 H4
Hillsborough U.S.A. 176 F9
Hillsborough, Cape Australia 149 F4
Hillsdale MI U.S.A. 173 I9
Hillsdale NY U.S.A. 177 L3
Hillsgrove U.S.A. 177 I4
Hillside Australia 150 B4
Hillsport Canada 168 C3
Hillston Australia 147 E3
Hillsville U.S.A. 176 E9
Hillswick U.K. 46 K3
Hilo U.S.A. 181 [inset] Z2
Hilton Australia 148 C4
Hilton U.S.A. 176 H2
Hilton Beach Canada 173 J4
Hilton Head Island U.S.A. 175 D5
Hilvan Turkey 107 D3
also known as Karacurun
Hilversum Neth. 48 C3
Ḩimā well Saudi Arabia 104 D4
Himachal Pradesh state India 96 C3
Ḩimā Ḑarīyah, Jabal mt. Saudi Arabia 104 C2
▶Himalaya mts Asia 97 C2
world [physical features] ➡ 8–9
asia [landscapes] ➡ 62–63
Himalchuli mt. Nepal 97 E3
Himanka Fin. 44 M2
Ḩimār, Wādī al watercourse Syria/Turkey 109 K1
also known as Hamra, Vâdii
Himarë Albania 59 A8
Ḩimār Umm Khunşur hill Saudi Arabia 109 M7
Himatangi Beach N.Z. 152 J8
Himatnagar India 96 B5
Himbirti Eritrea 104 B5
Himeji Japan 91 D7
Himekami-dake mt. Japan 90 G5
Himeville S. Africa 133 N6
Hime-zaki pt Japan 90 F5
Himi Japan 91 E6
Himora Eth. 128 C1
Ḩimş Syria see Homs
Ḩimş governorate Syria 109 J2
Ḩimş, Bahrat resr Syria see Qaţţīnah, Buḩayrat
Hinako i. Indon. 76 B2
Hinakura N.Z. 152 J9
Hinatuan Phil. 74 C4
Hinatuan Passage Phil. 74 C4
Hînceşti Moldova 58 J2
formerly known as Cotovsc or Kotovsk; formerly spelt Hănceşti or Khynchest' or Khynchesty
Hinche Haiti 187 E3
Hinchinbrook Island Australia 149 E3
Hinckley U.K. 47 K11
Hinckley IL U.S.A. 172 E9
Hinckley ME U.S.A. 177 P1
Hinckley MN U.S.A. 174 A2
Hinckley UT U.S.A. 183 L2
Hinckley Reservoir U.S.A. 177 J2
Hind, Wādī al watercourse Saudi Arabia 108 G8
Hinda Congo 126 B6
Hindan r. India 89 B6
Hindaun India 96 C4
Hindelang Germany 48 H8
Hindenburg Poland see Zabrze
Hindman U.S.A. 176 C8
Hindmarsh, Lake dry lake Australia 146 D4
Hindola India 95 E1
Hindoli India 96 B4
Hindoria India 96 C5
Hindri r. India 94 C3
Hinds N.Z. 153 F12
Hindu Kush mts Afgh./Pak. 101 F3
Hindupur India 94 C3
Hines Creek Canada 166 G3
Hinesville U.S.A. 175 D6
Hinganghat India 94 C1
Hingol r. Pak. 101 F5
Hingol r. Pak. see Girdar Dhor
Hinis Turkey 107 E3
Hinks Conservation Park nature res. Australia 146 C3
Hinnøya i. Norway 44 K1
Hino Japan 91 C7
Hinobaan Phil. 74 B4
Hinojedo mt. Spain 55 I3
Hinojosa del Duque Spain 54 F6
Hino-misaki pt Japan 91 C7
Hinsdale U.S.A. 177 M3
Hinterzarten Germany 48 F8
Hinthada Myanmar see Henzada
Hinton KY U.S.A. 176 A7
Hinton OK U.S.A. 179 C5
Hinton WV U.S.A. 176 E8
Hinuera N.Z. 152 J5
Hiort i. U.K. see Hirta
Hipólito Mex. 185 E3
Hipponium Italy see Vibo Valentia
Hippopotames, Réserve de nature res. Dem. Rep. Congo 126 F6
Hippopotames, Réserve de Faune des nature res. Dem. Rep. Congo 126 E5
Hippopotames de Sakania, Réserve de nature res. Dem. Rep. Congo 127 F8
Hippo Regius Alg. see Annaba
Hippo Zarytus Tunisia see Bizerte
Hirabit Dağ mt. Turkey 107 F3
Hirado Japan 91 A8
Hirado-shima i. Japan 91 A8
Hirafok Alg. 123 G5
Hirakud Reservoir India 97 D5
Hiraman watercourse Kenya 128 C5
Hirata Japan 91 C7
Hiré-Watta Côte d'Ivoire 124 D5
Hiriyur India 94 C3
Hîrlău Romania see Hârlău
Hiroo Japan 90 H3
Hirosaki Japan 90 G4
Hirose Japan 91 C7
Hiroshima Japan 91 C7
Hiroshima airport Japan 91 C7
Hiroshima pref. Japan 91 C7
Hiroo-wan b. Japan 90 G5
Hirschaid Germany 48 I6
Hirschberg Germany 48 I5
Hirschberg Poland see Jelenia Góra
Hirsingue France 51 N5
Hirson France 51 K3
Hirşova Romania see Hârşova
Hirta i. U.K. 46 D6
also known as Hiort
Hirtshals Denmark 45 J4
Hisai Japan 91 E7
Hisaka-jima i. Japan 91 A8
Hisar India 96 B3
also spelt Hissar
Hisar, Koh-i- mts Afgh. 101 F3
Hisarcık Turkey 59 K9
Hisarköy Turkey see Domaniç
Hisarönü Turkey 106 C2
Hisarönü Körfezi b. Turkey 59 I12
Hisb, Sha'īb watercourse Iraq 107 F5
Hişn al Fuḑūl Yemen 105 E4
Hisor Tajik. 101 G2
also known as Gissar
Hisor Tizmasi mts Tajik./Uzbek. see Gissar Range
Hispalis Spain see Seville
Hispania country Europe see Spain

▶Hispaniola i. Caribbean Sea 171 L7
Consists of the Dominican Republic and Haiti.

Hispur Glacier Jammu and Kashmir 96 B1
Hissar India see Hisar
Hisua India 97 E4
Hīt Iraq 107 E4
Hita Japan 91 B8
Hitachi Japan 91 G6
Hitachinaka Japan 91 G6
Hitachi-ōta Japan 91 G6
Hitoyoshi Japan 91 B8
Hitra i. Norway 44 J3
Hiuchi-nada b. Japan 91 C7
Hiva Oa i. Fr. Polynesia 221 I6
formerly known as Dominique
Hiwasa Japan 91 D8
Hixon Canada 166 F4
Hixson Cay reef Australia 149 G4
Hixton U.S.A. 172 B6
Hiyon watercourse Israel 108 G7
Hizan Turkey 107 E3
also known as Karasu
Hjallerup Denmark 45 J4
Hjälmaren l. Sweden 45 K4
Hjelle Norway 45 I3
Hjellestad Norway 46 R3
Hjelmeland Norway 45 I4
Hjerkinn Norway 44 J3
Hjo Sweden 45 K4
Hjørring Denmark 45 J4
Hjuvik Sweden 45 J4
Hka, Nam r. Myanmar 78 B3
Hkakabo Razi mt. Myanmar 78 B1
Hkok r. Myanmar 78 B3
Hkring Bum mt. Myanmar 78 B2
Hlabisa S. Africa 133 P5
Hlaing r. Myanmar 78 B4
Hlako Kangri mt. China see Lhagoi Kangri
Hlane Game Sanctuary nature res. Swaziland 133 P3
Hlatikulu Swaziland 133 P3
Hlazove Ukr. 43 O9
Hlegu Myanmar 78 B4
Hlinsko Czech Rep. 49 M6
Hlohlowane S. Africa 133 L5
Hlohovec Slovakia 49 O7
Hlotse Lesotho 133 M5
Hlučín Czech Rep. 49 P6
Hluhluwe S. Africa 133 Q5
Hluhluwe Game Reserve nature res. S. Africa 133 Q5
Hlukhiv Ukr. 41 E6
also spelt Glukhov
Hlung-Tan Myanmar 78 B3
Hlusha Belarus 43 J8
Hlusk Belarus 43 J9
Hlybokaye Belarus 42 I6
also spelt Glubokoye
Hnilec r. Slovakia 49 R7
Hnúšťa Slovakia 49 Q7
Ho Ghana 125 F5
Hoa Binh Vietnam 78 D3
Hoachanas Namibia 130 C4
Hoang Liên Sơn mts Vietnam 78 C3
Hoang Sa is S. China Sea see Paracel Islands
Hoanib watercourse Namibia 130 B3
Hoarusib watercourse Namibia 130 B3

▶Hobart Australia 147 E5
State capital of Tasmania.

Hobart U.S.A. 179 C5
Hobbs U.S.A. 179 B5
Hobbs Coast Antarctica 222 P1
Hobe Sound U.S.A. 175 D7
Hobhouse S. Africa 133 L6
Hobo Col. 198 C4
Hoboksar China 88 D2
Hobor China 85 G3
also known as Qahar Youyi Zhongqi
Hobot Xar Qi China see Xin Bulag
Hobro Denmark 45 J4
Hoburg Sweden 45 L4
Hoburgen pt Sweden 45 L4
Hobyo Somalia 128 F3
formerly spelt Obbia
Hochfeiler mt. Austria/Italy see Gran Pilastro
Hochfeld Namibia 130 C4
Hochgall mt. Austria/Italy see Collalto
Hochgolling mt. Austria 49 K8
Hochharz nat. park Germany 48 H4
Hô Chi Minh Vietnam see Ho Chi Minh City
Ho Chi Minh City Vietnam 79 D6
also known as Hô Chi Minh; formerly known as Saigon
Hochobir mt. Austria 49 L9
Hochschwab mt. Austria 49 M8
Hochtaunus nature res. Germany 48 F5
Hochtor mt. Austria 49 L8
Hocking r. U.S.A. 176 D6
Hôd reg. Mauritania 124 C2
Hodal India 96 C4
Hodda mt. Somalia 128 F2
Hodeidah Yemen 104 C5
also spelt Al Ḩudaydah
Hodein, Wâdi watercourse Egypt 121 G4
Hodgesville U.S.A. 176 E6
Hodgson Downs Australia 148 B2
Hodgson Downs Aboriginal Land res. Australia 148 B2
Hodh Ech Chargui admin. reg. Mauritania 124 D2
Hodh El Gharbi admin. reg. Mauritania 124 C2
Hódmezővásárhely Hungary 49 R9
Hodmo watercourse Somalia 128 E2
Hodna, Chott el salt l. Alg. 123 G2
Hodonín Czech Rep. 49 O7
Hodoşa Romania 58 F2
Hödrögö Mongolia 84 C1
Hodsons Peak Lesotho 133 N6
Hoek van Holland Neth. see Hook of Holland
Hoeryŏng N. Korea 82 C4
Hoeyang N. Korea 83 B5
Hof Germany 48 I5
Hoffman Mountain U.S.A. 177 L2
Hoffman's Cay i. Bahamas 186 D1
Hofmeyr S. Africa 133 J8
Höfn Iceland 44 [inset] D2
Hofors Sweden 45 L3
Hofsjökull ice cap Iceland 44 [inset] C2
Hofsós Iceland 44 [inset] C2
Hōfu Japan 91 B7
Hofüf Saudi Arabia see Al Hufūf
Höganäs Sweden 45 K4
Hogan Group is Australia 147 E4
Hogansburg U.S.A. 177 K1
Hoganthulla Creek r. Australia 149 E5
Hogg, Mount Canada 166 C2
▶Hoggar plat. Alg. 123 G5
also spelt Ahaggar
world [land cover] ➡ 18–19
Hog Island U.S.A. 177 J8
Högsby Sweden 45 L4
Hogste Breakulen mt. Norway 45 I3
Hogsty Reef Bahamas 187 E2
Högyész Hungary 49 P9
Hoh r. U.S.A. 180 A3
Hohenems Austria 48 G8
Hohenloher Ebene plain Germany 48 G6
Hohe Nock mt. Austria 49 L8
Hohensalza Poland see Inowrocław
Hohenwald U.S.A. 174 C5
Hohenwartetalsperre resr Germany 51 R2
Hoher Dachstein mt. Austria 49 K8
Hoh Ereg China see Wuchuan
Hoher Göll mt. Austria/Germany 49 K8
Hohe Rhön mts Germany 48 G5
Hohe Tauern mts Austria 49 J8
Hohe Tauern, Nationalpark nat. park Austria 49 J8
Hohe Venn moorland Belgium 51 M2
Hohhot China 85 F3
also spelt Huhhot; formerly spelt Huhehot
Hohoe Ghana 125 F5
Ho Hok Shan Hong Kong China 87 [inset]
Hōhoku Japan 91 B7
Hoh Xil Hu salt l. China 89 E5
Hoh Xil Shan mts China 80 D5
Hôi An Vietnam 78 E5
Hoima Uganda 128 A4
Hoisdorf Germany 48 H2
Hoisington U.S.A. 178 C4
Hoit Taria China 84 C4
Hôi Xuân Vietnam 78 D3
Hojagala Turkm. see Khodzha-Kala
Hojai India 97 G4
Hojambaz Turkm. see Khodzhambaz
Hōjo Japan 91 C8
Hökensås hills Sweden 45 K4
Hokio Beach N.Z. 152 J8
Hokitika N.Z. 153 E10
Hokkaidō i. Japan 81 O4
historically known as Ezo or Yezo
Hokkaidō pref. Japan 90 H3
Hokksund Norway 45 J4
Hokmābād Iran 100 D2
Hokonui N.Z. 153 C14
Hokonui Hills N.Z. 153 C13
Hokota Japan 91 G6
Hoktemberyan Armenia 107 F2
formerly spelt Oktemberyan
Hol Buskerud Norway 45 J3
Hol Nordland Norway 44 L1
Hola Kenya 128 C5
Holalkere India 94 C3
Holanda Bol. 200 D3
Holbæk Denmark 45 J5
Holberg Canada 166 D5
Holbrook Australia 147 E3
Holbrook U.S.A. 183 N7
Holcombe U.S.A. 172 B5
Holcombe Flowage resr U.S.A. 172 B5
Holden Canada 167 H4
Holden U.S.A. 183 L2
Holdenville U.S.A. 179 C5
Holdich Arg. 205 C7
Holdrege U.S.A. 178 C3
Hole Narsipur India 94 C3
Holgate watercourse S. Africa 132 A5
Holgate U.S.A. 176 A4
Holguín Cuba 186 D2
Holič Slovakia 49 O7
Höljes Sweden 45 K3
Hollabrunn Austria 49 N7
Holland country Europe see Netherlands
Holland MI U.S.A. 172 G8
Holland NY U.S.A. 176 G3
Hollandale U.S.A. 175 B5
Hollandia Indon. see Jayapura
Hollands Diep est. Neth. 48 B4
Hollick-Kenyon Peninsula Antarctica 222 T2
Hollick-Kenyon Plateau Antarctica 222 Q1
Hollis U.S.A. 179 C5
Hollister U.S.A. 182 C5
Hollóháza Hungary 49 S7
Hollola Fin. 45 N3
Hollum Neth. 48 C2
Holly U.S.A. 173 J8
Holly Springs U.S.A. 174 B5

index H

Hollywood U.S.A. 175 D7
Holm Norway 44 K2
Holman Canada 165 H2
also known as Uluqsaqtuuq
Holmdene S. Africa 133 N3
Holmes Reef Australia 149 E3
Holmestrand Norway 45 J4
Holmgard Rus. Fed. see Velikiy Novgorod
Holm Ø i. Greenland see Kiatassuaq
Holmöarna naturreservat nature res. Sweden 44 M3
Holmön i. Sweden 44 M3
Holmsund Sweden 44 M3
Holmudden pt Sweden 45 L4
Holod r. Romania 58 D2
Holon Israel 108 F5
also spelt Kholon
Holoog Namibia 130 C5
Holothuria Banks reef Australia 150 D2
Holovets'ko Ukr. 49 T6
Holroyd r. Australia 149 D2
Holroyd Bluff hills Australia 151 C5
Holspruit r. S. Africa 133 M4
Holstebro Denmark 45 J4
Holsted Denmark 45 J5
Holstein U.S.A. 178 D3
Holsteinsborg Greenland see Sisimiut
Holston r. U.S.A. 176 B9
Holston Lake U.S.A. 176 D9
Holt U.S.A. 173 I8
Holton KS U.S.A. 178 D4
Holton MI U.S.A. 172 G7
Holtville U.S.A. 183 I9
Holtwood U.S.A. 177 I6
Holy Cross, Mount of the U.S.A. 180 F5
Holyhead U.K. 47 H10
also known as Caergybi
Holy Island England U.K. 46 K8
also known as Lindisfarne
Holy Island Wales U.K. 47 H10
Holyoke CO U.S.A. 178 B3
Holyoke MA U.S.A. 177 M3
Holy See Europe see Vatican City
Holzkirchen Germany 48 I8
Holzminden Germany 48 G4
Hom watercourse Namibia 132 C5
Homa Bay Kenya 128 B5
Homalin Myanmar 78 A2
Homathko r. Canada 166 E5
Homāyūnshahr Iran see Khomeynīshahr
Homberg (Efze) Germany 48 G4
Hombetsu Japan see Honbetsu
Hombori Mali 125 E3
Hombre Muerto, Salar del salt flat Arg. 204 D2
Homburg Germany 48 E6
Home Bay Canada 165 M3
Home Hill Australia 149 E3
Home Point N.Z. 152 I3
Homer AK U.S.A. 164 D4
Homer GA U.S.A. 174 D5
Homer LA U.S.A. 179 D5
Homer MI U.S.A. 173 I8
Homer City U.S.A. 176 F5
Homerville U.S.A. 175 D6
Homestead Australia 149 E4
Homestead U.S.A. 175 D7
Homewood N.Z. 152 J9
Homewood U.S.A. 175 C5
Homnelvik Norway 44 J3
Homnabad India 94 C2
Homocea Romania 58 I2
Homodji well Niger 125 I2
Homoine Moz. 131 G4
Homs Libya see Al Khums
Homs Syria 109 H3
also spelt Ḥimṣ; historically known as Emesa
Homyel' Belarus 43 M9
also spelt Gomel'
Homyel Oblast admin. div. Belarus see Homyel'skaya Voblasts'
Homyel'skaya Voblasts' admin. div. Belarus 43 K9
English form Homyel Oblast or Gomel Oblast; also known as Gomel'skaya Oblast'
Honaker U.S.A. 176 D8
Honan prov. China see Henan
Honavar India 94 B3
Honaz Turkey 59 K11
historically known as Colossae
Hon Bai Canh i. Vietnam 79 D6
Honbetsu Japan 90 H3
also spelt Hombetsu
Hon Chông Vietnam 79 D6
Hon Chuôi i. Vietnam 79 D6
Honda Col. 198 C3
Honda India 97 E5
Honda, Bahía b. Col. 198 C1
Honda Bay Phil. 74 A4
Hondapa India 95 E1
Hondeblaf r. S. Africa 133 I7
Hondeklipbaai S. Africa 132 B7
Hondo r. Belize/Mex. 185 H5
Hondo Japan 91 B8
Hondo NM U.S.A. 181 F6
Hondo TX U.S.A. 179 C6
Hondo r. U.S.A. 181 F6
▶Honduras country Central America 186 B4
northamerica [countries] ➡ 158–159
Honduras, Gulf of Belize/Hond. 186 B3
Hønefoss Norway 45 J3
Honesdale U.S.A. 177 J4
Honey Brook U.S.A. 177 J5
Honey Lake U.S.A. 182 D1
Honfleur France 50 G3
Hông, Sông r. Vietnam see Red River
Hong'an China 87 E2
Hongch'ŏn S. Korea 83 B5
Hongde China 85 E4
Hông Gai Vietnam 78 D3
Honggouzi China 88 E4
Honggu China 84 D4
formerly known as Yaojie
Honghai Wan b. China 87 E4
Honghe China 86 B4
also known as Yisa
Hong He r. China 87 E1
Honghu China 87 E2
formerly known as Xindi
Hong Hu l. China 87 E2
Hongjialou China see Licheng
Hongjiang China 87 D3
Hongjiang China see Wangcang
▶Hong Kong Hong Kong China 87 [inset]
also known as Hsiang Kang or Xianggang
world [cities] ➡ 24–25
Hong Kong special admin. reg. China 87 [inset]
long form Xianggang Tebie Xingzhengqu
Hong Kong Harbour sea chan. Hong Kong China 87 [inset]
also known as Victoria Harbour
Hong Kong Island Hong Kong China 87 [inset]
also known as Hsiang Chang
Hongliu r. China 85 F4
Hongliu Daquan well China 84 C3
Hongliuwan China see Aksay
Hongliuyuan Gansu China 84 B3
Hongliuyuan Gansu China 84 D4
Hông Ngự Vietnam 79 D6
Hongor Mongolia 85 G2
Hongqiao China see Qidong
Hongqizhen China see Tongshi
Hongshan China 86 A2
formerly known as Mabating
Hongshui He r. China 87 D4
Hongtong China 85 F4
Hongū Japan 91 D8
Honguedo, Détroit d' sea chan. Canada 169 H3
Hongwansi China see Sunan
Hongwŏn N. Korea 83 B4
Hongyuan China 86 B1
also known as Qiongxi
Hongze China 87 F1
also known as Gaoliangjian
Hongze Hu l. China 87 F1

▶Honiara Solomon Is 145 E2
Capital of the Solomon Islands.

Honiton U.K. 47 I13
Honjō Japan 90 G5
Honkajoki Fin. 45 M3
Hon Khoai i. Vietnam 79 D6
Hon Mê i. Vietnam 78 D4
Hon Minh Hoa i. Vietnam 79 D6
Honnali India 94 B3
Honningsvåg Norway 44 N1
Honokaa U.S.A. 181 [inset] Z1

▶Honolulu U.S.A. 181 [inset] Z1
State capital of Hawaii.

Honor U.S.A. 172 G6
Hon Rai i. Vietnam 79 D6

▶Honshū i. Japan 91 F6
3rd largest island in Asia and 7th in the world.
asia [landscapes] ➡ 62–63

Honwad India 94 B2
Hood r. Canada 167 I1
Hood, Mount vol. U.S.A. 180 B3
Hood Point Australia 151 B7
Hood River U.S.A. 180 B3
Hoogeveen Neth. 48 D3
Hoogezand-Sappemeer Neth. 48 D2
Hooghly r. mouth India see Hugli
Hooker U.S.A. 178 B4
Hooker Creek Aboriginal Land res. Australia 148 A3
Hook Head Rep. of Ireland 47 F11
Hook of Holland Neth. 48 B4
also known as Hoek van Holland
Hook Reef Australia 149 F3
Hoolt Mongolia 84 D2
Hoonah U.S.A. 164 F4
Hoopa Valley Indian Reservation res. U.S.A. 180 B4
Hooper Bay U.S.A. 164 C3
Hooper Island U.S.A. 177 I7
Hoopstad S. Africa 133 J4
Hoorn Neth. 48 C3
Hoorn, Îles de is Wallis and Futuna Is see Futuna Islands
Hoorn Islands Wallis and Futuna Is see Futuna Islands
Hoosick U.S.A. 177 L3
Hoover Dam U.S.A. 183 J5
Hoover Memorial Reservoir U.S.A. 176 C5
Höövör Mongolia 84 D2
Hóp lag. Iceland 44 [inset] B2
Hopa Turkey 107 E2
Hope Canada 166 F5
Hope N.Z. 152 H9
Hope r. N.Z. 153 G10
Hope U.S.A. 179 D5
Hope, Lake salt flat S.A. Australia 146 C2
Hope, Lake salt flat W.A. Australia 151 C7
Hope, Point U.S.A. 164 C3
Hopedale Canada 169 I2
Hopefield S. Africa 132 C10
Hopei prov. China see Hebei
Hopelchén Mex. 185 H5
Hope Mountains Canada 169 I2
Hopen i. Svalbard 38 C2
Hopes Advance, Baie b. Canada 169 G1
Hopes Advance, Cap c. Canada 165 M3
Hopes Advance Bay Canada see Aupaluk
Hopetoun Vic. Australia 147 D3
Hopetoun W.A. Australia 151 C7
Hopetown S. Africa 132 I6
Hope Vale Aboriginal Reserve Australia 149 E2
Hope Valley U.S.A. 177 N4
Hopewell U.S.A. 177 H8
Hopewell Islands Canada 168 E1
Hopi Indian Reservation res. U.S.A. 183 N6
Hopin Myanmar 78 B2
Hopkins r. Australia 147 D4
Hopkins, Lake salt flat Australia 150 E5
Hopkinsville U.S.A. 174 C4
Hopland U.S.A. 182 A3
Hopong Myanmar 78 B3
Hopseidet Norway 44 N1
Hoquiam U.S.A. 180 B3
Hor Qinghai China 84 D5
Hor Xizang China 89 C6
also spelt Huoer
Horadiz Azer. 107 F3
also spelt Goradiz
Horasan Turkey 107 E2
Horažďovice Czech Rep. 49 K6
Horb am Neckar Germany 48 F7
Hörby Sweden 45 K5
Horcajo de Santiago Spain 55 I5
Horcasitas Mex. 184 D2
Horcón hill Spain 54 G6
Horcones r. Arg. 204 D2
Horda Norway 45 I4
Hordaland county Norway 45 I3
Horezu Romania 58 E3
Horgo Mongolia 84 C1
Horgoš Vojvodina, Srbija Yugo. 58 A2
Hörh Uul mts Mongolia 85 E3
Horia Romania 58 J3
Horicon U.S.A. 172 E7
Horinger China 85 F3
Horiult Mongolia 84 D2

▶Horizon Deep sea feature S. Pacific Ocean 220 G7
2nd deepest point in the world (Tonga Trench).

Horki Belarus 43 L7
also spelt Gorki
Horlick Mountains Antarctica 223 Q1
Horlivka Ukr. 41 F6
also spelt Gorlovka
Hormak Iran 101 E4
Hormoz i. Iran 100 D5
Hormoz, Kūh-e mt. Iran 100 C5
Hormozgan prov. Iran 100 D5
Hormūd-e Bāgh Iran 100 C5
Hormūd-e Mīr Khūnd Iran 100 C5
Hormuz, Strait of Iran/Oman 105 G2
Horn Austria 49 M7
Horn r. Canada 167 G2
Horn c. Iceland 44 [inset] B2
also known as Nord Kap

▶Horn, Cape Chile 205 D9
Most southerly point of South America. Also known as Hornos, Cabo de.

Hornád r. Slovakia 49 R7
also spelt Hernád (Hungary)
Hornavan l. Sweden 44 L2
Hornbrook U.S.A. 180 B4
Horndal Sweden 45 L3
Horne, Îles de is Wallis and Futuna Is see Futuna Islands
Hörnefors Sweden 44 L3
Hornell U.S.A. 176 H3
Hornepayne Canada 168 C3
Hornillos Mex. 184 C3
Hornindal Norway 45 I3
Horn Island U.S.A. 175 B6
Hornkranz Namibia 130 C4
Horn Mountains Canada 166 F2
Hornos, Cabo de c. Chile see Horn, Cape
Hornos, Parque Nacional de nat. park Chile 205 D9
Hornoy-le-Bourg France 51 H3
Horn Peak Canada 166 D2
Hornsby Australia 147 F3
Hornsea U.K. 47 L10
Hornslandet pen. Sweden 45 L3
Hornslet Denmark 45 J4
Hornstrandir reg. Iceland 44 [inset] B2
Horodenka Ukr. 41 C6
also spelt Gorodenka
Horodnya Ukr. 41 D6
Horodok Ukr. 41 C6
also spelt Gorodok
Horokanai Japan 90 H2
Horo Shan mts China 88 C3
Horoshiri-dake mt. Japan 90 H3
Horqin Shadi reg. China 85 I3
Horqin Youyi Qianqi China see Ulanhot
Horqin Zuoyi Houqi China see Ganjig
Horqin Zuoyi Zhongqi China see Baokang
Horqueta Para. 201 F5
Horru China 89 E6
Horse Creek r. U.S.A. 180 F4
Horsefly Canada 166 F4
Horseheads U.S.A. 177 I3
Horse Lake U.S.A. 182 D1
Horsens Denmark 45 J5
Horseshoe Bend Australia 148 B5
Horseshoe Reservoir U.S.A. 183 M7
Horsham Australia 147 D4
Horsham U.K. 47 L12
Horten Norway 45 J4
Hortobágyi nat. park Hungary 49 S8
Horton r. Canada 164 G3
Horwood Lake Canada 168 D3
Ho Sai Hu l. China 84 B5
Hosa'ina Eth. 128 C3
Hosdurga India 94 C3
Hose, Pegunungan mts Sarawak Malaysia 77 F2
Hosenofu well Libya 120 D4
Ḥoseynābād Iran 100 A3
Ḥoseynīyeh Iran 100 B4
Hoshab Pak. 101 E5
Hoshangabad India 96 C5
Hoshiarpur India 96 B3
Hōsh'īsa Egypt 108 B7
Höshööt Arhangay Mongolia 84 D1
Höshööt Bayan-Ölgiy Mongolia 84 A1
Hoskins P.N.G. 145 E2
Hoşköy Turkey 58 I8
Hospet India 94 C3
Hosséré Vokre mt. Cameroon 125 I4
Hosszúpályi Hungary 49 S8
Hoste, Isla i. Chile 205 C9
Hosur India 94 C3
Hotahudo East Timor see Hatohud
Hotan China 89 C4
formerly spelt Khotan
Hotan He watercourse China 88 C3
Hotazel S. Africa 132 G4
Hot Creek r. U.S.A. 183 H3
Hot Creek Range mts U.S.A. 183 H3
Hotham r. Australia 151 B7
Hotham, Cape Australia 148 A2
Hoting Sweden 44 L2
Hot Springs AR U.S.A. 179 D5
Hot Springs U.S.A. see Truth or Consequences
Hot Springs SD U.S.A. 178 B3
Hot Sulphur Springs U.S.A. 180 F4
Hottah Lake Canada 167 G1
Hottentots-Holland Nature Reserve S. Africa 132 C10
Hottentots Point Namibia 130 B5
Houaïlu New Caledonia 145 F4
Houdan France 50 H4
Houffalize Belgium 51 L2
Hougang Sing. 76 [inset]
Houghton MI U.S.A. 172 E3
Houghton NY U.S.A. 176 G3
Houghton Lake U.S.A. 173 I6
Houghton Lake l. U.S.A. 173 I6
Houghton le Spring U.K. 47 K9
Houie Moc, Phou mt. Laos 78 C3
Houlton U.S.A. 174 H2
Houma China 85 F5
Houma U.S.A. 175 B6
Houmen China 87 E4
Houmt Souk Tunisia 123 H2
Houndé Burkina 124 E4
Hourtin et de Carcans, Étang d' l. France 50 E7
Housatonic U.S.A. 177 L3
Housatonic r. U.S.A. 177 L4
House Range mts U.S.A. 183 K2
Housesteads tourist site U.K. 47 J8
historically known as Vercovicium
Houston Canada 166 E4
Houston MN U.S.A. 172 B7
Houston MO U.S.A. 174 B4
Houston MS U.S.A. 175 B5
Houston TX U.S.A. 179 D6
Hout Bay S. Africa 132 C11
Houtkraal S. Africa 132 I7
Houtman Abrolhos is Australia 151 A6
Houtskär Fin. 42 C1
Houwater S. Africa 132 H7
Houxia China 88 D3
Houzhai China see Nan'ao
Hov Denmark 45 J5
Hov Norway 45 J3
Hova Sweden 45 K4
Hovd Hovd Mongolia 84 A2
also known as Jargalant
Hovd Övörhangay Mongolia 84 D2
Hovd prov. Mongolia 84 B2
Hovden park Norway 45 I4
Hovd Gol r. Mongolia 84 B1
Hoveyzeh Iran 107 G5
Hovland U.S.A. 172 D3
Hovmantorp Sweden 45 K4
Hövsgöl Mongolia 85 F3
Hövsgöl prov. Mongolia 84 D1
Hövsgöl Nuur l. Mongolia 84 D1
Hövüün Mongolia 84 D3
Howa, Ouadi watercourse Chad/Sudan 120 D6
Howakil Bay Eritrea 104 C5
Howakil Island Eritrea 104 C5
Howar, Wadi watercourse Sudan 120 E5
Howard Australia 149 G5
Howard KS U.S.A. 178 C4
Howard SD U.S.A. 178 C2
Howard WI U.S.A. 172 E6
Howard City U.S.A. 172 H7
Howard Island Australia 148 B2
Howard Springs Australia 148 A2
Howden U.K. 47 L10
Howe, Cape Australia 147 F4
Howe, Mount Antarctica 223 O1
Howell U.S.A. 173 J8
Howes U.S.A. 180 G3
Howick S. Africa 133 O6
Howitt, Lake salt flat Australia 146 C1
Howland U.S.A. 174 G2

▶Howland Island N. Pacific Ocean 145 H1
United States Unincorporated Territory.
oceania [countries] ➡ 138–139

Howlong Australia 147 E3
Howrah India see Haora
Ḥowz well Iran 100 D3
Ḥowz-e Panj Iran 100 D4
Ḥowz-e Panj waterhole Iran 100 C3
Ḥowz-i-Khan well Iran 100 D3
Howz i-Mian i-Tak Iran 100 C3
Hoxie U.S.A. 178 B4
Höxter Germany 48 G4
Hoxtolgay China 88 D2
Hoxud China 88 D3
Hoy i. U.K. 46 I5
Høyanger Norway 45 I3
Hoyerswerda Germany 49 L4
Høylandet Norway 44 K2
Hoyle Canada 173 M2
Höytiäinen l. Fin. 44 O3
Hoyt Peak U.S.A. 183 M1
Hozat Turkey 107 D3
Hozha Belarus 42 E8
Hpa-an Myanmar see Pa-an
Hradec Králové Czech Rep. 49 M5
Hradiště hill Czech Rep. 49 K5
Hradyzanka Belarus 43 J8
Hrasnica Bos.-Herz. 56 K5
Hraun Iceland 44 [inset] B2
Hraun slope Iceland 44 [inset] D2
Hrawzhyshki Belarus 42 G7
Hrazdan Armenia 107 F2
also spelt Razdan; formerly known as Akhta
Hrazený hill Czech Rep. 49 L5
Hrebinka Ukr. 41 E6
also spelt Grebyonka; formerly known as Grebenkovskiy
Hrem"yach Ukr. 43 O9
Hristós Greece see Christos
Hrodna Belarus 42 E8
also known as Gardinas; also spelt Grodno
Hrodna Oblast admin. div. Belarus see Hrodzyenskaya Voblasts'
Hrodzyenskaya Voblasts' admin. div. Belarus 42 G8
English form Hrodna Oblast or Grodno Oblast; also known as Grodnenskaya Oblast'
Hron r. Slovakia 49 P8
Hrvatska country Europe see Croatia
Hrvatska Kostajnica Croatia 56 I3
Hsenwi Myanmar 78 B3
Hsiang Chang i. Hong Kong China see Hong Kong Island
Hsiang Kang Hong Kong China see Hong Kong
Hsi-hseng Myanmar 78 B3
Hsin, Nam r. Myanmar 78 B3
Hsin-chia-p'o country Asia see Singapore
Hsin-chia-p'o Sing. see Singapore
Hsinchu Taiwan 87 G3
also spelt Xinzhu
Hsinking China see Changchun
Hsinying Taiwan 87 G4
also spelt Xinying
Hsipaw Myanmar 78 B3
Hsi-sha Ch'un-tao is S. China Sea see Paracel Islands
Hsiyüp'ing Yü i. Taiwan 87 F4
Hsüeh Shan mt. Taiwan 87 G3
Hua'an China 87 F3
also known as Huafeng
Huab watercourse Namibia 130 B4
Huacaibamba Peru 200 A2
Huacaraje Bol. 201 E3
Huacaya Bol. 201 E5
Huacheng China 87 E3
Huachi Bol. 201 E3
Huachi China 85 F4
also known as Rouyuan; formerly known as Rouyuanchengzi
Huachinera Mex. 184 C2
Huacho Peru 200 A2
Huachón Peru 200 B2
Huachuan China 82 C3
also known as Yuelai
Huacrachuco Peru 200 A2
Huacullani Peru 200 C4
Huade China 85 G3
Huadian China 82 B4
Huadu China 87 E4
formerly known as Huaxian or Xinhua
Huafeng China see Hua'an
Huahaizi China 84 B4
Hua Hin Thai. 79 B5
Huai'an Hebei China 85 G3
also known as Chaigoubu
Huai'an Jiangsu China 87 F1
Huaibei China 87 F1
Huaibin China 87 E1
formerly known as Wulongji
Huaicheng China see Huaiji
Huaide China see Gongzhuling
Huaidian China see Shenqiu
Huai Had National Park Thai. 78 D4
Huai He r. China 87 F1
Huaihua China 87 D3
also known as Yushuwan
Huaiji China 87 E4
also known as Huaicheng
Huai-kha-khaeng Wildlife Reserve nature res. Thai. 79 B5
Huailai China 85 G3
also known as Shacheng
Huai Luang r. Thai. 78 C4
Huainan China 87 F1
Huaining China 87 F2
also known as Shipai
Huairen China 85 G4
Huairou China 85 H3
Huai Samran r. Thai. 79 D5
Huaiyang China 87 E1
Huaiyin Jiangsu China 87 F1
also known as Wangying
Huaiyin Jiangsu China 87 F1
formerly known as Qingjiang
Huaiyuan Anhui China 87 F1
Huaiyuan Guangxi China 87 D3
Huajialing China 84 E5
Huajuápan de León Mex. 185 F5
Huaki Indon. 75 C4
Hualahuises Mex. 185 F3
Hualapai Indian Reservation res. U.S.A. 183 K6
Hualapai Peak U.S.A. 183 K6
Hualfín Arg. 204 D2
Hualien Taiwan 87 G3
Hualla Peru 200 B3
Huallaga r. Peru 198 C6
Hualong China 84 D4
also known as Bayan
Huamachuco Peru 200 A1
Huamani Peru 200 B3
Huambo Angola 127 B8
formerly known as Nova Lisboa
Huambo prov. Angola 127 B8
Huams watercourse Namibia 132 B2
Huanan China 82 C3
Huancabamba r. Peru 198 B6
Huancache, Sierra mts Arg. 205 C6
Huancapi Peru 200 B3
Huancavelica Peru 200 B3
Huancavelica dept Peru 200 B3
Huancayo Peru 200 B3
Huancheng China see Huanxian
Huangbei China 87 E3
Huangcaoba China see Xingyi
Huangchuan China 87 E1
Huanggang China 87 E2
also known as Huangzhou
Huang He r. China see Yellow River
Huanghe Kou r. mouth China 85 H4
Huanghua China 85 H4
Huangjiajian China 87 G1
Huangling China 85 F5
also known as Qiaoshan
Huangliu China 87 D5
Huanglong China 85 F5
also known as Shipu
Huanglongsi China see Kaifeng
Huangmao Jian mt. China 87 F3
Huangmei China 87 E2
Huangnihe China 82 B4
Huangpi China 87 E2
Huangping China 87 C3
also known as Xinzhou
Huangqi China 87 F3
Huangshan China 87 F2
also known as Tunxi
Huang Shan mts China 87 F2
Huangshengguan China 86 B1
Huangshi China 87 E2
Huang Shui r. China 84 D4
Huangtu Gaoyuan plat. China 85 E4
Huangxian China 85 I4
Huangyan China 87 G2
Huangyangzhen China 84 D4
Huangyuan China 84 D4
Huangzhong China 84 D4
also known as Lushar
Huangzhou China see Huanggang
Huaning China 86 B3
also known as Ningzhou
Huanjiang China 87 D3
also known as Si'en
Huan Jiang r. China 85 E4
Huanren China 82 B4
Huanshan China see Yuhuan
Huanta Peru 200 B3
Huantai China 85 H4
also known as Suozhen
Huánuco Peru 200 A2
Huánuco dept Peru 200 A2
Huanuhuanu Peru 200 B3
Huanuni Bol. 200 D4
Huanxian China 85 E4
also known as Huancheng
Huaping China 86 B3
also known as Zhongxin
Huap'ing Yü i. Taiwan 87 G3
Huar Bol. 200 D4
Huaral Peru 200 A2
Huaráz Peru 200 A2
Huari Peru 200 A2
Huariaca Peru 200 A2
Huarmey Peru 200 A2
Huarochiri Peru 200 A3
Huaron Peru 200 A2
Huarong China 87 E2
Huasaga r. Peru 198 B5
Huascarán, Parque Nacional nat. park Peru 200 A2
Huasco Chile 204 C3
Hua Shan mt. China 87 D1
Huashaoying China 85 G3
Huashixia China 84 C5
also known as Zogainrawar
Huashugou China see Jingtieshan
Huatabampo Mex. 184 C3
Huatusco Mex. 185 F5
Huauchinango Mex. 185 F4
Huaura, Islas de is Peru 200 A2
Hautla Mex. 185 F5
Huaxian China see Huadu
Huaxian Henan China 85 G5
also known as Daokou
Huaxian Shaanxi China 87 D1
Huayacocotla Mex. 185 F4
Huayang China see Jixi
Huaylas Peru 200 A2
Huayuan China see Xiaochang
Huayuan China 87 D2
Huazangsi China see Tianzhu
Huazhaizi China 84 D4
Huazhou China 87 D4
Hubbard, Mount Canada/U.S.A. 166 B2
Hubbard, Pointe pt Canada 169 H1
Hubbard Lake U.S.A. 173 J6
Hubbart Point Canada 167 M3
Hubei prov. China 87 E2
English form Hupeh
Hubli India 94 B3
Hucal Arg. 204 D5
Huch'ang N. Korea 82 B4
Hückelhoven Germany 48 D4
Hudb Humar mts Saudi Arabia 104 B2
Huddersfield U.K. 47 K10
Huder China 85 I1
Hudiksvall Sweden 45 L3
Hudson MA U.S.A. 177 N3
Hudson MD U.S.A. 177 I7
Hudson MI U.S.A. 173 I9
Hudson NH U.S.A. 177 N3
Hudson NY U.S.A. 177 L3
Hudson, Baie d' sea Canada see Hudson Bay
Hudson, Cerro mt. Chile 205 B7
Hudson, Détroit d' strait Canada see Hudson Strait
Hudson Bay Canada 167 K4
Hudson Bay sea Canada 165 K4
also known as Hudson, Baie d'
Hudson Falls U.S.A. 177 L2
Hudson Island Tuvalu see Nanumanga
Hudson Land reg. Greenland 165 Q2
Hudson's Hope Canada 166 F3
Hudson Strait Canada 165 L3
also known as Hudson, Détroit d'
Huê Vietnam 78 D4
Huebra r. Spain 54 E4
Huechucuicui, Punta pt Chile 205 B6
Huedin Romania 58 E2
Huehuetán Mex. 185 G6
Huehuetenango Guat. 185 H6
Huehueto, Cerro mt. Mex. 184 D3
Huejuquilla Mex. 184 E4
Huejutla Mex. 185 F4
Huelgoat France 50 C4
Huelma Spain 55 H7
Huelva Spain 54 E7
Huelva r. Spain 54 E7
Huentelauquén Chile 204 C3
Huépac Mex. 184 C2
Huércal-Overa Spain 55 J7
Huerfano r. U.S.A. 181 F5
Huertecillas Mex. 185 E3
Huerva r. Spain 55 K3
Huesca Spain 55 K2
Huéscar Spain 55 I7
Huétamo Mex. 185 E5
Huete Spain 55 I4
Hueytown U.S.A. 175 C5
Huftarøy i. Norway 46 R3
Hugeilig l. Sudan 126 E2
Hugh watercourse Australia 148 B5
Hughenden Australia 149 E4
Hughes Australia 146 A2
Hughes r. Canada 167 K3
Hughes Bay Antarctica 222 T2
Hughesville MD U.S.A. 177 I7
Hughesville PA U.S.A. 177 I4
Hughson U.S.A. 182 D4
Hugli r. mouth India 97 E5
also spelt Hooghly
Hugli-Chunchura India 97 F5
Hugo CO U.S.A. 178 B4
Hugo OK U.S.A. 179 D5
Hugoton U.S.A. 178 B4
Huhehot China see Hohhot
Huhhot China see Hohhot
Huhucunya Venez. 199 E3
Huhudi S. Africa 133 I3
Huhus Fin. 44 O3
Hui'an China 87 F3
also known as Luocheng
Hui'anpu China 85 E4
Huiarau Range mts N.Z. 152 K6
Huib-Hoch Plateau Namibia 130 C5
Huichang China 87 E3
also known as Xiangjiang
Huichapán Mex. 185 F4
Huicheng China see Shexian
Huicheng China see Huilai
Huich'ŏn N. Korea 83 B4
Huidong Guangdong China 87 E4
also known as Pingshan
Huidong Sichuan China 86 B3
Huifa r. China 82 B4
Huihe China 85 H1
Huiji r. China 87 E1
Huila prov. Angola 127 B8
Huila dept Col. 198 C4
Huila, Nevado de vol. Col. 198 C4
Huilai China 87 F4
also known as Huicheng
Huila Plateau Angola 127 B8
Huili China 86 B3
Huilongzhen China see Qidong
Huimanguillo Mex. 185 G5
Huimin China 85 H4
Huinahuaca Arg. 200 D5
Huiñaimarca, Lago de l. Bol./Peru 200 C4
Huinan China 82 B4
also known as Chaoyang
Huinan China see Nanhui
Huinca Renancó Arg. 204 D4
Huining China 84 E5
also known as Huishi
Huishi China see Huining
Huishui China 86 C3
also known as Heping
Huisne r. France 50 G4
Huiten Nur l. China 89 E5
Huitong China 87 D3
also known as Lincheng
Huittinen Fin. 45 M3
Huixian Gansu China 86 C1
Huixian Henan China 85 G5
Huixtla Mex. 185 G6
Huiyang China see Huizhou
Huize China 86 B3
also known as Zhongping
Huizhou China 87 E4
also known as Huiyang
Hujirt Arhangay Mongolia 84 D1
Hujirt Övörhangay Mongolia 84 D2
Hujirt Töv Mongolia 84 E2
Hukanui N.Z. 152 J8
Hukawng Valley Myanmar 78 B2
Hukou China 87 F2
also known as Shuangzhong
Hukuntsi Botswana 130 D4
Hulan China 82 B3
Hulan r. China 82 B3
Hulan Ergi China 85 I2
Ḥulayfah Saudi Arabia 104 C2
Ḥulayḥilah well Syria 109 J3
Hulbert U.S.A. 173 H4
Hulbert Lake U.S.A. 173 H4
Hulen U.S.A. 176 B9
Hulilao China see Dabu
Hulin China 82 D3
Hull Canada 168 F4
Hull U.K. see Kingston upon Hull
Hull U.S.A. 177 O3
Hull Island Kiribati see Orona
Hullo Estonia 42 E3
Hultsfred Sweden 45 K4
Hulu r. China 85 F5
Huludao China 85 I3
Hulun China see Hailar
Hulun Nur l. China 85 H1
Ḥulwān Egypt see Ḥelwān
Hulyaypole Ukr. 41 F7
Huma China 82 B2
Huma r. China 82 B2
Humacao Puerto Rico 187 G3
Humaita Bol. 200 D2
Humaitá Brazil 201 E1
Humaitá Para. 201 F6
Humansdorp S. Africa 133 I11
Humay Peru 200 B3
Humaym well U.A.E. 105 F3
Humayyān, Jabal hill Saudi Arabia 104 D2
Humbe Angola 127 B9
Humbe, Serra do mts Angola 127 B8
Humber, Mouth of the U.K. 47 M10
Humberside airport U.K. 47 L10
Humberstone Chile 200 C5
Humberto de Campos Brazil 202 D2
Humboldt Canada 167 J4
Humboldt AZ U.S.A. 183 L7
Humboldt NE U.S.A. 178 D3
Humboldt NV U.S.A. 182 F1
Humboldt TN U.S.A. 174 B5
Humboldt r. U.S.A. 182 F1
Humboldt, Mont mt. New Caledonia 145 F4
Humboldt Bay U.S.A. 180 A4
Humboldt Gletscher glacier Greenland see Sermersuaq
Humboldt Lake U.S.A. 182 F1
Humboldt Mountain mts N.Z. 153 C12
Humboldt Range mts U.S.A. 182 F1
Humboldt Salt Marsh U.S.A. 182 G2
Hume r. Canada 166 D1
Humeburn Australia 147 E1
Humeda plain Arg. 204 E5
Hu Men sea chan. China 87 E4
Humenné Slovakia 49 S7
Hume Reservoir Australia 147 E3
Humina reg. Bos.-Herz. 56 J5
Humka, Gora hill Croatia 56 I3
Humos, Cabo c. Chile 204 B4
Humpata Angola 127 B8
Humphrey Island atoll Cook Is see Manihiki
Humphreys, Mount U.S.A. 182 F4
Humphreys Peak U.S.A. 183 M6
Humpolec Czech Rep. 49 M6
Humppila Fin. 45 M3
Humpty Doo Australia 148 A2

Hun r. China 85 I3
Hūn Libya 120 B2
Húnaflói b. Iceland 44 [inset] B2
Hunan prov. China 87 D3
Hunchun China 82 C4
Hunchun r. China 82 C4
Hundorp Norway 45 J3
Hundred U.S.A. 176 E6
Hunedoara Romania 58 D3
Hünfeld Germany 48 G5
▶Hungary country Europe 49 P8
known as Magyar Köztársaság in Hungarian
europe [countries] ▶ 32–35
Hungerford Australia 147 E2
Hungerford U.K. 47 K12
Hung Fa Leng hill Hong Kong China see Robin's Nest
Hüngiy Gol r. Mongolia 84 B1
Hŭngnam N. Korea 83 B5
Hungry Horse Reservoir U.S.A. 180 D2
Hung Shui Kiu Hong Kong China 87 [inset]
Hungund India 94 C2
Hunissout Pan salt pan S. Africa 132 D7
Hunjiang China see Baishan
Hun Jiang r. China 82 B4
Hunnebostrand Sweden 45 J4
Huns Mountains Namibia 132 B4
Hunstanton U.K. 47 M11
Hunsur India 94 C3
Hunta Canada 173 L1
Hunte r. Germany 48 F2
Hunter r. Australia 147 F3
Hunter N.Z. 153 F12
Hunter r. N.Z. 153 D12
Hunterganj India 97 E4
Hunter Island Australia 147 E5
Hunter Island Canada 166 D5
Hunter Island S. Pacific Ocean 145 G4
Hunter Islands Australia 147 E5
Hunter Mountains N.Z. 153 B13
Hunter's Bay Myanmar 78 A4
Huntingdon U.K. 47 L11
Huntingdon PA U.S.A. 176 H5
Huntingdon TN U.S.A. 174 B4
Huntington IN U.S.A. 174 C3
Huntington UT U.S.A. 183 N2
Huntington WV U.S.A. 176 C7
Huntington Beach U.S.A. 182 F8
Huntington Creek r. U.S.A. 183 I1
Huntly N.Z. 152 J5
Huntly U.K. 46 J6
Hunt Mountain U.S.A. 180 F3
Hunt Peninsula Australia 146 C2
Huntsville Canada 168 E4
Huntsville AL U.S.A. 174 C5
Huntsville AR U.S.A. 179 D4
Huntsville MO U.S.A. 178 D4
Huntsville TX U.S.A. 179 D6
Hunucmá Mex. 185 H4
Hunyani r. Moz./Zimbabwe see Manyame
Hunyuan China 85 G4
Hunza Jammu and Kashmir 96 B1
Hunza reg. Jammu and Kashmir 96 B1
Hunza r. Pak. 101 H3
Hunze r. Neth. 48 D2
Huocheng China 88 C2
also known as Shuiding
Huoer China see Hor
Huojia China 85 G5
Huolin r. China 85 J2
Huolongmen China 82 B2
Huolu China see Luquan
Hương Thuy Vietnam 78 D4
Huon Peninsula P.N.G. 73 K8
Huonville Australia 147 E5
Huoqiu China 87 F1
Huoshan China 87 F2
Huo Shan mt. China 87 F2
Huoshao Tao i. Taiwan see Lü Tao
Huotsaus waterhole Namibia 130 B4
Huoxian China see Huozhou
Huozhou China 85 F4
formerly known as Huoxian
Hupeh prov. China see Hubei
Hupnik r. Turkey 109 H1
Ḩūr Iran 100 D4
Hurault, Lac l. Canada 169 G2
Huraymilā Saudi Arabia 105 D2
Huraysān reg. Saudi Arabia 105 D3
Hurbanovo Slovakia 49 P8
Hurd, Cape Canada 168 D4
Hurd Island Kiribati see Arorae
Hurdiyo Somalia 128 F2
Hure China 85 I3
also known as Hure Qi
Hüremt Mongolia 84 D1
Hürent Mongolia 84 D2
Hure Qi China see Hure
Hurghada Egypt 121 G3
also known as Al Ghardaqah
Huri mt. Kenya 128 C4
Huriel France 51 I6
Hurkett Canada 172 E2
Hurley U.S.A. 177 K4
Hurlock U.S.A. 177 J7
Huron CA U.S.A. 182 D5
Huron SD U.S.A. 178 C2

▶Huron, Lake Canada/U.S.A. 173 J5
2nd largest lake in North America and 4th in the world.
northamerica [landscapes] ▶ 156–157

Huron Bay U.S.A. 172 E4
Huron Beach U.S.A. 173 I5
Huronian Canada 172 C2
Huron Mountains hills U.S.A. 172 F4
Hurricane U.S.A. 183 K4
Hurricane Flats sea feature Bahamas 175 E8
Hurtado Chile 204 C3
Hurung, Gunung mt. Indon. 77 F2
Hurunui r. N.Z. 153 H10
Hurup Denmark 45 J4
Husain Nika Pak. 101 G4
Húsavík Norðurland eystra Iceland 44 [inset] C2
Húsavík Vestfirðir Iceland 44 [inset] B2
Husayn reg. Yemen 105 D4
Huseyinabat Turkey see Alaca
Huseyınli Turkey see Kızılırmak
Hushan China see Wuyi
Hushan China see Cixi
Husheib Sudan 121 G6
Huşi Romania 58 J2
Huskvarna Sweden 45 K4
Husn Jordan see Al Ḩişn
Ḩuşn Āl 'Abr Yemen 105 D4
Husnes Norway 45 I4
Husøy i. Norway 46 Q2
Hussainabad India 97 E4
Hustopeče Czech Rep. 49 N7
Husum Germany 48 G1
Husum Sweden 44 L3
Husvik S. Georgia 205 [inset]
Hutag Mongolia 84 D1
Hūtak Iran 100 D4
Hutanopan Indon. 76 B2
Hutaym, Ḩarrat lava field Saudi Arabia 104 C2
Hutchinson S. Africa 132 H8
Hutchinson KS U.S.A. 178 C4
Hutchinson MN U.S.A. 178 D2
Hutch Mountain U.S.A. 183 M7
Ḩūth Yemen 104 C4
Hutou China 82 D3
Huttah Kulkyne National Park Australia 147 D3
Hutton, Mount hill Australia 149 F5
Hutton Range hills Australia 151 C5
Hutubi China 88 D2
Hutubi He r. China 88 D2
Hutuo r. China 85 H4
Hutup watercourse Namibia 132 B2
Hưu Đô Vietnam 78 D3
Huvadhu Atoll Maldives 93 D10
Hūvār Iran 101 E5
Hüvek Turkey see Bozova
Hūvīān, Kūh-e mts Iran 101 D5
Huwār i. The Gulf 105 E2
also spelt Hawar
Ḩuwaymī, Sha'īb al watercourse Iraq 109 P7
Huwaytat reg. Saudi Arabia 107 D5
Huxi China 87 E3
Huxian China 87 D1
also known as Ganting
Huxley, Mount hill Australia 150 D3
Huxley, Mount N.Z. 153 D12
Huy Belgium 51 L2
Hūzgān Iran 100 B4
Huzhen China 87 G2
Huzhou China 87 G2
formerly known as Wuxing
Huzhu China 84 D4
also known as Weiyuan
Huzurnagar India 94 C2
Hvalnes Iceland 44 [inset] D2
Hvammsfjörður inlet Iceland 44 [inset] B2
Hvannadalshnúkur vol. Iceland 44 [inset] C2
Hvar Croatia 56 I5
Hvar i. Croatia 56 I5
Hvardiys'ke Ukr. 41 E7
Hvarski Kanal sea chan. Croatia 56 I5
Hveragerði Iceland 44 [inset] B2
Hvide Sande Denmark 45 J4
Hvíta r. Iceland 44 [inset] B3
Hvítárvatn l. Iceland 44 [inset] C2
Hwadae N. Korea 83 C4
Hwange Zimbabwe 131 E3
formerly spelt Wankie
Hwange National Park Zimbabwe 131 E3
Hwang Ho r. China see Yellow River
Hwangju N. Korea 83 B5
Hwayang S. Korea 91 A7
Hwedza Zimbabwe 131 F3
Hwlffordd U.K. see Haverfordwest
Hyannis MA U.S.A. 177 O4
Hyannis NE U.S.A. 178 B3
Hyargas Nuur salt l. Mongolia 84 B1
Hyco Lake U.S.A. 176 F9
Hyde N.Z. 153 E13
Hyden Australia 151 B7
Hyden U.S.A. 176 B8
Hyderabad India 94 C2
Hyderabad Pak. 101 G5
Hydra i. Greece see Ydra
Hyères France 51 M9
Hyères, Îles d' is France 51 M10
Hyermanavichy Belarus 42 I6
Hyesan N. Korea 82 C4
Hyland r. Canada 166 D3
Hyland, Mount Australia 147 G2
Hyland Bay Australia 148 A2
Hyland Post Canada 166 D3
Hyllekrog i. Denmark 48 I1
Hyllestad Norway 45 I3
Hyltebruk Sweden 45 K4
Hyndman U.S.A. 176 G6
Hyndman Peak U.S.A. 180 D4
Hyōgo pref. Japan 91 D7
Hyōno-sen mt. Japan 91 D7
Hyrcania Iran see Gorgān
Hyrra Banda Cent. Afr. Rep. see Ira Banda
Hyrynsalmi Fin. 44 O2
Hysham U.S.A. 180 F3
Hythe Canada 166 G4
Hyūga Japan 91 B8
Hyvinkää Fin. 45 N3

↓ I

Ia A Dun r. Vietnam 79 E5
Iacanga Brazil 206 D8
Iaciara Brazil 202 C5
Iaco r. Brazil 200 C2
Iacobeni Romania 58 F2
Iacobeni Romania 58 G1
Iacri Brazil 206 C8
Iaçu Brazil 202 D5
Iadera Croatia see Zadar
Iaeger U.S.A. 176 D8
Iakora Madag. 131 [inset] J4
Ialomiţa r. Romania 58 I4
Ialomiţei, Balta marsh Romania 58 I4
Ialoveni Moldova 58 J2
formerly known as Kutuzov; formerly spelt Yaloven'
Ialpug r. Moldova 58 J2
formerly spelt Yalpukh
Ianca Romania 58 I3
Ian Calder Lake Canada 167 L1
Iancu Jianu Romania 58 F4
Iapu Brazil 207 K6
Iara r. Romania 58 E2
Iarauarune, Serra mts Brazil 199 F4
Iargara Moldova 58 J2
formerly spelt Yargara
Iaşi Romania 58 I1
also known as Jassy; also spelt Yaş
Iasmos Greece 58 G7
Iba Phil. 74 A3
Ibadan Nigeria 125 F5
Ibagué Col. 198 C3
Ibaiti Brazil 206 C10
Ibanda Uganda 128 A5
Ibăneşti Romania 58 F2
Ibañeta, Puerto de pass Spain 55 J1
Ibanga Kasai Occidental Dem. Rep. Congo 127 D6
Ibanga Sud-Kivu Dem. Rep. Congo 126 E5
Ibapah U.S.A. 183 K1
Ibar r. Yugo. 58 B5
Ibara Japan 91 C7
Ibaraki pref. Japan 91 G6
Ibarra Ecuador 198 B4
Ibarreta Arg. 204 F2
Ibaté Brazil 206 F8
Ibb Yemen 104 D5
Ibb governorate Yemen 104 D5
Ibba watercourse Sudan 126 F3
Ibbenbüren Germany 48 E3
Ibdeqqene watercourse Mali 125 F2
Iberá, Esteros del marsh Arg. 204 F3
Iberá, Lago l. Arg. 204 F3
Iberia Loreto Peru 198 C6
Iberia Madre de Dios Peru 200 C2

▶Iberian Peninsula Europe 54
Consists of Portugal, Spain and Gibraltar.

Ibertioga Brazil 207 J8
Iberville, Lac d' l. Canada 169 F2
also known as Upper Seal Lake
Ibestad Norway 44 L1
Ibeto Nigeria 125 G4
Ibi Indon. 76 B1
Ibi Nigeria 125 H4
Ibi Spain 55 K6
Ibiá Brazil 206 G6
Ibiapaba, Serra da hills Brazil 202 D2
Ibias r. Spain 54 E1
Ibicaraí Brazil 202 E5
Ibicuí Bahia Brazil 207 N1
Ibicuí Rio Grande do Sul Brazil 204 F3
Ibicuí r. Brazil 203 A9
Ibigawa Japan 91 E7
Ibimirim Brazil 202 E4
Ibina r. Dem. Rep. Congo 126 F4
Ibiporã Brazil 206 B10
Ibirá Brazil 206 D8
Ibiraçu Brazil 207 M6
Ibiranhém Brazil 207 M4
Ibitiara Brazil 202 D5
Ibitinga Brazil 206 E8
Ibiúna Brazil 206 F10
Ibiza Spain 55 M6
also spelt Eivissa
Ibiza i. Spain 55 M5
also spelt Eivissa; formerly spelt Iviza; historically known as Ebusus
Iblei, Monti mts Sicilia Italy 57 G11
İblis Burnu pt Turkey 59 J12
Ibn Buşayyiş well Saudi Arabia 105 D2
Ibn Ḩādī Saudi Arabia 104 C4
Ibotirama Brazil 202 D5
Iboundji, Mont hill Gabon 126 A5
Ibrā' Oman 105 G3
Ibra, Wadi watercourse Sudan 126 E2
Ibrāt, Wādī watercourse Iraq 109 N2
Ibresi Rus. Fed. 40 H5
Ibrī Oman 105 G3
Ibu Indon. 75 C2
Ibuhos i. Phil. 74 B1
Ibusuki Japan 91 B9
Içá r. Brazil 198 E5
Ica Peru 200 B3
Ica dept Peru 200 B3
Icabarú Venez. 199 F3
Icaiché Mex. 185 H5
Içana Brazil 199 E4
Içana r. Brazil 198 E4
Icaraí Brazil 202 E2
Icaria i. Greece see Ikaria
Icatu Brazil 202 C2
Iceberg Canyon gorge U.S.A. 183 J5
İçel Turkey 106 C3
also known as Mersin
İçel prov. Turkey 108 E1

▶Iceland country Europe 44 [inset] B2
2nd largest island in Europe. Known as Ísland in Icelandic.
europe [landscapes] ▶ 30–31
europe [countries] ▶ 32–35
europe [environments] ▶ 36–37

Icem Brazil 206 D7
Ichak India 97 E4
Ichalkaranji India 94 B2
Ichchapuram India 95 E2
Ichihara Japan 91 G7
Ichilo r. Bol. 201 D4
Ichinoseki Japan 90 G5
Ichinskiy, Vulkan vol. Rus. Fed. 39 P4
Ichkeria aut. rep. Rus. Fed. see Chechenskaya Respublika
Ichkeul National Park Tunisia 57 B11
Ichnya Ukr. 41 E6
Ich'ŏn N. Korea 83 B5
Ich'ŏn S. Korea 83 B5
Ichuña Peru 200 C4
İçikler Turkey 59 J10
İçmeler Turkey 59 J12
Icó Brazil 202 E3
Iconha Brazil 207 M7
Iconium Turkey see Konya
Icosium Alg. see Algiers
Iculisma France see Angoulême
Icy Bay U.S.A. 166 A3
Icy Strait U.S.A. 166 C3
Ida, Mount N.Z. 153 E12
Idabdaba well Niger 125 H2
Idabel U.S.A. 179 D5
Idaga Hamus Eth. 104 B5
Ida Grove U.S.A. 178 D3
Idah Nigeria 125 G5
Idaho state U.S.A. 180 D3
Idaho City U.S.A. 180 D4
Idaho Falls U.S.A. 180 D4
Idalia National Park Australia 149 E5
Idanha-a-Nova Port. 54 D5
Idar India 96 B5
Idar-Oberstein Germany 48 E6
Ida Valley N.Z. 153 D13
Iday well Niger 125 H3
Iddan Somalia 128 F3
Idd el Asoda well Sudan 121 F6
Idd el Chanam Sudan 126 E2
Idd esh Shurak well Sudan 121 F5
Idefjorden inlet Norway/Sweden 45 J4
Ider Mongolia 84 C1
Ideriyn Gol r. Mongolia 84 D1
Idfina Egypt 108 B6
Idfu Egypt 121 G3
also spelt Edfu; historically known as Apollinopolis Magna
Idhān Awbārī des. Libya 120 A3
Idhān Murzūq des. Libya 120 B3
Idhra i. Greece see Ydra
Ídhras, Kólpos sea chan. Greece see Ydras, Kolpos
Idi Amin Dada, Lake Dem. Rep. Congo/Uganda see Edward, Lake
Idice r. Italy 56 D4
Idiofa Dem. Rep. Congo 126 C6
Idku Egypt 121 F2
Idlib Syria 109 H2
Idlib governorate Syria 109 H2
Idra i. Greece see Ydra
Idracowra Australia 148 B5
Idre Sweden 45 K3
Idrija Slovenia 56 G2
Idrijca r. Slovenia 56 F2
Idritsa Rus. Fed. 43 J5
Idstein Germany 48 F5
Idugala Tanz. 129 B6
Idukki India 94 C4
Idutywa S. Africa 133 M9
Idyllwild U.S.A. 183 H8
Idzhevan Armenia see Ijevan
Iecava Latvia 42 F5
Iecava r. Latvia 42 E5
Iepê Brazil 206 B9
Ieper Belgium 51 I2
also spelt Ypres
Ier r. Romania 49 T8
Ierapetra Greece 59 G13
Ierissou, Kolpos b. Greece 59 E8
Ifakara Tanz. 129 C7
'Ifāl, Wādī watercourse Saudi Arabia 104 A1
also known as Afal
Ifalik atoll Micronesia 73 J5
also spelt Ifaluk; formerly known as Wilson
Ifaluk atoll Micronesia see Ifalik
Ifanadiana Madag. 131 [inset] J4
Ifanirea Madag. 131 [inset] J4
Ife Nigeria 125 G5
Ifenat Chad 120 C6
Iferouâne Niger 125 H2
Ifetesene mt. Alg. 123 G4
Iffley Australia 149 D3
Ifjord Norway 44 N1
Ifôghas, Adrar des hills Mali 125 F2
also known as Iforas, Adrar des; short form Adrar
Ifon Nigeria 125 G5
Iforas, Adrar des hills Mali see Ifôghas, Adrar des
Ifould Lake salt flat Australia 146 B2
Ifrane Morocco 122 D2
Ifumo Dem. Rep. Congo 126 D5
Ifunda Tanz. 129 B7
Igan Sarawak Malaysia 72 D6
Igan r. Sarawak Malaysia 77 E2
Iganga Uganda 128 B4
Igarapava Brazil 206 F7
Igarape Açú Brazil 202 C2
Igarapé Grande Brazil 202 C3
Igarapé Miri Brazil 202 B2
Igaratá Brazil 207 G10
Igarité Brazil 202 D4
Igarka Rus. Fed. 39 I3
Igatpuri India 94 B2
Igbeti Nigeria 125 G4
Igboho Nigeria 125 F4
Iğdır Turkey 107 F3
Iggesund Sweden 45 L3
Ighiu Romania 58 E2
Iglesia Arg. 204 C3
Iglesias Sardegna Italy 57 A9
Igli Alg. 123 E3
Iglino Rus. Fed. 40 K5
Igloolik Canada 165 K3
Igluligaarjuk Canada see Chesterfield Inlet
'Igma, Gebel el plat. Egypt 108 E8
Ignace Canada 168 B3
Ignacio Zaragosa Mex. 184 D2
Ignacio Zaragoza Mex. 185 F4
Ignalina Lith. 42 H6
İğneada Turkey 106 A2
İğneada Burnu pt Turkey 106 B2
Igoma Tanz. 129 B6
Igombe r. Tanz. 129 A6
Igorevskaya Rus. Fed. 43 O6
Igoumenitsa Greece 59 B9
Igra Rus. Fed. 40 J4
Igrim Rus. Fed. 38 G3
Iguaçu r. Brazil 203 A8
Iguaçu, Parque Nacional do nat. park Brazil 203 A8
Iguaçu, Saltos do waterfall Arg./Brazil see Iguaçu Falls
Iguaçu Falls Arg./Brazil 204 G2
also known as Iguazú, Cataratas do or Iguaçu, Saltos do
Iguaí Brazil 202 D5
Iguaje, Mesa de hills Col. 198 C4
Iguala Mex. 185 F5
Igualada Spain 55 M3
Iguape Brazil 203 C8
Iguaraçu Brazil 206 B10
Iguarapé Brazil 207 I7
Iguatemi Brazil 203 A7
Iguatemi r. Brazil 203 A7
Iguatu Brazil 202 E3
Iguazú, Cataratas do waterfall Arg./Brazil see Iguaçu Falls
Iguazú, Parque Nacional del nat. park Arg. 204 G2
Iguéla Gabon 126 A5
Igueña Spain 54 E2
Iguetti, Sebkhet salt flat Mauritania 122 C4
Igunga Tanz. 129 B6
Iguobazuwa Nigeria 125 G5
Igusule Tanz. 129 B5
Iguvium Italy see Gubbio
Iharaña Madag. 131 [inset] K2
formerly known as Vohémar or Vohimarina
Ihavandhippolhu Atoll Maldives 94 B5
Ihbulag Mongolia 85 E3
Ihhayrhan Mongolia 85 E2
Ihiala Nigeria 125 G5
Ihirène, Oued watercourse Alg. 123 G5
Ihosy Madag. 131 [inset] J4
Ihsuuj Mongolia 85 E1
Ih Tal China 85 I3
Iida Japan 91 E7
Iide-san mt. Japan 90 F6
Iijoki r. Fin. 44 N2
Iisalmi Fin. 44 N3
Iitti Fin. 42 H1
Iiyama Japan 91 F6
Iizuka Japan 91 B8
Ijâfene des. Mauritania 122 C5
Ijara Kenya 128 D5
Ijebu-Ode Nigeria 125 F5
Ijevan Armenia 107 F2
also spelt Idzhevan
IJmuiden Neth. 48 B3
Ijnâouene well Mauritania 124 B2
Ijoubbâne des. Mali 122 D5
IJssel r. Neth. 48 C3
IJsselmeer l. Neth. 48 C3
formerly known as Zuider Zee
Ijuí Brazil 203 A9
Ijuí r. Brazil 203 A8
IJzer r. Belgium 51 I2
also known as Yser (France)
Ikaahuk Canada see Sachs Harbour
Ikaalinen Fin. 45 M3
Ikageleng S. Africa 133 K2
Ikageng S. Africa 133 L3
Ikahavo hill Madag. 131 [inset] J3
Ikalamavony Madag. 131 [inset] J4
Ikamatua N.Z. 153 F10
Ikang Nigeria 125 H5
Ikare Nigeria 125 G5
Ikaria i. Greece 59 H11
English form Icaria
Ikast Denmark 45 J4
Ikawai N.Z. 153 E12
Ikawhenua Range mts N.Z. 152 K6
Ikeda Hokkaidō Japan 90 H3
Ikeda Tokushima Japan 91 C7
Ikeja Nigeria 125 F5
Ikela Dem. Rep. Congo 126 D5
Ikelemba r. Dem. Rep. Congo 126 C4
Ikelenge Zambia 127 E7
Ikengo Dem. Rep. Congo 126 C5
Ikéngue Gabon 126 A5
Ikere Nigeria 125 G5
also spelt Ikerre
Ikerre Nigeria see Ikere
Ikhtiman Bulg. 58 E6
Ikhutseng S. Africa 133 I5
Iki i. Japan 91 A8
Iki-Burul Rus. Fed. 41 H7
Ikimba, Lake Tanz. 128 A5
Ikire Nigeria 125 G5
Iki-suidō sea chan. Japan 91 A8
Ikla Estonia 42 F4
Ikom Nigeria 125 H5
Ikoma Tanz. 128 B5
Ikongo Madag. 131 [inset] J4
formerly known as Fort Carnot
Ikopa r. Madag. 131 [inset] J3
Ikorodu Nigeria 125 F5
Ikosi Dem. Rep. Congo 126 E5
Ikot Ekpene Nigeria 125 G5
Ikouhaouene, Adrar mt. Alg. 123 H4
Iksan S. Korea 83 B6
formerly known as Iri
Ikungu Tanz. 129 B6
Ila Nigeria 125 G4
Ilaferh, Oued watercourse Alg. 123 F5
Ilagala Tanz. 129 A6
Ilagan Phil. 74 B2
Ilaisamis Kenya 128 C4
Ilaiyankudi India 94 C4
Ilaka Atsinanana Madag. 131 [inset] K3
Īlām Iran 100 A3
Īlām prov. Iran 100 A3
Ilam Nepal 97 E4
Ilan Taiwan 87 G3
also spelt Yilan
Ilanz Switz. 51 P6
Ilaro Nigeria 125 F5
Ilave Peru 200 C4
Iława Poland 49 Q2
Ilazārān, Kūh-e mt. Iran 100 D4
Il Bogd Uul mts Mongolia 84 C2
Ile r. China/Kazakh. 88 B3
Île-à-la-Crosse, Lac l. Canada 167 J4
Ilebo Dem. Rep. Congo 126 D6
formerly known as Port Francqui
Île-de-France admin. reg. France 51 I4
Ileje Tanz. 129 B7
Ilek Kazakh. 102 C2
Ilek r. Rus. Fed. 102 C2
also spelt Elek
Ilen r. Rep. of Ireland 47 C12
Ileret Kenya 128 C3
Ilesa Nigeria 125 G5
also spelt Ilesha
Ilesha Nigeria see Ilesa
Ilet' r. Rus. Fed. 40 I5
Ileza Rus. Fed. 40 G3
Ilford Canada 167 M3
Ilfracombe Australia 149 E4
Ilfracombe U.K. 47 H12
Ilgaz Turkey 106 C2
Ilgaz Dağları mts Turkey 106 C2
Ilgın Turkey 106 B3
Ilhabela Brazil 203 C7
Ilha Grande Brazil 199 E5
Ilha Grande, Baía da b. Brazil 207 I10
Ilha Grande, Represa resr Brazil 203 A7
Ilha Solteira, Represa resr Brazil 206 B7
Ílhavo Port. 54 C4
Ilhéus Brazil 202 E5
Ili Kazakh. see Kapchagay
Ilia Romania 58 D3
Iliamna Lake U.S.A. 164 D4
İliç Turkey 107 D3
Il'ich Kazakh. 103 G4
Il'ichevsk Azer. see Şärur
Ilici Spain see Elche
Ilig, Raas pt Somalia 128 F3
Iligan Phil. 74 C4
Iligan Bay Phil. 74 C4
Iligan Point Phil. 74 B2
Ilijaš Bos.-Herz. 56 K5
Ilimananngip Nunaa i. Greenland 165 Q2
also known as Milne Land
Ilimpeya r. Rus. Fed. 39 K3
Il'inka Kazakh. 102 D2
Il'inka Kaluzhskaya Oblast' Rus. Fed. 43 R7
Il'inka Respublika Altay Rus. Fed. 88 D1
Il'inka Respublika Buryatiya Rus. Fed. 85 E1
Il'inka Respublika Tyva Rus. Fed. 84 B1
Il'ino Rus. Fed. 43 M6
Il'inskiy Permskaya Oblast' Rus. Fed. 40 J4
Il'inskiy Respublika Kareliya Rus. Fed. 43 N1
Il'inskiy Sakhalin Rus. Fed. 82 F3
Il'insko-Podomskoye Rus. Fed. 40 H3
Il'inskoye Orlovskaya Oblast' Rus. Fed. 43 Q8
Il'inskoye Tverskaya Oblast' Rus. Fed. 43 S5
Il'inskoye Yaroslavskaya Oblast' Rus. Fed. 43 T4
Il'inskoye-Khovanskoye Rus. Fed. 43 U5
Ilin Strait Phil. 74 B3
Iliomar East Timor 75 C5
Ilion U.S.A. 177 J2
Ilirska Bistrica Slovenia 56 G3
Ilium tourist site Turkey see Troy
Iliya r. Belarus 42 I7
Iliysk Kazakh. see Kapchagay
Ilk Hungary 49 T7
Il'ka Rus. Fed. 85 F1
Ilkal India 94 C3
Ill r. France 51 N4
Illana Bay Phil. 74 B5
Illapel Chile 204 C3
Illapel r. Chile 204 C3
Illbillee, Mount hill Australia 146 B1
Ille r. France 50 E4
Illela Nigeria 125 G3
Iller r. Germany 48 G7
Illertissen Germany 48 H7
Illescas Spain 54 H4
Illescas Uruguay 204 G4
Illimani, Nevado de mt. Bol. 200 D4
Illinois r. U.S.A. 174 B4
Illinois state U.S.A. 174 B4
Illinois and Mississippi Canal U.S.A. 172 D9
Illizi Alg. 123 H4
formerly known as Fort de Polignac
Illogwa watercourse Australia 148 B5
Illueca Spain 55 J3
Ilm r. Germany 48 I4
Ilma, Lake salt flat Australia 151 D6
'Ilmān, Jabal al hill Saudi Arabia 104 D4
Il'men', Ozero l. Rus. Fed. 43 M3
Ilmenau Germany 48 H5
Ilmtal park Germany 48 I5
Ilo Peru 200 C4
Ilobu Nigeria 125 G5
Iloc i. Phil. 74 A4
Iloilo Phil. 74 B4
Iloilo Strait Phil. 74 B4
Ilomantsi Fin. 44 O3
Ilongero Tanz. 129 B6
Ilorin Nigeria 125 G4
Ilova r. Croatia 56 I3
Ilovatka Rus. Fed. 41 H6
Ilovik i. Croatia 56 G4
Ilovlya Rus. Fed. 41 G6
Ilovlya r. Rus. Fed. 41 G6
Iłowa Poland 49 M4
Il-Ponta ta' Benghajsa pt Malta see Benghisa Point
Il'pyrskiy Rus. Fed. 39 Q3
formerly known as Il'pyrskoye
Il'pyrskoye Rus. Fed. see Il'pyrskiy
Ilūkste Latvia 42 H6
Ilulissat Greenland 165 N3
also known as Jakobshavn
Ilunde Tanz. 129 B6
Ilungu Tanz. 129 B6
Ilva i. Italy see Elba, Isola d'
Il'ya Belarus 42 I7
Il'yaly Turkm. see Yylanly
Ilych r. Rus. Fed. 40 K3
Iłżanka r. Poland 49 S4
Imabari Japan 91 C7
Imabetsu Japan 90 G4
Imabū r. Brazil 199 G5
Imagane Japan 90 G3
Imaichi Japan 91 F6
Imala Moz. 131 H2
Imām al Ḩamzah Iraq 107 F5
Imam-baba Turkm. 103 E5
İmamoğlu Turkey 106 C3
Iman Rus. Fed. see Dal'nerechensk
Iman r. Rus. Fed. 82 D3
Imantau, Ozero l. Kazakh. 103 G1
Imari Japan 91 A8
Imasgo Burkina 125 E3
also spelt Imassogo
Imassogo Burkina see Imasgo
Imata Peru 200 C3
Imataca, Serranía de mts Venez. 199 F3
Imatra Fin. 45 O3
Imavere Estonia 42 G3
Imazu Japan 91 E7
Imbabura prov. Ecuador 198 B4
Imbaimadai Guyana 199 F3
Imbituba Brazil 203 B9
imeni 26 Bakinskikh Komissarov Azer. see 26 Bakı Komissarı
imeni 26 Bakinskikh Komissarov Turkm. 102 C5
imeni Babushkina Rus. Fed. 40 G4
imeni C. A. Niyazova Turkm. 103 E5
formerly known as imeni Chapayevka
imeni Chapayevka Turkm. see imeni C. A. Niyazova
imeni Gastello Rus. Fed. 39 O3
imeni Kalinina l. Tajik. 101 H2
imeni Kerbabayeva Turkm. 102 E5
formerly known as Karrychirla
imeni Khamzy Khakikmzade Uzbek. see Khamza
imeni Kirova Kazakh. see Kopbirlik
imeni Kuybysheva Turkm. 103 E5
also known as Kuybyshew Adyndaky
imeni Petra Stuchki Latvia see Aizkraukle
imeni Poliny Osipenko Rus. Fed. 82 E1
imeni Voroshilova Kyrg. see Eshanguzar
imeni Zhelyabova Rus. Fed. 43 R3
Imeri, Serra mts Brazil 199 E4
Imese Dem. Rep. Congo 126 C4
Īmī Eth. 128 D3
Imishli Azer. see İmişli
İmişli Azer. 107 G3
also spelt Imishli
Imit Jammu and Kashmir 96 B1
Imja-do i. S. Korea 83 B6
Imjin-gang r. N. Korea/S. Korea 83 B5
Imlay U.S.A. 182 F1
Imlay City U.S.A. 173 J7
Imlili W. Sahara 122 B5
Immokalee U.S.A. 175 D7
Imo state Nigeria 125 G5
Imola Italy 56 D4
Imotski Croatia 56 J5
Imperatriz Brazil 202 C3
Imperia Italy 56 A5
Imperial Peru 200 A3
Imperial CA U.S.A. 183 I9
Imperial NE U.S.A. 178 B3
Imperial Beach U.S.A. 183 G9
Imperial Dam U.S.A. 183 J9
Imperial Valley plain U.S.A. 183 I9
Imperieuse Reef Australia 150 B3
Impfondo Congo 126 C4
Imphal India 97 G4
formerly known as Manipur
İmralı Adası i. Turkey 58 J8
Imrān Yemen 104 D5
İmroz Turkey 106 A2
İmroz i. Turkey see Gökçeada
ımrun Turkey see Pütürge
Imsil S. Korea 83 B6
Imst Austria 48 H8
Imtān Syria 109 H5
Imuris Mex. 184 C2
Imuruan Bay Phil. 74 A4
Imzouren Morocco 54 H9
In r. Rus. Fed. 82 D2
Ina Japan 91 E7
Ina r. Poland 49 L2
I-n-Abangharit well Niger 125 G2
Inabu Japan 91 E7
In Afaleleh well Alg. 123 H5
Inagauan Phil. 74 A4
Inago Moz. 131 H2
Inahuaya Peru 200 B1
Inajá Brazil 202 E4
Inaja, Serra do hills Brazil 201 H2
I-n-Akhmed well Mali 125 E2
I-n-Alchi well Mali 125 E2
I-n-Aleï well Mali 124 E2
Inamba-jima i. Japan see Inanba-jima
Inambari Peru 200 C3
Inambari r. Peru 200 C3
I-n-Ameddé well Mali 124 D2
In Aménas Alg. 123 H3
In Amguel Alg. 123 G5
Inanba-jima i. Japan 91 F8
also spelt Inamba-jima
Inanda S. Africa 133 O6
Inangahua Junction N.Z. 153 F9
Inanwatan Indon. 73 H7
Iñapari Peru 200 C2
Inari Fin. 44 N1
also known as Aanaar or Anár
Inarigda Rus. Fed. 39 K3
Inarijärvi l. Fin. 44 N1
Inarijoki r. Fin./Norway 44 N1
I-n-Arouinat well Niger 125 G2
I-n-Atankarer well Mali 125 F2
Inauini r. Brazil 200 D2
Inawashiro-ko l. Japan 90 G6
I-n Azaoua well Alg. 123 G4
In-Azaoua well Alg. 123 G5
I-n-Azaoua watercourse Niger 125 G1
In Azar well Libya 120 A2
In Azāwah well Libya 120 A3
I-n-Azerraf well Mali 125 F2
In Belbel Alg. 123 F4
Inca Spain 55 N5
Inca de Oro Chile 204 C2
İnce Burnu pt Turkey 58 I8
İnce Burun pt Turkey 106 C2
İnceler Turkey 59 K11
Inchbonnie N.Z. 153 F10
Īncheh Iran 100 D2
Īnch'īnī Terara mt. Eth. 128 C3
Inchiri admin. reg. Mauritania 122 B5
Inch'ŏn S. Korea 83 B5
also known as Jinsen; formerly known as Chemulpo
Inchope Moz. 131 G3
I-n-Choumaguene well Mali 125 F2
Incirli Turkey see Karasu
İncirlik Turkey 108 G1
Incomati r. Moz. 131 G5
Incudine, Monte mt. France 56 B7
Inčukalns Latvia 42 F4
Indaiá r. Brazil 207 H5
Indaiá Grande r. Brazil 206 A6
Indaiatuba Brazil 206 F10
Indalsälven r. Sweden 44 L3
Indalstø Norway 45 I3
Indargarh Madhya Pradesh India 96 C4
Indargarh Rajasthan India 96 C4
Inda Silasē Eth. 128 C1
Indawgyi, Lake Myanmar 78 B2
Indé Mex. 184 D3
I-n-Délimane well Mali 125 F3
Independence CA U.S.A. 182 F5
Independence IA U.S.A. 174 B3
Independence KS U.S.A. 178 D4
Independence KY U.S.A. 176 A7
Independence MO U.S.A. 178 D4
Independence VA U.S.A. 176 D9
Independence WI U.S.A. 172 B6
Independence Fjord inlet Greenland 165 Q1
Independence Mountains U.S.A. 180 C4
Independencia Bol. 200 D4
Independenţa Romania 58 I4
Independenţa Romania 58 J5
Independenţa Romania 58 I3
Inder China 85 I2
also known as Jalaid
Inder, Ozero salt l. Kazakh. 102 B2
Inderborskiy Kazakh. 102 B2
Indi India 94 C2

▶India country Asia 93 E6
2nd most populous country in the world and in Asia. 3rd largest country in Asia and 7th in the world. Known as Bharat in Hindi.
world [countries] ▶ 10–11
world [population] ▶ 22–23
asia [landscapes] ▶ 62–63
asia [countries] ▶ 64–67

Indian r. U.S.A. 172 G4
Indiana U.S.A. 176 F5
Indiana state U.S.A. 174 C3

▶Indianapolis U.S.A. 174 C4
State capital of Indiana.

Indian Cabins Canada 167 G3
Indian Desert India/Pak. see Thar Desert
Indian Fields U.S.A. 176 B8
Indian Harbour Canada 169 J2
Indian Head Canada 167 K5
Indian Lake U.S.A. 177 K2
Indian Lake l. MI U.S.A. 172 G5
Indian Lake l. NY U.S.A. 177 K2
Indian Lake l. OH U.S.A. 176 B5
Indian Lake l. PA U.S.A. 176 G5

▶Indian Ocean 218 M7
3rd largest ocean in the world.
oceans [features] ▶ 210–211

Indianola IA U.S.A. 174 A3
Indianola MS U.S.A. 175 B5
Indian Peak U.S.A. 183 K3
Indian Springs U.S.A. 183 I5

I — index

Indian Wells U.S.A. 183 N6
Indiara Brazil 206 C4
Indiaroba Brazil 202 E4
Indibir Eth. 128 C2
Indiga Rus. Fed. 40 I2
Indigirka r. Rus. Fed. 39 O2
Indigskaya Guba b. Rus. Fed. 40 I2
Inđija Vojvodina, Srbija Yugo. 58 B3
Indin Myanmar 78 A3
Indin Lake Canada 167 H1
Indio r. Nicaragua 186 C5
Indio U.S.A. 183 H8
Indispensable Reefs Solomon Is 145 F3
Indo-China reg. Asia 72 C3
Indomanka r. Rus. Fed. 43 S1

▶Indonesia country Asia 72 D8
4th most populous country in the world and Asia. 5th largest country in Asia. Formerly known as Dutch East Indies.
world [population] ▶ 22–23
asia [countries] ▶ 64–67

Indore India 96 B5
Indragiri r. Indon. 76 C3
Indramayu Indon. 77 E4
Indramayu, Tanjung pt Indon. 77 E4
Indrapura, Gunung vol. Indon. see Kerinci, Gunung
Indrapura, Tanjung pt Indon. 76 C3
Indravati r. India 95 D2
Indre r. France 51 G5
Indulkana Australia 146 B1
Indur India see Nizamabad
Indura Belarus 42 E8
Indurti India 94 C2
Indus r. China/Pakistan 89 C5
also known as Shiquan He
Indus, Mouths of the Pak. 101 F5
Indwe S. Africa 133 L8
Indwe r. S. Africa 133 L9
Indzhe Voyvoda Bulg. 58 I6
In Ebeggi well Alg. 123 G5
İnebolu Turkey 106 C2
I-n-Échaï well Mali 123 E5
İnegöl Turkey 106 B2
In Ekker Alg. 123 G4
Inerie vol. Indon. 75 B5
Ineu Romania 58 C2
Inevi Turkey see Cihanbeyli
Inez U.S.A. 176 C8
In Ezzane well Alg. 123 H5
Infanta, Cape S. Africa 132 E11
Infantas Col. 187 E6
Infantes Spain see Villanueva de los Infantes
Infernao, Cachoeira waterfall Brazil 201 E2
Infielés, Punta pt Chile 204 C2
Infiernillo, Presa resr Mex. 185 E5
Infiesto Spain 54 F1
Ing, Mae Nam r. Thai. 78 C3
Inga Dem. Rep. Congo 127 B6
Ingå Fin. 45 N3
Ingabu Myanmar 78 A4
Ingal Niger 125 G2
Ingallanna watercourse Australia 148 B4
Ingalls, Mount U.S.A. 182 D2
Inganda Dem. Rep. Congo 126 D5
Ingelstad Sweden 45 K4
Ingende Dem. Rep. Congo 126 C5
Ingeniero Guillermo Nueva Juárez Arg. 201 E5
Ingeniero Jacobacci Arg. 204 C6
Ingenika r. Canada 166 E3
Ingenio r. Peru 200 B3
Ingersoll Canada 173 M7
Ingessana Hills Sudan 128 B2
Ingettolgoy Mongolia 84 D1
Ingezi Zimbabwe see Ngezi
Ingham Australia 149 E3
Ingichka Uzbek. 103 F5
formerly known as Rudnik Ingichka
Inglefield Land reg. Greenland 165 L2
Inglewood Qld Australia 147 F2
Inglewood Vic. Australia 147 D4
Inglewood N.Z. 152 I7
Inglewood U.S.A. 182 F8
Ingoda r. Rus. Fed. 85 G1
Ingoka Pum mt. Myanmar 78 B2
Ingolf Fjord inlet Greenland 165 R1
Ingolstadt Germany 48 I7
Ingomar Australia 146 B2
Ingonish Canada 169 I4
Ingraj Bazar India 97 F4
formerly known as English Bazar
Ingram VA U.S.A. 176 F9
Ingram WI U.S.A. 172 C5
Ingray Lake Canada 167 G1
Ingrid Christensen Coast Antarctica 223 F2
I-n-Guezzam Alg. 123 G6
I-n-Guita well Mali 125 F3
Inguiets Ukr. see Inhulets'
Ingulsvatn Norway 44 K2
Ingushetia aut. rep. Rus. Fed. see Ingushetiya, Respublika
Ingushetiya, Respublika aut. rep. Rus. Fed. 41 H8
English form Ingushetia or Ingush Republic
Ingush Republic aut. rep. Rus. Fed. see Ingushetiya, Respublika
Ingwavuma S. Africa 133 Q4
Ingwavuma r. Swaziland see Ngwavuma
Ingwe Zambia 127 E8
Inhaca Moz. 133 Q2
Inhaca, Peninsula pen. Moz. 131 G5
Inhafenga Moz. 131 G4
Inhambane Moz. 131 G4
Inhambane prov. Moz. 131 G4
Inhambupe Brazil 202 E4
Inhamitanga Moz. 131 G3
Inhapim Brazil 203 D6
Inharrime Moz. 131 G5
Inhassoro Moz. 131 G4
Inhaúmas Brazil 202 C5
I-n-Hihaou, Adrar hills Alg. 123 F5
Inhobim Brazil 207 M2
Inhulets' Ukr. 41 E7
also spelt Ingulets
Inhumas Brazil 206 D3
Inielika vol. Indon. 75 B5
Iniesta Spain 55 J5
Inimutaba Brazil 207 I5
Iniö Fin. 42 C1
Inírida r. Col. 198 E4
Inis Rep. of Ireland see Ennis
Inis Córthaidh Rep. of Ireland see Enniscorthy
Inishark i. Rep. of Ireland 47 B10
Inishbofin i. Rep. of Ireland 47 B10
Inishmore i. Rep. of Ireland 47 C10
Inishmurray i. Rep. of Ireland 47 D9
Inishowen pen. Rep. of Ireland 47 E8
Inishowen Head Rep. of Ireland 47 F8
Inishtrahull i. Rep. of Ireland 46 E8
Inishturk i. Rep. of Ireland 47 B10
Injgan Sum China 85 H2
Injibara Eth. 128 C2
Injune Australia 149 F5
Inkardar'ya Kazakh. 103 F3
I-n-Kerchef well Mali 124 D2
Inkerman Australia 149 D3
Inklin Canada 166 C3
Inklin r. Canada 166 C3
Inkylap Turkm. 103 E5
Inland Kaikoura Range mts N.Z. 153 H10
Inland Sea Japan see Seto-naikai
Inlet U.S.A. 177 K2
I-n-Milach well Mali 125 E2
Inn r. Europe 48 H9
Innaanganeq c. Greenland 165 M2
also known as York, Kap
Innai Japan 91 B8
Innamincka Australia 146 D1
Innamincka Regional Reserve nature res. Australia 146 D1
Inndyr Norway 44 K2
Inner Mongolia aut. reg. China see Nei Mongol Zizhiqu
Inner Sound sea chan. U.K. 46 G6
Innes National Park Australia 146 C3
Innisfail Australia 149 E3
Innisfail Canada 167 H4
Innokent'yevka Rus. Fed. 82 C2
Innoshima Japan 91 C7
Innsbruck Austria 48 I8
Innuksuak r. Canada 168 E1
Inny r. Rep. of Ireland 47 E10
Ino Japan 91 C8
Inobonto Indon. 75 C2
Inocência Brazil 206 B6
Inongo Dem. Rep. Congo 126 C5
Inoni Congo 126 B5
Inonias Peru 198 C5
İnönü Turkey 106 B3
Inosu Col. 198 D1
Inoucdjouac Canada see Inukjuak
Inovec mt. Slovakia 49 P7
Inowrocław Poland 49 P3
historically known as Hohensalza
Inquisivi Bol. 200 D4
In Salah Alg. 123 F4
also spelt Ain Salah

▶Inscription, Cape Australia 151 A5
Most westerly point of Oceania.

Insein Myanmar 78 B4
Insel Usedom park Germany 49 L2
Insko Poland 49 M2
In Sokki, Oued watercourse Alg. 123 F3
Insterburg Rus. Fed. see Chernyakhovsk
Instruch r. Rus. Fed. 42 C7
Însurăţei Romania 58 I4
Insuza r. Zimbabwe 131 E3
Inta Rus. Fed. 40 L2
I-n-Tadéra well Niger 125 H1
I-n-Tadrof well Niger 125 H2
In Takoufi, Oued watercourse Alg. 123 G4
I-n-Tassit well Mali 125 F2
I-n-Tebezas Mali 125 F2
I-n-Téguift well Mali 125 F2
I-n-Telli well Mali 125 F2
I-n-Témegui well Mali 125 F2
İntepe Turkey 59 H8
Interamna Italy see Teramo
Interlaken Switz. 51 N6
International Falls U.S.A. 174 A1
Interview Island India 95 G3
Intich'o Eth. 104 B5
Întorsura Buzăului Romania 58 H3
I-n-Touft well Mali 125 F2
Intracoastal Waterway canal U.S.A. 179 D6
Intutu Peru 198 C5
Inubō-zaki pt Japan 91 G7
Inukai Japan 91 B8
Inukjuak Canada 168 E1
formerly known as Port Harrison; formerly spelt Inoucdjouac
Inútil, Bahía b. Chile 205 C9
Inuvik Canada 164 F3
Inuya r. Peru 200 B2
In'va r. Rus. Fed. 40 K4
Inveraray U.K. 46 G7
Inverbervie U.K. 46 J7
Invercargill N.Z. 153 C14
Inverell Australia 147 F2
Inverleigh Australia 149 D3
Inverness Canada 169 I4
Inverness U.K. 46 H6
Inverness CA U.S.A. 182 B3
Inverness FL U.S.A. 175 D6
Inverurie U.K. 46 J6
Inverway Australia 148 A3
Investigator Channel Myanmar 79 B5
Investigator Group is Australia 146 B3
Investigator Strait Australia 146 C3
Inwood U.S.A. 176 G6
Inxu r. S. Africa 133 M8
Inya Rus. Fed. 88 D1
Inyanga Zimbabwe see Nyanga
Inyanga Mountains Zimbabwe 131 G3
Inyanga National Park Zimbabwe see Nyanga National Park
Inyangani mt. Zimbabwe 131 G3
Inyati Zimbabwe see Nyathi
Inyazura Zimbabwe see Nyazura
Inyokern U.S.A. 182 G6
Inyo Mountains U.S.A. 182 F4
Inyonga Tanz. 129 B6
Inza Rus. Fed. 41 H5
Inzer r. Rus. Fed. 40 K5
Inzhavino Rus. Fed. 41 G5
Ioannina Greece 59 B9
also spelt Yannina
Ioanninon, Limni l. Greece 59 B9
Iôf di Montasio mt. Italy 56 F2
Iō-jima i. Kazan-rettō Japan 73 J2
also known as Iō-tō; also spelt Iwo Jima
Iō-jima i. Japan 91 B9
also spelt Iō-shima
Iokanga r. Rus. Fed. 40 F2
Iola KS U.S.A. 178 D4
Iola WI U.S.A. 172 D6
Iolgo, Khrebet mts Rus. Fed. 88 D1
Iolotan' Turkm. see Yeloten
Iona Angola 127 B9
Iona Canada 169 I4
Iona i. U.K. 46 F7
Iona, Parque Nacional do nat. park Angola 127 B9
Iona Abbey tourist site U.K. 46 F7
Ione U.S.A. 182 G3
Ioneşti Romania 58 F4
Ionia U.S.A. 173 H8
Ionian Islands admin. reg. Greece see Ionioi Nisoi
Ionian Islands reg. Greece 59 A9
also known as Ionioi Nisoi
Ionian Sea Greece/Italy 59 A11
Ionioi Nisoi admin. reg. Greece 59 A10
English form Ionian Islands
Ionioi Nisoi reg. Greece see Ionian Islands
Iony, Ostrov i. Rus. Fed. 39 O4
Iordan Uzbek. 101 G1
also spelt Yordon; formerly spelt Yardan
Iori r. Georgia 107 F2
Ios Greece 59 G12
Ios i. Greece 59 G12
Iō-shima i. Japan see Iō-jima
Iō-tō i. Japan see Iō-jima
Iouik Mauritania 124 A2
Iowa r. U.S.A. 174 B3
Iowa state U.S.A. 174 A3
Iowa City U.S.A. 174 B3
Iowa Falls U.S.A. 174 A3
Ipameri Brazil 206 E4
Ipanema Brazil 203 D6
Ipanema r. Brazil 202 E4
Iparía Peru 200 B2
Ipatinga Brazil 203 D6
Ipatovo Rus. Fed. 41 G7
Ipauçu Brazil 206 D10
Ipeiros admin. reg. Greece 59 B9
English form Epirus; also spelt Ípiros
Ipel' r. Slovakia 49 P8
Ipelegeng S. Africa 133 J4
Ipiaçu Brazil 206 D5
Ipiales Col. 198 B4
Ipiaú Brazil 202 E5
Ipirá Brazil 202 E5
Ipiranga Amazonas Brazil 198 D5
Ipiranga Amazonas Brazil 199 F6
Ípiros admin. reg. Greece see Ipeiros
Ipixuna Brazil 200 B1
Ipixuna r. Amazonas Brazil 199 F6
Ipixuna r. Amazonas Brazil 200 B1
Ipoh Malaysia 76 C1
Ipoly r. Hungary/Slovakia 49 P8
Ipopeng S. Africa 133 J6
Iporá Brazil 206 B3
Ippy Cent. Afr. Rep. 126 D3
Ipsala Turkey 58 H8
Ipswich Australia 147 G1
Ipswich U.K. 47 N11
Ipswich U.S.A. 178 C2
Ipu Brazil 202 D3
Ipuã Brazil 206 E7
Ipueiras Brazil 202 D3
Ipuh Indon. 76 C3
Ipupiara Brazil 202 D4
Iput' r. Rus. Fed. 43 M9

▶Iqaluit Canada 165 M3
Territorial capital of Nunavut. Formerly known as Frobisher Bay.

Iqe He r. China 84 B4
Iquê r. Brazil 201 F3
also known as Languiaru
Iquique Chile 200 C5
Iquiri r. Brazil see Ituxi
Iquitos Peru 198 C5
Ira Banda Cent. Afr. Rep. 126 D3
formerly spelt Hyrra Banda
Iracoubo Fr. Guiana 199 H3
Īrafshān reg. Iran 101 E5
Irai Brazil 203 A8
Irai Island P.N.G. 149 F1
Irakleia Greece 58 E7
Irakleia i. Greece 59 G12
also spelt Iráklia
Irakleio Greece see Iraklion
Irakleiou, Kolpos b. Greece 59 G13
Iráklia i. Greece see Irakleia
Iraklion Greece 59 G13
also spelt Heraklion or Irakleio; historically known as Candia
Irala Para. 201 G6
Iramaia Brazil 202 D5
▶Iran country Asia 100 C4
formerly known as Persia
asia [countries] ▶ 64–67
Iran, Pegunungan mts Indon. 77 F2
Īrānshāh Iran 100 A2
Īrānshahr Iran 101 E5
Irapuato Mex. 185 E4
▶Iraq country Asia 107 E4
asia [countries] ▶ 64–67
Irarrarene reg. Alg. 123 G4
Irasville U.S.A. 177 M1
Iratapuru r. Brazil 199 H5
Irati Brazil 203 B8
Irati r. Spain 55 J2
Irayel' Rus. Fed. 40 J2
Irazu, Volcán vol. Costa Rica 186 C5
Irbe r. Latvia 42 D4
Irbes šaurums sea chan. Estonia/Latvia see Irbe Strait
Irbe Strait Estonia/Latvia 42 D4
also known as Irbe väin or Irbes šaurums or Kura kurk or Sõrve väin
Irbe väin sea chan. Estonia/Latvia see Irbe Strait
Irbid Jordan 108 G5
Irbīl Iraq see Arbīl
Irbit Rus. Fed. 38 G4
Irebu Dem. Rep. Congo 126 C5
Irecê Brazil 202 D4
Iregua r. Spain 55 I2

▶Ireland i. International Feature 47 C11
4th largest island in Europe.
europe [landscapes] ▶ 30–31

▶Ireland, Republic of country Europe 47 D10
known as Éire in Irish; formerly known as Irish Free State
europe [countries] ▶ 32–35

Iren' r. Rus. Fed. 40 K4
Irene Arg. 204 E5
Irene, Mount N.Z. 153 B13
Ireng r. Guyana/Venez. 199 G4
Iretama Brazil 206 A11
Irgiz Kazakh. 103 E2
also spelt Yrghyz
Irgiz r. Kazakh. 102 E2
Irharhar, Oued watercourse Alg. 123 G3
Irharhar, Oued watercourse Alg. 123 G5
Irherm Morocco 122 C3
Irhil M'Goun mt. Morocco 122 D3
Irhzer Ediessane watercourse Alg. 120 A3
Iri S. Korea see Iksan
Irian, Teluk b. Indon. see Cenderawasih, Teluk
Irian Barat prov. Indon. see Irian Jaya
Irian Jaya prov. Indon. 75 D3
also known as West Papua; formerly known as Dutch New Guinea or Irian Barat or West Irian
Irian Jaya reg. Indon. 73 I7
Iriba Chad 120 D6
Iricoumé, Serra hills Brazil 199 G4
Īrī Dāgh mt. Iran 100 A2
Iriga Phil. 74 B3
Iriklinskiy Rus. Fed. 102 D2
Iriklinskoye Vodokhranilische resr Rus. Fed. 102 D2
Iringa Tanz. 129 B6
Iringa admin. reg. Tanz. 129 B7
Iriri r. Brazil 199 H5
Iriri Novo r. Brazil 202 A4
Irish Free State country Europe see Ireland, Republic of
Irish Sea Rep. of Ireland/U.K. 47 G10
Irituia Brazil 202 C2
'Irj well Saudi Arabia 105 E2
Irkeshtam Kyrg. see Erkech-Tam
Irkut r. Rus. Fed. 84 D1
Irkutsk Rus. Fed. 80 G2
Irkutskaya Oblast' admin. div. Rus. Fed. 84 D1
English form Irkutsk Oblast
Irkutsk Oblast admin. div. Rus. Fed. see Irkutskaya Oblast'
Irma U.S.A. 172 D5
Irmak Turkey 106 C3
Irminio r. Sicilia Italy 57 G12
Irmo U.S.A. 175 D5
Irnijärvi l. Fin. 44 O2
Iro, Lac l. Chad 126 C2
Iroise, Mer d' g. France 50 B4
Iron Baron Australia 146 C3
Iron Bridge Canada 173 J4
Irondequoit U.S.A. 176 H2
Iron Junction U.S.A. 172 A3
Iron Knob Australia 146 C3
Iron Mountain U.S.A. 172 E5
Iron Mountain mt. U.S.A. 183 K4
Iron Range National Park Australia 149 D2
Iron River MI U.S.A. 172 E4
Iron River WI U.S.A. 172 B4
Ironton MO U.S.A. 174 B4
Ironton OH U.S.A. 176 C7
Ironwood U.S.A. 172 C4
Iroquois Canada 177 J1
Iroquois r. U.S.A. 172 F9
Iroquois Falls Canada 168 D3
Irosin Phil. 74 C3
Irō-zaki pt Japan 91 F7
Irpen' Ukr. see Irpin'
Irpin' Ukr. 41 D6
also spelt Irpen'
'Irqah Yemen 105 D5
'Irq al Harūrī des. Saudi Arabia 105 D2
'Irq al Mazhūr des. Saudi Arabia 104 C2
'Irq Banbān des. Saudi Arabia 105 D2
'Irq Jahām des. Saudi Arabia 105 D2
'Irq Subay des. Saudi Arabia 104 C3
Irramarne Aboriginal Land res. Australia 148 C4
Irrawaddy admin. div. Myanmar 78 A4
Irrawaddy r. Myanmar 78 A5
also spelt Ayeyarwady or Erawadi or Eyawadi
Irrawaddy, Mouths of the Myanmar 79 A5
Irsarybaba, Gory hills Turkm. 102 C4
also known as Ärsarybaba Erezi
Irshad Pass Afgh./Pak. 101 H2

▶Irtysh r. Kazakh./Rus. Fed. 38 G3
5th longest river in Asia and 10th in the world. Part of the 2nd longest river in Asia (Ob'-Irtysh). Also spelt Ertis.
asia [landscapes] ▶ 62–63

Irtyshsk Kazakh. 103 H1
also known as Ertis; formerly known as Irtyshskoye
Irtyshskoye Kazakh. see Irtyshsk
Iruma Japan 91 F7
Irumu Dem. Rep. Congo 126 F4
Irún Spain 55 J1
Iruña Spain see Pamplona
Irupana Bol. 200 D4
Irvine U.K. 46 H8
Irvine CA U.S.A. 182 G8
Irvine KY U.S.A. 176 B8
Irvine Glacier Antarctica 222 T2
Irving U.S.A. 179 C5
Irwin r. Australia 151 A6
Irwinton U.S.A. 175 D5
Isa Nigeria 125 G3
'Isá, Ra's pt Yemen 104 C5
Isaac r. Australia 149 F4
Isaac Lake Canada 166 F4
Isabela Negros Phil. 74 B4
Isabela Phil. 74 B5
Isabela, Cabo c. Dom. Rep. 187 F3
Isabelia, Cordillera mts Nicaragua 186 B4
Isabella U.S.A. 172 B3
Isabella Indian Reservation res. U.S.A. 173 I7
Isabella Lake U.S.A. 182 F6
Isabelle, Point U.S.A. 172 F3
Isabey Turkey 59 K11
Isaccea Romania 58 J3
Isachenko, Ostrov i. Rus. Fed. 39 I2
Isachsen, Cape Canada 165 I2
Ísafjarðardjúp est. Iceland 44 [inset] B2
Ísafjörður Iceland 44 [inset] B2
Isagarh India 96 C4
Isahaya Japan 91 B8
Isai Kalat Pak. 101 F5
Isa Khel Pak. 101 G3
Isakogorka Rus. Fed. 40 G2
Isakovo Rus. Fed. 43 P6
Işalniţa Romania 58 E4
Isana r. Col. 198 D4
Isanga Dem. Rep. Congo 126 D5
Isangano National Park Zambia 127 F7
Isaouane-n-Tifernine des. Alg. 123 G4
Isar r. Germany 48 J7
Isbister U.K. 46 K3
Iscar Spain 54 G3
Iscayachi Bol. 200 D5
Ischia Italy 57 F8
Ischia, Isola d' i. Italy 57 F8
Isdell r. Australia 150 D3
Ise Japan 91 E7
formerly known as Ujiyamada
Isefjord b. Denmark 45 J5
Iseke Tanz. 129 B6
Isel r. Austria 49 J9
Isengi Dem. Rep. Congo 126 E4
Iseo, Lago d' l. Italy 56 C3
Isère r. France 51 K8
Isère, Pointe pt Fr. Guiana 199 H3
Iserlohn Germany 48 E4
Isernhagen Germany 48 G3
Isernia Italy 56 G7
historically known as Aesernia
Ise-shima National Park Japan 91 E7
Ise-wan b. Japan 91 E7
Iseyin Nigeria 125 F5
Isfahan Iran see Eşfahān
Isfana Kyrg. 103 G5
Isfandaqeh Iran see Sangū'īyeh
Isfara Tajik. 101 G1
Isherim, Gora mt. Rus. Fed. 40 K3
Isherton Guyana 199 G4
Isheyevka Rus. Fed. 41 I5
Ishikari Japan 90 G3
Ishikari-gawa r. Japan 90 G3
Ishikari-wan b. Japan 90 G3
Ishikawa pref. Japan 91 E6
Ishim r. Kazakh./Rus. Fed. 103 F1
also known as Esil
Ishim Rus. Fed. 38 G4
Ishimbay Rus. Fed. 102 D1
Ishinomaki Japan 90 G5
Ishioka Japan 91 G6
Ishizuchi-san mt. Japan 91 C8
Ishkaft, Jabal hill Iraq 109 N1
Ishkoshim Tajik. 101 G2
Ishkuman Jammu and Kashmir 96 B1
Ishnya Rus. Fed. 43 U4
Ishpeming U.S.A. 172 F4
Ishtikhon Uzbek. see Ishtykhan
Ishtragh Afgh. 101 G2
Ishtykhan Uzbek. 103 F5
also spelt Ishtikhon
Ishurdi Bangl. 97 F4
Isiboro r. Bol. 200 D3
Isiboro Sécure, Parque Nacional nat. park Bol. 200 D4
Isigny-sur-Mer France 50 E3
Işıklı Turkey 106 B3
Isil'kul' Rus. Fed. 38 H4
Isimbira Tanz. 129 B6
Isinliví Ecuador 198 B5
Isiolo Kenya 128 C4
Isipingo S. Africa 133 O6
Isiro Dem. Rep. Congo 126 E4
formerly known as Paulis
Isisford Australia 149 E5
Iskabad Canal Afgh. 101 F2
Iskateley Rus. Fed. 40 J2
İskele Cyprus see Trikomon
İskenderun Turkey 106 D3
historically known as Alexandretta
İskenderun Körfezi b. Turkey 106 C3
İskilip Turkey 106 C2
Iski-Naukat Kyrg. see Eski-Nookat
Iskine Kazakh. 102 C3
Iskitim Rus. Fed. 80 C2
Iskra Rus. Fed. 43 U7
Iskŭr r. Bulg. 58 F5
Iskŭr, Yazovir resr Bulg. 58 E6
Iskushuban Somalia 128 F2
Iskut r. Canada 166 D3
Isla r. U.K. 46 I7
Isla, Wâdi watercourse Egypt 108 E9
Isla Cristina Spain 54 D7
Isla de Salamanca, Parque Nacional nat. park Col. 198 C2
Isla Gorge National Park Australia 149 F5
İslahiye Turkey 107 D3
Islamabad Jammu and Kashmir see Anantnag

▶Islamabad Pak. 101 H3
Capital of Pakistan.

Isla Magdalena, Parque Nacional nat. park Chile 205 B7
Islamkot Pak. 101 G5
Islamorada U.S.A. 175 D7
Islampur India 97 E4
Island r. Canada 166 F2
Ísland country Europe see Iceland
Island Bay Phil. 74 A4
Island Lagoon salt flat Australia 146 C2
Island Lake Canada 167 M4
Island Lake l. Canada 167 M4
Island Lake l. U.S.A. 172 A3
Island Magee pen. U.K. 47 G9
Island Pond U.S.A. 177 N1
Islands, Bay of N.Z. 152 I3
Islas Baleares aut. comm. Spain 55 N5
Islas de Bahá, Parque Nacional nat. park Hond. 186 B3
Islay i. U.K. 46 F8
Islaz Romania 58 F5
Isle r. France 50 F8

▶Isle of Man i. Irish Sea 47 H9
United Kingdom Crown Dependency.
europe [countries] ▶ 32–35

Isle of Wight U.S.A. 177 I9
Isle Royale National Park U.S.A. 172 E3
Isluga, Parque Nacional nat. park Chile 200 C4
Ismail Ukr. see Izmayil
Ismâ'ilîya Egypt 121 G2
also spelt Al Ismā'īlīyah
Ismā'īlīya governorate Egypt 108 D7
Ismâ'ilîya, Tir'at el canal Egypt 108 D7
Ismailly Azer. see İsmayıllı
İsmayıllı Azer. 107 G2
also spelt Ismailly
Isna Egypt 121 G3
Isoanala Madag. 131 [inset] J4
Isojoki Fin. 45 M3
Isoka Zambia 129 B7
Isokylä Fin. 44 N2
Isokyrö Fin. 44 M3
Isola del Liri Italy 56 F7
Isola di Capo Rizzuto Italy 57 J10
Isonzo r. Italy 56 F3
also known as Soča
Isopa Tanz. 129 A7
Isorana Madag. 131 [inset] J4
Iso-Syöte hill Fin. 44 N2
Ispahan Iran see Eşfahān
Isparta Turkey 106 B3
also known as Hamitabat
Isperikh Bulg. 58 H5
Ispica Sicilia Italy 57 G12
İspir Turkey 107 E2
Ispisar Tajik. see Khŭjand
▶Israel country Asia 108 F5
spelt Yizra'el in Hebrew or Isrā'īl in Arabic
asia [countries] ▶ 64–67
Israelândia Brazil 206 C3
Israelite Bay Australia 151 C7
Isrā'īl country Asia see Israel
Issa Croatia see Vis
Issa r. Rus. Fed. 43 J5
Issano Guyana 199 G3
Issia Côte d'Ivoire 124 D5
Issimu Indon. 75 B2
Issin tourist site Iraq 107 F5
Issoire France 51 J7
Issoudun France 51 H6
Issuna Tanz. 129 B6
Is-sur-Tille France 51 L5
Issyk-Kul' Kyrg. see Balykchy
Issyk-Kul', Ozero salt l. Kyrg. see Ysyk-Köl
Issyk-Kul Oblast admin. div. Kyrg. see Ysyk-Köl
Issyk-Kul'skaya Oblast' admin. div. Kyrg. see Ysyk-Köl
Ista r. Rus. Fed. 43 R8
İştabl 'Antar Saudi Arabia 104 B2
Iştablāt tourist site Iraq 107 E4
İstanbul Turkey 106 B2
historically known as Byzantium or Constantinople
İstanbul prov. Turkey 58 J7
İstanbul Boğazı sea chan. Turkey see Bosporus
İstanbul Boğazı strait Turkey see Bosporus
Isten dombja hill Hungary 49 N9
Istgāh-e Eznā Iran 100 B3
Isthilart Arg. 204 F3
Istiaia Greece 59 E10
Istik r. Tajik. 101 H2
Istmina Col. 198 B3
Istok Kosovo, Srbija Yugo. 58 B6
Istokpoga, Lake U.S.A. 175 D7
Istra pen. Croatia see Istria
Istra Rus. Fed. 43 R6
Istres France 51 K9
Istria pen. Croatia 56 F3
also spelt Istra
Istria Romania 58 J4
Istriţa, Dealul hill Romania 58 H3
Ist'ya r. Rus. Fed. 43 V7
Isuela r. Spain 55 J3
Iswaripur Bangl. 97 F5
Iswepe S. Africa 133 O3
Isyangulovo Rus. Fed. 102 D1
Isyk Kazakh. 103 I4
Itabaianinha Brazil 202 E4
Itabapoana Brazil 207 M8
Itabapoana r. Brazil 207 M8
Itaberá Brazil 206 D10
Itaberaba Brazil 202 D5
Itaberaí Brazil 206 D3
Itabira Brazil 203 D6
Itabirito Brazil 203 D7
Itaboca Brazil 199 F6
Itaboraí Brazil 207 K9
Itabuna Brazil 202 E5
Itacaiuna r. Brazil 202 B3
Itacajá Brazil 202 C4
Itacambira Brazil 207 J4
Itacarambi Brazil 202 C5
Itacaré Brazil 202 E5
Itacayunas, Serra hills Brazil 201 H1
Itacoatiara Brazil 199 G5
Itacuaí r. Brazil 198 D6
Itaetê Brazil 202 D5
Itagmatana Iran see Hamadān
Itagmirim Brazil 207 N3
Itaguaçu Brazil 203 D6
Itaguaí Brazil 207 J9
Itaguajé Brazil 206 B9
Itaguara Brazil 207 I7
Itahuania Peru 200 C3
Itaí Brazil 206 D10
Itaim r. Brazil 202 D3
Itaiópolis Brazil 203 B8
Itaipu, Represa de resr Brazil 203 A8
Itäisen Suomenlahden kansallispuisto nat. park Fin. 45 N3
Itaituba Brazil 199 G6
Itajá Brazil 206 B6
Itajaí Brazil 203 B8
Itajobi Brazil 206 D8
Itajubá Brazil 203 C7
Itaju de Colônia Brazil 207 N2
Itajuípe Brazil 202 E5
Itaki India 97 E5
Itala Nature Reserve S. Africa 133 P4
Italia country Europe see Italy

▶Italy country Europe 56 C4
5th most populous country in Europe. Known as Italia in Italian.
europe [countries] ▶ 32–35

Itamaracá, Ilha de i. Brazil 202 F3
Itamaraju Brazil 203 E6
Itamarandiba Brazil 203 D6
Itamataré Brazil 202 C2
Itambacuri Brazil 207 L5
Itambacuri r. Brazil 207 L5
Itambé Brazil 202 D5
Itambé, Pico de mt. Brazil 203 D6
Itami airport Japan 91 D7
Itamirim Brazil 207 K1
Itampolo Madag. 131 [inset] I5
Itanagar India 97 G4
Itanguari r. Brazil 207 H1
Itanhaém Brazil 206 G11
Itanhauã r. Brazil 199 F6
Itanhém Brazil 203 D6
Itanhém r. Brazil 203 E6
Itanhomi Brazil 207 L6
Itany r. Fr. Guiana/Suriname 199 H4
Itaobím Brazil 202 D6
Itaocara Brazil 207 K8
Itapaci Brazil 206 D1
Itapajipe Brazil 206 D6
Itaparaná r. Brazil 199 F6
Itaparica, Represa de resr Brazil 202 E4
Itapé Brazil 207 N1
Itapebi Brazil 202 E5
Itapebí Uruguay 204 F3
Itapecerica Brazil 207 H7
Itapemirim Brazil 203 D7
Itaperuna Brazil 203 D7
Itapetinga Brazil 202 D5
Itapetininga Brazil 206 E10
Itapeva Brazil 206 E10
Itapeva, Lago l. Brazil 203 B9
Itapi r. Brazil 199 G5
Itapicuru Brazil 202 D4
Itapicuru r. Brazil 202 C2
Itapicuru r. Brazil 202 E4
Itapicuru, Serra de hills Brazil 202 C3
Itapicuru Mirim Brazil 202 C2
Itapicuru Mirim r. Brazil 202 E4
Itapinima Brazil 199 F6
Itapipoca Brazil 202 E2
Itapira Brazil 206 G9
Itapiranga Brazil 199 G5
Itapirapuã Brazil 206 C2
Itapiúna Brazil 202 E3
Itápolis Brazil 206 E8
Itaporanga Paraíba Brazil 202 E3
Itaporanga São Paulo Brazil 206 D10
Itapuã Brazil 203 B9
Itapuranga Brazil 206 D2
Itaquaquecetuba Brazil 207 G10
Itaqui Brazil 204 F3
Itarana Brazil 207 M6
Itarantim Brazil 207 M2
Itararé Brazil 206 D11
Itararé r. Brazil 206 D10
Itarsi India 96 C5
Itarumã Brazil 206 B5
Itä-Suomi prov. Fin. 44 O3
Itatiaia Brazil 206 G10
Itatinga Brazil 206 E10
Itatuba Brazil 199 F6
Itatupã Brazil 199 I5
Itauçu Brazil 206 D3
Itaueira r. Brazil 202 D3
Itaúna Amazonas Brazil 199 E5
Itaúna Minas Gerais Brazil 203 C7
Itaúnas r. Brazil 207 N5
Itbayat i. Phil. 74 B1
Itchen Lake Canada 167 H1
Ite Peru 200 C4
Itea Greece 59 D10
Itebero Dem. Rep. Congo 126 F5
Itemgen, Ozero l. Kazakh. 103 G1
Itende Tanz. 129 B6
Itezhi-Tezhi Dam Zambia 127 E8
Ithaca Greece see Ithaki
Ithaca i. Greece see Ithaki
Ithaca MI U.S.A. 173 I7
Ithaca NY U.S.A. 177 I3
Ithaki Greece 59 B10
English form Ithaca; also known as Vathi
Ithaki i. Greece 59 B10
English form Ithaca
Ithakis, Steno sea chan. Greece 59 B10
Ith Hils ridge Germany 48 G3
Ithil, Wādī al watercourse Saudi Arabia 109 H9
Itigi Tanz. 129 B6
Itihusa-yama mt. Japan 91 B8
Itilleq Greenland 165 N3
Itimbiri r. Dem. Rep. Congo 126 D4
Itinga Brazil 202 D6
Itiquira Brazil 203 A6
Itiquira r. Brazil 201 F4
Itirapina Brazil 206 F9
Itirapuã Brazil 206 F7
Itiúba Brazil 202 E4
Itiúba, Serra de hills Brazil 202 E4
Itiyura r. Arg. 201 E5
Itkhari India 97 E4
Itmurinkol', Ozero l. Kazakh. 102 C2
Itō Japan 91 F7
Itoculo Moz. 131 I2
Itoigawa Japan 90 E6
Itoko Dem. Rep. Congo 126 D5
Iton r. France 50 H3
Itongafeno mt. Madag. 131 [inset] J4
Itororó Brazil 207 M2
Itsuki Japan 91 B8
Itsukushima Shrine tourist site Japan 91 C7
Ittiri Sardegna Italy 57 A8
Ittoqqortoormiit Greenland 165 Q2
also known as Scoresbysund

Itu Brazil 206 F10
Itu Nigeria 125 G5
Itu Abu Island S. China Sea 72 D4
Ituaçu Brazil 202 D5
Ituberá Brazil 202 E5
Ituí r. Brazil 198 D6
Ituiutaba Brazil 206 D5
Itula Dem. Rep. Congo 126 E5
Itumba Tanz. 129 B6
Itumbiara Brazil 206 D5
Itumbiara, Barragem resr Brazil 206 D5
Itungi Port Malawi 129 B7
Ituni Guyana 199 G3
Itupiranga Brazil 202 B3
Iturama Brazil 206 C6
Iturbe Para. 201 F6
Iturbide Campeche Mex. 185 H5
Iturbide Nuevo León Mex. 185 F3
Ituri r. Dem. Rep. Congo 126 E4
Iturup, Ostrov i. Rus. Fed. 82 G3
also known as Etorofu-tō
Itutinga Brazil 207 I8
Ituverava Brazil 206 F7
Ituxi r. Brazil 200 D1
also known as Iquiri
Ituzaingo Arg. 204 F2
Ityopia country Africa see **Ethiopia**
Itzehoe Germany 48 G2
Iuaretê Brazil 198 D4
Iuka U.S.A. 174 B5
Iul'tin Rus. Fed. 39 S3
Iuluti Moz. 131 H2
Iúna Brazil 207 L7
Iutica Brazil 198 D4
Ivaí r. Brazil 206 A10
Ivaiporã Brazil 206 B11
Ivakoany mt. Madag. 131 [inset] J4
Ivalo Fin. 44 N1
also known as Avveel or Avvil
Ivalojoki r. Fin. 44 N1
Ivanava Belarus 42 G9
also spelt Ivanovo
Ivanec Croatia 56 I2
Ivangorod Rus. Fed. 43 J2
Ivangrad Crna Gora Yugo. see **Berane**
Ivanhoe N.S.W. Australia 147 E3
Ivanhoe W.A. Australia 150 E2
Ivanhoe r. Canada 168 D3
Ivanhoe CA U.S.A. 182 E5
Ivanhoe MN U.S.A. 178 C2
Ivanhoe VA U.S.A. 176 E9
Ivanhoe Lake N.W.T. Canada 167 J2
Ivanhoe Lake Ont. Canada 173 K2
Ivanić-Grad Croatia 56 I3
Ivanishchi Rus. Fed. 43 V6
Ivanivka Ukr. 58 L2
Ivanjica Srbija Yugo. 58 B5
Ivankiv Ukr. 41 D6
Ivankovo Croatia 56 K3
Ivan'kovo Rus. Fed. 43 S7
Ivan'kovskiy Rus. Fed. 43 V5
Ivan'kovskoye Vodokhranilishche resr Rus. Fed. 43 R5
Ivankovtsy Rus. Fed. 82 D2
Ivano-Frankivs'k Ukr. 41 C6
also spelt Ivano-Frankovsk; formerly known as Stanislav
Ivano-Frankovsk Ukr. see **Ivano-Frankivs'k**
Ivanovka Kazakh. see **Kokzhayyk**
Ivanovka Amurskaya Oblast' Rus. Fed. 82 B2
Ivanovka Orenburgskaya Oblast' Rus. Fed. 102 C1
Ivanovo Belarus see **Ivanava**
Ivanovo tourist site Bulg. 58 G5
Ivanovo Ivanovskaya Oblast' Rus. Fed. 40 G4
Ivanovo Pskovskaya Oblast' Rus. Fed. 43 L5
Ivanovo Tverskaya Oblast' Rus. Fed. 43 S3
Ivanovo Oblast admin. div. Rus. Fed. see **Ivanovskaya Oblast'**
Ivanovskaya Oblast' admin. div. Rus. Fed. 43 U4
English form Ivanovo Oblast
Ivanovskiy Khrebet mts Kazakh. 88 C1
Ivanovskoye Orlovskaya Oblast' Rus. Fed. 43 R8
Ivanovskoye Yaroslavskaya Oblast' Rus. Fed. 43 U5
Ivanpah Lake U.S.A. 183 I6
Ivanšćica mts Croatia 56 H2
Ivanski Bulg. 58 I5
Ivanteyevka Rus. Fed. 102 B1
Ivantsevichi Belarus see **Ivatsevichy**
Ivato Madag. 131 [inset] J4
Ivatsevichy Belarus 42 G9
also spelt Ivantsevichi
Ivaylovgrad Bulg. 58 H7
Ivaylovgrad, Yazovir resr Bulg. 58 G7
Ivdel' Rus. Fed. 38 G3
Iveşti Romania 58 I3
Iveşti Romania 58 I2
Ivi, Cap c. Alg. 55 L8
Ivindo r. Gabon 126 B5
Ivinheima Brazil 203 A7
Ivittuut Greenland 165 O3
Iviza i. Spain see **Ibiza**
Ivohibe Madag. 131 [inset] J4
Ivolândia Brazil 206 C3
Ivolginsk Rus. Fed. 85 E1
Ivón Bol. 200 D2
Ivor U.S.A. 177 I9
Ivory Coast country Africa see **Côte d'Ivoire**
Ivösjön l. Sweden 45 K4
Ivot Rus. Fed. 43 P8
Ivrea Italy 51 N7
İvrindi Turkey 59 I9
Ivris Ugheltekhili pass Georgia 107 F2
Ivugivik Canada see **Ivujivik**
Ivujivik Canada 165 L3
formerly spelt Ivugivik
Ivuna Tanz. 129 B7
Ivvavik National Park Canada 164 F3
Ivyanyets Belarus 42 H8
Ivydale U.S.A. 176 D7
Iwaizumi Japan 90 G5
Iwaki Japan 90 G6
Iwaki-san vol. Japan 90 G4
Iwakuni Japan 91 C7
Iwamatsu Japan 91 C8
Iwamizawa Japan 90 G3
Iwan r. Indon. 77 F2
Iwanai Japan 90 G3
Iwanda Tanz. 129 B7
Iwanuma Japan 90 G5
Iwata Japan 91 E7
Iwate Japan 90 G5
Iwate pref. Japan 90 G5
Iwate-san vol. Japan 90 G5
Iwo Nigeria 125 G5
Iwo Jima i. Japan see **Iō-jima**
Iwupataka Aboriginal Land res. Australia 148 B4
Iwye Belarus 42 G8
Ixcamilpa Mex. 185 F5
Ixiamas Bol. 200 C3
Ixmiquilpán Mex. 185 F4
Ixopo S. Africa 133 O7
Ixtacomitán Mex. 185 G5
Ixtlán Nayarit Mex. 184 D4
Ixtlán Oaxaca Mex. 185 F5
Iya i. Indon. 75 B5
Iya r. Rus. Fed. 80 G1
Iyayi Tanz. 129 B7
İyirmi Altı Bakı Komissarı Azer. see **26 Bakı Komissarı**
Iyo Japan 91 C8
Iyomishima Japan 91 C8
Iyo-nada b. Japan 91 C8
Izabal, Lago de l. Guat. 185 H6
Izamal Mex. 185 H4
Izapa tourist site Mex. 185 G6
Izari-dake mt. Japan 90 G3
Izazi Tanz. 129 B6
Izbăşeşti hill Romania 58 F3
Izberbash Rus. Fed. 102 A4
Izdeshkovo Rus. Fed. 43 O6
Īzeh Iran 100 B4
Izgagane well Niger 125 H2
Izhevsk Rus. Fed. 40 J4
formerly known as Ustinov
Izhma Rus. Fed. 40 J2
Izhma Rus. Fed. see **Sosnogorsk**
Izhma r. Rus. Fed. 40 J2
Izkī Oman 105 G3
Izmail Ukr. see **Izmayil**
Izmalkovo Rus. Fed. 43 S9
Izmayil Ukr. 41 D7
also spelt Izmail; formerly spelt Ismail
Izmeny, Proliv sea chan. Japan/Rus. Fed. see **Notsuke-suidō**
İzmir Turkey 106 A3
historically known as Smyrna
İzmir prov. Turkey 59 I10
İzmir Körfezi g. Turkey 106 A3
İzmit Turkey see **Kocaeli**
İzmit Körfezi b. Turkey 106 B2
Izmorene Morocco 54 H9
Iznajar, Embalse de resr Spain 54 G7
Iznalloz Spain 55 H7
İznik Turkey 58 K8
historically known as Nicaea
İznik Gölü l. Turkey 106 B2
Iznoski Rus. Fed. 43 Q7
Izoard, Col d' pass France 51 M8
Izobil'noye Rus. Fed. see **Izobil'nyy**
Izobil'nyy Rus. Fed. 41 G7
formerly known as Izobil'noye
Izola Slovenia 56 F3
Izoplit Rus. Fed. 43 R5
Izozog Bajo Bol. 201 E4
Izra' Syria 108 H5
Iztochni Rodopi mts Bulg. 58 G7
Izúcar de Matamoros Mex. 185 F5
Izu-hantō pen. Japan 91 F7
Izuhara Japan 91 A7
Izumi Japan 91 B8
Izumisano Japan 91 D7
Izumo Japan 91 C7

▶**Izu-Ogasawara Trench** sea feature N. Pacific Ocean 220 D3
5th deepest trench in the world.

Izu-shotō is Japan 91 F7
Izu-tobu vol. Japan 91 F7
Izvestiy Tsentral'nogo Ispolnitel'nogo Komiteta, Ostrova Rus. Fed. 39 I2
Izvestkovyy Rus. Fed. 82 C2
Izvoarele Romania 58 G4
Izvoarele Romania 58 F4
Izvoarele Romania 58 H3
Izvoru Romania 58 G4
Izyaslav Ukr. 41 C6
Iz"yayu Rus. Fed. 40 K2
Izyndy Kazakh. 102 D3
Izyum Ukr. 41 F6

Jaama Estonia 42 I2
Ja'ar Yemen 105 D5
Jaba watercourse Iran 100 D3
Jabal as Sirāj Afgh. 101 G3
Jabal Dab Saudi Arabia 105 E3
Jabalón r. Spain 54 G6
Jabalpur India 96 C5
formerly spelt Jubbulpore
Jabbārah Fara Islands Saudi Arabia 104 C4
Jabbūl, Sabkhat al salt flat Syria 109 I2
Jabiluka Aboriginal Land res. Australia 148 B2
Jabir reg. Oman 105 G3
Jabiru Australia 148 B2
Jablah Syria 108 G2
Jablanica Bos.-Herz. 56 J5
Jablanica r. Yugo. 58 C5
Jablonec nad Nisou Czech Rep. 49 M5
Jabłonowo Pomorskie Poland 49 Q2
Jablunkov Czech Rep. 49 P6
Jaboticabal Brazil 206 E8
Jaboticatubas Brazil 207 J6
Jabuka i. Croatia 56 H5
Jabuka Vojvodina, Srbija Yugo. 58 B4
Jabung, Tanjung pt Indon. 76 D3
Jaburu Brazil 199 E6
Jabuti Brazil 199 G6
Jaca Spain 55 K2
Jacala Mex. 185 F4
Jacaraci Brazil 207 K1
Jacaré Mato Grosso Brazil 202 A5
Jacaré Rondônia Brazil 201 D2
Jacaré r. Brazil 199 F6
Jacaré r. Brazil 202 D4
Jacareacanga Brazil 199 G6
Jacareí Brazil 207 G10
Jacaretinga Brazil 201 F2
Jacarézinho Brazil 206 D10
Jáchal r. Arg. 204 D3
Jaciara Brazil 202 A5
Jacinto Brazil 202 D6
Jaciparaná Brazil 201 D2
Jaciparaná r. Brazil 201 D2
Jack r. Australia 149 E2
Jackfish Canada 172 G2
Jackfish Lake Canada 167 I4
Jack Lee, Lake resr U.S.A. 179 D5
Jacksboro TN U.S.A. 176 A9
Jacksboro TX U.S.A. 179 C5
Jackson Australia 149 F5
Jackson AL U.S.A. 175 C6
Jackson CA U.S.A. 182 D3
Jackson GA U.S.A. 175 D5
Jackson KY U.S.A. 176 B8
Jackson MI U.S.A. 173 I8
Jackson MN U.S.A. 178 D3
Jackson MO U.S.A. 174 B4

▶**Jackson** MS U.S.A. 175 B5
State capital of Mississippi.

Jackson NC U.S.A. 176 H9
Jackson OH U.S.A. 176 C6
Jackson TN U.S.A. 174 B5
Jackson WI U.S.A. 172 E7
Jackson WY U.S.A. 180 E4
Jackson, Cape N.Z. 152 I8
Jackson, Mount Antarctica 222 T2
Jackson Bay N.Z. 153 C11
Jackson Bay b. N.Z. 153 C11
also known as Okahu
Jackson Head N.Z. 153 C11
Jackson Island Rus. Fed. see **Dzheksona, Ostrov**
Jackson Lake U.S.A. 180 E4
Jacksonport U.S.A. 172 F6
Jacksons N.Z. 153 F10
Jackson's Arm Canada 169 J3
Jacksonville AL U.S.A. 175 C5
Jacksonville AR U.S.A. 179 D5
Jacksonville FL U.S.A. 175 D6
Jacksonville IL U.S.A. 174 B4
Jacksonville NC U.S.A. 174 E5
Jacksonville OH U.S.A. 176 C6
Jacksonville TX U.S.A. 179 D6
Jacksonville Beach U.S.A. 175 D6
Jack Wade U.S.A. 166 A1
Jacmel Haiti 187 E3
Jaco i. East Timor see **Jako**
Jacobabad Pak. 101 G4
Jacobina Brazil 202 D4
Jacob Lake U.S.A. 183 L5
Jacobsdal S. Africa 133 I6
Jacques-Cartier, Détroit de sea chan. Canada 169 H3
also known as Jacques Cartier Passage
Jacques Cartier, Mont mt. Canada 169 H3
Jacques Cartier Passage Canada see **Jacques-Cartier, Détroit de**
Jacquet River Canada 169 H4
Jacuba r. Brazil 206 A5
Jacuí Brazil 206 G8
Jacuí r. Brazil 203 B9
Jacuípe r. Brazil 202 E5
Jacunda Brazil 202 B3
Jacundá r. Brazil 202 B2
Jacupemba Brazil 207 M6
Jacupiranga Brazil 203 C8
Jacura Venez. 198 D2
Jadar r. Bos.-Herz. 56 L4
Jadar r. Yugo. 58 A4
Jadcherla India 94 C2
Jaddangi India 95 D2
Jaddi, Ras pt Pak. 101 E5
Jadebusen b. Germany 48 F2
Jadhdhānah Saudi Arabia 104 C4
Jādib Yemen 105 F4
J. A. D. Jensen Nunatakker nunataks Greenland 165 O3
Jadotville Dem. Rep. Congo see **Likasi**
Jadova r. Croatia 56 H4
Jadovnik mt. Bos.-Herz. 56 I4
Jaén Peru 198 B6
Jaen Phil. 74 B3
Jaén Spain 54 H7
Jæren reg. Norway 45 I4
Ja'farābād Ardabīl Iran 100 B2
Ja'farābād Khorāsan Iran 100 D2
Jaffa Israel see **Tel Aviv-Yafo**
Jaffa, Cape Australia 146 C4
Jaffna Sri Lanka 94 C4
Jaffrey U.S.A. 177 M3
Jafr, Qa' al imp. l. Jordan 109 H7
Jagadhri India 96 C3
Jägala r. Estonia 42 G2
Jagalur India 94 C3
Jagdalak Afgh. 101 G3
Jagdalpur India 94 D2
Jagdaqi China 85 J1
Jagdishpur India 89 C7
Jagdispur India 97 E4
Jagersfontein S. Africa 133 J6
Jaggang China 89 B5
Jaggayyapeta India 94 D2
Jaghīn Iran 100 D5
Jaghjaghah, Nahr r. Syria/Turkey 109 M1
Jagīn watercourse Iran 100 D5
Jagkolk Vloer salt pan S. Africa 132 E6
Jagodina Srbija Yugo. 58 C5
formerly known as Svetozarevo
Jagok Tso salt l. China see **Urru Co**
Jagsamka China see **Luding**
Jagst r. Germany 48 G6
Jagtial India 94 C2
Jaguapitã Brazil 206 B10
Jaguarão r. Brazil/Uruguay 204 G4
also known as Yaguarón
Jaguarão Uruguay 204 G4
Jaguarari Brazil 202 D4
Jaguaretama Brazil 202 E3
Jaguari Brazil 203 A9
Jaguariaíva Brazil 206 D11
Jaguaribe Brazil 202 E3
Jaguaripe Brazil 202 E5
Jaguaruana Brazil 202 E3
Jagüe Arg. 204 C3
Jagüey Grande Cuba 186 C2
Jahanabad India 97 E4
formerly spelt Jehanabad
Jahān Dāgh mt. Iran 100 B2
Jahleel, Point Australia 148 A1
Jahmah well Iraq 107 F5
Jahrom Iran 100 C4
Jāhyad Iran 100 D5
Jaicós Brazil 202 D3
Jaigarh India 94 B2
Jailolo Indon. 75 C2
Jailolo, Selat sea chan. Indon. 75 D3
Jailolo Gilolo i. Indon. see **Halmahera**
Jaiña Chile 200 C4
Jainca China 84 D5
also known as Magitang
Jaintiapur Bangl. 97 G4
Jaipur India 96 B4
Jaipurhat Bangl. 97 F4
Jais India 97 D4
Jaisalmer India 96 A4
Jaisinghnagar India 97 D5
Jaitaran India 96 B4
Jaitgarh hill India 94 C1
Jaitpur India 96 C4
Jajarkot Nepal 97 D3
Jajce Bos.-Herz. 56 J4
Jajnagar state India see **Orissa**
Jakar Bhutan 97 F4
also known as Byakar

▶**Jakarta** Indon. 77 D4
Capital of Indonesia. Formerly spelt Djakarta; historically known as Batavia or Sunda Kalapa.
world [cities] ▶ 24–25

Jakhan India 101 G6
Jakharrah Libya 120 D2
Jakin mt. Afgh. 101 F4
Jakkalsberg Namibia 130 C3
Jakkalsberg hills Namibia 132 A5
Jakkī Kowr Iran 101 E5
Jäkkvik Sweden 44 L2
Jakliat India 96 B3
Jako i. East Timor 75 C5
also known as Jaco
Jakobshavn Greenland see **Ilulissat**
Jakobstad Fin. 44 M3
also known as Pietersaari
Jakupica mts Macedonia 58 C7
Jal U.S.A. 179 B5
Jalaid China see **Inder**
Jalājil Saudi Arabia 105 D2
Jalālābād Afgh. 101 G3
Jalalabad Punjab India 96 B3
Jalalabad Uttar Pradesh India 96 C3
Jalalabad Uttar Pradesh India 96 C4
Jalal-Abad Kyrg. 103 H4
also spelt Dzhalal-Abad
Jalal-Abad admin. div. Kyrg. 103 H4
English form Jalal-Abad Oblast; also known as Dzhalal-Abadskaya Oblast'
Jalal-Abad Oblast admin. div. Kyrg. see **Jalal-Abad**
Jalalpur Gujarat India 94 B1
Jalalpur Uttar Pradesh India 97 D4
Jalāmid, Ḥazm al ridge Saudi Arabia 107 D5
Ja'lān, Jabal mts Oman 105 G3
Jalandhar India 96 B3
formerly spelt Jullundur
Jalan Kayu Sing. 76 [inset]
Jalapa Guat. 185 H6
Jalapa Mex. 185 G5
Jalapa Nicaragua 186 B4
Jalapa Enríquez Mex. 185 F5
also known as Xalapa
Jalapur Pak. 101 H3
Jalapur Pirwala Pak. 101 G4
Jalasjärvi Fin. 44 M3
Jalaun India 96 C4
Jalawlā' Iraq 107 F4
also spelt Jalūlā
Jalboi r. Australia 148 B2
Jaldak Afgh. 101 F4
Jaldhaka r. Bangl. 97 F4
Jaldrug India 94 C2
Jales Brazil 206 C7
Jalesar India 96 C4
Jaleshwar India 97 E5
Jaleshwar Nepal see **Jaleswar**
Jaleswar Nepal 97 E4
also spelt Jaleshwar
Jalgaon India 96 B5
Jalībah Iraq 107 F5
Jalingo Nigeria 125 H4
Jalisco state Mex. 184 D5
Jallābī Iran 100 D5
Jalna India 94 B2
Jālo Iran 101 E5
Jalón r. Spain 55 J3
Jalor India 96 B4
Jalostotitlán Mex. 185 E4
Jalovik Srbija Yugo. 58 A4
Jalpa Mex. 185 E4
Jalpaiguri India 97 F4
Jalpan Mex. 185 F4
Jalrez Afgh. 101 G3
Jālū Libya 120 D2
Jalūlā Iraq see **Jalawlā'**
Jālū Oasis Libya 120 D2
Jām r. Iran 101 E3
Jām reg. Iran 101 E3
Jamaica Cuba 187 E2
▶**Jamaica** country West Indies 186 D3
northamerica [countries] ▶ 158–159
Jamaica Channel Haiti/Jamaica 187 E3
Jämaja Estonia 42 D3
Jamalpur Bangl. 97 F4
Jamalpur India 97 E4
Jamanxim r. Brazil 199 G6
Jamari Brazil 201 E2
Jamba Angola 127 C8
Jambi Indon. 76 C3
also known as Telanaipura
Jambi prov. Indon. 76 C3
Jambin Australia 149 F5
Jambo India 96 B4
Jamboaye r. Indon. 76 B1
Jambongan i. Sabah Malaysia 77 G1
Jambuair, Tanjung pt Indon. 76 B1
Jambūr Iraq 109 P2
Jambusar India 96 B5
Jamekunte India 94 C2
James watercourse Australia 148 C4
James r. Canada 167 I1
James r. MO U.S.A. 178 D4
James r. ND/SD U.S.A. 178 C3
James r. VA U.S.A. 177 I8
James, Isla i. Chile 205 B7
Jamesabad Pak. 101 G5
James Bay Canada 168 D2
Jamesburg U.S.A. 177 K5
James Cistern Bahamas 186 D1
Jameson Land reg. Greenland 165 Q2
Jameson Range hills Australia 151 D5
James Peak N.Z. 153 C13
James Ranges mts Australia 148 B5
James Ross Island Antarctica 222 U2
James Ross Strait Canada 165 J3
Jamestown Australia 146 C3
Jamestown Canada see **Wawa**
Jamestown S. Africa 133 K8

▶**Jamestown** St Helena 216 N7
Capital of St Helena and Dependencies.

Jamestown CA U.S.A. 182 D4
Jamestown KY U.S.A. 174 C4
Jamestown ND U.S.A. 178 C2
Jamestown NY U.S.A. 176 F3
Jamestown PA U.S.A. 176 E4
Jamestown TN U.S.A. 176 A9
Jämijärvi Fin. 45 M3
Jamiltepec Mex. 185 F5
Jamkhandi India 94 B2
Jamkhed India 94 B2
Jammalamadugu India 94 C3
Jammerbugten b. Denmark 45 J4
Jammu Jammu and Kashmir 96 B2

▶**Jammu and Kashmir** terr. Asia 96 C2
Disputed territory (India/Pakistan). Short form Kashmir.
asia [countries] ▶ 64–67

Jamnagar India 96 A5
formerly known as Navangar
Jamner India 94 B1
Jamni r. India 96 C4
Jamno, Jezioro lag. Poland 49 N1
Jampang Kulon Indon. 77 D4
Jampur Pak. 101 G4
Jämsä Fin. 45 N3
Jämsänkoski Fin. 45 N3
Jamshedpur India 97 E5
Jamtara India 97 E5
Jamtari Nigeria 125 H5
Jämtland county Sweden 44 K3
Jamui India 97 E4
Jamuk, Gunung mt. Indon. 77 G2
Jamu Mare Romania 58 C3
Jamuna r. Bangl. 97 F5
Jamuna r. India 97 G4
Janā i. Saudi Arabia 105 E2
Janāb, Wādī al watercourse Jordan 109 H6
Janakpur India 97 D5
Janakpur Nepal 97 E4
Janaúba Brazil 202 D5
Jandaia Brazil 206 C4
Jandaia do Sul Brazil 206 B10
Jandaq Iran 100 C3
Jandiala India 96 B3
Jandiatuba r. Brazil 198 D5
Jandongi Dem. Rep. Congo 126 D4
Jandowae Australia 149 F5
Jándula r. Spain 54 G6
Jandulilla r. Spain 55 H7
Janeiro r. Brazil 202 C5
Janesville CA U.S.A. 182 D1
Janesville WI U.S.A. 172 D8
Jang, Tanjung pt Indon. 76 D3
Jangal Iran 101 D3
Jangamo Moz. 131 G5
Jangaon India 94 C2
Jangeldi Uzbek. see **Dzhangel'dy**
Jangipur India 97 F4
Jangnga Turkm. see **Dzhanga**
Jangngai Ri mts China 89 D5
Jangngai Zangbo r. China 89 D5
Jānī Beyglū Iran 100 A2
Janikowo Poland 49 P3
Janiópolis Brazil 206 A11
Janja Bos.-Herz. 56 L4
Janja r. Bos.-Herz. 56 L4
Janjevo Kosovo, Srbija Yugo. 58 C6
Jan Kempdorp S. Africa 133 I4
formerly known as Andalusia
Jankov Kamen mt. Yugo. 58 B5

▶**Jan Mayen** i. Arctic Ocean 224 X2
Part of Norway.

Jāņmuiža Latvia 42 G4
Jannatābād Iran 100 B3
Jañona mt. Spain 54 E4
Janos Mex. 184 C2
Jánoshalma Hungary 49 Q9
Jánossomorja Hungary 49 O8
Janów Lubelski Poland 49 T5
Jans Bay Canada 167 I4
Jansenville S. Africa 133 I9
Jânua Coeli Brazil 202 B2
Januária Brazil 202 C5
Janūbī, Al Fulayj al watercourse Saudi Arabia 105 D1
Janûb Sînâ' governorate Egypt 108 E8
English form South Sinai; also known as Sinai al Janûbîya
Janwada India 94 C2
Janzar mt. Pak. 101 E5
Janzé France 50 E5
Jaora India 96 B5

▶**Japan** country Asia 90 E5
9th most populous country in the world. Known as Nihon or Nippon in Japanese.
world [population] ▶ 22–23
asia [countries] ▶ 64–67

Japan, Sea of N. Pacific Ocean 83 D5
also known as East Sea or Nippon Hai
Japan Alps National Park Japan see **Chibu-Sangaku National Park**
Japón Hond. 186 B4
Japurá r. Brazil 198 E5
Japvo Mount India 97 G4
Jaqué Panama 186 D6
Jarabacoa Dom. Rep. 187 F3
Jarābulus Syria 109 J1
Jarad Saudi Arabia 104 C4
Jaraguá Brazil 206 D2
Jaraguá do Sul Brazil 203 B8
Jaraguari Brazil 203 A7
Jaraiz de la Vera Spain 54 F4
Jarama r. Spain 55 H4
Jarash Jordan 108 G5
Jarauçu r. Brazil 199 H5
Järbo Sweden 45 L3
Jarboesville U.S.A. see **Lexington Park**
Jar-bulak Kazakh. see **Kabanbay**
Jardim Ceará Brazil 202 E3
Jardim Mato Grosso do Sul Brazil 201 F5
Jardín r. Spain 55 I6
Jardine River National Park Australia 149 D1
Jardinópolis Brazil 206 F8
Jargalant Arhangay Mongolia 84 D2
Jargalant Bayanhongor Mongolia 84 C2
Jargalant Bayan-Ölgiy Mongolia 84 A2
Jargalant Dornod Mongolia 85 G2
Jargalant Govĭ-Altay Mongolia 84 C2
Jargalant Mongolia see **Hovd**
Jargalant Töv Mongolia 85 E1
Jargalant Hayrhan mt. Mongolia 84 B2
Jargalthaan Mongolia 85 F2
Jari r. Brazil 199 I5
Jaria Jhanjail Bangl. 97 F4
Jarmen Germany 49 K2
Järna Dalarna Sweden 45 K3
Järna Stockholm Sweden 45 L4
Jarnac France 50 F7
Jarocin Poland 49 O4
Jaroměř Czech Rep. 49 M5
Jarosław Poland 49 T5
Järpen Sweden 44 K3
Jarqŭrghon Uzbek. see **Dzharkurgan**
Jarrāḩ, Wādī watercourse Syria 109 M1
Jarrāhi watercourse Iran 100 B4
Jarratt U.S.A. 176 H9
Jarrettsville U.S.A. 177 I6
Jartai China 85 E4
Jartai Yanchi salt l. China 84 E4
Jarú Brazil 201 E2
Jarūb Yemen 105 F4
Jarud China see **Lubei**
Jarut mt. Yugo. 58 B5
Järvakandi Estonia 42 F3
Järvenpää Fin. 45 N3

▶**Jarvis Island** terr. N. Pacific Ocean 221 H6
United States Unincorporated Territory.
oceania [countries] ▶ 138–139

Järvsand Sweden 44 K2
Järvsö Sweden 45 L3
Jarwa India 97 D4
Jasdan India 96 A5
Jashpurnagar India 97 E5
Jasień Poland 49 M4
Jasiołka r. Poland 49 S6
Jäsk Iran 100 D5
Jäsk-e Kohneh Iran 100 D5
Jasliq Uzbek. see **Zhaslyk**
Jasło Poland 49 S6
Jašlūnai Lith. 42 G7
Jasmund pen. Germany 49 K1
Jasmund, Nationalpark nature res. Germany 49 K1
Jason Peninsula Antarctica 222 T2
Jasper Canada 166 G4
Jasper AL U.S.A. 175 C5
Jasper AR U.S.A. 179 D4
Jasper FL U.S.A. 175 D6
Jasper GA U.S.A. 174 C5
Jasper IN U.S.A. 174 C4
Jasper NY U.S.A. 176 H3
Jasper OH U.S.A. 176 B6
Jasper TN U.S.A. 174 C5
Jasper TX U.S.A. 179 D6
Jasper National Park Canada 167 G4
Jaşşān Iraq 107 F4
Jassy Romania see **Iaşi**
Jastarnia Poland 49 P1
Jastrebarsko Croatia 56 H3
Jastrowie Poland 49 N2
Jastrzębie-Zdrój Poland 49 P6
historically known as Bad Königsdorff
Jászárokszállás Hungary 49 Q8
Jászberény Hungary 49 Q8
Jataí Brazil 206 B4
Jatapu r. Brazil 199 G5
Jatara India 96 C4
Jati Pak. 101 G5
also known as Mughalbhin
Jatibarang Indon. 77 E4
Jatibonico Cuba 186 D2
Játiva Spain see **Xátiva**
Jatiwangi Indon. 77 E4
Jatobá Brazil 202 A5
Jatoi Pak. 101 G4
Jättendal Sweden 45 L3
Jatuarana Brazil 201 E1
Jaú Brazil 206 E9
Jaú r. Brazil 199 F5
Jaú, Parque Nacional do nat. park Brazil 199 F5
Jauaperi r. Brazil 199 F5
Jaua Sarisariñama, Parque Nacional nat. park Venez. 199 E3
Jauco Cuba 187 E2
Jauja Peru 200 B2
Jaumave Mex. 185 F4
Jauna r. Brazil 199 F6
Jaunanna Latvia 42 I4
Jaunay-Clan France 50 G6
Jaunjelgava Latvia 42 G5
Jaunkalsnava Latvia 42 G5
Jaunlutriņi Latvia 42 D5
Jaunmārupe Latvia 42 E5
Jaunpiebalga Latvia 42 H4
Jaunpils Latvia 42 E5
Jaunpur India 97 D4
Jaupaci Brazil 206 C3
Jauru Brazil 203 A6
Jauru r. Brazil 201 F4

▶**Java** i. Indon. 77 D5
5th largest island in Asia. Also spelt Jawa.
asia [landscapes] ▶ 62–63

Javadi Hills India 94 C3
Javaés r. Brazil see **Formoso**
Javaés, Serra dos hills Brazil 202 B4
Javalambre mt. Spain 55 K4
Javalambre, Sierra de mts Spain 55 J4
Javand Afgh. 101 F3
Javari r. Brazil 198 D6
also spelt Yavari
Javarthushuu Mongolia 85 G1
Java Sea Indon. 77 E4

▶**Java Trench** sea feature Indian Ocean 218 N6
Deepest point in the Indian Ocean.
oceans [features] ▶ 210–211

Jávea Spain 55 L6
Javier, Isla i. Chile 205 B7
Javor mts Yugo. 58 B5
Javořice hill Czech Rep. 49 M6
Javorie mt. Slovakia 49 Q7
Javornik mt. Slovenia 56 H2
Javorníky mts Slovakia 49 P6
Jävre Sweden 44 M2
Jawa i. Indon. see **Java**
Jawa Barat prov. Indon. 77 D4
Jawad India 96 B4
Jawai r. India 96 A4
Jawala Mukhi India 96 C3
Jawar India 96 C5
Jawa Tengah prov. Indon. 77 E4
Jawa Timur prov. Indon. 77 F4
Jawbān Bayk Syria 109 I1
Jawf, Wādī al watercourse Yemen 104 D5
Jawhar India 94 B2
Jawhar Somalia 128 E4
Jawor Poland 49 N4
Jaworzno Poland 49 Q5
Jawoyn Aboriginal Land res. Australia 148 B2
Jay U.S.A. 179 D4

▶**Jaya, Puncak** mt. Indon. 73 I7
Highest mountain in Oceania. Formerly known as Carstensz-top or Puntjak Sukarno.
oceania [landscapes] ▶ 136–137

Jayanca Peru 198 B6
Jayanti India 97 F4
Jayapura Indon. 73 J7
formerly known as Hollandia or Sukarnapura
Jayb, Wādī al watercourse Israel/Jordan 108 G6
Jaynagar Bihar India 97 E4
Jaynagar W. Bengal India 97 F5
Jaypur India 95 D2
Jayrūd Syria 109 H4
Jayton U.S.A. 179 B5
Jazīrat al Hamrā U.A.E. 105 F2
Jazminal Mex. 185 E3
Jbail Lebanon 108 G3
historically known as Biblos
J. C. Murphey Lake U.S.A. 172 F9
Jean U.S.A. 183 I6
Jeanerette U.S.A. 175 B6
Jean Marie River Canada 166 F2
Jebāl Bārez, Kūh-e mts Iran 100 D4
Jebel Libya 120 C2
Jebel Romania 58 C3
Jebel Turkm. see **Dzhebel**
Jebel Abyad Plateau Sudan 121 F5
Jebel Ali U.A.E. see **Mina Jebel Ali**
Jebel, Bahr el r. Sudan/Uganda see **White Nile**
Jeberos Peru 198 B6
Jebha Morocco 54 G9
Jebus Indon. 77 D3
Jedburgh U.K. 46 J8
Jeddah Saudi Arabia 104 B3
also spelt Jiddah
Jeddore Lake Canada 169 K3
Jedeida Tunisia 57 B12
Jędrzejów Poland 49 R5
Jedwabne Poland 49 T2
Jeetze r. Germany 48 I2
Jefferson IA U.S.A. 178 D3
Jefferson NC U.S.A. 176 D9
Jefferson OH U.S.A. 176 E4
Jefferson TX U.S.A. 179 D5
Jefferson WI U.S.A. 172 E7
Jefferson r. U.S.A. 180 E3
Jefferson, Mount U.S.A. 183 H3
Jefferson, Mount vol. U.S.A. 180 B3

▶**Jefferson City** MO U.S.A. 178 D4
State capital of Missouri.

Jefferson City TN U.S.A. 176 B9
Jeffersonton U.S.A. 176 H7
Jeffersonville IN U.S.A. 174 C4
Jeffersonville KY U.S.A. 176 B8
Jeffersonville OH U.S.A. 176 B6
Jeffrey U.S.A. 176 D8
Jeffrey's Bay S. Africa 133 I11
Jega Nigeria 125 G3
Jehanabad India see **Jahanabad**
Jēkabpils Latvia 42 G5
Jelbart Ice Shelf Antarctica 223 X2
Jelcz-Laskowice Poland 49 O4
Jeldēsa Eth. 128 D2
Jelenia Góra Poland 49 M5
historically known as Hirschberg
Jelep La pass China/India 89 E7
Jelgava Latvia 42 E5
Jellico U.S.A. 176 A9
Jellicoe Canada 168 C3
Jelloway U.S.A. 176 C5
Jelondí Tajik. see **Dzhilandy**
Jelow Gīr Iran 100 A3
Jemaja i. Indon. 77 D2
Jember Indon. 77 F5
Jemez Pueblo U.S.A. 181 F6
Jeminay China 88 D2
also known as Topterek
Jeminay Kazakh. 88 D2
Jemma Bauchi Nigeria 125 H4
Jemma Kaduna Nigeria 125 H4
Jemmel Tunisia 57 C13
Jemnice Czech Rep. 49 M6
Jempang, Danau l. Indon. 77 G3
Jena Germany 48 I5
Jena U.S.A. 179 D6
Jenda Malawi 129 B8
Jendouba Tunisia 123 H1
Jengish Chokusu mt. China/Kyrg. see **Pobeda Peak**
Jenīn West Bank 108 G5
Jenipapo Brazil 199 F6
Jenkinjones U.S.A. 176 D8
Jenkins U.S.A. 176 C8
Jenkintown U.S.A. 177 J5
Jenne Mali see **Djenné**
Jenner Canada 167 I5
Jennersdorf Austria 49 N9
Jennings r. Canada 166 C3
Jennings U.S.A. 179 D6
Jenpeg Canada 167 L4
Jepara Indon. 77 E4
Jeparit Australia 147 D4
Jeppo Fin. 44 M3
Jequié Brazil 202 D5
Jequitaí Brazil 203 C6
Jequitaí r. Brazil 207 I4
Jequitinhonha Brazil 202 D6
Jequitinhonha r. Brazil 207 O2
Jerba, Île de i. Tunisia 123 H2
Jerbar Sudan 128 A3
Jereh Iran 107 G5
Jérémie Haiti 187 E3
Jeremoabo Brazil 202 E4
Jerer Shet' watercourse Eth. 128 D3
Jereweh Indon. 77 G5
Jerez Mex. 185 E4
Jerez de la Frontera Spain 54 E8
Jerez de los Caballeros Spain 54 E6
Jerfojaur Sweden 44 L2
Jerggul Norway 44 N1
Jergucat Albania 59 B9
Jericho Australia 149 E4
Jericho West Bank 108 G6
also known as Arihā; also spelt Yeriḩo; historically known as Tell es-Sultan

Jerid, Chott el *salt l.* Tunisia **123** H2
Jerijih, Tanjong *pt Sarawak* Malaysia **77** E2
Jerilderie Australia **147** E3
Jermyn U.S.A. **177** J4
Jerome *AZ* U.S.A. **183** L7
Jerome *ID* U.S.A. **180** D4
Jerramungup Australia **151** B7

▶**Jersey** *terr.* Channel Is **50** D3
United Kingdom Crown Dependency.
europe [countries] ▶ 32–35

Jersey City U.S.A. **177** K5
Jerseyville U.S.A. **174** B4
Jerte *r.* Spain **54** E5
Jerumenha Brazil **202** D3

▶**Jerusalem** Israel/West Bank **108** G6
Capital of Israel. Also known as El Quds; also spelt Yerushalayim; historically known as Aelia Capitolina *or* Hierosolyma.
asia [issues] ▶ 66–67

Jerusalem N.Z. **152** J7
Jervis Bay Australia **147** F3
Jervis Bay Territory *admin. div.* Australia **147** F3
also known as Commonwealth Territory
Jervois Range *hills* Australia **148** B4
Jesenice Slovenia **56** G2
Jeseník Czech Rep. **49** O5
Jesi Italy **56** F5
Jesmond Canada **166** F5
Jesolo Italy **56** E3
Jesselton *Sabah* Malaysia *see* **Kota Kinabalu**
Jessen Germany **49** J4
Jessheim Norway **45** J3
Jessore Bangl. **97** F5
Jesu Maria Island P.N.G. *see* **Rambutyo Island**
Jesup U.S.A. **175** D6
Jesús Carranza Mex. **185** G5
Jesús María Arg. **204** D3
Jesús María, Barra *spit* Mex. **185** F3
Jetalsar India **96** A5
Jethro *tourist site* Saudi Arabia **104** A1
also known as Maghā'ir Shu'ayb
Jetmore U.S.A. **178** C4
Jevnaker Norway **45** J3
Jewett City U.S.A. **177** N4
Jewish Autonomous Oblast *admin. div.* Rus. Fed. *see* **Yevreyskaya Avtonomnaya Oblast'**
Jeyhun Turkm. *see* **Dzheykhun**
Jeziorak, Jezioro *l.* Poland **49** Q2
Jeziorany Poland **49** R2
Jeziorka *r.* Poland **49** S3
Jeziorsko, Jezioro *l.* Poland **49** P4
Jezzine Lebanon **108** G4
Jhabua India **96** B5
Jha Jha India **97** E4
Jhajjar India **96** C3
Jhajju India **96** B4
Jhal Pak. **101** F4
Jhalakati Bangl. **97** F5
Jhalawar India **96** C4
Jhalida India **97** E5
Jhalrapatan India **96** C4
Jhang Pak. **101** H4
Jhanjharpur India **97** E4
Jhansi India **96** C4
Jhanzi *r.* India **97** G4
Jhapa Nepal **97** E4
Jhargram India **97** E5
Jharia India **97** E5
Jharkhand *state* India **97** E5
Jharsuguda India **97** E5
Jhatpat Pak. **101** G4
Jhawani Nepal **97** E4
Jhelum *r.* India/Pak. **96** B3
Jhelum Pak. **101** H3
Jhenaidaha Bangl. *see* **Jhenida**
Jhenida Bangl. **97** F5
also known as Jhenaidaha
Jhinjhuvada India **96** A5
Jhinkpani India **97** E5
Jhudo Pak. **101** G5
Jhumritilaiya India **97** E4
Jhunjhunun India **96** B3
Jhusi India **97** D4
Jiachuan China **86** C1
formerly known as Jiachuanzhen
Jiachuanzhen China *see* **Jiachuan**
Jiading China *see* **Xinfeng**
Jiading China **87** G2
Jiahe China **87** E3
Jiajiang China **86** B2
Jialing Jiang *r.* China **86** C2
Jialu China *see* **Jiaxian**
Jialu *r.* China **87** E1
Jiamusi China **82** C3
Ji'an *Jiangxi* China **87** E3
also known as Dunhou
Ji'an *Jiangxi* China **87** E3
Ji'an *Jilin* China **83** B4
Jianchang China *see* **Nancheng**
Jianchang China **85** H3
Jianchuan China **86** A3
also known as Jinhua
Jiandaoyu China *see* **Zigui**
Jiande China **87** F2
Jiang'an China **86** C2
Jiangbei China *see* **Yubei**
Jiangcheng China **86** B4
also known as Menglie
Jiangchuan China **86** B3
also known as Dajie
Jiangcun China **87** D3
Jiangdu China **87** F1
formerly known as Xiannümiao
Jiange China **86** C2
also known as Pu'an
Jiangjiehe China **87** C3
Jiangjin China **86** C2
Jiangjunmiao China **88** E2
Jiangjunmu China **85** G4
Jiangjuntai China **84** C3
Jiangkou China *see* **Fengkai**
Jiangkou *Guizhou* China **87** D3
also known as Shuangjiang
Jiangkou *Shaanxi* China **86** C1
Jiangkou China *see* **Pingchang**
Jiangle China **87** F3
also known as Guyong
Jiangling China *see* **Jingzhou**
Jiangluozhen China **86** C1
Jiangmen China **87** E4
Jiangna China *see* **Yanshan**
Jiangning China **87** F2
also known as Dongshan
Jiangshan China **87** F2
Jiangsi China *see* **Dejiang**
Jiangsu *prov.* China **87** F1
English form Kiangsu
Jiangtaibu China **85** E5
Jiangxi *prov.* China **87** E3
English form Kiangsi
Jiangxia China *see* **Wuchang**
Jiangxian China **85** F5
Jiangxigou China **84** D4
Jiangyan China **87** G1
formerly known as Taixian
Jiangyin China **87** G2
Jiangyong China **87** D3
Jiangyou China **86** C2
formerly known as Zhongba
Jiangyu China **85** H4
Jiangzhesongrong China **89** D6
Jianhu China **87** F1
Jian Jiang *r.* China **87** D4
Jianjun China *see* **Yongshou**
Jianli China **87** E2
also known as Rongcheng
Jianning China **87** F3
also known as Suicheng
Jian'ou China **87** F3
Jianping *Liaoning* China **85** H3
also known as Yebaishou
Jianping *Liaoning* China **85** H3
Jianshe China **86** A1
Jianshe China *see* **Baiyü**
Jianshi China **87** D2
also known as Yezhou
Jianshui China **86** B4
also known as Lin'an
Jianxing China **86** C2
Jianyang *Fujian* China **87** F3
Jianyang *Sichuan* China **86** C2
Jiaochang China **86** B1
formerly known as Jiaochangba
Jiaochangba China *see* **Jiaochang**
Jiaocheng China *see* **Jiaoling**
Jiaocheng China **85** G4
Jiaohe *Hebei* China **85** H4
Jiaohe *Jilin* China **82** B4
Jiaojiang China *see* **Taizhou**
Jiaokou China **85** F4
Jiaokui China *see* **Yiliang**
Jiaolai *r.* China **85** H4
Jiaolai *r.* China **85** I3
Jiaoling China **87** F3
also known as Jiaocheng
Jiaonan China **85** H5
formerly known as Wanggezhuang
Jiaowei China **87** F3
Jiaozhou China **85** I4
Jiaozhou Wan *b.* China **85** I4
Jiaozuo China **85** G5
Jiapigou China **82** B4
Jiasa China **86** B3
Jiashan China *see* **Mingguang**
Jiashi China **88** B4
also known as Payzawat
Jia Tsuo La *pass* China **89** D6
Jiaxian *Henan* China **87** E1
Jiaxian *Shaanxi* China **85** F4
also known as Jialu
Jiaxiang China **85** H5
Jiaxing China **87** G2
Jiayi Taiwan *see* **Chiai**
Jiayin China **82** C2
also known as Chaoyang
Jiayu China **87** E2
also known as Yuyue
Jiayuguan China **84** C4
Jiazi China **87** F4
Jibou Romania **58** E1
Jibsh, Ra's *c.* Oman **105** G3
Jibuti *country* Africa *see* **Djibouti**
Jibuti Djibouti *see* **Djibouti**
Jicarilla Apache Indian Reservation *res.* U.S.A. **181** F5
Jičín Czech Rep. **49** M5
Jiddah Saudi Arabia *see* **Jeddah**
Jidong China **82** C3
Jiehkkevarri *mt.* Norway **44** L1
Jiehu China *see* **Yinan**
Jieshi China **87** E4
Jieshi Wan *b.* China **87** E4
Jieshou China **87** E1
Jiesia *r.* Lith. **42** F7
Ješjávri *l.* Norway **44** N1
Jiexi China **87** E4
also known as Hepo
Jiexiu China **85** F4
Jieyang China **87** F4
Jieznas Lith. **42** F7
Jigalong Aboriginal Reserve Australia **150** C4
Jigawa *state* Nigeria **125** H3
Jigerbent Turkm. *see* **Dzhigirbent**
Jiggalong Australia **150** C4
Jiggs U.S.A. **183** I1
Jiguaní Cuba **186** D2
Jigzhi China **86** B1
also known as Chugqênsumdo
Jihār, Wādī al *watercourse* Syria **109** I3
Jihlava Czech Rep. **49** M6
Jihlava *r.* Czech Rep. **49** N7
Jijel Alg. **123** G1
formerly spelt Djidjelli
Jijia *r.* Romania **58** J2
Jijiga Eth. **128** D2
Jijona Spain **55** K6
Jiju China **86** B2
Jil'ād *reg.* Jordan **108** G5
English form Gilead
Jilān ash Shuwayhiţīyah *esc.* Saudi Arabia **109** K7
Jilava Romania **58** H4
Jilbadji Nature Reserve Australia **151** B6
Jilf al Kabīr, Haḑabat al *plat.* Egypt *see* **Gilf Kebir Plateau**
Jilga *r.* Afgh. **101** G3
Jilh al 'Ishār *plain* Saudi Arabia **105** D2
Jilib Somalia **128** D4
Jili Hu *l.* China **88** D2
Jilin China **82** B4
also known as Kirin
Jilin *prov.* China **85** J3
English form Kirin
Jiling China **84** D4
Jilin Handa Ling *mts* China **82** B4
Jiloca *r.* Spain **55** J3
Jilong Taiwan *see* **Chilung**
Jima Eth. **128** C3
Jima Ali *well* Eth. **128** E3
Jimani Haiti **187** F3
Jimbo Tanz. **129** C6
Jimbolia Romania **58** B3
Jimda China *see* **Zindo**
Jimena de la Frontera Spain **54** F8
Jiménez *Chihuahua* Mex. **184** D3
Jiménez *Coahuila* Mex. **185** E2
Jiménez *Tamaulipas* Mex. **185** F3
Jimeta Nigeria **125** I4
Jimi *r.* P.N.G. **73** J7
Jim Jim Creek *r.* Australia **148** B2
Jimo China **85** I4
Jimsar China **88** E3
Jina Romania **58** E3
Jinan China **85** H4
formerly spelt Tsinan
Jin'an China *see* **Songpan**
Jinbi China *see* **Dayao**
Jinchang China **84** D4
formerly known as Jinchuan
Jincheng China **85** G5
Jincheng China *see* **Leibo**
Jincheng China *see* **Yilong**
Jincheng China *see* **Wuding**
Jinchengjiang China *see* **Hechi**
Jinchuan China *see* **Jinchang**
Jinchuan China *see* **Xingan**
Jinchuan China **86** B2
also known as Quqên
Jind India **96** C3
Jindřichův Hradec Czech Rep. **49** M6
Jin'e China *see* **Longchang**
Jinfosi China **84** C4
Jing China *see* **Jinghe**
Jing *r.* China **87** D1
Jing'an China *see* **Doumen**
Jingbian China **85** F4
also known as Zhangjiapan
Jingchuan China **85** E5
Jingde China **87** F2
also known as Jingyang
Jingdezhen China **87** F2
Jingdong China **86** B3
also known as Jinping
Jinggangshan China **87** E3
formerly known as Ciping
Jinggang Shan *hill* China **87** E3
Jinggongqiao China **87** F2
Jinggu China **86** B4
also known as Weiyuan
Jinghai China **85** H4
Jinghe China **88** C2
also known as Jing
Jinghong China **86** B4
formerly known as Yunjinghong
Jingjiang China **87** G1
Jingle China **85** G4
Jingmen China **87** E2
Jingning China **85** E5
Jingpeng China **85** H3
also known as Hexigten Qi
Jingpo Hu *resr* China **82** C4
Jingshan China **87** E2
also known as Xinshi
Jingtai China **84** D4
also known as Yitiaoshan
Jingtieshan China **84** C4
formerly known as Huashugou
Jingxi China **86** C4
also known as Xinjing
Jingxian China **87** F2
Jingxian China *see* **Jingzhou**
Jingxin China *see* **Yongshan**
Jingyan China **86** C2
also known as Yancheng
Jingyang China *see* **Jingde**
Jingyu China **82** B4
Jingyuan China **84** E4
Jingzhou *Hubei* China **87** E2
formerly known as Jiangling
Jingzhou *Hubei* China **87** E2
formerly known as Shashi
Jingzhou *Hunan* China **87** D3
also known as Quyang; *formerly known as* Jingxian
Jinhe China *see* **Jinping**
Jinhua China *see* **Jianchuan**
Jinhua China **87** F2
Jining *Nei Mongol* China **85** G3
also spelt Tsining
Jining *Shandong* China **85** H5
formerly known as Chining
Jinja Uganda **128** B4
Jinjiang *Fujian* China **87** F3
Jinjiang China *see* **Chengmai**
Jinjiang *Yunnan* China **86** B3
Jin Jiang *r.* China **87** D3
Jin Jiang *r.* China **87** E3
Jinka Eth. **128** C3
Jinkouhe China **86** B2
Jinmen Taiwan *see* **Chinmen**
Jinmu Jiao *pt* China **87** D5
Jinning China **86** B3
also known as Kunyang
Jinotega Nicaragua **186** B4
Jinotepe Nicaragua **186** B5
Jinping *Guizhou* China **87** D3
also known as Sanjiang
Jinping China *see* **Jingdong**
Jinping *Yunnan* China **86** B4
also known as Jinhe
Jinping China *see* **Qiubei**
Jinping Shan *mts* China **86** B3
Jinsen S. Korea *see* **Inch'ŏn**
Jinsha China **86** C3
Jinsha Jiang *r.* China **78** B1
Jinsha Jiang *r.* China *see* **Yangtze**
Jinshan *Nei Mongol* China **85** H3
also known as Harqin Qi
Jinshan *Shanghai* China **87** G2
also known as Zhujing
Jinshan China *see* **Lufeng**
Jinshi China **87** D2
Jinshi China *see* **Xinning**
Jinta China **84** C4
Jintan China **87** F2
Jintang China **86** C2
also known as Zhaozhen
Jintotolo Channel Phil. **74** B4
Jintur India **94** C2
Jinxi China **87** F3
also known as Xiugu
Jinxi China *see* **Lianshan**
Jin Xi *r.* China **87** F3
Jinxian China **87** F2
also known as Minhe
Jinxian China *see* **Linhai**
Jinxiang *Shandong* China **85** H5
Jinxiang *Zhejiang* China **87** G3
Jinxiu China **87** D3
Jinyang China **86** B3
also known as Tiandiba
Jinyuan China *see* **Dayi**
Jinyun China **87** G2
also known as Wuyun
Jinz, Qa' al *salt flat* Jordan **108** H7
Jinzhai China **87** E2
also known as Meishan
Jinzhong China **85** G4
Jinzhou *Liaoning* China **85** I3
Jinzhou *Liaoning* China **85** I4
Jinzhou Wan *b.* China **85** I4
Jinzhu China *see* **Daocheng**
Ji-Paraná Brazil **201** E2
Jiparaná *r.* Brazil **201** E2
Jipijapa Ecuador **198** A5
Jiquilisco El Salvador **185** H6
Jiquilpan de Juárez Mex. **185** E5
Jiquitaia Brazil **207** N4
Jirau Brazil **200** D2
Jirgatol Tajik. **101** G2
also spelt Dzhirgatal'
Jiri *r.* India **97** G4
Jirin Gol China **85** H2
Jirkov Czech Rep. **49** K5
Jīroft Iran **100** D4
also known as Sabzvārān
Jirriiban Somalia **128** F3
Jirwān Saudi Arabia **105** E3
Jirzah Egypt **108** C8
Jishan China **85** F5
Jishi China *see* **Xunhua**
Jishou China **87** D2
Jishui China *see* **Yongfeng**
Jisr ash Shughūr Syria **108** H2
Jitian China *see* **Lianshan**
Jitra Malaysia **76** C1
Jiu *r.* Romania **58** E5
Jiudengkou China **85** E4
Jiuding Shan *mt.* China **86** B2
Jiugong Shan *mt.* China **87** E2
Jiujiang *Jiangxi* China **87** E2
also known as Shahejie; *formerly known as* Shahezhen
Jiujiang *Jiangxi* China **87** F2
Jiulian China *see* **Mojiang**
Jiuling Shan *mts* China **87** E2
Jiulong *Hong Kong* China *see* **Kowloon**
Jiulong China **86** B2
also known as Gyaisi
Jiulong China *see* **Yuechi**
Jiuquan China **84** C4
formerly known as Suzhou
Jiutai China **82** B3
Jiuxian China **85** F4
Jiuxu China **87** C3
Jiuzhen China **87** F3
Jiwani Pak. **101** E5
Jiwen China **85** I1
Jixi *Anhui* China **87** F2
also known as Huayang
Jixi *Heilong.* China **82** C3
Jixian China *see* **Jizhou**
Jixian *Heilong.* China **82** C3
also known as Fuli; *formerly known as* Fulitun
Jixian China *see* **Weihui**
Jixian *Shanxi* China **85** F4
Jiyuan China **85** G5
Jiz, Wādī al *r.* Yemen **105** F4
Jīzān Saudi Arabia **104** C4
Jīzān *prov.* Saudi Arabia **104** C4
Jizera *r.* Czech Rep. **49** L5
Jizerské Hory *mts* Czech Rep. **49** M5
Jizhou China **85** G4
formerly known as Jixian
Jizl *watercourse* Saudi Arabia **104** B2
Jizō-zaki *pt* Japan **91** C7
Jizzakh Uzbek. *see* **Dzhizak**
Jizzakh Wiloyati *admin. div.* Uzbek. *see* **Dzhizakskaya Oblast'**
Joaçaba Brazil **203** B8
Joachimsthal Germany **49** K3
Joaíma Brazil **202** D6
Joal-Fadiout Senegal **124** A3
Joana Peres Brazil **202** B2
João Belo Moz. *see* **Xai-Xai**
João de Almeida Angola *see* **Chibia**
João Monlevade Brazil **207** J6
João Pessoa Brazil **202** F3
João Pinheiro Brazil **203** C6
Joaquim Felício Brazil **207** I4
Joaquín V. González Arg. **204** D2
Jobabo Cuba **186** D2
Jobat India **96** B5
Job Peak U.S.A. **182** F2
Jockfall Sweden **44** M2
Jocoli Arg. **204** C4
Joda India **97** E5
Jódar Spain **55** H7
Jodhpur India **96** B4
Jodiya India **96** A5
Joe Batt's Arm Canada **169** K3
Joensuu Fin. **44** O3
Joesjö Sweden **44** K2
Jōetsu Japan **90** F6
Jofane Moz. **131** G4
Joffre, Mount Canada **167** H5
Jogbani India **97** E4
Jogbura Nepal **96** D3
Jõgeva Estonia **42** H3
Jogighopa India **97** F4
Jogindarnagar India **96** C3
Jogjakarta Indon. *see* **Yogyakarta**
Jõgua Estonia **42** I3
Johannesburg S. Africa **133** L3
Johan Peninsula Canada **165** L2
Jōhen Japan **91** C8
Johilla *r.* India **96** D5
John Day U.S.A. **180** C3
John Day *r.* U.S.A. **180** B3
John Day, Middle Fork *r.* U.S.A. **180** C3
John Day, North Fork *r.* U.S.A. **180** C3
John d'Or Prairie Canada **167** H3
John F. Kennedy *airport* U.S.A. **177** L5
John H. Kerr Reservoir U.S.A. **176** G9
John Jay, Mount Canada/U.S.A. **166** D3
Johnny Hoe *r.* Canada **166** F1
John o'Groats U.K. **46** I5
Johnson U.S.A. **177** M1
Johnsonburg U.S.A. **176** G4
Johnson City *NY* U.S.A. **177** J3
Johnson City *TN* U.S.A. **176** C9
Johnson City *TX* U.S.A. **179** C6
Johnsondale U.S.A. **182** F6
Johnston U.S.A. **175** D5
Johnston, Lake *salt flat* Australia **151** C7
Johnston and Sand Islands *atoll* N. Pacific Ocean *see* **Johnston Atoll**

▶**Johnston Atoll** N. Pacific Ocean **220** G4
United States Unincorporated Territory. Also known as Johnston and Sand Islands.
oceania [countries] ▶ 138–139

Johnstone Lake Canada *see* **Old Wives Lake**
Johnstone Strait Canada **166** E5
Johnston Range *hills* Australia **151** B6
Johnstown *NY* U.S.A. **177** K2
Johnstown *OH* U.S.A. **176** C5
Johnstown *PA* U.S.A. **176** G5
Johor *state* Malaysia **76** C2
Johor, Selat *strait* Malaysia/Sing. **76** [inset]
Johor, Sungai Malaysia **76** [inset]
Johor Bahru Malaysia **76** C2
Jõhvi Estonia **42** I2
Joigny France **51** J5
Joinville Brazil **203** B8
Joinville France **51** L4
Joinville Island Antarctica **222** U2
Jojutla Mex. **185** F5
Jokela Fin. **42** F1
Jokelbugten *b.* Greenland **165** Q2
Jokioinen Fin. **45** M3
Jokiperä Fin. **44** M3
Jokkmokk Sweden **44** L2
Jökulbunga *hill* Iceland **44** [inset] B2
Jökulfirðir *inlet* Iceland **44** [inset] B2
Jökulsá á Dal *r.* Iceland **44** [inset] D2
Jökulsá á Fjöllum *r.* Iceland **44** [inset] C2
Jolarpettai India **94** C3
Jolfa Iran **107** G4
Joliet U.S.A. **174** B3
Joliet, Lac *l.* Canada **168** E3
Joliette Canada **169** F4
Jolly Lake Canada **167** H1
Jolo Phil. **74** B5
Jolo *i.* Phil. **74** B5
Jomala Fin. **42** A1
Jomalig *i.* Phil. **74** B3
Jomard Entrance *sea chan.* P.N.G. **149** F1
Jombang Indon. **77** F4
Jomda China **86** A2
also known as Gatong
Jømna Norway **45** J3
Jomsom Nepal **97** D3
Jonāḩ Iran **100** C5
Jonancy U.S.A. **176** C8
Jonathán Point Belize **185** H5
Jonava Lith. **42** F6
Jondal Norway **45** I3
Jonê China **86** B1
also known as Liulin
Jonesboro *AR* U.S.A. **174** B5
Jonesboro *IL* U.S.A. **174** B4
Jonesboro *LA* U.S.A. **179** D5
Jonesboro *TN* U.S.A. **176** C9
Jones Mills U.S.A. **176** F5
Jones Mountains Antarctica **222** R2
Jonesport U.S.A. **174** H2
Jones Sound *sea chan.* Canada **165** K2
Jonestown *KY* U.S.A. **176** A8
Jonestown *PA* U.S.A. **177** I5
Jonesville *LA* U.S.A. **175** B6
Jonesville *NC* U.S.A. **176** E9
Jonesville *VA* U.S.A. **176** B9
Jonglei Sudan **128** A3
Jonglei *state* Sudan **128** B3
Jonglei Canal Sudan **128** A3
Joniškėlis Lith. **42** F5
Joniškis Lith. **42** E5
Jonk *r.* India **97** D5
Jönköping Sweden **45** K4
Jönköping *county* Sweden **45** K4
Jonquière Canada **169** G3
Jonuta Mex. **185** G5
Jonzac France **50** F7
Joplin U.S.A. **178** D4
Joppa Israel *see* **Tel Aviv-Yafo**
Jora India **96** C4

▶**Jordan** *country* Asia **108** G7
known as Al 'Urdun in Arabic
asia [countries] ▶ 64–67

Jordan *r.* Asia **108** G6
Jordan *MT* U.S.A. **180** F3
Jordan *NY* U.S.A. **177** I2
Jordan *r. OR* U.S.A. **180** C4
Jordan *r. UT* U.S.A. **183** L1
Jordânia Brazil **207** M2
Jordet Norway **45** K3
Jorge Montt, Isla *i.* Chile **205** B8
Jorhat India **97** G4
Jorm Afgh. **101** G2
Jormvattnet Sweden **44** K2
Jörn Sweden **44** M2
Joroinen Fin. **44** N3
Jørpeland Norway **45** I4
Jos Nigeria **125** H4
Jose Abad Santos Phil. **74** C5
José Bonifácio *Rondônia* Brazil **201** E3
José Bonifácio *São Paulo* Brazil **206** D8
José Cardel Mex. **185** F5
José de Freitas Brazil **202** D3
José de San Martín Arg. **205** C7
José Enrique Rodó Uruguay **204** F4
Joselândia Brazil **201** F4
José Pañganiban Phil. **74** B3
José Pedro Varela Uruguay **204** G4
Joseph, Lac *l.* Canada **169** H2
Joseph Bonaparte Gulf Australia **150** E2
Joseph City U.S.A. **183** N7
Joshimath India **96** C3
Jōshinetsu-kōgen National Park Japan **91** F6
Joshipur India **97** E5
Joshua Tree U.S.A. **183** H7
Joshua Tree National Park U.S.A. **183** I8
Jos Plateau Nigeria **125** H4
Josselin France **50** D5
Jossund Norway **44** J2
Jostedalsbreen *glacier* Norway **45** I3
Jostedalsbreen Nasjonalpark *nat. park* Norway **45** I3
Josvainiai Lith. **42** E6
Jotunheimen *mts* Norway **45** J3
Jotunheimen Nasjonalpark *nat. park* Norway **45** J3
Joubertina S. Africa **132** H10
Jouberton S. Africa **133** K3
Joué-lès-Tours France **50** G5
Joukokylä Fin. **44** N2
Joûnié Lebanon **108** G4
Jourdanton U.S.A. **179** C6
Joussard Canada **167** H4
Joutsa Fin. **45** N3
Joutseno Fin. **45** O3
Joutsijärvi Fin. **44** N2
Jovellanos Cuba **186** C2
Jowai India **97** G4
Jowzjān *prov.* Afgh. **101** F2
Joy, Mount Canada **166** C2
Joya de Cerén *tourist site* El Salvador **185** H6
Jozini S. Africa **133** Q4
Jrayfiya *well* W. Sahara **122** B4
Jreïda Mauritania **124** A2
Juan Aldama Mex. **185** E3
Juancheng China **85** G5
Juan de Fuca Strait Canada/U.S.A. **164** G5
Juan de Garay Arg. **204** D5
Juan de Nova *i.* Indian Ocean **129** D9
Juan E. Barra Arg. **204** E5
Juan Escutia Mex. **184** D4
Juan Fernández, Archipiélago *is* S. Pacific Ocean *see* **Juan Fernández Islands**
Juan Fernández Islands S. Pacific Ocean **221** M8
also known as Juan Fernández, Archipiélago
Juangriego Venez. **199** F2
Juan Jorge Arg. **204** F3
Juanjuí Peru **200** A1
Juankoski Fin. **44** O3
Juan Mata Ortíz Mex. **184** C2
Juanshui China *see* **Tongcheng**
Juan Stuven, Isla *i.* Chile **205** B7
Juara Brazil **201** F2
Juaréz Mex. **185** E3
Juárez, Sierra de *mts* Mex. **184** A1
Juatinga, Ponta da *pt* Brazil **207** I10
Juàzeiro Brazil **202** D4
Juàzeiro do Norte Brazil **202** E3
Juazohn Liberia **124** C5
Juba *r.* Somalia *see* **Jubba**
Juba Sudan **128** A3
Juban Yemen **104** D5
Jubany *research station* Antarctica **222** U2
long form Teniente Jubany
Jubba *r.* Somalia **128** D5
also spelt Juba; *formerly spelt* Giuba
Jubbada Dhexe *admin. reg.* Somalia **128** D4
Jubbada Hoose *admin. reg.* Somalia **128** D4
Jubbah Saudi Arabia **104** C1
Jubbulpore India *see* **Jabalpur**
Jubilee Lake *salt flat* Australia **151** D6
Jubing Nepal **97** E4
Juby, Cap *c.* Morocco **122** B4
Júcar *r.* Spain **55** K5
Juçara Brazil **206** C2
Jucás Brazil **202** E3
Juchatengo Mex. **185** F5
Juchitán Mex. **185** G5
Juchitlán Mex. **184** D4
Jucurucu Brazil **203** E6
Jucuruçu *r.* Brazil **207** N4
Judaberg Norway **45** I4
Judaidat al Hamir Iraq **107** E5
Judaydah *waterhole* Iraq **109** M5
Judaydah Syria **109** K2
Judayyidat 'Ar'ar *well* Iraq **107** E5
Judenburg Austria **49** L8
Judian China **86** A3
Judith *r.* U.S.A. **180** E3
Judith Gap U.S.A. **180** E3
Juegang China *see* **Rudong**
Juego de Bolos *mt.* Spain **55** H6
Juelsminde Denmark **45** J5
Juerana Brazil **207** N4
Jufari *r.* Brazil **199** F5
Jugon-les-Lacs France **50** D4
Jugoslavija *country* Europe *see* **Yugoslavia**
Juh China **85** F4
Juhaynah *reg.* Saudi Arabia **104** B2
Juigalpa Nicaragua **186** B4
Juillac France **50** H7
Juillet, Lac *l.* Canada **169** I2
Juína Brazil **201** F2
Juína *r.* Brazil **201** F3
Juist *i.* Germany **48** E2
Juiz de Fora Brazil **203** D7
Jujuhan *r.* Indon. **76** C3
Jujuy *prov.* Arg. **200** D5
Jukkasjärvi Sweden **44** M2
also known as Čohkkiras
Julaca Bol. **200** D5
Julesburg U.S.A. **178** B3
Juli Peru **200** C4
Julia Brazil **199** E5
Juliaca Peru **200** C3
Julia Creek Australia **149** D4
Julian U.S.A. **183** H8
Julian, Lac *l.* Canada **168** E2
Julian Alps *mts* Slovenia *see* **Julijske Alpe**
Julianatop *mt.* Indon. *see* **Mandala, Puncak**
Juliana Top *mt.* Suriname **199** G4
Julianehåb Greenland *see* **Qaqortoq**
Julijske Alpe *mts* Slovenia **56** F2
English form Julian Alps
Julimes Mex. **184** D2
Júlio de Castilhos Brazil **203** A9
Juliomagus France *see* **Angers**
Júlio Mesquita Brazil **206** D9
Julius, Lake Australia **148** C4
Jullundur India *see* **Jalandhar**
Juma *r.* Brazil **199** E6
Juma *r.* China **85** G4
Juma Uzbek. *see* **Dzhuma**
Jumanggoin China **86** A1
Jumba Somalia **128** D5
Jumilla Spain **55** J6
Jumla Nepal **97** D3
Jumna *r.* India *see* **Yamuna**
Jump *r.* U.S.A. **172** B5
Jumprava Latvia **42** F5
Junagadh India **96** A5
Junagarh India **95** D2
Junan China **85** H5
also known as Shizilu
Jun Bulen China **85** H2
Junction *TX* U.S.A. **179** C6
Junction *UT* U.S.A. **183** L3
Junction Bay Australia **148** B1
Junction City *KS* U.S.A. **178** C4
Junction City *KY* U.S.A. **176** A8
Junction City *OR* U.S.A. **180** B3
Jundah Australia **149** D5
Jundiaí Brazil **206** G10

▶**Juneau** U.S.A. **164** F4
State capital of Alaska.

Juneau Icefield Canada **166** C3
Junee Australia **147** E3
Jūn el Khudr *b.* Lebanon **108** G4
Jungar Qi China *see* **Shagedu**
Jungfrau *mt.* Switz. **51** O6
Junggar Pendi *basin* China **88** D2
English form Dzungarian Basin
Jungshahi Pak. **101** F5
Juniata Sudan **128** B2
Juniata *r.* U.S.A. **177** H5
Junik *Kosovo, Srbija* Yugo. **58** B6
Junín Arg. **204** E4
Junín Peru **200** A2
Junín *dept* Peru **200** B2
Junior U.S.A. **176** F7
Juniper Mountains U.S.A. **183** K6
Junipero Serro Peak U.S.A. **182** C5
Junkerdalen Balvatnet *nature res.* Norway **44** K2
Junlian China **86** C2
Junnar India **94** B2
Junosuando Sweden **44** M2
Junqueirópolis Brazil **206** B8
Junsele Sweden **44** L3
Junshan Hu *l.* China **87** F2
Juntura U.S.A. **180** C4
Juntusranta Fin. **44** O2
Junxi China *see* **Datian**
Junxian China *see* **Danjiangkou**
Ju'nyung China **86** A1
formerly known as Ju'nyunggoin
Ju'nyunggoin China *see* **Ju'nyung**
Juodkrantė Lith. **42** C6
Juodšiliai Lith. **42** G7
Juodupė Lith. **42** G5
Juoksengi Sweden **44** M2
Juosta *r.* Lith. **42** F6
Juostininkai Lith. **42** F6
Juozapinės kalnas *hill* Lith. **42** G7
Jūpār Iran **100** D4
Juparanã, Lagoa *l.* Brazil **207** M6
Jupiá Brazil **206** B7
Jupiá, Represa *resr* Brazil **206** B8
Jupiter U.S.A. **175** D7
Juquiá Brazil **206** F11
Juquiá *r.* Brazil **206** F11
Juquitiba Brazil **206** F10
Jur *r.* Sudan **126** F2
Jura *mts* France/Switz. **51** L7
Jura *r.* Lith. **42** D6
Jura *i.* U.K. **46** G7
Jura, Sound of *sea chan.* U.K. **46** G8
Juradó Col. **198** B3
Juramento Brazil **207** J3
Juranda Brazil **206** A11
Jurbarkas Lith. **42** D6
Juremal Brazil **202** D4
Jurf ad Darāwīsh Jordan **108** G7
Jurgurra *r.* Australia **150** C3
Jurh China **85** I2
Jurhen Ul Shan *mts* China **97** F2
Jūri Estonia **42** F2
Jurien Australia **151** A6
Jurien Bay Australia **151** A6
Jurilovca Romania **58** J4
Juriti Velho Brazil **199** G5
Jūrmala Latvia **42** E5
Jurmu Fin. **44** N2
Jurong China **87** F2
Jurong Sing. **76** [inset]
Jurong, Selat *strait* Sing. **76** [inset]
Jurong, Sungai *r.* Sing. **76** [inset]
Jurong Island *reg.* Sing. **76** [inset]
Juruá Brazil **199** E5
Juruá *r.* Brazil **198** E5
Juruena Brazil **201** F3
Juruena *r.* Brazil **201** F1
Jurumirim, Represa de *resr* Brazil **206** E10
Jurupari *r.* Brazil **200** C1
Juruti Brazil **199** G5
Jurva Fin. **44** M3
Jūsan-ko *l.* Japan **90** G4
Jusepín Venez. **199** F2
Jūshqān Iran **100** D2
Jussarö *i.* Fin. **42** E2
Jussey France **51** L5
Justice U.S.A. **176** D8
Justo Daract Arg. **204** D4
Jutaí Brazil **198** D6
Jutaí *r.* Brazil **198** E5
Jüterbog Germany **49** K4
Juti Brazil **203** A7
Jutiapa Guat. **185** H6
Jutiapa Hond. **186** B4

Juticalpa Hond. 186 B4
Jutis Sweden 44 L2
Jutland pen. Denmark 45 J4
also spelt Jylland
Juuka Fin. 44 O3
Juupajoki Fin. 45 N3
Juurikorpi Fin. 42 H1
Juva Fin. 45 N3
Juwain Afgh. 101 E4
Juwana Indon. 77 E4
Juxian China 85 H5
also known as Chengyang
Juye China 85 H5
Jüymand Iran 100 D3
also known as Gonabad
Jüyom Iran 100 C4
Južnoukrajinsk Ukr. see Yuzhnoukrayinsk
Jwaneng Botswana 131 E5
Jylland pen. Denmark see Jutland
Jyrgalang Kyrg. 103 I4
also spelt Dzhergalan
Jyväskylä Fin. 44 N3

↓ K

K2 mt. China/Jammu and Kashmir 96 C2
2nd highest mountain in the world and in Asia. English form Godwin-Austen, Mount; also known as Qogir Feng.
world [physical features] 8–9

Ka r. Nigeria 125 G4
Kaabong Uganda 128 B4
Kaa-Iya, Parque Nacional nat. park Bol. 201 E4
Kaakhka Turkm. see Kaka
Kaalpan salt pan S. Africa 132 I6
Kaalrug S. Africa 133 P2
Kaamanen Fin. 44 N1
also known as Gámas
Kaambooni Kenya 128 D5
Kääpa Estonia 42 I4
Kaapamuiden S. Africa 133 P2
Kaapstad S. Africa see Cape Town
Kaarina Fin. 45 M3
Kaarta reg. Mali 124 C3
Kaavi Fin. 44 O3
Kaba China see Habahe
Kaba r. China/Kazakh. 88 D2
Kabaena i. Indon. 75 B4
Kabakly Turkm. 103 E5
also spelt Gabakly
Kabala Sierra Leone 124 C4
Kabale Uganda 128 A5
Kabalega Falls National Park Uganda see Murchison Falls National Park
Kabalo Dem. Rep. Congo 127 E6
Kabambare Dem. Rep. Congo 126 E6
Kabanbay Kazakh. 88 C2
also spelt Qabanbay; formerly known as Dzerzhinskoye or Jar-bulak or Zharbulak
Kabanga Dem. Rep. Congo 127 C6
Kabangu Dem. Rep. Congo 127 D7
Kabanjahe Indon. 76 B2
Kabansk Rus. Fed. 85 E1
Kabara i. Fiji 145 H3
also spelt Kambara; formerly known as Appalla
Kabardino-Balkarskaya A.S.S.R. aut. rep. Rus. Fed. see Kabardino-Balkarskaya Respublika
Kabardino-Balkarskaya Respublika aut. rep. Rus. Fed. 41 G8
formerly known as Kabardino-Balkarskaya A.S.S.R.
Kabardino-Balkarskiy Zapovednik nature res. Rus. Fed. 107 E2
Kabare Dem. Rep. Congo 126 F5
Kabarega National Park Uganda see Murchison Falls National Park
Kabasalan Phil. 74 B5
Kabaung r. Myanmar 78 B4
Kabaw Valley Myanmar 78 A3
Kabba Nigeria 125 G5
Kabbani r. India 94 C3
Kåbdalis Sweden 44 M2
Kabd aş Şārim reg. Syria 109 K3
Kabd Warqah reg. Syria 109 K3
Kabélawa Niger 125 I3
Kabenung Lake Canada 173 I2
Kaberneeme Estonia 42 G2
Kabertene Alg. 123 F3
Kab-hegy hill Hungary 49 O8
Kabinakagami r. Canada 168 C3
Kabinakagami Lake Canada 168 C3
Kabinda Dem. Rep. Congo 127 E6
Kabīr r. Syria 108 G2
Kabīrkūh mts Iran 100 A3
Kabirwala Pak. 101 G4
Käbli Estonia 42 F3
Kabneshwar India 96 C5
Kabo Cent. Afr. Rep. 126 C3
Kabompo Zambia 127 E8
Kabompo r. Zambia 127 D8
Kabondo-Dianda Dem. Rep. Congo 127 E7
Kabongo Dem. Rep. Congo 127 E6
Kabosa Island Myanmar 79 B5
Kabou Cent. Afr. Rep. 126 D3
Kabou Togo 125 F4
Kabozha Rus. Fed. 43 Q3
Kabrousse Senegal 124 A3
Kabshah, Jabal hills Saudi Arabia 104 C2
Kabūdeh Iran 101 E3
Kabūd Gonbad Iran 101 D2
also known as Kalāt
Kabūd Rāhang Iran 100 B3
Kabugao Phil. 74 B2

Kābul Afgh. 101 G3
Capital of Afghanistan. Historically known as Ortospana.

Kābul prov. Afgh. 101 G3
Kabul r. Afgh. 101 H3
Kabunda Dem. Rep. Congo 127 F8
Kabunduk Indon. 75 A5
Kaburuang i. Indon. 75 C2
Kabushiya Sudan 121 G5
Kabūtar Khān Iran 100 D4
Kabwe Zambia 127 F8
formerly known as Broken Hill
Kabyrga r. Kazakh. 103 E2
also spelt Qabyrgha
Kačanik Kosovo, Srbija Yugo. 58 C6
Kacepi Indon. 75 D3
Kacha Kuh mts Iran/Pak. 101 E4
Kachalinskaya Rus. Fed. 41 H6
Kachchh, Great Rann of marsh India see Kachchh, Rann of
Kachchh, Gulf of India 96 A5
formerly known as Kutch, Gulf of
Kachchh, Rann of marsh India 96 A4
also known as Kachchh, Great Rann of; also spelt Kutch, Rann of
Kachh Pak. 101 F4
Kachhola India 96 B4
Kachhwa India 97 D4
Kachia Nigeria 125 G4
Kachin state Myanmar 78 B2
Kachiry Kazakh. 103 I1
Kachīsī Eth. 128 C2
Kacholola Zambia 127 F8
Kachug Rus. Fed. 80 H2
Kachung Uganda 128 B4
Kaçkar Dağı mt. Turkey 107 E2
Kaczawa r. Poland 49 N4
Kada Japan 91 D7
Kadaingti Myanmar 78 B4
Kadaiyanallur India 94 C4
Kadam mt. Uganda 128 B4
Kadana Chad 120 D6
Kadanai r. Afgh./Pak. 101 F4
Kadan Kyun i. Myanmar 79 B5
also known as King Island
Kadapongan i. Indon. 77 F4
Kadarkút Hungary 49 O9
Kadaura India 96 C4
Kadavu i. Fiji 145 G3
also spelt Kantavu
Kadavu Passage Fiji 145 G3
also known as Kedairu Passage; also spelt Kandavu Passage
Kadaya Rus. Fed. 85 H1
Kaddam l. India 94 C2
Kade Ghana 125 E5
Kadéï r. Cent. Afr. Rep. 125 J6
Kadgo, Lake salt flat Australia 151 D5
Kādhimain Iraq see Al Kāẓimīyah
Kadi India 96 B5
Kadiana Mali 124 D4
Kadiapattanam India 94 C4
Kadijica mt. Bulg. see Kadiytsa
Kadıköy Turkey 58 H8
Kadıköy Turkey 106 B2
historically known as Chalcedon
Kadina Australia 146 C3
Kading r. Laos 78 C4
Kadınhanı Turkey 106 C3
also known as Saiteli
Kadiolo Mali 124 D4
Kadiri India 94 C3
Kadirli Turkey 106 D3
Kadiyevka Ukr. see Stakhanov
Kadiytsa mt. Bulg. 58 D7
also spelt Kadijica
Kadmat i. India 94 B4
Kadnikov Rus. Fed. 43 V2
Kado Nigeria 125 H5
Ka-do i. N. Korea 83 B5
Kadok Malaysia 76 C1
Kadoka U.S.A. 178 B3
Kadoma Zimbabwe 131 F3
formerly spelt Gatooma
Kadonkani Myanmar 78 A5
Kadrina Estonia 42 H2
Kadugli Sudan 126 F2
Kaduna Nigeria 125 G4
Kaduna r. Nigeria 125 G4
Kaduna state Nigeria 125 G4
Kadur India 94 C3
Kadusam mt. China/India 86 A2
Kaduy Rus. Fed. 43 S2
Kadyy Rus. Fed. 40 G4
Kadzherom Rus. Fed. 40 J2
Kadzhi-Say Kyrg. see Kajy-Say
Kaechon N. Korea 83 B5
Kaédi Mauritania 124 B2
Kaegudeck Lake Canada 169 K3
Kaélé Cameroon 125 I4
Kaena Point U.S.A. 181 [inset] Y1
Kaeng Krachan National Park Thai. 79 B5
Kaeo N.Z. 152 H3
Kaesŏng N. Korea 83 B5
Kafa Ukr. see Feodosiya
Kafakumba Dem. Rep. Congo 127 D7
Kafan Armenia see Kapan
Kafanchan Nigeria 125 H4
Kafferrivier S. Africa 133 K6
Kaffin-Hausa Nigeria 125 H3
Kaffir r. S. Africa 133 J6
Kaffrine Senegal 124 B3
Kafia Kingi Sudan 126 E2
Kafiau i. Indon. 75 D3
Kafireas, Akra pt Greece 59 F10
Kafireos, Steno sea chan. Greece 59 F11
Kafiristan reg. Pak. 101 G3
Kafirnigan Tajik. see Kofarnihon
Kåfjordbotn Norway 44 M1
Kafolo Côte d'Ivoire 124 D4
Kafr el Battikh Egypt 108 C6
Kafr el Dauwâr Egypt 108 B6
Kafr el Garâyda Egypt 108 C6
Kafr el Sheikh Egypt 121 F2
Kafr el Sheikh governorate Egypt 108 B6
Kafr el Zaiyât Egypt 108 B7
Kafret Rihama Egypt 121 E2
Kafr Silîm Egypt 108 B6
Kafu r. Uganda 128 B4
Kafue Zambia 127 F8
Kafue r. Zambia 127 F8
Kafue Flats marsh Zambia 127 E8
Kafue National Park Zambia 127 E8
Kaga Japan 91 E6
Kaga Bandoro Cent. Afr. Rep. 126 C3
formerly known as Fort Crampel
Kagan Uzbek. 103 F5
also spelt Kogon
Kagang China 84 D5
Kaganovich Rus. Fed. see Tovarkovskiy
Kaganovichabad Tajik. see Kolkhozobod
Kaganovichi Pervyye Ukr. see Polis'ke
Kagarlyk Ukr. see Kaharlyk
Kagawa pref. Japan 91 D7
Kagawong Canada 173 K5
Kåge Sweden 44 M2
Kagera admin. reg. Tanz. 128 A5
Kagera, Parc National de la nat. park Rwanda see Akagera National Park
Kagiso S. Africa 133 L3
Kağızman Turkey 107 E2
Kagmar Sudan 121 F6
Kagologolo Indon. 76 B3
Kagoshima Japan 91 B9
Kagoshima airport Japan 91 B9
Kagoshima pref. Japan 91 B9
Kagoshima-wan b. Japan 91 B9
Kagul Moldova see Cahul
Kāhak Iran 100 D2
Kahalīya, Gebel hill Egypt 108 D8
Kahama Tanz. 129 B5
Kaharlyk Ukr. 41 D6
also spelt Kagarlyk
Kahatola i. Indon. 75 C2
Kahawero waterhole Namibia 130 B4
Kahayan r. Indon. 77 F3
Kahemba Dem. Rep. Congo 127 C6
Kaherekoau Mountains N.Z. 153 B13
Kahla Germany 48 I5
Kahntah Canada 166 F3
Kahnu Iran see Kahnūj
Kahnūj Iran 100 D5
also known as Kahnu
Kahnwia Liberia 124 C5
Kahoe N.Z. 152 H3
Kahoka U.S.A. 174 B3
Kahoolawe i. U.S.A. 181 [inset] Z1
also spelt Kahulaui; formerly known as Tahaurawe
Kahperusvaarat mts Fin. 38 C3
Kahramanmaraş Turkey 107 D3
formerly known as Maraş; historically known as Germanicea
Kahror Pak. 101 G4
Kahta Turkey 107 D3
also known as Kölük
Kahugish well Iran 100 D3
Kahuku Point U.S.A. 181 [inset] Y1
Kahul, Ozero l. Ukr. 58 J3
Kahulaui i. U.S.A. see Kahoolawe
Kahului U.S.A. 181 [inset] Z1
Kahūrak Iran 101 D4
Kahurangi National Park N.Z. 152 G9
formerly known as North West Nelson Forest Park
Kahuta Pak. 101 H3
Kahuzi-Biega, Parc National du nat. park Dem. Rep. Congo 126 E5
Kai, Kepulauan is Indon. 73 H8
Kaia r. Sudan 128 A3
Kaiama Nigeria 125 F4
Kaiapit P.N.G. 73 K8
Kaiapoi N.Z. 153 G11
Kaibab U.S.A. 183 L5
Kaibamardang China 84 C4
Kaibara Japan 91 D7
Kai Besar i. Indon. 73 H8
Kaibito Plateau U.S.A. 183 M5
Kaidu He r. China 88 D3
also known as Karaxahar
Kaieteur Falls Guyana 199 G3
Kaifeng Henan China 87 E1
also known as Huanglongsi
Kaifeng Henan China 87 E1
Kaihu N.Z. 152 H3
Kaihua China see Wenshan
Kaihua China 87 F2
Kaiingveld reg. S. Africa 132 F6
Kaijiang China 87 C2
also known as Xinning
Kai Kecil i. Indon. 73 H8
Kai Keung Leng Hong Kong China 87 [inset]
Kaikohe N.Z. 152 H3
Kaikoura N.Z. 153 H10
Kaikoura Peninsula N.Z. 153 H10
Kailahun Sierra Leone 124 C4
Kailas mt. China see Kangrinboqê Feng
Kailas Range mts China see Gangdisê Shan
Kaili China 87 C3
Kailongong waterhole Kenya 128 B3
Kailu China 85 I3
Kailua U.S.A. 181 [inset] Z1
Kailua Kona U.S.A. 181 [inset] Z2
Kaimai-Mamaku Forest Park nature res. N.Z. 152 J5
Kaimai Range hills N.Z. 152 J5
Kaimana Indon. 73 H7
Kaimanawa Forest Park nature res. N.Z. 152 K6
Kaimanawa Mountains N.Z. 152 J7
Kaimar China 97 G2
Kaimganj India 96 C4
Kaimon-dake hill Japan 91 B9
Kaimur Range hills India 97 D4
Käina Estonia 42 D3
Kainan Tokushima Japan 91 D8
Kainan Wakayama Japan 91 D7
Kainda Kyrg. see Kayyngdy
Kaindy Kyrg. see Kayyngdy
Kaingaroa Forest N.Z. 152 K6
Kaingiwa Nigeria 125 F3
Kainji Lake National Park Nigeria 125 G4
Kainji Reservoir Nigeria 125 G4
Kaintaragarh India 95 E1
Kaipara Harbour N.Z. 152 I4
Kaiparowits Plateau U.S.A. 183 M4
Kaiping China 87 E4
Kaiping China see Dêqên
Kaipokok Bay Canada 169 J2
Kaira India see Kheda
Kairakau Beach N.Z. 152 K7
Kairala Fin. 44 N2
Kairana India 96 C3
Kairatu Indon. 75 D3
Kairouan Tunisia 123 H2
Kaisepakte Sweden 44 L1
Kaiserslautern Germany 48 E6
Kaiser Wilhelm II Land reg. Antarctica 223 F2
Kaishantun China 82 C4
Kaišiadorys Lith. 42 F7
Kait, Tanjung pt Indon. 77 D3
Kaitaia N.Z. 152 H3
Kaitangata N.Z. 153 D14
Kaitawa N.Z. 152 L6
Kaitha India 96 C5
Kaithal India 96 C3
Kaitong China see Tongyu
Kaitum Sweden 44 M2
Kaitumälven r. Sweden 44 M2
Kaiwatu Indon. 75 C5
Kaiwi Channel U.S.A. 181 [inset] Z1
Kaixian China 87 D2
also known as Hanfeng
Kaiyang China 86 C3
Kaiyuan Liaoning China 85 J3
Kaiyuan Yunnan China 86 B4
Kajaani Fin. 44 N2
Kajabbi Australia 149 D4
Kajaki Afgh. 101 F3
Kajang Malaysia 76 C2
Kajdar Iran 101 E5
Kajiado Kenya 128 C5
Kajo Kaji Sudan 128 A4
Kaju Iran 100 A2
Kajuligah Nature Reserve Australia 147 E3
Kajy-Say Kyrg. 103 I4
also spelt Kadzhi-Say
Kak, Ozero salt l. Kazakh. 103 F1
also known as Qaq Köli
Kaka Sudan 128 B2
Kaka Turkm. 102 D5
formerly spelt Kaakhka
Kakaban i. Indon. 77 G2
Kakabeka Falls Canada 168 B3
Kakabia i. Indon. 75 B4
Kakadu Aboriginal Land res. Australia 148 B2
Kakadu National Park Australia 148 B2
Kakagi Lake Canada 168 A3
Kakal r. Phil. 74 C5
Kakamas S. Africa 132 E5
Kakamega Kenya 128 B4
Kakamigahara Japan 91 E7
Kakamoéka Congo 126 A6
Kakana India 95 G4
Kakanj Bos.-Herz. 56 K4
Kakanui Mountains N.Z. 153 E13
Kakarahil well Niger 125 H3
Kakaramea N.Z. 152 I7
Kakaramea vol. N.Z. 152 J6
Kakata Liberia 124 C5
Kakatahi N.Z. 152 J7
Kakching India 97 G4
Kake Japan 91 C7
Kakenge Dem. Rep. Congo 126 D6
Kakesio Tanz. 128 B5
Kakhi Azer. see Qax
Kakhovs'ke Vodoskhovyshche resr Ukr. 41 E7
Kakhul Moldova see Cahul
Kākī Iran 100 B4
Kakinada India 95 D2
also spelt Cocanada
Kakinjës, Maja e mt. Albania 58 A6
Kakisa r. Canada 167 G2
Kakisa Lake Canada 167 G2
Kakiške Latvia 42 C5
Kakogawa Japan 91 D7
Kakonko Tanz. 128 A5
Kakpin Côte d'Ivoire 124 E4
Kakrala India 96 C4
Kakrima r. Guinea 124 B4
Kakshaal-Too mts China/Kyrg. see Kokshaal-Tau
Kakuda Japan 90 G6
Kakuma Kenya 128 B4
Kakus r. Sarawak Malaysia 77 F2
Kakwa r. Canada 166 G4
Kal hill Croatia 56 G3
Kala Nigeria 125 I3
Kala Tanz. 129 A7
Kalaå Kebira Tunisia 123 H2
Kalaallit Nunaat terr. N. America see Greenland
Kalabagh Pak. 101 G3
Kalabahi Indon. 75 C5
Kalabak mt. Bulg./Greece see Radomir
Kalabáka Greece see Kalampaka
Kalabakan Sabah Malaysia 77 G1
Kalabaydh Togdheer Somalia 128 E2
Kalabaydh Woqooyi Galbeed Somalia 128 D2
Kalabo Zambia 127 D8
Kalach Rus. Fed. 41 G6
Kalacha Dida Kenya 128 C4
Kalach-na-Donu Rus. Fed. 41 G6
Kaladan r. India/Myanmar 95 G1
Kaladar Canada 168 E4
Kaladgi India 94 B2
Kalaena r. Indon. 75 B3
Kalagwe Myanmar 78 B3
Kalahari Desert Africa 130 D4
world [population] 22–23
Kalahari Gemsbok National Park S. Africa 132 E2
Kalaikhum Tajik. see Qal'aikhum
Kalai-Khumb Tajik. see Qal'aikhum
Kala-I-Mor Turkm. 101 E3
also spelt Galaymor
Kalaiya Nepal 97 E4
Kalajoki Fin. 44 M2
Kalajoki r. Fin. 44 M2
Kalak Norway 44 N1
Kalakoch hill Bulg. 58 H5
Kalalé Benin 125 F4
Kalaliok Indon. 75 B3
Kalalusu i. Indon. 75 C1
Kalam India 94 C1
Kalam Pak. 101 H3
Kalámai Greece see Kalamata
Kalamaria Greece 58 D8
Kalamata Greece 59 D11
also known as Kalámai
Kalamazoo U.S.A. 172 H8
Kalamazoo r. U.S.A. 172 G8
Kalambau i. Indon. 77 F4
Kalamnuri India 94 C2
Kalamos i. Greece 59 B10
Kalamos, Akra pt Greece 59 G12
Kalampaka Greece 59 C9
also spelt Kalabáka
Kalana Estonia 42 D3
Kalana Mali 124 C4
Kalanaur Haryana India 89 B6
Kalanaur Punjab India 96 B3
Kalanchak Ukr. 41 E7
Kalandula Angola see Calandula
Kalangala Uganda 128 B5
Kalangali Tanz. 129 B6
Kalanguy Rus. Fed. 85 H1
Kalannie Australia 151 B6
Kalanwali India 96 B3
Kalao i. Indon. 75 B4
Kalaoa U.S.A. 181 [inset] Z2
Kalaong Phil. 74 C5
Kalaotoa i. Indon. 75 B4
Kala Oya r. Sri Lanka 94 C4
Kalapana U.S.A. 181 [inset] Z2
Kalar watercourse Iran 101 E5
Kalār Iraq 107 F4
Kalarash Moldova see Călăraşi
Kalasin Thai. 78 C4
Kalāt Iran 101 D5
Kalāt Iran see Kabūd Gonbad
Kalat Balochistan Pak. 101 F4
Kalat Balochistan Pak. 101 F5
Kalat, Küh-e mt. Iran 100 D3
Kalaus r. Rus. Fed. 41 H7
Kalavad India 96 A5
Kalavryta Greece 59 D10
Kalb, Ra's al c. Yemen 105 E5
Kalba U.A.E. 105 G2
Kälbäcär Azer. 107 F2
Kalbarri Australia 151 A5
Kalbarri National Park Australia 151 A5
Kalbaskraal S. Africa 132 C10
Kalbinskiy Khrebet mts Kazakh. 88 C1
also known as Qalbi Zhotasy
Kalbū Iran 100 D3
Kaldırım Turkey 108 G1
Kaldygayty r. Kazakh. 102 C2
Kale Turkey 106 B3
Kale Turkey 106 C2
Kaledupa i. Indon. 75 B4
Kalegauk Island Myanmar 79 B5
Kaleindaung inlet Myanmar 78 A4
Kalema Dem. Rep. Congo 126 E6
Kalémié Dem. Rep. Congo 127 F6
formerly known as Albertville
Kalemyo Myanmar 78 A3
Kalenoye Kazakh. 102 B2
Kalesija Bos.-Herz. 56 K4
Kalevala Rus. Fed. 44 O2
formerly known as Ukhta
Kalewa Myanmar 78 A3
Kaleybar Iran 100 A2
Kalga Rus. Fed. 85 H1
Kalgan r. Australia 151 B7
Kalgan China see Zhangjiakou
Kalghatgi India 94 B3
Kalgoorlie Australia 151 C6
Kalguéri Niger 125 H3
Kali Croatia 56 H4
Kali r. India/Nepal 96 D3
Kaliakra, Nos pt Bulg. 58 J5
Kalianda Indon. 77 D4
Kalibo Phil. 74 B4
Kaliet Indon. 76 B3
Kali Gandaki r. Nepal 97 E4
Kaligiri India 94 C3
Kalikino Rus. Fed. 43 U9
Kalima Dem. Rep. Congo 126 E5
Kalimantan reg. Indon. 77 E3
Kalimantan Barat prov. Indon. 77 E3
Kalimantan Selatan prov. Indon. 77 F3
Kalimantan Tengah prov. Indon. 77 F3
Kalimantan Timur prov. Indon. 77 G2
Kálimnos i. Greece see Kalymnos
Kalimpang India 97 F4
Kalinadi r. India 94 B3
Kali Nadi r. India 96 D4
Kalingapatnam India 95 E2
Kalinin Kyrg. see Eshanguzar
Kalinin Rus. Fed. see Tver'
Kalinin Turkm. see Boldumsaz
Kalininabad Tajik. see Kalininobod
Kaliningrad Rus. Fed. 42 B7
historically known as Königsberg
Kaliningrad Oblast admin. div. Rus. Fed. see Kaliningradskaya Oblast'
Kaliningradskaya Oblast' admin. div. Rus. Fed. 42 C7
English form Kaliningrad Oblast
Kaliningradskiy Zaliv b. Rus. Fed. 42 A7
Kalinino Armenia see Tashir
Kalinino Kostromskaya Oblast' Rus. Fed. 40 G4
Kalinino Omskaya Oblast' Rus. Fed. 103 H1
Kalinino Permskaya Oblast' Rus. Fed. 40 K4
Kalininobod Tajik. 101 G2
also spelt Kalininabad
Kalininsk Rus. Fed. 41 H6
formerly known as Balanda
Kalininskaya Rus. Fed. 41 F7
formerly known as Popovichskaya
Kalininskaya Oblast' admin. div. Rus. Fed. see Tverskaya Oblast'
Kalinjara India 96 B5
Kalinkavichy Belarus 43 K9
also spelt Kalinkovichi
Kalinkovichi Belarus see Kalinkavichy
Kalinovka Kazakh. 102 C2
Kaliro Uganda 128 B4
Kalis Somalia 128 F2
Kalisat Indon. 77 F5
Kalisch Poland see Kalisz
Kali Sindh r. India 99 J4
Kalispell U.S.A. 180 D2
Kalisz Poland 49 P4
historically known as Kalisch
Kalisz Pomorski Poland 49 M2
Kalitva r. Rus. Fed. 41 G6
Kaliua Tanz. 129 A6
Kalix Sweden 44 M2
Kalixälven r. Sweden 44 M2
Kalka India 96 C3
Kalkan Turkey 106 B3
Kalkaringi Australia 148 A3
Kalkaska U.S.A. 173 H6
Kalkfeld Namibia 130 C4
Kalkfonteindam dam S. Africa 133 J6
Kalkfontein Dam Nature Reserve S. Africa 133 J6
Kalkwerf S. Africa 132 F5
Kallakkurichchi India 94 C4
Kallakoopah Creek watercourse Australia 146 C1
Kallaktjåkkå mt. Sweden 44 L2
Kallam India 94 C2
Kallang Sing. 76 [inset]
Kallang r. Sing. 76 [inset]
Kallaste Estonia 42 I3
Kallavesi l. Fin. 44 N3
Kållberget Sweden 44 K3
Kallfjärden b. Sweden 44 M2
Kallifoni Greece 59 C9
Kallmet i Madh Albania 58 A7
Kalloni Greece 59 G11
Kallonis, Kolpos b. Greece 59 H9
Kallsjön l. Sweden 44 K3
Kallur India 94 C2
Kalmakkyrgan watercourse Kazakh. 103 F3
Kalmar Sweden 45 L4
Kalmar county Sweden 45 L4
Kalmarsund sea chan. Sweden 45 L4
Kalmthoutse Heide Natuurreservaat nature res. Belgium 51 K1
Kalmūkh Qal'eh Iran 100 D2
Kalmunai Sri Lanka 94 D5
Kalmykia aut. rep. Rus. Fed. see Kalmykiya - Khalm'g-Tangch, Respublika
Kalmykiya - Khalm'g-Tangch, Respublika aut. rep. Rus. Fed. 41 H7
English form Kalmykia; formerly known as Kalmytskaya Avtonomnaya Oblast'
Kalmykovo Kazakh. see Taypak
Kalmytskaya Avtonomnaya Oblast' aut. rep. Rus. Fed. see Kalmykiya - Khalm'g-Tangch, Respublika
Kalnai India 97 D5
Kalnciems Latvia 42 E5
Kalni r. Bangl. 97 F4
Kalnik mts Croatia 56 I2
Kalo Chorio Greece 59 G13
Kalocsa Hungary 49 P9
Kalodnaye Belarus 41 C6
Kaloko Dem. Rep. Congo 127 E6
Kalol Gujarat India 96 B5
Kalol Gujarat India 96 B5
Kaloma i. Indon. 75 C2
Kalomo Zambia 127 E9
Kalona U.S.A. 172 B9
Kalone Peak Canada 166 E4
Kalopanagiotis Cyprus 108 D3
Kalozhnoye, Ozero l. Rus. Fed. 44 O2
Kalpa India 96 C3
formerly known as Chini
Kalpeni i. India 94 B4
Kalpetta India 94 C4
Kalpi India 96 C4
Kalquduq Uzbek. see Kulkuduk
Kāl-Shūr, Rūd-e r. Iran 100 D2
Kaltanėnai Lith. 42 G6
Kaltenkirchen Germany 48 G2
Kaltinėnai Lith. 42 D6
Kaltukatjara Australia 148 A5
Kaltungo Nigeria 125 H4
Kalu India 96 B3
Kalu r. India 94 B2
Kaluderica Srbija Yugo. 58 B4
Kaluga Rus. Fed. 43 R7
Kaluga Oblast admin. div. Rus. Fed. see Kaluzhskaya Oblast'
Kalukalukuang i. Indon. 77 G4
Kaluku Indon. 75 A3
Kalulong, Bukit mt. Sarawak Malaysia 77 F2
Kalulushi Zambia 127 F8
Kalumburu Australia 150 D2
Kalumburu Aboriginal Reserve Australia 150 D2
Kalundborg Denmark 45 J5
Kalupis Falls Sabah Malaysia 77 G1
Kalur Kot Pak. 101 G3
Kalush Ukr. 41 C6
Kałuszyn Poland 49 S3
Kalutara Sri Lanka 94 C5
Kaluzhskaya Oblast' admin. div. Rus. Fed. 43 Q7
English form Kaluga Oblast
Kalvåg Norway 45 I3
Kalvan India 94 B1
Kalvarija Lith. 42 E7
Kalveliai Lith. 42 G7
Kälviä Fin. 40 B3
Kalvitsa Fin. 45 N3
Kalvola Fin. 45 N3
Kalwakurti India 94 C2
Kalyan India 94 B2
Kalyandurg India 94 C3
Kalyani India 94 C2
Kalyansingapuram India 95 D2
Kalyazin Rus. Fed. 43 S4
Kalymnos Greece 59 H12
Kalymnos i. Greece 59 H11
also spelt Kálimnos
Kalyshki Belarus 43 L6
Kama Dem. Rep. Congo 126 E5
Kama Myanmar 78 A4

Kama r. Rus. Fed. 40 J4
4th longest river in Europe.
europe [landscapes] 30–31

Kamaishi Japan 90 G5
Kamakura Japan 91 F7
Kamakusa Guyana 199 G3
Kamakwie Sierra Leone 124 B4
Kamal Chad 120 C4
Kamalapuram India 94 C3
Kamalia Pak. 101 H4
Kamamaung Myanmar 78 B4
Kaman India 96 C4
Kaman Turkey 106 C3
Kamanassie r. S. Africa 132 G10
Kamanassieberg mts S. Africa 132 G10
Kamaniskeg Lake Canada 173 P5
Kamanjab Namibia 130 B3
Kamaran Yemen 104 C5
Kamarān i. Yemen 104 C5
English form Kamaran Island
Kamarang Guyana 199 F3
Kamaran Island Yemen see Kamarān
Kamard reg. Afgh. 101 F3
Kamarde Latvia 42 F5
Kamareddi India 94 C2
Kamares Dytiki Ellas Greece 59 C10
Kamares Sifnos Greece 59 F12
Kamaria Falls Guyana 199 G3
Kamarlu Armenia see Artashat
Kamas U.S.A. 183 M1
Kamashi Uzbek. 103 F5
also spelt Qamashi
Kamativi Zimbabwe 131 E3
Kamba Nigeria 125 F4
Kamba Kota Cent. Afr. Rep. 126 C3
Kambalda Australia 151 C6
Kambam India 94 C4
Kambang Indon. 76 C3
Kambangan i. Indon. 77 E5
Kambara i. Fiji see Kabara
Kambarka Rus. Fed. 40 J4
Kambia Sierra Leone 124 B4
Kambing, Pulau i. East Timor see Atauro
Kambo-san mt. N. Korea see Kwanmo-bong
Kambove Dem. Rep. Congo 127 E7
Kamburovo Bulg. 58 H5
Kambût Libya 120 E2
Kamchatka r. Rus. Fed. 39 Q4
Kamchatka, Poluostrov pen. Rus. Fed. see Kamchatka Peninsula
Kamchatka Peninsula Rus. Fed. 39 P4
also known as Kamchatka, Poluostrov
asia [threats] 70–71
Kamchatskiy Proliv strait Rus. Fed. 39 Q4
Kamchatskiy Zaliv b. Rus. Fed. 39 Q4
Kamchiya r. Bulg. 58 I5
Kamchiyska Planina hills Bulg. 58 I6
Kamdesh Afgh. 101 G3
Kameia, Parque Nacional de nat. park Angola see Cameia, Parque Nacional da
Kamelik r. Rus. Fed. 102 B1
Kamen Bulg. 58 G5
Kamen', Gory mts Rus. Fed. 39 J3
Kamende Dem. Rep. Congo 127 E6
Kamenets-Podol'skiy Ukr. see Kam"yanets'-Podil's'kyy
Kamenitsa r. Bulg. 58 F5
Kamenjak, Rt pt Croatia 56 F4
Kamenka Kazakh. 102 B2
Kamenka Arkhangel'skaya Oblast' Rus. Fed. 40 H2
Kamenka Kaluzhskaya Oblast' Rus. Fed. 43 Q7
Kamenka Leningradskaya Oblast' Rus. Fed. 43 K1
Kamenka Lipetskaya Oblast' Rus. Fed. 43 T9
Kamenka Penzenskaya Oblast' Rus. Fed. 41 H5
Kamenka Primorskiy Kray Rus. Fed. 82 E3
Kamenka Smolenskaya Oblast' Rus. Fed. 43 N6
Kamenka-Bugskaya Ukr. see Kam"yanka-Buz'ka
Kamenka-Strumilovskaya Ukr. see Kam"yanka-Buz'ka
Kamenki Rus. Fed. 43 S5
Kamen'-na-Obi Rus. Fed. 80 C2
Kamenniki Rus. Fed. 43 T3
Kamennogorsk Rus. Fed. 43 K1
Kamennomostskiy Rus. Fed. 41 G7
Kamennoye, Ozero l. Rus. Fed. 44 O2
Kameno Bulg. 58 I6
Kamenongue Angola see Camanongue
Kamen'-Rybolov Rus. Fed. 82 D3
Kamenskiy Rus. Fed. 41 H6
Kamenskoye Koryakskiy Avtonomnyy Okrug Rus. Fed. 39 Q3
Kamenskoye Lipetskaya Oblast' Rus. Fed. 43 T9
Kamenskoye Ukr. see Dniprodzerzhyns'k
Kamensk-Shakhtinskiy Rus. Fed. 41 G6
Kamensk-Ural'skiy Rus. Fed. 38 G4
Kamenz Germany 49 L4
Kameoka Japan 91 D7
Kamet mt. China 89 B6
Kameyama Japan 91 E7
Kamëz Albania 58 A7
Kamiah U.S.A. 180 C3
Kamienna r. Poland 49 S4
Kamienna Gora Poland 49 N5
Kamień Pomorski Poland 49 L2
historically known as Cammin
Kamiesberg S. Africa 132 C7
Kamiesberge mts S. Africa 132 C7
Kamieskroon S. Africa 132 B7
Kamifurano Japan 90 H3
Kamikawa Japan 90 H3
Kamileroi Australia 149 D3
Kamina Dem. Rep. Congo 127 E7
Kamina Base Dem. Rep. Congo 127 E7
Kaminak Lake Canada 167 M2
Kaminokuni Japan 90 G4
Kaminoyama Japan 90 G5
Kaminške in Savinjske Alpe mts Slovenia 56 G2
Kaminuriak Lake Canada see Qamanirjuaq Lake
Kamioka Japan 91 E6
Kamiros Greece 59 I12
Kamishihoro Japan 90 H3
Kamitsushima Japan 91 A7
Kamituga Dem. Rep. Congo 126 F5
Kamkaly Kazakh. 103 G3
Kamla r. India 97 E4
Kamla r. India 97 F4
Kamloops Canada 166 F5
Kamloops Lake Canada 166 F5
Kammuri-yama mt. Japan see Kanmuri-yama
Kamnik Slovenia 56 G2
Kamo Armenia 107 F2
formerly known as Gavarr or Nor-Bayazet
Kamo Japan 90 F6
Kamob Sanha Sudan 121 H5
Kamoenai Japan 90 G3
Kamogawa Japan 91 G7
Kamoke Pak. 101 H4
Kamola Dem. Rep. Congo 127 E6
Kamonanira Tanz. 129 A6
Kamp r. Austria 49 M7

Kampala Uganda 128 B4
Capital of Uganda.

Kampanos, Akra pt Greece 59 F10
Kampar r. Indon. 76 C2
Kampar Malaysia 76 C1
Kamparkalns hill Latvia 42 D4
Kamparkiri r. Indon. 76 C2
Kampen Neth. 48 C3
Kampene Dem. Rep. Congo 126 E5
Kamphaeng Phet Thai. 78 B4
Kampi Katoto Tanz. 129 B6
Kampinoski Park Narodowy nat. park Poland 49 R3
Kampli India 94 C3
Kamp'o S. Korea 91 A7
Kampolombo, Lake Zambia 127 F7
Kâmpóng Cham Cambodia 79 D6
also spelt Kompong Cham
Kâmpóng Chhnăng Cambodia 79 D5
also spelt Kompong Chhnang
Kâmpóng Khleăng Cambodia 79 D5
also spelt Kompong Kleang
Kâmpóng Saôm Cambodia see Sihanoukville
Kâmpóng Spoe Cambodia 79 D6
also spelt Kompong Speu
Kâmpóng Thum Cambodia 79 D5
also spelt Kompong Thom
Kâmpôt Cambodia 79 D6
Kampuchea country Asia see Cambodia
Kamrau, Teluk b. Indon. 73 H7
Kamromskoye, Ozero l. Rus. Fed. 43 V1
Kamsack Canada 167 K5
Kamsar Guinea 124 B4
Kamskoye Vodokhranilishche resr Rus. Fed. 40 K4
Kamsuuma Somalia 128 D4
Kamtha India 96 C5
Kamui-dake mt. Japan 90 H3
Kamuli Uganda 128 B4
Kamungu Dem. Rep. Congo 127 E6
Kam"yanets'-Podil's'kyy Ukr. 41 C6
also spelt Kamenets-Podol'skiy
Kam"yanka-Buz'ka Ukr. 41 C6
also known as Kamenka-Bugskaya; formerly known as Kamenka-Strumilovskaya
Kam"yans'ke Ukr. 58 K3
Kamyanyets Belarus 42 E9
Kamyanyuki Belarus 42 E9
Kāmyārān Iran 100 A3
Kamyen' Belarus 43 J6
Kamyshin Rus. Fed. 41 H6

index K

Kamyshla Rus. Fed. 41 J5
Kamyshlybash Kazakh. 103 E3
also spelt Qamystybas; formerly spelt Kamyslybas
Kamysh-Samarskiye Ozera l. Kazakh. 102 B2
Kamysknoye Kazakh. 103 E2
Kamyslybas Kazakh. see Kamyshlybash
Kamyslybas, Ozero l. Kazakh. 103 E3
Kamyzyak Rus. Fed. 102 B3
Kamzar Oman 105 G2
Kan r. Rus. Fed. 80 F2
Kan Sudan 128 A2
Kana r. Zimbabwe 131 E3
Kana, Bukit mt. Sarawak Malaysia 77 F2
Kanaaupscow r. Canada 169 E2
Kanab U.S.A. 183 L4
Kanab Creek r. U.S.A. 183 L5
Kanagawa pref. Japan 90 F7
Kanagi Japan 90 G4
Kanaima Falls Guyana 199 F3
Kanairiktok r. Canada 169 J2
Kanakapura India 94 C3
Kanala Greece 59 F11
Kanallaki Greece 59 B9
Kanan Sweden 44 K2
Kanana S. Africa 133 K3
Kananga Dem. Rep. Congo 127 D6
formerly known as Luluabourg
Kanangra-Boyd National Park Australia 147 F3
Kanarak India see Konarka
Kanarraville U.S.A. 183 K4
Kanas watercourse Namibia 132 B4
Kanash Rus. Fed. 40 H5
Kanas Köl l. China 88 D1
Kanawha r. U.S.A. 176 C7
Kanazawa Japan 91 E6
Kanbalu Myanmar 78 A3
Kanchanaburi Thai. 79 B5
Kanchanjanga mt. India/Nepal see Kangchenjunga
Kanchipuram India 94 C3
Kańczuga Poland 49 T6
Kand mt. Pak. 101 F4
Kandahār Afgh. 101 F4
also spelt Qandahar; historically known as Alexandria Arachoton
Kandahār prov. Afgh. 101 F4
Kandahar India 94 C2
Kandalaksha Rus. Fed. 44 P2
Kandalakshskiy Zaliv g. Rus. Fed. 40 E2
Kandalakshskiy Zapovednik nature res. Rus. Fed. 44 P2
Kandang Indon. 76 B2
Kandangan Indon. 77 F3
Kandava Latvia 42 D4
Kandavu Passage Fiji see Kadavu Passage
Kandé Togo 125 F4
Kandhkot Pak. 101 G4
Kandi Benin 125 F4
Kandi, Tanjung pt Indon. 75 B2
Kandiaro Pak. 101 G5
Kandila Dytiki Ellas Greece 59 B10
Kandila Peloponnisos Greece 59 D11
Kandil Bouzou well Niger 125 H3
Kandıra Turkey 106 B2
Kandja Cent. Afr. Rep. 126 D3
Kandla India 96 A5
Kandos Australia 147 F3
Kandra India 95 E1
Kandreho Madag. 131 [inset] J3
Kandri India 97 D5
Kandrian P.N.G. 145 D2
Kandukur India 94 C3
Kandy Sri Lanka 94 D5
Kandyagash Kazakh. 102 D2
also spelt Qandyaghash; formerly known as Oktyabr' or Oktyabr'sk
Kane U.S.A. 176 G4
Kane Basin b. Greenland see Kane Bassin
Kane Bassin b. Greenland 165 M2
English form Kane Basin
Kaneh watercourse Iran 100 C5
Kanem pref. Chad 120 B6
Kaneohe U.S.A. 181 [inset] Z1
Kanevskaya Rus. Fed. 41 F7
Kaneyama Japan 90 G5
Kang Botswana 130 D4
Kanga r. Bangl. 97 F5
Kangaamiut Greenland 165 N3
Kangaarsussuaq c. Greenland 165 L2
also known as Parry, Kap
Kangaatsiaq Greenland 165 N3
Kangaba Mali 124 C4
Kangal Turkey 107 D3
Kangalassy Rus. Fed. 39 M3
Kangān Būshehr Iran 100 C5
Kangān Hormozgan Iran 100 D5
Kangan Aboriginal Reserve Australia 150 B4
Kangandala, Parque Nacional de nat. park Angola see Cangandala, Parque Nacional de
Kangar Malaysia 76 C1
Kangaré Mali 124 C4
Kangaroo Island Australia 146 C3
Kangaroo Point Australia 148 C3
Kangaruma Guyana 199 G3
Kangasala Fin. 45 N3
Kangaslampi Fin. 44 O3
Kangasniemi Fin. 45 N3
Kangāvar Iran 100 A3
Kangayam India 94 C4
Kangbao China 85 G3

▶Kangchenjunga mt. India/Nepal 97 F4
3rd highest mountain in the world and in Asia. Also spelt Kanchanjanga.
world [physical features] ➡ 8–9

Kangding China 86 B2
also known as Dardo or Lucheng
Kangean, Kepulauan is Indon. 77 F4
Kangen r. Sudan 128 B3
Kangeq c. Greenland 165 O3
also known as Cort Adelaer, Kap
Kangerluarsoruseq Greenland 165 N3
also known as Færingehavn
Kangerlussuaq Greenland 165 N3
also known as Søndre Strømfjord
Kangerlussuaq inlet Greenland 165 N2
also known as Giesecke Isfjord
Kangerlussuaq inlet Greenland 165 N3
also known as Søndre Strømfjord
Kangerlussuaq inlet Greenland 165 P3
Kangerlussuatsiaq inlet Greenland 165 O3
also known as Lindenow Fjord
Kangersuatsiaq Greenland 165 N2
also known as Prøven
Kangertittivaq sea chan. Greenland 165 Q2
also known as Scoresby Sund
Kangertittivatsiaq inlet Greenland 165 P3
Kangetet Kenya 128 C4
Kanggye N. Korea 83 B4
Kangikajik c. Greenland 165 Q2
also known as Brewster, Kap
Kangilinnguit Greenland 165 O3
also known as Grønnedal
Kangiqsualujjuaq Canada 169 H1
formerly known as Port-Nouveau-Québec
Kangiqsujuaq Canada 165 L3
formerly known as Maricourt or Wakeham
Kangirsuk Canada 165 L3
formerly known as Bellin or Payne
Kang Krung National Park Thai. 79 B6
Kangle China 84 D5
Kangle China see Wanzai
Kanglong China 86 A1
Kangmar China 89 E6
Kangnŭng S. Korea 83 C5
Kango Gabon 126 A4
Kangping China 85 I3
Kangra India 96 C2
Kangri Karpo Pass China/India 86 A2
Kangrinboqê Feng mt. China 89 C6
also known as Kailas
Kangsangdobdê China see Xainza
Kang Tipayan Dakula i. Phil. 74 B5
Kangto mt. China/India 89 F7
Kangtog China 89 D5
Kangxian China 86 C1
also known as Zuitai; formerly known as Zuitaizi
Kangxiwar China 89 B4
Kangyidaung Myanmar 78 A4
Kanhan r. India 96 C5
Kanhar r. India 97 D4
Kanhargaon India 94 C2
Kani Côte d'Ivoire 124 D4
Kani Myanmar 78 A3
Kaniama Dem. Rep. Congo 127 E6
Kanibadam Tajik. 101 G1
also spelt Konibodom
Kanibongan Sabah Malaysia 77 G1
Kaniere N.Z. 153 F10
Kanifing Gambia 124 A3
Kanigiri India 94 C3
Kanimekh Uzbek. 103 F4
also spelt Konimekh
Kanin, Poluostrov pen. Rus. Fed. 40 H2
Kanin Nos Rus. Fed. 40 G1
Kanin Nos, Mys c. Rus. Fed. 40 G1
Kaninskiy Bereg coastal area Rus. Fed. 40 G2
Kanita Japan 90 G4
Kaniva Australia 146 D4
Kanjiroba mt. Nepal 97 D3
Kanjiža Vojvodina, Srbija Yugo. 58 B2
also known as Magyarkanizsa
Kankaanpää Fin. 45 M3
Kankakee U.S.A. 174 C3
Kankakee r. U.S.A. 174 B3
Kankan Guinea 124 C4
Kankan, Réserve Naturelle de nature res. Guinea 124 C4
Kanker India 94 D1
Kankesanturai Sri Lanka 94 D4
Kankiya Nigeria 125 G3
Kankossa Mauritania 124 C3
Kanmaw Kyun i. Myanmar 79 B6
also known as Kisseraing Island
Kanmuri-yama mt. Japan 91 C7
also spelt Kammuri-yama
Kannad India 94 B1
Kannapolis U.S.A. 174 D5
Kannauj India 96 C4
also known as Kanyakubja
Kanniyakumari India 94 C4
Kanniya Kumari c. India see Comorin, Cape
Kannod India 96 C5
Kannonkoski Fin. 44 N3
Kannur India see Cannanore
Kannus Fin. 44 M3
Kannuskoski Fin. 42 I1
Kano Nigeria 125 H3
Kano r. Nigeria 125 H4
Kano state Nigeria 125 H4
Kanona Zambia 127 F8
Kanonerka Kazakh. 103 I2
Kan-onji Japan 91 C7
Kanonpunt pt S. Africa 132 F11
Kanor India 96 B4
Kanosh U.S.A. 183 L3
Kanovlei Namibia 130 C3
Kanowit Sarawak Malaysia 77 F2
Kanoya Japan 91 B9
Kanpur India 96 D4
formerly spelt Cawnpore
Kanpur Pak. 101 G4
Kanrach reg. Pak. 101 F5
Kansai airport Japan 91 D7
Kansanshi Zambia 127 E8
Kansas r. U.S.A. 178 D4
Kansas state U.S.A. 178 C4
Kansas City KS U.S.A. 178 D4
Kansas City MO U.S.A. 178 D4
Kansenia Dem. Rep. Congo 127 E7
Kansk Rus. Fed. 80 F1
Kansu China 88 A4
Kansu prov. China see Gansu
Kanta mt. Eth. 128 B3
Kantala Fin. 44 N3
Kantang Thai. 79 B7
Kantara hill Cyprus 108 E2
Kantaralak Thai. 79 D5
Kantavu i. Fiji see Kadavu
Kantchari Burkina 125 F3
Kantemirovka Rus. Fed. 41 F6
Kanth India 96 C3
Kanti India 97 E4
Kantilo India 95 E1
Kantishna r. U.S.A. 164 D3
Kanton i. Kiribati 145 H2
also known as Abariringa; formerly spelt Canton Island
Kan-Too, Pik mt. Kazakh./Kyrg. see Khan-Tengri, Pik
Kanto-sanchi mts Japan 91 F7
Kantserava Belarus 45 O5
Kanttaji Aboriginal Land res. Australia 148 B3
Kanturk Rep. of Ireland 47 D11
Kanturrpa Aboriginal Land res. Australia 148 B3
Kanuku Mountains Guyana 199 G4
Kanuma Japan 91 F6
Kanur India 94 C3
also known as Vajrakarur
Kanus Namibia 132 C4
Kanuwe r. P.N.G. 73 J8
Kanyakubja India see Kannauj
KaNyamazane S. Africa 133 P2
Kanye Botswana 131 E5
Kanyemba Zimbabwe 131 F2
Kanyutino Rus. Fed. 43 O6
Kao Indon. 75 C2
Kao Niger 125 G3
Kao i. Tonga 145 H3
Kao, Teluk b. Indon. 75 C2
Kaohsiung Taiwan 87 G4
also spelt Gaoxiong
Kaôh Tang i. Cambodia 79 C6
Kaokoveld plat. Namibia 130 B3
Kaolack Senegal 124 A3
Kaoma Zambia 127 E8
Kaouadja Cent. Afr. Rep. 126 D3
Kapaa U.S.A. 181 [inset] Y1
Kapaau U.S.A. 181 [inset] Z1
Kapal Kazakh. 103 I3
also spelt Qapal
Kapalabuaya Indon. 75 C3
Kapa Moračka mt. Yugo. 58 A6
Kapan Armenia 107 F3
formerly spelt Ghap'an or Kafan
Kapanga Dem. Rep. Congo 127 D7
Kapareli Greece 59 E10
Kapatkyevichy Belarus 43 J9
Kapatu Zambia 127 F7
Kapchagay Kazakh. 103 I4
also spelt Qapshagay; formerly known as Ili or Iliysk
Kapchagayskoye Vodokhranilishche resr Kazakh. 103 I4
also known as Qapshagay Bögeni
Kapchorwa Uganda 128 B4
Kapčiamiestis Lith. 42 E8
Kap Dan Greenland see Kulusuk
Kapellen Belgium 51 K1
Kapello, Akra pt Greece 59 E12
Kapellskär Sweden 45 L4
also spelt Kapelskär
Kapelskär Sweden see Kapellskär
Kapfenberg Austria 49 M8
Kapıdağı Yarımadası pen. Turkey 58 I8
Kapili r. India 97 F4
Kapingamarangi atoll Micronesia 145 E1
formerly known as Greenwich
Kapıorman Dağları mts Turkey 106 B2
Kapiri Mposhi Zambia 127 F8
Kāpīsā prov. Afgh. 101 G3
Kapisillit Greenland 165 N3
Kapiskau r. Canada 168 D2
Kapiskong Lake Canada 173 L3
Kapit Sarawak Malaysia 77 F2
Kapiti Island N.Z. 152 I8
Kapiting Brazil 199 H4
Kapka well Chad 120 D5
Kapka, Massif du mts Chad 120 D6
Kaplamada, Gunung mt. Indon. 75 C3
Kaplankyr, Chink hills Turkm./Uzbek. 102 C4
Kaplankyrskiy Gosudarstvennyy Zapovednik nature res. Turkm. 102 D4
Kaplice Czech Rep. 49 L7
Kapoe Thai. 79 B6
Kapoeta Sudan 128 B3
Kapondai, Tanjung pt Indon. 75 B5
Kaponga N.Z. 152 I7
Kapos r. Romania 49 P9
Kaposvár Hungary 49 O9
Kappar Pak. 101 E5
Kappeln Germany 48 G1
Kapran India 96 C4
Kapsabet Kenya 128 B4
Kap Salt Swamp Pak. 101 E5
Kapsan N. Korea 83 C4
Kapsha r. Rus. Fed. 43 O2
Kapsukas Lith. see Marijampolė
Kaptai Bangl. 97 G5
Kaptsegaytuy Rus. Fed. 85 H1
Kaptsevichy Belarus 43 J9
Kapuas r. Indon. 77 E3
Kapuas r. Indon. 77 F3
Kapuas Hulu, Pegunungan mts Indon./Malaysia 77 F2
also known as Boven Kapuas Mountains
Kapunda Australia 146 C3
Kapuriya India 96 B4
Kapurthala India 96 B3
Kapuskasing Canada 168 D3
Kapuskasing r. Canada 168 D3
Kapustin Yar Rus. Fed. 41 H6
Kaputa Zambia 127 F7
Kaputar mt. Australia 147 F2
Kaputir Kenya 128 B4
Kapuvár Hungary 49 O8
Kapydzhik, Gora mt. Armenia/Azer. see Qazangödağ
Kapyl' Belarus 42 I8
also spelt Kopyl'
Kap'yŏng S. Korea 83 B5
Kapyrevshchina Rus. Fed. 43 N6
Ka Qu r. China 89 F6
Kaqung China 88 B4
Kara India 97 D4
Kara r. Rus. Fed. 40 M1
Kara Togo 125 F4
Kara r. Turkey 107 E3
Kara Ada i. Turkey 59 H10
Karaali Turkey 106 C3
Kara Art Pass China 88 A4
Karaaul Kazakh. see Karaul
Kara-Balta Kyrg. 103 H4
Karabanovo Rus. Fed. 43 T5
Karabas Kazakh. 103 H2
also spelt Qarabas
Karabekaul Turkm. see Garabekevyul
Karabiga Turkey 106 A2
Karabil', Vozvyshennost' hills Turkm. 103 E5
also known as Garabil Belentligi
Kara-Bogaz-Gol Turkm. see Karabogazkel'
Kara-Bogaz-Gol, Proliv sea chan. Turkm. 102 C4
also known as Garabogazköl Bogazy
▶Kara-Bogaz-Gol, Zaliv b. Turkm. 102 C4
also known as Garabogazköl Aylagy
asia [changes] ➡ 68–69
Karabogazkel' Turkm. 102 C4
formerly spelt Kara-Bogaz-Gol
Karabük Turkey 106 C2
Karabulak Almatinskaya Oblast' Kazakh. 103 I3
also spelt Qarabulaq
Karabulak Vostochnyy Kazakhstan Kazakh. 88 D2
Karabulakskaya Kazakh. 103 H2
Karabura China see Yumin
Karaburun Turkey 106 A3
Karabutak Kazakh. 102 E2
also spelt Qarabutaq
Karacabey Turkey 106 B2
Karacadağ mts Turkey 106 C3
Karacakılavuz Turkey 58 I7
Karacaköy Turkey 106 B2
Karacalı Dağ mt. Turkey 107 D3
Karaçal Tepe mt. Turkey 108 D1
Karacasu Turkey 59 J11
Karaca Yarımadası pen. Turkey 108 B1
Karachay-Cherkess Republic aut. rep. Rus. Fed. see Karachayevo-Cherkesskaya Respublika
Karachayevo-Cherkesskaya A.S.S.R. aut. rep. Rus. Fed. see Karachayevo-Cherkesskaya Respublika
Karachayevo-Cherkesskaya Respublika aut. rep. Rus. Fed. 41 G8
English form Karachay-Cherkess Republic; formerly known as Karachayevo-Cherkesskaya A.S.S.R.
Karachayevsk Rus. Fed. 41 G8
formerly known as Klukhori
Karachev Rus. Fed. 43 P8
▶Karachi Pak. 101 F5
world [cities] ➡ 24–25
Karaçoban Turkey 107 E3
also known as Karaköprü
Karaçulha Turkey 59 K12
Karacurun Turkey see Hilvan
Karad India 94 B2
Kara Dağ hill Turkey 59 H8
Kara Dağ hill Turkey 109 J1
Kara Dağ mt. Turkey 106 C3
Kara-Darya r. Kyrg. 103 H4
also spelt Qoradaryo
Kara-Dar'ya Uzbek. see Payshanba
Kara Deniz sea Asia/Europe see Black Sea
Karaga Ghana 125 E4
Karaganda Kazakh. 103 H2
also spelt Qaraghandy
Karaganda Oblast admin. div. Kazakh. see Karagandinskaya Oblast'
Karagandinskaya Oblast' admin. div. Kazakh. 103 H2
English form Karaganda Oblast; also known as Qaraghandy Oblysy
Karagash Kazakh. 103 I3
Karagay Rus. Fed. 40 J4
Karagayly Kazakh. 103 H2
also spelt Qaraghayly
Karagez Turkm. 102 C5
Karaginskiy, Ostrov i. Rus. Fed. 39 Q4
Karagiye, Vpadina depr. Kazakh. 102 B4
Karaguzhikha Kazakh. 88 C1
also known as Qaraqozha
Karagwe Tanz. 128 A5
Karahalil Turkey 58 I7
Karahallı Turkey 59 K10
Karahasanlı Turkey 106 C3
Karahisar Turkey 59 J11
Karaidel' Rus. Fed. 40 K5
Karaikal India 94 C4
Karaikkudi India 94 C4
Kara Irtysh r. Kazakh. 88 D2
Karaisalı Turkey 106 C3
Karaj Iran 100 B3
Karak Jordan see Al Karak
Kara-Kala Turkm. see Garrygala
Karakalli Turkey see Özalp
Karakalpakistan, Respublika aut. rep. Uzbek. 102 D4
also known as Karakalpakskaya Respublika or Karakalpakstan or Qaraqalpaqstan Respublikasy or Qoraqalpoghiston Respublikasi
Karakalpakiya Uzbek. 102 D3
also known as Qoraqalpoghiston
Karakalpakskaya Respublika aut. rep. Uzbek. see Karakalpakistan, Respublika
Karakalpakstan aut. rep. Uzbek. see Karakalpakistan, Respublika
Kara Kara State Park nature res. Australia 147 D4
Karakatinskaya, Vpadina depr. Uzbek. 103 F4
Karakax China see Moyu
Karakax He r. China 89 C4
Karakax Shan mts China 89 C5
Karakeçi Turkey 107 D3
also known as Mizar
Karakeçili Turkey 106 C3
Karakelong i. Indon. 75 C1
Kara-Khol' Rus. Fed. 88 E1
Karaki China 89 C4
Karakitang i. Indon. 75 C2
Karaklis Armenia see Vanadzor
Karakoçan Turkey 107 E3
also known as Tepeköy
Karakoin salt l. Kazakh. see Karakoyyn, Ozero
Karakol' Kazakh. 102 C2
also spelt Qaraköl
Kara-Köl Kyrg. 103 H4
also spelt Kara Kul'
Karakol Ysyk-Köl Kyrg. 103 I4
also known as Karakolka
Karakol Ysyk-Köl Kyrg. 103 I4
formerly known as Przheval'sk
Karakolka Kyrg. see Karakol
Karaköprü Turkey see Karaçoban
Karakoram mts Asia 99 J2
Karakoram Pass China/Jammu and Kashmir 89 B5
Kara K'orē Eth. 128 C2
Karakoro r. Mali/Mauritania 124 B3
Karaköse Turkey see Ağrı
Karakoyyn, Ozero salt l. Kazakh. 103 G3
also known as Karakoin or Qaraqoyyn Köli
Karaksar Rus. Fed. 85 G1
Karakubbud Ukr. see Komsomol's'ke
Kara Kul' Kyrg. see Kara-Köl
Karakul' Bukharskaya Oblast' Uzbek. 103 E5
Karakul' Bukharskaya Oblast' Uzbek. 103 E5
Karakul', Ozero l. Tajik. see Qarokŭl
Kara-Kul'dzha Kyrg. see Kara-Kulja
Karakulino Rus. Fed. 40 J4
Kara-Kulja Kyrg. 103 H4
also spelt Kara-Kul'dzha
Karakum Kazakh. 103 I3
Karakum Desert Kazakh. 102 C3
also known as Garagum or Peski Karakum or Qaraqum
Karakum Desert Turkm. 102 E5
also known as Garagum or Peski Karakumy or Qaraqum
Karakumskiy Kanal canal Turkm. 103 E5
Karakurt Turkey 107 E2
Karakurt Turkey 59 I9
Karala Estonia 42 C3
Karalı Turkey 108 H1
Karalundi Australia 151 B5
Karama r. Indon. 75 A3
Karaman Turkey 106 C3
historically known as Laranda
Karaman prov. Turkey 108 D1
Karamanbeyli Geçidi pass Turkey 108 B1
Karamanlı Turkey 106 B3
Karamay China 88 D2
Karambar Pass Afgh./Pak. 101 H2
Karamea N.Z. 152 G9
Karamea r. N.Z. 152 G9
Karamea Bight b. N.Z. 152 F9
Karamet-Niyaz Turkm. 103 F5
also spelt Garamätnyyaz
Karamian i. Indon. 77 F4
Karamiran China 89 D4
Karamiran He r. China 89 D4
Karamiran Shankou pass China 89 D4
Karamken Rus. Fed. 39 P3
Karamürsel Turkey 58 K8
Karamyshevo Rus. Fed. 43 J4
Karan r. Afgh. 101 G2
Karan state Myanmar see Kayin
Karān i. Saudi Arabia 105 E2
Karang Senegal 124 A3
Karang, Tanjung pt Indon. 75 A3
Karangagung Indon. 76 D3
Karangan Indon. 76 D4
Karangarua N.Z. 153 D11
Karangasem Indon. 77 F5
Karangetang vol. Indon. 75 C2
Karangoua r. Congo 126 B4
Karanja India 94 C1
Karanja r. India 94 C2
Karanjia India 97 E5
Karanpura India 96 B3
Karaoba Kazakh. 103 I1
Karaova Turkey 59 I11
Karaoy Almatinskaya Oblast' Kazakh. 103 H3
Karaoy Almatinskaya Oblast' Kazakh. 103 H3
also spelt Qaraoy
Karapelit Bulg. 58 I5
Karapınar Turkey 106 C3
also known as Sultanıye
Karapürçek Turkey 59 J9
Karaqi China 88 B3
Karas admin. reg. Namibia 130 C5
Karas mts Namibia 132 B4
Karaşar Turkey 106 B2
Karasay China 89 C4
Kara-Say Kyrg. 103 I4
Karasburg Namibia 130 C6
Kara Sea Rus. Fed. 39 H2
also known as Karskoye More
Karash Rus. Fed. 43 U5
Karashoky Kazakh. 103 H2
Karašica r. Croatia 56 K3
Karasica r. Hungary/Romania 56 K3
Kárášjohka Norway 44 N1
also spelt Karasjok
Kárášjohka r. Norway 44 N1
also spelt Karasjokka
Karasjok Norway see Kárášjohka
Karasjokka r. Norway see Kárášjohka
Karasor, Ozero salt l. Karagandinskaya Oblast' Kazakh. 103 H2
Karasor, Ozero salt l. Pavlodarskaya Oblast' Kazakh. 103 H2
Kara Strait Rus. Fed. see Karskiye Vorota, Proliv
Karasu Karagandinskaya Oblast' Kazakh. 103 H3
Karasu Kustanayskaya Oblast' Kazakh. 103 E2
Karasu Kustanayskaya Oblast' Kazakh. 103 F1
also spelt Qarasū
Karasu r. Kazakh. 103 H1
Karasu r. Syria/Turkey 109 H1
also known as Qara Şū Chāy
Karasu Turkey see Hizan
Karasu Turkey 106 B2
also known as Incirli
Karasu r. Turkey 107 E3
Karasubazar Ukr. see Bilohirs'k
Kara-Sug Rus. Fed. 84 B1
Karasuk Rus. Fed. 80 B2
Karasulak r. Ukr. 58 J3
Kara-Suu Kyrg. 103 H4
Karāt Iran 101 E3
Karatan Kazakh. 88 D2
Karataş Turkey 106 C3
Karataş Burnu hd Turkey see Fener Burnu
Karatau Kazakh. 103 G4
also spelt Qaratau; formerly known as Chulaktau
Karatau, Khrebet mts Kazakh. 103 F3
also known as Qaratau Zhotasy
Karatayka Rus. Fed. 40 L1
Karathuri Myanmar 79 B6
Karativu i. Sri Lanka 94 C4
Karatj l. Sweden 44 L2
Karatobe Kazakh. 102 C2
also spelt Qaratöbe
Karatobe, Mys pt Kazakh. 102 D3
Karatogay Kazakh. 102 D2
also spelt Qaratoghay
Karatol r. Kazakh. 103 I3
Karatomarskoye Vodokhranilishche resr Kazakh. 103 E1
also known as Qaratomar Bögeni
Karaton Kazakh. 102 C3
also spelt Qaraton
Karatsu Japan 91 A8
Karatünggü China 84 A2
Karatup, Poluostrov pen. Kazakh. 102 D3
Kara-Turgey r. Kazakh. 103 F2
Karaul Kazakh. 103 I2
also spelt Qaraūyl; formerly known as Abay; formerly spelt Karaaul
Karaulbazar Uzbek. 103 F5
also spelt Qorowulbozor
Karauli India 96 C4
Karaulkel'dy Kazakh. see Bayganin
Karaurgan Turkey 107 E2
Karauzyak Uzbek. 102 D4
also spelt Qara Özek or Qoraŭzak
Karavan Kyrg. see Kerben
Karavas Greece 59 D12
Karavastasë, Gjiri i b. Albania 58 A8
Karavastasë, Laguna e lag. Albania 58 A8
Karavatsichy Belarus 43 L9
Karavayevo Rus. Fed. 43 V4
Karavi i. Greece 59 E12
Karavonisia i. Greece 59 H13
Karawa Dem. Rep. Congo 126 D4
Karawang Indon. 77 D4
Karaxahar r. China see Kaidu He
Karayılan Turkey 108 H1
Karayulgan China 88 C3
Karazhal Kazakh. 103 G2
also spelt Qarazhal
Karazhar Uzbek. 102 D4
Karazhingil Kazakh. 103 H3
Karbalā' Iraq 107 F4
also spelt Kerbela
Karbalā' governorate Iraq 107 E4
Karbushevka Kazakh. 103 H2
Karcag Hungary 49 R8
Kardam Bulg. 58 J5
Kardamaina Greece 59 I12
also spelt Kardhaámaina
Kardeljevo Croatia see Ploče
Kardhaámaina Greece see Kardamaina
Kardhítsa Greece see Karditsa
Kardis Sweden 44 M2
Karditsa Greece 59 C9
also spelt Kardhítsa
Kärdla Estonia 42 D3
Kardymovo Rus. Fed. 43 N7
Karee S. Africa 133 K5
Kareeberge mts S. Africa 132 F7
Kareebospoort pass S. Africa 132 G7
Kareedouw S. Africa 133 I10
Kareha, Jebel mt. Morocco 54 F9
Kareima Sudan 121 F5
Karelaksha Rus. Fed. 44 P2
Kareli India 96 C5
Karelia aut. rep. Rus. Fed. see Kareliya, Respublika
Karelichy Belarus 42 H8
Kareliya, Respublika aut. rep. Rus. Fed. 44 P3
English form Karelia; formerly known as Karel'skaya A.S.S.R.
Karel'skaya A.S.S.R. aut. rep. Rus. Fed. see Kareliya, Respublika
Karel'skiy Bereg coastal area Rus. Fed. 40 E2
Karema Dodoma Tanz. 129 B6
Karema Rukwa Tanz. 129 A6
Karen state Myanmar see Kayin
Karenga r. Rus. Fed. 81 J2
Karera India 96 C4
Karesuando Sweden 44 M1
Kārevāndar Iran 101 E5
Kargala Rus. Fed. 102 C2
Kargalinskaya Rus. Fed. 102 A4
also known as Kargalinski
Kargalinski Rus. Fed. see Kargalinskaya
Kargalinskoye Kazakh. 102 D2
formerly known as Zhilyanka
Kargapazarı Dağları mts Turkey 107 E3
Karghalik China see Yecheng
Kargı Turkey 106 C2
Kargil Jammu and Kashmir 96 C2
Kargilik China see Yecheng
Kargıpınarı Turkey 108 F1
Kargopol' Rus. Fed. 40 F3
Kargowa Poland 49 M3
Kargūshkī Iran 100 D5
Karhal India 96 C4
Kari Nigeria 125 H4
Karīān Iran 100 D5
Kariba Zimbabwe 131 F3
Kariba, Lake resr Zambia/Zimbabwe 127 E9
Kariba Dam Zambia/Zimbabwe 127 F9
Kariba-yama vol. Japan 90 F3
Karibib Namibia 130 B4
Kariega r. S. Africa 132 H10
Karīf Salāsil well Yemen 105 E4
Karigasniemi Fin. 44 N1
also known as Gáregasnjárga
Karijini National Park Australia 150 B4
Karikari, Cape N.Z. 152 H2
Karīmābād Iran 100 C3
Karimata i. Indon. 77 E3
Karimata, Pulau-pulau is Indon. 77 E3
Karimata, Selat strait Indon. 77 E3
Karimganj India 97 G4
Karim Khanch Iran 100 B3
Karimnagar India 94 C2
Karimun Besar i. Indon. 76 C2
Karimunjawa i. Indon. 77 E4
Karimunjawa, Pulau-pulau is Indon. 77 E4
Karin Somalia 128 E2
Karinainen Fin. 45 M3
Käringsjön Sweden 44 K3
Karino S. Africa 133 P2
Karioi hill N.Z. 152 I5
Karis Fin. 45 M3
also known as Karjaa
Karisimbi, Mont vol. Rwanda 126 F5
Káristos Greece see Karystos
Karit Iran 100 D3
Karitsa Greece 59 D8
Kariya Japan 91 E7
Kariyangwe Zimbabwe 131 E3
Karjaa Fin. see Karis
Karjalohja Fin. 42 E1
Karjan India 96 B5
Karjat India 94 B2
Karkai r. India 97 E5
Karkal India 94 B3
Karkamb India 94 B2
Karkams S. Africa 132 B7
Karkaralinsk Kazakh. 103 H2
also known as Qarqaraly
Karkaralong, Kepulauan is Indon. 75 C1
Karkar Island P.N.G. 73 K7
also known as Dampier Island
Karkas, Kūh-e mts Iran 100 B3
Karkh Pak. 101 F5
Karkheh, Rūdkhāneh-ye r. Iran 100 A4
Karkinits'ka Zatoka g. Ukr. 41 E7
Karkkila Fin. 45 N3
Kärkölä Fin. 45 N3
Karkonoski Park Narodowy nat. park Czech Rep./Poland see Krkonošský narodní park
Karksi-Nuia Estonia 42 G3
Karkūmā, Ra's hd Saudi Arabia 104 B2
Karlantijpa North Aboriginal Land res. Australia 148 B3
Karlantijpa South Aboriginal Land res. Australia 148 B4
Karlik Shan mt. China 84 B3
Karlino Poland 49 M1
Karlıova Turkey 107 E3
Karlivka Ukr. 41 E6
also spelt Karlovka
Karl Marks, Qullai mt. Tajik. 101 H2
Karl-Marx-Stadt Germany see Chemnitz
Karlovac Croatia 56 H3
Karlovka Ukr. see Karlivka
Karlovo Bulg. 58 F6
formerly known as Levskigrad
Karlovy Vary Czech Rep. 49 J5
historically known as Carlsbad
Karlsberg Sweden 45 K3
Karlsborg Sweden 45 K4
Karlsburg Romania see Alba Iulia
Karlshamn Sweden 45 K4
Karlskoga Sweden 45 K4
Karlskrona Sweden 45 K4
Karlsruhe Germany 48 F6
Karlstad Sweden 45 K4
Karlstadt Germany 48 G6
Karlyuk Turkm. 103 F5
Karma Belarus 43 L8
Karma Niger 125 F3
Karma, Ouadi watercourse Chad 120 C6
Karmala India 94 B2
Karmanovka Kazakh. 102 B2
Karmanovo Rus. Fed. 43 P6
Karmas Sweden 44 L2
Karmona Spain see Córdoba
Karnabchul', Step' plain Uzbek. 103 F5
Karnafuli Reservoir Bangl. 97 G5
Karnal India 96 C3
Karnali r. Nepal 97 D3
Karnaprayag India 96 C3
Karnataka state India 94 B3
formerly known as Mysore
Karnes City U.S.A. 179 C6
Karnobat Bulg. 58 H6
formerly known as Polyanovgrad
Karodi Pak. 101 F5
Karoi Zimbabwe 131 F3
Karokpi Myanmar 78 B5
Karo La pass China 89 E6
Karong India 97 G4
Karonga Malawi 129 B7
Karonie Australia 151 C6
Karoo National Park S. Africa 132 G9
Karoonda Australia 146 C3
Karor Pak. 101 G4
Karora Eritrea 121 H5
Káros i. Greece see Keros
Karossa Indon. 75 A3
Karossa, Tanjung pt Indon. 77 G5
Karotis Greece 58 H7
Karouassa well Mali 125 E2
Karpasia pen. Cyprus 108 F2
also known as Karpas Peninsula; also spelt Kırpaşa
Karpas Peninsula Cyprus see Karpasia
Karpathos Greece 59 I13
Karpathos i. Greece 59 I13
formerly known as Scarpanto
Karpathou, Steno sea chan. Greece 59 I12
Karpaty mts Europe see Carpathian Mountains
Karpenisi Greece 59 C10
Karpilovka Belarus see Aktsyabrski
Karpinsk Rus. Fed. 38 G4
Karpogory Rus. Fed. 40 H2
Karpovychi Ukr. 43 N9
Karpuz r. Turkey 108 C1
Karpuzlu Aydın Turkey 59 I11
Karpuzlu Edirne Turkey 58 H8
Karratha Australia 150 B4
Karrats Fjord inlet Greenland see Nuugaatsiaap Imaa
Karrī Iran 100 B4
Karringmelkspruit S. Africa 133 L7
Karroo plat. S. Africa see Great Karoo
Karroun Hill Nature Reserve Australia 151 B6
Karrukh Afgh. 101 E3
Karrychirla Turkm. see imeni Kerbabayeva
Kars Turkey 107 E2
Karsakpay Kazakh. 103 F3
also spelt Qarsaqbay
Kärsämäki Fin. 44 N3
Kārsava Latvia 42 I5
Karshi Turkm. 102 C4
also spelt Garshy
Karshi Uzbek. 103 F5
also spelt Qarshi; historically known as Nautaca
Karshinskaya Step' plain Uzbek. 103 F5
also known as Qarshi Chŭli
Karşıyaka Balıkesir Turkey 58 J8
Karşıyaka İzmir Turkey 59 I10
Karsiyang India 97 F4
Karskiye Vorota, Proliv strait Rus. Fed. 40 K1
English form Kara Strait
Karskoye More sea Rus. Fed. see Kara Sea
Karstädt Germany 48 I2
Karsu Turkey 109 H1
Karsun Rus. Fed. 41 H5
Kartal Turkey 106 B2
Kartala vol. Comoros 129 D7
Kartaly Rus. Fed. 103 E1

Kartarpur India 96 B3
Kartena Lith. 42 C6
Karthaus U.S.A. 176 G4
Kartsevo Rus. Fed. 43 L5
Kartsino, Akra pt Greece 59 F10
Karttula Fin. 44 N3
Kartuni Guyana 199 G3
Kartuzy Poland 49 P1
Karubwe Zambia 127 F8
Kārūkh, Jabal mt. Iraq 109 P1
Karumai Japan 90 G4
Karumba Australia 149 D3
Karun, Kūh-e hill Iran 100 B4
Kārūn, Rūd-e r. Iran 100 B4
Karunagapalli India 94 C4
Karungi Sweden 44 M2
Karungu Kenya 128 B5
Karuni Indon. 75 A5
Karunjie Australia 150 D3
Karup Denmark 45 J4
Karur India 94 C4
Karuzi Burundi 126 F5
Karvetnagar India 94 C3
Karvia Fin. 45 M3
Karviná Czech Rep. 49 P6
Karwar India 94 B3
Karwendelgebirge nature res. Austria 48 I8
Karwi India 96 D4
Karya Greece 59 B10
Karyagino Azer. see Füzuli
Karyes Greece 59 F8
Karymskoye Rus. Fed. 85 G1
Karynzharyk, Peski des. Kazakh. 102 C4
Karystos Greece 59 F10
also spelt Káristos
Kaş Turkey 106 B3
Kasa India 94 B2
Kasaba Turkey see Turgutlu
Kasaba Lodge Zambia 127 F7
Kasabonika Canada 168 B2
Kasai r. Dem. Rep. Congo 127 C5
Kasai Japan 91 D7
Kasai, Plateau du Dem. Rep. Congo 127 D6
Kasai Occidental prov. Dem. Rep. Congo 127 D6
Kasai Oriental prov. Dem. Rep. Congo 126 E6
Kasaji Dem. Rep. Congo 127 D7
Kasama Japan 91 G6
Kasama Zambia 127 F7
Kasan Uzbek. 103 F5
also spelt Koson
Kasane Botswana 131 E3
Kasanga Tanz. 129 A7
Kasangulu Dem. Rep. Congo 126 B6
Kasanka National Park Zambia 127 F8
Kasansay Uzbek. 103 G4
also spelt Kosonsoy
Kasanza Dem. Rep. Congo 127 C6
Kasar, Ras pt Sudan 121 H5
Kasaragod India 94 B3
Kasari r. Estonia 42 E3
Kasatkino Rus. Fed. 82 C2
Kasba Lake Canada 167 K2
Kasba Tadla Morocco 122 D2
Kasbi Uzbek. 103 F5
Kaseda Japan 91 B9
Kasempa Zambia 127 E8
Kasenga Katanga Dem. Rep. Congo 127 D7
Kasenga Katanga Dem. Rep. Congo 127 F7
Kasenye Dem. Rep. Congo 126 F4
Kasese Dem. Rep. Congo 126 E5
Kasese Uganda 128 A4
Kasevo Rus. Fed. see Neftekamsk
Kasganj India 96 C4
Kasha China see Gonjo
Kasha waterhole Kenya 128 D5
Kashabowie Canada 168 B3
Kāshān Iran 100 B3
Kashary Rus. Fed. 41 G6
Kashechewan Canada 168 D2
Kashgar China see Kashi
Kashi China 88 B4
formerly known as Kashgar or Kaxgar
Kashihara Japan 91 D7
Kashima Japan 91 B8
Kashima-nada b. Japan 91 G6
Kashin Rus. Fed. 43 S4
Kashinka r. Rus. Fed. 43 S4
Kashiobwe Dem. Rep. Congo 127 F7
Kashipur India 96 C3
Kashira Rus. Fed. 43 T7
Kashirka r. Rus. Fed. 43 T7
Kashiwazaki Japan 90 F6
Kashkadar'inskaya Oblast' admin. div. Uzbek. 103 F5
English form Kashkadarya Oblast; also known as Qashqadaryo Wiloyati
Kashkadar'ya r. Uzbek. 101 F2
also known as Qashqadaryo
Kashkadarya Oblast admin. div. Uzbek. see Kashkadar'inskaya Oblast'
Kashkanteniz Kazakh. 103 H3
also spelt Kashken-Teniz or Qashqantengiz
Kashken-Teniz Kazakh. see Kashkanteniz
Kashkurino Rus. Fed. 43 M6
Kāshmar Iran 100 D3
Kashmir terr. Asia see Jammu and Kashmir
Kashmir, Vale of valley India 96 B2
Kashmor Pak. 101 G4
Kashmund reg. Afgh. 101 G3
Kashyukulu Dem. Rep. Congo 127 E6
Kasi India see Varanasi
Kasia India 97 D4
Kasilovo Rus. Fed. 43 O8
Kasimbar Indon. 75 A3
Kasimov Rus. Fed. 40 G5
Kasingi Dem. Rep. Congo 126 F4
Kasiruta i. Indon. 75 C3
Kaskaskia r. U.S.A. 174 B4
Kaskattama r. Canada 167 N3
Kaskelen Kazakh. 103 I4
also spelt Qaskelen
Kaskinen Fin. 44 M3
also known as Kaskö
Kas Klong i. Cambodia see Kŏng, Kaôh
Kaskö Fin. see Kaskinen
Kaslo Canada 167 G5
Kasmere Lake Canada 167 K3
Kasnya r. Rus. Fed. 43 P6
Kasomeno Dem. Rep. Congo 127 F7
Kasongan Indon. 77 F3
Kasongo Dem. Rep. Congo 126 E6
Kasongo-Lunda Dem. Rep. Congo 127 C6
Kasonguele Dem. Rep. Congo 127 E6
Kasos i. Greece 59 H13
Kasou, Steno sea chan. Greece 59 I13
Kaspi Georgia 107 F2
Kaspīy Mangy Oypaty lowland Kazakh./Rus. Fed. see Caspian Lowland
Kaspiysk Rus. Fed. 102 A4
Kaspiyskiy Rus. Fed. see Lagan'
Kaspiyskoye More sea Asia/Europe see Caspian Sea
Kasplya Rus. Fed. 43 M7
Kasplya r. Rus. Fed. 43 L6
Kasrawad India 96 B5
Kasrik Turkey see Gürpınar
Kassa Slovakia see Košice
Kassaare laht b. Estonia 42 D3
Kassala Sudan 121 H6
Kassala state Sudan 121 G6
Kassandra pen. Greece 59 E8
Kassandras, Akra pt Greece 59 E9
Kassandras, Kolpos b. Greece 59 E8
Kassandreia Greece 59 E8
Kassel Germany 48 G4
Kasserine Tunisia 123 H2
Kassinga Angola see Cassinga
Kassouloua well Niger 125 H3
Kastamonu Turkey 106 C2
also known as Çandar
Kastelli Kriti Greece 59 E13
also known as Kastéllion
Kastelli Kriti Greece 59 G13
Kastéllion Greece see Kastelli
Kastellorizon i. Greece see Megisti
Kastellou, Akra pt Greece 59 I13
Kastoria Greece 58 C8
Kastorias, Limni l. Greece 58 C8
Kastornoye Rus. Fed. 41 F6
Kastos i. Greece 59 B10
Kastrakiou, Techniti Limni resr Greece 59 C10
Kastre Estonia 42 I3
Kastrova Belarus 43 J5
Kastsyukovichy Belarus 43 N8
also spelt Kostyukovichi
Kastsyukowka Belarus 43 L9
Kasugai Japan 91 E7
Kasuku Dem. Rep. Congo 126 E5
Kasulu Tanz. 129 A6
Kasumiga-ura l. Japan 91 G6
Kasumkent Rus. Fed. 102 B4
Kasungu Malawi 129 B8
Kasungu National Park Malawi 129 B8
Kasur Pak. 101 H4
Kataba Zambia 127 E9
Katagum Nigeria 125 H3
Katahdin, Mount U.S.A. 174 G2
Kataklik Jammu and Kashmir 96 C2
Katako-Kombe Dem. Rep. Congo 126 E5
Katakolo, Akra pt Greece 59 C11
Katakwi Uganda 128 B4
Katanda Dem. Rep. Congo 127 D6
Katanga prov. Dem. Rep. Congo 127 E7
formerly known as Shaba
Katangi Madhya Pradesh India 96 C5
Katangi Madhya Pradesh India 96 C5
Katangli Rus. Fed. 82 F2
Katanning Australia 151 B7
Kata Pusht Iran 100 B2
Katashin Rus. Fed. 43 N9
Katastari Greece 59 B11
Katavi National Park Tanz. 129 A6
Katawaz Afgh. 101 G3
Katawaz reg. Afgh. 101 F3
Katchall i. India 95 G5
Katchamba Togo 125 F4
Katea Dem. Rep. Congo 127 E6
Katerini Greece 59 D8
Katesh Tanz. 129 B6
Kate's Needle mt. Canada/U.S.A. 164 F4
Katete Zambia 129 B8
Katghora India 97 D5
Katha Myanmar 78 B2
Katherîna, Gebel mt. Egypt 121 G2
Katherine Australia 148 B2
Katherine r. Australia 148 A2
Katherine Gorge National Park Australia see Nitmiluk National Park
Kathi India 96 B5
Kathiawar pen. India 96 A5
Kathīb, Ra's al pt Yemen 104 C5
Kathîb el Henu des. Egypt 121 G2
Kathîb el Henu hill Egypt 108 D7
Kathîb el Makhâzin des. Egypt 108 D7
Kathleen Falls Australia 148 A2
Kathlehong S. Africa 133 M3

▶Kathmandu Nepal 97 E4
Capital of Nepal. English form Katmandu.

Kathu S. Africa 132 H4
Kathua Jammu and Kashmir 96 B2
Kathua watercourse Kenya 128 C5
Kati Mali 124 C3
Katibas r. Sarawak Malaysia 77 F2
Kati-ér r. Hungary 49 S8
Katihar India 97 E4
Katikati N.Z. 152 J5
Kati-Kati S. Africa 133 L9
Katima Mulilo Namibia 131 E3
Katimik Lake Canada 167 L4
Katino Rus. Fed. 43 U8
Katiola Côte d'Ivoire 124 D4
Kā Tiritiri o te Moana mts N.Z. see Southern Alps
Katiti Aboriginal Land res. Australia 148 A5
Katkop Hills S. Africa 132 E7
Katlabukh, Ozero l. Ukr. 58 J3
Katma China 88 D4
Katmai National Park and Preserve U.S.A. 164 D4
Katmandu Nepal see Kathmandu
Kato Achaïa Greece 59 C10
Kat O Chau i. Hong Kong China see Crooked Island
Katochi Greece 59 C10
Kato Figaleia Greece 59 C11
Kat O Hoi b. Hong Kong China see Crooked Harbour
Katol India 96 C5
Kåtölandet i. Fin. 44 M3
Katombe Dem. Rep. Congo 127 D6
Katompi Dem. Rep. Congo 127 E6
Katondwe Zambia 127 F8
Kato Nevrokopi Greece 58 E7
Katong Sing. 76 [inset]
Katonga r. Uganda 128 A4
Katon-Karagay Kazakh. 88 D1
also spelt Katonqaraghay
Katonqaraghay Kazakh. see Katon-Karagay
Katoomba Australia 147 F3
Katoposa, Gunung mt. Indon. 75 B3
Katosan India 96 B5
Kato Tithorea Greece 59 D10
Kåtotjåkka mt. Sweden see Godučohkka
Katowice Poland 49 Q5
formerly known as Stalinogród; historically known as Kattowitz
Katoya India 97 F5
formerly spelt Katwa
Katpur India 96 B5
Katrineholm Sweden 45 L4
Katse Dam Lesotho 133 M6
Katsepy Madag. 131 [inset] J2
Katsikas Greece 59 B9
Katsina Nigeria 125 G3
Katsina state Nigeria 125 G4
Katsina-Ala Nigeria 125 H5
Katsumoto Japan 91 A8
Katsuura Japan 91 G7
Katsuyama Japan 91 E6
Kattakurgan Uzbek. 103 F5
also spelt Kattaqŭrghon
Kattamudda Well Australia 150 D4
Kattaqŭrghon Uzbek. see Kattakurgan
Kattasang Hills Afgh. 101 F3
Kattavia Greece 59 I13
Kattegat strait Denmark/Sweden 45 J4
Kattisavan Sweden 44 L2
Kattowitz Poland see Katowice
Kattuputtur India 94 C4
Katumba Dem. Rep. Congo 127 E6
Katumbi Malawi 129 B7
Katun' r. Rus. Fed. 88 D1
Katunino Rus. Fed. 40 H4
Katunskiy Khrebet mts Rus. Fed. 88 D1
Katwa India see Katoya
Katwijk aan Zee Neth. 48 B3
Katyk Ukr. see Shakhtars'k
Katyn' Rus. Fed. 43 M7
Kąty Wrocławskie Poland 49 N4
Kauai i. U.S.A. 181 [inset] Y1
Kauai Channel U.S.A. 181 [inset] Y1
Kaudom Game Park nature res. Namibia 130 D3
Kaufbeuren Germany 48 H8
Kaufman U.S.A. 179 C5
Kauhajoki Fin. 44 M3
Kauhanevan-Pohjankankaan kansallispuisto nat. park Fin. 45 M3
Kauhava Fin. 44 M3
Kaukauna U.S.A. 172 E6
Kaukkwè Hills Myanmar 78 B2
Kaukonen Fin. 44 N2
Kauksi Estonia 42 I2
Kaulinranta Fin. 44 M2
Kaumajet Mountains Canada 169 I1
Kaunakakai U.S.A. 181 [inset] Z1
Kaunas Lith. 42 E7
formerly known as Kovno
Kaunata Latvia 42 I5
Kaundy, Vpadina depr. Kazakh. 102 C4
Kaunia Bangl. 97 F4
Kauno marios l. Lith. 42 F7
Kaupiri N.Z. 153 F10
Kaura-Namoda Nigeria 125 G3
Kau Sai Chau i. Hong Kong China 87 [inset]
Kaushany Moldova see Căușeni
Kaustinen Fin. 44 M3
Kautokeino Norway 44 M1
Kau-ye Kyun i. Myanmar 79 B6
Kavacha Rus. Fed. 39 Q3
Kavadarci Macedonia 58 D7
Kavajë Albania 58 A7
Kavak Turkey 58 H8
Kavak Turkey 106 D2
Kavak Dağı hill Turkey 59 H9
Kavaklıdere Manisa Turkey 59 J10
Kavaklıdere Muğla Turkey 59 J11
Kavala Greece 58 F8
Kavalas, Kolpos b. Greece 58 F8
Kavalerovo Rus. Fed. 82 D3
Kavali India 94 D3
Kavalpatnam India 94 C4
Kavalyova Belarus 43 L6
Kavanayen Venez. 199 F3
Kavār Iran 100 C4
Kavaratti India 94 B4
Kavaratti i. India 94 B4
Kavarna Bulg. 58 J5
Kavarskas Lith. 42 F6
Kavendou, Mont mt. Guinea 124 B4
Kaveri r. India 94 C4
Kaveripatnam India 94 C3
Kavi India 96 B5
Kavieng P.N.G. 145 E2
Kavīr Iran 100 B3
Kavīr, Dasht-e des. Iran 100 C3
Kavīr-e Abarkuh des. Iran 100 C4
Kavīr-i-Namak salt flat Iran 100 D3
Kavīr Kūshk well Iran 100 D3
Kavirondo Gulf Kenya see Winam Gulf
Kavkazskiy Zapovednik nature res. Rus. Fed. 41 G8
Kaw Fr. Guiana 199 H3
Kawabe Japan 90 G5
Kawachi-nagano Japan 91 D7
Kawagama Lake Canada 168 E4
Kawagoe Japan 91 F7
Kawaguchi Japan 91 F7
Kawahara Japan 91 D7
Kawai Japan 90 G5
Kawaihae U.S.A. 181 [inset] Z1
Kawaihoa Point U.S.A. 181 [inset] Y1
Kawakawa N.Z. 152 I3
Kawamata Japan 90 G6
Kawambwa Zambia 127 F7
Kawaminami Japan 91 B8
Kawana Zambia 127 E8
Kawangkoan Indon. 75 C2
Kawanishi Japan 91 D7
Kawardha India 96 D5
Kawartha Lakes Canada 168 E4
Kawasa Dem. Rep. Congo 127 F7
Kawasaki Japan 91 F7
Kawashiri-misaki pt Japan 91 B7
Kawato Indon. 75 B3
Kawaura Japan 91 B8
Kawawachikamach Canada 169 H2
Kawe i. Indon. 75 D2
Kaweah, Lake U.S.A. 182 F5
Kaweka Forest Park nature res. N.Z. 152 K7
Kaweka Range mts N.Z. 152 K7
Kawene Canada 172 B2
Kawerau N.Z. 152 K6
Kawhia N.Z. 152 I6
Kawich Peak U.S.A. 183 H4
Kawich Range mts U.S.A. 183 H4
Kawinaw Lake Canada 167 L4
Kawio i. Indon. 75 C1
Kawkabān Yemen 104 C5
Kawkareik Myanmar 78 B4
Kaw Lake U.S.A. 178 C4
Kawlin Myanmar 78 A3
Kawludo Myanmar 78 B4
Kawmapyin Myanmar 79 B5
Kawm Dafanah tourist site Egypt see Daphnae
Kawngmeum Myanmar 78 B3
Kawthaung Myanmar 79 B6
Kawthoolei state Myanmar see Kayin
Kawthule state Myanmar see Kayin
Kaxgar China see Kashi
Kaxgar He r. China 88 B4
Kax He r. China 88 C3
Kaxtax Shan mts China 89 C4
Kaya Burkina 125 E3
Kaya S. Korea 91 A7
Kayacı Dağı hill Turkey 59 H9
Kayadibi Turkey 107 D3
Kayah state Myanmar 78 B4
Kayambi Zambia 129 A7
Kayan r. Indon. 77 E3
Kayan r. Indon. 77 G2
Kayan Myanmar 78 B4
Kayanaza Burundi 126 F5
Kayangel atoll Palau 73 H5
also known as Ngcheangel
Kayankulam India 94 C4
Kayar India 94 C2
Kayasa Indon. 75 C2
Kaya-san National Park S. Korea 91 A7
Kaybagar, Ozero l. Kazakh. see Koybagar, Ozero
Kaydanovo Belarus see Dzyarzhynsk
Kayenta U.S.A. 183 N5
Kayes Mali 124 C3
Kayes admin. reg. Mali 124 C3
Kayga Kazakh. 103 F2
also known as Qayghy; formerly known as Kaygy
Kaygy Kazakh. see Kayga
Kayin state Myanmar 78 B4
also known as Karan; formerly known as Karen or Kawthoolei or Kawthule
Kaymanachikha Kazakh. 103 H1
Kaymaz Turkey 106 B3
Kaynar Kazakh. 103 I2
also spelt Qaynar
Kaynar Turkey 107 D3
Kaynarlı r. Turkey 58 I7
Kayoa i. Indon. 75 C2
Kayrakkum Tajik. see Qayroqqum
Kayrakkumskoye Vodokhranilishche resr Tajik. see Obanbori Qayroqqum
Kayrakty Kazakh. 103 H2
also spelt Qayraqty
Kayseri Turkey 106 C3
historically known as Caesarea Cappadociae or Mazaca
Kaysersberg France 51 N4
Kayuadi i. Indon. 75 B4
Kayuagung Indon. 76 D3
Kayuyu Dem. Rep. Congo 126 E5
Kayyerkan Rus. Fed. 39 I3
Kayyngdy Kyrg. 103 H4
formerly spelt Kainda or Kaindy; formerly known as Molotovsk
Kazachka Rus. Fed. 43 T8
Kazach'ye Rus. Fed. 39 N2
Kazakh Azer. see Qazax
Kazakhdar'ya Uzbek. 102 D4
also spelt Qozoqdaryo
Kazakhskaya S.S.R. country Asia see Kazakhstan
Kazakhskiy Melkosopochnik plain Kazakh. 103 G2
Kazakhskiy Zaliv b. Kazakh. 102 C4
also known as Qazaq Shyghanaghy

▶Kazakhstan country Asia 102 C2
4th largest country in Asia and 9th in the world. Also spelt Kazakstan or Qazaqstan in Kazakh; formerly known as Kazakhskaya S.S.R.
world [countries] ▶ 10–11
asia [countries] ▶ 64–67

Kazakhstan Kazakh. see Aksay
Kazaki Rus. Fed. 43 T9
Kazakstan country Asia see Kazakhstan
Kazalinsk Kazakh. 103 E3
also known as Qazaly
Kazan r. Canada 167 M2
Kazan' Rus. Fed. 40 I5
Kazanchunkur Kazakh. 103 J2
Kazancı Turkey 106 C3
Kazandzhik Turkm. see Gazandzhyk
Kazanje, Mal mt. Albania 59 B9
Kazanka r. Rus. Fed. 40 I5
Kazanketken Uzbek. 102 D4
also spelt Qozonketkan
Kazanlı Turkey 108 F1
Kazanlŭk Bulg. 58 G6
Kazanovka Rus. Fed. 43 T8
Kazanovo Rus. Fed. 85 G1
Kazan-rettō is N. Pacific Ocean see Volcano Islands
Kazatin Ukr. see Kozyatyn
Kazatskiy Kazakh. 102 D2
Kaza Wenz r. Eth. 128 C1

▶Kazbek mt. Georgia/Rus. Fed. 107 F2
4th highest mountain in Europe. Also known as Mqinvartsveri.
europe [landscapes] ▶ 30–31

Kaz Dağı mts Turkey 106 A3
Kāzerūn Iran 100 B4
Kazgorodok Kazakh. 103 G1
Kazhim Rus. Fed. 40 I3
Kazhmak r. Pak. 101 E5
Kazıkbelı Geçidi pass Turkey 59 K11
Kazi Magomed Azer. see Qazımämmäd
Kazimierza Wielka Poland 49 R5
Kazimierz Dolne Poland 49 S4
Kazincbarcika Hungary 49 R7
Kazinka Lipetskaya Oblast' Rus. Fed. 43 U9
formerly known as Novaya Zhizn
Kazinka Ryazanskaya Oblast' Rus. Fed. 43 U8
Kaziranga National Park India 97 G4
Kazlowshchyna Belarus 42 G8
Kazlowshchyna Belarus 42 J6
Kazlų Rūda Lith. 42 E7
Kazo Japan 91 F6
Kaztalovka Kazakh. 102 B2
Kazuma Pan National Park Zimbabwe 131 E3
Kazumba Dem. Rep. Congo 127 D6
Kazungula Zambia 127 E9
Kazuno Japan 90 G4
Kazy Turkm. 102 D5
Kazyany Belarus 43 K6
Kazygurt Kazakh. 103 G4
also spelt Qazyqurt; formerly known as Lenīn or Leninskoye
Kazym r. Rus. Fed. 38 G3
Kazymskiy Mys Rus. Fed. 38 G3
Kçirë Albania 58 A6
Kea Greece 59 F11
Kea i. Greece 59 F11
English form Ceos
Keaau U.S.A. 181 [inset] Z2
Keahole Point U.S.A. 181 [inset] Z2
Kealakekua Bay U.S.A. 181 [inset] Z2
Kealia U.S.A. 181 [inset] Z2
Keams Canyon U.S.A. 183 N6
Kéamu i. Vanuatu see Anatom
Kearney U.S.A. 178 C3
Kearneysville U.S.A. 176 H6
Kearny U.S.A. 183 N8
Keas, Steno sea chan. Greece 59 F11
Keate's Drift S. Africa 133 O5
Keban Turkey 107 D3
Keban Barajı resr Turkey 107 D3
Kebatu i. Indon. 77 E3
Kebbi state Nigeria 125 F3
Kébémèr Senegal 124 A3
Kébi r. Cameroon 125 I4
Kébi Côte d'Ivoire 124 D4
Kebili Tunisia 123 H2
Kebīr, Nahr al r. Lebanon/Syria 108 G3
Kebkabiya Sudan 120 E6
Kebnekaise mt. Sweden 44 L2
K'ebrī Dehar Eth. 128 E3
Kebumen Indon. 77 E4
Kecel Hungary 49 Q9
Kech reg. Pak. 101 E5
K'ech'a Terara mt. Eth. 128 C3
Kéché Cent. Afr. Rep. 126 D2
Kechika r. Canada 166 E3
Keçiborlu Turkey 106 B3
Kecskemét Hungary 49 Q9
Kedah state Malaysia 76 C1
Kėdainiai Lith. 42 E6
Kedairu Passage Fiji see Kadavu Passage
Kédédéssé Chad 126 C2
Kedgwick Canada 169 H4
Kedian China 87 E2
Kediri Indon. 77 F4
Kedong China 82 B3
Kédougou Senegal 124 B3
Kedva r. Rus. Fed. 40 J2
Kędzierzyn-Koźle Poland 49 P5
historically known as Heydebreck
Keele r. Canada 166 E1
Keele Peak Canada 166 D2
Keeley Lake Canada 167 I4
Keeling Islands terr. Indian Ocean see Cocos Islands
Keelung Taiwan see Chilung
Keenapusan i. Phil. 74 A5
Keene CA U.S.A. 182 F6
Keene NH U.S.A. 177 M3
Keene OH U.S.A. 176 D5
Keep r. Australia 148 A2
Keepit, Lake resr Australia 147 F2
Keep River National Park Australia 148 A2
Keeromsberg mt. Free State S. Africa 133 K5
Keeromsberg mt. W. Cape S. Africa 132 D10
Keer-weer, Cape Australia 149 D2
Keetmanshoop Namibia 130 C5
Keewatin Canada 167 M5
Keewatin U.S.A. 174 A2
Kefallinía i. Greece see Cephalonia
Kefallonia i. Greece see Cephalonia
Kefalos Greece 59 H12
Kefalos, Akra pt Greece 59 F11
Kefamenanu Indon. 75 C5
Kefe Ukr. see Feodosiya
Keffi Nigeria 125 G4
Keflavík Iceland 44 [inset] B2
Kegalla Sri Lanka 94 D5
Kegayli Uzbek. see Kegeyli
Kegen Kazakh. 103 I4
Kegeyli Uzbek. 102 D4
also spelt Kegayli
Keglo, Baie de b. Canada 169 H1
Keg River Canada 167 G3
Kegul'ta Rus. Fed. 41 H7
Ķegums Latvia 42 F5
Keheili Sudan 121 G5
Kehl Germany 48 E7
Kehoula well Mauritania 124 C2
Kehra Estonia 42 G2
Kehsi Mansam Myanmar 78 B3
Kehtna Estonia 42 F3
Keibab Plateau U.S.A. 183 L5
Keighley U.K. 47 K10
Keihoku Japan 91 D7
Keila Estonia 42 F2
Keila r. Estonia 42 F2
Keilak Sudan 126 F2
Keili Sudan 128 B2
Kei Ling Ha Hoi b. Hong Kong China see Three Fathoms Cove
Keimoes S. Africa 132 E5
Kei Mouth S. Africa 133 M9
Kei Road S. Africa 133 L9
Keiskama r. S. Africa 133 L10
Keiskammahoek S. Africa 133 L9
Keïta Niger 125 G3
Kéita, Bahr r. Chad 126 C2
Keitele Fin. 44 N3
Keitele l. Fin. 44 N3
Keith Australia 146 D4
Keith U.K. 46 J6
Keith, Cape Australia 148 A1
Keith Arm b. Canada 166 F1
Keithley Creek Canada 166 F4
Keithsburg U.S.A. 172 C9
Kejimkujik National Park Canada 169 H4
Kekaha U.S.A. 181 [inset] Y1
Këk-Art Kyrg. see Alaykuu
Ķekava Latvia 42 F5
Kĕkaygyr Kyrg. see Kök-Aygyr
Kekerengu N.Z. 153 H10
Kékes mt. Hungary 49 R8
Kekova Adası i. Turkey 108 A1
Kekra Rus. Fed. 39 O4
Kekri India 96 B4
Këk-Tash Kyrg. see Kök-Tash
K'elafo Eth. 128 E3
Kelai atoll Maldives 94 B5
Kelan China 85 F4
Kelang i. Indon. 75 C3
Kelang Malaysia 76 C2
formerly spelt Klang
Kelantan r. Malaysia 76 C1
Kelantan state Malaysia 76 C1
Kelārdasht Iran 100 B2
Kelawar i. Indon. 77 E3
Kelbia, Sebkhet salt pan Tunisia 57 C13
Kele Uganda 128 B4
Kelekçi Turkey 59 K11
Keles Turkey 59 K9
Keles Uzbek. 103 G4
Kelheim Germany 48 I7
Kelibia Tunisia 123 H1
Kelif Turkm. 103 F5
Kelifskiy Uzboy marsh Turkm. 103 E5
Kelkit Turkey 107 D2
also known as Çiftlik
Kelkit r. Turkey 107 D2
Kellavere hill Estonia 42 H2
Kéllé Congo 126 B5
Kellerberrin Australia 151 B6
Keller Lake Canada 166 F2
Kellerovka Kazakh. 103 G1
Kellett, Cape Canada 164 G2
Kelliher Canada 167 K5
Kellogg U.S.A. 180 C3
Kelloselkä Fin. 44 O2
Kells Rep. of Ireland 47 F10
also known as Ceanannus Mór
Kelly Lake Canada 166 E1
Kelly Range hills Australia 151 C5
Kelmė Lith. 42 D6
Kelo Chad 126 B2
Kelowna Canada 166 G5
Kelp Head Canada 166 E5
Kelsey U.S.A. 172 A3
Kelseyville U.S.A. 182 B3
Kelso N.Z. 153 D13
Kelso U.K. 46 J8
Kelso CA U.S.A. 183 I6
Kelso WA U.S.A. 180 B3
Kelti, Jebel mt. Morocco 54 F9
Keluang Malaysia 76 C2
formerly spelt Kluang
Kelujärvi Fin. 44 N2
Kelvington Canada 167 K4
Kelvin Island Canada 168 B3
Kelwara India 101 H5
Kem' Rus. Fed. 40 E2
Kem' r. Rus. Fed. 40 E2
Kema r. Rus. Fed. 43 S1
Ke Macina Mali see Massina
Kemah Turkey 107 D3
Kemal Turkey 58 H7
Kemaliye Turkey 107 D3
also known as Eğin
Kemalpaşa Turkey 59 I10
Kemano Canada 166 E4
Kembé Cent. Afr. Rep. 126 D3
Kembolcha Eth. 128 C2
Kemeneshát hills Hungary 49 O8
Kemer Antalya Turkey 106 B3
Kemer Antalya Turkey 108 A1
Kemer Muğla Turkey 106 B3
Kemer Barajı resr Turkey 106 B3
Kemerovo Rus. Fed. 80 D1
Kemerovo Oblast admin. div. Rus. Fed. see Kemerovskaya Oblast'
Kemerovskaya Oblast' admin. div. Rus. Fed. 80 D2
English form Kemerovo Oblast
Kemi Fin. 44 N2
Kemihaara Fin. 44 O2
Kemijärvi Fin. 44 N2
Kemijärvi l. Fin. 44 N2
Kemijoki r. Fin. 44 N2
Kemin Kyrg. 103 H4
formerly known as Bystrovka
Keminmaa Fin. 44 N2
Kemiö Fin. see Kimito
Kemir Turkm. 102 C5
formerly spelt Keymir
Kemlya Rus. Fed. 40 H5
Kemmerer U.S.A. 180 E4
Kemmuna i. Malta 57 G12
also known as Comino
Kémo pref. Cent. Afr. Rep. 126 C3
Kemp, Lake U.S.A. 179 C5
Kempazh r. Rus. Fed. 40 L2
Kempele Fin. 44 N2
Kempen reg. Belgium 51 K1
Kempendyay Rus. Fed. 39 L3
Kempisch Kanaal canal Belgium 51 L1
Kemp Land reg. Antarctica 223 D2
Kemp Peninsula Antarctica 222 U2
Kemp's Bay Bahamas 186 D1
Kempsey Australia 147 G2
Kempt, Lac l. Canada 169 F4
Kempten (Allgäu) Germany 48 H8
Kempton Australia 147 E5
Kempton Park S. Africa 133 M3
Kemptville Canada 173 R5
Kemujan i. Indon. 77 E4
Ken r. India 96 D4
Kenabeek Canada 173 N3
Kenai U.S.A. 164 D3
Kenai Fiords National Park U.S.A. 164 D4
Kenai Mountains U.S.A. 164 D4
Kenamu r. Canada 169 J2
Kenamuke Swamp Sudan 128 B3
Kenansville U.S.A. 174 E5
Kenawang, Bukit mt. Sarawak Malaysia 77 F2
Kenâyis, Râs el pt Egypt 121 E2
Kenbridge U.S.A. 176 G9
Kendal Indon. 77 E4
Kendal U.K. 47 J9
Kendall r. Australia 149 D2
Kendall U.S.A. 175 D7
Kendall, Cape Canada 167 O2
Kendall, Mount N.Z. 152 G9
Kendallville U.S.A. 172 H9
Kendari Indon. 75 B3
Kendawangan Indon. 77 E3
Kendawangan r. Indon. 77 E3
Kendégué Chad 126 C2
Kendhrikí Makedhonía admin. reg. Greece see Kentriki Makedonia
Kendraparha India 95 E1
Kendrew S. Africa 133 I9
Kendrick Peak U.S.A. 183 M6
Kendua Bangl. 97 F4
Kendujhargarh India 97 E5
Kendyktas mts Kazakh. 103 H4
Kendyrli-Kayasanskoye, Plato plat. Kazakh. 102 C4
Kendyrlisor, Solonchak salt l. Kazakh. 102 C4
Kenedy U.S.A. 179 C6
Keneka r. S. Africa 133 N7
Kenema Sierra Leone 124 C5
Kenepai, Gunung mt. Indon. 77 E2
Keneurgench Turkm. 102 D4
also spelt Köneürgench; formerly spelt Kunya-Urgench
Kenga Bhutan 97 F4
Kenge Dem. Rep. Congo 126 C6
Kengere Dem. Rep. Congo 127 E7
Keng Hkam Myanmar 78 B3
Kengis Sweden 44 M2
Keng Lap Myanmar 78 C3
Keng Lon Myanmar 78 B3
Keng-Peli Uzbek. 102 D4
Keng Tawng Myanmar 78 B3
Kengtung Myanmar 78 B3
Kenhardt S. Africa 132 F6
Kéniéba Mali 124 C3
Kéniébaoulé, Réserve de nature res. Mali 124 C3
Kénitra Morocco 122 D2
formerly known as Port-Lyautrey
Kenli China 85 H4
Kenmare Rep. of Ireland 47 C12
Kenmare U.S.A. 178 B1
Kenmare River inlet Rep. of Ireland 47 B12
Kenmaur Zimbabwe 131 F3
Kenmore U.S.A. 176 G3
Kenn Germany 48 D6
Kennebec U.S.A. 178 C3
Kennebec r. U.S.A. 174 G2
Kennebunk U.S.A. 177 O2
Kennebunkport U.S.A. 177 O2
Kennedy Australia 149 E3
Kennedy r. Australia 149 E2
Kennedy, Cape U.S.A. see Canaveral, Cape
Kennedy Range hills Australia 151 A5
Kennedy Range National Park Australia 151 A5
Kennedy's Vale S. Africa 133 O1
Kennedy Town Hong Kong China 87 [inset]
Kennedyville U.S.A. 177 J6
Kenner U.S.A. 175 B6
Kennet r. U.K. 47 L12
Kenneth Range hills Australia 150 B4
Kennett U.S.A. 174 B4
Kennewick U.S.A. 180 C3
Kenogami r. Canada 168 C3
Kenogami Lake Canada 173 M2
Kenogamissi Lake Canada 173 L2
Keno Hill Canada 166 C2
Kenora Canada 167 M5
Kenosha U.S.A. 172 F8
Kenova U.S.A. 176 C7
Kenozero, Ozero l. Rus. Fed. 40 F3
Kensington Canada 169 I4
Kent OH U.S.A. 176 D4
Kent TX U.S.A. 181 F7
Kent VA U.S.A. 176 D9
Kent WA U.S.A. 180 B3
Kentani S. Africa 133 M9
also spelt Centane
Kentau Kazakh. 103 G4
Kent Group is Australia 147 E4
Kentland U.S.A. 174 C3
Kenton MI U.S.A. 172 E4
Kenton OH U.S.A. 176 B5
Kenton-on-Sea S. Africa 133 K10
Kent Peninsula Canada 165 I3
Kentriki Makedonia admin. reg. Greece 58 E8
also spelt Kendhrikí Makedhonía
Kentucky r. U.S.A. 176 B8
Kentucky state U.S.A. 176 A8
Kentucky Lake U.S.A. 174 B4
Kentwood LA U.S.A. 175 B6
Kentwood MI U.S.A. 172 H8
▶Kenya country Africa 128 C4
africa [countries] ▶ 114–117

▶Kenya, Mount Kenya 128 C5
2nd highest mountain in Africa. Also known as Kirinyaga.
africa [landscapes] ▶ 112–113

Kenyir, Tasik resr Malaysia 76 C1
Kenzingen Germany 48 E7
Keokuk U.S.A. 174 B3
Keoladeo National Park India 96 C4
Keosauqua U.S.A. 174 B3
Keowee, Lake resr U.S.A. 174 D5
Kepa Rus. Fed. 44 P2
Kepa r. Rus. Fed. 44 P2
Kepahiang Indon. 76 C3
Kępice Poland 49 N1
Kepina r. Rus. Fed. 40 G2
Kepler Mountains N.Z. 153 B13
Kępno Poland 49 O4
Keppel Bay Australia 149 F4
Keppel Harbour sea chan. Sing. 76 [inset]
Keppel Island Tonga see Tafahi
Kepsut Turkey 106 B3
Kerala state India 94 B4
historically known as Chera
Kerang Australia 147 D3
Kerava Fin. 45 N3
Kerba Alg. 55 M8
Kerbau, Tanjung pt Indon. 76 C3
Kerbela Iraq see Karbalā'
Kerben Kyrg. 103 G4
also spelt Karavan
Kerbi r. Rus. Fed. 82 E1
Kerch Ukr. 41 F7
historically known as Panticapaeum
Kerchem'ya Rus. Fed. 40 J3
Kerchevskiy Rus. Fed. 40 K4
Kere Eth. 128 C3
Kerema P.N.G. 73 K8
Keremeos Canada 166 G5
Kerempe Burun pt Turkey 106 C2
Keren Eritrea 121 H6
Kerend Iran 100 A3
Kerepehi N.Z. 152 J5
Kerest' r. Rus. Fed. 43 M2
Keret' Rus. Fed. 44 P2
Keret' r. Rus. Fed. 44 P2
Keret', Ozero l. Rus. Fed. 44 P2
Kerewan Gambia 124 A3
Kerey watercourse Kazakh. 103 G2
formerly spelt Kirey
Kerey, Ozero salt l. Kazakh. 103 G2
formerly spelt Kirey, Ozero
Kergeli Turkm. 102 D5
Kerguélen, Îles is Indian Ocean 219 L9
English form Kerguelen Islands
Kerguelen Islands Indian Ocean see Kerguélen, Îles
Kericho Kenya 128 B5
Kerihun mt. Indon. 77 F2
Kerikeri N.Z. 152 H3
Kerimäki Fin. 44 O3
Kerinci, Danau l. Indon. 76 C3

Laholmsbukten b. Sweden 45 K4
Lahontan Reservoir U.S.A. 182 E2
Lahore Pak. 101 H4
La Horqueta Venez. 199 F3
La Hotte, Massif de mts Haiti 187 E3
Lahoysk Belarus 42 I7
Lahr (Schwarzwald) Germany 48 E7
Lahri Pak. 101 G4
Lahti Fin. 45 N3
La Huerta Mex. 184 D5
L'Ahzar, Vallée de watercourse Niger 125 F3
Laï Chad 126 C2
Lai'an China 87 F1
also known as Xin'an
Laibach Slovenia see Ljubljana
Laibin China 87 D4
Laie U.S.A. 181 [inset] Z1
Laifeng China 87 D2
also known as Xiangfeng
L'Aigle France 50 G4
Laihia Fin. 44 M3
Lai-hka Myanmar 78 B3
Lai-Hsak Myanmar 78 B3
Laingsburg S. Africa 132 E10
Laingsburg U.S.A. 173 I8
Lainioälven r. Sweden 44 M2
Lainsitz r. Austria 49 M7
Lair U.S.A. 176 A7
L'Aïr, Massif de mts Niger 125 H2
also known as Azbine
L'Aïr et du Ténéré, Réserve Naturelle Nationale de nature res. Niger 125 H2
Laird U.K. 46 H5
Lais Indon. 76 C3
Lais Phil. 74 C5
La Isabela Cuba 186 C2
Laisälven r. Sweden 44 L2
Laishevo Rus. Fed. 40 I5
La Isla Col. 198 B3
La Isla, Salar de salt flat Chile 204 C2
Laitila Fin. 45 M3
Laivera well Tanz. 129 C6
Laives Italy 56 D2
Laiwu China 85 H4
Laiwui Indon. 75 C3
Laixi China 85 I4
formerly known as Shuiji
Laiyang China 85 I4
Laiyuan China 85 G4
Laizhou China 85 H4
formerly known as Yexian
Laizhou Wan b. China 85 H4
La Jagua Col. 198 C2
Lajamanu Australia 148 A3
Lajanurpekhi Georgia 107 E2
also known as Ladzhanurges
Lajeado Brazil 203 B9
Lajedo Brazil 202 E4
Laje dos Santos i. Brazil 207 G11
Lajes Brazil 203 B8
Lajinha Brazil 207 L7
Lajkovac Srbija Yugo. 58 B4
La Jolla Peak hill U.S.A. 182 F7
Lajosmizse Hungary 49 Q8
La Joya Mex. 184 D3
La Joya Peru 200 C4
La Joya de los Sachas Ecuador 198 B5
Lajta r. Austria/Hungary 49 O8
La Junta Bol. 201 E3
La Junta Mex. 184 D2
La Junta U.S.A. 178 B4
La Juventud, Isla de i. Cuba 186 C2
formerly known as Pines, Isle of or Pinos, Isla de
Lakadiya India 96 A5
L'Akagera, Parc National de nat. park Rwanda see Akagera National Park
Lakathah Saudi Arabia 104 C4
Lakaträsk Sweden 44 M2
Lake KY U.S.A. 176 B8
Lake WY U.S.A. 180 E3
Lake Alice N.Z. 152 J8
Lake Andes U.S.A. 178 C3
Lake Arthur U.S.A. 179 D6
Lake Butler U.S.A. 175 D6
Lake Cargelligo Australia 147 E3
Lake Charles U.S.A. 179 D6
Lake City AR U.S.A. 174 B5
Lake City CO U.S.A. 181 F5
Lake City FL U.S.A. 175 D6
Lake City IA U.S.A. 178 D3
Lake City MN U.S.A. 168 A4
Lake City SC U.S.A. 175 E5
Lake City TN U.S.A. 176 A9
Lake Clark National Park and Preserve U.S.A. 164 D3
Lake Clear U.S.A. 177 K1
Lake Coleridge N.Z. 153 F11
Lake Cowichan Canada 166 E5
Lake District National Park U.K. 47 I9
Lake Eyre National Park Australia 146 C2
Lakefield Australia 149 E2
Lakefield Canada 168 E4
Lakefield National Park Australia 149 E2
Lake Fork r. U.S.A. 183 O1
Lake Frome Regional Reserve nature res. Australia 146 C2
Lake Gairdner National Park Australia 146 B2
Lake Geneva U.S.A. 172 E8
Lake Gilles Conservation Park nature res. Australia 146 C3
Lake Grace Australia 151 B7
Lake Gregory Aboriginal Reserve Australia 150 D4
Lake Harbour Canada see Kimmirut
Lake Havasu City U.S.A. 183 J7
Lakehurst U.S.A. 177 K5
Lake Isabella U.S.A. 182 F6
Lake Jackson U.S.A. 179 D6
Lake King Australia 151 B7
Lake King Nature Reserve Australia 151 B7
Lakeland Australia 149 E2
Lakeland FL U.S.A. 175 D7
Lakeland GA U.S.A. 175 D6
Lake Linden U.S.A. 172 E3
Lake Louise Canada 167 G5
Lake Mackay Aboriginal Land res. Australia 148 A4
Lake Magenta Nature Reserve Australia 151 B7
Lake Manyara National Park Tanz. 128 B5
Lake Mburo National Park Uganda 128 A5
Lake Mills U.S.A. 174 A3
Lake Nash Australia 148 C4
Lake Paringa N.Z. 153 D11
Lake Placid U.S.A. 177 L1
Lakeport CA U.S.A. 182 B2
Lakeport MI U.S.A. 173 K7
Lake Providence U.S.A. 175 B5
Lake Pukaki N.Z. 153 E12
La Kéran, Parc National de nat. park Togo 125 F4
Lake Range mts U.S.A. 182 E1
Lake River Canada 168 D2
Lake St Peter Canada 173 O5
Lakes Entrance Australia 147 F4
Lakeshore U.S.A. 182 E4
Lakeside AZ U.S.A. 183 O7
Lakeside CA U.S.A. 183 H9
Lakeside NJ U.S.A. 177 K4
Lake Sumner Forest Park nature res. N.Z. 153 G10
Lake Superior Provincial Park Canada 173 I3
Lake Tekapo N.Z. 153 E12
Lake Torrens National Park Australia 146 C2
Lake Traverse (Sisseton) Indian Reservation res. U.S.A. 178 C2
Lakeview OH U.S.A. 176 B5
Lakeview OR U.S.A. 180 B4
Lake Village U.S.A. 175 B5
Lakeville U.S.A. 174 A2
Lake Wales U.S.A. 175 D7
Lakewood CO U.S.A. 180 F5
Lakewood OH U.S.A. 176 D4
Lakewood WI U.S.A. 172 E5
Lakhdaria Alg. 55 O8
Lakhdenpokh'ya Rus. Fed. 45 O3
Lakheri India 96 C4
Lakhimpur India 96 D4
Lakhipur India 97 G4
Lakhisarai India see Luckeesarai
Lakhish r. Israel 108 F6
Lakhnadon India 96 C5
Lakhpat India 96 A5
Lakhtar India 96 A5
Lakhva r. Belarus 43 L8
Lakin U.S.A. 178 B4
Lakinsk Rus. Fed. 43 U5
formerly known as Lakinskiy
Lakinskiy Rus. Fed. see Lakinsk
Lakitusaki r. Canada 168 D2
Lakki Pak. 101 G3
Lakkoma Greece 59 G8
Lakonikos Kolpos b. Greece 59 D12
Lakor i. Indon. 75 D5
Lakota Côte d'Ivoire 124 D5
Lakota U.S.A. 178 C1
Laksefjorden sea chan. Norway 44 N1
Lakselv Norway 44 N1
Laksfors Norway 44 K2
Lakshadweep is India see Laccadive Islands
Lakshadweep union terr. India 94 B4
formerly known as Laccadive, Minicoy and Amindivi Islands
Laksham Bangl. 97 F5
Lakshettipet India 94 C2
Lakshmeshwar India 94 B3
Lakshmikantapur India 97 F5
Laktyshy Vodaskhovishcha resr Belarus 42 H9
Lala Phil. 74 B5
Lalago Tanz. 128 B5
La Laguna Arg. 204 E4
La Laguna, Picacho de mt. Mex. 184 C4
La Laguna Ojo de Liebre, Parque Natural de nature res. Mex. 184 B3
Lala Musa Pak. 101 H3
Lalapanzi Zimbabwe 131 F3
Lalapaşa Turkey 58 H7
Lalara Gabon 126 A4
Lalaua Moz. 131 H2
L'Albufera l. Spain 55 K5
La Léfini, Réserve de Chasse de nature res. Congo 126 B5
Laleham Australia 149 F4
Lāleh Zār, Kūh-e mt. Iran 100 D4
La Lékoli-Pandaka, Réserve de Faune de nature res. Congo 126 B4
Lalganj India 97 E4
Lalgudi India 94 C4
Lālī Iran 100 B3
Lalibela Eth. 128 C1
La Libertad Ecuador 198 A5
La Libertad El Salvador 185 H6
La Libertad Guat. 185 H5
La Libertad Nicaragua 186 B4
La Libertad dept Peru 200 A2
La Ligua Chile 204 C4
Laliki Indon. 75 C4
Lalimboee Indon. 75 B3
Lalin China 82 B3
Lalin r. China 82 B3
Lalín Spain 54 C2
Lalinde France 50 G8
La Línea de la Concepción Spain 54 F8
Lalitpur India 96 C4
Lalitpur Nepal see Patan
Lal-Lo Phil. 74 B2
Lalmanirhat Bangl. 97 F4
Lalmikor Uzbek. see Lyal'mikar
La Loche Canada 167 I3
La Loche, Lac l. Canada 167 I3
La Loire et de l'Allier, Plaines de plain France 51 J6
La Loma Bol. 201 D5
La Loma Negra, Planicie de plain Arg. 204 D5
La Loupe France 50 H4
La Louvière Belgium 51 K2
Lalpur India 96 A5
Lal'sk Rus. Fed. 40 H3
Lalsot India 96 C4
La Lufira, Lac de retenue de resr Dem. Rep. Congo 127 E7
Lalui i. Indon. 75 C3
Lalung La pass China 89 D6
Lama Bangl. 97 G5
La Macarena, Parque Nacional nat. park Col. 198 C4
La Maddalena Sardegna Italy 56 B7
La Madeleine, Îles de is Canada 169 I4
Lamag Sabah Malaysia 77 G1
La Maiko, Parc National de nat. park Dem. Rep. Congo 126 E5
Lamaing Myanmar 79 B5
La Malbaie Canada 169 G4
La Malinche, Parque Nacional nat. park Mex. 185 F5
La Mancha Mex. 185 E3
La Manche strait France/U.K. see English Channel
La Manga del Mar Menor Spain 55 K7
La Manika, Plateau de Dem. Rep. Congo 127 E7
La Máquina Mex. 184 D2
Lamar CO U.S.A. 178 B4
Lamar MO U.S.A. 178 D4
La Maraoué, Parc National de nat. park Côte d'Ivoire 124 D5
La Marche, Plateaux de France 50 H6
Lamard Iran 100 C5
La Margeride, Monts de mts France 51 J7
Lamarque Arg. 204 D5
La Marque U.S.A. 179 D6
La Martre, Lac l. Canada 167 G2
Lamas r. Turkey 108 F1
La Matanzilla, Pampa de plain Arg. 204 C5
La Mauricie, Parc National de nat. park Canada 169 F4
La Maya Cuba 186 E2
Lamballe France 50 D4
Lambaréné Gabon 126 A5
Lambayeque Peru 198 B6
Lambayeque dept Peru 198 B6
Lambay Island Rep. of Ireland 47 G10
Lambeng Indon. 77 F3
Lambert atoll Marshall Is see Ailinglapalap
Lambert, Cape Australia 150 B4

▶Lambert Glacier Antarctica 223 E2
Largest series of glaciers in the world.

Lambert's Bay S. Africa 132 C9
Lambertville U.S.A. 177 K5
Lambeth Canada 173 L8
Lambi India 96 B3
Lambina Australia 146 B1
Lambro r. Italy 56 B3
Lam Chi r. Thai. 78 D5
Lam Chi r. Thai. 79 C5
La Media Luna, Arrecife de reef Hond. 186 C4
La Medjerda, Monts de mts Alg. 57 A12
Lamego Port. 54 D3
La Mejorada Peru 200 B3
Lamen Vanuatu 145 F3
Lamèque, Île i. Canada 169 H4
La Merced Arg. 204 D3
La Merced Peru 200 B2
Lameroo Australia 146 D3
La Mesa U.S.A. 183 G9
Lamesa U.S.A. 179 B5
L'Ametlla de Mar Spain 55 L4
Lamezia Italy 57 I10
Lamhar Touil, Sabkhet imp. l. W. Sahara 122 A5
Lamia Greece 59 D10
Lamigan Point Phil. 74 C5
Lamington National Park Australia 147 G2
Lamir Iran 100 B2
La Mirada U.S.A. 182 F8
formerly known as Mirada Hills
La Misa Mex. 184 C2
La Misión Mex. 183 H9
Lamitan Phil. 74 B5
Lamma Island Hong Kong China 87 [inset]
also known as Pok Liu Chau
Lammerkop S. Africa 133 N2
Lammerlaw Range mts N.Z. 153 D13
Lammermuir Hills U.K. 46 J8
Lammhult Sweden 45 K4
Lammi Fin. 45 N3
Lammijärv lake channel Estonia/Rus. Fed. 42 I3
La Moille U.S.A. 172 D9
Lamoille r. U.S.A. 177 L1
La Moine r. U.S.A. 174 B4
La Mojonera Spain 55 I8
Lamon Bay Phil. 74 B3
Lamone r. Italy 56 E4
Lamongan Indon. 77 F4
Lamoni U.S.A. 174 A3
Lamont U.S.A. 182 F6
La Montagne d'Ambre, Parc National de nat. park Madag. 131 [inset] K2
La Montagne de Reims, Parc Naturel Régional de nature res. France 51 J3
La Morita Chihuahua Mex. 184 D2
La Morita Coahuila Mex. 179 B6
Lamotrek atoll Micronesia 73 K5
La Motte Canada 173 O2
Lamotte-Beuvron France 51 I5
La Motte-Servolex France 51 L7
La Mougalaba, Réserve de nature res. Gabon 126 A5
La Moure U.S.A. 178 C2
Lampa Peru 200 C3
Lampang Thai. 78 B4
Lam Pao Reservoir Thai. 78 C4
Lampasas U.S.A. 179 C6
Lampasas r. U.S.A. 179 C6
Lampazos Mex. 185 E3
Lampedusa, Isola di i. Sicilia Italy 57 E13
Lampeland Norway 45 J4
Lampeter U.K. 47 H11
also known as Llanbedr
Lamphun Thai. 78 B4
Lam Plai Mat r. Thai. 79 C5
Lampozhnya Rus. Fed. 40 H2
Lampsacus Turkey see Lâpseki
Lampung prov. Indon. 76 D4
Lampung, Teluk b. Indon. 76 D4
Lam Si Bai r. Thai. 79 D5
Lamta India 96 D5
Lam Tin Hong Kong China 87 [inset]
Lamu Kenya 128 D5
Lamu Myanmar 78 A4
La Muela mt. Spain 55 J5
La Mure France 51 L8
Lana Australia 149 D4
Lana Italy 56 D2
Lanai i. U.S.A. 181 [inset] Z1
also known as Ranai
Lanai City U.S.A. 181 [inset] Z1
La Nao, Cabo de c. Spain 55 L6
Lanao, Lake Phil. 74 C5
Lanark Canada 173 Q5
Lanark U.K. 46 I8
Lanark U.S.A. 172 D8
Lanas Sabah Malaysia 77 G1
Lanbi Kyun i. Myanmar 79 B6
also known as Sullivan Island
Lanboyan Point Phil. 74 B4
Lancang China 86 A4
also known as Menglang
Lancang Jiang r. China see Mekong
Lancaster U.K. 47 J9
Lancaster CA U.S.A. 182 F7
Lancaster KY U.S.A. 176 A8
Lancaster MO U.S.A. 174 A3
Lancaster NH U.S.A. 177 N1
Lancaster OH U.S.A. 176 C6
Lancaster PA U.S.A. 177 I5
Lancaster SC U.S.A. 174 D5
Lancaster VA U.S.A. 177 I8
Lancaster WI U.S.A. 172 C8
Lancaster Sound strait Canada 165 K2
Lancelin Australia 151 A6
Lanch'khut'i Georgia 107 E2
Lanchow China see Lanzhou
Lanciano Italy 56 G6
Lancing U.S.A. 176 A9
Lanco Chile 204 B5
Lancun China 85 I4
Łańcut Poland 49 T5
Lancy Switz. 51 M6
Landak r. Indon. 77 E3
Landana Angola see Cacongo
Landau an der Isar Germany 49 J7
Landau in der Pfalz Germany 48 F6
Landeck Austria 48 H8
Lander watercourse Australia 148 A4
Lander U.S.A. 180 E4
Landerneau France 50 B4
Landes reg. France 50 F8
Landes de Gascogne, Parc Naturel Régional des nature res. France 50 F8
Landes de Lanvaux reg. France 50 D5
Landes du Mené reg. France 50 D4
Landfall Island India 95 G3
Landik, Gunung mt. Indon. 76 C3
Landis Canada 167 I4
Landivisiau France 50 B4
Landless Corner Zambia 127 F8
Land O' Lakes U.S.A. 172 D4
Landön Sweden 44 K3
Landor Australia 151 B5
Landquart Switz. 51 P5
Landrienne Canada 173 P2
Landrum U.S.A. 174 D5
Landsberg Poland see Gorzów Wielkopolski
Landsberg am Lech Germany 48 H7
Landsborough r. N.Z. 153 D11
Land's End pt U.K. 47 G13
Landshut Germany 48 J7
Landskrona Sweden 45 K5
La Nedei mt. Romania 58 E3
La Negra Chile 200 C5
Lane Pool Reserve nature res. Australia 151 B7
La Neuveville Switz. 51 N5
Lanfeng China see Lankao
Lang, Nam r. Myanmar 78 B2
La Nga r. Vietnam 79 D6
Lan'ga Co l. China 89 C6
Langadhás Greece see Lagkadas
Langai r. India 97 G4
Långan r. Sweden 44 K3
Langao China 87 D1
Langar Badakhshān Afgh. 101 H2
Langar Parvān Afgh. 101 G3
Langar Iran 101 E3
Langar Uzbek. 103 F5
formerly spelt Lyangar
Langar Uzbek. see Lyangar
Langara Indon. 75 B4
Langberg mts S. Africa 132 G5
Langdon U.S.A. 178 C1
Langeac France 51 J7
Langeais France 50 G5
Langebaan S. Africa 132 C10
Langeberg mts S. Africa 132 D10
Langehorn S. Africa 133 I3
Langeland i. Denmark 45 J5
Langelands Bælt strait Denmark 45 J5
Längelmäki Fin. 45 N3
Längelmävesi l. Fin. 40 C3
Langen Germany 48 F2
Langenburg Canada 167 K5
Langenlois Austria 49 M7
Langenthal Switz. 51 N5
Langeoog Germany 48 E2
Langeoog i. Germany 48 E2
Langepas Rus. Fed. 38 H3
Langesund Norway 45 J4
Langfang China 85 H4
also known as Anci
Långfjallets naturreservat nature res. Sweden 45 K3
Langgapayung Indon. 76 C2
Langgar China 89 F6
Langgöns Germany 48 F5
Langham Canada 167 J4
Langhko Myanmar 78 B3
Langholm S. Africa 133 K10
Langholm U.K. 47 J8
Langjökull ice cap Iceland 44 [inset] B2
Langka Indon. 76 B1
Langkawi i. Malaysia 76 B1
Langkesi, Kepulauan is Indon. 75 C4
Lang Kha Toek, Khao mt. Thai. 79 B6
Langklip S. Africa 132 E5
Langkon Sabah Malaysia 77 G1
Langlade Canada 173 R2
Langley Canada 166 F5
Langley U.S.A. 176 C8
Langlo watercourse Australia 149 E5
Langmusi China see Dagcanglhamo
Langogne France 51 J8
Langon France 50 F8
Langong, Xé r. Laos 78 D4
Langøya i. Norway 44 K1
Langqi China 87 F3
Langreo Spain 54 F1
Langres France 51 L5
Langres, Plateau de France 51 K5
Langsa Indon. 76 B1
Langsa, Teluk b. Indon. 76 B1
Långsele Sweden 44 L3
Langshan China 85 E3
Lang Shan mts China 85 E3
Langslett Norway 44 M1
Lang Son Vietnam 78 D3
Langtang National Park Nepal 97 E3
Langtao Myanmar 78 B2
Långträsk Sweden 44 M2
Langtry TX U.S.A. 179 B6
Languan China see Lantian
Languedoc-Roussillon admin. reg. France 51 I10
Languiaru r. Brazil see Iquê
Languiñeo Arg. 205 C6
Langundu, Tanjung pt Indon. 77 G5
Langvinds bruk Sweden 45 L3
Langwedel Germany 48 G3
Langya Shan mt. China 85 G4
Langzhong China 86 C2
Laniel Canada 173 N3
Lanigan Canada 167 J5
Lanín, Parque Nacional nat. park Arg. 204 C5
Lanín, Volcán vol. Arg./Chile 204 C5
Lanjak, Bukit mt. Sarawak Malaysia 77 E2
Lanji India 96 D5
Lanka country Asia see Sri Lanka
Lankao China 87 E1
formerly known as Lanfeng
Länkäran Azer. 107 G3
also spelt Lenkoran'
Lan Kok Tsui pt Hong Kong China see Black Point
Lanlacuni Bajo Peru 200 C3
Lannemezan France 50 G9
Lannion France 50 C4
L'Annonciation Canada 169 F4
La Noria Bol. 201 E3
La Noria Mex. 184 D4
Lansdale U.S.A. 177 J5
L'Anse U.S.A. 172 E4
L'Anse-St-Jean Canada 169 G3
Lansford U.S.A. 177 J5
Lansing r. Canada 166 C2
Lansing IA U.S.A. 172 B7

▶Lansing MI U.S.A. 173 I8
State capital of Michigan.

Länsi-Suomi prov. Fin. 44 M3
Lansjärv Sweden 44 M2
Lanta, Ko i. Thai. 79 B7
Lantau Island Hong Kong China 87 [inset]
also known as Tai Yue Shan
Lantau Peak hill Hong Kong China 87 [inset]
also known as Fung Wong Shan
Lanterne r. France 51 M5
Lantian China see Lianyuan
Lantian China 87 D1
also known as Languan
Lanusei Sardegna Italy 57 B9
Lanuza Phil. 74 C4
Lanuza Bay Phil. 74 C4
Lanxi Heilong. China 82 B3
Lanxi Zhejiang China 87 F2
Lanxian China 85 F4
also known as Dongcun
Lanya Sudan 128 A3
Lanyi r. China 85 F4
Lan Yü i. Taiwan 87 G4
Lanzarote i. Canary Is 122 B3
Lanzhou China 84 D4
also spelt Lanchow
Lanzijing China 85 I2
Lanzo Torinese Italy 51 N7
Lao r. Italy 57 H9
Lao, Mae r. Thai. 78 B4
Laoag Phil. 74 B2
Laoang Phil. 74 C3
Laobie Shan mts China 86 A4
Laobukou China 87 D3
Lao Cai Vietnam 78 C3
Laodicea Syria see Latakia
Laodicea Turkey see Denizli
Laodicea ad Lycum Turkey see Denizli
Laodicea ad Mare Syria see Latakia
Laofengkou China 88 C2
Laoha r. China 85 I3
Laoheishan China 82 C4
Laohekou China 87 D1
formerly known as Guanghua
Laohutun China 85 I4
Laojunmiao China see Yumen
La Okapi, Parc National de nat. park Dem. Rep. Congo 126 E4
Lao Ling mts China 82 B4
Laolong China see Longchuan
Laon France 51 J3
Laona U.S.A. 172 E5
La Oroya Peru 200 B2
▶Laos country Asia 78 C4
asia [countries] ▶▶▶ 64–67
Laoshan China 85 I4
also known as Licun
Laotieshan Shuidao sea chan. China see Bohai Haixia
Laotougou China 82 C4
Laotuding Shan hill China 82 B4
Laou, Oued r. Morocco 54 F9
La Ouandja-Vakaga, Réserve de Faune de nature res. Cent. Afr. Rep. 126 D2
Laoudi-Ba Côte d'Ivoire 124 E4
L'Aouk-Aoakole, Réserve de Faune de nature res. Cent. Afr. Rep. 126 D2
Laowohi pass Jammu and Kashmir see Khardung La
Laoximiao China 84 D3
Laoye Ling mts China 82 C4
Lapa Brazil 203 B8
Lapac i. Phil. 74 B5
Lapachito Arg. 204 F2
Lapai Nigeria 125 G4
Lapalisse France 51 J6
La Palma i. Canary Is 122 A3
La Palma Panama 186 D5
La Palma U.S.A. 183 M9
La Palma del Condado Spain 54 E7
La Paloma Uruguay 204 G4
La Pampa prov. Arg. 204 D5
formerly known as Eva Perón
La Panza Range mts U.S.A. 182 D6
La Paragua Venez. 199 F3
La Paramera, Puerto de pass Spain 54 G4
La Paramera, Sierra de mts Spain 54 F4
Laparan i. Phil. 74 A5
La Parata, Pointe de pt Corse France 56 A7
La Paya, Parque Nacional nat. park Col. 198 C4
La Paz Entre Ríos Arg. 204 F3
La Paz Mendoza Arg. 204 D4

▶La Paz Bol. 200 C4
Official capital of Bolivia.
world [countries] ▶▶▶ 10–11
southamerica [contrasts] ▶▶▶ 194–195

La Paz dept Bol. 200 C3
La Paz Hond. 186 B4
La Paz Mex. 184 C3
La Paz Nicaragua 186 B4
Lapaz U.S.A. 172 G9
La Paz Venez. 198 C2
La Paz, Bahía b. Mex. 184 C3
La Pedrera Col. 198 D5
Lapeer U.S.A. 173 J7
La Pelada Arg. 204 E3
La Peña Panama 186 C5
La Pendjari, Parc National de nat. park Benin 125 F4
La Perla Mex. 184 D2
La Pérouse Strait Japan/Rus. Fed. 90 G2
also known as Sōya-kaikyō
La Pesca Mex. 185 F4
La Piedad Mex. 185 E4
La Pila, Sierra de mts Spain 55 J6
La Pine U.S.A. 180 B4
Lapinig Phil. 74 C3
Lapinlahti Fin. 44 N3
La Pintada Panama 186 C5
Laplace U.S.A. 175 B6
Lap Lae Thai. 78 C4
La Plaine Ouanga, Réserve de nature res. Gabon 126 A5
Laplandskiy Zapovednik nature res. Rus. Fed. 44 P2
La Plata Arg. 204 F4
formerly known as Eva Perón
La Plata MD U.S.A. 177 I7
La Plata MO U.S.A. 178 D3
La Plata, Río de sea chan. Arg./Uruguay 204 F4
La Plaza Spain 54 E1
La Plonge, Lac l. Canada 167 J4
Lapmežciems Latvia 42 E4
La Pobla de Segur Spain 55 L2
La Pola de Gordón Spain 54 F2
La Poma Arg. 200 D6
Lapominka Rus. Fed. 40 G2
La Porte U.S.A. 174 C3
Laporte U.S.A. 177 I4
Laporte, Mount Canada 166 E2
Laposo, Bukit mt. Indon. 75 A4
La Potherie, Lac l. Canada 169 F1
Lapovo Srbija Yugo. 58 C4
La Poyata Col. 198 C3
Lappajärvi l. Fin. 44 M3
Lappeenranta Fin. 45 O3
Lappi Fin. 45 M3
Lappi prov. Fin. 44 N2
Lappland reg. Europe 44 L2
Lappohja Fin. 42 E2
Lappträsk Sweden 44 M2
Laprida Arg. 204 E5
La Pryor U.S.A. 179 C6
Lâpseki Turkey 106 A2
historically known as Lampsacus
Laptevo Rus. Fed. see Yasnogorsk
Laptev Sea Rus. Fed. 39 M2
also known as Laptevykh, More
Laptevykh, More sea Rus. Fed. see Laptev Sea
Lapua Fin. 44 M3
Lapuanjoki r. Fin. 44 M3
La Puebla Spain see Sa Pobla
La Puebla del Río Spain 54 E7
La Puebla de Montalbán Spain 54 G5
La Puerta Catamarca Arg. 204 D3
La Puerta Córdoba Arg. 204 E3
La Puerta Venez. 198 D2
Lapu-Lapu Phil. 74 B4
La Punilla, Cordillera de mts Chile 204 C3
Lapurdum France see Bayonne
Lăpuşnicu Mare Romania 58 C4
Lapušnik Kosovo, Srbija Yugo. 58 B6
Łapy Poland 49 T3
Laqiya Arbain well Sudan 121 F4
La Quiaca Arg. 200 D5
L'Aquila Italy 56 F6
La Quinta U.S.A. 183 H8
Lār Iran 100 C5
Lara Australia 147 E4
Lara state Venez. 198 D2
Laracha Spain 54 C1
Larache Morocco 122 D2
formerly spelt El Araïche; historically known as Lixus
Laragne-Montéglin France 51 L8
Lārak i. Iran 100 D5
Laramie U.S.A. 180 F4
Laramie r. U.S.A. 180 F4
Laramie Mountains U.S.A. 180 F4
Laranda Turkey see Karaman
Laranjal Brazil 199 G6
Laranjal Paulista Brazil 206 F10
Laranjeiras Brazil 202 E4
Laranjeiras do Sul Brazil 203 A8
Laranjinha r. Brazil 206 C9
Larantuka Indon. 75 B5
Larat i. Indon. 73 H8
La Raygat reg. W. Sahara 122 B5
Larba Alg. 55 O8
L'Arbresle France 51 K7
Lärbro Sweden 45 L4
L'Archipel de Mingan, Réserve du Parc National de nat. park Canada 169 I3
Larchwood Canada 173 L4
L'Ardenne, Plateau de Belgium see Ardennes
Larder Lake Canada 173 N2
Larder Lake l. Canada 173 N2
Laredo Spain 55 H1
Laredo U.S.A. 179 C7
La Reforma Sonora Mex. 181 E7
La Reforma Veracruz Mex. 185 F4
La Reina Adelaida, Archipiélago de is Chile 205 B9
English form Queen Adelaide Islands
La Reine Canada 173 N2
La Réole France 50 F8
Largeau Chad see Faya
L'Argentière-la-Bessée France 51 M8
Largo U.S.A. 175 D7
Largo, Cayo i. Cuba 186 C2
Largs U.K. 46 H8
Lārī Iran 100 A2
L'Ariana Tunisia 123 H1
also spelt Aryanah
Lariang Indon. 75 A3
Lariang r. Indon. 75 A3
Larimore U.S.A. 178 C1
La Rinconada Spain 54 F7
Larino Italy 56 G7
La Rioja Arg. 204 D3
La Rioja prov. Arg. 204 D3
La Rioja aut. comm. Spain 55 I2
Larionovo Rus. Fed. 43 L1
Larisa Greece 59 D9
also known as Yenisehir; also spelt Larissa
Larissa Greece see Larisa
Laristan reg. Iran 100 D5
Larkana Pak. 101 G5
Lark Harbour Canada 169 J3
Lar Koh mt. Afgh. 101 E3
Lark Passage Australia 149 E2
L'Arli, Parc National de nat. park Burkina 125 F4
L'Arli, Réserve Partielle de nature res. Burkina 125 F4
Larnaca Cyprus 108 E3
also spelt Larnaka
Larnaka Cyprus see Larnaca
Larne U.K. 47 G9
Larned U.S.A. 178 C4
Laro Cameroon 125 I4
La Robe Noire, Lac de l. Canada 169 I3
La Robla Spain 54 F2
La Roche-en-Ardenne Belgium 51 L2
La Rochefoucauld France 50 G7
La Rochelle France 50 E6
La Roche-sur-Yon France 50 E6
La Roda Spain 55 I5
La Romana Dom. Rep. 187 F3
La Ronge Canada 167 J4
La Ronge, Lac l. Canada 167 J4
La Rosa Mex. 185 E3
La Rosa de Castilla Mex. 183 H9
La Rosita Mex. 185 E2
Larouco, Serra do mts Spain 54 D3
Larrey Point Australia 150 B3
Larrimah Australia 148 B2
Larrimah Aboriginal Land res. Australia 148 B2
also known as Wubalawun
Lars Christensen Coast Antarctica 223 E2
▶Larsen Ice Shelf Antarctica 222 T2
antarctica [features] ▶▶▶ 212–213
Larsnes Norway 44 I3
La Rubia Arg. 204 E3
Larvik Norway 45 J4
Lar'yak Rus. Fed. 39 I3
Larzac, Causse du plat. France 51 J8
La Sabana Arg. 204 F2
La Sabana Col. 198 D4
Las Adjuntas, Presa de resr Mex. 185 F4
La Sal U.S.A. 183 O3
La Sal, Cerros de mts Peru 200 B2
La Sal Junction U.S.A. 183 O3
La Salle Canada 169 F4
La Salle U.S.A. 174 B3
La Salonga Nord, Parc National de nat. park Dem. Rep. Congo 126 D5
La Salonga Sud, Parc National de nat. park Dem. Rep. Congo 126 D5
Las Animas U.S.A. 178 B4
Las Ánimas, Punta pt Mex. 184 B2
Las Anod Somalia see Laascaanood
La Sarre Canada 168 E3
La Sauvette hill France 51 M9
Las Aves, Islas is West Indies 187 G5
short form Aves
Las Avispas Arg. 204 E3
Las Avispas Mex. 184 C2
La Savonnière, Lac l. Canada 169 F2
Las Bonitas Venez. 199 E3
Las Breñas Arg. 204 E2
Las Chapas Arg. 205 D6
La Scie Canada 169 K3
Las Conchas Bol. 201 F4
Las Cruces Mex. 184 D2
Las Cruces CA U.S.A. 182 D7
Las Cruces NM U.S.A. 181 F6
La Selle mt. Haiti 187 E3
La Serena Chile 204 C3
La Serena, Embalse de resr Spain 54 F6
Las Esperanças Mex. 185 E3
Las Estancias, Sierra de mts Spain 55 I7
Las Flores Buenos Aires Arg. 204 F5
Las Flores Salta Arg. 201 E6
Lashburn Canada 167 I4
Las Heras Arg. 204 C4
Las Hermosas, Parque Nacional nat. park Col. 198 C4
Las Herreras Mex. 184 D3
Lashio Myanmar 78 B3
Lashkar Gāh Afgh. 101 F4
Las Horquetas Arg. 205 C8
La Sila reg. Italy 57 I9
Łasin Poland 49 Q2
Las Juntas Chile 204 C3
Las Lajas Arg. 204 C5
Las Lajitas Venez. 199 E3
Las Lavaderos Mex. 185 F4
Las Lomas Peru 198 A6
Las Lomitas Arg. 201 E6
Las Marismas marsh Spain 54 E7
Las Martinetas Arg. 205 D7
Las Médulas tourist site Spain 54 E2
Las Mercedes Venez. 199 E2
Las Mesteñas Mex. 184 D2
Las Minas Venez. 199 E2
Las Minas, Sierra de mts Guat. 185 H6
Las Mulatas is Panama see San Blas, Archipiélago de
Las Nieves Mex. 184 D3
Las Nopaleras, Cerro mt. Mex. 185 E3
La Solana Spain 55 H6
Lasolo, Teluk b. Indon. 75 B3
Las Orquídeas, Parque Nacional nat. park Col. 198 B3
La Souterraine France 50 H6
Las Ovejas Arg. 204 C5
Las Palmas watercourse Mex. 183 G9
Las Palmas Panama 186 C5

▶Las Palmas de Gran Canaria Canary Is 122 B3
Joint capital of the Canary Islands.

Las Perlas, Archipiélago de is Panama 186 D5
Las Petas Bol. 201 F4
La Spezia Italy 56 B4
Las Piedras Uruguay 204 F4
Las Piedras, Río de r. Peru 200 C3
Las Pipinas Arg. 204 F4
Las Planchas Hond. 186 B4
Las Plumas Arg. 205 D6
Laspur Pak. 101 H2
Las Rosas Arg. 204 E4
Las Rozas de Madrid Spain 54 H4
Las Salinas, Pampa de salt pan Arg. 204 D3
Lassance Brazil 207 I4
Lassay-les-Châteaux France 50 F4
Lassen Peak vol. U.S.A. 182 C1
Lassen Volcanic National Park U.S.A. 182 C1
Las Tablas Panama 186 C6
Las Tablas de Daimiel, Parque Nacional de nat. park Spain 55 H5
Lastarria, Parque Nacional de nat. park Chile 205 B7
Last Chance U.S.A. 178 B4
Las Termas Arg. 204 D2
Last Mountain Lake Canada 167 J5
Las Torres de Cotillas Spain 55 J6
Las Tórtolas, Cerro mt. Chile 204 C3

Leukas Greece *see* **Lefkada**
Leung Shuen Wan Chau *i. Hong Kong* China *see* **High Island**
Leunovo Rus. Fed. **40** G2
Leupp U.S.A. **183** N6
Leura Australia **149** F4
Leuser, Gunung *mt.* Indon. **76** B2
Leutkirch im Allgäu Germany **48** H8
Leuven Belgium **51** K2
also spelt Louvain
Levadeia Greece **59** D10
Levan Albania **58** A8
Levanger Norway **44** J3
Levante, Riviera di *coastal area* Italy **56** A4
Levanto Italy **56** B4
Levanzo, Isola di *i. Sicilia* Italy **57** E10
Levashi Rus. Fed. **102** A4
Levelland U.S.A. **179** B5
Levels N.Z. **153** F12
Leven U.K. **46** J7
Levens France **51** N9
Lévêque, Cape Australia **150** C3
Leverburgh U.K. **46** E6
also known as An t-Ob
Levering U.S.A. **173** I5
Leverkusen Germany **48** D4
Leverville Dem. Rep. Congo *see* **Lusanga**
Lévézou *mts* France **51** I8
Levice Slovakia **49** P7
Levidi Greece **59** D11
Levin N.Z. **152** J8
Lévis Canada **169** G4
Levitha *i.* Greece **59** H12
Levittown U.S.A. **177** K5
Levka Bulg. **58** H7
Levkás *i.* Greece *see* **Lefkada**
Levkímmi Greece *see* **Lefkimmi**
Levoča Slovakia **49** R6
Levočské vrchy *mts* Slovakia **49** R6
Levroux France **50** H6
Levski Bulg. **58** G5
Levskigrad Bulg. *see* **Karlovo**
Lev Tolstoy Rus. Fed. **43** U8
Levuka Fiji **145** G3
Lėvuo *r.* Lith. **42** F5
Lewa Indon. **75** A5
Lewe Myanmar **78** B4
Lewer *watercourse* Namibia **132** B2
Lewerberg *mt.* S. Africa **132** B6
Lewes U.K. **47** M13
Lewes U.S.A. **177** J7
Lewin Brzeski Poland **49** O5
Lewis U.S.A. **183** P4
Lewis *r.* U.S.A. **180** B3
Lewis, Isle of *i.* U.K. **46** F5
also known as Leodhais, Eilean
Lewis, Lake *salt flat* Australia **148** B4
Lewisburg *OH* U.S.A. **176** A6
Lewisburg *PA* U.S.A. **177** I5
Lewisburg *TN* U.S.A. **174** C5
Lewisburg *WV* U.S.A. **176** E8
Lewis Cass, Mount Canada/U.S.A. **166** D3
Lewis Hills *hill* Canada **169** J3
Lewis Inlet India **95** G3
Lewis Pass N.Z. **153** G10
Lewis Pass National Reserve *nature res.* N.Z. **153** G10
Lewisporte Canada **169** K3
Lewis Range *hills* Australia **150** E4
Lewis Range *mts* U.S.A. **180** D2
Lewis Smith, Lake U.S.A. **175** C5
Lewiston *CA* U.S.A. **182** B1
Lewiston *ID* U.S.A. **180** C3
Lewiston *ME* U.S.A. **177** O1
Lewiston *MN* U.S.A. **172** B7
Lewistown *IL* U.S.A. **174** B3
Lewistown *MT* U.S.A. **180** E3
Lewistown *PA* U.S.A. **176** H5
Lewisville U.S.A. **179** D5
Lewisville, Lake U.S.A. **179** C5
Lewitz *park* Germany **48** I2
Lewotobi, Gunung *vol.* Indon. **75** B5
Lexington *GA* U.S.A. **175** D5
Lexington *IL* U.S.A. **172** E10
Lexington *KY* U.S.A. **176** A7
Lexington *MI* U.S.A. **173** K7
Lexington *MO* U.S.A. **178** D4
Lexington *MS* U.S.A. **175** B5
Lexington *NC* U.S.A. **174** D5
Lexington *NE* U.S.A. **178** C3
Lexington *OH* U.S.A. **176** C5
Lexington *SC* U.S.A. **175** D5
Lexington *TN* U.S.A. **174** B5
Lexington *VA* U.S.A. **176** F8
Lexington Park U.S.A. **177** I7
formerly known as Jarboesville
Leyden Neth. *see* **Leiden**
Leye China **86** C3
also known as Tongle
Leyla Dāgh *mt.* Iran **100** A2
Leyte *i.* Phil. **74** C4
Leyte Gulf Phil. **74** C4
Leżajsk Poland **49** T5
Lèze *r.* France **50** H9
Lezha Rus. Fed. **43** V3
Lezha *r.* Rus. Fed. **43** V2
Lezhë Albania **58** A7
formerly known as Alessio
Lezhi China **86** C2
also known as Tianchi
Lézignan-Corbières France **51** I9
Lezuza Spain **55** I6
L'gov Rus. Fed. **41** E6
Lhagoi Kangri *mt.* China **89** D6
also known as Hlako Kangri
Lhari China **89** F6
also known as Sirdingka
Lharidon Bight *b.* Australia **151** A5
Lharigarbo China *see* **Amdo**
Lhasa China **89** E6
Lhasa He *r.* China **89** E6
Lhasoi China **89** F6
Lhatog China **86** A2
Lhazê *Xizang* China **89** D6
also known as Quxar
Lhazê *Xizang* China **97** G3
L'Herbaudière, Pointe de *pt* France **50** D5
Lhokseumawe Indon. **76** B1
Lhoksukon Indon. **76** B1
Lhorong China **97** G3
also known as Zito

▶**Lhotse** *mt.* China/Nepal **97** E3
4th highest mountain in the world and in Asia.
world [physical features] ▶ 8–9

Lhozhag China **89** E6
also known as Garbo
Lhuentse Bhutan **97** F4
Lhünzê China **89** F6
also known as Xingba
Lhünzhub China **89** E6
also known as Gaindaingoinkor
Liancheng China **87** F3
also known as Lianfeng
Liancheng China *see* **Qinglong**
Liancheng China *see* **Guangnan**
Liancourt Rocks *i.* N. Pacific Ocean **91** B6
also known as Take-shima *or* Tokdo *or* Tok-tō *or* Tokto-ri
Lianfeng China *see* **Liancheng**
Liang Indon. **75** B3
Lianga Phil. **74** C4
Lianga Bay Phil. **74** C4
Liangaz Hu *l.* China **87** E2
Liangcheng China **85** G3
Liangdang China **86** C1
Liangfeng China **87** D3
Lianghe China **86** A3
also known as Zhedao
Lianghekou *Gansu* China **86** C1
Lianghekou *Sichuan* China **86** B2
Liangjiayoufang China *see* **Youyu**
Liangping China **87** C2
also known as Liangshan
Liangpran, Bukit *mt.* Indon. **77** F2
Liangshan China *see* **Liangping**
Liang Shan *mt.* Myanmar **78** B2
Liangshi China *see* **Shaodong**
Liang Timur, Gunung *mt.* Malaysia **76** C2
Liangwang Shan *mts* China **86** B3
Liangzhen China **85** F4
Liangzhou China *see* **Wuwei**
Lianhe China *see* **Qianjiang**
Lianhua China **87** E3
also known as Qinting
Lianhua Shan *mts* China **87** E4
Lianjiang *Fujian* China **87** F3
also known as Fengcheng
Lianjiang *Guangdong* China **87** D4
Lianjiang China *see* **Xingguo**
Lianjiangkou China **87** E3
Lian Jiang *r.* China **78** D2
Liannan China **87** E3
also known as Sanjiang
Lianping China **87** E3
also known as Yuanshan
Lianran China *see* **Anning**
Lianshan *Guangdong* China **87** E3
also known as Jitian
Lianshan *Liaoning* China **85** I3
formerly known as Jinxi
Liant, Cape *pt* Thai. *see* **Samae San, Laem**
Liantang China *see* **Nanchang**
Liantuo China **87** D2
Lianxian China *see* **Lianzhou**
Lianyin China **82** A1
Lianyuan China **87** D3
formerly known as Lantian
Lianyungang China **87** F1
Lianzhou China **87** E3
formerly known as Lianxian
Lianzhou China *see* **Hepu**
Lianzhushan China **82** C3
Liao *r.* China **85** I3
Liaocheng China **85** G4
Liaodong Bandao *pen.* China **85** I3
Liaodong Wan *b.* China **85** I3
Liaodun China **84** B3
Liaodunzhan China **84** B3
Liaoning *prov.* China **85** I3
Liaoyang China **85** I3
Liaoyuan China **82** B4
Liaozhong China **85** I3
Liapades Greece **59** A9
Liaqatabad Pak. **101** G3
Liard *r.* Canada **166** F2
Liard Highway Canada **166** F2
Liard Plateau Canada **166** E2
Liard River Canada **166** E3
Liari Pak. **101** F5
Liat *i.* Indon. **77** D3
Liathach *mt.* U.K. **46** G6
Liban *country* Asia *see* **Lebanon**
Liban, Jebel *mts* Lebanon **108** H3
Libano Col. **198** C3
Libau Latvia *see* **Liepāja**
Libby U.S.A. **180** D2
Libenge Dem. Rep. Congo **126** C4
Liberal U.S.A. **178** B4
Liberdade Brazil **207** I9
Liberdade *r. Amazonas* Brazil **200** C1
Liberdade *r. Mato Grosso* Brazil **202** A4
Liberec Czech Rep. **49** M5
▶**Liberia** *country* Africa **124** C5
africa [countries] ▶ 114–117
Liberia Costa Rica **186** B5
Libertad Venez. **198** D2
Libertador General San Martín Arg. **201** D5
Liberty *AK* U.S.A. **166** A1
Liberty *IN* U.S.A. **176** A6
Liberty *KY* U.S.A. **176** A8
Liberty *ME* U.S.A. **177** P1
Liberty *MO* U.S.A. **178** D4
Liberty *NY* U.S.A. **177** K4
Liberty *TX* U.S.A. **179** D6
Libertyville U.S.A. **172** F8
Libmanan Phil. **74** B3
Libni, Gebel *hill* Egypt **108** E7
Libo China **87** C3
also known as Yuping
Libobo, Tanjung *pt* Indon. **75** D3
Libode S. Africa **133** N8
Libohovë Albania **59** B8
Liboi Kenya **128** D4
Libong, Ko *i.* Thai. **79** B7
Libourne France **50** F8
Libral Well Australia **150** D4
Librazhd Albania **58** B7
Libre, Sierra *mts* Mex. **184** C2

▶**Libreville** Gabon **126** A4
Capital of Gabon.

Libuganon *r.* Phil. **74** C5

▶**Libya** *country* Africa **120** B3
4th largest country in Africa. Spelt Al Lībīyah in Arabic.
africa [countries] ▶ 114–117

Libyan Desert Egypt/Libya **120** E3
Libyan Plateau Egypt **121** E2
Licantén Chile **204** B4
Licata *Sicilia* Italy **57** F11
Lice Turkey **107** E3
Lichas *pen.* Greece **59** D10
also spelt Likhás
Licheng China *see* **Xianyou**
Licheng China *see* **Lipu**
Licheng *Shandong* China **85** H4
also known as Hongjialou
Licheng *Shanxi* China **85** G4
Lichfield N.Z. **152** J6
Lichfield U.K. **47** K11
Lichinga Moz. **129** B8
formerly known as Vila Cabral
Lichte Germany **48** I5
Lichtenburg S. Africa **133** K3
Lichtenfels Germany **48** I5
Lichuan *Hubei* China **87** D2
Lichuan *Jiangxi* China **87** F3
also known as Rifeng
Licínio de Almeida Brazil **207** K1
Liciro Moz. **131** H3
Licking *r.* U.S.A. **176** A6
Lički Osik Croatia **56** H4
Licun China *see* **Laoshan**
Lid' *r.* Rus. Fed. **43** Q2
Lida Belarus **42** G8
Lidjombo Cent. Afr. Rep. **126** C4
Lidköping Sweden **45** K4
Lidsjöberg Sweden **44** K2
Lidumnieki Latvia **42** I5
Lidzbark Poland **49** Q2
Lidzbark Warmiński Poland **49** R1
Liebenbergs Vlei *r.* S. Africa **133** M4
Liebenwalde Germany **49** K3
Liebig, Mount Australia **148** A4
Liebling Romania **58** C3
▶**Liechtenstein** *country* Europe **51** P5
europe [countries] ▶ 32–35
Liège Belgium **51** L2
also known as Luik
Liegnitz Poland *see* **Legnica**
Lieksa Fin. **44** O3
Lielais Ludzas *l.* Latvia **42** I5
Lielupe *r.* Latvia **42** F4
Lielvārde Latvia **42** F5
Lien Sweden **44** L3
Lienz Austria **49** J9
Liepāja Latvia **42** C5
also spelt Liepaya; *formerly spelt* Libau
Liepaya Latvia *see* **Liepāja**
Liepna Latvia **42** I4
Liesjärven kansallispuisto *nat. park* Fin. **42** E1
Liestal Switz. **51** N5
Lieto Fin. **42** D1
Liétor Spain **55** J6
Lietuva *country* Europe *see* **Lithuania**
Liévin France **51** I2
Lièvre *r.* Canada **168** F4
Liezen Austria **49** L8
Lifamatola *i.* Indon. **75** C3
Lifanga Dem. Rep. Congo **126** D4
Liffey *r.* Rep. of Ireland **47** F10
Lifford Rep. of Ireland **47** E9
Liffré France **50** E4
Lifi Mahuida *mt.* Arg. **205** C6
Lifou *i.* New Caledonia **145** F4
also spelt Lifu; *formerly known as* Chabrol
Lifu *i.* New Caledonia *see* **Lifou**
Lifudzin Rus. Fed. *see* **Rudnyy**
Ligao Phil. **74** B3
Līgatne Latvia **42** G4
Lighthouse Reef Belize **185** I5
Lightning Ridge Australia **147** E2
Ligny-en-Barrois France **51** L4
Ligonha *r.* Moz. **131** H3
Ligonier *IN* U.S.A. **172** H9
Ligonier *PA* U.S.A. **176** F5
Ligoúrion Greece *see* **Lygourio**
Ligui Mex. **184** C3
Ligure, Mar *sea* France/Italy *see* **Ligurian Sea**
Liguria *admin. reg.* Italy **56** A4
Ligurian Sea France/Italy **51** O9
also known as Ligure, Mar *or* Ligurienne, Mer
Ligurienne, Mer *sea* France/Italy *see* **Ligurian Sea**
Ligurta U.S.A. **183** J9
Lihir Group *is* P.N.G. **145** E2
formerly known as Gerrit Denys
Lihou Reef and Cays Australia **149** F3
Lihue U.S.A. **181** [inset] Y1
Lihula Estonia **42** E3
Liivi laht *b.* Estonia/Latvia *see* **Riga, Gulf of**
Lijiang China **86** B3
also known as Dayan
Lijiang China *see* **Yuanjiang**
Lijiazhai China **87** E2
Lik, Nam *r.* Laos **78** C4
Lika *reg.* Croatia **56** H4
Likak Iran **100** B4
Likala Dem. Rep. Congo **126** C4
Likasi Dem. Rep. Congo **127** E7
formerly known as Jadotville
Likati Dem. Rep. Congo **126** D4
Likati *r.* Dem. Rep. Congo **126** E4
Likely Canada **166** F4
Likhachevo Ukr. *see* **Pervomays'kyy**
Likhachyovo Ukr. *see* **Pervomays'kyy**
Likhás *pen.* Greece *see* **Lichas**
Likhoslavl' Rus. Fed. **43** Q4
Likimi Dem. Rep. Congo **126** D4
Likino-Dulevo Rus. Fed. **43** T6
Likisia East Timor **75** C5
also spelt Liquiçá *or* Liquissa
Likma India **94** D1
Likolia Dem. Rep. Congo **126** D5
Likouala *admin. reg.* Congo **126** C4
Likouala *r.* Congo **126** C5
Likouala aux Herbes *r.* Congo **126** C5
Liku Indon. **77** E2
Liku *Sarawak* Malaysia **77** F1
Likupang Indon. **75** C2
L'Île d'Anticosti, Réserve Faunique de *nature res.* Canada **169** I3
L'Île-Rousse *Corse* France **51** O10
Lilienfeld Austria **49** M7
Lilienthal Germany **48** F2
Liling China **87** E3
Liljendal Fin. **42** H1
Lilla Pak. **101** H3
Lilla Edet Sweden **45** K4
Lilla Luleälven *r.* Sweden **44** M2
Lillblaiken *hill* Sweden **44** L2
Lille Belgium **51** K1
Lille France **51** J2
Lille Bælt *sea chan.* Denmark *see* **Little Belt**
Lillebonne France **50** G3
Lillehammer Norway **45** J3
Lillesand Norway **45** J4
Lillestrøm Norway **45** J4
Lilley U.S.A. **172** H7
Lillian, Point *hill* Australia **151** D5
Lillie Glacier Antarctica **223** L2
Lillington U.S.A. **174** E5
Lillooet Canada **166** F5
Lillooet *r.* Canada **166** F5
Lillooet Range *mts* Canada **166** F5
Lilo *r.* Dem. Rep. Congo **126** E5
Lilong India **97** G4

▶**Lilongwe** Malawi **129** B8
Capital of Malawi.

Lilo Viejo Arg. **204** E2
Liloy Phil. **74** B4
Lily U.S.A. **172** E5
Lim *r.* Yugo. **58** A5

▶**Lima** Peru **200** A3
Capital of Peru and 4th most populous city in South America.
world [cities] ▶ 24–25

Lima *dept* Peru **200** A2
Lima *MT* U.S.A. **180** D3
Lima *NY* U.S.A. **176** H3
Lima *OH* U.S.A. **176** A5
Limaão Brazil **199** F4
Lima Duarte Brazil **207** J8
Līmah Oman **105** G2
Lima Islands China *see* **Wanshan Qundao**
Liman Rus. Fed. **102** A3
Limanowa Poland **49** R6
Limar Indon. **75** C4
Limarí *r.* Chile **204** C3
Limas Indon. **76** D2
Limassol Cyprus **108** E3
also known as Lemesos
Limavady U.K. **47** F8
Limay *r.* Arg. **204** D5
Limay Mahuida Arg. **204** D5
Limbach-Oberfrohna Germany **49** J5
Limbang *r. Sarawak* Malaysia **77** F1
Limbani Peru **200** C3
Limbaži Latvia **42** F4
Limbdi India **96** A5
Limbe Cameroon **125** H5
formerly known as Victoria
Limboto Indon. **75** B2
Limboto, Danau *l.* Indon. **75** B2
Limbuè Moz. **131** H3
Limbungan Indon. **77** F3
Limbunya Australia **148** A3
Limburg an der Lahn Germany **48** F5
Lim Chu Kang Sing. **76** [inset]
Lim Chu Kang *hill* Sing. **76** [inset]
Lime Acres S. Africa **132** H5
Limehills N.Z. **153** C14
Limeira Brazil **206** F9
Limenaria Greece **58** F8
Limerick Rep. of Ireland **47** D11
also spelt Luimneach
Limestone U.S.A. **176** C9
Limestone Point Canada **167** L4
Limfjorden *sea chan.* Denmark **45** J4
Limia *r.* Spain **54** C3
Limin Chersonisou Greece **59** G13
Limingen Norway **44** K2
Limingen *l.* Norway **44** K2
Liminka Fin. **44** N2
Limmen Bight *b.* Australia **148** C2
Limmen Bight River *r.* Australia **148** B2
Limni Greece **59** E10
Limnos *i.* Greece **59** G9
also spelt Lemnos
Limoeiro Brazil **202** F3
Limoges France **50** H7
Limón Costa Rica **186** C5
Limón Hond. **186** B4
Limon U.S.A. **178** B4
Limonum France *see* **Poitiers**
Limoquije Bol. **200** D3
Limousin *admin. reg.* France **50** H7
Limousin, Plateaux du France **50** H7
Limoux France **51** I9
Limpopo *r.* S. Africa/Zimbabwe **131** G5
Limu China **87** D3
Limulunga Zambia **127** D8
Linaälven *r.* Sweden **44** M2
Līnah Saudi Arabia **104** C1
Linakeng Lesotho **133** M6
Linakhamari Rus. Fed. **44** O1
Lin'an China *see* **Jianshui**
Lin'an China **87** F2
Linao Bay Phil. **74** C5
Linapacan *i.* Phil. **74** A4
Linapacan Strait Phil. **74** A4
Linares Chile **204** C4
Linares Mex. **185** F3
Linares Spain **55** H6
Linas, Monte *mt. Sardegna* Italy **57** A9
Linau Balui *plat. Sarawak* Malaysia **77** F2
Lincang China **86** B4
also known as Fengxiang
Lincheng China *see* **Lingao**
Lincheng China *see* **Huitong**
Linchuan China **87** F3
formerly known as Fuzhou
Linck Nunataks Antarctica **222** R1
Lincoln Arg. **204** E4
Lincoln U.K. **47** L10
historically known as Lindum
Lincoln *CA* U.S.A. **182** C3
Lincoln *IL* U.S.A. **174** B3
Lincoln *KS* U.S.A. **178** C4
Lincoln *ME* U.S.A. **174** G2
Lincoln *MI* U.S.A. **173** J6

▶**Lincoln** *NE* U.S.A. **178** C3
State capital of Nebraska.

Lincoln City U.S.A. **180** A3
Lincoln Island Paracel Is **72** D3
Lincoln National Park Australia **146** B3
Lincoln Sea Canada/Greenland **165** O1
Lincolnshire Wolds *hills* U.K. **47** L10
Linda, Serra *hills* Brazil **202** D5
Lindas Norway **46** R3
Lindau (Bodensee) Germany **48** G8
Lindeman Group *is* Australia **149** F4
Linden Canada **167** H5
Linden Guyana **199** G3
formerly known as Mackenzie
Linden *AL* U.S.A. **175** C5
Linden *CA* U.S.A. **182** C3
Linden *NJ* U.S.A. **177** K5
Linden *TN* U.S.A. **174** C5
Linden *TX* U.S.A. **179** D5
Lindenow Fjord *inlet* Greenland *see* **Kangerlussuatsiaq**
Lindesberg Sweden **45** K4
Líndhos Greece *see* **Lindos**
Lindi *r.* Dem. Rep. Congo **126** E4
Lindi Tanz. **129** C7
Lindi *admin. reg.* Tanz. **129** C7
Lindian China **85** J2
Lindisfarne *i.* U.K. *see* **Holy Island**
Lindley S. Africa **133** L4
Lindóia Brazil **206** G9
Lindome Sweden **45** K4
Lindong China **85** H3
also known as Bairin Zuoqi
Lindos Greece **59** J12
also spelt Líndhos
Lindos, Akra *pt* Greece **59** J12
Lindsay Canada **168** E4
Lindsay *CA* U.S.A. **182** E5
Lindsborg U.S.A. **178** C4
Lindsdal Sweden **45** L4
Lindside U.S.A. **176** E8
Lindum U.K. *see* **Lincoln**
Line Islands S. Pacific Ocean **221** H5
Linets Rus. Fed. **43** Q9
Linfen China **85** F4
Lingamparti India **94** D2
Linganamakki Reservoir India **94** B3
Lingao China **87** D5
also known as Lincheng
Lingayen Phil. **74** B2
Lingayen Gulf Phil. **74** B2
Lingbao China **87** D1
formerly known as Guoluezhen
Lingbi China **87** F1
Lingcheng China *see* **Lingshan**
Lingcheng China *see* **Lingshui**
Lingcheng China *see* **Lingxian**
Lingchuan *Guangxi* China **87** D3
Lingchuan *Shanxi* China **85** G5
Lingelethu S. Africa **133** K9
Lingelihle S. Africa **133** J9
Lingen (Ems) Germany **48** E3
Lingga *i.* Indon. **76** D3
Lingga, Kepulauan *is* Indon. **76** D3
Linggo Co *l.* China **89** E5
Lingig Phil. **74** C5
Lingle U.S.A. **180** F4
Lingomo Dem. Rep. Congo **126** D4
Lingqiu China **85** G4
Lingshan China **87** D4
also known as Lingcheng
Lingshan Wan *b.* China **85** I5
Lingshi Bhutan *see* **Lingzhi**
Lingshi China **85** F4
Lingshui China **87** D5
also known as Lingcheng
Lingsugur India **94** C2
Lingtai China **85** E5
also known as Zhongtai
Linguère Senegal **124** B3
Lingui China **87** D3
Lingxi China *see* **Yongshun**
Lingxian China *see* **Yanling**
Lingxian China **85** H4
also known as Lingcheng
Lingxiang China **87** E2
Lingyuan China **85** H3
Lingyun China **86** C3
also known as Sicheng
Lingzhi Bhutan **97** F4
also spelt Lingshi
Lingzi Thang Plains *l.* Aksai Chin **89** B5
Linhai *Liaoning* China **85** I3
also known as Dalinghe; *formerly known as* Jinxian
Linhai *Zhejiang* China **87** G2
Linhares Brazil **203** D6
Linh Cam Vietnam **78** D4
Linhe China **85** E3
Linhpa Myanmar **78** A2
Linidis Valley N.Z. **153** D12
Linjiang China *see* **Shanghang**
Linjiang China **82** B4
Linköping Sweden **45** K4
Linkou China **82** C3
Linksness U.K. **46** I5
Linkuva Lith. **42** E5
Linli China **87** D2
Linlü Shan *mt.* China **85** G4
Linmingguan China *see* **Yongnian**
Linn U.S.A. **174** B4
Linn, Mount U.S.A. **182** B1
Linnansaaren kansallispuisto *nat. park* Fin. **44** O3
Linnhe, Loch *inlet* U.K. **46** G7
Linosa, Isola di *i. Sicilia* Italy **57** E13
Linova Belarus **42** F9
Linqing China **85** G4
Linru China *see* **Ruzhou**
Lins Brazil **206** D8
Linsan Guinea **124** B4
Linshui China **86** C2
also known as Dingping
Linta *r.* Madag. **131** [inset] J5
Lintah, Selat *sea chan.* Indon. **75** A5
Lintan China **86** B1
Lintao China **84** D5
also known as Taoyang
Linth *r.* Switz. **51** P5
Linthal Switz. **51** P6
Linton U.S.A. **178** B2
Lintong China **87** D1
also known as Lishan
Linville U.S.A. **176** D9
Linxi China **85** H3
Linxia China **84** D5
Linxian China *see* **Linzhou**
Linxian China **85** F4
Linxiang China **87** E2
Linyanti *r.* Botswana/Namibia **131** E3
Linyanti Swamp Namibia **130** D3
Linyi *Shandong* China **85** H4
Linyi *Shandong* China **85** H5
Linyi *Shanxi* China **85** F5
Linying China **87** E1
Linz Austria **49** L7
Linze China **84** D4
formerly known as Shahepu *or* Shahezhen
Linzhou China **85** G4
formerly known as Linxian
Lioma Moz. **131** H2
Lion, Golfe du *g.* France **51** J10
English form Lions, Gulf of
Lions, Gulf of France *see* **Lion, Golfe du**
Lions Den Zimbabwe **131** F3
Lion's Head Canada **173** L6
Lioua Chad **120** B6
Liouesso Congo **126** B4
Lipa Phil. **74** B3
Lipari *Isole Lipari* Italy **57** G10
Lipari, Isola *i. Isole Lipari* Italy **57** G10
Lipari, Isole *is* Italy **57** G10
Lipatkain Indon. **76** C2
Lipawki Belarus **42** I6
Liperi Fin. **44** O3
Lipetsk Rus. Fed. **43** U9
Lipetskaya Oblast' *admin. div.* Rus. Fed. **43** T9
English form Lipetsk Oblast
Lipetsk Oblast *admin. div.* Rus. Fed. *see* **Lipetskaya Oblast'**
Lipez, Cordillera de *mts* Bol. **200** D5
Lipiany Poland **49** L2
Lipin Bor Rus. Fed. **43** S1
Liping China **87** D3
also known as Defeng
Lipitsy Rus. Fed. **43** S8
Lipki Rus. Fed. **43** S8
Lipljan *Kosovo, Srbija* Yugo. **58** C6
Lipnaya Gorka Rus. Fed. **43** O2
Lipník nad Bečvou Czech Rep. **49** O6
Lipno Poland **49** Q3
Lipno, Vodní nádrž *resr* Czech Rep. **49** L7
Lipova Romania **58** C2
Lipovtsy Rus. Fed. **90** B2
Lipovu Romania **58** E4
Lippe *r.* Germany **48** D4
Lippstadt Germany **48** F4
Lipscomb U.S.A. **179** B4
Lipsk Poland **49** U2
Lipsko Poland **49** S4
Lipsoí *i.* Greece *see* **Leipsoi**
Lipti Lekh *pass* Nepal **96** D3
Liptovská Mara, Vodná nádrž *resr* Slovakia **49** Q6
Liptovský Hrádok Slovakia **49** Q6
Liptovský Mikuláš Slovakia **49** Q6
Liptrap, Cape Australia **147** E4
Liptsy Rus. Fed. **43** P6
Lipu China **87** D3
also known as Licheng
Lipusz Poland **49** O1
Liquiçá East Timor *see* **Likisia**
Liquissa East Timor *see* **Likisia**
Lira Uganda **128** B4
Liran *i.* Indon. **75** C4
Liranga Congo **126** C5
Liri *r.* Italy **56** F7
Liri, Jebel el *mt.* Sudan **128** A2
Lirung Indon. **75** C2
Lis Albania **58** B7
Lisa Romania **58** F3
Lisakovsk Kazakh. **103** E1
Lisala Dem. Rep. Congo **126** D4
L'Isalo, Massif de *mts* Madag. **131** [inset] J4
L'Isalo, Parc National de *nat. park* Madag. **131** [inset] J4
Lisboa Port. *see* **Lisbon**
Lisboa *admin. dist.* Port. **54** B5

▶**Lisbon** Port. **54** B6
Capital of Portugal. Also spelt Lisboa; historically known as Olisipo.

Lisbon *IL* U.S.A. **172** E9
Lisbon *ME* U.S.A. **177** O1
Lisbon *ND* U.S.A. **178** C2
Lisbon *NH* U.S.A. **177** N1
Lisbon *OH* U.S.A. **176** E5
Lisbon Falls U.S.A. **177** O2
Lisburn U.K. **47** F9
Liscannor Bay Rep. of Ireland **47** C11
Liscomb Game Sanctuary *nature res.* Canada **169** I4
Lisdoonvarna Rep. of Ireland **47** C10
Lisec *mt.* Macedonia **58** D7
L'Iseran, Col de *pass* France **51** N7
Lishan China *see* **Lintong**
Lishan Taiwan **87** G3
Lishe Jiang *r.* China **86** B3
Lishi China *see* **Dingnan**
Lishi China **85** F4
Līshtar-e Bālā Iran **100** B4
Lishu China **82** B4
Lishui *Jiangsu* China **87** F2
Lishui *Zhejiang* China **87** F2
Li Shui *r.* China **87** D2
Lisichansk Ukr. *see* **Lysychans'k**
Lisieux France **50** G3
Lisiy Nos Rus. Fed. **43** L1
Liskeard U.K. **47** H13
Liski Rus. Fed. **41** F6
formerly known as Georgiu-Dezh
L'Isle-en-Dodon France **50** G9
L'Isle-Jourdain France **50** H9
L'Isle-sur-la-Sorgue France **51** L9
L'Isle-sur-le-Doubs France **51** M5
Lismore Australia **147** G2
Lismore N.Z. **153** F11
Lismore Rep. of Ireland **47** E11
Lisne Ukr. **58** K2
Liss *mt.* Saudi Arabia **109** J6
Lissa Croatia *see* **Vis**
Lissa Poland *see* **Leszno**
Lisseri, Oued *watercourse* Tunisia **123** H2
Listafjorden *b.* Norway **45** I4
Lister, Mount Antarctica **223** K1
Listore *watercourse* Australia **148** C5
Listowel Canada **168** D5
Listowel Rep. of Ireland **47** C11
Listowel Downs Australia **149** E5
Listvyaga, Khrebet *mts* Kazakh./Rus. Fed. **88** D1
Listvyanka Rus. Fed. **84** E1
Liswarta *r.* Poland **49** P4
Lit Sweden **44** K3
Litang *Guangxi* China **87** D4
Litang *Sichuan* China **86** B2
also known as Gaocheng
Litang Qu *r.* China **86** B2
Litani *r.* Fr. Guiana/Suriname **199** H4
Līṭānī *r.* Lebanon **108** G4
Litchfield *CA* U.S.A. **182** D1
Litchfield *IL* U.S.A. **174** B4
Litchfield *MI* U.S.A. **173** I8
Litchfield *MN* U.S.A. **178** D2
Litembe Tanz. **129** D7
Litene Latvia **42** I4
Līth, Wādī al *watercourse* Saudi Arabia **104** C3
Lithgow Australia **147** F3
Lithino, Akra *pt* Greece **59** F14
▶**Lithuania** *country* Europe **42** E6
known as Lietuva in Lithuanian; *formerly known as* Litovskaya S.S.R.
europe [countries] ▶ 32–35
Litija Slovenia **56** G2
Lititz U.S.A. **177** I5
Litke, Mys *c.* Rus. Fed. **39** S2
Litochoro Greece **59** D8
Litoměřice Czech Rep. **49** L5
Litomyšl Czech Rep. **49** N6
Litovel Czech Rep. **49** O6
Litovko Rus. Fed. **82** D2
Litovskaya S.S.R. *country* Europe *see* **Lithuania**
Little *r. LA* U.S.A. **179** D6
Little *r. OK* U.S.A. **179** D5
Little *r. TX* U.S.A. **179** C6
Little Abaco *i.* Bahamas **186** D1
Little Abitibi *r.* Canada **168** D3
Little Abitibi Lake Canada **168** D3
Little Aden Yemen *see* **'Adan as Sughra**
Little Andaman *i.* India **95** G4
Little Bahama Bank *sea feature* Bahamas **186** D1
Little Barrier *i.* N.Z. **152** J4
Little Bay de Noc U.S.A. **172** F5
Little Belt *sea chan.* Denmark **45** J5
also known as Lille Bælt
Little Belt Mountains U.S.A. **180** E3
Little Bighorn *r.* U.S.A. **180** F3
Little Bitter Lake Egypt **108** D7
also known as Murrat el Sughra, Buheirat
Little Blue *r.* U.S.A. **178** C4
Little Bow *r.* Canada **167** H5
Little Buffalo *r.* Canada **167** H2
Little Cayman *i.* Cayman Is **186** C3
Little Churchill *r.* Canada **167** M3
Little Coco Island Cocos Is **79** A5
Little Colorado *r.* U.S.A. **183** M5
Little Creek Peak U.S.A. **183** L4
Little Current Canada **168** D4
Little Current *r.* Canada **168** C3
Little Desert National Park Australia **146** D4
Little Egg Harbor *inlet* U.S.A. **177** K6
Little Exuma *i.* Bahamas **186** E2
Little Falls *MN* U.S.A. **178** D2
Little Falls *NY* U.S.A. **177** K2
Littlefield *AZ* U.S.A. **183** K5
Littlefield *TX* U.S.A. **179** B5
Little Fish *r.* S. Africa **133** K10
Little Fork *r.* U.S.A. **174** A1
Little Fort Canada **166** F5
Little Grand Rapids Canada **167** M4
Little Grass Valley Reservoir U.S.A. **182** C2
Little Inagua Island Bahamas **187** E2
Little Kanawha *r.* U.S.A. **176** D6
Little Karas Berg *plat.* Namibia **132** C4
Little Karoo *plat.* S. Africa **132** E10
Little Lake U.S.A. **182** G6
Little Mecatina *r.* Canada **169** I3
also known as Petit Mécatina
Little Mecatina Island Canada *see* **Petit Mécatina, Île du**
Little Miami *r.* U.S.A. **176** A6
Little Minch *sea chan.* U.K. **46** E6
Little Missouri *r.* U.S.A. **178** B2
Little Muskingum *r.* U.S.A. **176** D6
Little Nicobar *i.* India **95** G5
Little Olifants *r.* S. Africa **133** N2
Little Pamir *mts* Afgh. **101** H2
Little Pic *r.* Canada **172** G2
Little Powder *r.* U.S.A. **180** F3
Little Rann *marsh* India **96** A5
Little Red *r.* U.S.A. **179** E5
Little Red River Canada **167** H3
Little River N.Z. **153** G11
Little River U.S.A. **175** E5

▶**Little Rock** U.S.A. **179** D5
State capital of Arkansas.

Littlerock U.S.A. **182** G7
Little Sable Point U.S.A. **172** G7
Little Sachigo Lake Canada **168** A2
Little Salmon Lake Canada **166** C2
Little Salt Lake U.S.A. **183** L4
Little Sandy Desert Australia **150** B4
Little San Salvador *i.* Bahamas **186** E1
Little Sioux *r.* U.S.A. **178** C3
Little Smoky Canada **167** G4
Little Smoky *r.* Canada **167** G4
Little Snake *r.* U.S.A. **180** E4
Littlestown U.S.A. **177** H6
Little Tibet *reg.* Jammu and Kashmir *see* **Ladakh**
Littleton *NC* U.S.A. **176** H9
Littleton *NH* U.S.A. **177** N1
Littleton *WV* U.S.A. **176** E6
Little Traverse Bay U.S.A. **173** H5
Little Tupper Lake U.S.A. **177** K1
Little Turtle Lake Canada **172** A2
Little Valley U.S.A. **176** G3
Little Wabash *r.* U.S.A. **174** B4
Little Wanganui N.Z. **152** G9
Little White *r.* U.S.A. **178** B3
Little Wichita *r.* U.S.A. **179** C5
Little Wind *r.* U.S.A. **180** E4
Little Wood *r.* U.S.A. **180** D4
Little Zab *r.* Iraq *see* **Zāb aş Şaghīr, Nahr az**
Littoral *prov.* Cameroon **125** H5
Litunde Moz. **129** B8
Lituya Bay U.S.A. **166** B3
Litvínov Czech Rep. **49** K5
Liu *r.* China **85** H3
Liu *r.* China **85** I3
Liu Estonia **42** F3
Liuba China **86** C1
Liuchiu Yü *i.* Taiwan **87** G4
Liuchong He *r.* China **86** C3
Liuchow China *see* **Liuzhou**
Liugong Dao *i.* China **85** I4
Liugu *r.* China **85** I3
Liuhe China **82** B4
Liuheng Dao *i.* China **87** G2
Liujiachang China **87** D2
Liujiang China **87** D3
also known as Labao
Liujiaxia China *see* **Yongjing**
Liujiaxia Shuiku *resr* China **84** D5
Liulin China *see* **Jonê**
Liulin China **85** F4
Liupai China *see* **Tian'e**
Liupan Shan *mts* China **85** E5
Liupanshui China *see* **Lupanshui**
Liupo Moz. **131** H2
Liure Hond. **186** B4
Liushuquan China **84** B3
Liuwa Plain Zambia **127** D8
Liuwa Plain National Park Zambia **127** D8
Liuyang China **87** E2
Liuyang He *r.* China **87** E2
Liuzhangzhen China *see* **Yuanqu**

Lowestoft U.K. 47 N11
Lowgar prov. Afgh. 101 G3
Łowicz Poland 49 Q3
Low Island Kiribati see Starbuck Island
Lowmoor U.S.A. 176 F8
Lowsville U.S.A. 176 E6
Lowville U.S.A. 177 J2
Loxton Australia 146 D3
Loxton S. Africa 132 G8
Loyalsock Creek r. U.S.A. 177 I4
Loyalton U.S.A. 182 D2
Loyalty Islands New Caledonia see Loyauté, Îles
Loyang China see Luoyang
Loyauté, Îles is New Caledonia 145 F4
English form Loyalty Islands
Loyd U.S.A. 172 C7
Loyengo Swaziland 133 P3
Loyev Belarus see Loyew
Loyew Belarus 41 D6
also spelt Loyev
Loyno Rus. Fed. 40 J4
Loyola, Punta pt Arg. 205 C8
Løypskardtinden mt. Norway 44 K2
Lozère, Mont mt. France 51 J8
Loznica Srbija Yugo. 58 A4
Loznitsa Bulg. 58 H5
Lozova Ukr. 41 F6
also spelt Lozovaya
Lozovaya Kazakh. see Lozovoye
Lozovaya Ukr. see Lozova
Lozovik Srbija Yugo. 58 C4
Lozovoye Kazakh. 103 I1
formerly known as Lozovaya
Loz'va r. Rus. Fed. 40 L3
Ltyentye Apurte Aboriginal Land res. Australia 148 B5
also known as Santa Teresa Aboriginal Land
Lu r. China 85 F4
Luabo Moz. 131 H3
Luacano Angola 127 D7
Luachimo r. Angola/Dem. Rep. Congo 127 D6
Lua Dekere r. Dem. Rep. Congo 126 C4
Luakila Dem. Rep. Congo 126 E6
Luala r. Moz. 131 H3
Luambe National Park Zambia 129 B8
Luampa r. Zambia 127 E8
Lu'an China 87 F2
Luanchuan China 87 D1
Luanco Spain 54 F1

▶Luanda Angola 127 B7
Capital of Angola.

Luanda prov. Angola 127 B7
Luando Angola 127 C7
Luando r. Angola 127 C7
Luando, Reserva Natural Integral do nature res. Angola 127 C7
Luang, Khao mt. Thai. 79 B6
Luanginga r. Zambia 127 D8
Luang Nam Tha Laos see Louang Namtha
Luang Prabang Laos see Louangphrabang
Luanguinga r. Angola 127 D8
Luangwa Zambia 127 F8
formerly known as Feira
Luangwa r. Zambia 127 F8
Luanhaizi China 84 B5
Luan He r. China 85 H4
Luannan China 85 H4
also known as Bencheng
Lua Nova Brazil 199 G6
Luanping China 85 H3
Luanshya Zambia 127 F8
Luanxian China 85 H4
also known as Luanzhou
Luanza Dem. Rep. Congo 127 F7
Luanzhou China see Luanxian
Luao Angola see Luau
Luapula prov. Zambia 127 F7
Luar, Danau l. Indon. 77 F2
Luarca Spain 54 E1
Luashi Dem. Rep. Congo 127 D7
Luatamba Angola 127 D8
Luau Angola 127 D7
formerly known as Teixeira de Sousa or Vila Teixeira de Sousa; formerly spelt Luao
Luba Equat. Guinea 125 H6
formerly known as San Carlos
Lubaczów Poland 49 U5
Lubalo Angola 127 C7
Lubań Poland 49 M4
Lubāna Latvia 42 I5
Lubānas ezers l. Latvia 42 H5
Lubang Phil. 74 B3
Lubang i. Phil. 74 B3
Lubang Islands Phil. 74 A3
Lubango Angola 127 B8
formerly known as Sá da Bandeira
Lubao Dem. Rep. Congo 127 E6
Lubartów Poland 49 T4
Lubawa Poland 49 Q2
Lübbecke Germany 48 F3
Lübben Germany 49 K4
Lübbenau Germany 49 K4
Lubbeskolk salt pan S. Africa 132 D6
Lubbock U.S.A. 179 B5
Lübeck Germany 48 H2
Lubeck U.S.A. 176 D6
Lübecker Bucht b. Germany 48 H1
Lubefu Dem. Rep. Congo 126 E6
Lubei China 85 I2
also known as Jarud
Lubelska, Wyżyna hills Poland 49 T4
Lüben Poland see Lubin
Lubenka Kazakh. 102 C2
Lubero Dem. Rep. Congo 126 F5
Lubéron, Montagne du ridge France 51 L9
Lubéron, Parc Naturel Régional du nature res. France 51 L9
Lubersac France 50 H7
Lubie, Jezioro l. Poland 49 M2
Lubienka r. Poland 49 P3
Lubień Kujawski Poland 49 Q3
Lubin Poland 49 N4
historically known as Lüben
Lubisi Dam resr S. Africa 133 L8
Lublin Poland 49 T4
Lubliniec Poland 49 P5
Lubnān country Asia see Lebanon
Lubny Ukr. 41 E6
Lubok Antu Sarawak Malaysia 77 E2
Luboń Poland 49 N3
Lubosalma Rus. Fed. 44 O3
Lubraniec Poland 49 P3
Lubrín Spain 55 I7
Lübtheen Germany 48 I2
Lubuagan Phil. 74 B2
Lubudi Dem. Rep. Congo 127 E7
Lubudi r. Dem. Rep. Congo 127 E7
Lubuklinggau Indon. 76 C3
Lubukpakam Indon. 76 B2
Lubuksikaping Indon. 76 C2
Lubumbashi Dem. Rep. Congo 127 E7
formerly known as Élisabethville
Lubunda Dem. Rep. Congo 127 E6
Lubungu Zambia 127 E8
Lubuta Zambia 127 D9
Lubutu Dem. Rep. Congo 126 E5
Lubutu r. Dem. Rep. Congo 126 E5
Lubwe Zambia 127 F7
Lubyanki Rus. Fed. 43 Q9
Lucala Angola 127 B7
Lucan Canada 173 L7
Lucanas Peru 200 B3
Lučani Srbija Yugo. 58 B5
Lucania, Mount Canada 166 A2
Lücaoshan China 84 B4
Lucapa Angola 127 D7
formerly known as Lukapa
Lucas Brazil 201 G3
Lucasville U.S.A. 176 C7
Lucca Italy 56 C5
Lucé France 50 H4
Lucea Jamaica 186 D3
Luce Bay U.K. 47 H9
Lucedale U.S.A. 175 B6
Lucélia Brazil 206 B8
Lucena Phil. 74 B3
Lucena Spain 54 G7
Lučenec Slovakia 49 Q7
Lucera Italy 56 H7
Lucerna Peru 200 C3
Lucerne Switz. 51 O5
also spelt Luzern
Lucerne U.S.A. 182 B2
Lucerne Valley U.S.A. 183 H7
Lucero Mex. 184 D2
Lucha r. Rus. Fed. 82 C1
Luchay Belarus 42 I6
Luchegorsk Rus. Fed. 82 D3
Lucheng China see Luchuan
Lucheng China 85 G4
Lucheng China see Kangding
Lucheringo r. Moz. 129 C7
Luchki Rus. Fed. 43 U5
Luchosa r. Belarus 43 L7
Lüchow Germany 48 I3
Luchuan China 87 D4
also known as Lucheng
Lüchun China 86 B4
also known as Daxing
Lucinda Australia 149 E3
Lucipara, Kepulauan is Indon. 75 C4
Lucira Angola 127 B8
Luciu Romania 58 I4
Luck Ukr. see Luts'k
Luck U.S.A. 172 A5
Luckau Germany 49 K4
Luckeesarai India 97 E4
also spelt Lakhisarai
Luckenwalde Germany 49 K3
Luckhoff S. Africa 133 I6
Lucknow Canada 173 L7
Lucknow India 96 D4
Luçon France 50 E6
Lücongpo China 87 D2
Lucunga Angola 127 B6
Lucusse Angola 127 D8
Lucy Creek Australia 148 C4
Lüda China see Dalian
Luda Kamchiya r. Bulg. 58 I5
Ludberg Croatia 56 I2
Lüdenscheid Germany 48 E4
Lüderitz Namibia 130 B5
Ludewa Tanz. 129 B7
Ludhiana India 96 B3
Ludian China 86 B3
also known as Wenping
Luding China 86 B2
also known as Jagsamka or Luqiao
Ludington U.S.A. 172 G7
Ludlow U.K. 47 J11
Ludlow CA U.S.A. 183 H7
Ludlow VT U.S.A. 177 M2
Ludogorie reg. Bulg. 58 H5
Ludogorsko Plato plat. Bulg. 58 H5
Ludoni Rus. Fed. 43 K3
Ludowici U.S.A. 175 D6
Luduș Romania 58 F2
Ludvika Sweden 45 K3
Ludwigsburg Germany 48 G7
Ludwigsfelde Germany 49 K3
Ludwigshafen am Rhein Germany 48 F6
Ludwigslust Germany 48 I2
Ludwigsort Rus. Fed. see Ladushkin
Ludza Latvia 42 I5
Luebo Dem. Rep. Congo 127 D6
Lueki Dem. Rep. Congo 126 E5
Lueki r. Dem. Rep. Congo 126 E5
Luembe Zambia 127 F8
Luena Angola 127 C7
formerly known as Luso
Luena Dem. Rep. Congo 127 E7
Luena Zambia 127 F7
Luena r. Zambia 127 D8
Luena Flats plain Zambia 127 D8
Luengé, Coutada Pública do nature res. Angola 127 D9
Luengue r. Angola 127 D9
Luenha r. Moz./Zimbabwe 131 G3
Luepa Venez. 199 F3
Lüeyang China 86 C1
Lufeng Guangdong China 87 E4
Lufeng China see Xupu
Lufeng Yunnan China 86 B3
also known as Jinshan
Lufira r. Dem. Rep. Congo 127 E7
Lufkin U.S.A. 179 D6
Lufu China see Lunan
Lug r. Yugo. 58 C4
Luga Rus. Fed. 43 K3
Luga r. Rus. Fed. 43 J2
Lugano Switz. 51 O6
Lugansk Ukr. see Luhans'k
Luganville Vanuatu 145 F3
Lugdunum France see Lyon
Lugela Moz. 131 H3
Lugela r. Moz. 131 H3
Lugenda r. Moz. 131 H1
Lugg r. U.K. 47 J11
Luggate N.Z. 153 D12
Luggudontsen mt. China 89 E6
Lughaye Somalia 128 D2
Lugo Italy 56 D4
Lugo Spain 54 D1
Lugoj Romania 58 C3
Lugovaya Rus. Fed. 43 S5
Lugovaya Proleyka Rus. Fed. see Primorsk
Lugovoy Kazakh. 103 H4
Lugovoye Kazakh. 103 H4
Lugus i. Phil. 74 B5
Luhanka Fin. 45 N3
Luhans'k Ukr. 41 F6
also spelt Lugansk; formerly known as Voroshilovgrad
Luhawskiya Belarus 43 L6
Luhe China 87 F1
Luḥfī, Wādī watercourse Jordan 109 H5
Luhin Sum China 85 H2
Luhit r. China/India see Zayü Qu
Luhit r. India 97 G3
Luhombero Tanz. 129 C7
Luhua China see Heishui
Luhuo China 86 B2
also known as Xindu or Zhaggo
Luhyny Ukr. 41 D6
Luia Angola 127 D7
Luia r. Angola 127 D6
Luia r. Moz. 131 G3
Luiana Angola 127 D9
Luiana r. Angola 127 D9
Luiana, Coutada Pública do nature res. Angola 127 D9
Luica Romania 58 H4
Luichow Peninsula China see Leizhou Bandao
Luik Belgium see Liège
Luilaka r. Dem. Rep. Congo 126 D5
Luimneach Rep. of Ireland see Limerick
Luing i. U.K. 46 G7
Luino Italy 56 A3
Luio r. Angola 127 D8
Luiro r. Fin. 44 N2
Luís Correia Brazil 202 D2
Luis Echeverría Álvarez Mex. 183 H9
Luís Gomes Brazil 202 E3
Luishia Dem. Rep. Congo 127 E7
Luis L. León, Presa resr Mex. 184 D2
Luis Moya Durango Mex. 184 E3
Luis Moya Zacatecas Mex. 185 E4
Luitpold Coast Antarctica 222 V1
Luiza Dem. Rep. Congo 127 D6
Luizi Dem. Rep. Congo 127 E6
Luján Arg. 204 F4
Luján de Cuyo Arg. 204 C4
Lujiang China 87 F2
Lukackek Rus. Fed. 82 D1
Lukala Dem. Rep. Congo 127 B6
Lukanga Dem. Rep. Congo 126 C6
Lukanga Swamps Zambia 127 E8
Lukapa Angola see Lucapa
Lukavac Bos.-Herz. 56 K4
Luke, Mount hill Australia 151 B5
Lukenga, Lac l. Dem. Rep. Congo 127 E7
Lukenie r. Dem. Rep. Congo 126 C5
Lukh r. Rus. Fed. 40 G4
Lukhovitsy Rus. Fed. 43 U7
Lŭki Bulg. 58 F7
Lukinskaya Rus. Fed. 43 P1
Luk Keng Hong Kong China 87 [inset]
Lukolela Equateur Dem. Rep. Congo 126 C5
Lukolela Kasai Oriental Dem. Rep. Congo 127 E6
Lukomskaye, Vozyera l. Belarus 43 K7
Lukou China see Zhuzhou
Lukovac r. Bos.-Herz. 56 L4
Lukovë Albania 59 A9
Lukovit Bulg. 58 F5
Lukovnikovo Rus. Fed. 43 P5
Łuków Poland 49 T4
Lukoyanov Rus. Fed. 40 H5
Luksagu Indon. 75 B3
Lukšiai Lith. 42 E7
Lukuga r. Dem. Rep. Congo 127 E6
Lukula Dem. Rep. Congo 127 B6
Lukuledi Tanz. 129 C7
Lukulu Zambia 127 D8
Lukumburu Tanz. 129 B7
Lukuni Dem. Rep. Congo 127 C6
Lukusashi r. Zambia 127 F8
Lukusuzi National Park Zambia 129 B8
Lula r. Dem. Rep. Congo 126 D5
Luleå Sweden 44 M2
Luleälven r. Sweden 44 M2
Lüleburgaz Turkey 106 A2
Lules Arg. 204 D2
Luliang China 86 B3
also known as Zhongshu
Lüliang Shan mts China 85 F4
Lulimba Dem. Rep. Congo 126 F6
Luling U.S.A. 179 C6
Lulong China 85 H4
Lulonga Dem. Rep. Congo 126 C4
Lulonga r. Dem. Rep. Congo 126 C4
Lulu r. Dem. Rep. Congo 126 D4
Luluabourg Dem. Rep. Congo see Kananga
Lülung China 89 D6
Lulworth, Mount hill Australia 151 B5
Lumachomo China 89 D6
Lumai Angola 127 D8
Lumajang Indon. 77 F5
Lumajangdong Co salt l. China 89 C5
Lümanda Estonia 42 D3
Lūmār Iran 107 F4
Lumbala Angola see Lumbala N'guimbo
Lumbala Angola see Lumbala Kaquengue
Lumbala Kaquengue Angola 127 D8
formerly known as Lumbala
Lumbala N'guimbo Angola 127 D8
formerly known as Gago Coutinho or Lumbala
Lumber r. U.S.A. 174 E5
Lumberton U.S.A. 174 E5
Lumbis Indon. 77 G1
Lumbrales Spain 54 E4
Lumding India 97 G4
Lumecha Tanz. 129 B7
Lumezzane Italy 56 C3
Lumi P.N.G. 73 J7
Lumijoki Fin. 44 N2
Lumina Romania 58 J4
Luminárias Brazil 207 I8
Lum-nan-pai Wildlife Reserve nature res. Thai. 78 B4
Lumparland Fin. 45 M3
Lumphăt Cambodia 79 D5
also spelt Lomphat
Lumpkin U.S.A. 175 C5
Lumsden Canada 167 J5
Lumsden N.Z. 153 C13
Lumut, Gunung mt. Indon. 77 F3
Lumut, Tanjung pt Indon. 77 D3
Lumwana Zambia 127 E7
Lün Mongolia 85 E2
Luna Phil. 74 B2
Luna hill Spain 54 F8
Luna r. Spain 54 F2
Lunan China 86 B3
also known as Lufu
Lunan Lake Canada 167 M1
Lunan Shan mts China 86 B3
Luna Pier U.S.A. 173 J9
Lunavada India 96 B5
Lunayyir, Ḥarrat lava field Saudi Arabia 104 B2
Lunca Romania 58 F5
Lunca Bradului Romania 58 G2
Lunca Ilvei Romania 58 F1
Luncavița Romania 58 F4
Lund Sweden 45 K5
Lund NV U.S.A. 183 I3
Lund UT U.S.A. 183 K3
Lunda Norte prov. Angola 127 C7
Lundar Canada 167 L5
Lunda Sul prov. Angola 127 D7
Lundazi Zambia 129 B8
Lundbreck Canada 167 H5
Lundi r. Zimbabwe see Runde
Lunds U.S.A. 172 E6
Lundu Tanz. 129 B7
Lundy Island U.K. 47 H12
Lune r. U.K. 47 J9
Lüneburg Germany 48 H2
Lüneburger Heide reg. Germany 48 H2
Lüneburger Heide, Naturpark nature res. Germany 48 G2
Lunel France 51 K9
Lünen Germany 48 E4
Lunenburg U.S.A. 176 G9
Lunestedt Germany 48 F2
Lunéville France 51 M4
Lunga Moz. 131 I2
Lunga r. Zambia 127 E8
Lunggar China 89 C6
Lunggar Shan mts China 89 C6
Lung Kwu Chau i. Hong Kong China 87 [inset]
Lungleh India see Lunglei
Lunglei India 97 G5
formerly spelt Lungleh
Lungmari mt. China 89 D6
Lungmu Co salt l. China 89 C5
Lungnaquilla Mountain hill Rep. of Ireland 47 F11
Lungro Italy 57 I9
Lungué-Bungo r. Angola 127 D8
Lungwebungu r. Zambia 127 D8
Lunh Nepal 97 D3
Luni r. India 96 A4
Luni r. Pak. 101 G4
Luninets Belarus see Luninyets
Lunino Rus. Fed. 41 H5
Luninyets Belarus 42 H9
also spelt Luninets
L'Union France 50 H9
Lunkaransar India 96 B3
Lunkha India 96 B3
Lunkho mt. Afgh./Pak. 101 H2
Lunkkaus Fin. 44 N2
Lunna Belarus 42 F8
Lunn Island P.N.G. 149 F1
Lunsar Sierra Leone 124 B4
Lunsemfwa r. Zambia 127 F8
Lunsklip S. Africa 131 F5
Luntai China 88 D3
also known as Bügür
Lunxhërisë, Mali i ridge Albania 59 B8
Lunyuk Indon. 77 G5
Lunzua Zambia 127 F7
Luo r. Henan China 87 E1
Luo r. Shaanxi China 87 D1
Luobei China 82 C3
also known as Fengxiang
Luobuzhuang China 88 E4
Luocheng China see Hui'an
Luocheng Gansu China 84 C4
Luocheng Guangxi China 87 D3
also known as Dongmen
Luochuan China 85 F5
also known as Fengqi
Luodian China 86 C3
also known as Longping
Luoding China 87 D4
Luodonselkä sea chan. Fin. 44 N2
Luodou Sha i. China 87 D4
Luohe China 87 E1
Luoma Hu l. China 87 F1
Luonan China 87 D1
Luoning China 87 D1
Luonnonsuojelualue nature res. Fin. 44 M3
Luonteri l. Fin. 45 N3
Luoping China 86 C3
also known as Luoxiong
Luopioinen Fin. 45 N3
Luoshan China 87 E1
Luotian China 87 E2
also known as Fengshan
Luovtejok Norway 44 O1
Luoxiao Shan mts China 87 E3
Luoxiong China see Luoping
Luoyang China see Boluo
Luoyang China 87 E1
formerly known as Loyang
Luoyang China see Taishun
Luoyuan China 87 F3
also known as Fengshan
Luozi Dem. Rep. Congo 126 B6
Luozigou China 82 C4
Lupa Market Tanz. 129 B7
Lupane Zimbabwe 131 E3
Lupanshui China 86 C3
also known as Shuicheng or Xiayingpan or Zhongshan; formerly spelt Liupanshui
Lupar r. Sarawak Malaysia 77 E2
Łupawa r. Poland 49 O1
L'Upemba, Parc National de nat. park Dem. Rep. Congo 127 E7
Lupeni Romania 58 G2
Lupeni Romania 58 E3
Luperón Dom. Rep. 187 F3
Lupilichi Moz. 129 B7
formerly known as Olivença
Lupire Angola 127 C8
Lupiro Tanz. 129 C7
Lupon Phil. 74 C5
Luppa Germany 49 J4
Lupton U.S.A. 183 O6
Lup'ya r. Rus. Fed. 40 J3
Luqiao China see Luding
Luqu China 86 B1
also known as Ma'ngê
Lu Qu r. China see Tao He
Luquan Hebei China 85 G4
formerly known as Huolu
Luquan Yunnan China 86 B3
also known as Pingshan
Luquembo Angola 127 C7
Lūrā Shīrīn Iran 107 F3
Luray U.S.A. 176 G7
Lure France 51 M5
Lure, Sommet de mt. France 51 L8
Lureco r. Moz. 129 C8
Luremo Angola 127 C7
Lurgan U.K. 47 F9
Lūrg-e Shotorān salt pan Iran 101 D3
Luribay Bol. 200 D4
Lurín Peru 200 A3
Luring China see Gêrzê
Lurio Moz. 131 I2
Lurio r. Moz. 131 I2
Lusaheia park Norway 45 I4
Lusahunga Tanz. 128 A5
Lusaka Dem. Rep. Congo 127 F6

▶Lusaka Zambia 127 F8
Capital of Zambia.

Lusaka prov. Zambia 127 F8
Lusambo Dem. Rep. Congo 126 D6
Lusancay Islands and Reefs P.N.G. 145 E2
Lusanga Dem. Rep. Congo 126 C6
formerly known as Leverville
Lusangi Dem. Rep. Congo 126 E6
Luseland Canada 167 I4
Lusenga Plain National Park Zambia 127 F7
Lusewa Tanz. 129 C7
Lush, Mount hill Australia 150 D3
Lushan China 86 B2
also known as Luyang
Lushar China see Huangzhong
Lushi China 87 D1
Lushnjë Albania 58 A8
Lushoto Tanz. 129 C6
Lüshun China 85 I4
formerly known as Port Arthur or Ryojun
Lüsi China 87 G1
Lusi r. Indon. 77 E4
Lusignan France 50 G6
Lusikisiki S. Africa 133 N8
Lusiwasi Zambia 127 F8
Lusk U.S.A. 180 F4
Luso Angola see Luena
Lussac-les-Châteaux France 50 G6
Lussusso Angola 127 B7
Lusushwana r. Swaziland 133 P3
Lusutufu r. Africa see Usutu
Lut, Bahrat salt l. Asia see Dead Sea
Lut, Dasht-e des. Iran 100 D4
Lutai China see Ninghe
Lü Tao i. Taiwan 87 G4
English form Green Island; also known as Huoshao Tao
Lutécia Brazil 206 C9
Luterskie, Jezioro l. Poland 49 R2
Lutetia France see Paris
Lūt-e Zangī Aḥmad des. Iran 100 D4
Luther Lake Canada 173 M7
Luthersburg U.S.A. 176 G4
Lutherstadt Wittenberg Germany 49 J4
also known as Wittenberg
Lutiba Dem. Rep. Congo 126 F5
Lütjenburg Germany 48 H1
Luton U.K. 47 L12
Lutong Sarawak Malaysia 77 F1
Lutope r. Zimbabwe 131 F3
Łutselk'e Canada 167 I2
formerly known as Snowdrift
Lutshi Dem. Rep. Congo 126 E6
Luts'k Ukr. 41 C6
formerly spelt Łuck
Luttig S. Africa 132 G9
Lutto r. Fin./Rus. Fed. see Lotta
Lutuai Angola 127 D8
Lutynia r. Poland 49 O3
Lutz U.S.A. 175 D6
Lützow-Holm Bay Antarctica 223 C2
Lutzputs S. Africa 132 E5
Lutzville S. Africa 132 C8
Luumäki Fin. 45 N3
Luuq Somalia 128 D4
Luve Swaziland 133 P3
Luverne AL U.S.A. 175 C6
Luverne MN U.S.A. 178 C3
Luvia Fin. 45 M3
Luvo Angola 127 B6
Luvozero Rus. Fed. 44 O2
Luvua r. Dem. Rep. Congo 127 E6
Luvuei Angola 127 D8
Luvuvhu r. S. Africa 131 F4
Luwegu r. Tanz. 129 C7
Luwero Uganda 128 B4
Luwingu Zambia 127 F7
Luwo i. Indon. 75 D2
Luwuk Indon. 75 B3
▶Luxembourg country Europe 51 L3
Letzeburgish form Lëtzebuerg; also spelt Luxemburg
europe [countries] ▶▶ 32–35

▶Luxembourg Lux. 51 M3
Capital of Luxembourg.

Luxemburg country Europe see Luxembourg
Luxemburg IA U.S.A. 172 B8
Luxemburg WI U.S.A. 172 F6
Luxeuil-les-Bains France 51 M5
Luxi Hunan China 87 D2
also known as Wuxi
Luxi Yunnan China 86 A3
also known as Mangshi
Luxi Yunnan China 86 B3
also known as Zhongshu
Luxian China 86 C2
also known as Fuji
Luxolweni S. Africa 133 J8
Luxor Egypt 121 G3
also spelt El Uqṣur or Al Uqṣur
Luyang China see Lushan
Luya Shan mts China 85 F4
Luy de France r. France 50 F9
Luyi China 87 E1
Luyuan China see Gaoling
Luz Brazil 207 H6
Luza Rus. Fed. 40 H3
Luza r. Rus. Fed. 40 H3
Luza r. Rus. Fed. 40 K2
Luzech France 50 H8
Lucern Switz. see Lucerne
Luzha r. Rus. Fed. 43 R7
Luzhai China 87 D3
Luzhi China 86 C3
also known as Xiayingpan
Luzhou China 86 C2
Luziânia Brazil 206 F3
Lužické Hory mts Czech Rep. 49 L5
Luzilândia Brazil 202 D2
Lūžņas Latvia 42 C4
Lužnice r. Czech Rep. 49 L6
Luzon i. Phil. 74 B3
Luzon Strait Phil. 74 B1
Luzy France 51 J6
Luzzi Italy 57 I9
L'viv Ukr. 41 C6
English form Lvov; also spelt L'vov; formerly spelt Lwów; historically known as Lemberg
L'vov Ukr. see L'viv
Lvov Ukr. see L'viv
L'vovskiy Rus. Fed. 43 S6
Lwów Ukr. see L'viv
Lwówek Poland 49 N3
Lyady Belarus 43 M7
Lyady Rus. Fed. 43 J3
Lyakhavichy Belarus 42 H8
also spelt Lyakhovichi
Lyakhovichi Belarus see Lyakhavichy
Lyakhovskiye Ostrova is Rus. Fed. 39 O2
Lyallpur Pak. see Faisalabad
Lyal'mikar Uzbek. 103 F5
also spelt Lal'mikor
Lyamtsa Rus. Fed. 40 F2
Lyangar Uzbek. see Langar
Lyangar Uzbek. 103 F4
also spelt Langar
Lyapin r. Rus. Fed. 40 L3
Lyaskelya Rus. Fed. 44 O3
Lyaskovets Bulg. 58 G5
Lyasnaya Belarus 42 G9
Lyasnaya r. Belarus 42 E9
Lyebster U.K. 46 I5
Lychkovo Rus. Fed. 43 N4
Lyck Poland see Ełk
Lycksele Sweden 44 L2
Lycopolis Egypt see Asyūṭ
Lydda Israel see Lod
Lyddan Island Antarctica 222 W2
Lydenburg S. Africa 133 O2
Lydia reg. Turkey 59 I10
Łydynia r. Poland 49 R3
Lyebyada r. Belarus 42 G8
Lyel'chytsy Belarus 41 D6
Lyell, Mount U.S.A. 182 E4
Lyell Island Canada 166 D4
Lyell Range mts N.Z. 153 G9
Lyenina Belarus 43 M9
Lyepyel' Belarus 43 J7
also spelt Lepel'
Lygourio Greece 59 E11
also known as Ligoúrion
Lygumai Lith. 42 E5
Lykens U.S.A. 177 I5
Lykoshino Rus. Fed. 43 O3
Lykso S. Africa 132 I4
Lyman Ukr. 58 K3
Lyman U.S.A. 180 E4
Lymans'ke Ukr. 58 K1
Lyme Bay U.K. 47 J13
Lymington U.K. 47 K13
Łyna r. Poland 49 S1
Lynch U.S.A. 176 C9
Lynchburg TN U.S.A. 174 C5
Lynchburg VA U.S.A. 176 F8
Lynches r. U.S.A. 175 E5
Lynch Station U.S.A. 176 F8
Lynchville U.S.A. 177 O1
Lynd r. Australia 149 D3
Lyndhurst Qld Australia 149 E3
Lyndhurst S.A. Australia 146 C2
Lyndon Australia 150 A4
Lyndon r. Australia 150 A4
Lyndon U.S.A. 178 D4
Lyndonville NY U.S.A. 176 G2
Lyndonville VT U.S.A. 177 M1
Lyngdal Norway 45 I4
Lyngen sea chan. Norway 44 M1
Lyngseidet Norway 44 M1
Lynher Reef Australia 150 C2
Lynn U.K. see King's Lynn
Lynn IN U.S.A. 176 A5
Lynn MA U.S.A. 177 O3
Lynn Canal sea chan. U.S.A. 166 C3
Lynndyl U.S.A. 183 L2
Lynn Haven U.S.A. 175 C6
Lynn Lake Canada 167 K3
Lynton U.K. 47 I12
Lyntupy Belarus 42 H6
Lynx Lake Canada 167 J2
Lynxville U.S.A. 172 B7
Lyon France 51 K7
English form Lyons; historically known as Lugdunum
Lyon Mountain U.S.A. 177 L1
Lyonnais, Monts du hills France 51 K7
Lyons Australia 146 B2
Lyons r. Australia 151 A5
Lyons France see Lyon
Lyons GA U.S.A. 175 D5
Lyons KS U.S.A. 178 C4
Lyons NY U.S.A. 177 I2
Lyons Falls U.S.A. 177 J2
Lyozna Belarus 43 L6
Lyra Reef P.N.G. 145 E2
Lysá Hora mt. Czech Rep. 49 P6
Lysekil Sweden 45 J4
Lyshchichi Rus. Fed. 43 N9
Łysica hill Poland 49 R5
Lyskovo Rus. Fed. 40 H4
Lys'va Rus. Fed. 40 K4
Lysychans'k Ukr. 41 F6
also spelt Lisichansk
Lysyye Gory Rus. Fed. 41 H6
Lytham St Anne's U.K. 47 I10
Lytkarino Rus. Fed. 43 S6
Lyttelton N.Z. 153 G11
Lytton Canada 166 F5
Lyuban' Belarus 42 J9
Lyuban' Rus. Fed. 43 M2
Lyubanskaye Vodaskhovishcha resr Belarus 42 J9
Lyubavichi Rus. Fed. 43 L7
Lyubazh Rus. Fed. 43 Q9
Lyubcha Belarus 42 H8
Lyubertsy Rus. Fed. 43 S6
Lyubeshiv Ukr. 41 C6
Lyubim Rus. Fed. 43 V3
Lyubimets Bulg. 58 H7
Lyubimovka Rus. Fed. 43 T8
Lyubishchytsy Belarus 42 G9
Lyubitovo Rus. Fed. 43 P3
Lyubokhna Rus. Fed. 43 P8
Lyubomirovo Rus. Fed. 43 T2
Lyubotin Ukr. see Lyubotyn
Lyubotyn Ukr. 53 J2
also spelt Lyubotin
Lyubyacha Belarus 42 I8
Lyubytino Rus. Fed. 43 O3
Lyudinovo Rus. Fed. 43 P8
Lyugovichi Rus. Fed. 43 O1
Lyulyakovo Bulg. 58 I6
Lyunda r. Rus. Fed. 40 H4
Lyusina Belarus 42 H9
Lyzha r. Rus. Fed. 40 K2
Lža r. Latvia 42 J4
Lzha r. Rus. Fed. 43 J4

↓ M

Ma r. Myanmar 78 B3
Ma, Nam r. Laos 78 C3
Ma, Sông r. Vietnam 78 D4
Maalhosmadulu Atoll Maldives 94 B5
Maamakundhoo i. Maldives see Makunudhoo
Maamba Zambia 127 E9
Ma'an Cameroon 125 H6
Ma'ān Jordan 108 G7
Maaninka Fin. 44 N3
Maaninkavaara Fin. 44 O2
Maanselkä Fin. 44 O3
Ma'anshan China 87 F2
Maanyt Bulgan Mongolia 84 D1
Maanyt Töv Mongolia 85 E2
Maardu Estonia 42 G2
Maarianhamina Fin. see Mariehamn
Ma'arrat an Nu'mān Syria 109 H2
Maartenshoop S. Africa 133 O1
Maas r. Neth. 48 B4
also spelt Meuse (Belgium/France)
Maaseik Belgium 51 L1
Maasin Phil. 74 C4
Maas-Schwalm-Nette nat. park Germany/Neth. 48 C4
Maastricht Neth. 48 C5
Maatsuyker Group is Australia 147 E5
Maba China 87 F1
Maba Indon. 75 D2
Maba, Ouadi watercourse Chad 120 D6
Mabalacat Phil. 74 B3
Mabalane Moz. 131 G4
Mabana Dem. Rep. Congo 126 F4
Mabanda Gabon 126 A5
Ma'bar Yemen 104 D5
Mabaruma Guyana 199 G2
Mabating China see Hongshan
Mabein Myanmar 78 B3
Mabel Creek Australia 146 B2
Mabel Downs Australia 150 D3
Mabella Canada 168 B3
Maberly Canada 173 Q6
Mabian China 86 B2
also known as Minjian
Mablethorpe U.K. 47 M10
Mably France 51 K6
Mabopane S. Africa 133 M2
Mabote Moz. 131 G4
Mabou Canada 169 I4
Mabrak, Jabal mt. Jordan 108 G7
Mabroûk well Mali 125 E2
Mabrous well Niger 125 I1
Mabuasehube Game Reserve nature res. Botswana 130 D5
Mabudis i. Phil. 74 B1
Mabula S. Africa 133 L1
Ma'būs Yūsuf oasis Libya 120 D3
Mabutsane Botswana 130 D5
Macá, Monte mt. Chile 205 B7
Macachín Arg. 204 E5
Macadam Plains Australia 151 B5
Macadam Range hills Australia 148 A2
Macaé Brazil 203 D7
Macael Spain 55 I7
Macaíba Brazil 202 F3
Macajalar Bay Phil. 74 C4
Macajuba Brazil 202 D5
Macaloge Moz. 129 B8
formerly known as Miranda or Vila Miranda
MacAlpine Lake Canada 167 K1
Macamic Canada 168 E3
Macan, Kepulauan atolls Indon. see Taka'Bonerate, Kepulauan
Macandze Moz. 131 G4
Macaneta, Ponta de pt Moz. 133 Q2
Macao China see Macau
Macapá Amapá Brazil 199 I4
Macapá Amazonas Brazil 200 D2
Macará Ecuador 198 B6
Macaracas Panama 186 C6
Macarani Brazil 202 D5
Macarena, Cordillera mts Col. 198 C4
Macareo, Caño r. Venez. 199 F2
Macas Ecuador 198 B5
Maçãs r. Port./Spain 54 E3
Macassar Indon. see Ujung Pandang
Macassar Strait Indon. see Makassar Strait
Macau Brazil 202 E3
Macau China 87 E4
also known as Aomen; also spelt Macao
Macauã r. Brazil 200 C2
Macaúba Brazil 202 B4
Macaúbas Brazil 202 D5
Macauley Island N.Z. 145 H5
Macayari Col. 198 C4
Macbride Head Falkland Is 205 F8
Maccaretane Moz. 131 G5
Macclenny U.S.A. 175 D6
Macclesfield U.K. 47 J10
Macclesfield Bank sea feature S. China Sea 72 D3
also known as Zhongsha Qundao
Macdiarmid Canada 168 B3
Macdonald, Lake salt flat Australia 150 E4
MacDonnell Creek watercourse Australia 146 C2
Macdonnell Ranges mts Australia 148 A4
MacDowell Lake Canada 167 M4
Macedo de Cavaleiros Port. 54 E3
Macedon country Europe see Macedonia
▶Macedonia country Europe 58 C7
spelt Makedonija in Macedonian; historically known as Macedon; long form Former Yugoslav Republic of Macedonia; short form F.Y.R.O.M.
europe [countries] ▶▶ 32–35
Maceió Brazil 202 F4
Maceio, Ponta da pt Brazil 202 E3
Macenta Guinea 124 C4
Macerata Italy 56 F5
Macfarlane, Lake salt flat Australia 146 C3

Malay Sary Kazakh. 103 I3
▶Malaysia country Asia 76 C1
formerly known as Federated Malay States
asia [countries] ▶▶ 64–67
Malaysia, Semenanjung pen. Malaysia see Peninsular Malaysia
Malazgirt Turkey 107 E3
Malbaie r. Canada 169 G4
Malbaza Niger 125 G3
Malbon Australia 149 D4
Malbork Poland 49 Q1
historically known as Marienburg
Malbrán Arg. 204 E3
Malchin Germany 49 J2
Malcolm Australia 151 C6
Malcolm, Point Australia 151 C7
Malcolm Inlet Oman see Ghazira, Ghubbat al
Maldegem Belgium 51 J1
Malden U.S.A. 174 B4
Malden Island Kiribati 221 H6
▶Maldives country Indian Ocean 93 D10
also known as Divehi
asia [countries] ▶▶ 64–67
Maldon U.K. 47 M12
Maldonado Uruguay 204 G4
Maldonado, Punta pt Mex. 185 F5

▶Male Maldives 93 D10
Capital of the Maldives.
world [countries] ▶▶ 10–11

Male Myanmar 78 B3
Maléa Guinea 124 C4
Maleas, Akra pt Lesbos Greece 59 H9
Maleas, Akra pt Greece 59 E12
Male Atoll Maldives 93 D10
Malebogo S. Africa 133 J5
Malegaon Maharashtra India 94 B1
Malegaon Maharashtra India 94 C2
Malei Moz. 131 H3
Malé Karpaty hills Slovakia 49 O7
Malek Siāh, Kūh-e mt. Afgh. 101 E4
Malela Maniema Dem. Rep. Congo 126 E5
Malela Maniema Dem. Rep. Congo 126 E6
Malélé Congo 126 B6
Malele Dem. Rep. Congo 127 B6
Malema Moz. 131 H2
formerly known as Entre Rios
Malendo watercourse Nigeria 125 G4
Malente Germany 48 H1
Maleoskop S. Africa 133 N2
Målerås Sweden 45 K4
Maler Kotla India 96 B3
Maleševske Planine mts Bulg./Macedonia 58 D7
Malesherbes France 51 I4
Malesina Greece 59 E10
Maleštān Afgh. 101 F3
Malestroit France 50 D5
Maleta Rus. Fed. 85 F1
Malevka Rus. Fed. 43 T8
Malgas S. Africa 132 E11
Malgobek Rus. Fed. 41 H8
Malgomaj l. Sweden 44 L2
Malha Sudan 121 E6
Malhada Brazil 202 D5
Malham Saudi Arabia 105 D2
Malhargarh India 96 B4
Malheur r. U.S.A. 180 C3
Malheur Lake U.S.A. 180 C4
Malheur National Wildlife Refuge nature res. U.S.A. 180 C4
▶Mali country Africa 124 E2
formerly known as French Sudan
africa [countries] ▶▶ 114–117
Mali Dem. Rep. Congo 126 E5
Mali Guinea 124 B3
Malia Greece 59 G13
also spelt Mallia
Malian r. China 85 E5
Maliana East Timor 75 C5
Malianjing Gansu China 84 B3
Malianjing Gansu China 84 D4
Malibamatso r. Lesotho 133 M6
Malibu U.S.A. 182 F7
Maligay Bay Phil. 74 B5
Malihabad India 89 C7
Mali Hka r. Myanmar 78 B2
Malikdin Afgh. 101 G3
Malik Naro mt. Pak. 101 E4
Maliku Indon. 75 B3
Mali Kyun i. Myanmar 79 B5
also known as Tavoy Island
Malili Indon. 75 B3
Mali Lošinj Croatia 56 G4
Malimba, Monts mts Dem. Rep. Congo 127 F6
Malin Rep. of Ireland 47 E8
Malin Ukr. see Malyn
Malindi Kenya 128 D5
Malines Belgium see Mechelen
Malinga Gabon 126 B5
Malin Head Rep. of Ireland 46 E8
Mălini Romania 58 H1
Malino Indon. 75 A4
Malino Rus. Fed. 43 T6
Malino, Gunung mt. Indon. 75 B2
Malinovka r. Rus. Fed. 82 D3
Malinovoye Ozero Rus. Fed. 103 I2
formerly known as Mikhaylovskiy
Malinyi Tanz. 129 C7
Malipo China 86 C4
Maliq Albania 58 B8
Mali Raginac mt. Croatia 56 H4
Malit, Qafa e pass Albania 58 B6
Malita Phil. 74 C5
Malitbog Phil. 74 C4
Maliwun Myanmar 79 B6
Maliya India 96 A5
Malka r. Rus. Fed. 41 H8
Malka Mary Kenya 128 D3
Malkapur Maharashtra India 94 B2
Malkapur Maharashtra India 94 C1
Malkara Turkey 106 A2
Mal'kavichy Belarus 42 H9
Malkhanskiy Khrebet mts Rus. Fed. 85 F1
Malko Tŭrnovo Bulg. 58 I7
Mallacoota Australia 147 F4
Mallacoota Inlet b. Australia 147 F4
Mallaig U.K. 46 G7
Mallanga well Chad 120 D5
Mallani reg. India 96 A4
Mallawi Egypt 121 F3
Mallee Cliffs National Park Australia 147 D3
Mållejus hill Norway 44 M1
Mallery Lake Canada 167 L1
Mallét Brazil 203 B8
Mallia Greece see Malia
Mallorca i. Spain see Majorca
Mallow Rep. of Ireland 47 D11
also spelt Mala
Mallowa Well Australia 150 D4
Malm Norway 44 J2
Malmberget Sweden 44 M2
Malmédy Belgium 51 M2
Malmesbury S. Africa 132 C10
Malmesbury U.K. 47 J12
Malmköping Sweden 45 L4
Malmö Sweden 45 K5
Malmö-Sturup airport Sweden 45 K5
Malmslätt Sweden 45 K4
Malmyzh Rus. Fed. 40 I4
Malo i. Indon. 75 C1
Maloarkhangel'sk Rus. Fed. 43 R9
Maloca Amazonas Brazil 199 F5
Maloca Pará Brazil 199 H4
Maloca Salamaim Brazil 201 E3
Malo Crniče Srbija Yugo. 58 C4
Malolos Phil. 74 B3
Malolotja Nature Reserve Swaziland 133 P3
Maloma Swaziland 133 P4
Malombe, Lake Malawi 129 B8
Malone U.S.A. 177 K1
Malong China 86 B3
also known as Tongquan
Malonga Dem. Rep. Congo 127 D7
Małopolska, Wyżyna hills Poland 49 R5
Maloshuyka Rus. Fed. 40 F3
Malovan pass Bos.-Herz. 56 J5
Malovăț Romania 58 D4
Malowera Moz. 131 F2
formerly spelt Maluera
Måløy Norway 44 I3
Maloyaroslavets Rus. Fed. 43 R6
Maloye Borisovo Rus. Fed. 43 R2
Malozemel'skaya Tundra lowland Rus. Fed. 40 I2
Malpelo, Isla de i. N. Pacific Ocean 198 A4
Malpica Spain 54 C1
Mālpils Latvia 42 F4
Malprabha r. India 94 C2
Malpura India 96 B4
Malše r. Czech Rep. 49 L7
Malsiras India 94 B2
▶Malta country Europe 57 G13
europe [countries] ▶▶ 32–35
Malta Latvia 42 I5
Malta r. Latvia 42 I5
Malta i. Malta 57 G13
Malta U.S.A. 180 F2
Maltahöhe Namibia 130 C5
Maltam Cameroon 125 I3
Maltion luonnonpuisto nature res. Fin. 44 O2
Malton U.K. 47 L9
Maluera Moz. see Malowera
Malukken is Indon. see Moluccas
Maluku is Indon. see Moluccas
Maluku prov. Indon. 75 D3
Ma'lūlā, Jabal mts Syria 109 H4
Malului, Vârful hill Romania 58 D2
Malumfashi Nigeria 125 G4
Malundano Zambia 127 E9
Malung Sweden 45 K3
Maluti Mountains Lesotho 133 M6
Malu'u Solomon Is 145 F2
Malvan India 94 B2
Malvasia Greece see Monemvasia
Malvern AR U.S.A. 179 D5
Malvern OH U.S.A. 176 D5
Malvérnia Moz. see Chicualacuala
Malvinas, Islas terr. S. Atlantic Ocean see Falkland Islands
Malwa reg. India 96 C5
Malwal Sudan 128 A2
Malxe r. Germany 49 L4
Malý Dunaj r. Slovakia 49 P8
Malykay Rus. Fed. 39 L3
Malyn Ukr. 41 D6
also spelt Malin
Malyy, Ostrov i. Rus. Fed. 43 J1
Malyy Anyuy r. Rus. Fed. 39 Q3
Malyye Soli Rus. Fed. 43 V4
Malyy Irgiz r. Rus. Fed. 41 I5
Malyy Kavkaz mts Asia see Lesser Caucasus
Malyy Kunaley Rus. Fed. 85 E1
Malyy Lyakhovskiy, Ostrov i. Rus. Fed. 39 O2
Malyy Taymyr, Ostrov i. Rus. Fed. 39 K2
Malyy Uzen' r. Kazakh./Rus. Fed. 102 B2
also known as Kishiözen
Malyy Yenisey r. Rus. Fed. 84 B1
Malyy Zelenchuk r. Rus. Fed. 107 E1
Mama r. Rus. Fed. 39 O3
Mamadysh Rus. Fed. 40 I5
Mamafubedu S. Africa 133 M4
Mamahabane S. Africa 133 L5
Mamaranui N.Z. 152 H3
Mamasa Indon. 75 A3
Mambahenauhan i. Phil. 74 A5
Mambai Brazil 202 C5
Mambajao Phil. 74 C4
Mambal Cameroon 125 I5
Mambali Tanz. 129 B6
Mambasa Dem. Rep. Congo 126 F4
Mambéré r. Cent. Afr. Rep. 126 C4
Mambéré-Kadéï pref. Cent. Afr. Rep. 126 B3
Mambi Indon. 75 A3
Mambili r. Congo 126 C4
Mambolo Sierra Leone 124 B4
Mamborê Brazil 206 A11
Mambrui Kenya 128 D5
Mamburao Phil. 74 B3
Mamelodi S. Africa 133 M2
Mamers France 50 G4
Mamfé Cameroon 125 H5
Mamiá Brazil 199 F6
Mamili National Park Namibia 130 D3
Mamiña Chile 200 C5
Mamison Pass Georgia/Rus. Fed. 107 E2
Mammoth U.S.A. 183 N9
Mammoth Cave National Park U.S.A. 174 C4
Mammoth Lakes U.S.A. 182 F4
Mammoth Reservoir U.S.A. 182 E4
Mamonas Brazil 207 K2
Mamonovo Kaliningradskaya Oblast' Rus. Fed. 42 A7
historically known as Heiligenbeil
Mamonovo Ryazanskaya Oblast' Rus. Fed. 43 U8
Mamontovo Rus. Fed. 103 J1
Mamoré r. Bol./Brazil 200 D2
Mamori Brazil 199 E5
Mamori, Lago l. Brazil 199 F5
Mamoriá Brazil 200 D1
Mamou Guinea 124 B4
Mamoudzou Mayotte 129 E8
also spelt Mamoutsou or Mamutzu
Mamoutsou Mayotte see Mamoudzou
Mampikony Madag. 131 [inset] J3
Mampong Ghana 125 E5
Mamre S. Africa 132 C10
Mamry, Jezioro l. Poland 49 S1
Mamuju Indon. 75 A3
Ma'mūl Oman 105 F4
Mamuno Botswana 130 D4
Mamuras Albania 58 A7
Mamurogawa Japan 90 G5
Mamutzu Mayotte see Mamoudzou
Man Côte d'Ivoire 124 D5
Man r. India 94 B2
Man U.S.A. 176 D8

▶Man, Isle of i. Irish Sea 47 H9
United Kingdom Crown Dependency.
europe [countries] ▶▶ 32–35

Mana Fr. Guiana 199 H3
Mana U.S.A. 181 [inset] Y1
Mana Bárbara Venez. 198 C2
Manabí prov. Ecuador 198 B5
Manacacías r. Col. 198 C3
Manacapuru Brazil 199 F5
Manacor Spain 55 O5
Manado Indon. 75 C2

▶Managua Nicaragua 186 B4
Capital of Nicaragua.

Managua, Lago de l. Nicaragua 186 B4
Manah Oman 105 G3
Manaia N.Z. 152 I7
Manakara Madag. 131 [inset] J4
Manakau mt. N.Z. 153 H10
Manākhah Yemen 104 C5
Manali India 96 C2

▶Manama Bahrain 105 E2
Capital of Bahrain. Also spelt Al Manāmah.
world [countries] ▶▶ 10–11

Manamadurai India 94 C4
Manambaho r. Madag. 131 [inset] J3
Manambondro Madag. 131 [inset] J4
Manamelkudi India 94 C4
Manam Island P.N.G. 73 K7
also known as Vulcan Island
Manamo, Caño r. Venez. 199 F2
Manamoc i. Phil. 74 B4
Mananantañana r. Madag. 131 [inset] J4
Mananara r. Madag. 131 [inset] J4
Mananara, Parc National de nat. park Madag. 131 [inset] K3
Mananara Avaratra Madag. 131 [inset] K3
Manangoora Australia 148 C3
Mananjary Madag. 131 [inset] K4
Manankoliva Madag. 131 [inset] J5
Manankoro Mali 124 D4
Manantali, Lac de l. Mali 124 C3
Manantavadi India 94 C4
Manantenina Madag. 131 [inset] J5
Mana Pass China/India 89 B6
Mana Pools National Park Zimbabwe 131 F3
Manapouri N.Z. 153 B13

▶Manapouri, Lake N.Z. 153 B13
Deepest lake in Oceania.

Manapparai India 94 C4
Manarantsandry Madag. 131 [inset] J3
Manas China 88 D2
Manas r. India 97 F4
Manas, Gora mt. Uzbek. 103 G4
Manasa India 96 B4
Manas He r. China 88 D2
Manas Hu l. China 88 D2
Manāṣīr reg. U.A.E. 105 F3

▶Manaslu mt. Nepal 97 E3
8th highest mountain in the world and in Asia.
world [physical features] ▶▶ 8–9

Manasquan U.S.A. 177 K5
Manassas U.S.A. 176 H7
Manastir Macedonia see Bitola
Manas Wildlife Sanctuary nature res. Bhutan 97 F4
Manatang Indon. 75 C5
Manatuto East Timor 75 C5
Man-aung Kyun i. Myanmar see Cheduba Island
Manaus Brazil 199 F5
Manavgat Turkey 106 B3
Manavgat r. Turkey 108 C1
Manawa U.S.A. 172 E6
Manawar India 96 B5
Manawaru N.Z. 152 J5
Manawashei Sudan 120 E6
Manawatu r. N.Z. 152 J8
Manawatu-Wanganui admin. reg. N.Z. 152 J7
Manay Phil. 74 C5
Manayenki Rus. Fed. 43 R8
Manbazar India 97 E5
Manbij Syria 109 I1
Mancelona U.S.A. 173 H6
Manchar India 94 B2
Manchester U.K. 47 J10
Manchester CT U.S.A. 177 M4
Manchester IA U.S.A. 174 B3
Manchester KY U.S.A. 176 B8
Manchester MD U.S.A. 177 I6
Manchester MI U.S.A. 173 I8
Manchester NH U.S.A. 177 N3
Manchester OH U.S.A. 176 B7
Manchester TN U.S.A. 174 C5
Manchhar Lake Pak. 101 F5
Manciano Italy 56 D6
Mancılık Turkey 107 D3
Mancınık Dağı mts Turkey 59 I9
Mancos r. U.S.A. 183 P5
Mand Pak. 101 E5
Mand, Rūd-e r. Iran 100 B4
also known as Qara Āghach
Manda Bangl. 97 F4
Manda Malawi 129 B7
Manda Tanz. 129 B6
Manda, Jebel mt. Sudan 126 E2
Manda, Parc National de nat. park Chad 126 C2
Mandabe Madag. 131 [inset] J4
Mandaguaçu Brazil 206 A10
Mandaguari Brazil 206 B10
Mandai Sing. 76 [inset]
Mandal Afgh. 101 E3
Mandal Gujarat India 96 A5
Mandal Rajasthan India 96 B4
Mandal Bulgan Mongolia 84 D1
Mandal Töv Mongolia 85 E1
Mandal Norway 45 I4

▶Mandala, Puncak mt. Indon. 73 J7
3rd highest mountain in Oceania. Formerly known as Julianatop.
oceania [landscapes] ▶▶ 136–137

Mandalay Myanmar 78 B3
also spelt Mandale
Mandalay admin. div. Myanmar 78 A3
also spelt Mandale
Mandale Myanmar see Mandalay
Mandale admin. div. Myanmar see Mandalay
Mandalgarh India 96 B4
Mandalgovi Mongolia 85 E2
Mandali Iraq 107 F4
Mandalt China 85 G3
also known as Sonid Zuoqi
Mandan U.S.A. 178 B2
Mandaon Phil. 74 B3
Mandapam India 94 C4
Mandar, Teluk b. Indon. 75 A3
Mandas Sardegna Italy 57 B9
Mandav Hills India 96 A5
Mandé, Mont de hill France 51 K6
Mandelieu-la-Napoule France 51 M9
Mandello del Lario Italy 56 B3
Manderes Kenya 128 D4
Manderfield U.S.A. 183 L3
Mandeville Jamaica 186 D3
Mandeville N.Z. 153 C13
Mandha India 96 A4
Mandheera Somalia 128 E2
Mandhoúdhion Greece see Mantoudi
Mandi India 96 C3
Mandiakui Mali 124 D3
Mandiana Guinea 124 C4
Mandi Burewala Pak. 101 H4
Mandidzuzure Zimbabwe see Chimanimani
Mandié Moz. 131 G3
Mandimba Moz. 131 G2
Manding, Monts mts Mali 124 C3
Mandioli i. Indon. 75 C3
Mandji Gabon 126 A5
Mandla India 96 D5
Mandor India 96 B4
Mandorah Australia 148 A2
Mandoro Dem. Rep. Congo 126 F3
Mandoto Madag. 131 [inset] J3
Mandor Reserve nature res. Indon. 77 E2
Mandouri Togo 125 F4
Mandra Greece 59 E10
Mandraki Greece 59 I12
Mandrare r. Madag. 131 [inset] J5
Mandrenska r. Bulg. see Sredetska Reka
Mandritsara Madag. 131 [inset] K2
Mandsaur India 96 B4
Mandul i. Indon. 77 G2
Mandurah Australia 151 A7
Manduria Italy 57 J8
Mandvi Gujarat India 96 A5
Mandvi Gujarat India 96 B5
Mandya India 94 C3
Manekwara India 96 A5
Manendragarh India 97 D5
Maner India 97 E4
Maner r. India 94 C2
Manerbio Italy 56 C3
Maneromango Tanz. 129 C6
Manesht Kūh mt. Iran 100 A3
Mănești Romania 58 G4
Maneva Madag. see Mahaboboka
Manevychi Ukr. 41 C6
Manfalût Egypt 121 F3
Manfredonia Italy 56 H7
Manfredonia, Golfo di g. Italy 56 I7
Manga Brazil 202 D5
Manga Burkina 125 E4
Mangabeiras, Serra das hills Brazil 202 C4
Manga Grande Angola 127 B6
Mangai Dem. Rep. Congo 126 C6
Mangai, Réserve de Faune des Hippopotames de nature res. Dem. Rep. Congo 126 C5
Mangaia i. Cook Is 221 H7
also spelt Mangea
Mangakino N.Z. 152 J6
Mangalagiri India 94 D2
Mangaldai India 97 G4
Mangalia Romania 58 J5
Mangalmé Chad 120 C6
Mangalore India 94 B3
Mangalvedha India 94 B2
Mangamaunu N.Z. 153 H10
Mangamuka N.Z. 152 H3
Mangania Dem. Rep. Congo 126 D4
Manganui r. N.Z. 152 H3
Mangaon India 94 B2
Mangapet India 94 D2
Mangarakau N.Z. 152 G8
Mangaratiba Brazil 207 I9
Mangareva Islands Fr. Polynesia see Gambier, Îles
Mangatainoka N.Z. 152 J8
Mangatawhiri N.Z. 152 J5
Mangaung S. Africa 133 K6
Mangawan India 97 D4
Mangaweka N.Z. 152 J7
Mangawhai N.Z. 152 I4
Mangde Chhu r. Bhutan see Trongsa Chhu
Mang'ê China see Luqu
Mangea i. Cook Is see Mangaia
Mangengenge Dem. Rep. Congo 126 E6
Manger Norway 45 I3
Manggar Indon. 77 E3
Mangghyshlaq Kazakh. see Mangistau
Mangghystaū Kazakh. see Mangistau
Mangghystaū Oblysy admin. div. Kazakh. see Mangistauskaya Oblast'
Manghyt Uzbek. see Mangit
Manghit Uzbek. see Mangit
Mangistau Kazakh. 102 B4
also spelt Mangghystaū; formerly known as Mangghyshlaq or Mangyshlak
Mangistau, Gory hills Kazakh. 102 B3
Mangistauskaya Oblast' admin. div. Kazakh. 102 C4
also known as Mangghystaū Oblysy; formerly known as Mangyshlak Oblast or Mangyshlakskaya Oblast'
Mangit Uzbek. 102 E4
also spelt Manghyt or Manghit
Mangkalihat, Tanjung pt Indon. 77 G2
Mangkutup r. Indon. 77 F3
Manglares, Punta pt Col. 198 B4
Mangnai China 88 E4
Mangnai Zhen China 88 E4
Mangoaka Madag. 131 [inset] K2
Mangochi Malawi 129 B8
formerly known as Fort Johnston
Mangodara Burkina 124 D4
Mangoky r. Toliara Madag. 131 [inset] I4
Mangoky r. Toliara Madag. 131 [inset] J4
Mangole i. Indon. 75 C3
Mangole, Selat sea chan. Indon. 75 C3
Mangoli India 94 B2
Mangombe Dem. Rep. Congo 126 E5
Mangonui N.Z. 152 H3
Mangoro r. Madag. 131 [inset] K3
Mangqystaū Shyghanaghy b. Kazakh. see Mangyshlakskiy Zaliv
Mangra China see Guinan
Mangral India 96 A5
Mangrol India 96 C4
Mangrul India 94 C1
Mangshi China see Luxi
Mangualde Port. 54 D4
Manguari Brazil 198 D5
Manguchar Pak. 101 F4
Mangueira, Lago l. Brazil 204 G4
Mangueirinha Brazil 203 A8
Manguéni, Plateau du Niger 123 H5
Mangui China 82 A2
Manguinha, Pontal do pt Brazil 202 E4
Mangula Zimbabwe see Mhangura
Mangum U.S.A. 179 C5
Mangunça, Ilha i. Brazil 202 C2
Mangut Rus. Fed. 85 G1
Mangyshlak Kazakh. see Mangistau
Mangyshlak, Poluostrov pen. Kazakh. 102 B3
also known as Tüpqaraghan Tübegi
Mangyshlak Oblast admin. div. Kazakh. see Mangistauskaya Oblast'
Mangyshlakskaya Oblast' admin. div. Kazakh. see Mangistauskaya Oblast'
Mangyshlakskiy Zaliv b. Kazakh. 102 B3
also known as Mangqystaū Shyghanaghy
Manhan Mongolia see Tögrög
Manhan Mongolia 84 C1
Manhattan U.S.A. 178 C4
Manhattan Beach U.S.A. 182 F8
Manhica Moz. 133 Q2
Manhoca Moz. 133 Q3
Manhuaçu Brazil 203 D7
Manhuaçu r. Brazil 207 L6
Manhumirim Brazil 207 L7
Mani Chad 120 B6
Mani well Chad 120 C5
Mani China 89 D5
Mani Col. 198 C3
Mani Nigeria 125 G3
Mānī', Wādī al watercourse Iraq 109 M3
Mania r. Madag. 131 [inset] J3
Maniago Italy 56 E2
Maniakoi Greece 58 C8
Maniari Tank resr India 97 D5
also known as Khuria Tank
Manica Moz. 131 G3
Manica prov. Moz. 131 G3
Manicaland prov. Zimbabwe 131 G3
Manicoré Brazil 199 F6
Manicoré r. Brazil 199 F6
Manicouagan Canada 169 G3
Manicouagan r. Canada 169 G3
Manicouagan, Réservoir Canada 169 G3
Manic Trois, Réservoir Canada 169 G3
Maniema prov. Dem. Rep. Congo 126 E5
Manīfah Saudi Arabia 105 E2
Maniganggo China 86 A2
Manigotagan Canada 167 L5
Manihari India 97 E4
Manihiki atoll Cook Is 221 H6
formerly known as Great Ganges or Humphrey Island
Maniitsoq Greenland 165 N3
also known as Sukkertoppen
Manji r. Pak. 101 F5
Manikchhari Bangl. 97 G5
Manikganj Bangl. 97 F5
Manikgarh India see Rajura
Manikpur India 96 D4

▶Manila Phil. 74 B3
Capital of the Philippines.
world [cities] ▶▶ 24–25

Manila U.S.A. 180 E4
Manila Bay Phil. 74 B3
Manilaid i. Estonia 42 F3
Manilla Australia 147 F2
Manily Rus. Fed. 39 Q3
Manimbaya, Tanjung pt Indon. 75 A3
Maningrida Australia 148 B2
Maninjau, Danau l. Indon. 76 C3
Manipa i. Indon. 75 C3
Manipa, Selat sea chan. Indon. 75 C3
Manipur India see Imphal
Manipur state India 97 G4
Manipur r. India/Myanmar 97 G5
Manisa Turkey 106 A3
Manisa prov. Turkey 59 J10
Manises Spain 55 K5
Manissauá Missu r. Brazil 202 A4
Manistee U.S.A. 172 G6
Manistee r. U.S.A. 172 G6
Manistique U.S.A. 172 G5
Manistique Lake U.S.A. 172 H4
Manitoba prov. Canada 167 L4
Manitoba, Lake Canada 167 L5
Manito Lake Canada 167 I4
Manitou Canada 167 L5
Manitou r. Canada 169 H3
Manitou, Lake Canada 168 D4
Manitou Beach U.S.A. 176 H2
Manitou Falls Canada 168 A3
Manitou Island U.S.A. 172 F3
Manitou Islands U.S.A. 172 G5
Manitoulin Island Canada 168 D4
Manitouwadge Canada 168 C3
Manitowaning Canada 173 L5
Manitowik Lake Canada 173 I2
Manitowish Waters U.S.A. 172 D4
Manitowoc U.S.A. 172 F6
Maniwaki Canada 168 F4
Manizales Col. 198 C3
Manja Madag. 131 [inset] J4
Manjacaze Moz. 131 G5
Manjak Madag. 131 [inset] J3
Manjam Umm Qurayyāt waterhole Egypt 104 A3
Manjarabad India 94 B3
Manjeri India 94 C4
Manjhand Pak. 101 G5
Man Jiang r. China 82 B4
Manjil Iran 100 B2
Manjimup Australia 151 B7
Manjo Cameroon 125 H5
Manjra r. India 94 C2
Man Kabat Myanmar 78 B2
Mankachar India 97 F4
Mankanza Dem. Rep. Congo see Makanza
Mankato KS U.S.A. 178 C4
Mankato MN U.S.A. 178 D2
Mankono Côte d'Ivoire 124 D4
Mankota Canada 167 J5
Manlleu Spain 55 N3
Manly U.S.A. 174 A3
Manmad India 94 B1
Mann r. Australia 148 B2
Mann, Mount Australia 148 A5
Manna Indon. 76 C4
Mannahill Australia 146 C3
Mannar Sri Lanka 94 C4
Mannar, Gulf of India/Sri Lanka 94 C4
Mannargudi India 94 C4
Manneru r. India 94 D3
Mannheim Germany 48 F6
Mannicolo Islands Solomon Is see Vanikoro Islands
Männikuste Estonia 42 F3
Manning Canada 167 G3
Manning ND U.S.A. 178 B2
Manning SC U.S.A. 175 D5
Manning Provincial Park Canada 166 F5
Mannington U.S.A. 176 E6
Männlifluh mt. Switz. 51 N6
Mann Ranges mts Australia 148 A5
Mannsville U.S.A. 177 I2
Mannu r. Sardegna Italy 57 A8
Mannu r. Sardegna Italy 57 A9
Mannu r. Sardegna Italy 57 B9
Mannu, Capo c. Sardegna Italy 57 A8
Mannville Canada 167 I4
Mano r. Liberia/Sierra Leone 124 C5
Manoa Bol. 200 D2
Man-of-War Rocks is U.S.A. see Gardner Pinnacles
Manoharpur India 89 B7
Manohar Thana India 96 C4
Manokotak U.S.A. 164 D4
Manokwari Indon. 73 H7
Manombo Atsimo Madag. 131 [inset] I4
Manompana Madag. 131 [inset] K3
Manono Dem. Rep. Congo 127 E6
Manora Head Pak. 101 F5
Mano River Liberia 124 C5
Manosque France 51 L9
Manouane, Lac l. Canada 169 G3
Mano-wan b. Japan 90 F6
Man Pan Myanmar 78 B3
Manp'o N. Korea 83 B4
Manpur India 96 B5
Manra i. Kiribati 145 H2
formerly known as Sydney Island
Manresa Spain 55 M3
Mansa Gujarat India 96 B5
Mansa Punjab India 96 B3
Mansa Zambia 127 F7
formerly known as Fort Rosebery
Mansabá Guinea-Bissau 124 B3
Mansa Konko Gambia 124 B3
Man Sam Myanmar 78 B3
Mansehra Pak. 101 H3
Mansel Island Canada 165 L3
Mansel'kya ridge Fin./Rus. Fed. 44 O2
Mansfield Australia 147 E4
Mansfield U.K. 47 K10
Mansfield AR U.S.A. 179 D5
Mansfield LA U.S.A. 179 D5
Mansfield MA U.S.A. 177 N3
Mansfield OH U.S.A. 176 C5
Mansfield PA U.S.A. 177 H4
Mansfield, Mount U.S.A. 177 M1
Man Si Myanmar 78 B2
Mansi Myanmar 78 A2
Mansidão Brazil 202 D4
Manso r. Brazil see Mortes, Rio das
Manso-Nkwanta Ghana 125 E5
Mansuela Indon. 75 D3
Mansurlu Turkey 106 C3
also known as Tapan
Manta Ecuador 198 A5
long form San Pablo de Manta
Mantalingajan, Mount Phil. 74 A4
Mantantale Dem. Rep. Congo 126 D5
Mantaro r. Peru 200 B3
Manteca U.S.A. 182 C4
Mantecal Venez. 198 D3
Mantehage i. Indon. 75 C2
Manteigas Port. 54 D4
Mantena Brazil 203 D6
Manteno U.S.A. 172 F9
Manteo U.S.A. 174 F5
Mantes-la-Jolie France 50 H4
Manthani India 94 C2
Manti U.S.A. 183 M2
Mantiqueira, Serra da mts Brazil 203 C7
Manto Hond. 186 B4
Manton U.S.A. 172 H6
Mantorville U.S.A. 168 A4
Mantos Blancos Chile 200 C5
Mantoudi Greece 59 E10
also known as Mandhoúdhion
Mantova Italy see Mantua
Mäntsälä Fin. 45 N3
Mänttä Fin. 45 N3
Mantua Cuba 186 B2
Mantua Italy 56 C3
also spelt Mantova
Mantua U.S.A. 176 D4
Mantuan Downs Australia 149 E5
Manturovo Rus. Fed. 40 H4
Mäntyharju Fin. 45 N3
Mäntyjärvi Fin. 44 N2
Manu r. Bol. see Mapiri
Manú r. Peru 200 C3
Manu, Parque Nacional nat. park Peru 200 B3
Manuae atoll Fr. Polynesia 221 H7
also known as Fenua Ura; formerly known as Scilly, Île
Manua Islands American Samoa 145 I3
Manubi S. Africa 133 M9
Manuel Alves r. Brazil 202 B4
Manuel J. Cobo Arg. 204 F4
Manuel Rodríguez, Isla i. Chile 205 B9
Manuel Urbano Brazil 200 C2
Manuel Vitorino Brazil 202 D5
Manuelzinho Brazil 202 A3
Manui i. Indon. 75 B3
Manūjān Iran 100 D5
Manukan Phil. 74 B4
Manukau N.Z. 152 I4
Manukau Harbour N.Z. 152 I5
Manuk Manka i. Phil. 74 A5
Manunda watercourse Australia 146 C3
Manupari r. Bol. 200 D2
Manurimi r. Bol. 200 D2
Manuripi r. Bol. 200 D2
Manusela National Park Indon. 75 D3
Manus Island P.N.G. 73 K7
Manutuke N.Z. 152 L6
Manvi India 94 C3
Manwat India 94 C2
Many U.S.A. 179 D6
Manyallaluk Aboriginal reserve res. Australia 148 B2
Manyame r. Moz./Zimbabwe 131 F2
formerly known as Hunyani
Manyara, Lake salt l. Tanz. 129 B5
Manyas Turkey 59 I8
Manyas Gölü l. Turkey see Kuş Gölü
Manyatseng S. Africa 133 L6
Manyberries Canada 167 I5
Manych-Gudilo, Ozero l. Rus. Fed. 41 G7
Many Farms U.S.A. 183 O5
Manyinga Zambia 127 E8
Many Island Lake Canada 167 I5
Manyoni Tanz. 129 B6
Many Peaks, Mount hill Australia 151 B7
Manzala, Bahra el lag. Egypt see Manzala, Lake
Manzala, Lake lag. Egypt 108 D6
also known as Manzala, Bahra el
Manzanal, Puerto del pass Spain 54 E2
Manzanares Spain 55 H5
Manzaneda, Cabeza de mt. Spain 54 D2
Manzanillo Cuba 186 D2
Manzanillo Mex. 184 D5
Manzanillo, Punta pt Panama 186 D5
Manzanza Dem. Rep. Congo 126 F6
Manzariyeh Iran 100 B3
Manzengele Dem. Rep. Congo 127 C6
Manzhouli China 85 H1
Manzini Swaziland 133 P3
formerly known as Bremersdorp
Manzini admin. dist. Swaziland 133 P3
Manzovka Rus. Fed. see Sibirtsevo
Mao Chad 120 B6
Mao Dom. Rep. 187 F3
formerly known as Valverde
Maó Spain see Mahón
Mao, Nam r. Myanmar see Shweli
Maoba Guizhou China 86 C3
Maoba Hubei China 87 D2
Maocifan China 87 E2
Mao'ergai China 86 B1
Maoke, Pegunungan mts Indon. 73 I7
Maokeng S. Africa 133 L4
Maokui Shan mt. China 83 A4
Maomao Shan mt. China 84 D4
Maoming China 87 D4
Ma On Shan hill Hong Kong China 87 [inset]
Maopi Cape Taiwan see Maopi T'ou
Maopi T'ou c. Taiwan 87 D4
English form Maopi Cape
Maopora i. Indon. 75 C4
Maotou Shan mt. China 86 B3
Maowen China see Maoxian
Maoxian China 86 B2
also known as Fengyi; formerly known as Maowen
Mapai Moz. 131 F4
Mapam Yumco l. China 89 C6
Mapane Indon. 75 B3
Mapanza Zambia 127 E9
Mapastepec Mex. 185 G6
Maphodi S. Africa 133 J7
Mapi r. Indon. 73 I8
Mapiche, Serranía mts Venez. 199 E3
Mapimí Mex. 184 E3
Mapimí, Bolsón de des. Mex. 184 D3
Mapin i. Phil. 74 A5
Mapinhane Moz. 131 G4
Mapire Venez. 199 E3
Mapireme Brazil 199 H4
Mapiri Bol. 200 C3
Mapiri r. Bol. 200 D2
also known as Manu
Mapirpán Col. 198 C4
Mapiu N.Z. 152 J6
Maple r. IA U.S.A. 178 D3
Maple r. MI U.S.A. 173 I8
Maple r. ND U.S.A. 178 C2
Maple r. ND U.S.A. 178 C2
Maple Creek Canada 167 I5
Maple Peak U.S.A. 183 O8
Mapleton IA U.S.A. 178 D3
Mapleton UT U.S.A. 183 M1
Maplewood U.S.A. 172 F6
Mapoon Australia 149 D1
Mapoon Aboriginal Reserve Australia 149 D2
Mapor i. Indon. 76 D2
Mapoteng Lesotho 133 L6
Maprik P.N.G. 73 J7
Mapuca India 94 B3
Mapuera r. Brazil 199 G5
Mapulanguene Moz. 131 G5
Mapunda Dem. Rep. Congo 127 E7

▶Maputo Moz. 131 G5
Capital of Mozambique. Formerly known as Lourenço Marques.

Maputo prov. Moz. 131 G5
Maputo r. Moz./S. Africa 133 Q3
Maputo, Baía de b. Moz. 133 Q3
Maputo Elephant Reserve nature res. Moz. 133 Q3
Maputsoe Lesotho 133 L5
Maqanshy Kazakh. see Makanchi
Maqar an Na'am well Iraq 107 E5
Maqat Kazakh. see Makat
Maqên China 86 B1
also known as Dawu
Maqên Gangri mt. China 86 A1
Maqla, Jabal al mt. Saudi Arabia 108 G9

Mataigou China see Taole
Matak i. Indon. 77 D2
Matak Kazakh. 103 H2
Matakana Island N.Z. 152 K5
Matakaoa Point N.Z. 152 M5
Matakitaki N.Z. 153 G9
Matala Angola 127 B8
Matale Sri Lanka 94 D5
Mataleng S. Africa 133 I5
Matâli', Jabal hill Saudi Arabia 104 C2
Matam Senegal 124 B3
Matamata N.Z. 152 J5
Mata-Mata S. Africa 132 E2
Matamau N.Z. 152 K8
Matamey Niger 125 H3
Matamoras U.S.A. 177 K4
Matamoros Campeche Mex. 185 H5
Matamoros Coahuila Mex. 185 E3
Matamoros Tamaulipas Mex. 185 F3
Ma'ţa Moûlana well Mauritania 124 B2
Matana, Danau l. Indon. 75 B3
Matanal Point Phil. 74 B5
Ma'ţan as Sārah well Libya 120 D4
Ma'ţan Bishrah well Libya 120 D4
Matandu r. Tanz. 129 C7
Matane Canada 169 H3
Matane, Réserve Faunique de nature res. Canada 169 H3
Mata Negra Venez. 199 F2
Matanga Madag. 131 [inset] J4
Matangi N.Z. 152 J5
Matanzas Cuba 186 C2
Matão Brazil 206 E8
Matão, Serra do hills Brazil 202 B4
Matapalo, Cabo c. Costa Rica 186 C5
Matapan, Cape pt Greece see Tainaro, Akra
Mata Panew r. Poland 49 P5
Matapédia, Lac l. Canada 169 H3
Mataporquera Spain 54 G2
Maţar well Saudi Arabia 105 D2
Matará Arg. 204 E3
Matara Sri Lanka 94 D5
also known as Matturai
Mataragka Greece 59 C10
also spelt Mataránga
Mataram Indon. 77 G5
Mataránga Greece see Mataragka
Mataranka Australia 148 B2
Matarinao Bay Phil. 74 C4
Matarka Morocco 123 E2
Matarma, Râs pt Egypt 108 D8
Mataró Spain 55 N3
Mataroa N.Z. 152 J7
Matarombea r. Indon. 75 B3
Matarraña r. Spain 55 L3
Mataruška Banja Srbija Yugo. 58 B5
Matasiri i. Indon. 77 F4
Matassi well Sudan 121 F5
Matassi Tanz. 129 C6
Matatiele S. Africa 133 M7
Matatila Dam India 96 C4
Matau N.Z. 152 I7
Mataura N.Z. 153 C14
Mataura r. N.Z. 153 C14

▶Matā'utu Wallis and Futuna Is 145 H3
Capital of Wallis and Futuna.

Matawai N.Z. 152 L6
Matawaia N.Z. 152 H3
Matawin r. Canada 169 F4
Matay Kazakh. 103 I3
Maţbakh, Ra's al pt Qatar 105 E2
Matcha Tajik. see Mastchoh
Matchi-Manitou, Lac l. Canada 173 P2
Mategua Bol. 201 E3
Matehuala Mex. 185 E4
Matei Romania 58 F2
Mateke Hills Zimbabwe 131 F4
Matelica Italy 56 F5
Matelot Trin. and Tob. 187 H5
Matemanga Tanz. 129 C7
Matende Angola 127 C9
Matera Italy 57 I8
Mateso, Monti del mts Italy 56 G7
Mátészalka Hungary 49 T8
Matetsi Zimbabwe 131 E3
Mateur Tunisia 57 B11
Mateus Leme Brazil 207 I6
Matewan U.S.A. 176 C8
Matha France 50 F7
Matheson Canada 168 D3
Mathews U.S.A. 177 I8
Mathias U.S.A. 176 G7
Mathis U.S.A. 179 C6
Mathraki i. Greece 59 A9
Mathura India 96 C4
Mati Phil. 74 C5
Matiacoali Burkina 125 F3
Matianxu China 87 E3
Matiari Pak. 101 G5
Matias Barbosa Brazil 207 J8
Matias Cardoso Brazil 202 D5
Matías Romero Mex. 185 G5
Matibane Moz. 131 I2
Matimekosh Canada 169 H2
Matina Costa Rica 186 C5
Matinicus Island U.S.A. 177 Q2
Matizi China 86 B1
Matjiesfontein S. Africa 132 E10
Matla r. India 97 F5
Matli Pak. 101 G5
Matlock U.K. 47 K10
Matlwangtlwang S. Africa 133 L4
Matna Sudan 104 A5
Mato r. Venez. 199 E3
Mato, Cerro mt. Venez. 199 E3
Matoaka U.S.A. 176 D8
Matobo Hills Zimbabwe 131 F4
also spelt Matopo Hills
Matobo National Park Zimbabwe 131 F4
formerly known as Rhodes Matopos National Park
Matogrossense, Pantanal marsh Brazil 201 G4
Mato Grosso Brazil 201 F3
▶Mato Grosso state Brazil 206 A2
southamerica [contrasts] 194–195
Mato Grosso, Planalto do plat. Brazil 202 A5
Mato Grosso do Sul state Brazil 206 A6
Matola Moz. 131 G5
Matondo Moz. 131 G3
Matope Malawi 129 B8
Matopo Hills Zimbabwe see Matobo Hills
Matos r. Bol. 200 D3
Matosinhos Port. 54 C3
Matou China see Pingguo
Mato Verde Brazil 207 K2
Matozinhos Brazil 207 I6
Mátra mts Hungary 49 Q8
Maţraḩ Oman 105 G3
Matrai park Hungary 49 R8
Matrei in Osttirol Austria 49 J9
Matroosberg S. Africa 132 D10
Matroosberg mt. S. Africa 132 D10
Matrooster S. Africa 133 K2
Maţrūḩ governorate Egypt 108 A8
Matsalu riiklik looduskaitseala nature res. Estonia 42 E3
Matsap S. Africa 132 G5
Matsesta Rus. Fed. 107 D2
Matsitama Botswana 131 E4
Matsudo Japan 91 F7
Matsue Japan 91 C7
Matsumae Japan 90 G4
Matsumoto Japan 91 E6
Matsusaka Japan 91 E7
Matsu Tao i. Taiwan 87 G3
Matsuura Japan 91 A8
Matsuyama Japan 91 C8
Matsuzaki Japan 91 F7

Mattagami r. Canada 168 D3
Mattamuskeet, Lake U.S.A. 174 E5
Mattawa Canada 168 E4
Matterhorn mt. Italy/Switz. 51 N7
Matterhorn mt. U.S.A. 180 D4
Mattersburg Austria 49 N8
Matthew atoll Kiribati see Marakei
Matthews U.S.A. 174 D5
Matthews Peak Kenya 128 C4
Matthews Ridge Guyana 199 F3
Matthew Town Bahamas 187 E2
Maţţī, Sabkhat salt pan Saudi Arabia 105 F3
Mattituck U.S.A. 177 M5
Mattmar Sweden 44 K3
Mattō Japan 91 E6
Mattoon U.S.A. 174 B4
Måttsund Sweden 44 M2
Matturai Sri Lanka see Matara
Matu Sarawak Malaysia 77 E2
Matua, Ostrov i. Rus. Fed. 81 Q3
Matucana Peru 200 A2
Matugama Sri Lanka 94 D5
Matuku i. Fiji 145 G3
Matumbo Angola 127 C8
Matun Afgh. see Khowst
Maturín Venez. 199 F2
Maturuca Brazil 199 F3
Matusadona National Park Zimbabwe 131 F3
Matutuang i. Indon. 75 C1
Matveyev, Ostrov i. Rus. Fed. 40 K1
Matveyevka Rus. Fed. 102 C1
Matwabeng S. Africa 133 L5
Matxitxako, Cabo c. Spain 55 I1
Maty Island P.N.G. see Wuvulu Island
Matyrskiy Rus. Fed. 43 U9
Mau Madhya Pradesh India 96 C4
Mau Uttar Pradesh India 97 D4
Mau Uttar Pradesh India 97 D4
Maúa Moz. 131 H2
Mau Aimma India 97 D4
Maubermé, Pic de mt. France/Spain 55 L2
Maubeuge France 51 J2
Maubin Myanmar 78 A4
Ma-ubin Myanmar 78 B2
Maubourguet France 50 G9
Mauchsberg S. Africa 133 O2
Maudaha India 96 D4
Maude Australia 147 E3
Mau-é-ele Moz. see Marão
Maués Brazil 199 G5
Maués r. Brazil 199 G5
Mauganj India 97 D4
Maug Islands N. Mariana Is 73 K2
Mauguio France 51 K9
Maui i. U.S.A. 181 [inset] Z1
Maukkadaw Myanmar 78 A3
Maule admin. reg. Chile 204 B4
Maule r. Chile 204 B4
Mauléon France 50 F6
Mauléon-Licharre France 50 F9
Maullín Chile 205 B6
Maulvi Bazar Bangl. 97 F4
also spelt Moulavibazar
Maumaupaki hill N.Z. 152 J5
Maumee U.S.A. 176 B4
Maumee r. U.S.A. 176 B4
Maumee Bay U.S.A. 176 B4
Maumere Indon. 75 B5
Maun Botswana 130 D3
Mauna Kea vol. U.S.A. 181 [inset] Z2
Mauna Loa vol. U.S.A. 181 [inset] Z2
Maun Game Sanctuary nature res. Botswana 130 D3
Maungatainiwha mt. N.Z. 152 K6
Maungatapere N.Z. 152 I3
Maungaturoto N.Z. 152 I4
Maungdaw Myanmar 78 A3
Maungmagan Islands Myanmar 79 B5
Maungmagon Myanmar 79 B5
Maupin U.S.A. 180 B3
Mau Rampur India 96 C4
Maurawan India 96 D4
Maurepas, Lake U.S.A. 175 B6
Maures, Massif des hills France 51 M9
Mauri r. Bol. 200 C4
Mauriac France 51 I7
Maurice country Indian Ocean see Mauritius
Maurice, Lake salt flat Australia 146 A2
▶Mauritania country Africa 122 B6
spelt Al Mūrītānīyah in Arabic or Mauritanie in French
world [countries] 10–11
africa [countries] 114–117
Mauritanie country Africa see Mauritania
▶Mauritius country Indian Ocean 218 K7
also known as Maurice
africa [countries] 114–117
Mauro, Monte mt. Italy 56 G7
Mauron France 50 D4
Mauros mt. Spain 54 D3
Maurs France 51 I8
Mauston U.S.A. 172 C7
Mauvezin France 50 G9
Mauzé-sur-le-Mignon France 50 F6
Mava Dem. Rep. Congo 126 E4
Mavaca r. Venez. 199 E4
Mavago Moz. 129 C8
Mavasjaure l. Sweden 44 L2
Mavengue Angola 127 C9
Mavinga Angola 127 D8
Mavisdale U.S.A. 176 C8
Mavita Moz. 131 G3
Mavra i. Greece 59 H12
Mavrothalassa Greece 58 E8
Mavrovo nat. park Macedonia 58 B7
Mavume Moz. 131 G4
Mavuya S. Africa 133 L8
Mawa, Bukit mt. Indon. 77 F2
Ma Wan i. Hong Kong China 87 [inset]
Māwān, Khashm hill Saudi Arabia 105 D3
Mawana India 96 C3
Mawanga Dem. Rep. Congo 127 C6
Mawasangka Indon. 75 B4
Mawdaung Pass Myanmar/Thai. 79 B6
Mawei China 87 F3
Mawhai Point N.Z. 152 M6
Mawheraiti N.Z. 153 F10
Māwheranui r. N.Z. see Grey
Māwiyah Yemen 104 D5
Mawjib, Wādī al r. Jordan 108 G6
also known as Arnon
Mawkhi Myanmar 78 B4
Mawkmai Myanmar 78 B3
Mawlaik Myanmar 78 A3
also known as Upper Chindwin
Mawlamyaing Myanmar see Moulmein
Mawlamyine Myanmar see Moulmein
Mawphlang India 97 F4
Mawqaq Saudi Arabia 104 C2
Mawshij Yemen 104 C5
Mawson research station Antarctica 223 E2
Mawson Coast Antarctica 223 E2
Mawson Escarpment Antarctica 223 E2
Mawson Peninsula Antarctica 223 K2
Maw Taung mt. Myanmar 79 B6
Mawza Yemen 104 C5
Maxaas Somalia 128 E3
Maxán Arg. 204 D3
Maxcanú Mex. 185 H4
Maxhamish Lake Canada 166 F3
Maxia, Punta mt. Sardegna Italy 57 A9
Măxineni Romania 58 I3
Maxixe Moz. 131 G4
Maxmo Fin. 44 M3
Maxwell N.Z. 152 I7
Maxwelton Australia 149 D4
Maya Chad 126 C3
Maya i. Indon. 77 E3
Maya r. Rus. Fed. 39 N3
Mayaguana i. Bahamas 187 E2
Mayaguana Passage Bahamas 187 E2

Mayagüez Puerto Rico 187 G3
Mayahi Niger 125 G3
Mayak Rus. Fed. 102 C2
Mayakovskogo mt. Tajik. 101 G2
also known as Mayakovskogo, Pik
Mayakovskogo, Pik mt. Tajik. see Mayakovskogo
Mayakum Kazakh. 103 G4
also spelt Mayaqum
Mayala Dem. Rep. Congo 127 C6
Mayama Congo 126 B5
Mayamba Dem. Rep. Congo 126 C6
Mayamey Iran 100 C2
Maya Mountains Belize/Guat. 185 H5
Mayan China see Mayanhe
Mayang China 87 D3
also known as Gaocun
Mayanhe China 86 C1
formerly known as Mayan
Mayaqum Kazakh. see Mayakum
Mayari Cuba 186 E2
Maya-san mt. Japan 90 F5
Maybeury U.S.A. 176 D8
Maybole U.K. 46 H8
Maych'ew Eth. 128 C1
Maydā Shahr Afgh. 101 G3
Maydh Somalia 128 E2
Maydos Turkey see Eceabat
Mayen Germany 48 E5
Mayenne France 50 F4
Mayenne r. France 50 F5
Mayer U.S.A. 183 L7
Mayêr Kangri mt. China 89 D5
Mayersville U.S.A. 175 B5
Mayerthorpe Canada 167 H4
Mayet France 50 G5
Mayfa'ah Yemen 105 D5
Mayfield N.Z. 153 F11
Mayfield KY U.S.A. 174 B4
Mayfield UT U.S.A. 183 M2
Mayhan Mongolia 84 D2
Mayi r. China 82 C3
Maykain Kazakh. 103 H2
also spelt Mayqayyng
Maykamys Kazakh. 103 I3
Maykhura Tajik. 101 G2
Maykop Rus. Fed. 41 G7
Mayluu-Suu Kyrg. 103 H4
formerly known as Mayly-Say
Mayly-Say Kyrg. see Mayluu-Suu
Maymak Kazakh. 103 G4
Maymyo Myanmar 78 B3
Mayna Rus. Fed. 80 E2
Mayna Rus. Fed. 41 H5
Maynardville U.S.A. 174 D4
Mayne watercourse Australia 149 D4
Mayni India 94 B2
Maynooth Canada 173 P5
Mayo Canada 166 C2
formerly known as Mayo Landing
Mayo r. Mex. 181 E8
Mayo r. Peru 198 B6
Mayo U.S.A. 175 D6
Mayo Alim Cameroon 125 I4
Mayo-Belwa Nigeria 125 I4
Mayo Darlé Cameroon 125 H5
Mayo-Kébbi pref. Chad 126 B2
Mayoko Congo 126 B5
Mayo Lake Canada 166 C2
Mayo Landing Canada see Mayo
Mayo Lara Cent. Afr. Rep. 126 B3
Mayon vol. Phil. 74 B3
Mayor, Puig mt. Spain see Major, Puig
Mayor Buratovich Arg. 204 E5
Mayor Island N.Z. 152 K5
Mayor Pablo Lagerenza Para. 201 E4

▶Mayotte terr. Africa 129 E8
French Territorial Collectivity.
africa [countries] 114–117

May Pen Jamaica 186 D3
Mayqayyng Kazakh. see Maykain
Mayraira Point Phil. 74 B2
Maysah, Tall al mt. Jordan 108 G6
Maysān governorate Iraq 107 F5
Mayskiy Amurskaya Oblast' Rus. Fed. 82 C1
Mayskiy Kabardino-Balkarskaya Respublika Rus. Fed. 41 H8
Mayskiy Permskaya Oblast' Rus. Fed. 40 J4
Mayskiy, Khrebet mt. Rus. Fed. 82 D1
Mayskoye Kazakh. 103 I2
Mays Landing U.S.A. 177 K6
Mayson Lake Canada 167 J3
Maysville KY U.S.A. 176 B7
Maysville MO U.S.A. 178 D4
Maytag China see Dushanzi
Mayu i. Indon. 75 C2
Mayu r. Myanmar 78 A3
Mayumba Gabon 126 A5
Mayum La pass China 89 C6
Mayuram India 94 C4
Mayville MI U.S.A. 173 J7
Mayville ND U.S.A. 178 C2
Maywood U.S.A. 178 B3
Mayya Rus. Fed. 39 N3
Maza Arg. 204 E5
Maza Rus. Fed. 43 R2
Mazabuka Zambia 127 E8
Mazaca Turkey see Kayseri
Mazagan Morocco see El Jadida
Mazagão Brazil 199 I5
Ma'zah, Jabal hill Syria 109 L2
Maza Jugla r. Latvia 42 F5
Mazamet France 51 I9
Mazán Peru 198 C5
Māzandarān prov. Iran 100 B2
Mazao Dem. Rep. Congo 127 D7
Mazapil Mex. 185 E3
Mazar China 89 B4
Mazar, Koh-i- mt. Afgh. 101 F3
Mazāra Oman 105 G3
Mazara, Val di valley Sicilia Italy 57 E11
Mazara del Vallo Sicilia Italy 57 E11
Mazār-e Sharīf Afgh. 101 F2
Mazarrón Spain 55 J7
Mazartag mt. China 88 B4
Mazaruni r. Guyana 199 G3
Mazatán Mex. 184 C2
Mazatenango Guat. 185 H6
Mazatlán Mex. 184 D4
Mazatzal Peak U.S.A. 183 M7
Mazāvī watercourse Iran 100 D5
Mazeepa Bay S. Africa 133 M9
Mažeikiai Lith. 42 D5
Mazelet well Niger 125 H2
Mazı Turkey 59 I11
Mazie U.S.A. 176 C7
Mazirbe Latvia 42 D4
Mazocahui Mex. 184 C2
Mazocruz Peru 200 C4
Mazomanie U.S.A. 172 D7
Mazomeno Dem. Rep. Congo 126 E6
Mazomora Tanz. 129 C6
Mazong Shan mt. China 84 C3
Mazong Shan mts China 84 B3
Mazowe r. Zimbabwe 131 G3
Mazrub well Sudan 121 F6
Mazsalaca Latvia 42 G4
Māzū Iran 100 B3
Mazunga Zimbabwe 131 F4
Mazurskie, Pojezierze reg. Poland 49 R2
Mazyr Belarus 43 K9
also spelt Mozyr'
Mazzouna Tunisia 123 H2
Mba Cameroon 125 H5

▶Mbabane Swaziland 133 P3
Capital of Swaziland.

Mbacké Senegal 124 B3
Mbaéré r. Cent. Afr. Rep. 126 C4

Mbagne Mauritania 124 B2
Mbahiakro Côte d'Ivoire 124 D5
Mbaïki Cent. Afr. Rep. 126 C4
Mbakaou Cameroon 125 I5
Mbakaou, Lac de l. Cameroon 125 I5
Mbala Zambia 127 F7
formerly known as Abercorn
Mbalabala Zimbabwe 131 F4
formerly spelt Balla Balla
Mbalam Cameroon 125 I6
Mbale Uganda 128 B4
Mbalmayo Cameroon 125 H6
Mbam r. Cameroon 125 H5
Mbamba Bay Tanz. 129 B7
Mbandaka Dem. Rep. Congo 126 C5
formerly known as Coquilhatville
Mbandjok Cameroon 125 H5
Mbang Cameroon 125 I6
Mbanga Cameroon 125 H5
M'banza Congo Angola 127 B6
formerly known as São Salvador or São Salvador do Congo
Mbanza-Ngungu Dem. Rep. Congo 127 B6
formerly known as Songololo or Thysville
Mbar Senegal 124 B3
Mbarangandu Tanz. 129 C7
Mbarara Uganda 128 A5
Mbari r. Cent. Afr. Rep. 126 D3
Mbarika Mountains Tanz. 129 C7
Mbaswana S. Africa 133 Q4
Mbata Cent. Afr. Rep. 126 C4
Mbati Zambia 127 F7
Mbé Cameroon 125 I5
Mbé Congo 126 B5
Mbemba Moz. 129 B8
Mbembesi Zimbabwe 131 F3
Mbemkuru r. Tanz. 129 C7
Mbéni Comoros 129 D7
Mbengué Côte d'Ivoire 124 D4
Mberengwa Zimbabwe 131 F4
formerly known as Belingwe
Mbereshi Zambia 127 F7
Mbeya Tanz. 129 B7
Mbeya admin. reg. Tanz. 129 B7
Mbi r. Cameroon 125 I5
Mbi r. Cent. Afr. Rep. 126 C3
Mbigou Gabon 126 A5
Mbinda Congo 126 B5
Mbinga Tanz. 129 B7
Mbini Equat. Guinea 125 H6
Mbini r. Equat. Guinea 125 H6
formerly known as Benito
Mbizi Zimbabwe 131 F4
Mbizi Mountains Tanz. 129 A7
Mbo Cent. Afr. Rep. 126 C2
Mboki Cent. Afr. Rep. 126 E3
Mbomo Congo 126 B4
Mbomou pref. Cent. Afr. Rep. 126 D3
Mbomou r. Cent. Afr. Rep./Dem. Rep. Congo 126 D3
Mbon Congo 126 B5
Mbouda Cameroon 125 H5
Mbour Senegal 124 A3
Mbout Mauritania 124 B2
Mbowela Zambia 127 E8
Mbozi Tanz. 129 B7
Mbrès Cent. Afr. Rep. 126 C3
Mbrostar Albania 58 A8
Mbuji-Mayi Dem. Rep. Congo 127 D6
Mbulu Tanz. 129 B5
Mbuluzi r. Swaziland 133 Q3
Mburucuyá Arg. 204 F3
Mbutini Hills Swaziland 133 P3
Mbuyuni Tanz. 129 C6
Mbwewe Tanz. 129 C6
McAdam Canada 169 H4
McAdoo U.S.A. 177 J5
McAlester U.S.A. 179 D5
McAllen U.S.A. 179 C7
McAllister U.S.A. 172 F5
McArthur r. Australia 148 C2
McArthur U.S.A. 176 C6
McArthur Mills Canada 173 P5
McArthur Wildlife Sanctuary nature res. Canada 166 C2
McBain U.S.A. 173 H6
McBride Canada 166 F4
McCall U.S.A. 180 C3
McCamey U.S.A. 179 B6
McCammon U.S.A. 180 D4
McCaslin Mountain hill U.S.A. 172 E5
McCauley Island Canada 166 D4
McClintock, Mount Antarctica 223 K1
McClintock Channel Canada 165 I2
McClintock Range hills Australia 150 D3
McClure, Lake U.S.A. 182 D4
McClure Strait Canada 165 H2
McClusky U.S.A. 178 B2
McComb MS U.S.A. 175 B6
McComb OH U.S.A. 176 B4
McConaughy, Lake U.S.A. 178 B3
McConnellsburg U.S.A. 176 H6
McConnelsville U.S.A. 176 D6
McCook U.S.A. 178 B3
McCormick U.S.A. 175 D5
McCoy U.S.A. 176 E8
McCrea r. Canada 167 H2
McCreary Canada 167 L5
McCullough Range mts U.S.A. 183 I6
McCullum, Mount Canada 166 B1
McCutchenville U.S.A. 176 B5
McDame Canada 166 D3
McDonald Islands Indian Ocean 219 L9
McDonald Peak U.S.A. 180 D3
McDouall Range hills Australia 148 B3
McDowell Peak U.S.A. 183 M8
McFarland CA U.S.A. 182 E6
McFarland WI U.S.A. 172 D7
McFarlane r. Canada 167 J3
McFarlane, Mount N.Z. 153 D11
McGill U.S.A. 183 J2
McGivney Canada 169 H4
McGrath AK U.S.A. 164 D3
McGrath MN U.S.A. 174 A2
McGregor r. Canada 166 F4
McGregor, Lake Canada 167 H5
McGregor Bay Canada 173 L4
McGregor Range hills Australia 147 D1
McGuire, Mount U.S.A. 180 D3
Mchinga Tanz. 129 C7
Mchinji Malawi 129 B8
formerly known as Fort Manning
McIlwraith Range hills Australia 149 D2
McInnes Lake Canada 167 M4
McIntosh U.S.A. 178 B2
McKay Range hills Australia 150 C4
McKean i. Kiribati 145 H2
formerly known as Drummond Island
McKee U.S.A. 176 A8
McKeesport U.S.A. 176 F5
McKees Rocks U.S.A. 176 E5
McKenney U.S.A. 176 H9
McKenzie U.S.A. 174 B4
McKenzie r. U.S.A. 180 B3
McKinlay Australia 149 D4
McKinlay r. Australia 149 D4

▶McKinley, Mount U.S.A. 164 D3
Highest mountain in North America.
northamerica [landscapes] 156–157

McKinney U.S.A. 179 C5
McKittrick U.S.A. 182 E6
McLeansboro U.S.A. 174 B4
McLennan Canada 167 G4
McLeod r. Canada 167 H4
McLeod Bay Canada 167 I2
McLeod Lake Canada 166 F4
McLeods Island Myanmar 79 B6
McMinns Creek watercourse Australia 148 B5

McMinnville OR U.S.A. 180 B3
McMinnville TN U.S.A. 174 C5
McMurdo research station Antarctica 223 L1
McMurdo Sound b. Antarctica 223 L1
McNary U.S.A. 183 O7
McNaughton U.S.A. 172 D5
McNaughton Lake Canada see Kinbasket Lake
McPhadyen r. Canada 169 H2
McPherson U.S.A. 178 C4
McPherson Range mts Australia 147 G2
McQuesten r. Canada 166 B2
McRae U.S.A. 175 D5
McTavish Arm b. Canada 167 G1
McVeytown U.S.A. 176 H5
McVicar Arm b. Canada 166 F1
Mda r. Rus. Fed. 43 N3
Mdantsane S. Africa 133 L9
M'Daourouch Alg. 123 G1
Mdiq Morocco 54 F9
formerly known as Rincon
Mead, Lake resr U.S.A. 183 J5
Meade U.S.A. 178 B4
Meade r. U.S.A. 164 D2
Meadow Australia 151 A5
Meadow U.S.A. 183 L3
Meadowbank r. Canada 167 L1
Meadow Bridge U.S.A. 176 E8
Meadow Lake Canada 167 I4
Meadow Lake Provincial Park Canada 167 I4
Meadow Valley Wash r. U.S.A. 183 J5
Meadowview U.S.A. 176 D9
Meadville MS U.S.A. 175 B6
Meadville PA U.S.A. 176 E4
Meaford Canada 173 M6
Meaken-dake vol. Japan 90 I3
Mealhada Port. 54 C4
Mealy Mountains Canada 169 J2
Meandarra Australia 147 F1
Meander River Canada 167 G3
Meares i. Indon. 75 C1
Mearim r. Brazil 202 C2
Meaux France 51 I4
Mebridege r. Angola 127 B6
Mebtoun, Oued el watercourse Alg. 55 K9
Mebu India 97 G3
Mebulu, Tanjung pt Indon. 77 F5
Mecanhelas Moz. 131 G2
Mecca Saudi Arabia 104 B3
also spelt Makkah
Mecca U.S.A. 181 C6
Mechanic Falls U.S.A. 177 O1
Mechanicsburg OH U.S.A. 176 B5
Mechanicsburg VA U.S.A. 176 E8
Mechanicsville U.S.A. 176 H8
Mechanicville U.S.A. 177 L3
Mechelen Belgium 51 K1
also known as Malines
Mecherchar i. Palau see Eil Malk
Mecheria Alg. 123 E2
Mechernich Germany 48 D5
Mechiméré Chad 120 B6
Mechka r. Bulg. 58 G6
Mecidiye Edirne Turkey 58 H8
Mecidiye Manisa Turkey 59 I10
Mecitözü Turkey 106 C2
Meckenheim Germany 48 E5
Mecklenburger Bucht b. Germany 48 I1
Mecklenburg-Vorpommern land Germany 49 J2
English form Mecklenburg - West Pomerania
Mecklenburg - West Pomerania land Germany see Mecklenburg-Vorpommern
Meconta Moz. 131 H2
Mecubúri Moz. 131 H2
Mecubúri r. Moz. 131 I2
Mecúfi Moz. 131 I2
Mecula Moz. 129 C8
Meda Port. 54 D4
Meda r. Australia 150 C3
Meda mt. Spain 54 D2
Medak India 94 C2
Medan Indon. 76 B2
Medang i. Indon. 77 G5
Médanos Buenos Aires Arg. 204 E5
Médanos Entre Ríos Arg. 204 F4
Medanosa, Punta pt Arg. 205 D8
Médanos de Coro, Parque Nacional nat. park Venez. 198 D2
Medarysville U.S.A. 172 G9
Medchal India 94 C2
Médéa Alg. 123 F1
also known as Lemdiyya
Medeiros Neto Brazil 207 M4
Medellín Col. 198 C3
Medenine Tunisia 123 H2
Meder Eritrea 104 C5
Mederdra Mauritania 124 B2
Medford NY U.S.A. 177 M5
Medford OK U.S.A. 178 C4
Medford OR U.S.A. 180 B4
Medford WI U.S.A. 172 C5
Medgidia Romania 58 J4
Mediadilet well Mali 125 E2
Media Luna Arg. 204 D4
Mediapolis U.S.A. 172 B9
Mediaş Romania 58 F2
Medicine Bow r. U.S.A. 180 F4
Medicine Bow Mountains U.S.A. 180 F4
Medicine Bow Peak U.S.A. 180 F4
Medicine Hat Canada 167 I5
Medicine Lake U.S.A. 180 F2
Medicine Lodge U.S.A. 178 C4
Medina Brazil 202 D6
Medina Col. 198 C3
Medina Saudi Arabia 104 B2
also spelt Al Madinah
Medina NY U.S.A. 176 G2
Medina OH U.S.A. 176 D4
Medina r. U.S.A. 179 C6
Medinaceli Spain 55 I3
Medina del Campo Spain 54 G3
Medina de Pomar Spain 55 H2
Medina de Rioseco Spain 54 F3
Medina Gounas Senegal 124 B3
Medina-Sidonia Spain 54 F8
Medinet 15 Mayo Egypt 108 C8
English form 15th of May City
Medinet el Amal Egypt 108 C8
Medinet el Obour Egypt 108 C7
Medinet el Sadat Egypt 108 B7
Medinipur India 97 E5
formerly spelt Midnapore
Mediolanum Italy see Milan
Mediterranean Sea 53 C4
Medje Dem. Rep. Congo 126 E4
Medjedel Alg. 55 O9
Mednogorsk Rus. Fed. 102 D2
Mednoye Rus. Fed. 43 Q5
Mednyy, Ostrov i. Rus. Fed. 220 F2
Médoc reg. France 50 E7
Mêdog China 97 G3
also known as Dongbo
Medora U.S.A. 178 B2
Médouneu Gabon 126 A4
Medstead Canada 167 I4
Medu Kongkar China see Maizhokunggar
Meduro atoll Marshall Is see Majuro
Medveđa Srbija Yugo. 58 C6
Medvedevo Rus. Fed. 40 H4
Medveditsa r. Rus. Fed. 41 G6
Medvednica mts Croatia 56 H3
Medvedok Rus. Fed. 40 I4
Medvėgalio kalnis hill Lith. 42 D6
Medvezh'i, Ostrova is Rus. Fed. 39 Q2
Medvezh'yegorsk Rus. Fed. 40 E3
Medyn' Rus. Fed. 43 Q7
Medzilaborce Slovakia 49 S6
Meeberrie Australia 151 A5
Meekatharra Australia 151 B5

Meeker CO U.S.A. 180 F4
Meeker OH U.S.A. 176 B5
Meeks Bay U.S.A. 182 D2
Meeladeen Somalia 128 F2
Meelberg mt. S. Africa 132 I9
Meelpaeg Reservoir Canada 169 J3
Meerane Germany 49 J5
Meerapalu Estonia 42 I3
Meerut India 96 C3
Mefta Sidi Boubekeur Alg. 55 K9
Mēga Eth. 128 C3
Mega i. Indon. 76 C3
Mega Escarpment Eth./Kenya 128 C3
Megali Panagia Greece 59 E8
Megalo Eth. 128 D3
Megalo Chorio Greece 59 I12
Megalopoli Greece 59 D11
Megalos Anthropofas i. Greece 59 H11
Meganisi i. Greece 59 B10
Mégantic, Lac l. Canada 169 G4
Megara Greece 59 E10
Megezez mt. Eth. 128 C2

▶Meghalaya state India 97 F4
Highest mean annual rainfall in the world.
world [climate and weather] 16–17

Meghasani mt. India 97 E5
Meghna r. Bangl. 97 F5
Meghri Armenia 107 F3
also spelt Megri
Megion Rus. Fed. 38 H3
Mégiscane, Lac l. Canada 173 R2
Megisti i. Greece 59 K12
formerly known as Kastellorizon
Megletsy Rus. Fed. 43 P3
Meglino, Ozero l. Rus. Fed. 43 Q3
Megra Rus. Fed. 43 Q1
Megrega Rus. Fed. 43 O1
Megri Armenia see Meghri
Megrozero Rus. Fed. 43 O1
Mehadica Romania 58 D3
Mehamn Norway 44 N1
Mehar Pak. 101 F5
Meharry, Mount Australia 150 B4
Mehdia Tunisia see Mahdia
Mehedeby Sweden 45 L3
Mehekar India 94 C1
Meherpur Bangl. 97 F5
Meherrin U.S.A. 176 G8
Meherrin r. U.S.A. 176 I9
Mehidpur India 96 B5
Mehlville U.S.A. 174 B4
Mehmadabad India 96 B5
Mehndawal India 97 D4
Mehrābān Iran 100 A2
Mehrān Iran 100 C5
Mehrān watercourse Iran 100 C5
Mehrān Iraq 107 F4
Mehtar Lām Afgh. 101 G3
Mehun-sur-Yèvre France 51 I5
Meia Ponte r. Brazil 206 D5
Meicheng China see Qianshan
Meicheng China see Minqing
Meichengzhen China 87 D2
Meidougou Cameroon 125 I5
Meiganga Cameroon 125 I5
Meighen Island Canada 165 J2
Meigu China 86 B2
also known as Bapu
Meihekou China 82 B4
formerly known as Hailong
Meijiang China see Ningdu
Mei Jiang r. China 87 E3
Meikeng China 87 E3
Meikle r. Canada 166 G3
Meiktila Myanmar 78 A3
Meilen Switz. 51 O5
Meilin China see Ganxian
Meilleur r. Canada 166 E2
Meilü China see Wuchuan
Meiningen Germany 48 H5
Meira Spain 54 D1
Meiringen Switz. 51 O6
Meiringspoort pass S. Africa 132 G10
Meishan China see Jinzhai
Meishan China 86 B2
also known as Dongpo
Meißen Germany 49 K4
Meißner-Kaufunger Wald, Naturpark nature res. Germany 48 G4
Meister r. Canada 166 D2
Meitan China 87 C3
also known as Yiquan
Meitingen Germany 48 H7
Meixi China 82 C3
Meixian China see Meizhou
Meixian China 87 C1
Meixing China see Xiaojin
Meizhou China 87 F3
formerly known as Meixian
Mej r. India 96 C4
Méjan, Sommet de mt. France 51 K8
Mejaouda well Mauritania 122 D5
Mejez el Bab Tunisia 57 B12
Mejicana mt. Arg. 204 D3
Mejillones Chile 200 C5
Mejillones del Sur, Bahía de b. Chile 200 C5
Mekadio well Sudan 121 G5
Mékambo Gabon 126 B4
Mek'elē Eth. 128 C1
Mekhbaza Rus. Fed. 43 O1
Mékhé Senegal 124 A3
Mekhtar Pak. 101 G4
Mekkaw Nigeria 125 F5
Meknès Morocco 122 D2
Mekong r. Asia 78 D4
also known as Lancang Jiang (China) or Mènam Khong (Laos/Thailand)
Mekong, Mouths of the Vietnam 79 D6
Méla, Mont hill Cent. Afr. Rep. 126 D2
Melaka Malaysia 76 C2
formerly spelt Malacca
Melaka state Malaysia 76 C2
formerly spelt Malacca
Melalo, Tanjung pt Indon. 77 D3
Melanesia is Oceania 220 E6
Melar Iceland 44 [inset] B2
Melawi r. Indon. 77 E2

▶Melbourne Australia 147 E4
State capital of Victoria. 2nd most populous city in Oceania.
world [cities] 24–25

Melbourne AR U.S.A. 174 B4
Melbourne FL U.S.A. 175 D6
Melbu Norway 44 K1
Melchor, Isla i. Chile 205 B7
Melchor de Mencos Guat. 185 H5
Melchor Ocampo Mex. 185 E3
Meldal Norway 44 J3
Meldola Italy 56 E4
Meldorf Germany 48 G1
Meldrum U.S.A. 176 B9
Meldrum Bay Canada 168 D4
Mele, Capo c. Italy 56 A5
Melech r. Rus. Fed. 43 R4
Melekess Rus. Fed. see Dimitrovgrad
Melenci Vojvodina, Srbija Yugo. 58 B3
Melendiz Dağı mt. Turkey 106 C3
Melenki Rus. Fed. 40 G5
Melet Turkey see Mesudiye
Meleuz Rus. Fed. 102 C1
Mélèzes, Rivière aux r. Canada 169 G1
Melfa U.S.A. 177 J8
Mélfi Chad 126 C2
Melfi Italy 56 H8
Melfort Canada 167 J4
Melgaço Brazil 202 B2
Melgar de Fernamental Spain 54 G2

index

M

Mosopo Botswana 133 J1
Mosor mts Croatia 56 I5
Mosquera Col. 198 B4
Mosquero U.S.A. 181 F6
Mosquitia reg. Hond. 186 C4
Mosquito Creek Lake U.S.A. 176 E4
Mosquito Lake Canada 167 K2
Mosquitos, Costa de coastal area Nicaragua 186 C4 also spelt Miskitos, Costa de
Moss Norway 45 J4
Mossaka Congo 126 C5
Mossâmedes Angola see Namibe
Mossâmedes Brazil 206 C3
Mossburn N.Z. 153 C13
Mosselbaai S. Africa see Mossel Bay
Mossel Bay S. Africa 132 G11 also spelt Mosselbaai
Mossel Bay b. S. Africa 132 G11
Mossendjo Congo 126 B5
Mossgiel Australia 147 E3
Mossman Australia 149 E3
Mossoró Brazil 202 E3
Moss Vale Australia 147 F3
Mossy r. Canada 167 K4
Most Bulg. 58 G7
Most Czech Rep. 49 K5
Mostaganem Alg. 123 F2 also spelt Mestghanem
Mostar Bos.-Herz. 56 J5
Mostardas Brazil 204 H3
Moşteni Romania 58 G4
Mostiştea r. Romania 58 H4
Móstoles Spain 54 H4
Mostoos Hills Canada 167 I4
Mostovskoy Rus. Fed. 41 G7
Mosty Belarus see Masty
Mosul Iraq 107 E3 also spelt Al Mawşil
Mosvatn Austfjell park Norway 45 J4
Mosvatnet l. Norway 45 J4
Mosvik Norway 44 J3
Mot'a Eth. 128 C2
Motaba r. Congo 126 C4
Mota del Cuervo Spain 55 I5
Motagua r. Guat. 185 H6
Motal' Belarus 42 G9
Motala Sweden 45 K4
Mota Lava i. Vanuatu 145 F3 also known as Saddle Island or Valua
Motaze Moz. 131 G5
Moţca Romania 58 H1
Motenge-Boma Dem. Rep. Congo 126 C4
Moteng Pass Lesotho 133 M5
Moth India 96 C4
Motherwell U.K. 46 I8
Mothibistat S. Africa 132 H4
Mothonaio, Akra pt Greece 59 E12
Motihari India 97 E4
Motilla hill Spain 54 F6
Motilla del Palancar Spain 55 J5
Motiti Island N.Z. 152 K5
Motian Ling hill China 83 A4
Motloutse r. Botswana 131 F4
Motokwe Botswana 130 D5
Motovskiy Zaliv sea chan. Rus. Fed. 44 P1
Motoyoshi Japan 90 G5
Motozintla Mex. 185 G6
Motril Spain 55 H8
Motru Romania 58 D4
Motru r. Romania 58 E4
Motshikiri S. Africa 133 L2
Mott U.S.A. 178 B2
Motueka N.Z. 152 H9
Motuhora Island N.Z. 152 K5 also known as Whale Island; formerly known as Moutohora Island
Motu Ihupuku i. N.Z. see Campbell Island
Motukarara N.Z. 153 G11
Motul Mex. 185 H4
Motupipi N.Z. 152 G8
Mouali Gbangba Congo 126 C4
Mouan, Nam r. Laos 78 D4
Mouaskar Alg. see Mascara
Moubray Bay Antarctica 223 L2
Mouchalagane r. Canada 169 G3
Mouchet, Mont mt. France 51 J8
Mouchoir Bank sea feature Turks and Caicos Is 187 F2
Mouchoir Passage Turks and Caicos Is 187 F2
Mouding China 86 B3 also known as Gonghe
Moudjéria Mauritania 124 B2
Moudon Switz. 51 M6
Moudros Greece 59 G9
Mougri well Mauritania 124 B2
Mouhijärvi Fin. 45 M3
Mouhoun r. Africa 124 E4 see Black Volta
Mouila Gabon 126 A5
Moul well Niger 125 I3
Moulamein Australia 147 E3
Moulamein Creek r. Australia 147 D3 also known as Billabong Creek
Moulavibazar Bangl. see Maulvi Bazar
Moule Guadeloupe 187 H3
Moulèngui Binza Gabon 126 A5
Moulentâr well Mali 124 D2
Moulhoulé Djibouti 128 D1
Moulins France 51 J6
Moulins-Engilbert France 51 J6
Moulle de Jaut, Pic du mt. France 50 F9
Moulmein Myanmar 78 B4 also known as Mawlamyaing or Mawlamyine
Moulmeingyun Myanmar 78 A4
Moulouya, Oued r. Morocco 122 E2
Moulton U.S.A. 174 C5
Moulton, Mount Antarctica 222 P1
Moultonborough U.S.A. 177 N2
Moultrie U.S.A. 175 D6
Moultrie, Lake U.S.A. 175 E5
Mounana Gabon 126 B5
Mound City KS U.S.A. 178 D4
Mound City MO U.S.A. 178 D3
Mound City SD U.S.A. 178 B2
Moundou Chad 126 C2
Moundsville U.S.A. 176 E6
Mounta, Akra pt Greece 59 B10
Mount Abu India 96 B4
Mountainair U.S.A. 181 F6
Mountain Brook U.S.A. 175 C5
Mountain City U.S.A. 176 D9
Mountain Grove U.S.A. 178 D4
Mountain Home AR U.S.A. 179 D4
Mountain Home ID U.S.A. 180 D4
Mountain Home UT U.S.A. 183 N1
Mountain Iron U.S.A. 172 A3
Mountain Lake Park U.S.A. 176 F6
Mountain Pass U.S.A. 183 I6
Mountain View AR U.S.A. 179 D5
Mountain View CA U.S.A. 182 B4
Mountain View HI U.S.A. 181 [inset] Z2
Mountain Village U.S.A. 164 C3
Mountain Zebra National Park S. Africa 133 J9
Mount Airy MD U.S.A. 177 H6
Mount Airy NC U.S.A. 176 E9
Mount Anderson Aboriginal Reserve Australia 150 C3
Mount Arapiles-Tooan State Park nature res. Australia 146 D4
Mount Aspiring National Park N.Z. 153 C12
Mount Assiniboine Provincial Park Canada 167 H5
Mount Augustus Australia 150 B5
Mount Ayliff S. Africa 133 N7
Mount Ayr U.S.A. 178 D3
Mount Baldy U.S.A. 182 G7
Mount Barker S.A. Australia 146 C3
Mount Barker W.A. Australia 151 B7
Mount Barnett Australia 150 D3
Mount Barnett Aboriginal Reserve Australia 150 D3
Mount Beauty Australia 147 E4
Mount Bellew Rep. of Ireland 47 D10
Mount Bruce N.Z. 152 J8
Mount Brydges Canada 173 L8
Mount Buffalo National Park Australia 147 E4
Mount Carmel IL U.S.A. 174 C4
Mount Carmel TN U.S.A. 176 C9
Mount Carmel Junction U.S.A. 183 L4
Mount Carroll U.S.A. 174 B3
Mount Clere Australia 151 B5
Mount Cook N.Z. 153 E11 also known as Aoraki
Mount Cook National Park N.Z. 153 E11
Mount Coolon Australia 149 E4
Mount Currie Nature Reserve S. Africa 133 N7
Mount Darwin Zimbabwe 131 F3
Mount Denison Australia 148 B4
Mount Desert Island U.S.A. 177 Q1
Mount Eba Australia 146 B2
Mount Eccles National Park Australia 146 D4
Mount Edziza Provincial Park Canada 166 D3
Mount Etna U.S.A. 172 H10
Mount Field National Park Australia 147 E5
Mount Fletcher S. Africa 133 M7
Mount Forest Canada 168 D5
Mount Frankland National Park Australia 151 B7
Mount Frere S. Africa 133 M7 also known as Kwabhaca
Mount Gambier Australia 146 D4
Mount Garnet Australia 149 E3
Mount Hagen P.N.G. 73 J8
Mount Holly U.S.A. 177 K6
Mount Holly Springs U.S.A. 177 H5
Mount Hope N.S.W. Australia 147 E3
Mount Hope S.A. Australia 146 B3
Mount Hope U.S.A. 176 D8
Mount Horeb U.S.A. 172 D7
Mount House Australia 150 D3
Mount Howitt Australia 149 D5
Mount Hutt N.Z. 153 F11
Mount Ida U.S.A. 179 D5
Mount Isa Australia 148 C4
Mount Jackson U.S.A. 176 G7
Mount James Aboriginal Reserve Australia 151 B5
Mount Jewett U.S.A. 176 G4
Mount Kaputar National Park Australia 147 F2
Mount Keith Australia 151 C5
Mount Kenya National Park Kenya 128 C5
Mount Lebanon U.S.A. 176 E5
Mount Lofty Range mts Australia 146 C3
Mount MacDonald Canada 173 M3
Mount Magnet Australia 151 B6
Mount Manara Australia 147 D3
Mount Manning Nature Reserve Australia 151 B6
Mount Maunganui N.Z. 152 K5
Mount McKinley National Park U.S.A. see Denali National Park and Preserve
Mount Meadows Reservoir U.S.A. 182 D1
Mount Molloy Australia 149 E3
Mount Moorosi Lesotho 133 L7
Mount Morgan Australia 149 F4
Mount Morris IL U.S.A. 172 D8
Mount Morris MI U.S.A. 173 J7
Mount Morris NY U.S.A. 176 H3
Mount Nebo U.S.A. 176 E7
Mount Olivet U.S.A. 176 A7
Mount Orab U.S.A. 176 B6
Mount Pearl Canada 169 K4
Mount Perry Australia 149 F5
Mount Pierre Aboriginal Reserve Australia 150 D3
Mount Pleasant Canada 169 H4
Mount Pleasant IA U.S.A. 174 B3
Mount Pleasant MI U.S.A. 173 I7
Mount Pleasant PA U.S.A. 176 F5
Mount Pleasant SC U.S.A. 175 E5
Mount Pleasant TX U.S.A. 179 D5
Mount Pleasant UT U.S.A. 183 M2
Mount Rainier National Park U.S.A. 180 B3
Mount Remarkable National Park Australia 146 C3
Mount Revelstoke National Park Canada 166 G5
Mount Richmond Forest Park nature res. N.Z. 152 H9
Mount Robson Provincial Park Canada 166 G4
Mount Rogers National Recreation Area park U.S.A. 176 D9
Mount Rupert S. Africa 133 I5
Mount St Helens National Volcanic Monument nat. park U.S.A. 180 B3
Mount Sanford Australia 148 A3
Mount's Bay U.K. 47 G13
Mount Shasta U.S.A. 180 B4
Mount Somers N.Z. 153 F11
Mount Sterling IL U.S.A. 174 B4
Mount Sterling KY U.S.A. 176 B7
Mount Sterling OH U.S.A. 176 B6
Mount Stewart S. Africa 133 I10
Mount Storm U.S.A. 176 F6
Mount Surprise Australia 149 E3
Mount Upton U.S.A. 177 J3
Mount Vernon Australia 150 B5
Mount Vernon GA U.S.A. 175 D5
Mount Vernon IA U.S.A. 172 B9
Mount Vernon IL U.S.A. 174 B4
Mount Vernon IN U.S.A. 174 C4
Mount Vernon KY U.S.A. 176 A8
Mount Vernon MO U.S.A. 178 D4
Mount Vernon OH U.S.A. 176 C5
Mount Vernon TX U.S.A. 179 D5
Mount Vernon WA U.S.A. 180 B2
Mount Wedge Australia 148 B4
Mount Welcome Aboriginal Reserve Australia 150 B4
Mount William National Park Australia 147 F5
Mount Willoughby Australia 146 B1
Moura Australia 149 F5
Moura Brazil 199 F5
Moura r. Brazil 200 B1
Moura Port. 54 D6
Mourão Port. 54 D6
Mouraya Chad 126 D2
Mourdi, Dépression du depr. Chad 120 D5
Mourdiah Mali 124 D3
Mourenx France 50 F9
Mourne Mountains hills U.K. 47 F9
Mourre de Chanier mt. France 51 M9
Mourtzeflos, Akra pt Greece 59 G9
Mousa i. U.K. 46 K3
Mouscron Belgium 51 J2
Mousgougou Chad 126 C2
Mousie U.S.A. 176 C8
Moussafoyo Chad 126 C2
Moussoro Chad 120 C6
Moutamba Congo 126 B5
Mouth of Wilson U.S.A. 176 D9
Moutiers France 51 M7
Moutohora Island N.Z. see Motuhora Island
Moutong Indon. 75 B2
Moutourwa Cameroon 125 I4
Mouydir, Monts du plat. Alg. 123 F4
Mouyondzi Congo 126 B5
Mouzaki Greece 59 C9
Mouzarak Chad 120 B6
Mouzon France 51 L3
Movas Mex. 184 C2
Movila Miresii Romania 58 I3
Movileni Romania 58 F4
Mowanjum Aboriginal Reserve Australia 150 C3 also known as Oubling
Mowbullan, Mount Australia 149 F5
Mowchadz' Belarus 42 G8
Moxahala U.S.A. 176 C6
Moxey Town Bahamas 186 D1
Moxico prov. Angola 127 C8
Moy r. Rep. of Ireland 47 C9
Moyahua Mex. 185 E4
Moyale Eth. 128 C4
Moyamba Sierra Leone 124 B4
Moyen Atlas mts Morocco 122 D2 English form Middle Atlas
Moyen-Chari pref. Chad 126 C2
Moyen Congo country Africa see Congo
Moyeni Lesotho 133 L7 also known as Quthing
Moyenne-Guinée admin. reg. Guinea 124 B4
Moyen-Ogooué prov. Gabon 126 A5
Moynalyk Rus. Fed. 88 F1
Moynaq Uzbek. see Muynak
Moyo i. Indon. 77 G5
Moyo Uganda 128 A4
Moyobamba Peru 198 B6
Moyowosi r. Tanz. 129 A6
Moysalen mt. Norway 44 K1
Moyto Chad 120 C6
Moyu China 89 B4 formerly known as Karakax
Moyum waterhole Kenya 128 C4
Moyynkum Kazakh. 103 H3 formerly known as Furmanovka
Moyynkum, Peski des. Kazakh. 103 F3 also known as Moinkum
Moyynty Kazakh. 103 H3 formerly spelt Mointy
Mozambique country Africa 131 G4 spelt Moçambique in Portuguese; historically known as Portuguese East Africa africa [countries] 114–117
Mozambique Channel Africa 131 I4
Mozarlândia Brazil 206 C1
Mozdok Rus. Fed. 41 H8
Mozdūrān Iran 101 E2
Mozelle U.S.A. 176 B8
Mozhaysk Rus. Fed. 43 R6
Mozhga Rus. Fed. 40 J4
Mozhong China 86 A1
Mozo Myanmar 78 A3
Mozyr' Belarus see Mazyr
Mpal Senegal 124 A3 formerly spelt Pal
Mpanda Tanz. 129 A6
Mpandamatenga Botswana 131 E3
Mpande Zambia 127 F7
Mpé Congo 126 B5
Mpemvana S. Africa 133 O4
Mpessoba Mali 124 D3
Mpigi Uganda 128 B4
Mpika Zambia 127 F7
Mpoko r. Cent. Afr. Rep. 126 C3
Mpolweni S. Africa 133 O6
Mpongwe Zambia 127 F8
Mporokoso Zambia 127 F7
Mposa S. Africa 133 Q5
Mpouya Congo 126 C5
Mpui Tanz. 129 A7
Mpulungu Zambia 127 F7
Mpumalanga S. Africa 133 O6
Mpumalanga prov. S. Africa 133 N3 formerly known as Eastern Transvaal
Mpwapwa Tanz. 129 C6
Mqanduli S. Africa 133 M8
Mqinvartsveri mt. Georgia/Rus. Fed. see Kazbek
Mrągowo Poland 49 S2
Mrewa Zimbabwe see Murehwa
Mrežnica r. Croatia 56 H3
Mrkonjić-Grad Bos.-Herz. 56 J4
Mrocza Poland 49 O2
Mroga r. Poland 49 Q4
M'Saken Tunisia 57 C13
Msambweni Kenya 129 C6
Msata Tanz. 129 C6
Mshinskaya Rus. Fed. 43 K2
M'Sila Alg. 123 G2
Msta Rus. Fed. 43 P4
Msta r. Rus. Fed. 43 M3
Mstinskiy Most Rus. Fed. 43 N3
Mstislavl' Belarus see Mstsislaw
Mstsislaw Belarus 43 M7 also spelt Mstislavl'
Msunduze r. S. Africa 133 Q4
Mszana Dolna Poland 49 R6
Mtama Tanz. 129 C7
Mt'at'ushet'is Nakrdzali nature res. Georgia 107 F2
Mtelo Kenya 128 B4
Mtera Reservoir Tanz. 129 B6
Mtoko Zimbabwe see Mutoko
Mtonjaneni S. Africa 133 P5
Mtorashanga Zimbabwe see Mutorashanga
Mtsensk Rus. Fed. 43 R8
Mts'khet'a Georgia 107 F2
Mtukula Tanz. 129 C7
Mtunzini S. Africa 133 P5
Mtwara Tanz. 129 D7
Mtwara admin. reg. Tanz. 129 C7
Mu r. Myanmar 78 A3
Mu hill Port. 54 C7
Mu'āb, Jibāl reg. Jordan see Moab
Muaguide Moz. 129 C8
Mualama Moz. 131 H3
Muana Brazil 202 B2
Muanda Dem. Rep. Congo 127 B6
Muang Khammouan Laos 78 D4
Muang Không Laos 79 D5
Muang Khôngxédôn Laos 79 D5
Muang Luang r. Thai. 79 B6
Muang Pakbeng Laos 78 C4
Muang Pakxan Laos 78 C4
Muang Phin Laos 78 D4
Muang Phôn-Hông Laos 78 C4
Muang Sam Sip Thai. 79 D5
Muang Sing Laos 78 C3
Muang Thai country Asia see Thailand
Muang Vangviang Laos 78 C4
Muang Xaignabouri Laos 78 C4 also known as Sayabouri
Muanza Moz. 131 G3
Muar Malaysia 76 C2
Muar r. Malaysia 76 C2
Muara Brunei 77 F1
Muaraancalong Indon. 77 G2
Muaraatap Indon. 77 G2
Muarabeliti Indon. 76 C3
Muarabungo Indon. 76 C3
Muaradua Indon. 76 D4
Muaraenim Indon. 76 C3
Muarainu Indon. 77 F3
Muarakaman Indon. 77 G3
Muaralesan Indon. 77 G2
Muararupit Indon. 76 C3
Muarasoma Indon. 76 B2
Muaras Reef Indon. 75 A2
Muaratebo Indon. 76 C3
Muaratembesi Indon. 76 C3
Muarateweh Indon. 77 F3
Muara Tuang Sarawak Malaysia see Kota Samarahan
Muarawahau Indon. 77 G2
Muari, Ras pt Pak. 101 F5 also known as Monze, Cape
Mu'aylā, Wādī al watercourse Iraq 109 M5
Muazzam India 96 B3
Mubārak, Jabal mt. Jordan/Saudi Arabia 108 G8
Mubarakpur India 97 D4
Mubarek Uzbek. 103 F5 also spelt Muborak
Mubarraz well Saudi Arabia 107 E5
Mubende Uganda 128 A4
Mubi Nigeria 125 I4
Muborak Uzbek. see Mubarek
Mubur i. Indon. 77 D2
Mucaba Angola 127 B6
Mucajá Brazil 199 G5
Mucajaí r. Brazil 199 F4
Mucajai, Serra do mts Brazil 199 F4
Mucalic r. Canada 169 H1
Mučanj mt. Yugo. 58 B5
Mucheng China see Wuzhi
Muchinga Escarpment Zambia 127 F8
Muchiri Bol. 201 E4
Muchuan China 86 B2 also known as Muxi
Muck i. U.K. 46 F7
Muckadilla Australia 149 F5
Muckaty Aboriginal Land res. Australia 148 B3
Muco r. Col. 198 D3
Mucojo Moz. 129 D8
Muconda Angola 127 D7 formerly known as Nova Chaves
Mucope Angola 127 B9
Mucubela Moz. 131 H3
Mucucuaú r. Brazil 199 F5
Mucuim r. Brazil 199 E6
Mucumbura Moz. 131 F3
Mucundi Angola 127 D8
Mucunha Angola 127 C8
Mucupia Moz. 131 H3
Mucur Turkey 106 C3
Mucura Brazil 199 F5
Mucuri Brazil 203 E6
Mucuri r. Brazil 207 N5
Mucurici Brazil 207 M5
Mucuripe Brazil 198 D5
Mucuripe, Ponta de pt Brazil 202 E2
Mucusso, Coutada Pública do nature res. Angola 127 D9
Mucussueje Angola 127 D7
Muda r. Malaysia 76 C1
Mudabidri India 94 B3
Mudanjiang China 82 C3
Mudan Jiang r. China 82 C3
Mudan Ling mts China 82 B4
Mudanya Turkey 106 B2
Mudayrah Kuwait 107 F5
Mudaysīsāt, Jabal al hill Jordan 108 H6
Muddebihal India 94 C2
Muddus nationalpark nat. park Sweden 44 L2
Muddy r. U.S.A. 183 J5
Muddy Boggy Creek r. U.S.A. 179 D5
Muddy Creek r. U.S.A. 183 N3
Muddy Gap Pass U.S.A. 180 F4
Muddy Peak U.S.A. 183 J5
Mūd-e-Dahanāb Iran 101 D3
Muden S. Africa 133 O5
Mudgal India 94 C3
Mudgee Australia 147 F3
Mudhol India 94 B2
Mudigere India 94 B3
Mudjatik r. Canada 167 J3
Mudkhed India 94 C2
Mudki India 96 B3
Mud Lake U.S.A. 183 G4
Mudon Myanmar 78 B4
Mudraya country Africa see Egypt
Mudug admin. reg. Somalia 128 E3
Mudukani Tanz. 129 B5
Mudumu National Park Namibia 130 D3
Mudurnu Turkey 106 B2
Mud'yuga Rus. Fed. 40 F3
Muecate Moz. 131 H2
Mueda Moz. 129 C7
Muela de Arés mt. Spain 55 K4
Mueller Range hills Australia 150 D3
Muende Moz. 131 G2
Muerto, Mar lag. Mex. 185 G5
Muertos Cays is Bahamas 186 C1
Mufu hill Sudan 121 G4
Muftyuga Rus. Fed. 40 H2
Mufulira Zambia 127 F8
Mufumbwe Zambia 127 E8
Mufu Shan mts China 87 E2
Muğan Düzü lowland Azer. 107 G3
Muge r. Port. 54 C5
Mugeba Moz. 131 H3
Mughalbhin Pak. see Jati
Mughal Sarai India 97 D4
Mūghār Iran 100 C3
Mughayrā' Saudi Arabia 107 D5
Mughayrā' well Saudi Arabia 105 D2
Mughshin Oman 105 F4
Mughsu r. Tajik. 101 G2 also spelt Muksu
Mugia Spain see Muxía
Mugila, Monts mts Dem. Rep. Congo 127 F6
Muğla Turkey 106 B3
Muğla prov. Turkey 59 J11
Mugodzharskaya Kazakh. 102 D2
Mugodzhary, Gory mts Kazakh. 102 D3
Mug Qu r. China 80 E6
Muguia Moz. 129 C8
Mugu Karnali r. Nepal 97 D3
Mugur-Aksy Rus. Fed. 84 A1
Mugxung China 89 F5
Mūḩ, Sabkhat imp. l. Syria 109 J3
Muhagiriya Sudan 126 E2
Muhala China see Yutian
Muhala Dem. Rep. Congo 127 F6
Muhammad, Râs pt Egypt 121 G3
Muhammadabad India 97 D4
Muhammad Qol Sudan 121 H4
Muhammarah Iran see Khorramshahr
Muḩayriqah Saudi Arabia 105 D3
Muhaysh, Wādī al watercourse Jordan 108 H8
Muḩaywīr tourist site Iraq 109 M4
Muheza Tanz. 129 C6
Mühlacker Germany 48 F7
Mühlberg Germany 49 K4
Mühldorf am Inn Germany 49 J7
Mühlhausen (Thüringen) Germany 48 H4
Mühlig-Hofmann Mountains Antarctica 223 A2
Muhos Fin. 44 N2
Muḩradah Syria 109 H2
Muhu i. Estonia 42 E3
Muhukuru Tanz. 129 B7
Muhula Moz. 131 H2
Muhulu Dem. Rep. Congo 126 E5
Mui Eth. 128 B3
Mui Bai Bung c. Vietnam see Mui Ca Mau
Mui Ca Mau c. Vietnam 79 D6 also known as Mui Bai Bung
Mui Dinh hd Vietnam 79 E6
Mui Độc pt Vietnam 78 D4
Muidumbe Moz. 129 C7
Mui Kê pt Vietnam 79 E6
Muiliyk i. Indon. 75 D3
Muineachán Rep. of Ireland see Monaghan
Muine Bheag Rep. of Ireland 47 F11
Muir U.S.A. 173 I8
Muir Glacier Canada/U.S.A. 166 B3
Muirkirk U.K. 46 H8
Mui Ron hd Vietnam 78 D4
Muite Moz. 131 H2
Mujeres, Isla i. Mex. 186 B2
Muji China 88 B4
Mujong r. Sarawak Malaysia 77 F2
Muju S. Korea 83 B5
Mujuí Joboti Brazil 199 H5
Mukačevo Ukr. see Mukacheve
Mukacheve Ukr. 49 T7 also spelt Mukachevo or Mukačevo; historically known as Munkács
Mukachevo Ukr. see Mukacheve
Mukah Sarawak Malaysia 77 F2
Mukah r. Sarawak Malaysia 77 F2
Mukalla Yemen 105 E5 also spelt Al Mukallā
Mukandgarh India 96 B4
Mukandwara India 96 C4 also spelt Mokundurra
Mukanga Dem. Rep. Congo 127 D6
Mukawa Japan 90 G3
Mu-kawa r. Japan 90 G3
Mukawwar, Gezirat i. Sudan 121 H4
Mukdahan Thai. 78 D4
Mukden China see Shenyang
Mukerian India 96 B3
Muketei r. Canada 168 C2
Mukhen Rus. Fed. 82 E2
Mukhino Rus. Fed. 82 B1
Mukhorshibir' Rus. Fed. 85 F1
Mukhtuya Rus. Fed. see Lensk
Mukinbudin Australia 151 B6
Mu Ko Chang National Park Thai. 79 C6
Mukomuko Indon. 76 C3
Mukono Uganda 128 B4
Mukoshi Zambia 127 F7
Mukry Turkm. 103 F5
Muksu r. Tajik. see Mughsu
Muktinath Nepal 97 D3
Muktsar India 96 B3
Mukuku Zambia 127 F8
Mukumbura Zimbabwe 131 F3 formerly spelt Mkumvura
Mukunsa Zambia 127 F7
Mukur Atyrauskaya Oblast' Kazakh. 102 C3 also spelt Muqyr
Mukur Vostochnyy Kazakhstan Kazakh. 103 J2
Mukutawa r. Canada 167 L4
Mukwonago U.S.A. 172 E8
Mula r. India 94 B2
Mula r. Pak. 101 F4
Mula Spain 55 J6
Mulakatholhu Maldives 93 D10 formerly known as Mulaku
Mulaku atoll Maldives see Mulakatholhu
Mulaly Kazakh. 103 I3 also spelt Molaly
Mulan China 82 C3
Mulanay Phil. 74 B3
Mulanje Malawi 129 B9
Mulapula, Lake salt flat Australia 146 C2
Mula-tupo Panama 186 D5
Mulayḩ salt pan Saudi Arabia 109 J8
Mulayjah Saudi Arabia 105 E2
Mulbagal India 94 C3
Mulbekh Jammu and Kashmir 96 C2
Mulberry AR U.S.A. 179 D5
Mulberry NC U.S.A. 176 D9
Mulchatna r. U.S.A. 164 D3
Mulchén Chile 204 B5
Mulde r. Germany 49 J4
Muleba Tanz. 128 A5
Mule Creek U.S.A. 180 F4
Mulegé Mex. 184 B3
Mulekatembo Zambia 129 B7
Mules i. Indon. 75 B5
Muleshoe U.S.A. 179 B5
Mulevala Moz. 131 H3
Mulga Park Australia 148 A5
Mulgathing Australia 146 B2
Mulhacén mt. Spain 55 H7
Mülheim an der Ruhr Germany 48 D4
Mulhouse France 51 N5 also known as Mülhausen
Muli China 86 B3 also known as Qiaowa; formerly known as Bowa
Muli Rus. Fed. see Vysokogorniy
Mulilansolo Zambia 129 B7
Muling Heilong. China 82 C3 formerly known as Bamiantong
Muling Heilong. China 82 C3
Muling r. China 82 D3
Mull i. U.K. 46 G7
Mulla Ali Iran 100 B2
Mullaaxe Beyle Somalia 128 E2
Mullaittivu Sri Lanka 94 D4
Muller watercourse Australia 148 B4
Muller, Pegunungan mts Indon. 77 F2
Mullett Lake U.S.A. 173 I5
Mullewa Australia 151 A6
Müllheim Germany 48 E8
Mullica r. U.S.A. 177 K6
Mulligan watercourse Australia 148 C5
Mullingar Rep. of Ireland 47 E10 also known as An Muileann gCearr
Mullins U.S.A. 175 E5
Mull of Galloway c. U.K. 47 H9
Mull of Kintyre hd U.K. 47 G8
Mull of Oa hd U.K. 46 F8
Mullrose Germany 49 L3
Mullsjö Sweden 45 K4
Mullutu laht l. Estonia 42 D3
Mulobezi Zambia 127 E9
Mulondo Angola 127 B8
Mulonga Plain Zambia 127 D9
Mulongo Dem. Rep. Congo 127 E6
Mulsanne France 50 G5
Mulshi Lake India 94 B2
Multai India 96 C5
Multān Iran 101 E5
Multan Pak. 101 G4
Multia Fin. 44 N3
Mulu, Gunung mt. Sarawak Malaysia 77 F1
Mulug India 94 C2
Mulumbe, Monts mts Dem. Rep. Congo 127 E7
Mulurulu Lake Australia 147 D3
Mulūşī, Wādī al watercourse Iraq 109 K4
Muma Dem. Rep. Congo 126 D4
Mūmān Iran 101 E5
Mumbai India 94 B2 2nd most populous city in Asia and 3rd in the world. Formerly known as Bombay. world [cities] 24–25
Mumbeji Zambia 127 D8
Mumbondo Angola 127 B7
Mumbwa Zambia 127 E8
Mumbwi Tanz. 129 C6
Mume Dem. Rep. Congo 127 E7
Muminabad Tajik. see Leningrad
Mū'minobod Tajik. see Leningrad
Mumoma Dem. Rep. Congo 127 D6
Mumra Rus. Fed. 102 A3
Mun, Mae Nam r. Thai. 79 D5
Muna i. Indon. 75 B4
Muna Mex. 185 H4
Muna r. Rus. Fed. 39 M3
Munabao Pak. 101 G5
Munaðarnes Iceland 44 [inset] B2
Munagala India 94 C2
Munakata Japan 91 B8
Munayly Kazakh. 102 C3
Munayshy Kazakh. 102 C4
Münchberg Germany 48 I5
München Germany see Munich
München-Gladbach Germany see Mönchengladbach
Munchique, Parque Nacional nat. park Col. 198 B4
Muncho Lake Canada 166 E3
Muncho Lake Provincial Park Canada 166 E3
Munch'ŏn N. Korea 83 B5
Muncie U.S.A. 174 C3
Muncoonie West, Lake salt flat Australia 148 C5
Muncy U.S.A. 177 I4
Munda Solomon Is 145 E2
Mundel Lake Sri Lanka 94 C5
Mundemba Cameroon 125 H5
Mundiwindi Australia 150 C4
Mundjura Creek r. Australia 149 D3
Mundo r. Spain 55 J6
Mundo Novo Brazil 202 D4
Mundra India 96 A5
Mundrabilla Australia 151 D6
Munds Park U.S.A. 183 M7
Mundubbera Australia 149 F5
Mundwa India 96 B4
Muneru r. India 94 D2
Munfordville U.S.A. 174 C4
Mungallala Australia 149 E5
Mungallala Creek r. Australia 147 E2
Mungana Australia 149 E3
Mungaoli India 96 C4
Mungári Moz. 131 G3
Mungaroona Range Nature Reserve Australia 150 B4
Mungbere Dem. Rep. Congo 126 F4
Mungeli India 97 D5
Munger India 97 E4 formerly spelt Monghyr
Munger U.S.A. 173 J7
Mungeranie Australia 146 C2
Mu Nggava i. Solomon Is see Rennell
Mungguresak, Tanjung pt Indon. 77 E2
Mungilli Aboriginal Reserve Australia 151 D5
Mungindi Australia 147 F2
Mungkarta Aboriginal Land res. Australia 148 B4
Mungla Bangl. 97 F5
Mungo Angola 127 C7
Mungo, Lake Australia 147 D3
Mungo National Park Australia 147 D3
Mungwi Zambia 127 F7
Mun'gyŏng S. Korea 83 B5
Munhango Angola 127 C8
Munhino Angola 127 B8
Munich Germany 48 I7 also known as München
Munising U.S.A. 172 G4
Muniz Freire Brazil 207 L7
Munkács Ukr. see Mukacheve
Munkedal Sweden 45 J4
Munkflohögen Sweden 44 K3
Munku-Sardyk, Gora mt. Mongolia/Rus. Fed. 84 D1
Munro, Mount Australia 147 F5
Munse Indon. 75 B4
Munshiganj Bangl. 97 F5
Münsingen Switz. 51 N6
Münster Niedersachsen Germany 48 H3
Münster Nordrhein-Westfalen Germany 48 E4
Munster reg. Rep. of Ireland 47 D11
Münsterland reg. Germany 48 E4
Münster-Osnabrück airport Germany 48 E3
Muntadgin Australia 151 B6
Munte Indon. 75 A2
Muntele Mare, Vârful mt. Romania 58 E2
Munteni Romania 58 I3
Mununga Zambia 127 F7
Munyal-Par sea feature India see Bassas de Pedro Padua Bank
Munyati r. Zimbabwe 131 F3
Munyu S. Africa 133 M8
Munzur Vadisi Milli Parkı nat. park Turkey 107 D3
Muodoslompolo Sweden 44 M2
Muojärvi l. Fin. 44 O2
Muonio Fin. 44 M2
Muonioälven r. Fin./Sweden 44 M2 also known as Muonionjoki
Muonionjoki r. Fin./Sweden see Muonioälven
Mupa Angola 127 B9
Mupa, Parque Nacional da nat. park Angola 127 B8
Mupfure r. Zimbabwe 131 F3 formerly known as Umfuli
Muping China 85 I4
Muqaddam watercourse Sudan 121 F5
Muqaybirah Yemen 105 D5
Muqaynimah well Saudi Arabia 105 E3
Muqdisho Somalia see Mogadishu
Muqniyāt Oman 105 G3
Muqshin, Wādī r. Oman 105 F4
Muquem Brazil 202 B5
Muqui Brazil 203 D7
Muqyr Kazakh. see Mukur
Mur r. Austria 49 N9 also spelt Mura
Mura r. Croatia/Slovenia 49 N9 also spelt Mur
Muradiye Turkey 59 I10
Muradiye Turkey 107 E3
Murai, Tanjong pt Sing. 76 [inset] also known as Bargiri
Murai Reservoir Sing. 76 [inset]
Murakami Japan 90 F5
Murallón, Cerro mt. Chile 205 B8
Muramvya Burundi 126 F5
Muráň r. Slovakia 49 R7
Muranga Kenya 128 C5 formerly known as Fort Hall
Muras Spain 54 D1
Murashi Rus. Fed. 40 I4
Murat France 51 I7
Murat r. Turkey 107 D3
Muratlı Turkey 106 A2
Murayama Japan 90 G5
Murayr, Jabal al hill Saudi Arabia 104 C2
Muraysah, Ra's al pt Libya 120 E2
Murça Port. 54 D3
Murcheh Khvort Iran 100 B3
Murchison Australia 147 E4
Murchison watercourse Australia 151 A5
Murchison N.Z. 153 G9
Murchison, Mount Antarctica 223 L2
Murchison, Mount hill Australia 151 B5
Murchison Falls Uganda 128 A4
Murchison Falls National Park Uganda 128 A4 also known as Kabalega Falls National Park or Kabarega National Park
Murchison Island Canada 168 B3
Murchison Mountains N.Z. 153 B13
Murchison Range hills Australia 148 B4
Murcia Spain 55 J7
Murcia aut. comm. Spain 55 J7
Murcielagos Bay Phil. 74 B4
Mûr-de-Bretagne France 50 D4
Murdo U.S.A. 178 B3
Murdochville Canada 169 H3
Murefte Turkey 106 A2
Muregi Nigeria 125 G4
Murehwa Zimbabwe 131 F3 formerly spelt Mrewa or Murewa
Mureş r. Romania 58 B2
Muret France 50 H9
Murewa Zimbabwe see Murehwa
Murfjället mt. Norway 44 K2
Murfreesboro AR U.S.A. 179 D5
Murfreesboro NC U.S.A. 177 H9
Murfreesboro TN U.S.A. 174 C5
Murgab Tajik. see Murghob
Murgab r. Tajik. 101 H2
Murgab Turkm. see Murgap
Murgab r. Turkm. see Murgap
Murgap Turkm. 103 E5 also spelt Murgab
Murgap r. Turkm. 103 E5 formerly spelt Murgab
Murgeni Romania 58 J2
Murge Tarantine hills Italy 57 J8
Murghab r. Afgh. 101 E3
Murghab reg. Afgh. 101 E3
Murgha Kibzai Pak. 101 G4

Ñancorainza Bol. 201 E5
Nancowry i. India 95 G5
Nancut Canada 166 E4
Nancy France 51 M4
Nancy U.S.A. 176 A8
Nanda Devi mt. India 96 D3
Nanda Kot mt. India 96 D3
Nandan China 87 C3
Nanded India 94 C2
formerly known as Nander
Nander India see Nanded
Nandewar Range mts Australia 147 F2
Nandgaon India 94 B1
Nandi Zimbabwe 131 F4
Nandigama India 94 D2
Nandikotkur India 94 C3
Nanding He r. China 86 A4
Nandod India 96 B5
Nandu Jiang r. China 87 D4
Nandura India 94 C1
Nandurbar India 96 B5
Nandyal India 94 C3
Nănești Romania 58 I3
Nanfeng Guangdong China 87 D4
Nanfeng Jiangxi China 87 F3
also known as Qincheng
Nang China 89 F6
Nangade Moz. 129 C7
Nanga Eboko Cameroon 125 I5
Nangah Dedai Indon. 77 E3
Nangahembaloh Indon. 77 F2
Nangahkemangai Indon. 77 F3
Nangahmau Indon. 77 E3
Nangahpinoh Indon. 77 E3
Nangahsuruk Indon. 77 F2
Nangahtempuai Indon. 77 F2
Nangalala Australia 148 B2
Nanganga Tanz. 129 C7
Nangang Shan mts China 82 C4

▶Nanga Parbat mt. Jammu and Kashmir 96 B2
9th highest mountain in the world and in Asia.
world [physical features] ▶ 8–9

Nangarhār prov. Afgh. 101 G3
Nangatayap Indon. 77 E3
Nangbéto, Retenue de resr Togo 125 F5
Nangin Myanmar 79 B6
Nangis France 51 J4
Nangnim N. Korea 83 B4
Nangnim-sanmaek mts N. Korea 83 B4
Nangō Japan 90 F6
Nangong China 85 G4
Nangqên China 86 A1
also known as Xangda
Nangulangwa Tanz. 129 C7
Nanguneri India 94 C4
Nanhe China 85 G4
also known as Heyang
Nanhu China 84 B4
Nanhua Gansu China 84 C4
Nanhua Yunnan China 86 B3
also known as Longchuan
Nanhui China 87 G2
also known as Huinan
Nani Afgh. 101 G3
Nanisivik Canada 165 K2
Nanjangud India 94 C3
Nanjian China 86 B3
Nanjiang China 86 C1
Nanjie China see Guangning
Nanjing Fujian China 87 F3
also known as Shancheng
Nanjing Jiangsu China 87 F1
formerly spelt Nanking
Nanji Shan i. China 87 G3
Nanka Jiang r. China 86 A4
Nankang China 87 E3
formerly known as Rongjiang
Nankang China see Xingzi
Nanking China see Nanjing
Nankoku Japan 91 C8
Nankova Angola 127 C9
Nanlan He r. China 86 A4
Nanle China 85 G4
Nanling China 87 F2
Nan Ling mts China 87 D3
Nanliu Jiang r. China 87 D4
Nanlong China see Nanbu
Nanma China see Yiyuan
Nanmulingzue China see Namling
Nannine Australia 151 B5
Nanning China 87 D4
Nannup Australia 151 A7
Na Noi Thai. 78 C4
Nanortalik Greenland 165 O3
Nanouki atoll Kiribati see Nonouti
Nanouti atoll Kiribati see Nonouti
Nanpan Jiang r. China 86 C3
Nanpara India 97 D4
Nanpi China 85 H4
Nanpiao China 85 I3
Nanping Fujian China 87 F3
Nanping Sichuan China 86 C1
also known as Yongle
Nanpu China see Pucheng
Nanpu Xi r. China 87 F3
Nanqiao China see Fengxian
Nanri Dao i. China 87 F3
Nansa r. Spain 54 G1
Nansebo Eth. 128 C3
Nansei-shotō is Japan see Ryukyu Islands
Nansenga Zambia 127 E8
Nansen Land reg. Greenland 165 O1
Nansen Sound sea chan. Canada 165 J1
Nanshan Island S. China Sea 72 E4
Nanshankou China 84 B3
Nansha Qundao is S. China Sea see Spratly Islands
Nansio Tanz. 128 B5
Nantawarrina Aboriginal Land res. Australia 146 C2
Nantes France 50 E5
Nantes à Brest, Canal de France 50 D5
Nanthi Kadal lag. Sri Lanka 94 D4
Nantiat France 50 H6
Nanticoke Canada 168 D5
Nanticoke MD U.S.A. 177 J7
Nanticoke PA U.S.A. 177 I4
Nanticoke r. U.S.A. 177 J7
Nanton Canada 167 H5
Nantong Jiangsu China 87 G1
Nantong Jiangsu China 87 G2
Nantou China 87 [inset]
Nant'ou Taiwan 87 G4
Nantucket U.S.A. 177 O4
Nantucket Island U.S.A. 177 P4
Nantucket Sound g. U.S.A. 177 O4
Nantulo Moz. 129 C8
Nanty Glo U.S.A. 176 G5
Nanumaga i. Tuvalu see Nanumanga
Nanumanga i. Tuvalu 145 G2
also spelt Nanumaga; formerly known as Hudson Island
Nanumea i. Tuvalu 145 G2
Nanuque Brazil 203 D6
Nanusa, Kepulauan is Indon. 75 C1
Nanutarra Roadhouse Australia 150 A4
Nanxi China 86 C2
Nanxian China 87 E2
also known as Nanzhou
Nanxiong China 87 E3
formerly known as Xiongzhou
Nanyandang Shan mt. China 87 G3
Nanyang China 87 E1
Nanyō Japan 90 G5
Nanyuki Kenya 128 C5
Nanzamu China 82 B4
Nanzhang China 87 D2
Nanzhao China see Zhao'an
Nanzhao China 87 E1
Nanzheng China 86 C1
also known as Zhoujiaping
Nanzhou China see Nanxian
Naogaon Bangl. 97 F4
Naokot Pak. 101 G5
Naoli r. China 82 D3
Naomid, Dasht-e des. Afgh./Iran 101 E3
Naousa Greece 58 D8
Napa U.S.A. 182 B3
Napak mt. Uganda 128 B4
Napaktulik Lake Canada 167 H1
also known as Takijuq Lake
Napanee Canada 168 E4
Napasar India 96 B4
Napasoq Greenland 165 N3
Naperville U.S.A. 174 B3
Napier N.Z. 152 K7
Napier S. Africa 132 D11
Napier Broome Bay Australia 150 D2
Napier Mountains Antarctica 223 D2
Napier Peninsula Australia 148 B2
Napier Range hills Australia 150 D3
Naples Italy 57 G8
also known as Napoli; historically known as Neapolis
Naples FL U.S.A. 175 D7
Naples ME U.S.A. 177 O2
Naples NY U.S.A. 177 H3
Naples UT U.S.A. 183 O1
Napo China 86 C4
Napo prov. Ecuador 198 B5
Napo r. Ecuador 198 C5
Napoleon ND U.S.A. 178 C2
Napoleon OH U.S.A. 176 A4
Napoleonville U.S.A. 175 B6
Napoli Italy see Naples
Napoli, Golfo di b. Italy 57 G8
Naposta Arg. 204 E5
Nappanee U.S.A. 172 H9
Napperby Australia 148 B4
Naqadeh Iran 100 A2
Naqb Malha mt. Egypt 108 D8
Naqūb Yemen 105 D5
Nara Japan 91 D7
Nara pref. Japan 90 D7
Nara Mali 124 D3
Nara r. Rus. Fed. 43 S7
Narach Belarus 42 H7
Narach r. Belarus 42 H7
Narach, Vozyera l. Belarus 42 H7
Naracoorte Australia 146 D4
Naradhan Australia 147 E3
Narail Bangl. 97 F5
Naraina India 96 B4
Naranbulag Dornod Mongolia 85 G1
Naranbulag Uvs Mongolia 84 B1
Narang Afgh. 101 G3
Naranjal Ecuador 198 B5
Naranjal Peru 198 C6
Naranjos Mex. 185 F4
Naran Sebstein Bulag spring China 84 C3
Narao Japan 91 A8
Naraq Iran 100 B3
Narasannapeta India 95 E2
Narasapatnam, Point India 94 D2
Narasapur India 94 D2
Narasaraopet India 94 D2
Narasinghapur India 95 E1
Narasun Rus. Fed. 85 G1
Narat China 88 D3
Narathiwat Thai. 79 C7
Narat Shan mts China 88 C3
Nara Visa U.S.A. 179 B5
Narayanganj Bangl. 97 F5
Narayanganj India 96 D5
Narayangaon India 94 B2
Narayanpet India 94 C2
Naray Kelay Afgh. 101 G3
Narbada r. India see Narmada
Narbo France see Narbonne
Narbonne France 51 J9
historically known as Narbo
Narbuvoll Norway 44 J3
Narcea r. Spain 54 E1
Narcondam Island India 95 G3
Nardin Iran 100 C2
Nardò Italy 57 K8
Nare Arg. 204 E3
Narechi r. Pak. 101 G4
Naregal India 94 B3
Narembeen Australia 151 B7
Nares Strait Canada/Greenland 165 L2
Naretha Australia 151 D6
Narew r. Poland 49 R3
Narewka r. Poland 42 E9
Nari r. Pak. 101 F4
Naria Bangl. 97 F5
Narib Namibia 130 C5
Narie, Jezioro l. Poland 49 R2
Nariep S. Africa 132 B7
Narimanov Rus. Fed. 102 A3
formerly known as Nizhnevolzhsk
Narimskiy Khrebet mts Kazakh. 88 D1
Narin Afgh. 101 G2
Narin reg. Afgh. 101 G2
Narin China 85 F4
Narince Turkey 107 D3
Narin Gol watercourse China 84 B4
Nariño dept Col. 198 B4
Narita Japan 91 G7
Nariu-misaki pt Japan 91 D7
Nariwa Japan 91 C7
Narizon, Punta pt Mex. 184 C3
Narkaus Fin. 44 N2
Narken Sweden 44 M2
Narmada r. India 96 B5
also known as Narbada
Narnaul India 96 C3
Narni Italy 56 E6
historically known as Narnia
Narnia Italy see Narni
Narodnaya, Gora mt. Rus. Fed. 40 L2
Naro-Fominsk Rus. Fed. 43 R6
Narok Kenya 128 B5
Narooma Australia 147 F4
Narowlya Belarus 41 D6
Närpes Fin. 44 M3
Narrabri Australia 147 F2
Narragansett Bay U.S.A. 177 N4
Narran r. Australia 147 E2
Narrandera Australia 147 E3
Narran Lake Australia 147 E2
Narrogin Australia 151 B7
Narromine Australia 147 F3
Narrow Hills Provincial Park Canada 167 J4
Narrows U.S.A. 176 E8
Narrowsburg U.S.A. 177 J4
Narsalik Greenland 165 O3
Narsapur India 94 C2
Narsaq Greenland 165 O3
Narsarsuaq Greenland 165 O3
Narsimhapur India 96 C5
Narsingdi Bangl. 97 F5
Narsinghgarh India 96 C5
Narsipatnam India 95 D2
Nart China 85 G3
Nart Mongolia 85 E1
Nartë Albania 58 A8
Nartkala Rus. Fed. 107 E2
formerly known as Dokshukino
Naruko Japan 90 G5
Naruto Japan 91 D7
Narva Estonia 43 J2
Narva r. Estonia/Rus. Fed. 42 J2
Narva Bay Estonia/Rus. Fed. 42 I2
also known as Narva laht or Narvskiy Zaliv
Narvacan Phil. 74 B2
Narva-Jõesuu Estonia 43 J2
Narva laht b. Estonia/Rus. Fed. see Narva Bay
Narva Reservoir Estonia/Rus. Fed. see Narvskoye Vodokhranilishche
Narva veehoidla resr Estonia/Rus. Fed. see Narvskoye Vodokhranilishche
Narvik Norway 44 L1
Narvskiy Zaliv b. Estonia/Rus. Fed. see Narva Bay
Narvskoye Vodokhranilishche resr Estonia/Rus. Fed. 43 J2
English form Narva Reservoir; also known as Narva veehoidla
Narwana India 96 C3
Narwar India 96 C4
Narwinbi Aboriginal Land res. Australia 148 C3
Nar'yan-Mar Rus. Fed. 40 J2
Naryn Kyrg. 103 H4
Naryn admin. div. Kyrg. 103 H4
English form Naryn Oblast; also known as Narynskaya Oblast'; formerly known as Tien Shan Oblast or Tyanshanskaya Oblast'
Naryn r. Kyrg./Uzbek. 103 H4
Naryn Rus. Fed. 84 B1
Narynkol Kazakh. 88 C3
also spelt Naryngol
Naryn Oblast admin. div. Kyrg. see Naryn
Narynqol Kazakh. see Narynkol
Narynskaya Oblast' admin. div. Kyrg. see Naryn
Naryshkino Rus. Fed. 43 Q9
Năsăud Romania 58 F1
Näsby Sweden 45 L4
Naseby N.Z. 153 E13
Nashik India 94 B1
also spelt Nasik
Nashua U.S.A. 177 N3
Nashville AR U.S.A. 179 D5
Nashville GA U.S.A. 175 D6
Nashville IL U.S.A. 174 B4
Nashville NC U.S.A. 174 E5
Nashville OH U.S.A. 176 C5

▶Nashville TN U.S.A. 174 C4
State capital of Tennessee.

Našice Croatia 56 K3
Nasielsk Poland 49 R3
Näsijärvi l. Fin. 45 M3
Nasik India see Nashik
Nasir Sudan 128 B2
Nasirabad Bangl. see Mymensingh
Nasirabad India 96 B4
Nasirabad Pak. 101 G4
Naskaupi r. Canada 169 I2
Nasmganj India 97 E4
Nasondoye Dem. Rep. Congo 127 E7
Nasonville U.S.A. 172 C6
Nasosnyy Azer. see Hacı Zeynalabdin
Nasr Egypt 108 B7
Naşrābād Eşfahan Iran 100 B3
Naşrābād Khorāsan Iran 101 D3
Naşrānī, Jabal an mts Syria 109 I4
Nasratabad Iran see Zābol
Naşrīān-e Pā'īn Iran 100 A3
Nass r. Canada 166 D4
Nassarawa Nigeria 125 G4
Nassarawa state Nigeria 125 H4
Nassau r. Australia 149 D2

▶Nassau Bahamas 186 D1
Capital of The Bahamas.

Nassau i. Cook Is 221 G6
formerly known as Mitchell Island
Nassau U.S.A. 177 L3
Nassau, Naturpark nature res. Germany 48 E5
Nassawadox U.S.A. 177 J8
Nasser, Lake resr Egypt 121 G4
Nassian Côte d'Ivoire 124 E4
Nässjö Sweden 45 K4
Nassuttooq inlet Greenland 165 N3
also known as Nordre Strømfjord
Nastapoca r. Canada 169 E1
Nastapoka Islands Canada 168 E1
Nastola Fin. 42 G1
Nasu-dake vol. Japan 90 F6
Nasugbu Phil. 74 B3
Nasva Rus. Fed. 43 L5
Nasva r. Rus. Fed. 43 L5
Nata Botswana 131 E4
Nata watercourse Botswana/Zimbabwe 131 E4
Nataboti Indon. 75 C3
Natal Amazonas Brazil 201 E1
Natal Rio Grande do Norte Brazil 202 F3
Natal Indon. 76 B2
Natal prov. S. Africa see Kwazulu-Natal
Natal Drakensberg National Park S. Africa 133 N6
Naṭanz Iran 100 B3
Natashquan Canada 169 I3
Natashquan r. Canada 169 I3
Natchez U.S.A. 175 B6
Natchitoches U.S.A. 179 D6
Nathalia Australia 147 E4
Nathana India 96 B3
Nathdwara India 96 B4
Nati, Punta pt Spain 55 O4
Natiaboani Burkina 125 F4
National City U.S.A. 183 G9
National Park N.Z. 152 J7
National West Coast Tourist Recreation Area park Namibia 130 B4
Natitingou Benin 125 F4
Natividad, Isla i. Mex. 184 B3
Natividade Rio de Janeiro Brazil 207 L8
Natividade Tocantins Brazil 202 C4
Natla r. Canada 166 D2
Natmauk Myanmar 78 A3
Natogyi Myanmar 78 A3
Nator Bangl. 97 F4
Nátora Mex. 181 E7
Natori Japan 90 G5
Natron, Lake salt l. Tanz. 128 C5
Nattai National Park Australia 147 F3
Nattalin Myanmar 78 A4
Nattam India 94 C4
Nattaung mt. Myanmar 78 B4
Nattavaara Sweden 44 M2
Na'tū Iran 101 E3
Natuna, Kepulauan is Indon. 77 D1
also known as Bunguran, Kepulauan
Natuna Besar i. Indon. 77 E1
also known as Bunguran, Pulau
Natural Bridge U.S.A. 176 F8
Natural Bridges National Monument nat. park U.S.A. 183 N4
Naturaliste, Cape Australia 151 A7
Naturaliste Channel Australia 151 A5
Nature's Valley S. Africa 132 H10
Nau Tajik. see Nov
Naubinway U.S.A. 172 H4
Naucelle France 51 I8
Nauchas Namibia 130 C4
Nau Co l. China 89 C5
Naudesberg Pass S. Africa 133 I9
Nauen Germany 49 J3
Naugatuck U.S.A. 177 L4
Nau Hissar Pak. 101 F4
Naujan Phil. 74 B3
Naujoji Akmenė Lith. 42 D5
Naukh India 96 B4
Naulila Angola 127 B9
Naumburg (Saale) Germany 48 I4
Naungpale Myanmar 78 B4
Na'ūr Jordan 106 C5
Naurskaya Rus. Fed. 107 F2
Nauru i. Nauru 145 F2
▶Nauru country S. Pacific Ocean 145 F2
oceania [countries] ▶ 138–139
Naushahro Firoz Pak. 101 G5
Naushara Pak. 101 G5
Naushki Rus. Fed. 85 E1
Naustdal Norway 45 I3
Nauta Peru 198 C6
Nautaca Uzbek. see Karshi
Naute Dam Namibia 132 B3
Nautla Mex. 185 F4
Nautonwa India 97 D4
Nautsi Rus. Fed. 44 O1
Nauvoo U.S.A. 172 B10
Nava r. Dem. Rep. Congo 126 E4
Navabad Tajik. see Novobod
Navacerrada, Puerto de pass Spain 54 H4
Navachica mt. Spain 54 H8
Navadrutsk Belarus 42 I6
Navadwip India 97 F5
formerly spelt Nabadwip
Navahermosa Spain 54 G5
Navahrudak Belarus 42 G8
also spelt Novogrudok
Navahrudskaye Wzvyshsha hills Belarus 42 G8
Navajo r. U.S.A. 181 F5
Navajo Indian Reservation res. U.S.A. 183 O6
Navajo Lake U.S.A. 181 F5
Navajo Mountain U.S.A. 183 N4
Naval Phil. 74 C4
Navalmoral de la Mata Spain 54 F5
Navalvillar de Pela Spain 54 F5
Navan Rep. of Ireland 47 F10
also known as An Uaimh
Navangar India see Jamnagar
Navapolatsk Belarus 43 J6
also spelt Novopolotsk
Navarin, Mys c. Rus. Fed. 39 R3
Navarino, Isla i. Chile 205 D9
Navarra aut. comm. Spain 55 J2
English form Navarre
Navarre aut. comm. Spain see Navarra
Navarrenx France 50 F9
Navarro Peru 198 C6
Navarro r. U.S.A. 182 A2
Navashino Rus. Fed. 40 G5
Navasota U.S.A. 179 C6
Navasota r. U.S.A. 179 C6

▶Navassa Island terr. West Indies 187 E3
United States Unincorporated Territory.
oceania [countries] ▶ 138–139

Navasyolki Belarus 43 J9
Navayel'nya Belarus 42 G8
Naver r. U.K. 46 H5
Navesnoye Rus. Fed. 43 S9
Navesti r. Estonia 42 F3
Navia Spain 54 E1
Navia r. Spain 54 E1
Navidad Chile 204 C4
Navidad r. U.S.A. 179 C6
Naviraí Brazil 203 A7
Navlakhi India 96 A5
Navlya Rus. Fed. 43 P9
Navlya r. Rus. Fed. 43 P9
Năvodari Romania 58 J4
Navoi Uzbek. 103 F4
also spelt Nawoiy; formerly known as Kermine
Navoiyskaya Oblast' admin. div. Uzbek. 103 E4
English form Navoy Oblast; also known as Nawoiy Wiloyati
Navojoa Mex. 184 C3
Navolato Mex. 184 D3
Navoy Oblast admin. div. Uzbek. see Navoiyskaya Oblast'
Návpaktos Greece see Nafpaktos
Návplion Greece see Nafplio
Nävragöl Sweden 45 K4
Navrongo Ghana 125 E4
Navşar Turkey see Şemdinli
Navsari India 94 B1
Navua Fiji 145 G3
Nawa India 96 B4
Nawá Syria 108 H5
Nawabganj Bangl. 97 F4
Nawabganj India 97 D4
Nawabshah Pak. 101 G5
Nawada India 97 E4
Nāwah Afgh. 101 F3
Nawakot Nepal 97 E4
Nawalgarh India 96 B4
Nawar, Dasht-i imp. l. Afgh. 101 F3
Nawashahr India 89 B6
Nawāşīf, Ḩarrāt lava field Saudi Arabia 104 C3
Nawnghkio Myanmar 78 B3
Nawngleng Myanmar 78 B3
Nawoiy Uzbek. see Navoi
Nawoiy Wiloyati admin. div. Uzbek. see Navoiyskaya Oblast'
Naws, Ra's c. Oman 105 F4
Naxçıvan Azer. 107 F3
also spelt Nakhichevan'
Naxi China 86 C2
Naxos Greece 59 G11
Naxos i. Greece 59 G11
Naya Col. 198 B4
Nayagarh India 95 E1
Nayak Afgh. 101 F3
Nayarit state Mex. 184 D4
Nāy Band, Kūh-e mt. Iran 100 D3
Nayfah oasis Saudi Arabia 105 E4
Nayong China 86 C3
also known as Yongxi
Nayoro Japan 90 H2
Nayt Yemen 105 F5
Nayuchi Malawi 129 B8
Nayudupeta India 94 C3
Nayyāl, Wādī watercourse Saudi Arabia 104 B1
Nazare Brazil 199 E4
Nazaré Brazil 199 H6
Nazareno Mex. 184 E3
Nazareth India 94 C4
Nazareth Israel 108 G5
Nazareth U.S.A. 177 J5
Nazário Brazil 206 D3
Nazas Mex. 184 D3
Nazas r. Mex. 184 D3
Nazca Peru 200 B3
Nāzīk Iran 100 A2
Nazilli Turkey 106 B3
Nazımiye Turkey 107 D3
Nazinon r. Burkina/Ghana 125 E4 see Red Volta
Nazira India 97 G4
Nazir Hat Bangl. 97 F5
Naziya Rus. Fed. 43 M2
Nazko Canada 166 F4
Nazko r. Canada 166 F4
Nazran' Rus. Fed. 41 H8
formerly known as Kosta-Khetagurovo
Nazrēt Eth. 128 C2
Nazwá Oman 105 G3
also spelt Nizwā
Nazyvayevsk Rus. Fed. 38 H4
formerly known as Novonazyvayevka
Nbâk Mauritania 124 B2
Ncanaha S. Africa 133 J10
Nchelenge Zambia 127 F7
Ncheu Malawi see Ntcheu
Ncora S. Africa 133 L8
Ncue Equat. Guinea 125 H6
Ndala Tanz. 129 B6
N'dalatando Angola 127 B7
formerly known as Salazar or Vila Salazar; formerly spelt Dalatando
Ndali Benin 125 F4
Ndanda Cent. Afr. Rep. 126 D3
Ndao i. Indon. 75 B5
Ndareda Tanz. 129 B6
Ndélé Cent. Afr. Rep. 126 D2
Ndélélé Cameroon 125 I5
Ndendé Gabon 126 A5
Ndende i. Solomon Is see Ndeni
Ndeni i. Solomon Is 145 F3
also spelt Ndende or Nitendi
Ndiael, Réserve de Faune du nature res. Senegal 124 A2
Ndikiniméki Cameroon 125 H5
Ndim Cent. Afr. Rep. 126 B3
N'Djamena Chad see Ndjamena

▶Ndjamena Chad 120 B6
Capital of Chad. Also spelt N'Djamena; formerly known as Fort Lamy.

Ndji r. Cent. Afr. Rep. 126 D3
Ndjim r. Cameroon 125 H5
Ndjolé Gabon 126 A5
Ndjouani i. Comoros see Nzwani
Ndjounou Gabon 126 B5
Ndofane Senegal 124 B3
Ndogo, Lagune lag. Gabon 126 A5
Ndoi i. Fiji see Doi
Ndok Cameroon 125 I5
Ndola Zambia 127 F8
Ndoto mt. Kenya 128 C4
Ndougou Gabon 126 A5
Nduke i. Solomon Is see Kolombangara
Ndumbwe Tanz. 129 C7
Ndumu S. Africa 133 Q3
Ndumu Game Reserve nature res. Moz. 133 Q3
Nduye Dem. Rep. Congo 126 F4
Ndwedwe S. Africa 133 O6
Nea Anchialos Greece 59 D9
Nea Apollonia Greece 58 E8
Nea Artaki Greece 59 E10
Neabul Creek r. Australia 147 E1
Neagh, Lough l. U.K. 47 F9
Neah Bay U.S.A. 180 A2
Neajlov r. Romania 58 G4
Nea Karvali Greece 58 F8
Neale, Lake salt flat Australia 148 A5
Neale Junction Nature Reserve Australia 151 D6
Neales watercourse Australia 146 C2
Nea Liosia Greece 59 E10
Nea Makri Greece 59 E10
Nea Moudania Greece 59 E8
Neamț r. Romania 58 H1
Nea Peramos Greece 58 F8
Neapoli Kriti Greece 59 G13
Neapoli Peloponnisos Greece 59 E12
Neapolis Italy see Naples
Nea Roda Greece 59 E8
Nea Santa Greece 58 D8
Neath U.K. 47 I12
also known as Castell-nedd
Nea Zichni Greece 58 E7
Nebbi Uganda 128 A4
Nebbou Burkina 125 E4
Nebesnaya, Gora mt. China 88 C3
Nebine Creek r. Australia 147 E2
Nebitdag Turkm. 102 C5
Nebo Australia 149 F4
Nebo, Mount U.S.A. 183 M2
Nebolchi Rus. Fed. 43 O2
Nebraska state U.S.A. 178 B3
Nebraska City U.S.A. 178 D3
Nebrodi, Monti mts Sicilia Italy 57 G11
Nebyloye Rus. Fed. 43 U5
Necedah U.S.A. 172 C6
Necedah National Wildlife Refuge nature res. U.S.A. 172 C6
Neches r. U.S.A. 179 D6
Nechí r. Col. 198 C2
Nechisar National Park Eth. 128 C3
Neckarsulm Germany 48 G6
Neckartal-Odenwald, Naturpark nature res. Germany 48 G6
Necker Island U.S.A. 221 H4
Necochea Arg. 204 F5
Necoclí Col. 198 B2
Nedelino Bulg. 58 G7
Nedelišće Croatia 56 I2
Nedel'noye Rus. Fed. 43 R7
Nederland country Europe see Netherlands
Nederlandse Antillen terr. West Indies see Netherlands Antilles
Neder Rijn r. Neth. 48 C4
Nedlouc, Lac l. Canada 169 F1
also known as Nedluk Lake
Nedluk Lake Canada see Nedlouc, Lac
Nêdong China 89 E6
Nedre Soppero Sweden 44 M1
Nedstrand Norway 45 I4
Needham U.S.A. 177 N3
Needles U.S.A. 183 J7
Needmore U.S.A. 176 G6
Neemuch India see Nimach
Neenah U.S.A. 172 E6
Neepawa Canada 167 L5
Neergaard Lake Canada 165 K2
Neftçala Azer. 107 G3
also spelt Neftechala
Neftechala Azer. see 26 Bakı Komissarı
Neftechala Azer. see Neftçala
Neftegorsk Sakhalin Rus. Fed. 82 F1
formerly known as Vostok
Neftegorsk Samarskaya Oblast' Rus. Fed. 102 B1
Neftekamsk Rus. Fed. 40 J4
formerly known as Kasevo
Neftekumsk Rus. Fed. 41 H7
Nefteyugansk Rus. Fed. 38 H3
formerly known as Ust'-Balyk
Neftezavodsk Turkm. see Seydi
Nefza Tunisia 57 B11
Negada Weyn well Eth. 128 E3
Negage Angola 127 B6
Negala Mali 124 C3
Negar Iran 100 D4
Negara Bali Indon. 77 F5
Negara Kalimantan Selatan Indon. 77 F3
Negara r. Indon. 77 F3
Negaunee U.S.A. 172 F4
Negēlē Oromia Eth. 128 C3
Negēlē Oromia Eth. 128 C3
Negeri Sembilan state Malaysia 76 C2
formerly spelt Negri Sembilan
Negev des. Israel 108 G7
also spelt HaNegev
Negomane Moz. 129 C7
Negombo Sri Lanka 94 C5
Negotin Srbija Yugo. 58 D4
Negotino Macedonia 58 D7
Negra, Cordillera mts Peru 200 A2
Negra, Lago l. Uruguay 204 G4
also known as Los Difuntios, Lago de
Negra, Punta pt Peru 198 A6
Negra, Serra mts Brazil 203 D6
Negra, Serranía de mts Bol. 201 E3
Negrais, Cape Myanmar 78 A5
Negratín, Embalse de resr Spain 55 I7
Negreira Spain 54 C2
Negreiros Chile 200 C4
Nègrepelisse France 50 H8
Negrești Romania 58 I2
Negri r. Australia 148 A3
Negri Romania 58 H2
Négrine Alg. 123 G2
Negri Sembilan state Malaysia see Negeri Sembilan
Negritos Peru 198 A6
Negro r. Arg. 204 E6
Negro r. Brazil 201 F4
Negro r. Para. 201 F6
Negro r. S. America 199 G5
Negro r. Uruguay 204 G4
Negro, Cabo c. Morocco 54 F9
Negroponte i. Greece see Evvoia
Negros i. Phil. 74 B4
Negru Vodă Romania 58 J5
Nehalem r. U.S.A. 180 B3
Nehavand Iran 100 B3
Nehbandān Iran 101 E4
Nehe China 85 J1
Nehoiu Romania 58 H3
Nehone Angola 127 C9
Neiafu Tonga 145 H3
Neiba Dom. Rep. 187 F3
Neijiang China 86 C2
Neilersdrif S. Africa 132 E5
Neill Island India 95 G4
Neillsville U.S.A. 172 C6
Nei Mongol Zizhiqu aut. reg. China 85 D3
English form Inner Mongolia
Neiqiu China 85 G4
Neiße r. Germany/Poland 49 L3
also known as Nysa Łużycka
Neiva Col. 198 C4
Neixiang China 87 D1
Nejanilini Lake Canada 167 L3
Nejapa Mex. 185 G5
Nejd reg. Saudi Arabia see Najd
Neka Iran 100 C2
Neka r. Iran 100 C2
Nek'emtē Eth. 128 C2
Nekhayevskaya Rus. Fed. 41 G6
formerly known as Nekhayevskiy
Nekhayevskiy Rus. Fed. see Nekhayevskaya
Neklyudovo Rus. Fed. 43 V6
Nekrasovskiy Rus. Fed. 43 S5
Nekrasovskoye Rus. Fed. 43 V4
Neksø Denmark 45 K5
Nela r. Spain 54 H2
Nelamangala India 94 C3
Nelas Port. 54 D4
Nelazskoye Rus. Fed. 43 S2
Nelia Australia 149 D4
Nelidovo Rus. Fed. 43 N5
Neligh U.S.A. 178 C3
Nel'kan Khabarovskiy Kray Rus. Fed. 39 N4
Nel'kan Respublika Sakha (Yakutiya) Rus. Fed. 39 O3
Nellie Lake Canada 173 M2
Nellim Fin. 44 O1
also spelt Njellim
Nellore India 94 C3
Nelluz watercourse Turkey 109 K1
Nelshoogte pass S. Africa 133 O2
Nelson Arg. 204 E3
Nelson Canada 166 G5
Nelson r. Canada 167 M3
Nelson N.Z. 152 H9
Nelson admin. reg. N.Z. 152 H9
Nelson AZ U.S.A. 183 K6
Nelson NE U.S.A. 178 C3
Nelson NV U.S.A. 183 J6
Nelson, Cape Australia 146 D4
Nelson, Estrecho strait Chile 205 B8
Nelson Bay Australia 147 G3
Nelson Creek N.Z. 153 F10
Nelson Forks Canada 166 F3
Nelson House Canada 167 L4
Nelson Lakes National Park N.Z. 153 G10
Nelspoort S. Africa 132 H9
Nelspruit S. Africa 133 O2
Nem r. Rus. Fed. 40 J3
Néma Mauritania 124 D2
Nema Rus. Fed. 40 I4
Nemadji r. U.S.A. 172 A4
Neman r. Belarus/Lith. see Nyoman
Neman Rus. Fed. 42 D6
Neman r. Rus. Fed. 42 D6
Ne'matābād Iran 100 D4
Nemausus France see Nîmes
Nembe Nigeria 125 G5
Nemda r. Rus. Fed. 40 G4
Nemea Greece 59 D11
Nemed Rus. Fed. 40 J3
Nemegos Canada 173 J3
Nemegosenda Lake Canada 173 J2
Nemenčine Lith. 42 G7
Nemetocenna France see Arras
Nemetskiy, Mys c. Rus. Fed. 44 O1
Nemirov Ukr. see Nemyriv
Némiscau r. Canada 168 E3
Nemor r. China 85 J1
Nemours Alg. see Ghazaouet
Nemours France 51 I4
Nemrut Dağı mt. Turkey 107 E3
Nemta r. Rus. Fed. 82 D2
Nemunas r. Lith. 42 C6
Nemunėlio Radviliškis Lith. 42 F5
Nemunėlis r. Lith. 42 G5
Nemuro Japan 90 I3
Nemuro-hantō pen. Japan 90 I3
Nemuro-kaikyō sea chan. Japan/Rus. Fed. 90 I3
also known as Kunashirskiy Proliv
Nemuro-wan b. Japan 90 I3
Nemyriv Ukr. 41 D6
also spelt Nemirov
Nenagh Rep. of Ireland 47 D11
also known as An tAonach
Nenana U.S.A. 164 E3
Nenashevo Rus. Fed. 43 S7
Nene r. U.K. 47 M11
Nenets Autonomous Okrug admin. div. Rus. Fed. see Nenetskiy Avtonomnyy Okrug
Nenetskiy Avtonomnyy Okrug admin. div. Rus. Fed. 40 J2
English form Nenets Autonomous Okrug
Nenjiang China 85 J2
Nen Jiang r. China 85 J2
also known as Nonni
Neo Japan 91 E7
Neochori Greece 59 C9
also known as Neokhórion
Neo Karlovasi Greece 59 H11
also known as Néon Karlovásion
Neokhórion Greece see Neochori
Neola U.S.A. 183 N1
Neo Monastiri Greece 59 D9
Néon Karlovásion Greece see Neo Karlovasi
Neopit U.S.A. 172 E6
Neosho U.S.A. 178 D4
Neosho r. U.S.A. 178 D4
Neos Marmaras Greece 59 E8
▶Nepal country Asia 97 D3
asia [countries] ▶ 64–67
Nepalganj Nepal 97 D3
Nepanagar India 96 C5
Nepean Canada 168 F4
Nephi U.S.A. 183 M2
Nephin hill Rep. of Ireland 47 C9
Nephin Beg Range hills Rep. of Ireland 47 C9
Nepisiguit r. Canada 169 H4
Nepryadva r. Rus. Fed. 43 T8
Neptune U.S.A. 177 K5
Ner r. Poland 49 P3
Nera r. Italy 56 E6
Nérac France 50 G8
Neral India 94 B2
Nerang Australia 147 G1
Nera Tso l. Xizang China 89 F6
Neravai Lith. 42 F7
Nerchinsk Rus. Fed. 85 H1
Nerchinskiy Zavod Rus. Fed. 85 H1
Nerekhta Rus. Fed. 43 V4
Nereta Latvia 42 G5
Neretva r. Bos.-Herz./Croatia 56 J5
Neretvanski Kanal sea chan. Croatia 56 J5
Neri India 94 C1
Nêri Pünco l. China 89 E6
Neriquinha Angola 127 D8
Neris r. Lith. 42 E7

index N

	river	length	location	page#
1 ▶	Nile	6 695km / 4 160miles	Africa	121 F2
2 ▶	Amazon	6 516km / 4 049miles	South America	202 B1
3 ▶	Yangtze	6 380km / 3 964miles	Asia	87 G2
4 ▶	Mississippi-Missouri	5 969km / 3 709miles	North America	179 E6
5 ▶	Ob'-Irtysh	5 568km / 3 459miles	Asia	38 G3
6 ▶	Yenisey-Angara-Selenga	5 550km / 3 448miles	Asia	39 I2
7 ▶	Yellow	5 464km / 3 395miles	Asia	85 H4
8 ▶	Congo	4 667km / 2 900miles	Africa	127 B6
9 ▶	Rio de la Plata-Paraná	4 500km / 2 796miles	South America	204 F4
10 ▶	Irtysh	4 440km / 2 759miles	Asia	38 G3

longest rivers

Ningxian China 85 E5
also known as Xinning
Ningxiang China 87 E2
Ningyang China 85 H5
Ningyuan China 87 D3
Ningzhou China see Huaning
Ninh Binh Vietnam 78 D3
Ninh Hoa Vietnam 79 E5
Ninigo Group is P.N.G. 73 J7
Ninnis Glacier Antarctica 223 J2
Ninnis Glacier Tongue Antarctica 223 K2
Ninohe Japan 90 G4
Ninualac, Canal sea chan. Chile 205 B7
Nioaque Brazil 201 G5
Niobrara r. U.S.A. 178 C3
Nioghalvfjerdsfjorden inlet Greenland 165 R2
Nioki Dem. Rep. Congo 126 C5
Niokolo Koba, Parc National du nat. park Senegal 124 B3
Niono Mali 124 D3
Nioro Mali 124 C3
Niort France 50 F6
Nioût well Mauritania 124 D3
Nipa P.N.G. 73 J8
Nipani India 94 B2
Nipanipa, Tanjung pt Indon. 75 B3
Nipawin Canada 167 J4
Niphad India 94 B1
Nipigon Canada 168 B3
Nipigon, Lake Canada 168 B3
Nipigon Bay Canada 172 F2
Nipiodi Moz. 131 H3
Nipishish Lake Canada 169 I2
Nipissing Canada 173 N4
Nipissing, Lake Canada 168 E4
Nipomo U.S.A. 182 D6
Nippon country Asia see Japan
Nippon Hai sea N. Pacific Ocean see Japan, Sea of
Nippur tourist site Iraq 107 F4
Niquelândia Brazil 202 B5
Niquero Cuba 186 D2
Nir Ardabīl Iran 100 A2
Nir Yazd Iran 100 C4
Nir, Jabal an hills Saudi Arabia 104 C2
Nira r. India 94 B2
Nirasaki Japan 91 F7
Nirji China 85 J1
also known as Morin Dawa
Nirmal India 94 C2
Nirmali India 97 E4
Nirmal Range hills India 94 C2
Nirzas l. Latvia 42 I5
Niš Srbija Yugo. 58 C5
historically known as Naissus
Nisa Port. 54 D5
Nişāb Yemen 105 D5
Nisah, Wādī watercourse Saudi Arabia 105 D2
Nišava r. Yugo. 58 C5
Niscemi Sicilia Italy 57 G11
Niseko Japan 90 G3
Nīshāpūr Iran see Neyshābūr
Nishcha r. Belarus 43 J6
Nishibetsu-gawa r. Japan 90 I3
Nishikawa Japan 90 G5
Nishinomiya Japan 91 D7
Nishino-omote Japan 91 B9
Nishino-shima i. Japan 91 C6
Nishino-shima vol. Japan 81 O7
Nishi-Sonogi-hantō pen. Japan 91 A8
Nishi-suidō sea chan. Japan/S. Korea 91 A7
also known as Chōsen-kaikyō
Nishiwaki Japan 91 D7
Nísia Floresta Brazil 202 F3
Nisibis Turkey see Nusaybin
Nisi-mera Japan 91 B8
Nisiros i. Greece see Nisyros
Niskanselkä l. Fin. 44 N2
Niskayuna U.S.A. 177 L3
Niskibi r. Canada 168 B1
Nisko Poland 49 T5
Nisling r. Canada 166 B2
Nisporeni Moldova 58 J1
Nissan r. Sweden 45 K4
Nisser l. Norway 45 J4
Nissum Bredning b. Denmark 45 J4
Nistru r. Moldova see Dniester
Nistrului Inferior, Cîmpia lowland Moldova 58 K1
Nisutlin r. Canada 166 C2
Nisyros i. Greece 59 I12
also spelt Nísiros
Nita Japan 91 C7
Nitchequon Canada 169 G2
Nitendi i. Solomon Is see Ndeni
Niterói Brazil 203 D7
Nith r. U.K. 47 I8
Niti Pass China 96 C3
Nitmiluk National Park Australia 148 B2
formerly known as Katherine Gorge National Park
Nitra Slovakia 49 P7
Nitra r. Slovakia 49 P8
Nitro U.S.A. 176 D7
Nittedal Norway 45 J3
Niuafo'ou i. Tonga 145 H3
also spelt Niuafu
Niuafu i. Tonga see Niuafo'ou
Niuatoputopu i. Tonga 145 H3
formerly known as Boscawen Island
Niubiziliang China 84 B4

▶Niue terr. S. Pacific Ocean 145 I3
Self-governing New Zealand Overseas Territory.
oceania [countries] ➡ 138–139

Niujing China see Binchuan
Niulakita i. Tuvalu 145 G3
formerly spelt Nurakita
Niulan Jiang r. China 86 B3
Niur, Pulau i. Indon. 76 C3
Niushan China see Donghai
Niutao i. Tuvalu 145 G2
Niutoushan China 87 F2
Niuzhuang China 85 I3
Nivala Fin. 44 N3
Nivastroy Rus. Fed. 44 P2
Nive watercourse Australia 149 E5
Nive r. France 50 E9
Nive Downs Australia 149 E5
Nivelles Belgium 51 K2
Nivnoye Rus. Fed. 43 N8
Nivskiy Rus. Fed. 44 P2
Niwai India 96 B4
Niwari India 96 C4
Niwas India 96 D5
Nixia China see Sêrxu
Nixon U.S.A. 182 E2
Niya China see Minfeng
Niya He r. China 89 C4
Niyut, Gunung mt. Indon. 77 E2
Niz Rus. Fed. 43 Q2
Nizamabad India 94 C2
also known as Indur
Nizampatnam India 94 D3
Nizam Sagar l. India 94 C2
Nizh Aydere Turkm. 102 D5
Nizhegorodskaya Oblast' admin. div. Rus. Fed. 40 H4
English form Nizhniy Novgorod Oblast; formerly known as Gor'kovskaya Oblast'
Nizhneangarsk Rus. Fed. 81 H1
Nizhnedevitsk Rus. Fed. 41 F6
Nizhnekamsk Rus. Fed. 40 I5
Nizhnekamskoye Vodokhranilishche resr Rus. Fed. 40 J5
Nizhnekolymsk Rus. Fed. 39 Q3
Nizhne-Svirskiy Zapovednik nature res. Rus. Fed. 43 O1
Nizhneudinsk Rus. Fed. 80 F2
Nizhnevartovsk Rus. Fed. 38 H3
Nizhnevolzhsk Rus. Fed. see Narimanov
Nizhneyansk Rus. Fed. 39 N2
Nizhneye Kuyto, Ozero l. Rus. Fed. 44 O2
Nizhni Irginski Rus. Fed. 40 K4
Nizhniy Baskunchak Rus. Fed. 102 A2
Nizhniy Chir Rus. Fed. 41 G6
Nizhniye Kresty Rus. Fed. see Cherskiy
Nizhniye Ustriki Poland see Ustrzyki Dolne
Nizhniy Lomov Rus. Fed. 41 G5
Nizhniy Novgorod Rus. Fed. 40 G4
formerly known as Gor'kiy
Nizhniy Novgorod Oblast admin. div. Rus. Fed. see Nizhegorodskaya Oblast'
Nizhniy Odes Rus. Fed. 40 J3
Nizhniy Pyandzh Tajik. see Panji Poyon
Nizhniy Tagil Rus. Fed. 38 F4
Nizhniy Yenangsk Rus. Fed. 40 H4
Nizhnyaya Mola Rus. Fed. 40 H2
Nizhnyaya Omra Rus. Fed. 40 J3
Nizhnyaya Pesha Rus. Fed. 40 H2
Nizhnyaya Pirenga, Ozero l. Rus. Fed. 44 P2
Nizhnyaya Poyma Rus. Fed. 80 F1
Nizhnyaya Suyetka Rus. Fed. 103 I1
Nizhnyaya Tunguska r. Rus. Fed. 39 I3
English form Lower Tunguska
Nizhnyaya Tura Rus. Fed. 38 F4
Nizhnyaya Zolotitsa Rus. Fed. 40 G2
Nizhyn Ukr. 41 D6
also spelt Nezhin
Nizina Mazowiecka reg. Poland 49 R3
Nizip Turkey 107 D3
Nizkabor"ye Belarus 43 L6
Nízke Beskydy hills Slovakia 49 S6
Nízke Tatry mts Slovakia 49 Q7
Nízke Tatry nat. park Slovakia 49 Q7
Nizmennyy, Mys pt Rus. Fed. 90 D3
Nizwā Oman see Nazwá
Nizza France see Nice
Nizza Monferrato Italy 56 A4
Njavve Sweden 44 L2
Njazidja i. Comoros 129 D7
also known as Grande Comore
Njegoš mts Yugo. 56 K6
Njellim Fin. see Nellim
Njinjo Tanz. 129 C7
Njombe Tanz. 129 B7
Njombe r. Tanz. 129 B6
Njutånger Sweden 45 L3
Nkai Zimbabwe see Nkayi
Nkambe Cameroon 125 H5
Nkandla S. Africa 133 P5
Nkasi Tanz. 129 A6
Nkawkaw Ghana 125 E5
Nkayi Zimbabwe 131 F3
formerly spelt Nkai
Nkhaïlé well Mauritania 124 D2
Nkhata Bay Malawi 129 B7
Nkhotakota Malawi 129 B8
Nkhotakota Game Reserve nature res. Malawi 129 B8
Nkomfap Nigeria 125 H5
Nkomi, Lagune lag. Gabon 126 A5
Nkondwe Tanz. 129 A6
Nkongsamba Cameroon 125 H5
Nkoranza Ghana 125 E5
Nkoteng Cameroon 125 I5
Nkululeko S. Africa 133 L8
Nkundi Tanz. 129 A6
Nkungwi Tanz. 129 A6
Nkurenkuru Namibia 130 C3
Nkwalini S. Africa 133 P5
Nkwanta Ghana 125 F4
Nkwenkwezi S. Africa 133 K10
Nmai Hka r. Myanmar 78 B2
Noa Dihing r. India 97 H4
Noakhali Bangl. 97 F5
Noamundi India 97 E5
Noatak r. U.S.A. 164 C3
Noatak National Preserve nature res. U.S.A. 164 D3
Nobeoka Japan 91 B8
Noblesville U.S.A. 174 C3
Nobokwe S. Africa 133 L8
Noboribetsu Japan 90 G3
Nobres Brazil 201 F3
Noccundra Australia 147 D1
Noce r. Italy 56 D2
Nocera Terinese Italy 57 I9
Nochistlán Mex. 185 E4
Nochixtlán Mex. 185 F5
Noci Italy 57 J8
Nockatunga Australia 147 D1
Nocoleche Nature Reserve Australia 147 E2
Nocona U.S.A. 179 C5
Noda Japan 91 F7
Nodaway r. U.S.A. 178 D4
Nodeland Norway 45 I4
Noel Kempff Mercado, Parque Nacional nat. park Bol. 201 E3
Noelville Canada 173 M4
Noenieput S. Africa 132 E4
Nogales Mex. 184 C2
also known as Heroica Nogales
Nogales U.S.A. 181 E7
Nogaro France 50 F9
Nogat r. Poland 49 Q1
Nōgata Japan 91 B8
Nogayty Kazakh. 102 C2
Nogent-le-Rotrou France 50 G4
Nogent-sur-Oise France 51 I3
Nogent-sur-Seine France 51 J4
Noginsk Evenkiyskiy Avtonomnyy Okrug Rus. Fed. 39 J3
Noginsk Moskovskaya Oblast' Rus. Fed. 43 T6
Nogliki Rus. Fed. 82 F2
Nogo r. Australia 149 F5
Nogoa r. Australia 149 F4
Nōgōhaku-san mt. Japan 91 E7
Nogoyá Arg. 204 F4
Nohar India 96 B3
Noheji Japan 90 G4
Nohfelden Germany 48 E6
Nohili Point U.S.A. 181 [inset] Y1
Nohur Turkm. see Nokhur
Noia Spain 54 C2
also spelt Noya
Noidore r. Brazil 206 A1
Noire r. Canada 173 Q5
Noire, Montagne mts France 51 I9
Noire, Pointe pt Morocco 55 H9
Noires, Montagnes hills France 50 C4
Noirmoutier, Île de i. France 50 D6
Noirmoutier-en-l'Île France 50 D5
Nojima-zaki c. Japan 91 F7
Nokesville U.S.A. 176 H7
Nokha India 96 B4
Nokhowch, Kūh-e mt. Iran 101 E5
Nokhur Turkm. 102 D5
also spelt Nohur
Nokia Fin. 45 M3
Nōkis Uzbek. see Nukus
Nok Kundi Pak. 101 E4
Nokomis Canada 167 J5
Nokomis Lake Canada 167 K3
Nokou Chad 120 B6
Nokrek Peak India 97 F4
Nola Cent. Afr. Rep. 126 C4
Nolichuky r. U.S.A. 176 B9
Nolinsk Rus. Fed. 40 I4
formerly known as Molotovsk
Noll S. Africa 132 G10
Nólsoy i. Faroe Is 46 F1
Noma-misaki pt Japan 91 B9
Nome U.S.A. 164 C3
Nomgon Mongolia 85 E3
Nomhon China 84 C4
Nomoi Islands Micronesia see Mortlock Islands
Nomonde S. Africa 133 K8
Nomo-zaki pt Japan 91 A8
Nomto Rus. Fed. 84 E1
Nomuka Tonga 145 H4
Nomzha Rus. Fed. 40 G4
Nonacho Lake Canada 167 I2
Nong'an China 82 B3
Nong Hong Thai. 79 C5
Nonghui China see Guang'an
Nong Khai Thai. 78 C4
Nongoma S. Africa 133 P4
Nongstoin India 97 F4
Nonni r. China see Nen Jiang
Nonoai Brazil 203 A8
Nonoava Mex. 184 D3
Nonouti atoll Kiribati 145 G2
also spelt Nanouki or Nanouti; formerly known as Sydenham
Nonsan S. Korea 83 B5
Nonthaburi Thai. 79 C5
Nontron France 50 G7
Nonzwakazi S. Africa 132 I7
Nõo Estonia 42 H3
Nookawarra Australia 151 B5
Noolyeanna Lake salt flat Australia 146 C1
Noonamah Australia 148 A2
Noondie, Lake salt flat Australia 151 B6
Noonkanbah Australia 150 D3
Noonkanbah Aboriginal Reserve Australia 150 D3
Noonthorangee Range hills Australia 147 D2
Noorama Creek watercourse Australia 147 E1
Noordbeveland i. Neth. 48 A4
Noorderhaaks i. Neth. 48 B3
Noordkaap S. Africa 133 P2
Noordkuil S. Africa 132 C9
Noordoewer Namibia 132 B5
Noordoost Polder Neth. 48 C3
Noordpunt pt Neth. Antilles 187 F4
Noormarkku Fin. 45 M3
Noorvik U.S.A. 164 C3
Nootka Island Canada 166 E5
Nóqui Angola 127 B6
Nora r. Rus. Fed. 82 C2
Norak Tajik. 101 G2
also spelt Nurek
Norala Phil. 74 C5
Noranda Canada 168 E3
Nor-Bayazet Armenia see Kamo
Norberg Sweden 45 K3
Nord prov. Cameroon 125 I4
Nord Greenland see Station Nord
Nord, Canal du France 48 A5
Nordaustlandet i. Svalbard 38 C2
Nordborg Denmark 48 G1
Nordbotn Norway 44 M1
Nordegg Canada 167 G4
Norden Germany 48 E2
Nordenshel'da, Arkhipelag is Rus. Fed. 39 J2
English form Nordenskjold Archipelago
Nordenskiold r. Canada 166 B2
Nordenskjold Archipelago is Rus. Fed. see Nordenshel'da, Arkhipelag
Norder Hever sea chan. Germany 48 F1
Norderney Germany 48 E2
Norderney i. Germany 48 E2
Norderstedt Germany 48 H2
Nordfjord Norway 44 O1
Nordfjord inlet Norway 44 I3
Nordfjordeid Norway 45 I3
Nordfold Norway 44 K2
Nordfriesische Inseln is Germany see North Frisian Islands
Nordhausen Germany 48 H4
Nordholz Germany 48 F2
Nordhorn Germany 48 E3
Nordhuglo Norway 45 I4
Nordingrå naturreservat nature res. Sweden 44 L3
Nord Kap c. Iceland see Horn
Nordkapp c. Norway see North Cape
Nord-Kivu prov. Dem. Rep. Congo 126 F5
Nord-Kvaløy i. Norway 44 L1
Nordkynhalvøya i. Norway 44 N1
Nordland county Norway 44 K2
Nordli Norway 44 K2
Nördliches Harzvorland park Germany 48 H4
Nördlingen Germany 48 H7
Nordmaling Sweden 44 L3
Nordmannvik Norway 44 M1
Nord- og Østgrønland, Nationalparken i nat. park Greenland 165 P2
Nordostrundingen c. Greenland see Northeast Foreland
Nord-Ostsee-Kanal canal Germany see Kiel Canal
Nord-Ouest prov. Cameroon 125 H5
Nord - Pas-de-Calais admin. reg. France 51 I2
Nord-Pas-de-Calais, Parc Naturel Régional du nature res. France 51 J2
Nordre Strømfjord inlet Greenland see Nassuttooq
Nordrhein-Westfalen land Germany 48 E4
English form North Rhine - Westphalia
Nordstrand i. Germany 48 F1
Nord-Trøndelag county Norway 44 K2
Norðurland eystra constituency Iceland 44 [inset] C2
Norðurland vestra constituency Iceland 44 [inset] B2
Nordvik Rus. Fed. 39 L2
Nordvika Norway 44 J3
Nore r. Rep. of Ireland 47 F11
Nore, Pic de mt. France 51 I9
Noreg country Europe see Norway
Noreikiškės Lith. 42 E7
Noresund Norway 45 J3
Norfolk NE U.S.A. 178 C3
Norfolk NY U.S.A. 177 K1
Norfolk VA U.S.A. 177 I9

▶Norfolk Island terr. S. Pacific Ocean 145 F4
Australian External Territory.
oceania [countries] ➡ 138–139

Norfork Lake U.S.A. 179 D4
Norge country Europe see Norway
Norheimsund Norway 45 I3
Noria Chile 200 C5
Norikura-dake vol. Japan 91 E6
Noril'sk Rus. Fed. 39 I3
Norkyung China see Bainang
Norland Canada 173 O6
Norlina U.S.A. 176 G9
Normal U.S.A. 174 B3
Norman r. Australia 149 D3
Norman U.S.A. 179 C5
Norman, Lake resr U.S.A. 174 D5
Normanby r. Australia 149 E2
Normanby N.Z. 152 I7
Normanby Island P.N.G. 145 E2
Normanby Range hills Australia 149 F4
Normandes, Îles is English Chan. see Channel Islands
Normandia Brazil 199 G4
Normandie reg. France see Normandy
Normandie, Collines de hills France 50 F4
Normandie-Maine, Parc Naturel Régional nature res. France 50 F4
Normandien S. Africa 133 N4
Normandy reg. France 50 F4
also spelt Normandie
Normanton Australia 149 D3
Norman Wells Canada 166 E1
Normétal Canada 173 N2
Norogachic Mex. 184 D3
Norquay Canada 167 K5
Ñorquinco Arg. 205 C6
Norråker Sweden 44 K2
Norra Kvarken strait Fin./Sweden 44 M3
Norrbotten county Sweden 44 L2
Nørre Nebel Denmark 45 J5
Norrent-Fontes France 51 I2
Norrfjärden Sweden 44 M2
Norrhult-Klavreström Sweden 45 K4
Norris U.S.A. 176 A9
Norris Lake U.S.A. 176 B9
Norristown U.S.A. 177 J5
Norrköping Sweden 45 L4
Norrsundet Sweden 45 L3
Norrtälje Sweden 45 L4
Norseman Australia 151 C7
Norsewood N.Z. 152 K8
Norsjö Sweden 44 L2
Norsk Rus. Fed. 82 C1
Norske Øer is Greenland 165 R2
Norsup Vanuatu 145 F3
Norte, Punta pt Buenos Aires Arg. 204 F5
Norte, Punta pt Arg. 205 C8
Norte, Punta pt Arg. 205 E6
Norte, Serra do hills Brazil 201 F2
Norte de Santander dept Col. 198 C2
Nortelândia Brazil 201 F3
North, Cape Antarctica 223 L2
North, Cape Canada 169 I4
North Adams U.S.A. 177 L3
Northallerton U.K. 47 K9
Northam Australia 151 B6
Northam S. Africa 133 L1
Northampton Australia 151 A6
Northampton U.K. 47 L11
Northampton MA U.S.A. 177 M3
Northampton PA U.S.A. 177 J5
Northampton Downs Australia 149 E5
North Andaman i. India 95 G3
North Anna r. U.S.A. 176 H8
North Anson U.S.A. 177 P1
North Arm b. Canada 167 H2
North Balabac Strait Phil. 74 A4
North Baltimore U.S.A. 176 B4
North Battleford Canada 167 I4
North Bay Canada 168 E4
North Bend OR U.S.A. 180 A4
North Bend PA U.S.A. 176 H4
North Bennington U.S.A. 177 L3
North Berwick U.K. 46 J7
North Berwick U.S.A. 177 O2
North Borneo state Malaysia see Sabah
North Bosque r. U.S.A. 179 C6
North Branch MI U.S.A. 173 J7
North Branch MN U.S.A. 172 A5
North Caicos i. Turks and Caicos Is 187 F2
North Canadian r. U.S.A. 179 D5
North Cape Canada 169 H4
North Cape Norway 44 N1
also known as Nordkapp
North Cape N.Z. 152 H2
North Cape S. Georgia 205 [inset]
North Caribou Lake Canada 168 B2
North Carolina state U.S.A. 176 F9
North Cascades National Park U.S.A. 180 B2
North Central Aboriginal Reserve Australia 150 D4
North Channel lake channel Canada 168 D4
North Channel str. Northern Ireland/Scotland U.K. 47 G9
North Charleston U.S.A. 175 E5
North Cheyenne Indian Reservation res. U.S.A. 180 F3
Northcliffe Australia 151 B7
Northcliffe Glacier Antarctica 223 G2
North Collins U.S.A. 176 G3
North Concho r. U.S.A. 179 B6
North Conway U.S.A. 177 N1
North Cowichan Canada 166 F5
North Creek U.S.A. 177 L2
North Dakota state U.S.A. 178 B2
North Downs hills U.K. 47 L12
North East admin. dist. Botswana 131 E4
North East MD U.S.A. 177 J6
North East PA U.S.A. 176 F3
North East Cay reef Australia 149 G4
North-Eastern prov. Kenya 128 D4

▶Northeast Foreland c. Greenland 165 R1
Most easterly point of North America. Also known as Nordostrundingen.

North-East Frontier Agency state India see Arunachal Pradesh
Northeast Point Bahamas 175 F8
Northeast Providence Channel Bahamas 186 D1
North Edwards U.S.A. 182 G6
Northeim Germany 48 G4
North End Point Bahamas 175 F7
Northern admin. reg. Ghana 125 E4
Northern admin. reg. Malawi 129 B7
Northern prov. S. Africa 133 M1
formerly known as Northern Transvaal
Northern prov. Sierra Leone 124 C4
Northern state Sudan 121 F4
Northern prov. Zambia 127 F7
Northern Aegean admin. reg. Greece see Voreio Aigaio
Northern Areas admin. div. Pak. 101 H2
Northern Bahr el Ghazal state Sudan 126 E2
Northern Cape prov. S. Africa 132 D6
Northern Darfur state Sudan 121 E5
Northern Donets r. Rus. Fed./Ukr. see Severskiy Donets
Northern Dvina r. Rus. Fed. see Severnaya Dvina
Northern Indian Lake Canada 167 L3
Northern Ireland prov. U.K. 47 F9
Northern Kordofan state Sudan 121 F6
Northern Lau Group is Fiji 145 H3
Northern Light Lake Canada 168 B3

▶Northern Mariana Islands terr. N. Pacific Ocean 73 J3
United States Commonwealth. Historically known as Ladrones.
oceania [countries] ➡ 138–139

Northern Rhodesia country Africa see Zambia
Northern Sporades is Greece see Voreioi Sporades
Northern Territory admin. div. Australia 148 B3
Northern Transvaal prov. S. Africa see Northern
North Fabius r. U.S.A. 174 B4
Northfield MA U.S.A. 177 M3
Northfield MN U.S.A. 174 A2
Northfield NJ U.S.A. 171 H3
Northfield VT U.S.A. 177 M1
Northfield WI U.S.A. 172 B6
North Foreland c. U.K. 47 N12
North Fork U.S.A. 182 E4
North Fork Pass Canada 166 B1
North Fox Island U.S.A. 172 H5
North French r. Canada 168 D3
North Frisian Islands Germany 48 F1
also known as Nordfriesische Inseln
North Geomagnetic Pole Arctic Ocean 224 T1
North Haven U.S.A. 177 M4
North Head N.Z. 152 I4
North Henik Lake Canada 167 L2
North Hero U.S.A. 177 L1
North Highlands U.S.A. 182 C3
North Horr Kenya 128 C4
North Hudson U.S.A. 177 L2
North Island India 94 B4

▶North Island N.Z. 152 H6
3rd largest island in Oceania.
oceania [landscapes] ➡ 136–137

North Island Phil. 74 B1
North Islet reef Phil. 74 B4
North Jadito Canyon gorge U.S.A. 183 N6
North Judson U.S.A. 172 G9
North Kazakhstan Oblast admin. div. Kazakh. see Severnyy Kazakhstan
North Kingsville U.S.A. 176 E4
North Knife r. Canada 167 M3
North Knife Lake Canada 167 L3
North Koel r. India 97 D4
North Komelik U.S.A. 183 M9

▶North Korea country Asia 83 B4
asia [countries] ➡ 64–67

North Lakhimpur India 97 G4
Northland admin. reg. N.Z. 152 I3
North Land is Rus. Fed. see Severnaya Zemlya
Northland Forest Park nature res. N.Z. 152 H3
North Las Vegas U.S.A. 183 I5
North Liberty U.S.A. 172 G9
North Little Rock U.S.A. 179 D5
North Loup r. U.S.A. 178 C3
North Luangwa National Park Zambia 129 B7
North Maalhosmadulu Atoll Maldives 94 B5
North Macmillan r. Canada 166 C2
North Magnetic Pole Canada 224 R1
North Mam Peak U.S.A. 180 F5
North Manchester U.S.A. 172 H10
North Middletown U.S.A. 176 A7
North Moose Lake Canada 167 K4
North Muiron Island Australia 150 A4
North Nahanni r. Canada 166 F2
North Ossetia aut. rep. Rus. Fed. see Severnaya Osetiya-Alaniya, Respublika
North Palisade mt. U.S.A. 182 F4
North Platte U.S.A. 178 B3
North Platte r. U.S.A. 178 B3
North Point Australia 151 A6
North Point Hong Kong China 87 [inset]
also known as Tsat Tsze Mui
North Pole Arctic Ocean 224 A1
Northport U.S.A. 175 C5
North Port U.S.A. 175 D7
North Reef Island India 95 G3
North Rhine - Westphalia land Germany see Nordrhein-Westfalen
North River Bridge Canada 169 I4
North Rona i. U.K. see Rona
North Ronaldsay i. U.K. 46 J4
North Saskatchewan r. Canada 167 J4
North Schell Peak U.S.A. 183 J2
North Sea Europe 46 N6
North Seal r. Canada 167 L3
North Sentinel Island India 95 G4
North Shoal Lake Canada 167 L5
North Shoshone Peak U.S.A. 183 G2
North Siberian Lowland Rus. Fed. 39 K2
also known as Severo-Sibirskaya Nizmennost'
North Simlipal National Park India 97 E5
North Sinai governorate Egypt see Shamāl Sīnā'
North Slope plain U.S.A. 164 E3
North Spirit Lake Canada 167 M4
North Stradbroke Island Australia 147 G1
North Stratford U.S.A. 177 N1
North Taranaki Bight b. N.Z. 152 I6
North Thompson r. Canada 166 F5
North Tonawanda U.S.A. 176 G2
North Trap reef N.Z. 153 B15
North Troy U.S.A. 177 M1
North Truro U.S.A. 177 O3
North Tuas Basin dock Sing. 76 [inset]
North Twin Island Canada 168 E2
North Twin Lake Canada 169 K3
North Ubian i. Phil. 74 B5
North Uist i. U.K. 46 E6
also known as Uibhist a' Tuath
Northumberland Isles Australia 149 F4
Northumberland National Park U.K. 46 J8
Northumberland Strait Canada 169 H4
North Umpqua r. U.S.A. 180 B4
North Vancouver Canada 166 F5
Northville U.S.A. 177 K2
North Wabasca Lake Canada 167 H3
North Walsham U.K. 47 N11
North Waterford U.S.A. 177 O1
Northway U.S.A. 166 A2
Northway Junction U.S.A. 166 A2
North West prov. S. Africa 133 J3
North West Cape Australia 150 A4
North-Western prov. Zambia 127 D8
North West Frontier prov. Pak. 101 G3
North West Nelson Forest Park nat. park N.Z. see Kahurangi National Park
Northwest Providence Channel Bahamas 186 D1
North West River Canada 169 J2
Northwest Territories admin. div. Canada 167 J2
North Wilkesboro U.S.A. 176 D9
North Windham U.S.A. 177 O2
Northwood IA U.S.A. 174 A3
Northwood ND U.S.A. 178 C2
Northwood NH U.S.A. 177 N2
Northwoods Beach U.S.A. 172 B5
North York Canada 173 N7
North York Moors moorland U.K. 47 L9
North York Moors National Park U.K. 47 L9
Norton Canada 169 H4
Norton KS U.S.A. 178 C4
Norton VT U.S.A. 174 G2
Norton de Matos Angola see Balombo
Norton Shores U.S.A. 172 G7
Norton Sound sea chan. U.S.A. 164 C3
Nortorf Germany 48 G1
Nort-sur-Erdre France 50 E5
Norvegia, Cape Antarctica 223 X2
Norwalk OH U.S.A. 176 C4
Norwalk WI U.S.A. 172 C7

▶Norway country Europe 45 J3
known as Norge or Noreg in Norwegian
europe [countries] ➡ 32–35

Norway U.S.A. 177 O1
Norway Bay Canada 173 Q5
Norway House Canada 167 L4
Norwegian Bay Canada 165 J2
Norwegian Sea N. Atlantic Ocean 224 A2
Norwich Canada 173 M8
Norwich U.K. 47 N11
Norwich CT U.S.A. 177 M4
Norwich NY U.S.A. 177 J3
Norwood MA U.S.A. 177 N3
Norwood NY U.S.A. 177 K1
Norwood OH U.S.A. 176 A6
Norzagaray Phil. 74 B3
Nose Lake Canada 167 I1
Noshappu-misaki hd Japan 90 G2
Noshiro Japan 90 G4
Noshul' Rus. Fed. 40 I3
Nosivka Ukr. 41 D6
also spelt Nosovka
Nosop watercourse Africa see Nossob
Nosovaya Rus. Fed. 40 J1
Nosovka Ukr. see Nosivka
Nosrātābād Iran 101 D4
Nossa Senhora da Glória Brazil 200 B1
Nossa Senhora do Livramento Brazil 201 F3
Nossen Germany 49 K4
Nossob watercourse Africa 132 E3
also spelt Nosop
Nossob Camp S. Africa 132 E2
Nosy Varika Madag. 131 [inset] K4
Nota r. Fin./Rus. Fed. 44 O1
Notakwanon r. Canada 169 I1
Notch Peak U.S.A. 183 K2
Noteć r. Poland 49 M3
Notikewin r. Canada 166 G3
Notio Aigaio admin. reg. Greece 59 H12
English form Southern Aegean; also spelt Nótion Aiyaíon
Nótion Aiyaíon admin. reg. Greece see Notio Aigaio
Notios Evvoïkos Kolpos sea chan. Greece 59 E10
Notio Steno Kerkyras sea chan. Greece 59 B9
Noto Sicilia Italy 57 H12
Noto Japan 90 E6
Noto, Golfo di g. Sicilia Italy 57 H12
Notodden Norway 45 J4
Noto-hantō pen. Japan 90 E6
Notre Dame, Monts mts Canada 169 G4
Notre Dame Bay Canada 169 K3
Notre-Dame-de-Koartac Canada see Quaqtaq
Notre-Dame-de-la-Salette Canada 173 R5
Notre-Dame-du-Laus Canada 173 R4
Notre-Dame-du-Nord Canada 173 N3
Notsé Togo 125 F5
Notsu Japan 91 B8
Notsuke-saki pt Japan 90 I3
Notsuke-suidō sea chan. Japan/Rus. Fed. 90 I3
also known as Izmeny, Proliv
Nottawasaga Bay Canada 173 M6
Nottaway r. Canada 168 E3
Nottingham U.K. 47 K11
Nottingham Island Canada 165 L3
Nottingham Road S. Africa 133 O6
Nottoway U.S.A. 176 G8
Nottoway r. U.S.A. 176 I9
Notukeu Creek r. Canada 167 J5
Nouâdhibou Mauritania 122 A5
formerly known as Port Étienne
Nouâdhibou, Râs c. Mauritania 122 A5

▶Nouakchott Mauritania 124 B2
Capital of Mauritania.

Noual well Mauritania 124 D2
Nouâmghâr Mauritania 124 A2
Nouei Vietnam 79 D5

▶Nouméa New Caledonia 145 F4
Capital of New Caledonia.

Noun r. Cameroon 125 H5
Nouna Burkina 124 E3
Noupoort S. Africa 133 I8
Noupoortsnek pass S. Africa 133 M5
Nousu Fin. 44 O2
Nouveau-Comptoir Canada see Wemindji
Nouvelle Anvers Dem. Rep. Congo see Makanza
Nouvelle Calédonie i. S. Pacific Ocean 145 F4
also known as New Caledonia
Nouvelle Calédonie terr. S. Pacific Ocean see New Caledonia
Nouvelles Hébrides country S. Pacific Ocean see Vanuatu
Nov Tajik. 101 G1
also spelt Nau
Nova Estonia 42 E2
Nova Almeida Brazil 207 M7
Nova América Brazil 206 D2
Nova Aurora Brazil 206 E5
Novabad Tajik. see Novobod
Novabad Tajik. see Novobod
Nová Baňa Slovakia 49 P7
Nova Chaves Angola see Muconda
Novaci Romania 58 E3
Nova Crnja Vojvodina, Srbija Yugo. 58 B3
Nova Cruz Brazil 202 F3
Nova Era Brazil 207 J6
Nova Esperança Angola see Buengas
Nova Esperança Brazil 206 A10
Nova Freixa Moz. see Cuamba
Nova Friburgo Brazil 203 D7
Nova Gaia Angola see Cambundi-Catembo
Nova Goa India see Panaji
Nova Gorica Slovenia 56 F3
Nova Gradiška Croatia 56 J3
Nova Granada Brazil 206 D7
Nova Iguaçu Brazil 203 D7
Nova Kakhovka Ukr. 41 E7
also spelt Novaya Kakhovka
Nova Lima Brazil 203 D6
Nova Lisboa Angola see Huambo
Nova Londrina Brazil 206 A9
Novalukoml' Belarus 43 K7
also spelt Novolukoml'
Nova Mambone Moz. 131 G4
Nova Nabúri Moz. 131 H3
Nova Odesa Ukr. 41 D7
also spelt Novaya Odessa
Nová Paka Czech Rep. 49 M5
Nova Paraiso Brazil 199 F4
Nova Pazova Vojvodina, Srbija Yugo. 58 B4
Nova Pilão Arcado Brazil 202 D4
Nova Ponte Brazil 206 F6
Nova Ponte, Represa resr Minas Gerais Brazil 206 F6
Nova Ponte, Represa resr Brazil 203 C6
Novara Italy 56 A3
Nova Remanso Brazil 202 D4
Nova Resende Brazil 206 G8
Nova Russas Brazil 202 D3
Nova Scotia prov. Canada 169 H5
historically known as Acadia
Nova Sento Sé Brazil 202 D4
Nova Serrana Brazil 207 I6
Nova Sintra Angola see Catabola
Nova Soure Brazil 202 E4
Novate Mezzola Italy 56 B2
Novato U.S.A. 182 B3
Nova Topola Bos.-Herz. 56 J3
Novator Rus. Fed. 40 H3
Nova Vandúzi Moz. 131 G3
Nova Varoš Srbija Yugo. 58 A5
Nova Venécia Brazil 203 D6
Nova Viçosa Brazil 207 N4
Nova Vida Amazonas Brazil 199 E5
Nova Vida Rondônia Brazil 201 E2
Nova Xavantino Brazil 206 A1
Novaya Kakhovka Ukr. see Nova Kakhovka
Novaya Kazanka Kazakh. 102 B2
also known as Zhanga Qazan
Novaya Ladoga Rus. Fed. 43 N1
Novaya Odessa Ukr. see Nova Odesa
Novaya Pismyanka Rus. Fed. see Leninogorsk
Novaya Sibir', Ostrov i. Rus. Fed. 39 O2

▶Novaya Zemlya is Rus. Fed. 40 J1
3rd largest island in Europe.
europe [landscapes] ➡ 30–31
arctic [features] ➡ 214–215

Novaya Zhizn Rus. Fed. see Kazinka
Nova Zagora Bulg. 58 H6
Novelda Spain 55 K6
Novellara Italy 56 C4
Nové Město nad Metují Czech Rep. 49 N5
Nové Mlýny, Vodní nádrž resr Czech Rep. 49 N7
Nové Zámky Slovakia 49 P8
Novgorod Rus. Fed. see Velikiy Novgorod
Novgorodka Rus. Fed. 43 J4
Novgorod Oblast admin. div. Rus. Fed. see Novgorodskaya Oblast'
Novgorod-Severskiy Ukr. see Novhorod-Sivers'kyy
Novgorodskaya Oblast' admin. div. Rus. Fed. 43 N3
English form Novgorod Oblast
Novgorod-Volynskiy Ukr. see Novohrad-Volyns'kyy
Novgradets Bulg. see Suvorovo

Paarl S. Africa **132** C10
Paasvere Estonia **42** H2
Paatsjoki *r.* Europe *see* **Patsoyoki**
Paauilo U.S.A. **181** [inset] Z1
Pabaigh *i.* U.K. *see* **Pabbay**
Paballelo S. Africa **132** F5
P'abal-li N. Korea **83** C4
Pabbay *i. Western Isles, Scotland* U.K. **46** E6
Pabbay *i. Western Isles, Scotland* U.K. **46** E7 *also spelt* Pabaigh
Pabianice Poland **49** Q4 *historically known as* Pabianitz
Pabianitz Poland *see* **Pabianice**
Pabna Bangl. **97** F4
Pabradė Lith. **42** G7
Pab Range *mts* Pak. **101** F5
Pacaás, Serra dos *hills* Brazil **201** D2
Pacaás Novos, Parque Nacional *nat. park* Brazil **201** E2
Pacaembu Brazil **206** B8
Pacahuaras *r.* Bol. **200** D2
Pacajus Brazil **202** E3
Pacaraimã, Serra *mts* S. America *see* **Pakaraima Mountains**
Pacaraima Mountains S. America *see* **Pakaraima Mountains**
Pacarán Peru **200** B3
Pacasmayo Peru **200** A1
Pacatuba Brazil **202** E2
Pacaya *r.* Peru **198** C6
Pacaya, Volcán de *vol.* Guat. **185** H6
Pacaya Samiria, Reserva Nacional *nature res.* Peru **198** C6
Paceco *Sicilia* Italy **57** E11
Pacheco *Chihuahua* Mex. **184** C2
Pacheco *Zacatecas* Mex. **185** E3
Pachia *i.* Greece **59** G12 *also spelt* Pakhiá
Pachía Peru **200** C4
Pachino *Sicilia* Italy **57** H12
Pachitea *r.* Peru **200** B2
Pachiza Peru **200** A1
Pachmarhi India **96** C5
Pachor India **96** C5
Pachora India **94** B1
Pachpadra India **96** B4
Pachuca Mex. **185** F4
Pacifica U.S.A. **182** B4
Pacific Grove U.S.A. **182** C5

▶**Pacific Ocean 220**
Largest ocean in the world.
oceans [features] ▶ 210–211

Paget, Mount S. Georgia **205** [inset]
Paget Cay *reef* Australia **149** G3
Paghman *mt.* Afgh. **101** G3
Pagiriai Lith. **42** F6
Pagiriai Lith. **42** G7
Pagon *i.* N. Mariana Is *see* **Pagan**
Pagosa Springs U.S.A. **181** F5
Pagouda Togo **125** F4
Pagqên China *see* **Gadê**
Pagri China **89** E7
Pagwachuan *r.* Canada **168** C3
Pagwi P.N.G. **73** J7
Pahala U.S.A. **181** [inset] Z2
Pahang *r.* Malaysia **76** C2
Pahang *state* Malaysia **76** C2
Paharpur *tourist site* Bangl. **97** F4
Paharpur Pak. **101** G3
Pahauman Indon. **77** E2
Pahia Point N.Z. **153** B14
Pahiatua N.Z. **152** J8
Pahlavī Dezh Iran *see* **Āq Qal'eh**
Pahlgam Jammu and Kashmir **96** B2
Pahokee U.S.A. **175** D7
Pahost Vodaskhovishcha *resr* Belarus **42** H9
Pahra Kariz Afgh. **101** E3
Pahranagat Range *mts* U.S.A. **183** I4
Pahranichny Belarus **42** E8 *formerly known as* Byerastavitsa
Pahrump U.S.A. **183** I5
Pahuj *r.* India **96** C4
Pahute Mesa *plat.* U.S.A. **183** H4
Paiaguás Brazil **201** F4
Paicines U.S.A. **182** C5
Paide Estonia **42** G3
Paignton U.K. **47** I13
Paihia N.Z. **152** I3
Paiján Peru **200** A1
Päijänne *l.* Fin. **45** N3
Paikü Co *l.* China **89** D6
Paila *r.* Bol. **201** D4
Pailing China *see* **Chun'an**
Paillaco Chile **204** B6
Paimio Fin. **45** M3
Paimpol France **50** C4
Painan Indon. **76** C3
Painavu India **94** C4
Paine Chile **204** C4
Paine, Cerro *mt.* Chile **205** B8
Paineiras Brazil **207** H5
Painesdale U.S.A. **172** E3
Painesville U.S.A. **176** D4
Pains Brazil **207** H7

oceans	ocean	area sq km	area sq miles	greatest depth	page#
1 ▶	Pacific	166 241 000	*64 186 000*	10 920m / *35 826ft*	220–221
2 ▶	Atlantic	86 557 000	*33 420 000*	8 605m / *28 231ft*	216–217
3 ▶	Indian	73 427 000	*28 350 000*	7 125m / *23 376ft*	218–219
4 ▶	Arctic	9 485 000	*3 662 000*	5 450m / *17 880ft*	224

Pacific Rim National Park Canada **166** E5
Pacijan *i.* Phil. **74** C4
Pacinan, Tanjung *pt* Indon. **77** F4
Pačir *Vojvodina, Srbija* Yugo. **58** A3
Pacitan Indon. **77** E5
Packsattel *pass* Austria **49** L9
Pacov Czech Rep. **49** M6
Pacoval Brazil **199** H5
Pacuí *r.* Brazil **207** I3
Paczków Poland **49** O5
Padada Phil. **74** C5
Padalere Indon. **75** B3
Padali Rus. Fed. *see* **Amursk**
Padamarang *i.* Indon. **75** B4
Padampur India **96** B3
Padang *Kalimantan Barat* Indon. **77** E3
Padang *Sumatra* Indon. **76** C3
Padang *i.* Indon. **76** C2
Padangpanjang Indon. **76** C3
Padangsidimpuan Indon. **76** B2
Padangtikar Indon. **77** E3
Padangtikar *i.* Indon. **77** E3
Padany Rus. Fed. **40** E3
Padarosk Belarus **42** F9
Padas *r. Sabah* Malaysia **77** F1
Padasjoki Fin. **45** N3
Padatha, Kūh-e *mt.* Iran **100** B3
Padauiri *r.* Brazil **199** E5
Padaung Myanmar **78** A4
Padcaya Bol. **201** D5
Paddington Australia **147** E3
Paden City U.S.A. **176** E6
Paderborn Germany **48** F4
Padeşu, Vârful *mt.* Romania **58** D3
Padilla Bol. **201** D4
Padina Romania **58** I4
Padina *Vojvodina, Srbija* Yugo. **58** B3
Padinska Skela *Srbija* Yugo. **58** B4
Padjelanta nationalpark *nat. park* Sweden **44** L2
Padluzhzha Belarus **43** M8
Padma *r.* Bangl. *see* **Ganges**
Padmanabhapuram India **94** C4
Padmapur India **96** D5
Padova Italy *see* **Padua**
Padra India **96** B5
Padrão, Ponta *pt* Angola **127** B6
Padrauna India **97** E4
Padre Bernardo Brazil **206** E2
Padre Caro *hill* Spain **54** E7
Padre Island U.S.A. **179** C7
Padre Island National Seashore *nature res.* U.S.A. **179** C7
Padre Paraíso Brazil **207** L4
Padrón Spain **54** C2
Padrone, Cape S. Africa **133** K10
Padsvillye Belarus **42** I6
Padua India **95** D2
Padua Italy **56** D3 *also spelt* Padova; *historically known as* Patavium
Paducah *KY* U.S.A. **174** B4
Paducah *TX* U.S.A. **179** B5
Padul Spain **55** H7
Padum Jammu and Kashmir **96** C2
Pădurea Craiului, Munţii *mts* Romania **58** D2
Paekakariki N.Z. **152** I8
Paekdu-san *mt.* China/N. Korea **82** C4
Paengnyŏng-do *i.* S. Korea **83** B5
Paerau N.Z. **153** D13
Paeroa N.Z. **152** J5
Paese Italy **56** E3
Paestum *tourist site* Italy **57** G8 *historically known as* Poseidonia
Paete Phil. **74** B3
Pafos Cyprus *see* **Paphos**
Pafúri Moz. **131** F4
Pag Croatia **56** H4
Pag *i.* Croatia **56** G4
Paga *r.* Rus. Fed. **40** L2
Paga Conta Brazil **199** H6
Pagadenbaru Indon. **77** D4
Pagadian Phil. **74** B5
Pagai Selatan *i.* Indon. **76** C3
Pagai Utara *i.* Indon. **76** C3
Pagalu *i.* Equat. Guinea *see* **Annobón**
Pagan *i.* N. Mariana Is **73** K3 *also spelt* Pagon
Pagaralam Indon. **76** C3
Pagasitikos Kolpos *b.* Greece **59** D9
Pagatan *Kalimantan Selatan* Indon. **77** F3
Pagatan *Kalimantan Tengah* Indon. **77** F3
Page U.S.A. **183** M5
Pagėgiai Lith. **42** C6
Pagerdewa Indon. **76** D3
Painted Desert U.S.A. **183** M5
Painted Rock Dam U.S.A. **183** K8
Paint Hills Canada *see* **Wemindji**
Paint Lake Canada **167** L4
Paint Lake Provincial Recreation Park Canada **167** L4
Paint Lick U.S.A. **176** A8
Paint Rock U.S.A. **179** C6
Paintsville U.S.A. **176** C8
Paipa Col. **198** C3
Pairi *r.* India **94** D1
Paisley Canada **173** L6
Paisley U.K. **46** H8
País Vasco *aut. comm.* Spain **55** I1 *English form* Basque Country
Paita Peru **198** A6
Paitan, Teluk *b. Sabah* Malaysia **77** G1
Paithan India **94** B2
Paitou China **87** G2
Paiva *r.* Port. **54** C3
Paiva Couceiro Angola *see* **Quipungo**
Paixban Mex. **185** H5
Paizhou China **87** E2
Pajala Sweden **44** M2
Pajan Ecuador **198** A5
Pajarito Col. **198** C3
Pájaros, Islotes Chile **204** C3
Pajęczno Poland **49** P4
Pakala India **94** C3
Pakanbaru Indon. *see* **Pekanbaru**
Pakapė Lith. **42** E6
Pakaraima Mountains S. America **199** F4 *English form* Pacaraima Mountains; *also known as* Pacaraimã, Serra *or* Paracaima, Sierra
Pakashkan Lake Canada **168** B3
Pakaur India **97** E4
Pakawau N.Z. **152** G8
Pakch'ŏn N. Korea **83** B5
Pakesley Canada **168** D4
Pakhachi Rus. Fed. **39** Q3
Pakhar' Kazakh. **102** D2
Pakhiá *i.* Greece *see* **Pachia**
Pakhoi China *see* **Beihai**
Pakhomovo Rus. Fed. **43** S7
Pakhtaabad Uzbek. **103** H4 *formerly known as* Kokankishlak

▶**Pakistan** *country* Asia **101** F4
5th most populous country in Asia and 7th in the world.
world [population] ▶ 22–23
asia [countries] ▶ 64–67

Pak Ka Shan *hill Hong Kong* China *see* **Parker, Mount**
Pakkat Indon. **76** B2
Paklenica *nat. park* Croatia **56** H4
Paknampho Thai. *see* **Nakhon Sawan**
Pakokku Myanmar **78** A3
Pakoštane Croatia **56** H5
Pakotai N.Z. **152** H3
Pakowki Lake *imp. l.* Canada **167** I5
Pakpattan Pak. **101** H4
Pak Phanang Thai. **79** C6
Pak Phayun Thai. **79** C7
Pakra *r.* Croatia **56** I3
Pakrac Croatia **56** J3
Pakruojis Lith. **42** E6
Paks Hungary **49** P9
Pakse Laos *see* **Pakxé**
Pak Tam Chung *Hong Kong* China **87** [inset]
Pak Thong Chai Thai. **79** C5
Paktīā *prov.* Afgh. **101** G3
Paktīkā *prov.* Afgh. **101** G3
Paku *r. Sarawak* Malaysia **77** F2
Pakue Indon. **75** B3
Pakwash Lake Canada **167** M5
Pakxé Laos **79** D5 *also spelt* Pakse
Pal Senegal *see* **Mpal**
Pala Chad **126** B2
Pala Myanmar **79** B5
Palabuhanratu Indon. **77** D4
Palabuhanratu, Teluk *b.* Indon. **77** D4
Palacios Bol. **200** D3
Palaestinia *reg.* Asia *see* **Palestine**
Palafrugell Spain **55** O3
Palagiano Italy **57** J8
Palagruža *i.* Croatia **56** I6
Palaia Fokaia Greece **59** E11
Palaikastro Greece **59** H13 *also known as* Palaiókastron
Palaiochora Greece **59** E13
Palaiókastron Greece *see* **Palaikastro**
Palairos Greece **59** B10
Palaiseau France **51** I4
Palakkat India *see* **Palghat**
Palamakoloi Botswana **130** D4
Palamas Greece **59** D9
Palamós Spain **55** O3
Palam Pur India **96** C2
Palana India **96** B4
Palana Rus. Fed. **39** P4
Palanan Phil. **74** B2
Palanan Point Phil. **74** B2
Palancia *r.* Spain **55** K5
Palandur India **94** D1
Palanga Lith. **42** C6
Palangān, Kūh-e *mts* Iran **101** E4
Palangkaraya Indon. **77** F3
Palani India **94** C4
Palanpur India **96** B4
Palanro Indon. **75** A4
Palantak Pak. **101** F5
Palapag Phil. **74** C3
Palapye Botswana **131** E4
Palar *r.* India **94** D3
Palasa Indon. **75** B2
Palasbari India **97** F4
Palas de Rei Spain **54** D2
Palata *r.* Belarus **43** J6
Palatka Rus. Fed. **39** P3
Palatka U.S.A. **175** D6
Palau *Sardegna* Italy **56** B7
▶**Palau** *country* N. Pacific Ocean **73** H5 *also spelt* Belau
asia [countries] ▶ 64–67
Palaui *i.* Phil. **74** B2
Palauig Phil. **74** A3
Palau Islands Palau **73** H5
Palauk Myanmar **79** B5
Palaw Myanmar **79** B5
Palawan *i.* Phil. **74** A4 *historically known as* Paragua
Palawan Passage *strait* Phil. **74** A4
Palayan Phil. **74** B3
Palayankottai India **94** C4
Palazzo, Punta *pt Corse* France **51** O10
Paldiski Estonia **42** F2
Pale Bos.-Herz. **56** K5
Paleleh Indon. **75** B2
Palembang Indon. **76** D3
Palena *Aisén* Chile **205** B6
Palena *Los Lagos* Chile **205** C6
Palencia Spain **54** G2
Palenque Mex. **185** G5
Palermo Arg. **201** D6
Palermo *Sicilia* Italy **57** F10 *historically known as* Panormus
Palermo Punta Raisi *airport Sicilia* Italy **57** F10
Palestine *reg.* Asia **108** G5 *historically known as* Palaestinia
Palestine U.S.A. **179** D6
Paletwa Myanmar **78** A3
Palghar India **94** B2
Palghat India **94** C4 *also spelt* Palakkat
Palgrave, Mount *hill* Australia **150** A4
Palhoca Brazil **203** B8
Pali *Madhya Pradesh* India **96** D5
Pali *Maharashtra* India **94** B2
Pali *Rajasthan* India **96** B4
Palik Belarus **43** J7

▶**Palikir** Micronesia **220** E5
Capital of Micronesia.

Palimbang Phil. **74** C5
Palinuro, Capo *c.* Italy **57** H8
Paliouri Greece **59** E9
Paliouri, Akra *pt* Greece **59** E9
Palisade U.S.A. **180** E5
Palitana India **96** A5
Palivere Estonia **42** E3
Palja *hill* Sweden **44** L2
Paljakka *hill* Fin. **44** O2
Pälkäne Fin. **45** N3
Palk Bay Sri Lanka **94** C4
Palkino Rus. Fed. **42** J4
Palkohda India **95** D2
Palkonda Range *mts* India **94** C3
Palkot India **97** E5
Palk Strait India/Sri Lanka **94** C4
Palladani India **94** C4
Pallapalla *mt.* Peru **200** B3
Pallas ja Ounastunturin kansallispuisto *nat. park* Fin. **44** M1
Pallasovka Rus. Fed. **102** A2
Pallavaram India **94** D3
Palleru *r.* India **94** D2
Pallinup *r.* Australia **151** B7
Pallisa Uganda **128** B4
Palliser, Cape N.Z. **152** J9
Palliser, Îles *is* Fr. Polynesia **221** I7
Palliser Bay N.Z. **152** J9
Pallu India **96** B3
Palma *r.* Brazil **202** C5
Palma Moz. **129** D7
Palma del Río Spain **54** F7
Palma de Mallorca Spain **55** N5
Palma di Montechiaro *Sicilia* Italy **57** F11
Palmaner India **94** C3
Palmanova Italy **56** F3
Palmares *Acre* Brazil **200** D2
Palmares *Pernambuco* Brazil **202** F4
Palmares do Sul Brazil **203** B9
Palmarito Venez. **198** D3
Palmarola, Isola *i.* Italy **57** E8
Palmarolle Canada **173** N2
Palmar Sur Costa Rica **186** C5
Palmas *Paraná* Brazil **203** B8
Palmas *Tocantins* Brazil **202** B4
Palmas, Cape Liberia **124** D5
Palmas, Golfo di *b. Sardegna* Italy **57** A10
Palma Soriano Cuba **186** E2
Palm Bay U.S.A. **175** D7
Palmdale U.S.A. **182** F7
Palm Desert U.S.A. **183** H8
Palmeira Brazil **203** B8
Palmeira das Missões Brazil **203** A8
Palmeira dos Índios Brazil **202** E4
Palmeirais Brazil **202** D3
Palmeiras *r.* Brazil **202** C5
Palmeiras de Goiás Brazil **206** D3
Palmeirinhas, Ponta das *pt* Angola **127** B7
Palmer *research station* Antarctica **222** T2
Palmer *r.* Australia **149** D3
Palmer *watercourse* Australia **148** B5
Palmer U.S.A. **164** E3
Palmer Land *reg.* Antarctica **222** T2
Palmerston Australia *see* **Darwin**
Palmerston Australia **148** A2
Palmerston Canada **173** M7
Palmerston *atoll* Cook Is **221** H7 *also known as* Avarau
Palmerston N.Z. **153** E13
Palmerston, Cape Australia **149** F4
Palmerston North N.Z. **152** J8
Palmerton U.S.A. **177** J5
Palmerville Australia **149** E2
Palmetto U.S.A. **175** D7
Palmi Italy **57** H10
Palmillas Mex. **185** F4
Palmira Col. **198** B4
Palmira Cuba **186** C2
Palmital Brazil **206** C9
Palmnicken Rus. Fed. *see* **Yantarnyy**
Palm Springs U.S.A. **183** H8
Palm Tree Creek *r.* Australia **149** F5
▶**Palm Valley** Australia **148** B5
oceania [features] ▶ 142–143
Palmyra Syria *see* **Tadmur**
Palmyra *NY* U.S.A. **177** H2
Palmyra *PA* U.S.A. **177** I5
Palmyra *VA* U.S.A. **176** G8

▶**Palmyra Atoll** N. Pacific Ocean **221** H5
United States Unincorporated Territory.
oceania [countries] ▶ 138–139

Palmyras Point India **95** E1
Palni Hills India **94** C4
Palo Phil. **74** C4
Palo Alto U.S.A. **182** B4
Palo Blanco Arg. **204** D2
Palo Blanco Mex. **185** E3
Palo Chino *watercourse* Mex. **181** D7
Palo de las Letras Col. **198** B3
Palo Duro *watercourse* U.S.A. **179** B5
Paloh *Sarawak* Malaysia **77** E2
Paloich Sudan **128** B2
Palojoensuu Fin. **44** M1
Palomaa Fin. **44** N1
Palomani *mt.* Peru **200** C3
Palomares Mex. **185** G5
Palomar Mountain U.S.A. **183** H8
Palomera, Sierra *mts* Spain **55** J4
Palomitas Arg. **200** D6
Paloncha India **94** D2 *also known as* Palwancha
Palo Pinto U.S.A. **179** C5
Palopo Indon. **75** B3
Palos, Cabo de *c.* Spain **55** K7
Palo Santo Arg. **204** F2
Palouse *r.* U.S.A. **180** C3
Palo Verde U.S.A. **183** J8
Palo Verde, Parque Nacional *nat. park* Costa Rica **186** B5
Palovesi *l.* Fin. **45** M3
Palpa *Ica* Peru **200** B3
Palpa *Lima* Peru **200** A2
Palpetu, Tanjung *pt* Indon. **75** C3
Palsana India **96** B5
Paltamo Fin. **44** N2
Paltaselkä *l.* Fin. **44** N2
Pal'tsevo Rus. Fed. **43** J1
Pal'tso Rus. Fed. **43** P8
Palu Indon. **75** A3
Palu *i.* Indon. **75** B5
Palu *r.* Indon. **75** A3
Palu Turkey **107** D3
Paluan Phil. **74** B3
Paluan Bay Phil. **74** B3
Pal'vart Turkm. **103** F5
Palwal India **96** C3
Palwancha India *see* **Paloncha**
Pal'yanovo Rus. Fed. **38** G3
Palyatskishki Belarus **42** G7
Palyavaam *r.* Rus. Fed. **39** R3
Palyeskaya Nizina *marsh* Belarus/Ukr. *see* **Pripet Marshes**
Palyessye Belarus **43** K9
Palyessye Belarus **43** M8
Pama Austria **49** O7
Pama Burkina **125** F4
Pama *r.* Cent. Afr. Rep. **126** C3
Pama, Réserve Partielle de *nature res.* Burkina **125** F4
Pamamaroo Lake Australia **147** D3

▶**Pamana** *i.* Indon. **75** B5
Most southerly point of Asia.

Pamanukan Indon. **77** D4
Pamar Col. **198** D5
Pamban Channel India **94** C4
Pambarra Moz. **131** G4
Pambula Australia **147** F4
Pamekasan Indon. **77** F4
Pameungpeuk Indon. **77** D4
Pamfylla Greece **59** H9
Pamidi India **94** C3
Pamiers France **50** H9
Pamir *r.* Afgh./Tajik. **101** H2
Pamir *mts* Asia **99** I2
Pamlico *r.* U.S.A. **174** E5
Pamlico Sound *sea chan.* U.S.A. **174** E5
Pampa Chile **200** C5
Pampa U.S.A. **179** B5
Pampa Chica Arg. **205** C7
Pampachiri Peru **200** B3
Pampa de Infierno Arg. **204** E2
Pampa Grande Bol. **201** D4
Pampanua Indon. **75** B4
▶**Pampas** *reg.* Arg. **204** D5
southamerica [landscapes] ▶ 190–191
Pampas Peru **200** B3
Pampas *r.* Peru **200** B3
Pampeluna Spain *see* **Pamplona**
Pampierstad S. Africa **133** I4
Pamplin U.S.A. **176** G8
Pamplona Col. **198** C3
Pamplona Phil. **74** B4
Pamplona Spain **55** J2 *also known as* Iruña; *historically known as* Pampeluna
Pamukan, Teluk *b.* Indon. **77** G3
Pamukçu Turkey **59** I9
Pamukkale Turkey **59** K11
Pamukova Turkey **106** B2
Pamunkey *r.* U.S.A. **177** I8
Pamzal Jammu and Kashmir **96** C2
Pana Gabon **126** B5
Pana U.S.A. **174** B4
Panabá Mex. **185** H4
Panabo Phil. **74** C5
Panabutan Bay Phil. **74** B5
Panaca U.S.A. **183** J4
Panache, Lake Canada **168** D4
Panaci Romania **58** G1
Panaeati Island P.N.G. **149** G1
Panagar India **96** D5
Panagia *i.* Greece **58** F8 *also spelt* Panayía
Panagiri India **94** C2
Panagtaran Point Phil. **74** A4
Panagyurishte Bulg. **58** F6
Panaitan *i.* Indon. **76** D4
Panaitolio Greece **59** C10
Panaji India **94** B3 *formerly known as* Panjim; *historically known as* Nova Goa
▶**Panama** *country* Central America **186** C5
northamerica [countries] ▶ 158–159
Panamá Panama *see* **Panama City**
Panamá, Bahía de *b.* Panama **186** D5
Panamá, Golfo de *g.* Panama *see* **Panama, Gulf of**
Panama, Gulf of Panama **186** D6 *also known as* Panamá, Golfo de
Panama Canal Panama **186** D5

▶**Panama City** Panama **186** D5
Capital of Panama. Also known as Panamá.

Panama City U.S.A. **175** C6
Panamint Range *mts* U.S.A. **183** G5
Panamint Valley U.S.A. **183** G5
Panao Peru **200** A2
Panaon *i.* Phil. **74** C4
Panapompom Island P.N.G. **149** G1
Panar *r.* India **97** F4
Panarea, Isola *i. Isole Lipari* Italy **57** H10
Panarik Indon. **77** E2
Panaro *r.* Italy **56** D4
Panarukan Indon. **77** F4
Panatinane Island P.N.G. **149** G1
Panay *i.* Phil. **74** B4
Panayarvi Natsional'nyy Park *nat. park* Rus. Fed. **44** O2
Panay Gulf Phil. **74** B4
Panayía *i.* Greece *see* **Panagia**
Panbult S. Africa **133** O3
Pancake Range *mts* U.S.A. **183** I3
Pancas Brazil **207** M6
Pančevo *Vojvodina, Srbija* Yugo. **58** B4 *also spelt* Pancsova
Panchagarh Bangl. **97** F4
Panch'iao Taiwan **87** G3
Pancingapan, Bukit *mt.* Indon. **77** F2
Panciu Romania **58** I3
Pâncota Romania **58** C2 *formerly spelt* Pîncota
Pancsova *Vojvodina, Srbija* Yugo. *see* **Pančevo**
Panda Moz. **131** G5
Pandan *Panay* Phil. **74** B4
Pandan Phil. **74** C3
Pandan, Selat *strait* Sing. **76** [inset]
Pandan Bay Phil. **74** B4
Pandan Reservoir Sing. **76** [inset]
Pandaria India **97** D5
Pandavapura India **94** C3
Pan de Azúcar Chile **204** C2
Pan de Azúcar, Parque Nacional *nat. park* Chile **204** C2
Pandeglang Indon. **77** D4
Pandeiros *r.* Brazil **207** I2
Pandėlys Lith. **42** G5
Pandhana India **96** C5
Pandharpur India **94** B2
Pandhurna India **96** C5
Pando *dept* Bol. **200** D2
Pando Uruguay **204** G4
Pandokrátor *hill* Greece *see* **Pantokratoras**
Pandora Costa Rica **186** C5
Pandora Entrance *sea chan.* Australia **149** E1
Pandrup Denmark **45** J4
Paneas Syria *see* **Bāniyās**
Panelas Brazil **201** E2
Panevėžys Lith. **42** F6
Panfilov Kazakh. *see* **Zharkent**
Pang *r.* China **82** B1
Pang, Nam *r.* Myanmar **78** B3
Panga Dem. Rep. Congo **126** E4
Panga Estonia **42** D3
Pangai Tonga **145** H3
Pangal *Andhra Pradesh* India **94** C2
Pangal *Andhra Pradesh* India **94** C2
Pangandaran Indon. **77** E4
Pangani Tanz. **129** C6 *also known as* Ruvu
Pangani *r.* Tanz. **129** C6
Pañganiban Phil. **74** C3
Pangar Djerem, Réserve du *nature res.* Cameroon **125** I5
Pangean Indon. **75** A3
Panghsang Myanmar **78** B3
Pangi Dem. Rep. Congo **126** E5
Pangi Range *mts* Pak. **101** H3
Pangjiabu China **85** G3
Pangkah, Tanjung *pt* Indon. **77** F4
Pangkajene Indon. **75** A4
Pangkalanbuun Indon. **77** E3
Pangkalanlunang Indon. **76** B2
Pangkalansusu Indon. **76** B1
Pangkal Kalong Malaysia **76** C1
Pangkalpinang Indon. **77** D3
Pangkalsiang, Tanjung *pt* Indon. **75** B3
Panglang Myanmar **78** B2
Panglao *i.* Phil. **74** B4
Pangman Canada **167** J5
Pangnirtung Canada **165** M3
Pango Aluquém Angola **127** B7
Pangody Rus. Fed. **38** H3
Pangonda Cent. Afr. Rep. **126** D3
Pangong Tso *salt l.* China/Jammu and Kashmir *see* **Bangong Co**
Pangrango *vol.* Indon. **77** D4
Pang Sida National Park Thai. **79** C5
Pang Sua, Sungai *r.* Sing. **76** [inset]
Pangtara Myanmar **78** B3
Panguipulli Chile **204** B5
Panguitch U.S.A. **183** L4
Panguru N.Z. **152** H3
Pangururan Indon. **76** B2
Pangutaran *i.* Phil. **74** B5
Pangutaran Group *is* Phil. **74** B5
Panhandle U.S.A. **179** B5
Pania-Mwanga Dem. Rep. Congo **127** F6
Pani Mines India **96** B5
Panino *Tverskaya Oblast'* Rus. Fed. **43** P5
Panino *Voronezhskaya Oblast'* Rus. Fed. **41** G6
Paninskaya Rus. Fed. **43** R1
Panipat India **96** C3
Panitan Phil. **74** A4
Panizowye Belarus **43** L7
Panj *r.* Afgh./Tajik. *see* **Pyandzh**
Panj Tajik. **101** G2 *also spelt* Pyandzh; *formerly known as* Kirovabad
Panjāb Afgh. **101** F3
Panjakent Tajik. **101** F2 *also spelt* Pendzhikent
Panjang Indon. **76** D4
Panjang *i.* Indon. **77** E2
Panjang *i.* Indon. **77** G2
Panjang, Bukit Sing. **76** [inset]
Panjang, Selat *sea chan.* Indon. **76** C2
Panjgur Pak. **101** F5
Panjhra *r.* India **96** B5
Panjim India *see* **Panaji**
Panjin China **85** I3 *also known as* Panshan
Panji Poyon Tajik. **101** G2 *also known as* Nizhniy Pyandzh
Panjkora *r.* Pak. **101** G3
Panjnad *r.* Pak. **101** G4
Pankakoski Fin. **44** O3
Pankovka Rus. Fed. **43** M3
Panlian China *see* **Miyi**
Pan Ling *mts* China **82** C4
Panlong China *see* **Queshan**
Panna India **96** D4
Pannawonica Australia **150** B4
Pannonhalma Hungary **49** O8 *formerly known as* Győrszentmárton
Pano Aqil Pak. **101** G5
Panopah Indon. **77** E3
Panoplis Egypt *see* **Akhmîm**
Panorama Brazil **206** B8
Panormus *Sicilia* Italy *see* **Palermo**
Panruti India **94** C4
Panshan China *see* **Panjin**
Panshi China **82** B4
Panshui China *see* **Pu'an**
Pantaicermin, Gunung *mt.* Indon. **76** C3

▶**Pantanal** *marsh* S. America **201** F4
Largest area of wetlands in the world.

Pantanal de São Lourenço *marsh* Brazil **201** F4
Pantanal do Taquarí *marsh* Brazil **201** F4
Pantanal Matogrossense, Parque Nacional do *nat. park* Brazil **201** F4
Pantar *i.* Indon. **75** C5
Pantelaria *Sicilia* Italy *see* **Pantelleria**
Pantelleria *Sicilia* Italy **57** D12 *historically known as* Pantelaria
Pantelleria, Isola di *i. Sicilia* Italy **57** E12
Pantemakassar East Timor **75** C5 *formerly known as* Ocussi
Pantha Myanmar **78** A3
Panticapaeum Ukr. *see* **Kerch**
Pantijan Aboriginal Reserve Australia **150** D3
Pantokratoras *hill* Greece **59** A9 *also known as* Pandokrátor
Pantoowarinna, Lake *salt flat* Australia **146** C1
Pantukan Phil. **74** C5
Panu Dem. Rep. Congo **126** C5
Pánuco Mex. **185** F4
Pánuco *r.* Mex. **185** F4
Panvel India **94** B2
Panwari India **96** C4
Panxian China **86** C3
Panyu China **87** E4 *also known as* Shiqiao
Panzhihua China **86** B3 *also known as* Dukou
Panzi Dem. Rep. Congo **127** C6
Panzos Guat. **185** H6
Pao *r.* Venez. **199** E2
Pão de Açúcar Brazil **202** E4
Paola Italy **57** I9
Paola U.S.A. **178** D4
Paoli U.S.A. **174** C4
Paoni Indon. **75** D3
Paonia U.S.A. **180** F5
Paoua Cent. Afr. Rep. **126** C3
Paôy Pêt Cambodia **79** C5
Pap Uzbek. **103** G4 *also spelt* Pop
Pápa Hungary **49** O8
Papa, Monte del *mt.* Italy **57** H8
Papadianika Greece **59** D12
Papagaio *r.* Brazil *see* **Sauêruiná**
Papagaios *Minas Gerais* Brazil **207** I6
Papagaios *Rondônia* Brazil **201** E2
Papagni *r.* India **94** C3
Papakura N.Z. **152** I5
Papallacta Ecuador **198** B5
Papamoa Beach N.Z. **152** K5
Papanasam *Tamil Nadu* India **94** C4
Papanasam *Tamil Nadu* India **94** C4
Papantla Mex. **185** F4
Paparhahandi India **95** D2
Paparoa N.Z. **152** I4
Paparoa National Park N.Z. **153** F10
Paparoa Range *mts* N.Z. **153** F10
Papas, Akra *pt* Greece **59** G11
Papa Stour *i.* U.K. **46** K3
Pápateszér Hungary **49** O8
Papatoetoe N.Z. **152** I4
Papatowai N.Z. **153** D14
Papa Westray *i.* U.K. **46** J4 *also known as* Papay
Papay *i.* U.K. *see* **Papa Westray**

▶**Papeete** Fr. Polynesia **221** I7
Capital of French Polynesia.

Papenburg Germany **48** E2
Papendorp S. Africa **132** C8
Paphos Cyprus **108** D3 *also spelt* Pafos; *historically known as* Paphus
Paphus Cyprus *see* **Paphos**
Papigochic *r.* Mex. **181** F7
Papikio *mt.* Bulg./Greece **58** G7
Papilė Lith. **42** D5
Papillion U.S.A. **178** C3
Papineau-Labelle, Réserve Faunique de *nature res.* Canada **168** F4
Papiya *hill* Bulg. **58** I6
Papoose Lake U.S.A. **183** I4
Paposo Chile **204** C2
Papua, Gulf of P.N.G. **73** J8

▶**Papua New Guinea** *country* Oceania **144** D2
2nd largest and 2nd most populous country in Oceania.
oceania [countries] ▶ 138–139

Papun Myanmar **78** B4
Papunya Australia **148** A4
Pará *r.* Brazil **203** C6
Pará *state* Brazil **199** I5
Para *i.* Indon. **75** C2
Para *r.* Rus. Fed. **41** G5
Pará, Rio do *r.* Brazil **202** B2
Paraburdoo Australia **150** B4
Paracaima, Sierra *mts* S. America *see* **Pakaraima Mountains**
Paracale Phil. **74** B3
Paracambi Brazil **207** J9
Paracas Peru **200** A3
Paracas, Península *pen.* Peru **200** A3
Paracatu Brazil **206** G4
Paracatu *r. Minas Gerais* Brazil **206** H3
Paracel Islands S. China Sea **72** D3 *also known as* Dao Tay Sa *or* Hoang Sa *or* Hsi-sha Ch'un-tao *or* Quan Dao Hoang Sa *or* Xisha Qundao
Parachilna Australia **146** C2
Parachinar Pak. **101** G3
Paraćin *Srbija* Yugo. **58** C5
Parada, Punta *pt* Peru **200** B3
Pará de Minas Brazil **203** C6
Paradis Canada **168** E3
Paradise *r.* Canada **169** J2
Paradise Guyana **199** G3
Paradise *CA* U.S.A. **182** C2
Paradise *MI* U.S.A. **173** H4
Paradise *NV* U.S.A. **183** I5
Paradise Gardens Canada **167** H2
Paradise Hill Canada **167** I4
Paradise Peak U.S.A. **182** G3
Paradise River Canada **169** J2
Paradise Valley U.S.A. **183** M8
Parado Indon. **77** G5
Paradwip India **95** E1
Paraetonium Egypt *see* **Marsa Matrûh**
Paraf"yanava Belarus **42** I7
Paragominas Brazil **202** C2
Paragould U.S.A. **174** B4
Paragua *r.* Bol. **201** E3
Paragua *i.* Phil. *see* **Palawan**
Paragua *r.* Venez. **199** F3
Paraguaçu Brazil **207** H8
Paraguai *r.* Brazil **201** F5
Paraguáipoa Venez. **198** D2
Paraguarí Para. **201** F6
Paraguay *r.* Arg./Para. **201** F6
▶**Paraguay** *country* S. America **201** F5
southamerica [countries] ▶ 192–193
Paraíba *r.* Brazil **202** F3
Paraíba *state* Brazil **202** E3
Paraíba do Sul Brazil **207** J9
Paraíba do Sul *r.* Brazil **203** D7
Paraibuna Brazil **207** H10
Parainen Fin. *see* **Pargas**
Paraíso Brazil **206** A6
Paraíso Mex. **185** G5
Paraíso do Norte Brazil **202** B4
Paraisópolis Brazil **207** H9
Parakka Sweden **44** M2
Parakou Benin **125** F4
Parakylia Australia **146** C2
Paralakhemundi India **95** E2 *formerly spelt* Parlakimedi
Paralia Greece **59** D10
Paramagudi India *see* **Paramakkudi**
Paramakkudi India **94** C4 *formerly spelt* Paramagudi

▶**Paramaribo** Suriname **199** H3
Capital of Suriname.

Paramillo *mt.* Col. **198** C3
Paramillo, Parque Nacional *nat. park* Col. **198** B3
Paramirim Brazil **202** D5
Paramirim *r.* Brazil **202** D4
Páramo *hill* Spain **54** D2
Páramo de Masa, Puerto del *pass* Spain **54** H2
Paramonga Peru **200** A2
Paramushir, Ostrov *i.* Rus. Fed. **39** P4
Paramythia Greece **59** B9
Paran *watercourse* Israel **108** G7
Paraná Arg. **204** E3
Paranã Brazil **202** C5
Paraná *r.* Brazil **202** B5
Paraná *state* Brazil **206** B11

Penasi, Pulau i. Indon. 76 A1
also known as Dedap
Peña Ubiña mt. Spain 54 F1
Peña Utrera hill Spain 54 E6
Pench r. India 96 C5
Pencheng China see Ruichang
Pench National Park India 96 C5
Penck, Cape Antarctica 223 F2
Pendé r. Cent. Afr. Rep. 126 C3
Pendembu Sierra Leone 124 B4
Pender U.S.A. 178 C3
Pender Bay Australia 150 C3
Pender Bay Aboriginal Reserve Australia 150 C3
Pendik Turkey 58 K8
Pendleton U.S.A. 180 C3
Pendleton Bay Canada 166 E4
Pendopo Indon. 76 C3
Pend Oreille r. U.S.A. 180 C2
Pend Oreille Lake U.S.A. 180 C2
Pendra India 97 D5
Penduv India 94 B2
Pendzhikent Tajik. see Panjakent
Penebangan i. Indon. 77 E3
Peneda Gerês, Parque Nacional da nat. park Port. 54 C3
Pene-Mende Dem. Rep. Congo 126 F6
Pénessoulou Benin 125 F4
Penetanguishene Canada 173 N6
Penfield U.S.A. 176 G4
Penfro U.K. see Pembroke
Peng'an China 86 C2
also known as Zhoukou
Penganga r. India 94 C2
Peng Chau i. Hong Kong China 87 [inset]
P'engchia Yu i. Taiwan 87 G3
Penge Dem. Rep. Congo 127 E6
P'enghu Ch'üntao is Taiwan 87 F4
English form Pescadores; also known as P'enghu Liehtao
P'enghu Liehtao is Taiwan see P'enghu Ch'üntao
P'enghu Tao i. Taiwan 87 F4
Pengiki i. Indon. 77 E2
Peng Kang hill Sing. 76 [inset]
Penglai China 85 I4
formerly known as Dengzhou
Pengshan China 86 B2
Pengshui China 87 D2
also known as Hanjia
Peng Siang, Sungai r. Sing. 76 [inset]
Pengwa Myanmar 78 A3
Pengxi China 86 C2
also known as Chicheng
Pengxian China see Pengzhou
Pengze China 87 F2
also known as Longcheng
Pengzhou China 86 B2
formerly known as Pengxian
Penhalonga Zimbabwe 131 G3
Penhoek Pass S. Africa 133 K8
Penhook U.S.A. 176 F9
Peniche Port. 54 B5
Penicuik U.K. 46 I8
Penida i. Indon. 77 F5
Peninga Rus. Fed. 40 E3
Peninsular Malaysia Malaysia 76 C2
also known as Malaya or Semenanjung Malaysia; formerly known as West Malaysia
Penitente, Serra do hills Brazil 202 C4
Pênjwin Iraq 107 F4
Penmarch France 50 B5
Penmarch, Pointe de pt France 50 B5
Penn U.S.A. see Penn Hills
Penna, Punta della pt Italy 56 G6
Penne Italy 56 F6
Pennell Coast Antarctica 223 L2
Penner r. India 94 D3
Penneshaw Australia 146 C3
Penn Hills U.S.A. 176 F5
formerly known as Penn
Pennine, Alpi mts Italy/Switz. 51 N7
English form Pennine Alps
Pennine Alps mts Italy/Switz. see Pennine, Alpi
Pennines hills U.K. 47 J9
Pennington S. Africa 133 O7
Pennington Gap U.S.A. 176 B9
Pennsboro U.S.A. 176 E6
Penns Grove U.S.A. 177 J6
Pennsville U.S.A. 177 J6
Pennsylvania state U.S.A. 176 G4
Penny Icecap Canada 165 M3
Penny Point Antarctica 223 K1
Peno Rus. Fed. 43 N5
Penobscot r. U.S.A. 177 Q1
Penobscot Bay U.S.A. 177 Q1
Penola Australia 146 D4
Peñón Blanco Mex. 184 D3
Penong Australia 146 B2
Penonomé Panama 186 C5
Penrhyn atoll Cook Is 221 H6
also known as Tongareva
Penrith Australia 147 F3
Penrith U.K. 47 J9
Pensacola U.S.A. 175 C6
Pensacola Bay i. U.S.A. 175 C6
Pensacola Mountains Antarctica 223 T1
Pensamiento Bol. 201 E3
Pensaukee U.S.A. 172 F6
Pentadaktylos Range mts Cyprus 108 E2
also known as Kyrenia Mountains or Beşparmak Dağları
Pentakota India 95 D2
Pentecost Island Vanuatu 145 F3
also known as Pentecôte, Île; formerly known as Whitsun Island
Pentecôte r. Canada 169 H3
Pentecôte, Île i. Vanuatu see Pentecost Island
Penteleu, Vârful mt. Romania 58 H3
Penticton Canada 166 G5
Pentire Point U.K. 47 G13
Pentland Australia 149 E4
Pentland Firth sea chan. U.K. 46 I5
Pentland Hills U.K. 46 I8
Pentwater U.S.A. 172 G7
Penukonda India 94 C3
Penunjok, Tanjong pt Malaysia 76 C1
Penwegon Myanmar 78 B4
Pen-y-Bont ar Ogwr U.K. see Bridgend
Penygadair hill U.K. 47 I11
Penylan Lake Canada 167 J2
Penyu, Kepulauan is Indon. 75 C4
Penza Rus. Fed. 41 H5
Penzance U.K. 47 G13
Penza Oblast admin. div. Rus. Fed. see Penzenskaya Oblast'
Penzenskaya Oblast' admin. div. Rus. Fed. 41 H5
English form Penza Oblast
Penzhinskaya Guba b. Rus. Fed. 39 Q3
Peoples Creek r. U.S.A. 180 E2
Peoria AZ U.S.A. 183 L8
Peoria IL U.S.A. 174 B3
Peoria Heights U.S.A. 172 D10
Pepeekeo U.S.A. 181 [inset] Z2
Pepel Sierra Leone 124 B4
Peper Sudan 128 B3
Pepworth S. Africa 133 N5
Pëqin Albania 58 A7
Pequi Brazil 207 I6
Pequop Mountains U.S.A. 183 J1
Pera Head Australia 149 D2
Peraitepuy Venez. 199 F3
Perak i. Malaysia 76 B1
Perak r. Malaysia 76 C1
Perak state Malaysia 76 C1
Perama Greece 59 F13
Perambalur India 94 C4
Perämeren kansallispuisto nat. park Fin. 44 N2
Perä-Posio Fin. 44 N2
Percé Canada 169 H3
Perche, Collines du hills France 50 G4
Percival Lakes salt flat Australia 150 D4
Percy France 50 E4
Percy U.S.A. 177 N1
Percy Isles Australia 149 F4
Percy Reach l. Canada 173 P6
Perdekop S. Africa 133 N4
Perdepoort pass S. Africa 132 H10
Perdida r. Brazil 202 C4
Perdido r. Brazil 201 F5
Perdido, Monte mt. Spain 55 L2
Perdiguère, Pic mt. France/Spain 55 L2
Perdika Greece 59 B9
Perdizes Brazil 206 F6
Perdões Brazil 207 H8
Perdu, Lac l. Canada 169 G3
Perechyn Ukr. 49 T7
Peregrebnoye Rus. Fed. 38 G3
Pereira Col. 198 C3
Pereira Barreto Brazil 206 B7
Pereira de Eça Angola see Ondjiva
Pereiro Brazil 202 E3
Perekhoda r. Rus. Fed. 43 M3
Perelyub Rus. Fed. 102 B2
Pere Marquette r. U.S.A. 172 G7
Peremetnoye Kazakh. 102 B2
Peremul Par reef India 94 B4
Peremyshl' Rus. Fed. 43 R7
Peremyshlyany Ukr. 41 C6
Perené r. Peru 200 B2
Perenjori Australia 151 B6
Pereshnoye, Ozero l. Rus. Fed. 43 T1
Pereslavl'-Zalesskiy Rus. Fed. 43 T5
Pereslavskiy Natsional'nyy Park nat. park Rus. Fed. 43 T5
Peretu Romania 58 G4
Perevolotskiy Rus. Fed. 102 C2
Pereyaslavka Rus. Fed. 82 D3
Pereyaslav-Khmel'nitskiy Ukr. see Pereyaslav-Khmel'nyts'kyy
Pereyaslav-Khmel'nyts'kyy Ukr. 41 D6
also spelt Pereyaslav-Khmel'nitskiy
Pérez Chile 204 C2
Perg Austria 49 L7
Pergamino Arg. 204 E4
Perge tourist site Turkey 108 B1
Pergola Italy 56 E5
Perhentian Besar i. Malaysia 76 C1
Perho Fin. 44 N3
Periam Romania 58 B2
Péribonca r. Canada 169 F3
Perico Arg. 200 D6
Pericos Mex. 184 D3
Peridot U.S.A. 183 N8
Perieni Romania 58 I2
Périers France 50 E3
Perigoso, Canal sea chan. Brazil 202 B2
Périgueux France 50 G7
Perijá, Parque Nacional nat. park Venez. 198 C2
Perija, Sierra de mts Venez. 198 C2
Perim Island Yemen see Barīm
Peringat Malaysia 76 C1
Peripava Romania 58 K3
Perişoru Romania 58 I4
Peristera i. Greece 59 E9
Peritoró Brazil 202 C4
Periteasca-Gura Portiței nature res. Romania 58 K4
Perito Moreno Arg. 205 C7
Perito Moreno, Parque Nacional nat. park Arg. 205 B7
Perivar r. India 94 C4
Perlas, Laguna de lag. Nicaragua 186 C4
Perlas, Punta de pt Nicaragua 186 C4
Perleberg Germany 48 I2
Perlis state Malaysia 76 C1
Perm' Rus. Fed. 40 K4
formerly known as Molotov
Permas Rus. Fed. 40 H4
Përmet Albania 59 B8
Perm Oblast admin. div. Rus. Fed. see Permskaya Oblast'
Permskaya Oblast' admin. div. Rus. Fed. 40 K4
English form Perm Oblast; formerly known as Molotovskaya Oblast'
Permuda i. Croatia 56 G4
Pernå Fin. 42 H1
Pernambuco Brazil see Recife
Pernambuco state Brazil 202 E4
Pernatty Lagoon salt flat Australia 146 C2
Pernem India 94 B3
Pernik Bulg. 58 E6
formerly known as Dimitrovo
Perniö Fin. 45 M3
Pernov Estonia see Pärnu
Perolândia Brazil 206 A4
Peron, Cape Australia 151 A5
Peron Islands Australia 148 A2
Péronnas France 51 L6
Péronne France 51 I3
Peron Peninsula Australia 151 A5
Perote Mex. 185 F5
Perpignan France 51 I10
Perrégaux Alg. see Mohammadia
Perris U.S.A. 183 G8
Perros-Guirec France 50 C4
Perry Canada 173 I3
Perry r. Canada 167 K1
Perry FL U.S.A. 175 D6
Perry GA U.S.A. 175 D5
Perry IA U.S.A. 178 D3
Perry MI U.S.A. 173 I8
Perry OK U.S.A. 179 C4
Perry Hall U.S.A. 177 I6
Perrymennyy, Cape Antarctica 223 G2
Perrysburg U.S.A. 176 B4
Perryton U.S.A. 179 B4
Perryville AR U.S.A. 179 D5
Perryville KY U.S.A. 176 A8
Persepolis tourist site Iran 100 C4
Persia country Asia see Iran
Persian Gulf Asia see The Gulf
Persis prov. Iran see Fārs
Pertek Turkey 107 D3
Perth Tas. Australia 147 E5
Perth W.A. Australia 151 A6
State capital of Western Australia. 4th most populous city in Oceania.
world [cities] 24–25
Perth Canada 168 E4
Perth U.K. 46 I7
Perth-Andover Canada 169 H4
Pertominsk Rus. Fed. 40 F2
Pertteli Fin. 42 E1
Pertuis France 51 L9
Pertuis Breton sea chan. France 50 E6
Pertuis d'Antioche sea chan. France 50 E6
Pertunmaa Fin. 45 N3
Pertusato, Capo c. Corse France 56 B7
Perú Bol. 200 D3
Peru atoll Kiribati see Beru
Peru country S. America 200 B2
3rd largest and 4th most populous country in South America.
southamerica [countries] 192–193
Peru IL U.S.A. 172 D9
Peru IN U.S.A. 174 C3
Peru NY U.S.A. 177 L1
Peručko Jezero l. Croatia 56 I5
Perugia Italy 56 E5
historically known as Perusia
Perugorría Arg. 204 F3
Peruhumpenai Mountains Reserve nature res. Indon. 75 B3
Peruíbe Brazil 206 G11
Peruru India 94 C3
Perushtitsa Bulg. 58 F6
Perusia Italy see Perugia
Péruwelz Belgium 51 J2
Pervoavgustovskiy Rus. Fed. 43 Q9
Pervomaisc Moldova 58 K2
Pervomay Kyrg. 103 H4
also known as Pervomayskoye; formerly known as Pervomayskiy
Pervomaysk Rus. Fed. 40 G5
formerly known as Tashino
Pervomays'k Ukr. 41 D6
formerly known as Ol'viopol'
Pervomayskiy Kazakh. 103 J2
Pervomayskiy Kyrg. see Pervomay
Pervomayskiy Rus. Fed. see Novodvinsk
Pervomayskiy Chitinskaya Oblast' Rus. Fed. 85 G1
Pervomayskiy Orenburgskaya Oblast' Rus. Fed. 102 C2
Pervomayskiy Smolenskaya Oblast' Rus. Fed. 43 N7
Pervomayskiy Tambovskaya Oblast' Rus. Fed. 41 G5
formerly known as Bogoyavlenskoye
Pervomayskiy Tul'skaya Oblast' Rus. Fed. 43 S7
Pervomayskoye Kyrg. see Pervomay
Pervomayskoye Rus. Fed. 82 B1
Pervomayskoye Rus. Fed. 43 K1
Pervomays'kyy Ukr. 41 F6
formerly known as Likhachevo or Likhachyovo
Pervorechenskiy Rus. Fed. 39 Q3
Per'yevo Rus. Fed. 43 U2
Pes' Rus. Fed. 43 R3
Pes' r. Rus. Fed. 43 Q2
Pesa r. Italy 56 D5
Pesaguan r. Indon. 77 E3
Pesaro Italy 56 E5
historically known as Pisaurum
Pescadero U.S.A. 182 B4
Pescadores is Taiwan see P'enghu Ch'üntao
Pescadores, Punta pt Peru 200 B4
Pescara Italy 56 G6
Pescara r. Italy 56 G6
Pescari Romania 58 C4
Peschanokopskoye Rus. Fed. 41 G7
Peschanoye Rus. Fed. see Yashkul'
Peschanyy, Mys pt Kazakh. 102 B4
Peschici Italy 56 I7
Pescia Italy 56 C5
Pesebre, Punta pt Canary Is 122 B3
Pesha r. Rus. Fed. 40 H2
Peshanjan Afgh. 101 E3
Peshawar Pak. 101 G3
Peshkopi Albania 58 B7
Peshnyye, Ostrova is Kazakh. see Bol'shiye Peshnyye, Ostrova
Peshtera Bulg. 58 F6
Peshtigo U.S.A. 172 F5
Peshtigo r. U.S.A. 172 F6
Peski Kazakh. 103 F1
Peski Moskovskaya Oblast' Rus. Fed. 43 T6
Peski Voronezhskaya Oblast' Rus. Fed. 41 G6
Peski Turkm. 103 E5
Peski Karakum des. Kazakh. see Karakum Desert
Peski Karakumy des. Turkm. see Karakum Desert
Peskovka Rus. Fed. 40 J4
Pesnica Slovenia 56 H2
Pesochnoye Rus. Fed. 43 U3
Pesochnya Rus. Fed. 43 O8
Peso da Régua Port. 54 D3
Pespire Hond. 186 B4
Pesqueira Brazil 202 E4
Pesqueira Mex. 184 C2
Pessac France 50 F8
Pessinki naturreservat nature res. Sweden 40 B2
Pestovo Rus. Fed. 43 Q3
Pestravka Rus. Fed. 102 B1
Pestyaki Rus. Fed. 40 G4
Petah Tiqwa Israel 108 F5
Petaihari Martapura Reserve nature res. Indon. 77 F3
Petäjävesi Fin. 44 N3
Petalidi Greece 59 C12
Petalioi i. Greece 59 F10
Petaluma U.S.A. 182 B3
Pétange Lux. 51 L3
Petangis Indon. 77 F3
Petare Venez. 199 E2
Petas Greece 59 C9
Petatlán Mex. 185 E5
Petauke Zambia 127 F8
Petawaga, Lac l. Canada 173 R4
Petawawa Canada 173 P5
Petén Itzá, Lago l. Guat. 185 H5
Petenwell Lake U.S.A. 172 D6
Peterbell Canada 168 D3
Peterborough S.A. Australia 146 C3
Peterborough Vic. Australia 147 D4
Peterborough Canada 168 E4
Peterborough U.K. 47 L11
Peterborough U.S.A. 177 N3
Peterhead U.K. 46 K6
Peter I Island Antarctica 222 R2
also known as Peter I Øy
Peter I Øy i. Antarctica see Peter I Island
Peter Lougheed Provincial Park Canada 167 H5
Petermann Aboriginal Land res. Australia 148 A5
Petermann Bjerg nunatak Greenland 165 Q2
Petermann Ranges mts Australia 148 A5
Peter Pond Lake Canada 167 I4
Petersburg S. Africa 133 I9
Petersburg AK U.S.A. 164 F4
Petersburg IL U.S.A. 174 B4
Petersburg IN U.S.A. 174 C4
Petersburg NY U.S.A. 177 L3
Petersburg OH U.S.A. 176 E5
Petersburg VA U.S.A. 176 H8
Petersburg WV U.S.A. 176 F7
Petershagen Germany 48 F3
Peters Mine Guyana 199 G3
Peterstown U.S.A. 176 E8
Petersville U.S.A. 164 D3
Peter the Great Bay Rus. Fed. see Petra Velikogo, Zaliv
Péterváárad Vojvodina, Srbija Yugo. see Petrovaradin
Peterwardein Vojvodina, Srbija Yugo. see Petrovaradin
Peth India 94 B2
Petilia Policastro Italy 57 I9
Petit Atlas mts Morocco see Anti Atlas
Petitcodiac Canada 169 H4
Petite Creuse r. France 51 H6
Petit-Goâve Haiti 187 E3
Petitjean Morocco see Sidi Kacem
Petit Lac Manicouagan l. Canada 169 H2
Petit-Loango, Réserve de nature res. Gabon 126 A5
Petit Maine r. France 50 E5
Petit Mécatina r. Canada see Little Mecatina
Petit Mécatina r. Canada 169 J3
Petit Mécatina, Île du i. Canada 169 J3
also known as Little Mecatina Island
Petit Morin r. France 51 J4
Petitot r. Canada 166 F2
Petit St-Bernard, Col du pass France 51 M7
Petkino Rus. Fed. 43 U5
Petkula Fin. 44 N2
Petlad India 96 B5
Petlawad India 96 B5
Peto Mex. 185 H4
Petoskey U.S.A. 173 I5
Petra tourist site Jordan 108 G7
also spelt Batrā'
Petras, Mount Antarctica 222 P1
Petra tou Romiou tourist site Cyprus see Aphrodite's Birthplace
Petra Velikogo, Zaliv b. Rus. Fed. 82 C4
English form Peter the Great Bay
Petre, Point Canada 173 P7
Petrich Bulg. 58 E7
Petrified Forest National Park U.S.A. 183 O6
Petrijevci Croatia 56 K3
Petrikau Poland see Piotrków Trybunalski
Petrikov Belarus see Pyetrykaw
Petrila Romania 58 E3
Petrinja Croatia 56 I3
Petro, Cerro de mt. Chile 204 C3
Petroaleksandrovsk Uzbek. see Turtkul'
Petrodvorets Rus. Fed. 43 K2
Petrograd Rus. Fed. see St Petersburg
Petrokov Poland see Piotrków Trybunalski
Petrokrepost' Rus. Fed. see Shlissel'burg
Petrokrepost', Bukhta b. Rus. Fed. 43 M1
Petrolândia Brazil 202 E4
Petrolia Canada 173 K8
Petrolina Amazonas Brazil 199 E5
Petrolina Pernambuco Brazil 202 D4
Petrolina de Goiás Brazil 206 D3
Petron, Limni l. Greece 58 C8
Petropavl Kazakh. see Petropavlovsk
Petropavlovka Kazakh. 103 J3
Petropavlovka Rus. Fed. 85 E1
Petropavlovka Rus. Fed. 41 G6
Petropavlovsk Kazakh. 38 G4
also known as Petropavl
Petropavlovsk Rus. Fed. see Petropavlovsk-Kamchatskiy
Petropavlovsk-Kamchatskiy Rus. Fed. 39 P4
historically known as Petropavlovsk
Petrópolis Brazil 207 J9
Petroșani Romania 58 E3
Petrovac Bos.-Herz. see Bosanski Petrovac
Petrovac Srbija Yugo. 58 C4
Petrovaradin Vojvodina, Srbija Yugo. 58 A3
also known as Péterváárad; historically known as Peterwardein
Petrovichi Rus. Fed. 43 N8
Petrovsk Rus. Fed. 41 H5
Petrovskiy Rus. Fed. 43 V5
Petrovskoye Moskovskaya Oblast' Rus. Fed. 43 R5
Petrovskoye Rus. Fed. see Svetlograd
Petrovskoye Yaroslavskaya Oblast' Rus. Fed. 43 U4
Petrovsk-Zabaykal'skiy Rus. Fed. 85 F1
Petrov Val Rus. Fed. 41 H6
Petrozavodsk Rus. Fed. 40 E3
Petru Rareș Romania 58 F1
Petrusburg S. Africa 133 J6
Petrus Steyn S. Africa 133 M4
Petrusville S. Africa 133 I7
Petsamo Rus. Fed. see Pechenga
Petsana S. Africa 133 M4
Pettau Slovenia see Ptuj
Petukhovo Rus. Fed. 38 G4
Petushki Rus. Fed. 43 U6
formerly known as Novyye Petushki
Peuetsagu, Gunung vol. Indon. 76 B1
Peurasuvanto Fin. 44 N2
Peureula Indon. 76 B1
Pevek Rus. Fed. 39 R3
Pexung China 89 F5
Peza r. Rus. Fed. 40 H2
Pézenas France 51 J9
Pezinok Slovakia 49 O7
Pfaffenhofen an der Ilm Germany 48 I7
Pfälzer Wald hills Germany 48 E6
Pfälzer Wald park Germany 48 E6
Pfarrkirchen Germany 49 J7
Pforzheim Germany 48 F7
Pfullendorf Germany 48 G8
Pfungstadt Germany 48 F6
Phagwara India 96 B3
Phahameng S. Africa 133 K5
Phalaborwa S. Africa 131 F4
Phalia Pak. 101 H3
Phalodi India 96 B4
Phalsbourg France 51 N4
Phalsund India 96 A4
Phaltan India 94 B2
Phalut Peak India/Nepal 97 F4
Phangan, Ko i. Thai. 79 C6
Phangnga Thai. 79 B6
Phan Rang Vietnam 79 E6
Phan Ri Vietnam 79 E6
Phan Thiêt Vietnam 79 E6
Phan Thiêt, Vinh b. Vietnam 79 E6
Phaphund India 96 C4
Phaplu Nepal 97 E4
Phat Diêm Vietnam 78 D3
Phatthalung Thai. 79 C7
Phayao Thai. 78 B4
Phek India 97 G4
Phelps r. U.S.A. 148 B2
Phelps NY U.S.A. 177 H3
Phelps WI U.S.A. 172 D4
Phen Thai. 78 C4
Phenix U.S.A. 176 G8
Phenix City U.S.A. 175 C5
Phephane watercourse S. Africa 132 G2
Phet Buri Thai. 79 B5
Phetchabun Thai. 78 C4
Phichit Thai. 78 C4
Philadelphia Jordan see 'Ammān
Philadelphia S. Africa 132 C10
Philadelphia Turkey see Alaşehir
Philadelphia MS U.S.A. 175 B5
Philadelphia NY U.S.A. 177 J1
Philadelphia PA U.S.A. 177 J6
Philae tourist site Egypt 121 G4
Philip U.S.A. 178 B2
Philip Atoll Micronesia see Sorol
Philippeville Alg. see Skikda
Philippeville Belgium 51 K2
Philippi U.S.A. 176 E6
Philippi, Lake salt flat Australia 148 C5
Philippines country Asia 74 A3
spelt Filipinas or Pilipinas in Filipino
asia [countries] 64–67
Philippine Sea N. Pacific Ocean 74 B2
Philippine Trench sea feature N. Pacific Ocean 220 C5
3rd deepest trench in the world.
Philippolis S. Africa 133 J7
Philippolis Road S. Africa 133 J7
Philippopolis Bulg. see Plovdiv
Philipsburg Neth. Antilles 187 H3
Philipsburg U.S.A. 180 D3
Philip Smith Mountains U.S.A. 164 E3
Philipstown S. Africa 133 I7
Phillip Island Australia 147 E4
Phillips ME U.S.A. 177 O1
Phillips WI U.S.A. 172 C5
Phillips Arm Canada 166 E5
Phillipsburg KS U.S.A. 178 C4
Phillipsburg NJ U.S.A. 177 J5
Phillips Inlet Canada 165 K1
Phillips Range hills Australia 150 D3
Phillipston U.S.A. 176 F5
Philmont U.S.A. 177 L3
Philomelium Turkey see Akşehir
Philpott Reservoir U.S.A. 176 F9
Phimun Mangsahan Thai. 79 D5
Phiritona S. Africa 133 L4
Phitsanulok Thai. 78 C4
Phlox U.S.A. 172 D5
Phnom Penh Cambodia 79 D6
Capital of Cambodia. Also spelt Phnum Pénh.
Phnum Pénh Cambodia see Phnom Penh
Pho, Laem pt Thai. 79 C7
Phoenicia U.S.A. 177 K3
Phoenix AZ U.S.A. 183 L8
State capital of Arizona.
Phoenix NY U.S.A. 177 I2
Phoenix Island Kiribati see Rawaki
Phoenix Islands Kiribati 145 H2
Phoenixville U.S.A. 177 J5
Phokwane S. Africa 133 N1
Phola S. Africa 133 N3
Phomolong S. Africa 133 L4
Phon Thai. 78 C5
Phong Nha Vietnam 78 D4
Phôngsali Laos 78 C3
also spelt Phong Saly
Phong Saly Laos see Phôngsali
Phong Thô Vietnam 78 C3
Phosphate Hill Australia 149 D4
Phrae Thai. 78 C4
Phra Nakhon Si Ayutthaya Thai. see Ayutthaya
Phrao Thai. 78 B4
Phra Saeng Thai. 79 B6
Phra Thong, Ko i. Thai. 79 B6
Phuchong-Nayoi National Park Thai. 79 D5
Phu Cuong Vietnam see Thu Dâu Môt
Phuduhudu Botswana 131 E4
Phuentsholing Bhutan 97 F4
also spelt Phuntsholing
Phuket Thai. 79 B7
Phuket, Ko i. Thai. 79 B7
Phu-Khieo Wildlife Reserve nature res. Thai. 78 C4
Phulabani India 95 E1
Phulpur India 97 D4
Phu Luang Wildlife Reserve nat. park Thai. 78 C4
Phu Ly Vietnam 78 D3
Phumĭ Chhuk Cambodia 79 D6
also known as Chhuk
Phumĭ Kâmpóng Trâlach Cambodia 79 D5
Phumĭ Mlu Prey Cambodia 79 D5
Phumĭ Prâmaôy Cambodia 79 C5
Phumĭ Sâmraông Cambodia 79 C5
also known as Samrong
Phuntsholing Bhutan see Phuentsholing
Phu Phac Mo mt. Vietnam 78 C3
Phu Phan National Park Thai. 78 C4
Phu Quôc, Đao i. Vietnam 79 C6
formerly known as Quan Phu Quoc
Phuthaditjhaba S. Africa 133 M5
Phu Tho Vietnam 78 D3
Phu Vinh Vietnam see Tra Vinh
Pia Aboriginal Reserve Australia 151 B5
Piabung, Gunung mt. Indon. 77 F2
Piaca Brazil 202 C3
Piacatu Brazil 206 C8
Piacenza Italy 56 B3
historically known as Placentia
Piacouadie, Lac l. Canada 169 G3
Piadena Italy 56 C3
Piagochioui r. Canada 168 E2
Pian r. Australia 147 F2
Piana di Catania plain Sicilia Italy 57 G11
Piangil Australia 147 D3
Pianguan China 85 F4
Pianoro Italy 56 D4
Pianosa, Isola i. Italy 56 C6
Piaseczno Poland 49 S3
Piaski Poland 49 T4
Piassabussu Brazil 202 E4
Piatã Brazil 202 D5
Piatra Romania 58 G5
Piatra Neamţ Romania 58 H2
Piatra Olt Romania 58 F4
Piatra Şoimului Romania 58 H2
Piauí r. Brazil 202 D3
Piauí state Brazil 202 D3
Piauí, Serra de hills Brazil 202 D4
Piave r. Italy 56 E3
Piazza Armerina Sicilia Italy 57 G11
Piazzi, Cima de' mt. Italy 56 C2
Piazzi, Isla i. Chile 205 B8
Pibor r. Sudan 128 B2
Pibor Post Sudan 128 B3
Pic r. Canada 168 C3
Pica Chile 200 C5
Picacho U.S.A. 183 M9
Picachos, Cerro dos mt. Mex. 184 B2
Picardie admin. reg. France 51 I3
Picardie reg. France see Picardy
Picardy reg. France 50 H3
also spelt Picardie
Picassent Spain 55 K5
Picayune U.S.A. 175 B6
Pichachic Mex. 184 D2
Pichanal Arg. 201 D5
Pichilemu Chile 204 B4
Pichilingue Mex. 184 C3
Pichi Mahuida Arg. 204 D5
Pichincha prov. Ecuador 198 B5
Pichor India 96 C4
Pichucalco Mex. 185 G5
Pic Island Canada 172 G2
Pickens U.S.A. 176 E7
Pickerel Lake Canada 172 B2
Pickering Canada 173 N7
Pickering U.K. 47 L9
Pickford U.S.A. 173 I4
Pickle Lake Canada 168 B3
Pico Bonito, Parque Nacional nat. park Hond. 186 B4
Pico da Neblina, Parque Nacional do nat. park Brazil 199 E4
Pico de Orizaba, Parque Nacional nat. park Mex. 185 F5
Pico de Tancítaro, Parque Nacional nat. park Mex. 185 E5
Picos Brazil 202 D3
Picos, Punta dos pt Spain 54 C3
Picota Peru 198 B6
Pico Truncado Arg. 205 D7
Pic River Canada 172 G2
Picton Australia 147 F3
Picton Canada 168 E5
Picton N.Z. 152 I9
Picton, Mount Australia 147 E5
Pictou Canada 169 I4
Picture Butte Canada 167 H5
Pictured Rocks National Lakeshore nature res. U.S.A. 172 G4
Picuí Brazil 202 E3
Picún Leufú Arg. 204 C5
Pidarak Pak. 101 E5
Pidurutalagala mt. Sri Lanka 94 D5
Piedade Brazil 206 F10
Pie de Palo, Sierra mts Arg. 204 C3
Piedimonte Matese Italy 56 G7
Piedmont admin. reg. Italy see Piemonte
Piedmont AL U.S.A. 175 C5
Piedmont MO U.S.A. 174 B4
Piedmont OH U.S.A. 176 D5
Piedmont Lake U.S.A. 176 D5
Piedra r. Spain 55 J3
Piedrabuena Spain 54 G5
Piedra de Aguila Arg. 204 C6
Piedrafita Spain see Pedrafita do Cebreiro
Piedrahita Spain 54 F4
Piedralaves Spain 54 G4
Piedras, Punta pt Arg. 204 F4
Piedras Blancas Spain 54 F1
Piedras Blancas Point U.S.A. 182 C6
Piedras Negras Guat. 185 H5
Piedras Negras Coahuila Mex. 185 E2
Piedras Negras Veracruz Mex. 185 F5
Pie Island Canada 172 D2
Pieksämäki Fin. 44 N3
Pielavesi Fin. 44 N3
Pielavesi l. Fin. 44 N3
Pielinen l. Fin. 44 O3
Pieljekaise nationalpark nat. park Sweden 44 L2
Piemonte admin. reg. Italy 56 A4
English form Piedmont
Pienaarsrivier S. Africa 133 M2
Pieniężno Poland 49 R1
Pieniński Park Narodowy nat. park Poland 49 R6
Pieninský nat. park Slovakia 49 R6
Pieńsk Poland 49 M4
Pierce U.S.A. 178 C3
Pierce Lake Canada 167 M4
Pierceland Canada 167 I4
Pierceton U.S.A. 172 H9
Pieria mts Greece 59 D8
Pierre U.S.A. 178 B2
State capital of South Dakota.
Pierre, Bayou r. U.S.A. 175 B6
Pierre Bayou r. U.S.A. 179 D6
Pierrelatte France 51 K8
Pieskehaure l. Sweden 44 L2
Piešťany Slovakia 49 O7
Pietermaritzburg S. Africa 133 O6
Pietersaari Fin. see Jakobstad
Pietersburg S. Africa 131 F4
also known as Polokwane
Piet Plessis S. Africa 133 I3
Pietraperzia Sicilia Italy 57 G11
Pietrasanta Italy 56 C5
Pietra Spada, Passo di pass Italy 57 I10
Piet Retief S. Africa 133 O4
Pietrosu, Vârful mt. Romania 58 G1
Pieve di Cadore Italy 56 E2
Pievepelago Italy 56 C4
Pigeon r. Canada/U.S.A. 174 B1
Pigeon Bay Canada 173 K9
Pigeon Lake Canada 167 H4
Pigeon River U.S.A. 172 D2
Pigg r. U.S.A. 176 F8
Piggott U.S.A. 174 B4
Pigg's Peak Swaziland 133 P2
Pigon, Limni l. Greece 59 C9
Pigs, Bay of Cuba 186 C2
also known as Cochinos, Bahía de
Pigüé Arg. 204 E5
Piguicas mt. Mex. 185 F4
Piha N.Z. 152 I4
Pihama N.Z. 152 H7
Pihani India 96 D4
Pi He r. China 87 F1
Pihkva järv l. Estonia/Rus. Fed. see Pskov, Lake
Pihlajavesi l. Fin. 45 O3
Pihlava Fin. 45 M3
Pihtipudas Fin. 44 N3
Piikkiö Fin. 42 D1
Piippola Fin. 44 N2
Piirissaar i. Estonia 42 I3
Piirsalu Estonia 42 F2
Piispajärvi Fin. 44 O2
Piji China see Puge
Pijijiapan Mex. 185 G6
Pikalevo Rus. Fed. 43 P2
Pike NY U.S.A. 176 G3
Pike WV U.S.A. 176 D6
Pikelot i. Micronesia 73 K5
formerly known as Coquille
Pikes Peak U.S.A. 180 F5
Piketberg S. Africa 132 C9
Piketon U.S.A. 176 B6
Pikeville KY U.S.A. 176 C8
Pikeville TN U.S.A. 174 C5
Pikihatiti b. N.Z. see Port Pegasus
Pikirakatahi mt. N.Z. see Earnslaw, Mount
Pikou China 85 I4
Pikounda Congo 126 C4
Pila Arg. 204 F5
Piła Poland 49 N2
historically known as Schneidemühl
Pila mt. Spain 55 J6
Pilagá r. Arg. 204 F2
Pilanesberg National Park S. Africa 133 L2
Pilani India 96 B3
Pilar Buenos Aires Arg. 204 F4
Pilar Córdoba Arg. 204 E3
Pilar Para. 201 F6
Pilar Phil. 74 C4
Pilar, Cabo c. Chile 205 B9
Pilar do Sul Brazil 206 F10
Pilas i. Phil. 74 B5
Pilas Spain 54 E7
Pilas Channel Phil. 74 B5
Pilat, Mont mt. France 51 K7
Pilat, Parc Naturel Régional du nature res. France 51 K7
Pilaya r. Bol. 201 D5
Pilcaniyeu Arg. 204 C6
Pilcomayo r. Bol./Para. 201 F6
Pilenkovo Georgia see Gant'iadi
Piler India 94 C3
Pili Greece see Pyli
Pili Phil. 74 B3
Pili, Cerro mt. Chile 200 D5
also known as Acamarachi
Piliakalnis hill Lith. 42 G6
Pilibangan India 96 B3
Pilibhit India 96 C3
Pilica r. Poland 49 S4
Piliga Nature Reserve Australia 147 F2
Pilipinas country Asia see Philippines
Pilisi park Hungary 49 P8
Pillau Rus. Fed. see Baltiysk
Pillcopata Peru 200 C3
Pilliga Australia 147 F2
Pillo, Isla del i. Arg. 204 E4
Pillsbury, Lake U.S.A. 182 B2
Pil'na Rus. Fed. 40 H5
Pil'nya, Ozero l. Rus. Fed. 40 K1
Pilões, Serra dos mts Brazil 206 F4
Pilón Cuba 186 D3
Pilón r. Mex. 179 C7
Pilos Greece see Pylos
Pilot Mountain hill U.S.A. 176 E9
Pilot Peak U.S.A. 182 G3
Pilot Point U.S.A. 164 D4
Pilot Rock U.S.A. 180 C3
Pilot Station U.S.A. 164 C3
Pilsen Czech Rep. see Plzeň
Pilsen U.S.A. 172 F6
Piltene Latvia 42 C4
Pilu, Nam r. Myanmar 78 B4
Pilvė r. Lith. 42 E7
Pilviškiai Lith. 42 E7
Pima U.S.A. 183 O9
Pimenta Bueno Brazil 201 E2
Pimpalner India 94 B1
Pimpri India 94 B1
Pimu Dem. Rep. Congo 126 D4
Pin r. Myanmar 78 A3
Pin r. Belarus 42 H9
Pinahat India 96 C4
Pinaleno Mountains U.S.A. 183 N9
Pinamalayan Phil. 74 B3
Pinamar Arg. 204 F5
Pinang Malaysia see George Town
Pinang i. Malaysia 76 C1
Pinang state Malaysia 76 C1
also known as Pulau Pinang; formerly spelt Penang
Pinar mt. Spain 54 F8
Pinar, Puerto del pass Spain 55 I6
Pınarbaşı Turkey 107 D3
also known as Aziziye
Pinar del Río Cuba 186 C2
Pinarhisar Turkey 106 A2

Polonnoye Ukr. see Polonne
Polotnyanyy Zavod Rus. Fed. 43 Q7
Polotsk Belarus see Polatsk
Polovinka Rus. Fed. see Ugleural'skiy
Polovragi Romania 58 E3
Pöls r. Austria 49 L8
Polska country Europe see Poland
Polski Trümbesh Bulg. 58 G5
Polson U.S.A. 180 D3
Polta r. Rus. Fed. 40 G2
Poltár Slovakia 49 Q7
Poltava Ukr. 41 E6
Poltavka Rus. Fed. 82 C3
Poltavskaya Rus. Fed. 41 F7
formerly known as Krasnoarmeyskaya
Poltoratsk Turkm. see Ashgabat
Põltsamaa Estonia 42 G3
Põltsamaa r. Estonia 42 H3
Polur India 94 C3
Põlva Estonia 42 I3
Polvadera U.S.A. 181 F6
Polvijärvi Fin. 44 O3
Polya r. Rus. Fed. 43 U6
Polyaigos i. Greece 59 F12
also spelt Poliaigos
Polyanovgrad Bulg. see Karnobat
Polyany Rus. Fed. 43 K1
Polyarnoye Rus. Fed. see Russkoye Ust'ye
Polyarnyy Chukotskiy Avtonomnyy Okrug Rus. Fed. 39 R3
Polyarnyy Murmanskaya Oblast' Rus. Fed. 44 P1
Polyarnyye Zori Rus. Fed. 44 P2
Polyarnyy Krug Rus. Fed. 44 P2
Polyarnyy Ural mts Rus. Fed. 40 L2
Polydroso Greece 59 D10
also known as Polidhrosos
Polygyros Greece 59 E8
Polyiagou-Folegandrou, Steno sea chan. Greece 59 F12
Polykastro Greece 58 D8
also known as Polikastron
Polynesia is Oceania 220 G5
Polynésie Française terr. S. Pacific Ocean see French Polynesia
Pomabamba Peru 200 A2
Pomahaka r. N.Z. 153 D14
Pomarance Italy 56 C5
Pomarkku Fin. 45 M3
Pomba r. Brazil 203 D7
Pombal Pará Brazil 199 H5
Pombal Paraíba Brazil 202 E3
Pombal Port. 54 C5
Pombas r. Brazil 199 F6
Pombas Cape Verde 124 [inset]
Pombo r. Brazil 206 A7
Pomene Moz. 131 G4
Pomeroy S. Africa 133 O5
Pomeroy OH U.S.A. 176 C6
Pomeroy WA U.S.A. 180 C3
Pomezia Italy 56 E7
Pomfret S. Africa 132 H2
Pomio P.N.G. 145 E2
Pomokaira reg. Fin. 44 N2
Pomona Namibia 130 B5
Pomona U.S.A. 182 G7
Pomorie Bulg. 58 I6
Pomorska, Zatoka b. Poland 49 L1
Pomorskie, Pojezierze reg. Poland 49 O2
Pomorskiy Bereg coastal area Rus. Fed. 40 E2
Pomorskiy Proliv sea chan. Rus. Fed. 40 I1
Pomos Point Cyprus 108 D2
also known as Pomou, Akra
Pomo Tso l. China see Puma Yumco
Pomou, Akra pt Cyprus see Pomos Point
Pompei Italy 57 G8
historically known as Pompeii
Pompéia Brazil 206 C9
Pompeii Italy see Pompei
Pompéu Brazil 203 C6
Pompton Lakes U.S.A. 177 K4
Ponape atoll Micronesia see Pohnpei
Ponask Lake Canada 167 M4
Ponazyrevo Rus. Fed. 40 H4
Ponca U.S.A. 178 C3
Ponca City U.S.A. 178 C4
Ponce Puerto Rico 187 G3
Ponce de Leon Bay U.S.A. 175 D7
Poncha Springs U.S.A. 181 F5
Ponda India 94 B3
Pondicherry India 94 C4
also spelt Pondichéry or Puduchcheri
Pondicherry union terr. India 95 C4
Pondichéry India see Pondicherry
Pond Inlet Canada 165 L2
also known as Mittimatalik; formerly known as Ponds Bay
Pondoland reg. S. Africa 133 N8
Ponds, Island of Canada 169 K2
Ponds Bay Canada see Pond Inlet
Poneloya Nicaragua 186 B4
Ponente, Riviera di coastal area Italy 56 A5
Ponferrada Spain 54 E2
Pongakawa N.Z. 152 K5
Pongara, Pointe pt Gabon 126 A4
Pongaroa N.Z. 152 K8
Pongo watercourse Sudan 126 E3
Pongo de Manseriche gorge Peru 198 B6
Pongola S. Africa 133 P4
Pongola r. S. Africa 133 Q3
Pongolapoort Dam l. S. Africa 133 P4
Pongolapoort Public Resort Nature Reserve S. Africa 133 P4
Poniatowa Poland 49 T4
Poniki, Gunung mt. Indon. 75 B2
Ponindilisa, Tanjung pt Indon. 75 B3
Ponizov'ye Rus. Fed. 43 M6
Ponnagyun Myanmar 78 A3
Ponnaivar r. India 94 C4
Ponnampet India 94 B3
Ponnani India 94 B4
Ponnani r. India 94 B4
Ponneri India 94 D3
Ponnyadaung Range mts Myanmar 78 A3
Ponoka Canada 167 H4
Ponomarevka Rus. Fed. 102 C1
Ponorogo Indon. 77 E4
Ponoy r. Rus. Fed. 40 G2
Pons r. Canada 169 G1
Pons France 50 F7
Pons Spain see Ponts
Ponsacco Italy 56 C5
Ponsul r. Port. 54 D5
Pontacq France 50 F9

▶Ponta Delgada Azores 216 M3
Capital of the Azores.

Ponta de Pedras Brazil 202 B2
Ponta dos Índios Brazil 199 I3
Ponta do Sol Cape Verde 124 [inset]
Ponta Grossa Brazil 203 B8
Pontal do Ipiranga Brazil 207 N6
Pontalina Brazil 206 D4
Pont-à-Mousson France 51 M4
Pontant Arg. 204 E5
Pontão Brazil 202 B3
Ponta Porã Brazil 201 G5
Pontarlier France 51 M6
Pontassieve Italy 56 D5
Pont-Audemer France 50 G3
Pont-Aven France 50 C5
Pontax r. Canada 168 E3
Pontchartrain, Lake U.S.A. 175 B6
Pontchâteau France 50 D5
Pont-d'Ain France 51 L7
Pont-de-Roide France 51 M5
Pont de Suert Spain 55 L2
Ponte Alta do Norte Brazil 202 C4
Ponteareas Spain 54 C2
also spelt Puenteareas
Pontebba Italy 56 F2
Ponte Branca Brazil 206 A3
Ponte-Ceso Spain 54 C1
Pontecorvo Italy 56 F7
Ponte de Pedra Brazil 201 F3
Pontedera Italy 56 C5
Ponte de Sor Port. 54 C5
Ponte do Rio Verde Brazil 203 A6
Ponte Firme Brazil 206 G5
Pontefract Canada 167 J5
Ponteland U.K. 47 K8
Ponte Nova Brazil 203 D7
Pontes-e-Lacerda Brazil 201 F3
Pontevedra Spain 54 C2
Pontevedra, Ría de est. Spain 54 C2
Ponthierville Dem. Rep. Congo see Ubundu
Pontiac IL U.S.A. 174 B3
Pontiac MI U.S.A. 173 J8
Pontiae is Italy see Ponziane, Isole
Pontianak Indon. 77 E3
Pontine Islands is Italy see Ponziane, Isole
Pontivy France 50 D4
Pont-l'Abbé France 50 B5
Pontoetoe Suriname 199 H4
Pontoise France 51 I3
Ponton watercourse Australia 151 C6
Ponton Canada 167 L4
Pontotoc U.S.A. 174 B5
Pontremoli Italy 56 B4
Ponts Spain 55 M3
also spelt Pons
Pont-St-Esprit France 51 K8
Pont-sur-Yonne France 51 J4
Pontypool Canada 173 O6
Pontypool U.K. 47 I12
Pontypridd U.K. 47 I12
Ponui Island N.Z. 152 J4
Ponyatovka Rus. Fed. 43 N8
Ponyri Rus. Fed. 43 R9
Ponza Italy 57 E8
Ponza, Isola di i. Italy 56 E8
Ponziane, Isole is Italy 56 E8
English form Pontine Islands; historically known as Pontiae
Poochera Australia 146 B3
Pool admin. reg. Congo 126 B5
Poole U.K. 47 K13
Poolowanna Lake salt flat Australia 148 C5
Poona India see Pune
Pooncarie Australia 147 D3
Poopelloe Lake Australia 147 E2
Poopó Bol. 200 D4
Poopó, Lago de l. Bol. 200 D4
Poor Knights Islands N.Z. 152 I3
Pop Uzbek. see Pap
Popa Mountain Myanmar 78 A3
Popayán Col. 198 B4
Pope Latvia 42 C4
Popes Creek U.S.A. 177 I7
Popigay r. Rus. Fed. 39 K2
Popilta Lake imp. l. Australia 146 D3
Popio Lake Australia 146 D3
Poplar r. Man. Canada 167 L4
Poplar r. N.W.T. Canada 166 G2
Poplar U.S.A. 172 B4
Poplar r. U.S.A. 180 F2
Poplar, West Fork r. U.S.A. 180 F2
Poplar Bluff U.S.A. 174 B4
Poplar Camp U.S.A. 176 E9
Poplar Plains U.S.A. 176 B7
Poplarville U.S.A. 175 B6
Poplevinskiy Rus. Fed. 43 U8

▶Popocatépetl, Volcán vol. Mex. 185 F5
5th highest mountain in North America.
northamerica [landscapes] 156–157
northamerica [threats] 160–161

Popoh Indon. 77 E5
Popokabaka Dem. Rep. Congo 127 C6
Popoli Italy 56 F6
Popondetta P.N.G. 145 D2
Popovača Croatia 56 I3
Popovichskaya Rus. Fed. see Kalininskaya
Popovka Vologod. Obl. Rus. Fed. 43 S2
Popovka Vologod. Obl. Rus. Fed. 43 U1
Popovo Bulg. 58 H5
Popovo Polje plain Bos.-Herz. 56 J6
Popovska Reka r. Bulg. 58 H6
Poppberg hill Germany 48 I6
Poppenberg hill Germany 48 H4
Poprad r. Poland 49 R6
Poprad Slovakia 49 R6
Poquis, Nevado de mt. Chile 200 D5
Poquoson U.S.A. 177 I8
Por r. Poland 49 U5
Porali r. Pak. 101 F5
Porangahau N.Z. 152 K8
Porangatu Brazil 202 B5
Porazava Belarus 42 F9
Porbandar India 96 A5
Porcher Island Canada 166 D4
Porciúncula Brazil 207 K7
Porco Bol. 200 D4
Porcsalma Hungary 49 T8
Porcuna Spain 54 G7
Porcupine r. Canada/U.S.A. 164 E3
Porcupine, Cape Canada 169 J2
Porcupine Creek r. U.S.A. 180 F2
Porcupine Gorge National Park Australia 149 E4
Porcupine Hills Canada 167 K4
Porcupine Mountains U.S.A. 172 D4
Porcupine Plain Canada 167 K4
Porcupine Provincial Forest nature res. Canada 167 K4
Pordenone Italy 56 E3
Pordim Bulg. 58 F5
Pore Col. 198 D3
Poreč Croatia 56 F3
Porecatu Brazil 206 B9
Porech'ye Moskovskaya Oblast' Rus. Fed. 43 Q6
Porech'ye Pskovskaya Oblast' Rus. Fed. 43 L5
Porech'ye Tverskaya Oblast' Rus. Fed. 43 R3
Porech'ye-Rybnoye Rus. Fed. 43 U4
Poretskoye Rus. Fed. 40 H5
Porga Benin 125 F4
Pori Fin. 45 M3
also known as Björneborg
Porirua N.Z. 152 I9
Porjus Sweden 44 L2
Porkhov Rus. Fed. 43 K4
Porkkalafjärden b. Fin. 42 F2
Porlamar Venez. 199 F2
Porma r. Spain 54 F2
Pormpuraaw Australia 149 D2
Pornainen Fin. 45 N3
Pornic France 50 D5
Poro i. Phil. 74 C4
Poro, Monte hill Italy 57 H10
Poronaysk Rus. Fed. 82 F2
Porong China see Baingoin
Pörong, Stœng r. Cambodia 79 D5
Poros Greece 59 E11
Poros i. Greece 59 E11
Porosozero Rus. Fed. 40 E3
Porpoise Bay Antarctica 223 I2
Porquerolles, Île de i. France 51 M10
Porquis Junction Canada 173 M2
Porrentruy Switz. 51 N5
Porriño Spain 54 C2
Porsangen sea chan. Norway 44 N1
Porsangerhalvøya pen. Norway 44 N1
Porsgrunn Norway 45 J4
Porsuk r. Turkey 106 B3
Portadown U.K. 47 F9
Portaferry U.K. 47 G9
Portage IN U.S.A. 172 F9
Portage MI U.S.A. 172 H8
Portage PA U.S.A. 176 G5
Portage WI U.S.A. 172 D7
Portage Lakes U.S.A. 176 D5
Portage la Prairie Canada 167 L5
Portal U.S.A. 178 B1
Port Alberni Canada 166 E5
Port Albert Australia 147 E4
Portalegre Port. 54 D5
Portalegre admin. dist. Port. 54 D5
Portales U.S.A. 179 B5
Port-Alfred Canada see La Baie
Port Alfred S. Africa 133 K10
Port Alice Canada 166 E5
Port Allegany U.S.A. 176 G4
Port Alma Australia 149 F4
Port Angeles U.S.A. 180 B2
Port Antonio Jamaica 186 D3
Portarlington Rep. of Ireland 47 E10
Port Arthur Australia 147 E5
Port Arthur China see Lüshun
Port Arthur U.S.A. 179 D6
Port Askaig U.K. 46 F8
Port Augusta Australia 146 C3
Port-au-Port Bay Canada 169 J3

▶Port-au-Prince Haiti 187 E3
Capital of Haiti.

Port aux Choix Canada 169 J3
Port Beaufort S. Africa 132 E11
Port Blair India 95 G4
Portbou Spain 55 O2
Port Bradshaw b. Australia 148 C2
Port Broughton Australia 146 C3
Port Burwell Canada 173 M8
Port Campbell Australia 147 D4
Port Campbell National Park Australia 147 D4
Port Canning India 97 F5
Port Carling Canada 173 N5
Port-Cartier Canada 169 H3
formerly known as Shelter Bay
Port Chalmers N.Z. 153 E13
Port Charles N.Z. 152 J4
Port Charlotte U.S.A. 175 D7
Port Clements Canada 166 C4
Port Clinton OH U.S.A. 176 C4
Port Clyde U.S.A. 177 P2
Port Colborne Canada 168 E5
Port Credit Canada 173 N7
Port Darwin b. Australia 148 A2
Port Davey b. Australia 147 E5
Port-de-Paix Haiti 187 E3
Port de Pollença Spain 55 O5
also spelt Puerto de Pollensa
Port Dickson Malaysia 76 C2
Port Douglas Australia 149 E3
Port Dover Canada 173 M8
Port Easington inlet Australia 148 A1
Porte des Morts lake channel U.S.A. 172 G5
Port Edward Canada 166 D4
Port Edward S. Africa 133 O8
Port Edwards U.S.A. 172 D6
Porteira Brazil 199 G5
Porteirinha Brazil 202 D5
Portel Brazil 202 B2
Portel Port. 54 D6
Portelândia Brazil 206 A4
Port Elgin N.B. Canada 169 H4
Port Elgin Ont. Canada 168 D4
Port Elizabeth S. Africa 133 J10
Port Ellen U.K. 46 F8
Port Erin Isle of Man 47 H9
Porter Lake N.W.T. Canada 167 J2
Porter Lake Sask. Canada 167 J3
Porter Landing Canada 166 D3
Porterville S. Africa 132 C10
Porterville U.S.A. 182 E5
Portes-lès-Valence France 51 K8
Port Étienne Mauritania see Nouâdhibou
Port Everglades U.S.A. see Fort Lauderdale
Port Fairy Australia 147 D4
Port Fitzroy N.Z. 152 J4
Port Francqui Dem. Rep. Congo see Ilebo
Port-Gentil Gabon 126 A5
Port Gibson U.S.A. 175 B6
Port Grosvenor S. Africa 133 N8
Port Harcourt Nigeria 125 G5
Port Hardy Canada 166 E5
Port Harrison Canada see Inukjuak
Port Hawkesbury Canada 169 I4
Porthcawl U.K. 47 I12
Port Hedland Australia 150 B4
Port Henry U.S.A. 177 L1
Port Herald Malawi see Nsanje
Porthmos Zakynthou sea chan. Greece 59 B11
Port Hope Canada 173 O7
Port Hope U.S.A. 173 K7
Port Hope Simpson Canada 169 K2
Port Hueneme U.S.A. 182 E7
Port Huron U.S.A. 173 K8
Port-İliç Azer. 107 G3
Portillo Cuba 186 D3
Portimão Port. 54 C7
Port Island Hong Kong China 87 [inset]
also known as Chek Chau
Port Jackson Australia see Sydney
Port Jackson inlet Australia 147 F3
Port Jefferson U.S.A. 177 L5
Port Kaituma Guyana 199 G3
Port Keats Australia see Wadeye
Port Kent U.S.A. 177 L1
Port Klang Malaysia see Pelabuhan Kelang
Port Láirge Rep. of Ireland see Waterford
Portland Australia 146 D4
Portland IN U.S.A. 176 A5
Portland ME U.S.A. 177 O2
Portland MI U.S.A. 173 I8
Portland OR U.S.A. 180 B3
Portland, Isle of pen. U.K. 47 J13
Portland Bay Australia 146 D4
Portland Bill hd U.K. see Bill of Portland
Portland Canal inlet Canada 166 D4
Portland Creek Pond l. Canada 169 J3
Portland Inlet Canada 166 D4
Portland Point Jamaica 186 D3
Portland Roads Australia 149 D2
Portlaoise Rep. of Ireland 47 E10
Port Lavaca U.S.A. 179 C6
Port Lincoln Australia 146 B3
Port Loko Sierra Leone 124 B4
Port Louis Guadeloupe 187 H3

▶Port Louis Mauritius 219 K7
Capital of Mauritius.

Port-Lyautrey Morocco see Kénitra
Port MacDonnell Australia 146 D4
Port Macquarie Australia 147 G2
Port Manvers inlet Canada 169 I1
Port McArthur b. Australia 148 C2
Port McNeill Canada 166 E5
Port-Menier Canada 169 H3
Port Moller b. U.S.A. 164 C4
Port Morant Jamaica 186 D3

▶Port Moresby P.N.G. 73 K8
Capital of Papua New Guinea.

Port Musgrave b. Australia 149 D1
Portnacroish U.K. 46 G7
Portnahaven U.K. 46 F8
Port Neches U.S.A. 179 D6
Port Neill Australia 146 C3
Port Nelson Bahamas 187 E2
Portneuf r. Canada 169 G3
Portneuf, Réserve Faunique de nature res. Canada 169 F4
Port Nis U.K. 46 F5
Port Nolloth S. Africa 132 A6
Port Norris U.S.A. 177 J6
Port-Nouveau-Québec Canada see Kangiqsualujjuaq
Porto Brazil 202 D2
Porto Port. see Oporto
Porto admin. dist. Port. 54 C3
Porto, Golfe de b. Corse France 51 O10
Porto Acre Brazil 200 D2
Porto Alegre Amazonas Brazil 200 D2
Porto Alegre Mato Grosso do Sul Brazil 203 A7
Porto Alegre Pará Brazil 199 H6
Porto Alegre Rio Grande do Sul Brazil 203 B9
Porto Alencastro Brazil 206 C6
Porto Alexandre Angola see Tombua
Porto Amarante Brazil 201 E3
Porto Amboim Angola 127 B7
also known as Gunza
Porto Amélia Moz. see Pemba
Porto Artur Brazil 201 G3
Porto Azzurro Italy 56 C6
Porto Belo Brazil 203 B8
Portobelo Panama 186 D5
Portobelo, Parque Nacional nat. park Panama 186 D5
Porto Camargo Brazil 203 A7
Porto Cavlo Brazil 202 F4
Porto da Fôlha Brazil 202 E4
Porto da Lontra Brazil 199 H6
Porto de Meinacos Brazil 202 A5
Porto de Moz Brazil 199 H5
Porto de Santa Cruz Brazil 207 L2
Porto do Barka Brazil 199 H6
Porto do Massacas Brazil 201 E3
Porto dos Gaúchos Óbidos Brazil 201 F2
Porto do Son Spain 54 B2
also spelt Puerto del Son
Porto Empedocle Sicilia Italy 57 F11
Porto Esperança Brazil 201 F4
Porto Esperidião Brazil 201 F3
Porto Estrêla Brazil 201 F3
Porto Feliz Brazil 206 F10
Portoferraio Italy 56 C6
Porto Ferreira Brazil 206 F8
Porto Firme Brazil 207 J7
Porto Franco Brazil 202 C3

▶Port of Spain Trin. and Tob. 187 H5
Capital of Trinidad and Tobago.

Porto Grande Brazil 199 I4
Portogruaro Italy 56 E3
Porto Inglês Cape Verde 124 [inset]
Porto Jofre Brazil 201 F4
Portola U.S.A. 182 D2
Porto Lucena Brazil 203 A8
Portomaggiore Italy 56 D4
Porto Mauá Brazil 203 A8
Porto Murtinho Brazil 201 F5
Porto Nacional Brazil 202 B4

▶Porto-Novo Benin 125 F5
Capital of Benin.

Porto Novo Cape Verde 124 [inset]
Porto Novo India see Parangipettai
Portopalo di Capo Passero Sicilia Italy 57 H12
Porto Primavera, Represa resr Brazil 206 A8
Port Orange U.S.A. 175 D6
Port Orchard U.S.A. 180 B3
Port Orford U.S.A. 180 A4
Porto Rincão Cape Verde 124 [inset]
Porto San Giorgio Italy 56 F5
Porto Santana Brazil 199 I5
Porto Sant'Elpidio Italy 56 F5
Porto Santo, Ilha de i. Madeira 122 A2
Portoscuso Sardegna Italy 57 A9
Porto Seguro Brazil 202 E6
Porto Tolle Italy 56 E4
Porto Torres Sardegna Italy 56 A8
historically known as Turris Libisonis
Porto Triunfo Brazil 201 E3
Porto União Brazil 203 B8
Porto-Vecchio Corse France 52 D3
Porto Velho Brazil 201 E2
Portoviejo Ecuador 198 A5
Porto Wálter Brazil 200 B2
Portpatrick U.K. 47 G9
Port Pegasus b. N.Z. 153 B15
also known as Pikihatiti
Port Perry Canada 173 O6
Port Phillip Bay Australia 147 E4
Port Pirie Australia 146 C3
Portree U.K. 46 F6
Port Renfrew Canada 166 E5
Port Rexton Canada 169 K3
Port Roper b. Australia 148 B2
Port Rowan Canada 173 M8
Port Royal U.S.A. 177 H7
Port Royal Sound inlet U.S.A. 175 D5
Port Said Egypt 121 G2
also known as Bûr Sa'îd
Port St Joe U.S.A. 175 C6
Port St Johns S. Africa 133 N8
Port St-Louis Madag. see Antsohimbondrona
Port-St-Louis-du-Rhône France 51 K9
Port Saint Lucie City U.S.A. 175 D7
Port Salvador Falkland Is 205 F8
Ports de Beseit mts Spain 55 L4
also spelt Puertos de Beceite
Port Severn Canada 173 N6
Port Shelter b. Hong Kong China 87 [inset]
also known as Ngau Mei Hoi
Port Shepstone S. Africa 133 O7
Port Simpson Canada see Lax Kw'alaams
Portsmouth Dominica 187 H4
Portsmouth U.K. 47 K13
Portsmouth NH U.S.A. 177 O2
Portsmouth OH U.S.A. 176 C7
Portsmouth VA U.S.A. 177 I9
Port Stanley Falkland Is see Stanley
Port Stephens Falkland Is 205 E9
Port Sudan Sudan 121 H5
also known as Bûr Sudan
Port Sulphur U.S.A. 175 B6
Port-sur-Saône France 51 M5
Port Swettenham Malaysia see Pelabuhan Kelang
Port Talbot U.K. 47 I12
Port Tambang b. Phil. 74 B3
Porttipahdan tekojärvi l. Fin. 44 N1
Port Townsend U.S.A. 180 B2
▶Portugal country Europe 54 C7
europe [countries] 32–35
Portugalete Spain 55 H1
Portugália Angola see Chitato
Portuguesa state Venez. 198 D2
Portuguese East Africa country Africa see Mozambique
Portuguese Guinea country Africa see Guinea-Bissau
Portuguese Timor terr. Asia see East Timor
Portuguese West Africa country Africa see Angola
Portumna Rep. of Ireland 47 D10
Portus Herculis Monoeci country Europe see Monaco
Port-Vendres France 51 J10
Port Victoria Australia 146 C3

▶Port Vila Vanuatu 145 F3
Capital of Vanuatu. Also known as Vila.

Portville U.S.A. 176 G3
Port Vladimir Rus. Fed. 44 P1
Port Waikato N.Z. 152 I5
Port Wakefield Australia 146 C3
Port Warrender Australia 150 D2
Port Washington U.S.A. 172 F7
Port Wing U.S.A. 172 B4
Porumamilla India 94 C3
Porus'ya r. Rus. Fed. 43 M4
Porvenir Pando Bol. 200 C2
Porvenir Santa Cruz Bol. 201 E3
Porvenir Chile 205 C9
Porvoo Fin. 45 N3
also known as Borgå
Porvoonjoki r. Fin. 42 G1
Por'ya Guba Rus. Fed. 44 P2
Poryŏng S. Korea 83 B5
formerly known as Taech'ŏn
Porzuna Spain 54 G5
Posada Sardegna Italy 57 B8
Posada r. Sardegna Italy 57 B8
Posada Spain 54 F1
Posadas Arg. 204 G2
Posadas Spain 54 G6
Posadowsky Bay Antarctica 223 G2
Posavina reg. Bos.-Herz./Croatia 56 I3
Poschiavo Switz. 51 Q6
Poseidonia Greece 59 F11
Poseidonia tourist site Italy see Paestum
Posen Poland see Poznań
Posen U.S.A. 173 J5
Poshekhon'ye Rus. Fed. 43 U3
formerly known as Poshekhon'ye-Volodarsk
Poshekhon'ye-Volodarsk Rus. Fed. see Poshekhon'ye
Posht watercourse Iran 100 D4
Posht-e Badam Iran 100 C3
Poshteh-ye Chaqvīr hill Iran 100 D4
Posht-e Kūh mts Iran 100 B3
Posht Kūh hill Iran 100 B2
Posio Fin. 44 O2
Poskam China see Zepu
Poso Indon. 75 B3
Poso r. Indon. 75 B3
Poso, Danau l. Indon. 75 B3
Poso, Teluk b. Indon. 75 B3
Posof Turkey 107 E2
Posorja Ecuador 198 A5
Pospelikha Rus. Fed. 103 J1
Posse Brazil 202 C5
Possession Islands Antarctica 223 L2
Pößneck Germany 48 I5
Post U.S.A. 179 B5
Poşta Călnău Romania 58 H3
formerly spelt Poşta Cîlnău
Poşta Cîlnău Romania see Poşta Călnău
Postavy Belarus see Pastavy
Poste-de-la-Baleine Canada see Kuujjuarapik
Postmasburg S. Africa 132 H5
Postojna Slovenia 56 G3
Poston U.S.A. 183 J7
Postville Canada 169 J2
Postville U.S.A. 174 B3
Post Weygand Alg. 123 F4
Postysheve Ukr. see Krasnoarmiys'k
Posušje Bos.-Herz. 56 J5
Pos'yet Rus. Fed. 82 C4
Pota Indon. 75 B5
Potamia Greece 58 F8
Potamos Greece 59 D12
Potanino Rus. Fed. 43 N1
Potchefstroom S. Africa 133 L3
Potcoava Romania 58 F4
Poté Brazil 203 D6
Poteau U.S.A. 179 D5
Potegaon India 94 D2
Potentia Italy see Potenza
Potenza Italy 57 H8
historically known as Potentia
Potenza r. Italy 56 F5
Poteriteri, Lake N.Z. 153 B14
Potfontein S. Africa 132 I7
Potgietersrus S. Africa 131 F5
Poti r. Brazil 202 D3
P'ot'i Georgia 107 E2
Potikal India 94 D2
Potiraguá Brazil 202 E5
Potiskum Nigeria 125 H4
Potnarvin Vanuatu 145 F3
Poto Peru 200 C3
Po Toi i. Hong Kong China 87 [inset]
also spelt Putoi
Potomac r. U.S.A. 177 I7
Potomac, South Branch r. U.S.A. 176 G6
Potomac, South Fork South Branch r. U.S.A. 176 F7
Potomana, Gunung mt. Indon. 75 C5
Potoru Sierra Leone 124 C5
Potosí Bol. 200 D4
Potosí dept Bol. 200 D5
Potosi U.S.A. 174 B4
Potosi Mountain U.S.A. 183 I6
Pototan Phil. 74 B4
Potrerillos Chile 204 C2
Potrero del Llano Mex. 184 D2
Potro r. Peru 198 B6
Potsdam Germany 49 K3
Potsdam U.S.A. 177 K1
Potsdamer Havelseengebiet park Germany 49 J3
Pottangi India 95 D2
Pottendorf Austria 49 N8
Potter U.S.A. 178 B3
Potter Valley U.S.A. 182 A2
Potterville U.S.A. 176 A3
Pottsville U.S.A. 177 I5
Potwar reg. Pak. 101 H3
Pouancé France 50 E5
Pouce Coupe Canada 166 F4
Pouch Cove Canada 169 K4
Poughkeepsie U.S.A. 177 L4
Poultney U.S.A. 177 L2
Pouma Cameroon 125 H6
Pound U.S.A. 176 C8
Poupan S. Africa 132 I7
Pourerere N.Z. 152 K8
Pouso Alegre Brazil 207 H9
Pouso Alegre, Serra mts Brazil 206 D2
Pouso Alto Brazil 206 A3
Poutasi Samoa 145 H3
Poŭthĭsăt Cambodia 79 C5
also spelt Pursat
Pouto N.Z. 152 I4
Pouzauges France 50 F6
Povarovo Rus. Fed. 43 S5
Považská Bystrica Slovakia 49 P6
Poved' r. Rus. Fed. 43 P4
Povenets Rus. Fed. 40 E3
Povlen mt. Yugo. 58 A4
Povoação Brazil 207 N6
Póvoa de Varzim Port. 54 C3
Povorino Rus. Fed. 41 G6
Povorotnyy, Mys hd Rus. Fed. 82 D4
Poway U.S.A. 183 G9
Powder r. MT U.S.A. 180 F3
Powder r. OR U.S.A. 180 C3
Powder, South Fork r. U.S.A. 180 F4
Powder River U.S.A. 180 F4
Powell U.S.A. 180 E3
Powell r. U.S.A. 176 B9
Powell, Lake resr U.S.A. 183 N4
Powell Creek watercourse Australia 149 D5
Powell Mountain U.S.A. 182 F3
Powell River Canada 166 E5
Powellsville U.S.A. 177 I9
Powers U.S.A. 172 F5
Powhatan U.S.A. 176 H8
Powhatan Point U.S.A. 176 E6
Powidzkie, Jezioro l. Poland 49 O3
Powo China 86 A1
Poxoréu Brazil 202 A5
Poyan, Sungai r. Sing. 76 [inset]
Poyang China see Boyang
Poyang Hu l. China 87 F2
Poyan Reservoir Sing. 76 [inset]
Poyarkovo Rus. Fed. 82 C2
Poygan, Lake U.S.A. 172 E6
Poynette U.S.A. 172 D7
Poyo, Cerro mt. Spain 55 I7
Poysdorf Austria 49 N7
Pöytyä Fin. 45 M3
Pozantı Turkey 106 C3
Požarevac Srbija Yugo. 58 C4
Poza Rica Mex. 185 F4
Požega Croatia 56 J3
formerly known as Slavonska Požega
Požega Srbija Yugo. 58 B5
Pozharskoye Rus. Fed. 90 D1
Pozhnya Rus. Fed. 43 M5
Pozhva Rus. Fed. 40 K4
Poznań Poland 49 N3
historically known as Posen
Pozo Alcón Spain 55 I7
Pozo Betbeder Arg. 204 D2
Pozoblanco Spain 54 G6
Pozo Colorado Para. 201 F5
Pozo del Tigre Arg. 201 E6
Pozo Hondo Arg. 204 D2
Pozohondo Spain 55 J6
Pozo Nuevo Mex. 184 C2
Pozos, Punta pt Arg. 205 D7
Pozo San Martin Arg. 204 E2
Pozsony Slovakia see Bratislava
Pozuzo Peru 200 B2
Pozzallo Sicilia Italy 57 G12
Pozzuoli Italy 57 G8
historically known as Puteoli
Pra r. Ghana 125 E5
Prabumulih Indon. 76 D3
Prabuty Poland 49 Q2
Prachatice Czech Rep. 49 L6
Prachi r. India 95 E2
Prachin Buri Thai. 79 C5
Prachuap Khiri Khan Thai. 79 B6
Pradairo mt. Spain 54 D1
Praděd mt. Czech Rep. 49 O5
Pradera Col. 198 B4
Prades France 51 I10
Prado Brazil 203 E6
Pradópolis Brazil 206 E8

▶Prague Czech Rep. 49 L5
Capital of the Czech Republic. Also known as Praha.

Praha Czech Rep. see Prague
Prahova r. Romania 58 H4

▶Praia Cape Verde 124 [inset]
Capital of Cape Verde.

Praia a Mare Italy 57 H9
Praia do Bilene Moz. 131 G5
Praia Grande Brazil 206 G11
Praia Rica Brazil 201 G3
Prainha Amazonas Brazil 201 E1
Prainha Pará Brazil 199 H5
Prairie Australia 149 E4
Prairie r. U.S.A. 174 A2
Prairie City U.S.A. 180 C3
Prairie Dog Town Fork r. U.S.A. 179 B5
Prairie du Chien U.S.A. 172 B7
Prairie River Canada 167 K4
Prakhon Chai Thai. 79 C5
Pram r. Austria 49 K7
Pramanta Greece 59 C9
Pran r. Thai. 79 C5
Pran Buri Thai. 79 B5
Prangli i. Estonia 42 G2
Pranhita r. India 94 C2
Prapat Indon. 76 B2
Prasonisi, Akra pt Greece 59 I13
Praszka Poland 49 P4
Prat i. Chile 205 B8
Prata Brazil 206 E6
Prata r. Goiás Brazil 206 A5
Prata r. Minas Gerais Brazil 206 D5
Prata r. Minas Gerais Brazil 207 G4
Pratapgarh India 96 B4
Pratas Islands China see Dongsha Qundao
Prat de Llobregat Spain see El Prat de Llobregat
Prathes Thai country Asia see Thailand
Pratinha Brazil 206 G6
Prato Italy 56 D5
Pratt U.S.A. 178 C4
Prattville U.S.A. 175 C5
Pravara r. India 94 B2
Pravda Bulg. 58 I5
Pravdinsk Rus. Fed. 42 C7
historically known as Friedland
Pravia Spain 54 E1
Praya Indon. 77 G5
Prazaroki Belarus 45 O5
Preah, Prêk r. Cambodia 79 D5
Preăh Vihear Cambodia 79 D5
Prechistoye Smolenskaya Oblast' Rus. Fed. 43 N6
Prechistoye Yaroslavskaya Oblast' Rus. Fed. 43 V3
Precipice National Park Australia 149 F5
Predazzo Italy 56 D2
Predeal Romania 58 G3
Preeceville Canada 167 K5
Pré-en-Pail France 50 F4
Preetz Germany 48 H1
Pregolya r. Rus. Fed. 42 B7
Preiļi Latvia 42 I5
Preissac, Lac l. Canada 173 O2
Prekornica mts Yugo. 58 A6
Prelate Canada 167 I5
Prémery France 51 J5
Premnitz Germany 49 J3
Prenj mts Bos.-Herz. 56 J5
Prentiss U.S.A. 175 B6
Prenzlau Germany 49 K2
Preobrazheniye Rus. Fed. 82 D4
Preparis Island Cocos Is 79 A5
Preparis North Channel Cocos Is 79 A5
Preparis South Channel Cocos Is 79 A5
Přerov Czech Rep. 49 O6
Presa de la Amistad, Parque Natural nature res. Mex. 185 E2
Presanella, Cima mt. Italy 56 C2
Presa San Antonio Mex. 185 E3
Prescott Canada 168 F4
Prescott AR U.S.A. 179 D5
Prescott AZ U.S.A. 183 L7
Prescott Valley U.S.A. 183 L7
Preservation Inlet N.Z. 153 A14
Preševo Srbija Yugo. 58 C6
Presidencia Roca Arg. 204 F2
Presidencia Roque Sáenz Peña Arg. 204 E2
Presidente Bernardes Brazil 206 B9
Presidente de la Plaza Arg. 204 F2
Presidente Dutra Brazil 202 C3
Presidente Eduardo Frei research station Antarctica 222 U2
Presidente Epitácio Brazil 206 A8
Presidente Hermes Brazil 201 E2
Presidente Jânio Quadros Brazil 207 L1
Presidente Juan Perón prov. Arg. see Chaco
Presidente Juscelino Brazil 207 I5
Presidente Olegário Brazil 206 G5
Presidente Prudente Brazil 206 B9
Presidente Venceslau Brazil 206 B8
Presidio U.S.A. 181 F7
Preslav Bulg. see Veliki Preslav
Prešov Slovakia 49 S7
Prespa, Lake Europe 58 C8
also known as Prespansko Ezero or Prespës, Liqeni i
Prespansko Ezero l. Europe see Prespa, Lake

Pyhäjärvi l. Fin. 44 N3
Pyhäjärvi l. Fin. 44 N3
Pyhäjärvi l. Fin. 44 O3
Pyhäjärvi l. Fin. 45 M3
Pyhäjoki Fin. 44 N2
Pyhäjoki r. Fin. 44 N2
Pyhältö Fin. 42 I1
Pyhäntä Fin. 44 N2
Pyhäranta Fin. 45 M3
Pyhäsalmi Fin. 44 N3
Pyhäselkä Fin. 44 O3
Pyhäselkä l. Fin. 44 O3
Pyhätunturin kansallispuisto nat. park Fin. 44 N2
Pyhtää Fin. 45 N3
Pyin Myanmar see Pyè
Pyingaing Myanmar 78 A3
Pyinmana Myanmar 78 B4
Pyli Greece 59 I12
also spelt Píli
Pyl'karamo Rus. Fed. 39 I3
Pylos Greece 59 C12
also spelt Pílos
Pymatuning Reservoir U.S.A. 176 E4
Pyŏksŏng N. Korea 83 B5
Pyŏktong N. Korea 83 B4
P'yŏnggang N. Korea 83 B5
P'yŏngsong N. Korea 83 B5
P'yŏngt'aek S. Korea 83 B5

▶P'yŏngyang N. Korea 83 B5
Capital of North Korea.

Pyŏnsan Bando National Park S. Korea 83 B6
Pyramid Lake U.S.A. 182 E1
Pyramid Lake Indian Reservation res. U.S.A. 182 E1
Pyramid Range mts U.S.A. 182 E2
Pyrenees mts Europe 55 N2
also spelt Pyrénées or Pirineos
Pyrénées mts Europe see Pyrenees
Pyrénées Occidentales, Parc National des nat. park France/Spain 55 K2
Pyrgetos Greece 59 D9
also spelt Piryetós
Pyrgi Greece 59 G10
also known as Piryíon
Pyrgos Greece 59 C11
also spelt Pírgos
Pyrton, Mount hill Australia 150 B4
Pyryatyn Ukr. 41 E6
also spelt Piryatin
Pyrzyce Poland 49 L2
Pyshchug Rus. Fed. 40 H4
Pyshna Belarus 43 J7
Pyszna r. Poland 49 P4
Pytalovo Rus. Fed. 42 I4
Pythonga, Lac l. Canada 173 Q4
Pyu Myanmar 78 B4
Pyxaria mt. Greece 59 E10
also spelt Pixariá

↓ Q

Qā', Wādī al watercourse Saudi Arabia 104 B2
Qaa Lebanon 109 H3
formerly spelt El Kaa
Qaanaaq Greenland see Thule
Qabanbay Kazakh. see Kabanbay
Qabātiya West Bank 108 G5
Qābil Oman 105 F3
Qabka China see Xaitongmoin
Qabnag China 89 F6
Qabqa China see Gonghe
Qabr Bandar tourist site Iraq 107 E5
Qabr Hūd Oman 105 E4
Qabyrgha r. Kazakh. see Kabyrga
Qacentina Alg. see Constantine
Qacha's Nek Lesotho 133 M7
Qaḍā' Chāy watercourse Iraq 109 P3
Qadamgāli Iran 100 D2
Qādes Afgh. 101 E3
Qaḍīmah Saudi Arabia 104 B3
Qādir Karam Iraq 107 F4
Qādisīyah, Buḩayrat al resr Iraq 109 N3
Qādisīyah, Sadd dam Iraq 107 E4
English form Qadisiyah Dam
Qadisiyah Dam Iraq see Qādisīyah, Sadd
Qādub Yemen 105 F5
Qa'emabad Iran 101 E4
Qā'emiyeh Iran 100 B4
Qagan China 85 H1
Qagan Ders China 85 E3
Qagan Nur Nei Mongol China 85 F4
Qagan Nur Nei Mongol China 85 G3
also known as Xulun Hobot Qagan Qi or Zhengxiangbai Qi
Qagan Nur Nei Mongol China 85 G3
Qagan Nur Qinghai China 84 C4
Qagan Nur l. China 85 J2
Qagan Nur resr China 85 G3
Qagan Teg China 85 G3
Qagan Tohoi China 84 B5
Qagan Us China see Dulan
Qagan Us He r. China 84 C4
Qagca China 86 A1
formerly known as Cacagoin
Qagchêng China see Xiangcheng
Qahar Youyi Houqi China see Bayan Qagan
Qahar Youyi Qianqi China see Togrog Ul
Qahar Youyi Zhongqi China see Hobor
Qā' Ḩaẕawẕā' depr. Saudi Arabia 107 D5
Qahd, Wādī watercourse Saudi Arabia 104 C2
Qahr, Jibāl al hills Saudi Arabia 104 D4
Qahremānshahr Iran see Kermānshāh
Qaḩṭān reg. Saudi Arabia 104 C3
Qaidam He r. China 84 B4
Qaidam Pendi basin China 84 B4
English form Tsaidam Basin
Qaidar China see Cêtar
Qainaqangma China 89 E5
Qaisar Afgh. 101 F3
Qaisar r. Afgh. 101 F2
Qaisar, Koh-i- mt. Afgh. 101 F3
Qalabotjha S. Africa 133 M4
Qalā Diza Iraq 107 F3
Qala'en Nahl Sudan 121 G6
Qala-i-Fateh Afgh. 101 E4
Qala-i-Kang Afgh. 101 E4
Qal'aikhum Tajik. 101 G2
also spelt Kalaikhum; formerly spelt Kalai-Khumb
Qalamat Abū Shafrah Saudi Arabia 105 F3
Qalamat Al Juḩaysh oasis Saudi Arabia 105 E3
Qalamat ar Rakabah oasis Saudi Arabia 105 F3
Qalamat Fāris oasis Saudi Arabia 105 E4
Qalamat Nadqān well Saudi Arabia 105 E3
Qalamat Shutfah well Saudi Arabia 105 F3
Qalansīyah Yemen 105 F5
Qala Shinia Takht Afgh. 101 F3
Qalāt Afgh. 101 F3
Qal'at al Aẓlam Saudi Arabia 104 A2
Qal'at al Ḩiṣn tourist site Syria 109 H3
Qal'at al Marqab tourist site Syria 108 G2
Qal'at al Mu'aẓẓam Saudi Arabia 104 B2
Qal'at Bīshah Saudi Arabia 104 C3
Qal'at Muqaybirah, Jabal mt. Syria 109 J2
Qal'at Ṣāliḩ Iraq 107 F5
Qala Vali Afgh. 101 E3
Qalbī Zhotasy mts Kazakh. see Kalbinskiy Khrebet
Qal'eh Iran 100 C2
Qal'eh Dāgh mt. Iran 100 A2
Qal'eh Tirpul Afgh. 101 E3
Qal 'eh-ye Bost Afgh. 101 F4
Qal 'eh-ye Now Afgh. 101 E3
Qal'eh-ye Shūrak well Iran 100 D3
Qalhāt Oman 105 G3
Qalīb Bāqūr well Iraq 107 F5
Qalqīlya West Bank 108 F5
Qalqutan Kazakh. see Koluton
Qalti el Adusa well Sudan 121 E5
Qalyûb Egypt 121 F2
Qalyûbîya governorate Egypt 108 C7
Qamalung China 86 A1
Qamanirjuaq Lake Canada 167 M2
also known as Kaminuriak Lake
Qamanittuaq Canada see Baker Lake
Qamar, Ghubbat al b. Yemen 105 F4
English form Qamar Bay
Qamar, Jabal al mts Oman 105 F4
Qamar Bay Yemen see Qamar, Ghubbat al
Qamashi Uzbek. see Kamashi
Qamdo China 86 A2
also spelt Chamdo
Qam Hadīl Saudi Arabia 104 C4
Qamīnis Libya 120 C2
Qamruddin Karez Pak. 101 G4
Qamṣar Iran 100 B3
Qamystybas Kazakh. see Kamyshlybash
Qanawt Oman 105 F4
Qandahar Afgh. see Kandahār
Qandala Somalia 128 F2
Qandaranbashi mt. Iran 100 A2
Qandyaghash Kazakh. see Kandyagash
Qangzê China 89 B6
Qanṭara, Gebel hill Egypt 108 B7
Qapal Kazakh. see Kapal
Qapan Iran 100 C2
Qapqal China 88 C3
Qapshagay Kazakh. see Kapchagay
Qapshagay Bögeni resr Kazakh. see Kapchagayskoye Vodokhranilishche
Qaq Köli salt l. Kazakh. see Kak, Ozero
Qaqortoq Greenland 165 O3
also known as Julianehåb
Qara Egypt 106 A5
Qarā', Jabal al mts Oman 105 F4
Qara Āghach r. Iran see Mand, Rūd-e
Qara Anjīr Iraq 109 P2
Qaraaoun Lebanon 108 G4
Qarabas Kazakh. see Karabas
Qarabulaq Kazakh. see Karabulak
Qarabutaq Kazakh. see Karabutak
Qaraçala Azer. 100 B2
Qarachōq, Jabal mts Iraq 107 E4
Qara Ertis r. China/Kazakh. see Ertix He
Qaraghandy Kazakh. see Karaganda
Qaraghandy Oblysy admin. div. Kazakh. see Karagandinskaya Oblast'
Qaraghayly Kazakh. see Karagayly
Qārah Saudi Arabia 107 E5
Qārah, Jabal al hill Saudi Arabia 104 D4
Qarah Bāgh Ghaznī Afgh. 101 G3
Qarah Bāgh Kābul Afgh. 101 G3
Qarak China 88 B4
Qaraköl Kazakh. see Karakol'
Qaranqu r. Iran 100 A2
Qaraoy Kazakh. see Karaoy
Qara Özek Uzbek. see Karauzyak
Qaraqalpaqstan Respublikasy aut. rep. Uzbek. see Karakalpakistan, Respublika
Qara Qōsh Iraq 109 O1
Qaraqoyyn Köli salt l. Kazakh. see Karakoyyn, Ozero
Qaraqozha Kazakh. see Karaguzhikha
Qaraqum des. Kazakh. see Karakum Desert
Qaraqum des. Turkm. see Karakum Desert
Qarasū Kazakh. see Karasu
Qara Şū Chāy r. Syria/Turkey see Karasu
Qara Tarai mt. Afgh. 101 F3
Qarataū Kazakh. see Karatau
Qarataū Zhotasy mts Kazakh. see Karatau, Khrebet
Qaratöbe Kazakh. see Karatobe
Qaratoghay Kazakh. see Karatogay
Qaratomar Bögeni resr Kazakh. see Karatomarskoye Vodokhranilishche
Qaraton Kazakh. see Karaton
Qaraūyl Kazakh. see Karaul
Qarazhal Kazakh. see Karazhal
Qardho Somalia 128 F2
Qardud Sudan 126 F2
Qareh Chāy r. Iran 100 B3
Qareh Dāgh mts Iran 100 A2
Qareh Qāch, Kūh-e mts Iran 100 C3
Qareh Sū r. Iran 100 A2
Qâret Gahannam hill Egypt 108 B8
Qarhan China 84 B4
Qarkilik China see Ruoqiang
Qarnayṭ, Jabal hill Saudi Arabia 104 C3
Qarnein i. U.A.E. 105 F2
Qarn el Kabsh, Gebel mt. Egypt 121 G2
Qarokŭl l. Tajik. 101 H2
also known as Karakul', Ozero
Qarqan China see Qiemo
Qarqan He r. China 88 D4
Qarqaraly Kazakh. see Karkaralinsk
Qarqi Xinjiang China 88 C3
Qarqi Xinjiang China 88 D3
Qārqi Iran 102 C5
Qarqīn Afgh. 101 F2
Qarrit, Qafa e pass Albania 58 B8
Qarsaqbay Kazakh. see Karsakpay
Qarshi Uzbek. see Karshi
Qarshi Chŭli plain Uzbek. see Karshinskaya Step'
Qartaba Lebanon 108 G3
Qārūh, Jazīrat i. Kuwait 107 G5
Qârûn Egypt 108 B8
Qaryat al Ulyā Saudi Arabia 105 D2
Qaşab, Wādī al watercourse Iraq 109 O2
Qasamī Iran 100 D3
Qasa Murg mts Afgh. 101 E3
Qasba India 97 E4
Qaşbah, Ras al pt Saudi Arabia 108 F9
Qāsemābād Khorāsan Iran 100 D3
Qāsemābād Khorāsan Iran 101 D2
Qashqadaryo r. Uzbek. see Kashkadar'ya
Qashqadaryo Wiloyati admin. div. Uzbek. see Kashkadar'inskaya Oblast'
Qash Qai reg. Iran 100 B4
Qashqantengiz Kazakh. see Kashkanteniz
Qasigiannguit Greenland 165 N3
also known as Christianshåb
Qasīm reg. Saudi Arabia 104 C2
Qaskelen Kazakh. see Kaskelen
Qasq China 85 F3
also known as Tumd Zuoqi
Qaşr ad Dayr, Jabal mt. Jordan 108 G7
Qaşr al Azraq Jordan 109 H6
Qasr al Ḩayr tourist site Syria 109 I3
Qasr al Khubbāz Iraq 107 E4
Qaşr 'Āmij Iraq 109 M4
Qaşr 'Amrah tourist site Jordan 109 H6
Qaşr aş Şabīyah Kuwait 107 G5
Qaşr Burqu' tourist site Jordan 109 I5
Qaşr-e-Qand Iran 101 E5
Qaşr-e Shīrīn Iran 107 F4
Qasr Farafra Egypt 121 E3
Qaşr Ḩimām Saudi Arabia 105 D3
Qaşr Larocu Libya 120 B3
Qaşr Shaqrah tourist site Iraq 107 F5
Qassimiut Greenland 165 O3
Qa'tabah Yemen 104 D5
Qaṭanā Syria 108 H4
▶Qatar country Asia 105 E2
asia [countries] ▶▶ 64–67
Qatlish Iran 100 D2
Qaṭrâni, Gebel esc. Egypt 121 F2
Qaṭrūyeh Iran 100 C4
Qaṭṭāfī, Wādī al watercourse Jordan 109 I6
Qattâra, Râs esc. Egypt 121 E2
Qattâra Depression Egypt 121 E2
also known as Qaṭṭārah, Munkhafaḍ al
Qaṭṭārah, Munkhafaḍ al depr. Egypt see Qattâra Depression
Qaṭṭīnah, Buḩayrat resr Syria 109 H3
also known as Ḩimş, Baḩrat
Qavāmābād Iran 100 D4
Qax Azer. 107 F2
also spelt Kakhi
Qāyen Iran 100 D3
Qayghy Kazakh. see Kayga
Qaynar Kazakh. see Kaynar
Qayraqty Kazakh. see Kayrakty
Qayroqqum Tajik. 101 G1
formerly spelt Kayrakkum
Qaysīyah, Qa' al imp. l. Jordan 109 H6
Qayyārah Iraq 107 E4
Qazaly Kazakh. see Kazalinsk
Qazangödağ mt. Armenia/Azer. 107 F3
also known as Kapydzhik, Gora
Qazaq Shyghanaghy b. Kazakh. see Kazakhskiy Zaliv
Qazaqstan country Asia see Kazakhstan
Qazax Azer. 107 F2
also spelt Kazakh
Qazi Ahmad Pak. 101 G5
Qazımämmäd Azer. 107 G2
also spelt Kazi Magomed
Qazvīn Iran 100 B2
Qazvīn prov. Iran 100 B2
Qazyqurt Kazakh. see Kazygurt
Qedir China 88 D3
Qeh China 84 D3
Qeisûm, Gezâ'ir is Egypt 104 A2
English form Qeisûm Islands; also spelt Geisûm, Gezâ'ir
Qeisûm Islands Egypt see Qeisûm, Gezâ'ir
Qelelevu i. Fiji 145 H3
also spelt Nggelelevu
Qena Egypt 121 G3
also spelt Qinā
Qena governorate Egypt 104 A2
Qena, Wâdi watercourse Egypt 121 G3
Qeqertarsuaq Greenland 165 N3
also known as Godhavn
Qeqertarsuaq i. Greenland 165 N3
also known as Disko
Qeqertarsuatsiaat Greenland 165 N3
also known as Fiskenæsset
Qeqertarsuatsiaq i. Greenland 165 N2
also known as Hareøen
Qeqertarsuup Tunua b. Greenland 165 N3
also known as Disko Bugt
Qeshlāq Iran 100 A3
Qeshm Iran 100 D5
Qeshm i. Iran 100 D5
Qeydār Iran 100 B2
Qeys i. Iran 100 C5
Qezel Owzan, Rūdkhāneh-ye r. Iran 100 B2
Qeẕi'ot Israel 108 F7
Qi r. China 85 G5
Qian r. China 87 C1
Qian'an Hebei China 85 H4
Qian'an Jilin China 85 J2
Qiancheng China 87 D3
Qiang r. China 87 F1
Qian Gorlos China see Qianguozhen
Qianguozhen China 82 B3
also known as Qian Gorlos
Qianjiang Chongqing China 87 D2
also known as Lianhe
Qianjiang Hubei China 87 E2
Qianjin China 82 D3
formerly known as Weidongmen
Qianning China 86 B2
also known as Gartar
Qianqihao China 85 I2
Qianshan China 87 F2
also known as Meicheng
Qian Shan mts China 85 I3
Qianshanlaoba China 88 D2
Qianwei China 86 B2
also known as Yujin
Qianxi Guizhou China 86 C3
Qianxi Hebei China 85 H3
also known as Xingcheng
Qianxian China 87 D1
Qianyang Hunan China 87 D3
also known as Anjiang
Qianyang Shaanxi China 86 C1
Qianyang Zhejiang China 87 F2
Qianyou China see Zhashui
Qiaocun China 85 G4
Qiaojia China 86 B3
also known as Xinhua
Qiaoshan China see Huangling
Qiaotou China see Datong
Qiaotou China 86 B3
Qiaowa China see Muli
Qiaowan China 84 C3
Qiaozhuang China see Qingchuan
Qibā' Saudi Arabia 104 D2
Qibing S. Africa 133 L6
Qibray Uzbek. see Kibray
Qichun China 87 E2
also known as Caohe; formerly known as Caojiahe
Qidong Hunan China 87 E3
formerly known as Hongqiao
Qidong Jiangsu China 87 G2
also known as Huilongzhen
Qiemo China 88 D4
formerly known as Cherchen or Qarqan
Qihe China 85 H4
also known as Yancheng
Qijiang China 86 C2
also known as Gunan
Qijiaojing China 88 E3
Qikiqtarjuaq Canada 165 M3
formerly known as Broughton Island
Qiktim China 88 E3
Qila Ladgasht Pak. 101 E5
Qilaotu Shan mts China 85 H3
Qila Safed Pak. 101 E4
Qila Saifullah Pak. 101 G4
Qili China see Shitai
Qilian China 84 D4
also known as Babao
Qilian Shan mt. China 84 C4
Qilian Shan mts China 84 C4
Qillak i. Greenland 165 P3
also known as Dannebrog Ø
Qīma Kazakh. see Kiyma
Qiman el 'Arûs Egypt 108 C8
Qimantag mts China 89 E4
Qimen China 87 F2
also known as Qishan
Qimusseriarsuaq b. Greenland 165 M2
also known as Melville Bugt
Qin r. China 87 E1
Qinā Egypt see Qena
Qināb, Wādī r. Yemen 105 E4
Qin'an China 86 C1
also known as Xingguo
Qincheng China see Nanfeng
Qing r. China 82 A4
Qing'an China 82 B3
Qingcheng China see Qingyang
Qingchengzi China 83 A4
Qingchuan China 86 C1
also known as Qiaozhuang
Qingdao China 85 I4
formerly spelt Tsingtao
Qinggang China 82 B3
Qinggil China see Qinghe
Qingguandu China 87 D2
Qinghai prov. China 84 C4
English form Tsinghai; formerly known as Chinghai
Qinghai Hu salt l. China 84 D4
Qinghai Nanshan mts China 84 C4
Qinghe Hebei China 85 G4
also known as Gexianzhuang
Qinghe Xinjiang China 84 A2
also known as Qinggil
Qinghua China see Bo'ai
Qingjian China 85 F4
also known as Xiuyan
Qingjiang China see Huaiyin
Qingjiang China see Zhangshu
Qing Jiang r. China 87 D2
Qingkou China see Ganyu
Qingliu China 87 F3
also known as Longjin
Qinglong Guizhou China 86 C3
also known as Liancheng
Qinglong Hebei China 85 H3
Qinglong r. China 85 H4
Qingpu China 87 G2
Qingquan China see Xishui
Qingshan China see Dedu
Qingshizui China 84 D4
Qingshui China see Qingshuipu
Qingshui China 86 C1
also known as Yongqing
Qingshuihe Nei Mongol China 85 F4
Qingshuihe Qinghai China 86 A1
also known as Domda
Qingshuihezi China 88 C2
Qingshuilang Shan mts China 86 A3
Qingshuipu China 84 C4
formerly known as Qingshui
Qingtian China 87 G2
also known as Hecheng
Qingtongxia China 85 E4
also known as Xiaoba
Qingxian China 85 H4
also known as Qingzhou
Qingxu China 85 G4
also known as Qingyuan
Qingyang Anhui China 87 F2
also known as Rongcheng
Qingyang Gansu China 85 E4
also known as Qingcheng
Qingyang China see Sihong
Qingyuan China see Weiyuan
Qingyuan Guangdong China 87 E4
Qingyuan China see Yizhou
Qingyuan Liaoning China 82 B4
Qingyuan China see Qingxu
Qingyuan Zhejiang China 87 F3
Qingyun China 85 H4
formerly known as Xiejiaji
Qingzang Gaoyuan plat. China see Tibet, Plateau of
Qingzhen China 86 C3
Qingzhou China see Qingxian
Qingzhou Hubei China 87 D2
Qingzhou Shandong China 85 H4
formerly known as Yidu
Qinhuangdao China 85 H4
Qinjiang China see Shicheng
Qin Ling mts China 87 C1
Qinshui China 85 G5
Qinting China see Lianhua
Qinxian China 85 G4
Qinyang China 85 G5
Qinyuan China 85 G4
Qinzhou China 87 D4
Qinzhou Wan b. China 87 D4
Qionghai China 87 D5
Qiongjiexue China see Qonggyai
Qionglai China 86 B2
Qionglai Shan mts China 86 B2
Qiongshan China 87 D5
Qiongxi China see Hongyuan
Qiongzhou Haixia strait China see Hainan Strait
Qiqihar China 85 I2
formerly spelt Tsitsihar
Qiquanhu China 88 E3
Qīr Iran 100 C4
Qira China 89 C4
Qîraîya, Wâdi watercourse Egypt 108 F7
Qiryat Gat Israel 108 F6
Qiryat Shemona Israel 108 G4
Qishan China see Qimen
Qishan China 87 C1
also known as Fengming
Qishn Yemen 105 E5
Qishon r. Israel 108 G5
Qishrān Island Saudi Arabia 104 C3
Qitab ash Shāmah vol. crater Saudi Arabia 107 D5
Qitai China 88 E3
Qitaihe China 82 C3
Qitbīt, Wādī r. Oman 105 F4
Qiubei China 86 C3
also known as Jinping
Qiujin China 87 E2
Qixia China 85 I4
Qixian Henan China 85 G5
formerly known as Zhaoge
Qixian Henan China 87 E1
Qixian Shanxi China 85 G4
Qixing r. China 82 D3
Qiyang China 87 D3
Qiying China 85 E4
Qizhou Liedao i. China 87 D5
Qızılağac Körfäzi b. Azer. 100 B2
formerly known as Kirova, Zaliv
Qizil-Art, Aghbai pass Kyrg./Tajik. see Kyzylart Pass
Qizilrabot Tajik. 101 H2
also spelt Kyzylrabot
Qizqetkan Uzbek. see Kyzketken
Qoboqobo S. Africa 133 M9
Qoghaly Kazakh. see Kugaly
Qogir Feng mt. China/Jammu and Kashmir see K2
Qog Qi China 85 E3
Qojūr Iran 100 A2
Qolora Mouth S. Africa 133 M9
Qoltag mts China 88 E3
Qom Iran 100 B3
Qom prov. Iran 100 B3
Qomdo China see Qumdo
Qomishēh Iran 100 B3
formerly known as Shahrezā
Qomolangma Feng mt. China/Nepal see Everest, Mount
Qonaqkänd Azer. 107 G2
Qonggyai China 89 E6
also known as Qiongjiexue; also spelt Chonggye
Qongj China 85 F3
Qongkol China 88 D3
Qongrat Uzbek. see Kungrad
Qongyrat Kazakh. see Kounradskiy
Qongyrat Kazakh. see Konyrat
Qongyröleng Kazakh. see Konyrolen
Qonj China 84 C4
Qonystanū Kazakh. see Konystanu
Qooriga Neegro b. Somalia 128 F3
Qoornoq Greenland 165 N3
Qoqek China see Tacheng
Qoqodala S. Africa 133 K8
Qoradaryo r. Kyrg. see Kara-Darya
Qoraghaty Kazakh. see Kuragaty
Qoraqalpoghiston Uzbek. see Karakalpakiya
Qoraqalpoghiston Respublikasi aut. rep. Uzbek. see Karakalpakistan, Respublika
Qoraūzak Uzbek. see Karauzyak
Qorday Kazakh. see Kurday
Qorghalzhyn Kazakh. see Kurgal'dzhinskiy
Qornet es Saouda mt. Lebanon 108 H3
Qorowulbozor Uzbek. see Karaulbazar
Qoroy, Gardaneh-ye pass Iran 100 B2
Qorveh Iran 100 A3
Qosh Tepe Iraq 107 E3
Qosshaghyl Kazakh. see Koschagyl
Qostanay Kazakh. see Kostanay
Qostanay Oblysy admin. div. Kazakh. see Kustanayskaya Oblast'
Qoṭbābād Iran 100 D5
Qoṭūr Iran 100 A2
Qozhaköl l. Kazakh. see Kozhakol', Ozero
Qozonketkan Uzbek. see Kazanketken
Qozoqdaryo Uzbek. see Kazakhdar'ya
Quabbin Reservoir U.S.A. 177 M3
Quadra Island Canada 166 E5
Quadros, Lago dos l. Brazil 203 B9
Quaggasfontein Poort pass S. Africa 132 E8
Quail Mountains U.S.A. 183 G6
Quairading Australia 151 B7
Quakenbrück Germany 48 E3
Quamby Australia 149 D4
Quanah U.S.A. 179 C5
Quanbao Shan mt. China 87 D1
Quân Đao Cô Tô is Vietnam 78 D3
Quan Dao Hoang Sa is S. China Sea see Paracel Islands
Quân Đao Nam Du i. Vietnam 79 D6
Quan Dao Truong Sa is S. China Sea see Spratly Islands
Quang Ngai Vietnam 79 E5
Quang Tri Vietnam 78 D4
Quang Yen Vietnam 78 D3
Quan He r. China 87 E1
Quanjiang China see Suichuan
Quan Long Vietnam see Ca Mau
Quannan China 87 E3
also known as Chengxiang
Quan Phu Quoc i. Vietnam see Phu Quôc, Đao
Quanshang China 87 F3
Quanwan Hong Kong China see Tsuen Wan
Quanzhou Fujian China 87 F3
Quanzhou Guangxi China 87 D3
Qu'Appelle r. Canada 167 K5
Quaqtaq Canada 165 M3
formerly known as Notre-Dame-de-Koartac; formerly spelt Koartac
Quaraí Brazil 204 F3
Quarry Bay Hong Kong China 87 [inset]
Quarryville U.S.A. 177 I6
Quarteira Port. 54 C7
Quartu Sant'Elena Sardegna Italy 57 B9
Quartzite Mountain U.S.A. 183 H4
Quartzsite U.S.A. 183 J8
Quaryat al Faw tourist site Saudi Arabia 105 D4
Quba Azer. 107 G2
also spelt Kuba
Quchan Iran 100 D2
Qudaysah well Oman 105 G4
Qudeni S. Africa 133 O5
Queanbeyan Australia 147 F3

▶Québec Canada 169 G4
Provincial capital of Québec.

Québec prov. Canada 169 F2
Quebra Anzol r. Brazil 206 F6
Quedas Moz. 131 G3
Quedlinburg Germany 48 I4
Queen Adelaide Islands Chile see La Reina Adelaida, Archipiélago de
Queen Alia airport Jordan 108 G6
Queen Anne U.S.A. 177 J7
Queen Bess, Mount Canada 166 E5
Queen Charlotte Canada 166 C4
Queen Charlotte Bay Falkland Is 205 E8
Queen Charlotte Islands Canada 166 C4
Queen Charlotte Sound sea chan. Canada 166 D5
Queen Charlotte Strait Canada 166 E5
Queen Creek U.S.A. 183 M8
Queen Elizabeth Islands Canada 165 I2
Queen Elizabeth National Park Uganda 128 A5
formerly known as Ruwenzori National Park
Queen Elizabeth Range mts Antarctica 223 K1
Queen Fabiola Mountains Antarctica 223 C2
Queen Mary Land reg. Antarctica 223 G2
Queen Maud Bird Sanctuary nature res. Canada 167 K1
Queen Maud Gulf Canada 165 I3
Queen Maud Land reg. Antarctica 223 A2
also known as Dronning Maud Land
Queen Maud Mountains Antarctica 223 O1
Queensburgh S. Africa 133 O6
Queens Channel Australia 148 A2
Queenscliff Australia 147 E4
Queensland state Australia 149 E4
Queenstown Australia 147 E5
Queenstown N.Z. 153 C13
Queenstown Rep. of Ireland see Cóbh
Queenstown S. Africa 133 K8
Queenstown Sing. 76 [inset]
Queenstown U.S.A. 177 I7
Queen Victoria Spring Nature Reserve Australia 151 C6
Quehua Bol. 200 D4
Quehué Arg. 204 D5
Queiba well Chad 120 D5
Queimada Brazil 201 E2
Queimada, Ilha i. Brazil 202 B2
also known as Serraria, Ilha
Queimadas Brazil 202 E4
Queiroz Brazil 206 C8
Quela Angola 127 C7
Quelimane Moz. 131 H3
Quelite Mex. 184 D4
Quellón Chile 205 B6
Quelpart Island S. Korea see Cheju-do
Queluz Brazil 207 I9
Quemada Grande, Ilha i. Brazil 206 G11
Quemado U.S.A. 181 E6
Quembo r. Angola 127 D8
Quemchi Chile 205 B6
Quemoy i. Taiwan see Chinmen Tao
Quemú-Quemú Arg. 204 E5
Quepem India 94 B3
Que Que Zimbabwe see Kwekwe
Quequén Arg. 204 F5
Querência Brazil 202 A5
Querétaro Mex. 185 E4
Querétaro state Mex. 185 F4
Querfurt Germany 48 I4
Querobabi Mex. 184 C2
Querpon Peru 198 B6
Quesada Spain 55 H7
Quesat watercourse W. Sahara 122 C4
Queshan China 87 E1
also known as Panlong
Quesnel Canada 166 F4
Quesnel r. Canada 166 F4
Quesnel Lake Canada 166 F4
Questembert France 50 D5
Quetena de Lipez r. Bol. 200 D5
Quetico Provincial Park Canada 172 B2
Quetta Pak. 101 F4
Queuco Chile 204 C5
Queulat, Parque Nacional nat. park Chile 205 B7
Queupán Arg. 204 D6
Queyras, Parc Naturel Régional du nature res. France 51 M8
Quezaltenango Guat. 185 H6
Quezaltepeque El Salvador 185 H6
Quezon Negros Phil. 74 B4
Quezon Palawan Phil. 74 A4

▶Quezon City Phil. 74 B3
Former capital of the Philippines.

Qufu China 85 H5
Qugayatang China 89 E6
Quibala Angola 127 B7
Quibaxe Angola 127 B7
Quibdó Col. 198 B3
Quiberon France 50 C5
Quiberon, Baie de b. France 50 C5
Quíbor Venez. 198 D2
Quicama, Parque Nacional do nat. park Angola 127 B7
also spelt Kisama, Parque Nacional de
Quiet Lake Canada 166 C2
Quihita Angola 127 B8
Quiindy Para. 201 F6
Quilá Mex. 184 D3
Quilalí Nicaragua 186 B4
Quilán, Cabo c. Chile 205 B6
Quilandi India 94 B4
Quilca Peru 200 B4
Quilenda Angola 127 B7
Quilengues Angola 127 B8
Quillacollo Bol. 200 D4
Quillan France 51 I10
Quill Lakes Canada 167 J5
Quillota Chile 204 C4
Quilmes Arg. 204 F4
Quilon India 94 C4
also known as Kollam
Quilpie Australia 149 E5
Quilpué Chile 204 C4
Quimbele Angola 127 C6
Quimilí Arg. 204 E2
Quimome Bol. 201 E4
Quimper France 50 B5
Quimperlé France 50 C5
Quinault r. U.S.A. 180 A3
Quinault Indian Reservation res. U.S.A. 180 A3
Quince Mil Peru 200 C3
Quincinetto Italy 51 N7
Quincy CA U.S.A. 182 D2
Quincy FL U.S.A. 175 C6
Quincy IL U.S.A. 174 B4
Quincy MI U.S.A. 173 I9
Quincy OH U.S.A. 176 B5
Quindio dept Col. 198 C3
Quines Arg. 204 D4
Quinga Moz. 131 I2
Quinhagak U.S.A. 164 C4
Quinhámel Guinea-Bissau 124 B4
Qui Nhon Vietnam 79 E5
Quinigua, Cerro mts Venez. 199 E3
Quiniluban i. Phil. 74 B4
Quinkan Aboriginal Holding res. Australia 149 E2
Quinn r. U.S.A. 180 C4
Quinn Canyon Range mts U.S.A. 183 I4
Quinnimont U.S.A. 176 D8
Quiñones Bol. 200 D2
Quintana Brazil 206 C9
Quintana de la Serena Spain 54 F6
Quintanar de la Orden Spain 55 H5
Quintanar del Rey Spain 55 J5
Quintana Roo state Mex. 185 H5
Quintin France 50 D4
Quinto r. Arg. 204 D4
Quinto Spain 55 K3
Quinzau Angola 127 B6
Quinze, Lac des l. Canada 173 N3
Quionga Moz. 129 D7
Quiotepec Mex. 185 F5
Quipapá Brazil 202 F4
Quipungo Angola 127 B8
formerly known as Paiva Couceiro; formerly spelt Kipungo
Quiquive r. Bol. 200 D3
Quiriguá tourist site Guat. 185 H6
Quirihue Chile 204 B5
Quirima Angola 127 C7
Quirindi Australia 147 F2
Quirinópolis Brazil 206 C5
Quirke Lake Canada 173 K4
Quiroga Bol. 200 D4
Quiroga Spain 54 D2
Quisiro Venez. 198 D2
Quissac France 51 K9
Quissamã Brazil 207 L9
Quitapa Angola 127 C7
Quita Sueño Bank sea feature Caribbean Sea 186 C4
Quiterajo Moz. 129 D7
Quitéria r. Brazil 206 B7
Quitexe Angola see Dange
Quitilipi Arg. 204 E2
Quitman GA U.S.A. 175 D6
Quitman MS U.S.A. 175 B5

▶Quito Ecuador 198 B5
Capital of Ecuador.

Quitovac Mex. 184 B2
Quitralco, Parque Nacional nat. park Chile 205 B7
Quixadá Brazil 202 E3
Quixeramobim Brazil 202 E3
Qujiang China see Quxian
Qu Jiang r. China 86 C2
Qujing China 86 B3
Quko S. Africa 133 M9
Qulaly Araly i. Kazakh. see Kulaly, Ostrov
Qul'ân, Gezâ'ir i. Egypt 104 A2
English form Gulân Islands
Qulandy Kazakh. see Kulandy
Qulanötpes watercourse Kazakh. see Kulanotpes
Qulbān Layyah well Iraq 107 F5
Quljuqtow Toghi hills Uzbek. see Kul'dzhuktau, Gory
Qulsary Kazakh. see Kul'sary
Qulûsana Egypt 106 B5
Qulzum, Baḩr el b. Egypt see Suez Bay
Qumar He r. China 84 B5
Qumarheyan China 84 B5
Qumarlêb China 84 B5
also known as Yiggêtang
Qumbu S. Africa 133 M8
Qumdo China 97 G3
formerly spelt Qomdo
Qumola watercourse Kazakh. see Kumola
Qumrha S. Africa 133 L9
Qunayy well Saudi Arabia 105 D3
Qunayyin, Sabkhat al salt marsh Libya 120 D2
Qunfudh Yemen 105 E4
Qŭnghirot Uzbek. see Kungrad
Qu'nyido China 86 A2
Quoich r. Canada 167 M1
Quoin Island Australia 148 A2
Quoin Point S. Africa 132 D11
Quong Muztag mt. China 89 C5
Quorn Australia 146 C3
Quoxo r. Botswana 131 E4
Quqên China see Jinchuan
Qŭqon Uzbek. see Kokand
Qurayat Oman 105 G3
Qurayyah tourist site Saudi Arabia 108 H9
Qurayyat al Milḩ l. Jordan 109 I6
Qŭrghonteppa Tajik. 101 G2
also spelt Kurgantyube
Qus Egypt 121 G3
Qusar Azer. 107 G2
also spelt Kusary
Quşay'ir Saudi Arabia 105 E5
Quseir Egypt 121 G3
Qushan China see Beichuan
Qūshchī Iran 100 A2
Qūsheh Dāgh mts Iran 100 A2
Qŭshkŭpir Uzbek. see Koshkupyr
Qŭshrabot Uzbek. see Koshrabad
Qusmuryn Kazakh. see Kushmurun
Qusmuryn Köli salt l. Kazakh. see Kushmurun, Ozero
Qusum Xizang China 89 B5
Qusum Xizang China 89 F6
also known as Xiajiang
Quthing Lesotho see Moyeni
Quthing r. Lesotho 133 L7
Quṭn, Jabal hill Saudi Arabia 104 C2

Red Bank NJ U.S.A. 177 K5
Red Bank TN U.S.A. 174 C5
Red Basin China see **Sichuan Pendi**
Red Bay Canada 169 J3
Redberry Lake Canada 167 J4
Red Bluff hill Australia 151 B5
Red Bluff U.S.A. 182 B1
Red Bluff Lake U.S.A. 179 B6
Red Butte mt. U.S.A. 183 L6
Redcar U.K. 47 K9
Redcliff Canada 167 I5
Red Cliff U.S.A. 172 C4
Redcliff Zimbabwe 131 F3
Redcliffe, Mount hill Australia 151 C6
Red Cliffs Australia 147 D3
Red Cloud U.S.A. 178 C3
Red Deer Canada 167 H4
Red Deer r. Alta/Sask. Canada 167 I5
Red Deer r. Man./Sask. Canada 167 K4
Red Deer Lake Canada 167 K4
Reddersburg S. Africa 133 K6
Redding U.S.A. 182 B1
Redditch U.K. 47 K11
Red Earth Creek Canada 167 H3
Redelinghuys S. Africa 132 C9
Redenção Pará Brazil 202 B3
Redenção Piauí Brazil 202 C4
Redeyef Tunisia 123 H2
Redfield U.S.A. 178 C2
Red Granite Mountain Canada 166 B2
Redhill Australia 146 C3
Red Hills U.S.A. 178 C4
Red Hook U.S.A. 177 L4
Red Idol Gorge China 89 E6
Red Indian Lake Canada 169 J3
Redkino Rus. Fed. 43 R5
Redknife r. Canada 166 G2
Red Lake Canada 167 M5
Red Lake l. Canada 167 M5
Red Lake U.S.A. 183 L6
Red Lake r. U.S.A. 178 C2
Red Lake Falls U.S.A. 178 C2
Red Lake Indian Reservation res. U.S.A. 178 D1
Red Lakes U.S.A. 178 D1
Redlands U.S.A. 183 G7
Red Lion NJ U.S.A. 177 K6
Red Lion PA U.S.A. 177 I6
Red Lodge U.S.A. 180 E3
Red Mercury Island N.Z. 152 J4
Redmond OR U.S.A. 180 B3
Redmond UT U.S.A. 183 M2
Red Oak U.S.A. 178 D3
Redojari waterhole Kenya 128 C5
Redon France 50 D5
Redonda i. Antigua and Barbuda 187 H3
Redondela Spain 54 C2
Redondo Port. 54 D6
Redondo Beach U.S.A. 182 F8
Red Peak U.S.A. 180 D3
Red River r. Vietnam 78 D3
also known as Hồng, Sông or Nui Con Voi
Red Rock Canada 168 B3
Red Rock AZ U.S.A. 183 M9
Red Rock PA U.S.A. 177 I4
Red Rock r. U.S.A. 180 D3
Red Sea Africa/Asia 104 A2
Red Sea state Sudan 121 G5
Redstone Canada 166 F4
Redstone r. N.W.T. Canada 166 E1
Redstone r. Ont. Canada 173 L2
Red Volta r. Burkina/Ghana 125 E4
also known as Nazinon (Burkina)
Redwater r. U.S.A. 180 F2
Redway U.S.A. 182 A1
Red Willow Creek r. U.S.A. 178 B3
Red Wine r. Canada 169 J2
Red Wing U.S.A. 174 A2
Redwood City U.S.A. 182 B4
Redwood Falls U.S.A. 178 D2
Redwood National Park U.S.A. 180 A4
Redwood Valley U.S.A. 182 A2
Ree, Lough l. Rep. of Ireland 47 E10
Reed City U.S.A. 172 H7
Reed Lake Canada 167 K4
Reedley U.S.A. 182 E5
Reedsburg U.S.A. 172 D7
Reedsport U.S.A. 180 A4
Reedsville OH U.S.A. 176 D6
Reedsville PA U.S.A. 176 H5
Reedville U.S.A. 177 I8
Reedy U.S.A. 176 D7
Reedy Creek watercourse Australia 149 E4
Reedy Glacier Antarctica 223 P1
Reefton N.Z. 153 F10
Reese U.S.A. 173 J7
Reese r. U.S.A. 183 H1
Refahiye Turkey 107 D3
Reform U.S.A. 175 B5
Reforma Mex. 185 G5
Refugio U.S.A. 179 C6
Rega r. Poland 49 M1
Regen Germany 49 K7
Regência Brazil 207 N6
Regensburg Germany 48 J6
historically known as Castra Regina or Ratisbon
Regenstauf Germany 51 S3
Regente Feijó Brazil 206 B9
Reggane Alg. 123 F4
Reggio Italy see **Reggio di Calabria**
Reggio Italy see **Reggio nell'Emilia**
Reggio di Calabria Italy 57 H10
historically known as Rhegium; short form Reggio
Reggio Emilia Italy see **Reggio nell'Emilia**
Reggio nell'Emilia Italy 56 C4
also known as Reggio Emilia; historically known as Regium Lepidum; short form Reggio
Reghin Romania 58 F2
Regi Afgh. 101 F3

Regina Canada 167 J5
Provincial capital of Saskatchewan.

Régina Fr. Guiana 199 H3
Registan reg. Afgh. 101 F4
Registro Brazil 206 F11
Registro do Araguaia Brazil 206 B2
Regium Lepidum Italy see **Reggio nell'Emilia**
Regozero Rus. Fed. 44 O2
Rehli India 96 C5
Rehoboth Namibia 130 C4
Rehoboth Bay U.S.A. 177 J7
Rehoboth Beach U.S.A. 177 J7
Rehovot Israel 108 F6
Reïbell Alg. see **Ksar Chellala**
Reichenbach Germany 49 J5
Reichshoffen France 51 N4
Reid Australia 151 E6
Reidsville GA U.S.A. 175 D5
Reidsville NC U.S.A. 176 F9
Reigate U.K. 47 L12
Reiley Peak U.S.A. 183 N9
Reims France 51 K3
English form Rheims; historically known as Durocortorum or Remi
Reinach Switz. 51 N5
Reinbek Germany 48 H2
Reindeer r. Canada 167 K4
Reindeer Island Canada 167 L4
Reindeer Lake Canada 167 K3
Reine Norway 44 K2
Reinersville U.S.A. 176 D6
Reineskarvet mt. Norway 45 J3
Reinga, Cape N.Z. 152 G2
Reinosa Spain 54 G2
Reinsfeld Germany 48 D6
Reipholsfjöll hill Iceland 44 [inset] B2
Reisa Nasjonalpark nat. park Norway 44 M1
Reisjärvi Fin. 44 N3
Reisterstown U.S.A. 177 I6
Reitz S. Africa 133 M4
Reitzburg S. Africa 133 L4
Reiu r. Estonia 42 F3
Reivilo S. Africa 132 I4
Rejowiec Fabryczny Poland 49 U4
Rekapalle India 94 D2
Rekohua i. S. Pacific Ocean see **Chatham Island**
Rekovac Srbija Yugo. 58 C5
Rėkyvos ežeras l. Lith. 42 E6
Reliance Canada 167 I2
Relizane Alg. 123 F2
Rellano Mex. 184 D3
Relli India 95 D2
Remada Tunisia 123 H2
Remarkable, Mount hill Australia 146 C3
Rembang Indon. 77 E4
Remedios Cuba 186 D2
Remedios, Punta pt El Salvador 185 H6
Remel el Abiod des. Tunisia 123 H3
Remennikovo Rus. Fed. 43 J5
Remeshk Iran 100 D5
Remeskylä Fin. 44 N3
Remi France see **Reims**
Remington U.S.A. 176 H7
Rémire Fr. Guiana 199 H3
Remiremont France 51 M4
Remmel Mountain U.S.A. 180 B2
Remo Glacier Jammu and Kashmir 96 C2
Remontnoye Rus. Fed. 41 G7
Rempang i. Indon. 76 D2
Remscheid Germany 48 E4
Remus U.S.A. 173 H7
Rena Norway 45 J3
Rena r. Norway 45 J3
Renabie Canada 173 J2
Renaix Belgium see **Ronse**
Renapur India 94 C2
Renard Islands P.N.G. 149 G1
Rende China see **Xundian**
Rende Italy 57 I9
Rend Lake U.S.A. 174 B4
Rendsburg Germany 48 G1
Renedo Spain 54 H1
René-Levasseur, Île i. Canada 169 G3
Renens Switz. 51 M6
Renews Canada 169 K4
Renfrew Canada 168 E4
Rengat Indon. 76 C3
Rengo Chile 204 C4
Ren He r. China 87 D1
Renheji China 87 E2
Renhou China see **Tangxian**
Renhua China 87 E3
Renhuai China 86 C3
Reni Ukr. 41 D7
Renick U.S.A. 176 E8
Renigunta India 94 C3
Renko Fin. 42 F1
Renland reg. Greenland see **Tuttut Nunaat**
Renmark Australia 146 D3
Rennell i. Solomon Is 145 F3
also known as Mu Nggava
Rennell, Islas is Chile 205 B8
Rennerod Germany 48 F5
Renner Springs Australia 148 B3
Rennes France 50 E4
Rennes, Bassin de basin France 50 E4
Rennick Glacier Antarctica 223 K2
Rennie Canada 167 M5
Reno r. Italy 56 E4
Reno MN U.S.A. 172 B7
Reno NV U.S.A. 182 E2
Renoster r. S. Africa 133 K3
Renoster watercourse S. Africa 132 E8
Renosterkop S. Africa 132 G9
Renovo U.S.A. 176 H4
Renqiu China 85 H4
Renshou China 86 C2
also known as Wenlin
Rensselaer IN U.S.A. 174 C3
Rensselaer NY U.S.A. 177 L3
Rentjärn Sweden 44 L2
Renton U.S.A. 180 B3
Renukut India 97 D4
Renwick N.Z. 152 H9
Renya r. Rus. Fed. 43 S3
Réo Burkina 124 E3
Reo Indon. 75 B5
Repartimento Brazil 199 G5
Repembe r. Moz. 131 G4
Repetek Turkm. 103 E5
Repetekskiy Zapovednik nature res. Turkm. 103 E5
Repino Rus. Fed. 43 N6
Repokaira reg. Fin. 44 N1
Repolka Rus. Fed. 43 K2
Reporoa N.Z. 152 K6
Reposaari Fin. 45 M3
Republic OH U.S.A. 176 B4
Republic WA U.S.A. 180 C2
Republican r. U.S.A. 178 C4
Republican, South Fork r. U.S.A. 178 B3
Republika Srpska aut. div. Bos.-Herz. 56 J4
Repulse Bay b. Australia 149 F4
Repulse Bay Canada 165 K3
Repvåg Norway 44 N1
Requena Peru 198 C6
Requena Spain 55 J5
Réquista France 51 I8
Reriutaba Brazil 202 D3
Reşadiye Turkey 107 E3
also known as Sorp
Reşadiye Turkey 107 D2
Reşadiye Yarımadası pen. Turkey 59 I12
Resag, Gunung mt. Indon. 76 D4
Resava r. Yugo. 58 C4
Resavica Srbija Yugo. 58 C4
Resen Macedonia 58 C7
Resende Brazil 207 I9
Reserva Brazil 203 B8
Reserve U.S.A. 181 E6
Reshetnikovo Rus. Fed. 43 R5
Reshi China 87 D2
Resia, Passo di pass Austria/Italy 48 H9
Resistencia Arg. 204 F2
Reşita Romania 58 C3
Resko Poland 49 M2
Resolute Bay Canada 165 J2
Resolution Island Canada 165 M3
Resolution Island N.Z. 153 A13
Resplendor Brazil 207 L6
Ressa r. Rus. Fed. 43 Q7
Ressano Garcia S. Africa 133 P2
Resseta r. Rus. Fed. 43 Q8
Restefond, Col de pass France 51 M8
Restelica Kosovo, Srbija Yugo. 58 B7
Restinga de Marambaia coastal area Brazil 207 I10
Restinga Seca Brazil 203 A9
Restrepo Col. 198 C3
Resülayn Turkey see **Ceylanpınar**
Retalhuleu Guat. 185 H6
Retem, Oued er watercourse Alg. 123 G2
Retén Llico Chile 204 B4
Retezat, Parcul Național nat. park Romania 58 D3
Retford U.K. 47 L10
also known as East Retford
Rethel France 51 K3
Réthimnon Greece see **Rethymno**
Rethymno Greece 59 F13
also known as Réthimnon
Retiers France 50 E5
Retortillo tourist site Spain 54 G2
Rettikhovka Rus. Fed. 90 C2
Retuerta mt. Spain 55 J4

Réunion terr. Indian Ocean 218 K7
French Overseas Department. Historically known as Bourbon.
africa [countries] 114–117

Reus Spain 55 M3
Reusam, Pulau i. Indon. 76 B2
Reutlingen Germany 48 G7
Reutov Rus. Fed. 43 S6
Reval Estonia see **Tallinn**
Revda Rus. Fed. 44 P2
Reveille Peak U.S.A. 183 H4
Revel Estonia see **Tallinn**
Revel France 51 I9
Revelganj India 97 E4
Revelstoke Canada 166 G5
Reventazón Peru 198 A6
Revermont reg. France 51 L7
Reviga Romania 58 I4
Reviga r. Romania 58 I4
Revigny-sur-Ornain France 51 K4
Revillagigedo, Islas is Mex. 184 B5
Revillagigedo Island U.S.A. 164 F4
Revna r. Rus. Fed. 43 P9
Revolyutsii, Pik mt. Tajik. see **Revolyutsiya, Qullai**
Revolyutsiya, Qullai mt. Tajik. 101 H2
also known as Revolyutsii, Pik
Revsnes Norway 44 L1
Revúca Slovakia 49 R7
Revuè r. Moz. 131 G3
Revyakino Rus. Fed. 43 S7
Rewa India 97 D4
Rewari India 96 C3
Rex, Mount Antarctica 222 S2
Rexburg U.S.A. 180 E4
Rexton Canada 169 H4
Rey, Isla del i. Panama 186 D5
Reyes Bol. 200 D3
Reyes, Point U.S.A. 182 A3
Reyes, Punta pt Col. 198 B4
Reyhanlı Turkey 109 H1
Reykir Iceland 44 [inset] B2
Reykjanes constituency Iceland 44 [inset] B3
Reykjanestá pt Iceland 44 [inset] B3

Reykjavík Iceland 44 [inset] B2
Capital of Iceland. English form Reykjavik.

Reykjavik Iceland see **Reykjavík**
Reynolds Range mts Australia 148 B4
Reynosa Mex. 185 F3
Reyssouze r. France 51 K6
Rezā, Kūh-e hill Iran 100 B3
Reẓā'īyeh Iran see **Urmia**
Reẓā'īyeh, Daryācheh-ye salt l. Iran see **Urmia, Lake**
Rēzekne Latvia 42 I5
Rēzekne r. Latvia 42 I5
Rezinjski vrh mt. Slovenia 56 G3
Rezovska Reka r. Bulg./Turkey 58 J7
Rezvāndeh Iran see **Rezvānshahr**
Rezvānshahr Iran 100 B2
formerly known as Rezvāndeh
R. F. Magón Mex. see **Ricardo Flores Magón**
Rgotina Srbija Yugo. 58 D4
Rharbi, Oued el watercourse Alg. 123 F3
Rhegium Italy see **Reggio di Calabria**
Rheims France see **Reims**
Rhein r. Germany 48 D4 see **Rhine**
Rheine Germany 48 E3
Rheinland-Pfalz land Germany 48 E6
English form Rhineland-Palatinate
Rheinsberg Germany 49 J2
Rhein-Taunus, Naturpark nature res. Germany 48 F5
Rheinwaldhorn mt. Switz. 51 P6
Rhemilès well Alg. 122 D3
Rheris, Oued watercourse Morocco 122 D3
Rhin r. France 51 N4 see **Rhine**
Rhine r. Europe 48 D4
also spelt Rhein (Germany) or Rhin (France)
Rhinebeck U.S.A. 177 L4
Rhinelander U.S.A. 172 D5
Rhineland-Palatinate land Germany see **Rheinland-Pfalz**
Rhinluch marsh Germany 49 J3
Rhino Camp Uganda 128 A4
Rhinow Germany 49 J3
Rhir, Cap c. Morocco 122 C3
Rho Italy 56 B3
Rhode Island state U.S.A. 177 N4
Rhodes Greece 59 J12
also spelt Rodos
Rhodes i. Greece 59 J12
also spelt Rodos or Ródhos; formerly known as Rodi; historically known as Rhodus
Rhodesia country Africa see **Zimbabwe**
Rhodes Inyanga National Park Zimbabwe see **Nyanga National Park**
Rhodes Matopos National Park Zimbabwe see **Matobo National Park**
Rhodes Peak U.S.A. 180 D3
Rhodope Mountains mts Bulg. 58 E7
Rhodope Mountains Bulg./Greece 58 E7
also known as Rodopi Planina
Rhodus i. Greece see **Rhodes**
Rhône r. France/Switz. 51 K9
Rhône-Alpes admin. reg. France 51 L7
Rhube, Oasis of Syria see **Ruḥbah**
Rhuthun U.K. see **Ruthin**
Rhyl U.K. 47 I10
Riaba Equat. Guinea 125 H6
Riachão Brazil 202 C3
Riachão das Neves Brazil 202 C4
Riacho de Santana Brazil 202 D5
Riacho dos Machados Brazil 207 J2
Ri'al Fuhah hill Saudi Arabia 108 H9
Rialma Brazil 206 D2
Rialp, Pantà de resr Spain 55 M3
Rialto U.S.A. 183 G7
Riangnom Sudan 126 F2
Riaño, Embalse de resr Spain 54 F2
Rianópolis Brazil 206 D2
Riansáres r. Spain 55 H5
Riasi Jammu and Kashmir 96 B2
Riau prov. Indon. 76 C2
Riau, Kepulauan is Indon. 76 D2
Riaza r. Spain 55 H3
Ribadavia Spain 54 C2
Ribadeo Spain 54 D1
Ribadesella Spain 54 F1
Ribas de Fresser Spain see **Ribes de Freser**
Ribas do Rio Pardo Brazil 203 A7
Ribat Afgh. 101 G2
Ribat-i-Shur waterhole Iran 100 D3
Ribáuè Moz. 131 H2
Ribble r. U.K. 47 J10
Ribe Denmark 45 J5
Ribeirão Branco Brazil 206 E11
Ribeirão das Neves Brazil 207 I6
Ribeirão do Pinhal Brazil 206 C10
Ribeirão Preto Brazil 206 F8
Ribera Sicilia Italy 57 F11
Ribérac France 50 G7
Riberalta Bol. 200 D2
Ribes de Freser Spain 55 N2
also spelt Ribas de Fresser
Ribnica Slovenia 56 G3
Rîbnița Moldova 41 D7
formerly spelt Râbnita or Rybnitsa
Ribnitz-Damgarten Germany 49 J1
Ribnovo Bulg. 58 E7
Rica Aventura Chile 200 C5
Říčany Czech Rep. 49 L6
Ricardo Flores Magón Mex. 184 D2
short form R. F. Magón
Riccione Italy 56 E4
Rice CA U.S.A. 183 J7
Rice VA U.S.A. 176 G8
Rice Lake l. Ont. Canada 168 E4
Rice Lake l. Ont. Canada 173 K3
Rice Lake U.S.A. 172 B5
Riceville U.S.A. 176 G8
Richards Bay S. Africa 133 Q5
Richards Inlet Antarctica 223 L1
Richards Island Canada 164 F3
Richardson r. Canada 167 I3
Richardson Island Canada 167 G1
Richardson Lakes U.S.A. 177 O1
Richardson Mountains Canada 164 F3
Richardson Mountains N.Z. 153 C12
Richard Toll Senegal 124 B2
Richelieu France 50 G5
Richfield U.S.A. 183 L3
Richfield Springs U.S.A. 177 K3
Richford NY U.S.A. 177 I3
Richford VT U.S.A. 177 M1
Richgrove U.S.A. 182 E6
Richibucto Canada 169 H4
Rich Lake Canada 167 I4
Richland U.S.A. 180 C3
Richland Center U.S.A. 172 C7
Richlands U.S.A. 176 D8
Richmond N.S.W. Australia 147 F3
Richmond Qld Australia 149 D4
Richmond Ont. Canada 173 R5
Richmond Que. Canada 169 F4
Richmond N.Z. 152 H9
Richmond Kwazulu-Natal S. Africa 133 O6
Richmond N. Cape S. Africa 132 H8
Richmond U.K. 47 K9
Richmond CA U.S.A. 182 B4
Richmond IL U.S.A. 172 E8
Richmond IN U.S.A. 176 A6
Richmond KY U.S.A. 176 A8
Richmond ME U.S.A. 177 P1
Richmond MI U.S.A. 173 K8
Richmond TX U.S.A. 179 D6

Richmond VA U.S.A. 176 H8
State capital of Virginia.

Richmond VT U.S.A. 177 M1
Richmond, Mount N.Z. 152 H9
Richmond Dale U.S.A. 176 C6
Richmond Hill Canada 168 E5
Richmond Hill U.S.A. 175 D6
Richmond Range hills Australia 147 G2
Richmond Range mts N.Z. 152 H9
Richmondville U.S.A. 177 K3
Rich Square U.S.A. 176 H9
Richtersveld National Park S. Africa 132 B5
Richvale U.S.A. 182 C2
Richwood OH U.S.A. 176 B5
Richwood WV U.S.A. 176 E7
Ricklean r. Sweden 44 M2
Ricobayo, Embalse de resr Spain 54 F3
also known as Esla, Embalse de
Ricomagus France see **Riom**
Riddell Nunataks Antarctica 223 E2
Ridder Kazakh. see **Leninogorsk**
Riddlesburg U.S.A. 176 G5
Rideau r. Canada 173 R5
Rideau Lakes Canada 168 E4
Ridge r. Canada 168 C3
Ridgecrest U.S.A. 182 G6
Ridgefield U.S.A. 177 L4
Ridgeland MS U.S.A. 175 B5
Ridgeland SC U.S.A. 175 D5
Ridgeland WI U.S.A. 172 B5
Ridgetown Canada 173 L8
Ridgeway U.S.A. 176 F9
Ridgway U.S.A. 176 G4
Riding Mountain National Park Canada 167 K5
Ridley r. Australia 150 B4
Riebeek-Kasteel S. Africa 132 C10
Riebeek-Oos S. Africa 133 K10
Riebeek Wes S. Africa 132 C10
Riecito Venez. 198 D2
Ried im Innkreis Austria 49 K7
Riedlingen Germany 48 G7
Riekertsdam S. Africa 133 K2
Rieppesgai'sa mt. Norway 44 M1
Riesa Germany 49 K4
Riesco, Isla i. Chile 205 B9
Riesi Sicilia Italy 57 G11
Rieste Germany 48 F3
Riet r. S. Africa 133 H6
Riet watercourse S. Africa 132 E8
Rietavas Lith. 42 C6
Rietberg Germany 48 F4
Rietbron S. Africa 132 H9
Rietfontein S. Africa 132 E3
Riethuiskraal S. Africa 132 F11
Rieti Italy 56 E6
historically known as Reate
Rietpoort S. Africa 132 C7
Rietschen Germany 49 L4
Riet se Vloer salt pan S. Africa 132 E7
Rietvlei S. Africa 133 O6
Rieumes France 50 H9
Rifā'ī, Tall mt. Jordan/Syria 109 H5
Rifaina Brazil 206 F7
Rifeng China see **Lichuan**
Rifle U.S.A. 180 F5
Rift Valley prov. Kenya 128 B4
Rift Valley Lakes National Park Eth. see **Abijatta-Shalla National Park**

Rīga Latvia 42 F5
Capital of Latvia. English form Riga.

Riga Latvia see **Rīga**
Riga, Gulf of Estonia/Latvia 42 E4
also known as Liivi laht or Rīgas jūras līcis or Riia laht
Rigacikun Nigeria 125 G4
Rigaio Greece 59 D9
Rigān Iran 100 D4
Rīgas jūras līcis b. Estonia/Latvia see **Riga, Gulf of**
Rigby U.S.A. 180 E4
Rig-Rig Chad 120 B6
Riguel r. Spain 55 J2
Riia laht b. Estonia/Latvia see **Riga, Gulf of**
Riihimäki Fin. 45 N3
Riiser-Larsen Ice Shelf Antarctica 223 W2
Riisipere Estonia 42 F2
Riisitunturin kansallispuisto nat. park Fin. 44 O2
Riito Mex. 184 B1
Rijau Nigeria 125 G4
Rijeka Croatia 56 G3
formerly known as Fiume
Rijecki Zaljev b. Croatia 56 G3
Rijm al Mudhari hill Iraq 109 K5
Rikā, Wādī ar watercourse Saudi Arabia 104 D3
Rikubetsu Japan 90 H3
Rikuchū-kaigan National Park Japan 90 H5
Rikuzen-takata Japan 90 G5
Rila Bulg. 58 E6
Rila mts Bulg. 58 E6
Rila China 89 D6
Riley U.S.A. 180 C4
Rileyville U.S.A. 176 G7
Rillieux-la-Pape France 51 K7
Rillito U.S.A. 183 M9
Rima watercourse Niger/Nigeria 125 G3
Rimah, Wādī al watercourse Saudi Arabia 104 C2
Rimau, Pulau i. Indon. 76 D3
Rimava r. Slovakia 49 R7
Rimavská Sobota Slovakia 49 R7
Rimbey Canada 167 H4
Rimbo Sweden 45 L4
Rimersburg U.S.A. 176 F4
Rimetea Romania 58 E2
Rimforsa Sweden 45 K4
Rimini Italy 56 E4
historically known as Ariminum
Rîmnicu Sărat Romania see **Râmnicu Sărat**
Rîmnicu Vîlcea Romania see **Râmnicu Vâlcea**
Rimouski Canada 169 G3
Rimouski, Réserve Faunique de nature res. Canada 169 G3
Rimutaka Forest Park nature res. N.Z. 152 J9
Rinbung China 89 E6
also known as Deji
Rinca i. Indon. 75 A5
Rincão Brazil 206 E8
Rincon Morocco see **Mdiq**
Rincón, Cerro del mt. Chile 200 D6
Rinconada Arg. 200 D5
Rincón del Bonete, Lago Artificial de resr Uruguay 204 F4
Rincón de los Sauces Arg. 204 C5
Rincón de Romos Mex. 185 E4
Rind r. India 96 D4
Rinda r. Latvia 42 C4
Rindal Norway 44 J3
Rineia i. Greece 59 G11
also spelt Rinía
Riner U.S.A. 176 E8
Ringarooma Bay Australia 147 E5
Ringas India 96 B4
Ringe Denmark 45 J5
Ringebu Norway 45 J3
Ringgold U.S.A. 174 C5
Ringim Nigeria 125 H3
Ringkøbing Denmark 45 J4
Ringkøbing Fjord lag. Denmark 45 J5
Ringsted Denmark 45 J5
Ringvassøy i. Norway 44 L1
Ringwood U.K. 47 K13
Ringwood U.S.A. 177 K4
Rinía i. Greece see **Rineia**
Rinópolis Brazil 206 C8
Rinteln Germany 48 G3
Rinya r. Romania 49 O9
Rio IL U.S.A. 172 C9
Rio WI U.S.A. 172 D7
Rio Alegre Brazil 201 F4
Riobamba Ecuador 198 B5
Rio Bananal Brazil 207 M6
Río Blanco U.S.A. 180 F5
Rio Bonito Brazil 207 K9
Rio Branco Brazil 200 D2
Rio Branco state Brazil see **Roraima**
Rio Branco, Parque Nacional do nat. park Brazil 199 F4
Río Bravo, Parque Internacional del nat. park Mex. 185 E2
Rio Brilhante Brazil 203 A7
Rio Bueno Chile 204 B6
Río Caribe Venez. 199 F2
Río Casca Brazil 203 D7
Río Chico Arg. 205 C8
Río Chico Venez. 199 E2
Rio Claro Rio de Janeiro Brazil 207 I9
Rio Claro São Paulo Brazil 206 F9
Rio Claro Trin. and Tob. 187 H5
Río Claro Venez. 187 F5
Río Colorado Arg. 204 D5
Río Corrientes Ecuador 198 B5
Río Cuarto Arg. 204 D4
Rio das Almas r. Brazil 201 H3
Rio das Pedras Moz. 131 G4

Rio de Janeiro Brazil 203 D7
3rd most populous city in South America. Former capital of Brazil.
world [cities] 24–25

Rio de Janeiro state Brazil 203 D7
Río de Jesús Panama 186 C6

Río de la Plata - Paraná r. S. America 204 F4
2nd longest river in South America and 9th in the world.
southamerica [landscapes] 190–191

Rio Dell U.S.A. 180 A4
Rio do Sul Brazil 203 B8
Río Formoso Brazil 202 F4
Río Frío Costa Rica 186 C5
Río Gallegos Arg. 205 C8
Río Grande Arg. 205 D9
Río Grande Bol. 200 D5
Rio Grande Brazil 204 G4
Río Grande Mex. 185 E4
Rio Grande r. Mex./U.S.A. 185 F3
also known as Bravo del Norte, Río
Río Grande, Salar de salt flat Arg. 204 C2
Rio Grande City U.S.A. 179 C7
Rio Grande do Norte state Brazil 202 E3
Rio Grande do Sul state Brazil 203 A9
Riohacha Col. 198 C2
Río Hato Panama 186 C5
Río Hondo, Embalse resr Arg. 204 D2
Rioja Peru 198 B6
Río Lagartos Mex. 185 H4
Rio Largo Brazil 202 F4
Riom France 51 J7
historically known as Ricomagus
Rio Maior Port. 54 C5
Riom-ès-Montagnes France 51 I7
Río Muerto Arg. 204 E2
Río Mulatos Bol. 200 D4
Río Muni reg. Equat. Guinea 125 H6
Río Negro prov. Arg. 204 D5
Rio Negro Brazil 203 B8
Río Negro Chile 204 B6
Rionero in Vulture Italy 56 H8
Rioni r. Georgia 107 E2
Rio Novo Brazil 207 J8
Rio Novo do Sul Brazil 207 M7
Rio Pardo de Minas Brazil 202 D5
Río Plátano, Reserva Biósfera del nature res. Hond. 186 B4
Rio Pomba Brazil 207 J8
Rio Preto Brazil 207 J9
Rio Preto, Serra do hills Brazil 206 G3
Rio Rancho U.S.A. 181 F6
Ríos Spain 54 D3
Riosucio Col. 198 B3
Río Tercero Arg. 204 D4
Río Tigre Ecuador 198 B5
Rio Tinto Brazil 202 F3
Rio Tuba Phil. 74 A4
Riou, Oued watercourse Alg. 55 L9
Riou Lake Canada 167 J3
Rio Verde Brazil 206 C4
Río Verde Chile 205 C9
Rioverde Ecuador 198 B4
Río Verde Quintana Roo Mex. 185 H5
Río Verde San Luis Potosí Mex. 185 F4
Rio Verde de Mato Grosso Brazil 203 A6
Rio Vermelho Brazil 207 J5
Rio Vista U.S.A. 182 C3
Riozinho Brazil 200 D2
Riozinho r. Amazonas Brazil 199 E5
Riozinho r. Mato Grosso do Sul Brazil 201 F4
Ripanj Srbija Yugo. 58 B4
Ripats Sweden 44 M2
Ripky Ukr. 41 D6
Ripley MS U.S.A. 174 B5
Ripley NY U.S.A. 176 F3
Ripley OH U.S.A. 176 B7
Ripley TN U.S.A. 174 B5
Ripley WV U.S.A. 176 D7
Ripoll Spain 55 N2
Ripon U.K. 47 K9
Ripon CA U.S.A. 182 C4
Ripon WI U.S.A. 172 E7
Riposto Sicilia Italy 57 H11
Risalpur Pak. 101 H3
Risān 'Aneiza hill Egypt 108 E7
Risaralda dept Col. 198 C3
Risasi Dem. Rep. Congo 126 E5
Risbäck Sweden 44 K2
Riscle France 50 F9
Risco Plateado mt. Arg. 204 C4
Risha, Birket Umm salt l. Egypt 108 B7
Rishā', Wādī ar watercourse Saudi Arabia 104 D2
Rishikesh India 96 C3
Rishiri-Rebun-Sarobetsu National Park Japan 90 G2
Rishiri-tō i. Japan 90 G2
Rishiri-zan vol. Japan 82 F3
Rishon Le Ziyyon Israel 108 F6
Rising Sun IN U.S.A. 176 A7
Rising Sun MD U.S.A. 177 I6
Risle r. France 50 G3
Risnjak nat. park Croatia 56 G3
Rişnov Romania see **Râşnov**
Rison U.S.A. 179 D5
Risør Norway 45 J4
Rissa Norway 44 J3
Rissington N.Z. 152 K7
Rişşu, Gebel hill Egypt 108 B8
Ristiina Fin. 45 N3
Ristijärvi Fin. 44 O2
Ristikent Rus. Fed. 44 O1
Risum China 89 B5
Ritan r. Indon. 77 F2
Ritausma Latvia 42 F5
Ritchie S. Africa 133 I6
Ritchie's Archipelago is India 95 G3
Ritch Island Canada 167 G1
Ritscher Upland mts Antarctica 223 X2
Ritsem Sweden 44 L2
Ritsis Nakrdzali nature res. Georgia 107 E2
Ritter, Mount U.S.A. 182 E4
Ritupe r. Latvia 42 I5
Ritzville U.S.A. 180 C3
Riu, Mount hill P.N.G. 149 G1
Rīva r. Latvia 42 C5
Rivadavia Buenos Aires Arg. 204 E4
Rivadavia Mendoza Arg. 204 C4
Rivadavia Salta Arg. 201 E6
Rivadavia Chile 204 C3
Riva del Garda Italy 56 C3
Riva Palacio Mex. 181 F7
Rivarolo Canavese Italy 51 N7
Rivas Nicaragua 186 B5
Rivash Iran 100 D3
Rive-de-Gier France 51 K7
Rivera Arg. 204 E5
Rivera Uruguay 204 G3
River Cess Liberia 124 C5
Riverdale U.S.A. 182 E5
Riverhead U.S.A. 177 M5
Riverina Australia 151 C6
Riverina reg. Australia 147 E3
Rivero, Isla i. Chile 205 B7
Rivers state Nigeria 125 G5
Riversdale N.Z. 153 C13
Riversdale S. Africa 132 F11
Riversdale Beach N.Z. 152 K9
Riverside S. Africa 133 N7
Riverside CA U.S.A. 182 G8
Riverside IA U.S.A. 172 B9
Riversleigh Australia 148 C3
Riverton Canada 167 L5
Riverton N.Z. 153 C14
also known as Aparima
Riverton S. Africa 133 I5
Riverton UT U.S.A. 183 M1
Riverton VA U.S.A. 176 G7
Riverton WY U.S.A. 180 E4
Riverview Canada 169 H4
River View S. Africa 133 Q5
Rives France 51 L7
Rivesaltes France 51 I10
Rivesville U.S.A. 176 E6
Rivière-au-Renard Canada 169 H3
Rivière Bleue Canada 169 G4
Rivière-du-Loup Canada 169 G4
Rivière-Pentecôte Canada 169 H3
Rivière-Pigou Canada 169 H3
Rivière-Pilote Martinique 187 H4
Riviersonderend S. Africa 132 D11
Riviersonderend Mountains S. Africa 132 D11
Rivne Ukr. 41 C6
also spelt Rovno; formerly spelt Równe
Rivoli Italy 51 N7
Rivulets S. Africa 133 O2
Rivungo Angola 127 D9
Riwaka N.Z. 152 G9
Riwoqê China 86 A2

Riyadh Saudi Arabia 105 D2
Capital of Saudi Arabia. Also spelt Ar Riyāḍ.

Riyan Yemen 105 E5
Riyue Shankou pass China 84 D4
Riza well Iran 100 C3
Rizal Phil. 74 B3
Rize Turkey 107 E2
Rizhao Shandong China 85 H5
formerly known as Shijiusuo
Rizhao Shandong China 85 H5
Rizokarpaso Cyprus see **Rizokarpason**
Rizokarpason Cyprus 108 F2
also known as Dipkarpaz or Rizokarpaso
Rizū well Iran 100 D3
Rīzū'īyeh Iran 100 D4
Rjukan Norway 45 J4
Rkîz, Lac l. Mauritania 124 B2
Roa Norway 45 J3
Roa Spain 54 H3
Roach Lake U.S.A. 183 I6
Roads U.S.A. 176 C6

Road Town Virgin Is (U.K.) 187 G3
Capital of the British Virgin Islands.

Roan Norway 44 J2
Roan Cliffs ridge U.S.A. 183 O2
Roan Fell hill U.K. 47 J8
Roan High Knob mt. U.S.A. 176 C9
Roan Mountain U.S.A. 176 C9
Roanne France 51 K6
Roanoke AL U.S.A. 175 C5
Roanoke IL U.S.A. 172 D10
Roanoke VA U.S.A. 176 F8
Roanoke r. U.S.A. 176 I9
Roanoke Rapids U.S.A. 176 H9
Roan Plateau U.S.A. 183 O2
Roaringwater Bay Rep. of Ireland 47 C12
Roatán Hond. 186 B3
also known as Coxen Hole
Robāt r. Afgh. 101 E4
Robāt Iran 100 D4
Robāt-e Khān Iran 100 D3
Robāt-e Shahr-e Bābak Iran 100 C4
Robāt-e Tork Iran 100 B3
Robāt-e Ţoroq Iran 100 D2
Robāt Karīm Iran 100 B3
Robāt-Sang Iran 101 D3
Robat Thana Pak. 101 E4
Robb Canada 167 G4
Robben Island S. Africa 132 C10
Robbins Island Australia 147 E5
Robbinsville U.S.A. 174 D5
Robe r. Australia 150 A4
Robe, Mount hill Australia 146 D2
Röbel Germany 49 J2
Robert Glacier Antarctica 223 D2
Robert Lee U.S.A. 179 B6
Roberts U.S.A. 180 D4
Roberts, Mount Australia 147 G2
Robertsburg U.S.A. 176 D7
Roberts Butte mt. Antarctica 223 K2
Roberts Creek Mountain U.S.A. 183 H2
Robertsfors Sweden 44 M2
Robertsganj India 97 D4

San Carlos de la Ràpita Spain see Sant Carles de la Ràpita
San Carlos del Zulia Venez. 198 D2
San Carlos Indian Reservation res. U.S.A. 183 N8
San Carlos Lake U.S.A. 183 N8
San Cataldo Sicilia Italy 57 F11
San Cayetano Arg. 204 F5
San Celoni Spain see Sant Celoni
Sancerre France 51 I5
Sancerrois, Collines du hills France 51 I5
San Cesario di Lecce Italy 57 K8
Sancha Gansu China 86 C1
Sancha Shanxi China 85 F4
Sanchahe China see Fuyu
Sancha He r. China 86 C3
Sanchakou China 88 B4
Sanchi India 96 C5
San Chien Pau mt. Laos 78 C3
Sanchor India 96 A4
Sanchuan r. China 85 F4
Sanchursk Rus. Fed. 40 H4
San Ciro de Acosta Mex. 185 F4
San Clemente Chile 204 C4
San Clemente Spain 55 I5
San Clemente U.S.A. 182 G8
San Clemente del Tuyú Arg. 204 F5
San Clemente Island U.S.A. 182 F9
Sancoins France 51 I6
Sanco Point Phil. 74 C4
San Cristóbal Arg. 204 E3
San Cristóbal Potosí Bol. 200 D5
San Cristóbal Santa Cruz Bol. 201 E3
San Cristóbal Col. 198 C5
San Cristóbal Dom. Rep. 187 F3
San Cristóbal i. Solomon Is 145 F3
also known as Arossi, or Makira
San Cristóbal Venez. 198 C3
San Cristóbal, Volcán vol. Nicaragua 186 B4
San Cristóbal de las Casas Mex. 185 G5
San Cristobal Wash watercourse U.S.A. 183 K9
Sancti Spíritus Cuba 186 D2
Sand Norway 45 I4
Sand r. Free State S. Africa 133 K5
Sand r. Northern S. Africa 131 F4
Sanda Japan 91 D7
Sandagou Rus. Fed. 90 D3
Sandai Indon. 77 E3
Sandakan Sabah Malaysia 77 G1
Sandakphu Peak India 97 F4
Sandane Norway 45 I3
Sandanski Bulg. 58 E7
Sandaohezi China see Shawan
Sandaré Mali 124 C3
Sanday i. U.K. 46 J4
Sandberg S. Africa 132 C9
Sandbukt Norway 44 M1
Sand Cay reef India 94 B4
Sande Sogn og Fjordane Norway 45 I3
Sande Vestfold Norway 45 J4
Sandefjord Norway 45 J4
Sandefjord (Torp) airport Norway 45 J4
Sandercock Nunataks Antarctica 223 D2
Sanders U.S.A. 183 O6
Sanderson U.S.A. 179 B6
Sandersville U.S.A. 175 D5
Sandfire Roadhouse Australia 150 C3
Sandfloeggi mt. Norway 45 I4
Sand Hill r. U.S.A. 178 C2
Sand Hills U.S.A. 178 B3
Sandhornøy i. Norway 44 K2
Sandi India 96 D4
Sandia Peru 200 C3
San Diego Mex. 181 E7
San Diego CA U.S.A. 183 G9
San Diego TX U.S.A. 179 C7
San Diego, Cabo c. Arg. 205 D9
San Diego, Sierra mts Mex. 184 C2
San Diego de Cabrutica Venez. 199 E2
Sandıklı Turkey 106 B3
Sandila India 96 D4
Sanding i. Indon. 76 C3
Sand Island U.S.A. 172 C4
Sandivey r. Rus. Fed. 40 K2
Sand Lake Canada 168 C4
Sand Lake l. Canada 167 M5
Sandnes Norway 45 I4
Sandnessjøen Norway 44 K2
Sando i. Faroe Is see Sandoy
Sandoa Dem. Rep. Congo 127 D7
Sandomierz Poland 49 S5
Sândominic Romania 58 G2
formerly spelt Sîndominic
San Domino, Isole i. Italy 56 H6
Sandoná Col. 198 B4
San Donà di Piave Italy 56 E3
Sandover watercourse Australia 148 C4
Sandovo Rus. Fed. 43 R3
Sandow, Mount Antarctica 223 G2
Sandoway Myanmar 78 A4
also known as Thandwè
Sandoy i. Faroe Is 46 F2
also spelt Sandø
Sandpoint U.S.A. 180 C2
Sandray i. U.K. 46 E7
also spelt Sanndraigh
Sandringham Australia 148 C5
Sand River Reservoir Swaziland 133 P3
Sandsele Sweden 44 L2
Sandspit Canada 166 D4
Sand Springs IA U.S.A. 172 B8
Sand Springs OK U.S.A. 179 C4
Sand Springs Salt Flat U.S.A. 182 F2
Sandspruit r. S. Africa 133 K4
Sandstone Australia 151 B5
Sandstone U.S.A. 174 A2
Sand Tank Mountains U.S.A. 183 L9
Sandton S. Africa 133 M3
Sandu Guizhou China 87 C3
also known as Sanhe
Sandu Hunan China 87 E3
Sandur India 94 C3
Sandusky MI U.S.A. 173 K7
Sandusky OH U.S.A. 176 C4
Sandusky Bay U.S.A. 176 C4
Sandveld mts S. Africa 132 C8
Sandveld Nature Reserve S. Africa 133 J4
Sandverhaar Namibia 132 B3
Sandvika Akershus Norway 45 J4
Sandvika Nord-Trøndelag Norway 44 K3
Sandviken Sweden 45 L3
Sandvlakte S. Africa 133 I10
Sandwich U.S.A. 177 O4
Sandwich Bay Canada 169 J2
Sandwich Island Vanuatu see Éfaté
Sandwip Bangl. 97 F5
Sandwip Channel Bangl. 97 F5
Sandy U.S.A. 183 M1
Sandy r. U.S.A. 177 P1
Sandy Bay Canada 167 K4
Sandy Bight b. Australia 151 C7
Sandy Cape Qld Australia 149 G5
Sandy Cape Tas. Australia 147 E5
Sandy Creek r. Australia 148 C3
Sandy Island Australia 150 C2
Sandykachi Turkm. 103 E5
Sandykly Gumy des. Turkm. see Sundukli, Peski
Sandy Lake Alta Canada 167 H4
Sandy Lake Ont. Canada 167 M4
Sandy Lake l. Canada 167 M4
Sandy Springs U.S.A. 175 C5
Sandyville U.S.A. 176 D7
Sân el Hagar Egypt 108 C7
San Estanislao Para. 201 F6
San Esteban Hond. 186 B4
San Esteban, Isla i. Mex. 184 B2
San Fabián de Alico Chile 204 C5
San Felipe Chile 204 C4
San Felipe Baja California Norte Mex. 184 B2
San Felipe Chihuahua Mex. 184 D3
San Felipe Guanajuato Mex. 185 E4
San Felipe mt. Spain 55 J4
San Felipe Venez. 198 D2
San Felipe, Cayos de is Cuba 186 C2
San Feliú de Guíxols Spain see Sant Feliu de Guíxols
San Félix, Isla i. S. Pacific Ocean 221 M7
San Fernando Arg. 204 F4
San Fernando Chile 204 C4
San Fernando Baja California Norte Mex. 184 B2
San Fernando Tamaulipas Mex. 185 F3
San Fernando Luzon Phil. 74 B2
San Fernando Luzon Phil. 74 B3
San Fernando Spain 54 E8
San Fernando Trin. and Tob. 187 H5
San Fernando U.S.A. 182 F7
San Fernando de Apure Venez. 199 E3
San Fernando de Atabapo Venez. 199 E3
San Filipe Creek watercourse U.S.A. 183 I8
Sånfjället nationalpark nat. park Sweden 45 K3
Sanford r. Australia 151 A5
Sanford FL U.S.A. 175 D6
Sanford ME U.S.A. 177 O2
Sanford MI U.S.A. 173 I7
Sanford NC U.S.A. 174 E5
San Francisco Arg. 204 E3
San Francisco Bol. 200 D3
San Francisco Mex. 184 B2
▶San Francisco U.S.A. 182 B4
world [cities] 24–25
world [communications] 26–27
San Francisco r. U.S.A. 181 E6
San Francisco, Paso de pass Arg. 204 C2
San Francisco, Sierra mts Mex. 184 B3
San Francisco Bay inlet U.S.A. 182 B4
San Francisco del Oro Mex. 184 D3
San Francisco de Macorís Dom. Rep. 187 F3
San Francisco de Paula, Cabo c. Arg. 205 D8
San Francisco Gotera El Salvador 185 H6
San Francisco Javier Spain 55 M6
Sanga Dem. Rep. Congo 127 F6
San Gabriel Ecuador 198 B4
San Gabriel, Punta pt Mex. 184 B2
San Gabriel Mountains U.S.A. 182 F7
Sangachaly Azer. see Sanqaçal
Sangai, Parque Nacional nat. park Ecuador 198 B5
Sangaigerong Indon. 76 D3
Sa'ngain China 86 A2
San Gallan, Isla i. Peru 200 A3
Sangam India 94 C3
Sangameshwar India 94 B2
Sangamner India 94 B2
Sangamon r. U.S.A. 174 B3
Sangān Iran 101 D3
Sangan, Koh-i- mt. Afgh. 101 F3
Sangar r. Pak. 101 G4
Sangar Rus. Fed. 39 M3
Sangaréa Guinea 124 B4
Sangareddi India 94 C2
Sangaredi Guinea 124 B4
Sangaria India 96 B3
Sangasanga Indon. 77 G3
Sanga Sanga i. Phil. 74 A5
Sangasso Mali see Zangasso
Sangaste Estonia 42 H4
San Gavino Monreale Sardegna Italy 57 A9
Sangay, Volcán vol. Ecuador 198 B5
Sang Bast Iran 101 D3
Sangbé Cameroon 125 I5
Sangboy Islands Phil. 74 B5
Sangbur Afgh. 101 E3
Sangeang i. Indon. 77 G5
Sangejing China 85 E3
Sângeorgiu de Pădure Romania 58 F2
formerly spelt Sîngeorgiu de Pădure
Sângeorz-Băi Romania 58 F1
formerly spelt Sîngeorz-Băi
Sangequanzi China 88 E3
Sânger Romania 58 F2
Sanger U.S.A. 182 E5
Sângera Moldova see Sîngera
Sangerfield U.S.A. 177 J3
Sangerhausen Germany 48 I4
San Germán Puerto Rico 187 G3
Sanggan r. China 85 G3
Sanggar, Teluk b. Indon. 77 G5
Sanggarmai China 86 B1
Sanggau Indon. 77 E2
Sanggou Wan b. China 85 I4
Sangha admin. reg. Congo 126 B4
Sangha r. Congo 126 C5
Sangha-Mbaéré pref. Cent. Afr. Rep. 126 C4
Sanghar Pak. 101 G5
San Gil Col. 198 C3
Sangilen, Nagor'ye mts Rus. Fed. 84 B1
San Giovanni in Fiore Italy 57 I9
San Giovanni Rotondo Italy 56 H7
San Giovanni Suegiu Sardegna Italy 57 A9
Sangir India 96 B5
Sangir i. Indon. 75 C2
Sangir, Kepulauan is Indon. 75 C2
Sangiran tourist site Indon. 77 E4
San Giuliano Terme Italy 56 C5
San Giustino Italy 56 E5
Sangiyn Dalay Mongolia 84 E2
Sangiyn Dalay Nuur salt l. Mongolia 84 C1
Sangju S. Korea 83 C5
Sangkapura Indon. 77 F4
Sangkarang, Kepulauan is Indon. 75 A4
Sângke, Stœng r. Cambodia 79 C5
Sangkulirang Indon. 77 G2
Sangkulirang, Teluk b. Indon. 77 G2
Sangla Pak. 101 H4
Sangli India 94 B2
San Glorio, Puerto de pass Spain 54 G1
Sangmélima Cameroon 125 H6
Sango Zimbabwe 131 F4
formerly known as Vila Salazar or Villasalazar
Sangod India 96 C4
Sangole India 94 B2
San Gorgonio Mountain U.S.A. 183 H7
Sangowo Indon. 75 D2
Sangpi China see Xiangcheng
Sang Qu r. China 86 A2
Sangre de Cristo Range mts U.S.A. 181 F5
San Gregorio de Polanca Uruguay 204 G4
Sangre Grande Trin. and Tob. 187 H5
Sangri China 89 F6
also known as Xueba
Sangro r. Italy 56 G6
Sangrur India 96 B3
Sangsang China 89 D6
Sangu r. Bangl. 97 F5
Sangue r. Brazil 201 F2
Sangüesa Spain 55 J2
San Guiliano Milanese Italy 56 B3
Sangū'īyeh Iran 100 D4
also known as Isfandaqeh
Sangyuan China see Wuqiao
Sangzhi China 87 D2
also known as Liyuan
Sanhe China see Sandu
Sanhe China 85 I1
Sanhezhen China 87 F2
San Hilario Mex. 184 C3
San Hipólito, Punta pt Mex. 184 B3
Sanhūr Egypt 121 F2
San Ignacio Belize 185 H5
San Ignacio Beni Bol. 200 D3
San Ignacio Santa Cruz Bol. 201 E4
San Ignacio Santa Cruz Bol. 201 E4
San Ignacio Baja California Sur Mex. 184 B3
San Ignacio Sonora Mex. 184 C2
San Ignacio Para. 201 F6
San Ignacio Peru 198 B6
San Ignacio, Laguna l. Mex. 184 B3
Sanikiluaq Canada 168 E1
San Ildefonso Peninsula Phil. 74 B2
Sanin-kaigan National Park Japan 91 D7
Sanipas pass S. Africa 133 N6
Sanislău Romania 49 T8
Sanitz Germany 49 J1
Sāniyat al Fawākhir well Libya 120 C3
San Jacinto Col. 198 C2
San Jacinto Phil. 74 B3
San Jacinto U.S.A. 183 H8
San Jacinto Peak U.S.A. 183 H8
Sanjai r. India 97 E5
San Jaime Arg. 204 F3
San Javier Arg. 204 F3
San Javier Beni Bol. 200 D3
San Javier Santa Cruz Bol. 201 E4
San Javier Spain 55 K7
San Javier de Loncomilla Chile 204 C4
Sanjawi Pak. 101 G4
Sanjbod Iran 100 B2
San Jerónimo Mex. 185 E5
San Jerónimo Peru 200 B1
Sanjiang China see Liannan
Sanjiang China 87 D3
also known as Guyi
Sanjiang China see Jinping
Sanjiaocheng China see Haiyan
Sanjiaoping China 87 D2
Sanjie China 87 G2
Sanjō Japan 90 F6
San Joaquín Bol. 200 D3
San Joaquín Para. 201 F6
San Joaquin U.S.A. 182 D5
San Joaquin r. U.S.A. 182 C3
San Joaquin Valley U.S.A. 182 D4
San Jon U.S.A. 178 B5
San Jorge Arg. 204 E3
San Jorge, Golfo de g. Arg. 205 D7
San Jorge, Golfo de g. Spain see Sant Jordi, Golf de
San José Col. 199 D4
▶San José Costa Rica 186 B5
Capital of Costa Rica.
San José watercourse Mex. 181 D8
San Jose Luzon Phil. 74 B3
San Jose Mindoro Phil. 74 B3
San Jose Mindoro Phil. 74 B3
San Jose CA U.S.A. 182 C4
San Jose NM U.S.A. 181 F6
San Jose watercourse U.S.A. 181 F6
San José Venez. 199 E2
San José, Cabo c. Arg. 205 D7
San José, Cuchilla de hills Uruguay 204 F3
San José, Golfo g. Arg. 205 D6
San José, Isla i. Mex. 184 C3
San José, Volcán vol. Chile 204 C4
San José de Amacuro Venez. 199 F2
San José de Bavicora Mex. 184 D2
San José de Buenavista Phil. 74 B4
San José de Chiquitos Bol. 201 E4
San José de Comondú Mex. 184 C3
San José de Gracia Baja California Sur Mex. 184 B3
San José de Gracia Sonora Mex. 184 C2
San José de Guaribe Venez. 187 G5
San José de Jáchal Arg. 204 C3
San José de la Brecha Mex. 184 C3
San José de la Dormida Arg. 204 E3
San José de la Mariquina Chile 204 B5
San José del Boquerón Arg. 204 E2
San José del Cabo Mex. 184 C4
San José del Guaviare Col. 198 C4
San José de Mayo Uruguay 204 F4
San José de Ocuné Col. 198 D3
San José de Primas Mex. 181 E7
San José de Raíces Mex. 185 E3
San Juan Arg. 204 C3
San Juan prov. Arg. 204 C3
San Juan Bol. 201 E4
San Juan Col. 198 B3
San Juan r. Col. 198 B3
San Juan r. Costa Rica/Nicaragua 186 C5
San Juan mt. Cuba 186 C2
San Juan Dom. Rep. 187 F3
San Juan Chihuahua Mex. 184 D3
San Juan Coahuila Mex. 185 E3
San Juan Peru 200 B3
San Juan Phil. 74 C4
▶San Juan Puerto Rico 187 G3
Capital of Puerto Rico.
San Juan r. CA U.S.A. 182 D6
San Juan r. UT U.S.A. 183 N4
San Juan Venez. 199 E3
San Juan, Cabo c. Arg. 205 E9
San Juan, Cabo c. Equat. Guinea 125 H6
San Juan, Punta pt El Salvador 186 A4
San Juan Bautista Para. 201 F6
San Juan Bautista Spain 55 M5
San Juan Bautista U.S.A. 182 C5
San Juan Bautista Tuxtepec Mex. 185 F5
San Juan Capistrano U.S.A. 182 G8
San Juancito Hond. 186 B4
San Juan de César Col. 198 C2
San Juan de Guadalupe Mex. 185 E3
San Juan dela Costa Chile 204 B6
San Juan de la Peña, Sierra de mts Spain 55 K2
San Juan del Norte Nicaragua 186 C5
San Juan del Norte, Bahía de b. Nicaragua 186 C5
San Juan de los Cayos Venez. 198 D2
San Juan de los Morros Venez. 199 E2
San Juan del Río Durango Mex. 184 D3
San Juan del Río Querétaro Mex. 185 F4
San Juan del Sur Nicaragua 186 B5
San Juan de Salvamento Arg. 205 E9
San Juan Evangelista Mex. 185 G5
San Juan Islands U.S.A. 180 B2
San Juanito Mex. 184 D3
San Juanito, Isla i. Mex. 184 D4
San Juan Mountains U.S.A. 181 F5
San Juan y Martínez Cuba 186 C2
San Julián Arg. 205 D8
San Just mt. Spain 55 K4
San Justo Arg. 204 E3
Sankarani r. Côte d'Ivoire/Guinea 124 C4
Sankarankovil India 94 C4
Sankeshwar India 94 B2
Sankh r. India 97 E5
Sankosh r. Bhutan see Sunkosh
Sankra Chhattisgarh India 94 D1
Sankra Rajasthan India 96 A4
Sankt Andrä Austria 49 L9
Sankt Gallen Switz. 51 P5
Sankt Gotthard Hungary see Szentgotthárd
Sankt Johann im Pongau Austria 49 K8
Sankt Moritz Switz. 51 P6
Sankt-Peterburg Rus. Fed. see St Petersburg
Sankt Peter-Ording Germany 48 F1
Sankt Pölten Austria 49 M7
Sankt Veit an der Glan Austria 49 L9
Sankt Wendel Germany 48 E6
Sankuru r. Dem. Rep. Congo 126 D6
San Lázaro Para. 201 F5
San Lázaro, Cabo c. Mex. 184 B3
San Leandro U.S.A. 182 B4
San Leonardo in Passiria Italy 56 D2
Şanlıurfa Turkey 107 D3
formerly known as Urfa; historically known as Edessa
Şanlıurfa prov. Turkey 109 J1
San Lorenzo Corrientes Arg. 204 F3
San Lorenzo Santa Fé Arg. 204 E4
San Lorenzo Beni Bol. 200 D3
San Lorenzo Pando Bol. 200 D2
San Lorenzo Tarija Bol. 200 D5
San Lorenzo Ecuador 198 B4
San Lorenzo Hond. 186 B4
San Lorenzo Mex. 184 D2
San Lorenzo Peru 200 C2
San Lorenzo mt. Spain 55 I2
San Lorenzo, Cabo c. Ecuador 198 A5
San Lorenzo, Cerro mt. Arg./Chile 205 B7
San Lorenzo, Isla i. Mex. 184 B2
San Lorenzo, Isla i. Peru 200 A3
Sanlúcar de Barrameda Spain 54 E8
San Lucas Bol. 200 D5
San Lucas Baja California Sur Mex. 184 B3
San Lucas Baja California Sur Mex. 184 C4
San Lucas, Cabo c. Mex. 184 C4
San Lucas, Serranía de mts Col. 198 C3
San Luis Arg. 204 D4
San Luis prov. Arg. 204 D4
San Luis Brazil 200 D2
San Luis Cuba 186 E2
San Luis Guat. 185 H5
San Luis Mex. 185 E5
San Luis Peru 198 C5
San Luis AZ U.S.A. 183 J9
San Luis AZ U.S.A. 183 M9
San Luis CO U.S.A. 181 F5
San Luis Venez. 198 D2
San Luis, Isla i. Mex. 184 B2
San Luis, Sierra de mts Arg. 204 D4
San Luis de la Paz Mex. 185 E4
San Luis del Palmar Arg. 204 F2
San Luis Gonzaga Mex. 184 C3
San Luisito Mex. 184 B2
San Luis Obispo U.S.A. 182 D6
San Luis Obispo Bay U.S.A. 182 D6
San Luis Potosí Mex. 185 E4
San Luis Potosí state Mex. 185 E4
San Luis Reservoir U.S.A. 182 C4
San Luis Río Colorado Mex. 184 B1
Sanluri Sardegna Italy 57 A9
San Manuel U.S.A. 183 N9
San Marcello Pistoiese Italy 56 C4
San Marcial, Punta pt Mex. 184 C3
San Marco, Capo c. Sardegna Italy 57 A9
San Marco, Capo c. Sicilia Italy 57 F11
San Marcos Chile 204 C3
San Marcos Col. 198 C2
San Marcos Guat. 185 H6
San Marcos Hond. 186 B4
San Marcos Mex. 185 F5
San Marcos Peru 200 A1
San Marcos U.S.A. 179 C6
San Marcos r. U.S.A. 179 C6
San Marcos, Isla i. Mex. 184 B3
▶San Marino country Europe 56 E5
europe [countries] 32–35
▶San Marino San Marino 56 E5
Capital of San Marino.
San Martín research station Antarctica 222 T2
long form General San Martín
San Martín Catamarca Arg. 204 D3
San Martín Mendoza Arg. 204 C4
San Martín r. Bol. 201 E3
San Martín dept Peru 200 A1
San Martín, Lago l. Arg./Chile 205 B8
San Martín, Volcán vol. Mex. 185 G5
San Martín de los Andes Arg. 204 C6
San Martín de Valdeiglesias Spain 54 G4
San-Martino-di-Lota Corse France 51 P10
San Mateo Peru 198 D5
San Mateo U.S.A. 182 B4
San Mateo Venez. 199 E2
San Matías Bol. 201 F4
San Matías, Golfo g. Arg. 204 D6
San Mauricio Venez. 199 E2
Sanmen China 87 G2
also known as Haiyou
Sanmen Wan b. China 87 G2
Sanmenxia China 87 D1
San Miguel Arg. 204 F3
San Miguel Bol. 201 E3
San Miguel r. Bol. 201 E3
San Miguel r. Col. 198 C4
San Miguel El Salvador 185 H6
San Miguel Panama 186 D5
San Miguel Peru 200 B3
San Miguel U.S.A. 182 D6
San Miguel r. U.S.A. 181 E5
San Miguel Bay Phil. 74 B3
San Miguel de Allende Mex. 185 E4
San Miguel de Cruces Mex. 184 D3
San Miguel de Horcasitas r. Mex. 184 C2
San Miguel de Huachi Bol. 200 D3
San Miguel del Monte Arg. 204 F4
San Miguel de Tucumán Arg. 204 D2
short form Tucumán
San Miguel do Araguaia Brazil 202 B5
San Miguel el Alto Mex. 185 E4
San Miguel Island U.S.A. 182 D7
San Miguel Islands Phil. 74 A5
San Miguelito Panama 186 D5
San Miguel Sola de Vega Mex. 185 F5
Sanming China 87 F3
San Miniato Italy 56 C5
Sanna r. Poland 49 S5
San Narciso Phil. 74 B3
Sannaspos S. Africa 133 K6
Sanndatti India 94 B3
Sanndraigh i. U.K. see Sandray
Sannicandro Garganico Italy 56 H7
San Nicolás Mex. 185 F3
San Nicolas Phil. 74 B2
San Nicolás, Bahía b. Peru 200 B3
San Nicolás de los Arroyos Arg. 204 E4
San Nicolás del Presidio Mex. 184 D3
San Nicolas Island U.S.A. 182 E8
Sânnicolau Mare Romania 58 B2
formerly spelt Sînnicolau Mare
Sannieshof S. Africa 133 J3
Sanniquellie Liberia 124 C5
Sannohe Japan 90 G4
Sañogasta, Sierra de mts Arg. 204 D3
Sanok Poland 49 T6
San Onofre Col. 198 C2
San Pablo Arg. 205 D9
San Pablo Potosí Bol. 200 D5
San Pablo Santa Cruz Bol. 201 E3
San Pablo r. Bol. 201 E3
San Pablo Col. 198 D3
San Pablo Mex. 185 F4
San Pablo Phil. 74 B3
San Pablo U.S.A. 182 B4
San Pablo de Manta Ecuador see Manta
San Pedro Buenos Aires Arg. 204 F4
San Pedro Catamarca Arg. 204 D2
San Pedro Jujuy Arg. 200 D6
San Pedro Misiones Arg. 204 G2
San Pedro Belize 185 I5
San Pedro Beni Bol. 200 D3
San Pedro Santa Cruz Bol. 201 E4
San Pedro r. Bol. 200 D4
San-Pédro Côte d'Ivoire 124 D5
San Pedro r. Cuba 186 D2
San Pedro Mex. 184 C4
San Pedro r. Mex. 181 F7
San Pedro Peru 200 C2
San Pedro Phil. 74 B3
San Pedro watercourse U.S.A. 183 N9
San Pedro, Punta pt Costa Rica 186 C5
San Pedro, Sierra de mts Spain 54 D5
San Pedro Carchá Guat. 185 H6
San Pedro Channel U.S.A. 182 F8
San Pedro de Atacama Chile 200 C5
San Pedro de las Colonias Mex. 185 E3
San Pedro de Lloc Peru 200 A1
San Pedro del Pinatar Spain 55 K7
San Pedro de Macorís Dom. Rep. 187 F3
San Pedro de Ycuamandyyú Para. 201 F6
San Pedro el Saucito Mex. 184 C2
San Pedro Martir, Parque Nacional nat. park Mex. 184 B2
San Pedro Sula Hond. 186 A4
San Pietro, Isola di i. Sardegna Italy 57 A9
San Pietro in Cariano Italy 56 C3
San Pitch r. U.S.A. 183 M2
Sanqaçal Azer. 107 G2
also spelt Sangachaly
Sanquhar U.K. 46 I8
Sanquianga, Parque Nacional nat. park Col. 198 B4
San Quintín, Cabo c. Mex. 184 A2
San Rafael Arg. 204 C4
San Rafael Bol. 201 E4
San Rafael U.S.A. 182 B4
San Rafael r. U.S.A. 183 N3
San Rafael Venez. 198 D2
also known as San Rafael del Moján
San Rafael del Moján Venez. see San Rafael
San Rafael del Norte Nicaragua 186 B4
San Rafael del Yuma Dom. Rep. 187 F3
San Rafael Knob mt. U.S.A. 183 N3
San Rafael Mountains U.S.A. 182 D7
San Ramón Beni Bol. 200 D3
San Ramón Santa Cruz Bol. 201 E4
San Remo Italy 51 N9
San Rodrigo watercourse Mex. 179 B6
San Román, Cabo c. Venez. 198 D1
San Roque Andalucía Spain 54 F8
San Roque Galicia Spain 54 C1
San Roque Galicia Spain 54 C2
San Roque, Punta pt Mex. 184 B3
San Saba U.S.A. 179 C6
San Saba r. U.S.A. 179 C6
Sansalé Guinea 124 B4
San Salvador Arg. 204 F3
San Salvador i. Bahamas 187 E1
formerly known as Watling Island
▶San Salvador El Salvador 185 H6
Capital of El Salvador.
San Salvador Peru 198 D5
San Salvador de Jujuy Arg. 200 D6
San Salvo Italy 56 G6
Sansané Haoussa Niger 125 F3
Sansanné-Mango Togo 125 F4
San Sebastián Arg. 205 C9
San Sebastián hill Spain 54 C2
San Sebastián, Bahía de b. Arg. 205 C9
San Sebastián de los Reyes Spain 55 H4
Sansepolcro Italy 56 E5
San Severino Marche Italy 56 F5
San Severo Italy 56 H7
Sansha China 87 G3
San Silvestre Bol. 200 C2
San Silvestre Venez. 198 D2
San Simon U.S.A. 183 O9
Sanski Most Bos.-Herz. 56 I4
Sanson N.Z. 152 J8
Sansoral Islands Palau see Sonsorol Islands
Sansui China 87 D3
also known as Bagong
Santa Peru 200 A2
Santa r. Peru 200 A1
Santa Adélia Brazil 206 E8
Santa Ana Arg. 204 D2
Santa Ana La Paz Bol. 200 D3
Santa Ana Santa Cruz Bol. 201 F4
Santa Ana El Salvador 185 H6
Santa Ana Mex. 184 C2
Santa Ana U.S.A. 182 G8
Santa Ana de Yacuma Bol. 200 D3
Santa Anita Mex. 184 C4
Santa Anna U.S.A. 179 C6
Santa Bárbara Brazil 201 F3
Santa Bárbara Cuba see La Demajagua
Santa Bárbara Hond. 186 A4
Santa Bárbara Mex. 184 D3
Santa Bárbara mt. Spain 55 I7
Santa Bárbara mt. Spain 55 J6
Santa Barbara U.S.A. 182 E7
Santa Bárbara Amazonas Venez. 199 E4
Santa Bárbara Barinas Venez. 198 D3
Santa Bárbara, Ilha i. Brazil 207 O4
Santa Bárbara, Parque Nacional nat. park Hond. 186 A4
Santa Bárbara, Serra de hills Brazil 203 A7
Santa Barbara Channel U.S.A. 182 D7
Santa Bárbara d'Oeste Brazil 206 F9
Santa Bárbara do Sul Brazil 203 A9
Santa Barbara Island U.S.A. 182 E8
Santa Catalina Chile 204 C2
Santa Catalina Panama 186 C5
Santa Catalina Phil. 74 B5
Santa Catalina Venez. 199 F2
Santa Catalina, Gulf of U.S.A. 182 G8
Santa Catalina, Isla i. Mex. 184 C3
Santa Catalina de Armada Spain 54 C1
Santa Catalina Island U.S.A. 182 F8
Santa Catarina state Brazil 203 B8
Santa Catarina Baja California Norte Mex. 184 B2
Santa Catarina Nuevo León Mex. 185 E3
Santa Catarina Neth. Antilles 187 F4
also spelt Santa Catharina
Santa Catarina, Ilha de i. Brazil 203 B8
Santa Catharina Neth. Antilles see Santa Catarina
Santa Clara Col. 198 D5
Santa Clara Cuba 186 D2
Santa Clara r. Mex. 181 F7
Santa Clara CA U.S.A. 182 C4
Santa Clara UT U.S.A. 183 K4
Santa Clara r. U.S.A. 182 E7
Santa Clara, Barragem de resr Port. 54 C7
Santa Clarita U.S.A. 182 F7
Santa Clotilde Peru 198 C5
Santa Coloma de Farners Spain 55 N3
Santa Coloma de Gramanet Spain 55 N3
Santa Comba Angola see Waku-Kungo
Santa Comba Dão Port. 54 C4
Santa Croce Camerina Sicilia Italy 57 G12
Santa Cruz prov. Arg. 205 C8
Santa Cruz r. Arg. 205 C8
Santa Cruz Bol. 201 E4
Santa Cruz dept Bol. 201 E4
Santa Cruz Espírito Santo Brazil 207 M6
Santa Cruz Pará Brazil 199 H5
Santa Cruz Pará Brazil 202 B2
Santa Cruz Costa Rica 186 B5
Santa Cruz Mex. 184 C2
Santa Cruz Peru 198 C6
Santa Cruz Luzon Phil. 74 A3
Santa Cruz Luzon Phil. 74 B2
Santa Cruz Luzon Phil. 74 B3
Santa Cruz mt. Spain 55 J3
Santa Cruz U.S.A. 182 B5
Santa Cruz watercourse U.S.A. 183 L8
Santa Cruz, Isla i. Mex. 184 C3
Santa Cruz, Puerto inlet Arg. 205 C8
Santa Cruz Barillas Guat. 185 H6
Santa Cruz Cabrália Brazil 202 E6
Santa Cruz das Palmeiras Brazil 206 F8
Santa Cruz de Goiás Brazil 206 E4
Santa Cruz de la Palma Canary Is 122 A3
Santa Cruz del Quiché Guat. 185 H6
Santa Cruz del Sur Cuba 186 D2
Santa Cruz de Mudela Spain 55 H6
▶Santa Cruz de Tenerife Canary Is 122 A3
Joint capital of the Canary Islands.
Santa Cruz de Yojoa Hond. 186 B4
Santa Cruz do Rio Pardo Brazil 206 D9
Santa Cruz do Sul Brazil 203 A9
Santa Cruz Island U.S.A. 182 E7
Santa Cruz Islands Solomon Is 145 F3
Santa Efigênia de Minas Brazil 207 K5
Santa Elena Buenos Aires Arg. 204 F4
Santa Elena Entre Ríos Arg. 204 F3
Santa Elena Bol. 200 D5
Santa Elena Peru 198 C6
Santa Elena Venez. 199 F4
Santa Elena, Cabo c. Costa Rica 186 B5
Santa Elena, Punta pt Ecuador 198 A5
Santa Eufemia, Golfo di g. Italy 57 I10
Santa Eugenia Spain 54 C2
Santa Eulalia del Río Spain 55 M6
Santa Fé Arg. 204 E3
Santa Fé prov. Arg. 204 E3
Santa Fé Cuba 186 C2
Santa Fé Panama 186 C5
Santa Fe Phil. 74 B3
Santa Fe Spain 54 H7
▶Santa Fe U.S.A. 181 F6
State capital of New Mexico.
Santa Fé de Bogotá Col. see Bogotá
Santafé de Bogotá municipality Col. 198 C4
Santa Fé de Minas Brazil 202 C6
Santa Fé do Sul Brazil 206 C7
Santa Filomena Brazil 202 C4
Sant'Agata di Militello Sicilia Italy 57 G10
Santa Helena Brazil 202 C2
Santa Helena de Goiás Brazil 206 C4
Santai Sichuan China 86 C2
also known as Tongchuan
Santai Xinjiang China 88 C2
Santa Inês Bahia Brazil 202 E5
Santa Inês Maranhão Brazil 202 C2
Santa Inés, Isla i. Chile 205 B9
Santa Isabel Arg. 204 D5
Santa Isabel Bol. 200 D5
Santa Isabel Brazil 201 E3
Santa Isabel Equat. Guinea see Malabo
Santa Isabel i. Solomon Is 145 E2
formerly spelt Santa Ysabel
Santa Isabel, Ilha Grande de i. Brazil 202 D2
Santa Isabel, Sierra mts Mex. 184 B2
Santa Isabel de Sihuas Peru 200 B4
Santa Isabel do Araguaia Brazil 201 H1
Santa Juliana Brazil 206 F6
Santalpur India 96 A5
Santa Lucia Chile 200 C5
Santa Lucía Ecuador 198 B5
Santa Lucia Guat. 185 H6
Santa Lucía, Cerro de mt. Spain 54 G7
Santa Lucia Range mts U.S.A. 182 C5
Santa Luzia Maranhão Brazil 202 C3
Santa Luzia Paraíba Brazil 202 E3
Santa Luzia i. Cape Verde 124 [inset]
Santa Magdalena Arg. 204 E4
Santa Margarita Arg. 204 E3
Santa Margarita Spain 55 O5
Santa Margarita U.S.A. 182 D6
Santa Margarita, Isla i. Mex. 184 C3
Santa María Arg. 204 D2
Santa Maria Bol. 201 E3
Santa Maria Amazonas Brazil 199 F5
Santa Maria Amazonas Brazil 199 G5
Santa Maria Pará Brazil 199 H5
Santa Maria Rio Grande do Sul Brazil 203 A9
Santa Maria r. Brazil 203 A9
Santa Maria r. Brazil 206 G1
Santa Maria Cape Verde 124 [inset]
Santa María Mex. 185 H5
Santa María r. Mex. 184 D2
Santa Maria U.S.A. 182 D7
Santa Maria r. U.S.A. 183 K7
Santa María Venez. 199 E3
Santa Maria, Cabo de c. Moz. 131 G5
Santa Maria, Cabo de c. Port. 54 D8
Santa Maria, Cape Bahamas 175 F8
Santa María, Cayo i. Cuba 186 D2
Santa Maria, Chapadão de hills Brazil 202 C5
Santa María, Isla i. Chile 204 B5
Santa María, Punta pt Peru 200 B3
Santa Maria, Serra de hills Brazil 206 G1
Santa Maria Capua Vetere Italy 56 G7
Santa Maria das Barreiras Brazil 202 B4
Santa Maria da Vitória Brazil 202 C5
Santa María de Ipire Venez. 199 E2
Santa María del Oro Mex. 184 D3
Santa María del Río Mex. 185 E4
Santa Maria di Leuca, Capo c. Italy 57 K9
Santa Maria do Salto Brazil 207 M3
Santa Maria do Suaçuí Brazil 203 D6
Santa Maria Island Vanuatu 145 F3
Santa Maria Mountains U.S.A. 183 L7
Santa Marina Salina Isole Lipari Italy 57 G10
Santa Marinella Italy 56 D6
Santa Marta Col. 198 C2
Santa Marta, Cabo de c. Angola 127 B8
Santa Marta, Serra de mts Brazil see Divisões, Serra das
Santa Marta Grande, Cabo de c. Brazil 203 B9
Santa Martha, Cerro mt. Mex. 185 G5
Santa Maura i. Greece see Lefkada
Santa Monica U.S.A. 182 F7
Santa Monica Bay U.S.A. 182 F8
Santan Indon. 77 G3
Santana Amazonas Brazil 199 E4
Santana Bahia Brazil 202 D5
Santana r. Brazil 206 B6
Sântana Romania 58 C2
Santana da Boa Vista Brazil 203 A9
Santana do Acarau Brazil 202 D2
Santana do Araguaia Brazil 202 B4
Santana do Cariri Brazil 202 E3
Santana do Livramento Brazil 204 G3
Santander Col. 198 B4
Santander dept Col. 198 C3
Santander Spain 54 H1
Santa Nella U.S.A. 182 C4
Sant'Angelo in Lizzola Italy 56 E5
Sant'Angelo Lodigiano Italy 56 B3
Santanghu China 84 B2
Santanilla, Islas is Caribbean Sea see Swan Islands
Santan Mountain hill U.S.A. 183 M8
Sant'Anna, Ilha de i. Brazil 207 L9
Sant'Antioco Sardegna Italy 57 A9
historically known as Sulci or Sulcis
Sant'Antioco, Isola di i. Sardegna Italy 57 A9
Santañy Spain see Santanyí
Santanyí Spain 55 O5
also spelt Santañy
Santa Paula U.S.A. 182 E7
Santapilly India 95 D2
Santa Pola Spain 55 K6
Santa Pola, Cabo de c. Spain 55 K6
Santaquin U.S.A. 183 M2
Santa Quitéria Brazil 202 D3
Sant Arcangelo Italy 57 I8
Santarém Brazil 199 H5
Santarém Port. 54 C5
Santarém admin. dist. Port. 54 C5
Santa Rita Mato Grosso Brazil 201 F1
Santa Rita Paraíba Brazil 202 F3
Santa Rita Col. 198 C4
Santa Rita Mex. 185 E3
Santa Rita Guárico Venez. 199 E2
Santa Rita Zulia Venez. 198 D2
Santa Rita de Cassia Brazil 202 C4
Santa Rita do Araguaia Brazil 203 A6
Santa Rita do Pardo Brazil 206 A8
Santa Rita do Sapucaí Brazil 207 H9
Santa Rita do Weil Brazil 198 D5
Santa Rosa Corrientes Arg. 204 F3
Santa Rosa La Pampa Arg. 204 D5
Santa Rosa Río Negro Arg. 204 D6
Santa Rosa Salta Arg. 200 D6
Santa Rosa Bol. 200 D3
Santa Rosa Acre Brazil 200 C2
Santa Rosa Rio Grande do Sul Brazil 203 A8
Santa Rosa Col. 198 D4

index S

Santa Rosa Ecuador 198 B5
Santa Rosa Mex. 185 H5
Santa Rosa Para. 201 F6
Santa Rosa *Loreto* Peru 198 C5
Santa Rosa *Puno* Peru 200 C3
Santa Rosa *CA* U.S.A. 182 B3
Santa Rosa *NM* U.S.A. 181 F6
Santa Rosa Venez. 199 E4
Santa Rosa de Copán Hond. 186 A4
Santa Rosa de la Roca Bol. 201 E4
Santa Rosa del Conlara Arg. 204 D4
Santa Rosa del Palmar Bol. 201 E4
Santa Rosa de Osos Col. 198 C3
Santa Rosa de Viterbo Brazil 206 F8
Santa Rosa Island U.S.A. 182 D8
Santa Rosalía Mex. 184 B3
Santa Rosa Mountains U.S.A. 183 H8
Santa Rosa Range *mts* U.S.A. 180 C4
Santa Rosa Wash *watercourse* U.S.A. 183 L8
Santa Sylvina Arg. 204 E2
Santa Teresa Australia 148 B5
Santa Teresa Brazil 207 M6
Santa Teresa *r.* Brazil 202 B4
Santa Teresa Mex. 185 F3
Santa Teresa, Embalse de *resr* Spain 54 F4
Santa Teresa Aboriginal Land *res.* Australia *see* Ltyentye Apurte Aboriginal Land
Santa Teresa di Gallura *Sardegna* Italy 56 B7
Santa Terezinha Brazil 202 B4
Santa Vitória Brazil 206 C5
Santa Vitória do Palmar Brazil 204 G4
Santa Vittoria, Monte *mt. Sardegna* Italy 57 B9
Santa Ynez *r.* U.S.A. 182 D7
Santa Ysabel *i.* Solomon Is *see* Santa Isabel
Sant Carles de la Ràpita Spain 55 L4
also spelt San Carlos de la Rápita
Sant Celoni Spain 55 N3
also spelt San Celoni
Santee U.S.A. 183 H9
Santee *r.* U.S.A. 175 E5
Santeramo in Colle Italy 57 I8
Santerno *r.* Italy 56 D4
Sant Feliu de Guíxols Spain 55 O3
also spelt San Feliú de Guíxols
Santiago Brazil 203 A9

▶Santiago Chile 204 C4
Capital of Chile.
southamerica [countries] ▶▶ 192–193

Santiago *admin. reg.* Chile 204 C4
Santiago Dom. Rep. 187 F3
long form Santiago de los Caballeros
Santiago *Baja California Sur* Mex. 184 C4
Santiago *Nuevo León* Mex. 185 E3
Santiago Panama 186 C5
Santiago Para. 201 F6
Santiago Peru 200 B3
Santiago *r.* Peru 198 B6
Santiago Phil. 74 B2
Santiago, Cabo *c.* Chile 205 B8
Santiago, Cerro *mt.* Panama 186 C5
Santiago, Rio Grande de *r.* Mex. 184 D4
Santiago, Sierra de *hills* Bol. 201 F4
Santiago Astata Mex. 185 G5
Santiago de Cao Peru 200 A1
Santiago de Compostela Spain 54 C2
Santiago de Cuba Cuba 186 E2
Santiago de la Espada Spain 55 I6
Santiago del Estero Arg. 204 D2
Santiago del Estero *prov.* Arg. 204 E2
Santiago de los Caballeros Dom. Rep. *see* Santiago
Santiago de Mendez Ecuador 198 B5
Santiago de Pacaguaras Bol. 200 C3
Santiago do Cacém Port. 54 C6
Santiago Ixcuintla Mex. 184 D4
Santiago Peak U.S.A. 182 G8
Santiago Temple Arg. 204 E3
Santiago Vazquez Uruguay 204 F4
Santiaguillo, Laguna de *l.* Mex. 184 D3
Santillana Spain 54 G1
San Timoteo Venez. 198 D2
Santipur India *see* Shantipur
Santisteban del Puerto Spain 55 H6
Sant Jordi, Golf de *g.* Spain 55 L4
also spelt San Jorge, Golfo de
Sant Llorenç del Munt i de la Serra de L'Obac, Parque Natural de *nature res.* Spain 55 M3
Santo Amaro Brazil 202 E5
Santo Amaro de Campos Brazil 207 L8
Santo Anastácio *r.* Brazil 206 A8
Santo André Brazil 206 G10
Santo André Port. 54 C6
Santo Angelo Brazil 203 A9

▶Santo Antão *i.* Cape Verde 124 [inset]
Most westerly point of Africa.

Santo Antônio *Amazonas* Brazil 199 F5
Santo Antônio *Maranhão* Brazil 202 C3
Santo Antônio *Rio Grande do Norte* Brazil 202 F3
Santo Antônio *r.* Brazil 203 D6
Santo António São Tomé and Príncipe 125 G6
Santo Antônio, Ponta *pt* Brazil 207 O3
Santo Antônio da Barra Brazil 206 C4
Santo Antônio da Cachoeira Brazil 199 H5
Santo Antônio da Platina Brazil 206 C10
Santo Antônio de Jesus Brazil 202 E5
Santo Antônio de Leverger Brazil 201 F3
Santo Antônio de Pádua Brazil 207 K8
Santo Antônio do Amparo Brazil 207 I7
Santo Antônio do Içá Brazil 199 E5
Santo Antônio do Jacinto Brazil 207 M3
Santo Antônio do Monte Brazil 207 H7
Santo Antônio do Rio Verde Brazil 206 F4
Santo Antônio dos Cavaleiros Port. 54 B6
Santo António do Zaire Angola *see* Soyo
Santo Corazón Bol. 201 F4
Santo Domingo Cuba 186 C2

▶Santo Domingo Dom. Rep. 187 F3
Capital of the Dominican Republic. Formerly known as Ciudad Trujillo.

Santo Domingo *Baja California Norte* Mex. 184 B2
Santo Domingo *San Luis Potosí* Mex. 185 E4
Santo Domingo Nicaragua 186 B4
Santo Domingo Peru 200 C3
Santo Domingo *country* West Indies *see* Dominican Republic
Santo Domingo de la Calzada Spain 55 I2
Santo Domingo Pueblo U.S.A. 181 F6
Santo Domingo Tehuantepec Mex. 185 G5
Santo Eduardo Brazil 207 L8
Santo Hipólito Brazil 207 I5
Santo Inácio Brazil 206 B9
Santo Tomé Venez. 199 E2
Santoña Spain 55 H1
Santong *r.* China 82 B4
Santo Niño *i.* Phil. 74 C4
Santorini *i.* Greece *see* Thira
Santos Brazil 207 G10
Santos Dumont Brazil 207 J8
Santos Mercado Bol. 200 D2
Santo Stefano di Camastra *Sicilia* Italy 57 G10
Santo Tirso Port. 54 C3
Santo Tomás *Chihuahua* Mex. 181 F7
Santo Tomás *Sonora* Mex. 181 D7
Santo Tomás Nicaragua 186 B4
Santo Tomás Peru 200 B3
Santo Tomé Arg. 204 F3
Santrampur India 96 B5
Sanup Plateau U.S.A. 183 K5
San Valentín, Cerro *mt.* Chile 205 B7
San Vicente El Salvador 185 H6
San Vicente Mex. 184 A2
San Vicente Phil. 74 B2
San Vicente de Cañete Peru 200 A3
San Vicente de la Barquera Spain 54 G1
San Vicente del Caguán Col. 198 C4
San Vicente del Raspeig Spain 55 K6
San Vincenzo Italy 56 C5
San Vito, Capo *c. Sicilia* Italy 57 E10
San Vito al Tagliamento Italy 56 E3
San Vito Chietino Italy 56 G6
San Vito dei Normanni Italy 57 J8
San Vito lo Capo *Sicilia* Italy 57 E10
Sanwer India 96 B5
Sanya China 87 D5
formerly known as Yaxian
San Yanaro Col. 198 D4
Sanyati *r.* Zimbabwe 131 F3
Sanyuan China 87 D1
Sanza Pombo Angola 127 C6
Sao, Phou *mt.* Laos 78 C4
São Bartolomeu *r.* Brazil 206 F3
São Benedito Brazil 202 D3
São Bento *Amazonas* Brazil 200 D1
São Bento *Maranhão* Brazil 202 C2
São Bento *Roraima* Brazil 199 F4
São Bento do Norte Brazil 202 F3
São Bernardo Brazil 202 D2
São Bernardo do Campo Brazil 206 G10
São Borja Brazil 204 F3
São Carlos *Rondônia* Brazil 201 D2
São Carlos *Rondônia* Brazil 201 E2
São Carlos *São Paulo* Brazil 206 F9
São Desidério Brazil 202 C5
São Domingos Brazil 202 C5
São Domingos *r. Mato Grosso do Sul* Brazil 203 A7
São Domingos *r. Minas Gerais* Brazil 206 C6
São Domingos *r.* Brazil 206 G2
São Domingos do Norte Brazil 207 M6
São Felipe, Serra de *hills* Brazil 202 C5
São Félix *Bahia* Brazil 202 E5
São Félix *Mato Grosso* Brazil 202 B4
São Félix *Pará* Brazil 199 H6
São Fidélis Brazil 203 D7
São Filipe Cape Verde 124 [inset]
São Francisco *Acre* Brazil 200 C2
São Francisco *Amazonas* Brazil 199 F6
São Francisco *Minas Gerais* Brazil 202 C5
São Francisco *r.* Brazil 200 D2
also known as Espalha

▶São Francisco *r.* Brazil 207 H4
5th longest river in South America.
southamerica [landscapes] ▶▶ 190–191

São Francisco, Ilha de *i.* Brazil 203 B8
São Francisco de Assis Brazil 203 A9
São Francisco de Goiás Brazil 206 D2
São Francisco de Paula Brazil 203 B9
São Francisco de Sales Brazil 206 D6
São Francisco do Sul Brazil 203 B8
São Gabriel Brazil 203 A9
São Gabriel da Palha Brazil 207 M6
São Gabriel de Goiás Brazil 206 F2
São Gonçalo Brazil 203 D7
São Gonçalo do Abaeté Brazil 203 C6
São Gotardo Brazil 207 H6
Sao Hill Tanz. 129 B7
São Jerônimo da Serra Brazil 206 C10
São João Brazil 199 E5
São João, Ilhas de *is* Brazil 202 C2
São João, Serra de *hills* Brazil 201 E2
São João da Aliança Brazil 202 C5
São João da Barra Brazil 203 D7
São João da Boa Vista Brazil 206 G8
São João da Madeira Port. 54 C4
São João da Ponte Brazil 207 I2
São João das Duas Pontas Brazil 206 C7
São João del Rei Brazil 203 C7
São João de Meriti Brazil 207 J9
São João do Araguaia Brazil 202 B3
São João do Caiuá Brazil 206 A9
São João do Cariri Brazil 202 E3
São João do Paraíso Brazil 202 D5
São João do Piauí Brazil 202 D4
São João dos Patos Brazil 202 D3
São João do Sul Angola 127 B8
São João Evangelista Brazil 207 K5
São Joaquim *Amazonas* Brazil 199 E4
São Joaquim *Santa Catarina* Brazil 203 B9
São Jorge da Mina Ghana *see* Elmina
São José *Amazonas* Brazil 199 E5
São José *Santa Catarina* Brazil 203 B8
São José do Anauá Brazil 199 F4
São José de Belmonte Brazil 202 E3
São José do Divino Brazil 207 L5
São José do Egito Brazil 202 E3
São José do Jacuri Brazil 207 K5
São José do Norte Brazil 204 G4
São José do Peixe Brazil 202 D3
São José do Rio Pardo Brazil 206 G8
São José do Rio Preto Brazil 206 D7
São José dos Campos Brazil 207 H10
São José dos Dourados *r.* Brazil 206 B7
São José dos Pinhais Brazil 203 B8
São Lourenço Brazil 207 H9
São Lourenço *r.* Brazil 201 F4
São Lourenço do Sul Brazil 204 H3
São Lucas Angola 127 C7
São Luís Brazil 202 C2
São Luís Brazil 199 G6
São Luís de Montes Belos Brazil 206 C3
São Luís do Paraitinga Brazil 207 H10
São Luís do Quitunde Brazil 202 F4
São Luís Gonzaga Brazil 203 A9
São Manuel Brazil 206 E9
São Marceline Brazil 199 E4
São Marcos *r.* Brazil 206 F5
São Marcos, Baía de *b.* Brazil 202 C2
São Martinho Brazil 199 G6
São Mateus Brazil 203 E6
São Mateus *r.* Brazil 207 N5
São Mateus do Sul Brazil 203 B8
São Miguel *i.* Azores 216 M3
São Miguel *r.* Brazil 206 G3
São Miguel Arcanjo Brazil 206 F10
São Miguel do Tapuio Brazil 202 D3
São Miguel Jesuit Missions *tourist site* Brazil 203 A9
Saona, Isla *i.* Dom. Rep. 187 F3
Saône *r.* France 51 K7
São Nicolau Angola *see* Bentiaba
São Nicolau *i.* Cape Verde 124 [inset]

▶São Paulo Brazil 206 G10
Most populous city in South America and 4th in the world.
world [cities] ▶▶ 24–25

São Paulo *state* Brazil 206 E9
São Paulo de Olivença Brazil 198 D5
São Pedro *Amazonas* Brazil 199 G6
São Pedro *Mato Grosso do Sul* Brazil 206 B6
São Pedro *Rondônia* Brazil 201 E2
São Pedro *São Paulo* Brazil 206 F9
São Pedro da Aldeia Brazil 203 D7
São Pedro do Desterro Brazil 200 D2
São Pedro do Ivaí Brazil 206 B10
São Pedro do Sul Brazil 203 A9
São Pedro do Sul Port. 54 C4
São Pedro e São Paulo *is* N. Atlantic Ocean 216 M5
English form St Peter and St Paul Rocks
São Pires *r.* Brazil *see* Teles Pires
São Raimundo das Mangabeiras Brazil 202 C3
São Raimundo Nonato Brazil 202 D4
São Romão *Amazonas* Brazil 199 E6
São Romão *Minas Gerais* Brazil 202 C6
São Roque Brazil 206 F10
São Roque de Minas Brazil 206 G7
São Salvador Angola *see* M'banza Congo
São Salvador do Congo Angola *see* M'banza Congo
São Sebastião *Amazonas* Brazil 200 C1
São Sebastião *Pará* Brazil 199 H6
São Sebastião *Rondônia* Brazil 201 E2
São Sebastião *São Paulo* Brazil 203 C7
São Sebastião, Ilha do *i.* Brazil 203 C7
São Sebastião da Amoreira Brazil 206 C10
São Sebastião da Boa Vista Brazil 202 B2
São Sebastião do Paraíso Brazil 206 G7
São Simão *Mato Grosso do Sul* Brazil 201 F5
São Simão *Minas Gerais* Brazil 206 C5
São Simão, Barragem de *resr* Brazil 206 C6
São Simão, Represa de *resr* Brazil 206 D5
Sao-Siu Indon. 75 C2
São Tiago Brazil 207 I7
São Tiago *i.* Cape Verde 124 [inset]

▶São Tomé São Tomé and Príncipe 125 G6
Capital of São Tomé and Príncipe.

São Tomé *i.* São Tomé and Príncipe 125 G6
São Tomé, Cabo de *c.* Brazil 203 D7
São Tomé, Pico de *mt.* São Tomé and Príncipe 125 G6
▶São Tomé and Príncipe *country* Africa 125 G6
africa [countries] ▶▶ 114–117
Saoura, Oued *watercourse* Alg. 123 E3
São Vicente Brazil 206 G10
São Vicente *i.* Cape Verde 124 [inset]
São Vicente, Cabo de *c.* Port. 54 C7
English form St Vincent, Cape
São Vicente Ferrer Brazil 202 C2
Sápai Greece *see* Sapes
Sapallanga Peru 200 B3
Sapanca Turkey 106 B2
Sapão *r.* Brazil 202 C4
Saparua Indon. 75 D3
Saparua *i.* Indon. 75 D3
Sape, Selat *sea chan.* Indon. 75 A5
Sape, Teluk *b.* Indon. 77 G5
Sapele Nigeria 125 G5
Sapes Greece 58 G7
also known as Sápai
Şaphane Turkey 59 K9
Sapientza *i.* Greece 59 C12
Sapo, Serranía del *mts* Panama 186 D6
Sa Pobla Spain 55 O5
also spelt La Puebla
Sapo National Park Liberia 124 C5
Sapopema Brazil 206 C10
Sapotskin Belarus 42 E8
Sapouy Burkina 125 E4
Sapozhok Rus. Fed. 41 G5
Sappa Creek *r.* U.S.A. 178 C3
Sapporo Japan 90 G3
Saptamukhi *r.* India 97 F5
Sapucaí *r. Minas Gerais* Brazil 207 H8
Sapucaí *r. São Paulo* Brazil 206 E7
Sapucaia Brazil 199 G5
Sapudi *i.* Indon. 77 F4
Sapulpa U.S.A. 179 C4
Sapulut *Sabah* Malaysia 77 G1
Sāq, Jabal *hill* Saudi Arabia 104 C2
Saqi Iran 101 D3
Saqqaq Greenland 165 N2
Saqqez Iran 100 A2
Sara Bangl. 97 F4
Sarā Iran 100 A2
Sarāb Iran 100 A2
Sarabit el Khâdim *tourist site* Egypt 108 E8
Sara Buri Thai. 79 C5
Saracá, Lago *l.* Brazil 199 G5
Saraf Dougous Chad 120 C6
Saragossa Spain *see* Zaragoza
Saraguro Ecuador 198 B5
Saraikela India 97 E5
Sarai Sidhu Pak. 101 H4
Sărăisniemi Fin. 44 N2

▶Sarajevo Bos.-Herz. 56 K5
Capital of Bosnia-Herzegovina. Historically known as Bosna Saray.

Sarakhs Turkm. 102 E5
Sarakiniko, Akra *pt* Greece 59 E10
Sarakino *i.* Greece 59 F10
Saraktash Rus. Fed. 102 D2
Saraland U.S.A. 175 B6
Saralzhin Kazakh. 102 C2
Saramati *mt.* India/Myanmar 97 G4
Saramerіza Peru 198 B6
Saran' France 51 H5
Saran' Kazakh. 103 H2
Saran, Gunung *mt.* Indon. 77 E3
Saranac *r.* U.S.A. 177 L1
Saranac Lake U.S.A. 177 K1
Sarandë Albania 59 B9
Sarandi *Paraná* Brazil 206 B10
Sarandi *Rio Grande do Sul* Brazil 203 A8
Sarandib *country* Asia *see* Sri Lanka
Sarandi del Yi Uruguay 204 G4
Sarandi Grande Uruguay 204 F4
Sarangani *i.* Phil. 74 C5
Sarangani Bay Phil. 74 C5
Sarangani Islands Phil. 74 C5
Sarangani Strait Phil. 74 C5
Sarangarh India 97 D5
Sarangpur India 96 C5
Saransk Rus. Fed. 41 H5
Sara Peak Nigeria 125 H4
Sarapul Rus. Fed. 40 J4
Sarasota U.S.A. 175 D7
Saraswati *r.* India 96 A5
Sărata *r.* Moldova 58 J2
Sărata *r.* Romania 58 H4
Sarata Ukr. 41 D7
Sarata *r.* Ukr. 58 K3
Saratoga *CA* U.S.A. 182 B4
Saratoga *WY* U.S.A. 180 F4
Saratoga Springs U.S.A. 177 L2
Saratok *Sarawak* Malaysia 77 E2
Saratov Rus. Fed. 41 H6
Saratov Oblast *admin. div.* Rus. Fed. *see* Saratovskaya Oblast'
Saratovskaya Oblast' *admin. div.* Rus. Fed. 102 A2
English form Saratov Oblast
Saratovskoye Vodokhranilishche *resr* Rus. Fed. 102 A1
Saravan Iran 101 E5
Saravan Laos 79 D5
Sarawa *r.* Myanmar 79 B5
Sarawak *state* Malaysia 77 E2
Saray Turkey 106 A2
Saraya Guinea 124 C4
Saraya Senegal 124 C3
Saraya, Pulau *reg.* Sing. 76 [inset]
Saraycık Turkey 59 K10
Sarayköy Turkey 106 B3
Saraylar Turkey 58 I8
Sarayönü Turkey 106 C3
Sarbāz Iran 101 E5
Sarbāz *r.* Iran 101 E5
Sarbāz *reg.* Iran 101 E5
Sârbeni Romania 58 G4
Sarbhang Bhutan 97 F4
Sarbisheh Iran 101 D3
Sárbogárd Hungary 49 P9
Sarbulak China 84 A2
Sarcham Iran 100 B2
Sarco Chile 204 C3
Sarda *r.* India/Nepal 99 K4
Sardab Pass Afgh. 101 G2
Sardarpur India 96 B5
Sardarshahr India 96 B3
Sar Dasht Iran 100 A2
Sardasht *Būshehr* Iran 100 B4
Sardasht *Khūzestān* Iran 100 B3
Sardegna *admin. reg.* Italy 57 B8
Sardegna *i.* Italy *see* Sardinia
Sardica Bulg. *see* Sofia
Sardinata Col. 198 C2
Sardinia Costa Rica 186 B5
Sardinia *i.* Italy 57 A8
also spelt Sardegna
Sardis U.S.A. 174 B5
Sardis Lake *resr* U.S.A. 174 B5
Sardoal Port. 54 C5
Sareb, Rās-as- *pt* U.A.E. 105 E2
Sareks nationalpark *nat. park* Sweden 44 L2
Sarektjåkkå *mt.* Sweden 44 L2
Sarempaka, Gunung *mt.* Indon. 77 F3
Sar-e Pol Afgh. 101 F2
Sar-e Pol *prov.* Afgh. 101 F2
Sar Eskandar Iran *see* Hashtrud
Sare Yazd Iran 100 C4
Sarezskoye Ozero *l.* Tajik. *see* Sarez, Kŭli
Sarez, Kŭli *l.* Tajik. 101 H2
also known as Sarezskoye Ozero
Sargasso Sea Europe 216 J4
Sargentu Loros Peru 198 C5
Sargodha Pak. 101 H3
Sarh Chad 126 C2
formerly known as Fort Archambault
Sarhad *reg.* Iran 101 E4
Sarhro, Jbel *mt.* Morocco 122 D3
Sārī Iran 100 C2
Saria *i.* Greece 59 I13
Sar-i-Bum Afgh. 101 F3
Sáric Mex. 184 C2
Sarichioi Romania 58 J4
Sarigan *i.* N. Mariana Is 73 K3
Sarıgöl Turkey 106 B3
Sarıkamış Turkey 107 E2
Sarikei *Sarawak* Malaysia 77 E2
Sarıkemer Turkey 59 I11
Sarıköy Turkey 59 I8
Sarikŭl, Qatorkŭhi *mts* China/Tajik. *see* Sarykol Range
Sarila India 96 C4
Sarimbun Reservoir Sing. 76 [inset]
Sarina Australia 149 F4
Sariñena Spain 55 K3
Sarıoğlan Turkey *see* Belören
Sar-i Pīrān *mt.* Iraq 100 A2
Sar-i-Pul Afgh. 101 F3
Sārī Qamish Iran 100 C2
Sariqamish Kuli *salt l.* Turkm./Uzbek. *see* Sarykamyshkoye Ozero
Sarīr Tibesti *des.* Libya 120 C4
Sarir Water Wells Field Libya 120 D3
Sarishabari Bangl. 97 F4
Sarita U.S.A. 179 C7
Sarıveliler Turkey 108 D1
Sariwŏn N. Korea 83 B5
Sarıyer Turkey 106 B2
Sarız Turkey 107 D3
Sark *i.* Channel Is 50 D3
Sarkad Hungary 49 S9
Sarkand Kazakh. 103 I3
also spelt Sarqant
Sarkari Tala India 96 A4
Şarkikaraağaç Turkey 106 B3
Sărkisalo Fin. 42 D1
Şarkışla Turkey 107 D3
Şarkör *watercourse* Iran 101 E5
Şarköy Turkey 106 A2
Sarlath Range *mts* Afgh./Pak. 101 F4
Sarlat-la-Canéda France 50 H8
Sarmanovo Rus. Fed. 40 J5
Sărmaşag Romania 58 D1
Sărmaşu Romania 58 F2
Sarmente *r.* Italy 57 I8
Sarmi Indon. 73 I7
Sarmiento Arg. 205 C7
Särna Sweden 45 K3
Sarnate Latvia 42 C4
Sarneh Iran 100 A3
Sarnen Switz. 51 O6
Sarni India *see* Amla
Sarnia Canada 168 D5
Sarny Ukr. 41 C6
Sarolangun Indon. 76 C3
Saronikos Kolpos *g.* Greece 59 E11
Saros Körfezi *b.* Turkey 106 A2
Sárospatak Hungary 49 S7
Sarotra India 96 B4
Sarova Rus. Fed. 40 G5
Sarowbī Afgh. 101 G3
Sarpa, Ozero *l.* Rus. Fed. 41 H7
Sarpan *i.* N. Mariana Is *see* Rota
Šar Planina *mts* Macedonia/Yugo. 58 B7
Sarpsborg Norway 45 J4
Sarqant Kazakh. *see* Sarkand
Sarre *r.* France 51 N3
Sarrebourg France 51 N4
Sarreguemines France 51 N3
Sarre-Union France 51 N4
Sarria Spain 54 D2
Sarrión Spain 55 K4
Sarro Mali 124 D3
Sarroch *Sardegna* Italy 57 B9
Sars Rus. Fed. 40 K4
Sartana Ukr. 41 F7
formerly known as Prymors'ke
Sartène *Corse* France 56 A7
Sarthe *r.* France 50 F5
Sarti Greece 59 E8
Sartininkai Lith. 42 C6
Sartu China *see* Daqing
Sarud, Rūdkhāneh-ye *r.* Iran 100 B3
Saruhanlı Turkey 59 I10
Saruna *r.* Pak. 101 F5
Sarupsar India 96 B3
Şärur Azer. 107 F3
also spelt Sharur; *formerly known as* Il'ichevsk
Saru Tara *tourist site* Afgh. 101 E4
Sarvābād Iran 100 A3
Sarvani Georgia *see* Marneuli
Sárvár Hungary 49 N8
Sarvestān Iran 100 C4
Sárvíz *r.* Romania 49 P9
Sarwar India 96 B4
Sarya *r.* India 94 B2
Saryagach Kazakh. 103 G4
Sary-Bulak Kyrg. 103 H4
Sarydhaz *r.* Kyrg. *see* Sary-Jaz
Sarydzhas Kazakh. *see* Saryzhaz
Sarygamysh Köli *salt l.* Turkm./Uzbek. *see* Sarykamyshkoye Ozero
Sary-Ishikotrau, Peski *des.* Kazakh. *see* Saryyesik-Atyrau, Peski
Sary-Jaz *r.* Kyrg. 103 I4
also spelt Sarydhaz
Sarykamys Kazakh. 102 C3
also spelt Saryqamys
Sarykamyshkoye Ozero *salt l.* Turkm./Uzbek. 102 D4
also known as Sariqamish Kuli or Sarygamysh Köli
Sarykemer Kazakh. 103 G4
formerly known as Mikhaylovka
Sarykiyak Kazakh. 103 H2
Sarykol Range *mts* China/Tajik. 88 A4
also known as Sarikŭl, Qatorkŭhi
Sarymoyyn, Ozero *salt l.* Kazakh. 103 F2
Saryozek Kazakh. 103 I3
Saryqamys Kazakh. *see* Sarykamys
Saryshagan Kazakh. 103 H3
Sarysu *watercourse* Kazakh. 103 F3
formerly known as Zhaksy Sarysu
Sary-Tash Kyrg. 103 H5
Saryter, Gora *mt.* Kyrg. 103 I4
Sarыumir Kazakh. 102 B2
Sary Yazikskoye Vodokhranilishche *resr* Turkm. 103 E5
Saryyesik-Atyrau, Peski *des.* Kazakh. 103 H3
formerly known as Sary-Ishikotrau, Peski
Saryzhal Kazakh. *see* Sarzhal
Saryzhaz Kazakh. 103 I4
also spelt Sarydzhas
Sarzana Italy 56 B4
Sarzeau France 50 D5
Sarzhal Kazakh. 103 I2
also spelt Saryzhal
Sasak Indon. 76 B2
Sasar, Tanjung *pt* Indon. 75 A5
Sasaram India 97 E4
Sásd Hungary 49 P9
Sasebo Japan 91 A8
Saskatchewan *prov.* Canada 167 J4
Saskatchewan *r.* Canada 167 K4
Saskatoon Canada 167 J4
Saskylakh Rus. Fed. 39 L2
Saslaya *mt.* Nicaragua 186 B4
Saslaya, Parque Nacional *nat. park* Nicaragua 186 B4
Sasnovy Bor Belarus 43 K9
also spelt Sosnovyy Bor; *formerly known as* Golyashi
Sasolburg S. Africa 133 L3
Sasovo Rus. Fed. 41 G5
Sass *r.* Canada 167 H2
Sassandra Côte d'Ivoire 124 D5
Sassandra *r.* Côte d'Ivoire 124 D5
Sassari *Sardegna* Italy 57 A8
Sassnitz Germany 49 K1
Sassoferrato Italy 56 E5
historically known as Sentinum
Sasso Marconi Italy 56 D4
Sass Rigais *mt.* Italy 56 D2
Sass Town Liberia 124 C5
Sassuolo Italy 56 C4
Sastobe Kazakh. 103 G4
also spelt Saztöbe
Sastre Arg. 204 E3
Sasvad India 94 B2
Sasykkol', Ozero *l.* Kazakh. 103 J3
also known as Sasyqköl
Sasyqköl *l.* Kazakh. *see* Sasykkol', Ozero
Satadougou Mali 124 C3
Satahual *i.* Micronesia *see* Satawal
Sata-misaki *c.* Japan 91 B9
Satana India 94 B1
Satara India 94 B2
Satara S. Africa 131 F5
Satawal *i.* Micronesia 73 K5
also spelt Satahual
Sātbaev Kazakh. *see* Satpayev
Satchinez Romania 58 C3
Satéma Cent. Afr. Rep. 126 D3
Satengar *i.* Indon. 77 G4
Säter Sweden 45 K3
Satevó Mex. 184 D3
Saticoy U.S.A. 182 E7
Satihaure *l.* Sweden 44 L2
Satilla *r.* U.S.A. 175 D6
Satipo Peru 200 B2
Satiri Burkina 124 D4
Satırlar Turkey *see* Yeşilova
Satka Rus. Fed. 38 F4
Satkania Bangl. 97 G5
Satkhira Bangl. 97 F5
Satluj *r.* India/Pak. *see* Sutlej
Satmala Range *hills* India 94 C2
Satna India 96 D4
Sátoraljaújhely Hungary 49 S7
Satorina *mt.* Croatia 56 H4
Satpayev Kazakh. 103 F3
also spelt Sātbaev; *formerly known as* Nikol'skiy
Satpura Range *mts* India 96 B5
Šatrijos kalnis *hill* Lith. 42 D6
Satsuma-hantō *pen.* Japan 91 B9
Satsunai-gawa *r.* Japan 90 H3
Sattahip Thai. 79 C5
Sattanen Fin. 44 N2
Sattenapalle India 94 D2
Satthwa Myanmar 78 A4
Satti Jammu and Kashmir 96 C2
Satu Mare Romania 53 G2
Satun Thai. 79 C7
Satwas India 96 C5
Saubi *i.* Indon. 77 F4
Sauce Arg. 204 F3
Sauceda Mountains U.S.A. 183 L9
Sauce de Luna Arg. 204 F3
Saucillo Mex. 184 D2
Sauda Norway 45 I4
Saudakent Kazakh. 103 G4
formerly known as Baykadam *or* Bayqadam
Sauðárkrókur Iceland 44 [inset] C2
▶Saudi Arabia *country* Asia 104 C3
known as Al 'Arabiyah as Sa'ūdīyah in Arabic
asia [landscapes] ▶▶ 62–63
asia [countries] ▶▶ 64–67
Saue Estonia 42 F2
Sauêruiná *r.* Brazil 201 F3
also known as Papagaio
Saug *r.* Phil. 74 C5
Saughān Afgh. 101 F3
Saugas *r.* Estonia 42 F3
Saugeen *r.* Canada 168 D4
Saugerties U.S.A. 177 L3
Saugues France 51 J8
Sāūjbolāgh Iran *see* Mahābād
Saujil Arg. 204 D2
Saujon France 50 F7
Saukas ezers *l.* Latvia 42 G5
Sauk Center U.S.A. 178 D2
Sauk City U.S.A. 172 D7
Saul Fr. Guiana 199 H4
Sauland Norway 45 J4
Sauldre *r.* France 51 H5
Saulgau Germany 48 G7
Saulieu France 51 K5
Saulkrasti Latvia 42 F4
Sault Sainte Marie Canada 168 C4
Sault Ste Marie U.S.A. 173 I4
Saumalkol' Kazakh. 103 G1
formerly known as Volodarskoye
Saumarez Reef Australia 149 G4
Saumlakki Indon. 73 H8
Saumur France 50 F5
Saunavaara Fin. 44 N2
Saunders, Mount *hill* Australia 148 A2
Saunders Coast Antarctica 222 O1
Saunders Island Falkland Is 205 E8
Saunemin U.S.A. 172 E10
Saungka Myanmar 78 B2
Sauquoit U.S.A. 177 J2
Saur, Khrebet *mts* China/Kazakh. 88 D2
Saurieši Latvia 42 F5
Saurimo Angola 127 D7
formerly known as Henrique de Carvalho
Sausalito U.S.A. 182 B4
Sausar India 96 C5
Sautar Angola 127 C7
Sava *r.* Europe 49 M9
Savá Hond. 186 B4
Sava Italy 57 J8
Savage U.S.A. 177 I6
Savage River Australia 147 E5
Savai'i *i.* Samoa 145 H3
historically known as Chatham Island
Savala *r.* Rus. Fed. 41 G6
Savalou Benin 125 F5
Savanat Iran *see* Eştahbān
Savane *r.* Canada 169 G3
Savane Moz. 131 G3
Savanna U.S.A. 174 B3
Savannah *GA* U.S.A. 175 D5
Savannah *MO* U.S.A. 178 D4
Savannah *OH* U.S.A. 176 C5
Savannah *TN* U.S.A. 174 B5
Savannah *r.* U.S.A. 175 D5
Savannah Sound Bahamas 186 D1
Savannakhét Laos 78 D4
Savanna-la-Mar Jamaica 186 D3
Savanne Canada 172 C2
Savant Lake Canada 168 B3
Savantvadi India *see* Vadi
Savanur India 94 B3
Sävar Sweden 44 M3
Săvârşin Romania 58 D2
Sävast Sweden 44 M2
Savaştepe Turkey 106 A3
Savè Benin 125 F4
Save *r.* France 50 H9
Save Moz. 131 G4
Save *r.* Moz./Zimbabwe 131 G4
formerly spelt Sabi
Sāveh Iran 100 B3
Savelugu Ghana 125 E4
Savenay France 50 E5
Saveretik Guyana 199 G3
Saverne France 51 N4
Savigliano Italy 51 N8
Săvineşti Romania 58 H2
Savinja *r.* Slovenia 56 H2
Savino Rus. Fed. 40 G4
Savinskiy Rus. Fed. 40 G3
Savinskoye Rus. Fed. 43 U6
Savio *r.* Italy 56 E4
Savitaipale Fin. 45 N3
Savitri *r.* India 94 B2
Sävja Sweden 45 L4
Šavnik *Crna Gora* Yugo. 58 A6
Savoie *reg.* France *see* Savoy
Savona Italy 56 A4
Savonlinna Fin. 45 O3
Savonranta Fin. 44 O3
Savoonga U.S.A. 164 B3
Savoy *reg.* France 51 M6
also spelt Savoie
Savozero, Ozero *l.* Rus. Fed. 43 O1
Şavşat Turkey 107 E2
Sävsjö Sweden 45 K4
Savu *i.* Indon. 75 B5
also spelt Sawu
Savudrija, Rt *pt* Croatia 56 F3
Savukoski Fin. 44 O2
Savur Turkey 107 E3
Savute *r.* Botswana 130 E3
Savuti Botswana 131 E3
Saw Myanmar 78 A3
Şawāb, Wādī aş *watercourse* Iraq 109 K4
Şawāb, Wādī aş *watercourse* Syria 109 L3
Sawahlunto Indon. 76 C3
Sawai, Teluk *b.* Indon. 75 D3
Sawai Madhopur India 96 C4
Sawan Indon. 77 F3
Sawan Myanmar 78 B2
Sawankhalok Thai. 78 B4
also known as Wang Mai Khon
Sawar India 96 B4
Sawara Japan 91 G7
Sawasaki-bana *pt* Japan 90 F6
Sawata Japan 90 F6
Sawatch Range *mts* U.S.A. 180 F5
Sawdā', Jabal as *hills* Libya 120 B2
Sawi, Ao *b.* Thai. 79 B6
Sawi Egypt 108 C8
Sawla Ghana 124 E4
Sawmills Zimbabwe 131 F3
Sawn China 86 A4
Şawqirah, Dawḩat *b.* Oman 105 G4
English form Şawqirah Bay
Şawqirah, Ra's *c.* Oman 105 G4
Şawqirah Bay Oman *see* Şawqirah, Dawḩat
Sawtell Australia 147 G2
Sawtooth Mountains *hills* U.S.A. 174 B2
Sawtooth Range *mts ID* U.S.A. 180 D3
Sawtooth Range *mts WA* U.S.A. 180 B2
Sawu Indon. 75 B5
Sawu *i.* Indon. *see* Savu
Sawu Sea Indon. 75 B5
Saxby *r.* Australia 149 D3
Saxnäs Sweden 44 K2
Saxony *land* Germany *see* Sachsen
Saxony-Anhalt *land* Germany *see* Sachsen-Anhalt
Saxton *KY* U.S.A. 176 A9
Saxton *PA* U.S.A. 176 G5
Say Mali 124 D3
Say Niger 125 F3
Sayabouri Laos *see* Muang Xaignabouri
Sayafi *i.* Indon. 75 D2
Sayak Kazakh. 103 I3
also spelt Sayaq
Sayalkudi India 94 C4
Sayam *well* Niger 125 I3
Sayán Peru 200 A2
Sayang *i.* Indon. 75 D2
Sayano-Shushenskoye Vodokhranilishche *resr* Rus. Fed. 80 E2
Sayaq Kazakh. *see* Sayak
Sayat Turkm. 103 E5
also spelt Sayot; *formerly spelt* Sayyod
Sayda Lebanon *see* Sidon
Sāyen Iran 100 C4
Sayer Island Thai. 79 B6
Sayghān Afgh. 101 G3
Sayḩ *well* Yemen 104 D4
Sayḩ al Aḩmar *reg.* Oman 105 G3
Sayḩūt Yemen 105 E5
Sayingpan China 86 B3
Saykhin Kazakh. 102 A2
also spelt Sayqyn
Sāylac Somalia 128 D2
Saylan *country* Asia *see* Sri Lanka
Saynshand Mongolia 85 F2
Sayn-Ust Mongolia 84 B2
Say-Ötesh Kazakh. *see* Say-Utes
Şayqal, Baḩr *imp. l.* Syria 109 I4
Sayqyn Kazakh. *see* Saykhin
Sayram Hu *salt l.* China 88 C2

Sayramskiy, Pik mt. Uzbek. 103 G4
Sayre OK U.S.A. 179 C5
Sayre PA U.S.A. 177 I4
Sayreville U.S.A. 177 K5
Sayula Jalisco Mex. 184 E5
Sayula Veracruz Mex. 185 G5
Say'ūn Yemen 105 E4
Say-Utes Kazakh. 102 C3
also spelt Say-Ötesh
Sayward Canada 166 E5
Sayy well Oman 105 G4
Sayyod Turkm. see Sayat
Sazan i. Albania 58 A8
Sázava r. Czech Rep. 49 L6
Sazonovo Rus. Fed. 43 Q2
Saztöbe Kazakh. see Sastobe
Sbaa Alg. 123 E3
Sbeitla Tunisia 123 H2
Sbiba Tunisia 57 B13
Scaddan Australia 151 C7
Scaër France 50 C4
Scafell Pike hill U.K. 47 I9
Scalea Italy 57 H9
Scaletta Zanclea Sicilia Italy 57 H10
Scalloway U.K. 46 K3
Scalpaigh, Eilean i. U.K. see Scalpay
Scalpay i. U.K. 46 F6
also known as Scalpaigh, Eilean
Scandicci Italy 56 D5
Scansano Italy 56 D6
Scânteia Romania 58 I4
Scanzano Jonico Italy 57 I8
Scapa Flow inlet U.K. 46 I5
Scarba i. U.K. 46 G7
Scarborough Canada 168 E5
Scarborough Trin. and Tob. 187 H5
Scarborough U.K. 47 L9
Scarborough Shoal sea feature S. China Sea 73 E3
Scargill N.Z. 153 G10
Scarinish U.K. 46 F7
Scarp i. U.K. 46 E5
Scarpanto i. Greece see Karpathos
Scaterie Island Canada 169 J4
Scawfell Shoal sea feature S. China Sea 77 D1
Sceale Bay Australia 146 B3
Šćedro i. Croatia 56 I5
Schaale r. Germany 48 H2
Schaalsee l. Germany 48 H2
Schaalsee park Germany 48 H2
Schaffhausen Switz. 51 O5
Schagen Neth. 48 B3
Schakalskuppe Namibia 130 C5
Schao watercourse Afgh./Iran 101 E4
Scharbeutz Germany 48 H1
Schärding Austria 49 K7
Scharhörn sea feature Germany 48 F2
Schaumburg U.S.A. 172 E8
Scheeßel Germany 48 G2
Schefferville Canada 169 H2
formerly known as Knob Lake
Scheibbs Austria 49 M7
Schell Creek Range mts U.S.A. 183 J3
Schellsburg U.S.A. 176 G5
Schellville U.S.A. 182 B3
Schenectady U.S.A. 177 L3
Schenefeld Germany 48 G2
Schertz U.S.A. 179 C6
Schesaplana mt. Austria/Switz. 51 P5
Scheßlitz Germany 48 I6
Schierling Germany 48 J7
Schiermonnikoog i. Neth. 48 D2
Schiermonnikoog Nationaal Park nat. park Neth. 48 D2
Schiers Switz. 51 P6
Schimatari Greece 59 E10
also known as Skhimatárion
Schio Italy 56 D3
Schirmeck France 51 N4
Schitu Duca Romania 58 I1
Schiza i. Greece 59 C12
also spelt Skhiza
Schkeuditz Germany 49 J4
Schladen Germany 48 H3
Schladming Austria 49 K8
Schlei r. Germany 48 H1
Schleiz Germany 48 I5
Schleswig Germany 48 G1
Schleswig-Holstein land Germany 48 G1
Schleswig-Holsteinisches Wattenmeer, Nationalpark nat. park Germany 48 F1
Schlosshof tourist site Austria 49 N7
Schloß Holte-Stukenbrock Germany 48 F4
Schluchsee Germany 48 F8
Schlüchtern Germany 48 G5
Schlüsselburg Rus. Fed. see Shlissel'burg
Schmallenberg Germany 48 F4
Schmidt Island Rus. Fed. see Shmidta, Ostrov
Schmidt Peninsula Rus. Fed. see Shmidta, Poluostrov
Schmidtsdrif S. Africa 132 I5
Schneidemühl Poland see Piła
Schneverdingen Germany 48 G2
Schoemanskloof pass S. Africa 133 O2
Schoharie U.S.A. 177 K3
Schokland tourist site Neth. 48 C3
Schombee S. Africa 133 J8
Schönebeck (Elbe) Germany 48 I3
Schönefeld airport Germany 49 K3
Schöningen Germany 48 H3
Schoodic Point U.S.A. 177 R1
Schoolcraft U.S.A. 172 H8
Schoonhoven Neth. 48 B4
Schöpfl hill Austria 49 M7
Schorfheide reg. Germany 49 K3
Schouten Island Australia 147 F5
Schouten Islands P.N.G. 73 J7
Schrankogel mt. Austria 48 I8
Schreiber Canada 168 C3
Schrems Austria 49 M7
Schrobenhausen Germany 48 I7
Schroon Lake U.S.A. 177 L2
Schröttersburg Poland see Płock
Schulenburg U.S.A. 179 C6
Schull Rep. of Ireland 47 C12
Schultz Lake Canada 167 L1
Schuyler U.S.A. 178 C3
Schuyler Lake U.S.A. 177 J3
Schuylerville U.S.A. 177 L2
Schuylkill Haven U.S.A. 177 I5
Schwaan Germany 49 J2
Schwabach Germany 48 I6
Schwäbische Alb mts Germany 48 F8
Schwäbisch-Fränkischer Wald, Naturpark nature res. Germany 48 G7
Schwäbisch Hall Germany 48 G6
Schwabmünchen Germany 48 H7
Schwalm r. Germany 51 P1
Schwanden Switz. 51 P5
Schwandorf Germany 48 J6
Schwaner, Pegunungan mts Indon. 77 F3
Schwangau Germany 48 H8
Schwartz Range mts Antarctica 223 D2
Schwarzenbek Germany 48 H2
Schwarzenberg Germany 49 J5
Schwarzer Mann hill Germany 48 D5
Schwarzrand mts Namibia 130 C5
Schwarzwald mts Germany see Black Forest
Schwaz Austria 48 I8
Schwedeneck Germany 48 H1
Schwedt an der Oder Germany 49 L2
Schweinfurt Germany 48 H5
Schweiz country Europe see Switzerland
Schweizer-Reneke S. Africa 133 J4
Schwerin Germany 48 I2
Schweriner See l. Germany 48 I2
Schweriner Seenlandschaft park Germany 48 I2
Schwyz Switz. 51 O5
Sciacca Sicilia Italy 57 F11
Scicli Sicilia Italy 57 G12
Science Hill U.S.A. 176 A8
Scilla Italy 57 H10
Scilly, Île atoll Fr. Polynesia see Manuae
Scilly, Isles of U.K. 47 F14
Scio U.S.A. 176 D5
Scioto r. U.S.A. 176 C7
Scipio U.S.A. 183 L2
Scobey U.S.A. 180 F2
Scodra Albania see Shkodër
Scofield Reservoir U.S.A. 183 M2
Scone Australia 147 F3
Scordia Sicilia Italy 57 G11
Scoresby Land reg. Greenland 165 Q2
Scoresbysund Greenland see Ittoqqortoormiit
Scoresby Sund sea chan. Greenland see Kangertittivaq
Scorniceşti Romania 58 F4
Scorpion Bight b. Australia 151 D7
Scorzè Italy 56 E3
Scotia Sea S. Atlantic Ocean 217 K9
▶Scotland admin. div. U.K. 46 I6
historically known as Caledonia
europe [environments] 36–37
Scotland U.S.A. 177 I7
Scotstown Canada 169 G4
Scott, Cape Australia 148 A2
Scott, Cape Canada 166 D5
Scott, Mount hill U.S.A. 179 C5
Scott Base research station Antarctica 223 L1
Scottburgh S. Africa 133 O7
Scott City U.S.A. 178 B4
Scott Coast Antarctica 223 K1
Scott Glacier Antarctica 223 Q2
Scott Glacier Antarctica 223 N1
Scott Inlet Canada 165 L2
Scott Island Antarctica 223 L2
Scott Islands Canada 166 D5
Scott Mountains Antarctica 223 D2
Scott Reef Australia 150 C2
Scottsbluff U.S.A. 178 B3
Scottsboro U.S.A. 174 C5
Scottsburg U.S.A. 174 C4
Scottsdale Australia 147 E5
Scotts Head Dominica 187 H4
Scottsville KY U.S.A. 174 C4
Scottsville VA U.S.A. 176 G8
Scottville U.S.A. 172 G7
Scourie U.K. 46 G5
Scranton U.S.A. 177 J4
Scugog, Lake Canada 168 E4
Scunthorpe U.K. 47 L10
Scuol Switz. 51 Q6
Scupi Macedonia see Skopje
Scutari Albania see Shkodër
Scutari, Lake Albania/Yugo. 58 A6
also known as Shkodrës, Liqeni i or Skadarsko Jezero
Seaboard U.S.A. 176 H9
Seabrook, Lake salt flat Australia 151 B6
Seaca Romania 58 F4
Seaford U.K. 47 M13
Seaford U.S.A. 177 J7
Seaforth Canada 173 L7
Seahorse Bank sea feature Phil. 74 A4
also known as Routh Bank
Seal r. Canada 167 M3
Seal, Cape S. Africa 132 H11
Sea Lake Australia 147 D3
Seal Bay Antarctica 223 X2
Seal Cove Canada 169 J3
Seal Island U.S.A. 177 Q2
Seal Lake Canada 169 I2
Sealy U.S.A. 179 C6
Seaman U.S.A. 176 B7
Seaman Range mts U.S.A. 183 I4
Searcy U.S.A. 174 B5
Searles Lake U.S.A. 183 G6
Searsport U.S.A. 177 Q1
Seascale U.K. 47 I9
Seaside CA U.S.A. 182 C5
Seaside OR U.S.A. 180 B3
Seaside Park U.S.A. 177 K6
Seaton Glacier Antarctica 223 D2
Seattle U.S.A. 180 B3
Sea View S. Africa 133 J11
Seaview Range mts Australia 149 E3
Seaville U.S.A. 177 K6
Seaward Kaikoura Range mts N.Z. 153 H10
Seba Indon. 75 B5
Sebaco Nicaragua 186 B4
Sebago Lake U.S.A. 177 O2
Sebakwe Recreational Park Zimbabwe 127 F9
Sebangan, Teluk b. Indon. 77 F3
Sebangka i. Indon. 76 D2
Sebastea Turkey see Sivas
Sebastian U.S.A. 175 D7
Sebastián Vizcaíno, Bahía b. Mex. 184 B2
Sebasticook r. U.S.A. 177 P1
Sebastopol Ukr. see Sevastopol'
Sebastopol U.S.A. 182 B3
Sebatik i. Indon. 77 G1
Sebauh Sarawak Malaysia 77 F2
Sebayan, Bukit mt. Indon. 77 E3
Seba Burkina 125 F3
Sebderat Eritrea 121 H6
Sebdou Alg. 123 E2
Sébékoro Mali 124 C3
Seben Turkey 106 B2
Sebenico Croatia see Šibenik
Sebennytos Egypt see Samannūd
Sebeş Romania 58 E3
Sebeş r. Romania 58 E2
Sebewaing U.S.A. 173 J7
Sebezh Rus. Fed. 43 J5
Şebinkarahisar Turkey 107 D2
Sebiş Romania 58 D2
Sebisseb, Oued r. Alg. 55 O9
Sebla r. Rus. Fed. 43 S3
Seblat, Gunung mt. Indon. 76 C3
Sebrell U.S.A. 177 H9
Sebring U.S.A. 175 D7
Sebuku i. Indon. 77 G3
Sebuku r. Indon. 77 G1
Sebuku, Teluk b. Indon. 77 G2
Sečanj Vojvodina, Srbija Yugo. 58 B3
Secaş r. Romania 58 E2
Secas, Islas is Panama 186 C6
Secchia r. Italy 56 D3
Seccia Mountains Eth. 128 C3
Sechelt Canada 166 F5
Sechenovo Rus. Fed. 40 H5
Sechura Peru 198 A6
Sechura, Bahía de b. Peru 198 A6
Second Cataract rapids Sudan see 2nd Cataract
Second Mesa U.S.A. 183 N6
Second Three Mile Opening sea chan. Australia 149 D2
Secos, Ilhéus is Cape Verde 124 [inset]
also known as Rombo, Ilhéus do
Sečovce Slovakia 49 S7
Secretary Island N.Z. 153 A13
Secunda S. Africa 133 N3
Secunderabad India 94 C2
Sécure r. Bol. 200 D3
Seda Latvia 42 G4
Seda r. Latvia 42 G4
Seda Lith. 42 D5
Seda r. Port. 54 C6
Sedalia U.S.A. 178 D4
Sedam India 94 C2
Sedan France 51 K3
Sedan U.S.A. 178 C4
Sedan Dip Australia 149 D3
Seddon N.Z. 153 I9
Seddonville N.Z. 153 F9
Sedeh Fārs Iran 100 C4
Sedeh Khorāsan Iran 101 D3
Sedgefield U.S.A. 176 F9
Sedgewick Canada 167 I4
Sedgwick U.S.A. 177 Q1
Sédhiou Senegal 124 B3
Sedico Italy 56 E2
Sedlčany Czech Rep. 49 L6
Sedlets Poland see Siedlce
Sedom Israel 108 G6
Sedona U.S.A. 183 M7
Sédrata Alg. 123 G1
Šeduva Lith. 42 E6
Sędziszów Poland 49 R5
Seebad Heringsdorf Germany 49 L2
Seeberg pass Austria/Slovenia 49 L9
Seehausen (Altmark) Germany 48 I3
Seeheim Namibia 130 C5
Seeheim-Jugenheim Germany 48 F6
Seekoegat S. Africa 132 G10
Seekoei r. S. Africa 133 I7
Seekoeivlei Nature Reserve S. Africa 133 N4
Seela Pass Canada 166 B1
Seeley U.S.A. 183 I9
Seelig, Mount Antarctica 222 R1
Seelow Germany 49 L3
Seenu Atoll Maldives see Addu Atoll
Sées France 50 G4
Seesen Germany 48 H4
Seevetal Germany 48 H2
Sefadu Sierra Leone 124 C4
also known as Koidu
Seferihisar Turkey 59 H10
Sefid, Küh-e mt. Iran 100 B3
Sefid, Küh-e mts Iran 100 B4
Sefophe Botswana 131 E4
Segala Mali 124 C3
Segalstad Norway 45 J3
Segama r. Sabah Malaysia 77 G1
Segamat Malaysia 76 C2
Segangane Morocco 55 H9
Şegarcea Romania 58 E4
Ségbana Benin 125 F4
Segen Wenz watercourse Eth. 128 C3
Segera Tanz. 129 C6
Segezha Rus. Fed. 40 E3
Segguer, Oued watercourse Alg. 123 F2
Seghnān Afgh. 101 G2
Seghouane Alg. 55 N8
Segiz, Ozero salt l. Kazakh. 103 F3
Segontia U.K. see Caernarfon
Segontium U.K. see Caernarfon
Segonzac France 50 F7
Segorbe Spain 55 K5
Ségou Mali 124 D3
Ségou admin. reg. Mali 124 D3
Segovia Col. 198 C3
Segovia r. Hond./Nicaragua see Coco
Segovia Spain 54 G4
Segozerskoye, Ozero resr Rus. Fed. 40 E3
Segré France 50 F5
Segre r. Spain 55 L3
Séguédine Niger 125 I1
Séguéla Côte d'Ivoire 124 D5
Séguéla Mali 124 D3
formerly spelt Sagala
Séguénéga Burkina 125 E3
Seguin U.S.A. 179 C6
Segura r. Spain 55 K6
Segura, Sierra de mts Spain 55 I7
Sehithwa Botswana 130 D4
Sehlabathebe Lesotho 133 N6
Sehlabathebe National Park Lesotho 133 N6
Seho i. Indon. 75 C3
Sehore India 96 C5
Sehwan Pak. 101 F5
Seiche r. France 50 E5
Seignelay r. Canada 169 G3
Seikpyu Myanmar 78 A3
Seiland i. Norway 44 M1
Seiling U.S.A. 179 C4
Seille r. France 51 K6
Seille r. France 51 M3
Šeimena r. Lith. 42 D7
Sein, Île de i. France 50 B4
Seinäjoki Fin. 44 M3
Seine r. Canada 168 B3
Seine r. France 51 G3
Seine, Baie de b. France 50 F3
Seine, Sources de la tourist site France 51 K5
Seine, Val de valley France 51 J4
Seipinang Indon. 77 F3
Seistan reg. Iran see Sīstān
Seitsemisen kansallispuisto nat. park Fin. 45 M3
Seival Brazil 204 G3
Sejny Poland 49 U1
Sekadau Indon. 77 E2
Sekanak, Teluk b. Indon. 76 D3
Sekatak Bengara Indon. 77 G2
Sekayu Indon. 76 C3
Sekčov r. Slovakia 49 S7
Seke China see Sêrtar
Seke-Banza Dem. Rep. Congo 127 B6
Sekhukhune S. Africa 133 O1
Seki Japan 91 E7
Seki Turkey 108 A1
Seki r. Turkey 108 A1
Sekicau, Gunung vol. Indon. 76 D4
Sekoma Botswana 131 D5
Sekondi Ghana 125 E5
Sek'ot'a Eth. 128 C1
Sekseül Kazakh. see Saksaul'skiy
Seküheh Iran 101 E4
Şela Rus. Fed. see Shali
Şelagan r. Indon. 76 C3
Selah U.S.A. 180 B3
Selangor state Malaysia 76 C2
Selargius Sardegna Italy 57 B9
Selaru i. Indon. 73 H8
Selatan, Tanjung pt Indon. 77 F4
Selatpanjang Indon. 76 C2
Selawik U.S.A. 164 C3
Selbjørnsfjorden sea chan. Norway 46 Q4
Selbu Norway 44 J3
Selby U.K. 47 K10
Selby U.S.A. 178 B2
Selbyville U.S.A. 177 J7
Selçuk Turkey 59 I11
also known as Akıncılar
Sele r. Italy 57 G8
Selebi-Phikwe Botswana 131 E4
formerly spelt Selebi-Pikwe
Selebi-Pikwe Botswana see Selebi-Phikwe
Selečka Planina mts Macedonia 58 C7
Selemdzha r. Rus. Fed. 82 C1
Selemdzhinskiy Khrebet mts Rus. Fed. 82 D1
Selendi Turkey 59 J10
Selenduma Rus. Fed. 85 E1
▶Selenga r. Rus. Fed. 85 E1
Part of the Yenisey-Angara-Selenga, 3rd longest river in Asia.
asia [landscapes] 62–63
Selenge Dem. Rep. Congo 126 C5
Selenge Mongolia 84 D1
Selenge prov. Mongolia 85 E1
Selenge Mörön r. Mongolia 85 E1
Selenginsk Rus. Fed. 85 E1
Selenicë Albania 58 A8
Sélestat France 51 N4
Seletar Sing. 76 [inset]
Seletar, Pulau i. Sing. 76 [inset]
Seletar Reservoir Sing. 76 [inset]
Seletinskoye Kazakh. 103 H1
also known as Sileti
Selety r. Kazakh. see Sileti
Seletyteniz, Ozero salt l. Kazakh. see Siletiteniz, Ozero
Seleucia Turkey see Silifke
Seleucia Pieria Turkey see Samandağı
Seleznevo Rus. Fed. 43 J1
Selezni Rus. Fed. 43 M6
Selfoss Iceland 44 [inset] B3
Sel'gon Stantsiya Rus. Fed. 82 D2
Selib Rus. Fed. 40 I3
Sélibabi Mauritania 124 B3
Seligenstadt Germany 48 F5
Seliger, Ozero l. Rus. Fed. 43 O4
Seligman U.S.A. 183 L6
Selikhino Rus. Fed. 82 E2
Selima Oasis Sudan 121 F4
Selimiye Turkey 59 I11
Sélingué, Lac de l. Mali 124 C4
Selinnkegni Mali 124 C3
Selinous r. Greece 59 D10
Selinsgrove U.S.A. 177 I5
Selinunte tourist site Sicilia Italy 57 E11
Selishche Rus. Fed. 43 O5
Selishchi Rus. Fed. 41 G5
Selitrennoye Rus. Fed. 102 A3
Seliu i. Indon. 77 D3
Selizharovo Rus. Fed. 43 O5
Selje Norway 44 I3
Seljord Norway 45 J4
Selkirk Canada 167 L5
Selkirk U.K. 46 J8
Selkirk Mountains Canada 167 G4
Selkopp Norway 44 N1
Sellia Marina Italy 57 I10
Sellore Island Myanmar see Saganthit Kyun
Selma AL U.S.A. 175 C5
Selma CA U.S.A. 182 E5
Selmer U.S.A. 174 B5
Selmet Wielki, Jezioro l. Poland 49 T2
Selong Indon. 77 G5
Selongey France 51 L5
Selonsrivier S. Africa 133 N2
Sélouma Guinea 124 C4
Selous, Mount Canada 166 C2
Selous Game Reserve nature res. Tanz. 129 C7
Selseleh-ye Pīr Shūrān mts Iran 101 E4
Selsey Bill hd U.K. 47 L13
Sel'tso Bryanskaya Oblast' Rus. Fed. 43 P8
Sel'tso Bryanskaya Oblast' Rus. Fed. 43 P8
Selty Rus. Fed. 40 J4
Seluan i. Indon. 77 D1
Selukwe Zimbabwe see Shurugwi
Selvagens, Ilhas is Madeira 122 B3
Selvāna Iran 100 A2
Selvas reg. Brazil 199 D6
Selvíria Brazil 206 B7
Selway r. U.S.A. 180 D3
Selwyn Lake Canada 167 J2
Selwyn Mountains Canada 166 D1
Selwyn Range hills Australia 149 C4
Seman r. Albania 58 A8
Semangka, Teluk b. Indon. 76 D4
Semarang Indon. 77 E4
Sematan Sarawak Malaysia 77 E2
Semau i. Indon. 75 B5
Sembakung r. Indon. 77 G2
Sembawang Sing. 76 [inset]
Sembawang, Sungai r. Sing. 76 [inset]
Sembé Congo 126 B4
Şemdinli Turkey 107 F3
also known as Navşar
Semendire Srbija Yugo. see Smederevo
Semendua Dem. Rep. Congo 126 C5
Semendyayevo Rus. Fed. 43 T4
Semenic, Vârful mt. Romania 58 D3
Semenivka Ukr. 41 E5
also spelt Semenovka
Semenov Rus. Fed. 40 H4
Semenovka Ukr. see Semenivka
Semenovskoye Rus. Fed. 43 U3
Semeru, Gunung vol. Indon. 77 F5
Semey Kazakh. see Semipalatinsk
Semhar prov. Eritrea 104 B5
Semibratovo Rus. Fed. 43 U4
Semidi Islands U.S.A. 164 D4
Semigorodnyaya Rus. Fed. 43 V2
Semikarakorsk Rus. Fed. 41 G7
Semiluki Rus. Fed. 41 F6
Semily Czech Rep. 49 M5
Seminoe Reservoir U.S.A. 180 F4
Seminole U.S.A. 179 B5
Seminole, Lake U.S.A. 175 C6
Semiozernoye Kazakh. 103 F1
Semipalatinsk Kazakh. 103 J2
also known as Semey
Semirara i. Phil. 74 B3
Semirara Islands Phil. 74 B4
Semirom Iran 100 B4
Semitau Indon. 77 E2
Semiyarka Kazakh. 103 I2
Semizbuga Kazakh. 103 H2
also known as Semizbughy
Semizbughy Kazakh. see Semizbuga
Semkhoz Rus. Fed. 43 T5
Sem Kolodezey Ukr. see Lenine
Semlac Romania 58 B2
Semlevo Smolenskaya Oblast' Rus. Fed. 43 O6
Semlevo Smolenskaya Oblast' Rus. Fed. 43 O6
Semnān Iran 100 C3
Semnān prov. Iran 100 B3
Sêmnyi China 84 D4
Semois r. Belgium 51 K3
Semonkong Lesotho 133 M6
Sempach Switz. 51 O5
Semporna Sabah Malaysia 77 G1
Sempu i. Indon. 77 F5
Sem Tripa Brazil 199 H6
Semtsy Rus. Fed. 43 O9
Semyonovskoye Rus. Fed. see Bereznik
Semyonovskoye Rus. Fed. see Ostrovskoye
Sên, Stœng r. Cambodia 79 D5
Sena Bol. 200 D2
Senador Canedo Brazil 206 D3
Senador Pompeu Brazil 202 E3
Senafe Eritrea 104 B5
Senaki Georgia 107 E2
formerly known as Mikha Tskhakaia or Tskhakaia
Sena Madureira Brazil 200 C2
Senanayake Samudra l. Sri Lanka 94 D5
Senanga Zambia 127 D9
Sénas France 51 L9
Senatobia U.S.A. 174 B5
Sendai Kagoshima Japan 91 B9
Sendai Miyagi Japan 90 G5
Sendai-wan b. Japan 90 G5
Sendelingsfontein S. Africa 133 K3
Senden Germany 48 H7
Sendhwa India 96 B5
Senduruhan Indon. 77 E3
Sêndo China see Chido
Sendurjana India 96 C5
Sêndo China see Chido
Senebui, Tanjung pt Indon. 76 C2
Seneca IL U.S.A. 172 E9
Seneca KS U.S.A. 178 C4
Seneca OR U.S.A. 180 C3
Seneca PA U.S.A. 176 F4
Seneca Lake U.S.A. 177 I3
Seneca Rocks U.S.A. 176 F7
Senecaville Lake U.S.A. 176 D6
▶Senegal country Africa 124 B3
world [countries] 10–11
africa [countries] 114–117
Sénégal r. Mauritania/Senegal 124 A2
Seneka, Mys hd Rus. Fed. 82 E1
Senekal S. Africa 133 L5
Seney National Wildlife Refuge nature res. U.S.A. 172 G4
Senftenberg Germany 49 L4
Senga Malawi 129 B8
Senga Hill Zambia 127 F7
Sengar r. India 96 C4
Sengata Indon. 77 G2
Sengerema Tanz. 128 B5
Sengés Brazil 206 D11
Sengeyskiy, Ostrov i. Rus. Fed. 40 I1
Sengiley Rus. Fed. 41 I5
Sengirli, Mys pt Kazakh. see Syngyrli, Mys
Sengirli, Mys pt Kazakh. 102 C4
also spelt Syngyrli, Mys
Sêngli Co l. China 89 D6
Senguerr r. Arg. 205 C7
Sengwa r. Zimbabwe 131 F3
Senhit prov. Eritrea 104 B5
Senhor do Bonfim Brazil 202 D4
Senica Slovakia 49 O7
Senigallia Italy 56 F5
Senj Croatia 56 G4
Senja i. Norway 44 L1
Senjehopen Norway 44 L1
Şenkaya Turkey 107 E2
also known as Örtülü
Senko Guinea 124 C4
Senkobo Zambia 127 E9
Sen'kove Ukr. 41 F6
Sen'kovo Rus. Fed. 43 L6
Şenköy Turkey 108 H1
Senku Jammu and Kashmir 96 C2
Senlac S. Africa 132 H2
Senlin Shan mt. China 82 C4
Senlis France 51 I3
Senmonorom Cambodia 79 D5
Sennar Sudan 121 G6
Sennar state Sudan 121 G6
Senneterre Canada 168 E3
Senno Belarus see Syanno
Senonches France 50 H4
Senorbì Sardegna Italy 57 B9
Senqu r. Lesotho 133 L7
Sens France 51 J4
Sensuntepeque El Salvador 185 H6
Senta Vojvodina, Srbija Yugo. 58 B3
also spelt Zenta
Sentinel Peak Canada 166 F4
Sentinel Range mts Antarctica 222 S1
Sentinum Italy see Sassoferrato
Sentosa i. Sing. 76 [inset]
formerly known as Blakang Mati, Pulau
Şenyurt Turkey 107 E3
also known as Derbesiye
Seo de Urgell Spain see La Seu d'Urgell
Seonath r. India 97 D5
Seondha India 96 C4
Seoni India 96 C5
Seoni Chhapara India 96 C5
Seoni-Malwa India 96 C5
▶Seoul S. Korea 83 B5
Capital of South Korea. Also spelt Sŏul.
world [cities] 24–25
Séoune r. France 50 G8
Sepanjang i. Indon. 77 F4
Separation Point N.Z. 152 G8
Separation Well Australia 150 C4
Separ Shāhābād Iran 100 A3
Sepasu Indon. 77 G2
Sepatini r. Brazil 200 D1
Sepetiba, Baía de b. Brazil 207 I10
Sepik r. P.N.G. 73 J7
Sepinang Indon. 77 G2
Sepino Italy 56 G7
Sep'o N. Korea 83 B5
Sępólno Krajeńskie Poland 49 O2
Sepotuba r. Brazil 201 F3
Seppa India 97 G4
Şepreuş Romania 58 C2
Septèmes-les-Vallons France 51 L9
Sept-Îles Canada 169 H3
also known as Seven Islands
Sept-Îles-Port-Cartier, Réserve Faunique de nature res. Canada 169 H3
Sepupa Botswana 130 D3
Seputih r. Indon. 77 D4
Sequillo r. Spain 54 F3
Sequoia National Park U.S.A. 182 F5
Serae prov. Eritrea 104 B5
Serafimovich Rus. Fed. 41 G6
Sêraitang China see Baima
Seram i. Indon. 75 D3
English form Ceram
Seram Sea Indon. 75 D3
English form Ceram Sea
Serang Indon. 77 D4
Serangoon, Pulau i. Sing. 76 [inset]
also known as Coney Island
Serangoon, Sungai r. Sing. 76 [inset]
Serangoon Harbour b. Sing. 76 [inset]
Serapeum Egypt 108 D7
Serapong, Mount hill Sing. 76 [inset]
Serasan i. Indon. 77 E2
Serasan, Selat sea chan. Indon. 77 E2
Seraya i. Indon. 77 E2
Serbâl, Gebel mt. Egypt 108 E9
Serbia aut. rep. Yugo. see Srbija
Sêrbug Co l. China 89 E5
Sêrca China 97 G3
Serdica Bulg. see Sofia
Serdo Eth. 128 D2
Serdoba r. Rus. Fed. 41 H5
Serdobsk Rus. Fed. 41 H5
Serebryanka Rus. Fed. 40 J3
Serebryansk Kazakh. 88 C1
Serebryanyye Prudy Rus. Fed. 43 T7
Sered' Slovakia 49 O7
Sereda Moskovskaya Oblast' Rus. Fed. 43 Q6
Sereda Yaroslavskaya Oblast' Rus. Fed. 43 V4
Seredeyskiy Rus. Fed. 43 Q7
Seredka Rus. Fed. 43 J3
Serednikovo Rus. Fed. 43 U6
Seredniy Kuyal'nyk r. Ukr. 58 L2
Seredyna-Buda Rus. Fed. 43 P9
Seret r. Ukr. 49 T7
Şereflikoçhisar Turkey 106 C3
Şerein r. France 51 J5
Seremban Malaysia 76 C2
Serengeti National Park Tanz. 128 B5
Serengeti Plain Tanz. 128 B5
Serenje Zambia 127 F8
Serere Uganda 128 B4
Serezha r. Rus. Fed. 40 G5
Serezha r. Rus. Fed. 43 L5
Sergach Rus. Fed. 40 H5
Sergeikha Rus. Fed. 43 V5
Sergelen Dornod Mongolia 85 G1
Sergelen Sühbaatar Mongolia 85 F2
Sergen Turkey 58 I7
Sergeyavka Rus. Fed. 90 C3
Sergeyevka Akmolinskaya Oblast' Kazakh. 103 G2
Sergeyevka Severnyy Kazakhstan Kazakh. 103 F1
Sergino Rus. Fed. 38 G3
Sergipe state Brazil 202 E4
Sergiyev Posad Rus. Fed. 43 T5
formerly known as Zagorsk
Sergiyevskiy Rus. Fed. see Fakel
Sergiyevskoye Rus. Fed. 43 S9
Sergo Ukr. see Stakhanov
Serhiyivka Ukr. 58 L2
Seria Brunei 77 F1
Serian Sarawak Malaysia 77 E2
Seribu, Kepulauan is Indon. 77 D4
Seribudolok Indon. 76 B2
Serifos Greece 59 F11
Serifos i. Greece 59 F11
Serifou, Steno sea chan. Greece 59 F11
Sérignan France 51 J9
Sérigny r. Canada 169 G2
Sérigny, Lac l. Canada 169 G2
Serik Turkey 106 B3
Serikbuya China 88 B4
Serikkembelo Indon. 75 C3
Sèrinama Madag. 131 [inset] J3
Seringa, Serra da hills Brazil 199 I6
Seringapatam Reef Australia 150 C2
Serinhisar Turkey 59 K11
Serio r. Italy 56 B3
Serio, Parco del park Italy 56 B3
Sêrkang China see Nyainrong
Sermata i. Indon. 75 D5
Sermata, Kepulauan is Indon. 75 D5
Sermersuaq glacier Greenland 165 M2
also known as Humboldt Gletscher
Sermersuaq glacier Greenland 165 N2
also known as Steenstrup Gletscher
Sērmūkši Latvia 42 G4
Sernovodsk Rus. Fed. 41 I5
Sernur Rus. Fed. 40 I4
Sernyy Zavod Turkm. see Kukurtli
Serón Spain 55 I7
Seronga Botswana 130 D3
Serouenout well Alg. 123 G4
Serov Rus. Fed. 38 G4
Serowe Botswana 131 E4
Serpa Port. 54 D7
Serpa Pinto Angola see Menongue
Serpent r. Canada 169 G3
Serpent, Vallée du watercourse Mali 124 C3
Serpentine r. Australia 151 A7
Serpentine Lakes salt flat Australia 146 A2
Serpent's Mouth sea chan. Trin. and Tob./Venez. 187 H5
Serpeysk Rus. Fed. 43 Q7
Serpis r. Spain 55 K6
Serpneve Ukr. 58 K2
Serpukhov Rus. Fed. 43 S7
Serra Brazil 203 D7
Serra Bonita Brazil 206 G2
Serra da Bocaina, Parque Nacional da nat. park Brazil 203 C7
Serra da Canastra, Parque Nacional da nat. park Brazil 206 G7
Serra da Capivara, Parque Nacional da nat. park Brazil 202 D4
Serra da Estrela, Parque Natural da nature res. Port. 54 D4
Serra da Mesa, Represa resr Brazil 202 B5
Serra das Araras Brazil 207 H2
Serra de Outes Spain 54 C2
Serradilla Spain 54 E5
Serra do Divisor, Parque Nacional da nat. park Brazil 200 B2
Serra do Navio Brazil 199 H4
Serra dos Aimorés Brazil 207 M4
Serra do Salitre Brazil 206 G6
Sérrai Greece see Serres
Serramanna Sardegna Italy 57 A9
Serrana Brazil 206 F8
Serrana Bank sea feature Caribbean Sea 186 C4
Serranía de la Neblina, Parque Nacional nat. park Venez. 199 E4
Serranilla Bank sea feature Caribbean Sea 186 D4
Serrano i. Chile 205 B8
Serranópolis Brazil 206 A5
Serraria, Ilha i. Brazil see Queimada, Ilha
Serra San Bruno Italy 57 I10
Serras de Aire e Candeeiros, Parque Natural das nature res. Port. 54 C5
Serra Talhada Brazil 202 E3
Serravalle Scrivia Italy 56 A4
Serre r. France 51 J3
Serres Greece 58 E7
also known as Sérrai
Serrezuela Arg. 204 D3
Serrinha Brazil 202 E4
Serrita Brazil 202 E3
Sêrro Brazil 203 D6
Serrota mt. Spain 54 F4
Sers Tunisia 57 A12
Sersou, Plateau du Alg. 55 M9
Sertã Port. 54 C5
Sertânia Brazil 202 E4
Sertãozinho Brazil 206 B10
Sertão de Camapuã reg. Brazil 206 A6
Sertãozinho Brazil 206 F8
Sêrtar China 86 B1
also known as Seke
Sertavul Geçidi pass Turkey 108 E1
Sertolovo Rus. Fed. 43 L1
Serua vol. Indon. 75 D4
Serui Indon. 73 I7
Serule Botswana 131 E4
Seruto i. Indon. 77 E3
Seruyan r. Indon. 77 F3
Servach r. Belarus 42 I7
Servia Greece 59 D8
Servol r. Spain 55 L4
also spelt Cerbol
Serwaru Indon. 75 C5
Sêrxu China 86 A1
also known as Nixia
Sesayap Indon. 77 G2
Sesayap r. Indon. 77 G2
Sese Dem. Rep. Congo 126 E4
Sesekinika Canada 173 M2
Sesel country Indian Ocean see Seychelles
Sesepe Indon. 75 C3
Sesfontein Namibia 130 B3
Seshachalam Hills India 94 C3
Seshcha Rus. Fed. 43 O8
Sesheke Zambia 127 E9
Sesia r. Italy 56 A3
Seskar Furö i. Sweden 44 M2
Seskilo i. Greece 59 I12
Sesostris Bank sea feature India 94 A3
S'Espalmador i. Spain 55 M6
also known as Espalmador, Isla
Sessa Angola 127 D8
Ses Salines, Cap de c. Spain 55 O5
also spelt Salines, Cabo de
Sestra r. Rus. Fed. 43 S5
Sestri Levante Italy 56 B4
Sestroretsk Rus. Fed. 43 K1
Sestrunj i. Croatia 56 G4
Sestu Sardegna Italy 57 B9
Šešupė r. Lith./Rus. Fed. 42 D6
Sesvete Croatia 56 I3
Set r. Spain 55 L3
Set, Phou mt. Laos 79 D5
Sète France 51 J9
Sete Barras Brazil 206 F11
Šetekšna r. Lith. 42 G6
Sete Lagoas Brazil 203 C6
Setermoen Norway 44 L1
Setesdal valley Norway 45 I4
Seti r. Nepal 97 D3
Seti r. Nepal 97 E4
Setia Italy see Sezze
Sétif Alg. 123 G1
also spelt Stif
Setit r. Africa 121 H6
Seto Japan 91 E7
Seto-naikai sea Japan 91 C8
English form Inland Sea
Seto-naikai National Park Japan 91 C7
Setsan Myanmar 78 A4
Settat Morocco 122 D2
Setté Cama Gabon 126 A5
Settepani, Monte mt. Italy 56 A4
Settimo Torinese Italy 51 N7
Settle U.K. 47 J9
Settlement Creek r. Australia 148 C3
Settlers S. Africa 133 M1
Setúbal Port. 54 B6
Setúbal r. Brazil 207 K3
Setúbal Port. 54 C6
Setúbal admin. dist. Port. 54 C6
Setúbal, Baía de b. Port. 54 B6
Setubinha Brazil 207 K4
Seugne r. France 50 F7
Seul, Lac l. Canada 168 A3
Seurre France 51 L5
Sev r. Rus. Fed. 43 P9

index

S

Shiggaon India **94** B3
Shigong China **88** F3
Shigony Rus. Fed. **41** I5
Shiguai China **85** F3
formerly known as Shiguaigou
Shiguaigou China see **Shiguai**
Shiḩan Yemen **105** F4
Shiḩan, Wādī r. Oman **105** F4
Shihezi China **88** D2
Shihkiachwang China see **Shijiazhuang**
Shiikh Somalia **128** E2
Shijak Albania **58** A7
Shijiao China see **Fogang**
Shijiazhuang China **85** G4
formerly spelt Shihkiachwang
Shijiu Hu l. China **87** F2
Shijiusuo China see **Rizhao**
Shikabe Japan **90** G3
Shikag Lake Canada **168** B3
Shikar r. Pak. **101** E4
Shikarpur India **94** B3
Shikarpur Pak. **101** G5
Shikengkong mt. China **87** E3
Shikhany Rus. Fed. **102** A1
Shikohabad India **96** C4
Shikoku i. Japan **91** C8
Shikoku-sanchi mts Japan **91** C8
Shikotan, Ostrov i. Rus. Fed. **82** G4
also known as Shikotan-tō
Shikotan-tō i. Rus. Fed. see **Shikotan, Ostrov**
Shikotsu vol. Japan **90** G3
also known as Tarumae-san
Shikotsu-Tōya National Park Japan **90** G3
Shil'da Rus. Fed. **102** D2
Shilega Rus. Fed. **40** H2
Shiliguri India **97** F4
also spelt Siliguri
Shilipu China **87** E2
Shiliu China see **Changjiang**
Shilka Rus. Fed. **85** H1
Shilla mt. Jammu and Kashmir **96** C2
Shillelagh Rep. of Ireland **47** F11
Shillington Canada **173** M2
Shillo r. Israel **108** F5
Shillong India **97** F4
Shilou China **85** F4
Shilovo Ryazanskaya Oblast' Rus. Fed. **41** G5
Shilovo Tul'skaya Oblast' Rus. Fed. **43** T8
Shilüüstey Mongolia see **Balgatay**
Shimabara Japan **91** B8
Shimabara-wan b. Japan **91** B8
Shimada Japan **91** F7
Shimamaki Japan **90** G3
Shimane pref. Japan **91** C7
Shimane-hantō pen. Japan **91** C7
Shimanovsk Rus. Fed. **82** B1
Shimbiris mt. Somalia **128** E2
also known as Surud Ad
Shimbirre waterhole Kenya **128** D4
Shimen China **87** D2
Shimian China **86** B2
also known as Xinmian
Shimizu Hokkaidō Japan **90** H3
Shimizu Shizuoka Japan **91** F7
Shimla India **96** C3
formerly spelt Simla
Shimminato Japan see **Shinminato**
Shimoda Japan **91** F7
Shimodate Japan **91** F6
Shimoga India **94** B3
Shimokawa Japan **90** H2
Shimokita-hantō pen. Japan **90** G4
Shimoni Kenya **129** C6
Shimonoseki Japan **91** B8
formerly known as Akamagaseki
Shimotsuma Japan **91** F6
Shimsha r. India **94** C3
Shimshal Jammu and Kashmir **96** B1
Shimsk Rus. Fed. **43** L3
Shin, Loch l. U.K. **46** H5
Shināfīyah Iraq see **Ash Shanāfīyah**
Shinan China **87** D4
Shīndand Afgh. **101** E3
also known as Sabzawar
Shingbwiyang Myanmar **78** B2
Shinghshal Pass Pak. **101** H2
Shinglehouse U.S.A. **176** G4
Shingleton U.S.A. **172** G4
Shingletown U.S.A. **182** C1
Shing Mun Reservoir Hong Kong China **87** [inset]
also known as Ngan Hei Shui Tong
Shingozha Kazakh. **103** J3
also spelt Shyngqozha
Shingū Japan **91** E8
Shingwedzi S. Africa **131** F4
Shining Tree Canada **173** L3
Shinjō Japan **90** G5
Shinkai Hills Afgh. **101** G3
Shīnkāy Afgh. **101** F4
Shinminato Japan **91** E6
also spelt Shimminato
Shinnan-yō Japan **91** B7
Shinnston U.S.A. **176** E6
Shinshiro Japan **91** E7
Shintoku Japan **90** H3
Shinyanga Tanz. **128** B5
Shinyanga admin. reg. Tanz. **129** B5
Shiogama Japan **90** G5
Shiojiri Japan **91** E6
Shiono-misaki c. Japan **91** D8
Shioya-zaki pt Japan **90** G6
Shipai China see **Huaining**
Ship Chan Cay i. Bahamas **175** E7
Shipchenski Prokhod pass Bulg. **58** G6
Shipilovo Rus. Fed. **43** T4
Shiping China **86** B4
also known as Yilong
Shipki Pass China/India **89** B6
Shipman U.S.A. **176** G8
Shippegan Canada **169** H4
Shippegan Island Canada **169** H4
Shippensburg U.S.A. **176** H5
Shippenville U.S.A. **176** F4
Shiprock U.S.A. **183** P5
Shiprock Peak U.S.A. **183** P5
Shipu China see **Huanglong**
Shipu China **87** G2
Shipunskiy, Mys hd Rus. Fed. **39** Q4
Shiqian China **87** D3
Shiqiao China see **Panyu**
Shiqizhen China see **Zhongshan**
Shiqqat al Kharītah des. Saudi Arabia **105** D4
Shiquan China **87** D1
Shiquanhe China see **Ali**
Shiquanhe China see **Gar**
Shiquanh He r. China see **Indus**
Shi'r, Jabal hill Saudi Arabia **104** C2
Shirā'awh i. Qatar **105** F2
Shīrābād Iran **100** B2
Shirakami-misaki pt Japan **90** G4
Shirakawa Fukushima Japan **90** G6
Shirakawa Gifu Japan **91** E6
Shirane-san mt. Japan **91** F7
Shirane-san vol. Japan **90** F6
Shiranuka Japan **90** I3
Shiraoi Japan **90** G3
Shirase Coast Antarctica **223** O1
Shirase Glacier Antarctica **223** C2
Shirataki Japan **90** H3
Shirati Tanz. **128** B5
Shīrāz Iran **100** C4
Shirbîn Egypt **108** C6
Shire r. Malawi **129** B9
Shireet Mongolia **85** G2
Shirega Rus. Fed. **43** V1
Shiretoko-hantō pen. Japan **90** I3
Shiretoko-misaki c. Japan **90** I2
Shiretoko National Park Japan **90** I2
Shirin Uzbek. **103** G4
Shirinab r. Pak. **101** F4
Shīrīn Tagāb Afgh. **101** F2
Shiriya-zaki c. Japan **90** G4
Shirkala reg. Kazakh. **102** D3
Shīr Kūh mt. Iran **100** C4
Shiroishi Japan **90** G6
Shirone Japan **90** F6
Shiroro Reservoir Nigeria **125** G4
Shirotori Japan **91** E7
Shirpur India **96** B5
Shirten Höloy Gobi des. China **84** C3
Shīrvān Iran **100** D2
Shisanjianfang China **88** E3
Shisanzhan China **82** B2
Shiselweni admin. dist. Swaziland **133** P4
Shishaldin Volcano U.S.A. **164** C4
Shisha Pangma mt. China see **Xixabangma Feng**
Shishou China **87** E2
Shishovka Rus. Fed. **43** T3
Shitai China **87** F2
also known as Qili
Shitan China **87** E3
Shitang China **87** G2
Shitanjing China **85** E4
Shithāthah Iraq **109** O5
Shiv India **96** A4
Shiveluch, Sopka vol. Rus. Fed. **39** Q4
Shivpuri India **96** C4
Shivta tourist site Israel **108** F7
also known as Subeita
Shivwits U.S.A. **183** K4
Shivwits Plateau U.S.A. **183** K5
Shiwan Dashan mts China **87** C4
Shiwa Ngandu Zambia **127** F7
Shixing China **87** E3
also known as Taiping
Shiyan China **87** D1
Shizhu China **87** D2
also known as Nanbin
Shizilu China see **Junan**
Shizipu China **87** F2
Shizong China **86** B3
also known as Danfeng
Shizugawa Japan **90** G5
Shizuishan China **85** E4
also known as Dawukou
Shizukuishi Japan **90** G5
Shizuoka Japan **91** F7
historically known as Sumpu
Shizuoka pref. Japan **91** F7
▶**Shkhara** mt. Georgia/Rus. Fed. **107** E2
3rd highest mountain in Europe.
europe [landscapes] ▶ 30–31
Shklov Belarus see **Shklow**
Shklow Belarus **43** L7
also spelt Shklov
Shkodër Albania **58** A6
formerly known as Scutari; historically known as Scodra
Shkodrës, Liqeni i l. Albania/Yugo. see **Scutari, Lake**
Shkotovo Rus. Fed. **90** C3
Shkumbin r. Albania **58** A7
Shlina r. Rus. Fed. **43** P4
Shlino, Ozero l. Rus. Fed. **43** O4
Shlissel'burg Rus. Fed. **43** M2
also spelt Schlüsselburg; formerly known as Petrokrepost'
Shmidta, Ostrov i. Rus. Fed. **39** J1
English form Schmidt Island
Shmidta, Poluostrov pen. Rus. Fed. **82** F1
English form Schmidt Peninsula
Shmoylovo Rus. Fed. **43** J4
Shoalhaven r. Australia **147** F3
Shoal Lake Man. Canada **167** K5
Shoal Lake Sask. Canada **167** K4
Shoals U.S.A. **174** C4
Shoalwater Bay Australia **149** F4
Shōbara Japan **91** C7
Shōdo-shima i. Japan **91** D7
Shoemakersville U.S.A. **177** J5
Shofirkon Uzbek. see **Shafirkan**
Shoghlābād Iran **100** D2
Shoh Tajik. see **Shakh**
Shohi Pass Pak. see **Tal Pass**
Shokanbetsu-dake mt. Japan **90** G3
Shokotsu-gawa r. Japan **90** H2
Shokpar Kazakh. see **Chokpar**
Shola r. Rus. Fed. **43** S1
Sholaksay Kazakh. **103** F2
also spelt Sholaqsay
Sholapur India see **Solapur**
Sholaqorghan Kazakh. see **Shollakorgan**
Sholaqsay Kazakh. see **Sholaksay**
Shollakorgan Kazakh. **103** G4
also spelt Sholaqorghan; formerly spelt Chulakkurgan
Shomba r. Rus. Fed. **40** E2
Shongar Bhutan **97** F4
Shonzha Kazakh. see **Chundzha**
Shopsha Rus. Fed. **43** U4
Shoptykol' Kazakh. **103** H2
Shoqpar Kazakh. see **Chokpar**
Shoranur India **94** C4
Shorap Pak. **101** F5
Shorapur India **94** C2
Shorawak reg. Afgh. **101** F4
Shor Barsa-Kel'mes salt marsh Uzbek. **102** D4
Shorghun Uzbek. see **Shargun'**
Shorkot Pak. **101** H4
Shorkozakhly, Solonchak depr. Turkm. **102** D4
Shornaq Kazakh. see **Chernak**
Shorobe Botswana **130** D3
Shortandy Kazakh. **103** G2
Shortsville U.S.A. **177** H3
Shosambetsu Japan see **Shosanbetsu**
Shosanbetsu Japan **90** G2
also spelt Shosambetsu
Shosha r. Rus. Fed. **43** R5
Shoshone CA U.S.A. **183** H6
Shoshone ID U.S.A. **180** D4
Shoshone r. U.S.A. **180** E3
Shoshone Mountains U.S.A. **183** G2
Shoshone Peak U.S.A. **183** H5
Shoshong Botswana **131** E4
Shoshoni U.S.A. **180** E4
Shostka Ukr. **41** E6
Shouguang China **85** H4
Shouxian China **87** F1
Shouyang China **85** G4
Shouyang Shan mt. China **87** D1
Showak Sudan **121** G6
Show Low U.S.A. **183** N7
Shoyna Rus. Fed. **40** H2
Shpakovskoye Rus. Fed. **41** G7
formerly known as Mikhaylovskoye
Shpola Ukr. **41** D6
Shqipërisë, Republika e country Europe see **Albania**
Shreve U.S.A. **176** C5
Shreveport U.S.A. **179** D5
Shrewsbury U.K. **47** J11
Shrigonda India **94** B2
Shri Lanka country Asia see **Sri Lanka**
Shri Mohangarh India **96** A4
Shrirampur India **97** F5
Shrirangapattana India **94** C3
Shtefan-Vode Moldova see **Ştefan Vodă**
Shtërmen Albania **58** B8
Shtiqën Albania **58** B6
Shu r. China **87** F1
Shu Kazakh. **103** H4
formerly spelt Chu
Shu'ab, Ghubbat b. Yemen **105** F5
Shu'ab, Ra's pt Yemen **105** F5
Shu'aiba Iraq **107** F5
Shuajingsi China **86** B1
Shuangbai China **86** B3
also known as Tuodian
Shuangcheng China see **Zherong**
Shuangcheng China **82** B3
Shuanghe China **87** E2
Shuanghechang China **87** C2
Shuanghedagang China **82** C2
Shuanghuyu China see **Zizhou**
Shuangjiang China see **Jiangkou**
Shuangjiang China see **Tongdao**
Shuangjiang China **86** A4
also known as Mengmeng
Shuangjiang China see **Eshan**
Shuangliao China **85** I3
formerly known as Zhengjiatun
Shuangpai China **87** D3
Shuangshipu China see **Fengxian**
Shuangyang China **82** B4
Shuangyashan China **82** C3
Shuangzhong China see **Hukou**
Shu'ayt, Wādī r. Yemen **105** E4
Shubarkuduk Kazakh. **102** D2
Shubarshi Kazakh. **102** D2
Shubayḩ well Saudi Arabia **109** J7
Shubrâ el Kheima Egypt **121** F2
Shubrāmīyāh well Saudi Arabia **104** C3
Shucheng China **87** F2
Shucushuyacu Peru **198** C6
Shufu China **88** A4
Shuganu India **97** G4
Shughnon, Qatorkŭhi mts Tajik. **101** G2
also known as Shugnanskiy Khrebet
Shugnanskiy Khrebet mts Tajik. see **Shughnon, Qatorkŭhi**
Shugozero Rus. Fed. **43** P2
Shugur Rus. Fed. **38** G3
Shuicheng China see **Lupanshui**
Shuiding China see **Huocheng**
Shuidong China see **Dianbai**
Shuihu China see **Changfeng**
Shuiji China **87** F3
Shuiji China see **Laixi**
Shuijing China **86** C1
Shuikou Guangdong China **87** E4
Shuikou Hunan China **87** D3
also known as Tuojiang
Shuikouguan China **86** C4
Shuikoushan China **87** E3
Shuiluocheng China see **Zhuanglang**
Shuiquanzi China **84** D4
Shuituo He r. China **86** B3
Shuizhai China see **Wuhua**
Shujaabad Pak. **101** G4
Shulan China **82** B3
Shule China **88** B4
Shule He r. China **84** B3
Shule Nanshan mts China **84** C4
Shulinzhao China **85** F3
also known as Dalad Qi
Shul'mak Tajik. see **Novobod**
Shulu China see **Xinji**
Shum Rus. Fed. **43** M2
Shumagin Islands U.S.A. **164** C4
Shumanay Uzbek. **102** D4
formerly known as Taza-Bazar
Shumarinai-ko l. Japan **90** H2
Shumen Bulg. **58** H5
formerly known as Kolarovgrad
Shumensko Plato nat. park Bulg. **58** H5
Shumerlya Rus. Fed. **40** H5
Shumikha Rus. Fed. **38** G4
Shumilina Belarus **43** K6
Shumshu, Ostrov i. Rus. Fed. **39** P4
Shumyachi Rus. Fed. **43** N8
Shunak, Gora mt. Kazakh. **103** H3
Shūnat Nimrīn Jordan **108** G6
Shunde China **87** E4
also known as Daliang
Shunga Rus. Fed. **43** V4
Shunyi China **85** H3
Shuolong China **86** C4
Shuoxian China see **Shuozhou**
Shuozhou China **85** G4
formerly known as Shuoxian
Shupiyan Jammu and Kashmir **89** A5
Shuqqat Najrān depr. Saudi Arabia **105** D4
Shuqrah Yemen **105** D5
Shūr r. Iran **100** C4
Shūr r. Iran **100** C4
Shūr r. Iran **101** E3
Shūr r. Iran **101** E4
Shūr watercourse Iran **100** C4
Shūr watercourse Iran **100** C4
Shūr watercourse Iran **100** C5
Shur watercourse Iran **100** D3
Shūrāb Chahār Maḩāll va Bakhtīārī Iran **100** B3
Shūr Āb Iran **100** B3
Shūrāb Khorāsan Iran **100** D3
Shūrāb Yazd Iran **100** C3
Shūr Āb watercourse Iran **100** C4
Shurab Tajik. see **Shŭrob**
Shurchi Uzbek. **103** F5
Shureghestan Iran **100** C3
Shūr Gaz Iran **101** D4
Shūrjestān Iran **100** C4
Shurma Rus. Fed. **40** I4
Shŭrob Tajik. **101** G1
also spelt Shurab
Shūrū Iran **101** E4
Shurugwi Zimbabwe **131** F3
formerly spelt Selukwe
Shuruppak tourist site Iraq **107** F5
Shusf Iran **101** E4
Shūsh Iran **100** B3
Shusha Azer. see **Şuşa**
Shushicë r. Albania **59** A8
Shushkodom Rus. Fed. **43** V3
Shushtar Iran **100** B3
Shuswap Lake Canada **166** G5
Shutar Khun Pass Afgh. **101** F3
Shuwaysh, Tall ash hill Jordan **109** I6
Shuya Ivanovskaya Oblast' Rus. Fed. **40** G4
Shuya Respublika Kareliya Rus. Fed. **40** E3
Shuyak Island U.S.A. **164** D4
Shuyang China **87** F1
Shuyskoye Rus. Fed. **43** V2
Shvartsevskiy Rus. Fed. **43** S7
Shwebandaw Myanmar **78** A4
Shwebo Myanmar **78** A3
Shwedaung Myanmar **78** A4
Shwedwin Myanmar **78** A2
Shwegun Myanmar **78** B4
Shwegyin Myanmar **78** B4
Shwelaung r. Myanmar **78** A4
Shweli r. Myanmar **78** B3
also known as Mao, Nam
Shwenyaung Myanmar **78** B3
Shweudaung mt. Myanmar **78** B3
Shyghanaq Kazakh. see **Chiganak**
Shyghys Qazaqstan Oblysy admin. div. Kazakh. see **Vostochnyy Kazakhstan**
Shyghys-Qongyrat Kazakh. see **Shygys Konyrat**
Shygys Konyrat Kazakh. **103** H3
also spelt Shyghys-Qongyrat; formerly known as Vostochno-Kounradskiy
Shymkent Kazakh. **103** G4
formerly spelt Chimkent
Shynggyrlaū Kazakh. see **Chingirlau**
Shyngqozha Kazakh. see **Shingozha**
Shyok r. India **96** B2
Shyok Jammu and Kashmir **96** C2
Shypuvate Ukr. **41** F6
Shyshchytsy Belarus **42** I8
Si, Laem pt Thai. **79** B6
Sia Indon. **73** H8
Siabu Indon. **76** B2
Siachen Glacier Jammu and Kashmir **96** C2
Siahan Range mts Pak. **101** E5
Sīah Chashmeh Iran **100** A2
Siahgird Afgh. **101** F2
Siah Koh mts Afgh. **101** F3
Sīāh Kūh mts Iran **100** C3
Siak r. Indon. **76** C2
Siak Sri Inderapura Indon. **76** C2
Sialkot Pak. **101** H3
Siam country Asia see **Thailand**
Sian China see **Xi'an**
Sianów Poland **49** N1
Siantan i. Indon. **77** D2
Siapa r. Venez. **199** E4
Siargao i. Phil. **74** C4
Siasconset U.S.A. **177** P4
Siasi Phil. **74** B5
Siasi i. Phil. **74** B5
Siatista Greece **59** C8
Siaton Phil. **74** B4
Siau i. Indon. **75** C2
Šiauliai Lith. **42** E6
Siavonga Zambia **127** F9
Siayan i. Phil. **74** B1
Siazan' Azer. see **Siyäzän**
Sib Iran **101** E5
Sīb Oman **105** G3
Sibanicú Cuba **186** D2
Sibati China see **Xibet**
Sibay i. Phil. **74** B4
Sibay Rus. Fed. **102** D1
Sibayi, Lake S. Africa **133** Q4
Sibbald, Cape Antarctica **223** L2
Sibbo Fin. **45** N3
Sibbofjärden b. Fin. **42** G1
Šibenik Croatia **56** H5
formerly spelt Sebenico
Siberia Rus. Fed. see **Central Siberian Plateau**
Siberut i. Indon. **76** B3
Siberut, Selat sea chan. Indon. **76** B3
Siberut National Park Indon. **76** B3
Sibi Pak. **101** F4
Sibidiri P.N.G. **73** J8
Sibigo Indon. **76** A2
Sibiloi National Park Kenya **128** C4
Sibirtsevo Rus. Fed. **82** D3
formerly known as Manzovka
Sibiryakova, Ostrov i. Rus. Fed. **39** H2
Sibiti Congo **126** B5
Sibiu Romania **58** F3
Sibley U.S.A. **178** D3
Siboa Indon. **75** B2
Sibolga Indon. **76** B2
Siborongborong Indon. **76** B2
Sibowe r. Swaziland **133** P3
Sibsagar India **97** G4
Sibu Sarawak Malaysia **77** E2
Sibuco Phil. **74** B5
Sibuco Bay Phil. **74** B5
Sibuguey r. Phil. **74** B5
Sibuguey Bay Phil. **74** B5
Sibut Cent. Afr. Rep. **126** C3
Sibutu i. Phil. **74** A5
Sibutu Passage Phil. **74** A5
Sibuyan i. Phil. **74** B3
Sibuyan Sea Phil. **74** B3
Sic Romania **58** E2
Sicamous Canada **166** G5
Sicapoo mt. Phil. **74** B2
Sicca Veneria Tunisia see **Le Kef**
Siccus watercourse Australia **146** C2
Sicheng China see **Lingyun**
Sichon Thai. **79** B6
Sichuan prov. China **86** B2
English form Szechwan
Sichuan Pendi basin China **86** C2
English form Red Basin
Sicié, Cap c. France **51** L9
Sicilia admin. reg. Italy **57** G11
Sicilia i. Italy see **Sicily**
Sicilian Channel Italy/Tunisia **57** E11
Sicily i. Italy **57** G10
also known as Sicilia
Sicuani Peru **200** C3
Šid Vojvodina, Srbija Yugo. **58** A3
Sidangoli Indon. **75** C2
Siddhapur India **96** B5
also spelt Sidhpur
Siddharthanagar Nepal see **Bhairawa**
Siddipet India **94** C2
Sideby Fin. **45** M3
also known as Siipyy
Sideia Island P.N.G. **149** F1
Sid el Na'âm, Gebel hill Egypt **108** C8
Sidenreng, Danau l. Indon. **75** A3
Sidensjö Sweden **44** L3
Sidéradougou Burkina **124** D4
Sideros, Akra pt Greece **59** H13
Sidesaviwa S. Africa **132** G9
Sidhauli India **96** D4
Sidhi India **97** D4
Sidhirókastron Greece see **Sidirokastro**
Sidhpur India see **Siddhapur**
Sidi Aïssa Alg. **55** O9
Sidi Ali Alg. **55** L8
Sidi Ameur Alg. **55** O9
Sidi Barrani Egypt **121** E2
Sidi Bel Abbès Alg. **123** E2
Sidi Bennour Morocco **122** C2
Sidi Bou Sa'id Tunisia see **Sidi Bouzid**
Sidi Bouzid Tunisia **123** H2
also known as Sidi Bou Sa'id
Sidi El Hani, Sebkhet de salt pan Tunisia **123** H2
Sidi el Mokhtâr well Mali **124** E2
Sidi Ifni Morocco **122** C3
Sidi Kacem Morocco **122** D2
formerly known as Petitjean
Sidikalang Indon. **76** B2
Sidi Khaled Alg. **123** G2
Sidi Ladjel Alg. **55** N9
Sidi Mannsour well Alg. **123** E3
Sidi Mhamed well W. Sahara **122** B5
Sidi Okba Alg. **123** G2
Sidirokastro Greece **58** E7
also known as Sidhirókastron
Sidi Saâd, Barrage dam Tunisia **57** B13
Sidi Sâlim Egypt **108** B6
Sidi-Smaïl Morocco **122** C2
Sid Lake Canada **167** J2
Sidlaw Hills U.K. **46** I7
Sidley, Mount Antarctica **222** P1
Sidmouth U.K. **47** I13
Sidmouth, Cape Australia **149** D2
Sidnaw U.S.A. **172** E4
Sidney Canada **166** F5
Sidney IA U.S.A. **178** D3
Sidney MT U.S.A. **180** F3
Sidney NE U.S.A. **178** B3
Sidney NY U.S.A. **177** J3
Sidney OH U.S.A. **176** A5
Sidney Lanier, Lake U.S.A. **174** D5
Sido Mali **124** D4
Sidoan Indon. **75** B2
Sidoarjo Indon. **77** F4
Sidoktaya Myanmar **78** A3
Sidon Lebanon **108** G4
also spelt Saïda or Sayda
Sidorovo Rus. Fed. **43** V3
Sidra r. Poland **49** U2
Sidri, Wâdi watercourse Egypt **108** E9
Sidrolândia Brazil **203** A7
Sidvokodvo Swaziland **133** P3
Sidwadweni S. Africa **133** M8
Sidzhak Uzbek. **103** G4
also spelt Sijjak; formerly spelt Sydzhak
Siebe Norway **44** M1
Siedlce Poland **49** T3
historically known as Sedlets
Sieg r. Germany **48** E5
Siegen Germany **48** F5
Siemianówka, Jezioro l. Poland **49** T3
Siemiatycze Poland **49** T3
Siĕmréab Cambodia **79** C5
also spelt Siem Reap
Siem Reap Cambodia see **Siĕmréab**
Si'en China see **Huanjiang**
Siena Italy **56** D5
historically known as Saena Julia
Sieniawa Poland **49** T5
Sieppijärvi Fin. **44** M2
Sieradz Poland **49** P4
Sieraków Poland **49** N3
Sierpc Poland **49** Q3
Sierpienica r. Poland **49** Q3
Sierra Bahoruco nat. park Dom. Rep. **187** F3
Sierra Blanca U.S.A. **181** F7
Sierra Chica Arg. **204** E5
Sierra Colorada Arg. **204** D6
Sierra de Cazorla Segurla y las Villas park Spain **55** I6
Sierra del Gistral mts Spain see **Xistral, Serra do**
Sierra Grande Arg. **205** D6
▶**Sierra Leone** country Africa **124** B4
africa [countries] ▶ 114–117
Sierra Madre Mountains U.S.A. **182** D6
Sierra Mojada Mex. **184** E3
Sierra Nevada, Parque Nacional nat. park Venez. **198** D2
Sierra Nevada de Santa Marta, Parque Nacional nat. park Col. **198** C2
Sierraville U.S.A. **182** D2
Sierra Vista U.S.A. **181** E7
Sierre Switz. **51** N6
Siesartis r. Lith. **42** D7
Siesartis r. Lith. **42** F6
Şieu Romania **58** F1
Şieu r. Romania **58** F1
Sieve r. Italy **56** D5
Sievi Fin. **44** N3
Sifang Ling mts China **87** C4
Sīfenī Eth. **128** D1
Sifié Côte d'Ivoire **124** D5
Sifnos i. Greece **59** F11
Sifnou, Steno sea chan. Greece **59** F11
Sig Alg. **123** E2
formerly known as St-Denis-du-Sig
Sig, Ozero l. Rus. Fed. **43** O4
Sigani well Saudi Arabia **105** F4
Sigatoka Fiji **145** G3
also spelt Singatoka
Sigave Wallis and Futuna Is **145** H3
also known as Leava; also spelt Singave
Sigean France **51** I9
Sigep, Tanjung pt Indon. **76** B3
Sigguup Nunaa pen. Greenland **165** N2
also known as Svartenhuk Halvø
Sighişoara Romania **58** F2
Sigiriya Sri Lanka **94** D5
Siglap Sing. **76** [inset]
Sigli Indon. **76** A1
Siglufjörður Iceland **44** [inset] C2
Sigma Phil. **74** B4
Sigmaringen Germany **48** G7
Signal de Mailhebiau mt. France **51** J8
Signal de Randon mt. France **51** J8
Signal du Pic hill France **50** H7
Signal Peak U.S.A. **183** J8
Signy-l'Abbaye France **51** K3
Sigoga S. Africa **133** M7
Sigoisooinan Indon. **76** B3
Sigourney U.S.A. **174** A3
Sigri, Akra pt Greece **59** G9
Siguatepeque Hond. **186** B4
Sigüeiro Spain **54** C2
Sigüenza Spain **55** I3
Siguiri Guinea **124** C4
Sigulda Latvia **42** F4
Sigurd U.S.A. **183** M3
Sihanoukville Cambodia **79** C6
formerly known as Kâmpóng Saôm or Kompong Som
Sihanoukville, Chhâk b. Cambodia **79** C6
formerly known as Kompong Som Bay
Sihaung Myauk Myanmar **78** A3
Sihawa India **94** D1
Sihhoya Swaziland **133** P2
Sihong China **87** F1
also known as Qingyang
Sihora Madhya Pradesh India **96** D5
Sihora Maharashtra India **96** C5
Sihou China see **Changdao**
Sihuas Peru **200** A2
Sihui China **87** E4
Siikainen Fin. **45** M3
Siikajoki Fin. **44** N2
Siikajoki r. Fin. **44** N2
Siilinjärvi Fin. **44** N3
Siipyy Fin. see **Sideby**
Siirt Turkey **107** E3
historically known as Tigranocerta
Sijjak Uzbek. see **Sidzhak**
Sijunjung Indon. **76** C3
Sika India **96** A5
Sikakap Indon. **76** C3
Sikandra Rao India **96** C4
Sikanni Chief Canada **166** F3
Sikanni Chief r. Canada **166** F3
Sikar India **96** B4
Sikaram mt. Afgh. **101** G3
Sikasso Mali **124** D4
Sikasso admin. reg. Mali **124** D4
Sikaw Myanmar **78** B3
Sikea Greece **59** E8
Sikeli Indon. **75** B4
Sikeston U.S.A. **174** B4
Sikhote-Alin' mts Rus. Fed. **82** D4
Sikhote-Alinskiy Zapovednik nature res. Rus. Fed. **82** E3
Sikinos Greece **59** G12
Sikinos i. Greece **59** G12
Sikirevci Croatia **56** K3
Sikkim state India **97** F4
Siklós Hungary **56** K3
Sikongo Zambia **127** D8
Siksjö Sweden **44** L2
Sikta India **97** E4
Sikuaishi China see **Changhai**
Sikuati Sabah Malaysia **77** G1
Şila' i. Saudi Arabia **104** A2
Silago Phil. **74** C4
Šilalė Lith. **42** D6
Silandro Italy **56** C2
Si Lanna National Park Thai. **78** B4
Silao Mex. **185** E4
Sila Point Phil. **74** C3
Silawaih Agam vol. Indon. **76** A1
Silay Phil. **74** B4
Silba i. Croatia **56** G4
Silchar India **97** G4
Şile Turkey **58** K7
Šilene Latvia **42** H6
Siler City U.S.A. **174** E5
Sileru r. India **94** D2
Silesia reg. Czech Rep./Poland **49** N5
Silet Alg. **123** G5
Sileti Kazakh. see **Seletinskoye**
Sileti r. Kazakh. **103** H1
formerly spelt Selety
Siletiteniz, Ozero salt l. Kazakh. **103** H1
formerly spelt Seletyteniz, Ozero
Silgadi Nepal see **Silgarhi**
Silgarhi Nepal **96** D3
also spelt Silgadi
Silghat India **97** G4
Siliana Tunisia **123** H1
Silifke Turkey **106** C3
historically known as Seleucia
Siliguri India see **Shiliguri**
Sililo Zambia **127** E9
Siling Co salt l. China **89** E6
Silipur India **96** C4
Silisili, Mount Samoa **145** H3
Silistat Turkey see **Bozkır**
Siliştea Romania **58** G4
Siliştea Nouă Romania **58** F4
Silistra Bulg. **58** I4
historically known as Dorostol or Durostorum or Silistria
Silistria Bulg. see **Silistra**
Silivri Turkey **106** B2
Siljan Norway **45** J4
Siljan l. Sweden **45** K3
Silkaatskop S. Africa **133** K2
Silkeborg Denmark **45** J4
Silla Spain **55** K5
Sillamäe Estonia **42** I2
Sillaro r. Italy **56** D4
Sille Turkey **106** C3
Silleda Spain **54** C2
Silleiro, Cabo c. Spain **54** C2
Sillé-le-Guillaume France **50** F4
Silli India **97** E5
Sillod India **94** B1
Sillon de Talbert pen. France **50** C4
Siloam Springs U.S.A. **179** D4
Silobela S. Africa **133** O3
Silovayakha r. Rus. Fed. **40** L2
Silsbee U.S.A. **179** D6
Silsby Lake Canada **167** M4
Siltaharju Fin. **44** N2
Siltakylä Fin. **42** H1
Siltou well Chad **120** B5
Siluas Indon. **77** E2
Sīlūp r. Iran **101** E5
Šilutė Lith. **42** C6
Silutshana S. Africa **133** O5
Šiluva Lith. **42** E6
Silva Jardim Brazil **207** K9
Silvan Turkey **107** E3
Silvânia Brazil **206** E3
Silvassa India **94** B1
Silver Bank sea feature Turks and Caicos Is **187** F2
Silver Bank Passage Turks and Caicos Is **187** F2
Silver Bay U.S.A. **174** B2
Silver City Canada **166** B2
Silver City U.S.A. **181** E6
Silver Creek U.S.A. **176** F3
Silver Creek r. U.S.A. **183** N7
Silverdale N.Z. **152** I4
Silver Islet Canada **172** E2
Silver Lake U.S.A. **172** D6
Silver Lake l. CA U.S.A. **183** H6
Silver Lake l. MI U.S.A. **172** F4
Silvermine Mountains hills Rep. of Ireland **47** D11
Silver Peak Range mts U.S.A. **182** G4
Silver Spring U.S.A. **177** I7
Silver Springs U.S.A. **182** E2
Silverthrone Mountain Canada **166** E5
Silvertip Mountain Canada **180** B2
Silverton Australia **146** D2
Silverton Canada **166** G5
Silverton CO U.S.A. **181** F5
Silverton TX U.S.A. **179** B5
Silver Water Canada **173** K5
Silves Brazil **199** G5
Silves Port. **54** C7
Silvia Col. **198** B4
Silvies r. U.S.A. **180** C4
Silvituc Mex. **185** H5
Silvretta Gruppe mts Switz. **51** Q6
Sim r. Rus. Fed. **40** K5
Sima Comoros **129** E8
Sima Rus. Fed. **43** U5
Simao China **86** B4
Simão Dias Brazil **202** E4
Simaraña Venez. **199** F3
Simàrd, Lac l. Canada **173** O3
Simaria Jharkhand India **97** E4
Simaria Madhya Pradesh India **96** D4
Simatang i. Indon. **75** B2
Simav Turkey **106** B3
Simav Dağları mts Turkey **106** B3
Sīmayr i. Saudi Arabia **104** C4
Simba Dem. Rep. Congo **126** D4
Simbirsk Rus. Fed. see **Ul'yanovsk**
Simbruini, Monti mts Italy **56** F7
Simbukhovo Rus. Fed. **43** R6
Simcoe Canada **168** D5
Simcoe, Lake Canada **168** E4
Simdega India **97** E5
Simeä Sweden **45** L3
Simēn Mountain National Park Eth. **128** C1
Simēn Mountains Eth. **128** C1
Simeonovgrad Bulg. **58** G6
formerly known as Maritsa
Simeria Romania **58** E3
Simeto r. Sicilia Italy **57** H11
Simeuluë i. Indon. **76** B2
Simferopol' Ukr. **41** E7
Sími i. Greece see **Symi**
Simikot Nepal **97** D3
Simindou Cent. Afr. Rep. **126** D3
Siminy mt. Slovakia **49** R6
Simitli Bulg. **58** E7
Simi Valley U.S.A. **182** F7
Simla India see **Shimla**
Şimleu Silvaniei Romania **58** D1
Simmern (Hunsrück) Germany **48** E6
Simmesport U.S.A. **175** B6
Simm's Bahamas **187** E2
Simnas Lith. **42** E7
Simo Fin. **44** N2
Simojärvi l. Fin. **44** N2
Simonette r. Canada **166** G4
Simonhouse Canada **167** K4
Šimonka mt. Slovakia **49** S7
Simons U.S.A. **176** E4
Simon's Town S. Africa **132** C11
Simontornya Hungary **49** P9
Simon Wash watercourse U.S.A. **183** O9
Simpang Indon. **76** D3
Simpang Mangayau, Tanjong pt Sabah Malaysia **77** G1
Simplício Mendes Brazil **202** D3
Simplon Pass Switz. **51** O6
Simpson Canada **167** J5
Simpson Desert Australia **148** C5
Simpson Desert Conservation Park nature res. Australia **148** C5
Simpson Desert National Park Australia **148** C5
Simpson Desert Regional Reserve nature res. Australia **146** C1
Simpson Hill hill Australia **151** D5
Simpson Island Canada **172** F2
Simpson Islands Canada **167** H2
Simpson Park Mountains U.S.A. **183** H2
Simpson Peninsula Canada **165** K3
Simpsonville U.S.A. **174** D5
Simra Nepal **97** E4
Simrishamn Sweden **45** K5
Simuk i. Indon. **76** B3
Simulubek Indon. **76** B3
Simunjan Sarawak Malaysia **77** E2
Simunul i. Phil. **74** A5
Simushir, Ostrov i. Rus. Fed. **81** Q3
Sina r. India **94** B2
Sīnā', Shibh Jazīrat pen. Egypt see **Sinai**
Sinabang Indon. **76** B2
Sinabung vol. Indon. **76** B2
Sina Dhaqa Somalia **128** E3
▶**Sinai** pen. Egypt **121** G2
also known as Sīnā', Shibh Jazīrat
world [physical features] ▶ 8–9
Sinai, Mont hill France **51** K3
Sinai, Mount Egypt **108** E9
also known as Mûsa, Gebel
Sinaia Romania **58** G3
Sinai al Janûbîya governorate Egypt see **Janûb Sînâ'**
Sinai ash Shamâlîya governorate Egypt see **Shamâl Sînâ'**
Si Nakarin Reservoir Thai. **79** B5

Soča r. Slovenia 56 F3
Sochaczew Poland 49 R3
Sochi Rus. Fed. 41 F8
Sŏch'ŏn S. Korea 83 B5
Sochos Greece 58 E8
also spelt Sokhós
Société, Archipel de la is Fr. Polynesia see Society Islands
▶Society Islands Fr. Polynesia 221 H7
also known as Société, Archipel de la
oceania [issues] ▶ 140–141
Socol Romania 58 C4
Socompa Chile 200 C6
Soconusco, Sierra de mts Mex. see Madre, Sierra
Socorro Brazil 206 G9
Socorro Col. 198 C3
Socorro U.S.A. 181 F6
Socorro, Isla i. Mex. 184 C5
Socota Peru 198 B6
Socotra i. Yemen 105 F5
also spelt Suquṭrā
Socovos Spain 55 J6
Soc Trăng Vietnam 79 D6
formerly known as Khan Hung
Socuéllamos Spain 55 I5
Soda Lake CA U.S.A. 182 E6
Soda Lake CA U.S.A. 183 H6
Sodankylä Fin. 44 N2
Soda Plains Aksai Chin 89 B5
Soda Springs U.S.A. 180 E4
Söderhamn Sweden 45 L3
Söderköping Sweden 45 L4
Södermanland county Sweden 45 L4
Södertälje Sweden 45 L4
Sodiri Sudan 121 F6
Sodium S. Africa 132 H7
Sodo Eth. 128 C3
Södra Kvarken strait Fin./Sweden 45 L3
Sodus U.S.A. 177 H2
Sodwana Bay National Park S. Africa 133 Q4
Soë Indon. 75 C5
Soekmekaar S. Africa 131 F4
Soela väin sea chan. Estonia 42 D3
Soerabaia Indon. see Surabaya
Soest Germany 48 F4
Soetdoring Nature Reserve S. Africa 133 K5
Soetendalsvlei l. S. Africa 132 D11
Sofades Greece 59 D9
Sofala Moz. 131 G4
Sofala prov. Moz. 131 G3
formerly known as Beira
Sofala, Baía de b. Moz. 131 G4

▶Sofia Bulg. 58 E6
Capital of Bulgaria. Also spelt Sofiya; historically known as Sardica or Serdica or Sredets.

Sofia r. Madag. 131 [inset] J2
Sofiko Greece 59 E11
Sofiya Bulg. see Sofia
Sofiyevka Ukr. see Vil'nyans'k
Sofiysk Khabarovskiy Kray Rus. Fed. 82 D1
Sofiysk Khabarovskiy Kray Rus. Fed. 82 E2
Sofporog Rus. Fed. 44 O2
Sofrino Rus. Fed. 43 S5
Softa Kalesi tourist site Turkey 108 D1
Sōfu-gan i. Japan 81 O7
English form Lot's Wife
Sog China 89 F6
also known as Garqêntang
Sogamoso Col. 198 C3
Sogat China 88 D3
formerly spelt Süget
Sogda Rus. Fed. 82 D2
Sogma China 89 C5
Sogne Norway 45 I4
Sognefjorden inlet Norway 45 I3
Sogn og Fjordane county Norway 45 I3
Sogo Rus. Fed. 39 M2
Sogod Phil. 74 C4
Sogod Bay Phil. 74 C4
Sogo Hills Kenya 128 C4
Sogolle well Chad 120 B6
Sogo Nur l. China 84 D3
Sogozha r. Rus. Fed. 43 U3
Söğüt Turkey 106 B2
Söğüt Dağı mts Turkey 106 B3
Sŏgwip'o S. Korea 83 B6
Sohâg Egypt 121 F3
also spelt Sūhāj
Sohagpur India 96 C5
Sohalinskiy Kazakh. 103 G2
Sohan r. Pak. 101 G3
Sohano P.N.G. 145 E2
Sohar Oman see Ṣuḥār
Sohela India 97 D5
Sohna India 96 C3
Sohng Gwe, Khao hill Myanmar/Thai. 79 B5
Soignies Belgium 51 K2
Soila China 86 A2
Soini Fin. 44 N3
Soissons France 51 J3
Sōja Japan 91 C7
Sojat India 96 B4
Sojat Road India 96 B4
Sojoton Point Phil. 74 B4
Sok r. Rus. Fed. 41 I5
Sokch'o S. Korea 83 C5
Söke Turkey 106 A3
Sokele Dem. Rep. Congo 127 E7
Sokhondo, Gora mt. Rus. Fed. 85 F1
Sokhor, Gora mt. Rus. Fed. 85 E1
Sokhós Greece see Sochos
Sokhumi Georgia 107 E2
also known as Aq"a; also spelt Sukhumi; historically known as Dioscurias or Sukhum-Kale
Sokiryany Ukr. see Sokyryany
Sokkuram Grotto tourist site S. Korea 90 A7
Soknedal Norway 44 J3
Sokobanja Srbija Yugo. 58 C5
Sokodé Togo 125 F4
Soko Islands Hong Kong China 87 [inset]
also known as Shekka Ch'ün-Tao
Sokol Rus. Fed. 82 F3
Sokol Rus. Fed. 43 V2
Sokolac Bos.-Herz. 56 K5
Sokółka Poland 49 U2
Sokol'niki Tul'skaya Oblast' Rus. Fed. 43 T7
Sokol'niki Tverskaya Oblast' Rus. Fed. 43 P5
Sokolo Mali 124 D3
Sokolov Czech Rep. 49 J5
Sokolovka Rus. Fed. 90 C3
Sokołów Małopolski Poland 49 T5
Sokołów Podlaski Poland 49 T3
Sokolozero, Ozero l. Rus. Fed. 44 O2
Sokone Senegal 124 A3
Sokosti hill Fin. 44 O1
Sokoto Nigeria 125 G3
Sokoto r. Nigeria 125 G4
Sokoto state Nigeria 125 G3
Sokourala Guinea 124 C4
Sokyryany Ukr. 41 C6
also spelt Sokiryany
Sola Cuba 186 D2
Sola r. Poland 49 Q6
Sola i. Tonga see Ata
Solan India 96 C3
Solana Beach U.S.A. 183 G9
Solander Island N.Z. 153 A14
Solanet Arg. 204 F5
Solano Phil. 74 B2
Solano Venez. 199 E4
Solapur India 94 B2
formerly spelt Sholapur
Soldado Bartra Peru 198 C5
Soldotna U.S.A. 164 D3
Solec Kujawski Poland 49 P2
Soledad Arg. 204 E3
Soledad U.S.A. 182 C5
Soledad Venez. 199 F2
Soledad de Doblado Mex. 185 F5
Soledade Brazil 203 A9
Søla mt. Norway 45 J3
Solenoye Rus. Fed. 41 G7
Solenzo Burkina 124 D3
Solfjellsjøen Norway 44 K2
Solginskiy Rus. Fed. 40 G3
Solhan Turkey 107 E3
Soligalich Rus. Fed. 40 G4
Soligorsk Belarus see Salihorsk
Solihull U.K. 47 K11
Solikamsk Rus. Fed. 40 K4
Sol'-Iletsk Rus. Fed. 102 C2
Soliman Tunisia 57 C12
Solimón, Punta pt Mex. 185 I5
Solingen Germany 48 E4
Solita Col. 198 C4
Solita Venez. 187 F5
Sol-Karmala Rus. Fed. see Severnoye
Sölktäler nature res. Austria 49 K8
Sollefteå Sweden 44 L3
Sollentuna Sweden 45 L4
Söller Spain 55 N5
Sollerön Sweden 45 K3
Solling hills Germany 48 G4
Solnechnogorsk Rus. Fed. 43 R5
Solnechnyy Rus. Fed. 82 E2
Solnechnyy Rus. Fed. see Gornyy
Solo r. Java Indon. 77 F4
Solo r. Sulawesi Indon. 75 B3
Solofra Italy 57 G8
Solok Indon. 76 C3
Sololá Guat. 185 H6
Solomon U.S.A. 183 O9
Solomon r. U.S.A. 178 C4
Solomon, North Fork r. U.S.A. 178 C4
Solomon, South Fork r. U.S.A. 178 C4

▶Solomon Islands country S. Pacific Ocean 145 F2
4th largest and 5th most populous country in Oceania. Formerly known as British Solomon Islands.
oceania [countries] ▶ 138–139

Solomon Sea P.N.G./Solomon Is 145 E2
Solon China 85 I2
Solon U.S.A. 172 B9
Solor i. Indon. 75 B5
Solor, Kepulauan is Indon. 75 B5
Solotcha Rus. Fed. 43 U7
Solothurn Switz. 51 N5
Solovetskiy Rus. Fed. 40 E2
formerly known as Kreml'
Solovetskiye Ostrova is Rus. Fed. 40 E2
Solovetskoye Rus. Fed. 40 H4
Solov'yevo Rus. Fed. 43 N7
Solov'yevsk Mongolia 85 G1
Solov'yevsk Rus. Fed. 82 B1
Solsona Spain 55 M3
Solt Hungary 49 Q9
Šolta i. Croatia 56 I5
Solṭānābād Khorāsan Iran 100 D2
Solṭānābād Kermān Iran 101 D3
Solṭānābād Tehrān Iran 100 B3
Soltān-e Bakva Afgh. 101 E3
Solṭānī, Khowr-e b. Iran 100 B4
Solṭanqolī Iran 100 A3
Soltau Germany 48 G3
Sol'tsy Rus. Fed. 43 L3
Soltüstik Qazaqstan Oblysy admin. div. Kazakh. see Severnyy Kazakhstan
Soltvadkert Hungary 49 Q9
Solunska Glava mt. Macedonia 58 C7
Solvang U.S.A. 182 D7
Solvay U.S.A. 177 I2
Sölvesborg Sweden 45 K4
Sol'vychegodsk Rus. Fed. 40 H3
Solway Firth est. U.K. 47 I9
Solwezi Zambia 127 E8
Sōma Japan 90 G6
Soma Turkey 106 A3
Somabhula Zimbabwe 131 F3
formerly spelt Somabula
Somabula Zimbabwe see Somabhula
Somali admin. reg. Eth. 128 D3
▶Somalia country Africa 128 E4
spelt Soomaaliya in Somali; long form Somali Republic
africa [countries] ▶ 114–117
Somali Republic country Africa see Somalia
Somanga Tanz. 129 C7
Somanya Ghana 125 E5
Sombang, Gunung mt. Indon. 77 G2
Sombo Angola 127 D7
Sombor Vojvodina, Srbija Yugo. 58 A3
also spelt Zombor
Sombrerete Mex. 184 E4
Sombrero i. Anguilla 187 H3
Sombrero Chile 205 C9
Sombrero Channel India 95 G5
Somdari India 96 B4
Somero Fin. 45 M3
Somerset KY U.S.A. 176 A8
Somerset MA U.S.A. 177 N4
Somerset MI U.S.A. 173 I8
Somerset OH U.S.A. 176 C6
Somerset PA U.S.A. 176 F6
Somerset East S. Africa 133 J9
Somerset Island Canada 165 J2
Somerset West S. Africa 132 C11
Somersworth U.S.A. 177 O2
Somerton U.S.A. 183 J9
Sōmeru Estonia 42 H2
Somerville NJ U.S.A. 177 K5
Somerville TN U.S.A. 174 B5
Somerville Reservoir U.S.A. 179 C6
Someşan, Podişul plat. Romania 58 E2
Someşu Cald r. Romania 58 E2
Someşul Mare r. Romania 58 E1
Someşu Mic r. Romania 58 E1
Somesville U.S.A. 177 Q1
Someydeh Iran 100 A3
also spelt Samaida
Somino Rus. Fed. 43 P2
Somkele S. Africa 133 Q5
Sommarøy Norway 44 L1
Somme r. France 50 H2
Sommen l. Sweden 45 K4
Sömmerda Germany 48 I4
Sommet, Lac du l. Canada 169 G2
Somnath India 94 A1
also known as Patan
Somogyszob Hungary 49 O9
Somosomo Fiji 145 H3
Somotillo Nicaragua 186 B4
Somoto Nicaragua 186 B4
Somovo Orlovskaya Oblast' Rus. Fed. 43 Q9
Somovo Tul'skaya Oblast' Rus. Fed. 43 R8
Sompeta India 95 E2
Sompolno Poland 49 P3
Somport, Col du pass France/Spain 55 K2
Šomrda hill Yugo. 58 C4
Somuncurá, Mesa Volcánica de plat. Arg. 204 D6
Somvarpet India 94 B3
Son r. India 96 E4
Soná Panama 186 C6
Sonag China see Zêkog
Sonai r. India 97 G4
Sonai r. India 97 G4
Sonakhan India 97 D5
Sonala India 94 C1
Sonaly Kazakh. 103 G2
Sonamukhi India 97 E5
Sonapur India 95 D1
Sonari India 97 G4
Sŏnch'ŏn N. Korea 83 B5
Sondalo Italy 56 C2
Sønderå r. Denmark 48 F1
Sønderborg Denmark 45 J5
Sondershausen Germany 48 H4
Sønderup Denmark 45 J4
Søndre Strømfjord Greenland see Kangerlussuaq
Søndre Strømfjord inlet Greenland see Kangerlussuaq
Søndre Upernavik Greenland see Upernavik Kujalleq
Sondrio Italy 56 B2
Sonepet India 94 C2
Song Nigeria 125 I4
Songa Indon. 75 C3
Songad India 96 A5
Songbai China see Shennongjia
Songbu China 87 E2
Sông Cau Vietnam 79 E5
Songcheng China see Xiapu
Sông Da, Hô resr Vietnam 78 D3
Songea Tanz. 129 B7
Sŏnggan N. Korea 83 B4
Songhua Hu resr China 82 B4
Songhua Jiang r. China 82 D3
English form Sungari
Songjiachuan China see Wubu
Songjiang Jilin China 82 C4
formerly known as Antu
Songjiang Shanghai China 87 G2
formerly known as Sungkiang
Songjianghe China 82 B4
Sŏngjin N. Korea see Kimch'aek
Sŏngju S. Korea 91 A7
Songkan China 86 C2
Songkhla Thai. 79 C7
also known as Singora
Song Khram, Mae Nam r. Thai. 78 D4
Songköl l. Kyrg. 103 H4
also known as Sonkël', Ozero
Songling China 85 I2
Song Ling mts China 85 H3
Songmai China see Dêrong
Songming China 86 B3
also known as Songyang
Sŏngnam S. Korea 83 B5
Songnim N. Korea 83 B5
Songni-san National Park S. Korea 83 B5
Songo Angola 127 B6
Songo Moz. 131 G2
Songololo Dem. Rep. Congo 127 B6
Songololo Dem. Rep. Congo see Mbanza-Ngungu
Songpan China 86 B1
also known as Jin'an or Sungqu
Songsak India 97 F4
Sŏngsan S. Korea 83 B6
Songshan China see Ziyun
Song Shan mt. China 87 E1
Songtao China 87 D2
Songxi China 87 F3
also known as Songyuan
Songxian China 87 E1
Songyang China see Songming
Songyuan China see Songxi
Songyuan China 82 B3
also known as Ningjiang; formerly known as Fuyu
Songzi China 87 D2
formerly known as Xinjiangkou
Sonhat India 97 D5
Sonid Youqi China see Saihan Tal
Sonid Zuoqi China see Mandalt
Sonipat India 96 C3
Sonkach India 96 C5
Sonkajärvi Fin. 44 N3
Sonkël', Ozero l. Kyrg. see Songköl
Sonkovo Rus. Fed. 43 S4
Son La Vietnam 78 C3
Sonmiani Bay Pak. 101 F5
Sonneberg Germany 48 I5
Sonnenjoch mt. Austria 48 J8
Sono r. Minas Gerais Brazil 203 C6
Sono r. Tocantins Brazil 202 B4
Sonoita watercourse Mex. 181 D7
Sonoma U.S.A. 182 B3
Sonoma Peak U.S.A. 182 G1
Sonora r. Mex. 184 C2
Sonora state Mex. 184 C2
Sonora CA U.S.A. 182 D4
Sonora TX U.S.A. 179 B6
Sonora Peak U.S.A. 182 E3
Sonqor Iran 100 A3
Sonseca Spain 54 H5
Son Servera Spain 55 O5
Sonsón Col. 198 C3
Sonsonate El Salvador 185 H6
Sonsorol Islands Palau 73 H5
also spelt Sansoral Islands
Sonstraal S. Africa 132 G4
Son Tây Vietnam 78 D3
Sonthofen Germany 48 H8
Sonwabile S. Africa 133 M8
Soochow China see Suzhou
Soodla r. Estonia 42 G2
Soomaaliya country Africa see Somalia
Soperton U.S.A. 175 D5
Sopi, Tanjung pt Indon. 75 D2
Sopo watercourse Sudan 126 E2
Sopot Bulg. 58 F6
Sopot Poland 49 P1
Sopot Srbija Yugo. 58 B4
Sopron Hungary 49 N8
historically known as Ödenburg
Sopu-Korgon Kyrg. 88 A3
also known as Sufi-Kurgan
Sopur Jammu and Kashmir 96 B2
Soputan, Gunung vol. Indon. 75 C2
Sor r. Port. 54 C5
Sôr r. Port. 54 C6
Sor r. Spain 54 D1
Sora Italy 56 F7
Sorab India 94 B3
Soråker Sweden 44 L3
Sŏrak-san mt. S. Korea 83 C5
Sŏrak-san National Park S. Korea 83 C5
Sorata Bol. 200 C3
Sør-Audnedal Norway 45 I4
Sorbas Spain 55 I7
Sorbe r. Spain 55 H4
Sor Donyztau dry lake Kazakh. 102 D3
Sorel Canada 169 F4
Sorell Australia 147 E5
Soreq r. Israel 108 F6
Sørfjorden inlet Norway 45 I3
Sorgono Sardegna Italy 57 B8
Sorgues France 51 K8
Sorgues r. France 51 I9
Sorgun Yozgat Turkey 106 C3
also known as Yesilova
Sorgun r. Turkey 108 F1
Soria Spain 55 I3
Sorikmarapi vol. Indon. 76 B2
Sørkappøya i. Svalbard 38 B2
Sor Kaydak dry lake Kazakh. 102 C3
Sorkh, Kūh-e mts Iran 100 C3
Sorkheh Iran 100 C3
Sørland Norway 44 K2
Sørli Norway 44 K2
Sor Mertvyy Kultuk dry lake Kazakh. 102 C3
also known as Öli Qoltyq Sory
Sörmjöle Sweden 44 M3
Sørø Denmark 45 J5
Soro India 97 E5
Soro, Monte mt. Sicilia Italy 57 G11
Soroca Moldova 41 D6
formerly spelt Soroki
Sorocaba Brazil 206 F10
Sorochinsk Rus. Fed. 102 C1
Soroki Moldova see Soroca
Sorokino Rus. Fed. 43 K4
Sorol atoll Micronesia 73 J5
formerly known as Philip Atoll
Sorong Indon. 73 H7
Sororó r. Brazil 202 B3
Sororoca Brazil 199 F4
Sorot' r. Rus. Fed. 43 J4
Soroti Uganda 128 B4
Sørøya i. Norway 44 M1
Sørøysundet sea chan. Norway 44 M1
Sorp Turkey see Reşadiye
Sorraia r. Port. 54 C5
Sørreisa Norway 44 L1
Sorrento Italy 56 G8
Sorsakoski Fin. 44 N3
Sorsatunturi hill Fin. 44 O2
Sorsele Sweden 44 L2
Sorso Sardegna Italy 57 A8
Sorsogon Phil. 74 C3
Sortavala Rus. Fed. 45 O3
Sortland Norway 44 K1
Sortot Sudan 121 F5
Sør-Trøndelag county Norway 44 J3
Sørvær Norway 44 M1
Sørvågen Norway 44 K2
Sõrve väin sea chan. Estonia/Latvia see Irbe Strait
Sŏsan S. Korea 83 B5
Sosedno Rus. Fed. 43 J3
Sosenskiy Rus. Fed. 43 Q7
Soshanguve S. Africa 133 M2
Soskovo Rus. Fed. 43 Q9
Sosna r. Rus. Fed. 43 T9
Sosnogorsk Rus. Fed. 40 J3
formerly known as Izhma
Sosnovka Kazakh. 103 I2
Sosnovka Arkhangel'skaya Oblast' Rus. Fed. 40 H3
Sosnovka Murmanskaya Oblast' Rus. Fed. 40 G2
Sosnovka Tambovskaya Oblast' Rus. Fed. 41 G5
Sosnovka Vologod. Obl. Rus. Fed. 43 S3
Sosnovka Vologod. Obl. Rus. Fed. 43 U2
Sosnovo Rus. Fed. 43 L1
Sosnovoborsk Rus. Fed. 41 H5
Sosnovo-Ozerskoye Rus. Fed. 81 I2
Sosnovyy Rus. Fed. 44 P2
Sosnovyy Bor Belarus see Sasnovy Bor
Sosnovyy Bor Rus. Fed. 43 K2
Sosnowiec Poland 49 Q5
historically known as Sosnowitz
Sosnowitz Poland see Sosnowiec
Sosny Belarus 42 I9
Sosso Cent. Afr. Rep. 126 B4
Sos'va Rus. Fed. 38 G4
Sot' r. Rus. Fed. 43 V4
Sota r. Benin 125 F4
Sotang China 97 G3
Sotério r. Brazil 201 D2
Sotillo r. Spain 54 F6
Sotkamo Fin. 44 O2
Soto Arg. 204 D3
Soto la Marina Mex. 185 F4
Sotouboua Togo 125 F4
Sotteville-lès-Rouen France 50 H3
Sottunga Fin. 45 M3
Sotuta Mex. 185 H4
Souanké Congo 126 B4
Soubré Côte d'Ivoire 124 D5
Soucis, Cape N.Z. 152 H9
Souda Greece 59 F13
also spelt Soúdha
Soudan Australia 148 C4
Soudas, Ormos b. Greece 59 F13
Soúdha Greece see Souda
Soufli Greece 58 H7
Soufrière St Lucia 187 H4
Soufrière vol. St Vincent 199 F1
Soufrière Hills Montserrat 187 H3
Souguéta Guinea 124 B4
Sougueur Alg. 55 M9
Souillac France 50 H8
Souk Ahras Alg. 123 G1
Souk el Arbaâ du Rharb Morocco 122 D2
Souk el Had el Rharbia Morocco 54 F9
Souk el Kella Morocco 54 F9
Souk Khemis du Sahel Morocco 54 E9
Soukoukoutane Niger 125 F3
Souk Tleta Taghramet Morocco 54 F9
Souk-Tnine-de-Sidi-el-Yamani Morocco 54 F9
Sŏul S. Korea see Seoul
Soulac-sur-Mer France 50 E7
Sounding Creek r. Canada 167 I4
Sounfat well Mali see Tessoûnfat
Sounio nat. park Greece 59 F11
Soûr Lebanon see Tyre
Sourdeval France 50 F4
Soure Brazil 202 B2
Sour el Ghozlane Alg. 55 O8
Souris Man. Canada 167 K5
Souris P.E.I. Canada 169 I4
Souris r. Canada 167 L5
Souriya country Asia see Syria
Souroumelli well Mauritania 124 C2
Sous, Oued watercourse Morocco 122 C3
Sousa Brazil 202 E3
Sousa Lara Angola see Bocoio
Sousel Port. 54 D6
Sousse Tunisia 123 H2
also spelt Susah; historically known as Hadrumetum
Soussellem, Oued watercourse Alg. 55 N9
Soustons France 50 E9
Sout r. S. Africa 132 C8
Sout watercourse S. Africa 132 E5
South Africa country Africa see South Africa, Republic of
▶South Africa, Republic of country Africa 130 D6
known as Suid-Afrika in Afrikaans; short form South Africa
africa [countries] ▶ 114–117
South Alligator r. Australia 148 B2
Southampton Canada 168 D4
Southampton U.K. 47 K13
historically known as Hamwic
Southampton U.S.A. 177 M5
Southampton Island Canada 167 O1
South Andaman i. India 95 G4
South Anna r. U.S.A. 176 H8
South Aulatsivik Island Canada 169 I1
South Australia state Australia 146 B2
Southaven U.S.A. 174 B5
South Baldy mt. U.S.A. 181 F6
South Bay U.S.A. 175 D7
South Bend IN U.S.A. 174 C3
South Bend WA U.S.A. 180 B3
South Bluff pt Bahamas 187 E2
South Boston U.S.A. 176 G9
Southbridge N.Z. 153 G11
Southbridge U.S.A. 177 M3
South Brook Canada 169 J3
South Burlington U.S.A. 177 L1
Southburn N.Z. 153 F12
South Carolina state U.S.A. 175 D5
South Charleston OH U.S.A. 176 B6
South Charleston WV U.S.A. 176 D7
South China Sea N. Pacific Ocean 72 E4
South Coast Town Australia see Gold Coast
South Dakota state U.S.A. 178 B2
South Deerfield U.S.A. 177 M3
South Downs hills U.K. 47 L13
South East admin. dist. Botswana 133 J2
South East Cape Australia 147 E5
South East Isles Australia 151 C7
Southend Canada 167 K3
Southend-on-Sea U.K. 47 M12
Southern admin. reg. Malawi 129 B8
Southern prov. Sierra Leone 124 B5
Southern prov. Zambia 127 E9
Southern Aegean admin. reg. Greece see Notio Aigaio
Southern Alps mts N.Z. 153 E11
also known as Kā Tiritiri o te Moana
Southern Central Aboriginal Reserve Australia 151 D5
Southern Cross Australia 151 B6
Southern Darfur state Sudan 126 E2
Southern Indian Lake Canada 167 L3
Southern Kordofan state Sudan 128 A2
Southern Lau Group is Fiji 145 H3
Southern National Park Sudan 126 F3
Southern Ocean 222 F3
Southern Pines U.S.A. 174 E5
Southern Rhodesia country Africa see Zimbabwe
Southern Uplands hills U.K. 46 H8
Southern Urals mts Rus. Fed. see Yuzhnyy Ural
Southern Ute Indian Reservation res. U.S.A. 181 F5
South Esk Tableland reg. Australia 150 D3
Southey Canada 167 J5
Southeyville S. Africa 133 L8
South Fabius r. U.S.A. 178 E4
Southfield U.S.A. 173 J8
Southfields U.S.A. 177 K4
South Fork CA U.S.A. 182 A1
South Fork CO U.S.A. 181 F5
South Fork PA U.S.A. 176 G5
South Fox Island U.S.A. 172 H5
Southgate r. Canada 166 E5
South Geomagnetic Pole (2000) Antarctica 223 H1

▶South Georgia and South Sandwich Islands terr. S. Atlantic Ocean 217 L9
United Kingdom Overseas Territory.
southamerica [countries] ▶ 192–193

South Gillies Canada 172 D2
South Grand r. U.S.A. 178 D4
South Hatia Island Bangl. 97 F5
South Haven U.S.A. 172 G8
South Head N.Z. 152 I4
South Head N.Z. 152 I4
South Henik Lake Canada 167 L2
South Hero U.S.A. 177 L1
South Hill U.S.A. 176 G9
South Horr Kenya 128 C4
South Indian Lake Canada 167 L3
South Island India 94 B4

▶South Island N.Z. 153 G12
2nd largest island in Oceania. Also known as Te Waipounamu.
oceania [landscapes] ▶ 136–137

South Islet reef Phil. 74 A4
South Junction Canada 167 M5
South Kazakhstan Oblast admin. div. Kazakh. see Yuzhnyy Kazakhstan
South Kitui National Reserve nature res. Kenya 128 C5
South Koel r. India 97 E5
▶South Korea country Asia 83 B5
asia [countries] ▶ 64–67
South Lake Tahoe U.S.A. 182 D3
Southland admin. reg. N.Z. 153 B13
South Loup r. U.S.A. 178 C3
South Luangwa National Park Zambia 127 F8
South Macmillan r. Canada 166 C2
South Magnetic Pole (2000) Antarctica 223 J2
South Manitou Island U.S.A. 173 G5
South Mills U.S.A. 177 I9
Southminster U.K. 47 M12
South Moose Lake Canada 167 K4
South Mountains hills U.S.A. 177 H6
South Muiron Island Australia 150 A4
South Nahanni r. Canada 166 D1
South Negril Point Jamaica 186 D3
South New Berlin U.S.A. 177 J3
South Orkney Islands S. Atlantic Ocean 222 V2
South Paris U.S.A. 177 O1
South Passage Australia 151 A5
South Patrick Shores U.S.A. 175 D6
South Platte r. U.S.A. 178 B3
South Point pt U.S.A. 181 [inset] Z2
South Pole Antarctica 223 T1
South Porcupine Canada 173 L2
Southport Australia 147 E5
Southport U.K. 47 I10
Southport NC U.S.A. 175 E5
Southport NY U.S.A. 177 I3
South Portland U.S.A. 177 O2
South River Canada 173 N5
South Ronaldsay i. U.K. 46 J5
South Royalton U.S.A. 177 M2
South Salt Lake U.S.A. 183 M1
South San Francisco U.S.A. 182 B4
South Saskatchewan r. Canada 167 J4
South Seal r. Canada 167 L3
South Shetland Islands Antarctica 222 U2
South Shields U.K. 47 K8
South Sinai governorate Egypt see Janûb Sînâ'
South Skunk r. U.S.A. 174 A3
South Taranaki Bight b. N.Z. 152 I7
South Tent mt. U.S.A. 183 M2
South Tons r. India 97 D4
South Tucson U.S.A. 183 N9
South Turkana Nature Reserve Kenya 128 B4
South Twin Island Canada 168 E2
South Twin Lake Canada 169 K3
South Uist i. U.K. 46 E6
also known as Uibhist a' Deas
South Umpqua r. U.S.A. 180 B4
South Wellesley Islands Australia 148 C3
South-West Africa country Africa see Namibia
South West Cape Australia 147 E5
South West Cape N.Z. 153 B15
also known as Puhiwaero
South West Cay reef Australia 149 G4
Southwest Conservation Area nature res. Australia 147 E5
South West Entrance sea chan. P.N.G. 149 F1
Southwest Harbor U.S.A. 177 Q1
South West Island Australia 149 F3
South West National Park Australia 147 E5
South West Rocks Australia 147 G2
South Whitley U.S.A. 172 H9
South Williamson U.S.A. 176 C8
South Williamsport U.S.A. 177 I4
South Windham U.S.A. 177 O2
Southwold U.K. 47 N11
Southwood National Park Australia 147 F1
South Zanesville U.S.A. 176 C6
Soutpansberg mts S. Africa 131 F4
Souttouf, Adrar mts W. Sahara 122 B5
Souvigny France 51 J6
Sovata Romania 58 G2
Soveja Romania 58 H2
Soverato Italy 57 I10
Sovet Tajik. 101 G2
also known as Sovetskiy
Sovetabad Uzbek. see Khanabad
Sovetsk Kaliningradskaya Oblast' Rus. Fed. 42 C6
historically known as Tilsit
Sovetsk Kirovskaya Oblast' Rus. Fed. 40 I4
Sovetsk Tul'skaya Oblast' Rus. Fed. 43 S8
Sovetskaya Rus. Fed. 107 F1
Sovetskaya Gavan' Rus. Fed. 82 F2
Sovetskiy Khanty-Mansiyskiy Avtonomnyy Okrug Rus. Fed. 38 G3
Sovetskiy Leningradskaya Oblast' Rus. Fed. 43 J1
Sovetskiy Respublika Mariy El Rus. Fed. 40 I4
Sovetskiy Tajik. see Sovet
Sovetskiye Rus. Fed. see Shatoy
Sovetskoye Rus. Fed. 102 A2
Sovetskoye Rus. Fed. see Zelenokumsk
Soviči Bos.-Herz. 56 J5
Sowa Botswana 131 E4
Sowa China 86 A2
formerly known as Dagxoi
Sowa Pan salt pan Botswana 131 E4
Soweto S. Africa 133 L3
Sōya-kaikyō strait Japan/Rus. Fed. see La Pérouse Strait
Soyaló Mex. 185 G5
Sōya-misaki c. Japan 90 G2
Soyana r. Rus. Fed. 40 G2
Soyang-ho l. S. Korea 83 B5
Soyaux France 50 G7
Sōya-wan b. Japan 90 G2
Soylan Armenia see Vayk'
Soyma r. Rus. Fed. 40 I2
Soyo Angola 127 B6
formerly known as Santo António do Zaire
Sozaq Kazakh. see Suzak
Sozh r. Europe 43 L9
Sozimskiy Rus. Fed. 40 J4
Sozopol Bulg. 58 I6
historically known as Apollonia
Spaatz Island Antarctica 222 T2
Spadafora Sicilia Italy 57 H10

▶Spain country Europe 54 F4
4th largest country in Europe. Known as España in Spanish; historically known as Hispania.
europe [countries] ▶ 32–35

Spalato Croatia see Split
Spalatum Croatia see Split
Spalding Australia 146 C3
Spalding U.K. 47 L11
Spaniard's Bay Canada 169 K4
Spanish Canada 168 D4
Spanish r. Canada 168 D4
Spanish Fork U.S.A. 183 M1
Spanish Guinea country Africa see Equatorial Guinea
Spanish Netherlands country Europe see Belgium
Spanish Point Rep. of Ireland 47 C11
Spanish Sahara terr. Africa see Western Sahara
Spanish Town Jamaica 186 D3
Spanish Wells Bahamas 175 E7
Sparagio, Monte mt. Sicilia Italy 57 E10
Sparks U.S.A. 182 E2
Sparta Greece see Sparti
Sparta GA U.S.A. 175 D5
Sparta MI U.S.A. 172 H7
Sparta NC U.S.A. 176 D9
Sparta TN U.S.A. 174 C5
Sparta WI U.S.A. 172 C7
Spartanburg U.S.A. 174 D5
Spartansburg U.S.A. 176 F4
Spartel, Cap c. Morocco 54 F9
Sparti Greece 59 D11
historically known as Lacedaemon or Sparta
Spartivento, Capo c. Sardegna Italy 57 A10
Spartivento, Capo c. Italy 57 I11
Sparwood Canada 167 H5
Spas-Demensk Rus. Fed. 43 P7
Spas-Klepiki Rus. Fed. 43 V6
Spass Rus. Fed. 43 Q6
Spasskaya Polist' Rus. Fed. 43 M3
Spassk-Dal'niy Rus. Fed. 82 D3
Spasskoye Kazakh. 103 G1
Spasskoye-Lutovinovo Rus. Fed. 43 R8
Spas-Ugol Rus. Fed. 43 S5
Spatha, Akra pt Greece 59 E13
Spatsizi Plateau Wilderness Provincial Park Canada 166 D3
Spean Bridge U.K. 46 H7
Spearfish U.S.A. 178 B2
Spearman U.S.A. 179 B4
Speers Canada 167 J4
Speightstown Barbados 187 I4
Speikkogel mt. Austria 49 M8
Speke Gulf Tanz. 128 B5
Spence Bay Canada see Taloyoak
Spencer IA U.S.A. 178 D3
Spencer ID U.S.A. 180 D3
Spencer IN U.S.A. 174 C4
Spencer MA U.S.A. 177 N3
Spencer NY U.S.A. 177 I3
Spencer VA U.S.A. 176 E9
Spencer, Cape Australia 146 C3
Spencer, Cape U.S.A. 166 B3
Spencer, Point U.S.A. 39 T3
Spencer Gulf est. Australia 146 C3
Spencer Range hills N.T. Australia 148 A2
Spencer Range hills N.T. Australia 148 B2
Spences Bridge Canada 166 F5
Spenser Mountains N.Z. 153 G10
Spercheios r. Greece 59 D10
also spelt Sperkhiós
Sperkhiós r. Greece see Spercheios
Spermezeu Romania 58 F1
Sperrin Mountains hills U.K. 47 E9
Sperryville U.S.A. 176 G7
Spétsai i. Greece see Spetses
Spetses Greece 59 E11
Spetses i. Greece 59 E11
also known as Spétsai
Spey r. U.K. 46 I6
Speyer Germany 48 F6
Spezand Pak. 101 F4
Spice Islands Indon. see Moluccas
Spiekeroog i. Germany 48 E2
Spiez Switz. 51 N6
Spijkenisse Neth. 48 B4
Spil Dağı Milli Parkı nat. park Turkey 59 I10
Spilimbergo Italy 56 E2
Spīn Būldak Afgh. 101 F4
Spioenkop Dam Nature Reserve S. Africa 133 N5
Spirit Lake U.S.A. 178 D3
Spiritwood Canada 167 J4
Spirovo Rus. Fed. 43 P4
Spišská Nová Ves Slovakia 49 R7
Spitak Armenia 107 F2
Spiti r. India 96 C3
Spit Point Australia 150 B4

▶Spitsbergen i. Svalbard 38 B2
5th largest island in Europe. Also spelt Spitzbergen.
europe [landscapes] ▶ 30–31

Spitskop mt. S. Africa 132 G10
Spitskopvlei S. Africa 133 J8
Spitsyno Rus. Fed. 42 I3
Spittal an der Drau Austria 49 K9
Spitzbergen i. Svalbard see Spitsbergen
Split Croatia 56 I5
formerly known as Spalato; historically known as Spalatum
Split Lake Canada 167 L3
Split Lake l. Canada 167 L3
Spokane U.S.A. 180 C3
Spokane r. U.S.A. 180 C3
Spokane Indian Reservation res. U.S.A. 180 C3
Spoon r. U.S.A. 174 B3
Spooner U.S.A. 172 B5
Spot Bay Cayman Is 186 D3
Spotsylvania U.S.A. 176 H7
Spragge Canada 173 K4
Sprague r. U.S.A. 180 B4
Spranger, Mount Canada 166 F4
Spratly Island S. China Sea 72 D5
Spratly Islands S. China Sea 72 D5
also known as Nansha Qundao or Quan Dao Truong Sa or Truong Sa

Sucre *state* Venez. **199** F2
Sucuaro Col. **198** D3
Sucumbíos *prov.* Ecuador **198** B5
Sucunduri *r.* Brazil **199** G6
Sucuriú *r.* Brazil **206** B7
Suczawa Romania *see* **Suceava**
Sud *prov.* Cameroon **125** H6
Sud, Rivière du *r.* Canada **177** L1
Suda Rus. Fed. **43** S2
Suda *r.* Rus. Fed. **43** S2
Sudak Ukr. **41** E7

▶**Sudan** *country* Africa **121** E5
Largest country in Africa and 10th largest in the world. Historically known as Anglo-Egyptian Sudan.
world [countries] 10–11
africa [countries] 114–117

Suday Rus. Fed. **40** G4
Sudayr *reg.* Saudi Arabia **105** D2
Sudayr, Sha'īb *watercourse* Iraq **107** F5
Sudbishchi Rus. Fed. **43** S9
Sud'bodarovka Rus. Fed. **102** C1
Sudbury Canada **168** D4
Sudbury U.K. **47** M11
Sudd *swamp* Sudan **126** F3
Suddie Guyana **199** G3
Sude *r.* Germany **48** H2
Sudest Island P.N.G. *see* **Tagula Island**
Sudetenland *mts* Czech Rep./Poland *see* **Sudety**
Sudety *mts* Czech Rep./Poland **49** M5
historically known as Sudetenland
Sudimir Rus. Fed. **43** P8
Sudislavl' Rus. Fed. **40** G4
Sud-Kivu *prov.* Dem. Rep. Congo **126** F5
Sudlersville U.S.A. **177** J6
Sudogda Rus. Fed. **40** G5
Sudomskiye Vysoty *hills* Rus. Fed. **43** K4
Sudost' *r.* Rus. Fed. **43** O9
Sud-Ouest *prov.* Cameroon **125** H5
Sudr Egypt **121** G2
Sudr, Râs el *pt* Egypt **108** D8
Suðurland *constituency* Iceland **44** [inset] B2
Suðuroy *i.* Faroe Is **46** F2
Suðuroyarfjørður *sea chan.* Faroe Is **46** F2
Sue *watercourse* Sudan **126** F3
Sueca Spain **55** K5
Süedinenie Bulg. **58** F6
Suez Egypt **121** G2
also spelt El Suweis *or* As Suways
Suez, Gulf of Egypt **121** G2
also known as Suweis, Khalîg el *or* Suways, Khalīj as
Suez Bay Egypt **108** D8
also known as Qulzum, Baḥr el
Suez Canal Egypt **121** G2
also known as Suweis, Qanâ el
Şufaynah Saudi Arabia **104** C3
Suffolk U.S.A. **177** I9
Sūfīān Iran **100** A2
Sufi-Kurgan Kyrg. *see* **Sopu-Korgon**
Sug-Aksy Rus. Fed. **88** E1
Sugar *r.* U.S.A. **172** D8
Sugarbush Hill *hill* U.S.A. **172** E5
Sugar Grove *NC* U.S.A. **176** D9
Sugar Grove *OH* U.S.A. **176** C6
Sugarloaf Mountain U.S.A. **174** G2
Sugarloaf Point Australia **147** G3
Sugar Notch U.S.A. **173** R9
Sugbuhan Point Phil. **74** C4
Süget China *see* **Sogat**
Sugi *i.* Indon. **76** C2
Sugun China **88** B4
Sugut *r.* *Sabah* Malaysia **77** G1
Sugut, Tanjong *pt* *Sabah* Malaysia **77** G1
Suhaia Romania **58** G5
Suhai Hu *l.* China **84** B4
Suhait China **84** E4
Sūhāj Egypt *see* **Sohâg**
Şuḥār Oman **105** G2
English form Sohar
Sühbaatar Mongolia **85** E1
Sühbaatar *prov.* Mongolia **85** G2
Suheli Par *i.* India **94** B4
Suhl Germany **48** H5
Suhopolje Croatia **56** J3
Suhul *reg.* Saudi Arabia **105** D3
Suhūl al Kidan *plain* Saudi Arabia **105** F3
Suhum Ghana **125** E5
Şuhut Turkey **106** B3
Suiá Missur *r.* Brazil **202** A4
Sui'an China *see* **Zhangpu**
Suibin China **82** C3
Suichang China **87** F2
also known as Miaogao
Suicheng China *see* **Jianning**
Suicheng China *see* **Suixi**
Suichuan China **87** E3
also known as Quanjiang
Suid-Afrika *country* Africa *see* **South Africa, Republic of**
Suide China **85** F4
also known as Mingzhou
Suidzhikurmsy Turkm. *see* **Madau**
Suifen *r.* China **82** C4
Suifenhe China **82** C3
Suigam India **96** A4
Suihua China **82** B3
Suijiang China **86** B2
also known as Zhongcheng
Suileng China **82** B3
Suining *Hunan* China **87** D3
also known as Changpu
Suining *Jiangsu* China **87** F1
Suining *Sichuan* China **86** C2
Suiping China **87** E1
also known as Zhuoyang
Suippes France **51** K3
Suir *r.* Rep. of Ireland **47** E11
Suisse *country* Europe *see* **Switzerland**
Suixi *Anhui* China **87** F1
Suixi *Guangdong* China **87** D4
also known as Suicheng
Suixian China **87** E1
Suixian China *see* **Suizhou**
Suiyang China **87** C3
also known as Yangchuan
Suizhai China *see* **Xiancheng**
Suizhong China **85** I3
Suizhou China **87** E2
formerly known as Suixian
Sujangarh India **96** B4
Sujawal Pak. **101** G5
Sukabumi Indon. **77** D4
Sukadana *Kalimantan Barat* Indon. **77** E3
Sukadana *Sumatra* Indon. **77** D4
Sukadana, Teluk *b.* Indon. **77** E3
Sukagawa Japan **90** G6
Sukaramai Indon. **77** E3
Sukarnapura Indon. *see* **Jayapura**
Sukarno, Puntjak *mt.* Indon. *see* **Jaya, Puncak**
Suket India **96** C4
Sukeva Fin. **44** N3
Sukhanovka Rus. Fed. **90** C1
Sukhary Belarus **43** L8
Sukhinichi Rus. Fed. **43** Q7
Sukhodol'skoye, Ozero *l.* Rus. Fed. **43** L1
Sukhodrev *r.* Rus. Fed. **43** Q7
Sukhona *r.* Rus. Fed. **43** V2
Sukhothai Thai. **78** B4
Sukhoverkovo Rus. Fed. **43** Q5
Sukhumi Georgia *see* **Sokhumi**
Sukhum-Kale Georgia *see* **Sokhumi**
Sukkertoppen Greenland *see* **Maniitsoq**
Sukkozero Rus. Fed. **40** E3
Sukkur Pak. **101** G5
Sukkur Barrage Pak. **101** G5
Sukma India **94** D2
Sukpay Rus. Fed. **82** E3
Sukpay *r.* Rus. Fed. **82** E3
Sukri *r.* India **96** B4
Sukromlya Rus. Fed. **43** P5
Sukromny Rus. Fed. **43** R4
Sukses Namibia **130** C4
Suktel *r.* India **95** D1
Sukumo Japan **91** C8
Sukun *i.* Indon. **75** B5
Sul, Canal do *sea chan.* Brazil **202** B2
Sul, Pico do *mt.* Brazil **207** J7
Sula *i.* Norway **46** Q2
Sula *r.* Rus. Fed. **40** I2
Sula, Kepulauan *is* Indon. **75** C3
Sula, Ozero *l.* Rus. Fed. **44** O3
Sulabesi *i.* Indon. **75** C3
Sulaiman Ranges *mts* Pak. **101** G4
Sulak Rus. Fed. **102** A4
Sulak *r.* Rus. Fed. **102** A4
Sūlār Iran **100** B4
Sula Sgeir *i.* U.K. **46** F4
Sulasih, Gunung *vol.* Indon. **76** C3
Sulat Phil. **74** C4
Sulawesi *i.* Indon. *see* **Celebes**
Sulawesi Selatan *prov.* Indon. **75** A3
Sulawesi Tengah *prov.* Indon. **75** B3
Sulawesi Tenggara *prov.* Indon. **75** B4
Sulawesi Utara *prov.* Indon. **75** C2
Sulaymān Beg Iraq **107** F4
Sulayyimah Saudi Arabia **105** D3
Sulci *Sardegna* Italy *see* **Sant'Antioco**
Sulcis *Sardegna* Italy *see* **Sant'Antioco**
Sulechów Poland **49** M3
Sulęcin Poland **49** M3
Suledeh Iran **100** B2
Sulejów Poland **49** Q4
Sulejowskie, Jezioro *l.* Poland **49** Q4
Suleman, Teluk *b.* Indon. **75** A2
Sule Skerry *i.* U.K. **46** H4
Sule Stack *i.* U.K. **46** H4
Süleymanlı Turkey **107** D3
Suliki Indon. **76** C3
Sulima Sierra Leone **124** C5
Sulina Romania **58** K3
Sulina, Braţul *watercourse* Romania **58** K3
Suliskongen *mt.* Norway **44** L2
Sulitjelma Norway **44** L2
Sulkava Fin. **45** N3
Sullana Peru **198** A6
Süller Turkey **59** K10
Sullivan *IL* U.S.A. **174** B4
Sullivan *IN* U.S.A. **174** C4
Sullivan Bay Canada **166** E5
Sullivan Island Myanmar *see* **Lanbi Kyun**
Sullivan Lake Canada **167** I5
Sully-sur-Loire France **51** I5
Sulmo Italy *see* **Sulmona**
Sulmona Italy **56** F6
historically known as Sulmo
Suloğlu Turkey **58** H7
Sulphur *LA* U.S.A. **179** D6
Sulphur *OK* U.S.A. **179** C5
Sulphur *r.* U.S.A. **179** D5
Sulphur Draw *watercourse* U.S.A. **179** B5
Sulphur Springs U.S.A. **179** D5
Sulphur Springs Draw *watercourse* U.S.A. **179** B5
Sultan Canada **168** D4
Sultan Libya **120** D2
Sultan, Koh-i- *mts* Pak. **101** E4
Sultanabad India *see* **Osmannagar**
Sultanabad Iran *see* **Arāk**
Sultanbeyli Turkey **58** K8
Sultanhanı Turkey **106** C3
Sultanhisar Turkey **59** J11
Sultaniça Turkey **58** H8
Sultaniye Turkey *see* **Karapınar**
Sultanpur India **97** D4
Sultansandzharskoye Vodokhranilische *resr* Turkm. **103** E4
Sulu Dem. Rep. Congo **126** E6
Suluan *i.* Phil. **74** C4
Sulu Archipelago *is* Phil. **74** B5
Sülüklü Turkey **106** C3
Sülüktü Kyrg. **103** G5
also spelt Sulyukta
Suluntah Libya **120** D1
Sulūq Libya **120** D2
Suluru India **94** D3
Sulu Sea N. Pacific Ocean **74** A4
Sulyukta Kyrg. *see* **Sülüktü**
Sulzbach-Rosenberg Germany **48** I6
Sulzberger Bay Antarctica **222** N1
Sumaco, Volcán *vol.* Ecuador **198** B5
Šumadija *reg.* Yugo. **58** B4
Sumāil Oman **105** G3
Sumalata Indon. **75** B2
Sumampa Arg. **204** E3
Sumangat, Tanjong *pt* *Sabah* Malaysia **74** A5
Sumapaz, Parque Nacional *nat. park* Col. **198** C4
Sumatera *i.* Indon. *see* **Sumatra**
Sumatera Barat *prov.* Indon. **76** C3
Sumatera Selatan *prov.* Indon. **76** C3
Sumatera Utara *prov.* Indon. **76** B2

▶**Sumatra** *i.* Indon. **76** B2
2nd largest island in Asia and 6th in the world. Also spelt Sumatera.
asia [landscapes] 62–63

Sumaúma Brazil **201** E1
Šumava *mts* Czech Rep. **49** K6
Šumava *nat. park* Czech Rep. **49** K6
Sumba *i.* Indon. **75** B5
Sumba, Île *i.* Dem. Rep. Congo **126** C4
Sumba, Selat *sea chan.* Indon. **75** A5
Sumbar *r.* Turkm. **102** C5
Sumbawa *i.* Indon. **77** G5
Sumbawabesar Indon. **77** G5
Sumbawanga Tanz. **129** A6
Sumbay Peru **200** C3
Sumbe Angola **127** B7
formerly known as Ngunza *or* Ngunza-Kabolu *or* Novo Redondo
Sumbing, Gunung *vol.* Indon. **76** C3
Sumbu Zambia **127** F7
Sumbu National Park Zambia **127** F7
also spelt Nsumbu National Park
Sumburgh U.K. **46** K4
Sumburgh Head U.K. **46** K4
Sumbuya Sierra Leone **124** C5
Sumdo Aksai Chin **89** B5
Sumdo China **86** B2
Sumdum, Mount U.S.A. **166** C3
Sumé Brazil **202** E3
Sumedang Indon. **77** D4
Sume'eh Sarā Iran **100** B2
Sümeg Hungary **49** O9
Sumeih Sudan **126** E2
Sumenep Indon. **77** F4
Sumerpur India **96** B4
Sumgait Azer. *see* **Sumqayıt**
Sumisu-jima *i.* Japan **91** G9
Sümiyn Bulag Mongolia **85** G1
Summēl Iraq **107** E3
Summer Beaver Canada **168** B2
Summerdown Namibia **130** C4
Summerford Canada **169** K3
Summer Island U.S.A. **172** G5
Summerland Canada **166** G5
Summerside Canada **169** I4
Summersville U.S.A. **176** E7
Summersville Lake U.S.A. **176** E7
Summerville *GA* U.S.A. **174** C5
Summerville *SC* U.S.A. **175** D5
Summit Lake *B.C.* Canada **166** E3
Summit Lake *B.C.* Canada **166** F4
Summit Mountain U.S.A. **183** H2
Summit Peak U.S.A. **181** F5
Sumnal Aksai Chin **89** B5
Sumner U.S.A. **174** B5
Sumner, Lake N.Z. **153** G10
Sumner Strait U.S.A. **166** C3
Sumon-dake *mt.* Japan **90** F6
Sumoto Japan **91** D7
Sumpangbinangae Indon. **75** A4
Šumperk Czech Rep. **49** N6
Sumprabum Myanmar **78** B2
Sumpu Japan *see* **Shizuoka**
Sumqayıt Azer. **107** G2
also spelt Sumgait
Sumqayıt *r.* Azer. **107** G2
Sumsar Kyrg. **103** G4
Sumskiy Posad Rus. Fed. **40** E2
Sumter U.S.A. **175** D5
Sumur Jammu and Kashmir **96** C2
Sumy Ukr. **41** E6
Sun *r.* U.S.A. **180** E3
Suna Rus. Fed. **40** I4
Sunagawa Japan **90** G3
Sunam India **96** B3
Sunamganj Bangl. **97** F4
Sunan China **84** C4
also known as Hongwansi
Sunan N. Korea **83** B5
Şunaynah Oman **105** F3
Sunaysilah *salt l.* Iraq **109** M2
Sunbright U.S.A. **176** A9
Sunbula Kuh *mts* Iran **100** A3
Sunbury Australia **147** E4
Sunbury *NC* U.S.A. **177** I9
Sunbury *OH* U.S.A. **176** C5
Sunbury *PA* U.S.A. **177** I5
Sunchales Arg. **204** E3
Suncho Corral Arg. **204** E2
Sunch'ŏn N. Korea **83** B5
Sunch'ŏn S. Korea **83** B6
Sun City S. Africa **133** L2
Sun City U.S.A. **183** L8
Suncook U.S.A. **177** N2
Sund Fin. **42** B1
Sunda, Selat *strait* Indon. **77** D4
English form Sunda Strait
Sunda Kalapa Indon. *see* **Jakarta**
Sundance U.S.A. **180** F3
Sundarbans *reg.* Bangl./India **97** F5
Sundarbans National Park Bangl./India **97** F5
Sundargarh India **97** E5
Sundarnagar India **96** C3
Sunda Strait Indon. *see* **Sunda, Selat**
Sundays *r.* *E. Cape* S. Africa **133** J10
Sundays *r.* *Kwazulu-Natal* S. Africa **133** O5
Sunday Strait Australia **150** C3
Sunderland U.K. **47** K9
Sündiken Dağları *mts* Turkey **106** B3
Sundre Canada **167** H5
Sundridge Canada **168** E4
Sundsvall Sweden **45** L3
Sundukli, Peski *des.* Turkm. **103** E5
also known as Sandykly Gumy
Sundumbili S. Africa **133** P6
Sunel India **96** C4
Sunga Tanz. **129** C6
Sungaiapit Indon. **76** C2
Sungaiguntung Indon. **76** C2
Sungailiat Indon. **77** D3
Sungaipenuh Indon. **76** C3
Sungaipinyuh Indon. **77** E2
Sungai Tuas Basin *dock* Sing. **76** [inset]
Sungari *r.* China *see* **Songhua Jiang**
Sungei Petani Malaysia **76** C1
Sungei Seletar Reservoir Sing. **76** [inset]
Sungguminasa Indon. **75** A4
Sungikai Sudan **121** F6
Sungkiang China *see* **Songjiang**
Sung Kong *i.* *Hong Kong* China **87** [inset]
Sungo Moz. **131** G3
Sungqu China *see* **Songpan**
Sungurlare Bulg. **58** H6
Sungurlu Turkey **106** C2
Sunja Croatia **56** I3
Sunkar, Gora *mt.* Kazakh. **103** H3
Sunkosh *r.* Bhutan **97** F4
also spelt Sankosh
Sun Kosi *r.* Nepal **97** E4
Sunndal Norway **45** I3
Sunndalsøra Norway **44** J3
Sunne Sweden **45** K4
Sunnyside *UT* U.S.A. **183** N2
Sunnyside *WA* U.S.A. **180** C3
Sunnyvale U.S.A. **182** B4
Sun Prairie U.S.A. **172** D7
Sunsas, Sierra de *hills* Bol. **201** F4
Sunset House Canada **167** G4
Sunset Peak *hill* *Hong Kong* China **87** [inset]
also known as Tai Tung Shan
Sunshine Island *Hong Kong* China **87** [inset]
also known as Chau Kung To
Suntar Rus. Fed. **39** L3
Suntsar Pak. **101** E5
Suntu Eth. **128** C2
Sunwi-do *i.* N. Korea **83** B5
Sunwu China **82** B2
Sunyani Ghana **124** E5
Suojanperä Fin. **44** O1
Suolahti Fin. **44** N3
Suolijärvet *l.* Fin. **40** D2
Suoločielgi Fin. *see* **Saariselkä**
Suoluvuobmi Norway **44** M1
Suomenniemi Fin. **45** N3
Suomi Canada **172** D2
Suomi *country* Europe *see* **Finland**
Suomusjärvi Fin. **42** E1
Suomussalmi Fin. **44** O2
Suō-nada *b.* Japan **91** B8
Suonenjoki Fin. **44** N3
Suŏng Cambodia **79** D6
Suong *r.* Laos **78** C4
Suontee Fin. **44** N3
Suontienselkä *l.* Fin. **44** N3
Suoyarvi Rus. Fed. **40** E3
Suozhen China *see* **Huantai**
Supa India **94** B3
Supai U.S.A. **183** L5
Supaul India **97** E4
Superfosfatnyy Uzbek. **103** F5
Superior *AZ* U.S.A. **183** M8
Superior *MT* U.S.A. **180** D3
Superior *NE* U.S.A. **178** C3
Superior *WI* U.S.A. **172** A4
Superior, Laguna *lag.* Mex. **185** G5

▶**Superior, Lake** Canada/U.S.A. **172** F3
Largest lake in North America and 2nd in the world.
northamerica [landscapes] 156–157

Supetar Croatia **56** I5
Suphan Buri Thai. **79** C5
Süphan Dağı *mt.* Turkey **107** E3
Supiori *i.* Indon. **73** I7
Suponevo Rus. Fed. **43** P8
Support Force Glacier Antarctica **223** V1
Supraśl Poland **49** U2
Supraśl *r.* Poland **49** U2
Sup'sa *r.* Georgia **107** E2
Supung N. Korea **83** B4
Sūq al Inān Yemen **104** D4
Sūq ar Rubū' Saudi Arabia **104** C3
Sūq ash Shuyūkh Iraq **107** F5
Suqian China **87** F1
Sūq Suwayq Saudi Arabia **104** B2
Suquṭrā *i.* Yemen *see* **Socotra**
Sur *r.* Ghana **125** E4
Sur Hungary **49** P8
Şūr Oman **105** G3
Sur, Point U.S.A. **182** C5
Sur, Punta *pt* Arg. **204** F5
Sura Rus. Fed. **41** H5
Sura *r.* Rus. Fed. **41** H4
Şuraabad Azer. **107** G2
Surab Pak. **101** F4
Surabaya Indon. **77** F4
formerly spelt Soerabaia
Surajpur India **97** D5
Sūrak Iran **100** D5
Surakarta Indon. **77** E4
Suramana Indon. **75** A3
Şura Mare Romania **58** F3
Sūrān Iran **101** E5
Şūrān Syria **109** H2
Surat Australia **147** F1
Surat India **96** B5
Suratgarh India **96** B3
Surat Thani Thai. **79** B6
also known as Ban Don
Suraż Poland **49** T3
Surazh Belarus **43** L6
Surazh Rus. Fed. **43** N8
Surbiton Australia **149** E4
Sürdäsh Iraq **107** F4
Surdila-Greci Romania **58** I3
Surduc Romania **58** E1
Surdulica *Srbija* Yugo. **58** D6
Sûre *r.* Germany/Lux. **51** M3
Surendranagar India **96** A5
formerly known as Wadhwan
Suretka Costa Rica **186** C5
Surf U.S.A. **182** D7
Surgana India **94** B1
Surgères France **50** F6
Surgidero de Batabanó Cuba **186** C2
Surgut Rus. Fed. **38** H3
Suri India *see* **Siuri**
Suriapet India **94** C2
also spelt Suryapet
Surigao Phil. **74** C4
Surigao Strait Phil. **74** C4
Surimena Col. **198** C4
Surin Thai. **79** C5
Surinam *country* S. America *see* **Suriname**
▶**Suriname** *country* S. America **199** G3
also spelt Surinam; *formerly known as* Dutch Guiana
southamerica [countries] 192–193
Suriname *r.* Suriname **199** H3
Suripá Venez. **198** D3
Suriyān Iran **100** C4
Surkhābād Iran **100** C3
Surkhandar'inskaya Oblast' *admin. div.* Uzbek. **103** F5
English form Surkhandarya Oblast; *also known as* Surkhondaryo Wiloyati
Surkhandar'ya *r.* Uzbek. **103** F5
also spelt Surkhondaryo
Surkhandarya Oblast *admin. div.* Uzbek. *see* **Surkhandar'inskaya Oblast'**
Surkhet Nepal **97** D3
also known as Birendranagar
Surkhob *r.* Tajik. **101** G2
Surkhondaryo *r.* Uzbek. *see* **Surkhandar'ya**
Surkhondaryo Wiloyati *admin. div.* Uzbek. *see* **Surkhandar'inskaya Oblast'**
Surmāq Iran **100** C4
Sürmene Turkey **107** E2
Surnadalsøra Norway **44** J3
Sürnevo Bulg. **58** G6
Surovikino Rus. Fed. **41** G6
Surprise Canada **166** C3
Surprise Lake Canada **166** C3
Surrey Canada **166** F5
Surskoye Rus. Fed. **41** H5
Surt Libya *see* **Sirte**
Surt, Khalīj *g.* Libya *see* **Sirte, Gulf of**
Surtsey *i.* Iceland **44** [inset] B3
Sürü Iran **100** D5
Suru, Vârful *mt.* Romania **58** F3
Surubiú *r.* Brazil **202** B2
Sürüç Turkey **107** D3
Surud, Raas *pt* Somalia **128** E2
Surud Ad *mt.* Somalia *see* **Shimbiris**
Suruga-wan *b.* Japan **91** F7
Surulangun Indon. **76** C3
Surumú *r.* Brazil **199** F4
Surup Phil. **74** C5
Suryapet India *see* **Suriapet**
Şuşa Azer. **107** F3
also spelt Shusha
Susa Italy **51** N7
Susa Japan **91** B7
Sušac *i.* Croatia **56** I6
Susah Tunisia *see* **Sousse**
Susak *i.* Croatia **56** G4
Susaki Japan **91** C8
Susami Japan **91** D8
Susan U.S.A. **177** I8
Süsangerd Iran **100** B4
Susanville U.S.A. **182** D1
Suşehri Turkey **107** D2
Sushitsa Bulg. **58** G5
Sushui *r.* China **87** D1
Sušice Czech Rep. **49** K6
Suškova Latvia **43** J5
Susner India **96** C5
Susong China **87** F2
Susquehanna U.S.A. **177** J4
Susquehanna *r.* U.S.A. **177** I6
Susquehanna, West Branch *r.* U.S.A. **176** I5
Susques Arg. **200** D5
Sussex Canada **169** H4
Sussex U.S.A. **172** K4
Susua Indon. **75** B3
Susuman Rus. Fed. **39** O3
Susupu Indon. **75** C2
Susurluk Turkey **106** B3
Šušvė *r.* Lith. **42** E6
Suswa, Mount Kenya **128** B5
Susz Poland **49** Q2
Sutak Jammu and Kashmir **96** C2
Sutaşı Turkey **108** G1
Sutay Uul *mt.* Mongolia **84** B2
Sutherland Australia **147** F3
Sutherland S. Africa **132** E9
Sutherland *NE* U.S.A. **178** B3
Sutherland *VA* U.S.A. **176** H8
Sutherland Range *hills* Australia **151** D5
Sutjeska *nat. park* Bos.-Herz. **56** K5
Sutlej *r.* India/Pak. **96** A3
also spelt Satluj
Sutlepa meri *l.* Estonia **42** E2
Sütlüce Turkey **108** E1
Sütlüce Turkey **58** I7
Sutter U.S.A. **182** C2
Sutter Creek U.S.A. **182** D3
Sutton *r.* Canada **168** D2
Sutton N.Z. **153** E13
Sutton *NE* U.S.A. **178** C3
Sutton *WV* U.S.A. **176** E7
Sutton Coldfield U.K. **47** K11
Sutton Lake Canada **168** C2
Sutton Lake U.S.A. **176** E7
Suttor *r.* Australia **149** E4
Suttsu Japan **90** G3
Sutwik Island U.S.A. **164** D4
Sutyr' *r.* Rus. Fed. **82** D2
Suugant Mongolia **85** E2
Suurberg *mt.* S. Africa **133** J8
Suurberg *mts* S. Africa **133** J10
Suurbraak S. Africa **132** E11
Suure-Jaani Estonia **42** G3
Suuremõisa Estonia **42** D3
Suur katel *b.* Estonia **42** D3
Suur-Pakri *i.* Estonia **42** E2
Suurpea Estonia **42** G2
Suur väin *sea chan.* Estonia **42** E3

▶**Suva** Fiji **145** G3
Capital of Fiji.

Suvalki Poland *see* **Suwałki**
Suva Reka *Kosovo, Srbija* Yugo. **58** B6
Suvarov *atoll* Cook Is *see* **Suwarrow**
Suvorov Rus. Fed. **43** R7
Suvorove Ukr. **58** J3
Suvorovo Bulg. **58** I5
formerly known as Novgradets
Suvorovo Moldova *see* **Ştefan Vodă**
Suwa Japan **91** F6
Suwakong Indon. **77** F3
Suwałki Poland **49** T1
formerly spelt Suvalki
Suwannaphum Thai. **79** C5
Suwannee *r.* U.S.A. **175** D6
Suwanose-jima *i.* Japan **83** C7
Suwaran, Gunung *mt.* Indon. **77** G2
Suwarrow *atoll* Cook Is **221** H6
also known as Anchorage Island; *also spelt* Suvorov
Suwaylih Jordan **108** G5
also spelt Suweilih
Suwayqiyah, Hawr as *imp. l.* Iraq **107** F4
Suwayr *well* Saudi Arabia **107** E5
Suways, Khalīj as *g.* Egypt *see* **Suez, Gulf of**
Suweilih Jordan *see* **Suwaylih**
Suweis, Khalîg el *g.* Egypt *see* **Suez, Gulf of**
Suweis, Qanâ el *canal* Egypt *see* **Suez Canal**
Suwŏn S. Korea **83** B5
Suxu China **87** D4
Suykbulak Kazakh. **103** J2
also spelt Sūyqbulaq
Suyo Peru **198** A6
Sūyqbulaq Kazakh. *see* **Suykbulak**
Suz, Mys *pt* Kazakh. **102** C4
Sūzā Iran **100** D5
Suzak Kazakh. **103** G3
also spelt Sozaq
Suzaka Japan **91** F6
Suzdal' Rus. Fed. **43** V5
Suzemka Rus. Fed. **43** P9
Suzhou *Anhui* China **87** F1
Suzhou China *see* **Jiuquan**
Suzhou *Jiangsu* China **87** G2
formerly spelt Soochow
Suzi *r.* China **82** B4
Suzu Japan **90** E6
Suzuka Japan **91** E7
Suzu-misaki *pt* Japan **83** E5
Suzzara Italy **56** C4
Sværholthalvøya *pen.* Norway **44** N1

▶**Svalbard** *terr.* Arctic Ocean **38** A2
Part of Norway.

Svalenik Bulg. **58** H5
Svanstein Sweden **44** M2
Svapa *r.* Rus. Fed. **43** Q9
Svappavaara Sweden **44** M2
also known as Veaikevárri
Svapushcha Rus. Fed. **43** N4
Svärdsjö Sweden **45** K3
Svarta *r.* Fin. **42** G1
Svartälven *r.* Sweden **45** K4
Svartbyn Sweden **44** M2
Svartenhuk Halvø *pen.* Greenland *see* **Sigguup Nunaa**
Svartlå Sweden **44** M2
Svatove Ukr. **41** F6
Svay Riěng Cambodia **79** D6
Svecha Rus. Fed. **40** H4
Svėdasai Lith. **42** G6
Sveg Sweden **45** K3
Svegsjön *l.* Sweden **45** K3
Sveio Norway **45** I4
Sveki Latvia **42** H4
Švėkšna Lith. **42** C6
Svelgen Norway **45** I3
Svellingen Norway **44** J3
Švenčionėliai Lith. **42** G7
Švenčionys Lith. **42** H6
Svendborg Denmark **45** J5
Svenljunga Sweden **45** K4
Svenstavik Sweden **44** K3
Šventoji *r.* Lith. **42** F6
Sverchkovo Rus. Fed. **43** Q6
Sverdlovsk Rus. Fed. *see* **Yekaterinburg**
Sverdlovs'k Ukr. **41** F6
Sverdlovsk Uzbek. **103** F5
Sverdlovskaya Oblast' *admin. div.* Rus. Fed. **40** L4
English form Sverdlovsk Oblast
Sverdlovsk Oblast *admin. div.* Rus. Fed. *see* **Sverdlovskaya Oblast'**
Sverdrup Channel Canada **165** J2
Sverdrup Islands Canada **165** J2
Sverige *country* Europe *see* **Sweden**
Sveta Andrija *i.* Croatia **56** H5
Švėtė *r.* Lith. **42** E5
Sveti Ivan Zelina Croatia *see* **Zelina**
Sveti Jure *mt.* Croatia **56** J5
Sveti Nikole Macedonia **58** C7
Svetlaya Rus. Fed. **82** E3
Svetlodarskoye Rus. Fed. **82** F2
Svetlogorsk Belarus *see* **Svyetlahorsk**
Svetlogorsk *Kaliningradskaya Oblast'* Rus. Fed. **42** B7
historically known as Rauschen
Svetlogorsk *Krasnoyarskiy Kray* Rus. Fed. **39** I3
Svetlograd Rus. Fed. **41** G7
formerly known as Petrovskoye
Svetlopolyansk Rus. Fed. **40** J4
Svetlovodsk Ukr. *see* **Svitlovods'k**
Svetlyy Rus. Fed. **42** B7
historically known as Zimmerbude
Svetlyy Rus. Fed. **103** E2
Svetlyy Yar Rus. Fed. **41** H6
Svetogorsk Rus. Fed. **43** J1
Svetozarevo *Srbija* Yugo. *see* **Jagodina**
Svētupe *r.* Latvia **42** F4
Sviahnúkar *vol.* Iceland **44** [inset] C2
Svidník Slovakia **49** S6
Sviibi Estonia **42** E3
Svilaja *mts* Croatia **56** I5
Svilajnac *Srbija* Yugo. **58** C4
Svilengrad Bulg. **58** H7
Svinecea Mare, Vârful *mt.* Romania **58** D4
Svino *i.* Faroe Is *see* **Svínoy**
Svínoy *i.* Faroe Is **46** F1
also spelt Svinø
Svintsovyy Rudnik Turkm. **103** F5
Svir Belarus **42** H7
Svir' *r.* Rus. Fed. **43** P1
Svir, Vozyera *l.* Belarus **42** H7
Sviritsa Rus. Fed. **43** N1
Svirskaya Guba *b.* Rus. Fed. **43** N1
Svir'stroy Rus. Fed. **43** O1
Svishtov Bulg. **58** G5
Svislach *Hrodzyenskaya Voblasts'* Belarus **42** F8
Svislach *Minskaya Voblasts'* Belarus **42** I8
Svislach *r.* Belarus/Poland **42** F8
also spelt Świsłocz
Svislach *r.* Belarus **42** J8
also spelt Svisloch
Svisloch Belarus *see* **Svislach**
Svisloch *r.* Belarus *see* **Svislach**
Svisloch *r.* Belarus *see* **Svislach**
Svit Slovakia **49** R6
Svitava *r.* Czech Rep. **49** N7
Svitavy Czech Rep. **49** N6
Svitlovods'k Ukr. **41** E6
also spelt Svetlovodsk; *formerly known as* Khrushchev *or* Kremges
Svizzera *country* Europe *see* **Switzerland**
Svoboda Rus. Fed. **42** C7
Svobodnyy Rus. Fed. **82** C2
Svoge Bulg. **58** E6
Svol'nya *r.* Belarus **43** J6
Svolvær Norway **44** K1
Svratka *r.* Czech Rep. **49** N6
Svrljig *Srbija* Yugo. **58** D5
Svrljiške Planine *mts* Yugo. **58** D5
Svyantsyanskiya Hrady *hills* Belarus **42** H7
Svyatoy Nos, Mys *c.* Rus. Fed. **40** I2
Svyatsk Rus. Fed. **43** M9
Svyetlahorsk Belarus **43** K9
also spelt Svetlogorsk; *formerly known as* Shatilki
Svyha *r.* Ukr. **43** O9
Swabi Pak. **101** H3
Swaershoek S. Africa **133** J9
Swaershoekpas *pass* S. Africa **133** J9
Swain Reefs Australia **149** G4
Swainsboro U.S.A. **175** D5
Swains Island American Samoa **145** H3
also known as Olosenga
Swakop *watercourse* Namibia **130** B4
Swakopmund Namibia **130** B4
Swale *r.* U.K. **47** K9
Swallow Islands Solomon Is **145** F3
Swampy *r.* Canada **169** G1
Swan *r.* Australia **151** A6
Swan *r.* *Man./Sask.* Canada **167** K4
Swan *r.* *Ont.* Canada **168** D2
Swanage U.K. **47** K13
Swana-Mume Dem. Rep. Congo **127** E7
Swandale U.S.A. **176** E7
Swanepoelspoort *mt.* S. Africa **132** H10
Swan Hill Australia **147** D3
Swan Hills Canada **167** H4
Swan Islands *is* Caribbean Sea **186** C3
also known as Santanilla, Islas
Swan Lake *B.C.* Canada **166** D4
Swan Lake *Man.* Canada **167** K4
Swan Lake U.S.A. **178** D2
Swanlinbar Rep. of Ireland **47** E9
Swanquarter U.S.A. **174** E5
Swanquarter National Wildlife Refuge *nature res.* U.S.A. **174** E5
Swan Reach Australia **146** C3
Swan River Canada **167** K4
Swansea Australia **147** F5
Swansea U.K. **47** I12
also known as Abertawe
Swansea Bay U.K. **47** I12
Swans Island U.S.A. **177** Q1
Swanton *CA* U.S.A. **182** B4
Swanton *VT* U.S.A. **177** L1
Swartberg S. Africa **133** N7
Swartberg *mt.* S. Africa **132** D11
Swartbergpas *pass* S. Africa **132** F10
Swartdoorn *r.* S. Africa **132** B7
Swart Kei *r.* S. Africa **133** L9
Swartkolkvloer *salt pan* S. Africa **132** E7
Swartkops *r.* S. Africa **133** J10
Swart Nossob *watercourse* Namibia *see* **Black Nossob**
Swartplaas S. Africa **133** K3
Swartputs S. Africa **132** H5
Swartput se Pan *salt pan* Namibia **132** D3
Swartruggens S. Africa **133** K2
Swartruggens *mts* S. Africa **133** K2
Swartz Creek U.S.A. **173** J8
Swarzędz Poland **49** O3
Swasey Peak U.S.A. **183** K2
Swastika Canada **173** M2
Swat *r.* Pak. **101** G3
Swat Kohistan *reg.* Pak. **101** H3
Swatow China *see* **Shantou**
▶**Swaziland** *country* Africa **133** P3
known as Ngwane in Swazi
africa [countries] 114–117

▶**Sweden** *country* Europe **45** K4
5th largest country in Europe. Known as Sverige in Swedish.
europe [countries] 32–35

Swedesburg U.S.A. **172** B9
Sweet Briar U.S.A. **176** F8
Sweet Home U.S.A. **180** B3
Sweet Springs U.S.A. **176** E8
Sweetwater U.S.A. **179** B5
Sweetwater *r.* U.S.A. **180** F4
Swellendam S. Africa **132** E11
Swempoort S. Africa **133** L8
Świder *r.* Poland **49** S3
Świdnica Poland **49** N5
Świdnik Poland **49** T4
Świdwin Poland **49** M2
Świebodzice Poland **49** N5
Świebodzin Poland **49** M3
Świecie Poland **49** P2
Świętokrzyskie, Góry *hills* Poland **49** R5
Świętokrzyski Park Narodowy *nat. park* Poland **49** R5
Swift *r.* U.S.A. **177** O1
Swift Current Canada **167** J5
Swiftcurrent Creek *r.* Canada **167** J5
Swilly, Lough *inlet* Rep. of Ireland **47** E8
Swindon U.K. **47** K12
Swinkpan *imp. l.* S. Africa **133** J5
Świnoujście Poland **49** L2
Swiss Confederation *country* Europe *see* **Switzerland**
Swiss National Park Switz. **51** Q6
Świsłocz *r.* Belarus *see* **Svislach**
▶**Switzerland** *country* Europe **51** N6
known as Schweiz in German or Suisse in French or Svizzera in Italian; also known as Swiss Confederation; long form Confoederatio Helvetica
europe [countries] 32–35
Swords Rep. of Ireland **47** F10
Swords Range *hills* Australia **149** D4
Syalyets Belarus **43** L8
Syalyets Vodaskhovishcha *resr* Belarus **42** F9
Syamozero, Ozero *l.* Rus. Fed. **40** E3
Syamzha Rus. Fed. **43** V2
Syang Nepal **97** D3
Syanno Belarus **43** K7
also spelt Senno
Syarednenemanskaya Nizina *lowland* Belarus/Lith. **42** F8
Syas' *r.* Rus. Fed. **43** N1
Syas'troy Rus. Fed. **43** N1
Sybrandskraal S. Africa **133** M2
Sycamore U.S.A. **172** E9
Sychevka Rus. Fed. **43** P6
Sychevo Rus. Fed. **43** R6
Syców Poland **49** O4
Sydenham *atoll* Kiribati *see* **Nonouti**

▶**Sydney** Australia **147** F3
State capital of New South Wales. Most populous city in Oceania. Historically known as Port Jackson.
world [cities] 24–25
oceania [features] 142–143

Sydney Canada **169** I4
Sydney Island Kiribati *see* **Manra**
Sydney Lake Canada **167** M5
Sydney Mines Canada **169** I4
Sydzhak Uzbek. *see* **Sidzhak**
Syedra *tourist site* Turkey **108** D1
Syeverodonets'k Ukr. **41** F6
also spelt Severodonetsk; *formerly known as* Leskhimstroy
Sykesville U.S.A. **176** G4
Sykkylven Norway **44** I3
Syktyvkar Rus. Fed. **40** I3
Sylacauga U.S.A. **175** C5
Sylhet Bangl. **97** F4
Sylhet *admin. div.* Bangl. **97** F4
Sylt *i.* Germany **48** F1
Sylva *r.* Rus. Fed. **40** K4
Sylva U.S.A. **174** D5
Sylvania *GA* U.S.A. **175** D5
Sylvania *OH* U.S.A. **176** B4
Sylvan Lake Canada **167** H4
Sylvester U.S.A. **175** D6
Sylvester, Lake *salt flat* Australia **148** B3
Sylvia, Mount Canada **166** E3

Tanafjorden inlet Norway 44 O1
also known as Deanuvuotna
Tanagro r. Italy 57 H8
Tanah, Tanjung pt Indon. 77 E4
T'ana Hāyk' l. Eth. see Tana, Lake
Tanahbala i. Indon. 76 B3
Tanahgrogot Indon. 77 G3
Tanahjampea i. Indon. 75 B4
Tanahmasa i. Indon. 76 B3
Tanahmerah Indon. 77 G2
Tanahputih Indon. 76 C2
Tanakeke i. Indon. 75 A4
Tanakpur India 96 D3
Tanambung Indon. 75 A3
Tanami Australia 148 A3
Tanami Desert Australia 148 A3
Tanami Downs Aboriginal Land res. Australia 148 A4
Tân An Vietnam 79 D6
Tananarive Madag. see Antananarivo
Tanandava Madag. 131 [inset] I4
Tanāqib, Ra's pt Saudi Arabia 105 E2
Tanaro r. Italy 56 A3
Tanauan Phil. 74 C4
Tanbar Australia 149 D5
Tancheng China see Pingtan
Tancheng China 87 F1
Tanch'ŏn N. Korea 83 C4
Tanda Côte d'Ivoire 124 E5
Tanda Uttar Pradesh India 96 C3
Tanda Uttar Pradesh India 97 D4
Tandag Phil. 74 C4
Țăndărei Romania 58 I4
Tandaué Angola 127 C9
Tandek Sabah Malaysia 77 G1
formerly known as Taritipan
Tandi India 96 C2
Tandil Arg. 204 F5
Tandjilé pref. Chad 126 C2
Tando Adam Pak. 101 G5
Tando Alahyar Pak. 101 G5
Tando Bago Pak. 101 G5
Tando Muhammmad Khan Pak. 101 G5
Tandou Lake imp. l. Australia 147 D3
Tandsjöborg Sweden 45 K3
Tandubatu i. Phil. 74 B5
Tandula r. India 96 D5
Tandur Andhra Pradesh India 94 C2
Tandur Andhra Pradesh India 94 C2
Taneatua N.Z. 152 K6
Tanega-shima i. Japan 91 B9
Taneichi Japan 90 G4
Tanen Taunggyi mts Thai. 78 B4
Taneti i. Indon. 75 C3
Tanew r. Poland 49 T5
Taneytown U.S.A. 177 H6
Tanezrouft reg. Alg./Mali 123 E5
Tanezrouft Tan-Ahenet reg. Alg. 123 E5
Ţanf, Jabal aţ hill Syria 109 J4
Tang, Ra's-e pt Iran 101 D5
Tanga Rus. Fed. 85 F1
Tanga Tanz. 129 C6
Tanga admin. reg. Tanz. 129 C6
Tangaehe N.Z. 152 I4
Tangail Bangl. 97 F4
Tanga Islands P.N.G. 145 E2
Tangalla Sri Lanka 94 D5
Tanganyika country Africa see Tanzania

▶Tanganyika, Lake Africa 127 F6
Deepest and 2nd largest lake in Africa and 7th largest in the world.
africa [landscapes] 112–113

Tangar Iran 100 C2
Tangasseri India 94 C4
Tangdan China 86 B3
formerly known as Dongshuan
Tangeli Iran 100 C2
Tange Promontory hd Antarctica 223 D2
Tanger Morocco see Tangier
Tangerang Indon. 77 D4
Tangermünde Germany 48 I3
Tang-e Sarkheh Iran 101 D5
Tanggor China 86 B1
Tanggu China 85 H4
Tanggulashan China see Tuotuoheyan
Tanggula Shan mt. China 89 E5
Tanggula Shan mts China 89 E5
also known as Dangla Shan
Tanggula Shankou pass China 89 E5
Tangguo China 89 D6
Tanghe China 87 E1
Tang He r. China 87 E1
Tangi Pak. 101 G3
Tangier Morocco 122 D2
also spelt Tanger or Tanjah; historically known as Tingis
Tangimoana N.Z. 152 J8
Tangkittebak, Gunung mt. Indon. 76 D4
Tang La pass China 89 E7
Tanglag China 86 A1
Tanglin Sing. 76 [inset]
Tangmai China 97 G3
Tango Japan 91 D7
Tangorin Australia 149 E4
Tangra Yumco salt l. China 89 D6
Tangse Indon. 76 A1
Tangshan China 85 H4
Tangsyq Kazakh. see Tansyk
Tangte mt. Myanmar 78 B3
Tangub Mindanao Phil. 74 B4
Tangub Negros Phil. 74 B4
Tanguieta Benin 125 F4
Tangwan China 87 D3
Tangwang r. China 82 C3
Tangwanghe China 82 C2
Tangxian China 85 G4
also known as Renhou
Tangxianzhen China 87 E2
Tang-yan Myanmar 78 B3
Tangyan He r. China 87 D2
Tangyin China 85 G5
Tangyuan China 82 C3
Tanhaçu Brazil 202 D5
Tanhua Fin. 44 N2
Taniantaweng Shan mts China 86 A2
Tanimbar, Kepulauan is Indon. 73 H8
Taninthari Myanmar see Tenasserim
Tanintharyi Myanmar see Tenasserim
Tanintharyi admin. div. Myanmar see Tenasserim
Taninthayi Myanmar see Tenasserim
Taniwel Indon. 75 D3
Tanjah Morocco see Tangier
Tanjay Phil. 74 B4
Tanjore India see Thanjavur
Tanjung Kalimantan Selatan Indon. 77 F3
Tanjung Sumatra Indon. 76 D3
Tanjungbalai Sumatra Indon. 76 B2
Tanjungbalai Sumatra Indon. 76 C2
Tanjungbaliha Indon. 75 C3
Tanjungbatu Kalimantan Timur Indon. 77 G2
Tanjungbatu Sumatra Indon. 76 C2
Tanjungbuayabuaya, Pulau i. Indon. 77 G2
Tanjunggaru Indon. 77 G3
Tanjungkarang-Telukbetung Indon. 76 D4
also known as Telukbetung; formerly known as Bandar Lampung
Tanjungpandan Indon. 77 D3
Tanjungpinang Indon. 76 D2
Tanjungpura Indon. 76 B2
Tanjung Puting National Park Indon. 77 F3
Tanjungraja Indon. 76 D3
Tanjungredeb Indon. 77 G2
Tanjungsaleh i. Indon. 77 E3
Tanjungsatai Indon. 77 E3
Tanjungselor Indon. 77 G2
Tank Pak. 101 G3
Tankara India 96 A5
Tankavaara Fin. 44 N1
Tankhala India 96 B5
Tankhoy Rus. Fed. 85 E1
Tankse Jammu and Kashmir 96 C2
Tankuhi India 97 E4
Tankwa r. S. Africa 132 D9
Tankwa-Karoo National Park S. Africa 132 D9
Tanlwe r. Myanmar 78 A4
Tanna i. Vanuatu 145 F3
also spelt Tana
Tännäs Sweden 44 K3
Tanner, Mount Canada 166 G5
Tannila Fin. 44 N2
Tannu-Ola, Khrebet mts Rus. Fed. 84 A1
Tannu Tuva aut. rep. Rus. Fed. see Tyva, Respublika
Tano Japan 91 B9
Tañon Strait Phil. 74 B4
Tanot India 96 A4
Tanout Niger 125 H3
Tanquian Mex. 185 F4
Tansen Nepal 97 D4
Tanshui Taiwan 87 G3
also spelt Danshui
Tansilla Burkina 124 D3
Tansyk Kazakh. 103 I3
also spelt Tangsyq
Tanta Egypt 121 F2
Tantabin Pegu Myanmar 78 B4
Tantabin Sagaing Myanmar 78 A3
Tan-Tan Morocco 122 C3
Tantoyuca Mex. 185 F4
Tantpur India 96 C4
Tantu China 85 I2
Tantura Israel 108 F5
Tanuku India 94 D2
Tanumshede Sweden 45 J4
Tanwakka, Sabkhat well W. Sahara 122 B5
▶Tanzania country Africa 129 B6
formerly known as Tanganyika
africa [countries] 114–117
Tanzilla r. Canada 166 D3
Tao, Ko i. Thai. 79 B6
Tao'an China see Taonan
Taocheng China see Yongchun
Taocheng China see Daxin
Taodeni Mali see Taoudenni
Tao'er r. China 85 I2
Tao He r. China 84 D5
also known as Lu Qu
Taohong China see Longhui
Taohuaping China see Longhui
Taojiang China 87 E2
Taolanaro Madag. see Tôlañaro
Taole China 85 E4
also known as Mataigou
Taonan China 85 I2
formerly known as Tao'an
Taongi atoll Marshall Is 220 F5
Taormina Sicilia Italy 57 H11
Taos U.S.A. 181 F5
Taouârdeï well Mali 125 F2
Taoudenni Mali 122 E5
also spelt Taodeni
Taounate Morocco 122 D2
Taounnant well Mali 123 E5
formerly known as Tin Tounnant
Taourirt Morocco 123 E2
Taoxi China 87 F3
Taoyang China see Lintao
Taoyuan China 87 D2
T'aoyüan Taiwan 87 G3
formerly known as Sinchu
Taozhou China see Guangde
Tapa Estonia 42 G2
Tapaan Passage Phil. 74 B5
Tapachula Mex. 185 G6
Tapajós r. Brazil 199 H5
Tapaktuan Indon. 76 B2
Tapalqué Arg. 204 E5
Tapan Indon. 76 C3
Tapan Turkey see Mansurlu
Tapanahoni r. Suriname 199 H3
Tapanatepec Mex. 185 G5
Tapanuli, Teluk b. Indon. 76 B2
Tapará, Ilha Grande do i. Brazil 199 H5
Tapara, Serra do hills Brazil 199 H5
Tapat i. Indon. 75 C3
Tapauá Brazil 199 E6
Tapauá r. Brazil 199 E6
Tapawera N.Z. 152 G9
Tapera Rio Grande do Sul Brazil 203 A9
Tapera Roraima Brazil 199 F5
Tapera Chile 205 C7
Taperoá Brazil 202 E5
Tapes Brazil 203 B9
Tapeta Liberia 124 C5
Tapi r. India 96 B5
Tapia, Sierra de hills Bol. 201 F4
Tapi Aike Arg. 205 C8
Tapiantana i. Phil. 74 B5
Tapiau Rus. Fed. see Gvardeysk
Tapiche r. Peru 198 C6
Tápió r. Hungary 49 R8
Tapiocanga, Chapada do hills Brazil 206 F3
Tápiószecső Hungary 49 Q8
Tapira Brazil 206 G6
Tapiracanga Brazil 202 C5
Tapiraí Brazil 206 F10
Tapirapé r. Brazil 202 B4
Tapirapecó, Sierra mts Brazil/Venez. 199 E4
Tapirapuã Brazil 201 F3
Tapis mt. Malaysia 76 C1
Tapisuelas Mex. 184 C3
Taplejung Nepal 97 E4
Tap Mun Chau i. Hong Kong China 87 [inset]
Tapoa watercourse Burkina 125 F3
Tapol Chad 126 B2
Tapolca Hungary 49 O9
Ta-pom Myanmar 78 B3
Tappahannock U.S.A. 177 I8
Tappal India 96 C3
Tappeh, Kūh-e hill Iran 100 B3
Tappi-zaki pt Japan 90 G4
Taprobane country Asia see Sri Lanka
Tapuaenuku mt. N.Z. 153 H9
Tapul Phil. 74 B5
Tapul Group is Phil. 74 B5
Tapulonanjing mt. Indon. 76 B2
Tapung r. Indon. 76 C2
Tapurú Brazil 199 F6
Tapurucuara Brazil 199 E5
Taputeouea atoll Kiribati see Tabiteuea
Taqar mt. Yemen 104 D5
Ţaqţaq Iraq 107 F4
Taquara Brazil 203 B9
Taquaral, Serra do hills Brazil 206 A2
Taquari Brazil 203 A6
Taquari r. Brazil 201 F4
Taquaritinga Brazil 206 E8
Taquarituba Brazil 206 D10
Taquaruçu r. Brazil 206 A8
Tara Australia 147 F1
Tara r. Bos.-Herz./Yugo. 56 K5
Tara nat. park Yugo. 58 A5
Taraba r. Nigeria 125 H4
Taraba state Nigeria 125 H4
Tarabai Brazil 206 B9
Tarabuco Bol. 200 D4
Ţarābulus Libya see Tripoli
Taraclia Moldova 58 J3
formerly spelt Tarakliya
Taraco Peru 200 C3
Taracua Brazil 198 D4
Tarādale N.Z. 152 K7
Tarāghin Libya 120 B3
Tarai reg. India 97 E4
Taraira r. Brazil see Traíra
Tarairí Bol. 201 E5
Tarakan Indon. 77 G2
Tarakan i. Indon. 77 G2
Tarakki reg. Afgh. 101 F3
Taraklı Turkey 106 B2
Tarakliya Moldova see Taraclia
Tarakua Fiji 145 H3
Taran, Mys pt Rus. Fed. 42 A7
Tarana India 96 C5
Taranagar India 96 B3
Taranaki admin. reg. N.Z. 152 H7
Taranaki, Mount vol. N.Z. 152 I7
also known as Egmont, Mount
Tarancón Spain 55 H4
Tarangambadi India 94 C4
Tarangara Chad 126 C2
Tarangire National Park Tanz. 129 C6
Tarangul l. Kazakh. see Tarankol', Ozero
Tarankol', Ozero l. Kazakh. 103 G1
formerly known as Tarangul
Taranovskoye Kazakh. 103 E1
formerly known as Viktorovka
Taranto Italy 57 J8
historically known as Tarentum
Taranto, Golfo di g. Italy 57 J8
Tarapacá admin. reg. Chile 200 C4
Tarapacá Col. 198 D5
Tarapoto Peru 198 B6
Ţaraq an Na'jah reg. Syria 109 K3
Tarare France 51 K7
Tararua Forest Park nature res. N.Z. 152 J8
Tararua Range mts N.Z. 152 J8
Tarascon-sur-Ariège France 50 H10
Tarashcha Ukr. 41 D6
Tarasht Iran 100 D3
Tarasovskiy Rus. Fed. 41 G6
Tarat Alg. 123 H4
Tarata Peru 200 C4
Tarauacá Brazil 200 C2
Tarauacá r. Brazil 198 D6
Taravo r. Corse France 56 A7
Tarawa atoll Kiribati 145 G1
formerly known as Cook Atoll or Knox Atoll
Tarawera N.Z. 152 K7
Tarawera, Lake N.Z. 152 K6
Tarawera, Mount N.Z. 152 K6
Taraz Kazakh. 103 G4
formerly known as Dzhambul or Zhambyl; historically known as Auliye Ata
Tarazona Spain 55 J3
Tarazona de la Mancha Spain 55 J5
Tarbagatay Kazakh. 103 J3
Tarbagatay Rus. Fed. 85 E1
Tarbagatay, Khrebet mts Kazakh. 88 C2
Tarbat Ness pt U.K. 46 I6
Tarbert Rep. of Ireland 47 C11
Tarbert Argyll and Bute, Scotland U.K. 46 G8
Tarbert Western Isles, Scotland U.K. 46 F6
also spelt Tairbeart
Tarbes France 50 G9
Tarbet U.K. 46 H7
Tarboro U.S.A. 174 E5
Tarcoola Australia 146 B2
Tarcoon Australia 147 E2
Tarcoonyinna watercourse Australia 146 B1
Tarcului, Munții mts Romania 58 D3
Tardes r. France 51 I6
Tardoire r. France 50 G7
Tardoki-Yani, Gora mt. Rus. Fed. 82 E2
Taree Australia 147 G2
Tareifing Sudan 128 B2
Tarendö Sweden 44 M2
Tarentum Italy see Taranto
Tareya Rus. Fed. 39 J2
Ţarfā, Ra's aţ pt Saudi Arabia 104 C4
Tarfaya Morocco 122 B4
formerly known as Cabo Yubi or Cape Juby or Villa Bens
Targa well Niger 125 G2
Targan Kazakh. see Targyn
Targhee Pass U.S.A. 180 E3
Târgoviște Romania 58 G4
formerly spelt Tîrgoviște
Târgu Bujor Romania 58 I3
formerly spelt Tîrgu Bujor
Târgu Cărbunești Romania 58 E4
formerly spelt Tîrgu Cărbunești
Târgu Frumos Romania 58 H1
formerly spelt Tîrgu Frumos
Targuist Morocco 122 D2
Târgu Jiu Romania 58 E3
formerly spelt Tîrgu Jiu
Târgu Lăpuș Romania 58 E1
formerly spelt Tîrgu Lăpuș
Târgu Mureș Romania 58 F2
also known as Marosvásárhely; formerly spelt Tîrgu Mureș
Târgu Neamț Romania 58 H1
formerly spelt Tîrgu Neamț
Târgu Ocna Romania 58 H2
formerly spelt Tîrgu Ocna
Târgu Secuiesc Romania 58 H2
formerly spelt Tîrgu Secuiesc
Targyailing China 89 D6
Targyn Kazakh. 88 C1
formerly spelt Targan
Tarhān Iran 100 A3
Tarhmanant well Mali see Taghmanant
Tarhūnah Libya 120 B1
Tari P.N.G. 73 J8
Tarian Gol China 85 F4
Tarib, Wādī watercourse Saudi Arabia 104 C4
Tarif U.A.E. 105 F2
Tarifa Spain 54 F8
Tarifa, Punta de pt Spain 54 F8
Tarigtig Point Phil. 74 B2
Tarija Bol. 201 D5
Tarija dept Bol. 201 D5
Tarikere India 94 B3
Tariku r. Indon. 73 I7
Tarim Yemen 105 E4
Tarim Basin China 88 C4
also known as Tarim Pendi
Tarime Tanz. 128 B5
Tarim He r. China 88 D3
Tarim Liuchang China 88 D3
Tarim Pendi basin China see Tarim Basin
Taringuiti Bol. 201 E5
Tarin Kowt Afgh. 101 F3
Taritatu r. Indon. 73 I7
Taritipan Sabah Malaysia see Tandek
Tarjīl Iraq 109 P2
Tarka r. S. Africa 133 J9
Tarka, Vallée de watercourse Niger 125 G3
Tarkastad S. Africa 133 K9
Tarkio U.S.A. 178 D3
Tarko-Sale Rus. Fed. 39 H3
Tarkwa Ghana 125 E5
Tarlac Phil. 74 B3
Tarlac r. Phil. 74 B2
Tarlo River National Park Australia 147 F3
Tarlton U.S.A. 176 C6
Tarma Junín Peru 200 B2
Tarma Loreto Peru 198 D5
Tarn r. France 51 H8
Tarna r. Hungary 49 Q8
Tärnaby Sweden 44 K2
Tarnak r. Afgh. 101 F4
Târnava Mare r. Romania 58 E2
Târnava Mică r. Romania 58 E2
Târnăveni Romania 58 F2
formerly spelt Tîrnăveni
Tarnica mt. Poland 49 T6
Tarnobrzeg Poland 49 S5
Tarnogród Poland 49 T5
Tarnogskiy Gorodok Rus. Fed. 40 G3
Tarnopol Ukr. see Ternopil'
Tarnos France 50 E9
Târnova Romania 58 D3
Tarnów Poland 49 R5
Tarnowitz Poland see Tarnowskie Góry
Tarnowskie Góry Poland 49 P5
historically known as Tarnowitz
Tårnvik Norway 44 K2
Taro r. Italy 56 C4
Tarō Japan 90 G5
Taro Co salt l. China 89 C6
Ţārom Iran 100 C4
Taroom Australia 149 F5
Taroudannt Morocco 122 C3
Tarpasa Bangl. 97 F5
Tarpaulin Swamp Australia 148 C3
Tarpon Springs U.S.A. 175 D6
Tarpum Bay Bahamas 175 E7
Tarq Iran 100 B3
Tarquinia Italy 56 D6
historically known as Corneto or Tarquinii
Tarquinii Italy see Tarquinia
Tarrabool Lake salt flat Australia 148 B3
Tarracina Italy see Terracina
Tarraco Spain see Tarragona
Tarragona Spain 55 M3
historically known as Tarraco
Tårrajaur Sweden 44 L2
Tarraleah Australia 147 E5
Tarrant Point Australia 148 C3
Tarras N.Z. 153 D12
Tarrasa Spain see Terrassa
Tàrrega Spain 55 M3
Tarrong China see Nyêmo
Tarso Ahon mt. Chad 120 C4
Tarso Emissi mt. Chad 120 C4
Tarso Kobour mt. Chad 120 C4
Tarsus Turkey 106 C3
Tarta Turkm. see Darta
Tartagal Salta Arg. 201 E5
Tartagal Santa Fé Arg. 204 F3
Tärtär Azer. 107 F2
also spelt Terter; formerly known as Mir-Bashir
Tartas France 50 F9
Tartu Estonia 42 H3
formerly known as Yuryev; historically known as Dorpat
Ţarţūs Syria 108 G3
Ţarţūs governorate Syria 108 H2
Tarumae-san vol. Japan see Shikotsu
Tarumirim Brazil 207 L6
Tarumizu Japan 91 B9
Tarumovka Rus. Fed. 102 A3
Tarung Hka r. Myanmar 78 B2
Tarusa Rus. Fed. 43 S7
Tarusa r. Rus. Fed. 43 S7
Tarūt Saudi Arabia 105 E2
Tarutung Indon. 76 B2
Tarutyne Ukr. 58 K2
Tarvisio Italy 56 F2
Tarvisium Italy see Treviso
Tarvo Bol. 201 E3
Tarz Iran 100 D4
Tasaral Kazakh. 88 A2
Tasbuget Kazakh. 103 F3
Taschereau Canada 173 O2
Taseko Mountain Canada 166 F5
Tasendjanet, Oued watercourse Alg. 123 F4
Tasgaon India 94 B2
Tashauz Turkm. see Dashkhovuz
Tashauzskaya Oblast' admin. div. Turkm. see Dashkhovuzskaya Oblast'
Tashbunar r. Ukr. 58 J3
Tashi China 84 B3
Tashi Chho Bhutan see Thimphu
Tashigang Bhutan see Trashigang
Tashino Rus. Fed. see Pervomaysk
Tashir Armenia 107 F2
formerly known as Kalinino
Tashk, Daryācheh-ye l. Iran 100 C4

▶Tashkent Uzbek. 103 G4
Capital of Uzbekistan. Also spelt Toshkent.

Tashkent Oblast admin. div. Uzbek. see Tashkentskaya Oblast'
Tashkentskaya Oblast' admin. div. Uzbek. 103 G4
English form Tashkent Oblast; also known as Toshkent Wiloyati
Tashkepri Turkm. 103 E5
also spelt Dashköpri
Tash-Kömür Kyrg. 103 H4
also spelt Tash-Kumyr
Tash-Kumyr Kyrg. see Tash-Kömür
Tashla Rus. Fed. 102 C2
Tāshqurghān Afgh. see Kholm
Tasialujjuaq, Lac l. Canada 169 F1
Tasiat, Lac l. Canada 169 F1
Tasiilap Karra c. Greenland 165 P3
also known as Gustav Holm, Kap
Tasiilaq Greenland see Ammassalik
Tasikmalaya Indon. 77 E4
Tasiujaq Canada 169 G1
formerly known as Baie-aux-Feuilles or Leaf Bay
Tasiusaq Greenland 165 N2
Tåsjö Sweden 44 K2
Task well Niger 125 H3
Tasker Niger 125 H3
Taskesken Kazakh. 103 J3
Taşköprü Turkey 106 C2
Taşlıçay Turkey 107 E3
Tasman N.Z. 152 H9
Tasman admin. reg. N.Z. 152 G9
Tasman r. N.Z. 153 E12
Tasman, Mount N.Z. 153 E11
Tasman Bay N.Z. 152 H9

▶Tasmania state Australia 147 E5
4th largest island in Oceania. Historically known as Van Diemen's Land.
oceania [landscapes] 136–137

Tasman Mountains N.Z. 152 G9
Tasman Peninsula Australia 147 F5
Tasman Sea S. Pacific Ocean 145 G6
Tășnad Romania 58 D1
Taşova Turkey 107 D2
also known as Yemişenbükü
Tassara Niger 125 G2
Tasselot, Mont hill France 51 K5
Tassi Gabon 126 A5
Tassialouc, Lac l. Canada 169 F1
Tassili du Hoggar plat. Alg. 123 G5
Tassili n'Ajjer plat. Alg. 123 G4
Tassin-la-Demi-Lune France 51 K7
Tåstrup Denmark 45 K5
Tas-Tumus Rus. Fed. 39 M3
Tasty Kazakh. 103 G3
Tasty-Taldy Kazakh. 103 F2
Tasu Canada 166 C4
Taşucu Turkey 108 E1
Tas-Yuryakh Rus. Fed. 39 L3
Tata Hungary 49 P8
Tata Morocco 122 D3
Tataba Indon. 75 B3
Tatabánya Hungary 49 P8
Tatamagouche Canada 169 I4
Tata Mailau, Gunung mt. East Timor 75 C5
Tatanagar India 97 E5
Tataouine Tunisia 123 H2
Tatarbunary Ukr. 41 D7
Tatarka Belarus 43 J8
Tatarpur India 96 C4
Tatarsk Rus. Fed. 80 B1
Tatarsk Rus. Fed. 43 M7
Tatarskaya A.S.S.R. aut. rep. Rus. Fed. see Tatarstan, Respublika
Tatarskiy Proliv strait Rus. Fed. 82 F2
English form Tatar Strait
Tatarstan, Respublika aut. rep. Rus. Fed. 40 I5
formerly known as Tatarskaya A.S.S.R.
Tatar Strait Rus. Fed. see Tatarskiy Proliv
Tătăruși Romania 58 H1
Tatau Sarawak Malaysia 77 F2
Tatavi r. Iran 100 A2
Tate r. Australia 149 D3
Tatebayashi Japan 91 F6
Tateyama Japan 91 F7
Tate-yama vol. Japan 91 E6
Tathlina Lake Canada 167 G2
Tathlīth Saudi Arabia 104 C4
Tathlīth, Wādī watercourse Saudi Arabia 104 D3
Tathra Australia 147 F4
Tati Botswana 131 E4
Tātīlt well Mauritania 124 B2
Tatishchevo Rus. Fed. 41 H6
Tatkon Myanmar 78 B3
Tatla Lake Canada 166 E5
Tatlatui Provincial Park Canada 166 E3
Tatlayoko Lake Canada 166 E5
Tatlıkbulak China 88 D4
Tatnam, Cape Canada 167 N3
Tatra Mountains Poland/Slovakia 49 Q6
also known as High Tatras or Tatry
Tatrang China 88 D4
Tatranský nat. park Slovakia 49 R6
Tatry mts Poland/Slovakia see Tatra Mountains
Tatrzański Park Narodowy nat. park Poland 49 Q6
Tatsenshenri r. Canada 166 B3
Tatshenshini-Alsek Provincial Wilderness Park Canada 166 B3
Tatsuno Japan 91 D7
Tatta Pak. 101 F5
Tatti Kazakh. 103 H4
Tatty Kazakh. see Tatti
Tatuí Brazil 206 F10
Tatuk Mountain Canada 166 E4
Tatula r. Lith. 42 F5
Tatum NM U.S.A. 178 B5
Tatum TX U.S.A. 179 D5
Tatvan Turkey 107 E3
Ta'ū i. American Samoa 145 I3
Taua Brazil 202 D3
Tauapeçaçu Brazil 199 F5
Tauariã Brazil 199 F6
Taubaté Brazil 203 C7
Tauber r. Germany 48 G6
Tauberbischofsheim Germany 48 G6
Tauchik Kazakh. 102 B3
also spelt Taūshyq
Taufkirchen (Vils) Germany 48 J7
Tauhara mt. N.Z. 152 K6
Tauhoa N.Z. 152 I4
Tauini r. Brazil 199 G4
Taukum, Peski des. Kazakh. 103 H3
Taumarunui N.Z. 152 J6
Taumaturgo Brazil 200 B2
Taunay Brazil 201 G5
Taung S. Africa 133 I4
Taungbon Myanmar 79 B5
Taungdwingyi Myanmar 78 A3
Taunggyi Myanmar 78 B3
Taunglau Myanmar 78 B3
Taungnyo Range mts Myanmar 78 B4
Taungtha Myanmar 78 A3
Taungup Myanmar 78 A4
Taunsa Pak. 101 G4
Taunton U.K. 47 I12
Taunton U.S.A. 177 N4
Taunus hills Germany 48 E5
Taupiri N.Z. 152 J5
Taupo N.Z. 152 K6
Taupo, Lake N.Z. 152 J6
Tauragė Lith. 42 D6
Tauralaukis Lith. 42 C6
Tauramena Col. 198 C3
Tauranga N.Z. 152 K5
Taurasia Italy see Turin
Taureau, Réservoir Canada 169 F4
Taurianova Italy 57 I10
Taurikura N.Z. 152 I3
Taurion r. France 50 H7
Tauroa Point N.Z. 152 H3
Taurus Mountains Turkey 106 C3
also known as Toros Dağları
Taūshyq Kazakh. see Tauchik
Tauste Spain 55 J3
Tauu Islands P.N.G. 145 E2
formerly known as Mortlock Islands
Tauwhareparae N.Z. 152 M6
Tauyskaya Guba g. Rus. Fed. 39 P4
Tauz Azer. see Tovuz
Tavagnacco Italy 56 F2
Tavankut Vojvodina, Srbija Yugo. 58 A2
Tavares U.S.A. 175 D6
Tavas Turkey 106 B3
also known as Yarangüme
Tavastehus Fin. see Hämeenlinna
Tavda Rus. Fed. 38 G4
Tavelsjö Sweden 44 M2
Tavernes de la Valldigna Spain 55 K5
also spelt Tabernes de Valldigna
Taveuni i. Fiji 145 H3
Tavgetos mts Greece 59 D11
also known as Taÿetos Óros
Taviano Italy 57 K9
Tavignano r. Corse France 56 B6
Tavil'dara Tajik. 101 G2
also spelt Tovil'-Dora
Tavira Port. 54 D7
Tavistock Canada 173 M7
Tavistock U.K. 47 H13
Tavolara, Isola i. Sardegna Italy 56 B8
Tavolzhan Kazakh. 103 I1
also spelt Tobylzhan
Távora r. Spain 54 D3
Tavoy Myanmar 79 B5
also known as Dawei; also spelt Tawè
Tavoy r. Myanmar 79 B5
also known as Dawei
Tavoy Island Myanmar see Mali Kyun
Tavoy Point Myanmar 79 B5
Tavrichanka Rus. Fed. 90 B3
Tavricheskoye Kazakh. 103 J2
also known as Tavrīl
Tavrīl Kazakh. see Tavricheskoye
Tavşanlı Turkey 106 B3
Tavua Fiji 145 G3
Taw r. U.K. 47 H12
Tawakoni, Lake U.S.A. 179 D5
Tawallah Range hills Australia 148 B2
Tawang India 97 F4
Tawas Bay U.S.A. 173 J6
Tawas City U.S.A. 173 J6
Tawau Sabah Malaysia 77 G1
Tawau, Telukan b. Sabah Malaysia 77 G1
Tawè Myanmar see Tavoy
Taweisha Sudan 121 E6
Tawi r. India 96 B2
Ţawī Ḩafīr well U.A.E. 105 F2
Tawila Sudan 120 E6
Ţawīlah, Gezā'ir is Egypt 104 A2
English form Tawila Islands
Tawila Islands Egypt see Ţawīlah, Gezā'ir
Ţawī Murra well U.A.E. 105 F2
Tawitawi i. Phil. 74 A5
Tawmaw Myanmar 78 B2
Tawu Taiwan 87 G4
also spelt Dawu
Taxco Mex. 185 F5
Taxkorgan China 88 A4
Tay r. Canada 166 C2
Tay r. U.K. 46 I7
Tay, Firth of est. U.K. 46 I7
Tay, Lake salt flat Australia 151 C7
Tay, Loch l. U.K. 46 H7
Tayabamba Peru 200 A2
Tayabas Bay Phil. 74 B3
Tayan Indon. 77 E2
Tayeeglow Somalia 128 E3
Tayga Rus. Fed. 80 D1
Taygan Mongolia 84 C2
Taykanskiy Khrebet mts Rus. Fed. 82 D1
Taylor Canada 166 F3
Taylor AZ U.S.A. 183 N7
Taylor NE U.S.A. 178 C3
Taylor TX U.S.A. 179 C6
Taylor, Mount N.Z. 153 F11
Taylor, Mount U.S.A. 181 F6
Taylorsville U.S.A. 174 C4
Taylorville U.S.A. 174 B4
Taymā' Saudi Arabia 104 B2
Taymura r. Rus. Fed. 39 J3
Taymyr, Ozero l. Rus. Fed. 39 K2
Taymyr, Poluostrov pen. Rus. Fed. see Taymyr Peninsula
Taymyr Peninsula Rus. Fed. 39 I2
also known as Taymyr, Poluostrov
Tây Ninh Vietnam 79 D6
Taypak Kazakh. 102 B2
also spelt Taypaq; formerly known as Kalmykovo
Taypaq Kazakh. see Taypak
Tayport U.K. 46 J7
Tayshet Rus. Fed. 80 F1
Taysoygan, Peski des. Kazakh. 102 C2
Tayspun tourist site Iraq see Ctesiphon
Taytan Turkey 59 J10
Taytay Luzon Phil. 74 B3
Taytay Palawan Phil. 74 A4
Taytay Bay Phil. 74 A4
Tayu Indon. 77 E4
Tayuan China 82 B2
Tayyebād Iran 101 E3
Tayynsha Kazakh. 103 G1
formerly known as Krasnoarmeysk
Taz r. Rus. Fed. 39 H3
Taza Morocco 122 E2
Taza-Bazar Uzbek. see Shumanay
Tāza Khurmātū Iraq 107 F4
Taze Myanmar 78 A3
Tazeh Kand Azer. 107 F3
Tazenakht Morocco 122 D3
Tazewell TN U.S.A. 176 B9
Tazewell VA U.S.A. 176 D8
Tazin r. Canada 167 I2
Tāzirbū Libya 120 D3
Tazirbu Water Wells Field Libya 120 D3
Tazizilet well Niger 125 H2
Tazlău Romania 58 H2
Tazlău r. Romania 58 H2
Tazmalt Alg. 55 P8
Tazoghrane Tunisia 57 C12
Tazouikert hill Mali 123 E5
Tazovskaya Guba sea chan. Rus. Fed. 39 H3
Tazovskiy Rus. Fed. 39 H3
Tazrouk Alg. 123 G5
Tazzarine Morocco 122 D3
Tazzouguert Morocco 122 E2
Tbessa Alg. see Tébessa

▶T'bilisi Georgia 107 F2
Capital of Georgia. English form Tbilisi; historically known as Tiflis.

Tbilisi Georgia see T'bilisi
Tchabal Mbabo mt. Cameroon 125 I5
Tchad country Africa see Chad
Tchamba Togo 125 F4
Tchaourou Benin 125 F4
Tchetti Benin 125 F5
Tchibanga Gabon 126 A5
Tchidoutene watercourse Niger 125 G2
Tchié well Chad 120 C5
Tchigaï, Plateau du Niger 123 I5
Tchikala-Tcholohanga Angola 127 C8
formerly known as Vila Nova
Tchin-Tabaradene Niger 125 G3
Tcholliré Cameroon 125 I4
Tczew Poland 49 P1
historically known as Dirschau
Te, Prêk r. Cambodia 79 D5
Tea r. Brazil 199 E5
Teacapán Mex. 184 D4
Teague, Lake salt flat Australia 151 C5
Te Anau N.Z. 153 B13
Te Anau, Lake N.Z. 153 B13
Te Anga N.Z. 152 I6
Teano Italy 56 G7
historically known as Teanum Sidicinum
Teano Range mts Australia 150 B5
Teanum Sidicinum Italy see Teano
Teapa Mex. 185 G5
Te Araroa N.Z. 152 M5
Te Aroha N.Z. 152 J5
Te Aroha, Mount hill N.Z. 152 J5
Teate Italy see Chieti
Te Awamutu N.Z. 152 J6
Tébarat Niger 125 G3
Tebedu Sarawak Malaysia 77 E2
Teberda Rus. Fed. 41 G8
Teberdinskiy Zapovednik nature res. Rus. Fed. 107 E2
Tebesjuak Lake Canada 167 L2
Tébessa Alg. 123 H2
also spelt Tbessa; historically known as Theveste
Tébessa, Monts de mts Alg. 123 H2
Tebicuary Para. 201 F6
Tebicuary r. Para. 201 F6
Tebingtinggi Sumatra Indon. 76 B2
Tebingtinggi Sumatra Indon. 76 C3
Tebo r. Indon. 76 C3
Tébourba Tunisia 57 B12
Téboursouk Tunisia 57 B12
Tebulos Mt'a Georgia/Rus. Fed. 41 H8
Tecalitlán Mex. 185 E5
Tecate Mex. 184 A1
Tece Turkey 108 F1
Tech r. France 51 J10
Techiman Ghana 125 E5
Techirghiol Romania 58 J4
Tecka Arg. 205 C6
Tecka r. Arg. 205 C6
Tecoh Mex. 185 H4
Tecolutla Mex. 185 F4
Tecomán Mex. 184 E5
Tecopa U.S.A. 183 H6
Tecoripa Mex. 184 C2
Técpan Mex. 185 E5
Tecuala Mex. 184 D4
Tecuci Romania 58 I3
Tecumseh MI U.S.A. 173 J9
Tecumseh NE U.S.A. 178 C3
Ted Somalia 128 D3
Tedzhen Turkm. 102 E5
also spelt Tejen
Tedzhen r. Turkm. 102 E5
Tedzhenstroy Turkm. 102 E5
Teec Nos Pos U.S.A. 183 O5
Teekloof Pass S. Africa 132 F9
Teel Mongolia 84 D1
Teeli Rus. Fed. 84 A1
Tees r. U.K. 47 K9
Teeswater Canada 173 L6
Tefé Brazil 199 E5
Tefé r. Brazil 199 E5
Tefé, Lago l. Brazil 199 E5
Tefedest mts Alg. 123 G4
Téfoûlet well Mali 125 F2
Tegal Indon. 77 E4
Tegel airport Germany 49 K3
Tegina Nigeria 125 G4

▶Tegucigalpa Hond. 186 B4
Capital of Honduras.

Teguidda-n-Tessoumt Niger 125 G2
Tehachapi U.S.A. 182 F6
Tehachapi Mountains U.S.A. 182 E7
Tehachapi Pass U.S.A. 182 F6
Te Hana N.Z. 152 I4
Te Hauke N.Z. 152 K7
Tehek Lake Canada 167 M1
Teheran Iran see Tehrān
Tehery Lake Canada 167 M1
Téhini Côte d'Ivoire 124 E4
Tehran Iran see Tehrān

	city	population	location		page#
largest cities					
1 ▶	Tōkyō	26 444 000	Japan **Asia**	➡	91 F7
2 ▶	Mexico City	18 131 000	Mexico **North America**	➡	185 F5
3 ▶	Mumbai (Bombay)	18 066 000	India **Asia**	➡	94 B2
4 ▶	São Paulo	17 755 000	Brazil **South America**	➡	206 G10
5 ▶	New York	16 640 000	USA **North America**	➡	177 L5
6 ▶	Lagos	13 427 000	Nigeria **Africa**	➡	125 F5
7 ▶	Los Angeles	13 140 000	USA **North America**	➡	182 F7
8 ▶	Kolkata (Calcutta)	12 918 000	India **Asia**	➡	97 F5
9 ▶	Shanghai	12 887 000	China **Asia**	➡	87 G2
10 ▶	Buenos Aires	12 560 000	Argentina **South America**	➡	204 F4

323

⬇ V

325 ←

index

V

▶**Vanuatu** country S. Pacific Ocean 145 F3 formerly known as New Hebrides or Nouvelles Hébrides oceania [countries] 138–139 oceania [features] 142–143
Vanua Valavo i. Fiji see **Vanua Balavu**
Van Wert U.S.A. 176 A5
Van Wyksdorp S. Africa 132 F10
Vanwyksvlei S. Africa 132 F7
Vanwyksvlei l. S. Africa 132 F7
Van Zylsrus S. Africa 132 G3
Vao, Embalse de resr Spain 54 D2 also spelt Bao, Embalse del
Var r. France 51 N9
Vara Estonia 42 H3
Vara Sweden 45 K4
Varada r. India 94 C3
Varadero Cuba 186 C2
Varahi India 96 A5
Varaita r. Italy 51 N8
Varakļāni Latvia 42 H5
Varalé Côte d'Ivoire 124 E4
Varallo Italy 56 A3
Varāmīn Iran 100 B3
Varanasi India 97 D4 formerly known as Benares; historically known as Kasi
Varandey Rus. Fed. 40 K1
Varangerfjorden sea chan. Norway 44 O1
Varangerhalvøya pen. Norway 44 O1 also known as Várnjárg
Varano, Lago di lag. Italy 56 H7
Varapayeva Belarus 42 I6
Varaždin Croatia 56 I2
Varazze Italy 56 A4
Varberg Sweden 45 K4
Varbla Estonia 42 E3
Varda Greece 59 C10
Vardak prov. Afgh. 101 G3
Vardannapet India 94 C2
Vardar r. Macedonia 58 D7
Varde Denmark 45 J5
Vardenis Armenia 107 F2 formerly known as Basargechar
Vårdö Fin. 42 B1
Vardø Norway 44 O1
Varduva r. Lith. 42 D5
Varegovo Rus. Fed. 43 U4
Varel Germany 48 F2
Varela Arg. 204 D4
Varėna Lith. 42 F7
Vareš Bos.-Herz. 56 K4
Varese Italy 56 A3
Varfolomeyevka Rus. Fed. 82 D3
Vårgårda Sweden 45 K4
Vargas Arg. 204 C4
Vargem r. Brazil 202 E4
Vargem Alta Brazil 207 L7
Vargem Grande Brazil 202 D2
Vargem Grande do Sul Brazil 206 G8
Varginha Brazil 203 C7
Varhaug Norway 45 I4
Varkana Iran see **Gorgān**
Varkaus Fin. 44 N3
Varkhi Belarus 43 K6
Varmahlíð Iceland 44 [inset] C2
Varmeln l. Sweden 45 K4
Värmland county Sweden 45 K4
Värmlandsnäs i. Sweden 45 K4
Varna Bulg. 58 I5 formerly known as Stalin; historically known as Odessus
Varna r. India 94 B2
Varna Rus. Fed. 103 E1
Värnamo Sweden 45 K4
Värnäs Sweden 45 K3
Varnavino Rus. Fed. 40 H4
Varnek Rus. Fed. 40 L1
Varniai Lith. 42 D6
Varnja Estonia 42 I3
Várnjárg pen. Norway see **Varangerhalvøya**
Varnyany Belarus 42 H7
Varosha Cyprus see **Varosia**
Varosia Cyprus 108 E2 also known as Maraş; also spelt Varosha
Varoška Rijeka Bos.-Herz. 56 I3
Varpaisjärvi Fin. 44 N3
Várpalota Hungary 49 P8
Värriön luonnonpuisto nature res. Fin. 44 O2
Vărşag Romania 58 G2
Varsaj Afgh. 101 G2
Vărşand Romania 58 C2
Varsh, Ozero l. Rus. Fed. 40 H2
Varsinais-Suomi reg. Fin. 45 M3 also known as Egentliga Finland
Värska Estonia 42 I4
Vartashen Azer. see **Oğuz**
Vartdalsfjorden inlet Norway 44 I3
Vartholomio Greece 59 C11
Varto Turkey 107 E3 also known as Gümgüm
Vârtop Romania 58 E4
Vârtop, Pasul pass Romania 58 D2
Värtsilä Fin. 44 O3
Var'yegan Rus. Fed. 38 H3
Varzaneh Iran 100 C3
Várzea Alegre Brazil 202 E3
Várzea da Palma Brazil 203 C6
Várzea Grande Brazil 202 D3
Varzelândia Brazil 207 I2
Varzo Italy 56 A2
Varzob Tajik. 101 G2
Varzuga Rus. Fed. 40 F2
Vasa Fin. see **Vaasa**
Vasa Barris r. Brazil 202 E4
Vasai India 94 B2
Vasalemma Estonia 42 F2
Vasalemma r. Estonia 42 F2
Vásárosnamény Hungary 49 T7
Vascão r. Port. 54 D7
Vaşcău Romania 58 D2
Vashka r. Rus. Fed. 40 H2
Vasht Iran see **Khāsh**
Vasilika Greece 58 E8
Vasilkov Ukr. see **Vasyl'kiv**
Vasilyevichy Belarus 43 K9
Vasil'yevo Rus. Fed. 42 I4
Vasil'yevskiy Mokh Rus. Fed. 43 Q4
Vas'kavichy Belarus 43 L8
Vaskivesi Fin. 45 M3
Vasknarva Estonia 42 I2
Vaslui Romania 58 I2
Vassar U.S.A. 173 J7
Vassenden Norway 45 I3
Vassfaret og Vidalen park Norway 45 J3
Vas-Soproni-síkság hills Hungary 49 N8
Vassouras Brazil 207 J9
Vastan Turkey see **Gevaş**
Västana Sweden 44 L3
Västanfjärd Fin. 42 D1
Västansjö Sweden 44 L2
Vastemõisa Estonia 42 G3
Vastenjaure l. Sweden 44 L2
Västerås Sweden 45 L4
Västerbotten county Sweden 44 K2
Västerdalälven r. Sweden 45 K3
Västerhaninge Sweden 45 L4
Västernorrland county Sweden 44 L3
Västervik Sweden 45 L4
Västmanland county Sweden 45 K4
Vasto Italy 56 G6
Västra Götaland county Sweden 45 K4
Västra Ormsjö Sweden 44 L2
Vastse-Kuuste Estonia 42 H3
Vasvár Hungary 49 N8
Vasyl'kiv Ukr. 41 D6 also spelt Vasilkov
Vatan France 50 H5
Väte Sweden 45 L4
Vaté i. Vanuatu see **Éfaté**
Vatersay i. U.K. 46 E7
Vathi Greece see **Ithaki**
Vathí Greece see **Vathy**
Vathia Greece 59 D12
Vathy Notio Aigaio Greece 59 H12
Vathy Voreio Aigaio Greece 59 H11 also spelt Vathí
▶**Vatican City** Europe 56 E7 Independent papal state, the smallest country in the world. English form Holy See; known as Città del Vaticano in Italian world [countries] 10–11 europe [countries] 32–35
Vaticano, Capo c. Italy 57 H10
Vaticano, Città del Europe see **Vatican City**
Vatio Greece 59 I12
Vatnajökull ice cap Iceland 44 [inset] C2
Vatne Norway 44 I3
Vatoa i. Fiji 145 H3 also known as Turtle Island
Vatomandry Madag. 131 [inset] K3
Vatoussa Greece 59 H9
Vatra Dornei Romania 58 G1
Vätter, Lake Sweden see **Vättern**
Vättern l. Sweden 45 K4 English form Vätter, Lake
Vattrång Sweden 45 L3
Vatulele i. Fiji 145 G3
Vaucluse, Monts de mts France 51 L9
Vaucouleurs France 51 L4
Vaughan Springs Australia 148 A4
Vaughn U.S.A. 181 F6
Vaulx-en-Velin France 51 K7
Vaupés dept Col. 198 D4
Vaupés r. Col. 198 D4
Vauquelin r. Canada 168 E2
Vauvert France 51 K9
Vauxhall Canada 167 H5
Vav India 96 A4
Vavatenina Madag. 131 [inset] K3
Vava'u i. Tonga 145 H3
Vava'u Group is Tonga 145 H3
Vavitao i. Fr. Polynesia see **Raivavae**
Vavoua Côte d'Ivoire 124 D5
Vavozh Rus. Fed. 40 I4
Vavuniya Sri Lanka 94 D4
Vawkalata Belarus 42 I7
Vawkavichy Belarus 43 L8 also known as Volkovichi
Vawkavysk Belarus 42 F8 also known as Volkovysk
Vawkavyskaye Wzvyshsha hills Belarus 42 F8 also known as Volkovyskiye Vysoty
Växjö Sweden 45 K4
Vây, Đao i. Vietnam 79 C6
Vayalpad India 94 C3
Vayenga Rus. Fed. see **Severomorsk**
Vaygach, Ostrov i. Rus. Fed. 40 K1
Vayittiri India 94 C4
Vayk' Armenia 107 F3 formerly known as Azizbekov or Soylan
Vazante Brazil 206 G4
Vazáš Sweden see **Vittangi**
Vazobe mt. Madag. 131 [inset] J3
Vazuza r. Rus. Fed. 43 P6
Vazuzskoye Vodokhranilishche resr Rus. Fed. 43 P6
Veaikevárri Sweden see **Svappavaara**
Vecht r. Neth. 48 D3 also known as Vechte (Germany)
Vechta Germany 48 F3
Vechte r. Germany 48 D3 also known as Vecht (Neth.)
Vecmikeļi Latvia 42 E5
Vecumnieki Latvia 42 F5
Vedana Rus. Fed. see **Vedeno**
Vedaranniyam India 94 C4
Vedasandur India 94 C4
Veddige Sweden 45 K4
Vedea Romania 58 F4
Vedea Romania 58 G5
Vedea r. Romania 58 G5
Vedeno Rus. Fed. 107 F2 also known as Vedana
Vedi Armenia 107 F3
Vedia Arg. 204 E4
Vedlozero Rus. Fed. 40 E3
Vedrych r. Belarus 43 L9
Veendam Neth. 48 D2
Veenendaal Neth. 48 C3
Vega i. Norway 44 J2
Vega U.S.A. 179 B5
Vegadeo Spain 54 D1
Vegarshei Norway 45 J4
Vegoritis, Limni l. Greece 58 C8
Vegreville Canada 167 H4
Végueta Peru 200 A2
Vehkalahti Fin. 42 I1
Vehmaa Fin. 45 M3
Vehoa r. Pak. 101 G4
Veidnes Norway 44 N1
Veinticinco de Mayo Arg. see **25 de Mayo**
Veinticinco de Mayo Arg. see **25 de Mayo**
Veinticinco de Mayo Arg. see **25 de Mayo**
Veiros Brazil 199 H5
Veisiejis Lith. 42 E7
Veitsiluoto Fin. 44 N2
Vejer de la Frontera Spain 54 F8
Vejle Denmark 45 J5
Velachha India 96 B5
Vela Luka Croatia 56 I6
Velardena Mex. 184 E3
Vèlas, Cabo c. Costa Rica 186 B5
Velasco, Sierra de mts Arg. 204 D3
Vela Vrata, Kanal sea chan. Croatia 56 G3
Velázquez Uruguay 204 G4
Velbŭzhdki Prokhod pass Macedonia 58 D6 also known as Deve Bair
Velddrif S. Africa 132 C9
Velden am Wörther See Austria 49 L9
Veldhoven Neth. 48 C4
Veldurti India 94 C3
Velebit mts Croatia 56 G4
Velebitski Kanal sea chan. Croatia 56 G3
Veleka r. Bulg. 58 I6
Velen Germany 48 D4
Velenje Slovenia 56 H2 formerly known as Titovo Velenje
Veles Macedonia 58 C7 formerly known as Titov Veles
Velës, Mali i mt. Albania 58 A7
Velež mts Bos.-Herz. 56 J5
Vélez Col. 198 C3
Vélez-Málaga Spain 54 G8
Vélez-Rubio Spain 55 I7
Velhas r. Minas Gerais Brazil 203 C6
Velhas r. Minas Gerais Brazil 206 F6
Velia tourist site Italy 57 H8
Velibaba Turkey see **Aras**
Velichayevskoye Rus. Fed. 41 H7
Velika Drenova Srbija Yugo. 58 C5
Velika Gorica Croatia 56 I3
Velika Kapela mts Croatia 56 G3
Velika Kladuša Bos.-Herz. 56 H3
Velika Mlaka Croatia 56 I3
Velika Morava canal Yugo. 58 C4
Velika Plana Srbija Yugo. 58 C4
Velikaya Rus. Fed. 40 I4
Velikaya r. Rus. Fed. 39 R3
Velikaya r. Rus. Fed. 40 I4
Velikaya r. Rus. Fed. 43 J4
Velikaya Guba Rus. Fed. 40 E3
Velikaya Kema Rus. Fed. 82 E3
Veliki Drvenik i. Croatia 56 I5
Veliki Jastrebac mts Yugo. 58 C5
Veliki Preslav Bulg. 58 H5 formerly known as Preslav
Veliki Risnjak mt. Croatia 56 G3
Veliki Šiljegovac Srbija Yugo. 58 C5
Veliki Šturac mt. Yugo. 58 B4
Velikiye Luki Rus. Fed. 43 L5
Velikiy Novgorod Rus. Fed. 43 M3 formerly known as Novgorod; historically known as Holmgard
Velikiy Ustyug Rus. Fed. 40 H3
Velikonda Range hills India 94 C3
Velikooktyabr'skiy Rus. Fed. 43 O4
Veliko Tŭrnovo Bulg. 58 G5 formerly known as Tŭrnovo
Velikoye Vologod. Obl. Rus. Fed. 43 R2
Velikoye Yaroslavskaya Oblast' Rus. Fed. 43 U4
Velikoye, Ozero l. Rus. Fed. 43 R4
Velikoye, Ozero l. Rus. Fed. 43 V6
Vélingara Senegal 124 B3
Vélingara Senegal 124 B3
Velingrad Bulg. 58 F6
Velino r. Italy 56 E6
Velino, Monte mt. Italy 56 F6
Veliuona Lith. 42 E6
Velizh Rus. Fed. 43 M6
Velká Bíteš Czech Rep. 49 N6
Veľká Domaša, Vodná nádrž resr Slovakia 49 S6
Veľká Fatra mts Slovakia 49 P7
Velká Javořina hill Czech Rep./Slovakia 49 O7
Veľké Kapušany Slovakia 49 T7
Velké Meziříčí Czech Rep. 49 N6
Velkua Fin. 42 C1
Veľký Krtíš Slovakia 49 Q7
Veľký Meder Slovakia 49 O8 formerly known as Čalovo
Vella Lavella i. Solomon Is 145 E2
Vellar r. India 94 C4
Velletri Italy 56 E7
Vellinge Sweden 45 K5
Vellore India 94 C3
Vel'mo r. Rus. Fed. 39 J3
Velopoula i. Greece 59 E12
Vel'sk Rus. Fed. 40 G3
Velsuna Italy see **Orvieto**
Vel't Rus. Fed. 40 I1
Velten Germany 49 K3
Veluwezoom, Nationaal Park nat. park Neth. 48 C3
Velvendos Greece 59 D8
Vel'ye, Ozero l. Rus. Fed. 43 N4
Velyka Mykhaylivka Ukr. 58 K1
Velykodolyns'ke Ukr. 58 L2
Velykyy Tokmak Ukr. see **Tokmak**
Vel'yu r. Rus. Fed. 40 J3
Vemalwada India 94 C2
Vembanad Lake India 94 C4
Vemor'ye Rus. Fed. 82 F3
Vempalle India 94 C3
Venado Tuerto Arg. 204 E4
Venafro Italy 56 G7
Venamo r. Guyana/Venez. 199 F3
Venamo, Cerro mt. Venez. 199 F3
Venarey-les-Laumes France 51 K5
Venaria Italy 51 N7
Vencedor Brazil 199 F6
Venceslau Bráz Brazil 206 D10
Venciūnai Lith. 42 F7
Venda Nova Brazil 207 L7
Vendenheim France 51 N4
Vendeuvre-sur-Barse France 51 K4
Vendinga Rus. Fed. 40 H3
Vendôme France 50 H5
Vendrell Spain see **El Vendrell**
Venecia Col. 198 C4
Venegas Mex. 185 E4
Veneta, Laguna lag. Italy 56 E3
Venetia Italy see **Venice**
Veneto admin. reg. Italy 56 D3
Venev Rus. Fed. 43 T7
Venezia Italy see **Venice**
Venezia, Golfo di g. Europe see **Venice, Gulf of**
▶**Venezuela** country S. America 199 E3 5th most populous country in South America. southamerica [countries] 192–193
Venezuela, Golfo de g. Venez. 198 D2
Vengurla India 94 B3
Veniaminof Volcano U.S.A. 164 D4
Venice Italy 56 E3 also known as Venezia; historically known as Venetia
Venice FL U.S.A. 175 D7
Venice LA U.S.A. 179 E6
Venice, Gulf of Europe 56 E3 also known as Venezia, Golfo di
Vénissieux France 51 K7
Venjan Sweden 45 K3
Venkatagiri India 94 C3
Venkatapuram India 94 D2
Venlo Neth. 48 D4
Vennesla Norway 45 I4
Venosa Italy 56 H8 historically known as Venusia
Venosta, Val valley Italy 56 C2
Venray Neth. 48 C4
Venta r. Latvia/Lith. 42 D5
Venta Lith. 42 D5
Venta de Baños Spain 54 G3
Ventania Brazil 206 C11
Ventersburg S. Africa 133 L5
Ventersdorp S. Africa 133 K3
Venterstad S. Africa 133 J7
Ventimiglia Italy 51 N9
Ventisquero mt. Arg. 205 C6
Ventnor U.K. 47 K13
Ventotene, Isola i. Italy 57 F8
Ventoux, Mont mt. France 51 L8
Ventspils Latvia 42 C4 historically known as Windau
Ventuari r. Venez. 199 E3
Ventura U.S.A. 182 E7
Venus Bay Australia 147 E4
Venusia Italy see **Venosa**
Venustiano Carranza, Presa resr Mex. 185 E3
Venzone Italy 56 F2
Vepsovskaya Vozvyshennost' hills Rus. Fed. 43 P1
Vera Arg. 204 E3
Vera Spain 55 J7
Verá, Lago l. Para. 201 F6
Vera Cruz Amazonas Brazil 200 D2
Vera Cruz São Paulo Brazil 206 D9
Vera Cruz Mex. see **Veracruz**
Veracruz Mex. 185 F5 also spelt Vera Cruz
Veracruz state Mex. 185 F4
Vera de Bidasoa Spain 55 J1
Veranópolis Brazil 203 B9
Veraval India 94 A1
Verbania Italy 56 A3
Verbilki Rus. Fed. 43 S5
Verbovskiy Rus. Fed. 40 G5
Vercelli Italy 56 A3
Vercors reg. France 51 L8
Vercors, Parc Naturel Régional du nature res. France 51 L8
Vercovicium tourist site U.K. see **Housesteads**
Verda r. Rus. Fed. 43 V8
Verdalsøra Norway 44 J3
Verde r. Arg. 205 D6
Verde r. Bahia Brazil 202 D4
Verde r. Goiás Brazil 206 C5
Verde r. Goiás/Minas Gerais Brazil 206 F5
Verde r. Mato Grosso Brazil 201 G2
Verde r. Mato Grosso do Sul Brazil 206 B8
Verde r. Minas Gerais Brazil 206 C6
Verde r. Minas Gerais Brazil 206 D6
Verde r. Minas Gerais Brazil 207 H8
Verde r. Brazil 206 E2
Verde r. Mex. 184 D3
Verde r. Para. 201 F5
Verde r. U.S.A. 183 M8
Verde, Cabo c. Senegal see **Vert, Cap**
Verde, Península pen. Arg. 204 E5
Verde Grande r. Brazil 202 D5
Verde Island Passage Phil. 74 B3
Verden (Aller) Germany 48 G3
Verde Pequeno r. Brazil 202 D5
Verdi U.S.A. 182 E2
Verdigris r. U.S.A. 178 D5
Verdikoussa Greece 59 C9
Verdinho r. Brazil 206 C4
Verdinho, Serra do mts Brazil 206 B5
Verdon r. France 51 L9
Verdun France 51 L3
Verdun-sur-Garonne France 50 H9
Vereeniging S. Africa 133 L3
Verena S. Africa 133 N2
Vereshchagino Rus. Fed. 40 J4
Verestovo, Ozero l. Rus. Fed. 43 R4
Vereya Rus. Fed. 43 R6
Verfeil France 50 H9
Verga, Cap c. Guinea 124 B4
Vergara Uruguay 204 G4
Vergeleë S. Africa 133 I2
Vergennes U.S.A. 177 L1
Vergina Greece 58 D8 also spelt Veryína
Véria Greece see **Veroia**
Verigino Rus. Fed. 43 T5
Verín Spain 54 D3
Veriora Estonia 42 I3
Veríssimo Brazil 206 E6
Veríssimo Sarmento Angola see **Camissombo**
Verkeerdevlei S. Africa 133 K5
Verkhne-Avzyan Rus. Fed. 102 D1
Verkhne-berezovskiy Kazakh. 88 C1
Verkhnedneprovsk Ukr. see **Verkhn'odniprovs'k**
Verkhnedneprovskiy Rus. Fed. 43 O7
Verkhneimbatsk Rus. Fed. 39 I3
Verkhnekolvinsk Rus. Fed. 40 K2
Verkhneruzskoye Vodokhranilishche resr Rus. Fed. 43 Q6
Verkhnespasskoye Rus. Fed. 40 H4
Verkhnetulomskiy Rus. Fed. 44 O1
Verkhnetulomskoye Vodokhranilishche resr Rus. Fed. 44 O1
Verkhneural'sk Rus. Fed. 102 D1
Verkhnevilyuysk Rus. Fed. 39 M3
Verkhnevolzhskoye Vodokhranilishche resr Rus. Fed. 43 N4
Verkhneyarkeyevo Rus. Fed. 40 J5
Verkhneye Kuyto, Ozero l. Rus. Fed. 44 O2
Verkhnezeysk Rus. Fed. 82 C1
Verkhniy At-Uryakh Rus. Fed. 39 P3
Verkhniy Baskunchak Rus. Fed. 102 A2
Verkhniye Koshevichi Rus. Fed. 43 M6
Verkhniye Mokhovichi Rus. Fed. 43 M6
Verkhniy Lomovets Rus. Fed. 43 T9
Verkhniy Mamon Rus. Fed. 41 G6
Verkhniy Shergol'dzhin Rus. Fed. 85 F1
Verkhniy Tatyshly Rus. Fed. 40 J4
Verkhniy Vyalozerskiy Rus. Fed. 40 E2
Verkhn'odniprovs'k Ukr. 41 E6 also spelt Verkhnedneprovsk
Verkhnyaya Inta Rus. Fed. 40 L2
Verkhnyaya Pakhachi Rus. Fed. 39 Q3
Verkhnyaya Taymyra r. Rus. Fed. 39 J2
Verkhnyaya Toyma Rus. Fed. 40 H3
Verkhnyaya Troitsa Rus. Fed. 43 S4
Verkhnyaya Tunguska r. Rus. Fed. see **Angara**
Verkhnyaya Yelovka Kazakh. 88 D1
Verkhoshizhem'ye Rus. Fed. 40 I4
Verkhovazh'ye Rus. Fed. 40 G3
Verkhov'ye Rus. Fed. 43 S9
Verkhoyanskiy Khrebet mts Rus. Fed. 39 M2
Verkhuba Kazakh. 88 C1
Verknė r. Lith. 42 F7
Verkola Rus. Fed. 40 H3
Verkykerskop S. Africa 133 N4
Verlatekloof pass S. Africa 132 E9
Verma Norway 44 J3
Vermaaklikheid S. Africa 132 F11
Vermelha, Serra hills Brazil 206 C10
Vermelho r. Mato Grosso Brazil 206 B1
Vermelho r. Pará Brazil 202 B3
Vermelho r. Tocantins Brazil 202 C3
Vermenton France 51 J5
Vermeş Romania 58 C3
Vermilion Canada 167 I4
Vermilion r. U.S.A. 174 B3
Vermilion Bay U.S.A. 179 E6
Vermilion Cliffs esc. AZ U.S.A. 183 L5
Vermilion Cliffs esc. UT U.S.A. 183 L4
Vermilion Lake U.S.A. 174 A2
Vermilion Range hills U.S.A. 172 A3
Vermillion U.S.A. 178 C3
Vermillion r. U.S.A. 178 C3
Vermillion Bay Canada 168 A3
Vermillon r. Canada 174 F2
Vermont state U.S.A. 177 M1
Vernadsky research station Antarctica 222 T2 long form Academician Vernadskiy
Vernal U.S.A. 183 O1
Verner Canada 168 D4
Verneuil-sur-Avre France 50 G4
Verneuk Pan salt pan S. Africa 132 F6
Vernier Switz. 51 M6
Vernio Italy 56 D4
Vernon Canada 166 G5
Vernon France 50 H3
Vernon AL U.S.A. 175 B5
Vernon TX U.S.A. 179 C5
Vernon, Mount hill Australia 150 B5
Vernon Islands Australia 148 A2
Vernoye Rus. Fed. 82 C2
Vernyy Kazakh. see **Almaty**
Vero Beach U.S.A. 175 D7
Veroia Greece 58 D8 also spelt Véria; historically known as Beroea
Verona Italy 56 C3
Verona VA U.S.A. 176 F7
Verona WI U.S.A. 172 D8
Verres Italy 51 N7
Versailles France 51 I4
Versailles IN U.S.A. 174 C4
Versailles KY U.S.A. 176 A7
Versailles MO U.S.A. 178 D4
Versailles OH U.S.A. 176 A5
Versalles Bol. 201 E3
Versec Vojvodina, Srbija Yugo. see **Vršac**
Verseka r. Lith. 42 F7
Versmold Germany 48 F3
Versoix Switz. 51 M6
Vert, Cap c. Senegal 124 A3 also known as Verde, Cabo
Vert, Île i. Canada 169 G3
Vertentes r. Brazil 202 B4
Vertesi park Hungary 49 P8
Vertientes Cuba 186 D2
Vertou France 50 E5
Vertus France 51 K4
Verulam S. Africa 133 P6
Verulamium U.K. see **St Albans**
Verviers Belgium 51 L2
Vervins France 51 J3
Verwoerdburg S. Africa see **Centurion**
Verwood Canada 167 J5
Veryína Greece see **Vergina**
Vesanto Fin. 44 N3
Vescovato Corse France 51 P10
Vesele Ukr. 41 E7
Veselevo Rus. Fed. 43 R6
Veselina r. Bulg. 58 G5
Veselí nad Lužnicí Czech Rep. 49 L6
Veselí nad Moravou Czech Rep. 49 O7
Veselovskoye Vodokhranilishche resr Rus. Fed. 41 G7
Veseloyarsk Rus. Fed. 88 C1
Veselyy Rus. Fed. 41 G7
Veselyy Podol Kazakh. 103 F1
Veshenskaya Rus. Fed. 41 G6
Vesijärvi l. Fin. 45 N3
Vesle r. France 51 J3
Veslyana r. Rus. Fed. 40 J3
Vesontio France see **Besançon**
Vesoul France 51 M5
Vesselyy Yar Rus. Fed. 90 D3
Vest-Agder county Norway 45 I4
Vesterålen is Norway 44 K1
Vesterålsfjorden sea chan. Norway 44 K1
Vestfirðir constituency Iceland 44 [inset] B2
Vestfjorddalen valley Norway 45 J4
Vestfjorden sea chan. Norway 44 K2
Vestfold county Norway 45 J4
Vestfold Hills Antarctica 223 F2
Vestmanna Faroe Is 46 E1
Vestmannaeyjar is Iceland 44 [inset] B3 English form Westman Islands
Vestnes Norway 44 I3
Vestre Jakobselv Norway 44 O1
Veststraumen Glacier Antarctica 223 X2
Vesturland constituency Iceland 44 [inset] B2
Vestvågøy i. Norway 44 K1
Vesuvio vol. Italy see **Vesuvius**
Vesuvio, Parco Nazionale del nat. park Italy 57 G8
Vesuvius vol. Italy 57 G8 also spelt Vesuvio
Ves'yegonsk Rus. Fed. 43 S3
Veszprém Hungary 49 O8
Vésztő Hungary 49 S9
Vet r. S. Africa 133 J4
Vetauua i. Fiji 145 H3
Veteli Fin. 44 M3
Veteran Canada 167 I4
Veternik Vojvodina, Srbija Yugo. 58 A3
Vetlanda Sweden 45 K4
Vetlefjorden Norway 45 I3
Vetluga Rus. Fed. 40 H4
Vetluga r. Rus. Fed. 40 H4
Vetluzhskiy Kostromskaya Oblast' Rus. Fed. 38 E4 formerly known as Golyshi
Vetluzhskiy Nizhegorodskaya Oblast' Rus. Fed. 40 H4
Vet'ma r. Rus. Fed. 43 O8
Vetovo Bulg. 58 H5
Vetralla Italy 56 E6
Vetren Bulg. 58 I6 formerly known as Zhitarovo
Vetrişoaia Romania 58 J2
Vetsikko Fin. 44 N1
Vettasjärvi Sweden 44 M2
Vettore, Monte mt. Italy 56 F6
Veurne Belgium 51 I1 also known as Furnes
Vevay U.S.A. 174 C4
Veveno r. Sudan 128 B3
Vevey Switz. 51 M6
Veydelevka Rus. Fed. 41 F6
Veyle r. France 51 K6
Veynes France 51 L8
Veyo U.S.A. 183 K4
Veys Iran 100 B4
Vėžaičiai Lith. 42 C6
Vézère r. France 50 G8
Vezhen mt. Bulg. 58 F6
Vezirköprü Turkey 106 C2
Via r. Liberia 124 C5
Viacha Bol. 200 C4
Viadana Italy 56 C4
Vialar Alg. see **Tissemsilt**
Viamao Brazil 203 B9
Viamonte Arg. 205 D9
Viana Angola 127 B7
Viana Espírito Santo Brazil 207 M7
Viana Maranhão Brazil 202 C2
Viana del Bollo Spain see **Viana do Bolo**
Viana do Alentejo Port. 54 D6
Viana do Bolo Spain 54 D2 also spelt Viana del Bollo
Viana do Castelo Port. 54 C3
Viana do Castelo admin. dist. Port. 54 C3
Vianden Lux. 51 M3
Viangchan Laos see **Vientiane**
Viangphoukha Laos 78 C3
Viaño Pequeno Spain 54 C1
Vianópolis Brazil 206 E3
Viar r. Spain 54 F7
Viareggio Italy 56 C5
Viaur r. France 51 H8
Viborg Denmark 45 J4
Viborg Rus. Fed. see **Vyborg**
Vibo Valentia Italy 57 I10 historically known as Hipponium
Vic Spain 55 N3 also spelt Vich
Vicam Mex. 184 C3
Vicdessos r. France 50 H10
Vicecomodoro Marambio research station Antarctica see **Marambio**
Vic-en-Bigorre France 50 G9
Vicente, Point U.S.A. 182 F8
Vicente Guerrero Mex. 184 A2
Vicenza Italy 56 D3
Vic-Fezensac France 50 G9
Vich Spain see **Vic**
Vichada dept Col. 198 D3
Vichada r. Col. 198 E3
Vichadero Uruguay 204 G3
Vichuga Rus. Fed. 40 G4
Vichy France 51 J6
Vicksburg AZ U.S.A. 183 K8
Vicksburg MI U.S.A. 172 H8
Vicksburg MS U.S.A. 175 B5
Vic-le-Comte France 51 J7
Vico, Lago di l. Italy 56 E6
Viçosa Alagoas Brazil 202 E4
Viçosa Minas Gerais Brazil 203 D7
Vic-sur-Cère France 51 I8
Victor, Mount Antarctica 223 C2
Victor Harbor Australia 146 C3
Victoria Arg. 204 E4
Victoria r. Australia 148 A2
Victoria state Australia 147 E4
Victoria Cameroon see **Limbe**
▶**Victoria** Canada 166 F5 Provincial capital of British Columbia.
Victoria La Araucania Chile 204 B5
Victoria Magallanes Chile 205 C9
Victoria Hond. 186 B4
Victoria Malaysia see **Labuan**
Victoria Malta 57 G12 also known as Rabat
Victoria Phil. 74 B3
Victoria Romania 58 I4
Victoria Romania 58 F3
▶**Victoria** Seychelles 218 K6 Capital of the Seychelles.
Victoria TX U.S.A. 179 C6
Victoria VA U.S.A. 176 G9
Victoria, Isla i. Chile 205 B7
▶**Victoria, Lake** Africa 128 B5 Largest lake in Africa and 3rd in the world. africa [landscapes] 112–113
Victoria, Lake Australia 146 D3
Victoria, Mount Myanmar 78 A3
Victoria, Mount N.Z. 153 G10
Victoria, Mount P.N.G. 73 K8
Victoria and Albert Mountains Canada 165 L2
▶**Victoria Falls** waterfall Zambia/Zimbabwe 127 E9 africa [locations] 118–119
Victoria Falls Zimbabwe 131 E3
Victoria Falls National Park Zimbabwe 131 E3 also known as Mosi-oa-Tunya National Park
Victoria Fjord inlet Greenland 165 O1
Victoria Forest Park nature res. N.Z. 153 G9
Victoria Harbour sea chan. Hong Kong China see **Hong Kong Harbour**
▶**Victoria Island** Canada 165 H2 3rd largest island in North America and 9th in the world. northamerica [landscapes] 156–157
Victoria Lake Canada 169 J3
Victoria Land coastal area Antarctica 223 K2
Victoria Peak hill Hong Kong China 87 [inset] also known as Shan Teng
Victoria Range mts N.Z. 153 G10
Victoria River Australia 148 A2
Victoria River Downs Australia 148 A3
Victoria Valley N.Z. 152 H3
Victoriaville Canada 169 G4
Victoria West S. Africa 132 H8
Victorica Arg. 204 D5
Victorino Venez. 199 E4
Víctor Rosales Mex. 185 E4
Victorville U.S.A. 183 G7
Victory U.S.A. 177 I2
Victory Downs Australia 148 B5
Vicuña Chile 204 C3
Vicuña Mackenna Arg. 204 D4
Vidal, Isla i. Chile 205 B8
Vidalia U.S.A. 175 B6
Vidal Junction U.S.A. 183 J7
Vidamlya Belarus 42 E9
Videle Romania 58 G4
Viden mt. Bulg. 58 D6
Vidigueira Port. 54 D6
Vidima r. Bulg. 58 G6
Vidin Bulg. 58 D5
Vidisha India 96 C5
Vidlitsa Rus. Fed. 40 E3
Vidnoye Rus. Fed. 43 S6 formerly known as Rastorguyevo
Vidourle r. France 51 K9
Vidova Gora hill Croatia 56 I5
Vidsel Sweden 44 M2
Viduklė Lith. 42 D6
Viduša mts Bos.-Herz. 56 K6
Vidzemes Centrālā Augstiene hills Latvia 42 G5
Vidzy Belarus 42 H6
Viechtach Germany 49 J6
Viedgesville S. Africa 133 M8
Viedma Arg. 204 E6
▶**Viedma, Lago** l. Arg. 205 B8 southamerica [landscapes] 190–191
Viehberg mt. Austria 49 L7
Viejo, Cerro mt. Mex. 184 B2
Viekšniai Lith. 42 D5
Vielha Spain 55 L2 also spelt Viella
Viella Spain see **Vielha**
Vielsalm Belgium 51 L2
Vienenburg Germany 48 H4
▶**Vienna** Austria 49 N7 Capital of Austria. Also known as Wien; historically known as Vindobona.
Vienna GA U.S.A. 175 D5
Vienna IL U.S.A. 174 B4
Vienna MD U.S.A. 177 J7
Vienna MO U.S.A. 174 B4
Vienna WV U.S.A. 176 D6
Vienne France 51 K7
Vienne r. France 50 G5
▶**Vientiane** Laos 78 C4 Capital of Laos. Also spelt Viangchan.
Vieques i. Puerto Rico 187 G3
Vieremä Fin. 44 N3
Viersen Germany 48 D4
Vierwaldstätter See l. Switz. 51 O5
Vierzon France 51 I5
Viesca Mex. 185 E3
Viesīte Latvia 42 G5
Vieste Italy 56 I7
Viešvilės rezervatas nature res. Lith. 42 D6
Vietas Sweden 44 L2
▶**Vietnam** country Asia 78 D4 also spelt Viet Nam asia [countries] 64–67
Viet Nam country Asia see **Vietnam**
Viêt Tri Vietnam 78 D3
Vieux Comptoir, Lac du l. Canada 168 E2
Vieux-Fort Canada 169 J3
Vieux Fort St Lucia 187 H4
Vieux Poste, Pointe du pt Canada 169 I3
Vievis Lith. 42 F7
Vigala r. Estonia 42 F3
Vigan Phil. 74 B2
Vigeois France 50 H7
Vigevano Italy 56 A3
Vigia Brazil 202 B2
Vigia hill Port. 54 C7
Vigía Chico Mex. 185 I5
Viglio, Monte mt. Italy 56 F7
Vignemale mt. France 50 F10
Vignola Italy 56 D4
Vigny France 51 H3
Vigo Spain 54 C2
Vigo, Ría de est. Spain 54 C2
Vigors, Mount Australia 150 B4
Vihanti Fin. 44 N2
Vihari Pak. 101 H4
Vihiers France 50 F5
Vihorlat mt. Slovakia 49 T7
Vihterpalu r. Estonia 42 E2
Vihti Fin. 45 N3
Viiala Fin. 45 M3
Viipuri Rus. Fed. see **Vyborg**

Viirinkylä Fin. 44 N2
Viitasaari Fin. 44 N3
Viitka Estonia 42 I4
Vijainagar India 96 B3
Vijapur India 96 B5
Vijayadurg India 94 B2
Vijayanagar India see Hampi
Vijayapati India 94 C4
Vijayawada India 94 D2
also known as Bezwada
Vík Iceland 44 [inset] C3
Vik Norway 44 K2
Vikajärvi Fin. 44 N2
Vikarabad India 94 C2
Vikedal Norway 45 I4
Vikeke East Timor 75 C5
also known as Viqueque
Vikersund Norway 45 J4
Vikhra r. Rus. Fed. 43 M7
Vikhren mt. Bulg. 58 E7
Viking Canada 167 I4
Vikna i. Norway 44 J2
Vikos-Aoos nat. park Greece 59 B9
Vikøyri Norway 45 I3
Vikran Norway 44 L1
Viktorovka Kazakh. see Taranovskoye
Vila Spain 54 C3
Vila Vanuatu see Port Vila
Vila Alferes Chamusca Moz. see Guija
Vila Arriaga Angola see Bibala
Vila Bittencourt Brazil 198 D5
Vila Braga Brazil 199 G6
Vila Bugaço Angola see Camanongue
Vila Cabral Moz. see Lichinga
Vila Caldas Xavier Moz. see Muende
Vilacaya Bol. 200 D4
Vila Coutinho Moz. see Ulongue
Vila da Ponte Angola see Kuvango
Vila da Ribeira Brava Cape Verde 124 [inset]
Vila de Aljustrel Angola see Cangamba
Vila de Almoster Angola see Chiange
Vila de João Belo Moz. see Xai-Xai
Vila de Junqueiro Moz. see Gurué
Vila de Sal Rei Cape Verde 124 [inset]
Vila de Sena Moz. 131 G3
Vila de Trego Morais Moz. see Chókwé
Vila do Conde Port. 54 C3
Vila do Tarrafal Cape Verde 124 [inset]
Vila Flor Port. 54 D3
Vila Fontes Moz. see Caia
Vilafranca del Penedès Spain 55 M3
also spelt Villafranca del Penedès
Vila Franca de Xira Port. 54 C6
Vilagarcía de Arousa Spain 54 C2
also spelt Villagarcía de Arosa
Vila Gomes da Costa Moz. 131 G5
Vila Gouveia Moz. see Catandica
Vilaine r. France 50 D5
Vilaka Latvia 42 I4
Vilalba Spain 54 D1
Vila Luísa Moz. see Marracuene
Vila Marechal Carmona Angola see Uíge
Vila Miranda Moz. see Macaloge
Vila Murtinho Brazil 200 D2
Vilanandro, Tanjona pt Madag. 131 [inset] J3
formerly known as St-André, Cap
Vilanculos Moz. 131 G4
Viļāni Latvia 42 H5
Vila Nova Angola see Tchikala-Tcholohanga
Vila Nova da Fronteira Moz. 131 G3
Vilanova de Arousa Spain 54 C2
also spelt Villanueva de Arosa
Vila Nova de Foz Côa Port. 54 D3
Vila Nova de Gaia Port. 54 C3
Vila Nova de Ourém Port. 54 C5
Vila Nova de Paiva Port. 54 D4
Vila Nova do Seles Angola see Uku
Vilanova i la Geltrú Spain 55 M3
also spelt Villanueva-y-Geltrú
Vila Nova Sintra Cape Verde 124 [inset]
Vila Paiva de Andrada Moz. see Gorongosa
Vila Pery Moz. see Chimoio
Vila Pouca de Aguiar Port. 54 D3
Vila Real Port. 54 D3
Vila Real admin. dist. Port. 54 D3
Vila-real de los Infantes Spain 55 K5
also spelt Villareal de los Infantes; formerly known as Villareal
Vilar Formoso Port. 54 E4
Vila Salazar Angola see N'dalatando
Vila Salazar Zimbabwe see Sango
Vila Teixeira de Sousa Angola see Luau
Vilavankod India 94 C4
Vila Velha Amapá Brazil 199 I4
Vila Velha Espírito Santo Brazil 203 D7
formerly known as Espírito Santo
Vila Velha de Ródão Port. 54 D5
Vila Verde Port. 54 C3
Vilcabamba, Cordillera mts Peru 200 B3
Vilcanota, Cordillera de mts Peru 200 C3
Vil'cheka, Zemlya i. Rus. Fed. 38 G1
English form Wilczek Land
Viled' r. Rus. Fed. 40 H3
Vileyka Belarus see Vilyeyka
Vil'gort Permskaya Oblast' Rus. Fed. 40 K3
Vil'gort Respublika Komi Rus. Fed. 40 I3
Vilhelmina Sweden 44 L2
Vilhena Brazil 201 E3
Viliya r. Belarus/Lith. 42 G7
Viljandi Estonia 42 G3
Viljoenskroon S. Africa 133 K4
Vilkaviškis Lith. 42 E7
Vilkija Lith. 42 E6
Vil'kitskogo, Ostrov i. Rus. Fed. 39 H2
Vil'kitskogo, Proliv strait Rus. Fed. 39 J2
Villa Abecia Bol. 200 D5
Villa Adriana tourist site Italy 56 E7
Villa Ahumada Mex. 184 D2
Villa Alba Arg. 204 E5
Villa Altagracia Dom. Rep. 187 F3
Villa Ana Arg. 204 F3
Villa Ángela Arg. 204 E2
Villa Bella Bol. 200 D2
Villa Bens Morocco see Tarfaya
Villablino Spain 54 E2
Villacañas Spain 55 H5
Villacarrillo Spain 55 H6
Villach Austria 49 K9
also known as Beljak
Villacidro Sardegna Italy 57 A9
Villa Cisneros W. Sahara see Ad Dakhla
Villa Constitución Arg. 204 E4
Villa Constitución Mex. see Ciudad Constitución
Villa de Álvarez Mex. 184 E5
Villa de Cos Mex. 185 E4
Villa de Cura Venez. 199 E2
Villa de Guadalupe Mex. 185 H5
Villa del Rosario Arg. 204 E3
Villa del Totoral Arg. 204 D3
Villa Diego Arg. 204 E4
Villadiego Spain 54 G2
Villa Dolores Arg. 204 D3
Villadossola Italy 56 A2
Villa Flores Mex. 185 G5
Villafranca Spain 55 J2
Villafranca del Bierzo Spain 54 E2
Villafranca del Cid Spain 55 K4
Villafranca de los Barros Spain 54 E6
Villafranca del Penedès Spain see Vilafranca del Penedès
Villafranca di Verona Italy 56 C3
Villagarcía de Arosa Spain see Vilagarcía de Arousa
Villa Gesell Arg. 204 F5
Villagrán Mex. 185 F3
Villaguay Arg. 204 F3
Villa Guillermina Arg. 204 F3
Villa Hayes Para. 201 F6
Villahermosa Mex. 185 G5
Villa Hidalgo Mex. 181 E7
Villa Huidobro Arg. 204 D4
Villaines-la-Juhel France 50 F4
Villa Insurgentes Mex. 184 C3
Villa Iris Arg. 204 E5
Villajoyosa Spain 55 K6
Villa Juárez Mex. 181 E8
Villaldama Mex. 185 E3
Villalonga Arg. 204 E5
Villa María Arg. 204 E4
Villa María Grande Arg. 204 F3
Villa Martín Bol. 200 D5
Villamartín Spain 54 F8
Villa Matoque Arg. 204 E2
Villa Montes Bol. 201 E5
Villanova Monteleone Sardegna Italy 57 A8
Villa Nueva Arg. 204 E4
Villanueva Col. 198 C2
Villanueva Mex. 185 E4
Villanueva de Arosa Spain see Vilanova de Arousa
Villanueva de Córdoba Spain 54 G6
Villanueva de la Serena Spain 54 F6
Villanueva de los Castillejos Spain 54 D7
Villanueva de los Infantes Spain 55 I6
formerly known as Infantes
Villanueva-y-Geltrú Spain see Vilanova i la Geltrú
Villa Ocampo Arg. 204 F3
Villa Ocampo Mex. 184 D3
Villa O'Higgins Chile 205 B8
Villa Ojo de Agua Arg. 204 E3
Villa O. Pereyra Mex. see Villa Orestes Pereyra
Villa Orestes Pereyra Mex. 184 D3
short form Villa O. Pereyra
Villa Oropeza Bol. 200 D4
Villa Pesqueira Mex. 181 E7
Villaputzu Sardegna Italy 57 B9
Villar del Rey Spain 54 E5
Villareal Spain see Vila-real de los Infantes
Villarreal de los Infantes Spain see Vila-real de los Infantes
Villarrica Chile 204 B5
Villarrica Para. 201 F6
Villarrica, Lago l. Chile 204 B5
Villarrica, Parque Nacional nat. park Chile 204 C5
Villarrobledo Spain 55 I5
Villarrubia de los Ojos Spain 55 H5
Villas U.S.A. 177 K6
Villasalazar Zimbabwe see Sango
Villasana de Mena Spain 55 H1
Villa San Giovanni Italy 57 H10
Villa Sanjurjo Morocco see Al Hoceïma
Villa San Martín Arg. 204 D3
Villasboas Uruguay 204 F4
Villa Serrano Bol. 201 D4
Villasimius Sardegna Italy 57 B9
Villa Unión Arg. 204 C3
Villa Unión Coahuila Mex. 185 E2
Villa Unión Durango Mex. 184 D4
Villa Unión Sinaloa Mex. 184 D4
Villa Valeria Arg. 204 D4
Villa Vásquez Dom. Rep. 187 F3
Villavicencio Col. 198 C3
Villaviciosa Spain 54 F1
Villaviciosa de Córdoba Spain 54 F6
Villa Viscarra Bol. 200 D4
Villazon Bol. 200 D5
Villedieu-les-Poêles France 50 E4
Villefranche-de-Lauragais France 50 H9
Villefranche-de-Rouergue France 51 I8
Villefranche-sur-Saône France 51 K7
Ville-Marie Canada see Montréal
Ville-Marie Canada 173 N3
Villemontel Canada 173 O2
Villemur-sur-Tarn France 50 H9
Villena Spain 55 K6
Villenauxe-la-Grande France 51 J4
Villeneuve-de-Marsan France 50 F9
Villeneuve-sur-Lot France 50 G8
Villeneuve-sur-Yonne France 51 J4
Ville Platte U.S.A. 179 D6
Villers-Bocage France 50 F3
Villers-Cotterêts France 51 J3
Villeta Para. 201 F6
Villeurbanne France 51 K7
Villicun, Sierra mts Arg. 204 C3
Villiers S. Africa 133 M4
Villingen Germany 48 F7
Villupuram India see Viluppuram
Vilna Canada 167 I4
Vilna Lith. see Vilnius

▶Vilnius Lith. 42 G7
Capital of Lithuania. Formerly known as Wilno; historically known as Vilna.

Vil'nyans'k Ukr. 41 E7
also spelt Vol'nyansk; formerly known as Chervonoarmeyskoye or Sofiyevka
Vilppula Fin. 45 N3
Vils r. Germany 48 I6
Vils r. Germany 49 K7
Vilsandi i. Estonia 42 C3
Vilsandi nature res. Estonia 42 C3
Vilsbiburg Germany 49 J7
Vilshofen Germany 49 K7
Viluppuram India 94 C4
also spelt Villupuram
Vilvoorde Belgium 51 K2
Vilyeyka Belarus 42 H7
also spelt Vileyka
Vilyeyskaye, Vozyera l. Belarus 42 I7
Vilyuy r. Rus. Fed. 39 M3
Vilyuyskoye Vodokhranilishche resr Rus. Fed. 39 L3
Vimbe mt. Zambia 127 F8
Vimercate Italy 56 B3
Vimianzo Spain 54 B1
Vimioso Port. 54 E3
Vimmerby Sweden 45 K4
Vimoutiers France 50 G4
Vimpeli Fin. 44 M3
Vimperk Czech Rep. 49 K6
Vina r. Cameroon 125 I5
also spelt Wina
Vina U.S.A. 182 B2
Viña del Mar Chile 204 C4
Vinalhaven U.S.A. 177 Q1
Vinalopó r. Spain 55 K6
Vinanivao Madag. 131 [inset] K2
Vinaròs Spain 55 L4
also spelt Vinaroz
Vinaroz Spain see Vinaròs
Vincelotte, Lac l. Canada 169 F2
Vincennes U.S.A. 174 C4
Vincennes Bay Antarctica 223 H2
Vinces r. Ecuador 198 B5
Vinchina Arg. 204 C3
Vinchos Peru 200 B3
Vindelälven r. Sweden 44 L3
Vindelfjällens naturreservat nature res. Sweden 44 K2
Vindeln Sweden 44 L2
Vindhya Range hills India 96 B5
Vindobona Austria see Vienna
Vineland U.S.A. 177 J6
Vinga Romania 58 C2
Vingăi, Câmpia plain Romania 58 C2
Vingåker Sweden 45 K4
Vinh Vietnam 78 D4
Vinhais Port. 54 E3
Vinh Long Vietnam 79 D6
Vinh Thuc, Đao i. Vietnam 78 D3
Vinh Yên Vietnam 78 D3
Vinica Macedonia 58 D7
Vinita U.S.A. 178 D4
Vinjhan India 96 A5
Vinju Mare Romania see Vânju Mare
Vinkovci Croatia 56 K3
Vinland i. Canada see Newfoundland
Vinni Estonia 42 H2
Vinnitsa Ukr. see Vinnytsya
Vinnitsy Rus. Fed. 43 P1
Vinnytsya Ukr. 41 D6
also spelt Vinnitsa
Vinogradovo Rus. Fed. 43 T6

▶Vinson Massif mt. Antarctica 222 S1
Highest mountain in Antarctica.
antarctica [features] 212–213

Vinstra Norway 45 J3
Vintar Phil. 74 B2
Vinton U.S.A. 174 A3
Vinukonda India 94 C2
Vinza Congo 126 B5
Viola CA U.S.A. 182 C1
Viola IL U.S.A. 172 C9
Violeta Cuba see Primero de Enero
Violet Valley Aboriginal Reserve Australia 150 D3
Vioolsdrif S. Africa 132 B5
Viphya Mountains Malawi 129 B8
Vipiteno Italy 56 D2
Viqueque East Timor see Vikeke
Vir i. Croatia 56 H4
Virac Phil. 74 C3
Virac Point Phil. 74 C3
Viramgam India 96 B5
Viranşehir Turkey 107 D3
Virarajendrapet India 94 B3
Virawah Pak. 101 G5
Virawlya Belarus 43 K6
Vircava r. Latvia/Lith. 42 E5
Virchow, Mount hill Australia 150 B4
Virdáánjarga Fin. see Virtaniemi
Virden Canada 167 K5
Vire France 50 F4
Virei Angola 127 B8
Virful Highiş hill Romania 58 C2
Virgenes, Cabo c. Arg. 205 C9
Virgilina U.S.A. 176 G9
Virgin r. U.S.A. 183 J5
Virginatown Canada 173 N2
Virgin Gorda i. Virgin Is (U.K.) 187 G3
Virginia S. Africa 133 K5
Virginia U.S.A. 174 A2
Virginia state U.S.A. 176 G8
Virginia Beach U.S.A. 177 J9
Virginia City MT U.S.A. 180 E3
Virginia City NV U.S.A. 182 E2
Virginia Falls Canada 166 E2

▶Virgin Islands (U.K.) terr. West Indies 187 G3
United Kingdom Overseas Territory.
oceania [countries] 138–139

▶Virgin Islands (U.S.A.) terr. West Indies 187 G3
United States Unincorporated Territory.
oceania [countries] 138–139

Virgin Mountains U.S.A. 183 J5
Virginópolis Brazil 203 D6
Virje Croatia 56 J2
Virkkala Fin. 45 N3
Virmasvesi l. Fin. 44 N3
Virôchey Cambodia 79 D5
Virolahti Fin. 45 N3
Viroqua U.S.A. 172 C7
Virovitica Croatia 56 J3
Virpe Latvia 42 D4
Virrat Fin. 44 M3
Virserum Sweden 45 K4
Virtaniemi Fin. 44 O1
also known as Virdáánjarga
Virton Belgium 51 L3
Virtsu Estonia 42 E3
Virú Peru 200 A2
Virudunagar India 94 C4
Virunga, Parc National des nat. park Dem. Rep. Congo 126 F5
formerly known as Albert, Parc National
Virvytė r. Lith. 42 D5
Vis Croatia 56 I5
also known as Issa or Lissa
Vis i. Croatia 56 I5
Visaginas Lith. 42 H6
formerly known as Sniečkus
Visakhapatnam India see Vishakhapatnam
Visalia U.S.A. 182 E5
Visavadar India 96 A5
Visayan Sea Phil. 74 B4
Visby Sweden 45 L4
Visconde do Rio Branco Brazil 207 K8
Viscount Melville Sound sea chan. Canada 165 H2
Vise, Ostrov i. Rus. Fed. 39 H2
Višegrad Bos.-Herz. 56 L5
Viseu Brazil 202 C2
Viseu Port. 54 D4
Viseu admin. dist. Port. 54 D4
Vishakhapatnam India 95 D2
also spelt Visakhapatnam; formerly spelt Vizagapatam
Vishegrad hill Bulg. 58 H7
Vishera r. Rus. Fed. 40 J3
Vishera r. Rus. Fed. 40 K3
Vishera r. Rus. Fed. 43 M3
Vishneva Belarus 42 H7
Vishnevka Kazakh. 103 H2
Visikums Latvia 42 I4
Vişina Romania 58 G4
Viški Latvia 42 H5
Viški Kanal sea chan. Croatia 56 I5
Visnagar India 96 B5
Viso, Monte mt. Italy 51 N8
Viso del Marqués Spain 55 H6
Visoko Bos.-Herz. 56 K5
Visp Switz. 51 N6
Visrivier S. Africa 133 J8
Vissannapeta India 94 D2
Vista U.S.A. 183 G8
Vista Alegre Amazonas Brazil 199 D4
Vista Alegre Amazonas Brazil 199 D6
Vista Alegre Amazonas Brazil 199 F6
Vista Alegre Mato Grosso do Sul Brazil 201 F4
Vista Alegre Roraima Brazil 199 F4
Vista Lake U.S.A. 182 E6
Vistonida, Limni lag. Greece 58 G7
Vistula r. Poland 49 P1
also spelt Wisła
Vištytis Lith. 42 D7
Vit r. Bulg. 58 F5
Vita r. Col. 198 E3
Vitao mt. Yugo. 56 K5
Vitebsk Belarus see Vitsyebsk
Vitebskaya Oblast' admin. div. Belarus see Vitsyebskaya Voblasts'
Vitebsk Oblast admin. div. Belarus see Vitsyebskaya Voblasts'
Viterbo Italy 56 E6
Vitez Bos.-Herz. 56 J4
Vitez pass Bos.-Herz. 56 K5
Vitigudino Spain 54 E3
Viti Levu i. Fiji 145 G3
Vitim r. Rus. Fed. 81 I1
Vitimskoye Ploskogor'ye plat. Rus. Fed. 81 I2
Vitina Kosovo, Srbija Yugo. 58 C6
Vitomirica Kosovo, Srbija Yugo. 58 B6
Vitor Peru 200 C4
Vitor r. Peru 200 B4
Vitória Espírito Santo Brazil 203 D7
Vitória Pará Brazil 199 H5
Vitoria Spain see Vitoria-Gasteiz
Vitória da Conquista Brazil 202 D5
Vitoria-Gasteiz Spain 55 I2
also known as Gasteiz or Vitoria
Vitosha nat. park Bulg. 58 E6
Vitré France 50 E4
Vitrolles France 51 L9
Vitry-en-Artois France 51 I2
Vitry-le-François France 51 K4
Vitsyebsk Belarus 43 L6
English form Vitebsk
Vitsyebskaya Voblasts' admin. div. Belarus 43 J6
English form Vitebsk Oblast; also known as Vitebskaya Oblast'
Vittangi Sweden 44 M2
also known as Vazáš
Vitteaux France 51 K5
Vittel France 51 L4
Vittoria Sicilia Italy 57 G12
Vittorio Veneto Italy 56 E3
Vivarais, Monts du mts France 51 K8
Viveiro Spain 54 D1
also spelt Vivero
Vivero Spain see Viveiro
Vivian U.S.A. 179 D5
Vivo S. Africa 131 F4
Vivonne France 50 G6
Vivorată Arg. 204 F5
Vivorillo, Cayos is Hond. 186 C4
Vizagapatam India see Vishakhapatnam
Vizcaíno Mex. 181 D8
Vizcaíno, Desierto de des. Mex. 184 B3
Vizcaíno, Sierra mts Mex. 184 B3
Vize Turkey 106 A2
Vizhas r. Rus. Fed. 40 H2
Vizianagaram India 95 D2
Vizinga Rus. Fed. 40 I3
Viziru Romania 58 I3
Vizzini Sicilia Italy 57 G11
V. J. José Perez Bol. 200 C3
Vjosë r. Albania 59 A8
Vlaardingen Neth. 48 B4
Vlădeasa, Vârful mt. Romania 58 D2
Vladičin Han Srbija Yugo. 58 D6
Vladikavkaz Rus. Fed. 41 H8
also known as Dzaudzhikau; formerly known as Ordzhonikidze
Vladimir Rus. Fed. 90 D3
Vladimir Rus. Fed. 43 V5
historically known as Lodomeria
Vladimiro-Aleksandrovskoye Rus. Fed. 82 D4
Vladimir Oblast admin. div. Rus. Fed. see Vladimirskaya Oblast'
Vladimirovka Kazakh. 103 F1
formerly known as Vladimirovskiy
Vladimirovo Bulg. 58 E5
Vladimirovskiy Kazakh. see Vladimirovka
Vladimirskaya Oblast' admin. div. Rus. Fed. 43 V6
English form Vladimir Oblast
Vladimirskiy Tupik Rus. Fed. 43 O6
Vladimir-Volynskiy Ukr. see Volodymyr-Volyns'kyy
Vladivostok Rus. Fed. 82 C4
Vladychnoye Rus. Fed. 43 U3
Vlăhița Romania 58 G2
Vlajna mt. Yugo. 58 C6
Vlasenica Bos.-Herz. 56 K4
Vlašić Planina mts Yugo. 58 A4
Vlašim Czech Rep. 49 L6
Vlasotince Srbija Yugo. 58 D6
Vlasovo Rus. Fed. 43 U6
Vlas'yevo Rus. Fed. 82 F1
Vlazovichi Rus. Fed. 43 N8
Vleesbaai b. S. Africa 132 F11
Vlieland i. Neth. 48 B2
Vlissingen Neth. 48 A4
historically known as Flushing
Vlorë Albania 58 A8
also known as Aulon or Valona; historically known as Avlona
Vlorës, Gjiri i b. Albania 58 A8
Vlotslavsk Poland see Włocławek
Vltava r. Czech Rep. 49 L5
Vnina r. Rus. Fed. 43 R2
Vöcklabruck Austria 49 K7
Vodice Croatia 56 H5
Vodlozero, Ozero l. Rus. Fed. 40 F3
Vodňany Czech Rep. 49 L6
Vodnjan Croatia 56 F4
Vodopyanovo Rus. Fed. see Donskoye
Voël r. S. Africa 133 J10
Vogan Togo 125 F5
Vogelkop Peninsula Indon. see Doberai, Jazirah
Vogelsberg hills Germany 48 F5
Voghera Italy 56 B4
Vognill Norway 44 J3
Vogošća Bos.-Herz. 56 K5
Vohburg an der Donau Germany 48 I7
Vohémar Madag. see Iharaña
Vohibinany Madag. see Ampasimanolotra
Vohilava Fianarantsoa Madag. 131 [inset] J4
Vohilava Fianarantsoa Madag. 131 [inset] K4
Vohimarina Madag. see Iharaña
Vohimena, Tanjona c. Madag. 131 [inset] J5
formerly known as Ste-Marie, Cap
Vohipeno Madag. 131 [inset] J4
Võhma Estonia 42 G3
Voi Kenya 128 C5
Voikoski Fin. 45 N3
Voinesa Romania 58 E3
Voinești Romania 58 I1
Voinjama Liberia 124 C4
Voin Pervyy Rus. Fed. 43 R8
Voiron France 51 L7
Voitsberg Austria 49 M8
Vojvodina prov. Yugo. 58 A3
Voka Estonia 42 I2
Vokhma Rus. Fed. 40 H4
Vokhtoga Rus. Fed. 43 V3
Vokhnavolok Rus. Fed. 44 O2
Voko Cameroon 125 I4
Vol' r. Rus. Fed. 40 J3
Volaterrae Italy see Volterra
Volcán Arg. 200 D5
Volcán, Cerro vol. Bol. 200 D5
Volcán Barú, Parque Nacional nat. park Panama 186 C5
Volcano Bay Japan see Uchiura-wan

▶Volcano Islands N. Pacific Ocean 220 D4
Part of Japan. Also known as Kazan-rettō.

Volcans d'Auvergne, Parc Naturel Régional des nature res. France 51 I7
Volchas r. Belarus 43 M8
Volchikha Rus. Fed. 103 J1
Volchina r. Rus. Fed. 43 Q4
Volchiy Nos, Mys pt Rus. Fed. 43 N1
Volda Norway 44 I3
Vol'dino Rus. Fed. 40 J3
Volens U.S.A. 176 F9
Volga Rus. Fed. 43 T4

▶Volga r. Rus. Fed. 43 Q5
Longest river in Europe.
europe [landscapes] 30–31

Volga r. U.S.A. 172 B8
Volga Upland hills Rus. Fed. see Privolzhskaya Vozvyshennost'
Volgodonsk Rus. Fed. 41 G7
Volgograd Rus. Fed. 41 H6
formerly known as Stalingrad; historically known as Tsaritsyn
Volgograd Oblast admin. div. Rus. Fed. see Volgogradskaya Oblast'
Volgogradskaya Oblast' admin. div. Rus. Fed. 41 H6
English form Volgograd Oblast; formerly known as Stalingradskaya Oblast'
Volgogradskoye Vodokhranilishche resr Rus. Fed. 41 H6
Volissos Greece 59 G10
Völkermarkt Austria 49 L9
Volkhov Rus. Fed. 43 N2
Volkhov r. Rus. Fed. 43 N1
Volkhovskaya Guba b. Rus. Fed. 43 N1
Volkhovskiy Rus. Fed. 43 M3
Völklingen Germany 48 D6
Volkovichi Belarus see Vawkavichy
Volkovo Rus. Fed. 43 L7
Volkovysk Belarus see Vawkavysk
Volkovyskiye Vysoty hills Belarus see Vawkavyskaye Wzvyshsha
Volksrust S. Africa 133 N4
Vol'no-Nadezhdinskoye Rus. Fed. 82 C4
Volnovakha Ukr. 41 F7
Vol'nyansk Ukr. see Vil'nyans'k
Volochanka Rus. Fed. 39 J2
Volochayevka-Vtoraya Rus. Fed. 82 D2
Volochisk Ukr. see Volochys'k
Volochys'k Ukr. 41 C6
also spelt Volochisk
Volodars'ke Ukr. 41 F7
Volodarskiy Rus. Fed. 102 B3
Volodarskoye Kazakh. see Saumalkol'
Volodymyr-Volyns'kyy Ukr. 41 C6
also spelt Vladimir-Volynskiy
Vologda Rus. Fed. 43 U2
Vologda r. Rus. Fed. 43 V2
Vologda Oblast admin. div. Rus. Fed. see Vologodskaya Oblast'
Vologodskaya Oblast' admin. div. Rus. Fed. 43 T1
English form Vologda Oblast
Volokolamsk Rus. Fed. 43 Q5
Volokonovka Rus. Fed. 41 F6
Volokoslavinskoye Rus. Fed. 43 T2
Volop S. Africa 132 G5
Volos Greece 59 D9
Voloshka Rus. Fed. 40 G3
Volosovo Rus. Fed. 43 K2
Volot Rus. Fed. 43 L4
Volovo Lipetskaya Oblast' Rus. Fed. 43 S9
Volovo Tul'skaya Oblast' Rus. Fed. 43 T8
Voloye Rus. Fed. 43 P7
Volozhin Belarus see Valozhyn
Volsini, Monti mts Italy 56 D6
Volsinii Italy see Orvieto
Vol'sk Rus. Fed. 102 A1
Volstruisleegte S. Africa 132 H10
Volstruispoort pass S. Africa 132 G7
Volta admin. reg. Ghana 125 F5
Volta r. Ghana 125 F5
Volta Blanche watercourse Burkina/Ghana see White Volta

▶Volta, Lake resr Ghana 125 F5
5th largest lake in Africa.
africa [landscapes] 112–113

Voltaire, Cape Australia 150 D2
Volta Noire r. Africa see Black Volta
Volta Redonda Brazil 203 C7
Volterra Italy 56 C5
historically known as Volaterrae
Voltoya r. Spain 54 G3
Volturino, Monte mt. Italy 57 H8
Volturno r. Italy 56 F7
Volubilis tourist site Morocco 122 D2
Voluntari Romania 58 H4
Volunteer Point Falkland Is 205 F8
Volvi, Limni l. Greece 58 E8
Volzhsk Rus. Fed. 40 I5
Volzhskiy Samarskaya Oblast' Rus. Fed. 41 I5
formerly known as Bol'shaya Tsarevshchina
Volzhskiy Volgogradskaya Oblast' Rus. Fed. 41 H6
Vomano r. Italy 56 G6
Vondanka Rus. Fed. 40 H4
Vondrozo Madag. 131 [inset] J4
Vonga Rus. Fed. 40 G2
Vonitsa Greece 59 B10
Võnnu Estonia 42 I3
Vonozero Rus. Fed. 43 P1
Vontimitta India 94 C3
Voorheesville U.S.A. 177 L3
Voosi kurk sea chan. Estonia 42 E2
Vop' r. Rus. Fed. 43 N7
Vopnafjörður Iceland 44 [inset] D2
Vopnafjörður b. Iceland 44 [inset] D2
Vörå Fin. 44 M3
also spelt Vöyri
Voran' Belarus 43 J6
Voranava Belarus 42 G7
Vordingborg Denmark 45 J5
Vordorf Germany 48 H3
Vorë Albania 58 A7
Voreio Aigaio admin. reg. Greece 59 G9
English form Northern Aegean
Voreioi Sporades is Greece 59 E9
English form Northern Sporades; also spelt Vorioi Sporádhes
Voreios Evvoïkos Kolpos sea chan. Greece 59 E10
Vorga Rus. Fed. 43 N8
Vorgashor Rus. Fed. 40 L2
Vorioi Sporádhes is Greece see Voreioi Sporades
Vorjing mt. India 97 G3
Vorkuta Rus. Fed. 40 M2
Vormedalsheia park Norway 45 I4
Vormsi i. Estonia 42 E2
Vorob'yevka Lipetskaya Oblast' Rus. Fed. 43 U9
Vorob'yevka Voronezhskaya Oblast' Rus. Fed. 41 G6
Vorob"yivka Ukr. 43 O9
Vorogovo Rus. Fed. 39 I3
Vorona r. Rus. Fed. 41 G6
Voronezh Rus. Fed. 41 F6
Voronezh r. Rus. Fed. 43 U9
Voronezh Oblast admin. div. Rus. Fed. see Voronezhskaya Oblast'
Voronezhskaya Oblast' admin. div. Rus. Fed. 41 G6
English form Voronezh Oblast
Voronov, Mys pt Rus. Fed. 40 G2
Voronov, Mys pt Rus. Fed. 43 N1
Voronovo Rus. Fed. 43 S6
Vorontsovka Kazakh. 103 J2
Vorontsovo Rus. Fed. 43 J4
Vorontsovo-Aleksandrovskoye Rus. Fed. see Zelenokumsk
Voron'ye Rus. Fed. 40 G4
Voroshilov Rus. Fed. see Ussuriysk
Voroshilovgrad Ukr. see Luhans'k
Voroshilovsk Rus. Fed. see Stavropol'
Voroshilovsk Ukr. see Alchevs'k
Vorot'kovo Rus. Fed. 43 O6
Vorotynets Rus. Fed. 40 H4
Vorotynsk Rus. Fed. 43 R7
Vorozhba Ukr. 41 E6
Vorpommersche Boddenlandschaft, Nationalpark nat. park Germany 49 J1
Vorposten Peak Antarctica 223 B2
Vorskla r. Rus. Fed. 41 E6
Vorstershoop S. Africa 132 H2
Vørterkaka Nunatak mt. Antarctica 223 B2
Võrtsjärv l. Estonia 42 G3
Võru Estonia 42 I4
Vorukh Tajik. 101 G2
Vorya r. Rus. Fed. 43 P7
Vosburg S. Africa 132 G7
Vose Tajik. 101 G2
formerly known as Aral
Vosges mts France 51 M5
Vosges du Nord, Parc Naturel Régional des nature res. France 51 N4
Voshchazhnikovo Rus. Fed. 43 U4
Voskresensk Rus. Fed. 43 T6
Voskresenskoye Lipetskaya Oblast' Rus. Fed. 43 T8
Voskresenskoye Respublika Bashkortostan Rus. Fed. 102 D1
Voskresenskoye Tul'skaya Oblast' Rus. Fed. 43 S7
Voskresenskoye Vologod. Obl. Rus. Fed. 43 S2
Voskresenskoye Yaroslavskaya Oblast' Rus. Fed. 43 S4
Voss Norway 45 I3
Vostochnaya Litsa Rus. Fed. 40 F1
Vostochno-Kazakhstanskaya Oblast' admin. div. Kazakh. see Vostochnyy Kazakhstan
Vostochno-Kounradskiy Kazakh. see Shygys Konyrat
Vostochno-Sakhalinskiy Gory mts Rus. Fed. 82 F2
Vostochno-Sibirskoye More sea Rus. Fed. see East Siberian Sea
Vostochnyy Rus. Fed. 40 J4
Vostochnyy Chink Ustyurta esc. Uzbek. 102 D4
Vostochnyy Kazakhstan admin. div. Kazakh. 103 I2
English form East Kazakhstan Oblast; also known as Shyghys Qazaqstan Oblysy; long form Vostochno-Kazakhstanskaya Oblast'
Vostochnyy Sayan mts Rus. Fed. 80 E2
English form Eastern Sayan Mountains

▶Vostok research station Antarctica
Lowest recorded screen temperature in the world.
world [climate and weather] 16–17

Vostok Rus. Fed. 82 D3
Vostok Rus. Fed. see Neftegorsk
Vostok Island Kiribati 221 H6
Vostretsovo Rus. Fed. 82 D3
Vostroye Rus. Fed. 40 H3
Võsu Estonia 42 G2
Votkinsk Rus. Fed. 40 J4
Votkinskoye Vodokhranilishche resr Rus. Fed. 40 J4
Votorantim Brazil 206 F10
Votrya r. Rus. Fed. 43 N6
Votuporanga Brazil 206 D7
Voudi, Akra pt Greece 59 J12
Vouga Angola see Cunhinga
Vouga r. Port. 54 C4
Vouillé France 50 G6
Voula Greece 59 E11
Vourinos mt. Greece 59 C8
Vouziers France 51 K3
Voves France 50 H4
Vovodo r. Cent. Afr. Rep. 126 E3
Voxna Sweden 45 K3
Voxnan r. Sweden 45 L3
Voya r. Rus. Fed. 40 I4
Voyageurs National Park U.S.A. 174 A1
Voykar r. Rus. Fed. 40 M2
Voynitsa Rus. Fed. 44 O2
Vöyri Fin. see Vörå
Voyvozh Respublika Komi Rus. Fed. 40 J2
Voyvozh Respublika Komi Rus. Fed. 40 J3
Vozdvizhenskoye Moskovskaya Oblast' Rus. Fed. 43 R5
Vozdvizhenskoye Moskovskaya Oblast' Rus. Fed. 43 T5
Vozha r. Rus. Fed. 43 U7
Vozhayel' Rus. Fed. 40 I3
Vozhd' Proletariata Rus. Fed. 43 U6
Vozhe, Ozero l. Rus. Fed. 43 T1
Vozhega Rus. Fed. 43 V1
Vozhega r. Rus. Fed. 43 U1
Vozhgora Rus. Fed. 40 I2
Voznesenka Kazakh. 103 G1
Voznesens'k Ukr. 41 D7
Voznesen'ye Rus. Fed. 43 Q1
Vozrovdenye Uzbek. 102 D3
Vozrozhdeniya, Ostrov i. Uzbek. 102 D3
also known as Wozrojdeniye Oroli
Vozzhayevka Rus. Fed. 82 C2
Vrå Denmark 45 J4
Vrabevo Bulg. 58 F6
Vrachionas hill Greece 59 B11
also known as Vrakhíonas Óros
Vrachnaiika Greece 59 C10
also spelt Vrakhnaiika
Vrådal Norway 45 J4
Vrakhíonas Óros hill Greece see Vrachionas
Vrakhnaiika Greece see Vrachnaiika
Vran mt. Bos.-Herz. 56 J5
Vrana r. Bulg. 58 H5
Vrangel' Rus. Fed. 82 D4
Vrangelya, Mys pt Rus. Fed. 82 E1
Vrangelya, Ostrov i. Rus. Fed. see Wrangel Island
Vranjak Bos.-Herz. 56 K4
Vranje Srbija Yugo. 58 C6
Vranjska Banja Srbija Yugo. 58 D6
Vranov, Vodní nádrž resr Czech Rep. 49 M7
Vranov nad Topľou Slovakia 49 S7
Vrapčište Macedonia 58 B7
Vrasidas, Akra pt Greece 58 F8
Vratnik pass Bulg. 58 H6
Vratsa Bulg. 58 E5
Vrbanja r. Bos.-Herz. 56 J4
Vrbas r. Bos.-Herz. 56 J3
Vrbas Vojvodina, Srbija Yugo. 58 A3
formerly known as Titov Vrbas
Vrbno pod Pradědem Czech Rep. 49 O5
Vrbovec Croatia 56 I3
Vrbovsko Croatia 56 H3
Vrchlabí Czech Rep. 49 M5
Vrede S. Africa 133 M4
Vredefort S. Africa 133 L3
Vredenburg S. Africa 132 B9
Vredendal S. Africa 132 C8
Vredeshoop Namibia 132 D4
Vreed-en-Hoop Guyana 199 G3
Vrela Kosovo, Srbija Yugo. 58 B6
Vrhnika Slovenia 56 G3
Vriddhachalam India 94 C4
Vrigstad Sweden 45 K4
Vrindavan India 89 B7
Vrnjačka Banja Srbija Yugo. 58 B5
Vrolijkheid Nature Reserve S. Africa 132 D10
Vrrin Albania 58 A7
Vršac Vojvodina, Srbija Yugo. 58 C3
also known as Versec
Vryburg S. Africa 133 I3
Vryheid S. Africa 133 O4
Vsetín Czech Rep. 49 O6
Vsevolozhsk Rus. Fed. 43 L1
Vskhody Rus. Fed. 43 P7
Vtáčnik mt. Slovakia 49 P7
Vtáčnik mts Slovakia 49 P7
Vůcha r. Bulg. 58 F7
Vučica r. Croatia 56 K3
Vučitrn Kosovo, Srbija Yugo. 58 B6
Vuka r. Croatia 56 L3
Vuktyl' Rus. Fed. 40 K3
Vukuzakhe S. Africa 133 N4
Vulcan Canada 167 H5
Vulcan Romania 58 E3
Vulcănești Moldova 58 J3
formerly spelt Vulkaneshty
Vulcan Island P.N.G. see Manam Island
Vulcano, Isola i. Isole Lipari Italy 57 G10
Vülchedrŭm Bulg. 58 E5
Vülchidol Bulg. 58 I5
Vulkaneshty Moldova see Vulcănești
Vulture Mountains U.S.A. 183 K8
Vung Dung Quat b. Vietnam 79 E5

Xingan China **87** E3
also known as Jinchuan
Xingba China see **Lhünzê**
Xingcheng China see **Qianxi**
Xingcheng China **85** I3
Xingdi China **88** D3
Xinge Angola **127** C7
Xingguo China see **Qin'an**
Xingguo China **87** E3
also known as Lianjiang
Xinghai China **84** C5
also known as Ziketan
Xinghua China **87** F1
Xinghua Wan b. China **87** F3
Xingkai China **82** D3
Xingkai Hu l. China/Rus.Fed. see **Khanka, Lake**
Xinglong Hebei China **85** H3
Xinglong Heilong. China **82** B2
Xinglongzhen China **82** B3
Xingning China **87** E3
Xingou China **87** E2
Xingping China **87** D1
Xingren China **86** C3
Xingrenbu China **84** E4
Xingsagoinba China **86** B1
Xingshan China see **Majiang**
Xingshan China **87** D2
also known as Gufu
Xingtai China **85** G4
Xingtang China **85** G4
Xingu r. Brazil **199** H5
Xingu, Parque Indígena do res. Brazil **202** A4
Xinguara Brazil **202** B3
Xingxian China **85** F4
Xingxingxia China **84** B3
Xingyang China **87** E1
Xingyi China **86** C3
also known as Huangcaoba
Xingzi China **87** F2
also known as Nankang
Xinhe Hebei China **85** G4
Xinhe Xinjiang China **88** C3
also known as Toksu
Xin Hot China **85** G3
also known as Abag Qi
Xinhua China see **Huadu**
Xinhua China **87** D3
Xinhua China see **Qiaojia**
Xinhua China see **Funing**
Xinhuacun China **84** D4
Xinhuang China **87** D3
Xinhui China **85** H3
also known as Aohan Qi
Xining China **84** D4
formerly spelt Sining
Xinji China **85** G4
formerly known as Shulu
Xinji China see **Xinxian**
Xinjian China **87** E2
also known as Changleng
Xinjiang China **85** F5
Xinjiang aut. reg. China see **Xinjiang Uygur Zizhiqu**
Xin Jiang r. China **87** F2
Xinjiangkou China see **Songzi**
Xinjiang Uygur Autonomous Region aut. reg. China see **Xinjiang Uygur Zizhiqu**
Xinjiang Uygur Zizhiqu aut. reg. China **84** B3
English form Sinkiang Uighur Autonomous Region or Xinjiang Uygur Autonomous Region; short form Sinkiang or Xinjiang; formerly known as Chinese Turkestan
Xinjie China **85** F4
Xinjie China see **Yuanyang**
Xinjin China see **Pulandian**
Xinjin China **86** B2
also known as Wujin
Xinjing China see **Jingxi**
Xinkai r. China **85** I3
Xinling China see **Badong**
Xinlong China **86** B2
also known as Nyagrong or Rulong
Xinmi China **87** E1
formerly known as Mixian
Xinmian China see **Shimian**
Xinmin China **85** I3
Xinning China see **Ningxian**
Xinning China see **Fusui**
Xinning China **87** D3
also known as Jinshi
Xinning China see **Wuning**
Xinning China see **Kaijiang**
Xinping China **86** B3
also known as Guishan
Xinqing China **82** C2
Xinquan China **87** F3
Xinshan China see **Anyuan**
Xinshao China **87** D3
also known as Niangxi
Xinshi China see **Jingshan**
Xinshiba China see **Ganluo**
Xintai China **85** H5
Xintanpu China **87** E2
Xintian China **87** E3
Xinxian China **87** E2
also known as Xinji
Xinxiang China **85** G5
Xinxing China **87** E4
also known as Xincheng
Xinyang China **87** E1
Xinyang Gang r. China **87** G1
Xinye China **87** E1
Xinye r. China **87** F1
Xinyi Guangdong China **87** D4
Xinyi Jiangsu China **87** F1
Xinying China **87** D5
Xinying Taiwan see **Hsinying**
Xinyu China **87** E3
Xinyuan China see **Tianjun**
Xinyuan China **88** C3
also known as Künes
Xinzhangfang China **85** I1
Xinzheng China **87** E1
Xinzhou China see **Longlin**
Xinzhou China see **Huangping**
Xinzhou Hubei China **87** E2
Xinzhou Shanxi China **85** G4
Xinzhu Taiwan see **Hsinchu**
Xinzo de Limia Spain **54** D2
also spelt Ginzo de Limia
Xiongshan China see **Zhenghe**
Xiongzhou China see **Nanxiong**
Xipamanu r. Bol./Brazil **200** D2
Xiping Henan China **87** D1
also known as Baicheng
Xiping Henan China **87** E1
Xiqing Shan mts China **86** B1
Xique Xique Brazil **202** D4
Xiro hill Greece **59** E10
Xirokampo Greece **59** H11
Xiruá r. Brazil **198** E6
Xisa China see **Xichou**
Xishanzui China **85** F3
also known as Urad Qianqi
Xisha Qundao is S. China Sea see **Paracel Islands**
Xishuangbanna reg. China **86** B4
Xishui Guizhou China **86** C2
Xishui Hubei China **87** E2
also known as Qingquan
Xistral, Serra do mts Spain **54** D1
also spelt Sierra del Gistral
Xi Taijnar Hu l. China **84** B4
Xitole Guinea-Bissau **124** B4
Xiucaiwan China see **Fengdu**
Xiugu China see **Jinxi**
Xi Ujimqin Qi China see **Bayan Ul Hot**
Xiuning China **87** F2
also known as Haiyang
Xiushan China **87** D2
also known as Zhonghe
Xiushan China see **Tonghai**
Xiushui China **87** E2
also known as Yining
Xiu Shui r. China **87** E2
Xiuwen China **86** C3
Xiuwu China **85** G5
Xiuyan China **85** I3
Xiuyan China see **Qingjian**
Xiuying China **87** D4
Xiwanzi China see **Chongli**
Xiwu China **86** A1
Xixabangma Feng mt. China **89** D6
also known as Shisha Pangma; formerly known as Gosainthan
Xixia China **87** D1
Xixian Henan China **87** E1
Xixian Shanxi China **85** F4
Xixiang China **87** C1
Xixón Spain see **Gijón**
Xiyang China **85** G4
Xiyang Dao i. China **87** G3
Xiyang Jiang r. China **86** C3
Xizang aut. reg. China see **Xizang Zizhiqu**
Xizang Gaoyuan plat. China see **Tibet, Plateau of**
Xizang Zizhiqu aut. reg. China **86** A2
English form Tibet or Tibet Autonomous Region; short form Xizang
Xizhong Dao i. China **85** I4
Xocavänd Azer. **107** F3
also spelt Khodzhavend
Xodoto, Akra pt Greece **59** H12
Xoi China see **Qüxü**
Xolobe S. Africa **133** L9
Xom An Lôc Vietnam **79** D6
Xom Duc Hanh Vietnam **79** D6
Xonxa Dam S. Africa **133** L8
Xorkol China **88** E4
Xuancheng China see **Xuanzhou**
Xuan'en China **87** D2
also known as Zhushan
Xuanhan China **87** C2
also known as Dongxiang
Xuanhua China **85** G3
Xuân Lôc Vietnam **79** D6
Xuanwei China **86** C3
Xuanzhou China **87** F2
formerly known as Xuancheng
Xuchang Henan China **87** E1
Xucheng China see **Xuwen**
Xudat Azer. **107** G2
also spelt Khudat
Xuddur Somalia **128** D3
Xudun Somalia **128** E2
Xueba China see **Sangri**
Xuefeng China see **Mingxi**
Xuefeng Shan mts China **87** D3
Xuehua Shan hill China **87** D1
Xue Shan mts China **86** A3
Xugou China **87** F1
Xugui China **84** B5
Xuguit Qi China see **Yakeshi**
Xujiang China see **Guangchang**
Xulun Hobot Qagan Qi China see **Qagan Nur**
Xulun Hoh Qi China see **Dund Hot**
Xümatang China **86** A1
Xun r. China **82** C2
Xundian China **86** B3
also known as Rende
Xungba China **89** C5
also known as Xangdoring
Xungmai China **89** E6
Xung Qu r. China **89** F6
Xungru China **89** D6
Xunhe China **82** B2
Xun He r. China **87** D1
Xunhua China **84** D5
also known as Jishi
Xun Jiang r. China **87** D4
Xunke China **82** C2
Xunwu China **87** E3
also known as Changning
Xunxian China **85** G5
Xunyang China **87** D1
Xunyi China **85** F5
Xupu China **87** D3
also known as Lufeng
Xuru Co salt l. China **89** D6
Xushui China **85** G4
also known as Ansu
Xuwen China **87** D4
also known as Xucheng
Xuyang China see **Rongxian**
Xuyi China **87** F1
Xuyong China **86** C2
also known as Yongning
Xuzhou China see **Tongshan**
Xylagani Greece **58** G8
also spelt Xilagani
Xylokastro Greece **59** D10
also known as Xilókastron
Xylopoli Greece **58** E8
also known as Xilópolis

Y

Ya'an China **86** B2
Yaapeet Australia **147** D3
Yabanabat Turkey see **Kızılcahamam**
Yabassi Cameroon **125** H5
Yabēlo Eth. **128** C3
Yabēlo Wildlife Sanctuary nature res. Eth. **128** C3
Yablanitsa Bulg. **58** F5
Yablanovo Bulg. **58** H6
Yablonovyy Khrebet mts Rus. Fed. **85** F1
Yabo Nigeria **125** G3
Yabrai Shan mts China **84** D4
Yabrai Yanchang China **84** D4
Yabrīn reg. Saudi Arabia **105** E3
Yabrūd Syria **109** H4
Yabuli China **82** C3
Yabuyanos Peru **198** C5
Yacha China see **Baisha**
Yacheng China **87** D5
Yachi He r. China **86** C3
Yaciretá, Isla i. Para. **201** F6
Yaciretá Apipé, Embalse resr Para. **201** F6
Yacuiba Bol. **201** E5
Yacurai Venez. **199** E3
Yadé, Massif du mts Cent. Afr. Rep. **126** B3
Yadgir India **94** C2
Yadiki India **94** C3
Yadkin r. U.S.A. **174** D5
Yadkinville U.S.A. **176** E9
Yadong China **89** E7
also known as Xarsingma; formerly known as Chomo
Yadrin Rus. Fed. **40** H5
Yaeyama-rettō is Japan **81** K8
Yafa Israel see **Tel Aviv-Yafo**
Yafran Libya **120** B1
Yagaba Ghana **125** E4
Yagaing state Myanmar see **Arakan**
Yağcılı Turkey **59** I9
Yağda Turkey see **Erdemli**
Yagman Turkm. **102** C5
Yagmo China **89** D6
Yagnitsa Rus. Fed. **43** S3
Yago Mex. **184** D4
Yagoda Bulg. **58** G6
Yagodnaya Polyana Rus. Fed. **41** H6
Yagodnoye Kaluzhskaya Oblast' Rus. Fed. **43** Q8
Yagodnoye Magadanskaya Oblast' Rus. Fed. **39** O3
Yagodnyy Rus. Fed. **82** E2
Yagoua Cameroon **125** I4
Yagra China **89** C6
Yagradagzê Shan mt. China **84** B5
Yaguajay Cuba **186** D2
Yaguarón r. Brazil/Uruguay see **Jaguarão**
Yaguas r. Peru **198** D5
Yaha Thai. **79** C7
Yahk Canada **167** G5
Yahualica Mex. **185** E4
Yahyalı Turkey **98** B2
also known as Gazibenli
Yahya Wana Afgh. **96** A3
Yai, Khao hill Thai. **79** B5
Yaita Japan **90** F6
Yaizu Japan **91** F7
Yajiang China **86** B2
also known as Hekou or Nyagquka
Yakacık Turkey **108** H1
Yakapınar Turkey **108** G1
Yakeshi China **85** I1
formerly known as Xuguit Qi
Yakhab waterhole Iran **100** D3
Yakhehal Afgh. **101** F4
Yakhroma Rus. Fed. **43** S5
Yakima U.S.A. **180** B3
Yakima r. U.S.A. **180** C3
Yakima Indian Reservation res. U.S.A. **180** B3
Yakinish Iran **100** C3
Yakkabag Uzbek. **103** F5
formerly known as Stantsiya-Yakkabag
Yakmach Pak. **101** E4
Yako Burkina **125** E3
Yakobi Island U.S.A. **166** B3
Yakoma Dem. Rep. Congo **126** D3
Yakoruda Bulg. **58** E6
Yakovlevka Rus. Fed. **82** D3
Yakumo Japan **90** G3
Yaku-shima i. Japan **91** B9
Yakutat U.S.A. **166** B3
Yakutat Bay U.S.A. **164** E4
Yakutsk Rus. Fed. **39** M3
Yakymivka Ukr. **41** E7
Yala Ghana **125** E4
Yala Thai. **79** C7
Yalai China **89** D6
Yalakdere Turkey **58** K8
Yala National Park Sri Lanka see **Ruhuna National Park**
Yalan Dünya Mağarası tourist site Turkey **108** D1
Yalata Aboriginal Lands res. Australia **146** A2
Yale Canada **166** F5
Yale U.S.A. **173** K7
Yalgoo Australia **151** B6
Yalıkavak Turkey **59** I11
Yalıköy Turkey **58** J7
Yalinga Cent. Afr. Rep. **126** D3
Yalizava Belarus **43** K8
Yalkubul, Punta pt Mex. **185** H4
Yalleroi Australia **149** E5
Yallo Burkina **124** E3
Yallourn Australia **147** E4
Yaloké Cent. Afr. Rep. **126** C3
Yalong Jiang r. China **86** B3
Yalova Turkey **106** B2
Yalova prov. Turkey **58** K8
Yaloven' Moldova see **Ialoveni**
Yalpirakinu Aboriginal Land res. Australia **148** B4
Yalpuh, Ozero l. Ukr. **58** J3
Yalpukh r. Moldova see **Ialpug**
Yalta Ukr. **41** E7
Yaltins'kyy Zapovidnyk nature res. Ukr. **106** C1
Yalu Jiang r. China **85** I2
Yalu Jiang r. China/N. Korea **83** B4
also known as Amnok-kang
Yalutorovsk Rus. Fed. **38** G4
Yalvaç Turkey **106** B3
Yām reg. Saudi Arabia **105** D4
Yamada Japan **90** G5
Yamaga Japan **91** B8
Yamagata Iwate Japan **90** G4
Yamagata Yamagata Japan **90** G5
Yamagata pref. Japan **90** F5
Yamaguchi Japan **91** B7
Yamaguchi pref. Japan **91** B7
Yamal, Poluostrov pen. Rus. Fed. see **Yamal Peninsula**
Yam Alin', Khrebet mts Rus. Fed. **82** D1
Yamal Peninsula Rus. Fed. **38** G2
also known as Yamal, Poluostrov
Yamanashi pref. Japan **90** F7
Yamanie Falls National Park Australia **149** E3
Yamankhalinka Kazakh. see **Makhambet**
Yamanovka Rus. Fed. **85** F1
Yamasaki Japan **91** D7
Yamatsuri Japan **90** G6
Yamba Australia **147** G2
Yambacoona Australia **147** D4
Yambarran Range hills Australia **148** A2
Yambéring Guinea **124** B4
Yambi, Mesa de hills Col. **198** D4
Yambio Sudan **126** F3
Yambol Bulg. **58** H6
Yambrasbamba Peru **198** B6
Yamdena i. Indon. **73** H8
Yame Japan **91** B8
Yamethin Myanmar **78** B3
Y'ami i. Phil. **74** B1

▶**Yamin, Puncak** mt. Indon. **73** I7
4th highest mountain in Oceania.
oceania [landscapes] 136–137

Yamizo-san mt. Japan **90** G6
Yamkanmardi India **94** B2
Yamkhad Syria see **Aleppo**
Yamkino Rus. Fed. **43** K4
Yamm Rus. Fed. **43** J3
Yamma Yamma, Lake salt flat Australia **149** D5
also known as Mackillop, Lake

▶**Yamoussoukro** Côte d'Ivoire **124** D5
Capital of Côte d'Ivoire.

Yampil' Ukr. **41** D6
also spelt Yampol'
Yampol' Ukr. see **Yampil'**
Yamuna r. India **96** D4
English form Jumna
Yamunanagar India **96** C3
Yamzho Yumco l. China **89** E6
Yan r. China **85** F4
Yan r. Rus. Fed. **39** N2
Yanac Australia **146** D4
Yanachaga-Chemillen, Parque Nacional nat. park Peru **200** B2
Yanadani Japan **91** C8
Yanai Japan **91** C8
Yanam India **95** D2
formerly known as Yanaon
Yan'an China **85** F4
Yanaoca Peru **200** C3
Yanaon India see **Yanam**
Yanaul Rus. Fed. **40** J4
Yanavichy Belarus **43** L6
Yanayacu Peru **198** C5
Yanbian China **86** B3
also known as Dapingdi
Yanbu' al Baḩr Saudi Arabia **104** B2
Yanbu' an Nakhl reg. Saudi Arabia **104** B2
Yanceyville U.S.A. **176** F9
Yanchang China **85** F4
Yancheng China **87** G1
Yancheng China see **Qihe**
Yancheng China see **Jingyan**
Yanchep Australia **151** A6
Yanchi Ningxia China **85** E4
Yanchi Xinjiang China **84** B3
Yanchuan China **85** F4
Yanco Creek r. Australia **147** E3
Yanco Glen Australia **146** D2
Yanda watercourse Australia **147** E2
Yandama Creek watercourse Australia **146** D2
Yandang Shan mts China **87** G3
Yandao China see **Yingjing**
Yandaxkak China **88** E4
Yandeyarra Aboriginal Reserve Australia **150** B4
Yandil Australia **151** B5
Yandina Solomon Is **145** E2
Yandja Dem. Rep. Congo **126** C5
Yandoon Myanmar **78** A4
Yandun China **84** B3
Yanega Rus. Fed. **43** O1
Yanfolila Mali **124** C4
Yang r. China **85** G3
Yangalia Cent. Afr. Rep. **126** D3
Yangambi Dem. Rep. Congo **126** E4
Ya'ngamdo Xizang China **89** F6
Ya'ngamdo Xizang China **89** F6
Yangasso Mali **124** D3
Yangbajain China **89** E6
Yangbi China **86** A3
also known as Shangjie
Yangcheng China see **Yangshan**
Yangcheng China **85** G5
Yangchuan China see **Suiyang**
Yangchun China **87** D4
Yangcun China **87** E4
Yangcun China see **Wuqing**
Yangdok N. Korea **83** B5
Yanggao China **85** G3
Yanggu China **85** G4
Yanghe China see **Yongning**
Yang Hu l. China **89** D5
Yangiaryk Uzbek. **102** E4
Yangi Davan pass Aksai Chin/China **89** B5
Yangi-Nishan Uzbek. **103** F5
Yangi Qal'eh Afgh. **101** G2
Yangirabad Uzbek. **103** F4
Yangiyul' Uzbek. **103** G4
Yangjialing China **85** F4
Yangjiang China **87** D4
Yangjiaogou China **85** H4
Yangôn Myanmar see **Rangoon**
Yangôn admin. div. Myanmar **78** B4
English form Rangoon; also spelt Rangôn
Yangping China **87** D2
Yangquan China **85** G4
Yangshan China **87** E3
also known as Yangcheng
Yangshuo China **87** D3
Yang Talat Thai. **78** C4
Yangtouyan China **86** B3

▶**Yangtze** r. China **87** G2
Longest river in Asia and 3rd in the world. Also known as Yangtze Kiang or Chang Jiang or Jinsha Jiang or Tongtian He or Zhi Qu.
asia [landscapes] 62–63

Yangtze Kiang r. China **87** F2
also known as Yangtze
Yangtze, Mouth of the China **87** G2
also known as Changjiang Kou
Yangudi Rassa National Park Eth. **128** D2
Yangweigang China **87** F1
Yangxian China **87** C1
Yangyang S. Korea **83** C5
Yangyuan China **85** G3
also known as Xicheng
Yangzhou China see **Hanjiang**
Yanhe China **87** D2
also known as Heping
Yanhu China **88** E3
Yaninee, Lake salt flat Australia **146** B3
Yanishpole Rus. Fed. **40** E3
Yanis"yarvi, Ozero l. Rus. Fed. **44** O3
Yanji China **82** C4
Yanjin Henan China **85** G5
Yanjin Yunnan China **86** C2
also known as Yanjing
Yanjing China see **Yanyuan**
Yanjing China **86** A2
also known as Xiayanjing; formerly known as Caka'lho
Yanjing China see **Yanjin**
Yankara National Park Nigeria **125** H4
Yankavichy Belarus **43** J6
Yankou China see **Wusheng**
Yankton U.S.A. **178** C3
Yankton Indian Reservation res. U.S.A. **178** C3
Yanling Henan China **87** E1
also known as Anling
Yanling Hunan China **87** E3
formerly known as Lingxian
Yannina Greece see **Ioannina**
Yano-Indigirskaya Nizmennost' lowland Rus. Fed. **39** O2
Yanovo Rus. Fed. **43** N7
Yanov-Stan Rus. Fed. **39** I3
Yan Oya r. Sri Lanka **94** D4
Yanqi China **88** D3
Yanqing China **85** G3
Yanqul Oman **105** G3
Yanrey r. Australia **150** A4
Yanshan Hebei China **85** H4
Yanshan Jiangxi China **87** F2
also known as Hekou
Yanshan Yunnan China **86** C4
also known as Jiangna
Yan Shan mts China **85** H3
Yanshi China **87** E1
Yanshiping China **97** G2
Yanshou China **82** C3
Yanskiy Zaliv g. Rus. Fed. **39** N2
Yantabulla Australia **147** E2
Yantai China **85** I4
formerly known as Chefoo
Yántales, Cerro mt. Chile **205** B6
Yantarnyy Rus. Fed. **42** A7
historically known as Palmnicken
Yanting China **86** C2
also known as Yunxi
Yantongshan China **82** B4
Yantou China **87** G2
Yantra r. Bulg. **58** G5
Yanūfi, Jabal al hill Saudi Arabia **104** C3
Yany-Kurgan Kazakh. see **Zhanakorgan**
Yanyuan China **86** B3
also known as Yanjing
Yanzhou China **85** H5
Yao'an China **86** B3
also known as Dongchuan
Yaodu China see **Dongzhi**
Yaojie China see **Honggu**
Yaoli China **87** F2

▶**Yaoundé** Cameroon **125** H6
Capital of Cameroon.

Yaoxian China **87** D1
Yao Yai, Ko i. Thai. **79** B6
Yaozhen China **85** F4
Yap i. Micronesia **73** I5
formerly spelt Eap
Yapacana, Parque Nacional nat. park Venez. **199** E4
Yapacani r. Bol. **201** D3
Yapen i. Indon. **73** I7
Yapen, Selat sea chan. Indon. **73** I7
Yappar r. Australia **149** D3
Yapukarri Guyana **199** G4
Yapuparra Aboriginal Reserve Australia **151** D5
Yaqui r. Mex. **184** C3
Yar Rus. Fed. **40** J4
Yara Cuba **186** D2
Yaracal Venez. **198** D2
Yaracuy state Venez. **198** D2
Yaradzha Turkm. see **Yaradzhi**
Yaradzhi Turkm. **102** D5
formerly spelt Yaradzha
Yaraka Australia **149** E5
Yarangüme Turkey see **Tavas**
Yaransk Rus. Fed. **40** H4
Yardan Uzbek. see **Iordan**
Yardea Australia **146** B3
Yardımcı Burnu pt Turkey **106** B3
also known as Gelidonya Burnu
Yardımlı Azer. **107** G3
also spelt Yardymly
Yardley U.S.A. **177** K5
Yardoi China **89** E6
Yardymly Azer. see **Yardımlı**
Yare r. U.K. **47** N11
Yarega Rus. Fed. **40** J3

▶**Yaren** Nauru **145** F2
Capital of Nauru.
world [countries] 10–11

Yarenga r. Rus. Fed. **40** I3
Yarensk Rus. Fed. **40** I3
Yargara Moldova see **Iargara**
Yari r. Col. **198** C5
also known as Engaños, Río de los
Yariga-take mt. Japan **91** E6
Yarīm Yemen **104** D5
Yarımca Turkey see **Körfez**
Yaringa watercourse Australia **148** C4
Yaripo Brazil **199** H4
Yaris well Niger **125** G3
Yaritagua Venez. **187** F5
Yarkand China see **Shache**
Yarkant China see **Shache**
Yarkant He r. China **88** B4
Yarker Canada **173** Q6
Yarkhun r. Pak. **101** H2
Yarlovo Bulg. **58** E6
Yarlung Zangbo r. China **89** D6 see **Brahmaputra**
Yarmouth Canada **169** H5
Yarmouth U.K. see **Great Yarmouth**
Yarmouth U.S.A. **177** O2
Yarmūk r. Asia **108** G5
Yarnell U.S.A. **183** L7
Yaroslavichi Rus. Fed. **43** P1
Yaroslavl' Rus. Fed. **43** U4
Yaroslavl Oblast admin. div. Rus. Fed. see **Yaroslavskaya Oblast'**
Yaroslavskaya Oblast' admin. div. Rus. Fed. **43** U4
English form Yaroslavl Oblast
Yaroslavskiy Rus. Fed. **82** D3
Yarqon r. Israel **108** F5
Yarrabah Aboriginal Reserve Australia **149** E3
Yarra Junction Australia **147** E4
Yarralin Aboriginal Land res. Australia **148** A3
Yarram Australia **147** E4
Yarraman Australia **149** F5
Yarrawonga Australia **147** E4
Yarra Yarra Lakes salt flat Australia **151** A6
Yarrie Australia **150** C4
Yarronvale Australia **149** E5
Yarrowmere Australia **149** E4
Yartsevo Krasnoyarskiy Kray Rus. Fed. **39** I3
Yartsevo Smolenskaya Oblast' Rus. Fed. **43** N6
Yaru r. China **89** D6
Yarumal Col. **198** C3
Yarwa China **86** A2
Yary Rus. Fed. **40** M1
Yarzhong China **86** A2
Yaş Romania see **Iaşi**
Yasa Dem. Rep. Congo **126** D5
Yasai r. India **95** E1
Yasawa Group is Fiji **145** G3
Yasenkovo Bulg. **58** H5
Yashi Nigeria **125** G3
Yashikera Nigeria **125** F4
Yashilkŭl l. Tajik. **101** H2
Yashkino Rus. Fed. **41** J5
Yashkul' Rus. Fed. **41** H7
formerly known as Peschanoye
Yasin Jammu and Kashmir **96** B1
Yaskavichy Belarus **42** I9
Yasna Polyana Bulg. **58** I6
Yasnogorsk Rus. Fed. **43** S7
formerly known as Laptevo
Yasnyy Amurskaya Oblast' Rus. Fed. **82** C1
Yasnyy Orenburgskaya Oblast' Rus. Fed. **102** D2
Yasothon Thai. **78** D5
Yass Australia **147** F3
Yass r. Australia **147** F3
Yassı Burnu c. Cyprus see **Plakoti, Cape**
Yasski Rus. Fed. **43** L4
Yasugi Japan **91** C7
Yāsūj Iran **100** B4
Yasuni nat. park Ecuador **198** C5
Yasur vol. Vanuatu **145** F3
Yat well Niger **125** I1
Yata r. Bol. **200** D2
Yata r. Cent. Afr. Rep. **126** D2
Yatağan Turkey **106** B3
Yatakala Niger **125** F3
Yata Plateau Kenya **128** C5
Yaté New Caledonia **145** F4
Yates r. Canada **167** H2
Yates Center U.S.A. **178** D4
Yathkyed Lake Canada **167** L2
Yathong Nature Reserve Australia **147** E3
Yatolema Dem. Rep. Congo **126** E4
Yatou China see **Rongcheng**
Yatsuga-take vol. Japan **91** F7
Yatsushiro Japan **91** B8
Yatsushiro-kai b. Japan **91** B8
Yatta West Bank **108** G6
also spelt Yuta
Yauca Peru **200** B3
Yauco Puerto Rico **187** G3
Yauli Peru **200** A2
Yauna Maloca Col. **198** D5
Yauri Peru **200** C3
Yauricocha Peru **200** B3
Yau Tong b. Hong Kong China **87** [inset]
Yauyos Peru **200** B3
Yavan Tajik. see **Yovon**
Yavari r. Peru **198** D6
also spelt Javari
Yávaros Mex. **184** C3
Yavatmal India **94** C1
formerly spelt Yeotmal
Yavero r. Peru **200** B3
also known as Paucartambo
Yaví, Cerro mt. Venez. **199** E3
Yavr r. Fin./Rus. Fed. **44** O1
Yavuzlu Turkey **109** I1
Yawatahama Japan **91** C8
Yawatongguz He r. China **89** C4
Yawatongguzlangar China **89** C4
Yaw Chaung r. Myanmar **78** A3
Yawng-hwe Shan Myanmar **78** B3
Yaxchilan tourist site Guat. **185** H5
Yaxian China see **Sanya**
Yayladağı Turkey **108** H2
also known as Ordu
Yayva Rus. Fed. **40** K4
Yazagyo Myanmar **78** A3
Yazd Iran **100** C4
Yazd prov. Iran **100** C4
Yazdān Iran **101** E3
Yazd-e Khvāst Iran **100** C4
also known as Samirum
Yazgulemskiy Khrebet mts Tajik. see **Yazgulom, Qatorkŭhi**
Yazgulom, Qatorkŭhi mts Tajik. **101** G2
also known as Yazgulemskiy Khrebet
Yazhelbitsy Rus. Fed. **43** N3
Yazıhan Turkey **107** D3
also known as Fethiye
Yazıkent Turkey **59** J11
Yazoo r. U.S.A. **175** B5
Yazoo City U.S.A. **175** B5
Yaz'va r. Rus. Fed. **40** K3
Ybakoura well Chad **120** B4
Y Bala U.K. see **Bala**
Ybbs r. Austria **49** M7
Ybbs an der Donau Austria **49** M7
Ybycuí Para. **201** F6
Yding Skovhøj hill Denmark **45** J5
Ydra Greece **59** E11
Ydra i. Greece **59** E11
English form Hydra; also spelt Idhra or Idra
Ydras, Kolpos sea chan. Greece **59** E11
also spelt Ídhras, Kólpos
Y Drenewydd U.K. see **Newtown**
Ye Myanmar **79** B5
Ye r. Myanmar **79** B5
Yebaishou China see **Jianping**
Yebawmi Myanmar **78** A2
Yebbi-Bou Chad **120** C4
Yebekshi Kazakh. **103** G4
Yecheng China **88** B4
also known as Karghalik or Kargilik
Yecla Spain **55** J6
Yécora Mex. **184** C2
Yedashe Myanmar **78** B4
Yedatore India **94** C3
Yedi Burun Başı pt Turkey **59** K12
Yedoma Rus. Fed. **40** H3
Yedri well Chad **120** C4
Yedrovo Rus. Fed. **43** O4
Yedy Belarus **42** I6
Yeed Eth. **128** D3
Yeeda River Australia **150** C3
Yeelanna Australia **146** B3
Yefimovskiy Rus. Fed. **43** P2
Yefremov Rus. Fed. **43** T8
Yêgainnyin China see **Henan**
Yeggueba well Niger **125** I2
Yeghegnadzor Armenia **107** F3
formerly known as Mikoyan; formerly spelt Yekhegnadzor
Yegindybulak Kazakh. **103** I2
also spelt Egindibulaq
Yegorlyk r. Rus. Fed. **41** G7
Yegorlykskaya Rus. Fed. **41** G7
Yegorova, Mys pt Rus. Fed. **82** E3
Yegor'ye Rus. Fed. **43** O6
Yegor'yevsk Rus. Fed. **43** U6
Yégué Togo **125** F4
Yei Sudan **128** A3
Yei r. Sudan **128** A3
Yeina Island P.N.G. **149** G1
Yeji China **87** E2
also known as Yejiaji
Yeji Ghana **125** E4
Yejiaji China see **Yeji**
Yekaterinburg Rus. Fed. **38** G4
formerly known as Sverdlovsk
Yekaterinodar Rus. Fed. see **Krasnodar**
Yekaterinoslav Ukr. see **Dnipropetrovs'k**
Yekaterinoslavka Rus. Fed. **82** C2
Yekaterinovka Lipetskaya Oblast' Rus. Fed. **43** T9
Yekaterinovka Saratovskaya Oblast' Rus. Fed. **41** H5
Yekhegnadzor Armenia see **Yeghegnadzor**
Yekimovichi Rus. Fed. **43** O7
Yekokora r. Dem. Rep. Congo **126** D4
Yelabuga Rus. Fed. **82** D2
Yelabuga Rus. Fed. **40** I5
Yelan' Rus. Fed. **41** G6
Yelbarsli Turkm. **102** E5
Yeleğen Turkey **59** J10
Yelenovskiye Kar'yery Ukr. see **Dokuchayevs'k**
Yelenskiy Rus. Fed. **43** Q8
Yelets Rus. Fed. **43** T9
Yeletskiy Rus. Fed. **40** M2
Yeligovo Rus. Fed. **43** O3
Yélimané Mali **124** C3
Yelino Rus. Fed. **43** U7
Yelizavetgrad Ukr. see **Kirovohrad**
Yelizovo Rus. Fed. **39** P4
Yelkhovka Rus. Fed. **41** I5
Yell i. U.K. **46** K3
Yellabina Regional Reserve nature res. Australia **146** B2
Yellandu India **94** D2
Yellapur India **94** B3
Yellareddi India **94** C2

▶**Yellow** r. China **85** H4
4th longest river in Asia and 7th in the world. Also known as Huang He or Ma Qu; formerly spelt Hwang Ho.
asia [landscapes] 62–63

Yellow r. U.S.A. **172** C7
Yellow Bluff hd Canada **167** O1
Yellowdine Australia **151** B6
Yellowhead Pass Canada **166** G4

▶**Yellowknife** Canada **167** H2
Capital of Northwest Territories.

Yellowknife r. Canada **167** H2
Yellow Mountain hill Australia **147** E3
Yellow Sea N. Pacific Ocean **83** B6
Yellow Springs U.S.A. **176** B6
Yellowstone r. U.S.A. **178** B2
Yellowstone Lake U.S.A. **180** E3
▶**Yellowstone National Park** U.S.A. **180** E3
northamerica [environments] 162–163
Yell Sound strait U.K. **46** K3
Yellville U.S.A. **179** D4
Yelm U.S.A. **180** B3
Yel'nya Rus. Fed. **43** O7
Yeloten Turkm. **103** E5
also spelt Yolöten; formerly spelt Iolotan'
Yelovo Rus. Fed. **40** J4
Yel'sk Belarus **41** D6
Yel'tsy Rus. Fed. **43** O5
Yelva r. Rus. Fed. **40** I3
Yelverton Bay Canada **165** K1
Yelwa Nigeria **125** H4
Yema Nanshan mts China **84** B4
Yema Shan mts China **84** B4
Yematan China **84** C4
Yembo Eth. **128** C2
▶**Yemen** country Asia **104** D5
asia [countries] 64–67
Yemetsk Rus. Fed. **40** G3
Yemişenbükü Turkey see **Taşova**
Yemmiganur India see **Emmiganuru**
Yemtsa Rus. Fed. **40** G3
Yemva Rus. Fed. **40** I3
formerly known as Zheleznodorozhnyy
Yena Rus. Fed. **44** O2
Yenagoa Nigeria **125** G5
Yenakiyeve Ukr. **41** F6
also spelt Yenakiyevo; formerly known as Rykovo
Yenakiyevo Ukr. see **Yenakiyeve**
Yenangyat Myanmar **78** A3
Yenangyaung Myanmar **78** A3
Yenanma Myanmar **78** A4
Yên Bai Vietnam **78** D3
Yendi Ghana **125** E4
Yêndum China see **Zhag'yab**
Yénéganou Congo **126** B5
Yenge r. Dem. Rep. Congo **126** D5
Yengejeh Iran **100** A2
Yengema Sierra Leone **124** C4

Zaire country Africa see Congo, Democratic Republic of
Zaire prov. Angola 127 B6
Zaïre r. Congo/Dem. Rep. Congo see Congo
Zaječar Srbija Yugo. 58 D5
Zaka Zimbabwe 131 F4
Zakamensk Rus. Fed. 84 D1
formerly known as Gorodok
Zakataly Azer. see Zaqatala
Zakháro Greece see Zacharo
Zakharovka Kazakh. 103 G2
Zakharovo Rus. Fed. 43 U7
Zakhmet Turkm. 103 E5
also spelt Zähmet
Zākhō Iraq 107 E3
Zakhodnyaya Dzvina r. Europe see Zapadnaya Dvina
Zakhrebetnoye Rus. Fed. 40 F1
Zákinthos i. Greece see Zakynthos
Zakopane Poland 49 Q6
Zakouma Chad 126 C2
Zakouma, Parc National de nat. park Chad 126 C2
Zakros Greece 59 H13
Zakwaski, Mount Canada 166 F5
Zakynthos Greece 59 B11
Zakynthos i. Greece 59 B11
also spelt Zákinthos; historically known as Zacynthus
Zala Angola 127 B6
Zala r. Romania 49 O9
Zalābiyah tourist site Syria 109 K2
Zalaegerszeg Hungary 49 N9
Zalai-domsag hills Hungary 49 N9
Zalakomár Hungary 49 O9
Zalamea de la Serena Spain 54 F6
Zalanga Nigeria 125 H4
Zalantun China 85 I2
also known as Butha Qi
Zalaszentgrót Hungary 49 O9
Zalău Romania 58 E1
Zalavas Lith. 42 H7
Žalec Slovenia 56 H2
Zalegoshch' Rus. Fed. 43 R9
Zaleski U.S.A. 176 C6
Zales'ye Rus. Fed. 43 R3
Zalewo Poland 49 Q2
Zalew Szczeciński b. Poland 49 L2
Zalew Wiślany b. Poland 49 Q1
Zalim Saudi Arabia 104 C3
Zalingei Sudan 120 D6
Zalmā, Jabal az mt. Saudi Arabia 104 B2
Zaltan, Jabal hills Libya 120 C2
Zaluch'ye Rus. Fed. 43 M4
Zama Japan 91 F7
Zama Niger 125 F3
Zama City Canada 166 G3
Zamakh Saudi Arabia 105 D4
Zamani S. Africa 133 N4
Zamanti r. Turkey 106 C3
Zambales Mountains Phil. 74 B3
Zambeze r. Africa 131 G2 see Zambezi

▶Zambezi r. Africa 131 G2
4th longest river in Africa. Also spelt Zambeze.
africa [landscapes] ▶▶ 112–113

Zambezi Zambia 127 D8
Zambézia prov. Moz. 131 H3
Zambezi Escarpment Zambia/Zimbabwe 127 E9
Zambezi National Park Zimbabwe 131 E3
▶Zambia country Africa 127 E8
formerly known as Northern Rhodesia
africa [countries] ▶▶ 114–117
Zamboanga Phil. 74 B5
Zamboanga Peninsula Phil. 74 B5
Zamboanguita Phil. 74 B4
Zambrów Poland 49 T3
Zambue Moz. 131 F2
Zamfara state Nigeria 125 G3
Zamfara watercourse Nigeria 125 G3
Zamlat Amagraj hills W. Sahara 122 B4
Zamogil'ye Rus. Fed. 42 I3
Zamora Ecuador 198 B6
Zamora r. Ecuador 198 B5
Zamora Spain 54 F3
Zamora-Chinchipe prov. Ecuador 198 B5
Zamora de Hidalgo Mex. 185 E5
Zamość Poland 53 G1
formerly known as Zamost'ye
Zamost'ye Poland see Zamość
Zamtang China 86 B1
also known as Rangke; formerly known as Gamda
Zamuro, Punta pt Venez. 187 F5
Zamuro, Sierra del mts Venez. 199 F3
Zamzam, Wādī watercourse Libya 120 B2
Zanaga Congo 126 B5
Zanatepec Mex. 185 G5
Záncara r. Spain 55 H5
Zancle Sicilia Italy see Messina
Zanda China 89 B6
also known as Toling
Zandamela Moz. 131 G5
Zanderij Suriname 199 H3
Zandvliet Belgium 51 K1
Zanesville U.S.A. 176 C6
Zangasso Mali 124 D3
formerly spelt Sangasso
Zangelan Azer. see Zängilan
Zängilan Azer. 107 F3
also spelt Zangelan; formerly known as Pirchevan
Zangla Jammu and Kashmir 96 C2
Zangsêr Kangri mt. China 89 D5
Zanhuang China 85 G4
Zanjān Iran 100 B2
Zanjān prov. Iran 100 B2
Zanjān Rūd r. Iran 107 F3
Zannah, Jabal az hill U.A.E. 105 F2
Zanskar reg. Jammu and Kashmir see Zaskar
Zanthus Australia 151 C6
Zantiébougou Mali 124 D4
Zanzibar Tanz. 129 C6
Zanzibar Channel Tanz. 129 C6
Zanzibar Island Tanz. 129 C6
Zanzibar North admin. reg. Tanz. 129 C6
also known as Unguja North
Zanzibar South admin. reg. Tanz. 129 C6
also known as Unguja South
Zanzibar West admin. reg. Tanz. 129 C6
also known as Unguja West
Zaokskiy Rus. Fed. 43 S7
Zaonia Mornag Tunisia 57 C12
Zaoro-Songou Cent. Afr. Rep. 126 C3
Zaoshi Hubei China 87 E2
Zaoshi Hunan China 87 D3
Zaouatallaz Alg. 123 H4
formerly known as Fort Gardel
Zaouet el Kahla Alg. see Bordj Omer Driss
Zaouiet Kounta Alg. 123 E4
Zaoyang China 87 E1
Zaoyangzhan China 87 E1
Zaō-zan vol. Japan 90 G5
Zaozernyy Kazakh. 103 G1
formerly known as Aysarinskoye or Aysary
Zaozernyy Rus. Fed. 80 E1
Zaozer'ye Rus. Fed. 43 T4
Zaozhuang China 87 F1
Zap r. Turkey 107 E3
Zapadna Morava r. Yugo. 58 C5
Zapadnaya Dvina r. Europe 43 L6
English form Western Dvina; also spelt Zakhodnyaya Dvina
Zapadnaya Dvina Rus. Fed. 43 N5
Zapadno-Kazakhstanskaya Oblast' admin. div. Kazakh. see Zapadnyy Kazakhstan
Zapadno-Sakhalinskiy Khrebet mts Rus. Fed. 82 F2
Zapadno-Sibirskaya Nizmennost' plain Rus. Fed. see West Siberian Plain
Zapadno-Sibirskaya Ravnina plain Rus. Fed. see West Siberian Plain
Zapadnyy Alamedin, Pik mt. Kyrg. 103 H4
Zapadnyy Berezovyy, Ostrov i. Rus. Fed. 43 J1
Zapadnyy Chink Ustyurta esc. Kazakh. 102 C4
Zapadnyy Kazakhstan admin. div. Kazakh. 102 B2
English form West Kazakhstan Oblast; also known as Batys Qazaqstan Oblysy; formerly known as Ural'skaya Oblast'; long form Zapadno-Kazakhstanskaya Oblast'
Zapadnyy Sayan reg. Rus. Fed. 80 D2
English form Western Sayan Mountains
Zapala Arg. 204 C5
Zapardiel r. Spain 54 F3
Zapata U.S.A. 179 C7
Zapata, Peninsula de pen. Cuba 186 C2
Zapatoca Col. 198 C3
Zapatón r. Spain 54 E6
Zapatoza, Ciénaga de l. Col. 198 C2
Zapiga Chile 200 C4
Zaplyus'ye Rus. Fed. 43 K3
Zăpodeni Romania 58 I2
Zapolyarnyy Murmanskaya Oblast' Rus. Fed. 44 O1
Zapolyarnyy Respublika Komi Rus. Fed. 40 L2
Zapol'ye Pskovskaya Oblast' Rus. Fed. 43 K3
Zapol'ye Vologod. Obl. Rus. Fed. 43 R2
Zaporizhzhya Ukr. 41 E7
also spelt Zaporozh'ye; formerly known as Aleksandrovsk or Oleksandrivs'k
Zaporozhskoye Rus. Fed. 43 L1
Zaporozh'ye Ukr. see Zaporizhzhya
Zapponeta Italy 56 H7
Zaprešić Croatia 56 H3
Zaprudnya Rus. Fed. 43 S5
Zaprudy Belarus 42 F9
Zapug China 89 C5
Zaqatala Azer. 107 F2
also spelt Zakataly
Zaqên China 97 G2
Zaqqui Libya 120 C2
Za Qu r. China 86 A2
Zaqungngomar mt. China 89 E5
Zara China see Moinda
Zara Croatia see Zadar
Zara Turkey 107 D3
Zarafshan Uzbek. 103 F4
also spelt Zarafshon
Zarafshon Tajik. 101 G2
also spelt Zeravshan
Zarafshon r. Tajik. 101 G2
also spelt Zeravshan
Zarafshon Uzbek. see Zarafshan
Zarafshon r. Uzbek. see Zeravshan
Zarafshon, Qatorkŭhi mts Tajik. 101 F2
also known as Zeravshanskiy Khrebet
Zaragoza Col. 198 C3
Zaragoza Mex. 185 E2
Zaragoza Spain 55 K3
English form Saragossa; historically known as Caesaraugusta
Zarand Kermān Iran 100 D4
Zarand Markazī Iran 100 B3
Zarandului, Munții hills Romania 58 D2
Zarang China 89 B6
Zaranj Afgh. 101 E4
Zarasai Lith. 42 H6
Zárate Arg. 204 F4
Zarautz Spain 55 I1
Zaraysk Rus. Fed. 43 T7
Zaraza Venez. 199 E2
Zarbdar Uzbek. 103 G4
Zärdab Azer. 107 F2
Zardak Iran 100 D3
Zard Kuh mts Iran 100 B3
Zarechensk Rus. Fed. 40 D2
Zarechka Belarus 42 G9
Zarechnyy Rus. Fed. 85 E1
Zarechnyy Rus. Fed. 43 U8
formerly known as Pobedinskiy
Zāreh Iran 100 B3
Zarembo Island U.S.A. 166 C3
Zarėnai Lith. 42 D6
Zarghat Saudi Arabia 104 C2
Zarghūn Shahr Afgh. 101 G3
Zargun mt. Pak. 101 F4
Zari Afgh. 101 F3
Zaria Nigeria 125 G4
Zariaspa Afgh. see Balkh
Zarichne Ukr. 41 C6
Zarīneh Rūd r. Iran 100 A2
Zaring China 89 E6
Zarmardan Afgh. 101 E3
Zărnești Romania 58 G3
Żarnowieckie, Jezioro l. Poland 49 P1
Zarqā' Jordan see Az Zarqā'
Zarqā', Nahr az r. Jordan 108 G5
Zarqān Iran 100 C4
Zarubino Rus. Fed. 43 O3
Zarubino Rus. Fed. 82 C4
Żary Poland 49 M4
Zarzaïtine Alg. 123 H3
Zarzal Col. 198 B3
Zarzis Tunisia 123 H2
Zasa Latvia 42 G5
Zashchita Kazakh. 88 C1
Zasheyek Rus. Fed. 44 O2
Zaskar r. India 96 C2
Zaskar reg. Jammu and Kashmir 96 C2
also spelt Zanskar
Zaskarki Belarus 43 J6
▶Zaskar Mountains India 96 C2
world [land images] ▶▶ 12–13
Zaslawkaye Vodaskhovishcha resr Belarus 42 I8
Zaslawye Belarus 42 I7
Zastron S. Africa 133 L7
Za'tarī, Wādī az watercourse Jordan 109 H5
Žatec Czech Rep. 49 K5
Zaterechnyy Rus. Fed. 107 F1
Zatobol'sk Kazakh. 103 E1
Zatoka Ukr. 58 L2
formerly known as Bugaz
Zatyshshya Ukr. 58 K1
Zaunguzskiye Karakumy des. Turkm. 102 D4
also known as Üngüz Angyrsyndaky Garagum
Zautla Mex. 185 F5
Zavadovskiy Island Antarctica 223 F2
Zavareh Iran 100 C3
Zavety Il'icha Rus. Fed. 82 F2
Zavidoviči Bos.-Herz. 56 K4
Zavidovskiy Zapovednik nature res. Rus. Fed. 43 R5
Zavitaya Rus. Fed. see Zavitinsk
Zavitinsk Rus. Fed. 82 C2
formerly known as Zavitaya
Zavodskoy Rus. Fed. see Komsomol'skiy
Zavolzhsk Rus. Fed. 40 G4
formerly known as Zavolzh'ye
Zavolzh'ye Rus. Fed. see Zavolzhsk
Závora, Ponta pt Moz. 131 G5
Zavutstsye Belarus 42 J6
Zavyachellye Belarus 43 J6
Zav'yalova, Ostrov i. Rus. Fed. 39 P4
Zav'yalovo Rus. Fed. 103 J1
Zawa Xinjiang China 96 C1
Zawa Qinghai China 84 D4
Zawadzkie Poland 49 P5
Zawgyi r. Myanmar 78 B3
Zawiercie Poland 49 Q5
Zawīlah Libya 120 B3
Zāwiyah, Jabal az hills Syria 109 H2
Zāwiyat Masūs Libya 120 D2
Zawlīyah, Jiddat az plain Oman 105 F3
Zawr, Ra's az pt Saudi Arabia 105 E2
Zâwyet Shammâs pt Egypt 106 A5
Zâwyet Sidi Ghâzi Egypt 108 B6
Zay r. Rus. Fed. 40 I5
Zaydī, Wādī az watercourse Syria 109 H5
Zaysan Kazakh. 88 D2
Zaysan, Lake Kazakh. 88 C1
also known as Zaysan, Ozero
Zaysan, Ozero l. Kazakh. see Zaysan, Lake
Zaytsevo Rus. Fed. 43 J4
Zayü Xizang China 86 A2
Zayü Xizang China 86 A2
also known as Gyigang
Zayü Qu r. China/India 86 A2
also known as Lohil or Luhit
Zayyr Uzbek. see Zair
Zazafotsy Madag. 131 [inset] J4
Zazir, Oued watercourse Alg. 123 G6
Zbąszynek Poland 49 M3
Zboriště mt. Yugo. 58 A5
Žďár nad Sázavou Czech Rep. 49 M6
Žďárské Vrchy hills Czech Rep. 49 M6
Zdolbuniv Ukr. 41 C6
also spelt Zdolbunov
Zdolbunov Ukr. see Zdolbuniv
Zduńska Wola Poland 49 P4
Zealand i. Denmark 45 J5
also spelt Sjælland
Zēbāk Afgh. 101 G2
Zeballos mt. Arg. 205 C7
Zeballos Canada 166 E5
Zēbār Iraq 107 F3
Zebargad, Gezîret i. Egypt 104 B3
English form Zebirget Island
Zebirget Island Egypt see Zebargad, Gezîret
Žebrák Czech Rep. 49 K6
Zebulon GA U.S.A. 175 C5
Zebulon KY U.S.A. 176 C8
Zebulon NC U.S.A. 174 E5
Zeebrugge Belgium 51 J1
Zeehan Australia 147 E5
Zeeland U.S.A. 172 G8
Zeerust S. Africa 133 K2
Zefat Israel 108 G5
also known as Safad; also spelt Tsefat
Zegrzyńskie, Jezioro l. Poland 49 S3
Zehdenick Germany 49 K3
Zeil, Mount Australia 148 B4
formerly spelt Ziel, Mount
Zeimelis Lith. 42 F5
Zeitz Germany 48 J4
Zêkog China 86 B1
also known as Sonag
Zela Turkey see Zile
Żelechów Poland 49 S4
Zelena Gora mt. Bos.-Herz. 56 J5
Zelenaya Roshcha Kazakh. 103 H1
Zelengora mts Bos.-Herz. 56 K5
Zelennik Rus. Fed. 40 H3
Zelenoborskiy Rus. Fed. 44 P2
Zelenodol'sk Rus. Fed. 40 I5
Zelenogorsk Rus. Fed. 43 K1
Zelenograd Rus. Fed. 43 S5
Zelenogradsk Rus. Fed. 42 B7
historically known as Cranz
Zelenokumsk Rus. Fed. 41 G7
formerly known as Sovetskoye or Vorontsovo-Aleksandrovskoye
Zelentsovo Rus. Fed. 40 H4
Zelenyy, Ostrov i. Rus. Fed. 82 G4
also known as Shibotsu-jima
Zelenyy Gay Kazakh. 103 G2
Železné Hory hills Czech Rep. 49 M6
Zelienople U.S.A. 176 E5
Želiezovce Slovakia 49 P7
Zelina Croatia 56 I3
also known as Sveti Ivan Zelina
Zelinggou China 84 C4
Želivka, Vodní nádrž resr Czech Rep. 49 L6
Željin mt. Yugo. 58 B5
Zell am See Austria 49 J8
Zellerrain pass Austria 49 M8
Zelów Poland 49 Q4
Zeltiņi Latvia 42 H4
Zel'va Belarus 42 F8
Žemaičių Naumiestis Lith. 42 C6
Žemaitijos nacionalinis parkas nat. park Lith. 42 C5
Zêmdasam China 86 B1
Zemen Bulg. 58 D6
Zemeș Romania 58 H2
Zemetchino Rus. Fed. 41 G5
Zémio Cent. Afr. Rep. 126 E3
Zemmora Alg. 55 L9
Zémongo, Réserve de Faune de nature res. Cent. Afr. Rep. 126 E3
Zempleni park Hungary 49 S7
Zemplínska šírava l. Slovakia 49 T7
Zempoaltépetl, Nudo de mt. Mex. 185 G5
Zemtsy Rus. Fed. 43 N5
Zemun Srbija Yugo. 58 B4
Zênda China 86 A1
Zengcheng China 87 E4
Zengfeng Shan mt. China 82 C4
Zenica Bos.-Herz. 56 J4
Zenifim watercourse Israel 108 F7
Zenta Vojvodina, Srbija Yugo. see Senta
Zentsūji Japan 91 C7
Zenyeh Afgh. 101 G3
Zenzach Alg. 55 O9
Žepče Bos.-Herz. 56 K4
Zephyr Cove U.S.A. 182 E2
Zepu China 88 B4
formerly known as Poskam
Zeraf, Bahr el r. Sudan 128 A2
Zeravshan Tajik. see Zarafshon
Zeravshan r. Tajik. see Zarafshon
Zeravshan r. Uzbek. 103 E5
also spelt Zarafshon
Zeravshanskiy Khrebet mts Tajik. see Zarafshon, Qatorkŭhi
Zerenda Kazakh. 103 G1
Zeribet el Oued Alg. 123 G2
Zerków Poland 49 O3
Zermatt Switz. 51 N6
Zernograd Rus. Fed. 41 G7
formerly known as Zernovoy
Zernovoy Rus. Fed. see Zernograd
Zestafoni Georgia see Zestap'oni
Zestap'oni Georgia 107 E2
also spelt Zestafoni
Zeta r. Yugo. 58 A6
Zêtang China 89 E6
Zetea Romania 58 G2
Zeulenroda Germany 48 I5
Zeven Germany 48 G2
Zevenaar Neth. 48 D4
Zevgolatio Greece 59 D11
Zeya Rus. Fed. 82 B1
Zeya r. Rus. Fed. 82 B2
Zeydābād Iran 100 C4
Zeydar Iran 100 D2
Zeynalābād Iran 100 D4
Zeyskiy Zapovednik nature res. Rus. Fed. 82 B1
Zeysko-Bureinskaya Vpadina depr. Rus. Fed. 82 C2
Zeyskoye Vodokhranilishche resr Rus. Fed. 82 B1
Zeytin Burnu c. Cyprus see Elaia, Cape
Zeytindağ Turkey 59 I10
Zêzere r. Port. 54 C5
Zgharta Lebanon 108 G3
Zgierz Poland 49 Q4
historically known as Sgiersch
Zhabdün China 89 D6
Zhabinka Belarus 42 F9
Zhadove Ukr. 43 N9
Zhaggo China see Luhuo
Zhaglag China 86 A1
Zhag'yab China 86 A2
also known as Yêndum
Zhailma Kazakh. 103 E2
also spelt Zhayylma
Zhaksy Kazakh. 103 F2
also spelt Zhaqsy; formerly spelt Dzhaksy
Zhaksy-Kon watercourse Kazakh. 103 G2
Zhaksykylysh, Ozero salt l. Kazakh. 103 E3
Zhaksy Sarysu watercourse Kazakh. see Sarysu
Zhalaghash Kazakh. see Dzhalagash
Zhalanash Kazakh. 103 I4
Zhalanash Kazakh. see Damdy
Zhalgyztöbe Kazakh. see Zhangiztobe
Zhalpaktal Kazakh. 102 B2
also spelt Zhalpaqtal; formerly known as Furmanovo
Zhalpaqtal Kazakh. see Zhalpaktal
Zhaltyr Kazakh. 103 G2
formerly spelt Dzhaltyr
Zhaltyr, Ozero l. Kazakh. 102 B3
Zhaludok Belarus 42 F8
Zhamanakkol', Ozero salt l. Kazakh. 103 E2
Zhamansor Kazakh. 102 C3
Zhambyl Kazakh. 103 G3
Zhambyl Kazakh. see Taraz
Zhambyl Oblast admin. div. Kazakh. see Zhambylskaya Oblast'
Zhambylskaya Oblast' admin. div. Kazakh. 103 H3
English form Zhambyl Oblast; formerly known as Dzhambulskaya Oblast'
Zhameuka Kazakh. 103 J3
Zhamo China see Bomi
Zhan r. China 82 C2
Zhanakorgan Kazakh. 103 F4
also spelt Zhangaqorghan; formerly known as Yany-Kurgan
Zhanakurylys Kazakh. 103 E3
Zhanang China 89 E6
also known as Chatang
Zhanaortalyk Kazakh. 103 H3
Zhanaozen Kazakh. 102 C4
also spelt Zhangaözen; formerly known as Novyy Uzen'
Zhanatala Kazakh. 103 I4
Zhanatas Kazakh. 103 G4
also spelt Zhangatas
Zhanbay Kazakh. 102 B3
Zhanbei China 82 B2
also known as Zhanhe
Zhang r. China 85 G4
Zhangaözen Kazakh. see Zhanaozen
Zhangaqazaly Kazakh. see Ayteke Bi
Zhanga Qazan Kazakh. see Novaya Kazanka
Zhangaqorghan Kazakh. see Zhanakorgan
Zhangatas Kazakh. see Zhanatas
Zhangbei China 85 G3
Zhangcheng China see Yongtai
Zhangcunpu China 87 F1
Zhangde China see Anyang
Zhangdian China see Zibo
Zhanggu China see Danba
Zhangguangcai Ling mts China 82 C3
Zhanghua Taiwan see Changhua
Zhangiztobe Kazakh. 103 J2
also known as Zhalgyztöbe
Zhangjiajie China see Dayong
Zhangjiakou China 85 G3
also known as Kalgan
Zhangjiapan China see Jingbian
Zhangla China 86 B1
Zhanglou China 87 F1
Zhangping China 87 F3
Zhangpu China 87 F3
also known as Sui'an
Zhangqiu China 85 H4
Zhangshu China 87 E2
formerly known as Qingjiang
Zhangwei Xinhe r. China 85 H4
Zhangwu China 85 I3
Zhangxian China 86 C1
Zhangye China 84 D4
Zhangzhou China 87 F3
formerly spelt Changchow
Zhangzi China 85 G4
Zhanhe China see Zhanbei
Zhanhua China 85 H4
also known as Fuguo
Zhänibek Kazakh. see Dzhanybek
Zhanjiang China 87 D4
formerly spelt Changkiang
Zhansügirov Kazakh. see Dzhansugurov
Zhanterek Kazakh. 102 C3
Zhanyi China 86 B3
Zhao'an China 87 F4
also known as Nanzhao
Zhaodong China 82 B3
Zhaoge China see Qixian
Zhaojue China 86 B2
also known as Xincheng
Zhaoliqiao China 87 E2
Zhaoping China 87 D3
Zhaoqing China 87 E4
Zhaoren China see Changwu
Zhaosu China 88 C3
also known as Mongolküre
Zhaosutai r. China 85 I3
Zhaotong China 86 B3
Zhaoxian China 85 G4
also known as Zhaozhou
Zhaoyuan Heilong. China 82 B3
Zhaoyuan Shandong China 85 I4
Zhaozhen China see Jintang
Zhaozhou China see Zhaoxian
Zhaozhou China 82 B3
Zhapo China 87 D4
Zhaqsy Kazakh. see Zhaksy
Zharbulak Kazakh. see Kabanbay
Zharbulak Kazakh. 88 C2
Zhardzyazhzha Belarus 42 I7
Zhari Namco salt l. China 89 D6
Zharkamys Kazakh. 102 D3
Zharkent Kazakh. 103 J3
formerly known as Panfilov; formerly spelt Dzharkent
Zharkovskiy Rus. Fed. 43 N6
Zharma Kazakh. 103 J2
Zharmysh Kazakh. 102 C3
Zharsuat Kazakh. 103 J3
Zharyk Kazakh. see Saken Seyfullin
Zhashkiv Ukr. 41 D6
also spelt Zhashkov
Zhashkov Ukr. see Zhashkiv
Zhashui China 87 D1
also known as Qianyou
Zhaslyk Uzbek. 102 D4
also spelt Jasliq
Zhastkovo Rus. Fed. 43 N8
Zhaxi China see Weixin
Zhaxi Co salt l. China 89 D5
Zhaxigang China 89 B5
Zhaxizê China 86 A2
Zhayrem Kazakh. 103 G2
Zhayü China 86 A2
Zhayylma Kazakh. see Zhailma
Zhayyq r. Kazakh./Rus. Fed. see Ural
Zhdanov Ukr. see Mariupol'
Zhdanovo Kazakh. 103 G3
Zhdanovo Rus. Fed. 43 O4
Zhdanovsk Azer. see Beyläqan
Zhecheng China 87 E1
Zhedao China see Lianghe
Zhêhor China 86 B2
Zhejiang prov. China 87 G2
English form Chekiang
Zhelang China 87 E4
Zhelaniya, Mys c. Rus. Fed. 39 G2
Zhelcha r. Rus. Fed. 42 I3
Zhelezinka Kazakh. 103 H1
Zheleznodorozhnyy Rus. Fed. 42 C7
historically known as Gerdauen
Zheleznodorozhnyy Rus. Fed. see Yemva
Zheleznodorozhnyy Uzbek. see Kungrad
Zheleznogorsk Rus. Fed. 43 Q9
Zheleznya Rus. Fed. 43 S7
Zhelou China see Ceheng
Zheltorangy Kazakh. 103 H3
Zheltyye Vody Ukr. see Zhovti Vody
Zhelyu Voyvoda Bulg. 58 H6
Zhem Kazakh. see Emba
Zhemgang Bhutan 97 F4
also spelt Shamgong
Zhen'an China 87 D1
also known as Yongle
Zhenba China 87 C1
Zheng'an China 87 C2
also known as Fengyi
Zhengding China 85 G4
Zhenghe China 87 F3
also known as Xiongshan
Zhengjiakou China see Gucheng
Zhengjiatun China see Shuangliao
Zhengkou China see Gucheng
Zhenglan Qi China see Dund Hot
Zhengning China 85 F5
also known as Shanhe
Zhengxiangbai Qi China see Qagan Nur
Zhengyang China 87 E1
also known as Zhenyang
Zhengzhou China 87 E1
also spelt Chengchow
Zhenhai China 87 G2
Zhenjiang China see Dantu
Zhenjiangguan China 86 B1
Zhenlai China 85 I2
Zhenning China 86 C3
Zhenping China 87 D2
Zhenwudong China see Ansai
Zhenxi China 85 I2
Zhenxiong China 86 C3
also known as Wufeng
Zhenyang China see Zhengyang
Zhenyuan Gansu China 85 E5
Zhenyuan Guizhou China 87 D3
also known as Wuyang
Zhenyuan Yunnan China 86 B4
also known as Enle
Zhenziling China 87 D2
Zherdevka Rus. Fed. 41 G6
formerly known as Chibizovka
Zherdevo Rus. Fed. 43 R8
Zherong China 87 F3
also known as Shuangcheng
Zheshart Rus. Fed. 40 I3
Zhestylevo Rus. Fed. 43 S5
Zhetibay Kazakh. see Zhetybay
Zhetikara Kazakh. see Zhitikara
Zhetisay Kazakh. see Zhetysay
Zhetybay Kazakh. 102 C4
also spelt Zhetibay
Zhety-Kol', Ozero l. Rus. Fed. 103 E2
Zhetysay Kazakh. 103 G4
also spelt Zhetisay; formerly spelt Dzhetysay
Zhexam China 89 D6
Zhexi Shuiku resr China 87 D2
Zhezdy Kazakh. 103 F2
formerly known as Marganets; formerly spelt Dzhezdy
Zhezkazgan Kazakh. 103 F3
also spelt Zhezqazghan; formerly spelt Dzhezkazgan
Zhezqazghan Kazakh. see Zhezkazgan
Zhicheng China see Changxing
Zhichitsy Rus. Fed. 43 M6
Zhidan China 85 F4
also known as Bao'an
Zhidoi China 97 G2
also known as Gyaijêpozhanggê
Zhigansk Rus. Fed. 39 M3
Zhigung China 89 E6
Zhijiang China 87 D3
Zhijin China 86 C3
Zhilevo Rus. Fed. 43 T7
Zhilino Rus. Fed. 43 R8
Zhilyanka Kazakh. see Kargalinskoye
Zhi Qu r. China see Yangtze
Zhirnovsk Rus. Fed. 41 H6
formerly known as Zhirnovskiy or Zhirnoye
Zhirnovskiy Rus. Fed. see Zhirnovsk
Zhirnoye Rus. Fed. see Zhirnovsk
Zhiryatino Rus. Fed. 43 O8
Zhitarovo Bulg. see Vetren
Zhitikara Kazakh. 103 E1
also spelt Zhetikara; formerly known as Dzhetygara
Zhitkovichi Belarus see Zhytkavichy
Zhitkovo Rus. Fed. 43 K1
Zhitkur Rus. Fed. 102 A2
Zhitomir Ukr. see Zhytomyr
Zhizdra Rus. Fed. 43 P8
Zhizdra r. Rus. Fed. 43 R7
Zhizhitsa Rus. Fed. 43 M5
Zhizhitskoye, Ozero l. Rus. Fed. 43 M5
Zhlobin Belarus 43 L9
Zhmerinka Ukr. see Zhmerynka
Zhmerynka Ukr. 41 D6
also spelt Zhmerinka
Zhob Pak. 101 G4
formerly known as Fort Sandeman
Zhob r. Pak. 101 G3
Zhodzina Belarus 43 J7
Zhokhova, Ostrov i. Rus. Fed. 39 P2
Zholnuskay Kazakh. 88 C1
Zholymbet Kazakh. 103 G2
Zhong'an China see Fuyuan
Zhongba China 87 E4
Zhongba China see Jiangyou
Zhongcheng China see Suijiang
Zhongdian China 86 A3
also known as Zhongxin
Zhongduo China see Youyang
Zhongguo country Asia see China
Zhongguo Renmin Gongheguo country Asia see China
Zhonghe China see Xiushan
Zhongmou China 87 E1
Zhongning China 85 E4
Zhongping China see Huize
Zhongshan research station Antarctica 223 F2
Zhongshan Guangdong China 87 E4
formerly known as Shiqizhen
Zhongshan Guangxi China 87 D3
Zhongshan China see Lupanshui
Zhongsha Qundao sea feature S. China Sea see Macclesfield Bank
Zhongshu China see Luxi
Zhongshu China see Luliang
Zhongtai China see Lingtai
Zhongtiao Shan mts China 87 D1
Zhongwei China 84 E4
Zhongxian China 87 D2
also known as Zhongzhou
Zhongxin China 87 E3
Zhongxin China see Zhongdian
Zhongxin China see Huaping
Zhongxing China see Siyang
Zhongxingji China 87 F2
Zhongyang China 85 F4
Zhongyicun China 86 B3
Zhongze China 87 D3
Zhongzhai China 86 C1
Zhongzhou China see Zhongxian
Zhosaly Kazakh. see Dzhusaly
Zhosaly Kazakh. 103 I2
Zhoujiajing China 84 D4
Zhoujiaping China see Nanzheng
Zhoukou China 87 E1
Zhoukou China see Peng'an
Zhouning China 87 F3
also known as Shicheng
Zhoushan China 87 G2
Zhoushan Dao i. China 87 G2
Zhoushan Qundao is China 87 G2
Zhouzhi China 87 D1
also known as Erqu
Zhovten' Ukr. 58 L1
Zhovti Vody Ukr. 41 E6
formerly known as Zheltyye Vody
Zhualy Kazakh. 103 E2
Zhuanghe China 85 I4
Zhuanglang China 85 E5
also known as Shuiluocheng
Zhuantobe Kazakh. 103 G3
Zhubgyügoin China 86 A1
Zhucheng China 85 H5
Zhudong Taiwan see Chutung
Zhugqu China 86 C1
Zhuhai China 87 E4
formerly known as Chuhai
Zhuji China see Shangqiu
Zhuji China 87 G2
Zhujia Chuan r. China 85 F4
Zhujing China see Jinshan
Zhukeng China 87 E4
Zhukopa r. Rus. Fed. 43 N5
Zhukovka Rus. Fed. 43 O8
Zhukovo Rus. Fed. 43 R6
formerly known as Ugodskiy Zavod
Zhukovskiy Rus. Fed. 43 T6
formerly known as Stakhanovo
Zhulong r. China 85 G4
Zhumadian China 87 E1
Zhumysker Kazakh. 102 B3
Zhuolu China 85 G3
Zhuoyang China see Suiping
Zhuozang r. China 85 G4
Zhuozhou China 85 H4
Zhuozi China 85 G3
also known as Zhuozishan
Zhuozishan China see Zhuozi
Zhuravlevka Kazakh. 103 G2
Zhurki Belarus 42 I6
Zhuryn Kazakh. 102 D2
formerly spelt Dzhurun
Zhusandala, Step' plain Kazakh. 103 H3
Zhushan China 87 D1
Zhushan China see Xuan'en
Zhuxi China 87 D1
Zhuyang China see Dazhu
Zhuzhou Hunan China 87 E3
also known as Lukou
Zhuzhou Hunan China 87 E3
Zhydachiv Ukr. 41 C6
Zhympity Kazakh. 102 C2
formerly known as Dzhambeyty
Zhyngyldy Kazakh. 102 B3
formerly known as Kuybyshevo
Zhytkavichy Belarus 42 I9
also spelt Zhitkovichi
Zhytomyr Ukr. 41 D6
also spelt Zhitomir
Zi r. China 85 H4
Ziama mt. Guinea 124 C4
Ziarat Iran 100 D2
Žiar nad Hronom Slovakia 49 P7
Zībā salt pan Saudi Arabia 109 J7
Zibār Iraq 107 E3
Zibo China 85 H4
formerly known as Zhangdian
Zichang China 85 F4
also known as Wayaobu
Zicheng China see Zijin
Zichtauer Berge und Klötzer Forst park Germany 48 I3
Ziddi Tajik. 101 G2
Zidi Pak. 101 F5
Ziębice Poland 49 O5
Ziel, Mount Australia see Zeil, Mount
Zielona Góra Poland 49 M4
historically known as Grünberg
Ziemelkursas Augstiene hills Latvia 42 D4
Ziemeris Latvia 42 I4
Ziemupe Latvia 42 C5
Ziesar Germany 49 J3
Zifta Egypt 121 F2
Zigaing Myanmar 78 A3
Zigê Tangco l. China 89 E5
Ziggurat of Ur tourist site Iraq 107 F5
Zighan Libya 120 D3
Zigon Myanmar 78 A4
Zigong China 86 C2
Ziguey Chad 120 B6
Zigui China 87 D2
also known as Jiandaoyu
Ziguinchor Senegal 124 A3
Žīguri Latvia 42 I4
Zihuatanejo Mex. 185 E5
Zijin China 87 E4
also known as Zicheng
Ziketan China see Xinghai
Zikeyevo Rus. Fed. 43 P8
Zikhron Ya'aqov Israel 108 F5
Zilair Rus. Fed. 102 D1
Zilaiskalns Latvia 42 G4
Zile Turkey 106 C2
historically known as Zela
Zilim r. Rus. Fed. 40 K5
Žilina Slovakia 49 P6
Zillah Libya 120 C2
Zillertaler Alpen mts Austria 48 I8
Zilupe Latvia 42 J5
Zima Rus. Fed. 80 G2
Zimapán Mex. 185 F4
Zimatlán Mex. 185 F5
Zimba Zambia 127 E9
▶Zimbabwe country Africa 131 F3
formerly known as Rhodesia or Southern Rhodesia
africa [countries] ▶▶ 114–117
Zimbabwe tourist site Zimbabwe see Great Zimbabwe National Monument
Zimkān, Rūdkhāneh-ye r. Iran 100 A3
Zimmerbude Rus. Fed. see Svetlyy
Zimmi Sierra Leone 124 C5
Zimnicea Romania 58 G5
Zimniy Bereg coastal area Rus. Fed. 40 F2
Zimovniki Rus. Fed. 41 G7
Zin watercourse Israel 108 G6
Zinave, Parque Nacional de nat. park Moz. 131 G4
Zinder Niger 125 H3
Zinder dept Niger 125 H3
Zindo China 86 B2
formerly known as Jimda
Zing Nigeria 125 H4
Zinga Mulike Tanz. 129 C7
Ziniaré Burkina 125 E3
Zinihu China 85 E4
Zinjibār Yemen 105 D5
Zinkwazi Beach S. Africa 133 P6
Zinovo Rus. Fed. 43 V5
Zinoyevsk Ukr. see Kirovohrad
Zinzana Mali 124 D3
Zion U.S.A. 172 F8
Zion National Park U.S.A. 183 K4
Ziqudukou China 97 G2
Zirab Iran 100 C2
Zirbitzkogel mt. Austria 49 L8
Zirc Hungary 49 O8
Žirje i. Croatia 56 H5
Zirkel, Mount U.S.A. 180 F4
Zirkūh i. U.A.E. 105 F2
Ziro India 97 G4
Zi Shui r. China 87 E2
Zistersdorf Austria 49 N7
Zitácuaro Mex. 185 E5
Zitava r. Slovakia 49 P8
Žitište Vojvodina, Srbija Yugo. 58 B3
Zitiua r. Brazil 202 C2
Zito China see Lhorong
Zitong China 86 C2
also known as Wenchang

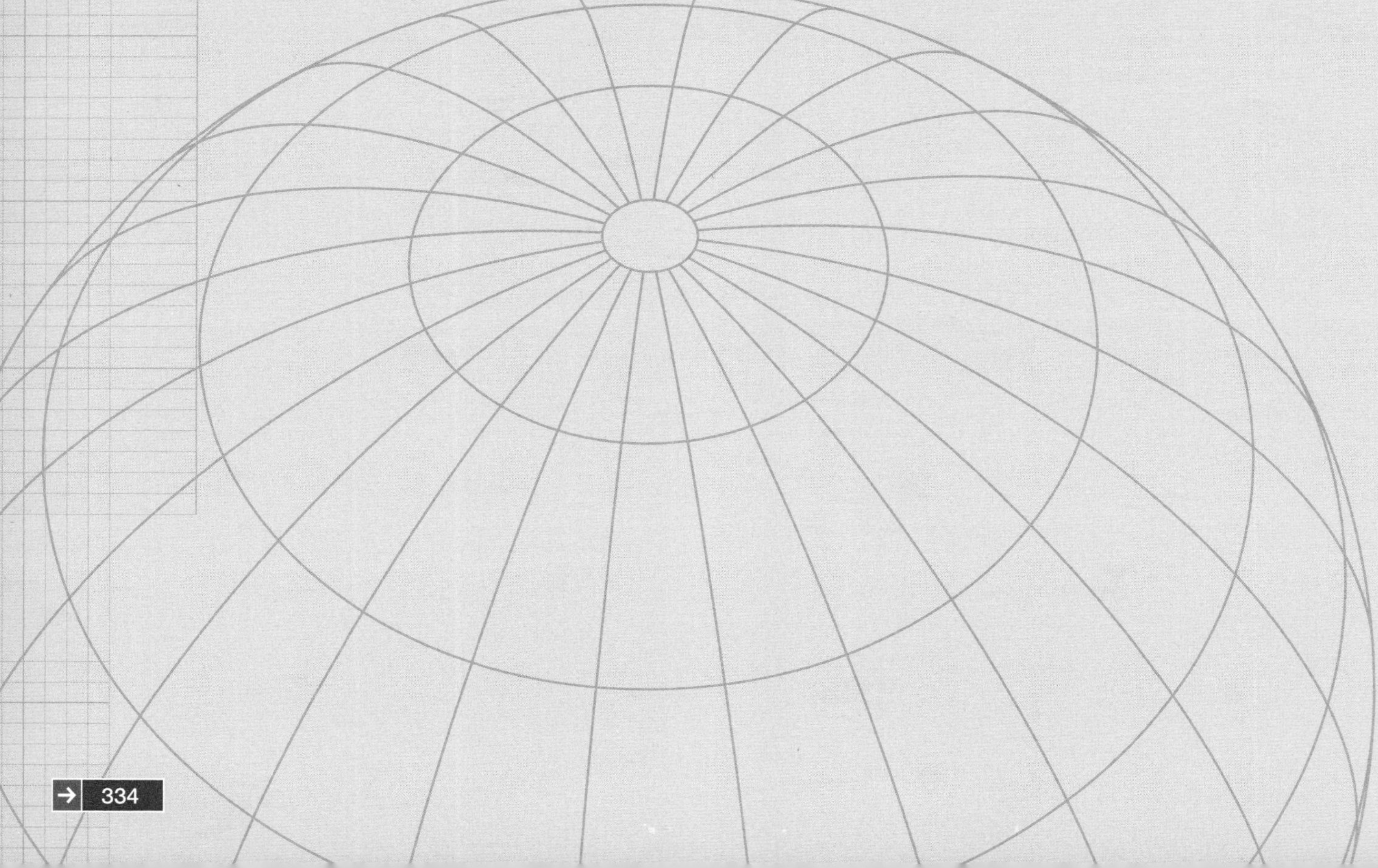

acknowledgements

MAPS AND DATA

General ➤➤

Maps designed and created by HarperCollins Cartographic, Glasgow, UK

Design: One O'Clock Gun Design Consultants Ltd, Edinburgh, UK

Continental perspective views (pp30–31, 62–63, 112–113, 136–137, 156–157, 190–191) and globes (pp 14–15, 26–27, 214): Alan Collinson Design, Llandudno, UK

The publishers would like to thank all national survey departments, road, rail and national park authorities, statistical offices and national place name committees throughout the world for their valuable assistance, and in particular the following:

British Antarctic Survey, Cambridge, UK

Bureau of Rural Sciences, Barton, ACT, Australia, a scientific agency of the Department of Agriculture, Fisheries and Forestry, Australia

Tony Champion, Professor of Population Geography, University of Newcastle upon Tyne, UK

Mr P J M Geelan, London, UK

International Boundary Research Unit, University of Durham, UK

The Meteorological Office, Bracknell, Berkshire, UK

Permanent Committee on Geographical Names, London, UK

Data ➤➤

Antarctica (pp222–223): Antarctic Digital Database (versions 1 and 2), © Scientific Committee on Antarctic Research (SCAR), Cambridge, UK (1993, 1998)

Bathymetric data: The GEBCO Digital Atlas published by the British Oceanographic Data Centre on behalf of IOC and IHO, 1994

Earthquakes data (pp14–15, 71): United States Geological Survey (USGS) National Earthquakes Information Center, Denver, USA

Coral reefs data (p141): UNEP World Conservation Monitoring Centre (UNEP-WCMC), Cambridge, UK. 'Reefs at Risk', 1998 Washington, DC, USA from World Resources Institute (WRI), the International Center for Living Aquatic Resources Management (ICLARM) and UNEP-WCMC

PHOTOGRAPHS AND IMAGES

page	image number	credit
3		NASA/Science Photo Library
6		NASA/Science Photo Library
7		NASA
8–9	1	NASA
	2	NASA/Science Photo Library
10–11	1	CNES, 1996 Distribution Spot Image/Science Photo Library
	2	US Geological Survey/Science Photo Library
	3	CNES, 1991 Distribution Spot Image/Science Photo Library
	4	CNES, 1986 Distribution Spot Image/Science Photo Library
12–13	1	NASA
	2	NASA/Science Photo Library
	3	NASA
	4	ImageState
	5	Bernhard Edmaier/Science Photo Library
	6	Earth Science Corporation/Science Photo Library
	7	CNES, 1996 Distribution Spot Image/Science Photo Library
	8	Digital image © 1996 CORBIS; Original image courtesy of NASA/CORBIS
14–15	1	Axiom Photographic Agency Ltd
	2	David Parker/Science Photo Library
	3	Chris Johns/NGS Image Collection
16–17	Fig. 1	Courtesy of NASA/JPL/Caltech
	Fig. 2	Courtesy of NASA/JPL/Caltech
	Fig. 3	Courtesy of NASA/JPL/Caltech
	Fig. 4	NRSC Ltd/Science Photo Library
	Fig. 9	NASA/Goddard Space Flight Center
	Fig. 10	Reproduced by permission of The Met Office, Bracknell, Berkshire
	Fig. 11	Reproduced by permission of The Met Office, Bracknell, Berkshire
18–19	1	Francois Suchel/Still Pictures
	2	Earth Satellite Corporation/Science Photo Library
	3	NRSC/Still Pictures
	4	M & C Denis-Huot/Still Pictures
	5	Pictor International - London
	6	Dick Ross/Still Pictures
	7	ImageState
	8	Klaus Andrews/Still Pictures
20–21	1	NASA/Science Photo Library
	2	Earth Satellite Corporation/Science Photo Library
	3	Daniel Dancer/Still Pictures
	4 left	NASA - Goddard Space Flight Center Scientific Visualization Studio
	4 right	NASA - Goddard Space Flight Center Scientific Visualization Studio
	5 left	NPA Group www.satmaps.com
	5 right	NPA Group www.satmaps.com
22–23	1	David Reed/Panos pictures
	2	Cities Revealed ® aerial photography © The GeoInformation ® Group, 1998
24–25	1	Earth Satellite Corporation/Science Photo Library
	2	Spaceimaging.com
	3	NRSC/Still Pictures
	4	NASA
26–27		NRSC/Still Pictures
	Fig. 1	TeleGeography, Inc, Washington D.C., USA www.telegeography.com
	Fig. 2	TeleGeography, Inc, Washington D.C., USA www.telegeography.com
28		© Marc Garanger/CORBIS
29		NASA
30–31	1	Digital image © 1996 CORBIS; Original image courtesy of NASA/CORBIS
	2	NASA
	3	NASA
32–33	1	P. Tatlow/Panos Pictures
	2	CNES, 1993 Distribution Spot Image/Science Photo Library
	3	CNES, 1991 Distribution Spot Image/Science Photo Library
34–35	1	Wim Van Cappellen/Still Pictures
	2	NASA
	3	Andrew Tatlow/Panos Pictures

page	image number	credit
36–37	1	Geoslides Photography
	2	Pictor International - London
	3	CNES, 1992 Distribution Spot Image/Science Photo Library
	4	ESA, Eurimage/Science Photo Library
	5	Dick Ross/Still Pictures
	6	NRSC/Science Photo Library
	7	Cities Revealed ® aerial photography © The GeoInformation ® Group, 1999
60		Pictures Colour Library Ltd
61		NASA
62–63	1	ImageState
	2	CNES, 1992 Distribution Spot Image/Science Photo Library
	3	CNES, 1987 Distribution Spot Image/Science Photo Library
64–65	1	Digital image © 1996 CORBIS; Original image courtesy of NASA/CORBIS
	2	Marc Schlossman/Panos pictures
	3	Georg Gerster/NGS Image Collection
66–67	1	NASA
	2	© Hanan Isachar/CORBIS
	3	Pictor International - London
68–69	1 top	© Wolfgang Kaehler/CORBIS
	1 middle	© Keren Su/CORBIS
	1 bottom	DERA/Still Pictures
	2 top	NASA
	2 bottom	NASA
	3 top	Science Photo Library
	3 bottom	CNES, 1987 Distribution Spot Image/Science Photo Library
70–71	1	NOAA
	2	NASA
	3	Shehzad Nooran/Still Pictures
	4	Digital image © 1996 CORBIS; Original image courtesy of NASA/CORBIS
	5	NASA
110		Pictures Colour Library Ltd
111		NASA
112–113	1	CNES, 1988 Distribution Spot Image/Science Photo Library
	2	© CORBIS
	3	NASA/JPL/Caltech
114–115	1	Peter Hering
	2	Libe Taylor/Panos pictures
116–117	1	NASA
	2	NASA
	3	Christian Aid/Glynn Griffiths/Still Pictures
	4	Mark Edwards/Still Pictures
	5 left	CNES, 1998 Distribution Spot Image/Science Photo Library
	5 right	CNES, 2001 Distribution Spot Image/Science Photo Library
118–119	1	Paul Springett/Still Pictures
	2	CNES, 1994 Distribution Spot Image/Science Photo Library
	3	Alan Collinson Design
	4	Pierre Gleizes/Still Pictures
	5	Voltchev-Unep/Still Pictures
	6	Spaceimaging.com
134		Pictures Colour Library Ltd
135		NASA
136–137	1	Pictor International - London
	2	CNES, 1986 Distribution Spot Image/Science Photo Library
	3	Mike Schroder/Still Pictures
138–139	1	The aerial photograph on page 138 is Copyright © Commonwealth of Australia, AUSLIG, Australia's national mapping agency. All rights reserved. Reproduced by permission of the General Manager, Autralian Surveying and Land Information Group, Department of Industry, Science and Resources, Canberra, ACT.
	2	eMAP Ltd
	3	eMAP Ltd
140–141	1 left	Pictor International - London
	1 right	NASA/Science Photo Library
	2	Bill van Aken © CSIRO Land and Water
	3 left	CNES, Distribution Spot Image/Science Photo Library
	3 right	Gerard & Margi Moss/Still Pictures
	Fig. 1	Bureau of Rural Sciences, Australia

page	image number	credit
142–143	1	NASA
	2	NASA
	3	ImageState
	4	Institute of Geological & Nuclear Sciences, New Zealand
	5	Spaceimaging.com
	6	NASA
	7	Image provided by ORBIMAGE © Orbital Imaging Corporation and processing by NASA Goddard Space Flight Center.
154		Pictures Colour Library Ltd
155		NASA
156–157	1	© Owen Franken/CORBIS
	2	© Lowell Georgia/CORBIS
	3	NASA
158–159	1	Gregor Turk
	2	NASA/Marshall Space Flight Center
	3	NASA
160–161	1	Infoterra Ltd
	2	© Roger Ressmeyer/CORBIS
	3	CNES, 1996 Distribution Spot Image/Science Photo Library
	4	NASA/Goddard Space Flight Center/Science Photo Library
	4 inset	NASA
162–163	1	NRSC/Still Pictures
	2	NASA
	3	Alex S. Maclean/Still Pictures
	4	NASA
	5	© David Muench/CORBIS
	6	Bernhard Edmaier/Science Photo Library
188		Pictures Colour Library Ltd
189		NASA
190–191	1	NASA
	2	© Yann Arthus-Bertrand/CORBIS
	3	NASA
192–193	1	Earth Satellite Corporation/Science Photo Library
	2	CNES, 1995 Distribution Spot Image/Science Photo Library
	3	NASA
194–195	1	Ron Giling/Still Pictures
	2	Jeremy Horner/Panos pictures
	3	NASA
	4	CNES, 1988 Distribution Spot Image/Science Photo Library
	5	Alan Collinson Design
	6	CNES, 1986 Distribution Spot Image/Science Photo Library
	7	Jacques Jangoux/Science Photo Library
	8	Digital image © 1996 CORBIS; Original image courtesy of NASA/CORBIS
	9	NASA
196–197	1	NASA/Science Photo Library
	2	Mark Edwards/Still Pictures
	3 top right	NASA/Goddard Space Flight Center/Science Photo Library
	3 left	Michael Nichols/NGS Image Collection
	3 bottom right	NASA/Goddard Space Flight Center/Science Photo Library
208		Pictures Colour Library Ltd
209		NASA
210–211	1	Alan Collinson Design
	2	WHF Smith, US National Oceanic and Atmospheric Administration (NOAA), USA
	Fig. 2	NASA/JPL
212–213	1	NASA
	2	Data provided by the EOS Distributed Active Archive Center (DAAC) procesed at the National Snow and Ice Data Center, University of Colorado, Boulder, CO.
	3	NASA
	4	Courtesy of the David Vaughan/BEDMAP Consortium
	5	RADARSAT data Canadian Space Agency/Agence Spatiale Canadienne 1997. Received by the Canada Centre for Remote Sensing. Processed and distributed by RADARSAT International.
214–215	1	B&C Alexander
	2	Data provided by the EOS Distributed Active Archive Center (DAAC) procesed at the National Snow and Ice Data Center, University of Colorado, Boulder, CO.
	3	Alan Collinson Design
	4 and 5	B&C Alexander
	6	NASA

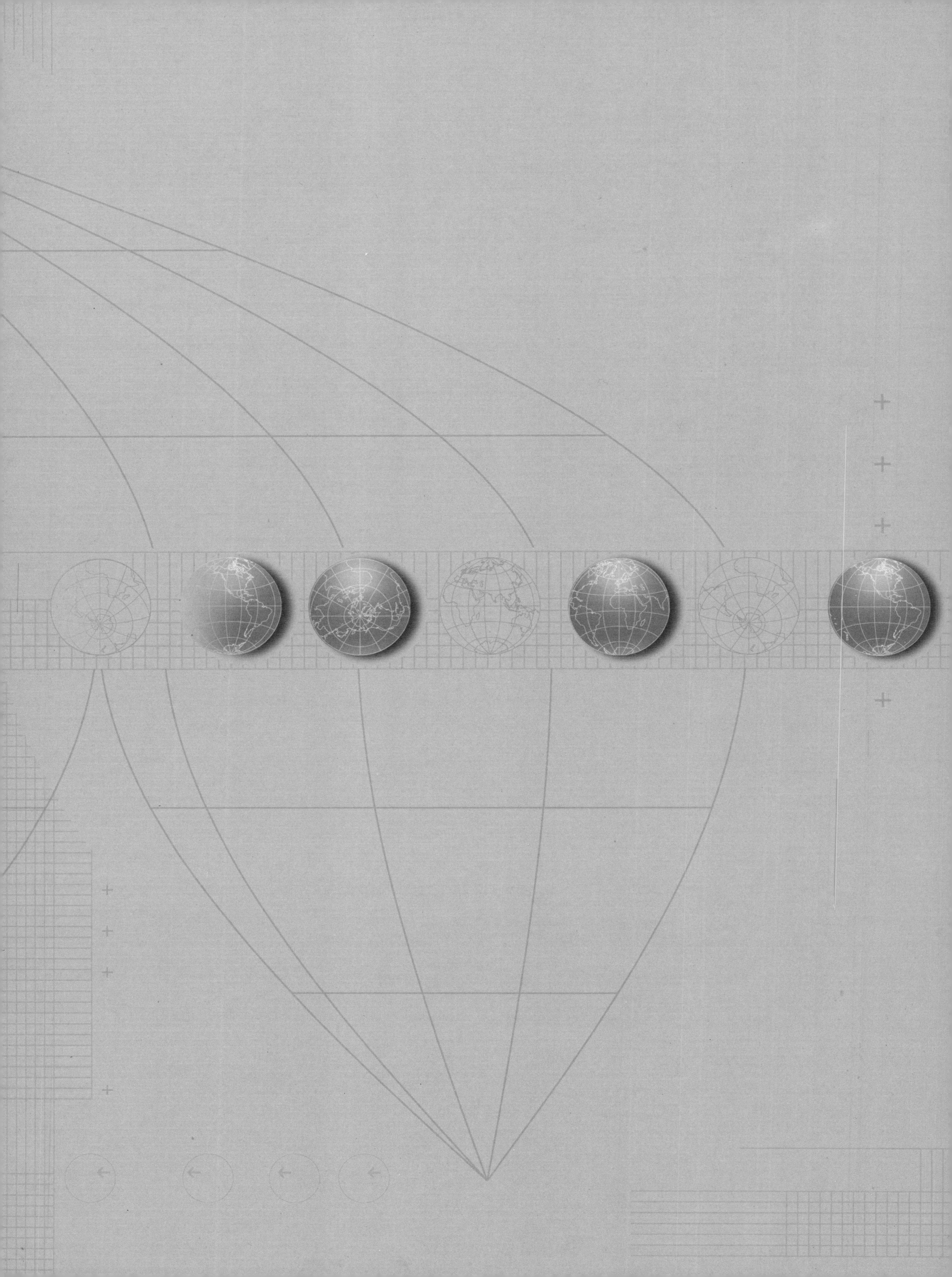